NE

ANNUAL 2004–2005

Published by Invincible Press, an imprint of HarperCollins*Publishers*, 77–85 Fulham Palace Road, Hammersmith, London W6 8JB

First published 1887

A CIP catalogue record for this book is available from the British Library

The HarperCollins website address is: www.harpercollins.co.uk

Editorial compilation by Hayters-Teamwork Image House, Station Road, London, N17 9LR

Typesetting by Letterpart Limited, Reigate, Surrey

Printed and bound in Great Britain by Clays Ltd, St Ives plc

Distributed by The Magazine Marketing Company, Octagon House, White Hart Meadows, Ripley, Woking, Surrey GU23 6HR. Telephone (01483) 211222

ISBN 0-00-719179-0

Cover picture: Copyright © Clive Mason/Getty Images

CONTENTS

A FOOTBALLING FAIRYTALE TO REMEMBER

BY CHRIS HATHERALL

EURO 2004 may not go down as one of the greatest footballing spectacles, but Greece's dramatic triumph in Lisbon will long be remembered as one of the game's most endearing fairytales. Sometimes, skills and thrills make a tournament memorable, none more so than in Brazil's immortal performance at the World Cup of 1970. But in the absence of players like Pele and Jairzinho, nothing beats a good giant-killing – and Greece's run to the Final was one of the best of its kind.

Otto Rehhagel's side were rated 100-1 to win by some bookmakers, but right from the opening day they proved their doubters wrong. The adventure began with a 2-1 victory over Portugal, thanks to goals from Georgios Karagounis and Angelos Basinas – and from that moment they never looked back.

It took a while for the critics to catch up, because at every step along the way Greece were rated as underdogs. They were expected to lose to France in the quarter-finals, but won 1-0 with a goal from Angelos Charisteas. Then there was a dramatic extra-time victory over the in-form Czech Republic, with a header from impressive defender Traianos Dellas.

Even in the Final, the Greeks were expected to lose. But they frustrated Portugal in midfield, soaked up every attack the hosts could muster and then claimed an unlikely but inspirational victory with another headed goal from Charisteas after 57 minutes.

The jubilant scenes that greeted the players when they returned home for an emotional reception in Athens confirmed just how special their victory had been. Nobody in the football world, including the Greek players themselves, had believed they would end up as European champions – but the truth is they deserved it. Portugal and the Czechs may have played the more attractive football and England, in Wayne Rooney, had perhaps the tournament's greatest discovery. But Greece played as a team, defended more effectively than any of their more-fancied rivals and in captain Theo Zagorakis had the official UEFA Player of the Tournament.

Much of the credit for must go to enigmatic coach Rehhagel, whose determination to stick to his own unique training methods and on-field tactics reaped rich dividends. He had his critics along the way, upsetting the purists who had yearned for a Portugal-Czech Republic Final and mourned the departure of Europe's big guns. But Greece's victory should go down as one of the greatest upsets in football history and their people celebrated it as such.

Euro 2004, however, will not only be remembered for giant-killing. Portugal's flowing, fluent play lit up the Finals, with midfielder Deco and Manchester United's Cristiano Ronaldo providing the tricks and flicks to thrill the home crowd. A carnival atmosphere in the streets of Lisbon and Porto ensured supporters from all over Europe enjoyed a trouble-free tournament, free from the outbreaks of hooliganism that have marred previous Finals.

As for England, again it was a summer of what might-have-been – one that began and ended in drama. In the opening game, Sven-Goran Eriksson's side were impressive as they led 1-0 against defending champions France with only a minute of normal time remaining. But a free-kick and a penalty from Zinedine Zidane turned a morale-boosting victory into defeat.

The response against Switzerland, a 3-0 win with two goals from Rooney, had the fans back on their feet. Then, a 4-2 victory over Croatia took Rooney's total to four for the tournament and ensured Roonmania swept the country. Unfortunately, the spectre of penalties lurking over the team was destined to quash the sudden outpouring of national pride and expectation.

England's quarter-final against Portugal was dramatic, thrilling, heartbreaking and exhausting – even though Eriksson's side failed to hit form and defended for 87 minutes after taking an early lead through Michael Owen. The real drama began when Portugal equalised through Helder Postiga with time running out, followed by Sol Campbell's headed goal disallowed for a foul on the goalkeeper. Both sides scored in extra-time –

Rui Costa and Frank Lampard – to set up a penalty shoot-out that Portugal won 6-5 thanks to goalkeeper Ricardo, who saved Darius Vassell's kick, then fired home the winner himself.

But England were not the only team to feel hard done-by. The Italians muttered about a fix after Sweden and Denmark delivered a 2-2 draw in their final group game – the only result that could send Italy home and put the Scandinavians through. Holland fans campaigned against coach Dick Advocaat after seeing their team throw away a 2-0 lead to lose 3-2 to the Czech Republic in possibly the game of the tournament. But they soon changed their minds as the Dutch went on to reach the semi-finals.

The Czechs played some of the most attractive football of the tournament and had the top scorer in Milan Baros, a perennial Liverpool substitute who proved Gerard Houllier wrong by scoring five times and taking his team to the last four. Just like Greece, it was a case of the underdog fighting back. And that is the memory most fans will have of Euro 2004 for many years to come.

EUROPEAN CHAMPIONSHIP 2002-04

HOW THEY QUALIFIED

(Portugal as hosts)

GROUP 1

	P	W	D	L	F	A	Pts
FRANCE	8	8	0	0	29	2	24
Slovenia	8	4	2	2	15	12	14
Israel	8	2	3	3	9	11	9
Cyprus	8	2	2	4	9	18	8
Malta	8	0	1	7	5	24	1

Results: Cyprus 1, France 2; Slovenia 3, Malta 0; France 5, Slovenia 0; Malta 0, Israel 2; Malta 0, France 4; Cyprus 2, Malta 1; Cyprus 1, Israel 1; France 6, Malta 0; Slovenia 4, Cyprus 1; Israel 1, France 2; Malta 1, Slovenia 3; Israel 2, Cyprus 0; Malta 1, Cyprus 2; Israel 0, Slovenia 0; France 5, Cyprus 0; Slovenia 3, Israel 1; Israel 2, Malta 2; Slovenia 0, France 2; Cyprus 2, Slovenia 2; France 3, Israel 0.

GROUP 2

	P	W	D	L	F	A	Pts
DENMARK	8	4	3	1	15	9	15
Norway	8	4	2	2	9	5	14
Romania	8	4	2	2	21	9	14
Bosnia-Herzegovina	8	4	1	3	7	8	13
Luxembourg	8	0	0	8	0	21	0

Results: Bosnia-Herzegovina 0, Romania 3; Norway 2, Denmark 2; Denmark 2, Luxembourg 0; Romania 0, Norway 1; Luxembourg 0, Romania 7; Norway 2, Bosnia-Herzegovina 0; Romania 2, Denmark 5; Bosnia-Herzegovina 2, Luxembourg 0; Denmark 0, Bosnia-Herzegovina 2; Luxembourg 0, Norway 2; Denmark 1, Norway; Romania 2, Bosnia-Herzegovina 0; Luxembourg 0, Denmark 2; Norway 1, Romania 1; Bosnia-Herzegovina 1, Norway 0; Romania 4, Luxembourg 0; Luxembourg 0, Bosnia-Herzegovina 1; Denmark 2, Romania 2; Norway 1, Luxembourg 0; Bosnia-Herzegovina 1, Denmark 1.

GROUP 3

	P	W	D	L	F	A	Pts
CZECH REPUBLIC	8	7	1	0	23	5	22
HOLLAND	8	6	1	1	20	6	19
Austria	8	3	0	5	12	14	9
Moldova	8	2	0	6	5	19	6
Belarus	8	1	0	7	4	20	3

Results: Austria 2, Moldova 0; Holland 3, Belarus 0; Belarus 0, Austria 2; Moldova 0, Czech Republic 2; Austria 0, Holland 3; Czech Republic 2, Belarus 0; Belarus 2, Moldova 1; Holland 1, Czech Republic 1; Czech Republic 4, Austria 0; Moldova 1, Holland 2; Moldova 1, Austria 0; Belarus 0, Holland 2; Czech Republic 5, Moldova 0; Austria 5, Belarus 0; Holland 3, Austria 1; Belarus 1, Czech Republic 3; Czech Republic 3, Holland 1; Moldova 2, Belarus 1; Austria 2, Czech Republic 3; Holland 5, Moldova 0.

GROUP 4

	P	W	D	L	F	A	Pts
SWEDEN	8	5	2	1	19	3	17
LATVIA	8	5	1	2	10	6	16
Poland	8	4	1	3	11	7	13
Hungary	8	3	2	3	15	9	11
San Marino	8	0	0	8	0	30	0

Results: Latvia 0, Sweden 0; San Marino 0, Poland 2; Poland 0, Latvia 1; Sweden 1, Hungary 1; Hungary 3, San Marino 0; San Marino 0, Latvia 1; Poland 0, Hungary 0; Poland 5, San Marino 0; Hungary 1, Sweden 2; Latvia 3, San Marino 0; San Marino 0, Sweden 6; Hungary 1, Latvia 1; San Marino 0, Hungary 5; Sweden 3, Poland 0; Latvia 0, Poland 2; Sweden 5, San Marino 0; Poland 0, Sweden 2; Latvia 3, Hungary 1; Sweden 0, Latvia 1; Hungary 1, Poland 2.

GROUP 5

	P	W	D	L	F	A	Pts
GERMANY	8	5	3	0	13	4	18
Scotland	8	4	2	2	12	8	14
Iceland	8	4	1	3	11	9	13
Lithuania	8	3	1	4	7	11	10
Faroe Islands	8	0	1	7	7	18	1

Results: Faroe Islands 2, **Scotland** 2; Lithuania 0, Germany 2; Iceland 0, **Scotland** 2; Lithuania 2, Faroe Islands 0; Germany 2, Faroe Islands 1; Iceland 3, Lithuania 0; **Scotland** 2, Iceland 1; Germany 1, Lithuania 1; Lithuania 1, **Scotland** 0; **Scotland** 1, Germany 1; Iceland 2, Faroe Islands 1; Faroe Islands 0, Germany 2; Lithuania 0, Iceland 1; **Scotland** 3, Faroe Islands 1; Iceland 0, Germany 0; Germany 2, **Scotland** 1; Faroe Islands 1, Lithuania 3; **Scotland** 1, Lithuania 0; Germany 3, Iceland 0.

GROUP 6

	P	W	D	L	F	A	Pts
GREECE	8	6	0	2	8	4	18
SPAIN	8	5	2	1	16	4	17
Ukraine	8	2	4	2	11	10	10
Armenia	8	2	1	5	7	16	7
Northern Ireland	8	0	3	5	0	8	3

Results: Armenia 2, Ukraine 2; Greece 0, Spain 2; Spain 3, **Northern Ireland** 0; Ukraine 2, Greece 0; Greece 2, Armenia 0; **Northern Ireland** 0, Ukraine 0; Armenia 1, **Northern Ireland** 0; Ukraine 2, Spain 2; **Northern Ireland** 0, Greece 2; Spain 3, Armenia 0; Ukraine 4, Armenia 3; Spain 0, Greece 1; **Northern Ireland** 0, Spain 0; Greece 1, Ukraine 0; Armenia 0, Greece 1; Ukraine 0, **Northern Ireland** 0; **Northern Ireland** 0, Armenia 1; Spain 2, Ukraine 1; Greece 1, **Northern Ireland** 0; Armenia 0, Spain 4.

GROUP 7

	P	W	D	L	F	A	Pts
ENGLAND	8	6	2	0	14	5	20
Turkey	8	6	1	1	17	5	19
Slovakia	8	3	1	4	11	9	10
Macedonia	8	1	3	4	11	14	6
Liechtenstein	8	0	1	7	2	22	1

Results: Turkey 3, Slovakia 0; Liechtenstein 1, Macedonia 1; Macedonia 1, Turkey 2; Slovakia 1, **England** 2; **England** 2, Macedonia 2; Turkey 5, Liechtenstein 0; Liechtenstein 0, **England** 2; Macedonia 0, Slovakia 2; Slovakia 4, Liechtenstein 0; **England** 2, Turkey 0; Macedonia 3, Liechtenstein 1; Slovakia 0, Turkey 1; **England** 2, Slovakia 1; Turkey 3, Macedonia 0; Liechtenstein 0, Turkey 3; Macedonia 1, **England** 2; **England** 2, Liechtenstein 0; Slovakia 1, Macedonia 1; Turkey 0, **England** 0; Liechtenstein 0, Slovakia 2.

GROUP 8

	P	W	D	L	F	A	Pts
BULGARIA	8	5	2	1	13	4	17
CROATIA	8	5	1	2	12	4	16
Belgium	8	5	1	2	11	9	16
Estonia	8	2	2	4	4	6	8
Andorra	8	0	0	8	1	18	0

Results: Belgium 0, Bulgaria 2; Croatia 0, Estonia 0; Andorra 0, Belgium 1; Bulgaria 2, Croatia 0; Bulgaria 2, Andorra 1; Estonia 0, Belgium 1; Croatia 4, Belgium 0; Estonia 0, Bulgaria 0; Croatia 2, Andorra 0; Andorra 0, Estonia 2; Estonia 2, Andorra 0; Bulgaria 2, Belgium 2; Estonia 0, Croatia 1; Belgium 3, Andorra 0; Bulgaria 2, Estonia 0; Andorra 0, Croatia 3; Belgium 2, Croatia 1; Andorra 0, Bulgaria 3; Croatia 1, Bulgaria 0; Belgium 2, Estonia 0.

GROUP 9

	P	W	D	L	F	A	Pts
ITALY	8	5	2	1	17	4	17
Wales	8	4	1	3	13	10	13
Serbia	8	3	3	2	11	11	12
Finland	8	3	1	4	9	10	10
Azerbaijan	8	1	1	6	5	20	4

Results: Azerbaijan 0, Italy 2; Finland 0, **Wales** 2; Finland 3, Azerbaijan 0; Italy 1, Serbia-Montenegro 1; **Wales** 2, Italy 1; Serbia-Montenegro 2, Finland 0; Azerbaijan 0, **Wales** 2; Serbia-Montenegro 2, Azerbaijan 2; **Wales** 4, Azerbaijan 0; Italy 2, Finland 1; Finland 3, Serbia-Montenegro 0; Azerbaijan 2, Serbia-Montenegro 1; Finland 1, Italy 2; Serbia-Montenegro 1, **Wales** 0; Italy 4, **Wales** 0; Azerbaijan 1, Finland 2; **Wales** 1, Finland 1; Serbia-Montenegro 1, Italy 1; Italy 4, Azerbaijan 0; **Wales** 2, Serbia-Montenegro 3.

GROUP 10

	P	W	D	L	F	A	Pts
SWITZERLAND	8	4	3	1	15	11	15
RUSSIA	8	4	2	2	19	12	14
Republic of Ireland	8	3	2	3	10	11	11
Albania	8	2	2	4	11	15	8
Georgia	8	2	1	5	8	14	7

Results: Russia 4, **Republic of Ireland** 2; Switzerland 4, Georgia 1; Albania 1, Switzerland 1; **Republic of Ireland** 1, Switzerland 2; Russia 4, Albania 1; Albania 3, Russia 1; Georgia 1, **Republic of Ireland** 2; Albania 0, **Republic of Ireland** 0; Georgia 0, Switzerland 0; Georgia 1, Russia 0; **Republic of Ireland** 2, Albania 1; Switzerland 2, Russia 2; **Republic of Ireland** 2, Georgia 0; Switzerland 3, Albania 3; **Republic of Ireland** 1, Russia 1; Georgia 3, Albania 0; Russia 4, Switzerland 1; Albania 3, Georgia 1; Russia 3, Georgia 1; Switzerland 2, **Republic of Ireland** 0.

PLAY-OFFS

First legs: Croatia 1, Slovenia 1; Latvia 1, Turkey 0; **Scotland** 1, Holland 0; Spain 2, Norway 1; Russia 0, **Wales** 0.

Second legs: Holland 6, **Scotland** 0 (Holland won 6-1 on agg); Norway 0, Spain 3 (Spain won 5-1 on agg); Slovenia 0, Croatia 1 (Croatia won 2-1 on agg); Turkey 2, Latvia 2 (Latvia won 3-2 on agg); **Wales** 0, Russia 1 (Russia won 1-0 on agg).

EUROPEAN CHAMPIONSHIP FINALS – 2004

GROUP A

Saturday, June 12 (Oporto – Dragao, 48,761)

PORTUGAL 1, GREECE 2

Portugal (4-2-3-1): Ricardo, Paulo Ferreira, Fernando Couto, Jorge Andrade, Rui Jorge, Costinha (Nuno Gomes 66), Maniche, Figo, Rui Costa (Deco 46), Simao (Ronaldo 46), Pauleta. **Scorer:** Ronaldo (90). **Booked:** Costinha, Pauleta.

Greece (4-2-3-1): Nikopolidis, Seitaridis, Dellas, Kapsis, Fyssas, Giannakopoulos (Nikolaidis 68), Zagorakis, Basinas, Karagounis (Katsouranis 46), Vryzas, Charisteas (Lakis 74). **Scorers:** Karagounis (7), Basinas (51 pen). **Booked:** Karagounis, Seitaridis.

Referee: P. Collina (Italy). **Half-time:** 0-1.

Saturday, June 12 (Faro Loule, 28,182)

SPAIN 1, RUSSIA 0

Spain (4-1-3-2): Iker Casillas, Puyol, Helguera, Marchena, Raul Bravo, Albelda, Etxeberria, Baraja (Xabi Alonso 59), Vicente, Raul (Fernando Torres 78), Morientes (Valeron 59). **Scorer:** Valeron (60). **Booked:** Baraja, Marchena, Albelda.

Russia (4-3-2-1): Ovchinnikov, Evseev, Smertin, Sharonov, Sennikov, Alenichev, Aldonin (Sychev 68), Mostovoi, Gusev (Radimov 46), Izmailov (Kariaka 74), Bulykin.

Booked: Gusev, Sharonov, Smertin, Aldonin, Radmov. **Sent-off:** Sharonov (88).

Referee: U. Meier (Switzerland). **Half-time:** 0-0.

Wednesday, June 16 (Oporto – Bessa, 25,444)

GREECE 1, SPAIN 1

Greece (4-2-3-1): Nikopolidis, Kapsis, Dellas, Katsouranis, Seitaridis, Zagorakis, Karagounis (Tsiartas 53), Fyssas (Venetidis 86), Giannakopoulos (Nikolaidis 49), Charisteas, Vryzas. **Scorer:** Charisteas (66). **Booked:** Katsouranis, Giannakopoulos, Karagounis, Zagorakis, Vryzas.

Spain (4-4-2): Iker Casillas, Puyol, Helguera, Marchena, Raul Bravo, Etxeberria (Joaquin 46), Albelda, Baraja, Vicente, Morientes (Valeron 65), Raul (Fernando Torres 80). **Scorer:** Morientes (28). **Booked:** Marchena, Helguera.

Referee: L. Michel (Slovakia). **Half-time:** 0-1.

Wednesday, June 16 (Lisbon – Luz, 59,273)

RUSSIA 0, PORTUGAL 2

Russia (4-1-3-2): Ovchinnikov, Evseev, Smertin, Bugayev, Sennikov, Aldonin (Malafeev 45), Alenichev, Loskov, Kariaka (Bulykin 79), Kerzhakov, Izmailov (Bystrov 72). **Booked:** Smertin, Evseev, Alenichev. **Sent-off:** Ovchinnikov (45).

Portugal (4-1-4-1): Ricardo, Miguel, Jorge Andrade, Ricardo Carvalho, Nuno Valente, Costinha, Figo (Ronaldo 78), Maniche, Deco, Simao (Rui Costa 63), Pauleta (Nuno Gomes 57). **Scorers:** Maniche (7), Rui Costa (89). **Booked:** Ricardo Carvalho, Deco.

Referee: T. Hauge (Norway). **Half-time:** 0-1.

Sunday, June 20 (Lisbon – Alvalade, 47,491)

SPAIN 0, PORTUGAL 1

Spain (4-2-3-1): Iker Casillas, Puyol, Juanito (Morientes 80), Helguera, Raul Bravo, Xabi Alonso, Albelda (Baraja 66), Joaquin (Luque 72), Raul, Vicente, Fernando Torres. **Booked:** Albelda, Juanito, Puyol.

Portugal (4-1-4-1): Ricardo, Miguel, Jorge Andrade, Ricardo Carvalho, Nuno Valente, Costinha, Figo (Petit 78), Maniche, Deco, Ronaldo (Fernando Couto 84), Pauleta (Nuno Gomes 46). **Scorer:** Nuno Gomes (57). **Booked:** Pauleta, Nuno Gomes.

Referee: A. Frisk (Sweden). **Half-time:** 0-0.

Sunday, June 20 (Faro Loule, 24,347)

RUSSIA 2, GREECE 1

Russia (4-3-1-2): Malafeev, Anuykov, Sharonov (Sennikov 56), Bugaev, Evseev, Gusev, Radimov, Kariaka (Semshov 46), Alenichev, Bulykin (Sychev 46), Kirichenko. **Scorers:** Kirichenko (2), Bulykin (17). **Booked:** Sharonov, Anuykov, Evseev, Kariaka, Alenichev, Radimov, Malafeev.

Greece (4-2-3-1): Nikopolidis, Seitaridis, Kapsis, Dellas, Venetidis (Fyssas 89), Zagorakis, Basinas (Tsiartas 43), Katsouranis, Padadopoulos (Nikolaidis 70), Vryzas, Charisteas. **Scorer:** Vryzas (44). **Booked:** Vryzas, Dellas.

Referee: G. Veissiere (France). **Half-time:** 2-1.

GROUP A TABLE

	P	W	D	L	F	A	Pts
PORTUGAL	3	2	0	1	4	2	6
GREECE	3	1	1	1	4	4	4
Spain	3	1	1	1	2	2	4
Russia	3	1	0	2	2	4	3

GROUP B

Sunday, June 13 (Leiria, 24,090)

SWITZERLAND 0, CROATIA 0

Switzerland (4-3-1-2): Stiel, Haas, M. Yakin, Muller, Spycher, Huggel, Vogel, Wicky (Henchoz 83), H. Yakin (Gygax 87), Frei, Chapuisat (Celestini 54). **Booked:** Vogel, Huggel, Stiel. **Sent-off:** Vogel (50).

Croatia (4-2-3-1): Butina, Simic (Srna 61), R. Kovac, Simunic, Zivkovic, N. Kovac, Bjelica (Rosso 74), Mornar, Prso, Olic (Rapaic 46), Sokota. **Booked:** Prso, Bjelica, Rapaic, Zivkovic, Mornar.

Referee: L. Bastista (Portugal). **Half-time:** 0-0.

Sunday, June 13 (Lisbon – Luz, 62,487)

FRANCE 2, ENGLAND 1

France (4-4-2): Barthez, Gallas, Thuram, Silvestre (Sagnol 79), Lizarazu, Pires (Wiltord 76), Vieira, Makelele, Zidane, Henry, Trezeguet. **Scorer:** Zidane (90, 90 pen). **Booked:** Pires, Silvestre.

England (4-4-2): James (Manchester City), G. Neville (Manchester Utd.), King (Tottenham), Campbell (Arsenal), Cole (Arsenal), Beckham (Real Madrid), Lampard (Chelsea), Gerrard (Liverpool), Scholes (Manchester Utd.) (Hargreaves, Bayern Munich, 76), Owen (Liverpool) (Vassell, Aston Villa, 69), Rooney (Everton) (Heskey, Birmingham City, 76). **Scorer:** Lampard (38). **Booked:** Scholes, Lampard, James.

Referee: M. Merk (Germany). **Half-time:** 0-1.

Thursday, June 17 (Coimbra, 28,214)

ENGLAND 3, SWITZERLAND 0

England (4-4-2): James (Manchester City), G. Neville (Manchester Utd.), Terry (Chelsea), Campbell (Arsenal), Cole (Arsenal), Beckham (Real Madrid), Lampard (Chelsea), Gerrard (Liverpool), Scholes (Manchester Utd.) (Hargreaves, Bayern Munich, 70), Rooney (Everton) (Dyer, Newcastle Utd., 83), Owen (Liverpool) (Vassell, Aston Villa, 72). **Scorers:** Rooney (23, 76), Gerrard (82). **Booked:** Rooney.

Switzerland (4-3-1-2): Stiel, Haas, Muller, M. Yakin, Spycher, Wicky, Celestini (Cabanas 53), Huggel, H.Yakin (Vonlanthen 83), Chapuisat (Gygax 46), Frei. **Booked:** Celestini, Haas. **Sent-off:** Haas (60).

Referee: V. Ivanov (Russia). **Half-time:** 1-0.

Thursday, June 17 (Leiria, 29,160)

CROATIA 2, FRANCE 2

Croatia (4-4-1-1): Butina, Simic, Tudor, R. Kovac, Simunic, Rosso, Bjelica (Leko 68), N. Kovac, Rapaic (Mornar 87), Prso, Sokota (Olic 73). **Scorers:** Rapaic (48 pen), Prso (52). **Booked:** Tudor, Rosso, Leko, R. Kovac.

France (4-4-2): Barthez, Gallas (Sagnol 81), Thuram, Desailly, Silvestre, Wiltord (Pires 70), Vieira, Dacourt (Pedretti 79), Zidane, Trezeguet, Henry. **Scorers:** Tudor (23 og), Trezeguet (64). **Booked:** Vieira, Dacourt.

Referee: K. Milton Nielsen (Denmark). **Half-time:** 0-1.

Monday, June 21 (Lisbon – Luz, 57,047)

CROATIA 2, ENGLAND 4

Croatia (4-4-2): Bulina, Zivkovic, Simic (Srna 67), R. Kovac (Mornar 46), Simunic, Rosso, Tudor, N. Kovac, Rapaic (Olic 55), Prso, Sokota. **Scorers:** N. Kovac (6), Tudor (74). **Booked:** Simic.

England (4-4-2): James (Manchester City), G. Neville (Manchester Utd.), Terry (Chelsea), Campbell (Arsenal), Cole (Arsenal), Beckham (Real Madrid), Lampard (Chelsea) (P. Neville, Manchester Utd., 84), Scholes (Manchester Utd.) (King, Tottenham, 70), Gerrard (Liverpool), Rooney (Everton) (Vassell, Aston Villa, 72), Owen (Liverpool). **Scorers:** Scholes (40), Rooney (45, 68), Lampard (79).

Referee: P. Collina (Italy). **Half-time:** 1-2.

Monday, June 21 (Coimbra, 28,111)

SWITZERLAND 1, FRANCE 3

Switzerland (4-2-3-1): Stiel, Henchoz (Magnin 86), M. Yakin, Muller, Spycher, Vogel, Cabanas, Gygax (Rama 86), H. Yakin (Huggel 60), Wicky, Vonlanthen. **Scorer:** Vonlanthen (26). **Booked:** H. Yakin, Wicky, Huggel.

France (4-4-2): Barthez, Sagnol (Gallas 46) (Boumsong 90), Thuram, Silvestre, Lizarazu, Makelele, Zidane, Vieira, Pires, Trezeguet (Saha 75), Henry. **Scorers:** Zidane (20), Henry (76, 84). **Booked:** Henry.

Referee: L. Michel (Slovakia). **Half-time:** 1-1.

GROUP B TABLE

	P	W	D	L	F	A	Pts
FRANCE	3	2	1	0	7	4	7
ENGLAND	3	2	0	1	8	4	6
Croatia	3	0	2	1	4	6	2
Switzerland	3	0	1	2	1	6	1

GROUP C

Monday, June 14 (Guimaraes, 19,595)

DENMARK 0, ITALY 0

Denmark (4-3-3): Sorensen, Helveg, Laursen, Henriksen, N. Jensen, Poulsen (Priske 76), Tomasson, D. Jensen, Jorgensen (Perez 72), Sand (C. Jensen 69), Rommedahl. **Booked:** Tomasson, Helveg.

Italy (4-2-3-1): Buffon, Panucci, Nesta, Cannavaro, Zambrotta, Zanetti (Gattuso 57), Perrotta, Camoranesi (Fiore 68), Totti, Del Piero (Cassano 64), Vieri. **Booked:** Cannavaro, Cassano, Gattuso, Totti.

Referee: M. Mejuto Gonzalez (Spain). **Half-time:** 0-0.

Monday, June 14 (Lisbon – Alvalade, 31,652)

SWEDEN 5, BULGARIA 0

Sweden (4-4-2): Isaksson, Lucic (Wilhelmsson 41), Jakobsson, Mellberg, Edman, Nilssson, Linderoth, Svensson (Kallstrom 77), Ljungberg, Ibrahimovic (Allback 82), Larsson. **Scorers:** Ljungberg (32), Larsson (57, 58), Ibrahimovic (78 pen), Allback (90). **Booked:** Linderoth, Ibrahimovich.

Bulgaria (4-4-1-1): Zdravkov, Ivanov, Kirilov, Pajin, I. Petkov, Peev, S. Petrov, Hristov, M. Petrov (Lazarov 84), Jankovic (Dimitrov 62), Berbatov (Manchev 77). **Booked:** I. Petkov, Kirilov, Jankovic, Ivanov.

Referee: M. Riley (England). **Half-time:** 1-0.

Friday, June 18 (Braga, 24,131)

BULGARIA 0, DENMARK 2

Bulgaria (4-4-1-1): Zdravkov, Ivanov (Lazarov 51), Kirilov, Stoianov, I. Petkov (Zagorcic 40), Peev, S. Petrov, Hristov, M.Petrov, Jankovic (M. Petkov 81), Berbatov. **Booked:** Kirilov, Stoianov, S. Petrov, Zagorcic, Hristov, M. Petrov. **Sent-off:** S. Petrov (83).

Denmark (4-3-3): Sorensen, Helveg, Laursen, Henriksen, N. Jensen, Gravesen, Tomasson, D. Jensen, Jorgensen (C. Jensen 72), Sand, Rommedahl (Gronkjaer 23). **Scorers:** Tomasson (44), Rommedahl (90). **Booked:** N. Jensen, Sand.

Referee: L. Batista (Portugal). **Half-time:** 0-1.

Friday, June 18 (Oporto – Dragao, 44,926)

ITALY 1, SWEDEN 1

Italy (4-3-1-2): Buffon, Panucci, Nesta, Cannavero, Zambrotta, Gattuso (Favalli 76), Pirlo, Perrotta, Cassano (Fiore 70), Del Piero (Camoranesi 82), Vieri. **Scorer:** Cassano (37). **Booked:** Gattuso, Cannavaro, Zambrotta.

Sweden (4-2-2): Isaksson, Nilsson, Mellberg, Jakobsson, Edman (Allback 76), Wilhelmsson (Jonson 65), Linderoth, Svensson (Kallstrom 55), Ljungberg, Ibrahimovic, Larsson. **Scorer:** Ibrahimovic (85). **Booked:** Edman, Linderoth.

Referee: U. Meier (Switzerland). **Half-time:** 1-0.

Tuesday, June 22 (Guimaraes, 16,002)

ITALY 2, BULGARIA 1

Italy (3-4-3): Buffon, Panucci, Materazzi (Di Vaio 83), Nesta, Perrotta (Oddo 68), Pirlo, Fiore, Zambrotta, Cassano, Corradi (Vieri 53), Del Piero. **Scorers:** Perrotta (48), Cassano (90). **Booked:** Materazzi.

Bulgaria (4-5-1): Zdravkov, Borimirov, Zagorcic, Pazin (Kotev 64), Stoianov, Lazarov, M. Petrov, Jankovic (Bojinov 46), Hristov (Dimitrov 79), M. Petkov, Berbatov. **Scorer:** M. Petrov (45 pen). **Booked:** M. Petrov, Bojinov, Stoianov, Lazarov.

Referee: V. Ivanov (Russia). **Half-time:** 0-1.

Tuesday, June 22 (Oporto – Bessa, 26,115)

DENMARK 2, SWEDEN 2

Denmark (4-2-3-1): Sorensen, Helveg, Laursen, Henriksen, N. Jensen (Bogelund 46), D. Jensen (Poulsen 65), Gravesen, Gronkjaer, Tomasson, Jorgensen (Rommedahl 57), Sand. **Scorer:** Tomasson (28, 66).

Sweden (4-1-3-2): Isaksson, Nilsson, Mellberg, Jakobsson, Edman, Andersson (Allback 81), Jonson, Kallstrom (Wilhelmsson 72), Ljungberg, Ibrahimovic, Larsson. **Scorers:** Larsson (47 pen), Jonson (90). **Booked:** Edman, Kallstrom.

Referee: M. Merk (Germany). **Half-time:** 1-0.

GROUP C TABLE

	P	W	D	L	F	A	Pts
SWEDEN	3	1	2	0	8	3	5
DENMARK	3	1	2	0	4	2	5
Italy	3	1	2	0	3	2	5
Bulgaria	3	0	0	3.	1	9	0

GROUP D

Tuesday, June 15 (Aveiro, 21,744)

CZECH REPUBLIC 2, LATVIA 1

Czech Republic (4-1-3-2): Cech, Grygera (Heinz 56) Ujfalusi, Bolf, Jankulovski, Galasek (Smicer 65), Poborksy, Rosicky, Nedved, Koller, Baros (Jiranek 87). **Scorers:** Baros (73), Heinz (85).

Latvia (4-1-3-2): Kolinko, Isakovs, Zemlinskis, Stepanovs, Blagonadezdins, Lobanovs (Rimkus 90), Bleidelis, Astafjevs, Rubins, Verpakovskis (Pahars 82), Prohorenkovs (Laizans 71). **Scorer:** Verpakovskis (45).

Referee: G. Veissiere (France). **Half-time:** 0-1.

Tuesday, June 15 (Oporto – Dragao, 48,197)

GERMANY 1, HOLLAND 1

Germany (4-4-1-1): Kahn, Friedrich, Worns, Nowotny, Lahm, Schneider (Schweinsteiger 68), Hamann, Baumann, Frings (Ernst 79), Ballack, Kuranyi (Bobic 85). **Scorer:** Frings (30). **Booked:** Kuranyi, Ballack.

Holland (4-4-1-1): Van der Sar, Heitinga (Van Hooijdonk 73), Stam, Bouma, Van Bronckhorst, Van der Meyde, Cocu, Davids (Sneijder 46), Zenden (Overmars 46), Van der Vaart, Van Nistelrooy. **Scorer:** Van Nistelrooy (81). **Booked:** Cocu, Stam.

Referee: A. Frisk (Sweden). **Half-time:** 1-0.

Saturday, June 19 (Oporto – Bessa, 22,344)

LATVIA 0, GERMANY 0

Latvia (4-4-2): Kolinko, Isakovs, Zemlinskis, Stepanovs, Blagonadezdins, Bleidelis, Lobanovs (Laizans 70), Astafjevs, Rubins, Verpakovskis (Zirnis 90), Prohorenkovs (Pahars 67). **Booked:** Isakovs, Astafjevs.

Germany (4-4-2): Kahn, Friedrich, Worns, Baumann, Lahm, Schneider (Schweinsteiger 46), Hamann, Ballack, Frings, Bobic (Klose 67), Kuranyi (Brdaric 76). **Booked:** Friedrich, Hamann, Frings.

Referee: M. Riley (England). **Half-time:** 0-0.

Saturday, June 19 (Aveiro, 29,935)

HOLLAND 2, CZECH REPUBLIC 3

Holland (3-4-3): Van der Sar, Stam, Cocu, Bouma, Heitinga, Seedorf (Van der Vaart 86), Davids, Van Bronckhorst, Van der Meyde (Reiziger 79), Van Nistelrooy, Robben (Bosvelt 59). **Scorers:** Bouma (4), Van Nistelrooy (19). **Booked:** Seedorf, Heitinga. **Sent-off:** Heitinga (75).

Czech Republic (4-1-3-2): Cech, Grygera (Smicer 25), Jiranek, Ujfalusi, Jankulovski, Galasaek (Heinz 62), Poborsky, Rosicky, Nedved, Koller (Rozehnal 75), Baros. **Scorers:** Koller (23), Baros (71), Smicer (88). **Booked:** Galasek

Referee: M. Mejuto Gonzalez (Spain). **Half-time:** 2-1.

Wednesday, June 23 (Lisbon – Alvalade, 46,849)

GERMANY 1, CZECH REPUBLIC 2

Germany (3-3-3-1): Kahn, Friedrich, Nowotny, Worns, Frings (Podolski 46), Hamann (Klose 79), Lahm, Schneider, Ballack, Schweinsteiger (Jeremies 86), Kuranyi. **Scorer:** Ballack (21). **Booked:** Nowotny, Lahm, Worns.

Czech Republic (4-1-3-2): Blazek, Jiranek, Bolf, Rozehnal, Mares, Galasek (Hubschman 46), Plasil (Poborsky 70), Tyce, Vachousek, Heinz, Lokvenc (Baros 59). **Scorers:** Heinz (30), Baros (77). **Booked:** Tyce.

Referee: T. Hauge (Norway). **Half-time:** 1-1.

Wednesday, June 23 (Braga, 27,904)

HOLLAND 3, LATVIA 0

Holland (4-1-2-3): Van der Sar, Reiziger, Stam, De Boer, Van Bronckhorst, Cocu, Seedorf, Davids (Sneijder 77), Van der Meyde (Overmars 63), Van Nistelrooy (Makaay 70), Robben. **Scorers:** Van Nistelrooy (27 pen, 35), Makaay (84).

Lartvia (4-4-2): Kolinko, Isakovs, Zemlinkis, Stepanovs, Blagonadezdins, Bleidelis (Stolcers 83), Lobanovs, Astafjevs, Rubins, Prohorenkovs (Laizans 74), Verpakovskis (Pahars 62). **Booked:** Lobanovs.

Referee: K. Milton Nielsen (Denmark). **Half-time:** 2-0.

GROUP D TABLE

	P	W	D	L	F	A	Pts
CZECH REPUBLIC	3	3	0	0	7	4	9
HOLLAND	3	1	1	1	6	4	4
Germany	3	0	2	1	2	3	2
Latvia	3	0	1	2	1	5	1

QUARTER-FINALS

Thursday, June 24 (Lisbon – Luz, 62,564)

PORTUGAL 2, ENGLAND 2 (aet, Portugal won 6-5 on pens)

Portugal (4-1-4-1): Ricardo, Miguel (Rui Costa 79), Jorge Andrade, Ricardo Carvalho, Nuno Valente, Costinha (Simao 63), Ronaldo, Maniche, Deco, Figo (Postiga 75), Nuno Gomes.
Scorers: Postiga (82), Rui Costa (110). **Booked:** Costinha, Deco, Ricardo Carvalho.

England (4-4-2): James (Manchester City), G. Neville (Manchester Utd.), Terry (Chelsea), Campbell (Arsenal), Cole (Arsenal), Beckham (Real Madrid), Lampard (Chelsea), Gerrard (Liverpool) (Hargreaves, Bayern Munich, 82), Scholes (Manchester Utd.) (P. Neville, Manchester Utd., 56), Owen (Liverpool), Rooney (Everton) (Vassell, Aston Villa, 27). **Scorers:** Owen (3), Lampard (115). **Booked:** Gerrard, G. Neville, P. Neville.

Penalty shoot-out: Beckham (missed), Deco (1-0), Owen (1-1), Simao (2-1), Lampard (2-2), Rui Costa (missed), Terry (2-3), Ronaldo (3-3), Hargreaves (3-4), Maniche (4-4), Cole (4-5), Postiga (5-5), Vassell (saved), Ricardo (6-5).

Referee: U. Meier (Switzerland). **Half-time:** 0-1.

Friday, June 25 (Lisbon – Alvalade, 45,390)

FRANCE 0, GREECE 1

France (4-4-2): Barthez, Gallas, Thuram, Silvestre, Lizarazu, Zidane, Makelele, Dacourt (Wiltord 70), Pires (Rothen 79), Trezeguet (Saha 70), Henry. **Booked:** Zidane, Saha.

Greece (4-2-3-1): Nikopolidis, Seitaridis, Kapsis, Dellas, Fyssas, Zagorakis, Basinas (Tsiartis 85), Karagounis, Katsouranis, Nikolaidis (Laksis 60), Charisteas. **Scorer:** Charisteas (65). **Booked:** Karagounis, Zagorakis.

Referee: A. Frisk (Sweden). **Half-time:** 0-0.

Saturday, June 26 (Faro Loule, 27,762)

SWEDEN 0, HOLLAND 0 (aet, Holland won 5-4 on pens)

Sweden (4-1-2-1-2): Isaksson, Ostlund, Mellberg, Jakobsson, Nilsson, Linderoth, Jonson (Wilhelmsson 65), Ljungberg, Svensson (Kallstrom 81), Ibrahimovic, Larsson. **Booked:** Ibrahimovic, Ostlund.

Holland (4-3-3): Van der Sar, Reiziger, Stam, De Boer (Bouma 36), Van Bronckhorst, Davids (Heitinga 62), Seedorf, Cocu, Van der Meyde (Makaay 87), Van Nistelrooy, Robben. **Booked:** De Boer, Van der Meyde, Makaay.

Penalty shoot-out: Kallstrom (1-0), Van Nistelrooy (1-1), Larsson (2-1), Heitinga (2-2), Ibrahimovic (missed), Reiziger (2-3), Ljungberg (3-3), Cocu (hit post), Wilhelmsson (4-3), Makaay (4-4), Mellberg (saved), Robben (4-5).

Referee: L. Michel (Slovakia). **Half-time:** 0-0.

Sunday, June 27 (Oporto – Dragao, 41,092)

CZECH REPUBLIC 3, DENMARK 0

Czech Republic (4-1-3-2): Cech, Jiranek (Grygera 39), Ujfalusi, Bolf (Rozehnal 65), Jankulovski, Galasek, Poborksy, Rosieky, Nedved, Koller, Baros (Heinz 71). **Scorers:** Koller (49), Baros (46, 65). **Booked:** Jankulovski, Ujfalusi, Nedved.

Denmark (4-3-3): Sorensen, Helveg, Laursen, Henriksen, Bogelund, Poulsen, C. Jensen (Madsen 71), Gravesen, Gronkjaer (Rommedahl 77), Tomasson, Jorgensen (Lovenkrands 85). **Booked:** Poulsen, Bogelund, Gravesen.

Referee: V. Ivanov (Russia). **Half-time:** 0-0.

SEMI-FINALS

Wednesday, June 30 (Lisbon – Alvalade, 46,679)

PORTUGAL 2, HOLLAND 1

Portugal (4-2-3-1): Ricardo, Miguel, Ricardo Carvalho, Jorge Andrade, Nuno Valente, Maniche (Fernando Couto 87), Costinha, Ronaldo (Petit 67), Deco, Figo, Pauleta (Nuno Gomes 75). **Scorers:** Ronaldo (26), Maniche (58). **Booked:** Ronaldo, Nuno Valente, Figo.

Holland (4-1-4-1): Van der Sar, Reiziger, Stam, Bouma (Van der Vaart 55), Van Bronckhorst, Cocu, Overmars (Makaay 46), Seedorf, Davids, Robben (Van Hooijdonk 81), Van Nistelrooy. **Scorer:** Jorge Andrade (63 og). **Booked:** Overmars, Robben.

Referee: A. Frisk (Sweden). **Half-time:** 1-0.

14

Thursday, July 1 (Oporto – Dragao, 42,449)

GREECE 1, CZECH REPUBLIC O (silver goal)

Greece (4-2-3-1): Nikopolidis, Seitaridis, Kapsis, Dellas, Fyssas, Zagorakis, Katsouranis, Basinas (Giannakopoulos 72), Vrygas (Tsiartas 90), Karagounis, Charisteas.
Scorer: Dellas (105). **Booked:** Seitaridis, Charisteas, Karagounis.

Czech Republic (4-1-3-2): Cech, Grygera, Ujfalusi, Bolf, Jankulovski, Galasek, Poborsky, Rosicky, Nedved (Smicer 40), Baros, Koller. **Booked:** Galasek, Smicer, Baros.

Referee: P. Collina (Italy). **Half-time:** 0-0.

FINAL

Sunday, July 4 (Lisbon – Luz, 62,865)

PORTUGAL O, GREECE 1

Portugal (4-2-3-1): Ricardo, Miguel (Paulo Ferreira 43), Jorge Andrade, Ricardo Carvalho, Nuno Valente, Manice, Costinha (Rui Costa 61), Ronaldo, Deco, Figo (capt), Pauleta (Nuno Gomes 74). **Booked:** Costinha, Nuno Valente. **Coach:** Luiz Felipe Scolari.

Greece (4-2-3-1): Nikopolidis, Seitaridis, Kapsis, Dellas, Fyssas, Katsouranis, Zagorakis (capt), Basinas, Giannakopoulos (Venetidis 76), Charisteas, Vryzas (Papadopoulos 81).
Scorer: Charisteas (57). **Booked:** Basinas, Seitaridis, Fyssas, Papadopoulos. **Coach:** Otto Rehhagel.

Referee: M. Merk (Germany). **Half-time:** 0-0. **Man-of-the-match:** Theo Zagorakis.

PREVIOUS FINALS

1960	*USSR	2	Yugoslavia	1	(Paris)
1964	Spain	2	USSR	1	(Madrid)
1968	***Italy	2	Yugoslavia	0	(Rome)
1972	West Germany	3	USSR	0	(Brussels)
1976	**Czechoslovakia	2	West Germany	2	(Belgrade)
1980	West Germany	2	Belgium	1	(Rome)
1984	France	2	Spain	0	(Paris)
1988	Holland	2	USSR	0	(Munich)
1992	Denmark	2	Germany	0	(Gothenburg)
1996	+Germany	2	Czech Republic	1	(Wembley)
2000	+France	2	Italy	1	(Rotterdam)

(***Replay after 1-1; **Czechoslovakia won 5-3 on pens; *After extra-time; +Golden goal winner)

Austria and Switzerland will be joint hosts for the 2008 Finals.

HENRY A DOUBLE RUNNER-UP

Arsenal's Thierry Henry was runner-up for both World and European Player of the Year awards. **World:** 1 Zidane (Real Madrid), 264 pts, 2 Henry 186, 3 Ronaldo (Real Madrid), 176, 4 Nedved (Juventus) 158, 5 Roberto Carlos (Real Madrid) 105, 6 Van Nistelrooy (Manchester Utd.) 86, 7 Beckham (Real Madrid) 74, 8 Raul (Real Madrid) 39, 9 Maldini (AC Milan) 37, 10 Shevchenko (AC Milan) 26.
   European: 1 Nedved 190, 2 Henry 128, 3 Maldini 123, 4 Shevchenko 67, 5 Zidane 64, 6 Van Nistelrooy 61, 7 Raul 32, 8 Roberto Carlos 27, 9 Buffon (Juventus) 19, 10 Beckham 17.

EURO 2004 FACTS AND FIGURES

- Greece lost their first two matches in the qualifying competition – 2-0 at home to Spain and 2-0 away to the Ukraine. They won the next six, including victories over Northern Ireland, to finish top of their group.

- Before the Finals, Greece were quoted upwards of 100-1 to win, never having won a match in a major Championship. Only Latvia had longer odds.

- Greece captain Theo Zagarakis, 32, was named UEFA's Player of the Tournament. Former Liverpool manager Gerard Houllier, a member of the selection panel, said: 'He was man of the match in the first game and the last. He showed leadership, skill and technique.' Zagorakis, who equalled the Greece record by winning his 95th cap in the Final, helped Leicester City reach the Worthington Cup Final in 2000, appearing in every round up to the Final. He was an unused sub when Leicester beat Tranmere 2-1 at Wembley.

- Three other Greece players from the Final have connections with English clubs. Midfielder Stylianos Giannakopoulos, who likes to be known as Stelios, was a regular for Bolton last season, scoring two goals in the Premiership, against Leeds and Blackburn, and two in the Carling Cup, against Gillingham and Aston Villa. In the Final which Bolton lost 2-1 to Middlesbrough, he went on as a late substitute. Defender Traianos Dellas had two seasons at Sheffield United from 1997, while striker Dimitrios Padadopoulos, came to Burnley in 2001 and stayed for two seasons. Squad member Nikos Dabizas was the first Greek to play in an F.A. Cup Final, for Newcastle in their 2-0 defeat by Arsenal in 1998. Last season he joined Leicester.

- Liverpool's Milan Baros was leading scorer in the Finals with five goals for the Czech Republic. England's Wayne Rooney and Holland's Ruud van Nistelrooy netted four, while Frank Lampard (England), Angelos Charisteas (Greece), Henrik Larsson (Sweden), Jon Dahl Tomasson (Denmark) and Zinedine Zidane (France) each scored three.

- England squad: 1 James (Manchester City), 2 Gary Neville (Manchester Utd.), 3 Ashley Cole (Arsenal), 4 Gerrard (Liverpool), 5 Terry (Chelsea), 6 Campbell (Arsenal), 7 Beckham (Real Madrid, capt), 8 Scholes (Manchester Utd.), 9 Rooney (Everton), 10 Owen (Liverpool), 11 Lampard (Chelsea), 12 Bridge (Chelsea), 13 Robinson (Tottenham), 14 Phil Neville (Manchester Utd.), 15 King (Tottenham), 16 Carragher (Liverpool), 17 Butt (Manchester Utd.), 18 Hargreaves (Bayern Munich), 19 Joe Cole (Chelsea), 20 Dyer (Newcastle Utd.), 21 Heskey (Birmingham City), 22 Walker (Leicester City), 23 Vassell (Aston Villa).

- England's Sven-Goran Eriksson was the only one of five coaches of big-name countries to remain in his job after their teams under-achieved in the Championship. Germany's Rudi Voller, Spain's Inaki Saez and Italy's Giovanni Trapattoni stepped down after failing to progress from the group stage. Jacques Santini had already decided to join Tottenham before France lost to Greece in the quarter-finals.

- England's penalty defeat by Portugal was their fourth in five major shoot-outs since 1990. Under Bobby Robson that year, they lost a World Cup semi-final to Germany in Turin 4-3 after the match finished 1-1, Stuart Pearce and Chris Waddle failing from the spot. In Euro 1996, when Terry Venables was in charge, England beat Spain 4-2 after their quarter-final at Wembley had finished goalless. But in the semi-finals, Gareth Southgate's penalty was saved as Germany won 6-5 at Wembley after the teams were locked on 1-1 after extra-time. Two years later in St Etienne, Glenn Hoddle's team lost 4-3 to Argentina in round two of the World Cup after a 2-2 scoreline, Paul Ince and David Batty having penalties saved. This time, in Lisbon, David Beckham missed and Darius Vassell had his spot-kick saved in a 6-5 defeat by Portugal after a 2-2 scoreline.

- Wayne Rooney was one of four England players named in UEFA's 23-strong, all-star squad. The squad was: **Goalkeepers** – Cech (Czech Republic), Nikopolidis (Greece). **Defenders** – Campbell (England), Ashley Cole (England), Dellas (Greece), Seitaridis (Greece), Mellberg (Sweden), Ricardo Carvalho (Portugal), Zambrotta (Italy). **Midfielders:** Figo (Portugal), Maniche (Portugal), Ballack (Germany), Lampard (England), Nedved (Czech Republic), Zagorakis (Greece), Zidane (France). **Strikers** – Baros (Czech Republic), Charisteas (Greece), Larsson (Sweden), Ronaldo (Portugal), Rooney (England), Tomasson (Denmark), Van Nistelrooy (Holland).

EURO 2004 QUOTE UNQUOTE

'If pushed, I would say maybe Greece. Otto Rehhagel is a cunning coach and has some quality players. They have nothing to lose' – **Arsene Wenger**, Arsenal manager, asked before the tournament who might prove to be the surprise team.

'This is the result of three years' work. It is has united Greeks all over the world, something politics is unable to do' – **Otto Rehhagel**, Greece coach.

'I am the only man in Athens who is allowed to drive in the bus lane. I don't know what will happen now' – **Otto Rehhagel**.

'Greece haven't come from the beach – they've come from nowhere' – **John Motson**, BBC commentator, drawing a parallel with 1992 surprise winners Denmark, who replaced war-torn Yugoslavia in the Finals at short notice.

'I felt I missed a great opportunity, not only for me but for my team-mates who had lived the competition so intensely and our fans' – **Luis Figo**, Portugal captain.

'It always seems to happen to us' – **Michael Owen** after another penalty shoot-out defeat for England, this time against Portugal in the quarter-finals.

'It was a clear foul by (John) Terry and if the situation occurred again I would do the same thing' – **Urs Meier**, Swiss referee, on his controversial decision to disallow Sol Campbell's 89th minute goal.

'I went to see the referee after the game. But I will not tell you what was said' – **Sven-Goran Eriksson**, England coach.

'If there is another penalty I will step up and take it. If I miss that, I will take another one' – **David Beckham**, England captain, after his failure from the spot against France.

'I don't think we've done as much conditioning work at Real Madrid as we used to do at Manchester United.' – **David Beckham** admitting he was not fully fit for the tournament.

'I'm not surprised by his comments. He's always making personal excuses. (Luis) Figo didn't go skiing while the team were still in the Champions League' – **Carlos Queiroz**, former Real Madrid manager now back as Sir Alex Ferguson's assistant at Old Trafford, responding to Beckham's comments.

'Dropping Wayne Rooney will give England the best chance of achieving the victory they need' – **Tony Adams**, former captain, offering advice before the game against Switzerland . . . . . . in which Rooney scored twice.

'I stand by that judgement 100 per cent. I would drop Rooney from the team to play Croatia' – **Tony Adams** before the match in which Rooney scored two more.

'We believe in sports ethics' – **Giovanni Trapattoni**, Italy coach, on the 2-2 group match draw between Denmark and Sweden which sent his team out of the tournament.

'Your suspicions are as ugly as your spitting' – **Lars Lagerback**, Sweden co-manager, on suggestions by Italy that the result was contrived.

SOCCER DIARY 2003-04

JULY 2003

1 Ken Bates sells control of **Chelsea** to Russian billionaire oil magnate **Roman Abramovich** for a reported £120m. **West Ham Utd.** manager Glenn Roeder returns to work ten weeks after collapsing with a brain tumour. FIFA order **Fulham** to pay **Lyon** the final £3.3m. of **Steve Marlet**'s £11.5m. transfer fee. **2 Birmingham City** sign **David Dunn** from **Blackburn Rov.** for a club-record £5.5m. **3 John Terry** signs a new four-year contract with **Chelsea**, but **Gianfranco Zola** turns down the chance to stay at Stamford Bridge to return to his native Sardinia with **Cagliari**. **4 Manchester Utd.** pay £3.5m. for Cameroon midfielder **Eric Djemba-Djemba** from **Nantes**. **8 Sven-Goran Eriksson** is forced to re-affirm his commitment to his job as **England** coach after it is revealed that he had a meeting with the new **Chelsea** owner **Roman Abramovich**. **9 Harry Kewell** leaves Leeds Utd. for Liverpool in an acrimonious £5m. transfer, of which £2m. goes to his agent. **10** Another cut-price departure from Elland Road, with **Olivier Dacourt** confirming a move to **Roma** for £3.5m. The F.A. also accept less than before in a new £300m., four-year TV deal with the BBC and Sky for England's home internationals and F.A. Cup ties. **13 Blackburn Rov.** follow up the £2.5m. signing of **Brett Emerton** from **Feyenoord** by paying **Rangers** £1.4m. for **Lorenzo Amoruso**. **14 Luton Town** go into administrative receivership. **15 Chelsea** launch a summer spending spree by paying **West Ham Utd.** £6m. for **Glen Johnson**. **16 Chelsea** sign midfielder **Geremi** from **Real Madrid** for £6.9m. **19** World Cup winner **Ronaldinho** rejects a move to **Manchester Utd.** and joins **Barcelona** from **Paris St-Germain** for £21m. **21 Chelsea** pay a club-record £17m. for **Damien Duff** from **Blackburn Rov.** and £7m. for **Southampton**'s **Wayne Bridge**, with **Graeme Le Saux** going in the opposite direction as part of that deal. **Manchester City** lose captain **Ali Benarbia**, who announces his retirement, but gain **Trevor Sinclair**, a £2.5m. buy from **West Ham Utd**. **23 Birmingham City** sign Argentine striker **Luciano Figueroa** from **Rosario Central** for £2.5m. **24 Arsenal** end their search for a replacement for **David Seaman** by signing **Jens Lehmann** from **Borussia Dortmund** for £1.5m. **25 Manchester City**'s **Alf-Inge Haaland** retires after a two-year battle against a knee injury. **28 Sammy McIlroy**, the **Northern Ireland** manager, agrees a two-year extension to his contract. **29 Graeme Souness**, the **Blackburn Rov.** manager, is fined £10,000 by the F.A. for improper conduct during a Worthington Cup tie at Wigan Athletic.

AUGUST 2003

1 Manchester Utd. are fined £1.65m. and the F.A. £158,000 by the Office of Fair Trading for 'fixing' the price of replica kits. JJB Sports (£8.37m.) and Umbro (£6.64m.) are among the sports goods firms fined. **Aston Villa** announce pre-tax losses of £11.6m. **4 Tottenham** sign **Freddie Kanoute** from **West Ham Utd.** for £3.5m. **5 Huddersfield Town** are released from administration by the Football League following the take-over by **Ken Davy**, chairman of Huddersfield Rugby League Club. **6 Chelsea** sign Joe Cole from **West Ham Utd.** for £6.6m. **Bradford City** sell Valley Parade to the trustees of a pension fund for £5m. **7 Chelsea** take their summer spending to nearly £60m. by paying **Manchester Utd.** £15m. for **Juan Sebastian Veron**. The Football League introduce an experimental scheme in Division Three to bring salaries under control. **8** The BBC pay £105m. to outbid ITV and restore *Match of the Day* to their Saturday night schedules for three years beginning in 2004-05. Sky pay £1.02bn. to retain live coverage of the Premiership, with an increase from 106 to 138 matches a season. **9** Football mourns **Ray Harford**, one of the country's most respected coaches, who dies of cancer aged 58, and the 21-year-old **Manchester Utd.** player Jimmy Davis, who is killed in a car crash. Davis was on loan at Watford, whose game against Coventry City is postponed. On the opening day of the season there are 3-1 away wins for League newcomers Yeovil Town, against Rochdale, and Doncaster Rov., at Leyton Orient. **10 Francis Jeffers** receives the 50th red card of **Arsene Wenger**'s seven years as **Arsenal** manager in the Community Shield, which

Manchester Utd. win on penalties. **11 Paolo Di Canio** joins **Charlton Athletic** on a free transfer, the 12th **West Ham Utd.** player to find a new club during the summer. **12 Manchester Utd.** make **Sporting Lisbon** winger **Cristiano Ronaldo** the most expensive teenager in British football in a £12.2m. deal, and pay **Paranaense** nearly £6m. for World Cup winner **Kleberson. Arsenal** also enjoy a good day, with **Patrick Vieira** signing a new four-year deal and **Robert Pires** extending his contract until 2006. **14** A £3.2m. fee takes **Kevin Phillips** from **Sunderland** to **Southampton**, the club that rejected him as a teenager. **15 Birmingham City** manager **Steve Bruce** signs a new five-year contract. His club, along with **Aston Aston Villa**, are fined £5,000 by the F.A. for a players' brawl last season. **16 Chelsea** pay £15.8m. for **Romania** striker **Adrian Mutu** from **Parma**, taking their spending spree to £75m. **18** Fears of an upsurge in hooliganism follow Home Office figures showing a 19% increase in football-related offences last season. **19 John O'Shea** scores his first goal for the **Republic of Ireland**, who beat **Australia** 2-1 in a friendly international. **Oldham Athletic** go into administration. **20 Wales** suffer their first Euro 2004 qualifying defeat, losing 1-0 to **Serbia & Montenegro**. **Frank Lampard** scores his first goal for **England** who mark their first-ever match at Ipswich by beating **Serbia & Montenegro** 3-1 in a friendly. **Scotland** draw 0-0 in **Norway**. **21 Darius Vassell** signs a new three-year contract with **Aston Villa**. **24 Glenn Roeder** becomes the first managerial casualty of the season, sacked by **West Ham Utd. 26 Chelsea** sign **Hernan Crespo** from **Inter Milan** for £16.8m and **Alexei Smertin** from **Bordeaux** for £3.45m. They also reach the group stage of the Champions League. **Smertin** joins **Portsmouth** on loan for the season. **27 Newcastle Utd.** lose on penalties to **Partizan Belgrade** and fail to qualify for the group stage of the Champions League. **Celtic** and **Rangers** win their qualifying games. **Neil Warnock**, the **Sheffield Utd.** manager, is given a four-match touchline ban and fined £300 by the F.A. for verbally abusing two referees last season. **29 Blackburn Rov.** pay **Rangers** £7.5m. for **Barry Ferguson. Claudio Reyna** leaves **Sunderland** for **Manchester City** for £2.5m. **Carlisle Utd.** sack manager **Roddy Collins**. **30 Steve McManaman** ends four years at **Real Madrid** by joining **Manchester City** on a free transfer. **31 Chelsea** complete an unprecedented summer spending spree of £111m. by signing **Claude Makelele** from **Real Madrid** for £16.6m.

SEPTEMBER 2003

1 Everton are the busiest club on transfer deadline day, buying **James McFadden** from **Motherwell** for £1.25m, **Kevin Kilbane** from **Sunderland** for £1m. and **Nigel Martyn** from **Leeds Utd.** for £500,000, selling **Mark Pembridge** to **Fulham** for £500,000 and bringing back **Francis Jeffers** to Goodison Park from **Arsenal** on loan. **2** The PFA warn of a possible conflict of interests for Premiership players on long-term loan deals. **3 Manchester Utd.** and **Real Madrid** are fined £13,500 each by UEFA over fans' disturbances at last season's Champions League game at the Bernabeu. **Newcastle Utd.** are fined £2,100 for five bookings against **Partizan Belgrade** in last month's qualifier. The Football League decide to continue to allow domestic transfer between their clubs, despite the closure of the worldwide transfer window. **4 Liverpool's El-Hadji Diouf** is fined £5,000 at Glasgow Sheriff Court for spitting at a **Celtic** fan during a UEFA Cup tie. **Rangers** post an annual loss of nearly £30m. **Millwall** striker **Richard Sadlier** is forced to retire, at 24, with a persistent knee injury. **5** Former **Leeds Utd.** chairman **Peter Ridsdale** takes over **Barnsley. 6 Wayne Rooney**, at 17 years 317 days, becomes the youngest-ever scorer for **England** in a 2-1 win in **Macedonia**, during which they face intense provocation on and off the pitch. The chances of **Wales** qualifying automatically for the Euro 2004 Finals recede in a 4-0 defeat by **Italy**. Other results: **Scotland** 3, **Faroe Islands** 1; **Ukraine** 0, **Northern Ireland** 0; **Republic of Ireland** 1, **Russia** 1. **7** The Football League give **Notts Co.** another three months to resolve financial problems threatening the existence of the club. **8 Chelsea** announce another major signing – **Manchester Utd.** chief executive **Peter Kenyon. 9** An injury-time goal by **Richard Dunne** gives the **Republic of Ireland** a 2-2 friendly international draw with **Turkey. England** lose 2-1 to **Portugal** and fail to qualify for the European U-21 Championship Finals. **10 Sven-Goran Eriksson** surpasses the record of **Alf Ramsey** by supervising an eighth successive **England** victory – 2-0 over **Liechtenstein**. **Northern Ireland** lose 1-0 to **Armenia** and are goalless for a European record 12th successive match. Other Euro 2004 qualifying results: **Germany** 2, **Scotland** 1; **Wales** 1, **Finland** 1. **Reading** manager **Alan Pardew** resigns after being refused permission to talk to **West Ham Utd.** about their vacancy. **11** **Alan Shearer** announces his intention to retire at the end of next season. **13** **Robert Earnshaw** scores four times in a 5-0 win by **Cardiff City** over **Gillingham**. **16** **Manchester Utd.** open their Champions League campaign with a 5-0 win over **Panathinaikos**. **17** **Arsenal** lose 3-0 at to **Inter Milan** in their first game. **18** **Alan Pardew** is cleared to become **West Ham Utd.** manager after **Reading** accept £380,000 compensation and drop an injunction aimed at preventing him taking over at Upton Park. **19** **Wimbledon** receive the go-ahead from the Football League to relocate to Milton Keynes. **Carlton Palmer** is sacked as **Stockport Co.** manager. **20** Goalkeeper **Mart Poom** heads a stoppage-time equaliser for **Sunderland** against his former club **Derby Co.** **21** **Tottenham** sack manager **Glenn Hoddle**. **22** **Crewe Alexandra**'s **Dario Gradi**, longest-serving manager in English football, has surgery to replace a heart valve. **Blackpool** take pride of place in round two of the Carling Cup by beating **Birmingham City** 1-0. **23** Another goalkeeper is on the mark in stoppage time – **Paul Robinson** heading an equaliser for **Leeds Utd.** against **Swindon Town** in the Carling Cup. He then makes two saves in a penalty shoot-out which his team win 4-3. **Michael Owen** overtakes **Ian Rush** as **Liverpool**'s leading scorer in Europe with his 21st goal against **Olimpija Ljubljana** in a UEFA Cup tie. **24** The Football League decide to deduct 10 points from any club falling into administration from next season. **Rangers** manager **Alex McLeish** signs a new four-year contract. **26** **Wolves** benefactor **Sir Jack Hayward** announces his intention to give away the club to any consortium guaranteeing a substantial investment. **27** Two managers are sacked – **Ray Mathias**, of **Tranmere Rov.**, and **Leyton Orient**'s **Paul Brush**. In their first match at Milton Keynes, **Wimbledon** draw 2-2 with **Burnley**. **29** **Northampton Town** dismiss manager **Martin Wilkinson**. An employment tribunal orders **Fulham** to pay former manager **Jean Tigana** £455,000 in unpaid wages. **30** As **Manchester Utd.** announce record annual pre-tax profits of £39m., **Sir Alex Ferguson** agrees a new four-year contract. **Wycome Wand.** sack their manager **Lawrie Sanchez**.

OCTOBER 2003

1 **Newcastle Utd.** inform the Stock Exchange that rumours of **Sir Bobby Robson**'s resignation as manager are unfounded. Manager **Barry Fry** buys **Peterborough Utd.** **2** A U-turn by **Leeds Utd.** means manager **Peter Reid** stays as manager. **4** The worst day ever for sendings-off in English League football with 17 red cards. Sixteen are in the Football League – another record. **6** **Rio Ferdinand** is left out of the **England** squad to play **Turkey** after failing to undergo a routine drugs test. **7** **England** players discuss the possibility of refusing to play the match. **Newcastle Utd.** player **Craig Bellamy** is fined £750 by Cardiff Magistrates for threatening behaviour outside a nightclub. **8** **England** players withdraw their threat of strike action. **Arsenal**'s **Sol Campbell** is fined £20,000 by the F.A. for kicking out at **Eric Djemba Djemba** in the Community Shield match against **Manchester Utd.** **Rufus Brevett**, of **West Ham Utd.**, is fined £1,000 for improper conduct against **Bolton Wand.** **Portsmouth** manager **Harry Redknapp** receives a two-match touchline ban and a fine of £3,000 for verbally abusing referee **Andy D'Urso**. **9** **Steve Coppell** leaves **Brighton & H.A.** to become **Reading** manager. **Tottenham** reserve coach **Colin Calderwood** is named manager of **Northampton Town**. Caretaker **Paul Simpson** is appointed **Carlisle Utd.** manager. **Rangers** defender **Fernando Ricksen** is fined £7,000 at Paisley Sheriff Court for assaulting a neighbour in a row over fireworks. **11** **David Beckham** misses a penalty and is physically and verbally abused by **Turkey** defender **Alpay**, but **England** qualify for the Euro 2004 Finals with a 0-0 draw in Istanbul. **Sven-Goran Eriksson** ends speculation about his immediate future by insisting he will lead them into the championship. **Scotland**, 1-0 winners over **Lithuania**, and **Wales**, beaten 3-2 by **Serbia & Montenegro**, make the play-offs. The **Republic of Ireland** miss out after a 2-0 defeat in **Switzerland**, while **Northern Ireland** end a goalless group campaign with a 1-0 defeat by **Greece**. **13** **Brian Little** is appointed manager of **Tranmere Rov.**, his eighth club. **14** **Sammy McIlroy** resigns as **Northern Ireland** manager to become manager of **Stockport Co.** **15** **Millwall** sack manager **Mark McGhee**. **Blackburn Rov.** lose to **Genclerbirligi**, **Southampton** are beaten by **Steaua Bucharest** and **Dundee** go down to **Perugia** in round one of the UEFA Cup.

16 Crystal Palace midfielder **Michael Hughes** wins compensation from **Birmingham City** for a year-long exile from club football. **18 Bobby Gould** resigns as **Cheltenham Town** manager. **19 Jan Molby** returns to **Kidderminster Harr.** as director of football following the sacking of manager **Ian Britton**. **20 Sir Alex Ferguson** receives a two-match touchline ban and a £10,000 fine from the F.A. for verbally abusing referee **Uriah Rennie** and fourth official **Jeff Winter** during **Manchester Utd.**'s game against **Newcastle Utd. Derby Co.** are sold to a consortium of businessmen. **22 Manchester Utd.** score their 50th Champions League win – a 1-0 success over **Rangers**. **23** Turkey defender **Alpay** has his contract terminated by **Aston Villa** – a legacy of the stormy Euro 2004 qualifier with **England. 24 Philip Don** is ousted as manager of the select group of Premier League referees. His assistant, **Keith Hackett**, takes over. **Reading** manager **Steve Coppell** is banned from the touchline for one match and fined £750 by the F.A. for verbally abusing referee **David Crick** while at **Brighton & H.A. 26 Macclesfield Town** sack manager **David Moss. 27 Tottenham** report a pre-tax loss for the year of £7.1m. **28 Leeds Utd.** announce a record annual loss of £49.5m. **Mark McGhee**, sacked by **Millwall**, becomes **Brighton & H.A.** manager. **Arsenal**'s youngest-ever side win a marathon shoot-out of 22 penalties 9-8 against **Rotherham Utd.** in round three of the Carling Cup. **29** Former **Arsenal** striker **Ian Wright** is racially abused by a spectator after celebrating a goal by his son **Shaun Wright-Phillips** for **Manchester City** at **Q.P.R. 30 Arsenal** are fined £175,000 by the F.A. following a fracas at the end of the goalless draw at Old Trafford. Players punished over incidents are **Lauren** (£40,000 and four-match ban), **Martin Keown** (£20,000 and three matches), **Patrick Vieira** (£20,000 and one match), **Ray Parlour** (£10,000 and one match) and **Ashley Cole** (£10,000). UEFA fine the F.A. £4,400 and the Turkish F.A. £13,300 for a tunnel fracas at the **Turkey-England** European Championship qualifier. **31 David Hodgson** replaces **Mick Tait** and becomes **Darlington** manager for the third time.

NOVEMBER 2003

3 Two more managers are sacked – **Steve Kember** at **Crystal Palace** and **Steve Wignall** at **Southend Utd. 4 Chelsea** deliver one of the best-ever results by a British side in the Champions League by beating **Lazio** 4-0 away from home. **Sunderland** announce pre-tax losses of £20.6m. **5** Former **Arsenal** and **England** stalwart **Tony Adams** is appointed manager of **Wycombe Wand. 6 John Ward**, former **Bristol City**, **Bristol Rov.** and **York City** manager, takes over at **Cheltenham Town. 8 Bradford City** sack manager **Nicky Law. 10 Leeds Utd.** manager **Peter Reid** is dismissed after eight months in the job. **11 Dennis Wise** is appointed **Millwall** manager after a successful spell as caretaker. **Steven Gerrard** signs a new contract keeping him at **Liverpool** until 2007. **12 Lincoln City** manager **Keith Alexander** collapses at home and is rushed to hospital for emergency brain surgery. **13 Leeds Utd.** striker **Alan Smith** is called up to the **England** squad to play **Denmark** – then sent home hours later after the F.A discover he had been arrested over a bottle-throwing incident. **14 England** captain **David Beckham** criticises the F.A. and chief executive **Mark Palios** over their handling of the affair. **15 Scotland** beat **Holland** 1-0 and **Wales** hold **Russia** to a goalless draw in first leg play-off matches for Euro 2004. **16 England** lose 3-2 at home to **Denmark** in a friendly. **17 Southampton**'s **Matt Oakley** is ruled out for the rest of the season by a knee injury. **18** The **Republic of Ireland** beat **Canada** 3-0 in a friendly. **19 Scotland**, thrashed 6-0 by **Holland**, and **Wales**, defeated 1-0 by **Russia**, fail to reach the Euro 2004 Finals. **Alan Smith** learns he will not be prosecuted for the bottle-throwing incident in **Leeds Utd.**'s Carling Cup tie against **Manchester Utd. 21 Jermaine Jenas** signs a new five-year contract with **Newcastle Utd. 24 Bryan Robson**, former **Middlesbrough** manager, is named **Bradford City**'s new boss. **25 Arsenal** give one of their best-ever performances in Europe, beating **Inter Milan** 5-1 away from home in the Champions League. **Dundee** dismiss 25 players and staff after going into administration with debts of around £20m. **Nott'm Forest** sell **Marlon Harewood** to **West Ham Utd.** for £500,000 and sign **Marlon King** from **Gillingham** for £950,000. **26 Manchester Utd.** and **Chelsea** qualify for the second phase of the Champions League. **Rangers** go out. **Mark Hughes** ends speculation about his future by announcing he will continue as **Wales** manager. **27 Liverpool** and **Newcastle Utd.** reach round three of the UEFA Cup, but **Manchester City** and **Hearts** are eliminated. The F.A. appoint **Trevor Brooking** director of football development. **28 Gordon Strachan**, linked with the manager's job at **Leeds Utd.**, says he is staying with **Southampton**. **29** A woman spectator suffers serious facial injuries when hit by a stray firework before the **Wolves-Newcastle Utd.** match. FIFA president **Sepp Blatter** criticises the F.A. and **Manchester Utd.** for allowing **Rio Ferdinand** to continue playing after being charged with failing to take a drugs test. **30 Partick Thistle** dismiss manager **Gerry Collins**.

DECEMBER 2003

1 On the day that **Manchester Utd.** launch a new £36m., four-year sponsorship deal with Vodafone, **Ryan Giggs** is fined £7,500 and **Cristiano Ronaldo** £4,000 by the F.A. for improper conduct during the fracas at the end of the match with **Arsenal**. The F.A. bring in former Olympic champion **Sebastian Coe** to advise on drug-testing procedures. **2 Joe Cole** is belatedly fined £15,000 and banned for two games by the F.A. for improper conduct during a fracas at **Bolton Wand.** last season when the **Chelsea** player was still with **West Ham Utd. 3 Notts Co.**, in administration for 18 months, are saved from expulsion from the Football League by an approved takeover by the Blenheim Consortium. Holders **Liverpool** lose to **Bolton Wand.** and beaten finalists **Manchester Utd.** are knocked out by **W.B.A.** in round four of the Carling Cup. **Wigan Athletic** manager **Paul Jewell** receives a two-match touchline ban and a £1,000 fine from the F.A. after being sent from the dug-out at **Reading**. **4** The **Manchester Utd.** manager **Sir Alex Ferguson** has hospital treatment to correct a minor heart problem. **5** **Aston Villa** terminate the contract of Croatian striker **Bosko Balaban**, who was signed for £5.8m. in August 2001 but did not start a Premiership game. **8 Sam Allardyce** and his **Bolton Wand.** captain **Jay-Jay Okocha** strike a blow for the lower reaches of the Premiership by winning the Barclaycard Manager and Player of the Month awards for November. **9 Rangers** finish bottom of their Champions League group and miss out on a UEFA Cup place. **10 Arsenal** complete their recovery from a dreadful start to their group by beating **Lokomotiv Moscow** to finish top. **Celtic** lose to disputed late penalty by **Lyon** and fail to qualify. **Newcastle Utd.** announce a £25m., five-year extension to their kit deal with Adidas. **Fulham's Luis Boa Morte** is fined £4,000 and banned for one match by the F.A. for stamping on the midriff of **Leicester City's Frank Sinclair**. **11 Tottenham** announce that **David Pleat** will continue as caretaker-manager until the end of the season. **Coventry City** manager **Gary McAllister** asks to be relieved of his duties because of his wife's illness. **12 Celtic** supporters win FIFA's annual Fair Play award for their conduct at the UEFA Cup Final against **FC Porto** in Seville. **Wimbledon** receive planning permission for a new 30,000-capacity stadium on the outskirts of Milton Keynes. **Barnsley** come out of administration. **13** A record total of 19 players are sent off – two in the Premiership and 17 in the Football League. **15 Arsenal's Thierry Henry** is runner-up to **Real Madrid's Zinedine Zidane** for the FIFA World Player of the Year award. **16** Sky lose their monopoly of live Premiership coverage by order of the European Commission. **Fulham** receive local council permission for a £5m. scheme to bring Craven Cottage up to Premiership standard for next season. Caretaker **John Askey** is appointed **Macclesfield Town** manager. **Bury** dismiss player-manager **Andy Preece**. **18 Geoff Horsfield** makes his second £1m. move in less than four months, joining **W.B.A.** from **Wigan Athletic**. **19 Manchester Utd.'s Rio Ferdinand** is banned for eight months and fined £50,000 by the F.A. for failing to take a drugs test. **Wolves** benefactor **Sir Jack Hayward** hands over control to his son Rick and writes off £40m. in loans to the club. **20 Iain Dowie** resigns as **Oldham Athletic** manager to take over at **Crystal Palace**. **22 Thierry Henry** is runner-up to **Pavel Nedved** (**Juventus**) as European Footballer of the Year. Caretaker **Martin Ling** is appointed **Leyton Orient** manager. **23 Cambridge Utd.** are saved from the threat of going under by supporters raising £100,000 to help pay off debts. **Plymouth Argyle** manager **Paul Sturrock** signs a new contract stretching to 2008. **24 Darlington** go into administration. **29** Businessman **Eddie Davies** takes over **Bolton Wand.** **30 Port Vale** are saved from administration by a £150,000 investment by supporters. **Alan Buckley**, manager of **Rochdale** for six months, is sacked. **31 Steve Parkin**, who resigned two years previously to join **Barnsley**, returns as **Rochdale** manager.

JANUARY 2004

1 Celtic manager **Martin O'Neill** receives an OBE in the New Year's Honours' List. **3** Celtic score a record 18th successive League win by beating **Rangers** 3-0. **5 Fulham** reject an offer of £8m. from **Manchester Utd.** for **Louis Saha. 6 Alan Smith** is banned for two games by the F.A. for throwing a plastic bottle back into the crowd during **Leeds Utd.**'s Carling Cup tie against **Manchester Utd. 7 Notts Co.** manager **Billy Dearden** resigns. **8** Caretaker **Graham Barrow** is appointed **Bury** manager until the end of the season. **9** Manager **Gordon Strachan** says he will leave **Southampton** at the end of the season. The red card **El-Hadji Diouf** received in **Liverpool**'s match at **Chelsea** is rescinded. **Coventry City** coach **Gary Mills** is appointed **Notts Co.** manager. **12** A month after asking to be relieved of his duties to look after his sick wife, **Gary McAllister** resigns as **Coventry City** manager. Senior **England** players **Gary Neville** and **David James** meet the F.A. to heal a rift over the **Rio Ferdinand** and **Alan Smith** selection affairs. **Manchester Utd.** sign Chinese striker **Dong Fangzhou** (18) from **Dalian Stride** for a fee rising to £3.5m. **13** Former **Arsenal** and **England** stalwart **David Seaman** announces his retirement at 40. **George Reynolds**, who built a new £25m. stadium for the club, steps down as **Darlington** chairman. **Wigan Athletic** pay a club-record £1.4m for **Jason Roberts** from **W.B.A. 14 Manchester City** replace **David Seaman** with **England** goalkeeper **David James**, signed from **West Ham Utd.** for £2m. **Birmingham City**'s **Christophe Dugarry** is banned for three matches by the F.A.for elbowing **Craig Short** in the match against **Blackburn Rov.** – an offence which went unpunished at the time. **15 Coventry City** appoint caretaker **Eric Black** as manager. **16 Rio Ferdinand** appeals against his eight-month ban for missing a drugs test. **17** Division One matches produce 54 goals – including **Ipswich Town** 6 **Crewe Alexandra** 4 – the highest total since reorganisation. **19** Manager **Ray Graydon** leaves **Bristol Rov.** by mutual consent. **20 Steve McMahon** changes his mind about resigning and stays as **Blackpool** manager. **21** Four months after being sacked by **Wycombe Wand.**, **Lawrie Sanchez** is appointed manager of **Northern Ireland. 22** The Scottish Premier League decide that clubs going into administration after this season will have 10 points deducted and be banned from signing new players. **Wolves** sign **Carl Cort** from **Newcastle Utd.** for £2m. **23 Manchester Utd.** sign **Louis Saha** from **Fulham** for £12.8m. **25 Frank de Boer** joins twin brother **Ronald** at **Rangers** on a free transfer from **Galatasaray. 26 Manchester Utd.** announce an internal investigation into transfer deals which had been questioned by the club's biggest shareholders, **John Magnier** and **J. P. McManus. 27 Bolton Wand.** reach the final of the Carling Cup with a 5-4 aggregate win over **Aston Villa. 28 Arsenal** sign 20-year-old forward **Jose Reyes** from Seville for a club-record fee rising eventually to £17.4m. **Manchester Utd.** manager **Sir Alex Ferguson** signs a new one-year rolling contract. **29** Premiership chairmen vote for a two-week winter break and for a nine-point penalty for clubs going into administration. **Leeds Utd.** are saved from administration by players agreeing to a wage deferral until the end of the season. **Ruud van Nistelrooy** signs a new four-and-a-half-year contract with **Manchester Utd. Aston Villa** pay **Newcastle Utd.** £1.5m. for **Nolberto Solano. 30 Chelsea** sign **Scott Parker** from **Charlton Athletic** for £10m. Two Premiership players – **Celestine Babayro (Chelsea)** and **Yakubu Ayegbeni (Portsmouth)** are sent home from **Nigeria**'s African Nations Cup team in Tunisia for disciplinary reasons.

FEBRUARY 2004

1 Bob Stokoe, who led **Sunderland** to their FA Cup Final win over **Leeds Utd.** in 1973, dies aged 73. Former **Scotland** manager **Ally McLeod** dies aged 72. **2** As the transfer window closes, the biggest deal takes **Jermain Defoe** from **West Ham Utd.** to **Tottenham** for £7m., with **Bobby Zamora** going in the opposite direction. **Birmingham City** pay £1.25m. for **Martin Taylor** from **Blackburn Rov.**, who sign **Jonathan Stead** from **Huddersfield Town** for £1m. **3 Middlesbrough** reach the final of the Carling Cup with a 3-1 aggregate win over **Arsenal**. UEFA reject an attempt by **Wales** to have **Russia** thrown out of the Euro 2004 Finals because one of their players failed a drugs test. A takeover of **Oldham Athletic** by a three-man business consortium is approved, paving the way for the club to come out of administration. **Livingston**, the Scottish Premier League club, go into adminstration. **5** Three British bids to stage the 2005 UEFA Cup Final – at St James' Park, the Stadium of Light and Hampden Park – are unsuccessful, with the match awarded to the Alvalade Stadium in Lisbon. **6** **Derby Co.** reveal debts of £34m. **7** Three months after life-saving brain surgery, **Lincoln City** manager Keith Alexander is back in charge of the team. **Nott'm Forest** sack manager **Paul Hart**. **8** **Chelsea** take their spending since last summer to £128m by agreeing a £7m. deal for **Rennes** goalkeeper Petr Cech. **9** Paul Groves is dismissed as manager of **Grimsby Town**. **Paul Merson** leaves **Walsall** for a spell to seek a cure for 'addiction' problems. **10** Joe Kinnear, former **Wimbledon** and **Luton Town** manager, takes over at **Nott'm Forest**. **12** **Port Vale** part company with manager **Brian Horton**. **Sheffield Wed.** declare debts of £23.6m. **13** Gordon Strachan steps down as **Southampton** manager three months early. **Charlton Athletic** manager Alan Curbishley ends speculation about his future by agreeing a new three-and-a-half-year contract. **Boston Utd.** manager **Neil Thompson** is sacked by new owner **John Sotnik**, a Staffordshire-based businessman. **Martin Foyle**, long-serving **Port Vale** player and coach, is appointed the club's new manager. **16** **Arsenal** goalkeeper Jens Lehmann is fined £10,000 by the F.A. for throwing the ball at **Kevin Phillips** seconds after the final whistle against **Southampton**. **18** After 13 barren matches, **Northern Ireland** score through **David Healy** against **Norway**, but not before their run extends to a world record 1,298 minutes without a goal. **Norway** win the game 4-1. **Robert Earnshaw** registers the first hat-trick for **Wales** for 12 years in a 4-0 win over **Scotland**. **Ledley King** scores his first **England** goal in a 1-1 draw with **Portugal**. The **Republic of Ireland** hold **Brazil** to a goalless draw. **Mark Viduka** is ruled out of **Leeds Utd.**'s match against **Manchester Utd.** by a FIFA ban imposed for missing **Australia**'s game in Venezuela. **20** **Fulham** pay £3.3m. to **Lyon** in settlement of the 2001 transfer of **Steve Marlet**. **21** John Charles, football's 'Gentle Giant', dies aged 72. **22** **Celtic** set a Scottish record of 24 successive League wins when beating **Partick Thistle** 4-1. **23** **Arsenal** announce the official go-ahead for their new £400m. stadium at Ashburton Grove. Former **Charlton Athletic** player **Matt Holmes** accepts damages of £250,000 for a tackle, which he claims ended his career, by **Kevin Muscat** during a match against **Wolves** in February, 1998. **Leicester City** manager **Micky Adams** is fined £500 by the F.A. for confronting referee **Mike Riley** at half-time of the game against **Birmingham City**. **24** Substitute **James Hayter** scores the fastest-ever Football League hat-trick in two minutes and 20 seconds after coming on in the 84th minute for **Bournemouth** against **Wrexham**. **Steve Evans** is appointed manager of **Boston Utd.** for the second time after serving a 20-month F.A. ban for impeding an investigation into contract irregularities at the club. **25** An administrative error over an outstanding suspension means **Lee Bowyer** cannot play in **Newcastle Utd.**'s next six European matches. **26** **Bradford City** are placed into administration for the second time in less than two years. Coca-Cola take over from Nationwide as title sponsor of the Football League in a three-year deal reported to be worth £15m. **27** Manager **Chris Coleman**, in hospital with a virus, picks the **Fulham** team to beat **Manchester Utd.** from his sickbed. **Hereford Utd.** equal the record Conference win when beating ten-man **Dagenham & Redbridge** 9-0 away from home. **28** A run of 11 successive wins in Division Two ends for **Bristol City** with a 1-0 defeat at **Sheffield Wed.** **29** **Middlesbrough** beat **Bolton Wand.** 2-1 in the Carling Cup Final for the first major trophy in the club's 128-year history.

MARCH 2004

1 **Chelsea** beat **Manchester Utd.** to the signature of **PSV Eindhoven** winger **Arjen Robben**, who moves to London in the summer in a £12m transfer. **Kevin Phillips** is fined £2,000 by the F.A. over an incident with **Jens Lehmann** in the Southampton-Arsenal game. **2** **Ken Bates**, the driving force behind **Chelsea** for 22 years, steps down as chairman. **3** Sir Alex Ferguson appoints former **Everton** manager Walter Smith as his assistant at **Manchester Utd.** until the end of the season. **Liverpool**, **Newcastle Utd.** and **Celtic** reach round four of the UEFA Cup. **4** **Southampton** name **Plymouth Argyle**'s **Paul Sturrock** as their new manager after **Glenn Hoddle** withdraws his interest in the job because of opposition from fans. **Barnsley** manager **Gudjon Thordarson** is sacked and replaced by **Paul Hart**, dismissed by **Nott'm Forest** a month earlier. **Nicky Law**, sacked by **Bradford City** in November, takes over as manager of **Grimsby Town** until the end of the season. Administrators put **Bradford City** up for sale. **5** **Michael Owen** reveals that, like his

Liverpool manager **Gerard Houllier**, he has received death threats. **6 Sir Alex Ferguson** ends his legal action against **Manchester Utd.**'s principal shareholder **John Magnier** over disputed stud fees for racehorse Rock of Gibraltar. **7 Leicester City** manager **Micky Adams** offers to resign after some of his players are arrested during a training break in Spain. **8 Brian Talbot** parts company with **Rushden & Diamonds** by mutual consent after seven years as manager. **9 Manchester Utd.** are beaten on aggregate by a last minute **FC Porto** goal and fail to reach the quarter-finals of the Champions League for the first time in eight years. **Chelsea** go through against **Stuttgart**. **10 Arsenal** qualify for the last eight by beating **Celta Vigo**. **Brian Talbot** is appointed manager of **Oldham Athletic**. The F.A. fine **Wolves** defender **Paul Butler** £3,000 for improper conduct following an incident in the players' tunnel at **Middlesbrough**. **11** World Cup winner **Christophe Dugarry** leaves **Birmingham City** by mutual agreement. Former player **Steve Tilson** is appointed **Southend Utd.** manager. **12 Sir Alex Ferguson** reveals he has had a pacemaker fitted because of a heart problem. **13 Brentford** sack manager **Wally Downes**. **14** Five weeks after going into administration, **Livingston** win their first major trophy by beating **Hibernian** 2-0 in the CIS Scottish Cup Final. **16** The F.A. announce plans to streamline their disciplinary system. **17 Cambridge Utd.** sack manager **John Taylor**. **Swansea City** manager **Brian Flynn** leaves by mutual agreement. **Martin Allen** resigns as **Barnet** manager to take over at **Brentford**. **18 Rio Ferdinand** is ruled out of the European Championship Finals after his appeal against an eight-month ban for failing to undergo a routine drugs test is dismissed. **19** The immediate future of **Leeds Utd.** is guaranteed by a local consortium's £30m. takeover. An appeal by **Wales** against the UEFA decision not to eject play-off winners **Russia** from the Euro 2004 Finals because one of their players failed a drugs test is turned down. **20** An **Everton** fan on his way to the Walkers Stadium for the match against **Leicester City** is killed by flying debris. **21 Blackpool** beat **Southend Utd.** 2-0 to win the LDV Vans Trophy for the second time in three years. **22 Oxford Utd.** suspend manager **Ian Atkins** over links with the vacant job at **Bristol Rov.** and appoint former **Chelsea** coach **Graham Rix** on a temporary basis. **23 Liverpool** turn down a £50m. injection of funds from building tycoon **Steve Morgan**. **Claude Le Roy**, former coach of **Cameroon** and **Senegal**, is appointed **Cambridge Utd.** manager. **24 Brian Laws**, the longest-serving manager in Division Three, leaves **Scunthorpe Utd.** after seven years in charge. **Burnley** manager **Stan Ternent** is given a four-match touchline ban and £3,000 fine by the F.A. for improper conduct after an F.A. Cup tie against **Gillingham**. **25 Celtic** beat **Barcelona** and **Newcastle Utd.** overcome **Mallorca** to reach the last eight of the UEFA Cup. **Liverpool** lose to **Marseille**. **26 Newcastle Utd.** manager **Sir Bobby Robson**, 71, signs a new one-year contract. **27** Speculation about the future of **Sven-Goran Eriksson** is brought to a head by a photograph of him visiting the home of **Chelsea** chief executive **Peter Kenyon**. **28** After talks with the F.A., the England coach agrees a two-year extension of his contract to 2008. **29** UEFA abandon an appeal to increase a one-match ban, imposed by their own disciplinary panel, on **Manchester Utd.**'s **Roy Keane**. **30 Manchester Utd.** announce pre-tax profits of £26.8m. – and a £2.4m. pay-off for **Fabien Barthez**. A £31m. scheme to raise the standard of the game in Scotland is launched by the Scottish F.A. **31 Northern Ireland** beat **Estonia** 1-0, their first win in 16 games stretching back two-and-a-half-years. The **Republic of Ireland** end a two-year unbeaten run by the **Czech Republic** with a 2-1 victory. **England** lose 1-0 in **Sweden**. **Wales** win 2-1 in **Hungary**. **Scotland** go down 2-1 to **Romania**.

APRIL 2004

1 Macclesfield Town bring in former **Port Vale** manager **Brian Horton**, demoting **John Askey** to assistant manager after three months in charge. **3 Manchester Utd.** beat **Arsenal** 1-0 with a **Paul Scholes** goal to reach the F.A. Cup Final. **4** They are joined by **Millwall**, winners by the same scoreline against **Sunderland** with a goal from **Tim Cahill**. **5 Duncan Ferguson** is fined £10,000 and banned for four matches by the F.A. for violent conduct after being sent off in **Everton**'s match against **Leicester City**. **Kenny Jackett**, assistant manager of **Q.P.R.**, is appointed manager of **Swansea City**. **6 Wayne Bridge** puts **Chelsea** into the semi-finals of the Champions League with an 87th minute winner against **Arsenal**. **7 Millwall**'s **Kevin Muscat** is ruled out of the F.A. Cup Final against **Manchester**

Utd. by a knee injury. **8** Manager **Kevin Keegan** is forced to prolong his absence from **Manchester City** by further complications with a back problem. **9 Claudio Ranieri** has more talks with **Chelsea** over his future. **12** Third Division **Doncaster Rov.** become the first side to be promoted. **13 Roy Keane** ends his international retirement by making himself available to play again for the **Republic of Ireland. John Gregory** reaches a settlement with **Derby Co.** over his dismissal as manager in May 2003. **14 Newcastle Utd.** reach the semi-finals of the UEFA Cup by beating **PSV Eindhoven. Celtic** are knocked out by **Villarreal.** Three weeks after losing his job in a boardroom power struggle, **Brian Laws** is reinstated as **Scunthorpe Utd.** manager. **Millwall** player-manager **Dennis Wise** is fined £3,000 by the F.A. for abusive comments towards referee **Frazer Stretton** after the game against **Sheffield Utd. 15 Kidderminster Harr.** manager **Jan Molby** receives a four-match touchline ban and £1,500 fine for abusive language towards the fourth official during the game against **Southend Utd. 16 Colin Lee** is sacked by **Walsall** after talking to **Plymouth Argyle** about their managerial vacancy. **17 Chester City** win the Conference title. **18 Celtic** regain the Scottish Premier League championship from **Rangers. 19 Bobby Williamson** leaves **Hibernian** to take over as manager of **Plymouth Argyle. 21 Celtic**'s bid to go through the League season unbeaten comes to an end when they lose 2-1 at home to **Aberdeen.** TV pundit **Ron Atkinson** resigns from ITV Sport after making a racist remark about **Chelsea**'s **Marcel Desailly.** Caretaker **Graham Rix** is confirmed as **Oxford Utd.** manager. **22** Former **Wimbledon** coach **Ernie Tippett** is named **Rusden & Diamonds** manager. **Stockport Co.** and **Brighton & H.A.** are fined £5,000 by the F.A. for a confrontation involving their players. **Lincoln City** manager **Keith Alexander** receives a three-match touchline ban for gesturing to spectators at **Bury.** Former chairman **George Reynolds**'s association with **Darlington** ends when new owners remove his name from the stadium he built. **23 Chelsea**'s **Marcel Desailly** receives a three-match ban from UEFA for elbowing **Fernando Morientes,** an offence that went unpunished in the Champions League semi-final against **Monaco. 24 Plymouth Argyle** become Second Division champions, their second title in three seasons. **York City** drop into the Conference. **25 Arsenal** are crowned unbeaten Premiership champions, and a few hours later **Thierry Henry** becomes the first man to be named PFA Player of the Year for the second year running. **26 Roy Keane** is ruled out of his **Republic of Ireland** comeback against **Poland** by a hamstring injury. **27 Arsenal** sign 20-year-old forward **Robin van Persie** from **Feyenoord** for £3m. **28** Friendly international results: **Denmark** 1, **Scotland** 0; **Northern Ireland** 1, **Serbia & Montenegro** 1; **Poland** 0, **Republic of Ireland** 0. **29 Chelsea**'s **Damien Duff** suffers a dislocated shoulder for the second time this season. **30 Marcel Desailly**'s three-match UEFA ban is reduced to two games on appeal. **Celtic**'s **Henrik Larsson** decides to come out of international retirement to play for Sweden in the European Championship Finals.

MAY 2004

1 Leicester City and **Wolves** are relegated from the Premiership. **Doncaster Rov.** win the Division Three title. **Carlisle Utd.** lose their League status. **2 Leeds Utd.** go down to Division One. **Newcastle Utd.**'s **Jonathan Woodgate** is ruled out of the **England** squad for Euro 2004 by a thigh injury. **Jackie McNamara,** of **Celtic,** is voted the Scottish Football Writers' Association Player of the Year. **3 Eric Black,** manager of **Coventry City** for less than four months, is sacked; two days after a 5-2 win at **Gillingham. 4 Stan Ternent,** third longest-serving manager in Division One, is dismissed by **Burnley** after six years in the job. **Norwich City** become First Division champions. **5 Chelsea** are beaten by **Monaco** in the Champions League semi-finals. **6** Former **Sunderland** and **Leeds Utd.** manager **Peter Reid** takes over at **Coventry City. 6 Newcastle Utd.** lose to **Marseille** in the semi-finals of the UEFA Cup. **7 Steve McMahon,** the **Blackpool** manager, leaves by mutual agreement. **8** A stoppage-time goal by **Chris Sutton** gives **Celtic** their fifth victory of the season over **Rangers** – four in the SPL and one in the Scottish Cup. **9 Thierry Henry** becomes the first player to win the Football Writers' Association Footballer of the Year award for the second successive season – as he did with the PFA accolade last month. **10 Liverpool**'s **Michael Owen** signs a new contract with his boot sponsors Umbro, reported to be worth £15m. over 15 years. **Leeds Utd.** tell caretaker-manager **Eddie Gray** his services are no longer required. **11** Caretaker **Paul Merson** is appointed manager of **Walsall,** despite going down. Relegated **Bradford City**, with debts of £31m., tell their entire playing staff to find new clubs. **12** Dennis **Bergkamp**, approaching his 35th birthday, gets a one-year extension to his contract from **Arsenal**. **Bolton Wand.** announce a new £10m., five-year contract with their sponsors, Reebok. **13** A final appeal by **Wales** to have **Russia** thrown out of Euro 2004 because one of their players failed a drugs test is rejected by the Court of Arbitration for Sport. **Paul Robinson** becomes the first player to leave crisis-club **Leeds Utd.**, moving to **Tottenham** for £2m., but **James Milner** turns down the chance to join him. **Blackburn Rov.** manager **Graeme Souness** is fined £10,000 by the F.A. for abusive language towards referee **Graham Poll** during the game against **Tottenham**. **14** **David Platt** is sacked as **England U21** manager for poor results. **Middlesbrough** manager **Steve McClaren** returns to the **England** coaching staff because of **Brian Kidd**'s illness. **15** Champions **Arsenal** complete the 38-match Premiership season without a defeat. **16** **Shrewsbury Town** regain League status at the first attempt, beating **Aldershot Town** on penalties in the Conference Play-off Final. **17** **David Beckham**, refused permission by **Real Madrid** to turn out in a sell-out testimonial for **Arsenal** stalwart **Martin Keown**, plays for three minutes before coming off at Highbury. **18** **Birmingham City** pay a club-record £6.25m. for **Liverpool**'s **Emile Heskey**. Less than two months after being appointed **Cambridge Utd.** manager, **Claude Le Roy** is replaced by his No 2 **Herve Renard**, with Le Roy becoming director of football. **Tottenham** director of football **David Pleat** is replaced by **PSV Eindhoven**'s **Frank Arnesen** in a sporting director capacity. **19** Jay-Jay **Okocha** signs a three-year contract with **Bolton Wand.** **20** **David Beckham** ends speculation about his future by announcing he is staying at **Real Madrid**. **22** **Ruud van Nistelrooy** scores twice as **Manchester Utd.** beat **Millwall** 3-0 in the F.A. Cup Final. **Henrik Larsson** gets two on his last competitive appearance for **Celtic** – a 3-1 win over **Dunfermline Athletic** in the Scottish Cup Final. **24** **Liverpool** sack manager **Gerard Houllier**. **Aberdeen** sack manager **Steve Paterson**. **Ipswich Town** coach **Tony Mowbray** is appointed manager of **Hibernian**. **25** Millionaire **Steve Parkin** pulls out of a takeover bid for **Leeds Utd.** After a review of transfer policy, **Manchester Utd.** decide not to do business again with agent **Jason Ferguson**, son of the manager. **26** On the day the club sell **Alan Smith** to **Manchester Utd.** for £7m, coach **Kevin Blackwell** is appointed **Leeds Utd.** manager. **27** Roy **Keane** makes his comeback for the **Republic of Ireland** in a 1-0 win over **Romania**. **Darren Fletcher**, at 20, becomes the youngest **Scotland** captain since 1886 in a 1-0 victory over **Estonia**. **Wales** share a goalless draw with **Norway**. **Scarborough**'s **Russell Slade** is appointed **Grimsby Town** manager. **Jimmy Calderwood** leaves **Dunfermline Athletic** to become **Aberdeen** manager. Conference club **Telford Utd.**, who reached the fourth round of the F.A. Cup in January, go into liquidation. **29** Crystal Palace beat **West Ham Utd.** 1-0 in the Division One Play-off Final. **Republic of Ireland** lose 3-0 to **Nigeria**. **30** Brighton & H.A. win the Division Two Play-off Final, 1-0 against **Bristol City**. **Paul Parry**'s first international goal gives **Wales** a 1-0 victory over **Canada**. **Nigel Quashie** scores his first for **Scotland** in a 4-1 victory over **Trinidad & Tobago**. **Mark Williams** is sent off as **Northern Ireland** draw 1-1 with **Barbados**. **31** After weeks of speculation, **Chelsea** announce the dismissal of **Claudio Ranieri**. **Huddersfield Town** beat **Mansfield Town** on penalties in the Third Division Play-off Final.

JUNE 2004

1 Fulham's **Junichi Inamoto** suffers a broken leg as **Japan** hold **England** to a 1-1 draw. **Steve Cotterill**, former **Cheltenham Town** and **Stoke City** manager, takes over at **Burnley**. **Livingston** manager **Davie Hay** is forced out by new owners of the club. **2** FC Porto coach **Jose Mourinho** becomes manager of **Chelsea**. The **Republic of Ireland** beat **Jamaica** 1-0. **3** Ten days before leading **France** into Euro 2004, **Jacques Santini** is appointed manager of **Tottenham**. **W.B.A.** pay a club-record £2.7m. for **Denmark** defender **Martin Albrechtsen** from **FC Copenhagen**. A knee injury forces **Charlton Athletic** defender **Richard Rufus** to retire at 29. **Juan Veron**, a £15m. signing from **Manchester Utd.** ten months ago, is the first player to leave **Chelsea**, joining **Inter Milan** on a year's loan. **4** **Bristol City** sack **Danny Wilson** and appoint **Brian Tinnion** player-manager. Coach **Allan Preston** is appointed manager of **Livingston** – at 34 the youngest in the Scottish Premier League. **5** Wayne **Bridge** scores his first international goal as **England** complete their warm-up for Euro

2004 by beating **Iceland** 6-1. **Holland** lose 1-0 at home to the **Republic of Ireland**. 6 **David Healy** becomes **Northern Ireland's** highest scorer on 14 with two goals in a 3-0 win over **Trinidad and Tobago**. 7 **Blackpool** appoint former **Scotland** defender **Colin Hendry** as their new manager. 8 After reaching a settlement with **Chelsea** over his dismissal, **Claudio Ranieri** returns to former club **Valencia** as coach. **Charlton Athletic** miss out on a UEFA cup place in the Fair Play League draw. 10 The Football League announce new titles for their three divisions – The Championship, League One and League Two. 11 **Manchester Utd.** pay £6m. for the **Paris St-Germain** defender, **Gabriel Heinze**. 12 **Trevor Brooking**, the F.A.'s director of football development, is knighted and **Wales** manager **Mark Hughes** receives an OBE in the Queen's Birthday Honours list. Euro 2004 opens with a surprise, **Greece** beating the hosts **Portugal** 2-1. 13 Two stoppage-time goals by **Zinedine Zidane** give **France** a 2-1 win over **England**. 16 **Rafael Benitez**, who led **Valencia** to the Spanish title and UEFA Cup last season, becomes **Liverpool** manager. **Bryan Robson** resigns as manager of relegated **Bradford City** after seven months in charge and is replaced by his assistant, **Colin Todd**. 17 **Wayne Rooney** makes history as the youngest player to score in the European Championship Finals and gets a second as **England** beat **Swizerland** 3-0. **Davie Hay**, who left **Livingston** at the beginning of the month, is appointed manager of **Dunfermline Athletic**. Assistant manager **Phil Thompson** follows **Gerard Houllier** out of Anfield. 21 **Wayne Rooney** hits two more goals as **England** beat **Croatia** 4-2 to qualify for the quarter-finals. But he is overtaken as the youngest scorer by **Johan Vonlanthen** of **Switzerland** in their 3-1 defeat by **France**. **Wimbledon** receive Football League permission to change their name to **Milton Keynes Dons**. 22 First Division champions **Inverness Caledonian Thistle** are accepted into the Scottish Premier League after initially being refused admission because of plans to groundshare with **Aberdeen**. The **Gillingham** manager, **Andy Hessenthaler**, receives a three-match touchline ban and a £1,000 fine from the F.A. for comments to referee **Tony Bates** after the last home game of the season against **Coventry City**. 23 **Chelsea** agree a £13m. fee for **FC Porto** defender **Paulo Ferreira**. 24 **England** lose on penalties to **Portugal** in the quarter-finals of Euro 2004 after **Sol Campbell** has a goal controversially disallowed. 28 **Steven Gerrard** turns down the chance to join **Chelsea** to stay with Liverpool. 29 **Birmingham City** manager **Steve Bruce** agrees a new five-year contract.

JULY 2004

1 **Liverpool** pay a club-record £14m. for **Auxerre** striker **Djibril Cisse**. **Charlton Athletic** sign **Denmark** Euro 2004 winger **Dennis Rommedahl** from **PSV Eindhoven** for £2m. **Milton Keynes Dons** come out of administration. 2 **James Milner** joins **Newcastle Utd.** from **Leeds Utd.** for a fee rising to £5m. 4 **Greece** are crowned the most unlikely European Championship winners after beating **Portugal** 1-0 in the Final. 5 **Fulham** manager **Chris Coleman** signs a three-year contract. 6 **Ipswich Town** manager **Joe Royle** is awarded £423,000 in the High Court over his sacking by **Manchester City** in May 2001. **Middlesbrough** sign **Holland** Euro 2004 defender **Michael Reiziger** on a free transfer from **Barcelona**. **Charlton Athletic** defender **Gary Rowett** is forced to retire at 30 because of a knee injury. **Middlesbrough** sign a multi-million pound sponsorship deal with 888.com. 7 **Wolves** manager **Dave Jones** is fined £1,000 by the F.A. for comments about referee **Uriah Rennie** after last season's game against **Bolton Wand.** The Football League break new ground by publishing details of payment by clubs to agents. 8 **Middlesbrough** sign **Mark Viduka** from **Leeds Utd.** for £4.5m. **Peter Taylor** is re-appointed as **England** U-21 coach after a gap of four years, this time while retaining the job as **Hull City** manager. 9 A busy day in the transfer market. **Sean Davis** joins **Tottenham** from **Fulham** for £3m., **Southampton** pay £2m for **Peter Crouch** from **Aston Villa** and **Chelsea** pair **Jimmy Floyd Hasselbaink** and **Mario Melchiot** leave on frees for **Middlesbrough** and **Birmingham City** respectively. **Helder Postiga** leaves **Tottenham** to rejoin **FC Porto**, with the Portuguese club's midfielder **Pedro Mendes** moving to White Hart Lane.

FOOTBALLER OF THE YEAR

(Original award by the Football Writers' Association to the 'player who, by precept and example, on the field and off, shall be considered to have done most for football').

1948 Stanley Matthews (Blackpool); **1949** Johnny Carey (Manchester Utd.); **1950** Joe Mercer (Arsenal); **1951** Harry Johnston (Blackpool); **1952** Billy Wright (Wolves); **1953** Nat Lofthouse (Bolton Wand.); **1954** Tom Finney (Preston N.E.); **1955** Don Revie (Manchester City); **1956** Bert Trautmann (Manchester City); **1957** Tom Finney (Preston N.E.); **1958** Danny Blanchflower (Tottenham); **1959** Syd Owen (Luton Town); **1960** Bill Slater (Wolves); **1961** Danny Blanchflower (Tottenham); **1962** Jimmy Adamson (Burnley); **1963** Stanley Matthews (Stoke City); **1964** Bobby Moore (West Ham Utd.); **1965** Bobby Collins (Leeds Utd.); **1966** Bobby Charlton (Manchester Utd.); **1967** Jack Charlton (Leeds Utd.); **1968** George Best (Manchester Utd.); **1969** Tony Book (Manchester City) & Dave Mackay (Derby Co.) – shared; **1970** Billy Bremner (Leeds Utd.); **1971** Frank McLintock (Arsenal); **1972** Gordon Banks (Stoke City); **1973** Pat Jennings (Tottenham); **1974** Ian Callaghan (Liverpool); **1975** Alan Mullery (Fulham); **1976** Kevin Keegan (Liverpool); **1977** Emlyn Hughes (Liverpool); **1978** Kenny Burns (Nott'm Forest); **1979** Kenny Dalglish (Liverpool); **1980** Terry McDermott (Liverpool); **1981** Frans Thijssen (Ipswich Town); **1982** Steve Perryman (Tottenham); **1983** Kenny Dalglish (Liverpool); **1984** Ian Rush (Liverpool); **1985** Neville Southall (Everton); **1986** Gary Lineker (Everton); **1987** Clive Allen (Tottenham); **1988** John Barnes (Liverpool); **1989** Steve Nicol (Liverpool); Special award to the Liverpool players for the compassion shown to bereaved families after the Hillsborough Disaster; **1990** John Barnes (Liverpool); **1991** Gordon Strachan (Leeds Utd.); **1992** Gary Lineker (Tottenham); **1993** Chris Waddle (Sheffield Wed.); **1994** Alan Shearer (Blackburn Rov.); **1995** Jurgen Klinsmann (Tottenham); **1996** Eric Cantona (Manchester Utd.); **1997** Gianfranco Zola (Chelsea); **1998** Dennis Bergkamp (Arsenal); **1999** David Ginola (Tottenham); **2000** Roy Keane (Manchester Utd.); **2001** Teddy Sheringham (Manchester Utd.); **2002** Robert Pires (Arsenal); **2003** Thierry Henry (Arsenal); **2004** Thierry Henry (Arsenal).

P.F.A. AWARDS

Player of the Year: 1974 Norman Hunter (Leeds Utd.); **1975** Colin Todd (Derby Co.); **1976** Pat Jennings (Tottenham); **1977** Andy Gray (Aston Villa); **1978** Peter Shilton (Nott'm Forest); **1979** Liam Brady (Arsenal); **1980** Terry McDermott (Liverpool); **1981** John Wark (Ipswich Town); **1982** Kevin Keegan (Southampton); **1983** Kenny Dalglish (Liverpool); **1984** Ian Rush (Liverpool); **1985** Peter Reid (Everton); **1986** Gary Lineker (Everton); **1987** Clive Allen (Tottenham); **1988** John Barnes (Liverpool); **1989** Mark Hughes (Manchester Utd.); **1990** David Platt (Aston Villa); **1991** Mark Hughes (Manchester Utd.); **1992** Gary Pallister (Manchester Utd.); **1993** Paul McGrath (Aston Villa); **1994** Eric Cantona (Manchester Utd.); **1995** Alan Shearer (Blackburn Rov.); **1996** Les Ferdinand (Newcastle Utd.); **1997** Alan Shearer (Newcastle Utd.); **1998** Dennis Bergkamp (Arsenal); **1999** David Ginola (Tottenham); **2000** Roy Keane (Manchester Utd.); **2001** Teddy Sheringham (Manchester Utd.); **2002** Ruud van Nistelrooy (Manchester Utd.); **2003** Thierry Henry (Arsenal); **2004** Thierry Henry (Arsenal).

Young Player of the Year: 1974 Kevin Beattie (Ipswich Town); **1975** Mervyn Day (West Ham Utd.); **1976** Peter Barnes (Manchester City); **1977** Andy Gray (Aston Villa); **1978** Tony Woodcock (Nott'm Forest); **1979** Cyrille Regis (W.B.A.); **1980** Glenn Hoddle (Tottenham); **1981** Gary Shaw (Aston Villa); **1982** Steve Moran (Southampton); **1983** Ian Rush (Liverpool); **1984** Paul Walsh (Luton Town); **1985** Mark Hughes (Manchester Utd.); **1986** Tony Cottee (West Ham Utd.); **1987** Tony Adams (Arsenal); **1988** Paul Gascoigne (Newcastle Utd.); **1989** Paul Merson (Arsenal); **1990** Matthew Le Tissier (Southampton); **1991** Lee Sharpe (Manchester Utd.); **1992** Ryan Giggs (Manchester Utd.); **1993** Ryan Giggs (Manchester Utd.); **1994** Andy Cole (Newcastle Utd.); **1995** Robbie Fowler (Liverpool); **1996** Robbie Fowler (Liverpool); **1997** David Beckham (Manchester Utd.); **1998** Michael Owen (Liverpool); **1999** Nicolas Anelka (Arsenal); **2000** Harry Kewell

(Leeds Utd.); **2001** Steven Gerrard (Liverpool); **2002** Craig Ballamy (Newcastle Utd.); **2003** Jermaine Jenas (Newcastle Utd.); **2004** Scott Parker (Chelsea).

Merit Awards: **1974** Bobby Charlton & Cliff Lloyd; **1975** Denis Law; **1976** George Eastham; **1977** Jack Taylor; **1978** Bill Shankly; **1979** Tom Finney; **1980** Sir Matt Busby; **1981** John Trollope; **1982** Joe Mercer; **1983** Bob Paisley; **1984** Bill Nicholson; **1985** Ron Greenwood; **1986** England 1966 World Cup-winning team; **1987** Sir Stanley Matthews; **1988** Billy Bonds; **1989** Nat Lofthouse; **1990** Peter Shilton; **1991** Tommy Hutchison; **1992** Brian Clough; **1993** Manchester Utd., 1968 European Champions; Eusebio (Benfica & Portugal); **1994** Billy Bingham; **1995** Gordon Strachan; **1996** Pele; **1997** Peter Beardsley; **1998** Steve Ogrizovic; **1999** Tony Ford; **2000** Gary Mabbutt; **2001** Jimmy Hill; **2002** Niall Quinn; **2003** Sir Bobby Robson; **2004** Dario Gradi.

MANAGER OF THE YEAR (1)

(Chosen by a panel including managers, players, media, fan representatives, referees, the England coach and representatives of the Premier League and Football Association.)

1966 Jock Stein (Celtic); **1967** Jock Stein (Celtic); **1968** Matt Busby (Manchester Utd.); **1969** Don Revie (Leeds Utd.); **1970** Don Revie (Leeds Utd.); **1971** Bertie Mee (Arsenal); **1972** Don Revie (Leeds Utd.); **1973** Bill Shankly (Liverpool); **1974** Jack Charlton (Middlesbrough); **1975** Ron Saunders (Aston Villa); **1976** Bob Paisley (Liverpool); **1977** Bob Paisley (Liverpool); **1978** Brian Clough (Nott'm Forest); **1979** Bob Paisley (Liverpool); **1980** Bob Paisley (Liverpool); **1981** Ron Saunders (Aston Villa); **1982** Bob Paisley (Liverpool); **1983** Bob Paisley (Liverpool); **1984** Joe Fagan (Liverpool); **1985** Howard Kendall (Everton); **1986** Kenny Dalglish (Liverpool); **1987** Howard Kendall (Everton); **1988** Kenny Dalglish (Liverpool); **1989** George Graham (Arsenal); **1990** Kenny Dalglish (Liverpool); **1991** George Graham (Arsenal); **1992** Howard Wilkinson (Leeds Utd.); **1993** Alex Ferguson (Manchester Utd.); **1994** Alex Ferguson (Manchester Utd.); **1995** Kenny Dalglish (Blackburn Rov.); **1996** Alex Ferguson (Manchester Utd.); **1997** Alex Ferguson (Manchester Utd.); **1998** Arsene Wenger (Arsenal); **1999** Alex Ferguson (Manchester Utd.); **2000** Sir Alex Ferguson (Manchester Utd.); **2001** George Burley (Ipswich Town); **2002** Arsene Wenger (Arsenal); **2003** Sir Alex Ferguson (Manchester Utd.); **2004** Arsene Wenger (Arsenal).

MANAGER OF THE YEAR (2)

(As chosen by the League Managers' Association and awarded to 'the manager who has made best use of the resources available to him'.)

1993 Dave Bassett (Sheffield Utd.); **1994** Joe Kinnear (Wimbledon); **1995** Frank Clark (Nott'm Forest); **1996** Peter Reid (Sunderland); **1997** Danny Wilson (Barnsley); **1998** David Jones (Southampton); **1999** Alex Ferguson (Manchester Utd.); **2000** Alan Curbishley (Charlton Athletic); **2001** George Burley (Ipswich Town); **2002** Arsene Wenger (Arsenal); **2003** David Moyes (Everton); **2004** Arsene Wenger (Arsenal).

SCOTTISH FOOTBALL WRITERS' ASSOCIATION

Player of the Year: **1965** Billy McNeill (Celtic); **1966** John Greig (Rangers); **1967** Ronnie Simpson (Celtic); **1968** Gordon Wallace (Raith); **1969** Bobby Murdoch (Celtic); **1970** Pat Stanton (Hibernian); **1971** Martin Buchan (Aberdeen); **1972** David Smith (Rangers); **1973** George Connelly (Celtic); **1974** World Cup Squad; **1975** Sandy Jardine (Rangers); **1976** John Greig (Rangers); **1977** Danny McGrain (Celtic); **1978** Derek Johnstone (Rangers); **1979** Andy Ritchie (Morton); **1980** Gordon Strachan (Aberdeen); **1981** Alan Rough (Partick Thistle); **1982** Paul Sturrock (Dundee Utd.); **1983** Charlie Nicholas (Celtic); **1984** Willie Miller (Aberdeen); **1985** Hamish McAlpine (Dundee Utd.); **1986** Sandy Jardine (Hearts); **1987** Brian McClair (Celtic); **1988** Paul McStay (Celtic); **1989**

Richard Gough (Rangers); **1990** Alex McLeish (Aberdeen); **1991** Maurice Malpas (Dundee Utd.); **1992** Ally McCoist (Rangers); **1993** Andy Goram (Rangers); **1994** Mark Hateley (Rangers); **1995** Brian Laudrup (Rangers); **1996** Paul Gascoigne (Rangers); **1997** Brian Laudrup (Rangers); **1998** Craig Burley (Celtic); **1999** Henrik Larsson (Celtic); **2000** Barry Ferguson (Rangers); **2001** Henrik Larsson (Celtic); **2002** Paul Lambert (Celtic); **2003** Barry Ferguson (Rangers); **2004** Jackie McNamara (Celtic).

SCOTTISH P.F.A. AWARDS

Player of the Year: 1978 Derek Johnstone (Rangers); **1979** Paul Hegarty (Dundee Utd.); **1980** Davie Provan (Celtic); **1981** Mark McGhee (Aberdeen); **1982** Sandy Clarke (Airdrieonians); **1983** Charlie Nicholas (Celtic); **1984** Willie Miller (Aberdeen); **1985** Jim Duffy (Morton); **1986** Richard Gough (Dundee Utd.); **1987** Brian McClair (Celtic); **1988** Paul McStay (Celtic); **1989** Theo Snelders (Aberdeen); **1990** Jim Bett (Aberdeen); **1991** Paul Elliott (Celtic); **1992** Ally McCoist (Rangers); **1993** Andy Goram (Rangers); **1994** Mark Hateley (Rangers); **1995** Brian Laudrup (Rangers); **1996** Paul Gascoigne (Rangers); **1997** Paolo Di Canio (Celtic) **1998** Jackie McNamara (Celtic); **1999** Henrik Larsson (Celtic); **2000** Mark Viduka (Celtic); **2001** Henrik Larsson (Celtic); **2002** Lorenzo Amoruso (Rangers); **2003** Barry Ferguson (Rangers); **2004** Chris Sutton (Celtic).

Young Player of Year: 1978 Graeme Payne (Dundee Utd.); **1979** Ray Stewart (Dundee Utd.); **1980** John McDonald (Rangers); **1981** Charlie Nicholas (Celtic); **1982** Frank McAvennie (St. Mirren); **1983** Paul McStay (Celtic); **1984** John Robertson (Hearts); **1985** Craig Levein (Hearts); **1986** Craig Levein (Hearts); **1987** Robert Fleck (Rangers); **1988** John Collins (Hibernian); **1989** Billy McKinlay (Dundee Utd.); **1990** Scott Crabbe (Hearts); **1991** Eoin Jess (Aberdeen); **1992** Phil O'Donnell (Motherwell); **1993** Eoin Jess (Aberdeen); **1994** Phil O'Donnell (Motherwell); **1995** Charlie Miller (Rangers); **1996** Jackie McNamara (Celtic); **1997** Robbie Winters (Dundee Utd.); **1998** Gary Naysmith (Hearts); **1999** Barry Ferguson (Rangers) ; **2000** Kenny Miller (Hibernian); **2001** Stilian Petrov (Celtic); **2002** Kevin McNaughton (Aberdeen); **2003** James McFadden (Motherwell); **2004** Stephen Pearson (Celtic).

SCOTTISH MANAGER OF THE YEAR

1987 Jim McLean (Dundee Utd.); **1988** Billy McNeill (Celtic); **1989** Graeme Souness (Rangers); **1990** Andy Roxburgh (Scotland); **1991** Alex Totten (St. Johnstone); **1992** Walter Smith (Rangers); **1993** Walter Smith (Rangers); **1994** Walter Smith (Rangers); **1995** Jimmy Nicholl (Raith); **1996** Walter Smith (Rangers); **1997** Walter Smith (Rangers); **1998** Wim Jansen (Celtic); **1999** Dick Advocaat (Rangers); **2000** Dick Advocaat (Rangers); **2001** Martin O'Neill (Celtic); **2002** John Lambie (Partick Thistle); **2003** Alex McLeish (Rangers); **2004** Martin O'Neill (Celtic).

EUROPEAN FOOTBALLER OF THE YEAR

(Poll conducted by *France Football*) 1956 Stanley Matthews (Blackpool); **1957** Alfredo di Stefano (Real Madrid); **1958** Raymond Kopa (Real Madrid); **1959** Alfredo di Stefano (Real Madrid); **1960** Luis Suarez (Barcelona); **1961** Omar Sivori (Juventus); **1962** Josef Masopust (Dukla Prague); **1963** Lev Yashin (Moscow Dynamo); **1964** Denis Law (Manchester Utd.); **1965** Eusebio (Benfica); **1966** Bobby Charlton (Manchester Utd.); **1967** Florian Albert (Ferencvaros); **1968** George Best (Manchester Utd.); **1969** Gianni Rivera (AC Milan); **1970** Gerd Muller (Bayern Munich); **1971** Johan Cruyff (Ajax); **1972** Franz Beckenbauer (Bayern Munich); **1973** Johan Cruyff (Barcelona); **1974** Johan Cruyff (Barcelona); **1975** Oleg Blokhin (Dynamo Kiev); **1976** Franz Beckenbauer (Bayern Munich); **1977** Allan Simonsen (Borussia Moenchengladbach); **1978** Kevin Keegan (SV Hamburg); **1979** Kevin Keegan (SV Hamburg); **1980** Karl-Heinz Rummenigge (Bayern Munich); **1981** Karl-Heinz Rummenigge (Bayern Munich); **1982** Paolo Rossi (Juventus); **1983** Michel Platini (Juventus); **1984** Michel Platini (Juventus); **1985** Michel Platini

(Juventus); **1986** Igor Belanov (Dynamo Kiev); **1987** Ruud Gullit (AC Milan); **1988** Marco van Basten (AC Milan); **1989** Marco van Basten (AC Milan); **1990** Lothar Matthaus (Inter Milan); **1991** Jean-Pierre Papin (Marseille); **1992** Marco van Basten (AC Milan); **1993** Roberto Baggio (Juventus); **1994** Hristo Stoichkov (Barcelona); **1995** George Weah (AC Milan); **1996** Matthias Sammer (Borussia Dortmund); **1997** Ronaldo (Inter Milan); **1998** Zinedine Zidane (Juventus); **1999** Rivaldo (Barcelona); **2000** Luis Figo (Real Madrid); **2001** Michael Owen (Liverpool); **2002** Ronaldo (Real Madrid); **2003** Pavel Nedved (Juventus).

FIFA WORLD FOOTBALLER OF YEAR

(Voted by national coaches): **1991** Lothar Matthaus (Inter Milan and Germany); **1992** Marco van Basten (AC Milan and Holland); **1993** Roberto Baggio (Juventus and Italy); **1994** Romario (Barcelona and Brazil); **1995** George Weah (AC Milan and Liberia); **1996** Ronaldo (Barcelona and Brazil); **1997** Ronaldo (Inter Milan and Brazil); **1998** Zinedine Zidane (Juventus and France); **1999** Rivaldo (Barcelona and Brazil); **2000** Zinedine Zidane (Juventus and France); **2001** Luis Figo (Real Madrid and Portugal); **2002** Ronaldo (Real Madrid and Brazil); **2003** Zinedine Zidane (Real Madrid and France).

QUOTE – UNQUOTE

'While one or two players may indeed leave, the outward movement will not be drastic' – **Terence Brown**, West Ham chairman, after relegation from the Premiership.

'If we hadn't sold players, cheques would have started bouncing. People are saying I should have been more open when the club went down. But my former colleagues in the Premiership would have smelled blood' – **Terence Brown** on a host of departures from Upton Park.

'At the moment it's like having a new-born baby. You want to hold it all the time. But after a while you give it less attention' – **Roberto Carlos**, Real Madrid defender, on new team-mate David Beckham.

'I challenge the little worms at the FSA in the most robust way to come out from under their stone and justify their action' – **Ken Bates**, while Chelsea chairman, criticising the Financial Services Authority's decision to investigate the ownership of the club prior to Roman Abramovich's takeover.

'At Chelsea he can be the conductor of the orchestra. At United he is just the lead musician' – **Pini Zahavi**, agent, on Juan Sebastian Veron's move from Old Trafford to Stamford Bridge.

'It's frightening. You don't know who's going to turn up next' – **Damien Duff**, one of Chelsea's many signings.

'The reserve team car park will be impressive' – **Arsene Wenger**, Arsenal manager, on Chelsea's expanding squad.

'Any manager who has been in the Premier League for ten years and can't afford a £3m. house is a fool' – **Harry Redknapp**, Portsmouth manager.

'We subscribe to the view that sporting success is achieved by people who want to play together, share a common goal and are committed to the club' – **Rupert Lowe**, Southampton chairman, granting the transfer request of Wayne Bridge who joined Chelsea.

'I have been a fighter all my life, but this one has beaten me' – **Ray Harford**, one of the game's most respected coaches, shortly before dying of cancer.

THE STORY OF THE PREMIERSHIP SEASON 2003-04

AUGUST

16 An eventful start to the season with records, red cards, plenty of goals and some impressive debuts. Ruud van Nistelrooy sets a new mark by scoring for the ninth successive Premiership game as Manchester United open their defence of the title with a 4-0 win over Bolton, which features an impressive first appearance by record teenage signing Cristiano Ronaldo. Despite having Sol Campbell sent off, Arsenal beat Everton 2-1, scoring for a record 41st successive home game. There are mixed fortunes for the promoted sides. Teddy Sheringham and Patrik Berger launch their Portsmouth careers with goals in the 2-1 win over Aston Villa, who have Gareth Barry dismissed. Kevin Phillips gets one on his first appearance for Southampton, who come from two down to draw at Leicester. But Wolves lose 5-1 at Blackburn, for whom Brett Emerton and Lorenzo Amoruso make scoring debuts. Birmingham's record-signing David Dunn is also on the mark with the spot-kick winner against Tottenham.

17 Juan Sebastian Veron, sold by Manchester United, hits Chelsea's first in a 2-1 victory at Anfield, and there is immediate successive, too, for Manchester City newcomer Antoine Sibierski in the 3-0 win at Charlton.

23 Sir Alex Ferguson watches the rest of Manchester United's 2-1 success at Newcastle Utd. in Sir Bobby Robson's office after being sent from the touchline for foul language. Riccardo Scimeca and Alan Rogers are sent off in Leicester's 2-1 defeat by Chelsea, who have Geremi dismissed. Charlton score four times in the first 33 minutes to win 4-0 at Molineux. Matt Jansen scores his first League goal for Blackburn since a life-threatening holiday accident in a 2-2 draw with Bolton. David Sommeil's last-minute header earns Manchester City a point against Portsmouth in the first game at their new stadium.

24 Steve McClaren, whose managerial career at Middlesbrough started with a 4-0 home defeat by Arsenal two years ago, sees his side on the receiving end of the same scoreline.

26 A hat-trick by 37-year-old Teddy Sheringham against Bolton puts Portsmouth on top of the table for 24 hours after a 4-0 win.

27 John O'Shea's first goal for Manchester United inflicts Wolves' third successive defeat, but a record 11th successive Premiership strike proves beyond Ruud van Nistelrooy.

30 Two goals by Michael Owen lift Liverpool spirits in the Merseyside derby at Goodison, while two by Juan Pablo Angel for Aston Villa against Leicester double his tally for the whole of the previous season. Also 3-0 winners are Fulham, at Tottenham. Referee Matt Messias accidentally flattens Birmingham's Robbie Savage with an elbow during their 1-0 win at Newcastle.

31 An 88th minute header by James Beattie for Southampton inflicts Manchester United's first defeat in the League since Boxing Day. So Arsenal, who come from behind to beat Manchester City 2-1, end the month on top.

SEPTEMBER

13 On a day of controversy littered with red cards and penalties, Gerard Houllier criticises Lucas Neill for the tackle which fractures Jamie Carragher's right leg during Liverpool's 3-1 win at Blackburn. Gary Naysmith (Everton) and Laurent Robert (Newcastle) are dismissed in a 2-2 draw at Goodison, where three of the goals come from the spot, two by Alan Shearer and one from Duncan Ferguson. Robert Pires is accused of diving for the Thierry Henry penalty which gives Arsenal a fortuitous point against Portsmouth, and Wolves are unhappy about the way Kevin Phillips goes to ground for the first of James Beattie's two goals in Southampton's 2-0 victory. Also sent off is Charlton's Jason Euell in the 2-0 home defeat by Manchester United.

14 More sendings-off and more penalties. Darren Purse (Birmingham) and Sylvain Legwinski (Fulham) see red at St Andrews, where on-loan Mikael Forssell, scores twice on his debut for the home team in a 2-2 result. Nicolas Anelka's hat-trick, including two penalties, enables Manchester City to beat Aston Villa 4-1 after trailing at half-time.

20 James Beattie scores twice in Southampton's 3-1 win at White Hart Lane, a match which proves to be Glenn Hoddle's last as Tottenham manager. Injury-dogged Paulo Wanchope's stoppage-time equaliser for Manchester City against Fulham is his first goal since he scored for Costa Rica against Brazil in the World Cup. Paul Robinson pulls off a brilliant save from David Dunn's penalty, but is controversially ruled to have moved from his line and Robbie Savage scores with the re-taken spot kick in Birmingham's 2-0 win at Leeds. Hernan Crespo opens his account for Chelsea with two goals in the 5-0 win at Wolves. Alpay and Jlloyd Samuel score for the first time for Aston Villa, who beat Charlton 2-1.

21 Patrick Vieira is sent off for a Premiership-record eighth time and Arsenal players later taunt and jostle Ruud van Nistelrooy after he misses a stoppage-time penalty in the goalless draw at Old Trafford. There is also trouble during Middlesbrough's 1-0 win over Everton, with a touchline confrontation between managers Steve McClaren and David Moyes.

26 At the end of a troubled week for the club, a late penalty by Thierry Henry enables Arsenal to stay on top with a 3-2 win over Newcastle.

27 Ruud van Nistelrooy scores a hat-trick in Manchester United's 4-1 victory at Leicester. Southampton suffer their first defeat – 1-0 at home to Middlesbrough – and have Kevin Phillips sent off.

28 Two more hat-tricks – by Kevin Lisbie in Charlton's 3-2 victory over Liverpool and Steve Watson for Everton, who beat Leeds 4-0.

OCTOBER

4 Alan Shearer's 250th League goal gives Newcastle their first win of the season, against Southampton. Wolves' first victory, by the same 1-0 scoreline, comes against Manchester City. Birmingham have goalkeeper Maik Taylor sent off and lose for the first time – 3-0 to Manchester United. Arsenal come from behind to win 2-1 at Liverpool with a spectacular strike by Robert Pires. Tottenham continue to improve under caretaker David Pleat, scoring three times in six minutes either side of half-time to beat Everton 3-0.

14 Chelsea are goalless for the first time this season, but a point gained at Birmingham is enough to put them top for a few days.

18 Arsenal reclaim pole position and are left as the only unbeaten side as goals by Edu and Thierry Henry account for Chelsea 2-1. Patrik Berger scores against his old club to give Portsmouth victory over fading Liverpool, while Shola Ameobi's strike at The Riverside enables Newcastle to prevail in the north-east derby. Shaun Wright-Phillips hits two in Manchester City's 6-2 romp against Bolton, but is then sent off for a tackle on Simon Charlton.

19 South African Mbulelo Mabizela equalises with one of his first touches in a Tottenham shirt and Freddie Kanoute gets a last-minute winner at Leicester.

21 Newcastle are 2-0 down in eight minutes at Fulham, but Alan Shearer's double continues their resurgence in a 3-2 win.

25 Fulham shock the Premiership's biggest-ever crowd – 67,727 – by overcoming Manchester United 3-1 at Old Trafford. Sharing pride of place are Wolves, who retrieve a 3-0 half-time deficit to beat Leicester 4-3, Colin Cameron netting twice. Florent Sinama-Pongolle scores his first Liverpool goal in a 3-1 win over Leeds and another French 19-year-old, Leandre Griffit, gets one on his debut for Southampton, who defeat Blackburn 2-0.

26 Thierry Henry's free-kick cancels out Paolo Di Canio's penalty and a 1-1 draw at against Charlton is enough to put Arsenal back on top.

NOVEMBER

1 At the end of a week in which there are fines and bans for club and players for the fracas at Old Trafford, Arsenal win 4-1 at struggling Leeds. Two players score in the Premiership for the first time, Cristiano Ronaldo, in Manchester United's 3-0 win over Portsmouth, and Gaizka Mendieta for Middlesbrough who beat Wolves 2-0. Tottenham lose for the first time under David Pleat, Kevin Nolan's goal giving Bolton victory at White Hart Lane.

2 Steve Howey gets his first goal for Leicester, who deepen Blackburn's woes 2-0, while Danny Murphy's last-minute penalty gives Liverpool victory at Fulham.

3 Matt Holland is also on the mark for the first time for Charlton, scoring both goals in a 2-1 success at Birmingham.

8 Gary O'Neill scores twice on his Premiership debut for Portsmouth, whose 6-1 crushing of Leeds proves to be Peter Reid's last match as manager. Arsenal come from behind to beat Tottenham 2-1, while Alan Curbishley celebrates his 46th birthday by watching Charlton climb to fourth with first-of-the-season goals by Jonatan Johansson (2) and Graham Stuart against Fulham.

9 Two from Ryan Giggs sets up Manchester United's 2-1 win at Anfield. Chelsea crush ten-man Newcastle 5-0 and Liverpool manager Gerard Houllier admits the top three places are virtually tied up.

10 Markus Babbel's first goal for the club helps Blackburn end a run of five successive defeats with a 2-1 win over fellow-strugglers Everton.

22 Arsenal's 3-0 win at Birmingham stretches their unbeaten start to the season to 13 matches – a Premiership record. A new record crowd of 67,748 see Manchester United beat Blackburn 2-1, Kleberson scoring his first goal for the club. Southampton's attendance of 32,149 for the 1-0 defeat by Chelsea, inflicted by a rare goal for Mario Melchiot, is a new high for St Mary's.

29 Alan Curbishley's 400th match in sole charge of Charlton is spoiled by Leeds, who upset the form book by winning 1-0 at The Valley. Blackburn manager Graeme Souness is sent to the stands by Graham Poll for comments during the 1-0 victory over Tottenham.

30 Frank Lampard's penalty against Manchester United settles the season's biggest game so far, enabling Chelsea to finish the month on top. Arsenal's goalless draw with Fulham ends a 46-match run of scoring in every League game at Highbury.

DECEMBER

6 Arsenal concede a last-minute equaliser to Leicester's Craig Hignett and Chelsea are also held 1-1, at Leeds. So Manchester United steal a march on their rivals by beating Aston Villa 4-0. Robbie Keane's hat-trick points Tottenham to a 5-2 win over Wolves, while Barry Ferguson and 19-year-old Paul Gallagher register their first Premiership goals as improving Blackburn score four times in the last quarter of the match at Birmingham.

7 Watched by England coach Sven-Goran Eriksson, Scott Parker scores two spectacular goals for Charlton, but Brett Ormerod's second for Southampton gives his side a 3-2 success.

13 A last-minute own goal by John Terry gives Bolton a shock 2-1 win at Stamford Bridge. Two headers by Paul Scholes help United beat City 3-1 in the Manchester derby, and two spectacular strikes by Laurent Robert highlight Newcastle's 4-0 defeat of Tottenham. Leicester's run of improved form ends horribly, with captain Matt Elliott and goalkeeper Ian Walker shown red cards and manager Micky Adams sent to the stands by Mike Riley during the 2-0 home defeat by Birmingham.

14 Arsenal resume pole position thanks to a Dennis Bergkamp goal against Blackburn, while Leeds continue to improve with a 3-2 win over Fulham.

20 A record crowd at The Reebok – 28,003 – see a late goal by Henrik Pedersen earn Bolton a point against Arsenal. Stefan Moore's first goal of the season helps Aston Villa to their first away win – 2-0 at Blackburn. Two matches are controversially called off because of the weather – Birmingham v Middlesbrough and Wolves v Liverpool.

21 Jason Dodd scores his first goal for three years and Marian Pahars his first for 15 months as Southampton beat Portsmouth 3-0 in the clubs' first top-flight League derby for 16 years.

26 A goal after 42 seconds by Hermann Hreidarsson sets Charlton on the way to a 4-2 win over Chelsea in front of the biggest crowd – 26,768 – since the club returned to the Valley 11 years ago. Thierry Henry completes a 'full-set' of current Premiership teams he has scored against with two goals in the 3-0 victory over Wolves. Portsmouth beat Tottenham 2-0, both coming from Patrik Berger, but lose Tim Sherwood for the rest of the season with a broken leg. Other two-goal marksmen are Blackburn's Markus Babbel and Middlesbrough's Juninho in their teams' 2-2 draw, and Louis Saha in Fulham's 2-0 win over Southampton.

28 Quinton Fortune's shot, deflected in by Danny Mills, gives Manchester United victory at Middlesbrough and puts them on top at the end of 2003. Wolves remain bottom, despite two goals by Steffen Iversen in a 3-1 win over Leeds. Darius Vassell, without a goal at Villa Park since New Year's Day, gets two in a 3-0 success against Fulham, while Robbie Fowler scores a 90th minute equaliser for Manchester City against former club Liverpool. Blackburn's 1-0 win at Newcastle is marred when Barry Ferguson sustains a fractured kneecap and is ruled out for the rest of the season.

29 Arsenal close to within a point of Manchester United as Robert Pires repeats his F.A. Cup winner against Southampton.

JANUARY

7 Bruno Cheyrou registers his first Premiership goal to give Liverpool victory at Chelsea. Arsenal are punished by one of their own players, on-loan Francis Jeffers setting up an Everton equaliser for Tomasz Radzinski. Stephane Dalmat scores twice as Tottenham beat Birmingham 4-1 after four successive defeats.

10 Kevin Nolan is on target after 14 seconds and goes on to hit the winner for Bolton, who come from 3-1 down to beat Blackburn 4-3. Jason Euell marks his 100th appearance for Charlton with both goals in the defeat of Wolves. Robbie Keane's winner for Tottenham piles on the pressure for his former club Leeds.

11 Referee Paul Durkin publicly admits he was wrong to deny Newcastle's Alan Shearer a penalty after being tripped by Manchester United goalkeeper Tim Howard. A fixture which normally produces plenty of goals ends 0-0. Chelsea bounce back with a 4-0 win at Leicester.

17 Kenny Miller's first Premiership goal enables Wolves to turn the table on its head by beating Manchester United. Helder Postiga scores his first in the League for Tottenham, who defeat Liverpool 2-1. Middlesbrough score twice in stoppage time to salvage a 3-3 draw with Leicester.

18 Two controversial Thierry Henry goals, one a quickly-taken free-kick and the second a penalty, account for Aston Villa and put Arsenal back on top. Chelsea stumble again, held to a goalless draw at home by Birmingham.

31 A bad day for goalkeepers Ian Walker and Paul Robinson. Walker grapples with a fan on the pitch during Leicester's 5-0 home defeat by Aston Villa. Robinson is sent off for bringing down Michael Ricketts as Middlesbrough win 3-0 at Leeds. Louis Saha scores on his debut for Manchester United, who beat Southampton 3-2 in front of a new record crowd of 67,758. Another new boy, Brian McBride, gets the winner for Fulham against Tottenham. Everton goalkeeper Nigel Martyn stars in a goalless Merseyside derby. United are top by a point – but only for a day.

FEBRUARY

1 Nicolas Anelka is sent off after a last-minute incident with Ashley Cole as Arsenal beat Manchester City 2-1. Chelsea win 3-2 at Blackburn with an 88th minute goal from Glen Johnson.

7 Gary Speed becomes the first player to make 400 Premiership appearances, in Newcastle's 3-1 win over Leicester. Ruud van Nistelrooy claims his 100th and 101st goals in all competitions for Manchester United, the second a last-minute winner after

Everton retrieve a 3-0 half-time deficit. Jon Stead nets the only goal of the game on his Blackburn debut at Middlesbrough. Jermain Defoe scores on his Tottenham debut in a 4-3 win over Portsmouth.

10 Thierry Henry scores his 100th and 101st Premiership goals – both disputed – for Arsenal, who beat Southampton 2-0. Leeds end a run of six successive League defeats by beating Wolves 4-1.

11 Two headed goals by Juninho pave the way for a shock 3-2 win by Middlesbrough at Old Trafford. Scott Parker opens his account for Chelsea in their 2-0 success at Portsmouth. Michael Owen ends a run of nine games without a goal in Liverpool's 2-1 victory over Manchester City.

21 Arsenal take charge of the title race. They concede a goal after 27 seconds, but win 2-1 at Stamford Bridge. Manchester United, meanwhile, are held 1-1 by Leeds. Two goals by Robbie Fowler set up Manchester City's first victory in 15 League games – 3-1 at Bolton. Blackburn goalkeeper Brad Friedel scores a 90th minute equaliser but is then beaten by Claus Jensen's shot which makes it 3-2 for Charlton.

22 After leading 3-1 at half-time, Tottenham need an 89th minute goal from Jermain Defoe, his second of the afternoon, to draw 4-4 with ten-man Leicester. Another late equaliser, from Stern John, earns Birmingham a 2-2 draw with Aston Villa, who surrender a 2-0 advantage.

28 Arsenal extend their lead to nine points as two goals in the first four minutes gives them a 2-1 win over Charlton. Manchester United falter again, held by Fulham despite an early goal against his former club from Louis Saha. Substitute Tomasz Radzinski sparks Everton, who win for the first time in the League in 2004, 2-0 against Aston Villa.

29 Newcastle are frustrated by one of their own players, on-loan Lomana LuaLua scoring an 88th minute equaliser for Portsmouth. A goal by Milan Baros on his Premiership return after nearly six months out with a broken ankle earns Liverpool a point at Leeds.

MARCH

6 After beating Middlesbrough 3-1 in midweek, Birmingham complete a double over the Carling Cup finalists with a 2-0 victory against Bolton.

13 A traumatic week for Leicester after incidents at a training camp in Spain ends on a much-needed high note with their first League win in 14 matches, Les Ferdinand scoring the only goal at Birmingham. Arsenal, who began to lose their grip on the championship the previous season when beaten at Blackburn, make no mistake this time, winning 2-0 despite having a goal disallowed when Thierry Henry intercepts an attempted clearance by goalkeeper Brad Friedel.

14 Manchester United's title hopes are effectively ended by Manchester City, whose 4-1 victory is their biggest local derby success since 1989. Paul Sturrock makes a winning start as manager of Southampton, who beat Liverpool 2-0. Juan Pablo Angel scores twice as Aston Villa win 4-0 at Wolves. .

20 Arsenal beat Bolton 2-1 to set a Premiership record of 31 successive games unbeaten. Two last-minute goals influence results for teams struggling against relegation. Marcus Bent earns Leicester a point against Everton. Wolves lose to Sami Hyypia's header for Liverpool. New boy Jon Stead scores for the third time in four games as Blackburn ease relegation worries with a 2-0 win at Aston Villa, only their second in 10 games.

21 A goal by the Nigerian striker Aiyegbeni Yakubu is enough to give Portsmouth their first win over arch-rivals Southampton at Fratton Park since 1963.

22 In their first match since a takeover secured the club's immediate future, Leeds move off the bottom with a 2-1 success against Manchester City, earned by Mark Viduka's controversial penalty.

27 Jimmy Floyd Hasselbaink comes off the bench to score his 100th Premiership goal on the way to a hat-trick in 13 minutes for Chelsea who beat Wolves 5-2. A goal eight minutes from time by Yakubu gives Portsmouth their first away win – 2-1 at Blackburn. Rory Delap savours his first goal for two years – a spectacular overhead volley to give Southampton victory over Tottenham.

28 Arsenal stretch their unbeaten run from the start of the season to a record 30 games in a 1-1 draw with Manchester United, Thierry Henry's 25-yard rocket being cancelled out by Louis Saha. They end the month seven points clear of Chelsea.

APRIL

3 On his 250th League appearance for Southampton spanning eight seasons, Claus Lundekvam scores for the first time in a 4-1 win at Wolves. Kevin Phillips nets twice and so does Alan Shearer in Newcastle's 4-2 victory over Everton.
5 Alan Smith hits the winner for Leeds after fellow-strugglers Leicester retrieve a 2-0 deficit. But Mark Viduka's sending-off is a blow.
9 Arsenal regroup after going out of the F.A. Cup to Manchester United and the Champions League to Chelsea, beating Liverpool 4-2 with a hat-trick by Thierry Henry. Everton's under-fire defenders David Unsworth, Gary Naysmith and Joseph Yobo turn match-winners with the goals that account for Tottenham.
10 Teenager Collins John, on only his second substitute appearance, scores both goals to give Fulham victory at Leicester. In games between relegation-threatened sides, a last-minute Shaun Wright-Phillips strike salvages a 3-3 draw for Manchester City against Wolves, while on-loan Stephen Caldwell scores in a 2-1 win by Leeds at Blackburn.
12 Collins John scores two more for Fulham, this time on his full debut, but Blackburn win a thriller 4-3. Chelsea's championship chances are virtually ended by a 3-2 defeat at Aston Villa. Charlton beat Liverpool at Anfield for the first time since 1954, thanks to the only goal of the game from Shaun Bartlett. Birmingham goalkeeper Maik Taylor is sent off for handling outside his area in a 3-1 setback at Portsmouth.
16 Thierry Henry gets four in a 5-0 romp against Leeds, becoming the first player to claim back-to-back hat-tricks at Highbury for more than half a century.
17 Steve Stone's goal on his 400th career appearance gives Portsmouth victory over Manchester United, takes their tally to 13 points from five games and moves them away from the relegation zone. Manager Kevin Keegan returns to the Manchester City dug-out after surgery on his back, but two goals for Kevin Phillips in Southampton's 3-1 success makes it 10 in 12 matches for him.
24 For the third time in four seasons, Danny Murphy gives Liverpool a 1-0 win at Manchester United, this time from the penalty spot. David James saves Paul Dickov's controversial penalty to keep Manchester City heads above water and virtually condemn Leicester to relegation in a 1-1 result. Blackburn climb to safety with the only goal at Everton, Jon Stead's fifth in 10 games.
25 After Chelsea go down 2-1 at Newcastle, Arsenal clinch the title in their 34th unbeaten game, against Tottenham who salvage some pride with a last-minute Robbie Keane penalty for 2-2. Portsmouth are safe after a 2-1 win which leaves Leeds on the brink.

MAY

1 Despite beating Everton 2-1, Wolves go down. So do Leicester after a 2-2 draw at Charlton, where Nikos Dabizas receives a red card which referee Rob Styles later rescinds. Paulo Wanchope's winner against Newcastle, his first goal for six months, leaves Manchester City safe. Martin Cranie, 17, concedes an own goal on his debut for Southampton, who lose 4-0 at Chelsea.
2 Leeds are relegated after a 4-1 defeat at Bolton Wand., where Mark Viduka is sent off for the second time in a month. Juan Pablo Angel's fifth minute header against Tottenham furthers Aston Villa's European ambitions.
4 Jose Antonio Reyes claims his first Premiership goal as Arsenal close in on an unbeaten season with a 1-1 draw at Portsmouth, for whom Aiyegbeni Yukubu scores for the seventh time in eight games.
8 Chelsea clinch the runners-up spot to Arsenal by holding Manchester United to 1-1 at Old Trafford. Liverpool, with another inspired performance from Steven Gerrard, move clear in the race for the fourth Champions League place with a 3-0 victory at

Birmingham. Paul Dickov scores one goal and has a hand in two more as Leicester beat Portsmouth 3-1 for their first home win for six months. Two by Youri Djorkaeff give Bolton their first League win at Everton since 1961.

9 Arsenal's Jose Antonio Reyes punishes an error by goalkeeper Edwin van der Sar to score the only goal against Fulham in the home side's final match at Loftus Road before returning to a redeveloped Craven Cottage.

12 Newcastle concede fourth place to Liverpool when held 3-3 at Southampton.

15 Arsenal come from behind to beat Leicester 2-1 with goals from Thierry Henry (pen) and Patrick Vieira and complete the season unbeaten. Chelsea fans bid an emotional farewell to coach Claudio Ranieri after his last match in charge against Leeds. Denis Irwin makes his 902nd, and final, career appearance as Wolves finish bottom after a 2-0 home defeat by Tottenham. Newcastle claim a UEFA Cup spot with a 1-1 draw at Liverpool. They move above Aston Villa after Villa lose 2-0 to Manchester United, who have Cristiano Ronaldo and Darren Fletcher sent off. Aiyegbeni Yakubu scores four times in Portsmouth's 5-1 defeat of Middlesbrough.

QUOTE – UNQUOTE

'There are some things he does with the ball that make me touch my head and wonder how he did it' – **Luis Figo** on his young Portuguese compatriot and new Manchester United signing Cristiano Ronaldo

'They've got the footballing brains collectively of a rocking horse' – **Keith Curle**, Mansfield Town manager, after his team conceded a last-minute equaliser against Leyton Orient.

'You can get booked for sneezing at players these days' – **Glenn Hoddle**, while Tottenham manager.

'We're in a dog-fight, but the fight in the dog will get us out of it' – **Sir Bobby Robson** after a sticky start to the season by his Newcastle side.

'Don't talk about my wife like that' – **David Beckham** to Sir Alex Ferguson during one of the rows which led to the England captain leaving Old Trafford for Real Madrid.

'He wanted a £200,000 bonus if we got into the Champions League. I said I would give him £2 million' – **Harry Redknapp**, Portsmouth manager, after an unsuccessful attempt to sign Argentinian Juan Sorin.

'I thought I was good in the air, but I've never headed one like that. It was awesome' – **Mick McCarthy**, Sunderland manager, after goalkeeper Mart Poom's spectacular stoppage-time equaliser against Derby.

'There are no excuses. What makes it worse is the fact it was senior players' – **Peter Hill-Wood**, Arsenal chairman, on shameful scenes at the end of the game against Manchester United at Old Trafford.

'We at Manchester United have to hope we win titles without any help' – **Sir Alex Ferguson** suggesting the F.A. did not punish Arsenal sufficiently

'For some people, even if you hang us, it will not be enough because you should hang us twice' – **Arsene Wenger**, Arsenal manager.

'As Gordon Strachan says, it's nice to see yourselves on the first page of Teletext' – **Alan Curbishley**, Charlton manager, on his side's climb into the top half of the table.

'I didn't know you were a Tottenham supporter' – **Graeme Souness** to referee Graham Poll, who was not amused and sent the Blackburn manager to the stands during the match against Tottenham.

HOW WENGER LET HIS TEAM DO THE TALKING

BY NEIL MARTIN

At approximately 4.26pm on Saturday May 15 there was a sense of predictability inside Highbury as Patrick Vieira supplied the finishing touches to a flowing Arsenal move to secure the Gunners a place in history. The Frenchman's goal, to put the home side 2-1 up against already relegated Leicester City, ensured Arsenal completed their entire League season without defeat and by that hazy, early summer day the result was totally expected.

However, it is important not to forget that expectations at the start of the amazing season were much lower, with major doubts over manager Arsene Wenger's transfer dealings.

Arsenal's pre-season tour was dominated by talk that he had added only goalkeeper Jens Lehmann – to replace David Seaman – to a squad that had finished runners-up to Manchester United in the previous campaign after stumbling badly in the home straight.

United, meanwhile, were parading more than £25m. worth of new talent after signing the likes of Cristiano Ronaldo, Kleberson and Tim Howard. And across London at Chelsea, Roman Abramovich spent a phenomenal £100m.-plus on a star-studded squad that many believed would overtake the static Gunners.

But the Premiership season started brightly for Wenger, not least because he had a 'new' signing in the centre of defence. With Martin Keown in the twilight of his career and the likes of Pascal Cygan and Igors Stepanovs unconvincing, the heart of the back-line again looked to be a weak spot. One journalist even dared to bet Wenger that his side would concede more than the 42 goals they had shipped in 2002-03.

But the man heralded for his transformation of unknown players into world stars, had the answer up his sleeve as he moved energetic full-back Kolo Toure alongside Sol Campbell in a move which formed the bedrock of their unbeaten run. Toure's athleticism and enthusiasm was the perfect foil to Campbell's no-nonsense tackling and power in the air, and the pair were virtually ever-present as Arsenal conceded just 26 League goals all season – costing that media man an expensive meal in the process.

Wenger's tactical genius was highlighted in a gruelling four-match Premiership run in autumn that brought consecutive fixtures against Manchester United, Newcastle, Liverpool and Chelsea – all sandwiched around two tough Champions League ties.

Arsenal drew with United in that tempestous clash at Old Trafford, but used the resulting furore to refocus their efforts and win the other three League matches to start whispers about the possibility of an unbeaten season.

However, Wenger had been down that road before and was still smarting. Midway through the 2002-03 season, he was reported as saying he would not be surprised if his side went through the season unbeaten. He was accused of arrogance and, although he rightly insisted he had been misquoted, in the wake of their October defeat to Wayne Rooney's Everton, there were T-shirts on sale depicting him as 'Comical Wenger' in a reference to the Iraqi Minister of Information who made outrageous statements during the second Gulf War.

Therefore, the Frenchman was naturally wary this time around, refusing to even utter the word 'unbeaten' despite the fact his side marched on relentlessly. Christmas, New Year and even Leap Day all came and went without any team seriously worrying the north Londoners, let alone scoring more goals than them. But Wenger refused to believe the amazing feat could be achieved until the aptly-named Good Friday fixture against Liverpool.

Arsenal went into the lunchtime match on the back of defeats against Manchester United and Chelsea in the FA Cup and Champions League that had ended their hopes of the Treble. And at half-time they were 2-1 down, fearing that for a second successive season they could throw the title away after dominating for so long.

However, Thierry Henry ripped the Merseysiders to shreds after the break and the resulting 4-2 victory finally convinced his manager that the remaining seven Premiership matches could be negotiated without loss.

That proved to be the case, even though the players visibly took their foot off the pedal when clinching the title with more than three weeks to spare.

The manager understandably enjoyed the hour-long post-match celebrations which marked the end of the 38th Premiership game against Leicester and was even photographed holding one of those 'Comical Wenger' shirts – along with the trophy – on the lap of honour. 'I was just a season too early,' he joked afterwards.

ARSENAL'S RECORD SEASON – P38 W26 D12 LO

AUGUST

16 Arsenal 2 (Henry 35 pen, Pires 58), Everton 1 (Radzinski 84). Att: 38,014.
24 Middlesbrough 0, Arsenal 4 (Henry 5, Gilberto Silva 13, Wiltord 22, 60). Att: 29,450.
27 Arsenal 2 (Campbell 57, Henry 90), Aston Villa 0. Att: 38,010.
31 Manchester City 1 (Lauren 10 og), Arsenal 2 (Wiltord 48, Ljungberg 72). Att: 46,436.

SEPTEMBER

13 Arsenal 1 (Henry 40 pen), Portsmouth 1 (Sheringham 26). Att: 38,052.
21 Manchester Utd. 0, Arsenal 0. Att: 67,639.
26 Arsenal 3 (Henry 18, 80 pen, Gilberto Silva 67), Newcastle Utd. 2 (Robert 26, Bernard 71). Att: 38,112.

OCTOBER

4 Liverpool 1 (Kewell 14), Arsenal 2 (Hyypia 31 og, Pires 68). Att: 44,374.
18 Arsenal 2 (Edu 5, Henry 75), Chelsea 1 (Crespo 8). Att: 38,172.
26 Charlton Athletic 1 (Di Canio 28 pen), Arsenal 1 (Henry 39). Att: 26,660.

NOVEMBER

1 Leeds Utd. 1 (Smith 64), Arsenal 4 (Henry 8, 33, Pires 17, Gilberto Silva 50). Att: 36,491.
8 Arsenal 2 (Pires 69, Ljungberg 79), Tottenham 1 (Anderton 5). Att: 38,101.
22 Birmingham City 0, Arsenal 3 (Ljungberg 4, Bergkamp 80, Pires 88). Att: 29,588.
30 Arsenal 0, Fulham 0. Att: 38,063.

DECEMBER

6 Leicester City 1 (Hignett 90), Arsenal 1 (Gilberto Silva 60). Att: 32,108.
14 Arsenal 1 (Bergkamp 11), Blackburn Rov. 0. Att: 37,677.
20 Bolton Wand. 1 (Pedersen 83), Arsenal 1 (Pires 57). Att: 28,003.
26 Arsenal 3 (Craddock 13 og, Henry 20, 89), Wolves 0. Att: 38,003.
29 Southampton 0, Arsenal 1 (Pires 35). Att: 32,151.

JANUARY

7 Everton 1 (Radzinksi 75), Arsenal 1 (Kanu 29). Att: 38,726.
10 Arsenal 4 (Henry 38 pen, Queudrue 45 og, Pires 57, Ljungberg 68), Middlesbrough 1 (Maccarone 86 pen). Att: 38,117.
18 Aston Villa 0, Arsenal 2 (Henry 29, 53 pen). Att: 39,380.

FEBRUARY

1 Arsenal 2 (Tarnat 39 og, Henry 83), Manchester City 1 (Anelka 89). Att: 38,103.
7 Wolves 1 (Ganea 26), Arsenal 3 (Bergkamp 9, Henry 58, Toure 63). Att: 29,392.
10 Arsenal 2 (Henry 31, 90), Southampton 0. Att: 38,007.
21 Chelsea 1 (Gudjohnsen 1), Arsenal 2 (Vieira 15, Edu 21). Att: 41,847.
28 Arsenal 2 (Pires 2, Henry 4), Charlton Athletic 1 (Jensen 59). Att: 38,137.

MARCH

13 Blackburn Rov 0, Arsenal 2 (Henry 53, Pires 86). Att: 28,627.
20 Arsenal 2 (Pires 16, Bergkamp 24), Bolton Wand. 1 (Campo 41). Att: 38,053.
28 Arsenal 1 (Henry 50), Manchester Utd. 1 (Saha 86). Att: 38,184.

APRIL

9 Arsenal 4 (Henry 31, 50, 78, Pires 49), Liverpool 2 (Hyypia 5, Owen 42). Att: 38,119.
11 Newcastle Utd. 0 Arsenal 0. Att: 52,141.
16 Arsenal 5 (Pires 6, Henry 27, 33 pen, 50, 67), Leeds Utd. 0. Att: 38,094.
25 Tottenham 2 (Redknapp 61, Keane 90 pen), Arsenal 2 (Vieira 2, Pires 34). Att: 36,097.

MAY

1 Arsenal 0 Birmingham City 0. Att: 38,061.
4 Portsmouth 1 (Yakubu 30), Arsenal 1 (Reyes 50). Att: 20,140.
9 Fulham 0 Arsenal 1 (Reyes 9). Att: 18,102.
15 Arsenal 2 (Henry 47 pen, Vieira 66), Leicester City 1 (Dickov 26). Att: 38,419.

CHELSEA'S PREVIOUS RUSSIAN TAKEOVER

The Roman Abramovich takeover last season was the second time Russia had written its name indelibly in Chelsea history. The first was 58 years earlier, on the afternoon of Tuesday, November 13, 1945, when Chelsea played Moscow Dynamo in the first big international club friendly after the war. The 3–3 draw pulled the biggest crowd ever to watch football at Stamford Bridge — 74,496 was the official attendance, but an estimated 100,000 packed the stadium. The exact figure could not be ascertained because thousands burst into the ground after the gates were closed an hour before kick-off.

REFEREES COME AND GO AT CARDIFF

All three match officials had a spell as referee during Cardiff's 3-2 home defeat by Reading. Mark Warren, who started in charge, limped off with a hamstring strain and was replaced by assistant referee Steve Habgood, with fourth official Brendan Malone taking over from Habgood. Malone's duties were assumed at half-time by the spectating League of Wales referee Anthony Jones. Habgood then went off with a calf injury and was replaced in the middle by the second appointed assistant Richard Smith. Jones took over on the line from Smith, with Habgood acting as fourth official until the end.

ALL THE FOURS AT CHESTERFIELD

When Chesterfield and Grimsby drew 4-4 at the Recreation Ground last season the attendance was . . . . . . 4,444.

FOOTBALL'S CHANGING HOMES

Work is now well under way after years of wrangling over a new 60,000-seater stadium for **Arsenal** at Ashburton Grove. Following problems with planning permission and worries over financing for the £400m. project, the builders are now on site and the foundations in place. Arsenal are confident the stadium will be open in time for the start of the 2006-2007 season when they will complete the move from their historic home at Highbury. As part of the relocation, Highbury will be turned into flats, with the pitch converted into a garden for the residents. **Manchester United**, the club Arsenal are trying to compete with financially, have started work on raising the Old Trafford capacity from 67,500 to 75,000 by filling in the corners of the massive north stand at a cost of £45m.

After two seasons sharing Loftus Road with Queens Park Rangers, **Fulham** return to a refurbished Craven Cottage for the new season. The club have spent £8m. bringing it up to Premiership requirements, with a capacity of 22,000. Seating has been installed on the enclosure terraces in front of the Stevenage Road stand and at both ends of the ground. In order for all the new seating to be under cover, a new roof has been built at the Putney end and the existing roof at the Hammersmith end extended. The original floodlights have been replaced and 'pods' of executive boxes built in three corners.

Charlton Athletic have unveiled plans to turn The Valley, current capacity 26,875, into a 40,000-plus stadium in a staggered development. A new upper tier on the east stand would increase the capacity to just over 30,000. Redevelopment of the Jimmy Seed stand, including the south-east and south-west corners, would raise it to more than 37,000. A third tier on the south stand would complete the transformation.

Premiership newcomers **Norwich City**, who unveiled a new 8,000-seater south stand last season, are to further boost the capacity of Carrow Road to 26,000 because of the demand for tickets. A full corner in-fill will be built between the new stand and the Norwich and Peterborough stand.

John Sillett, manager of the 1987 F.A. Cup-winning team, drove in the first stake at what will be the centre point of the pitch as work finally began on a new 32,000-seater stadium for **Coventry City**. The Arena project, which has been plagued with problems, is on the site of a former gasworks near the M6 and includes hotel, conference and music venue facilities. It was saved when Coventry City Council put in £21m. Scheduled opening date is August 2005.

Liberal Democrats, biggest party on the local council, have assured **Cardiff City** that plans for a new £100m. stadium opposite Ninian Park will receive their backing. There were concerns that if Labour lost control in the June elections, it could be shelved. **Wimbledon**, now known as **Milton Keynes Dons**, moved to the National Hockey Stadium early last season after 12 years of sharing Selhurst Park with Crystal Palace. Their first game at the new venue was a 2-2 draw against Burnley on September 27, watched by a crowd of 5,639. The club, now out of administration, hope eventually to build a permanent new home on the outskirts of Milton Keynes with a capacity of up to 30,000.

Swindon Town announced plans to move from the County Ground into an out-of-town, 22,000-seater stadium, incorporating a sports village and costing upwards of £20m. **Shrewsbury Town**, back in the Football League after winning the Conference Play-off Final, plan a new 10,000-capacity ground on the outskirts of the town for the 2005-06 season, with Gay Meadow being sold for luxury housing overlooking the river.

Cambridge United have received planning permission, subject to some conditions, to redevelop their Abbey Stadium, including a new all-seater stand to replace the Newmarket Road end terrace, together with hotel and commercial facilities. The west stand and north terrace at Brisbane Road were demolished during the close season as **Leyton Orient** moved towards a modern, 10,500-capacity ground incorporating residential development.

In Scotland, **Inverness Caledonian Thistle** will play their Premier League home matches 100 miles away at Aberdeen's Pittodrie ground because they do not have enough seating. The Division One champions were initially refused permission by the SPL to move up, but a second ballot of clubs gave approval.

F.A. BARCLAYCARD PREMIERSHIP RESULTS 2003-04

Column abbreviations (away teams): ARS = Arsenal, AVL = Aston Villa, BIR = Birmingham City, BLB = Blackburn Rov., BOL = Bolton Wand., CHA = Charlton Athletic, CHE = Chelsea, EVE = Everton, FUL = Fulham, LEE = Leeds Utd., LEI = Leicester City, LIV = Liverpool, MCI = Manchester City, MUN = Manchester Utd., MID = Middlesbrough, NEW = Newcastle Utd., POR = Portsmouth, SOU = Southampton, TOT = Tottenham, WOL = Wolves.

Home \ Away	ARS	AVL	BIR	BLB	BOL	CHA	CHE	EVE	FUL	LEE	LEI	LIV	MCI	MUN	MID	NEW	POR	SOU	TOT	WOL
Arsenal	–	2-0	0-0	1-0	2-1	2-1	2-1	1-1	2-1	5-0	1-1	4-2	2-1	1-1	4-1	3-2	1-1	2-0	2-1	3-0
Aston Villa	0-0	–	2-2	0-2	2-1	2-1	3-2	2-0	1-0	2-0	3-1	0-0	1-1	0-0	0-2	0-0	2-1	2-0	1-0	3-2
Birmingham City	0-3	0-0	–	0-4	2-0	1-2	0-0	3-0	2-2	4-1	0-1	0-3	1-1	1-2	2-1	1-1	2-1	2-1	2-1	2-2
Blackburn Rov.	0-2	0-2	0-4	–	3-4	0-1	2-3	2-1	3-1	1-2	1-0	1-3	2-3	1-0	2-2	1-2	1-2	0-1	0-1	5-1
Bolton Wand.	1-1	2-2	1-1	2-2	–	0-0	0-2	2-0	2-0	4-1	1-1	2-2	6-2	4-0	2-0	0-0	4-0	1-2	0-1	1-1
Charlton Athletic	1-1	1-2	0-1	3-2	0-0	–	4-2	1-0	2-1	1-0	2-2	2-2	1-1	2-0	0-0	3-1	1-2	3-2	0-1	2-0
Chelsea	1-2	1-0	0-0	2-2	1-2	4-2	–	0-0	2-1	1-0	0-0	0-1	1-0	1-1	1-2	5-0	0-2	4-0	0-0	5-2
Everton	1-1	2-0	1-0	0-1	1-2	1-0	0-1	–	3-1	4-0	3-2	0-3	0-0	3-4	1-1	2-2	1-0	0-0	3-0	2-0
Fulham	0-1	1-2	0-2	3-4	1-2	0-1	0-1	2-1	–	2-0	2-0	1-2	0-0	1-0	2-1	2-3	0-0	2-2	2-0	0-0
Leeds Utd.	1-4	0-0	0-2	2-1	0-2	2-0	1-1	1-1	2-0	–	2-2	2-2	2-1	0-1	2-3	1-0	1-2	0-1	2-1	4-1
Leicester City	1-1	0-5	0-2	2-0	1-1	3-3	1-1	1-1	3-2	4-0	–	0-0	1-1	1-4	0-3	1-1	2-1	2-2	4-4	0-0
Liverpool	1-2	1-0	3-1	4-0	3-1	0-1	1-2	0-0	0-0	3-1	0-0	–	2-1	1-2	0-1	1-1	3-0	3-1	2-1	0-0
Manchester City	1-2	4-1	3-0	1-1	6-2	1-1	1-0	5-1	0-0	1-1	1-3	2-2	–	1-4	0-1	2-3	4-2	3-2	4-2	3-3
Manchester Utd.	0-0	4-0	3-0	2-1	4-0	2-0	1-1	3-2	1-3	1-1	1-0	4-1	1-1	–	2-3	0-0	3-0	3-2	2-1	1-0
Middlesbrough	0-4	1-2	5-3	0-0	2-0	0-0	1-2	1-0	2-3	2-3	0-3	0-0	0-1	2-3	–	0-1	5-1	3-1	3-0	2-0
Newcastle Utd.	0-0	1-1	1-1	1-0	0-0	3-1	2-1	4-2	3-1	1-0	1-1	1-1	2-3	1-2	2-2	–	1-1	3-1	4-0	1-1
Portsmouth	0-1	2-1	3-1	1-2	4-0	1-2	0-2	1-0	0-0	6-1	2-1	1-3	4-2	1-0	5-1	1-1	–	0-0	1-0	0-0
Southampton	0-1	1-1	0-0	2-0	1-2	3-2	0-1	3-3	0-0	0-1	0-0	2-0	0-2	1-0	0-1	3-3	3-0	–	1-0	2-0
Tottenham	2-2	2-1	4-1	1-0	0-1	0-1	0-1	2-1	2-1	2-1	4-4	2-1	1-1	1-2	2-1	4-0	4-3	1-3	–	5-2
Wolves	1-3	0-4	1-1	2-2	1-2	0-4	0-5	2-1	2-1	3-1	4-3	1-1	1-0	0-1	2-0	1-1	0-0	1-4	0-2	–

Read across for home results, down for away.

44

NATIONWIDE LEAGUE RESULTS 2003-04 – FIRST DIVISION

Home \ Away	Bradford City	Burnley	Cardiff City	Coventry City	Crewe Alexandra	Crystal Palace	Derby Co.	Gillingham	Ipswich Town	Millwall	Norwich City	Nott'm. Forest	Preston N.E.	Reading	Rotherham Utd.	Sheffield Utd.	Stoke City	Sunderland	Walsall	Watford	W.B.A.	West Ham Utd.	Wigan Athletic	Wimbledon
Bradford City	–	1-2	2-0	1-0	2-2	0-1	3-2	1-0	3-1	3-1	0-1	0-1	1-0	2-2	1-2	2-0	1-0	3-0	1-0	1-0	2-0	1-0	1-0	2-1
Burnley	4-0	–	2-0	4-0	3-1	0-0	2-3	2-1	4-2	1-1	3-5	1-3	2-1	3-0	2-3	3-2	2-1	0-2	0-1	0-1	2-3	1-1	0-2	2-0
Cardiff City	0-2	2-0	–	0-1	3-0	2-1	4-1	5-0	2-3	1-3	2-1	0-0	2-2	2-3	1-0	0-1	3-1	4-0	4-1	0-1	0-1	0-0	0-2	1-1
Coventry City	0-0	4-0	0-1	–	3-1	2-1	3-0	1-1	2-1	1-0	2-1	3-1	1-1	2-3	0-0	0-2	4-2	2-1	2-1	0-1	1-2	0-3	1-1	1-1
Crewe Alexandra	2-2	3-1	3-0	3-1	–	2-3	1-1	1-0	2-2	1-1	1-3	3-1	4-1	2-3	1-0	0-1	6-3	3-0	0-1	2-0	1-2	0-3	2-3	1-0
Crystal Palace	0-1	0-0	2-1	2-1	2-3	–	1-1	2-1	1-1	1-0	0-4	4-2	1-0	2-3	0-1	0-3	0-1	1-3	3-0	3-1	1-2	1-2	2-3	3-1
Derby Co.	3-2	2-2	1-3	1-1	2-0	2-1	–	0-0	2-2	2-1	1-2	1-0	0-1	2-3	1-0	2-0	6-3	0-1	3-0	3-2	0-3	0-1	0-3	3-1
Gillingham	1-0	2-1	1-2	2-5	1-3	3-4	1-2	–	1-1	4-3	1-2	1-2	2-0	0-1	0-3	3-0	1-0	1-3	3-0	4-1	2-3	2-1	0-3	1-2
Ipswich Town	3-1	6-1	1-1	1-3	1-1	0-0	0-0	0-0	–	2-2	0-1	1-1	2-0	2-3	3-0	3-0	2-1	3-1	1-0	1-2	4-1	1-1	1-2	2-1
Millwall	3-1	6-1	6-4	1-1	0-0	3-1	0-0	2-1	4-3	–	1-2	2-0	0-1	3-1	2-1	0-3	1-0	0-2	2-1	1-2	4-0	1-3	2-0	3-1
Norwich City	0-1	2-0	2-0	0-4	2-0	4-0	0-1	1-2	2-0	2-0	–	0-0	2-0	2-0	2-1	1-1	1-0	2-0	3-0	1-2	1-0	2-1	2-1	3-2
Nott'm. Forest	3-1	1-1	0-4	1-1	1-2	0-0	2-1	1-2	1-1	2-0	3-1	–	0-1	5-1	2-2	2-2	0-1	0-2	5-0	1-2	0-3	3-3	2-0	3-2
Preston N.E.	1-0	5-3	1-2	4-2	0-0	4-1	3-2	2-0	1-3	0-1	2-0	2-2	–	2-1	4-1	3-3	1-0	0-1	2-0	1-1	3-0	0-2	2-4	2-0
Reading	2-2	2-2	2-1	2-0	0-3	3-1	3-1	2-1	1-0	3-1	0-1	0-1	0-1	–	4-1	2-1	2-1	0-2	2-0	2-1	3-0	2-0	1-0	6-0
Rotherham Utd.	1-2	3-0	2-2	2-0	0-2	1-2	2-1	1-1	1-3	2-0	0-0	2-2	3-2	5-1	–	0-2	3-0	1-2	2-0	2-0	3-0	1-3	0-3	0-3
Sheffield Utd.	2-0	0-0	5-3	2-0	1-2	0-3	3-1	3-0	3-0	3-0	4-4	4-1	3-0	1-2	5-0	–	0-1	0-0	0-2	2-0	2-0	0-2	1-1	3-1
Stoke City	1-0	2-3	2-3	1-0	0-1	3-1	2-1	1-0	2-1	1-0	0-1	1-0	1-0	2-1	2-0	2-0	–	1-1	2-0	0-2	0-2	0-2	0-3	2-1
Sunderland	3-0	1-1	2-3	2-0	0-1	0-1	2-1	3-2	3-2	0-1	1-3	3-3	3-3	3-0	0-2	2-1	3-1	–	0-2	2-2	4-1	3-3	1-0	2-1
Walsall	1-0	0-1	1-1	1-6	1-1	0-0	1-1	2-1	2-0	2-1	0-1	4-1	0-1	2-0	0-1	0-2	1-1	0-1	–	3-2	0-1	0-2	2-1	1-0
Watford	1-0	0-1	2-1	1-1	1-5	2-0	2-1	4-1	3-2	1-2	1-1	1-1	2-1	0-2	1-0	0-2	3-0	2-2	3-2	–	1-0	0-1	2-1	4-0
W.B.A	2-0	4-1	3-0	3-0	1-1	1-5	2-1	2-2	4-1	2-0	1-0	0-2	1-1	3-0	1-0	0-2	0-2	1-1	0-1	1-0	–	3-4	2-1	-01
West Ham Utd.	1-0	2-2	2-0	2-0	4-2	3-0	0-0	2-1	2-1	4-1	0-1	1-1	2-1	1-0	2-0	0-2	1-0	3-3	3-0	4-0	3-4	–	4-0	5-0
Wigan Athletic	1-0	0-2	3-0	2-0	2-3	3-0	0-0	1-2	1-1	0-0	2-0	1-1	1-2	0-2	1-2	1-1	0-1	2-1	1-1	2-1	0-0	1-1	–	0-1
Wimbledon	2-1	2-2	0-1	0-3	3-1	1-0	1-0	1-2	1-2	0-1	0-1	0-1	3-3	0-3	1-2	1-2	0-1	0-2	1-0	1-3	0-0	1-1	2-4	–

Read across for home results, down for away.

NATIONWIDE LEAGUE RESULTS 2003-04 – SECOND DIVISION

	Barnsley	Blackpool	Bournemouth	Brentford	Brighton & H.A.	Bristol City	Chesterfield	Colchester Utd.	Grimsby Town	Hartlepool Utd.	Luton Town	Notts Co.	Oldham Athletic	Peterborough Utd.	Plymouth Argyle	Port Vale	Q.P.R.	Rushden & D's	Sheffield Wed.	Stockport Co.	Swindon Town	Tranmere Rov.	Wrexham	Wycombe Wand.
Barnsley	–	3-0	1-1	0-2	3-1	1-0	0-1	1-0	0-1	2-2	0-0	1-1	1-1	1-1	1-0	0-0	3-3	2-0	1-1	3-3	1-1	2-0	2-1	0-0
Blackpool	0-2	–	1-2	0-2	1-0	1-0	2-2	0-1	0-1	4-0	6-3	2-1	1-0	1-4	1-3	2-1	2-3	1-3	4-1	3-3	2-2	1-5	0-1	3-2
Bournemouth	2-2	1-2	–	1-0	0-0	1-4	2-2	4-0	0-1	1-0	6-3	2-3	1-0	0-3	2-1	3-1	2-2	2-3	2-1	0-0	2-2	1-5	6-0	1-0
Brentford	2-1	0-0	1-0	–	4-0	0-0	2-2	0-1	4-0	2-1	6-3	2-3	2-1	0-3	1-3	3-2	1-3	3-1	2-2	0-0	0-2	1-5	1-0	1-0
Brighton & H.A.	1-0	4-0	3-0	1-0	–	1-4	4-0	2-1	1-0	2-0	4-2	5-0	2-2	0-3	1-1	1-0	2-2	0-0	2-1	2-0	2-0	3-0	2-0	4-0
Bristol City	3-0	3-1	3-1	3-1	1-1	–	2-1	2-1	3-0	2-5	2-2	2-1	2-1	0-3	1-1	2-1	1-2	3-2	3-1	0-2	0-3	3-0	2-0	1-1
Chesterfield	0-2	1-1	1-0	1-2	0-2	1-1	–	1-0	4-4	1-2	2-2	4-1	3-3	0-0	1-0	4-2	2-2	2-0	2-0	0-2	3-0	2-2	2-1	2-1
Colchester Utd.	1-1	0-2	1-1	1-0	0-2	1-2	1-0	–	2-0	0-2	3-2	4-0	2-0	0-0	0-2	1-1	1-4	2-0	2-0	1-1	0-1	1-1	3-1	2-2
Grimsby Town	6-1	0-2	1-3	0-1	2-1	1-1	1-0	1-2	–	8-1	4-3	4-0	3-3	0-0	1-4	2-0	1-4	1-3	2-0	2-2	0-3	1-1	3-3	3-1
Hartlepool Utd.	1-2	2-1	2-1	2-0	2-0	3-2	1-0	2-0	1-2	–	3-1	4-0	1-1	1-2	2-1	1-2	1-3	3-1	1-1	2-2	0-2	2-2	1-3	3-1
Luton Town	0-1	3-2	1-1	4-1	2-0	2-3	1-2	0-0	8-1	1-1	–	4-0	1-1	2-0	2-0	2-1	3-3	3-2	2-1	2-1	2-3	0-1	3-2	1-1
Notts Co.	1-1	4-1	3-2	1-1	1-3	0-1	0-0	3-0	3-1	3-4	1-1	–	1-1	3-0	1-2	1-4	3-3	3-2	2-0	4-1	0-3	1-1	0-1	2-3
Oldham Athletic	2-3	0-1	1-1	0-0	3-3	1-1	6-0	0-2	3-0	2-5	1-2	5-2	–	2-0	0-0	2-3	0-0	2-1	2-2	2-2	4-2	1-0	6-1	2-1
Peterborough Utd.	2-0	1-0	1-0	2-0	3-3	1-0	1-2	0-0	3-1	2-1	2-1	1-0	1-0	–	4-1	3-1	1-4	3-2	3-0	2-1	4-2	0-0	0-0	2-0
Plymouth Argyle	2-0	1-0	1-0	1-1	2-1	4-3	3-0	3-0	5-1	2-5	1-0	3-2	1-0	2-0	–	4-1	1-2	3-2	3-0	1-0	2-3	6-0	2-0	2-1
Port Vale	3-1	2-1	3-1	2-1	0-1	2-1	2-0	4-1	3-0	2-5	1-1	1-0	4-1	0-0	1-5	–	3-2	3-3	3-0	1-1	4-2	0-0	6-1	1-1
Q.P.R.	4-0	2-3	2-3	2-1	2-1	2-0	2-0	3-0	3-0	2-5	1-1	3-2	1-0	3-0	3-0	3-0	–	3-3	2-1	2-1	3-3	6-1	0-0	0-0
Rushden & D's	2-3	0-1	0-3	1-1	1-3	4-0	1-1	2-0	1-2	2-2	2-2	2-1	2-2	2-0	4-1	2-1	3-3	–	2-2	1-1	1-1	1-1	2-0	2-0
Sheffield Wed.	2-3	0-1	1-1	2-0	1-1	0-1	2-0	0-0	1-0	1-0	0-0	2-1	1-0	3-0	1-3	0-2	1-3	0-0	–	1-1	1-0	2-3	0-1	2-0
Stockport Co.	2-3	1-3	3-2	1-1	2-1	1-3	2-0	2-0	1-2	2-1	3-2	4-0	2-2	2-1	2-3	0-0	1-1	4-2	2-2	–	1-0	2-0	3-2	2-1
Swindon Town	1-1	2-2	2-1	2-1	1-0	0-1	2-0	2-0	3-0	4-0	2-1	4-0	2-1	2-4	0-0	1-0	1-1	4-2	2-2	3-2	–	2-0	0-3	2-1
Tranmere Rov.	2-0	0-1	2-1	4-1	2-1	2-1	2-3	1-1	3-0	4-0	1-0	4-0	2-1	1-2	2-3	1-0	2-1	1-1	1-2	1-0	1-0	–	2-1	2-1
Wrexham	1-0	4-2	0-1	1-0	0-2	0-0	1-1	1-2	3-0	1-2	2-1	0-1	1-2	2-3	3-0	2-1	0-2	1-1	1-2	3-2	1-0	0-1	–	2-1
Wycombe Wand.	1-2	0-3	2-0	1-2	1-1	3-3	1-2	3-4	4-1	0-0	0-0	2-5	2-1	1-2	2-1	2-2	2-2	0-2	1-2	1-0	0-3	1-2	1-1	–

Read across for home results, down for away.

46

NATIONWIDE LEAGUE RESULTS 2003-04 – THIRD DIVISION

	Boston Utd.	Bristol Rov.	Bury	Cambridge Utd.	Carlisle Utd.	Cheltenham Town	Darlington	Doncaster Rov.	Huddersfield Town	Hull City	Kidderminster Harr.	Leyton Orient	Lincoln City	Macclesfield Town	Mansfield Town	Northampton Town	Oxford Utd.	Rochdale	Scunthorpe Utd.	Southend Utd.	Swansea City	Torquay Utd.	Yeovil Town	York City
Boston Utd.	–	1-0	1-2	1-2	1-0	3-1	1-0	0-0	2-2	1-2	3-1	3-0	3-1	1-1	1-2	1-2	1-0	0-0	1-0	0-2	1-2	4-0	3-2	2-0
Bristol Rov.	2-0	–	1-2	0-2	1-0	2-0	0-3	1-3	1-0	2-2	0-0	1-4	0-0	1-3	3-0	1-2	0-4	0-2	3-2	1-1	2-0	2-2	2-1	3-0
Bury	1-3	0-0	–	0-0	1-3	2-1	1-0	3-3	3-1	0-2	2-1	3-0	0-2	3-2	2-4	4-3	2-0	3-2	1-4	1-2	2-1	1-1	1-4	2-0
Cambridge Utd.	0-1	3-1	1-2	–	2-0	2-1	2-1	0-0	4-0	3-1	5-0	2-1	1-2	0-1	4-2	2-3	0-0	2-1	2-2	0-0	3-4	3-1	2-0	2-0
Carlisle Utd.	1-0	0-2	2-1	0-0	–	2-1	3-1	0-0	3-3	1-1	1-1	1-1	0-0	4-0	1-3	0-0	2-0	1-0	3-2	3-2	1-2	1-0	3-2	1-2
Cheltenham Town	3-0	1-2	4-1	0-3	2-1	–	4-2	0-0	6-2	2-2	3-0	1-2	0-3	1-4	2-1	0-4	2-1	0-1	1-0	0-0	3-0	1-0	1-0	1-1
Darlington	3-0	0-4	1-3	0-1	1-0	2-1	–	1-0	2-2	2-3	1-1	1-1	1-3	3-2	4-1	1-2	4-2	1-1	4-2	3-2	2-1	0-1	0-0	3-1
Doncaster Rov.	2-0	2-1	2-0	2-2	2-0	3-3	4-1	–	0-1	0-2	1-0	1-2	2-2	3-1	0-3	3-0	2-1	1-0	5-0	2-1	2-1	1-0	2-3	0-1
Huddersfield Town	2-1	2-1	0-2	2-2	2-1	0-0	1-0	3-1	–	3-1	6-1	3-0	3-1	4-0	3-0	0-0	0-0	0-1	3-2	1-0	2-1	1-3	4-1	1-1
Hull City	2-0	0-2	2-1	2-1	2-1	2-0	1-1	0-0	4-2	–	1-1	3-0	1-2	2-1	2-0	0-0	2-0	2-1	1-1	2-2	3-0	2-1	2-0	4-1
Kidderminster Harr.	1-3	1-0	2-0	2-1	0-3	1-4	1-1	3-1	0-1	2-1	–	3-0	1-1	2-4	2-1	2-3	2-0	0-1	1-2	2-1	2-1	2-1	2-3	3-0
Leyton Orient	1-1	3-1	2-1	2-2	1-1	3-0	3-1	4-1	2-1	1-1	1-1	–	0-0	3-2	4-1	0-4	4-2	1-0	1-1	0-0	1-1	1-3	2-0	0-0
Lincoln City	0-0	2-1	5-3	0-1	2-3	4-0	3-1	1-1	1-0	1-5	0-1	0-0	–	3-2	0-3	0-4	0-0	1-0	5-0	1-0	1-1	2-1	0-1	1-0
Macclesfield Town	2-1	3-2	3-2	2-1	2-0	0-1	3-1	0-0	0-1	1-0	0-1	1-3	1-3	–	2-1	1-2	2-2	2-2	3-2	2-2	3-0	2-1	0-1	3-1
Mansfield Town	0-0	0-0	3-2	2-0	3-1	1-1	3-1	0-0	1-1	1-1	0-1	3-0	0-3	3-2	–	3-0	1-1	3-1	3-2	1-0	0-0	1-1	1-3	0-0
Northampton Town	1-0	2-2	0-0	2-1	1-0	4-2	4-1	2-0	1-1	2-2	0-1	4-2	1-0	1-0	1-0	–	1-1	2-2	3-2	2-1	2-0	1-2	1-0	0-0
Oxford Utd.	0-1	1-2	1-0	2-3	1-2	5-2	3-0	0-0	1-1	2-2	3-0	1-1	1-3	1-0	0-0	0-1	–	4-0	4-2	2-3	2-1	1-2	0-2	1-2
Rochdale	0-2	1-0	0-0	0-0	4-2	3-0	3-2	4-0	2-2	2-3	3-0	1-1	2-2	1-0	4-2	4-2	2-0	–	0-2	2-3	2-1	1-2	0-2	0-0
Scunthorpe Utd.	2-0	4-0	3-0	4-1	3-1	3-1	1-1	3-1	0-1	1-1	1-1	3-0	2-0	4-1	1-0	3-1	0-0	1-3	–	1-2	3-0	1-2	0-2	1-2
Southend Utd.	2-0	4-0	4-1	3-0	0-1	0-2	0-2	1-0	1-1	0-2	2-0	1-2	3-1	0-2	3-0	0-2	1-1	1-2	2-0	–	1-1	1-2	2-2	3-0
Swansea City	1-1	2-1	1-1	2-0	1-0	2-1	1-1	1-0	2-1	2-1	2-1	1-2	0-3	1-0	2-1	3-1	1-0	3-1	1-0	2-0	–	2-1	2-1	1-2
Torquay Utd.	4-0	4-1	1-1	3-0	3-0	0-2	1-1	2-1	2-2	0-2	1-0	2-1	3-1	2-0	1-0	0-2	2-2	1-2	3-2	4-0	0-0	–	0-0	1-1
Yeovil Town	1-1	1-1	2-2	4-1	2-2	0-2	1-1	1-0	0-1	0-2	1-0	1-2	3-1	0-2	1-2	1-0	2-2	1-2	2-0	0-0	0-0	0-0	–	1-2
York City	1-1	2-0	1-2	0-2	4-0	0-2	1-1	1-0	2-0	0-2	1-1	1-2	1-4	0-2	1-2	1-0	2-2	1-2	1-3	3-0	0-0	0-0	1-2	–

Read across for home results, down for away.

47

FINAL TABLES 2003-04

F.A. BARCLAYCARD PREMIERSHIP

		P	HOME					AWAY					Pts	GD
			W	D	L	F	A	W	D	L	F	A		
1	Arsenal	38	15	4	0	40	14	11	8	0	33	12	90	+47
2	Chelsea	38	12	4	3	34	13	12	3	4	33	17	79	+37
3	Manchester Utd.	38	12	4	3	37	15	11	2	6	27	20	75	+29
4	Liverpool	38	10	4	5	29	15	6	8	5	26	22	60	+18
5	Newcastle Utd.	38	11	5	3	33	14	2	12	5	19	26	56	+12
6	Aston Villa	38	9	6	4	24	19	6	5	8	24	25	56	+4
7	Charlton Athletic	38	7	6	6	29	29	7	5	7	22	22	53	0
8	Bolton Wand.	38	6	8	5	24	21	8	3	8	24	35	53	-8
9	Fulham	38	9	4	6	29	21	5	6	8	23	25	52	+6
10	Birmingham City	38	5	6	8	26	24	4	9	6	17	24	50	-5
11	Middlesbrough	38	8	4	7	25	23	5	5	9	19	29	48	-8
12	Southampton	38	8	6	5	24	17	4	5	10	20	28	47	-1
13	Portsmouth	38	10	4	5	35	19	2	5	12	12	35	45	-7
14	Tottenham	38	9	4	6	33	27	4	2	13	14	30	45	-10
15	Blackburn Rov.	38	5	4	10	25	31	7	4	8	26	28	44	-8
16	Manchester City	38	5	9	5	31	24	4	5	10	24	30	41	+1
17	Everton	38	8	5	6	27	20	1	7	11	18	37	39	-12
18	Leicester City	38	3	10	6	19	28	3	5	11	29	37	33	-17
19	Leeds Utd.	38	5	7	7	25	31	3	2	14	15	48	33	-39
20	Wolves	38	5	7	5	23	35	0	7	12	15	42	33	-39

(Arsenal and Chelsea go straight into the Champions League group stage; Manchester Utd. and Liverpool into the third qualifying round. Newcastle Utd., Middlesbrough and Millwall go into the UEFA Cup.)

Prize-money: 1 £10.90m, 2 £10.35m, 3 £9.81m, 4 £9.26m, 5 £8.72m, 6 £8.17m, 7 £7.63m, 8 £7.08m, 9 £6.54m, 10 £5.99m, 11 £5.45m, 12 £4.90m, 13 £4.36m, 14 £3.81m, 15 £3.27m, 16 £2.72m, 17 £2.18m, 18 £1.63m, 19 £1.09m, 20 £545,000.

Biggest win: Arsenal 5, Leeds Utd. 0; Chelsea 5, Newcastle Utd. 0; Leicester City 0, Aston Villa 5; Portsmouth 6, Leeds Utd. 1; Wolves 0, Chelsea 5.

Highest attendance: 67,758 (Manchester Utd. v Southampton).

Lowest attendance: 13,981 (Fulham v Blackbun Rov.).

Manager of Year: Arsene Wenger (Arsenal).

Player of Year: Thierry Henry (Arsenal).

Golden Boot: 30 Thierry Henry.

Golden Glove: Jens Lehmann (Arsenal).

Football Writers' Association Footballer of Year: Thierry Henry.

PFA Player of Year: Thierry Henry.

PFA Young Player of Year: Scott Parker (Chelsea).

PFA divisional team: Howard (Manchester Utd.), Lauren (Arsenal), Campbell (Arsenal), Terry (Chelsea), Cole (Arsenal), Gerrard (Liverpool), Lampard (Chelsea), Pires (Arsenal), Vieira (Arsenal), Henry (Arsenal), Van Nistelroov (Manchester Utd.).

Fair Play award: Arsenal

Leading scorers (all club competitions): 39 Henry (Arsenal); 30 Van Nistelrooy (Manchester Utd.); 28 Shearer (Newcastle Utd.); 24 Anelka (Manchester City), Stead (Blackburn Rov.) – 18 for Huddersfield Town; 23 Angel (Aston Villa); 22 Defoe (Tottenham) – 15 for West Ham Utd.); Saha (Manchester Utd.) – 15 for Fulham; 19 Forssell (Birmingham City), Owen (Liverpool), Pires (Arsenal), Yakubu (Portsmouth); 17 Beattie (Southampton), Hasselbaink (Chelsea); 16 Keane (Tottenham); 15 Lampard (Chelsea); 14 Scholes (Manchester Utd.); 13 Dickov (Leicester City), Ferdinand (Leicester City), Gudjohnsen (Chelsea), Phillips (Southampton); 12 Crespo (Chelsea), Heskey (Liverpool), Kanoute (Tottenham), Nolan (Bolton Wand.), Robert (Newcastle Utd.), Viduka (Leeds Utd.).

NATIONWIDE LEAGUE

FIRST DIVISION

			HOME				AWAY						
		P	W	D	L	F	A	W	D	L	F	A	Pts	GD
1	Norwich City	46	18	3	2	44	15	10	7	6	35	24	94	+40
2	W.B.A.	46	14	5	4	34	16	11	6	6	30	26	86	+22
3	Sunderland	46	13	8	2	33	15	9	5	9	29	30	79	+17
4	West Ham Utd.	46	12	7	4	42	20	7	10	6	25	25	74	+22
5	Ipswich Town	46	12	3	8	49	36	9	7	7	35	36	73	+12
6	Crystal Palace*	46	10	8	5	34	25	11	2	10	38	36	73	+11
7	Wigan Athletic	46	11	8	4	29	16	7	9	7	31	29	71	+15
8	Sheffield Utd.	46	11	6	6	37	25	9	5	9	28	31	71	+9
9	Reading	46	11	6	6	29	25	9	4	10	26	32	70	−2
10	Millwall	46	11	8	4	28	15	7	7	9	27	33	69	+7
11	Stoke City	46	11	7	5	35	24	7	5	11	23	31	66	+3
12	Coventry City	46	9	9	5	34	22	8	5	10	33	32	65	+13
13	Cardiff City	46	10	6	7	40	25	7	8	8	28	33	65	+10
14	Nott'm Forest	46	8	9	6	33	25	7	6	10	28	33	60	+3
15	Preston N.E.	46	11	7	5	43	29	4	7	12	26	42	59	−2
16	Watford	46	9	8	6	31	28	6	4	13	23	40	57	−14
17	Rotherham Utd.	46	8	8	7	31	27	5	7	11	22	34	54	−8
18	Crewe Alexandra	46	11	3	9	33	26	3	8	12	24	40	53	−9
19	Burnley	46	9	6	8	37	32	4	8	11	23	45	53	−17
20	Derby Co.	46	11	5	7	39	33	2	8	13	14	34	52	−14
21	Gillingham	46	10	1	12	28	34	4	8	11	20	33	51	−19
22	Walsall	46	8	7	8	29	31	5	5	13	16	34	51	−20
23	Bradford City	46	6	3	14	23	35	4	3	16	15	34	36	−31
24	Wimbledon	46	3	4	16	21	40	5	1	17	20	49	29	−48

(* Also promoted via play-offs)

Biggest win: Nott'm Forest 6, Wimbledon 0.
Highest attendance: 36,278 (Sunderland v Walsall).
Lowest attendance: 1,054 (Wimbledon v Wigan Athletic).
Manager of Year: Nigel Worthington (Norwich City).
Player of Year: Darren Huckerby (Norwich City).
Top League scorer: 27 Andrew Johnson (Crystal Palace).
PFA divisional team: Green (Norwich City), Jagielka (Sheffield Utd.), Gabbidon (Cardiff City), Mackay (Norwich City), Arca (Sunderland), Cahill (Millwall), Carrick (West Ham Utd.), Koumas (W.B.A.), Reid (Nott'm Forest), Earnshaw (Cardiff City), Johnson (Crystal Palace).
Fair Play award: Crewe Alexandra.
Leading scorers (all club competitions): 32 Johnson (Crystal Palace); 26 Earnshaw (Cardiff City), Harewood (West Ham Utd.) – 12 for Nott'm Forest; 22 Blake (Burnley), McKenzie (Norwich City) – 13 for Peterborough Utd.; 21 McSheffrey (Coventry City) – 9 for Luton Town; 20 Ashton (Crewe Alexandra); 19 Ellington (Wigan Athletic), Fuller (Preston N.E.); 17 Bent (Ipswich Town), Kuqi (Ipswich Town) – 5 for Sheffield Wed., Lowe (Coventry City) – 16 for Rushden & Diamonds; 16 Jones, S (Crewe Alexandra), Kitson (Reading) – 11 for Cambridge Utd., Kyle (Sunderland), Stewart (Sunderland); 15 Butler (Rotherham Utd.), Freedman (Crystal Palace), Healy (Preston N.E.), Huckerby (Norwich City) – 1 for Manchester City, Lester (Sheffield Utd.); 14 Connolly (West Ham Utd.), Goater (Reading), Horsfield (W.B.A.) – 7 for Wigan Athletic.

SECOND DIVISION

		P	W	D	L	F	A	W	D	L	F	A	Pts	GD
			HOME					**AWAY**						
1	Plymouth Argyle	46	17	5	1	52	13	9	7	7	33	28	90	+44
2	Q.P.R.	46	16	7	0	47	12	6	10	7	33	33	83	+35
3	Bristol City	46	15	6	2	34	12	8	7	8	24	25	82	+21
4	Brighton & H.A.*	46	17	4	2	39	11	5	7	11	25	32	77	+21
5	Swindon Town	46	12	7	4	41	23	8	6	9	35	35	73	+18
6	Hartlepool Utd.	46	10	8	5	39	24	10	5	8	37	37	73	+15
7	Port Vale	46	15	6	2	45	28	6	4	13	28	35	73	+10
8	Tranmere Rov.	46	13	7	3	36	18	4	9	10	23	38	67	+3
9	Bournemouth	46	11	8	4	35	25	6	7	10	21	26	66	+5
10	Luton Town	46	14	6	3	44	27	3	9	11	25	39	66	+3
11	Colchester Utd.	46	11	8	4	33	23	6	5	12	19	33	64	−4
12	Barnsley	46	7	12	4	25	19	8	5	10	29	39	62	−4
13	Wrexham	46	9	6	8	27	21	8	3	12	23	39	60	−10
14	Blackpool	46	9	5	9	31	28	7	6	10	27	37	59	−7
15	Oldham Athletic	46	9	8	6	37	25	3	13	7	29	35	57	+6
16	Sheffield Wed.	46	7	9	7	25	26	6	5	12	23	38	53	−16
17	Brentford	46	9	5	9	34	38	5	6	12	18	31	53	−17
18	Peterborough Utd.	46	5	8	10	36	33	7	8	8	22	25	52	0
19	Stockport Co.	46	6	8	9	31	36	5	11	7	31	34	52	−8
20	Chesterfield	46	9	7	7	34	31	3	8	12	15	40	51	−22
21	Grimsby Town	46	10	5	8	36	26	3	6	14	19	55	50	−26
22	Rushden & Diamonds	46	9	5	9	37	34	4	4	15	23	40	48	−14
23	Notts Co.	46	6	9	8	32	27	4	3	16	18	51	42	−28
24	Wycombe Wand.	46	5	7	11	31	39	1	12	10	19	36	37	−25

(* Also promoted via play-offs)

Biggest win: Hartlepool Utd. 8, Grimsby Town 1; Plymouth Argyle 7, Chesterfield 0.

Highest attendance: 29,313 (Sheffield Wed. v Q.P.R.).

Lowest attendance: 2,513 (Colchester Utd. v Stockport Co.).

Manager of Year: Paul Sturrock (Plymouth Argyle – now Southampton).

Player of Year: Graham Coughlan (Plymouth Argyle).

Top League scorer: 25 Leon Knight (Brighton & H.A.), Stephen McPhee (Port Vale).

PFA divisional team: Phillips (Bristol City), Carey (Bristol City), Coughlan (Plymouth Argyle), Cullip (Brighton & H.A.), Padula (Q.P.R.), Edwards (Wrexham), Friio (Plymouth Argyle), Tinnion (Bristol City), Wellens (Blackpool), Knight (Brighton & H.A.), Taylor (Blackpool).

Fair Play award: Hartlepool Utd.

Leading scorers (all club competitions): 27 Knight (Brighton & H.A.), McPhee (Port Vale), Taylor (Blackpool); 23 Parkin (Swindon Town); 21 Heffernan (Notts Co.); 20 Mooney (Swindon Town); 19 Dadi (Tranmere Rov.); 17 Gallen (Q.P.R.), McGleish (Colchester Utd.); 16 Boyd (Hartlepool Utd.) – 4 for Boston Utd., Furlong (Q.P.R.), Howard (Luton Town), Peacock (Bristol City); 15 Friio (Plymouth Argyle); 14 Andrews (Colchester Utd.), Evans (Plymouth Argyle), Forbes (Luton Town), Hayter (Bournemouth), Hume (Tranmere Rov.), Paynter (Port Vale), Thorpe (Q.P.R.) – 3 for Luton Town, Vernon (Oldham Athletic), Williams (Hartlepool Utd.).

THIRD DIVISION

			HOME					AWAY						
		P	W	D	L	F	A	W	D	L	F	A	Pts	GD
1	Doncaster Rov.	46	17	4	2	47	13	10	7	6	32	24	92	+42
2	Hull City	46	16	4	3	50	21	9	9	5	32	23	88	+38
3	Torquay Utd.	46	15	6	2	44	18	8	6	9	24	26	81	+24
4	Huddersfield Town*	46	16	4	3	42	18	7	8	8	26	34	81	+16
5	Mansfield Town	46	13	5	5	44	25	9	4	10	32	37	75	+14
6	Northampton Town	46	13	4	6	30	23	9	5	9	28	28	75	+7
7	Lincoln City	46	9	11	3	36	23	10	6	7	32	24	74	+21
8	Yeovil Town	46	14	3	6	40	19	9	2	12	30	38	74	+13
9	Oxford Utd.	46	14	8	1	34	13	4	9	10	21	31	71	+11
10	Swansea City	46	9	8	6	36	26	6	6	11	22	35	59	−3
11	Boston Utd.	46	11	7	5	35	21	5	4	14	15	33	59	−4
12	Bury	46	10	7	6	29	26	5	4	14	25	38	56	−10
13	Cambridge Utd.	46	6	7	10	26	32	8	7	8	29	35	56	−12
14	Cheltenham Town	46	11	4	8	37	38	3	10	10	20	33	56	−14
15	Bristol Rov.	46	9	7	7	29	26	5	6	12	21	35	55	−11
16	Kidderminster Harr.	46	9	5	9	28	29	5	8	10	17	30	55	−14
17	Southend Utd.	46	8	4	11	27	29	6	8	9	24	34	54	−12
18	Darlington	46	10	4	9	30	28	4	7	12	23	33	53	−8
19	Leyton Orient	46	8	9	6	28	27	5	5	13	20	38	53	−17
20	Macclesfield Town	46	8	8	6	28	25	5	4	14	26	44	52	−15
21	Rochdale	46	7	8	8	28	26	5	6	12	21	32	50	−9
22	Scunthorpe Utd.	46	7	10	6	36	27	4	6	13	33	45	49	−3
23	Carlisle Utd.	46	8	5	10	23	27	4	4	15	23	42	45	−23
24	York City	46	7	6	10	22	29	3	8	12	13	37	44	−31

(* Also promoted via play-offs)

Biggest win: Doncaster Rov. 5, Kidderminster Harr. 0; Doncaster Rov. 5, Leyton Orient 0; Hull City 6, Kidderminster Harr. 1; Mansfield Town 5, Scunthorpe Utd. 0.
Highest attendance: 23,495 (Hull City v Huddersfield Town).
Lowest attendance: 1,513 (Macclesfield Town v Swansea City).
Manager of Year: Dave Penney (Doncaster Rov.).
Player of Year: Michael McIndoe (Doncaster Rov.).
Top League scorer: 23 Steven MacLean (Scunthorpe Utd.).
PFA divisional team: Weale (Yeovil Town), Stanton (Scunthorpe Utd.), Crosby (Oxford Utd.), Sodje (Huddersfield Town), Dawson (Hull City), Beagrie (Scunthorpe Utd.), Lawrence (Mansfield Town), McIndoe (Doncaster Rov.), Russell (Torquay Utd.), Graham (Torquay Utd.), Trundle (Swansea City).
Fair Play award: Macclesfield Town.
Leading scorers (all club competitions): 25 Constantine (Southend Utd.), MacLean (Scunthorpe Utd.); 23 Graham (Torquay Utd.); 22 Lawrence (Mansfield Town), Trundle (Swansea City); 20 Blundell (Doncaster Rov.); 19 Fletcher (Lincoln City), Tipton (Macclesfield Town); 18 Burgess (Hull City); 16 Alexander (Leyton Orient); 15 Allsopp (Hull City), Basham (Oxford Utd.), Smith (Northampton Town), Torpey (Scunthorpe Utd.); 14 Booth (Huddersfield Town), Conlon (Darlington), Elliott (Hull City); 13 Mendes (Mansfield Town), Williams (Yeovil Town), Yeo (Lincoln City); 12 Beagrie (Scunthorpe Utd.), Fortune-West (Doncaster Rov.), Guttridge (Cambridge Utd.), McCann (Cheltenham Town), Tait (Bristol Rov.), Townson (Rochdale).

NATIONWIDE LEAGUE PLAY-OFFS 2004

Crystal Palace, Brighton and Hove Albion and Huddersfield Town won tight, tense Finals which produced just two goals, the lowest since the end-of-season play-offs were introduced to decide final promotion issues.

One of them, scored by much-travelled striker Neil Shipperley against West Ham United, secured the most unlikely of Premiership places for Palace, who were languishing 19th in the table when Iain Dowie left Oldham Athletic to become their manager – and transform their season.

It came in the wake of a stoppage-time header by substitute Darren Powell which had sent their semi-final against Sunderland into extra-time and set up eventual victory in a penalty shoot-out. With 62 minutes gone, Stephen Bywater parried Andrew Johnson's shot and Shipperley tapped in a goal reckoned to be worth more than £20m. to the south London club.

West Ham, denied an immediate return to Division One and faced with the need to cut their wage bill as a result, had efforts by David Connolly and Bobby Zamora ruled out for offside. Nico Vaesen's save also denied Steve Lomas, but overall Palace played with greater purpose – midfield man Michael Hughes was outstanding – and deserved the result.

Brighton made an immediate return to Division One in a poor game against Bristol City which looked set for extra-time until Danny Coles lunged at Chris Iwelumo in the penalty box. Leon Knight, who had earlier hit the crossbar with a free-kick in one of the few bright moments, scored his 27th goal of the season from the spot six minutes from time.

Huddersfield also went back up at the first attempt by winning the Division Three decider against Mansfield Town in a much livelier affair, despite a blank scoreline. Both could have won it in normal time and the extra half-hour, before the Yorkshire side's nerves held much better in the penalty shoot-out which they won 4-1.

A third team to revive their fortunes 12 months after going down were Shrewsbury Town, who beat Aldershot Town 3-0 on penalties in the Conference Final to join champions Chester City back in the Football League.

SEMI-FINALS, FIRST LEG

DIVISION 1

Crystal Palace 3 (Shipperley 52, Butterfield 64, Johnson 87), **Sunderland** 2 (Stewart 51 pen, Kyle 85). Att: 25,287. **Ipswich Town** 1 (Bent 57), **West Ham Utd**. 0. Att: 28,435.

DIVISION 2

Hartlepool Utd. 1 (Porter 74), **Bristol City** 1 (Rougier 5). Att: 7,211. **Swindon Town** 0, **Brighton & H.A.** 1 (Carpenter 72). Att: 14,034.

DIVISION 3

Lincoln City 1 (Fletcher 51), **Huddersfield Town** 2 (Onuora 5, Mirfin 72). Att: 9,202. **Northampton Town** 0, **Mansfield Town** 2 (Day 40, Mendes 67). Att: 6,960.

CONFERENCE

Aldershot Town 1 (D'Sane 45 pen), **Hereford Utd.** 1 (Brown 7). Att: 6,379. **Barnet** 2 (Strevens 11 pen, Clist 90), **Shrewsbury Town** 1 (Rodgers 43 pen). Att: 4,171.

SEMI-FINALS, SECOND LEG

DIVISION 1

Sunderland 2 (Kyle 42, Stewart 45), **Crystal Palace** 1 (Powell 90). Att: 34,536 (aet, agg 4-4, **Crystal Palace** won 5-4 on pens). **West Ham Utd.** 2 (Etherington 50, Dailly 71), **Ipswich Town** 0. Att: 34,002. (**West Ham Utd.** won 2-1 on agg).

DIVISION 2

Brighton & H.A. 1 (Virgo 120), **Swindon Town** 2 (Parkin 81, Fallon 97). Att: 6,876 (aet, agg 2-2, **Brighton & H.A.** won 4-3 on pens). **Bristol City** 2 (Goodfellow 88, Roberts 90), **Hartlepool Utd.** 1 (Sweeney 63). Att: 18,434 (**Bristol City** won 3-2 on agg).

DIVISION 3

Huddersfield Town 2 (Schofield 60 pen, Edwards 83), **Lincoln City** 2 (Butcher 38, Bailey 39). Att: 19,467 (**Huddersfield Town** won 4-3 on agg). **Mansfield Town** 1 (Curtis 68), **Northampton Town** 3 (Richards 36, Hargreaves 42, Smith 46). Att: 9,243 (aet, agg 3-3, **Mansfield Town** won 5-4 on pens).

CONFERENCE

Hereford Utd. 0, **Aldershot Town** 0. Att: 7,044 (aet, agg 1-1, **Aldershot Town** won 4-2 on pens). **Shrewsbury Town** 1 (Rodgers 44 pen), **Barnet** 0. Att: 7,012 (aet, agg 2-2, **Shrewsbury Town** won 5-3 on pens)

FINALS – MILLENNIUM STADIUM

DIVISION 1 – MAY 29, 2004

Crystal Palace 1 (Shipperley 62), **West Ham Utd.** 0. Att: 72,523.
Crystal Palace (4-4-2): Vaesen, Butterfield (Powell 70), Leigertwood, Popovic, Granville, Routledge, Riihilahti, Hughes, Derry, Johnson, Shipperley. **Subs not used:** Berthelin, Black, Watson, Freedman. **Booked:** Derry, Hughes, Routledge. **Manager:** Iain Dowie.
West Ham Utd. (4-4-2): Bywater, Repka, Dailly, Melville, Mullins, Harewood (Reo-Coker 69), Carrick, Lomas, Etherington, Zamora (Deane 68), Connolly (Hutchison 74). **Subs not used:** Srnicek, Brevett. **Booked:** Repka, Harewood, Mullins, Etherington. **Manager:** Alan Pardew.
Referee: G. Poll (Herts). **Half-time:** 0-0.

DIVISION 2 – MAY 30, 2004

Brighton & H.A. 1 (Knight 84 pen), **Bristol City** 0. Att: 65,167.
Brighton & H.A. (4-4-2): Roberts, Virgo, Cullip, Butters, Harding, Hart, Oatway, Carpenter (Reid 62), Jones (Piercy 78), Knight, Iwelumo. **Subs not used:** Kuipers, Mayo, Hinshelwood. **Booked:** Virgo. **Manager:** Mark McGhee.
Bristol City (4-4-2): Phillips, Carey, Butler (Goodfellow 88), Coles, Hill, Rougier, Doherty, Tinnion (Wilkshire 82), Woodman, Miller (Murray 62), Roberts. **Subs not used:** Stowell, Burnell. **Manager:** Danny Wilson.
Referee: R. Beeby (Northants). **Half-time:** 0-0.

DIVISION 3 – MAY 31, 2004

Huddersfield Town 0, **Mansfield Town** 0. Att: 37,298 (aet, **Huddersfield Town** won 4-1 on pens).
Huddersfield Town (3-5-2): Rachubka, Mirfin, Sodje, Yates, Holdsworth, Carss, Worthington (Fowler 85), Schofield, Lloyd (Edwards 112), Booth, Abbott (McAliskey 91). **Subs not used:** Senior, Brown. **Booked:** Sodje. **Manager:** Peter Jackson.

Mansfield Town (4-4-2): Pilkington, Hassell, Day, Baptiste, Eaton, Lawrence, Williamson (Mackenzie 98), Curtis, Corden, Disley (Larkin 60), Mendes (D'Jaffo 69). **Subs not used:** Coates, Artell. **Booked:** Eaton. **Manager:** Keith Curle.
Referee: M. Clattenburg (Co Durham). **Half-time:** 0-0.

FINAL – BRITANNIA STADIUM

CONFERENCE – MAY 16, 2004

Aldershot Town 1 (McLean 35), **Shrewsbury Town** 1 (Darby 43). Att: 19,216 (aet, **Shrewsbury Town** won 3-0 on pens).
Aldershot Town (4-4-2): Bull, Downer (Hooper 66), Warburton, Giles, Sterling, Gosling, Challinor, Antwi, Miller, D'Sane (Charles 85), McLean (Sills 60). **Subs not used:** Barnard, Chewins. **Booked:** Sterling. **Manager:** Terry Brown.
Shrewsbury Town (4-4-2): Howie, Sedgemore, Tinson (Lawrence 91), Ridler, Challis, Lowe, O'Connor (Street 84), Tolley, Aiston, Darby (Cramb 93), Rodgers. **Subs not used:** Edwards, Hart. **Booked:** Lowe, O'Connor, Ridler. **Manager:** Jimmy Quinn.
Referee: K. Stroud (Dorset). **Half-time:** 1-1.

PLAY-OFF FINALS – HOME & AWAY

1987 Divs. 1/2: Charlton Athletic beat Leeds Utd. 2-1 in replay (Birmingham City) after 1-1 agg (1-0h, 0-1a). Charlton Athletic remained in Div. 1. Losing semi-finalists: Ipswich Town and Oldham Athletic. **Divs. 2/3: Swindon Town** beat Gillingham 2-0 in replay (Crystal Palace) after 2-2 agg (0-1a, 2-1h). Swindon Town promoted to Div. 2. Losing semi-finalists: Sunderland and Wigan Athletic; Sunderland relegated to Div. 3. **Divs. 3/4: Aldershot** beat Wolves 3-0 on agg (2-0h, 1-0a) and promoted to Div. 3. Losing semi-finalists: Bolton Wand. and Colchester Utd.; Bolton Wand. relegated to Div.4.

1988 Divs. 1/2: Middlesbrough beat Chelsea 2-1 on agg (2-0h, 0-1a) and promoted to Div. 1; Chelsea relegated to Div. 2. Losing semi-finalists: Blackburn Rov. and Bradford City. **Divs. 2/3: Walsall** beat Bristol City 4-0 in replay (h) after 3-3 agg (3-1a, 0-2h) and promoted to Div. 2. Losing semi-finalists: Sheffield Utd. and Notts Co; Sheffield Utd. relegated to Div. 3. **Divs. 3/4: Swansea City** beat Torquay Utd. 5-4 on agg (2-1h, 3-3a) and promoted to Div. 3. Losing semi-finalists: Rotherham Utd. and Scunthorpe Utd.; Rotherham Utd. relegated to Div.4.

1989 Div. 2: Crystal Palace beat Blackburn Rov. 4-3 on agg (1-3a, 3-0h). Losing semi-finalists: Watford and Swindon Town. **Div. 3: Port Vale** beat Bristol Rov. 2-1 on agg (1-1a, 1-0h). Losing semi-finalists: Fulham and Preston N.E. **Div.4: Leyton Orient** beat Wrexham 2-1 on agg (0-0a, 2-1h). Losing semi-finalists: Scarborough and Scunthorpe Utd.

PLAY-OFF FINALS AT WEMBLEY

1990 Div. 2: Swindon Town 1, Sunderland 0 (att: 72,873). Swindon Town promoted, then demoted for financial irregularities; Sunderland promoted. Losing semi-finalists: Blackburn Rov. and Newcastle Utd. **Div. 3: Notts Co.** 2, Tranmere Rov. 0 (att: 29,252). Losing semi-finalists: Bolton Wand. and Bury. **Div.4: Cambridge Utd.** 1, Chesterfield 0 (att: 26,404). Losing semi-finalists: Maidstone and Stockport Co.

1991 Div. 2: Notts Co. 3, Brighton & H.A. 1 (att: 59,940). Losing semi-finalists: Middlesbrough and Millwall. **Div. 3: Tranmere Rov.** 1, Bolton Wand. 0 (att: 30,217). Losing semi-finalists: Brentford and Bury. **Div.4: Torquay Utd.** 2, Blackpool 2 – Torquay Utd. won 5-4 on pens (att: 21,615). Losing semi-finalists: Burnley and Scunthorpe Utd.

1992 Div. 2: Blackburn Rov. 1, Leicester City 0 (att: 68,147). Losing semi-finalists: Derby Co. and Cambridge Utd. **Div. 3: Peterborough Utd.** 2, Stockport Co. 1 (att: 35,087). Losing semi-finalists: Huddersfield Town and Stoke City. **Div.4: Blackpool** 1, Scunthorpe Utd. 1 – Blackpool won 4-3 on pens (att: 22,741). Losing semi-finalists: Barnet and Crewe Alexandra.

1993 Div. 1; Swindon Town 4, Leicester City 3 (att: 73,802). Losing semi-finalists: Portsmouth and Tranmere Rov. **Div. 2: W.B.A.** 3, Port Vale 0 (att: 53,471). Losing semi-finalists: Stockport Co. and Swansea City. **Div. 3: York City** 1, Crewe Alexandra 1 – York City won 5-3 on pens (att: 22,416). Losing semi-finalists: Bury and Walsall.

1994 Div. 1: Leicester City 2, Derby Co. 1 (att: 73,671). Losing semi-finalists: Millwall and Tranmere Rov. **Div. 2: Burnley** 2, Stockport Co. 1 (att: 44,806). Losing semi-finalists: Plymouth Argyle and York City. **Div. 3: Wycombe Wand.** 4, Preston N.E. 2 (att: 40,109). Losing semi-finalists: Carlisle Utd. and Torquay Utd.

1995 Div. 1: Bolton Wand. 4, Reading 3 (att: 64,107). Losing semi-finalists: Tranmere Rov. and Wolves. **Div. 2: Huddersfield Town** 2, Bristol Rov. 1 (att: 59,175). Losing semi-finalists: Brentford and Crewe Alexandra. **Div. 3: Chesterfield** 2, Bury 0 (att: 22,814). Losing semi-finalists: Mansfield Town and Preston N.E.

1996 Div. 1: Leicester City 2, Crystal Palace 1, aet (att: 73,573). Losing semi-finalists: Charlton Athletic and Stoke City. **Div. 2: Bradford City** 2, Notts Co. 0 (att: 39,972). Losing semi-finalists: Blackpool and Crewe Alexandra. **Div. 3: Plymouth Argyle** 1, Darlington 0 (att: 43,431). Losing semi-finalists: Colchester Utd. and Hereford.

1997 Div. 1: Crystal Palace 1, Sheffield Utd. 0, (att: 64,383). Losing semi-finalists: Ipswich Town and Wolves. **Div. 2: Crewe Alexandra** 1, Brentford 0 (att: 34,149). Losing semi-finalists: Bristol City and Luton Town. **Div. 3: Northampton Town** 1, Swansea City 0 (att: 46,804). Losing semi-finalists: Cardiff City and Chester City.

1998 Div. 1: Charlton Athletic 4, Sunderland 4, aet Charlton Athletic won 7-6 on pens. (att: 77, 739). Losing semi-finalists: Ipswich Town and Sheffield United. **Div. 2: Grimsby Town** 1, Northampton Town 0 (att: 62,988). Losing semi-finalists: Bristol Rov. and Fulham. **Div. 3: Colchester Utd.** 1, Torquay Utd. 0 (att: 19,486). Losing semi-finalists: Barnet and Scarborough.

1999 Div. 1: Watford 2, Bolton Wand. 0, (att. 70,343). Losing semi-finalists: Ipswich Town and Birmingham City. **Div. 2: Manchester City** 2, Gillingham 2, aet Manchester City won 3-1 on pens. (att. 76,935). Losing semi-finalists: Preston N.E. and Wigan Athletic. **Div. 3: Scunthorpe Utd.** 1, Leyton Orient 0, (att. 36,985). Losing semi-finalists: Rotherham Utd. and Swansea City.

2000 Div. 1: Ipswich Town 4, Barnsley 2 (att: 73,427). Losing semi-finalists: Birmingham City and Bolton Wand. **Div. 2: Gillingham** 3, Wigan Athletic 2, aet (att: 53,764). Losing semi-finalists: Millwall and Stoke City. **Div. 3: Peterborough Utd.** 1, Darlington 0 (att: 33,383). Losing semi-finalists: Barnet and Hartlepool Utd.

PLAY-OFF FINALS AT MILLENNIUM STADIUM

2001 Div. 1: Bolton Wand. 3, Preston N.E. 0 (att: 54,328). Losing semi-finalists: Birmingham City and W.B.A. **Div. 2: Walsall** 3, Reading 2, aet (att: 50,496). Losing semi-finalists: Stoke City and Wigan Athletic. **Div. 3: Blackpool** 4, Leyton Orient 2 (att: 23,600). Losing semi-finalists: Hartlepool Utd. and Hull City.

2002 Div 1: Birmingham City 1, Norwich City 1, aet Birmingham City won 4-2 on pens. (att: 71,597). Losing semi-finalists: Millwall and Wolves. **Div 2: Stoke City** 2, Brentford

0 (att: 42,523). Losing semi-finalists: Cardiff City and Huddersfield Town. **Div 3: Cheltenham Town** 3, Rushden & Diamonds 1 (att: 24,368). Losing semi-finalists: Hartlepool Utd. and Rochdale.

2003 Div 1: Wolves 3, Sheffield Utd. 0 (att: 69,473). Losing semi-finalists: Nott'm Forest and Reading. **Div 2: Cardiff City** 1, Q.P.R. 0 aet (att: 66,096). Losing semi-finalists: Bristol City and Oldham Athletic. **Div 3: Bournemouth** 5, Lincoln City 2 (att: 32,148). Losing semi-finalists: Bury and Scunthorpe Utd.

HISTORY OF THE PLAY-OFFS

Play-off matches were introduced by the Football League to decide final promotion and relegation issues at the end of season 1986-87.

A similar series styled "Test Matches" had operated between Divisions One and Two for six seasons from 1893-98, and was abolished when both divisions were increased from 16 to 18 clubs.

Eighty-eight years later, the play-offs were back in vogue. In the first three seasons (1987-88-89), the Finals were played home-and-away, and since they were made one-off matches in 1990, they have featured regularly in Wembley's spring calendar, until the old stadium closed its doors and the action switched to the Millennium Stadium in Cardiff in 2001.

Through the years, these have been the ups and downs of the play-offs:

1987 Initially, the 12 clubs involved comprised the one that finished directly above those relegated in Divisions One, Two and Three and the three who followed the sides automatically promoted in each section. Two of the home-and-away Finals went to neutral-ground replays, in which **Charlton Athletic** clung to First Division status by denying Leeds Utd. promotion while **Swindon Town** beat Gillingham to complete their climb from Fourth Division to Second in successive seasons, via the play-offs, Sunderland fell into the Third and Bolton Wand. into Division Four, both for the first time. **Aldershot** went up after finishing only sixth in Division Four; in their Final, they beat Wolves, who had finished nine points higher and missed automatic promotion by one point.

1988 Chelsea were relegated from the First Division after losing on aggregate to **Middlesbrough**, who had finished third in Division Two. So Middlesbrough, managed by Bruce Rioch, completed the rise from Third Division to First in successive seasons, only two years after their very existence had been threatened by the bailiffs. Also promoted via the play-offs: **Walsall** from Division Three and **Swansea City** from the Fourth. Relegated, besides Chelsea: Sheffield Utd. (to Division Three) and Rotherham Utd. (to Division Four).

1989 After two seasons of promotion-relegation play-offs, the system was changed to involve the four clubs who had just missed automatic promotion. That format has remained. Steve Coppell's **Crystal Palace**, third in Division Two, returned to the top flight after eight years, beating Blackburn Rov. 4-3 on aggregate after extra time. Similarly, **Port Vale** confirmed third place in Division Three with promotion via the play-offs. For **Leyton Orient**, promotion seemed out of the question in Division Four when they stood 15th. on March 1. But eight wins and a draw in the last nine home games swept them to sixth in the final table, and two more home victories in the play-offs completed their season in triumph.

1990 The play-off Finals now moved to Wembley over three days of the Spring Holiday week-end. On successive afternoons, **Cambridge Utd.** won promotion from Division Four and **Notts County** from the Third. Then, on Bank Holiday Monday, the biggest crowd for years at a Football League fixture (72,873) saw Ossie Ardiles' **Swindon Town** beat Sunderland 1-0 to reach the First Division for the first time. A few weeks later, however,

Wembley losers **Sunderland** were promoted instead, by default; Swindon were found guilty of "financial irregularities" and stayed in Division Two.

1991 Again, the season's biggest League crowd (59,940) gathered at Wembley for the First Division Final in which **Notts Co.** (having missed promotion by one point) still fulfilled their ambition, beating Brighton & H.A. 3-1. In successive years, County had climbed from Third Division to First via the play-offs – the first club to achieve double promotion by this route. Bolton Wand. were denied automatic promotion in Division Three on goal difference, and lost at Wembley to an extra-time goal by **Tranmere Rov.** The Fourth Division Final made history, with Blackpool beaten 5-4 on penalties by **Torquay Utd.** – first instance of promotion being decided by a shoot-out. In the table, Blackpool had finished seven points ahead of Torquay.

1992 Wembley that Spring Bank Holiday was the turning point in the history of **Blackburn Rov.** Bolstered by Kenny Dalglish's return to management and owner Jack Walker's millions, they beat Leicester City 1-0 by Mike Newell's 45th-minute penalty to achieve their objective – a place in the new Premier League. Newell, who also missed a second-half penalty, had recovered from a broken leg just in time for the play-offs. In the Fourth Division Final **Blackpool** (denied by penalties the previous year) this time won a shoot-out 4-3 against Scunthorpe Utd., who were unlucky in the play-offs for the fourth time in five years. **Peterborough Utd.** climbed out of the Third Division for the first time, beating Stockport Co. 2-1 at Wembley.

1993 The crowd of 73,802 at Wembley to see **Swindon Town** beat Leicester City 4-3 in the First Division Final was 11,000 bigger than that for the F.A. Cup Final replay between Arsenal and Sheffield Wed. Leicester rallied from three down to 3-3 before Paul Bodin's late penalty wiped away Swindon Town's bitter memories of three years earlier, when they were denied promotion after winning at Wembley. In the Third Division Final, **York City** beat Crewe Alexandra 5-3 in a shoot-out after a 1-1 draw, and in the Second Division decider, **W.B.A.** beat Port Vale 3-0. This was tough on Vale, who had finished third in the table with 89 points – the highest total never to earn promotion in any division. They had beaten Albion twice in the League, too.

1994 Wembley's record turn-out of 158,586 spectators at the three Finals started with a crowd of 40,109 to see Martin O'Neill's **Wycombe Wand.** beat Preston N.E. 4-2. They thus climbed from Conference to Second Division with successive promotions. **Burnley's** 2-1 victory in the Second Division Final was marred by the sending-off of two Stockport Co. players, and in the First Division decider **Leicester City** came from behind to beat Derby Co. and end the worst Wembley record of any club. They had lost on all six previous appearances there – four times in the F.A. Cup Final and in the play-offs of 1992 and 1993.

1995 Two months after losing the Coca-Cola Cup Final to Liverpool, Bruce Rioch's **Bolton Wand.** were back at Wembley for the First Division play-off Final. From two goals down to Reading in front of a crowd of 64,107, they returned to the top company after 15 years, winning 4-3 with two extra-time goals. **Huddersfield Town** ended the first season at their new £15m. home with promotion to the First Division via a 2-1 victory against Bristol Rov. – manager Neil Warnock's third play-off success (after two with Notts Co.). Of the three clubs who missed automatic promotion by one place, only **Chesterfield** achieved it in the play-offs, comfortably beating Bury 2-0.

1996 Under new manager **Martin O'Neill** (a Wembley play-off winner with Wycombe Wand. in 1994), **Leicester City** returned to the Premiership a year after leaving it. They had finished fifth in the table, but in the Final came from behind to beat third-placed Crystal Palace by Steve Claridge's shot in the last seconds of extra time. In the Second Division **Bradford City** came sixth, nine points behind Blackpool (3rd), but beat them (from two down in the semi-final first leg) and then clinched promotion by 2-0 v Notts Co. at Wembley. It was City's greatest day since they won the Cup in 1911. **Plymouth**

Argyle beat Darlington in the Third Division Final to earn promotion a year after being relegated. It was manager Neil Warnock's fourth play-off triumph in seven seasons after two with Notts Co. (1990 and 1991) and a third with Huddersfield Town in 1995.

1997 High drama at Wembley as **Crystal Palace** left it late against Sheffield Utd. in the First Division play-off final. The match was scoreless until the last 10 seconds when David Hopkin lobbed Blades' keeper Simon Tracey from 25 yards to send the Eagles back to the Premiership after two seasons of Nationwide action. In the Second Division play-off final, **Crewe Alexandra** beat Brentford 1-0 courtesy of a Shaun Smith goal. **Northampton Town** celebrated their first Wembley appearance with a 1-0 victory over Swansea City thanks to John Frain's injury-time free-kick in the Third Division play-off final.

1998 In one of the finest games ever seen at Wembley, **Charlton Athletic** eventually triumphed 7-6 on penalties over Sunderland. For Charlton Athletic, Wearside-born Clive Mendonca scored a hat-trick and Richard Rufus his first career goal in a match that lurched between joy and despair for both sides as it ended 4-4. Sunderland defender Michael Gray's superb performance ill deserved to end with his weakly struck spot kick being saved by Sasa Ilic. In the Third Division, the penalty spot also had a role to play, as **Colchester Utd.**'s David Gregory scored the only goal to defeat Torquay Utd., while in the Second Division a Kevin Donovan goal gave **Grimsby Town** victory over Northampton Town.

1999: Elton John, watching via a personal satellite link in Seattle, saw his **Watford** side overcome Bolton Wand. 2-0 to reach the Premiership. Against technically superior opponents, Watford prevailed with application and teamwork. They also gave Bolton a lesson in finishing through match-winners by Nick Wright and Allan Smart. **Manchester City** staged a remakarble comeback to win the Second Division Final after trailing to goals by Carl Asaba and Robert Taylor for Gillingham. Kevin Horlock and Paul Dickov scored in stoppage time and City went on to win on penalties. A goal by Spaniard Alex Calvo-Garcia earned **Scunthorpe Utd.** a 1-0 success against Leyton Orient in the Third Division Final.

2000: After three successive play-off failures, **Ipswich Town** finally secured a place in the Premiership. They overcame the injury loss of leading scorer David Johnson to beat Barnsley 4-2 with goals by 36-year-old Tony Mowbray, Marcus Stewart and substitutes Richard Naylor and Martijn Reuser. With six minutes left of extra-time in the Second Division Final, **Gillingham** trailed Wigan Athletic 2-1. But headers by 38-year-old player-coach Steve Butler and fellow substitute Andy Thomson gave them a 3-2 victory. Andy Clarke, approaching his 33rd birthday, scored the only goal of the Third Division decider for **Peterborough Utd.** against Darlington.

2001: **Bolton Wand.**, unsuccessful play-off contenders in the two previous seasons, made no mistake at the third attempt. They flourished in the new surroundings of the Millennium Stadium to beat Preston N.E. 3-0 with goals by Gareth Farrelly, Michael Ricketts – his 24th of the season – and Ricardo Gardner to reach the Premiership. **Walsall**, relegated 12 months earlier, scored twice in a three-minute spell of extra time to win 3-2 against Reading in the Second Division Final, while **Blackpool** capped a marked improvement in the second half of the season by overcoming Leyton Orient 4-2 in the Third Division Final.

2002: Holding their nerve to win a penalty shoot-out 4-2, **Birmingham City** wiped away the memory of three successive defeats in the semi-finals of the play-offs to return to the top division after an absence of 16 years. Substitute Darren Carter completed a fairy-tale first season as a professional by scoring the fourth spot-kick against Norwich City. **Stoke City** became the first successful team to come from the south dressing room in 12 finals since football was adopted by the home of Welsh rugby, beating Brentford 2-0 in the Second Division Final with Deon Burton's strike and a Ben Burgess own goal.

Julian Alsop's 26th goal of the season helped **Cheltenham Town** defeat League newcomers Rushden & Diamonds 3-1 in the Third Division decider.

2003: Wolves benefactor Sir Jack Hayward finally saw his £60m. investment pay dividends when the club he first supported as a boy returned to the top flight after an absence of 19 years by beating Sheffield Utd. 3-0. It was also a moment to savour for manager Dave Jones, who was forced to leave his previous club Southampton because of child abuse allegations, which were later found to be groundless. **Cardiff City**, away from the game's second tier for 18 years, returned with an extra-time winner from substitute Andy Campbell against Q.P.R after a goalless 90 minutes in the Division Two Final. **Bournemouth**, relegated 12 months earlier, became the first team to score five in the end-of-season deciders, beating Lincoln City 5-2 in the Division Three Final.

PLAY-OFF CROWDS YEAR BY YEAR

YEAR	MATCHES	AGG. ATT.
1987	20	310,000
1988	19	305,817
1989	18	234,393
1990	15	291,428
1991	15	266,442
1992	15	277,684
1993	15	319,907
1994	15	314,817
1995	15	295,317
1996	15	308,515
1997	15	309,085
1998	15	320,795
1999	15	372,969
2000	15	333,999
2001	15	317,745
2002	15	327,894
2003	15	374,461
2004	15	388,675 (record)
	282	5,669,943

RECORD NUMBER OF PLAYERS SENT OFF

A record 19 players were sent off in English League football on December 13, 2003, two more than the previous highest figure two months earlier. Two in the Premiership were Leicester's Matt Elliott and Ian Walker against Birmingham. There were five reds in Division One and seven in Division Two. Of the five dismissals in Division Three, three were Southend players – Dave McSweeney, Jay Smith and Mark Gower.

FLITCROFT BROTHERS ALL ON LOSING SIDE

The footballing Flitcroft brothers all ended on the losing side in F.A. Cup third round ties. Garry was in the Blackburn side beaten 4-0 by Birmingham; David was on the bench during Macclesfield's 2-1 defeat at Swansea City; Steve and his Accrington team lost 2-1 in a replay at Colchester.

LEAGUE CLUB MANAGERS

Figure in brackets = number of managerial changes at club since the War.
Date present manager took over shown on right.
Dario Gradi, appointed by Crewe Alexandra in June, 1983, currently has the longest service with one club.

BARCLAYS PREMIERSHIP

Arsenal (11)	Arsene Wenger	October 1996
Aston Villa (18)	David O'Leary	May 2003
Birmingham City (21)	Steve Bruce	December 2001
Blackburn Rov. (21)	Graeme Souness	March 2000
Bolton Wand. (17)	Sam Allardyce	October 1999
Charlton Athletic (12)	Alan Curbishley	July 1991
Chelsea (19)	Jose Mourinho	June 2004
Crystal Palace (31)	Iain Dowie	December 2003
Everton (16)	David Moyes	March 2002
Fulham (23)	Chris Coleman	May 2003
Liverpool (10)	Rafael Benitez	June 2004
Manchester City (24)	Kevin Keegan	May 2001
Manchester Utd. (8)	Sir Alex Ferguson	November 1986
Middlesbrough (16)	Steve McClaren	June 2001
Newcastle Utd. (17)	Sir Bobby Robson	September 1999
Norwich City (21)	Nigel Worthington	January 2001
Portsmouth (21)	Harry Redknapp	March 2002
Southampton (15)	Paul Sturrock	March 2004
Tottenham (17)	Jacques Santini	June 2004
W.B.A. (24)	Gary Megson	March 2000

COCA-COLA LEAGUE – CHAMPIONSHIP

Brighton & H.A (26)	Mark McGhee	October 2003
Burnley (20)	Steve Cotterill	June 2004
Cardiff City (25)	Lennie Lawrence	February 2002
Coventry City (25)	Peter Reid	May 2004
Crewe Alexandra (17)	Dario Gradi	June 1983
Derby Co. (17)	George Burley	June 2003
Gillingham (16)	Andy Hessenthaler	June 2000
Ipswich Town (9)	Joe Royle	October 2002
Leeds Utd. (20)	Kevin Blackwell	May 2004
Leicester City (18)	Micky Adams	April 2002
Millwall (22)	Dennis Wise	November 2003
Nott'm Forest (13)	Joe Kinnear	February 2004
Plymouth Argyle (26)	Bobby Williamson	April 2004
Preston N.E. (21)	Craig Brown	April 2002
Q.P.R. (21)	Ian Holloway	February 2001
Reading (16)	Steve Coppell	October 2003
Rotherham Utd. (18)	Ronnie Moore	May 1997
Sheffield Utd. (29)	Neil Warnock	December 1999
Stoke City (20)	Tony Pulis	November 2002
Sunderland (19)	Mick McCarthy	March 2003
Watford (23)	Ray Lewington	July 2002
West Ham Utd. (9)	Alan Pardew	September 2003
Wigan Athletic (15)	Paul Jewell	June 2001
Wolves (18)	Dave Jones	January 2001

(Number of changes since elected to Football League: Wigan Athletic 1978).

LEAGUE ONE

Barnsley (17)	Paul Hart	March 2004
Blackpool (22)	Colin Hendry	June 2004
Bournemouth (18)	Sean O'Driscoll	August 2000
Bradford City (28)	Colin Todd	June 2004
Brentford (25)	Martin Allen	March 2004
Bristol City (19)	Brian Tinnion	June 2004
Chesterfield (16)	Roy McFarland	May 2003
Colchester Utd. (20)	Phil Parkinson	February 2003
Doncaster Rov. (-)	Dave Penney	January 2002
Hartlepool Utd. (27)	Neale Cooper	June 2003
Huddersfield Town (21)	Peter Jackson	June 2003
Hull City (21)	Peter Taylor	October 2002
Luton Town (19)	Mike Newell	June 2003
Notts Co. (26)	Gary Mills	January 2004
Oldham Athletic (20)	Brian Talbot	March 2004
Peterborough Utd. (20)	Barry Fry	May 1996
Port Vale (18)	Martin Foyle	February 2004
Sheffield Wed. (22)	Chris Turner	November 2002
Stockport Co. (30)	Sammy McIlroy	October 2003
Swindon Town (20)	Andy King	December 2001
Tranmere Rov. (16)	Brian Little	October 2003
Walsall (28)	Paul Merson	May 2004
Wimbledon (10)	Stuart Murdoch	June 2002
Wrexham (17)	Denis Smith	October 2001

(Number of changes since elected to Football League: Peterborough Utd. 1960; Wimbledon 1977; since Doncaster Rov. returned in 2003).

LEAGUE TWO

Boston Utd. (2)	Steve Evans+	February 2004
Bristol Rov. (21)	Ian Atkins	April 2004
Bury (20)	Graham Barrow	January 2004
Cambridge Utd. (15)	Herve Renard	May 2004
Cheltenham Town (3)	John Ward	November 2003
Chester City (-)	Mark Wright	January 2002
Darlington (30)	David Hodgson	November 2003
Grimsby Town (27)	Russell Slade	May 2004
Kidderminster Harr. (2)	Jan Molby+	October 2003
Leyton Orient (20)	Martin Ling	October 2003
Lincoln City (23)	Keith Alexander	May 2002
Macclesfield Town (5)	Brian Horton	April 2004
Mansfield Town (22)	Keith Curle	December 2002
Northampton Town (25)	Colin Calderwood	October 2003
Oxford Utd. (18)	Graham Rix	April 2004
Rochdale (28)	Steve Parkin+	December 2003
Rushden & Diamonds (1)	Ernie Tippett	April 2004
Scunthorpe Utd. (21)	Brian Laws++	February 1997
Shrewsbury Town (-)	Jimmy Quinn	May 2003
Southend Utd. (26)	Steve Tilson	March 2004
Swansea City (27)	Kenny Jackett	April 2004
Torquay Utd. (28)	Leroy Rosenior	May 2002
Wycombe Wand. (5)	Tony Adams	November 2003
Yeovil Town (-)	Gary Johnson	June 2001

+ Second spell at club. ++ Reinstated (Apr. 2004) three weeks after leaving (Number of changes since elected to Football League: Oxford Utd. 1962; Wycombe Wand. 1993; Macclesfield Town 1997; Cheltenham Town 1999; Kidderminster Harr. 2000; Boston Utd. 2002, Yeovil Town 2003; since Chester City and Shrewsbury Town returned in 2004).

OTHER COMPETITIONS 2003-04

LDV VANS TROPHY

FIRST ROUND

Northern: Blackpool 3, Tranmere Rov. 2; Carlisle Utd. 2, Rochdale 0; Chester City 0, Doncaster Rov. 1; Chesterfield 2, Macclesfield Town 1; Darlington 1, Hull City 3; Halifax Town 2, York City 1; Lincoln City 3, Telford Utd. 1; Mansfield Town 1, Stockport Co. 2; Notts Co. 0, Barnsley 0 (aet, Barnsley won 4-2 on pens); Oldham Athletic 3, Hartlepool Utd. 3 (aet, Oldham Athletic won 5-3 on pens); Scarborough 2, Port Vale 1; Scunthorpe Utd. 2, Shrewsbury Town 1; Sheffield Wed. 1, Grimsby Town 1 (aet, Sheffield Wed. won 5-4 on pens); Wrexham 4, Morecambe 1.
Southern: Barnet 3, Brentford 3 (aet, Brentford won 3-1 on pens); Boston Utd. 2, Swindon Town 1; Brighton & H.A. 2, Forest Green Rov. 0; Cheltenham Town 1, Colchester Utd. 3; Dagenham & Redbridge 4, Leyton Orient 1; Hereford Utd. 2, Exeter City 0; Oxford Utd. 0, Rushden & Diamonds 1; Peterborough Utd. 3, Torquay Utd. 2; Plymouth Argyle 4, Bristol City 0; Q.P.R. 2, Kiddermninster Harriers 0; Southend Utd. 2, Bristol Rov. 1; Stevenage Borough 0, Luton Town 1; Wycombe Wand. 1, Cambridge Utd. 0; Yeovil Town 2, Bournemouth 0.

SECOND ROUND

Northern: Blackpool 1, Doncaster Rov. 0; Bury 2, Oldham Athletic 1; Carlisle Utd. 2, Huddersfield Town 0; Hull City 1, Scunthorpe Utd. 3; Lincoln City 4, Chesterfield 3 (aet, silver goal); Scarborough 0, Halifax Town 1; Sheffield Wed. 1, Barnsley 0; Stockport Co. 5, Wrexham 4 (aet, silver goal).
Southern: Brighton & H.A. 3, Boston Utd. 1 (aet, silver goal); Hereford Utd. 1, Northampton Town 1 (aet, Northampton Town won 4-3 on pens); Peterborough Utd. 3, Brentford 2; Plymouth Argyle 2, Wycombe Wand. 2 (aet, Wycombe Wand. won 4-2 on pens); Q.P.R. 2, Dagenham & Redbridge 1; Rushden & Diamonds 1, Luton Town 2; Swansea City 1, Southend Utd. 2; Yeovil Town 2, Colchester Utd. 2 (aet, Colchester Utd. won 4-2 on pens).

QUARTER-FINALS

Northern: Bury 0, Scunthorpe Utd. 1 (aet, silver goal); Carlisle Utd. 0, Sheffield Wed. 3; Stockport Co. 0, Blackpool 1; Halifax Town 1, Lincoln City 0.
Southern: Q.P.R. 2, Brighton & H.A. 1; Northampton Town 2, Peterborough Utd. 1 (aet, silver goal); Southend Utd. 3, Luton Town 0; Wycombe Wand. 2, Colchester Utd. 3 (aet).

SEMI-FINALS

Northern: Blackpool 3, Halifax Town 2; Sheffield Wed. 4, Scunthorpe Utd. 0.
Southern: Northampton Town 2, Colchester Utd. 3 (aet, silver goal); Southend Utd. 4, Q.P.R. 0.

AREA FINALS

Northern first leg: Blackpool 1 (Taylor 82), Sheffield Wed. 0. Att: 7,482. **Second leg:** Sheffield Wed. 0, Blackpool 2 (Sheron 20, Southern 31). Att: 21,390 (Blackpool won 3-0 on agg).
Southern first leg: Colchester Utd. 2 (Pinault 7, Andrews 75), Southend Utd. 3 (Constantine 17, Broughton 42, Bramble 68). Att: 5,401. **Second leg:** Southend Utd. 1 (Broughton 45), Colchester Utd. 1 (Izzet 3). Att: 9,603 (Southend Utd. won 4-3 on agg).

BLACKPOOL 2, SOUTHEND UNITED 0
Millennium Stadium, (34,031), Sunday, March 21, 2004

Blackpool (4-4-2): Jones, Grayson, Flynn, Elliott, Jaszczun, Bullock (Richardson 90), Dinning, Wellens (McMahon 90), Coid, Murphy, Sheron (Blinkhorn 74). **Subs not used:** Barnes, Davis. **Scorers:** Murphy (2), Coid (55). **Booked:** Jaszczun. **Manager:** Steve McMahon.

Southend Utd. (4-4-2): Flahavan, Jupp, Cort, Warren, Wilson (Bramble 64), Gower (Jenkins 86), Hunt, Maher, Pettefer, Broughton, Constantine. **Subs not used:** Emberson, McSweeney, Stuart. **Booked:** Maher. **Manager:** Steve Tilson.

Referee: R. Pearson (Co Durham). **Half-time:** 1-0.

FINALS – RESULTS

Associated Members' Cup
1984   (Hull City) Bournemouth 2, Hull City 1
Freight Rover Trophy
1985   (Wembley) Wigan Athletic 3, Brentford 1
1986   (Wembley) Bristol City 3, Bolton Wand. 0
1987   (Wembley) Mansfield Town 1, Bristol City 1 (aet; Mansfield Town won 5-4 on pens.)
Sherpa Van Trophy
1988   (Wembley) Wolves 2, Burnley 0
1989   (Wembley) Bolton Wand. 4, Torquay Utd. 1
Leyland Daf Cup
1990   (Wembley) Tranmere Rov. 2, Bristol Rov. 1
1991   (Wembley) Birmingham City 3, Tranmere Rov. 2
Autoglass Trophy
1992   (Wembley) Stoke City 1, Stockport Co. 0
1993   (Wembley) Port Vale 2, Stockport Co. 1
1994   (Wembley) Huddersfield Town 1, Swansea City 1 (aet; Swansea City won 3-1 on pens.)
Auto Windscreens Shield
1995   (Wembley) Birmingham City 1, Carlisle Utd. 0 (Birmingham City won in sudden-death overtime)
1996   (Wembley) Rotherham Utd. 2, Shrewsbury Town 1
1997   (Wembley) Carlisle Utd. 0, Colchester Utd. 0 (aet; Carlisle Utd. won 4-3 on pens.)
1998   (Wembley) Grimsby Town 2, Bournemouth 1 (Grimsby Town won with golden goal in extra time)
1999   (Wembley) Wigan Athletic 1, Millwall 0
2000   (Wembley) Stoke City 2, Bristol City 1
LDV Vans Trophy
2001   (Millennium Stadium) Port Vale 2, Brentford 1
2002   (Millennium Stadium) Blackpool 4, Cambridge Utd. 1
2003   (Millennium Stadium) Bristol City 2, Carlisle Utd. 0
2004   (Millennium Stadium) Blackpool 2, Southend Utd. 0

OTHER LEAGUE CLUBS' CUP COMPETITIONS

FINALS – AT WEMBLEY

Full Members' Cup (Discontinued after 1992)
1985-86   Chelsea 5, Manchester City 4
1986-87   Blackburn Rov. 1, Charlton Athletic 0

Simod Cup
1987-88   Reading 4, Luton Town 1
1988-89   Nott'm. Forest 4, Everton 3
Zenith Data Systems Cup
1989-90   Chelsea 1, Middlesbrough 0
1990-91   Crystal Palace 4, Everton 1
1991-92   Nott'm Forest 3, Southampton 2

ANGLO-ITALIAN CUP (Discontinued after 1996: * Home club)

1970   *Napoli 0, Swindon Town 3
1971   *Bologna 1, Blackpool 2 (aet)
1972   *AS Roma 3, Blackpool 1
1973   *Fiorentina 1, Newcastle Utd. 2
1993   Derby Co. 1, Cremonese 3 (at Wembley)
1994   Notts Co. 0, Brescia 1 (at Wembley)
1995   Ascoli 1, Notts Co. 2 (at Wembley)
1996   Port Vale 2, Genoa 5 (at Wembley)

F.A. CHALLENGE VASE FINALS

At Wembley
1975   Hoddesdon Town 2, Epsom & Ewell 1
1976   Billericay Town 1, Stamford 0*
1977   Billericay Town 2, Sheffield 1 (replay Nottingham, after a 1-1 draw at Wembley)
1978   Blue Star 2, Barton Rov. 1
1979   Billericay Town 4, Almondsbury Greenway 1
1980   Stamford 2, Guisborough Town 0
1981   Whickham 3, Willenhall Town 2*
1982   Forest Green Rov. 3, Rainworth Miners' Welfare 0
1983   V.S. Rugby 1, Halesowen Town 0
1984   Stansted 3, Stamford 2
1985   Halesowen Town 3, Fleetwood Town 1
1986   Halesowen Town 3, Southall 0
1987   St. Helens Town 3, Warrington Town 2
1988   Colne Dynamoes 1, Emley 0*
1989   Tamworth 3, Sudbury Town 0 (replay Peterborough Utd., after a 1-1 draw at Wembley)
1990   Yeading 1, Bridlington 0 (replay Leeds Utd., after 0-0 draw at Wembley)
1991   Guiseley 3, Gresley Rov. 1 (replay Bramall Lane, Sheffield, after a 4-4 draw at Wembley)
1992   Wimborne Town 5, Guiseley 3
1993   Bridlington Town 1, Tiverton Town 0
1994   Diss Town 2, Taunton Town 1*
1995   Arlesey Town 2, Oxford City 1
1996   Brigg Town 3, Clitheroe 0
1997   Whitby Town 3, North Ferriby Utd. 0
1998   Tiverton Town 1, Tow Law Town 0
1999   Tiverton Town 1, Bedlington Terriers 0
2000   Deal Town 1, Chippenham Town 0
At Villa Park
2001   Taunton Town 2, Berkhamsted 1
2002   Whitley Bay 1, Tiptree Utd. 0*
At Upton Park
2003   Brigg Town 2, AFC Sudbury 1
At St Andrews
2004   Winchester City 2, AFC Sudbury 0

                              * After extra time

F.A. TROPHY

THIRD ROUND

Altrincham 2, Runcorn 1; *Barnet 3, Dover 2; Bishop's Stortford 1, Aldershot 3; Blyth 1 Barrow 0; Burscough 0, Tamworth 1; Burton 4 Accrington 2; Canvey Island 6, Farnborough 0; Chester City 1 Halifax 2; Dagenham & Redbridge 0, Crawley 0; Dorchester 2 Margate 2; Exeter 3 Hereford 2; Folkestone 1, Stevenage 3; Forest Green 4 Sutton 0; Gravesend 2, Weston-super-Mare 2; Guiseley 0, Worksop 2; Hayes 2, Arlesey 2; Hednesford 2, Gresley 0; Histon 1, Maidenhead 3; Hornchurch 2, Aylesbury 0; Hucknall 1, Bradford PA 0; Kettering 0, Woking 1; King's Lynn 3, Basingstoke 1; *Leigh RMI 1, Stalybridge 1; Lewes 5, Weymouth 8; Marine 1, Northwich 0; Marlow 3, Ford 1; Scarborough 1, Stafford 2; Shrewsbury 2, Morecambe 0; Staines 1, Bath 0; Telford 2, Alfreton 0; Wealdstone 3, Thurrock 2; Worthing 2, Taunton 0. **Replays:** Arlesey 1, Hayes 1 (aet, Arlesey won 4-3 on pens); Crawley 1, Dagenham & Redbridge 2 (aet); Margate 2, Dorchester 0; Weston-super-Mare 1, Gravesend 0; Woking 2, Kettering 3. (*expelled for fielding ineligible player)

FOURTH ROUND

Blyth 1, Aldershot 3; Burton 1, Kettering 1; Dagenham & Redbridge 3, Arlesey 3; Forest Green 3, Dover 3; Halifax 1, Staines 1; Hednesford 1, Worthing 1; Hornchurch 1, Stevenage 0; King's Lynn 0, Exeter 3; Maidenhead 5, Wealdstone 3; Margate 2, Worksop 0; Marlow 0, Tamworth 4; Shrewsbury 2, Hucknall 1; Stafford 0, Canvey Island 2; Stalybridge 1, Marine 1; Telford 4, Weston-super-Mare 2; Weymouth 0, Altrincham 2. **Replays:** Arlesey 4, Dagenham & Redbridge 2; Dover 2, Forest Green 1; Kettering 1, Burton 2 (aet); Marine 0, Stalybridge 1; Staines 2, Halifax 3 (aet); Worthing 1, Hednesford 2.

FIFTH ROUND

Aldershot 1, Tamworth 1; Altrincham 0, Shrewsbury 1; Exeter 3, Arlesey 0; Halifax 0, Maidenhead 2; Hednesford 1, Dover 0; Hornchurch 2, Burton 1; Stalybridge 0, Canvey Island 0; Telford 3, Margate 0. **Replays:** Canvey Island 4, Stalybridge 0; Tamworth 0, Aldershot 2.

SIXTH ROUND

Aldershot 2, Exeter 1; Canvey Island 4, Maidenhead 0; Hednesford 3, Hornchurch 1; Shrewsbury 1, Telford 1. **Replay:** Telford 2, Shrewsbury 1.

SEMI-FINALS

First leg: Aldershot 0, Hednesford 2; Telford 0, Canvey Island 0
Second leg: Hednesford 1, Aldershot 1 (Hednesford won 3-1 on agg); Canvey Island 2, Telford 2 (aet, agg 2-2, Canvey Island won 4-2 on pens).

FINAL

CANVEY ISLAND 2, HEDNESFORD TOWN 3

Villa Park, (6,635), Sunday, May 23, 2004

Canvey Island (3-5-2): Potter, Cowan, Chenery, Ward, Kennedy, Gooden (Dobinson 89), Midgley (Berquez 74), Minton, Duffy, Gregory (McDougald 80), Boylan. **Subs not used:** Theobald, Harrison. **Scorers:** Boylan (46), Brindley (47 og). **Booked:** Chenery. **Manager:** Jeff King.

Hednesford Town (4-4-2): Young, Simkin, Brindley, Ryder (Barrow 59), Hines, Maguire, King, Palmer, Charie (Evans 55), Anthrobus, Danks (Pearce 77). **Subs not used:** Evans, McGhee. **Scorers:** Maguire (27), Hines (53), Brindley (86). **Booked:** Anthrobus, Danks. **Manager:** Barry Powell.

Referee: M. Dean (Wirral). **Half-time:** 1-0.

F.A. CHALLENGE TROPHY FINALS

At Wembley

1970	Macclesfield Town 2, Telford Utd. 0
1971	Telford Utd. 3, Hillingdon Borough 2
1972	Stafford Rangers 3, Barnet 0
1973	Scarborough 2, Wigan Athletic 1*
1974	Morecambe 2, Dartford 1
1975	Matlock Town 4, Scarborough 0
1976	Scarborough 3, Stafford Rangers 2*
1977	Scarborough 2, Dagenham 1
1978	Altrincham 3, Leatherhead 1
1979	Stafford Rangers 2, Kettering Town 0
1980	Dagenham 2, Mossley 1
1981	Bishop's Stortford 1, Sutton Utd. 0
1982	Enfield 1, Altrincham 0*
1983	Telford Utd. 2, Northwich Victoria 1
1984	Northwich Victoria 2, Bangor City 1 (replay Stoke City, after a 1-1 draw at Wembley)
1985	Wealdstone 2, Boston Utd. 1
1986	Altrincham 1, Runcorn 0
1987	Kidderminster Harriers 2, Burton Albion 1 (replay W.B.A., after a 0-0 draw at Wembley)
1988	Enfield 3, Telford Utd. 2 (replay W.B.A., after a 0-0 draw at Wembley)
1989	Telford Utd. 1, Macclesfield Town 0*
1990	Barrow 3, Leek Town 0
1991	Wycombe Wand. 2, Kidderminster Harriers 1
1992	Colchester Utd. 3, Witton Albion 1
1993	Wycombe Wand. 4, Runcorn 1
1994	Woking 2, Runcorn 1
1995	Woking 2, Kidderminster 1
1996	Macclesfield Town 3, Northwich Victoria 1
1997	Woking 1, Dagenham & Redbridge 0*
1998	Cheltenham Town 1, Southport 0
1999	Kingstonian 1, Forest Green Rov. 0
2000	Kingstonian 3, Kettering Town 2

At Villa Park

2001	Canvey Island 1, Forest Green Rov. 0
2002	Yeovil Town 2, Stevenage Borough 0
2003	Burscough 2, Tamworth 1
2004	Hednesford Town 3, Canvey Island 2

(* After extra-time)

F.A. YOUTH CUP WINNERS

Year	Winners	Runners-up	Aggregate
1953	Manchester Utd.	Wolves	9-3
1954	Manchester Utd.	Wolves	5-4
1955	Manchester Utd.	W.B.A.	7-1
1956	Manchester Utd.	Chesterfield	4-3
1957	Manchester Utd.	West Ham Utd.	8-2
1958	Wolves	Chelsea	7-6
1959	Blackburn Rov.	West Ham Utd.	2-1
1960	Chelsea	Preston N.E.	5-2
1961	Chelsea	Everton	5-3
1962	Newcastle Utd.	Wolves	2-1

1963	West Ham Utd.	Liverpool	6-5
1964	Manchester Utd.	Swindon Town	5-2
1965	Everton	Arsenal	3-2
1966	Arsenal	Sunderland	5-3
1967	Sunderland	Birmingham City	2-0
1968	Burnley	Coventry City	3-2
1969	Sunderland	W.B.A.	6-3
1970	Tottenham	Coventry City	4-3
1971	Arsenal	Cardiff City	2-0
1972	Aston Villa	Liverpool	5-2
1973	Ipswich Town	Bristol City	4-1
1974	Tottenham	Huddersfield Town	2-1
1975	Ipswich Town	West Ham Utd.	5-1
1976	W.B.A.	Wolves	5-0
1977	Crystal Palace	Everton	1-0
1978	Crystal Palace	Aston Villa	*1-0
1979	Millwall	Manchester City	2-0
1980	Aston Villa	Manchester City	3-2
1981	West Ham Utd.	Tottenham	2-1
1982	Watford	Manchester Utd.	7-6
1983	Norwich City	Everton	6-5
1984	Everton	Stoke City	4-2
1985	Newcastle Utd.	Watford	4-1
1986	Manchester City	Manchester Utd.	3-1
1987	Coventry City	Charlton Athletic	2-1
1988	Arsenal	Doncaster Rov.	6-1
1989	Watford	Manchester City	2-1
1990	Tottenham	Middlesbrough	3-2
1991	Millwall	Sheffield Wed.	3-0
1992	Manchester Utd.	Crystal Palace	6-3
1993	Leeds Utd.	Manchester Utd.	4-1
1994	Arsenal	Millwall	5-3
1995	Manchester Utd.	Tottenham	†2-2
1996	Liverpool	West Ham Utd.	4-1
1997	Leeds Utd.	Crystal Palace	3-1
1998	Everton	Blackburn Rov.	5-3
1999	West Ham Utd.	Coventry City	9-0
2000	Arsenal	Coventry City	5-1
2001	Arsenal	Blackburn Rov.	6-3
2002	Aston Villa	Everton	4-2
2003	Manchester Utd.	Middlesbrough	3-1
2004	Middlesbrough	Aston Villa	4-0

(* One match only; † Manchester Utd. won 4-3 on pens.)

WELSH CUP FINAL

Rhyl 1, TNS 0 (at Newtown).

WOMEN'S F.A. CUP FINAL

Arsenal 3, Charlton Athletic 0 (at Loftus Road).

WOMEN'S PREMIER LEAGUE CUP FINAL

Charlton Athletic 1, Fulham 0 (at Underhill, Barnet).

F.A. SUNDAY CUP FINAL

Nicosia (Liverpool) 3, UK Flooring (Bristol) 1 (at Anfield).

F.A. COMMUNITY SHIELD

ARSENAL 1, MANCHESTER UNITED 1
(Manchester Utd. won 4-3 on pens)
Millennium Stadium, (59,293), Sunday, August 10, 2003

Arsenal (4-4-2): Lehmann, Lauren, Toure, Campbell, Cole, Parlour (Pires 46), Gilberto Silva (Edu 60), Vieira, Ljungberg (Van Bronckhorst 64), Bergkamp (Jeffers 60), Henry (Wiltord 46). **Scorer:** Henry (20). **Booked:** Cole, Vieira. **Sent-off:** Jeffers (74).

Manchester Utd. (4-2-3-1): Howard, P. Neville (Forlan 79), Ferdinand, Silvestre, Fortune (O'Shea 69), Butt (Djemba-Djemba 60), Keane, Solskjaer, Giggs, Scholes, Van Nistelrooy. **Scorer:** Silvestre (15). **Booked:** P. Neville, Scholes, Fortune.

Referee: S. Bennett (Kent). **Half-time:** 1-1.

CHARITY SHIELD RESULTS

Year	Winners	Runners-up	Score
1908	Manchester Utd.	Q.P.R.	4-0
			(after 1-1 draw)
1909	Newcastle Utd.	Northampton Town	2-0
1910	Brighton & H.A.	Aston Villa	1-0
1911	Manchester Utd.	Swindon Town	8-4
1912	Blackburn Rov.	Q.P.R.	2-1
1913	Professionals	Amateurs	7-2
1920	W.B.A.	Tottenham	2-0
1921	Tottenham	Burnley	2-0
1922	Huddersfield Town	Liverpool	1-0
1923	Professionals	Amateurs	2-0
1924	Professionals	Amateurs	3-1
1925	Amateurs	Professionals	6-1
1926	Amateurs	Professionals	6-3
1927	Cardiff City	Corinthians	2-1
1928	Everton	Blackburn Rov.	2-1
1929	Professionals	Amateurs	3-0
1930	Arsenal	Sheffield Wed.	2-1
1931	Arsenal	W.B.A.	1-0
1932	Everton	Newcastle Utd.	5-3
1933	Arsenal	Everton	3-0
1934	Arsenal	Manchester City	4-0
1935	Sheffield Wed.	Arsenal	1-0
1936	Sunderland	Arsenal	2-1
1937	Manchester City	Sunderland	2-0
1938	Arsenal	Preston N.E.	2-1
1948	Arsenal	Manchester Utd.	4-3
1949	Portsmouth	Wolves	*1-1
1950	England World Cup XI	F.A. Canadian Tour Team	4-2
1951	Tottenham	Newcastle Utd.	2-1
1952	Manchester Utd.	Newcastle Utd.	4-2
1953	Arsenal	Blackpool	3-1
1954	Wolves	W.B.A.	*4-4
1955	Chelsea	Newcastle Utd.	3-0
1956	Manchester Utd.	Manchester City	1-0
1957	Manchester Utd.	Aston Villa	4-0
1958	Bolton Wand.	Wolves	4-1
1959	Wolves	Nott'm. Forest	3-1

1960	Burnley	Wolves	*2-2
1961	Tottenham	F.A. XI	3-2
1962	Tottenham	Ipswich Town	5-1
1963	Everton	Manchester Utd.	4-0
1964	Liverpool	West Ham Utd.	*2-2
1965	Manchester Utd.	Liverpool	*2-2
1966	Liverpool	Everton	1-0
1967	Manchester Utd.	Tottenham	*3-3
1968	Manchester City	W.B.A.	6-1
1969	Leeds Utd.	Manchester City	2-1
1970	Everton	Chelsea	2-1
1971	Leicester City	Liverpool	1-0
1972	Manchester City	Aston Villa	1-0
1973	Burnley	Manchester City	1-0
1974	Liverpool	Leeds Utd.	1-1

(Liverpool won 6-5 on penalties)

1975	Derby Co.	West Ham Utd.	2-0
1976	Liverpool	Southampton	1-0
1977	Liverpool	Manchester Utd.	*0-0
1978	Nott'm. Forest	Ipswich Town	5-0
1979	Liverpool	Arsenal	3-1
1980	Liverpool	West Ham Utd.	1-0
1981	Aston Villa	Tottenham	*2-2
1982	Liverpool	Tottenham	1-0
1983	Manchester Utd.	Liverpool	2-0
1984	Everton	Liverpool	1-0
1985	Everton	Manchester Utd.	2-0
1986	Everton	Liverpool	*1-1
1987	Everton	Coventry City	1-0
1988	Liverpool	Wimbledon	2-1
1989	Liverpool	Arsenal	1-0
1990	Liverpool	Manchester Utd.	*1-1
1991	Arsenal	Tottenham	*0-0
1992	Leeds Utd.	Liverpool	4-3
1993	Manchester Utd.	Arsenal	1-1

(Manchester Utd. won 5-4 on penalties)

1994	Manchester Utd.	Blackburn Rov.	2-0
1995	Everton	Blackburn Rov.	1-0
1996	Manchester Utd.	Newcastle Utd.	4-0
1997	Manchester Utd.	Chelsea	1-1

(Manchester Utd. won 4-2 on penalties)

1998	Arsenal	Manchester Utd.	3-0
1999	Arsenal	Manchester Utd.	2-1
2000	Chelsea	Manchester Utd.	2-0
2001	Liverpool	Manchester Utd.	2-1

COMMUNITY SHIELD RESULTS

Year	Winners	Runners-up	Score
2002	Arsenal	Liverpool	1-0
2003	Manchester Utd.	Arsenal	1-1

(Manchester Utd. won 4-3 on penalties)

(Fixture played at Wembley since 1974. Millennium Stadium since 2001.
*Trophy shared)

ATTENDANCES 2003-04

The Football League reported their biggest crowds for 40 years last season. Nearly 16 million spectators watched matches in the three divisions, an increase of more than a million on the 2002-03 campaign. Division Three saw attendances up by 21%, helped by Hull City's first full season at their 25,000-capacity Kingston Communications Stadium. Gates there averaged 16,846, better than every club in Division Two apart from Sheffield Wednesday and more than 15 Division One grounds.

End-of-season Play-offs attracted record crowds, while those in the Carling Cup and LDV Vans Trophy also rose. 'These figures demonstrate the passion for the game that exists among supporters at all levels of the Football League,' said chairman Sir Brian Mawhinney. 'Week-in, week-out throughout the season, they go to tremendous lengths to support their clubs.'

Premiership crowds, totalling 13.3 million, fell slightly from the previous season's record high. Bolton Wanderers, at The Reebok, Leicester City, at The Walkers Stadium, and Southampton, at St Mary's, all had new highs. In their first season at the City of Manchester Stadium, Manchester City recorded a best of 47,304.

LEAGUE CROWDS SINCE 1980

	Total	Div. One	Div. Two	Div. Three	Div. Four
1979-80	24,623,975	12,163,002	6,112,025	3,999,328	2,349,620
1980-81	21,907,569	11,392,894	5,175,442	3,637,854	1,701,379
1981-82	20,006,961	10,420,793	4,750,463	2,836,915	1,998,790
1982-83	18,766,158	9,295,613	4,974,937	2,943,568	1,552,040
1983-84	18,358,631	8,711,448	5,359,757	2,729,942	1,557,484
1984-85	17,849,835	9,761,404	4,030,823	2,667,008	1,390,600
1985-86	16,498,868	9,037,854	3,555,343	2,495,991	1,409,680
1986-87	17,383,032	9,144,676	4,168,131	2,354,784	1,715,441
1987-88	17,968,887	8,094,571	5,350,754	2,751,275	1,772,287
1988-89	18,477,565	7,809,993	5,827,805	3,048,700	1,791,067
1989-90	19,466,826	7,887,658	6,884,439	2,803,551	1,891,178
1990-91	19,541,341	8,618,709	6,297,733	2,847,813	1,777,086
1991-92	20,487,273	9,989,160	5,809,787	2,993,352	1,694,974

New format	Total	Premier	Div. One	Div. Two	Div. Three
1992-93	20,657,327	9,759,809	5,874,017	3,483,073	1,540,428
1993-94	21,693,889	10,655,059	6,487,104	2,972,702	1,579,024
1994-95	21,856,223	11,213,371	6,044,293	3,037,752	1,560,807
1995-96	21,844,416	10,469,107	6,566,349	2,843,652	1,965,308
1996-97	22,791,527	10,804,762	6,804,606	3,332,451	1,849,708
1997-98	24,679,527	11,091,773	8,330,018	3,503,264	1,767,220
1998-99	25,435,981	11,620,765	7,543,369	4,169,697	2,102,150
1999-2000	25,342,478	11,668,222	7,811,420	3,700,433	2,162,403
2000-01	26,067,729	12,503,732	7,912,046	3,490,250	2,161,701
2001-02	27,835,107	13,043,118	8,402,142	3,981,252	2,408,595
2002-03	28,340,946	13,468,965	8,519,866	3,892,400	2,459,715
2003-04	29,196,787	13,307,037	8,771,259	4,143,691	2,974,800

All-time record Football League attendance aggregate: 41,271,414 in season 1948-49 (88 clubs). The average was 22,333.

FAMILY DAY AT TORQUAY

Each manager's son was in action when Torquay drew 2-2 at home with Yeovil last season. Torquay's Leroy Rosenior brought on Liam – on loan from Fulham – as a substitute in the 29th minute. Lee Johnson, son of Yeovil manager Gary, played the whole game.

HONOURS LIST

F.A. PREMIER LEAGUE

	First	Pts.	Second	Pts.	Third	Pts.
1992-3a	Manchester Utd.	84	Aston Villa	74	Norwich City	72
1993-4a	Manchester Utd.	92	Blackburn Rov.	84	Newcastle Utd.	77
1994-5a	Blackburn Rov.	89	Manchester Utd.	88	Nott'm Forest	77
1995-6b	Manchester Utd.	82	Newcastle Utd.	78	Liverpool	71
1996-7b	Manchester Utd.	75	Newcastle Utd.	68	Arsenal	68
1997-8b	Arsenal	78	Manchester Utd.	77	Liverpool	65
1998-9b	Manchester Utd.	79	Arsenal	78	Chelsea	75
1999-00b	Manchester Utd.	91	Arsenal	73	Leeds Utd.	69
2000-01b	Manchester Utd.	80	Arsenal	70	Liverpool	69
2001-02b	Arsenal	87	Liverpool	80	Manchester Utd.	77
2002-03b	Manchester Utd.	83	Arsenal	78	Newcastle Utd.	69
2003-04b	Arsenal	90	Chelsea	79	Manchester Utd.	75

Maximum points: a, 126; b, 114.

FOOTBALL LEAGUE

FIRST DIVISION

1992-3	Newcastle Utd.	96	West Ham Utd.	88	††Portsmouth	88
1993-4	Crystal Palace	90	Nott'm Forest	83	††Millwall	74
1994-5	Middlesbrough	82	††Reading	79	Bolton Wand.	77
1995-6	Sunderland	83	Derby Co.	79	††Crystal Palace	75
1996-7	Bolton Wand.	98	Barnsley	80	††Wolves	76
1997-8	Nott'm Forest	94	Middlesbrough	91	††Sunderland	90
1998-9	Sunderland	105	Bradford City	87	††Ipswich Town	86
1999-00	Charlton Athletic	91	Manchester City	89	Ipswich Town	87
2000-01	Fulham	101	Blackburn Rov.	91	Bolton Wand.	87
2001-02	Manchester City	99	W.B.A.	89	††Wolves	86
2002-03	Portsmouth	98	Leicester City	92	††Sheffield Utd.	80
2003-04	Norwich City	94	W.B.A.	86	††Sunderland	79

Maximum points: 138. ††Not promoted after play-offs.

SECOND DIVISION

1992-3	Stoke City	93	Bolton Wand.	90	††Port Vale	89
1993-4	Reading	89	Port Vale	88	††Plymouth Argyle	85
1994-5	Birmingham City	89	††Brentford	85	††Crewe Alexandra	83
1995-6	Swindon Town	92	Oxford Utd.	83	††Blackpool	82
1996-7	Bury	84	Stockport Co.	82	††Luton Town	78
1997-8	Watford	88	Bristol City	85	Grimsby Town	72
1998-9	Fulham	101	Walsall	87	Manchester City	82
1999-00	Preston N.E.	95	Burnley	88	Gillingham	85
2000-01	Milwall	93	Rotherham Utd.	91	††Reading	86
2001-02	Brighton & H.A.	90	Reading	84	††Brentford	83
2002-03	Wigan Athletic	100	Crewe Alexandra	86	††Bristol City	83
2003-04	Plymouth Argyle	90	Q.P.R.	83	††Bristol City	82

Maximum points: 138. †† Not promoted after play-offs.

THIRD DIVISION

1992-3a	Cardiff City	83	Wrexham	80	Barnet	79
1993-4a	Shrewsbury Town	79	Chester City	74	Crewe Alexandra	73

	First		Second		Third	
1994-5a	Carlisle Utd.	91	Walsall	83	Chesterfield	81
1995-6b	Preston N.E.	86	Gillingham	83	Bury	79
1996-7b	Wigan Athletic	87	Fulham	87	Carlisle Utd.	84
1997-8b	Notts County	99	Macclesfield Town	82	Lincoln City	75
1998-9b	Brentford	85	Cambridge Utd.	81	Cardiff City	80
1999-00b	Swansea City	85	Rotherham Utd.	84	Northampton Town	82
2000-01b	Brighton & H.A.	92	Cardiff City	82	*Chesterfield	80
2001-02b	Plymouth Argyle	102	Luton Town	97	Mansfield Town	79
2002-03b	Rushden & Diamonds	87	Hartlepool Utd.	85	Wrexham	84
2003-04b	Doncaster Rov.	92	Hull City	88	Torquay Utd.	81

Maximum points: a, 126; b, 138; * Deducted 9 points for financial irregularities.

FOOTBALL LEAGUE 1888-1992

	First	Pts.	Second	Pts.	Third	Pts.
1888-89a	Preston N.E.	40	Aston Villa	29	Wolves	28
1889-90a	Preston N.E.	33	Everton	31	Blackburn Rov.	27
1890-1a	Everton	29	Preston N.E.	27	Notts Co.	26
1891-2b	Sunderland	42	Preston N.E.	37	Bolton Wand.	36

OLD FIRST DIVISION

	First	Pts.	Second	Pts.	Third	Pts.
1892-3c	Sunderland	48	Preston N.E.	37	Everton	36
1893-4c	Aston Villa	44	Sunderland	38	Derby Co.	36
1894-5c	Sunderland	47	Everton	42	Aston Villa	39
1895-6c	Aston Villa	45	Derby Co.	41	Everton	39
1896-7c	Aston Villa	47	Sheffield Utd.	36	Derby Co.	36
1897-8c	Sheffield Utd.	42	Sunderland	39	Wolves	35
1898-9d	Aston Villa	45	Liverpool	43	Burnley	39
1899-1900d	Aston Villa	50	Sheffield Utd.	48	Sunderland	41
1900-1d	Liverpool	45	Sunderland	43	Notts Co.	40
1901-2d	Sunderland	44	Everton	41	Newcastle Utd.	37
1902-3d	The Wednesday	42	Aston Villa	41	Sunderland	41
1903-4d	The Wednesday	47	Manchester City	44	Everton	43
1904-5d	Newcastle Utd.	48	Everton	47	Manchester City	46
1905-6e	Liverpool	51	Preston N.E.	47	The Wednesday	44
1906-7e	Newcastle Utd.	51	Bristol City	48	Everton	45
1907-8e	Manchester Utd.	52	Aston Villa	43	Manchester City	43
1908-9e	Newcastle Utd.	53	Everton	46	Sunderland	44
1909-10e	Aston Villa	53	Liverpool	48	Blackburn Rov.	45
1910-11e	Manchester Utd.	52	Aston Villa	51	Sunderland	45
1911-12e	Blackburn Rov.	49	Everton	46	Newcastle Utd.	44
1912-13e	Sunderland	54	Aston Villa	50	Sheffield Wed.	49
1913-14e	Blackburn Rov.	51	Aston Villa	44	Middlesbrough	43
1914-15e	Everton	46	Oldham Athletic	45	Blackburn Rov.	43
1919-20f	W.B.A.	60	Burnley	51	Chelsea	49
1920-1f	Burnley	59	Manchester City	54	Bolton Wand.	52
1921-2f	Liverpool	57	Tottenham	51	Burnley	49
1922-3f	Liverpool	60	Sunderland	54	Huddersfield Town	53
1923-4f	*Huddersfield Town	57	Cardiff City	57	Sunderland	53
1924-5f	Huddersfield Town	58	W.B.A.	56	Bolton Wand.	55
1925-6f	Huddersfield Town	57	Arsenal	52	Sunderland	48
1926-7f	Newcastle Utd.	56	Huddersfield Town	51	Sunderland	49
1927-8f	Everton	53	Huddersfield Town	51	Leicester City	48
1928-9f	Sheffield Wed.	52	Leicester City	51	Aston Villa	50
1929-30f	Sheffield Wed.	60	Derby Co.	50	Manchester City	47
1930-1f	Arsenal	66	Aston Villa	59	Sheffield Wed.	52
1931-2f	Everton	56	Arsenal	54	Sheffield Wed.	50

Season	Winner	Pts	Runner-up	Pts	Third	Pts
1932-3f	Arsenal	58	Aston Villa	54	Sheffield Wed.	51
1933-4f	Arsenal	59	Huddersfield Town	56	Tottenham	49
1934-5f	Arsenal	58	Sunderland	54	Sheffield Wed.	49
1935-6f	Sunderland	56	Derby Co.	48	Huddersfield Town	48
1936-7f	Manchester City	57	Charlton Athletic	54	Arsenal	52
1937-8f	Arsenal	52	Wolves	51	Preston N.E.	49
1938-9f	Everton	59	Wolves	55	Charlton Athletic	50
1946-7f	Liverpool	57	Manchester Utd.	56	Wolves	56
1947-8f	Arsenal	59	Manchester Utd.	52	Burnley	52
1948-9f	Portsmouth	58	Manchester Utd.	53	Derby Co.	53
1949-50f	*Portsmouth	53	Wolves	53	Sunderland	52
1950-1f	Tottenham	60	Manchester Utd.	56	Blackpool	50
1951-2f	Manchester Utd.	57	Tottenham	53	Arsenal	53
1952-3f	*Arsenal	54	Preston N.E.	54	Wolves	51
1953-4f	Wolves	57	W.B.A.	53	Huddersfield Town	51
1954-5f	Chelsea	52	Wolves	48	Portsmouth	48
1955-6f	Manchester Utd.	60	Blackpool	49	Wolves	49
1956-7f	Manchester Utd.	64	Tottenham	56	Preston N.E.	56
1957-8f	Wolves	64	Preston N.E.	59	Tottenham	51
1958-9f	Wolves	61	Manchester Utd.	55	Arsenal	50
1959-60f	Burnley	55	Wolves	54	Tottenham	53
1960-1f	Tottenham	66	Sheffield Wed.	58	Wolves	57
1961-2f	Ipswich Town	56	Burnley	53	Tottenham	52
1962-3f	Everton	61	Tottenham	55	Burnley	54
1963-4f	Liverpool	57	Manchester Utd.	53	Everton	52
1964-5f	*Manchester Utd.	61	Leeds Utd.	61	Chelsea	56
1965-6f	Liverpool	61	Leeds Utd.	55	Burnley	55
1966-7f	Manchester Utd.	60	Nott'm Forest	56	Tottenham	56
1967-8f	Manchester City	58	Manchester Utd.	56	Liverpool	55
1968-9f	Leeds Utd.	67	Liverpool	61	Everton	57
1969-70f	Everton	66	Leeds Utd.	57	Chelsea	55
1970-1f	Arsenal	65	Leeds Utd.	64	Tottenham	52
1971-2f	Derby Co.	58	Leeds Utd.	57	Liverpool	57
1972-3f	Liverpool	60	Arsenal	57	Leeds Utd.	53
1973-4f	Leeds Utd.	62	Liverpool	57	Derby Co.	48
1974-5f	Derby Co.	53	Liverpool	51	Ipswich Town	51
1975-6f	Liverpool	60	Q.P.R.	59	Manchester Utd.	56
1976-7f	Liverpool	57	Manchester City	56	Ipswich Town	52
1977-8f	Nott'm Forest	64	Liverpool	57	Everton	55
1978-9f	Liverpool	68	Nott'm Forest	60	W.B.A.	59
1979-80f	Liverpool	60	Manchester Utd.	58	Ipswich Town	53
1980-1f	Aston Villa	60	Ipswich Town	56	Arsenal	53
1981-2g	Liverpool	87	Ipswich Town	83	Manchester Utd.	78
1982-3g	Liverpool	82	Watford	71	Manchester Utd.	70
1983-4g	Liverpool	80	Southampton	77	Nott'm Forest	74
1984-5g	Everton	90	Liverpool	77	Tottenham	77
1985-6g	Liverpool	88	Everton	86	West Ham Utd.	84
1986-7g	Everton	86	Liverpool	77	Tottenham	71
1987-8h	Liverpool	90	Manchester Utd.	81	Nott'm Forest	73
1988-9j	†Arsenal	76	Liverpool	76	Nott'm Forest	64
1989-90j	Liverpool	79	Aston Villa	70	Tottenham	63
1990-1j	Arsenal	83	Liverpool	76	Crystal Palace	69
1991-2g	Leeds Utd.	82	Manchester Utd.	78	Sheffield Wed.	75

Maximum points: a, 44; b, 52; c, 60; d, 68; e, 76; f, 84; g, 126; h, 120; j, 114.
*Won on goal average. †Won on goal diff. No comp. 1915-19 – 1939-46

OLD SECOND DIVISION 1892-1992

	First	Pts.	Second	Pts.	Third	Pts.
1892-3a	Small Heath	36	Sheffield Utd.	35	Darwen	30
1893-4b	Liverpool	50	Small Heath	42	Notts Co.	39
1894-5c	Bury	48	Notts County	39	Newton Heath	38
1895-6c	*Liverpool	46	Manchester City	46	Grimsby Town	42
1896-7c	Notts Co.	42	Newton Heath	39	Grimsby Town	38
1897-8c	Burnley	48	Newcastle Utd.	45	Manchester City	39
1898-9d	Manchester City	52	Glossop	46	Leicester Fosse	45
1899-1900d	The Wednesday	54	Bolton Wand.	52	Small Heath	46
1900-1d	Grimsby Town	49	Small Heath	48	Burnley	44
1901-2d	W.B.A.	55	Middlesbrough	51	Preston N.E.	42
1902-3d	Manchester City	54	Small Heath	51	Woolwich Arsenal	48
1903-4d	Preston N.E.	50	Woolwich Arsenal	49	Manchester Utd.	48
1904-5d	Liverpool	58	Bolton Wand.	56	Manchester Utd.	53
1905-6e	Bristol City	66	Manchester Utd.	62	Chelsea	53
1906-7e	Nott'm Forest	60	Chelsea	57	Leicester Fosse	48
1907-8e	Bradford City	54	Leicester Fosse	52	Oldham Athletic	50
1908-9e	Bolton Wand.	52	Tottenham	51	W.B.A.	51
1909-10e	Manchester City	54	Oldham Athletic	53	Hull City	53
1910-11e	W.B.A.	53	Bolton Wand.	51	Chelsea	49
1911-12e	*Derby Co.	54	Chelsea	54	Burnley	52
1912-13e	Preston N.E.	53	Burnley	50	Birmingham City	46
1913-14e	Notts County	53	Bradford City P.A.	49	Woolwich Arsenal	49
1914-15e	Derby Co.	53	Preston N.E.	50	Barnsley	47
1919-20f	Tottenham	70	Huddersfield Town	64	Birmingham City	56
1920-1f	*Birmingham City	58	Cardiff City	58	Bristol City	51
1921-2f	Nott'm Forest	56	Stoke City	52	Barnsley	52
1922-3f	Notts County	53	West Ham Utd.	51	Leicester City	51
1923-4f	Leeds Utd.	54	Bury	51	Derby Co.	51
1924-5f	Leicester City	59	Manchester Utd.	57	Derby Co.	55
1925-6f	Sheffield Wed.	60	Derby Co.	57	Chelsea	52
1926-7f	Middlesbrough	62	Portsmouth	54	Manchester City	54
1927-8f	Manchester City	59	Leeds Utd.	57	Chelsea	54
1928-9f	Middlesbrough	55	Grimsby Town	53	Bradford City	48
1929-30f	Blackpool	58	Chelsea	55	Oldham Athletic	53
1930-1f	Everton	61	W.B.A.	54	Tottenham	51
1931-2f	Wolves	56	Leeds Utd.	54	Stoke City	52
1932-3f	Stoke City	56	Tottenham	55	Fulham	50
1933-4f	Grimsby Town	59	Preston N.E.	52	Bolton Wand.	51
1934-5f	Brentford	61	Bolton Wand.	56	West Ham Utd.	56
1935-6f	Manchester Utd.	56	Charlton Athletic	55	Sheffield Utd.	52
1936-7f	Leicester City	56	Blackpool	55	Bury	52
1937-8f	Aston Villa	57	Manchester Utd.	53	Sheffield Utd.	53
1938-9f	Blackburn Rov.	55	Sheffield Utd.	54	Sheffield Wed.	53
1946-7f	Manchester City	62	Burnley	58	Birmingham City	55
1947-8f	Birmingham City	59	Newcastle Utd.	56	Southampton	52
1948-9f	Fulham	57	W.B.A.	56	Southampton	55
1949-50f	Tottenham	61	Sheffield Wed.	52	Sheffield Utd.	52
1950-1f	Preston N.E.	57	Manchester City	52	Cardiff City	50
1951-2f	Sheffield Wed.	53	Cardiff City	51	Birmingham City	51
1952-3f	Sheffield Utd.	60	Huddersfield Town	58	Luton Town	52
1953-4f	*Leicester City	56	Everton	56	Blackburn Rov.	55
1954-5f	*Birmingham City	54	Luton Town	54	Rotherham Utd.	54
1955-6f	Sheffield Wed.	55	Leeds Utd.	52	Liverpool	48
1956-7f	Leicester City	61	Nott'm Forest	54	Liverpool	53
1957-8f	West Ham Utd.	57	Blackburn Rov.	56	Charlton Athletic	55
1958-9f	Sheffield Wed.	62	Fulham	60	Sheffield Utd.	53

74

1959-60*f*	Aston Villa	59	Cardiff City	58	Liverpool	50
1960-1*f*	Ipswich Town	59	Sheffield Utd.	58	Liverpool	52
1961-2*f*	Liverpool	62	Leyton Orient	54	Sunderland	53
1962-3*f*	Stoke City	53	Chelsea	52	Sunderland	52
1963-4*f*	Leeds Utd.	63	Sunderland	61	Preston N.E.	56
1964-5*f*	Newcastle Utd.	57	Northampton Town	56	Bolton Wand.	50
1965-6*f*	Manchester City	59	Southampton	54	Coventry City	53
1966-7*f*	Coventry City	59	Wolves	58	Carlisle Utd.	52
1967-8*f*	Ipswich Town	59	Q.P.R.	58	Blackpool	58
1968-9*f*	Derby Co.	63	Crystal Palace	56	Charlton Athletic	50
1969-70*f*	Huddersfield Town	60	Blackpool	53	Leicester City	51
1970-1*f*	Leicester City	59	Sheffield Utd.	56	Cardiff City	53
1971-2*f*	Norwich City	57	Birmingham City	56	Millwall	55
1972-3*f*	Burnley	62	Q.P.R.	61	Aston Villa	60
1973-4*f*	Middlesbrough	65	Luton Town	50	Carlisle Utd.	49
1974-5*f*	Manchester Utd.	61	Aston Villa	58	Norwich City	53
1975-6*f*	Sunderland	56	Bristol City	53	W.B.A.	53
1976-7*f*	Wolves	57	Chelsea	55	Nott'm Forest	52
1977-8*f*	Bolton Wand.	58	Southampton	57	Tottenham	56
1978-9*f*	Crystal Palace	57	Brighton & H.A.	56	Stoke City	56
1979-80*f*	Leicester City	55	Sunderland	54	Birmingham City	53
1980-1*f*	West Ham Utd.	66	Notts Co.	53	Swansea City	50
1981-2*g*	Luton Town	88	Watford	80	Norwich City	71
1982-3*g*	Q.P.R.	85	Wolves	75	Leicester City	70
1983-4*g*	†Chelsea	88	Sheffield Wed.	88	Newcastle Utd.	80
1984-5*g*	Oxford Utd.	84	Birmingham City	82	Manchester City	74
1985-6*g*	Norwich City	84	Charlton Athletic	77	Wimbledon	76
1986-7*g*	Derby Co.	84	Portsmouth	78	††Oldham Athletic	75
1987-8*h*	Millwall	82	Aston Villa	78	Middlesbrough	78
1988-9*j*	Chelsea	99	Manchester City	82	Crystal Palace	81
1989-90*j*	†Leeds Utd.	85	Sheffield Utd.	85	†† Newcastle Utd.	80
1990-1*j*	Oldham Athletic	88	West Ham Utd.	87	Sheffield Wed.	82
1991-2*j*	Ipswich Town	84	Middlesbrough	80	†† Derby Co.	78

Maximum points: *a*, 44; *b*, 56; *c*, 60; *d*, 68; *e*, 76; *f*, 84; *g*, 126; *h*, 132; *j*, 138. * Won on goal average. † Won on goal difference. †† Not promoted after play-offs.

THIRD DIVISION 1958-92

	First	Pts.	Second	Pts.	Third	Pts.
1958-9	Plymouth Argyle	62	Hull City	61	Brentford	57
1959-60	Southampton	61	Norwich City	59	Shrewsbury Town	52
1960-1	Bury	68	Walsall	62	Q.P.R.	60
1961-2	Portsmouth	65	Grimsby Town	62	Bournemouth	59
1962-3	Northampton Town	62	Swindon Town	58	Port Vale	54
1963-4	*Coventry City	60	Crystal Palace	60	Watford	58
1964-5	Carlisle Utd.	60	Bristol City	59	Mansfield Town	59
1965-6	Hull City	69	Millwall	65	Q.P.R.	57
1966-7	Q.P.R.	67	Middlesbrough	55	Watford	54
1967-8	Oxford Utd.	57	Bury	56	Shrewsbury Town	55
1968-9	*Watford	64	Swindon Town	64	Luton Town	61
1969-70	Orient	62	Luton Town	60	Bristol Rov.	56
1970-1	Preston N.E.	61	Fulham	60	Halifax Town	56
1971-2	Aston Villa	70	Brighton & H.A.	65	Bournemouth	62
1972-3	Bolton Wand.	61	Notts Co.	57	Blackburn Rov.	55
1973-4	Oldham Athletic	62	Bristol Rov.	61	York City	61
1974-5	Blackburn Rov.	60	Plymouth Argyle	59	Charlton Athletic	55
1975-6	Hereford	63	Cardiff City	57	Millwall	56
1976-7	Mansfield Town	64	Brighton & H.A.	61	Crystal Palace	59
1977-8	Wrexham	61	Cambridge Utd.	58	Preston N.E.	56

1978-9	Shrewsbury Town 61	Watford 60	Swansea City 60
1979-80	Grimsby Town 62	Blackburn Rov. ... 59	Sheffield Wed. 58
1980-1	Rotherham Utd. 61	Barnsley 59	Charlton Athletic ... 59
†1981-2	*Burnley 80	Carlisle Utd. 80	Fulham 78
†1982-3	Portsmouth 91	Cardiff City 86	Huddersfield Town .. 82
†1983-4	Oxford Utd. 95	Wimbledon 87	Sheffield Utd. 83
†1984-5	Bradford City 94	Millwall 90	Hull City 87
†1985-6	Reading 94	Plymouth Argyle ... 87	Derby Co. 84
†1986-7	Bournemouth 97	Middlesbrough 94	Swindon Town 87
†1987-8	Sunderland 93	Brighton & H.A. .. 84	Walsall 82
†1988-9	Wolves 92	Sheffield Utd. 84	Port Vale 84
†1989-90	Bristol Rov. 93	Bristol City 91	Notts Co. 87
†1990-1	Cambridge Utd. 86	Southend Utd. 85	Grimsby Town 83
†1991-2	Brentford 82	Birmingham City 81	††Huddersfield T ... 78

* Won on goal average. † Maximum points 138 (previously 92). †† Not promoted after play-offs.

FOURTH DIVISION 1958-92

	First	Pts.	Second	Pts.	Third	Pts.	Fourth	Pts.
1958-9	Port Vale	64	Coventry City	60	York City	60	Shrewsbury Town	58
1959-60	Walsall	65	Notts Co.	60	Torquay Utd.	60	Watford	57
1960-1	Peterborough Utd.	66	Crystal Palace	64	Northampton Town	60	Bradford P.A.	60
1961-2	Millwall	56	Colchester Utd.	55	Wrexham	53	Carlisle Utd.	52
1962-3	Brentford	62	Oldham Athletic	59	Crewe Alexandra	59	Mansfield Town	57
1963-4	*Gillingham	60	Carlisle Utd.	60	Workington	59	Exeter City	58
1964-5	Brighton & H.A.	63	Millwall	62	York City	62	Oxford Utd.	61
1965-6	*Doncaster Rov.	59	Darlington	59	Torquay Utd.	58	Colchester Utd.	56
1966-7	Stockport Co.	64	Southport	59	Barrow	59	Tranmere Rov.	58
1967-8	Luton Town	66	Barnsley	61	Hartlepool Utd.	60	Crewe Alexandra	58
1968-9	Doncaster Rov.	59	Halifax Town	57	Rochdale	56	Bradford City	56
1969-70	Chesterfield	64	Wrexham	61	Swansea City	60	Port Vale	59
1970-1	Notts Co.	69	Bournemouth	60	Oldham Athletic	59	York City	56
1971-2	Grimsby Town	63	Southend Utd.	60	Brentford	59	Scunthorpe Utd.	57
1972-3	Southport	62	Hereford	58	Cambridge Utd.	57	Aldershot	56
1973-4	Peterborough Utd.	65	Gillingham	62	Colchester Utd.	60	Bury	55
1974-5	Mansfield Town	68	Shrewsbury Town	62	Rotherham Utd.	58	Chester City	57
1975-6	Lincoln City	74	Northampton Town	68	Reading	60	Tranmere Rov.	58
1976-7	Cambridge Utd.	65	Exeter City	62	Colchester Utd.	59	Bradford City	59
1977-8	Watford	71	Southend Utd.	60	Swansea City	56	Brentford	59
1978-9	Reading	65	Grimsby Town	61	Wimbledon	61	Barnsley	61
1979-80	Huddersfield Town	66	Walsall	64	Newport	61	Portsmouth	60
1980-1	Southend Utd.	67	Lincoln City	65	Doncaster Rov.	56	Wimbledon	55
†1981-2	Sheffield Utd.	96	Bradford City	91	Wigan Athletic	91	Bournemouth	88
†1982-3	Wimbledon	98	Hull City	90	Port Vale	88	Scunthorpe Utd.	83
†1983-4	York City	101	Doncaster Rov.	85	Reading	82	Bristol City	82
†1984-5	Chesterfield	91	Blackpool	86	Darlington	85	Bury	84
†1985-6	Swindon Town	102	Chester City	84	Mansfield Town	81	Port Vale	79
†1986-7	Northampton Town	99	Preston N.E.	90	Southend Utd.	80	††Wolves	79
†1987-8	Wolves	90	Cardiff City	85	Bolton Wand.	78	††Scunthorpe Utd.	77
†1988-9	Rotherham Utd.	82	Tranmere Rov.	80	Crewe Alexandra	78	††Scunthorpe Utd.	77
†1989-90	Exeter City	89	Grimsby Town	79	Southend Utd.	75	††Stockport Co.	74
†1990-1	Darlington	83	Stockport Co.	82	Hartlepool Utd.	82	Peterborough Utd.	80
1991-2a	Burnley	83	Rotherham Utd.	77	Mansfield Town	77	Blackpool	76

* Won on goal average. Maximum points: †, 138; a, 126; previously 92. †† Not promoted after play-offs.

THIRD DIVISION – SOUTH 1920-58

	First	Pts.	Second	Pts.	Third	Pts.
1920-1a	Crystal Palace	59	Southampton	54	Q.P.R.	53
1921-2a	*Southampton	61	Plymouth Argyle	61	Portsmouth	53
1922-3a	Bristol City	59	Plymouth Argyle	53	Swansea City	53
1923-4a	Portsmouth	59	Plymouth Argyle	55	Millwall	54
1924-5a	Swansea City	57	Plymouth Argyle	56	Bristol City	53
1925-6a	Reading	57	Plymouth Argyle	56	Millwall	53
1926-7a	Bristol City	62	Plymouth Argyle	60	Millwall	56
1927-8a	Millwall	65	Northampton Town	55	Plymouth Argyle	53
1928-9a	*Charlton Athletic	54	Crystal Palace	54	Northampton Town	52
1929-30a	Plymouth Argyle	68	Brentford	61	Q.P.R.	51
1930-31a	Notts Co.	59	Crystal Palace	51	Brentford	50
1931-2a	Fulham	57	Reading	55	Southend Utd.	53
1932-3a	Brentford	62	Exeter City	58	Norwich City	57
1933-4a	Norwich City	61	Coventry City	54	Reading	54
1934-5a	Charlton Athletic	61	Reading	53	Coventry City	51
1935-6a	Coventry City	57	Luton Town	56	Reading	54
1936-7a	Luton Town	58	Notts Co.	56	Brighton & H.A.	53
1937-8a	Millwall	56	Bristol City	55	Q.P.R.	53
1938-9a	Newport	55	Crystal Palace	52	Brighton & H.A.	49
1946-7a	Cardiff City	66	Q.P.R.	57	Bristol City	51
1947-8a	Q.P.R.	61	Bournemouth	57	Walsall	51
1948-9a	Swansea City	62	Reading	55	Bournemouth	52
1949-50a	Notts Co.	58	Northampton Town	51	Southend Utd.	51
1950-1d	Nott'm Forest	70	Norwich City	64	Reading	57
1951-2d	Plymouth Argyle	66	Reading	61	Norwich City	61
1952-3d	Bristol Rov.	64	Millwall	62	Northampton Town	62
1953-4d	Ipswich Town	64	Brighton & H.A.	61	Bristol City	56
1954-5d	Bristol City	70	Leyton Orient	61	Southampton	59
1955-6d	Leyton Orient	66	Brighton & H.A.	65	Ipswich Town	64
1956-7d	*Ipswich Town	59	Torquay Utd.	59	Colchester Utd.	58
1957-8d	Brighton & H.A.	60	Brentford	58	Plymouth Argyle	58

THIRD DIVISION – NORTH 1921-58

	First	Pts.	Second	Pts.	Third	Pts.
1921-2b	Stockport Co.	56	Darlington	50	Grimsby Town	50
1922-3b	Nelson	51	Bradford P.A.	47	Walsall	46
1923-4a	Wolves	63	Rochdale	62	Chesterfield	54
1924-5a	Darlington	58	Nelson	53	New Brighton	53
1925-6a	Grimsby Town	61	Bradford P.A.	60	Rochdale	59
1926-7a	Stoke City	63	Rochdale	58	Bradford P.A.	57
1927-8a	Bradford P.A.	63	Lincoln City	55	Stockport Co.	54
1928-9a	Bradford City	63	Stockport Co.	62	Wrexham	52
1929-30a	Port Vale	67	Stockport Co.	63	Darlington	50
1930-1a	Chesterfield	58	Lincoln City	57	Wrexham	54
1931-2c	*Lincoln City	57	Gateshead	57	Chester City	50
1932-3a	Hull City	59	Wrexham	57	Stockport Co.	54
1933-4a	Barnsley	62	Chesterfield	61	Stockport Co.	59
1934-5a	Doncaster Rov.	57	Halifax Town	55	Chester City	54
1935-6a	Chesterfield	60	Chester City	55	Tranmere Rov.	54
1936-7a	Stockport Co.	60	Lincoln City	57	Chester City	53
1937-8a	Tranmere Rov.	56	Doncaster Rov.	54	Hull City	53
1938-9a	Barnsley	67	Doncaster Rov.	56	Bradford City	52
1946-7a	Doncaster Rov.	72	Rotherham Utd.	64	Chester City	56
1947-8a	Lincoln City	60	Rotherham Utd.	59	Wrexham	50
1948-9a	Hull City	65	Rotherham Utd.	62	Doncaster Rov.	50
1949-50a	Doncaster Rov.	55	Gateshead	53	Rochdale	51

1950-1*d*	Rotherham Utd.	71	Mansfield Town	64	Carlisle Utd.	62
1951-2*d*	Lincoln City	69	Grimsby Town	66	Stockport Co.	59
1952-3*d*	Oldham Athletic	59	Port Vale	58	Wrexham	56
1953-4*d*	Port Vale	69	Barnsley	58	Scunthorpe Utd.	57
1954-5*d*	Barnsley	65	Accrington	61	Scunthorpe Utd.	58
1955-6*d*	Grimsby Town	68	Derby Co.	63	Accrington	59
1956-7*d*	Derby Co.	63	Hartlepool Utd.	59	Accrington	58
1957-8*d*	Scunthorpe Utd.	66	Accrington	59	Bradford City	57

Maximum points: *a*, 84; *b*, 76; *c*, 80; *d*, 92. * Won on goal average.

CHAMPIONSHIP WINNERS

F.A. PREMIER LEAGUE
Manchester Utd. 8
Arsenal 3
Blackburn Rov. 1

FOOTBALL LEAGUE
DIV.1 (NEW)
Sunderland 2
Bolton Wand. 1
Charlton Athletic 1
Crystal Palace 1
Fulham 1
Manchester City 1
Middlesbrough 1
Newcastle Utd. 1
Norwich City 1
Nott'm Forest 1
Portsmouth 1

DIV.1 (ORIGINAL)
Liverpool 18
Arsenal 10
Everton 9
Aston Villa 7
Manchester Utd. 7
Sunderland 6
Newcastle Utd. 4
Sheffield Wed. 4
Huddersfield Town 3
Leeds Utd. 3
Wolves 3
Blackburn Rov. 2
Burnley 2
Derby Co. 2

Manchester City 2
Portsmouth 2
Preston N.E. 2
Tottenham 2
Chelsea 1
Ipswich Town 1
Nott'm Forest 1
Sheffield Utd. 1
W.B.A. 1

DIV.2 (NEW)
Birmingham City 1
Brighton & H.A. 1
Bury 1
Fulham 1
Millwall 1
Plymouth Argyle 1
Preston N.E. 1
Reading 1
Stoke City 1
Swindon Town 1
Watford 1
Wigan Athletic 1

DIV.2 (ORIGINAL)
Leicester City 6
Manchester City 6
Sheffield Wed. 5
Birmingham City 4
Derby Co. 4
Liverpool 4
Ipswich Town 3
Leeds Utd. 3
Middlesbrough 3

Notts County 3
Preston N.E. 3
Aston Villa 2
Bolton Wand. 2
Burnley 2
Chelsea 2
Grimsby Town 2
Manchester Utd. 2
Norwich City 2
Nott'm Forest 2
Stoke City 2
Tottenham 2
W.B.A. 2
West Ham Utd. 2
Wolves 2
Blackburn Rov. 1
Blackpool 1
Bradford City 1
Brentford 1
Bristol City 1
Bury 1
Coventry City 1
Crystal Palace 1
Everton 1
Fulham 1
Huddersfield Town 1
Luton Town 1
Millwall 1
Newcastle Utd. 1
Oldham Athletic 1
Oxford Utd. 1
Q.P.R. 1
Sheffield Utd. 1
Sunderland 1

APPLICATIONS FOR RE-ELECTION
(System discontinued 1987)

14	Hartlepool Utd.	8	Darlington	5	Accrington
12	Halifax Town	8	Exeter City	5	Gillingham
11	Barrow	7	Chester City	5	Lincoln City
11	Southport	7	Walsall	5	New Brighton
10	Crewe Alexandra	7	Workington	4	Bradford P.A.
10	Newport	7	York City	4	Northampton Town
10	Rochdale	6	Stockport Co.	4	Norwich City

3 Aldershot	2 Colchester Utd.	1 Brighton & H.A.
3 Bradford City	2 Durham C.	1 Bristol Rov.
3 Crystal Palace	2 Gateshead	1 Cambridge Utd.
3 Doncaster Rov.	2 Grimsby Town	1 Cardiff City
3 Hereford	2 Millwall	1 Carlisle Utd.
3 Merthyr Tyd.	2 Nelson	1 Charlton Athletic
3 Swindon Town	2 Oldham Athletic	1 Mansfield Town
3 Torquay Utd.	2 Q.P.R.	1 Port Vale
3 Tranmere Rov.	2 Rotherham Utd.	1 Preston N.E.
2 Aberdare	2 Scunthorpe Utd.	1 Shrewsbury Town
2 Ashington	2 Southend Utd.	1 Swansea City
2 Bournemouth	2 Watford	1 Thames
2 Brentford	1 Blackpool	1 Wrexham

RELEGATED CLUBS (TO 1992)

1892-3	In Test matches, Darwen and Sheffield Utd. won promotion in place of Accrington and Notts Co.
1893-4	Tests, Liverpool and Small Heath won promotion. Darwen and Newton Heath relegated.
1894-5	After Tests, Bury promoted, Liverpool relegated.
1895-6	After Tests, Liverpool promoted, Small Heath relegated.
1896-7	After Tests, Notts Co. promoted, Burnley relegated.
1897-8	Test system abolished after success of Burnley and Stoke City, League extended. Blackburn Rov. and Newcastle Utd. elected to First Division. Automatic promotion and relegation introduced.

FIRST DIVISION TO SECOND DIVISION

1898-9	Bolton Wand., Sheffield Wed.
1899-00	Burnley, Glossop
1900-1	Preston N.E., W.B.A.
1901-2	Small Heath, Manchester City
1902-3	Grimsby Town, Bolton Wand.
1903-4	Liverpool, W.B.A.
1904-5	League extended. Bury and Notts Co., two bottom clubs in First Division, re-elected.
1905-6	Nott'm Forest, Wolves
1906-7	Derby Co., Stoke City
1907-8	Bolton Wand., Birmingham City
1908-9	Manchester City, Leicester Fosse
1909-10	Bolton Wand., Chelsea
1910-11	Bristol City, Nott'm Forest
1911-12	Preston N.E., Bury
1912-13	Notts Co., Woolwich Arsenal
1913-14	Preston N.E., Derby Co.
1914-15	Tottenham, *Chelsea
1919-20	Notts Co., Sheffield Wed.
1920-1	Derby Co., Bradford P.A.
1921-2	Bradford City, Manchester Utd.
1922-3	Stoke City, Oldham Athletic
1923-4	Chelsea, Middlesbrough
1924-5	Preston N.E., Nott'm Forest
1925-6	Manchester City, Notts Co.
1926-7	Leeds Utd., W.B.A.
1927-8	Tottenham, Middlesbrough
1928-9	Bury, Cardiff City
1929-30	Burnley, Everton
1930-1	Leeds Utd., Manchester Utd.

1931-2	Grimsby Town, West Ham Utd.
1932-3	Bolton Wand., Blackpool
1933-4	Newcastle Utd., Sheffield Utd.
1934-5	Leicester City, Tottenham
1935-6	Aston Villa, Blackburn Rov.
1936-7	Manchester Utd., Sheffield Wed.
1937-8	Manchester City, W.B.A.
1938-9	Birmingham City, Leicester City
1946-7	Brentford, Leeds Utd.
1947-8	Blackburn Rov., Grimsby Town
1948-9	Preston N.E., Sheffield Utd.
1949-50	Manchester City, Birmingham City
1950-1	Sheffield Wed., Everton
1951-2	Huddersfield Town, Fulham
1952-3	Stoke City, Derby Co.
1953-4	Middlesbrough, Liverpool
1954-5	Leicester City, Sheffield Wed.
1955-6	Huddersfield Town, Sheffield Utd.
1956-7	Charlton Athletic, Cardiff City
1957-8	Sheffield Wed., Sunderland
1958-9	Portsmouth, Aston Villa
1959-60	Luton Town, Leeds Utd.
1960-61	Preston N.E., Newcastle Utd.
1961-2	Chelsea, Cardiff City
1962-3	Manchester City, Leyton Orient
1963-4	Bolton Wand., Ipswich Town
1964-5	Wolves, Birmingham City
1965-6	Northampton Town, Blackburn Rov.
1966-7	Aston Villa, Blackpool
1967-8	Fulham, Sheffield Utd.
1968-9	Leicester City, Q.P.R.
1969-70	Sheffield Wed., Sunderland
1970-1	Burnley, Blackpool
1971-2	Nott'm Forest, Huddersfield Town
1972-3	W.B.A., Crystal Palace
1973-4	Norwich City, Manchester Utd., Southampton
1974-5	Chelsea, Luton Town, Carlisle Utd.
1975-6	Sheffield Utd., Burnley, Wolves
1976-7	Tottenham, Stoke City, Sunderland
1977-8	Leicester City, West Ham Utd., Newcastle Utd.
1978-9	Q.P.R., Birmingham City, Chelsea
1979-80	Bristol City, Derby Co., Bolton Wand.
1980-1	Norwich City, Leicester City, Crystal Palace
1981-2	Leeds Utd., Wolves, Middlesbrough
1982-3	Manchester City, Swansea City, Brighton & H.A.
1983-4	Birmingham City, Notts Co., Wolves
1984-5	Norwich City, Sunderland, Stoke City
1985-6	Ipswich Town, Birmingham City, W.B.A.
1986-7	Leicester City, Manchester City, Aston Villa
1987-8	Chelsea**, Portsmouth, Watford, Oxford Utd.
1988-9	Middlesbrough, West Ham Utd., Newcastle Utd.
1989-90	Sheffield Wed., Charlton Athletic, Millwall
1990-1	Sunderland, Derby Co.
1991-2	Luton Town, Notts Co., West Ham Utd.

* Subsequently re-elected to First Division when League extended after the war.
** Relegated after play-offs.

SECOND DIVISION TO THIRD DIVISION

1920-1	Stockport Co.
1921-2	Bradford City, Bristol City
1922-3	Rotherham Utd., Wolves
1923-4	Nelson, Bristol City
1924-5	Crystal Palace, Coventry City
1925-6	Stoke City, Stockport Co.
1926-7	Darlington, Bradford City
1927-8	Fulham, South Shields
1928-9	Port Vale, Clapton Orient
1929-30	Hull City, Notts County
1930-1	Reading, Cardiff City
1931-2	Barnsley, Bristol City
1932-3	Chesterfield, Charlton Athletic
1933-4	Millwall, Lincoln City
1934-5	Oldham Athletic, Notts Co.
1935-6	Port Vale, Hull City
1936-7	Doncaster Rov., Bradford City
1937-8	Barnsley, Stockport Co.
1938-9	Norwich City, Tranmere Rov.
1946-7	Swansea City, Newport
1947-8	Doncaster Rov., Millwall
1948-9	Nott'm Forest, Lincoln City
1949-50	Plymouth Argyle, Bradford P.A.
1950-1	Grimsby Town, Chesterfield
1951-2	Coventry City, Q.P.R.
1952-3	Southampton, Barnsley
1953-4	Brentford, Oldham Athletic
1954-5	Ipswich Town, Derby Co.
1955-6	Plymouth Argyle, Hull City
1956-7	Port Vale, Bury
1957-8	Doncaster Rov., Notts Co.
1958-9	Barnsley, Grimsby Town
1959-60	Bristol City, Hull City
1960-1	Lincoln City, Portsmouth
1961-2	Brighton & H.A., Bristol Rov.
1962-3	Walsall, Luton Town
1963-4	Grimsby Town, Scunthorpe Utd.
1964-5	Swindon Town, Swansea City
1965-6	Middlesbrough, Leyton Orient
1966-7	Northampton Town, Bury
1967-8	Plymouth Argyle, Rotherham Utd.
1968-9	Fulham, Bury
1969-70	Preston N.E., Aston Villa
1970-1	Blackburn Rov., Bolton Wand.
1971-2	Charlton Athletic, Watford
1972-3	Huddersfield Town, Brighton & H.A.
1973-4	Crystal Palace, Preston N.E., Swindon Town
1974-5	Millwall, Cardiff City, Sheffield Wed.
1975-6	Portsmouth, Oxford Utd., York City
1976-7	Carlisle Utd., Plymouth Argyle, Hereford Utd.
1977-8	Hull City, Mansfield Town, Blackpool
1978-9	Sheffield Utd., Millwall, Blackburn Rov.
1979-80	Fulham, Burnley, Charlton Athletic
1980-1	Preston N.E., Bristol City, Bristol Rov.
1981-2	Cardiff City, Wrexham, Orient
1982-3	Rotherham Utd., Burnley, Bolton Wand.
1983-4	Derby Co., Swansea City, Cambridge Utd.

1984-5	Notts Co., Cardiff City, Wolves
1985-6	Carlisle Utd., Middlesbrough, Fulham
1986-7	Sunderland**, Grimsby Town, Brighton & H.A.
1987-8	Sheffield Utd.**, Reading, Huddersfield Town
1988-9	Shrewsbury Town, Birmingham City, Walsall
1989-90	Bournemouth, Bradford City, Stoke City
1990-1	W.B.A., Hull City
1991-2	Plymouth Argyle, Brighton & H.A., Port Vale

** Relegated after play-offs.

THIRD DIVISION TO FOURTH DIVISION

1958-9	Rochdale, Notts Co., Doncaster Rov., Stockport Co.
1959-60	Accrington, Wrexham, Mansfield Town, York City
1960-1	Chesterfield, Colchester Utd., Bradford City, Tranmere Rov.
1961-2	Newport, Brentford, Lincoln City, Torquay Utd.
1962-3	Bradford P.A., Brighton & H.A., Carlisle Utd., Halifax Town
1963-4	Millwall, Crewe Alexandra, Wrexham, Notts Co.
1964-5	Luton Town, Port Vale, Colchester Utd., Barnsley
1965-6	Southend Utd., Exeter City, Brentford, York City
1966-7	Doncaster Rov., Workington, Darlington, Swansea City
1967-8	Scunthorpe Utd., Colchester Utd., Grimsby Town, Peterborough Utd. (demoted)
1968-9	Oldham Athletic, Crewe Alexandra, Hartlepool Utd., Northampton Town
1969-70	Bournemouth, Southport, Barrow, Stockport Co.
1970-1	Gillingham, Doncaster Rov., Bury, Reading
1971-2	Mansfield Town, Barnsley, Torquay Utd., Bradford City
1972-3	Scunthorpe Utd., Swansea City, Brentford, Rotherham Utd.
1973-4	Cambridge Utd., Shrewsbury Town, Rochdale, Southport
1974-5	Bournemouth, Watford, Tranmere Rov., Huddersfield Town
1975-6	Aldershot, Colchester Utd., Southend Utd., Halifax Town
1976-7	Reading, Northampton Town, Grimsby Town, York City
1977-8	Port Vale, Bradford City, Hereford, Portsmouth
1978-9	Peterborough Utd., Walsall, Tranmere Rov., Lincoln City
1979-80	Bury, Southend Utd., Mansfield Town, Wimbledon
1980-1	Sheffield Utd., Colchester Utd., Blackpool, Hull City
1981-2	Wimbledon, Swindon Town, Bristol City, Chester City
1982-3	Reading, Wrexham, Doncaster Rov., Chesterfield
1983-4	Scunthorpe Utd., Southend Utd., Port Vale, Exeter City
1984-5	Burnley, Orient, Preston N.E., Cambridge Utd.
1985-6	Lincoln City, Cardiff City, Wolves, Swansea City
1986-7	Bolton Wand.**, Carlisle Utd., Darlington, Newport
1987-8	Doncaster Rov., York City, Grimsby Town, Rotherham Utd.**
1988-9	Southend Utd., Chesterfield, Gillingham, Aldershot
1989-90	Cardiff City, Northampton Town, Blackpool, Walsall
1990-1	Crewe Alexandra, Rotherham Utd., Mansfield Town
1991-2	Bury, Shrewsbury Town, Torquay Utd., Darlington

** Relegated after plays-offs.

DEMOTED FROM FOURTH DIVISION TO CONFERENCE

1987	Lincoln City
1988	Newport
1989	Darlington
1990	Colchester Utd.
1991	No demotion
1992	No demotion

DEMOTED FROM THIRD DIVISION TO CONFERENCE

1993	Halifax Town
1994-6	No demotion
1997	Hereford
1998	Doncaster Rov.
1999	Scarborough
2000	Chester City
2001	Barnet
2002	Halifax Town
2003	Exeter City, Shrewsbury Town
2004	Carlisle Utd., York City

RELEGATED CLUBS (SINCE 1993)

1993

Premier League to Div. 1: Crystal Palace, Middlesbrough, Nott'm Forest
Div. 1 to Div. 2: Brentford, Cambridge Utd., Bristol Rov.
Div. 2 to Div. 3: Preston N.E., Mansfield Town, Wigan Athletic, Chester City

1994

Premier League to Div. 1: Sheffield Utd., Oldham Athletic, Swindon Town
Div. 1 to Div. 2: Birmingham City, Oxford Utd., Peterborough Utd.
Div. 2 to Div. 3: Fulham, Exeter City, Hartlepool Utd., Barnet

1995

Premier League to Div. 1: Crystal Palace, Norwich City, Leicester City, Ipswich Town
Div. 1 to Div. 2: Swindon Town, Burnley, Bristol City, Notts Co.
Div. 2 to Div. 3: Cambridge Utd., Plymouth Argyle, Cardiff City, Chester City, Leyton Orient

1996

Premier League to Div. 1: Manchester City, Q.P.R., Bolton Wand.
Div. 1 to Div. 2: Millwall, Watford, Luton Town
Div. 2 to Div. 3: Carlisle Utd., Swansea City, Brighton & H.A., Hull City

1997

Premier League to Div. 1: Sunderland, Middlesbrough, Nott'm Forest
Div. 1 to Div. 2: Grimsby Town, Oldham Athletic, Southend Utd.
Div. 2 to Div. 3: Peterborough Utd., Shrewsbury Town, Rotherham Utd., Notts Co.

1998

Premier League to Div. 1: Bolton Wand., Barnsley, Crystal Palace
Div. 1 to Div. 2: Manchester City, Stoke City, Reading
Div. 2 to Div. 3: Brentford, Plymouth Argyle, Carlisle Utd., Southend Utd.

1999

Premier League to Div. 1: Charlton Athletic, Blackburn Rov., Nott'm Forest
Div. 1 to Div. 2: Bury, Oxford Utd., Bristol City
Div. 2 to Div. 3: York City, Northampton Town, Lincoln City, Macclesfield Town

2000

Premier League to Div. 1: Wimbledon, Sheffield Wed., Watford
Div. 1 to Div. 2: Walsall, Port Vale, Swindon Town
Div. 2 to Div. 3: Cardiff City, Blackpool, Scunthorpe Utd., Chesterfield

2001

Premier League to Div. 1: Manchester City, Coventry City, Bradford City
Div. 1 to Div. 2: Huddersfield Town, Q.P.R., Tranmere Rov.
Div. 2 to Div. 3: Bristol Rov., Luton Town, Swansea City, Oxford Utd.

2002

Premier League to Div. 1: Ipswich Town, Derby Co., Leicester City
Div. 1 to Div. 2: Crewe Alexandra, Barnsley, Stockport Co.
Div. 2 to Div. 3: Bournemouth, Bury, Wrexham, Cambridge Utd.

2003

Premier League to Div. 1: West Ham Utd., W.B.A., Sunderland
Div. 1 to Div. 2: Sheffield Wed., Brighton & H.A., Grimsby Town
Div. 2 to Div. 3: Cheltenham Town, Huddersfield Town, Mansfield Town, Northampton Town

2004

Premier League to Div. 1: Leicester City, Leeds Utd., Wolves
Div. 1 to Div. 2: Walsall, Bradford City, Wimbledon
Div. 2 to Div. 3: Grimsby Town, Rushden & Diamonds, Notts Co., Wycombe Wand.

QUOTE – UNQUOTE

'It is our opinion the organisation we represent have not only let down one of our team-mates but the England squad and its manager. We feel they have failed us very badly' – **England** players' statement criticising the F.A.'s handling of the Rio Ferdinand drugs test affair.

'The threat not to play in the (Turkey) game was real. The thought about being chucked out of Euro 2004 was the main factor in pulling us back' – **Paul Scholes**, one of England's senior players.

'We are very well aware of our duties in this respect, but have no doubt we have acted entirely properly during this difficult and complex issue' – **Mark Palios**, F.A. chief executive.

'A very good example of how not to handle doping' – **Sepp Blatter**, FIFA president.

'The F.A. are really pushing the players' loyalty to the limit. You wouldn't treat a dog like this' – **Gordon Taylor**, chief executive of the PFA, after Alan Smith was called up to the England squad to play Denmark, then sent home when officials discovered he had been arrested over a bottle-throwing incident.

F.A. CUP 2003-04

FIRST ROUND

Accrington Stanley 1 Huddersfield Town 0
Barnet 2, Stalybridge Celtic 2
Blackpool 4, Boreham Wood 0
Bournemouth 1, Bristol Rov. 0
Bradford P.A. 2, Bristol City 5
Brentford 7, Gainsborough Trinity 1
Bury 1, Rochdale 2
Cheltenham Town 3, Hull City 1
Chester City 0, Gravesend & Northfleet 1
Colchester Utd. 1, Oxford Utd. 0
Farnborough Town 0, Weston-S-Mare 1
Grantham Town 1, Leyton Orient 2
Gray's Athletic 1, Aldershot Town 2
Grimsby Town 1, Q.P.R. 0
Hartlepool Utd. 4, Whitby Town 0
Hornchurch 2, Darlington 0
Kidderminster Harr. 2 Northwich 1
Lancaster City 1, Cambridge Utd. 2
Lincoln City 3, Brighton & H.A. 1
Macclesfield Town 3, Boston Utd. 0
Mansfield Town 6, Bishop's Stortford 0
Northampton Town 3, Plymouth Argyle 2
Notts Co. 7, Shildon 2
Oldham Athletic 3, Carlisle Utd. 0
Peterborough Utd. 2, Hereford Utd. 0
Port Vale 2, Ford Utd. 2
Scarborough 1, Doncaster Rov. 0
Scunthorpe Utd. 2, Shrewsbury Town 1
Sheffield Wed. 4, Salisbury 0
Southend Utd. 1, Canvey Island 1
Stevenage Borough 2 Stockport Co. 1
Swansea City 3, Rushden & Diamonds 0
Telford Utd. 3, Crawley Town 2
Thurrock 1, Luton Town 1
Torquay Utd. 1, Burton Albion 2
Tranmere Rov. 3, Chesterfield 2
Woking 3, Histon 1
Wycombe Wand. 4, Swindon Town 1
Yeovil Town 4, Wrexham 1
York City 1, Barnsley 2

FIRST ROUND REPLAYS

Canvey Island 2, Southend Utd. 3
Ford Utd. 1, Port Vale 2 (aet)
Luton Town 3, Thurrock 1
Stalybridge Celtic 0, Barnet 2

SECOND ROUND

Bournemouth 1, Accrington Stanley 1
Bristol City 0, Barnsley 0
Burton Albion 0, Hartlepool Utd. 1
Cheltenham Town 3, Leyton Orient 1
Colchester Utd. 1, Aldershot Town 0
Gravesend & Northfleet 1, Notts Co. 2
Hornchurch 0, Tranmere Rov. 1
Macclesfield Town 1, Cambridge Utd. 1
Northampton Town 4, Weston-S-Mare 1
Oldham Athletic 2, Blackpool 5
Peterborough Utd. 3, Grimsby Town 2
Port Vale 0, Scarborough 1
Rochdale 0, Luton Town 2
Scunthorpe Utd. 2, Sheffield Wed. 2
Southend Utd. 3, Lincoln City 0
Swansea City 2, Stevenage Borough 1
Telford Utd. 3, Brentford 0
Woking 0, Kidderminster Harr. 3
Wycombe Wand. 1, Mansfield Town 1
Yeovil Town 5, Barnet 1

SECOND ROUND REPLAYS

Accrington Stanley 0, Bournemouth 0
(aet, Accrington won 5-3 on pens)
Barnsley 2, Bristol City 1
Cambridge Utd. 2, Macclesfield Town 2
(aet, Macclesfield won 4-2 on pens)
Mansfield Town 3, Wycombe Wand. 2
Sheffield Wed. 0, Scunthorpe Utd. 0
(aet, Scunthorpe Utd. won 3-1 on pens)

MANCHESTER UNITED WIN F.A. CUP FOR 11TH TIME

THIRD ROUND	FOURTH ROUND	FIFTH ROUND	SIXTH ROUND	SEMI-FINALS	FINAL
Manchester Utd. 2	Manchester Utd. 3				
*Aston Villa 1		*Manchester Utd. 4			
*Northampton Town .. 1:1	*Northampton Town .. 0				
Rotherham Utd 1:2			*Manchester Utd. 2		
*Manchester City .. 2:3	*Manchester City .. 1:4				
Leicester City 2:1		Manchester City 2			
*Tottenham 3	Tottenham 1:3				
Crystal Palace 0				Manchester Utd. 1	
Norwich City 1	*Everton 1:1				
*Everton 3		*Fulham 0:3			
*Fulham 2	Fulham ...... 1:†2				
Cheltenham Town 1			Fulham 1		
*Kidderminster Harr. .. 1:0	*Wolves 1				
Wolves 1:2		West Ham Utd. 0:0			
*Wigan Athletic 1	West Ham Utd. 3				
West Ham Utd. 3					Manchester Utd. 3
*Yeovil Town 0	*Liverpool 2				
Liverpool 2		*Liverpool 1:0			
*Southampton 1	Newcastle Utd. 1				
Newcastle Utd. 3			*Portsmouth 1		
*Portsmouth 2	Portsmouth 2				
Blackpool 1		Portsmouth 1:1			
Scunthorpe Utd. 0:0	Scunthorpe Utd. 1				
*Barnsley 0:2				Arsenal 0	
Arsenal 4	*Arsenal 4				
*Leeds Utd. 1		*Arsenal 2			
*Middlesbrough 2	Middlesbrough 1				
Notts Co. 0			Arsenal 5		
*Southend 1:0	*Scarborough 0				
Scarborough 1:1		Chelsea 1			
*Watford 2:0	Chelsea 1				
Chelsea 2:4					

Round 1

*Ipswich Town	3
Derby Co.	0
Hartlepool Utd.	1
Birmingham City	4
Blackburn Rov.	0
Wimbledon	1:1
Stoke City	1:0
Nott'm Forest	1
W.B.A.	0
Cardiff City	1
Sheffield Utd.	0
Coventry City	2
Peterborough Utd.	0:1
Accrington Stanley	0:1
Colchester Utd.	0:2
Bradford City	1
Luton Town	2
Tranmere Rov.	1:†2
Bolton Wand.	1:1
Swansea City	2
Macclesfield Town	1
Preston N.E.	3:2
Reading	3:1
Mansfield Town	0
Burnley	3
Gillingham	1
Charlton Athletic	0
Crewe Alexandra	0
Telford Utd.	1
Walsall	1
*Millwall	2

Round 2

*Ipswich Town	1
Sunderland	2
*Birmingham City	1
Wimbledon	0
*Nott'm Forest	0
Sheffield Utd.	3
*Coventry City	1:1
Colchester Utd.	1:3
*Luton Town	0
Tranmere Rov.	1
*Swansea City	1
Preston N.E.	1
*Burnley	3
Gillingham	1
*Telford Utd.	0
*Millwall	1

Round 3

*Sunderland	1:†2
Birmingham City	1:0
*Sheffield Utd.	1
Colchester Utd.	0
*Tranmere Rov.	2
Swansea City	1
Burnley	0
*Millwall	1

Round 4

*Sunderland	1
Sheffield Utd.	0
Tranmere Rov.	0:1
*Millwall	0:2

Round 5

Sunderland	0
Millwall	1

Winner

Millwall	0

* Drawn at home. † After extra-time. Semi-finals: Manchester Utd. v Arsenal at Villa Park; Millwall v Sunderland at Old Trafford.

ROUND BY ROUND HIGHLIGHTS

FIRST ROUND

A stoppage-time goal by substitute Andy Gouck gives Accrington victory over Huddersfield – one of four victories by Conference sides over League opposition. Scarborough also beat Doncaster by the only goal of the tie, while Burton and Stevenage record 2-1 wins over Torquay and Stockport respectively. Hornchurch fly the flag for the Ryman Premier League by putting out Darlington 2-0. There are four hat-tricks – Brentford's Matt Harrold against Gainsborough (7-1), Mansfield's Neil MacKenzie against Bishop's Stortford (6-0), Adam Proudlock in Sheffield Wednesday's 4-0 win over Salisbury and Adrian Forbes for Luton in a 3-1 replay win over Thurrock.

SECOND ROUND

Telford's Christian Moore takes pride of place with all three goals in the 3-0 win over Brentford. Scarborough are not far behind, winning 1-0 at Port Vale, while Accrington put out Bournemouth on penalties in a replay. There are also hat-tricks for Blackpool's John Taylor at Oldham (5-2) and Mansfield's Liam Lawrence in a replay against Wycombe (3-2), two of his coming from the penalty spot.

THIRD ROUND

Telford and Scarborough march on. A second minute goal by Lee Mills gives Telford victory at Crewe. An 83rd minute strike by Mark Quayle takes Scarborough through in a replay against Southend. Arsenal begin their defence of the trophy with a 4-1 win at Leeds. Two Premiership sides go out to lower division opposition, Charlton losing 4-2 to Gillingham after scoring in the first minute, and Bolton beaten 2-1 by an extra-time goal by Tranmere's Canadian international Iain Hume in a replay. Birmingham reverse a Premiership scoreline of a month earlier when knocking out Blackburn 4-0. Kieron Dyer, without a goal all season, gets two as Newcastle win 3-0 at Southampton. Freddie Kanoute scores all three for Tottenham, who defeat Crystal Palace 3-0. Biggest crowd of the round, over 40,000, see Sunderland score a 1-0 win over Hartlepool, who are cheered on by 10,000 fans, nearly twice their home gate.

FOURTH ROUND

Ten-man Manchester City deliver one of the competition's greatest-ever comebacks, retrieving a 3-0 half-time deficit to beat Tottenham 4-3 at White Hart Lane with a last-minute goal by Jon Macken. Scarborough bow out with flying colours, restricting Chelsea to a goal by John Terry. Telford's run also ends. After two postponements, they lose 2-0 at home to Millwall. Colchester upset Coventry in another replay, winning 3-1 with a hat-trick from Rowan Vine. Bruno Cheyrou's double for Liverpool accounts for Newcastle in the big match of the round.

FIFTH ROUND

Record-signing Jose Antonio Reyes marks his F.A. Cup debut for Arsenal with his first goals for the club in a 2-1 win over Chelsea. Despite having Gary Neville sent off for butting Steve McManaman, United beat City 4-2 in the Manchester derby. Shaka Hislop, on his 35th birthday, saves a Michael Owen penalty as Portsmouth beat Liverpool 1-0 in a replay with a goal by substitute Richard Hughes. Tranmere reach the quarter-finals for the third time in five years with a 2-1 victory over Swansea.

SIXTH ROUND

Arsenal emphatically end Portsmouth's run, Thierry Henry and Freddie Ljungberg each scoring twice in a 5-1 success at Fratton Park. Two by Ruud van Nistelrooy earn Manchester United victory after Fulham lead with a Steed Malbranque penalty.

Sunderland's Tommy Smith gets the only goal against Sheffield United. John Achterberg saves Kevin Muscat's penalty to earn Tranmere a goalless draw at the Den, but Millwall win the replay 2-1.

SEMI-FINALS

Arsenal's bid to reach the Final for the fourth successive season is ended by a 32nd minute goal by Paul Scholes which rescues Manchester United's season. By the time Arsene Wenger brings on Thierry Henry with 57 minutes gone, United have a grip on the match. Five days after winning his first cap for Australia, Tim Cahill scores the only goal (26mins) for Millwall against Sunderland, who have Jason McAteer sent off for a second yellow card.

FINAL

The only surprise on an afternoon when everything else went according to the form book was the choice, by England coach Sven-Goran Eriksson, of Ruud van Nistelrooy as official man-of-the match. Admittedly, the Manchester United striker's two second half goals underlined the one-sided nature of the Final. But the vast majority watching would surely have plumped for 19-year-old Cristiano Ronaldo, who headed his side's first, tormented defenders with his trickery and whose growing maturity provided the biggest single reason why United can look forward with some optimism after a generally disappointing season by their high standards.

Millwall worked hard to stifle superior opponents and for 44 minutes succeeded, with the help of an excellent tip-over save by Andy Marshall from Roy Keane's 25-yard volley and Darren Ward's clearance from near the line after the goalkeeper could only partially halt the pace of a shot by Ronaldo following Van Nistelrooy's knock-down. But they were found wanting after Britain's most expensive teenage footballer started and finished off a move which opened up the game.

Ronaldo fed a short corner to 20-year-old Darren Fletcher, another player destined for a key role in United's emerging new team. The ball then went via Ryan Giggs on to Keane, who spread it wide into the path of Gary Neville's run. As Neville's cross came over, the Millwall player-manager Dennis Wise was caught ball-watching and Ronaldo punished him by heading in firmly.

Wise later blamed his striker Neil Harris for a wrong call, but could have no argument that United were well worth the lead. Nor could he complain about the way his side were overrun after the interval. Van Nistelrooy converted a 65th minute penalty after Giggs was brought down by David Livermore, and the Dutchman touched in a driven Giggs cross for the third, which had a hint of offside about it, with 81 minutes gone.

In addition, Marshall made another fine save, this time low down from a Paul Scholes shot, while Wise stopped a goal-bound Mikael Silvestre header from Ronaldo's far-post corner. By contrast, Tim Howard did not have a single effort to deal with and made way for Roy Carroll in the final ten minutes. Early on, Paul Ifill had raised Millwall spirits when galloping past John O'Shea. But it was a rare moment of concern for the United defence. With Danny Dichio suspended, Harris was an isolated figure up front, starved of support and service.

Millwall exceeded all expectations by reaching the Final and there was certainly no disgrace in the scoreline. Yet for a side whose First Division Play-off chances fell apart after their semi-final win over Sunderland, the thought lingered that they might have been better served by pursuing a place in the Premiership with no extra responsibilities.

MANCHESTER UNITED 3, MILLWALL 0
Millennium Stadium, (71,350), Saturday, May 22, 2004

Manchester Utd. (4-2-3-1): Howard (Carroll 83), G. Neville, Brown, Silvestre, O'Shea, Fletcher (Butt 83), Keane (capt), Ronaldo (Solskjaer 83), Scholes, Giggs, Van Nistelrooy. **Subs not used:** P. Neville, Djemba-Djemba. **Scorers:** Ronaldo (44), Van Nistelrooy (65, pen, 81). **Manager:** Sir Alex Ferguson.

Millwall (4-1-4-1): Marshall, Elliott, Lawrence (capt), Ward, Ryan (Cogan 74), Wise (Weston 89), Ifill, Cahill, Livermore, Sweeney, Harris (McCammon 74). **Subs not used:** Gueret, Dunne. **Booked:** Wise. **Manager:** Dennis Wise.

Referee: J. Winter (Cleveland). **Half-time:** 1-0. **Man-of-the-match:** Ruud van Nistelrooy. **Presentation:** Sven-Goran Eriksson.

HOW THEY REACHED THE FINAL

MANCHESTER UNITED

Round 3: 2-1 away to Aston Villa (Scholes 2)
Round 4: 3-0 away to Northampton Town (Silvestre, Hargreaves og, Forlan)
Round 5: 4-2 home to Manchester City (Van Nistelrooy 2, Scholes, Ronaldo)
Round 6: 2-1 home to Fulham (Van Nistelrooy 2)
Semi-final (Villa Park): 1-0 v Arsenal (Scholes)

MILLWALL

Round 3: 2-1 home to Walsall (Braniff, Cahill)
Round 4: 2-0 away to Telford (Ifill, Wise)
Round 5: 1-0 home to Burnley (Dichio)
Round 6: 0-0 home to Tranmere Rov.; 2-1 away to Tranmere Rov. (Cahill, Harris)
Semi-final (Old Trafford): 1-0 v Sunderland (Cahill)

LEADING SCORERS (FROM FIRST ROUND PROPER)

6 Taylor (Blackpool), Van Nistelrooy (Manchester Utd.)
5 Forbes (Luton Town), Trundle (Swansea City)
4 Anelka (Manchester City), Bennett (Kidderminster Harr.), Ljungberg (Arsenal), Scholes (Manchester Utd.), Smith (Sunderland), Vine (Colchester Utd.).

FINAL FACTS AND FIGURES

• Manchester United extended their record number of wins in the competition to 11.

• Roy Keane was playing in his sixth Final, a post-war record. He has four wins and a defeat with Manchester United and one defeat with Nottingham Forest.

• Sir Alex Ferguson extended his record number of wins as manager to five.

• Tim Howard became the first American to collect a winner's medal.

• Manchester United players donned 'Jimmy Davis' shirts for the presentation ceremony in memory of United player Jimmy Davis killed in a car crash in August 2003

• United's win was the biggest in the Final since they beat Chelsea 4-0 in 1994.

• Millwall substitue Curtis Weston, at 17 years and 119 days, became the youngest player to appear in an F.A. Cup Final.

• Millwall reached the Final without playing a Premiership team.

• The BBC's John Motson was commentating on his 25th F.A. Cup Final.

• Jeff Winter was refereeing his last match before retiring at the compulsory age of 48.

F.A. CUP FINAL TEAMS 1900-2004

1900 BURY – Thompson; Darrock, Davidson, Pray, Leeming, Ross, Richards, Wood, McLuckie, Sagar, Plant. **SOUTHAMPTON** – Robinson; Meehan, Durber, Meston, Chadwick, Petrie, Turner, Yates, Farrell, Wood, Milward. **Scorers:** Bury – McLuckie 2, Wood, Plant.

1901 TOTTENHAM – Clawley; Erentz, Tait, Norris, Hughes, Jones, Smith, Cameron, Brown, Copeland, Kirwan. **SHEFFIELD UTD.** – Foulke; Thickett, Boyle, Johnson, Morren, Needham, Bennett, Field, Hedley, Priest, Lipsham. **Scorers:** (first match) Tottenham – Brown 2, Sheff. Utd. – Bennett, Priest. **Scorers:** (second match) Tottenham – Cameron, Smith, Brown, Sheff. Utd. – Priest.

1902 SHEFFIELD UTD. – Foulke; Thickett, Boyle, Needham, Wilkinson, Johnson, Barnes, Common, Hedley, Priest, Lipsham. (Bennett injured in first match and Barnes took his place in the replay). **SOUTHAMPTON** – Robinson; C. B. Fry, Molyneux, Bowman, Lee, A. Turner, Wood, Brown, Chadwick, J. Turner, Metson. **Scorers:** (first match) Sheff. Utd. – Common, Southampton – Wood. **Scorers:** (second match) Sheff. Utd. – Hedley, Barnes, Southampton – Brown.

1903 BURY – Monteith; Lindsey, McEwan, Johnson, Thorpe, Ross, Richards, Wood, Sagar, Leeming, Plant. **DERBY CO.** – Fryer; Methven, Morris, Warren, Goodall (A.), May, Warrington, York, Boag, Richards, Davis. **Scorers:** Bury – Ross, Sagar, Leeming 2, Wood, Plant.

1904 MANCHESTER CITY – Hillman; McMahon, Burgess, Frost, Hynde, S. B. Ashworth, Meredith, Livingstone, Gillespie, Turnbull (A.), Booth. **BOLTON WAND.** – D. Davies; Brown, Struthers, Clifford, Greenhalgh, Freebairn, Stokes, Marsh, Yenson, White, Taylor. **Scorer:** Manchester City – Meredith.

1905 ASTON VILLA – George; Spencer, Miles, Pearson, Leake, Windmill, Brawn, Garratty, Hampton, Bache, Hall. **NEWCASTLE UTD.** – Lawrence; McCombie, Carr, Gardner, Aitken, McWilliam, Rutherford, Howie, Appleyard, Veitch, Gosnell. **Scorer:** Aston Villa – Hampton 2.

1906 EVERTON – Scott; Balmer (W.), Crelly, Makepeace, Taylor, Abbott, Sharp, Bolton, Young, Settle, H. P. Hardman. **NEWCASTLE UTD.** – Lawrence; McCombie, Carr, Gardner, Aitken, McWilliam, Rutherford, Howie, Veitch, Orr, Gosnell. **Scorer:** Everton – Young.

1907 SHEFFIELD WED. – Lyall; Layton, Burton, Brittleton, Crawshaw, Bartlett, Chapman, Bradshaw, Wilson, Stewart, Simpson. **EVERTON** – Scott; Balmer (W.), Balmer (R.), Makepeace, Taylor, Abbott, Sharp, Bolton, Young, Settle, H. P. Hardman. **Scorers:** Sheff. Wed. – Stewart, Simpson, Everton – Sharp.

1908 WOLVES – Lunn; Jones, Collins, Rev. K. R. G. Hunt, Wooldridge, Bishop, Harrison, Shelton, Hedley, Radford, Pedley. **NEWCASTLE UTD.** – Lawrence; McCracken, Pudan, Gardner, Veitch, McWilliam, Rutherford, Howie, Appleyard, Speedie, Wilson. **Scorers:** Wolves – Hunt, Hedley, Harrison, Newcastle Utd. – Howie.

1909 MANCHESTER UTD. – Moger; Stacey, Hayes, Duckworth, Roberts, Bell, Meredith, Halse, Turnbull (J.), Turnbull (A.), Wall. **BRISTOL CITY** – Clay; Annan, Cottle, Hanlin, Wedlock, Spear, Staniforth, Hardy, Gilligan, Burton, Hilton. **Scorer:** Manchester Utd. – Turnbull (A.).

1910 NEWCASTLE UTD. – Lawrence; McCracken, Carr, Veitch, Low, McWilliam, Rutherford, Howie, Shepherd, Higgins, Wilson. (Whitson was injured in first match and Carr took his place in the replay). **BARNSLEY** – Mearns; Downs, Ness, Glendinning, Boyle, Utley, Bartrop, Gadsby, Lillycrop, Tufnell, Forman. **Scorers:** (first match) Newcastle Utd. – Rutherford, Barnsley – Tufnell. **Scorer:** (second match) Newcastle Utd. – Shepherd 2 (1 pen.).

1911 BRADFORD CITY – Mellors; Campbell, Taylor, Robinson, Torrance, McDonald, Logan, Spiers, O'Rourke, Devine, Thompson. (Gildea played centre half in the first match). **NEWCASTLE UTD.** – Lawrence; McCracken, Whitson, Veitch, Low, Willis, Rutherford, Jobey, Stewart, Higgins, Wilson. **Scorer:** Bradford City – Spiers.

1912 BARNSLEY – Cooper; Downs, Taylor, Glendinning, Bratley, Utley, Bartrop, Tufnell, Lillycrop, Travers, Moore. **W.B.A.** – Pearson; Cook, Pennington, Baddeley, Buck, McNeal, Jephcott, Wright, Pailor, Bower, Shearman. **Scorer:** Barnsley – Tufnell.

1913 ASTON VILLA – Hardy; Lyons, Weston, Barber, Harrop, Leach, Wallace, Halse, Hampton, Stephenson (C.), Bache. **SUNDERLAND** – Butler; Gladwin, Ness, Cuggy, Thompson, Low, Mordue, Buchan, Richardson, Holley, Martin. **Scorer:** Aston Villa – Barber.

1914 BURNLEY – Sewell; Bamford, Taylor, Halley, Boyle, Watson, Nesbit, Lindley, Freeman, Hodgson, Mosscrop. **LIVERPOOL** – Campbell; Longworth, Pursell, Fairfoul, Ferguson, McKinlay, Sheldon, Metcalfe, Miller, Lacey, Nicholl. **Scorer:** Burnley – Freeman.

1915 SHEFFIELD UTD. – Gough; Cook, English, Sturgess, Brelsford, Utley, Simmons, Fazackerley, Kitchen, Masterman, Evans. **CHELSEA** – Molyneux; Bettridge, Harrow, Taylor, Logan, Walker, Ford, Halse, Thompson, Croal, McNeil. **Scorers:** Sheff. Utd. – Simmons, Fazackerley, Kitchen.

1920 ASTON VILLA – Hardy; Smart, Weston, Ducat, Barson, Moss, Wallace, Kirton, Walker, Stephenson (C.), Dorrell. **HUDDERSFIELD TOWN** – Mutch; Wood, Bullock, Slade, Wilson, Watson, Richardson, Mann, Taylor, Swan, Islip. **Scorer:** Aston VIlla – Kirton.

1921 TOTTENHAM – Hunter; Clay, McDonald, Smith, Walters, Grimsdell; Banks, Seed, Cantrell, Bliss, Dimmock. **WOLVES** – George; Woodward, Marshall, Gregory, Hodnett, Riley, Lea, Burrill, Edmonds, Potts, Brooks. **Scorer:** Tottenham – Dimmock.

1922 HUDDERSFIELD TOWN – Mutch; Wood, Wadsworth, Slade, Wilson, Watson, Richardson, Mann, Islip, Stephenson, Smith (W.H.). **PRESTON N.E.** – J. F. Mitchell; Hamilton, Doolan, Duxbury, McCall, Williamson, Rawlings, Jefferis, Roberts, Woodhouse, Quinn. **Scorer:** Huddersfield Town – Smith (pen.).

1923 BOLTON WAND. – Pym; Haworth, Finney, Nuttall, Seddon, Jennings, Butler, Jack, Smith (J. R.), Smith (J.), Vizard. **WEST HAM UTD.** – Hufton; Henderson, Young, Bishop, Kay, Tresadern, Richards, Brown, Watson (V.), Moore, Ruffell. **Scorers:** Bolton Wand. – Jack, Smith (J. R.).

1924 NEWCASTLE UTD. – Bradley; Hampson, Hudspeth, Mooney, Spencer, Gibson, Low, Cowan, Harris, McDonald, Seymour. **ASTON VILLA** – Jackson; Smart, Mort, Moss, Dr. V. E. Milne, Blackburn, York, Kirton, Capewell, Walker, Dorrell. **Scorers:** Newcastle Utd. – Harris, Seymour.

1925 SHEFFIELD UTD. – Sutcliffe; Cook, Milton, Pantling, King, Green, Mercer, Boyle, Johnson, Gillespie, Tunstall. **CARDIFF CITY** – Farquharson; Nelson, Blair, Wake, Keenor, Hardy, Davies (W.), Gill, Nicholson, Beadles, Evans (J.). **Scorer:** Sheff. Utd. – Tunstall.

1926 BOLTON WAND. – Pym; Haworth, Greenhalgh, Nuttall, Seddon, Jennings, Butler, Jack, Smith (J. R.), Smith (J.), Vizard. **MANCHESTER CITY** – Goodchild; Cookson, McCloy, Pringle, Cowan, McMullan, Austin, Browell, Roberts, Johnson, Hicks. **Scorer:** Bolton Wand. – Jack.

1927 CARDIFF CITY – Farquharson; Nelson, Watson, Keenor, Sloan, Hardy, Curtis, Irving, Ferguson, Davies (L.), McLachlan. **ARSENAL** – Lewis; Parker, Kennedy, Baker, Butler, John, Hulme, Buchan, Brain, Blyth, Hoar. **Scorer:** Cardiff City – Ferguson.

1928 BLACKBURN ROV. – Crawford; Hutton, Jones, Healless, Rankin, Campbell, Thornewell, Puddefoot, Roscamp, McLean, Rigby. **HUDDERSFIELD TOWN** – Mercer; Goodall, Barkas, Redfern, Wilson, Steele, Jackson (A.), Kelly, Brown, Stephenson, Smith (W.H.). **Scorers:** Blackburn Rov. – Roscamp 2, McLean, Huddersfield Town – Jackson.

1929 BOLTON WAND. – Pym; Haworth, Finney, Kean, Seddon, Nuttall, Butler, McClelland, Blackmore, Gibson, Cook (W.). **PORTSMOUTH** – Gilfillan; Mackie, Bell, Nichol, McIlwaine, Thackeray, Forward, Smith (J.), Weddle, Watson, Cook (F.). **Scorers:** Bolton Wand. – Butler, Blackmore.

1930 ARSENAL – Preedy; Parker, Hapgood, Baker, Seddon, John, Hulme, Jack, Lambert, James, Bastin. **HUDDERSFIELD TOWN** – Turner; Goodall, Spence, Naylor, Wilson, Campbell, Jackson (A.), Kelly, Davies, Raw, Smith (W. H.). **Scorers:** Arsenal – James, Lambert.

1931 W.B.A. – Pearson; Shaw, Trentham, Magee, Richardson (W.), Edwards, Glidden, Carter, Richardson (W. G.), Sandford, Wood. **BIRMINGHAM CITY** – Hibbs; Liddell, Barkas, Cringan, Morrall, Leslie, Briggs, Crosbie, Bradford, Gregg, Curtis. **Scorers:** W.B.A. – Richardson (W. G.) 2, Birmingham City – Bradford.

1932 NEWCASTLE UTD. – McInroy; Nelson, Fairhurst, McKenzie, Davidson, Weaver, Boyd, Richardson, Allen, McMenemy, Lang. **ARSENAL** – Moss; Parker, Hapgood, Jones

(C.), Roberts, Male, Hulme, Jack, Lambert, Bastin, John. **Scorers:** Newcastle Utd. – Allen 2, Arsenal – John.

1933 EVERTON – Sagar; Cook, Cresswell, Britton, White, Thomson, Geldard, Dunn, Dean, Johnson, Stein. **MANCHESTER CITY** – Langford; Cann, Dale, Busby, Cowan, Bray, Toseland, Marshall, Herd, McMullan, Brook. **Scorers:** Everton – Stein, Dean, Dunn.

1934 MANCHESTER CITY – Swift; Barnett, Dale, Busby, Cowan, Bray, Toseland, Marshall, Tilson, Herd, Brook. **PORTSMOUTH** – Gilfillan; Mackie, Smith (W.), Nichol, Allen, Thackeray, Worrall, Smith (J.), Weddle, Easson, Rutherford. **Scorers:** Manchester City – Tilson 2, Portsmouth – Rutherford.

1935 SHEFFIELD WED. – Brown; Nibloe, Catlin, Sharp, Millership, Burrows, Hooper, Surtees, Palethorpe, Starling, Rimmer. **W.B.A.** – Pearson; Shaw, Trentham, Murphy, Richardson (W.), Edwards, Glidden, Carter, Richardson (W. G.), Sandford, Boyes. **Scorers:** Sheff. Wed. – Rimmer 2, Palethorpe, Hooper, W.B.A. – Boyes, Sandford.

1936 ARSENAL – Wilson; Male, Hapgood, Crayston, Roberts, Copping, Hulme, Bowden, Drake, James, Bastin. **SHEFFIELD UTD.** – Smith; Hooper, Wilkinson, Jackson, Johnson, McPherson, Barton, Barclay, Dodds, Pickering, Williams. **Scorer:** Arsenal – Drake.

1937 SUNDERLAND – Mapson; Gorman, Hall, Thomson, Johnston, McNab, Duns, Carter, Gurney, Gallacher, Burbanks. **PRESTON N.E.** – Burns; Gallimore, Beattie (A.), Shankly, Tremelling, Milne, Dougal, Beresford, O'Donnell (F.), Fagan, O'Donnell (H). **Scorers:** Sunderland – Gurney, Carter, Burbanks, Preston N.E. – O'Donnell (F.).

1938 PRESTON N.E. – Holdcroft; Gallimore, Beattie (A.), Shankly, Smith, Batey, Watmough, Mutch, Maxwell, Beattie (R.), O'Donnell (H.). **HUDDERSFIELD TOWN** – Hesford; Craig, Mountford, Willingham, Young, Boot, Hulme, Isaac, McFadyen, Barclay, Beasley. **Scorer:** Preston N.E. – Mutch (pen.).

1939 PORTSMOUTH – Walker; Morgan, Rochford, Guthrie, Rowe, Wharton, Worrall, McAlinden, Anderson, Barlow, Parker. **WOLVES** – Scott; Morris, Taylor, Galley, Cullis, Gardiner, Burton, McIntosh, Westcott, Dorsett, Maguire. **Scorers:** Portsmouth – Barlow, Anderson, Parker 2, Wolves – Dorsett.

1946 DERBY CO. – Woodley; Nicholas, Howe, Bullions, Leuty, Musson, Harrison, Carter, Stamps, Doherty, Duncan. **CHARLTON ATHLETIC** – Bartram; Phipps, Shreeve, Turner (H.), Oakes, Johnson, Fell, Brown, A. A. Turner, Welsh, Duffy. **Scorers:** Derby Co. – Turner (H.) (o.g.), Doherty, Stamps 2, Charlton Athletic – Turner (H.).

1947 CHARLTON ATHLETIC – Bartram; Croker (P.), Shreeve, Johnson, Phipps, Whittaker, Hurst, Dawson, Robinson (W.), Welsh, Duffy. **BURNLEY** – Strong; Woodruff, Mather, Attwell, Brown, Bray, Chew, Morris, Harrison, Potts, F. P. Kippax. **Scorer:** Charlton Athletic – Duffy.

1948 MANCHESTER UTD. – Crompton; Carey, Aston, Anderson, Chilton, Cockburn, Delaney, Morris, Rowley, Pearson, Mitten. **BLACKPOOL** – Robinson; Shimwell, Crosland, Johnston, Hayward, Kelly, Matthews, Munro, Mortensen, Dick, Rickett. **Scorers:** Manchester Utd. – Rowley 2, Pearson, Anderson, Blackpool – Shimwell (pen.), Mortensen.

1949 WOLVES – Williams; Pritchard, Springthorpe, Crook (W.), Shorthouse, Wright, Hancocks, Smyth, Pye, Dunn, Mullen. **LEICESTER CITY** – Bradley; Jelly, Scott, Harrison (W.), Plummer, King, Griffiths, Lee, Harrison (J.), Chisholm, Adam. **Scorers:** Wolves – Pye 2, Smyth, Leicester City – Griffiths.

1950 ARSENAL – Swindin; Scott, Barnes, Forbes, Compton (L.), Mercer, Cox, Logie, Goring, Lewis, Compton (D.). **LIVERPOOL** – Sidlow; Lambert, Spicer, Taylor, Hughes, Jones, Payne, Baron, Stubbins, Fagan, Liddell. **Scorer:** Arsenal – Lewis 2.

1951 NEWCASTLE UTD. – Fairbrother; Cowell, Corbett, Harvey, Brennan, Crowe, Walker, Taylor, Milburn, Robledo (G.), Mitchell. **BLACKPOOL** – Farm; Shimwell, Garrett, Johnston, Hayward, Kelly, Matthews, Mudie, Mortensen, W. J. Slater, Perry. **Scorer:** Newcastle Utd. – Milburn 2.

1952 NEWCASTLE UTD. – Simpson; Cowell, McMichael, Harvey, Brennan, Robledo (E.), Walker, Foulkes, Milburn, Robledo (G.), Mitchell. **ARSENAL** – Swindin; Barnes, Smith (L.), Forbes, Daniel, Mercer, Cox, Logie, Holton, Lishman, Roper. **Scorer:** Newcastle Utd. – Robledo (G.).

1953 BLACKPOOL – Farm; Shimwell, Garrett, Fenton, Johnston, Robinson, Matthews, Taylor, Mortensen, Mudie, Perry. **BOLTON WAND.** – Hanson; Ball, Banks (R.), Wheeler,

Barrass, Bell, Holden, Moir, Lofthouse, Hassall, Langton. **Scorers:** Blackpool – Mortensen 3, Perry, Bolton Wand. – Lofthouse, Moir, Bell.

1954 W.B.A. – Sanders; Kennedy, Millard, Dudley, Dugdale, Barlow, Griffin, Ryan, Allen, Nicholls, Lee. **PRESTON N.E.** – Thompson; Cunningham, Walton, Docherty, Marston, Forbes, Finney, Foster, Wayman, Baxter, Morrison. **Scorers:** W.B.A. – Allen 2 (1 pen.), Griffin, Preston N.E. – Morrison, Wayman.

1955 NEWCASTLE UTD. – Simpson; Cowell, Batty, Scoular, Stokoe, Casey, White, Milburn, Keeble, Hannah, Mitchell. **MANCHESTER CITY** – Trautmann; Meadows, Little, Barnes, Ewing, Paul, Spurdle, Hayes, Revie, Johnstone, Fagan. **Scorers:** Newcastle Utd. – Milburn, Mitchell, Hannah, Manchester City – Johnstone.

1956 MANCHESTER CITY – Trautmann; Leivers, Little, Barnes, Ewing, Paul, Johnstone, Hayes, Revie, Dyson, Clarke. **BIRMINGHAM CITY** – Merrick; Hall, Green, Newman, Smith, Boyd, Astall, Kinsey, Brown, Murphy, Govan. **Scorers:** Manchester City – Hayes, Dyson, Johnstone, Birmingham City – Kinsey.

1957 ASTON VILLA – Sims; Lynn, Aldis, Crowther, Dugdale, Saward, Smith, Sewell, Myerscough, Dixon, McParland. **MANCHESTER UTD.** – Wood; Foulkes, Byrne, Colman, Blanchflower, Edwards, Berry, Whelan, Taylor (T.), Charlton, Pegg. **Scorers:** Aston Villa – McParland 2, Manchester Utd. – Taylor.

1958 BOLTON WANDERERS – Hopkinson; Hartle, Banks (T.), Hennin, Higgins, Edwards, Birch, Stevens, Lofthouse, Parry, Holden. **MANCHESTER UTD.** – Gregg; Foulkes, Greaves, Goodwin, Cope, Crowther, Dawson, Taylor (E.), Charlton, Viollet, Webster. **Scorer:** Bolton Wand. – Lofthouse 2.

1959 NOTT'M FOREST – Thomson; Whare, McDonald, Whitefoot, McKinlay, Burkitt, Dwight, Quigley, Wilson, Gray, Imlach. **LUTON TOWN** – Baynham; McNally, Hawkes, Groves, Owen, Pacey, Bingham, Brown, Morton, Cummins, Gregory. **Scorers:** Nott'm. Forest – Dwight, Wilson, Luton Town – Pacey.

1960 WOLVES – Finlayson; Showell, Harris, Clamp, Slater, Flowers, Deeley, Stobart, Murray, Broadbent, Horne. **BLACKBURN ROV.** – Leyland; Bray, Whelan, Clayton, Woods, McGrath, Bimpson, Dobing, Dougan, Douglas, MacLeod. **Scorers:** Wolves – McGrath (o.g.), Deeley 2.

1961 TOTTENHAM – Brown; Baker, Henry, Blanchflower, Norman, Mackay, Jones, White, Smith, Allen, Dyson. **LEICESTER CITY** – Banks; Chalmers, Norman, McLintock, King, Appleton, Riley, Walsh, McIlmoyle, Keyworth, Cheesebrough. **Scorers:** Tottenham – Smith, Dyson.

1962 TOTTENHAM – Brown; Baker, Henry, Blanchflower, Norman, Mackay, Medwin, White, Smith, Greaves, Jones. **BURNLEY** – Blacklaw; Angus, Elder, Adamson, Cummings, Miller, Connelly, McIlroy, Pointer, Robson, Harris. **Scorers:** Tottenham – Greaves, Smith, Blanchflower (pen.), Burnley – Robson.

1963 MANCHESTER UTD. – Gaskell; Dunne, Cantwell, Crerand, Foulkes, Setters, Giles, Quixall, Herd, Law, Charlton. **LEICESTER CITY** – Banks; Sjoberg, Norman, McLintock, King, Appleton, Riley, Cross, Keyworth, Gibson, Stringfellow. **Scorers:** Manchester Utd. – Law, Herd 2, Leicester City – Keyworth.

1964 WEST HAM UTD. – Standen; Bond, Burkett, Bovington, Brown, Moore, Brabrook, Boyce, Byrne, Hurst, Sissons. **PRESTON N.E.** – Kelly; Ross, Smith, Lawton, Singleton, Kendall, Wilson, Ashworth, Dawson, Spavin, Holden. **Scorers:** West Ham Utd. – Sissons, Hurst, Boyce, Preston N.E. – Holden, Dawson.

1965 LIVERPOOL – Lawrence; Lawler, Byrne, Strong, Yeats, Stevenson, Callaghan, Hunt, St. John, Smith, Thompson. **LEEDS UTD.** – Sprake; Reaney, Bell, Bremner, Charlton, Hunter, Giles, Storrie, Peacock, Collins, Johanneson. **Scorers:** Liverpool – Hunt, St. John, Leeds Utd. – Bremner.

1966 EVERTON – West; Wright, Wilson, Gabriel, Labone, Harris, Scott, Trebilcock, Young, Harvey, Temple. **SHEFFIELD WED.** – Springett; Smith, Megson, Eustace, Ellis, Young, Pugh, Fantham, McCalliog, Ford, Quinn. **Scorers:** Everton – Trebilcock 2, Temple, Sheff. Wed. – McCalliog, Ford.

1967 TOTTENHAM – Jennings; Kinnear, Knowles, Mullery, England, Mackay, Robertson, Greaves, Gilzean, Venables, Saul. **CHELSEA** – Bonetti; Harris (A.), McCreadie, Hollins, Hinton, Harris (R.), Cooke, Baldwin, Hateley, Tambling, Boyle. **Scorers:** Tottenham – Robertson, Saul, Chelsea – Tambling.

1968 W.B.A. – Osborne; Fraser, Williams, Brown, Talbut, Kaye (Clarke), Lovett, Collard, Astle, Hope, Clark. **EVERTON** – West; Wright, Wilson, Kendall, Labone, Harvey, Husband, Ball, Royle, Hurst, Morrissey. **Scorer:** W.B.A. – Astle.

1969 MANCHESTER CITY – Dowd; Book, Pardoe, Doyle, Booth, Oakes, Summerbee, Bell, Lee, Young, Coleman. **LEICESTER CITY** – Shilton; Rodrigues, Nish, Roberts, Woollett, Cross, Fern, Gibson, Lochhead, Clarke, Glover (Manley). **Scorer:** Manchester City – Young.

1970 CHELSEA – Bonetti; Webb, McCreadie, Hollins, Dempsey, Harris (R.) (Hinton), Baldwin, Houseman, Osgood, Hutchinson, Cooke. **LEEDS UTD.** – Sprake; Madeley, Cooper, Bremner, Charlton, Hunter, Lorimer, Clarke, Jones, Giles, Gray. **Scorers:** Chelsea – Houseman, Hutchinson, Leeds Utd. – Charlton, Jones. **Replay: CHELSEA** – Bonetti; Harris (R.), McCreadie, Hollins, Dempsey, Webb, Baldwin, Cooke, Osgood (Hinton), Hutchinson, Houseman. **LEEDS UTD.** – Harvey; Madeley, Cooper, Bremner, Charlton, Hunter, Lorimer, Clarke, Jones, Giles, Gray. **Scorers:** Chelsea – Osgood, Webb, Leeds Utd. – Jones.

1971 ARSENAL – Wilson; Rice, McNab, Storey (Kelly), McLintock, Simpson, Armstrong, Graham, Radford, Kennedy, George. **LIVERPOOL** – Clemence; Lawler, Lindsay, Smith, Lloyd, Hughes, Callaghan, Evans (Thompson), Heighway, Toshack, Hall. **Scorers:** Arsenal – Kelly, George, Liverpool – Heighway.

1972 LEEDS UTD. – Harvey; Reaney, Madeley, Bremner, Charlton, Hunter, Lorimer, Clarke, Jones, Giles, Gray. **ARSENAL** – Barnett; Rice, McNab, Storey, McLintock, Simpson, Armstrong, Ball, Radford (Kennedy), George, Graham. **Scorer:** Leeds Utd. – Clarke.

1973 SUNDERLAND – Montgomery; Malone, Guthrie, Horswill, Watson, Pitt, Kerr, Hughes, Halom, Porterfield, Tueart. **LEEDS UTD.** – Harvey; Reaney, Cherry, Bremner, Madeley, Hunter, Lorimer, Clarke, Jones, Giles, Gray (Yorath). **Scorer:** Sunderland – Porterfield.

1974 LIVERPOOL – Clemence; Smith, Lindsay, Thompson, Cormack, Hughes, Keegan, Hall, Heighway, Toshack, Callaghan. **NEWCASTLE UTD.** – McFaul; Clark, Kennedy, McDermott, Howard, Moncur, Smith (Gibb), Cassidy, Macdonald, Tudor, Hibbitt. **Scorers:** Liverpool – Keegan (2), Heighway.

1975 WEST HAM UTD. – Day; McDowell, Lampard, Bonds, Taylor (T.), Lock, Jennings, Paddon, Taylor (A.), Brooking, Holland. **FULHAM** – Mellor; Cutbush, Fraser, Mullery, Lacy, Moore, Mitchell, Conway, Busby, Slough, Barrett. **Scorer:** West Ham Utd. – Taylor (A.) 2.

1976 SOUTHAMPTON – Turner; Rodrigues, Peach, Holmes, Blyth, Steele, Gilchrist, Channon, Osgood, McCalliog, Stokes. **MANCHESTER UTD.** – Stepney; Forsyth, Houston, Daly, Greenhoff (B.), Buchan, Coppell, McIlroy, Pearson, Macari, Hill (McCreery). **Scorer:** Southampton – Stokes.

1977 MANCHESTER UTD. – Stepney; Nicholl, Albiston, McIlroy, Greenhoff (B.), Buchan, Coppell, Greenhoff (J.), Pearson, Macari, Hill (McCreery). **LIVERPOOL** – Clemence; Neal, Jones, Smith, Kennedy, Hughes, Keegan, Case, Heighway, McDermott, Johnson (Callaghan). **Scorers:** Manchester Utd. – Pearson, Greenhoff (J.), Liverpool – Case.

1978 IPSWICH TOWN – Cooper; Burley, Mills, Talbot, Hunter, Beattie, Osborne (Lambert), Wark, Mariner, Geddis, Woods. **ARSENAL** – Jennings; Rice, Nelson, Price, O'Leary, Young, Brady (Rix), Sunderland, Macdonald, Stapleton, Hudson. **Scorer:** Ipswich Town – Osborne.

1979 ARSENAL – Jennings; Rice, Nelson, Talbot, O'Leary, Young, Brady, Sunderland, Stapleton, Price (Walford), Rix. **MANCHESTER UTD.** – Bailey; Nicholl, Albiston, McIlroy, McQueen, Buchan, Coppell, Greenhoff (J.), Jordan, Macari, Thomas. **Scorers:** Arsenal – Talbot, Stapleton, Sunderland, Manchester Utd. – McQueen, McIlroy.

1980 WEST HAM UTD. – Parkes; Stewart, Lampard, Bonds, Martin, Devonshire, Allen, Pearson, Cross, Brooking, Pike. **ARSENAL** – Jennings; Rice, Devine (Nelson), Talbot, O'Leary, Young, Brady, Sunderland, Stapleton, Price, Rix. **Scorer:** West Ham Utd. – Brooking.

1981 TOTTENHAM – Aleksic; Hughton, Miller, Roberts, Perryman, Villa (Brooke), Ardiles, Archibald, Galvin, Hoddle, Crooks. **MANCHESTER CITY** – Corrigan; Ranson, McDonald, Reid, Power, Caton, Bennett, Gow, Mackenzie, Hutchison (Henry), Reeves. **Scorer:** Tottenham – Hutchison (o.g.), Manchester City – Hutchison. **Replay: TOTTENHAM** – Aleksic; Hughton, Miller, Roberts, Perryman, Villa, Ardiles, Archibald, Galvin, Hoddle,

Crooks. **MANCHESTER CITY** – Corrigan; Ranson, McDonald (Tueart), Reid, Power, Caton, Bennett, Gow, Mackenzie, Hutchison, Reeves. **Scorers:** Tottenham – Villa 2, Crooks, Manchester City – Mackenzie, Reeves (pen.).

1982 TOTTENHAM – Clemence; Hughton, Miller, Price, Hazard (Brooke), Perryman, Roberts, Archibald, Galvin, Hoddle, Crooks. **Q.P.R.** – Hucker; Fenwick, Gillard, Waddock, Hazell, Roeder, Currie, Flanagan, Allen (Micklewhite), Stainrod, Gregory. **Scorers:** Tottenham – Hoddle, Q.P.R. – Fenwick. **Replay: TOTTENHAM** – Clemence; Hughton, Miller, Price, Hazard (Brooke), Perryman, Roberts, Archibald, Galvin, Hoddle, Crooks. **Q.P.R.** – Hucker; Fenwick, Gillard, Waddock, Hazell, Neill, Currie, Flanagan, Micklewhite (Burke), Stainrod, Gregory. **Scorer:** Tottenham – Hoddle (pen.).

1983 MANCHESTER UTD. – Bailey; Duxbury, Albiston, Wilkins, Moran, McQueen, Robson, Muhren, Stapleton, Whiteside, Davies. **BRIGHTON & H.A.** – Moseley; Ramsey (Ryan), Pearce, Grealish, Gatting, Stevens, Case, Howlett, Robinson, Smith, Smillie. **Scorers:** Manchester Utd. – Stapleton, Wilkins, Brighton & H.A. – Smith, Stevens. **Replay: MANCHESTER UTD.** – Bailey; Duxbury, Albiston, Wilkins, Moran, McQueen, Robson, Muhren, Stapleton, Whiteside, Davies. **BRIGHTON & H.A.** – Moseley; Gatting, Pearce, Grealish, Foster, Stevens, Case, Howlett (Ryan), Robinson, Smith, Smillie. **Scorers:** Manchester Utd. – Robson 2, Whiteside, Muhren (pen.).

1984 EVERTON – Southall; Stevens, Bailey, Ratcliffe, Mountfield, Reid, Steven, Heath, Sharp, Gray, Richardson. **WATFORD** – Sherwood; Bardsley, Price (Atkinson), Taylor, Terry, Sinnott, Callaghan, Johnston, Reilly, Jackett, Barnes. **Scorers:** Everton – Sharp, Gray.

1985 MANCHESTER UTD. – Bailey; Gidman, Albiston (Duxbury), Whiteside, McGrath, Moran, Robson, Strachan, Hughes, Stapleton, Olsen. **EVERTON** – Southall; Stevens, Van den Hauwe, Ratcliffe, Mountfield, Reid, Steven, Sharp, Gray, Bracewell, Sheedy. **Scorer:** Manchester Utd. – Whiteside. **Sent-off:** Moran.

1986 LIVERPOOL – Grobbelaar; Lawrenson, Beglin, Nicol, Whelan, Hansen, Dalglish, Johnston, Rush, Molby, MacDonald. **EVERTON** – Mimms; Stevens (Heath), Van den Hauwe, Ratcliffe, Mountfield, Reid, Steven, Lineker, Sharp, Bracewell, Sheedy. **Scorers:** Liverpool – Rush 2, Johnston, Everton – Lineker.

1987 COVENTRY CITY – Ogrizovic; Phillips, Downs, McGrath, Kilcline (Rodger), Peake, Bennett, Gynn, Regis, Houchen, Pickering. **TOTTENHAM** – Clemence; Hughton (Claesen), Thomas (M.), Hodge, Gough, Mabbutt, Allen (C.), Allen (P.), Waddle, Hoddle, Ardiles (Stevens). **Scorers:** Coventry City – Bennett, Houchen, Mabbutt (o.g.), Tottenham – Allen (C.), Mabbutt.

1988 WIMBLEDON – Beasant; Goodyear, Phelan, Jones, Young, Thorn, Gibson (Scales), Cork (Cunningham), Fashanu, Sanchez, Wise. **LIVERPOOL** – Grobbelaar; Gillespie, Ablett, Nicol, Spackman (Molby), Hansen, Beardsley, Aldridge (Johnston), Houghton, Barnes, McMahon. **Scorer:** Wimbledon – Sanchez.

1989 LIVERPOOL – Grobbelaar; Ablett, Staunton (Venison), Nicol, Whelan, Hansen, Beardsley, Aldridge (Rush), Houghton, Barnes, McMahon. **EVERTON** – Southall; McDonald, Van den Hauwe, Ratcliffe, Watson, Bracewell (McCall), Nevin, Steven, Sharp, Cottee, Sheedy (Wilson). **Scorers:** Liverpool – Aldridge, Rush 2, Everton – McCall 2.

1990 MANCHESTER UTD. – Leighton; Ince, Martin (Blackmore), Bruce, Phelan, Pallister (Robins), Robson, Webb, McClair, Hughes, Wallace. **CRYSTAL PALACE** – Martyn; Pemberton, Shaw, Gray (Madden), O'Reilly, Thorn, Barber (Wright), Thomas, Bright, Salako, Pardew. **Scorers:** Manchester Utd. – Robson, Hughes 2, Crystal Palace – O'Reilly, Wright·2. **Replay: MANCHESTER UTD.** – Sealey; Ince, Martin, Bruce, Phelan, Pallister, Robson, Webb, McClair, Hughes, Wallace. **CRYSTAL PALACE** – Martyn; Pemberton, Shaw, Gray, O'Reilly, Thorn, Barber (Wright), Thomas, Bright, Salako (Madden), Pardew. **Scorer:** Manchester Utd. – Martin.

1991 TOTTENHAM – Thorstvedt; Edinburgh, Van den Hauwe, Sedgley, Howells, Mabbutt, Stewart, Gascoigne (Nayim), Samways (Walsh), Lineker, Allen. **NOTT'M FOREST** – Crossley; Charles, Pearce, Walker, Chettle, Keane, Crosby, Parker, Clough, Glover (Laws), Woan (Hodge). **Scorers:** Tottenham – Stewart, Walker (o.g.), Nott'm. Forest – Pearce.

1992 LIVERPOOL – Grobbelaar; Jones (R.), Burrows, Nicol, Molby, Wright, Saunders, Houghton, Rush (I.), McManaman, Thomas. **SUNDERLAND** – Norman; Owers, Ball,

Bennett, Rogan, Rush (D.) (Hardyman), Bracewell, Davenport, Armstrong (Hawke), Byrne, Atkinson. **Scorers:** Liverpool – Thomas, Rush (I.).

1993 ARSENAL – Seaman; Dixon, Winterburn, Linighan, Adams, Parlour (Smith), Davis, Merson, Jensen, Wright (O'Leary), Campbell. **SHEFFIELD WED.** – Woods; Nilsson, Worthington, Palmer, Hirst, Anderson (Hyde), Waddle (Bart-Williams), Warhurst, Bright, Sheridan, Harkes. **Scorers:** Arsenal – Wright, Sheff. Wed. – Hirst. **Replay: ARSENAL** – Seaman; Dixon, Winterburn, Linighan, Adams, Davis, Jensen, Merson, Smith, Wright (O'Leary), Campbell. **SHEFFIELD WED.** – Woods; Nilsson (Bart-Williams), Worthington, Palmer, Hirst, Wilson (Hyde), Waddle, Warhurst, Bright, Sheridan, Harkes. **Scorers:** Arsenal – Wright, Linighan, Sheff. Wed. – Waddle.

1994 MANCHESTER UTD. – Schmeichel; Parker, Bruce, Pallister, Irwin (Sharpe), Kanchelskis (McClair), Keane, Ince, Giggs, Cantona, Hughes. **CHELSEA** – Kharine; Clarke, Johnsen, Kjeldbjerg, Sinclair, Burley (Hoddle), Newton, Wise, Peacock, Stein (Cascarino), Spencer. **Scorers:** Manchester Utd. – Cantona 2 (2 pens.), Hughes, McClair.

1995 EVERTON – Southall; Jackson, Watson, Unsworth, Ablett, Horne, Parkinson, Hinchcliffe, Stuart, Limpar (Amokachi), Rideout (Ferguson). **MANCHESTER UTD.** – Schmeichel; Neville (G.), Bruce (Giggs), Pallister, Irwin, Butt, Keane, Ince, Sharpe (Scholes), McClair, Hughes. **Scorer:** Everton – Rideout.

1996 MANCHESTER UTD. – Schmeichel; Irwin, May, Pallister, Neville (P.), Beckham (Neville, G.), Keane, Butt, Giggs, Cantona, Cole (Scholes). **LIVERPOOL** – James; McAteer, Scales, Wright, Babb, Jones (Thomas), McManaman, Redknapp, Barnes, Collymore (Rush), Fowler. **Scorer:** Manchester Utd. – Cantona.

1997 CHELSEA – Grodas; Sinclair, Leboeuf, Clarke, Minto, Petrescu, Di Matteo, Newton, Wise, Zola (Vialli), Hughes (M.). **MIDDLESBROUGH** – Roberts; Blackmore, Pearson, Festa, Fleming, Stamp, Emerson, Mustoe (Vickers), Hignett (Kinder), Juninho, Ravanelli, (Beck). **Scorers:** Chelsea – Di Matteo, Newton.

1998 ARSENAL – Seaman; Dixon, Adams, Keown, Winterburn, Parlour, Petit, Vieira, Overmars, Wreh (Platt), Anelka. **NEWCASTLE** – Given; Barton (Watson), Dabizas, Howey, Pearce (Andersson), Pistone, Batty, Lee, Speed, Shearer, Ketsbaia (Barnes). **Scorers:** Arsenal – Overmars, Anelka.

1999 MANCHESTER UTD. – Schmeichel; Neville (G.), Johnsen, May, Neville (P.); Beckham, Scholes (Stam), Keane (Sheringham), Giggs; Cole (Yorke), Solskjaer. **NEWCASTLE UTD.** – Harper; Griffin, Charvet, Dabizas, Domi; Lee, Hamann (Ferguson), Speed, Solano (Maric); Ketsbaia (Glass), Shearer. **Scorers:** Manchester Utd. – Sheringham, Scholes.

2000 CHELSEA – De Goey; Melchiot, Desailly, Leboeuf, Babayaro, Di Matteo, Wise, Deschamps, Poyet, Weah (Flo), Zola (Morris). **ASTON VILLA** – James; Ehiogu, Southgate, Barry, Delaney. Taylor (Stone), Boateng, Merson, Wright (Hendrie), Dublin, Carbone (Joachim). **Scorer:** Chelsea – Di Matteo.

2001 LIVERPOOL – Westerveld; Babbel, Henchoz, Hyypia, Carragher, Murphy (Berger), Hamann (McAllister), Gerrard, Smicer (Fowler), Heskey, Owen. **ARSENAL** – Seaman; Dixon (Bergkamp), Keown, Adams, Cole, Ljungberg (Kanu), Grimandi, Vieira, Pires, Henry, Wiltord (Parlour). **Scorers:** Liverpool – Owen 2, Arsenal – Ljungberg.

2002 ARSENAL – Seaman; Lauren, Campbell, Adams, Cole, Wiltord (Keown), Parlour, Vieira, Ljungberg, Bergkamp (Edu), Henry (Kanu). **CHELSEA** – Cudicini; Melchiot, Desailly, Gallas, Babayaro (Terry), Gronkjaer, Lampard, Petit, Le Saux, Hasselbaink (Zola), Gudjohnsen. **Scorers:** Arsenal – Parlour, Ljungberg.

2003 ARSENAL – Seaman; Lauren, Keown, Luzhny, Cole, Ljungberg, Parlour, Gilberto Silva, Pires, Bergkamp (Wiltord), Henry. **SOUTHAMPTON** – Niemi (Jones); Baird (Fernandes), Lundekvam, Svensson (M.), Bridge, Telfer, Oakley, Svensson (A.) (Tessem), Marsden, Beattie, Ormerod. **Scorer:** Arsenal – Pires.

2004 MANCHESTER UTD. – Howard (Carroll), G. Neville, Brown, Silvestre, O'Shea, Fletcher (Butt), Keane, Ronaldo (Solskjaer), Scholes, Giggs, Van Nistelrooy. **MILLWALL:** Marshall, Elliott, Lawrence, Ward, Ryan (Cogan), Wise (Weston), Ifill, Cahill, Livermore, Sweeney, Harris (McCammon). **Scorers:** Manchester Utd. – Van Nistelrooy (2), Ronaldo.

F.A. CUP FINALS – COMPLETE RESULTS

AT KENNINGTON OVAL
1872 The Wanderers beat Royal Engineers (1-0)

AT LILLIE BRIDGE, LONDON
1873 The Wanderers beat Oxford University (2-1)

AT KENNINGTON OVAL
1874 Oxford University beat Royal Engineers (2-0)
1875 Royal Engineers beat Old Etonians (2-0 after a 1-1 draw)
1876 The Wanderers beat Old Etonians (3-0 after a 0-0 draw)
1877†† The Wanderers beat Oxford University (2-1)
1878* The Wanderers beat Royal Engineers (3-1)
1879 Old Etonians beat Clapham Rov. (1-0)
1880 Clapham Rov. beat Oxford University (1-0)
1881 Old Carthusians beat Old Etonians (3-0)
1882 Old Etonians beat Blackburn Rov. (1-0)
1883†† Blackburn Olympic beat Old Etonians (2-1)
1884 Blackburn Rov. beat Queen's Park (Glasgow) (2-1)
1885 Blackburn Rov. beat Queen's Park (Glasgow) (2-0)
1886†a Blackburn Rov. beat W.B.A. (2-0 after a 0-0 draw)
1887 Aston Villa beat W.B.A. (2-0)
1888 W.B.A. beat Preston N.E. (2-1)
1889 Preston N.E. beat Wolves (3-0)
1890 Blackburn Rov. beat Sheffield Wed. (6-1)
1891 Blackburn Rov. beat Notts Co. (3-1)
1892 W.B.A. beat Aston Villa (3-0)

AT FALLOWFIELD, MANCHESTER
1893 Wolves beat Everton (1-0)

AT GOODISON PARK
1894 Notts Co. beat Bolton Wand. (4-1)

AT CRYSTAL PALACE
1895 Aston Villa beat W.B.A. (1-0)
1896 Sheffield Wed. beat Wolves (2-1)
1897 Aston Villa beat Everton (3-2)
1898 Nott'm. Forest beat Derby Co. (3-1)
1899 Sheffield Utd. beat Derby Co. (4-1)
1900 Bury beat Southampton (4-0)
1901††† Tottenham beat Sheffield Utd. (3-1 after a 2-2 draw)
1902 Sheffield Utd. beat Southampton (2-1 after a 1-1 draw)
1903 Bury beat Derby Co. (6-0)
1904 Manchester City beat Bolton Wand. (1-0)
1905 Aston Villa beat Newcastle Utd. (2-0)
1906 Everton beat Newcastle Utd. (1-0)
1907 Sheffield Wed. beat Everton (2-1)
1908 Wolves beat Newcastle Utd. (3-1)
1909 Manchester Utd. beat Bristol City (1-0)
1910** Newcastle Utd. beat Barnsley (2-0 after a 1-1 draw)
1911b Bradford City beat Newcastle Utd. (1-0 after a 0-0 draw)
1912c Barnsley beat W.B.A. (1-0 after a 0-0 draw)
1913 Aston Villa beat Sunderland (1-0)
1914 Burnley beat Liverpool (1-0)

AT OLD TRAFFORD
1915   Sheffield Utd. beat Chelsea (3-0)

AT STAMFORD BRIDGE
1920††   Aston Villa beat Huddersfield Town (1-0)
1921   Tottenham beat Wolves (1-0)
1922   Huddersfield Town beat Preston N.E. (1-0)

AT WEMBLEY
1923   Bolton Wand. beat West Ham Utd. (2-0)
1924   Newcastle Utd. beat Aston Villa (2-0)
1925   Sheffield Utd. beat Cardiff City (1-0)
1926   Bolton Wand. beat Manchester City (1-0)
1927   Cardiff City beat Arsenal (1-0)
1928   Blackburn Rov. beat Huddersfield Town (3-1)
1929   Bolton Wand. beat Portsmouth (2-0)
1930   Arsenal beat Huddersfield Town (2-0)
1931   W.B.A. beat Birmingham City (2-1)
1932   Newcastle Utd. beat Arsenal (2-1)
1933   Everton beat Manchester City (3-0)
1934   Manchester City beat Portsmouth (2-1)
1935   Sheffield Wed. beat W.B.A. (4-2)
1936   Arsenal beat Sheffield Utd. (1-0)
1937   Sunderland beat Preston N.E. (3-1)
1938††   Preston N.E. beat Huddersfield Town (1-0)
1939   Portsmouth beat Wolves (4-1)
1946††   Derby Co. beat Charlton Athletic (4-1)
1947††   Charlton Athletic beat Burnley (1-0)
1948   Manchester Utd. beat Blackpool (4-2)
1949   Wolves beat Leicester City (3-1)
1950   Arsenal beat Liverpool (2-0)
1951   Newcastle Utd. beat Blackpool (2-0)
1952   Newcastle Utd. beat Arsenal (1-0)
1953   Blackpool beat Bolton Wand. (4-3)
1954   W.B.A. beat Preston N.E. (3-2)
1955   Newcastle Utd. beat Manchester City (3-1)
1956   Manchester City beat Birmingham City (3-1)
1957   Aston Villa beat Manchester Utd. (2-1)
1958   Bolton Wand. beat Manchester Utd. (2-0)
1959   Nott'm. Forest beat Luton Town (2-1)
1960   Wolves beat Blackburn Rov. (3-0)
1961   Tottenham beat Leicester City (2-0)
1962   Tottenham beat Burnley (3-1)
1963   Manchester Utd. beat Leicester City (3-1)
1964   West Ham Utd. beat Preston N.E. (3-2)
1965††   Liverpool beat Leeds Utd. (2-1)
1966   Everton beat Sheffield Wed. (3-2)
1967   Tottenham beat Chelsea (2-1)
1968††   W.B.A. beat Everton (1-0)
1969   Manchester City beat Leicester City (1-0)
1970††•   Chelsea beat Leeds Utd. (2-1 after a 2-2 draw)
1971††   Arsenal beat Liverpool (2-1)
1972   Leeds Utd. beat Arsenal (1-0)
1973   Sunderland beat Leeds Utd. (1-0)
1974   Liverpool beat Newcastle Utd. (3-0)
1975   West Ham Utd. beat Fulham (2-0)

1976	Southampton beat Manchester Utd. (1-0)
1977	Manchester Utd. beat Liverpool (2-1)
1978	Ipswich Town beat Arsenal (1-0)
1979	Arsenal beat Manchester Utd. (3-2)
1980	West Ham Utd. beat Arsenal (1-0)
1981	Tottenham beat Manchester City (3-2 after a 1-1 draw)
1982	Tottenham beat Q.P.R. (1-0 after a 1-1 draw)
1983	Manchester Utd. beat Brighton & H.A. (4-0 after a 2-2 draw)
1984	Everton beat Watford (2-0)
1985††	Manchester Utd. beat Everton (1-0)
1986	Liverpool beat Everton (3-1)
1987††—	Coventry City beat Tottenham (3-2)
1988	Wimbledon beat Liverpool (1-0)
1989††	Liverpool beat Everton (3-2)
1990	Manchester Utd. beat Crystal Palace (1-0 after a 3-3 draw)
1991††	Tottenham beat Nott'm. Forest (2-1)
1992	Liverpool beat Sunderland (2-0)
1993††	Arsenal beat Sheffield Wed. (2-1 after a 1-1 draw)
1994	Manchester Utd. beat Chelsea (4-0)
1995	Everton beat Manchester Utd. (1-0)
1996	Manchester Utd. beat Liverpool (1-0)
1997	Chelsea beat Middlesbrough (2-0)
1998	Arsenal beat Newcastle Utd. (2-0)
1999	Manchester Utd. beat Newcastle Utd. (2-0)
2000	Chelsea beat Aston Villa (1-0)

AT MILLENNIUM STADIUM

2001	Liverpool beat Arsenal (2-1)
2002	Arsenal beat Chelsea (2-0)
2003	Arsenal beat Southampton (1-0)
2004	Manchester Utd. beat Millwall (3-0)

†† After extra time. * Won outright but restored to the Association. *a* Replayed at Baseball Ground, Derby Co. † A special trophy was awarded for the third consecutive win. ††† Replayed at Burnden Park, Bolton Wand. ** Replayed at Goodison Park, Liverpool. *b* Replayed at Old Trafford, Manchester, new trophy provided. *c* Replayed at Bramall Lane, Sheffield. • Replayed at Old Trafford.
(All replays since 1981 played at Wembley.)

SUMMARY OF F.A. CUP WINS

Manchester Utd.	11	Chelsea	3	Charlton Athletic	1
Arsenal	9	Sheffield Wed.	3	Clapham Rov.	1
Tottenham	8	West Ham Utd.	3	Coventry City	1
Aston Villa	7	Bury	2	Derby Co.	1
Blackburn Rov.	6	Nott'm Forest	2	Huddersfield Town	1
Liverpool	6	Old Etonians	2	Ipswich Town	1
Newcastle Utd.	6	Preston N.E.	2	Leeds Utd.	1
Everton	5	Sunderland	2	Notts Co.	1
The Wanderers	5	Barnsley	1	Old Carthusians	1
W.B.A.	5	Blackburn Olympic	1	Oxford University	1
Bolton Wand.	4	Blackpool	1	Portsmouth	1
Manchester City	4	Bradford City	1	Royal Engineers	1
Sheffield Utd.	4	Burnley	1	Southampton	1
Wolves	4	Cardiff City	1	Wimbledon	1

APPEARANCES IN FINALS

(Figures do not include replays)

Arsenal	16	Derby Co.	4	Notts Co.	2
Manchester Utd.	16	Leeds Utd.	4	Queen's Park (Glas.)	2
Newcastle Utd.	13	Leicester City	4	Blackburn Olympic*	1
Everton	12	Oxford University	4	Bradford City*	1
Liverpool	12	Royal Engineers	4	Brighton & H.A.	1
Aston Villa	10	Southampton	4	Bristol City	1
W.B.A.	10	Sunderland	4	Coventry City*	1
Tottenham	9	West Ham Utd.	4	Crystal Palace	1
Blackburn Rov.	8	Blackpool	3	Fulham	1
Manchester City	8	Burnley	3	Ipswich Town*	1
Wolves	8	Nott'm Forest	3	Luton Town	1
Bolton Wand.	7	Portsmouth	3	Middlesbrough	1
Chelsea	7	Barnsley	2	Millwall	1
Preston N.E.	7	Birmingham City	2	Old Carthusians*	1
Old Etonians	6	Bury*	2	Q.P.R.	1
Sheffield Utd.	6	Cardiff City	2	Watford	1
Sheffield Wed.	6	Charlton Athletic	2	Wimbledon*	1
Huddersfield Town	5	Clapham Rov.	2	(* Denotes undefeated)
The Wanderers*	5				

APPEARANCES IN SEMI-FINALS

(Figures do not include replays)

Arsenal 24, Everton 23, Manchester Utd. 23, Liverpool 21, Aston Villa 19, W.B.A. 19, Tottenham 17, Blackburn Rov. 16, Newcastle Utd. 16, Sheffield Wed. 16, Chelsea 15, Wolves 14, Bolton Wand. 13, Derby Co. 13, Sheffield Utd. 13, Nott'm Forest 12, Sunderland 12, Southampton 11, Manchester City 10, Preston N.E. 10, Birmingham City 9, Burnley 8, Leeds Utd. 8, Huddersfield Town 7, Leicester City 7, Fulham 6, Old Etonians 6, Oxford University 6, West Ham Utd. 6, Notts Co. 5, Portsmouth 5, The Wanderers 5, Luton Town 4, Millwall 4, Queen's Park (Glasgow) 4, Royal Engineers 4, Watford 4, Blackpool 3, Cardiff City 3, Clapham Rov. 3, *Crystal Palace 3, Ipswich Town 3, Norwich City 3, Old Carthusians 3, Oldham Athletic 3, Stoke City 3, The Swifts 3, Barnsley 2, Blackburn Olympic 2, Bristol City 2, Bury 2, Charlton Athletic 2, Grimsby Town 2, Middlesbrough 2, Swansea City Town 2, Swindon Town 2, Wimbledon 2, Bradford City 1, Brighton & H.A. 1, Cambridge University 1, Chesterfield 1, Coventry City 1, Crewe Alexandra 1, Darwen 1, Derby Co. Junction 1, Hull City 1, Marlow 1, Old Harrovians 1, Orient 1, Plymouth Argyle 1, Port Vale 1, Q.P.R. 1, Rangers (Glasgow) 1, Reading 1, Shropshire Wand. 1, Wycombe Wand. 1, York City 1.
(*A previous and different Crystal Palace club also reached the semi-final in season 1871-72)

MIDDLESBROUGH END 128-YEAR WAIT FOR TROPHY

THIRD ROUND	FOURTH ROUND	FIFTH ROUND	SEMI-FINALS	FINAL
*Bolton Wand. 2				
Gillingham 0	Bolton Wand. 3			
*Blackburn Rov. 3		*Bolton Wand. †1		
Liverpool 4	*Liverpool 2			
*Bristol City 0			*Bolton Wand. 5:0	
Southampton 3	*Southampton 2			
*Nott'm Forest 2		Southampton 0		
Portsmouth †4	Portsmouth 0			Bolton Wand. 1
*Aston Villa 1				
Leicester City 0	*Aston Villa 3			
*Blackpool 1		*Aston Villa 2		
Crystal Palace 3	Crystal Palace 0			
*Reading 1			Aston Villa 2:2	
Huddersfield Town 0	*Reading 0			
*Chelsea 4		Chelsea 1		
Notts Co. 2	Chelsea 1			
*Newcastle Utd. 1				
W.B.A. †2	*W.B.A. 2			
*Leeds Utd. 2		*W.B.A. 0		
Manchester Utd. †3	Manchester Utd. 0			
*Arsenal †A1			*Arsenal 0:1	
Rotherham Utd. 1	*Arsenal 5			
*Wolves 2		Arsenal 2		
Burnley 0	Wolves 1			

*Tottenham .... †1
West Ham Utd. 0

*Q.P.R. 0
Manchester City 3

*Everton 1
Charlton Athletic 0

*Wigan Athletic 1
Middlesbrough 2

*Tottenham 3
Manchester City 1

*Everton 0
Middlesbrough .... †B0

*Tottenham 1
Middlesbrough .... †C1

*Tottenham 1
Middlesbrough 1:2

Middlesbrough 2

*Drawn at home; in semi-finals drawn at home in first leg. † After extra-time. A – Arsenal won 9-8 on pens. B – Middlesbrough won 5-4 on pens. C – Middlesbrough won 5-4 on pens.

FIRST ROUND: Barnsley 1, Blackpool 2; Boston Utd. 1, Reading 3; Bradford City 0, Darlington 0 (aet, Darlington won 5-3 on pens); Bristol City 4, Swansea City 1; Bristol Rov. 0, Brighton & H.A. 1; Cambridge Utd. 1, Gillingham 2; Cardiff City 4, Leyton Orient 1; Cheltenham Town 1, Q.P.R. 2; Chesterfield 0, Burnley 0 (aet, Burnley won 3-2 on pens); Colchester Utd. 2, Plymouth Argyle 1; Coventry City 2, Peterborough Utd. 0; Crewe Alexandra 2, Wrexham 0; Doncaster Rov. 3, Grimsby Town 2; Huddersfield Town 2, Derby Co. 1; Ipswich Town 1, Kidderminster Harr. 0 (aet); Lincoln City 0, Stockport Co. 1; Luton Town 4, Yeovil Town 1; Macclesfield Town 1, Mansfield Town 1, Sunderland 0 (aet); Millwall 0, Oxford Utd. 1; Northampton Town 1, Norwich City 0; Port Vale 0, Nott'm Forest 0; (aet, Nott'm Forest won 3-2 on pens); Preston N.E. 0, Notts Co. 0; (aet, Notts Co. won 7-6 on pens); Rotherham Utd. 2, York City 1; Scunthorpe Utd. 2, Oldham Athletic 1; Sheffield Wed. 2, Hartlepool Utd. 2 (aet, Hartlepool Utd. won 5-4 on pens); Southend Utd. 2, Swindon Town 3; Stoke City 2, Rochdale 1; Torquay Utd. 1, Crystal Palace 1 (aet, Crystal Palace won 3-1 on pens); Tranmere Rov. 1, Bury 0; Walsall 2, Carlisle Utd. 1; Watford 1, Bournemouth 0 (aet); W.B.A. 4, Brentford 0; West Ham Utd. 3, Rushden & Diamonds 1; Wigan Athletic 2, Hull City 0; Wycombe Wand. 2, Wimbledon 0.

SECOND ROUND: Blackpool 1, Birmingham City 0; Bolton Wand. 3, Walsall 1; Bristol City 1, Watford 0; Cardiff City 2, West Ham Utd. 3; Charlton Athletic 4, Luton Town 4 (aet, Charlton Athletic won 8-7 on pens); Coventry City 0, Tottenham 3; Crystal Palace 2, Doncaster Rov. 1; Everton 3, Stockport Co. 0; Hartlepool Utd. 1, W.B.A. 2; Leeds Utd. 2, Swindon Town 2; (aet, Leeds Utd. won 4-3 on pens); Leicester City 1, Crewe Alexandra 0; Middlesbrough 1, Brighton & H.A. 0; Notts Co. 2, Portsmouth 5; Northampton Town 2, Rotherham Utd. 1, Colchester Utd. 0; Scunthorpe Utd. 2, Burnley 3; Ipswich Town 1, Oxford Utd. 1, Reading 3; Sheffield Utd. 0, Q.P.R. 2; Stoke City 0, Gillingham 2; Sunderland 2, Huddersfield Town 4; Tranmere Rov. 0, Nott'm Forest 0 (aet, Nott'm Forest won 4-1 on pens); Wigan Athletic 1, Fulham 0; Wolves 2, Darlington 0; Wycombe Wand. 0, Aston Villa 5.

CARLING CUP FINAL

BOLTON WANDERERS 1, MIDDLESBROUGH 2

Millennium Stadium, (72,634), Sunday, February 29, 2004

Bolton Wand. (4-1-4-1): Jaaskelainen, Hunt (Giannakopoulos 87), Thome, N'Gotty, Charlton, Campo, Nolan (Moreno 78), Frandsen (Pedersen 64), Okocha (capt), Djorkaeff, Davies. **Subs not used:** Poole, Barness. **Scorer:** Davies (21). **Booked:** Frandsen, Campo. **Manager:** Sam Allardyce.

Middlesbrough (4-4-1-1): Schwarzer, Mills, Ehiogu, Southgate (capt), Queudrue, Mendieta, Boateng, Doriva, Zenden, Juninho, Job (Ricketts 66). **Subs not used:** Jones, Riggott, Maccarone, Downing. **Scorers:** Job (2), Zenden (7 pen). **Booked:** Boateng, Ricketts. **Manager:** Steve McClaren.

Referee: M. Riley (West Yorks). **Half-time:** 1-2. **Man-of-the-match:** Gaizka Mendieta.

Middlesbrough's 128-year wait for a major trophy ended with two goals in the first seven minutes of a match which showed that the best finals are not always the prerogative of the most glamorous teams. Success in a thoroughly entertaining and absorbing affair was accompanied by controversy, Sam Allardyce complaining with some justification that two crucial penalty box decisions went against his side. At the same time, the Bolton manager admitted they never really recovered from such a poor start.

Steve McClaren thus became the first English manager to land a trophy since Brian Little led Aston Villa to the Coca Cola Cup in 1996. For McClaren's chairman, Steve Gibson, it was the reward for the millions he ploughed into the club after seeing it almost go out of existence ten years earlier. Gibson has never been one for the spotlight, but here he was so overcome by the occasion that his exuberance at the final whistle matched that of his players.

McClaren was still on his way from the dressing room when the influential Spaniard Gaizka Mendieta, twice a Champions League finalist with Valencia, released Holland's Boudewijn Zenden, whose cross was turned in by the Cameroon striker Joseph-Desire Job with two minutes on the clock. Five minutes later, as Bolton continued to struggle to establish a foothold in the game, Job was brought down in the penalty area by Emerson Thome. Approaching the penalty, Zenden nudged the ball with his right boot before converting the spot kick with his left. But the offence went unnoticed by referee Mike Riley.

A mistake by Mark Schwarzer, who allowed a shot by Kevin Davies to slip through his grasp at the near post, put Bolton back in the game on 21 minutes. Later, the goalkeeper went some way to redeeming the error with quality saves from Youri Djorkaeff, Jay-Jay Okocha and Kevin Nolan. Then, with a minute remaining, Riley was again the centre of attention, ruling that a shot driven by substitutute Stelios Giannakopoulos against the left hand of Ugo Ehiogu was not a penalty.

HOW THEY REACHED THE FINAL

BOLTON WANDERERS

Round 2: 3-1 home to Walsall (Jardel 2, Nolan)
Round 3: 2-0 home to Gillingham (Giannakopoulos, Pedersen)
Round 4: 3-2 away to Liverpool (Djorkaeff pen, Jardel, Okocha)
Round 5: 1-0 home to Southampton (Pedersen)
Semi-finals: v Aston Villa – first leg, 5-2 home (Okocha 2, Giannakopoulos, N'Gotty, Nolan); second leg, 0-2 away – won 5-4 on agg.

MIDDLESBROUGH

Round 2: 1-0 home to Brighton (Christie)
Round 3: 2-1 away to Wigan (Maccarone, Mendieta)
Round 4: 0-0 home to Everton – won 5-4 on pens
Round 5: 1-1 away to Tottenham (Ricketts) – won 5-4 on pens
Semi-finals: v Arsenal – first leg 1-0 away (Juninho); second leg 2-1 home (Zenden, Reyes og) – won 3-1 on agg.

LEADING SCORERS

7 – Angel (Aston Villa)
5 – Earnshaw (Cardiff)
4 – Aliadiere (Arsenal), Defoe (West Ham), Forster (Reading), Johnson (Crystal Palace)
3 – Beattie (Southampton), Hulse (W.B.A.), Jardel (Bolton), Kyle (Sunderland), Okocha (Bolton), Parkin (Swindon), Roberts (Portsmouth), Taylor (Blackpool).

QUOTE – UNQUOTE

'They are lions. We wish for the same success in the European Championship' – **Sven-Goran Eriksson**, England coach, on England's rugby World Cup triumph.

'I've got my wife on my arm, my son in the dug-out and my grandson on my knee. What more could I ask for on a Sunday afternoon?' – **Brian Clough** watching Nigel's team Burton Albion play Hartlepool in the F.A. Cup.

'His nose is pointing in a different direction to what it was at three o'clock' – **Graeme Souness**, Blackburn manager, after his defender Craig Short was elbowed by Birmingham's Christophe Dugarry.

'Everyone knows that boy's not right in the head' – **Terence Brown**, West Ham chairman, on striker Jermain Defoe.

'The difference between the top three and the rest is huge. Chelsea, Arsenal and Manchester United basically inhabit another league' – **James Beattie**, Southampton striker.

'They say goalkeepers are mad and he was' – **Micky Adams**, Leicester manager, after Ian Walker was sent off for handling outside his area.

'It takes ten years to build a great club and five minutes of nonsense to destroy it' – **Arsene Wenger**, Arsenal manager, dismissing Chelsea's interest in Thierry Henry.

'What I really need is a goalkeeper, right back, maybe a centre-half, a left-back, a couple of midfield players and a couple of forwards' – **Tony Adams**, manager of struggling Wycombe.

'When I don't put Damien in the squad my mother, who is 84, says 'Why Claudio, why?'' – **Claudio Ranieri**, Chelsea manager, under pressure from his mum to pick Damien Duff for every match.

'The management and players of this football club are given Rolls Royce treatment, but we are not getting Rolls Royce performances from them in return' – **Freddie Shepherd**, Newcastle chairman.

'His strike rate is phenomenal, but I keep telling him that he hasn't beaten my record yet. I scored 45 goals in 51 games for Dunfermline one season' – **Sir Alex Ferguson** reminds Manchester United marksman Ruud van Nistelrooy that he too once packed a punch in front of goal.

LEAGUE CUP – COMPLETE RESULTS

LEAGUE CUP FINALS
1961*	Aston Villa beat Rotherham Utd. 3-2 on agg. (0-2a, 3-0h)
1962	Norwich City beat Rochdale 4-0 on agg. (3-0a, 1-0h)
1963	Birmingham City beat Aston Villa 3-1 on agg. (3-1h, 0-0a)
1964	Leicester City beat Stoke City 4-3 on agg. (1-1a, 3-2h)
1965	Chelsea beat Leicester City 3-2 on agg. (3-2h, 0-0a)
1966	W.B.A. beat West Ham Utd. 5-3 on agg. (1-2a, 4-1h)

AT WEMBLEY
1967	Q.P.R. beat W.B.A. (3-2)
1968	Leeds Utd. beat Arsenal (1-0)
1969*	Swindon Town beat Arsenal (3-1)
1970*	Manchester City beat W.B.A. (2-1)
1971	Tottenham beat Aston Villa (2-0)
1972	Stoke City beat Chelsea (2-1)
1973	Tottenham beat Norwich City (1-0)
1974	Wolves beat Manchester City (2-1)
1975	Aston Villa beat Norwich City (1-0)
1976	Manchester City beat Newcastle Utd. (2-1)
1977†*	Aston Villa beat Everton (3-2 after 0-0 and 1-1 draws)
1978††	Nott'm. Forest beat Liverpool (1-0 after 0-0 draw)
1979	Nott'm. Forest beat Southampton (3-2)
1980	Wolves beat Nott'm. Forest (1-0)
1981†††	Liverpool beat West Ham Utd. (2-1 after 1-1 draw)

MILK CUP
1982*	Liverpool beat Tottenham (3-1)
1983*	Liverpool beat Manchester Utd. (2-1)
1984**	Liverpool beat Everton (1-0 after *0-0 draw)
1985	Norwich City beat Sunderland (1-0)
1986	Oxford Utd. beat Q.P.R. (3-0)

LITTLEWOODS CUP
1987	Arsenal beat Liverpool (2-1)
1988	Luton Town beat Arsenal (3-2)
1989	Nott'm. Forest beat Luton Town (3-1)
1990	Nott'm. Forest beat Oldham Athletic (1-0)

RUMBELOWS CUP
1991	Sheffield Wed. beat Manchester Utd. (1-0)
1992	Manchester Utd. beat Nott'm. Forest (1-0)

COCA-COLA CUP
1993	Arsenal beat Sheffield Wed. (2-1)
1994	Aston Villa beat Manchester Utd. (3-1)
1995	Liverpool beat Bolton Wand. (2-1)
1996	Aston Villa beat Leeds Utd. (3-0)
1997	Leicester City beat Middlesbrough (*1-0 after *1-1 draw) ★
1998	Chelsea beat Middlesbrough (2-0)

WORTHINGTON CUP (AT MILLENNIUM STADIUM FROM 2001)

1999	Tottenham beat Leicester City (1-0)
2000	Leicester City beat Tranmere Rov. (2-1)
2001	Liverpool beat Birmingham City (5-4 on pens after *1-1 draw)
2002	Blackburn Rov. beat Tottenham (2-1)
2003	Liverpool beat Manchester Utd. (2-0)

CARLING CUP

2004	Middlesbrough beat Bolton Wand. (2-1)

* After extra time. † First replay at Hillsborough, second replay at Old Trafford. †† Replayed at Old Trafford. ††† Replayed at Aston Villa Park. ** Replayed at Maine Road. ★ Replayed at Hillsborough

SUMMARY OF LEAGUE CUP WINNERS

Liverpool	7	Norwich City	2	Middlesbrough	1
Aston Villa	5	Wolves	2	Oxford Utd.	1
Nott'm Forest	4	Blackburn Rov.	1	Q.P.R.	1
Leicester City	3	Birmingham City	1	Sheffield Wed.	1
Tottenham	3	Leeds Utd.	1	Stoke City	1
Arsenal	2	Luton Town	1	Swindon Town	1
Chelsea	2	Manchester Utd.	1	W.B.A.	1
Manchester City	2				

LEAGUE CUP FINAL APPEARANCES

9 Liverpool; **7** Aston Villa; **6** Nott'm. Forest; **5** Arsenal, Leicester City, Tottenham Manchester Utd.; **4** Norwich City; **3** Chelsea, Manchester City, Middlesbrough, W.B.A.; **2** Birmingham City, Bolton Wand., Everton, Leeds Utd., Luton Town, Q.P.R., Sheffield Wed., Stoke City, West Ham Utd., Wolves; **1** Blackburn Rov., Newcastle Utd., Oldham Athletic, Oxford Utd., Rochdale, Rotherham Utd., Southampton, Sunderland, Swindon Town, Tranmere Rov. **(Figures do not include replays).**

LEAGUE CUP SEMI-FINAL APPEARANCES

12 Aston Villa, Liverpool; **10** Arsenal, Tottenham; **8** Manchester Utd.; **7** Chelsea, West Ham Utd.; **6** Nott'm Forest; **5** Leeds Utd., Leicester City, Manchester City, Middlesbrough, Norwich City; **4** Birmingham City, Blackburn Rov., Bolton Wand., Sheffield Wed., W.B.A.; **3** Burnley, Crystal Palace, Everton, Ipswich Town, Q.P.R., Sunderland, Swindon Town, Wolves; **2** Bristol City, Coventry City, Luton Town, Oxford Utd., Plymouth Argyle, Southampton, Stoke City, Tranmere Rov., Wimbledon; **1** Blackpool, Bury, Cardiff City, Carlisle Utd., Chester City, Derby Co., Huddersfield Town, Newcastle Utd., Oldham Athletic, Peterborough, Rochdale, Rotherham Utd., Sheffield Utd., Shrewsbury Town, Stockport Co., Walsall, Watford. **(Figures do not include replays).**

VICTORY FOR EIGHT-MAN SOUTHEND

Despite having three players sent off, Southend finished 3-2 winners at Swansea. David McSweeney saw red in the first half, followed by Jay Smith and Mark Gower in the last five minutes of normal time, along with coach Paul Brush for protesting. Mark Warren made it 3-1 in stoppage time and Southend held out despite James Thomas pulling one back.

SCOTTISH FINAL TABLES 2003-04

BANK OF SCOTLAND PREMIER LEAGUE

		P	HOME W	D	L	F	A	AWAY W	D	L	F	A	Pts	GD
1	Celtic	38	15	2	2	62	15	16	3	0	43	10	98	+80
2	Rangers	38	16	0	3	48	11	9	6	4	28	22	81	+43
3	Hearts	38	12	5	2	32	17	7	6	6	24	23	68	+16
4	Dunfermline Athletic	38	9	7	3	28	19	4	10	17	33	53		−7
5	Dundee Utd.	38	8	6	5	28	27	5	4	10	19	33	49	−13
6	Motherwell	38	7	5	5	25	22	5	3	11	27	27	46	−7
7	Dundee	38	8	3	8	21	20	4	7	8	27	37	46	−9
8	Hibernian	38	6	5	8	25	28	5	6	8	16	32	44	−19
9	Livingston	38	6	9	4	24	18	4	11	24	39	43		−9
10	Kilmarnock	38	8	3	8	29	31	4	3	12	22	43	42	−23
11	Aberdeen	38	5	3	11	22	29	4	4	11	17	34	34	−24
12	Partick Thistle	38	6	4	10	24	32	1	4	14	15	35	26	−28

(After 33 matches League split into top six and bottom six teams, each playing five further games. No relegation.)

Leading scorers (all club competitions): 41 Larsson (Celtic); 28 Sutton (Celtic); 25 Novo (Dundee); 18 Grady (Partick Thistle), Lilley (Liingston), Riordan (Hibernian); 17 Crawford (Dunfermline Athletic); 16 De Vries (Heats); 15 Arveladze (Rangers), Boyd (Kilmarnock); 14 Clarkson (Motherwell); 13 Lovenkrands (Rangers), McMenamin (Livingston)) − 5 for Falkirk, Thompson (Celtic). **Player of Year:** Chris Sutton. **Manager of Year:** Martin O'Neil (Celtic).

BELL'S FIRST DIVISION

		P	HOME W	D	L	F	A	AWAY W	D	L	F	A	PtS	GD
1	Inverness CT	36	13	4	1	37	12	8	3	7	30	21	70	+34
2	Clyde	36	11	4	3	34	17	9	5	4	30	23	69	+24
3	St Johnstone	36	8	5	5	34	27	7	7	4	25	18	57	+14
4	Falkirk	36	8	4	6	20	16	7	6	5	23	21	55	+6
5	Queen of South	36	9	6	3	24	16	6	3	9	22	32	54	−2
6	Ross Co.	36	8	6	4	24	17	4	7	7	25	24	49	+8
7	St Mirren	36	6	9	3	27	23	5	5	10	12	23	41	−7
8	Raith Rov.	36	5	5	8	18	28	3	5	10	19	29	34	−20
9	Ayr Utd.	36	4	7	7	21	29	2	6	10	16	29	31	−21
10	Brechin City	36	5	3	10	21	33	1	6	11	16	40	27	−36

Leading scorers (all club competitions): 23 Ritchie (Inverness CT); 17 Bingham (Inverness CT); 16 Burke (Queen of the South), Sutton (Raith Rov.); 15 Harty (Clyde), O'Connor (Queen of the South); 14 Hislop (Inverness CT), Paatelainen (St Johnstone), Wilson (Inverness CT); 13 Keogh (Clyde), Winters (Ross Co.); 12 Smith (Clyde). **Player of Year:** Paul Ritchie. **Manager of Year:** John Robertson (Inverness CT).

BELL'S SECOND DIVISION

			HOME					AWAY						
		P	W	D	L	F	A	W	D	L	F	A	Pts	GD
1	Airdrie Utd.	36	10	6	2	36	19	10	4	4	28	17	70	+28
2	Hamilton Acad.	36	9	3	6	32	21	9	5	4	38	26	62	+23
3	Dumbarton	36	12	3	3	31	13	6	3	9	25	28	60	+15
4	Morton	36	8	8	2	37	30	8	3	7	29	28	59	+8
5	Berwick Rangers	36	8	2	8	31	31	6	4	8	30	36	48	−6
6	Forfar Athletic	36	7	4	7	25	30	5	7	6	24	27	47	−8
7	Alloa Athletic	36	6	6	6	33	26	6	2	10	22	29	44	0
8	Arbroath	36	5	6	7	17	27	4	8	24	30	43	−16
9	East Fife	36	7	2	9	24	24	4	6	8	14	21	41	−7
10	Stenhousemuir	36	4	1	13	12	29	3	3	12	16	36	25	−37

Leading scorers (all club competitions): 25 Hutchison (Berwick Rangers), Tosh (Forfar Athletic); 23 McPhee (Hamilton Acad.); 20 Weatherson (Morton); 17 McGlashan (Arbroath), Williams (Morton); 16 Carrigan (Hamilton Acad.); 15 Coyle (Airdrie Utd.); 14 Hamilton (Alloa Athletic), McCutcheon (Berwick Rangers); 13 Shields (Forfar Athletic). **Player of Year:** Paul Tosh. **Manager of Year:** Sandy Stewart (Airdrie Utd.)

BELL'S THIRD DIVISION

			HOME					AWAY						
		P	W	D	L	F	A	W	D	L	F	A	Pts	GD
1	Stranraer	36	13	2	3	51	14	11	5	2	36	16	79	+57
2	Stirling Albion	36	10	5	3	37	12	13	3	2	41	15	77	51
3	Gretna	36	9	5	4	29	18	11	3	4	30	21	68	+20
4	Peterhead	36	10	5	3	38	13	8	2	8	29	24	61	+30
5	Cowdenbeath	36	7	3	8	25	27	8	7	3	21	12	55	+7
6	Montrose	36	7	4	7	31	34	5	8	5	21	29	48	−11
7	Queen's Park	36	5	5	8	20	24	5	6	7	21	29	41	−12
8	Albion Rov.	36	6	2	10	36	35	6	2	10	30	40	40	−9
9	Elgin City	36	4	5	9	23	34	2	2	14	25	59	25	−45
10	East Stirling	36	2	2	14	12	51	0	0	18	8	67	8	−88

Leading scorers (all club competitions): 27 Moore (Stranraer); 22 McLean (Stirling Albion); 20 McManus (Albion Rov.); 19 Graham (Stranraer); 18 Bavidge (Peterhead), Johnston (Peterhead); 17 Cameron (Gretna); 16 Michie (Montrose); 15 Bone (Elgin City), Shields (Cowdenbeath); 13 Stevens (Gretna). **Player of Year:** Michael Moore. **Manager of Year:** Neil Watt (Stranraer).

ANOTHER DEBUT GOAL FOR DEFOE

Jermain Defoe continued his run of scoring debuts with a goal for Tottenham in the 4-3 win over Portsmouth. The £7m. signing had previously netted in his first matches for West Ham, Bournemouth on loan and the England U21 side.

SAME AGAIN FOR HENRY

Thierry Henry scored his first Premiership goal for Arsenal against Southampton in September 1999 – and claimed his 100th against the same side in last season's 2-0 win at Highbury.

SCOTTISH HONOURS LIST

PREMIER DIVISION

	First	Pts.	Second	Pts.	Third	Pts.
1975-6	Rangers	54	Celtic	48	Hibernian	43
1976-7	Celtic	55	Rangers	46	Aberdeen	43
1977-8	Rangers	55	Aberdeen	53	Dundee Utd.	40
1978-9	Celtic	48	Rangers	45	Dundee Utd.	44
1979-80	Aberdeen	48	Celtic	47	St Mirren	42
1980-81	Celtic	56	Aberdeen	49	Rangers	44
1981-2	Celtic	55	Aberdeen	53	Rangers	43
1982-3	Dundee Utd.	56	Celtic	55	Aberdeen	55
1983-4	Aberdeen	57	Celtic	50	Dundee Utd.	47
1984-5	Aberdeen	59	Celtic	52	Dundee Utd.	47
1985-6	*Celtic	50	Hearts	50	Dundee Utd.	47
1986-7	Rangers	69	Celtic	63	Dundee Utd.	60
1987-8	Celtic	72	Hearts	62	Rangers	60
1988-9	Rangers	56	Aberdeen	50	Celtic	46
1989-90	Rangers	51	Aberdeen	44	Hearts	44
1990-1	Rangers	55	Aberdeen	53	Celtic	41
1991-2	Rangers	72	Hearts	63	Celtic	62
1992-3	Rangers	73	Aberdeen	64	Celtic	60
1993-4	Rangers	58	Aberdeen	55	Motherwell	54
1994-5	Rangers	69	Motherwell	54	Hibernian	53
1995-6	Rangers	87	Celtic	83	Aberdeen	55
1996-7	Rangers	80	Celtic	75	Dundee Utd.	60
1997-8	Celtic	74	Rangers	72	Hearts	67

PREMIER LEAGUE

	First	Pts.	Second	Pts.	Third	Pts.
1998-99	Rangers	77	Celtic	71	St Johnstone	57
1999-2000	Rangers	90	Celtic	69	Hearts	54
2000-01	Celtic	97	Rangers	82	Hibernian	66
2001-02	Celtic	103	Rangers	85	Livingston	58
2002-03	*Rangers	97	Celtic	97	Hearts	63
2003-04	Rangers	98	Rangers	81	Hearts	68

Maximum points: 72 except 1986-8 (88), 1991-4 (88), 1994-2000 (108), 2001-04 (114).
* Won on goal difference.

FIRST DIVISION (Scottish Championship until 1975-76)

	First	Pts.	Second	Pts.	Third	Pts.
1890-1a	††Dumbarton	29	Rangers	29	Celtic	24
1891-2b	Dumbarton	37	Celtic	35	Hearts	30
1892-3a	Celtic	29	Rangers	28	St Mirren	23
1893-4a	Celtic	29	Hearts	26	St Bernard's	22
1894-5a	Hearts	31	Celtic	26	Rangers	21
1895-6a	Celtic	30	Rangers	26	Hibernian	24
1896-7a	Hearts	28	Hibernian	26	Rangers	25
1897-8a	Celtic	33	Rangers	29	Hibernian	22
1898-9a	Rangers	36	Hearts	26	Celtic	24
1899-1900a	Rangers	32	Celtic	25	Hibernian	24
1900-1c	Rangers	35	Celtic	29	Hibernian	25
1901-2a	Rangers	28	Celtic	26	Hearts	22
1902-3b	Hibernian	37	Dundee	31	Rangers	29

1903-4d	Third Lanark	43	Hearts	39	Rangers	38
1904-5a	†Celtic	41	Rangers	41	Third Lanark	35
1905-6a	Celtic	46	Hearts	39	Rangers	38
1906-7f	Celtic	55	Dundee	48	Rangers	45
1907-8f	Celtic	55	Falkirk	51	Rangers	50
1908-9f	Celtic	51	Dundee	50	Clyde	48
1909-10f	Celtic	54	Falkirk	52	Rangers	49
1910-11f	Rangers	52	Aberdeen	48	Falkirk	44
1911-12f	Rangers	51	Celtic	45	Clyde	42
1912-13f	Rangers	53	Celtic	49	Hearts	41
1913-14g	Celtic	65	Rangers	59	Hearts	54
1914-15g	Celtic	65	Hearts	61	Rangers	50
1915-16g	Celtic	67	Rangers	56	Morton	51
1916-17g	Celtic	64	Morton	54	Rangers	53
1917-18f	Rangers	56	Celtic	55	Kilmarnock	43
1918-19f	Celtic	58	Rangers	57	Morton	47
1919-20h	Rangers	71	Celtic	68	Motherwell	57
1920-1h	Rangers	76	Celtic	66	Hearts	56
1921-2h	Celtic	67	Rangers	66	Raith	56
1922-3g	Rangers	55	Airdrieonians	50	Celtic	40
1923-4g	Rangers	59	Airdrieonians	50	Celtic	41
1924-5g	Rangers	60	Airdrieonians	57	Hibernian	52
1925-6g	Celtic	58	Airdrieonians	50	Hearts	50
1926-7g	Rangers	56	Motherwell	51	Celtic	49
1927-8g	Rangers	60	Celtic	55	Motherwell	55
1928-9g	Rangers	67	Celtic	51	Motherwell	50
1929-30g	Rangers	60	Motherwell	55	Aberdeen	53
1930-1g	Rangers	60	Celtic	58	Motherwell	56
1931-2g	Motherwell	66	Rangers	61	Celtic	48
1932-3g	Rangers	62	Motherwell	59	Hearts	50
1933-4g	Rangers	66	Motherwell	62	Celtic	47
1934-5g	Rangers	55	Celtic	52	Hearts	50
1935-6g	Celtic	68	Rangers	61	Aberdeen	61
1936-7g	Rangers	61	Aberdeen	54	Celtic	52
1937-8g	Celtic	61	Hearts	58	Rangers	49
1938-9f	Rangers	59	Celtic	48	Aberdeen	46
1946-7f	Rangers	46	Hibernian	44	Aberdeen	39
1947-8g	Hibernian	48	Rangers	46	Partick	46
1948-9i	Rangers	46	Dundee	45	Hibernian	39
1949-50i	Rangers	50	Hibernian	49	Hearts	43
1950-1i	Hibernian	48	Rangers	38	Dundee	38
1951-2i	Hibernian	45	Rangers	41	East Fife	37
1952-3i	*Rangers	43	Hibernian	43	East Fife	39
1953-4i	Celtic	43	Hearts	38	Partick	35
1954-5f	Aberdeen	49	Celtic	46	Rangers	41
1955-6f	Rangers	52	Aberdeen	46	Hearts	45
1956-7f	Rangers	55	Hearts	53	Kilmarnock	42
1957-8f	Hearts	62	Rangers	49	Celtic	46
1958-9f	Rangers	50	Hearts	48	Motherwell	44
1959-60f	Hearts	54	Kilmarnock	50	Rangers	42
1960-1f	Rangers	51	Kilmarnock	50	Third Lanark	42
1961-2f	Dundee	54	Rangers	51	Celtic	46
1962-3f	Rangers	57	Kilmarnock	48	Partick	46
1963-4f	Rangers	55	Kilmarnock	49	Celtic	47
1964-5f	*Kilmarnock	50	Hearts	50	Dunfermline	49
1965-6f	Celtic	57	Rangers	55	Kilmarnock	45
1966-7f	Celtic	58	Rangers	55	Clyde	46
1967-8f	Celtic	63	Rangers	61	Hibernian	45

1968-9f	Celtic	54	Rangers	49	Dunfermline 45
1969-70f	Celtic	57	Rangers	45	Hibernian 44
1970-1f	Celtic	56	Aberdeen	54	St Johnstone 44
1971-2f	Celtic	60	Aberdeen	50	Rangers 44
1972-3f	Celtic	57	Rangers	56	Hibernian 45
1973-4f	Celtic	53	Hibernian	49	Rangers 48
1974-5f	Rangers	56	Hibernian	49	Celtic 45

* Won on goal average. †Won on deciding match. ††Title shared.
Competition suspended 1940-46 (Second World War).

SCOTTISH CHAMPIONSHIP WINS

Rangers	*50	Hibernian	4	Kilmarnock	1
Celtic	39	Dumbarton	*2	Motherwell	1
Aberdeen	4	Dundee	1	Third Lanark	1
Hearts	4	Dundee Utd.	1	(* Incl. 1 shared)

FIRST DIVISION

(Since formation of Premier Division)

	First	Pts.	Second	Pts.	Third	Pts.
1975-6d	Partick	41	Kilmarnock	35	Montrose	30
1976-7j	St Mirren	62	Clydebank	58	Dundee	51
1977-8j	*Morton	58	Hearts	58	Dundee	57
1978-9j	Dundee	55	Kilmarnock	54	Clydebank	54
1979-80j	Hearts	53	Airdrieonians	51	Ayr	44
1980-1j	Hibernian	57	Dundee	52	St Johnstone	51
1981-2j	Motherwell	61	Kilmarnock	51	Hearts	50
1982-3j	St Johnstone	55	Hearts	54	Clydebank	50
1983-4j	Morton	54	Dumbarton	51	Partick	46
1984-5j	Motherwell	50	Clydebank	48	Falkirk	45
1985-6j	Hamilton	56	Falkirk	45	Kilmarnock	44
1986-7k	Morton	57	Dunfermline	56	Dumbarton	53
1987-8k	Hamilton	56	Meadowbank	52	Clydebank	49
1988-9j	Dunfermline	54	Falkirk	52	Clydebank	48
1989-90j	St Johnstone	58	Airdrieonians	54	Clydebank	44
1990-1j	Falkirk	54	Airdrieonians	53	Dundee	52
1991-2k	Dundee	58	Partick	57	Hamilton	57
1992-3k	Raith	65	Kilmarnock	54	Dunfermline	52
1993-4k	Falkirk	66	Dunfermline	65	Airdrieonians	54
1994-5l	Raith	69	Dunfermline	68	Dundee	68
1995-6l	Dunfermline	71	Dundee Utd.	67	Greenock Morton	67
1996-7l	St Johnstone	80	Airdrieonians	60	Dundee	58
1997-8l	Dundee	70	Falkirk	65	Raith	60
1998-9l	Hibernian	89	Falkirk	66	Ayr	62
1999-2000l	St Mirren	76	Dunfermline	71	Falkirk	68
2000-01l	Livingston	76	Ayr Utd.	69	Falkirk	68
2001-02l	Partick Thistle	66	Airdie	56	Ayr Utd.	52
2002-03l	Falkirk	81	Clyde	72	St Johnstone	67
2003-04l	Inverness CT	70	Clyde	69	St Johnstone	57

Maximum points: a, 36; b, 44; c, 40; d, 52; e, 60; f, 68; g, 76; h, 84; i, 60; j, 78; k, 88; l, 108. * Won on goal difference.

SECOND DIVISION

	First	Pts.	Second	Pts.	Third	Pts.
1921-2a	Alloa	60	Cowdenbeath	47	Armadale	45

1922-3a	Queen's Park	57	Clydebank	52	St Johnstone	50
1923-4a	St Johnstone	56	Cowdenbeath	55	Bathgate	44
1924-5a	Dundee Utd.	50	Clydebank	48	Clyde	47
1925-6a	Dunfermline	59	Clyde	53	Ayr	52
1926-7a	Bo'ness	56	Raith	49	Clydebank	45
1927-8a	Ayr	54	Third Lanark	45	King's Park	44
1928-9b	Dundee Utd.	51	Morton	50	Arbroath	47
1929-30a	*Leith Athletic	57	East Fife	57	Albion	54
1930-1a	Third Lanark	61	Dundee Utd.	50	Dunfermline	47
1931-2a	*East Stirling	55	St Johnstone	55	Stenhousemuir	46
1932-3c	Hibernian	55	Queen of South	49	Dunfermline	47
1933-4c	Albion	45	Dunfermline	44	Arbroath	44
1934-5c	Third Lanark	52	Arbroath	50	St Bernard's	47
1935-6c	Falkirk	59	St Mirren	52	Morton	48
1936-7c	Ayr	54	Morton	51	St Bernard's	48
1937-8c	Raith	59	Albion	48	Airdrieonians	47
1938-9c	Cowdenbeath	60	Alloa	48	East Fife	48
1946-7d	Dundee Utd.	45	Airdrieonians	42	East Fife	31
1947-8e	East Fife	53	Albion	42	Hamilton	40
1948-9e	*Raith	42	Stirling	42	Airdrieonians	41
1949-50e	Morton	47	Airdrieonians	44	St Johnstone	36
1950-1e	*Queen of South	45	Stirling	45	Ayr	36
1951-2e	Clyde	44	Falkirk	43	Ayr	39
1952-3e	Stirling	44	Hamilton	43	Queen's Park	37
1953-4e	Motherwell	45	Kilmarnock	42	Third Lanark	36
1954-5e	Airdrieonians	46	Dunfermline	42	Hamilton	39
1955-6b	Queen's Park	54	Ayr	51	St Johnstone	49
1956-7b	Clyde	64	Third Lanark	51	Cowdenbeath	45
1957-8b	Stirling	55	Dunfermline	53	Arbroath	47
1958-9b	Ayr	60	Arbroath	51	Stenhousemuir	46
1959-60b	St Johnstone	53	Dundee Utd.	50	Queen of South	49
1960-1b	Stirling	55	Falkirk	54	Stenhousemuir	50
1961-2b	Clyde	54	Queen of South	53	Morton	44
1962-3b	St Johnstone	55	East Stirling	49	Morton	48
1963-4b	Morton	67	Clyde	53	Arbroath	46
1964-5b	Stirling	59	Hamilton	50	Queen of South	45
1965-6b	Ayr	53	Airdrieonians	50	Queen of South	47
1966-7b	Morton	69	Raith	58	Arbroath	57
1967-8b	St Mirren	62	Arbroath	53	East Fife	49
1968-9b	Motherwell	64	Ayr	53	East Fife	48
1969-70b	Falkirk	56	Cowdenbeath	55	Queen of South	50
1970-1b	Partick	56	East Fife	51	Arbroath	46
1971-2b	*Dumbarton	52	Arbroath	52	Stirling	50
1972-3b	Clyde	56	Dunfermline	52	Raith	47
1973-4b	Airdrieonians	60	Kilmarnock	58	Hamilton	55
1974-5b	Falkirk	54	Queen of South	53	Montrose	53

SECOND DIVISION (MODERN)

	First	Pts.	Second	Pts.	Third	Pts.
1975-6d	*Clydebank	40	Raith	40	Alloa	35
1976-7f	Stirling	55	Alloa	51	Dunfermline	50
1977-8f	*Clyde	53	Raith	53	Dunfermline	48
1978-9f	Berwick Rangers	54	Dunfermline	52	Falkirk	50
1979-80f	Falkirk	50	East Stirling	49	Forfar	46
1980-1f	Queen's Park	50	Queen of South	46	Cowdenbeath	45
1981-2f	Clyde	59	Alloa	50	Arbroath	50
1982-3f	Brechin	55	Meadowbank	54	Arbroath	49
1983-4f	Forfar	63	East Fife	47	Berwick Rangers	43

	First	Pts.	Second	Pts.	Third	Pts.
1984-5f	Montrose	53	Alloa	50	Dunfermline	49
1985-6f	Dunfermline	57	Queen of South	55	Meadowbank	49
1986-7f	Meadowbank	55	Raith	52	Stirling	52
1987-8f	Ayr	61	St Johnstone	59	Queen's Park	51
1988-9f	Albion	50	Alloa	45	Brechin	43
1989-90f	Brechin	49	Kilmarnock	48	Stirling	47
1990-1f	Stirling	54	Montrose	46	Cowdenbeath	45
1991-2f	Dumbarton	52	Cowdenbeath	51	Alloa	50
1992-3f	Clyde	54	Brechin	53	Stranraer	53
1993-4f	Stranraer	56	Berwick Rangers	48	Stenhousemuir	47
1994-5g	Greenock Morton	64	Dumbarton	60	Stirling	58
1995-6g	Stirling	81	East Fife	67	Berwick Rangers	60
1996-7g	Ayr	77	Hamilton	74	Livingston	64
1997-8g	Stranraer	61	Clydebank	60	Livingston	59
1998-9g	Livingston	77	Inverness Cal.	72	Clyde	53
1999-2000g	Clyde	65	Alloa	64	Ross County	62
2000-01g	Partick Thistle	75	Arbroath	58	Berwick Rangers	54
2001-02g	Queen of South	67	Alloa Athletic	59	Forfar Athletic	53
2002-03g	Raith Rov.	59	Brechin City	55	Airdrie Utd.	54
2003-04g	Airdrie Utd.	70	Hamilton	62	Dumbarton	60

Maximum points: *a*, 76; *b*, 72; *c*, 68; *d*, 52; *e*, 60; *f*, 78; *g*, 108. * Won on goal average.

THIRD DIVISION (MODERN)

	First	Pts.	Second	Pts.	Third	Pts.
1994-5	Forfar	80	Montrose	67	Ross County	60
1995-6	Livingston	72	Brechin	63	Caledonian Th.	57
1996-7	Inverness Cal.T.	76	Forfar	67	Ross County	77
1997-8	Alloa	76	Arbroath	68	Ross County	67
1998-9	Ross County	77	Stenhousemuir	64	Brechin	59
1999-2000	Queen's Park	69	Berwick Rangers	66	Forfar	61
2000-01	*Hamilton	76	Cowdenbeath	76	Brechin	72
2001-02	Brechin City	73	Dumbarton	61	Albion Rov.	59
2002-03	Morton	72	East Fife	71	Albion Rov.	70
2003-04	Stranraer	79	Stirling	77	Gretna	68

Maximum points: 108. * Won on goal difference.

RELEGATED FROM PREMIER DIVISION

1975-6	Dundee, St Johnstone	1990-1	No relegation
1976-7	Kilmarnock, Hearts	1991-2	St Mirren, Dunfermline
1977-8	Ayr, Clydebank	1992-3	Falkirk, Airdrieonians
1978-9	Hearts, Motherwell	1993-4	St J'stone, Raith, Dundee
1979-80	Dundee, Hibernian	1994-5	Dundee Utd.
1980-1	Kilmarnock, Hearts	1995-6	Falkirk, Partick Thistle
1981-2	Partick, Airdrieonians	1996-7	Raith
1982-3	Morton, Kilmarnock	1997-8	Hibernian
1983-4	St Johnstone, Motherwell	1998-9	Dunfermline
1984-5	Dumbarton, Morton	1999-2000	No relegation
1985-6	No relegation	2000-01	St Mirren
1986-7	Clydebank, Hamilton	2001-02	St Johnstone
1987-8	Falkirk, Dunfermline, Morton	2002-03	No relegation
1988-9	Hamilton	2003-04	Partick Thistle
1989-90	Dundee		

RELEGATED FROM FIRST DIVISION

1975-6	Dunfermline, Clyde	1990-1	Clyde, Brechin
1976-7	Raith, Falkirk	1991-2	Montrose, Forfar
1977-8	Alloa, East Fife	1992-3	Meadowbank, Cowdenbeath
1978-9	Montrose, Queen of South	1993-4	Dumbarton, Stirling Alb.,
1979-80	Arbroath, Clyde		Clyde, Morton, Brechin
1980-1	Stirling, Berwick Rangers	1994-5	Ayr, Stranraer
1981-2	East Stirling, Queen of South	1995-6	Hamilton, Dumbarton
1982-3	Dunfermline, Queen's Park	1996-7	Clydebank, East Fife
1983-4	Raith, Alloa	1997-8	Partick, Stirling Alb.
1984-5	Meadowbank, St Johnstone	1998-9	Hamilton, Stranraer
1985-6	Ayr, Alloa	1999-2000	Clydebank
1986-7	Brechin, Montrose	2000-01	Morton, Alloa
1987-8	East Fife, Dumbarton	2001-02	Raith Rov.
1988-9	Kilmarnock, Queen of South	2002-03	Alloa Athletic, Arbroath
1989-90	Albion, Alloa	2003-04	Ayr, Brechin

RELEGATED FROM SECOND DIVISION

1993-4	Alloa, Forfar, E. Stirling,	1997-8	Stenhousemuir, Brechin
	Montrose, Queen's Park,	1998-9	East Fife, Forfar
	Arbroath, Albion,	1999-2000	Hamilton
	Cowdenbeath	2000-01	Queen's Park, Stirling Alb.
1994-5	Meadowbank, Brechin	2001-02	Morton
1995-6	Forfar, Montrose	2002-03	Stranraer, Cowdenbeath
1996-7	Dumbarton, Berwick Rangers	2003-04	East Fife, Stenhousemuir

QUOTE – UNQUOTE

'If I was playing in red it would have been a definite penalty' – **Alan Shearer** after being brought down by goalkeeper Tim Howard in the Manchester United-Newcastle match.

'I'm a bit disappointed from a professional point of view because we like to get the big decisions right' – **Paul Durkin** publicly admitting that he was wrong not to award Newcastle a spot kick.

'The bottom line is I'm glad we are out' – **Sam Allardyce**, Bolton manager, after losing to Tranmere in an F.A. Cup third round replay.

'Sometimes we lose two (players) in a week – two for the price of one. I'm always the last to know and there's nothing I can do about it' – **Stuart Murdoch**, Wimbledon manager, on seeing half his team sold by the club's administrators.

'He's a good man who has conducted himself with a great deal of dignity in difficult times' – **Iain Dowie**, Crystal Palace manager, echoing the thoughts of many in the game about Stuart Murdoch.

'Long after we are all dead and buried, people will still be talking about this game' – **Kevin Keegan** after his ten-man Manchester City side came back from 3-0 down to win 4-3 at Tottenham in an F.A. Cup fourth round replay.

'People call the Prime Minister a liar over weapons of mass destruction, so what have I got to worry about?' – **Gordon Strachan**, before stepping down as Southampton manager, on the prospect of F.A. action for criticising match officials after defeat at Arsenal.

'He made a bit of a boo-boo, but he held his hands up about it' – **Alan Pardew**, West Ham manager, after the team coach driver got lost and took ten hours to reach Bradford for a match.

SCOTTISH LEAGUE RESULTS 2003-04

BANK OF SCOTLAND PREMIER LEAGUE

	Aberdeen	Celtic	Dundee	Dundee Utd.	Dunfermline	Hearts	Hibernian	Kilmarnock	Livingston	Motherwell	Partick Thistle	Rangers
Aberdeen	–	1-3	2-2	0-1	1-2	0-1	3-1	3-1	0-3	0-3	2-1	2-3
	–		1-2	3-0	2-0	–	0-1	–	1-2	0-2	0-0	1-1
Celtic	4-0	–	3-2	5-0	5-0	5-0	6-0	5-1	5-1	3-0	3-1	3-0
	1-2	–	–	2-1	1-2	2-2	–	–	5-1	1-1	–	1-0
	–	–	–	2-1	–	–	–	–	–	–	–	–
Dundee	2-0	0-1	–	2-1	0-2	1-2	1-1	1-2	2-1	0-1	1-0	0-2
	1-1	1-2	–	–	0-1	–	2-2	2-0	1-0	–	2-1	–
	–	–	–	–	–	–	–	–	–	2-0	–	–
Dundee Utd.	3-2	1-5	1-1	–	1-0	2-1	1-2	1-1	2-0	0-2	0-0	1-3
	–	–	2-2	–	3-2	0-2	0-0	4-1	–	1-0	–	2-0
	–	–	–	–	–	–	–	–	–	–	–	3-3
Dunfermline	2-2	0-0	2-0	2-0	–	2-1	0-0	2-3	2-2	1-0	2-1	2-0
	–	1-4	–	1-1	–	0-0	1-1	2-1	–	3-0	1-0	2-3
Hearts	2-0	0-1	2-2	3-0	1-0	–	2-0	2-1	3-1	0-0	2-0	0-4
	1-0	1-1	3-1	3-1	2-1	–	–	–	1-1	3-2	–	1-1
Hibernian	1-1	1-2	1-1	2-2	1-2	1-0	–	3-1	0-2	0-2	3-2	0-1
	0-1	0-4	1-0	–	–	1-1	–	3-0	3-1	3-3	1-2	–
Kilmarnock	1-3	0-5	1-1	0-2	1-1	0-2	0-2	–	0-3	2-0	2-1	2-3
	3-1	0-1	4-2	–	–	1-1	2-0	–	4-2	–	2-1	–
	4-0	–	–	–	–	–	–	–	–	–	–	–
Livingston	1-1	0-2	1-1	0-0	0-0	2-3	1-0	1-2	–	1-1	2-0	0-0
	2-0	–	–	2-3	0-0	–	4-1	1-1	–	3-1	2-2	1-1
Motherwell	1-0	0-2	0-3	3-1	2-2	1-1	0-1	2-1	1-1	–	2-2	1-1
	–	1-1	5-3	0-1	1-0	1-1	–	1-0	–	–	3-0	0-1
Partick Thistle	0-3	1-2	1-2	0-2	4-1	1-4	0-1	2-4	1-1	1-0	–	0-1

	2-0	1-4	0-1	1-1	–	1-0	1-1	2-2	5-2	–	–	–
Rangers	3-0	0-1	3-1	2-1	4-0	2-1	5-2	4-0	1-0	1-0	3-1	–
	–	1-2	4-0	–	4-1	0-1	3-0	2-0	–	4-0	2-0	–

Read across for home results, down for away. After 33 matches, League split into top six and bottom six teams, each playing five further games.

BELL'S FIRST DIVISION

	Ayr Utd.	Brechin City	Clyde	Falkirk	Inverness CT	Queen of South	Raith Rov.	Ross Co.	St Johnstone	St Mirren
Ayr Utd.	–	3-2	2-2	1-1	0-3	1-4	1-0	1-3	1-1	0-2
	–	1-2	1-1	2-3	1-1	1-1	1-0	1-2	1-1	2-0
Brechin City	3-1	–	1-3	2-2	0-2	0-1	0-3	4-2	0-1	1-1
	0-3	–	2-5	0-1	2-4	2-1	1-1	1-0	0-2	2-0
Clyde	3-0	2-1	–	1-2	1-0	3-1	0-0	2-2	2-0	2-0
	2-1	0-0	–	4-2	1-2	2-0	4-1	1-0	2-3	2-2
Falkirk	0-1	3-0	0-2	–	2-1	0-0	3-2	0-2	0-3	0-0
	0-0	5-0	1-1	–	2-1	0-2	1-0	2-0	0-1	1-0
Inverness CT	1-0	5-0	0-0	1-2	–	4-1	2-1	3-3	1-0	2-0
	2-1	1-0	3-1	0-0	–	4-1	3-0	1-0	3-1	1-1
Queen of South	1-0	1-0	4-1	2-0	3-2	–	0-2	1-0	1-1	1-2
	0-0	2-2	1-2	1-0	2-1	–	1-1	1-1	1-1	1-0
Raith Rov.	1-1	2-1	0-1	0-1	1-3	0-1	–	1-7	1-4	1-1
	2-1	1-1	0-3	2-0	0-1	3-1	–	0-0	1-1	2-0
Ross Co.	2-2	4-0	0-1	1-2	1-1	1-0	3-2	–	0-3	2-0
	1-1	2-1	0-0	1-1	1-0	1-2	1-1	–	2-0	1-0
St Johnstone	1-1	3-1	3-0	0-4	1-2	4-1	0-1	1-1	–	1-0
	3-0	2-2	1-3	2-1	3-2	2-2	5-2	1-1	–	1-3
St Mirren	3-2	0-0	2-1	0-0	0-4	1-2	2-1	1-1	1-1	–
	4-1	3-3	2-3	1-1	0-0	3-1	1-1	2-0	1-1	–

Read across from home results, down for away.

BELL'S SECOND DIVISION

	Airdrie Utd.	Alloa Athletic	Arbroath	Berwick Rangers	Dumbarton	East Fife	Forfar Athletic	Morton	Hamilton Acad.	Stenhousemuir
Airdrie Utd.	–	1-0	2-1	1-1	2-0	1-1	3-3	1-6	3-0	2-0
	–	2-1	0-1	6-0	1-1	2-1	2-2	2-0	1-1	4-0
Alloa Athletic	1-4	–	2-2	2-3	1-2	2-0	1-1	0-1	1-3	2-2
	0-1	–	4-0	4-2	3-0	1-1	4-0	3-3	1-1	1-0
Arbroath	1-1	3-1	–	1-0	2-1	0-1	0-0	0-4	2-2	2-1
	0-4	2-1	–	1-2	0-3	0-0	0-1	2-2	0-2	1-1
Berwick Rangers	0-1	3-2	3-0	–	1-4	0-2	0-4	2-3	3-1	2-1
	1-1	3-1	1-3	–	1-2	1-1	3-1	2-0	2-4	3-0
Dumbarton	2-0	1-0	1-1	1-1	–	3-1	2-1	1-0	0-3	0-1
	1-2	3-1	1-0	4-1	–	1-0	1-1	3-0	2-0	4-0
East Fife	3-1	0-1	0-1	3-1	1-0	–	2-3	0-0	2-3	3-2
	0-1	0-1	1-2	2-2	1-3	–	2-0	1-0	2-3	1-0
Forfar Athletic	1-1	1-1	2-2	1-5	3-1	0-1	–	2-3	4-3	2-0
	1-3	2-0	1-2	0-2	1-0	1-0	–	2-1	0-4	1-1
Morton	3-1	2-2	6-4	1-3	2-2	2-1	1-1	–	1-1	5-2
	1-1	2-1	1-0	2-1	3-2	1-1	1-1	–	2-2	1-4
Hamilton Acad.	2-1	3-4	2-0	2-2	2-0	2-2	1-2	1-2	–	2-0
	0-1	0-1	2-2	2-0	2-1	1-0	2-1	6-1	–	0-1
Stenhousemuir	0-1	1-3	1-0	0-3	1-1	3-0	2-0	0-2	0-3	–
	0-3	0-1	0-3	3-1	1-2	0-1	0-2	0-1	0-2	–

Read across for home results, down for away.

BELL'S THIRD DIVISION

	Albion Rov.	Cowdenbeath	East Stirling	Elgin City	Gretna	Montrose	Peterhead	Queen's Park	Stirling Albion	Stranraer
Albion Rov.	–	1–2	5–0	1–2	1–3	0–1	2–0	3–1	0–3	1–1
	–	2–4	5–1	1–2	1–2	3–0	3–3	3–1	3–5	1–4
Cowdenbeath	1–4	–	2–1	3–2	0–1	3–3	2–0	0–1	2–0	0–1
	1–1	–	2–0	2–0	1–2	0–0	0–3	5–1	0–5	1–2
East Stirling	3–4	1–1	–	3–1	0–1	1–1	1–2	1–2	2–4	1–4
	1–8	0–1	–	2–1	2–4	1–4	0–3	2–4	0–3	1–2
Elgin City	1–5	0–4	3–1	–	3–3	2–3	2–3	2–2	0–2	1–3
	1–2	0–0	3–0	–	1–1	2–1	1–0	1–3	0–1	0–0
Gretna	3–1	1–0	2–1	2–2	–	1–1	3–2	1–1	0–1	1–1
	3–0	0–1	5–1	2–1	–	1–2	3–2	0–1	1–0	0–0
Montrose	1–0	1–3	5–1	3–3	2–0	–	0–1	0–0	2–3	2–4
	3–1	1–1	1–0	4–3	1–4	–	2–1	1–1	1–4	1–4
Peterhead	2–1	0–1	2–0	5–1	2–0	0–0	–	4–1	2–2	1–2
	5–0	0–0	6–0	3–1	2–1	1–2	–	1–1	0–0	2–0
Queen's Park	1–1	0–0	3–0	5–2	0–1	1–1	0–2	–	0–2	0–4
	0–1	1–2	1–0	4–0	1–1	1–1	1–0	–	1–4	0–2
Stirling Albion	2–1	0–0	5–1	3–0	0–1	3–0	3–1	1–0	–	1–0
	3–0	1–1	6–0	6–1	0–1	1–1	0–2	0–0	–	2–2
Stranraer	5–0	2–0	4–0	4–3	1–2	2–0	0–2	1–0	0–1	–
	4–0	1–0	7–1	6–0	3–2	6–0	1–1	3–1	1–1	–

Read across for home results, down for away.

SCOTTISH LEAGUE CUP FINALS

1946	Aberdeen beat Rangers (3-2)
1947	Rangers beat Aberdeen (4-0)
1948	East Fife beat Falkirk (4-1 after 0-0 draw)
1949	Rangers beat Raith Rov. (2-0)
1950	East Fife beat Dunfermline Athletic (3-0)
1951	Motherwell beat Hibernian (3-0)
1952	Dundee beat Rangers (3-2)
1953	Dundee beat Kilmarnock (2-0)
1954	East Fife beat Partick Thistle (3-2)
1955	Hearts beat Motherwell (4-2)
1956	Aberdeen beat St Mirren (2-1)
1957	Celtic beat Partick Thistle (3-0 after 0-0 draw)
1958	Celtic beat Rangers (7-1)
1959	Hearts beat Partick Thistle (5-1)
1960	Hearts beat Third Lanark (2-1)
1961	Rangers beat Kilmarnock (2-0)
1962	Rangers beat Hearts (3-1 after 1-1 draw)
1963	Hearts beat Kilmarnock (1-0)
1964	Rangers beat Morton (5-0)
1965	Rangers beat Celtic (2-1)
1966	Celtic beat Rangers (2-1)
1967	Celtic beat Rangers (1-0)
1968	Celtic beat Dundee (5-3)
1969	Celtic beat Hibernian (6-2)
1970	Celtic beat St Johnstone (1-0)
1971	Rangers beat Celtic (1-0)
1972	Partick Thistle beat Celtic (4-1)
1973	Hibernian beat Celtic (2-1)
1974	Dundee beat Celtic (1-0)
1975	Celtic beat Hibernian (6-3)
1976	Rangers beat Celtic (1-0)
1977†	Aberdeen beat Celtic (2-1)
1978†	Rangers beat Celtic (2-1)
1979	Rangers beat Aberdeen (2-1)
1980	Dundee Utd. beat Aberdeen (3-0 after 0-0 draw)
1981	Dundee Utd. beat Dundee (3-0)
1982	Rangers beat Dundee Utd. (2-1)
1983	Celtic beat Rangers (2-1)
1984†	Rangers beat Celtic (3-2)
1985	Rangers beat Dundee Utd. (1-0)
1986	Aberdeen beat Hibernian (3-0)
1987	Rangers beat Celtic (2-1)
1988†	Rangers beat Aberdeen (5-3 on pens. after 3-3 draw)
1989	Rangers beat Aberdeen (3-2)
1990†	Aberdeen beat Rangers (2-1)
1991†	Rangers beat Celtic (2-1)
1992	Hibernian beat Dunfermline Athletic (2-0)
1993†	Rangers beat Aberdeen (2-1)
1994	Rangers beat Hibernian (2-1)
1995	Raith Rov. beat Celtic (6-5 on pens. after 2-2 draw)
1996	Aberdeen beat Dundee (2-0)
1997	Rangers beat Hearts (4-3)
1998	Celtic beat Dundee Utd. (3-0)
1999	Rangers beat St Johnstone (2-1)

```
2000    Celtic beat Aberdeen (2-0)
2001    Celtic beat Kilmarnock (3-0)
2002    Rangers beat Ayr Utd. (4-0)
2003    Rangers beat Celtic (2-1)
2004    Livingston beat Hibernian (2-0)
```

(† After extra time; Skol Cup 1985-93, Coca-Cola Cup 1995-97, CIS Insurance 1999)

SUMMARY OF SCOTTISH LEAGUE CUP WINNERS

Rangers	23	Dundee	3	Livingston	1
Celtic	12	East Fife	3	Motherwell	1
Aberdeen	6	Dundee Utd.	2	Partick Thistle	1
Hearts	4	Hibernian	2	Raith Rov.	1

BELL'S SCOTTISH CHALLENGE CUP 2003-04

First round: Airdrie Utd. 2, Montrose 0; Albion Rov. 1, East Fife 0; Alloa Athletic 1, Clyde 2; Ayr Utd. 1 Stirling Alb. 2 (aet); Brechin City 1, Falkirk 0; Cowdenbeath 1, Ross Co. 2; East Stirling 2, Raith Rov. 5; Forfar Athletic 4, Elgin City 0; Gretna 0, Inverness CT 5; Hamilton Acad. 2 St Johnstone 3 (aet); Morton 4, Arbroath 3; St Mirren 3 Queen's Park 2 (aet); Stenhousemuir 0, Peterhead 3; Stranraer 2, Queen of the South 1.

Second round: Brechin City 3, Stirling Alb. 1; Clyde 0 St Johnstone 1; Forfar Athletic 4, Albion Rov. 2 (aet); Morton 1 Airdrie Utd 2; Peterhead 1, Inverness CT 2; Raith Rov. 2, Stranraer 0; Ross Co. 5, Dumbarton 0; St Mirren 2, Berwick Rangers 1.

Third round: Forfar Athletic 0, Airdrie Utd. 2; Inverness CT 1, Ross Co. 0; Raith Rov. 3, St Mirren 2; St Johnstone 1, Brechin City 2.

Semi-finals: Brechin City 1, Airdrie Utd. 2 (aet); Raith Rov. 0, Inverness CT 4;

FINAL

AIRDRIE UNITED 0, INVERNESS CALEDONIAN THISTLE 2
McDiarmid Park, (5,428), Sunday, October 26, 2003

Airdrie Utd. (4-3-3): McGeown, Docherty (Singbo 64), Stewart, McManus, W. Wilson, S. Wilson (Ronald 73), M. Wilson, Dunn, Vareille (McKeown 83), Roberts, Gow. **Subs not used:** Glancy, Hollis. **Manager:** Sandy Stewart.

Inverness CT (4-3-3): Brown, Tokely, McCaffery, Mann, Golabek, Duncan, Hart (Keogh 86), McBain, Ritchie (Hislop 58), B. Wilson, Bingham (Thomson 90). **Subs not used:** Munro, Fraser. **Scorers:** Bingham (79), Hislop (89). **Manager:** John Robertson.

Referee: W. Young. **Half-time:** 0-0.

FIRST MAJOR TROPHY FOR LIVINGSTON

SECOND ROUND	THIRD ROUND	FOURTH ROUND	SEMI-FINALS	FINAL
*Hibernian 9				
Montrose 0	*Hibernian 2			
*Ross Co. 0		*Hibernian 2		
Queen of the South 3	Queen of the South 1			
*Peterhead 2			Hibernian .... †C1	
Partick Thistle .... †A2	*Partick Thistle 0			
		Celtic 1		
● Bye	Celtic 2			
				Hibernian 0
● Bye	*Rangers 6			
		*Rangers 3		
*Forfar Athletic .... †B3	Forfar Athletic 0			
Motherwell 3			Rangers 1	
*St Johnstone .... †3	*St Johnstone 3			
Hamilton Acad. 2		St Johnstone 0		
*Dunfermline 2	Dunfermline 2			
Cowdenbeath 0				
*Clyde 2	*Clyde 2			
Airdrie Utd. 1		*Dundee 1		
● Bye	Dundee 5			
			Dundee 0	
● Bye	*Hearts 2			
		Hearts 0		
*Arbroath 3	Falkirk 1			
Falkirk .... †4				

Livingston 2

*Aberdeen 3
Dumbarton 0

*Aberdeen 5

*Brechin City 1
Kilmarnock 0

Brechin City 0

*Aberdeen 2

*Dundee Utd. 3
Morton 2

*Dundee Utd. 0

Livingston .... †3

*Queen's Park 1
Livingston 3

Livingston 1

FIRST ROUND: Arbroath 1, Raith Rov. 0; Ayr Utd. 1, Dumbarton 2; Cowdenbeath 3, Alloa Athletic 0; East Fife 0, East Stirling 1, Ross Co. 2; Elgin City 0, Brechin City 4; Forfar Athletic 1, Berwick Rangers 0; Gretna 1, Peterhead 2; Hamilton Acad. 3, Albion Rov. 2; Inverness CT 1, Queen's Park 2; Montrose 2, Stirling Albion 0; Morton 2, Stranraer 0; St Mirren 0, St Johnstone 2+; Stenhousemuir 1, Queen of the South 2.

*Drawn at home. +After extra-time. A – Partick Thistle won 4-3 on pens. B – Forfar Athletic won 4-2 on pens. C – Hibernian won 4-3 on pens. Semi-finals: Hibernian v Rangers at Hampden Park. Dundee v Livingston at Easter Road.

CIS INSURANCE CUP FINAL

HIBERNIAN 0, LIVINGSTON 2

Hampden Park, (45,500), Sunday, March 14, 2004

Hibernian (4-3-3): Andersson, Smith (McManus 62), Murdock, Doumbe, Edge, Caldwell, Thomson, Reid (Dobbie 69), Brown, O'Connor, Riordan. **Subs not used:** Brown, Whittaker, Nicol. **Booked:** Brown, Thomson. **Manager:** Bobby Williamson.

Livingston (3-5-2): McKenzie, Rubio, Andrews, Dorado, McNamee (McLaughlin 79), Makel, Lovell, O'Brien (McGovern 90), McAllister, Fernandez (Pasquinelli 88), Lilley. **Subs not used:** Main, Snowdon. **Scorers:** Lilley (50), McAllister (52). **Booked:** McAllister, Dorado. **Manager:** Davie Hay.

Referee: W. Young. **Half-time:** 0-0.

123

CELTIC COMPLETE LEAGUE AND CUP DOUBLE

THIRD ROUND	FOURTH ROUND	FIFTH ROUND	SEMI-FINALS	FINAL
*Celtic ... 2	Celtic ... 3	*Celtic ... 1	Celtic ... 3	Celtic ... 3
Ross Co. ... 0				
*Hearts ... 2	*Hearts ... 0			
Berwick Rangers ... 0				
*Raith Row. ... 1	*Kilmarnock ... 0	Rangers ... 0		
Kilmarnock ... 3				
*Hibernian ... 0	Rangers ... 2			
Rangers ... 2				
*Ayr Utd. ... 1	*Falkirk ... 0	*Aberdeen ... 1:0		
Falkirk ... 2				
*Aberdeen ... 0:3	Aberdeen ... 2		Livingston ... 1	
Dundee ... 0:2				
*Arbroath ... 1	*Spartans ... 0	Livingston ... 1:1		
Spartans ... 4				
*Livingston ... 1	Livingston ... 4			
Montrose ... 0				
*St Johnstone ... 0	*Motherwell ... 3	*Motherwell ... 0		
Motherwell ... 3				
*East Fife ... 0	Queen of the South ... 2		Inverness CT ... 1:2	
Queen of the South ... 1				
*St Mirren ... 2	*St Mirren ... 0	Inverness CT ... 1		
Airdrie Utd. ... 0				
*Inverness CT ... 5	Inverness CT ... 1			
Brechin City ... 1				

*Morton	0
Partick Thistle	3
	Dunfermline Athletic 1

*Partick Thistle	5

*Hamilton Acad.	2
Cowdenbeath	0

Hamilton Acad.	1
	*Partick Thistle	0

*Clyde	3
Gretna	0

	Dunfermline Athletic ...1:3

*Clyde	0

	Dunfermline Athletic 3

Dundee Utd.	1
*Dunfermline Athletic	3

FIRST ROUND: Clachnacuddin 0, Stranraer 5; Cowdenbeath 5, Edinburgh City 2; Elgin City 1, Peterhead 2; Forfar Athletic 1, East Fife 1; Gretna 4, Dumbarton 1; Montrose 1, Albion Rov. 1; Spartans 6, Buckie Thistle 1; Stirling Albion 3, Queen's Park 1.

REPLAYS: Albion Rov. 1, Montrose 3; East Fife 3, Forfar Athletic 3 (aet, East Fife won 4-1 on pens).

SECOND ROUND: Alloa Athletic 3, Spartans 3; Berwick Rangers 4, Huntly 2; East Stirling 0, Cowdenbeath 5; Gretna 5, Stenhousemuir 1; Inverurie Locos 1, Airdrie Utd. 5; Peterhead 0, East Fife 2; Stirling Albion 1, Arbroath 2; Montrose 1, Threave Rov. 0; Morton 4, Vale of Leithen 0; Stranraer 0, Hamilton Acad. 1.

REPLAY: Spartans 5, Alloa Athletic 3 (aet).
* Drawn at home. Semi-finals at Hampden Park (Inverness CT v Dunfermline Athletic replay at Pittodrie.).

TENNENTS SCOTTISH CUP FINAL

CELTIC 3, DUNFERMLINE ATHLETIC 1

Hampden Park, (50,846), Saturday, May 22, 2004

Celtic (4-4-2): Marshall, Agathe, Balde, Varga, McNamara, Petrov, Lennon, Pearson (Wallace 57), Thompson, Larsson, Sutton. **Subs not used:** McGovern, Lambert, Mjallby, Beattie. **Scorers:** Larsson (58, 71), Petrov (84). **Booked:** Lennon. **Manager:** Martin O'Neill.

Dunfermline Athletic (4-4-2): Stillie, Nicholson, Skerla, Labonte, Byrne (Tod 87), Derek Young, Darren Young, Mason (Grondin 81), Dempsey (Bullen 59), Crawford, Brewster. **Subs not used:** Thomson, Mehmet. **Scorer:** Skerla (40). **Booked:** Brewster, Darren Young. **Manager:** Jimmy Calderwood.

Referee: S. Dougal. **Half-time:** 0-1.

125

SCOTTISH F.A. CUP FINALS

1874	Queen's Park beat Clydesdale (2-0)
1875	Queen's Park beat Renton (3-0)
1876	Queen's Park beat Third Lanark (2-0 after 1-1 draw)
1877	Vale of Leven beat Rangers (3-2 after 0-0, 1-1 draws)
1878	Vale of Leven beat Third Lanark (1-0)
1879	Vale of Leven awarded Cup (Rangers withdrew after 1-1 draw)
1880	Queen's Park beat Thornlibank (3-0)
1881	Queen's Park beat Dumbarton (3-1)
1882	Queen's Park beat Dumbarton (4-1 after 2-2 draw)
1883	Dumbarton beat Vale of Leven (2-1 after 2-2 draw)
1884	Queen's Park awarded Cup (Vale of Leven withdrew from Final)
1885	Renton beat Vale of Leven (3-1 after 0-0 draw)
1886	Queen's Park beat Renton (3-1)
1887	Hibernian beat Dumbarton (2-1)
1888	Renton beat Cambuslang (6-1)
1889	Third Lanark beat Celtic (2-1)
1890	Queen's Park beat Vale of Leven (2-1 after 1-1 draw)
1891	Hearts beat Dumbarton (1-0)
1892	Celtic beat Queen's Park (5-1)
1893	Queen's Park beat Celtic (2-1)
1894	Rangers beat Celtic (3-1)
1895	St. Bernard's beat Renton (2-1)
1896	Hearts beat Hibernian (3-1)
1897	Rangers beat Dumbarton (5-1)
1898	Rangers beat Kilmarnock (2-0)
1899	Celtic beat Rangers (2-0)
1900	Celtic beat Queen's Park (4-3)
1901	Hearts beat Celtic (4-3)
1902	Hibernian beat Celtic (1-0)
1903	Rangers beat Hearts (2-0 after 0-0, 1-1 draws)
1904	Celtic beat Rangers (3-2)
1905	Third Lanark beat Rangers (3-1 after 0-0 draw)
1906	Hearts beat Third Lanark (1-0)
1907	Celtic beat Hearts (3-0)
1908	Celtic beat St. Mirren (5-1)
1909	Cup withheld because of riot after two drawn games in Final between Celtic and Rangers (2-2, 1-1)
1910	Dundee beat Clyde (2-1 after 2-2, 0-0 draws)
1911	Celtic beat Hamilton Academical (2-0 after 0-0 draw)
1912	Celtic beat Clyde (2-0)
1913	Falkirk beat Raith Rov. (2-0)
1914	Celtic beat Hibernian (4-1 after 0-0 draw)
1915-19	No competition (World War 1)
1920	Kilmarnock beat Albion Rov. (3-2)
1921	Partick Thistle beat Rangers (1-0)
1922	Morton beat Rangers (1-0)
1923	Celtic beat Hibernian (1-0)
1924	Airdrieonians beat Hibernian (2-0)
1925	Celtic beat Dundee (2-1)
1926	St. Mirren beat Celtic (2-0)
1927	Celtic beat East Fife (3-1)
1928	Rangers beat Celtic (4-0)
1929	Kilmarnock beat Rangers (2-0)
1930	Rangers beat Partick Thistle (2-1 after 0-0 draw)
1931	Celtic beat Motherwell (4-2 after 2-2 draw)
1932	Rangers beat Kilmarnock (3-0 after 1-1 draw)

1933	Celtic beat Motherwell (1-0)
1934	Rangers beat St. Mirren (5-0)
1935	Rangers beat Hamilton Academical (2-1)
1936	Rangers beat Third Lanark (1-0)
1937	Celtic beat Aberdeen (2-1)
1938	East Fife beat Kilmarnock (4-2 after 1-1 draw)
1939	Clyde beat Motherwell (4-0)
1940-6	No competition (World War 2)
1947	Aberdeen beat Hibernian (2-1)
1948†	Rangers beat Morton (1-0 after 1-1 draw)
1949	Rangers beat Clyde (4-1)
1950	Rangers beat East Fife (3-0)
1951	Celtic beat Motherwell (1-0)
1952	Motherwell beat Dundee (4-0)
1953	Rangers beat Aberdeen (1-0 after 1-1 draw)
1954	Celtic beat Aberdeen (2-1)
1955	Clyde beat Celtic (1-0 after 1-1 draw)
1956	Hearts beat Celtic (3-1)
1957†	Falkirk beat Kilmarnock (2-1 after 1-1 draw)
1958	Clyde beat Hibernian (1-0)
1959	St. Mirren beat Aberdeen (3-1)
1960	Rangers beat Kilmarnock (2-0)
1961	Dunfermline Athletic beat Celtic (2-0 after 0-0 draw)
1962	Rangers beat St. Mirren (2-0)
1963	Rangers beat Celtic (3-0 after 1-1 draw)
1964	Rangers beat Dundee (3-1)
1965	Celtic beat Dunfermline Athletic (3-2)
1966	Rangers beat Celtic (1-0 after 0-0 draw)
1967	Celtic beat Aberdeen (2-0)
1968	Dunfermline Athletic beat Hearts (3-1)
1969	Celtic beat Rangers (4-0)
1970	Aberdeen beat Celtic (3-1)
1971	Celtic beat Rangers (2-1 after 1-1 draw)
1972	Celtic beat Hibernian (6-1)
1973	Rangers beat Celtic (3-2)
1974	Celtic beat Dundee Utd. (3-0)
1975	Celtic beat Airdrieonians (3-1)
1976	Rangers beat Hearts (3-1)
1977	Celtic beat Rangers (1-0)
1978	Rangers beat Aberdeen (2-1)
1979†	Rangers beat Hibernian (3-2 after two 0-0 draws)
1980†	Celtic beat Rangers (1-0)
1981	Rangers beat Dundee Utd. (4-1 after 0-0 draw)
1982†	Aberdeen beat Rangers (4-1)
1983†	Aberdeen beat Rangers (1-0)
1984†	Aberdeen beat Celtic (2-1)
1985	Celtic beat Dundee Utd. (2-1)
1986	Aberdeen beat Hearts (3-0)
1987†	St. Mirren beat Dundee Utd. (1-0)
1988	Celtic beat Dundee Utd. (2-1)
1989	Celtic beat Rangers (1-0)
1990†	Aberdeen beat Celtic (9-8 on pens. after 0-0 draw)
1991†	Motherwell beat Dundee Utd. (4-3)
1992	Rangers beat Airdrieonians (2-1)
1993	Rangers beat Aberdeen (2-1)
1994	Dundee Utd. beat Rangers (1-0)
1995	Celtic beat Airdrieonians (1-0)
1996	Rangers beat Hearts (5-1)

1997	Kilmarnock beat Falkirk (1-0)
1998	Hearts beat Rangers (2-1)
1999	Rangers beat Celtic (1-0)
2000	Rangers beat Aberdeen (4-0)
2001	Celtic beat Hibernian (3-0)
2002	Rangers beat Celtic (3-2)
2003	Rangers beat Dundee (1-0)
2004	Celtic beat Dunfermline Athletic (3–1)

(† After extra time; Cup sponsored by Tennents since season 1989-90)

SUMMARY OF SCOTTISH CUP WINNERS

Celtic 32, Rangers 31, Queen's Park 10, Aberdeen 7, Hearts 6, Clyde 3, Kilmarnock 3, St. Mirren 3, Vale of Leven 3, Dunfermline Ath. 2, Falkirk 2, Hibernian 2, Motherwell 2, Renton 2, Third Lanark 2, Airdrieonians 1, Dumbarton 1, Dundee 1, Dundee Utd. 1, East Fife 1, Morton 1, Partick Thistle 1, St. Bernard's 1.

QUOTE – UNQUOTE

'Elsie thinks I'm an absolute nut. She says I should be out in the garden smelling the roses, or spending Saturday afternoons together in Tesco' – **Sir Bobby Robson** on his wife's thoughts about him continuing to manage Newcastle at the age of 71.

'I'd never heard about *Groundhog Day* before, but I'm going to have to see the film now'–**David Pleat**, caretaker-manager after his Tottenham team were involved in another high-scoring, roller-coaster match, this time against Leicester.

'I didn't think I would even get on the pitch' – **James Hayter**, Bournemouth striker, on scoring the fastest-ever Football League hat-trick in two minutes and 20 seconds after coming on against Wrexham.

'I want to buy Buckingham Palace, but that doesn't mean to say I can have it' – **Arsene Wenger**, Arsenal manager, dismisses another approach for Thierry Henry, this time from Barcelona.

'I don't normally get wrapped up in the celebrations. When I see other people getting involved I think 'Prat' – **Steve Gibson**, Middlesbrough chairman, after the club's Carling Cup victory, their first major trophy.

'Roman Abramovich has bought the toy shop, but I hope he respects the toys that the fans enjoy' – **Ken Bates**, resigning after 22 years as Chelsea chairman.

'I'd put money on them for the Boat Race' – **Harry Redknapp**, Portsmouth manager, after his side were beaten 5-1 by Arsenal in the F.A. Cup.

'I'm a southern softie coming up to the north where it's cold, I don't know anyone and where I've got it all to do' – **Brian Talbot** on leaving Rushden & Diamonds after seven years to become Oldham manager.

'It's not meltdown at Old Trafford' – **Sir Alex Ferguson** on Manchester United's modest, by their standards, season.

IRISH FOOTBALL 2003-04

EIRCOM LEAGUE
PREMIER DIVISION

		P	W	D	L	F	A	Pts
1	Shelbourne	36	19	12	5	52	28	69
2	Bohemians	36	18	10	8	58	37	64
3	Cork City	36	13	14	9	43	33	53
4	Longford Town	36	12	12	12	46	44	48
5	St Patrick's Ath.	36	10	16	10	48	48	46
6	Waterford Utd.	36	11	12	13	44	58	45
7	Shamrock Rov.	36	10	14	12	45	46	44
8	Drogheda Utd.	36	9	10	17	38	50	37
9	Derry City	36	7	15	14	33	51	36
10	U.C.D.	36	7	13	16	27	39	34

Leading Scorer: 21 Jason Byrne (Shelbourne). **Player of Year:** Jason Byrne. **Personality of Year:** Alan Mathews (Longford Town). **Goalkeeper of Year:** Steve Williams (Shelbourne).

FIRST DIVISION

		P	W	D	L	F	A	Pts
1	Dublin City	33	19	10	4	44	26	67
2	Bray Wand.	33	18	10	5	59	35	64
3	Finn Harps	33	17	11	5	52	24	62
4	Limerick	33	16	9	8	55	38	57
5	Kildare Co.	33	15	10	8	50	39	55
6	Sligo Rov.	33	11	13	9	39	39	46
7	Galway Utd.	33	10	13	10	48	53	43
8	Cobh Ramb.	33	9	11	13	33	45	38
9	Athlone Town	33	9	10	14	37	42	37
10	Dundalk	33	6	14	13	36	40	32
11	Monaghan Utd.*	33	3	9	21	28	60	15
12	Kilkenny City	33	2	6	25	25	65	12

* deducted 3 points

Leading scorer: 21 Alan Murphy (Galway Utd.). **Player of Year:** Alan Murphy.

FAI CARLSBERG CUP FINAL

Longford Town 2 (Francis, Barrett) **St Patrick's Athletic** 0 – Lansdowne Road, October 26, 2003

Longford Town: O'Brien, Murphy, McGovern, Ferguson, Dillon, Kirby (Lavine) Keogh, Perth, Prunty, Francis, Barrett.

St Patrick's Athletic: Adamson, Prenderville, Delaney (Foy), Foley, Maguire, Byrne (Donnelly), Fahey, Osam, Dunne, Bird, McPhee (Freeman). **Sent-off:** Fahey.

Referee: A. Kelly (Cork).

EIRCOM LEAGUE CUP FINAL

St Patrick's Athletic 1 (Freeman), **Longford Town** 0. Richmond Park, August 25, 2003

DAILY MIRROR IRISH LEAGUE

PREMIER DIVISION

		P	W	D	L	F	A	Pts
1	Linfield	30	22	7	1	67	16	73
2	Portadown	30	22	4	4	71	22	70
3	Lisburn Dist.	30	16	7	7	45	30	55
4	Coleraine	30	14	9	7	48	36	51
5	Glentoran	30	15	5	10	48	27	50
6	Ballymena Utd.	30	12	8	10	37	39	44
7	Limavady Utd.	30	12	5	13	41	44	41
8	Ards	30	9	11	10	35	45	38
9	Institute	30	10	7	13	42	49	37
10	Dungannon Swifts	30	10	6	14	34	47	36
11	Newry	30	8	9	13	35	53	33
12	Larne	30	7	8	15	41	49	29
13	Cliftonville	30	6	8	16	27	45	26
14	Glenavon	30	4	4	22	23	66	16

Leading Scorer: 25 Glenn Ferguson (Linfield). **Player of the Year:** Glenn Ferguson. **Young Player of the Year:** Chris Morrow (Crusaders). **Manager of the Year:** David Jeffrey (Linfield).

FIRST DIVISION

		P	W	D	L	F	A	Pts
1	Loughall	22	14	6	2	37	20	48
2	Armagh City	22	13	4	5	30	15	43
3	Ballyclare Com.	22	13	4	5	34	21	43
4	Bangor	22	11	6	5	35	19	39
5	Harland & Wolf	22	9	6	7	29	24	33
6	Ballymoney Utd.	22	7	8	7	22	26	29
7	Carrick Rgrs.	22	6	7	9	30	35	25
8	Donegal Celtic	22	5	8	9	28	27	23
9	Ballinamallard	22	5	6	11	20	31	21
10	Moyola Park	22	4	6	12	34	41	18
11	Lurgan Celtic	22	3	9	10	24	44	18
12	Brantwood	22	4	6	12	18	38	18

Leading Scorer: 15 Paul McVeigh (Donegal Celtic).

NATIONWIDE IRISH CUP FINAL

Coleraine 0 **Glentoran** 1 (Halliday) – Windsor Park, May 1, 2004

Coleraine: O'Hare, Clanachan, Flynn, Gaston, McAuley (Johnston), Beatty, Curran (Armstrong), Hamill, Tolan, Haveron, Gorman.

Glentoran: Morris, Nixon, Glendinning, Melaugh, Leeman, Smyth, McCann (Kilmartin), Lockhart, Smith, Halliday (Armour), Keegan (McCallion).

Referee: D. Malcolm (Bangor).

CIS LEAGUE CUP FINAL

Cliftonville 1 (Mulvenna) **Larne** 1 (Delaney) – **Cliftonville** won 5-4 on pens – Windsor Park, November 11, 2003

COUNTY ANTRIM SHIELD FINAL

Linfield 2 (Hunter og, Larmour), **Ards** 0 – The Oval, March 2, 2004

NATIONWIDE CONFERENCE

			HOME				AWAY						
		P	W	D	L	F	A	W	D	L	F	A	Pts	GD
1	Chester City	42	16	4	1	45	18	11	7	3	40	16	92	+51
2	Hereford	42	14	3	4	42	20	14	4	3	61	24	91	+59
3	Shrewsbury Town*	42	13	6	2	38	14	7	8	6	29	28	74	+25
4	Barnet	42	11	6	4	30	17	8	8	5	30	29	71	+14
5	Aldershot	42	12	6	3	40	24	8	4	9	40	43	70	+13
6	Exeter City	42	10	7	4	33	24	9	5	7	38	33	69	+14
7	Morecambe	42	14	4	3	43	25	6	3	12	23	41	67	0
8	Stevenage	42	10	5	6	29	22	8	4	9	29	30	63	+6
9	Woking	42	10	9	2	40	23	5	7	9	25	29	61	+13
10	Accrington	42	13	3	5	46	31	2	10	9	22	30	58	+7
11	Gravesend	42	7	6	8	34	35	7	9	5	35	31	57	+3
12	Telford	42	10	3	8	28	28	5	7	9	21	23	55	−2
13	Dag & Red	42	8	3	10	30	34	7	6	8	29	30	54	−5
14	Burton†	42	7	4	10	30	29	8	3	10	27	30	51	−2
15	Scarborough	42	8	9	4	32	25	4	6	11	19	29	51	−3
16	Margate	42	8	2	11	30	32	6	7	8	26	32	51	−8
17	Tamworth	42	9	6	6	32	30	4	4	13	17	38	49	−19
18	Forest Green	42	6	8	7	32	36	6	4	11	26	44	48	−22
19	Halifax Town	42	9	4	8	28	26	3	4	14	15	39	44	−22
20	Farnborough	42	7	6	8	31	34	3	3	15	22	40	39	−21
21	Leigh	42	4	6	11	26	44	3	2	16	20	53	29	−51
22	Northwich	42	2	8	11	15	38	2	3	16	15	42	23	−50

† Burton deducted 1 point for fielding ineligible player
* Also promoted via play-offs

Manager of Year: Mark Wright (Chester City). **Player of Year:** Daryl Clare (Chester City). **Goalscorer of Year:** 29 Daryl Clare. **Highest gate:** 8,256 (Exeter City v Accrington). **Relegated:** None – Telford into liquidation; Margate voluntary move into Conference South; no promotion from Unibond League because of ground requirements. **Promoted to Conference:** Canvey (Ryman League); Crawley (Dr Martens League). **Top scorers (all comps):** 30 Clare (Chester City); 29 Guinan (Hereford); 27 D'Sane (Aldershot); 26 Grazioli (Barnet), McNiven (Leigh); 25 Devine (Exeter City); 24 Mullin (Accrington); 21 Sills (Aldershot); 20 Stamp (Chester City); 19 Elding (Stevenage); 18 Brown (Hereford), James (Accrington); 17 Carlton (Morecambe).

CONFERENCE CHAMPIONS

1979-80	Altrincham	1992-93*	Wycombe Wand.
1980-81	Altrincham	1993-94	Kidderminster H.
1981-82	Runcorn	1994-95	Macclesfield Town
1982-83	Enfield	1995-96	Stevenage Borough
1983-84	Maidstone Utd.	1996-97*	Macclesfield Town
1984-85	Wealdstone	1997-98*	Halifax Town
1985-86	Enfield	1998-99*	Cheltenham Town
1986-87*	Scarborough	1999-2000*	Kidderminster Harriers
1987-88*	Lincoln City	2000-01*	Rushden & Diamonds
1988-89*	Maidstone Utd.	2001-02*	Boston Utd.
1989-90*	Darlington	2002-03*	Yeovil Town
1990-91*	Barnet	2003-04*	Chester City
1991-92*	Colchester Utd.		

(* Promoted to Football League)

Conference – Record Attendance: 9,432, Lincoln City v Wycombe Wand., May 2, 1988.

NATIONWIDE CONFERENCE RESULTS 2003-04

	Accrington	Aldershot	Barnet	Burton	Chester City	Dag & Red	Exeter City	Farnborough	Forest Green	Gravesend	Halifax Town	Hereford	Leigh	Margate	Morecambe	Northwich	Scarborough	Shrewsbury Town	Stevenage	Tamworth	Telford	Woking
Accrington	-	4-2	2-0	3-1	0-2	2-3	1-2	3-1	4-1	3-3	2-1	2-0	4-1	3-2	1-0	2-2	1-0	1-2	2-1	3-0	1-5	3-3
Aldershot	2-1	-	1-1	3-1	0-0	2-1	2-1	2-0	3-0	1-3	3-1	1-3	2-0	0-2	2-2	4-3	1-0	1-1	1-1	1-0	3-1	2-1
Barnet	0-0	2-1	-	1-0	0-0	2-4	2-3	0-2	5-0	2-2	4-1	4-1	2-0	3-1	2-1	1-0	0-0	0-1	0-0	1-0	2-0	0-0
Burton	1-1	1-4	2-3	-	1-0	0-1	3-4	3-2	2-3	1-0	2-0	0-0	3-2	3-1	2-1	0-1	0-0	0-1	1-1	1-0	2-0	2-1
Chester City	3-3	4-2	1-0	3-1	-	0-0	0-2	1-0	1-0	2-2	2-0	0-9	5-0	3-0	1-3	4-0	1-0	2-1	1-2	1-0	2-1	1-0
Dag & Red	0-1	2-3	5-2	2-0	0-0	-	1-2	1-1	5-2	0-4	1-1	0-1	1-2	0-1	4-0	2-0	0-0	5-0	1-0	3-2	0-3	1-0
Exeter City	3-2	2-1	1-1	2-0	1-2	1-2	-	2-2	2-2	2-2	1-0	0-1	3-1	2-1	1-3	2-0	1-2	1-3	1-0	3-3	2-1	1-0
Farnborough	1-1	4-0	1-1	2-1	1-2	1-3	1-2	-	1-3	1-2	1-0	0-5	1-1	1-1	4-0	2-0	1-2	1-3	2-0	3-3	2-1	2-2
Forest Green	2-1	3-1	1-1	1-2	1-2	2-5	2-2	1-1	-	1-2	1-0	1-7	2-1	2-4	1-2	2-0	4-0	1-3	2-0	2-1	2-1	1-0
Gravesend	0-0	1-3	1-2	1-2	0-4	0-4	2-0	1-1	1-1	-	1-0	2-5	3-1	1-2	6-0	0-0	1-1	0-3	2-3	1-2	1-3	2-2
Halifax Town	1-1	1-2	1-4	0-3	2-0	0-4	2-5	2-0	0-2	1-2	-	1-2	2-1	1-2	1-2	5-3	2-1	0-0	1-0	4-0	1-0	2-2
Hereford	1-0	4-3	2-0	1-2	0-3	0-0	5-1	0-2	5-1	2-5	7-1	-	0-1	3-0	3-0	1-0	1-1	2-2	1-1	2-1	0-1	0-1
Leigh	3-1	2-2	0-1	0-1	1-2	2-2	0-3	1-1	0-2	1-3	2-0	1-3	-	4-2	3-1	3-0	1-4	0-2	1-1	1-2	1-2	1-2
Margate	1-0	1-2	0-0	1-2	2-6	0-1	0-3	1-1	0-1	2-0	1-0	0-5	0-1	-	4-2	3-1	3-0	0-2	2-1	3-1	0-1	1-2
Morecambe	3-1	1-0	2-0	0-1	1-2	2-0	0-3	3-0	3-0	3-2	4-0	2-2	2-1	3-3	-	3-0	1-0	3-3	2-1	4-0	1-1	1-4
Northwich	3-3	2-0	1-3	1-0	0-4	1-1	2-3	1-1	0-4	0-0	0-0	1-5	0-1	0-3	1-0	-	2-0	1-1	2-1	0-1	1-0	1-0
Scarborough	0-0	1-2	2-2	1-2	2-2	2-1	2-3	3-0	2-2	2-1	1-0	3-3	4-1	0-1	2-0	3-1	-	3-3	1-1	3-1	1-1	1-1
Shrewsbury Town	2-1	1-0	1-0	1-0	0-0	0-2	2-1	3-2	3-2	2-2	1-0	4-1	3-1	4-2	2-3	3-1	2-2	-	2-0	2-1	0-1	1-0
Stevenage	1-3	3-3	1-2	1-1	0-0	2-0	2-1	1-0	1-0	2-0	2-0	0-2	4-3	1-1	2-3	0-0	0-0	2-0	-	2-2	1-2	2-2
Tamworth	1-0	2-5	1-2	2-2	1-5	2-0	2-1	2-4	4-3	1-3	1-3	1-3	5-0	3-1	2-3	2-1	2-1	1-1	1-2	-	0-1	2-0
Telford	2-2	2-2	2-2	1-0	0-2	0-3	1-0	3-2	3-2	2-2	2-2	0-1	5-0	1-1	2-1	0-1	0-1	3-3	0-2	4-0	-	1-0
Woking	2-2	2-1	0-0	2-1	1-0	0-1	1-0	2-2	1-0	2-2	0-1	0-1	1-2	2-1	1-4	1-0	1-2	3-3	1-1	4-0	3-1	-

RYMAN LEAGUE
PEMIER DIVISION

		P	W	D	L	F	A	Pts	GD
1	Canvey Island	46	32	8	6	106	42	104	+64
2	Sutton	46	25	10	11	94	56	85	+38
3	Thurrock	46	24	11	11	87	45	83	+42
4	Hendon	46	25	8	13	68	47	83	+21
5	Hornchurch*	46	24	11	11	63	35	82	+28
6	Grays	46	22	15	9	82	39	81	+43
7	Carshalton	46	24	9	13	66	55	81	+11
8	Hayes	46	21	11	14	56	46	74	+10
9	Kettering	46	20	11	15	63	63	71	0
10	Bognor Regis	46	20	10	16	69	67	70	+2
11	Bishop's Stortford	46	20	9	17	78	61	69	+17
12	Maidenhead	46	18	9	19	60	68	63	−8
13	Ford	46	16	14	16	69	63	62	+6
14	Basingstoke	46	17	9	20	58	64	60	−6
15	Bedford	46	14	13	19	62	63	55	−1
16	Heybridge	46	14	11	21	57	78	53	−21
17	Harrow	46	12	14	20	47	63	50	−16
18	Kingstonian	46	12	13	21	40	56	49	−16
19	St Albans	46	12	12	22	55	83	48	−28
20	Hitchin	46	13	8	25	55	89	47	−34
21	Northwood	46	12	9	25	65	95	45	−30
22	Billericay	46	11	11	24	51	66	44	−15
23	Braintree	46	11	6	29	41	88	39	−47
24	Aylesbury	46	5	14	27	41	101	29	−60

*Hornchurch deducted 1 point for fielding an ineligible player

DR MARTENS LEAGUE
PREMIER DIVISION

		P	W	D	L	F	A	Pts	GD
1	Crawley	42	25	9	8	77	43	84	+34
2	Weymouth	42	20	12	10	76	47	72	+29
3	Stafford	42	19	11	12	55	43	68	+12
4	Nuneaton	42	17	15	10	65	49	66	+16
5	Worcester	42	18	9	15	71	50	63	+21
6	Hinckley	42	15	14	13	55	46	59	+9
7	Newport	42	15	14	13	52	50	59	+2
8	Cambridge City	42	14	15	13	54	53	57	+1
9	Welling	42	16	8	18	56	58	56	−2
10	Weston SM	42	14	13	15	52	52	55	0
11	Eastbourne	42	14	13	15	48	56	55	−8
12	Havant and W	42	15	10	17	59	70	55	−11
13	Moor Green	42	14	12	16	42	54	54	−12
14	Merthyr	42	13	14	15	60	66	53	−6
15	Tiverton	42	12	15	15	63	64	51	−1
16	Bath	42	13	12	17	49	56	51	−7
17	Dorchester	42	14	9	19	56	69	51	−13
18	Chelmsford	42	11	16	15	46	53	49	−7
19	Dover	42	12	13	17	50	59	49	−9
20	Hednesford	42	12	12	18	56	69	48	−13
21	Chippenham	42	10	17	15	51	63	47	−12
22	Grantham	42	10	15	17	45	67	45	−22

UNIBOND LEAGUE

PREMIER DIVISION

		P	W	D	L	F	A	Pts	GD
1	Hucknall	44	29	8	7	83	38	95	+45
2	Droylsden	44	26	8	10	96	64	86	+32
3	Barrow	44	22	14	8	82	52	80	+30
4	Alfreton	44	23	9	12	73	43	78	+30
5	Harrogate	44	24	5	15	79	63	77	+16
6	Southport	44	20	10	14	71	52	70	+19
7	Worksop	44	19	13	12	69	50	70	+19
8	Lancaster	44	20	9	15	62	49	69	+13
9	Vauxhall	44	19	10	15	78	75	67	+3
10	Gainsborough	44	17	13	14	70	52	64	+18
11	Stalybridge	44	18	10	16	72	66	64	+6
12	Altrincham	44	16	15	13	66	51	63	+15
13	Runcorn	44	16	13	15	67	63	61	+4
14	Ashton	44	17	8	19	59	79	59	-20
15	Whitby	44	14	11	19	55	70	53	-15
16	Marine	44	13	12	19	62	74	51	-12
17	Bradford PA	44	12	14	18	48	62	50	-14
18	Spennymoor	44	14	6	24	55	93	48	-38
19	Burscough	44	10	15	19	47	67	45	-20
20	Radcliffe	44	12	6	26	74	99	42	-25
21	Blyth	44	10	10	24	54	74	40	-20
22	Frickley	44	11	7	26	51	83	40	-32
23	Wakefield	44	8	6	30	45	99	30	-54

WELSH PREMIER LEAGUE

		P	W	D	L	F	A	Pts	GD
1	Rhyl	32	23	8	1	76	26	77	+50
2	TNS	32	24	4	4	77	28	76	+49
3	Haverfordwest	32	17	11	4	40	23	62	+17
4	Aberystwyth	32	18	5	9	59	39	59	+20
5	Caersws	32	15	10	7	63	41	55	+22
6	Bangor	32	16	6	10	72	47	54	+25
7	Cwmbran	32	15	3	14	51	44	48	+7
8	Connah's Quay	32	11	9	12	58	55	42	+3
9	Caernarfon	32	11	9	12	65	65	42	0
10	Newtown	32	12	5	15	43	50	41	-7
11	Port Talbot	32	11	6	15	41	51	39	-10
12	Porthmadog	32	11	3	18	41	55	36	-14
13	Newi Cefn	32	11	2	19	44	59	35	-15
14	Afan Lido	32	8	8	16	31	54	32	-23
15	Welshpool	32	6	7	19	35	71	25	-36
16	Carmarthen	32	3	11	18	28	69	20	-41
17	Barry	32	3	7	22	30	77	16	-47

HIGHLAND LEAGUE

		P	W	D	L	F	A	Pts	GD
1	Clachnacuddin	28	21	3	4	61	25	66	+36
2	Buckie	28	18	7	3	56	32	61	+24
3	Fraserburgh	28	18	5	5	81	36	59	+45
4	Deveronvale	28	18	1	9	77	41	55	+36
5	Keith	28	17	2	9	70	36	53	+34
6	Huntly	28	16	5	7	73	47	53	+26
7	Inverurie	28	13	10	5	76	51	49	+25
8	Forres Mechs	28	13	4	11	63	49	43	+14
9	Nairn	28	9	5	14	40	60	32	−20
10	Cove	28	7	6	15	45	61	27	−16
11	Wick	28	6	5	17	42	65	23	−23
12	Brora	28	5	6	17	34	70	21	−36
13	Lossiemouth	28	4	8	16	41	74	20	−33
14	Rothes	28	2	9	17	19	62	15	−43
15	Fort William	28	3	4	21	20	89	13	−69

F.A. BARCLAYCARD PREMIERSHIP RESERVE LEAGUE

NORTH

		P	W	D	L	F	A	Pts	GD
1	Aston Villa	26	17	5	4	55	31	56	+24
2	Liverpool	26	14	8	4	41	21	50+	20
3	Manchester Utd.	26	13	8	5	55	39	47	+16
4	Manchester City	26	11	8	7	34	24	41	+10
5	Newcastle Utd.	25	12	4	9	47	41	40	+6
6	Blackburn Rov.	26	11	6	9	49	45	39	+4
7	Everton	26	10	8	8	37	33	38	+4
8	Leeds Utd.	26	10	7	9	40	40	37	0
9	Middlesbrough	26	8	10	8	33	33	34	0
10	Sunderland	25	8	7	10	36	43	31	−7
11	W.B.A	26	8	6	12	36	48	30	−12
12	Birmingham City	26	6	5	15	28	42	23	−14
13	Wolves	26	4	6	16	27	49	18	−22
14	Bolton Wand.	26	3	4	19	22	51	13	−29

SOUTH

		P	W	D	L	F	A	Pts	GD
1	Charlton Athletic	28	17	6	5	46	19	57	+27
2	Derby Co.	28	13	10	5	46	31	49	+15
3	Southampton	28	14	6	8	43	28	48	+15
4	West Ham Utd.	28	12	8	8	37	35	44	+2
5	Tottenham	28	11	9	8	42	35	42	+7
6	Arsenal	28	10	9	9	41	35	39	+6
7	Chelsea	28	11	6	11	37	33	39	+4
8	Leicester City	28	9	11	8	34	40	38	−6
9	Coventry City	28	9	10	9	38	40	37	−2
10	Wimbledon	28	9	5	14	35	47	32	−12
11	Watford	28	6	12	10	32	40	30	−8
12	Portsmouth	28	6	11	11	36	39	29	−3
13	Nott'm Forest	28	6	11	11	33	41	29	−8
14	Ipswich Town	28	8	4	16	34	44	28	−10
15	Fulham	28	6	8	14	27	54	26	−27

PONTIN'S HOLIDAYS LEAGUE

PREMIER DIVISION

		P	W	D	L	F	A	Pts	GD
1	Stoke City	22	13	4	5	45	31	43	+14
2	Tranmere Rov.	22	13	3	6	42	32	42	+10
3	Walsall	22	12	5	5	38	18	41	+20
4	Sheffield Utd.	22	11	4	7	28	26	37	+2
5	Hull City	22	9	6	7	39	32	33	+7
6	Bradford City	22	6	9	7	30	28	27	+2
7	Sheffield Wed.	22	8	3	11	32	33	27	−1
8	Preston N.E.	22	6	7	9	39	34	25	+5
9	Barnsley	22	6	7	9	31	37	25	−6
10	Rotherham Utd.	22	7	4	11	35	56	25	−21
11	Huddersfield Town	22	6	6	10	28	34	24	−6
12	Burnley	22	4	4	14	26	52	16	−26

DIVISION ONE WEST

		P	W	D	L	F	A	Pts	GD
1	Wigan Athletic	18	11	3	4	43	25	36	+18
2	Stockport Co.	18	10	3	5	31	23	33	+8
3	Carlisle Utd.	18	10	2	6	38	35	32	+3
4	Blackpool	18	7	5	6	29	25	26	+4
5	Oldham Athletic	18	7	5	6	24	24	26	0
6	Bury	18	7	3	8	22	25	24	−3
7	Shrewsbury Town	18	6	2	10	36	31	20	+5
8	Macclesfield Town	18	4	8	6	20	27	20	−7
9	Wrexham	18	5	4	9	36	46	19	−10
10	Rochdale	18	5	1	12	25	43	16	−18

DIVISION ONE EAST

		P	W	D	L	F	A	Pts	GD
1	Hartlepool Utd.	18	12	4	2	41	18	40	+23
2	Newcastle Utd.	18	9	3	6	38	28	30	+10
3	Scunthorpe Utd.	18	7	8	3	22	22	29	0
4	Boston Utd.	18	8	0	10	34	33	24	+1
5	Grimsby Town	18	5	7	6	28	27	22	+1
6	Notts Co.	18	6	4	8	25	26	22	−1
7	Darlington	18	6	4	8	29	34	22	−5
8	Doncaster Rov.	18	4	8	6	20	25	20	−5
9	York City	18	4	7	7	24	34	19	−10
10	Lincoln City	18	3	7	8	23	37	16	−14

F.A. WOMEN'S PREMIER LEAGUE

		P	W	D	L	F	A	Pts	GD
1	Arsenal	18	15	2	1	65	11	47	+54
2	Charlton Athletic	18	15	1	2	52	17	46	+35
3	Fulham	18	14	2	2	60	20	44	+40
4	Leeds Utd.	18	8	4	6	32	28	28	+4
5	Doncaster Rov.	18	8	3	7	41	40	27	+1
6	Everton	18	6	2	10	21	36	20	−15
7	Birmingham City	18	4	5	9	17	31	17	−14
8	Bristol Rov.	18	3	3	12	27	37	12	−10
9	Aston Villa	18	1	4	13	18	63	7	−45
10	Tranmere Rov.	18	1	4	13	13	63	7	−50

THE CHANGING FACE OF FOOTBALL

The **Football League** will have a new look for the new season after club chairmen approved new names for the three divisions during their summer meeting in Chester. Divisions One, Two and Three will be retitled The Championship, League One and League Two, a change coinciding with a new title sponsor, Coca-Cola, after the end of Nationwide's seven-season involvement. The League also have a redesigned logo as part of a widespread rebranding exercise aimed at strengthening perceptions of the competition. Further announcements will be made during the new season. Chairman Sir Brian Mawhinney said: 'The Championship is a term steeped in the history of the Football League. Reclaiming it for our leading clubs will place a new, enhanced emphasis on its status at the pinnacle of our competition. Not only is it the gateway to the Premiership, it is one of Europe's leading league competitions in terms of the standard of football being played, the high quality of stadia and the numbers of supporters attending.'

Following consultation with managers, referees and the P.F.A., the **Football Association** are introducing a new disciplinary system in the Premiership, Football League and Conference this season. Suspensions previously took 14 days to activate. Under this pilot scheme, players sent off will serve an immediate ban, unless a claim for wrongful dismissal is submitted by noon on the next working day. Bans incurred by the accumulation of five, ten or 15 yellow cards will operate seven days from the last caution, instead of 14 days as before.

The **Scottish Premier League** have changed the rule requiring a promoted club to have a 10,000-seater stadium. Officials hope that the new requirement of 6,000 seats will end the controversy involving Inverness Caledonian Thistle and Falkirk in the last two seasons. First Division champions Inverness will share Aberdeen's Pittodrie Stadium after a second vote of SPL clubs, who initially refused them entry to the top-flight. Relegated Partick Thistle protested, but were told by the Scottish F.A. they had no grounds for appeal. Twelve months earlier, bottom-of-the-table Motherwell won a reprieve when Division One champions Falkirk's bid to groundshare with Airdrie United was rejected.

Rule-makers at the **International Board** have decided that substitutions in friendly matches should be limited to six per team. In England's last friendly before the European Championship, Sven-Goran Eriksson replaced all his 11 starting players against Iceland. The gold and silver goal rule was scrapped after the Championship. Knock-out competition matches will now be decided on penalties if the score is level after extra-time. **FIFA** have reaffirmed that players removing their shirts in goal celebrations must be booked for unsporting behaviour. **UEFA** have clarified their disciplinary rules after Lee Bowyer, Newcastle United's former Leeds United midfielder, was forced to miss 12 European matches because of a registration mix-up.

'STREAKER' RED CARD RESCINDED

Common sense prevailed after Witton Albion player Brian Pritchard was sent off for violent conduct when tripping a streaker who ran on the pitch during the Cheshire Senior Cup Final against Woodley Sports. The red card was rescinded on appeal by an F.A. disciplinary commission.

PREMIERSHIP PAIR IN UEFA TEAM

Thierry Henry and Ruud van Nistelrooy were named in a UEFA team of the year chosen by a website poll. The team was: Buffon (Juventus), Ferreira (FC Porto), Nesta (AC Milan), Maldini (AC Milan), Roberto Carlos (Real Madrid), Figo (Real Madrid), Beckham (Real Madrid), Zidane (Real Madrid), Nedved (Juventus), Van Nistelrooy (Manchester Utd.), Henry (Arsenal). Coach: Jose Mourinho (FC Porto).

NATIONAL REFEREES 2004-05

FATHER AND SON FIRST FOR FOOTBALL LEAGUE

The Football League will have father and son match officials for the first time in the new season, with Clive and Michael Oliver, from Northumberland, promoted to the National List. Clive, 41, who takes charge of matches while his 19-year-old son will be an assistant referee, said: 'It was a real family celebration when we heard. This is probably as far as I will go, but Michael has time on his side and I expect him to go higher.' Michael is believed to be the League's youngest-ever official. Jim Ashworth, National Group Manager for Referees, said: 'If you are good enough you are old enough.' Clive Oliver is among ten new Football League referees. Mark Clattenburg has been promoted to the Premiership list which loses Graham Barber, Paul Durkin and Jeff Winter, who have reached the retirement age of 48.

SELECT GROUP

Barry, Neale (North Lincs)
Bennett, Steve (Kent)
*Clattenburg Mark (Tyne and Wear)
Dean, Mike (Wirral)
Dowd, Phil (Staffs)
Dunn, Steve (Gloucs)
D'Urso, Andy (Essex)
Foy, Chris (Merseyside)
Gallagher, Dermot (Oxon)
Halsey, Mark (Lancs)
Knight, Barry (Kent)

Messias, Matt (South Yorks)
Poll, Graham (Herts)
Rennie, Uriah (South Yorks)
Riley, Mike (West Yorks)
Styles, Rob (Hants)
Walton, Peter (Northants)
Webb, Howard (South Yorks)
Wiley, Alan (Staffs)

(*New appointment to Select Group)

NATIONAL GROUP

Armstrong, Paul (Berks)
Atkinson, Martin (West Yorks)
Bates, Tony (Staffs)
Beeby, Richard (Northants)
*Booth, Russell (Notts)
Boyeson, Carl (East Yorks)
Cable, Lee (Surrey)
Cowburn, Mark (Lancs)
Crossley, Phil (Kent)
Curson, Brian (Leics)
Danson, Paul (Leics)
*Drysdale, Darren (Lincs)
Evans, Eddie (Gtr Manchester)
Fletcher, Mick (Worcs)
Friend, Kevin (Leics)
*Graham, Fred (Essex)
Hall, Andy (West Midlands)
Hegley, Grant (Herts)
Hill, Keith (Herts)
Ilderton, Eddie (Tyne & Wear)
Jones, Michael (Cheshire)
Joslin, Phil (Notts)
Kaye, Alan (West Yorks)
Kettle, Trevor (Berks)
Laws, Graham (Tyne & Wear)
Leake, Tony (Lancs)
*Lewis, Gary (Cambs)
Marriner, Andre (West Midlands)
Mason, Lee (Lancs)

Mathieson, Scott (Cheshire)
*Melin, Paul (Surrey)
Miller, Nigel (Co Durham)
*Oliver, Clive (Northumberland)
Olivier, Ray (West Midlands)
Parkes, Trevor (West Midlands)
Penn, Andy (West Midlands)
Penton, Clive (Sussex)
Pike, Mike (Cumbria)
Probert, Lee (Gloucs)
Prosser, Phil (West Yorks)
Robinson, Paul (East Yorks)
Ross, Joe (London)
*Russell, Mike (Herts)
Ryan, Michael (Lancs)
Salisbury, Graham (Lancs)
*Singh, Jarnail (Middx)
*Stroud, Keith (Dorset)
Tanner, Steve (Somerset)
Taylor, Paul (Herts)
Thorpe, Mike (Suffolk)
Tomlin, Steve (East Sussex)
Warren, Mark (West Midlands)
Webster, Colin (Tyne & Wear)
Williamson, Iain (Berks)
*Woolmer, Andy (Northants)
Wright, Kevin (Cambs)

(* New appointments to National Group)

138

UEFA CHAMPIONS LEAGUE 2003-04

FIRST QUALIFYING ROUND, FIRST LEG

Bate Borisov 1 (Loshankov 24), **Bohemians** 0. Att: 4,500. **Glentoran** 0, HJK Helsinki 0. Att: 3,000. Vardar 3 (Dos Santos 37, 69, Ristovski 49), **Barry Town** 0. Att: 5,000.

FIRST QUALIFYING ROUND, SECOND LEG

Barry Town 2 (Jarman 1, Moralee 63), Vardar 1 (Oliveira 61). Att: 1,400 (Vardar won 4-2 on agg). HJK Helsinki 1 (Makela 73), **Glentoran** 0. Att: 4,270 (HJK Helsinki won 1-0 on agg). **Bohemians** 3 (Caffrey 37, Bryan 45, Crowe 58), Bate Borisov 0. Att: 6,000 (**Bohemians** won 3-1 on agg).

FIRST QUALIFYING ROUND (ON AGGREGATE)

FBK Kaunas 5, Torshavn 1; Leotar 2 Grevenmacher 0; Omonia Nicosia 2, Irtysh Pavlodar 1; Pyunik 2, KR 1; Sheriff Tiraspol 2, Flora Tallinn 1; SK Tirana 3, Dinamo Tbilisi 3 (SK Tirana won 4-2 on pens); Sliema Wanderers 3, Skonto Riga 3 (Sliema Wanderers won on away goals).

SECOND QUALIFYING ROUND, FIRST LEG

Bohemians 0, Rosenborg 1 (Karadas 35). Att: 8,500. FBK Kaunas 0, **Celtic** 4 (Larsson 13, Sutton 29, Maloney 54, Miller 85). Att: 3,000.

SECOND QUALIFYING ROUND, SECOND LEG

Celtic 1 (Gvildys 21 og), FBK Kaunas 0. Att: 40,284 (**Celtic** won 5-0 on agg). Rosenborg 4 (Karadas 43, Brattbakk 50, Strand 68, Johnsen 75), **Bohemians** 0. Att: 15,900 (Rosenborg won 5-0 on agg)

SECOND QUALIFYING ROUND (ON AGGREGATE)

Anderlecht 3, Rapid Bucharest 2; CSKA Sofia 3, Pyunik 0; Dinamo Zagreb 3, Maribor 2; FC Copenhagen 10, Sliema Wanderers 1; Graz 7, SK Tirana 2; MTK Hungaria 3, HJK Helsinki 2; Partizan Belgrade 3, Djurgarden 3 (Partizan Belgrade won on away goals); Shakhtar Donetsk 2, Sheriff Tiraspol 0; Slavia Prague 4, Leotar 1; Vardar Skopje 3, CSKA Moscow 2; Wisla Krakow 7, Omonia Nicosia 4; Zilina 2, Maccabi Tel Aviv 1.

THIRD QUALIFYING ROUND, FIRST LEG

MTK Hungaria 0, **Celtic** 4 (Larsson 19, Agathe 35, Petrov 68, Sutton 90). Att: 5,000. Partizan Belgrade 0, **Newcastle Utd.** 1 (Solano 39). Att: 32,500. **Rangers** 1 (Lovenkrands 7), FC Copenhagen 1 (Jonsson 51). Att: 47,401. Zilina 0, **Chelsea** 2 (Gudjohnsen 42, Drahno 75 og). Att: 6,160.

THIRD QUALIFYING ROUND, SECOND LEG

Celtic 1 (Sutton 13), MTK Hungaria 0. Att: 41,720 (**Celtic** won 5-0 on agg). **Chelsea** 3 (Johnson 32, Huth 67, Hasselbaink 78), Zilina 0. Att: 23,408. (**Chelsea** won 5-0 on agg); FC Copenhagen 1 (Dos Santos 83), **Rangers** 2 (Arteta 52 pen, Arveladze 86). Att: 35,519 (**Rangers** won 3-2 on agg). Newcastle Utd. 0, Partizan Belgrade 1 (Iliev 50). Att: 37,293 (aet, agg 1-1, Partizan Belgrade won 4-3 on pens).

THIRD QUALIFYING ROUND (ON AGGREGATE)

AEK Athens 3, Grasshoppers 2; Anderlecht 4, Wisla Krakow 1; Ajax 3, Graz 2; Bruges 3, Borussia Dortmund 3 (aet, Bruges won 4-2 on pens); Celta Vigo 3, Slavia Prague 2; Deportivo La Coruna 1, Rosenborg 0; Dynamo Kiev 5, Dinamo Zagreb 1; Galatasaray 6, CSKA Sofia 0; Lazio 4, Benfica 1; Lokomotiv Moscow 3, Shakhtar Donetsk 2; Marseille 1, Austria Vienna 0; Sparta Prague 5, Vardar Skopje 4

GROUP STAGE

GROUP A

September 17, 2003
Bayern Munich 2 (Makaay 73, 86), **Celtic** 1 (Thompson 56). Att: 48,500.
Celtic (3-5-2): Hedman, Varga, Balde, McNamara, Agathe, Lennon, Petrov, Sutton, Thompson, Larsson, Hartson (Miller 66).
Lyon 1 (Juninho 25 pen), **Anderlecht** 0. Att: 32,000.

September 30, 2003
Anderlecht 1 (Mornar 52), **Bayern Munich** 1 (Santa Cruz 73). Att: 21,788.
Celtic 2 (Miller 70, Sutton 78), **Lyon** 0. Att: 58,027.
Celtic (3-5-2): Hedman, Varga, Balde, McNamara, Agathe, Lennon, Sutton, Petrov, Thompson, Larsson, Hartson (Miller 63).

October 21, 2003
Anderlecht 1 (Dindane 72), **Celtic** 0. Att: 27,000.
Celtic (3-5-2): Hedman, Varga, Balde, McNamara (Valgaeren 46), Agathe, Petrov, Sutton, Lennon (Miller 80), Thompson, Hartson, Larsson.
Lyon 1 (Luyindula 88), **Bayern Munich** 1 (Makaay 25). Att: 38,145.

November 5, 2003
Bayern Munich 1 (Makaay 14), **Lyon** 2 (Juninho 6, Elber 53). Att: 59,000.
Celtic 3 (Larsson 12, Miller 17, Petrov 81), **Anderlecht** 1 (Aruna 77). Att: 59,057.
Celtic (4-4-2): Hedman, Agathe, Varga, Balde, McNamara, Miller (Gray 75), Lennon, Sutton, Petrov, Larsson, Hartson (Maloney 83, Sylla 90).

November 25, 2003
Anderlecht 1 (Tihinen 69), **Lyon** 0. Att: 20,779.
Celtic 0, **Bayern Munich** 0. Att: 59,506.
Celtic (3-5-2): Hedman, Varga, Balde, McNamara, Agathe (Miller 62), Lennon, Sutton, Petrov, Thompson, Larsson, Hartson (Sylla 86).

December 10, 2003
Bayern Munich 1 (Makaay 42 pen), **Anderlecht** 0. Att: 52,000.
Lyon 3 (Elber 6, Juninho 52, 86 pen), **Celtic** 2 (Hartson 24, Sutton 75). Att: 38,659.
Celtic (4-4-2): Hedman, Mjallby, Varga, Balde, Gray (Wallace 67), Miller, Lennon, Sutton, Petrov; Larsson, Hartson (Sylla 67).

FINAL TABLE

	P	W	D	L	F	A	Pts
LYON	6	3	1	2	7	7	10
BAYERN MUNICH	6	2	3	1	6	5	9
Celtic	6	2	1	3	8	7	7
Anderlecht	6	2	1	3	4	6	7

GROUP B

September 17, 2003
Arsenal 0, **Inter Milan** 3 (Cruz 22, Van der Meyde 24, Martins 41). Att: 34,393.
Arsenal (4-4-2): Lehmann, Lauren, Toure, Campbell, Cole, Ljungberg, Gilberto Silva
(Kanu 65), Vieira, Pires (Bergkamp 65), Wiltord (Parlour 79), Henry.
Dynamo Kiev 2 (Rincon 83, 90), **Lokomotiv Moscow** 0. Att: 79,500.

September 30, 2003
Inter Milan 2 (Adani 22, Vieri 90), **Dynamo Kiev** 1 (Fedorov 34). Att: 35,000.
Lokomotiv Moscow 0, **Arsenal** 0. Att: 27,000.
Arsenal (4-4-2): Lehmann, Lauren, Keown, Toure, Cole, Parlour, Gilberto Silva, Edu,
Pires, Wiltord, Henry.

October 21, 2003
Dynamo Kiev 2 (Shatskikh 27, Belkevich 64), **Arsenal** 1 (Henry 81). Att: 80,000.
Arsenal (4-3-1-2): Lehmann, Lauren, Toure, Campbell, Cole, Parlour (Ljungberg 72),
Gilberto Silva, Edu (Vieira 60), Pires, Wiltord (Kanu 72), Henry.
Lokomotiv Moscow 3 (Loskov 2, Ashvetia 50, Khokhlov 57), **Inter Milan** 0. Att: 25,000.

November 5, 2003
Arsenal 1 (Cole 88), **Dynamo Kiev** 0. Att: 34,419.
Arsenal (4-4-2): Lehmann, Lauren, Toure, Campbell, Cole, Ljungberg (Wiltord 69),
Parlour (Kanu 76), Gilberto Silva, Pires, Bergkamp (Edu 90), Henry.
Inter Milan 1 (Recoba 14), **Lokomotiv Moscow** 1 (Loskov 55). Att: 25,000.

November 25, 2003
Inter Milan 1 (Vieri 33), **Arsenal** 5 (Henry 25, 85, Ljungberg 49, Edu 87, Pires 89). Att:
50,000.
Arsenal (4-4-2): Lehmann, Toure, Campbell, Cygan, Cole, Ljungberg, Edu, Parlour,
Pires, Kanu (Gilberto Silva 73), Henry (Aliadiere 88).
Lokomotiv Moscow 3 (Buznikin 28, Ignashevich 45 pen, Parks 89). **Dynamo Kiev** 2
(Belkevich 37, Shatskikh 65). Att: 50,000.

December 10, 2003
Arsenal 2 (Pires 12, Ljungberg 67), **Lokomotiv Moscow** 0. Att: 35,343.
Arsenal (4-4-2): Lehmann, Toure, Campbell, Cygan, Cole, Ljungberg, Gilberto Silva,
Vieira, Pires, Bergkamp (Kanu 75), Henry.
Dynamo Kiev 1 (Rincon 85), **Inter Milan** 1 (Adani 68). Att: 30,000.

FINAL TABLE

	P	W	D	L	F	A	Pts
ARSENAL	6	3	1	2	9	6	10
LOK. MOSCOW	6	2	2	2	7	7	8
Inter Milan	6	2	2	2	8	11	8
Dynamo Kiev	6	2	1	3	8	8	7

GROUP C

September 17, 2003
AEK Athens 1 (Tsartas 85), **Deportivo La Coruna** 1 (Pandiani 12). Att: 16,000.
PSV Eindhoven 1 (Bouma 65), **Monaco** 2 (Morientes 31, Cisse 55). Att: 30,000.

September 30, 2003
Deportivo La Coruna 2 (Sergio 19, Pandiani 51 pen), **PSV Eindhoven** 0. Att: 24,300.
Monaco 4 (Giuly 23, Morientes 27, 57, Prso 86), **AEK Athens** 0. Att: 12,000.

October 21, 2003
AEK Athens 0, **PSV Eindhoven** 1 (Lucius 36). Att: 10,000.
Deportivo La Coruna 1 (Tristan 82), **Monaco** 0. Att: 22,000.

November 5, 2003
Monaco 8 (Rothen 2, Giuly 11, Prso 26, 30, 45, 49, Plasil 47, Cisse 68), **Deportivo La Coruna** 3 (Tristan 39, 53, Scaloni 45). Att: 6,000 (record Champions League aggregate score).
PSV Eindhoven 2 (Bouma 51, Robben 63), **AEK Athens** 0. Att: 28,000.

November 25, 2003
Deportivo La Coruna 3 (Hector 21, Valeron 51, Luque 71), **AEK Athens** 0. Att: 26,000.
Monaco 1 (Morientes 34), **PSV Eindhoven** 1 (Vennegoor 85). Att: 18,000.

December 10, 2003
AEK Athens 0, **Monaco** 0. Att: 4,000.
PSV Eindhoven 3 (De Jong 14, 90, Robben 48), **Deportivo La Coruna** 2 (Luque 58, Pandiani 83). Att: 32,000.

FINAL TABLE

	P	W	D	L	F	A	Pts
MONACO	6	3	2	1	15	6	11
DEP. LA CORUNA	6	3	1	2	12	12	10
PSV Eindhoven	6	3	1	2	8	7	10
AEK Athens	6	0	2	4	1	11	2

GROUP D

September 17, 2003
Juventus 2 (Del Piero 5, Ferrara 73), **Galatasaray** 1 (Hakan Sukur 19). Att: 14,420.
Real Sociedad 1 (Kovacevic 80 pen), **Olympiakos** 0. Att: 29,000.

September 30, 2003
Galatasaray 1 (Hakan Sukur 60), **Real Sociedad** 2 (Kovacevic 3, Alonso 71). Att: 55,000.
Olympiakos 1 (Stoltidis 11), **Juventus** 2 (Nedved 21, 79). Att: 16,000.

October 21, 2003
Galatasaray 1 (Haspolatli 9), **Olympiakos** 0. Att: 41,000.
Juventus 4 (Trezeguet 3, 63, Di Vaio 6, 45), **Real Sociedad** 2 (Tudor 67 og, De Pedro 80). Att: 17,246.

November 5, 2003
Olympiakos 3 (Mavrogenidis 6, Castillo 35, Giovanni 90), **Galatasaray** 0. Att: 14,000.
Real Sociedad 0, **Juventus** 0. Att: 29,000.

November 25, 2003
Olympiakos 2 (Stoltidis 59, Castillo 71), **Real Sociedad** 2 (Gabilondo 31, Schurrer 74). Att: 14,000.

December 2, 2003
Galatasaray 2 (Hakan Sukur 47, 90), **Juventus** 0. Att: 60,000.

December 10, 2003
Juventus 7 (Trezeguet 14, 25, Miccoli 19, Maresca 28, Di Vaio 63, Del Piero 67, Zalayeta 79), **Olympiakos** 0. Att: 12,578.
Real Sociedad 1 (De Paula 50), **Galatasaray** 1 (Hakan Sukur 25). Att: 30,000.

FINAL TABLE

	P	W	D	L	F	A	Pts
JUVENTUS	6	4	1	1	15	6	13
REAL SOCIEDAD	6	2	3	1	8	8	9
Galatasaray	6	2	1	3	6	8	7
Olympiakos	6	1	1	4	6	13	4

GROUP E

September 16, 2003
Manchester Utd. 5 (Silvestre 13, Fortune 15, Solskjaer 33, Butt 40, Djemba Djemba 83), **Panathinaikos** 0. Att: 66,520.
Manchester Utd. (4-4-1-1): Howard, G. Neville, Ferdinand, Silvestre, O'Shea (Fletcher 57), Solskjaer (Bellion 46), Butt (Djemba Djemba 57), P. Neville, Fortune, Giggs, Van Nistelrooy.
Rangers 2 (Nerlinger 74, Lovenkrands 79), **Stuttgart** 1 (Kuranyi 45). Att: 47,957.
Rangers (4-4-2): Klos, Ricksen (Ross 33), Berg, Khizanishvili, Ball, Emerson (Capucho 63), Arteta, Nerlinger, Vanoli (Lovenkrands 46), Arveladze, Mols.

October 1, 2003
Panathinaikos 1 (Konstantinidis 87), **Rangers** 1 (Emerson 35). Att: 13,718.
Rangers (4-4-2): Klos, Khizanishvili, Moore, Berg, Ball, Capucho, Emerson, Arteta, Lovenkrands (Vanoli 76), Arveladze (Nerlinger 84), Mols.
Stuttgart 2 (Szabics 50, Kuranyi 52), **Manchester Utd.** 1 (Van Nistelrooy 67 pen). Att: 50,348.
Manchester Utd. (4-4-1-1): Howard, G. Neville, Ferdinand (Forlan 82), Silvestre, O'Shea (Fortune 65), Scholes, Keane, P. Neville, Ronaldo (Fletcher 90), Giggs, Van Nistelrooy.

October 22, 2003
Rangers 0, **Manchester Utd.** 1 (P. Neville 5). Att: 48,730.
Rangers (4-4-1-1): Klos, Khizanishvili (Ross 86), Berg, Moore, Ball, Lovenkrands, Ricksen, Arteta, Vanoli (Nerlinger 67), Arveladze, Mols.
Manchester Utd. (4-4-1-1): Howard, G. Neville, Ferdinand, Silvestre, O'Shea, P. Neville (Butt 86), Keane, Fortune (Djemba Djemba 90), Scholes, Giggs, Van Nistelrooy.
Stuttgart 2 (Szabics 12, Soldo 25), **Panathinaikos** 0. Att: 50,000

November 4, 2003
Manchester Utd. 3 (Forlan 6, Van Nistelrooy 44, 60), **Rangers** 0. Att: 66,707.
Manchester Utd. (4-4-2): Howard, G. Neville, Ferdinand, Silvestre, Fortune, Ronaldo, P. Neville, Keane, Giggs (Kleberson 67), Forlan (Bellion 67), Van Nistelrooy (Fletcher 77).
Rangers (4-2-3-1): Klos, Khizanishvili, Berg, Moore (Ross 67), Ball, Arteta, Hughes, Lovenkrands, Arveladze, Vanoli (Burke 83), Mols (Capucho 57).
Panathinaikos 1 (Konstantinou 59), **Stuttgart** 3 (Fissas 68 og, Kuranyi 74, Hinkel 76). Att: 6,015.

November 26, 2003
Panathinaikos 0, **Manchester Utd.** 1 (Forlan 85). Att: 6,890.
Manchester Utd. (4-5-1): Howard, O'Shea, Ferdinand, Silvestre, Fortune, Ronaldo, Fletcher (Bellion 75), Butt, Kleberson, Giggs, Forlan.
Stuttgart 1 (Wenzel 45), **Rangers** 0. Att: 50,348.
Rangers (4-4-2): Klos, Ross (Ostenstad 76), Berg, Khizanishvili, Ball, Ricksen, Vanoli (Mols 55), Capucho, Hughes, Lovenkrands, Arveladze.

December 9, 2003
Manchester Utd. 2 (Van Nistelrooy 45, Giggs 58), **Stuttgart** 0. Att: 67,141.

Manchester Utd. (4-4-1-1): Carroll, G. Neville, Ferdinand, Silvestre, O'Shea, Fletcher, P. Neville, Scholes (Djemba Djemba 79), Fortune, Giggs (Bellion 71), Van Nistelrooy (Forlan 71).
Rangers 1 (Mols 28), **Panathinaikos** 3 (Zutautas 32, Basinas 62, Konstantinou 80). Att: 48,588.
Rangers (4-4-2): Klos, Moss (Duffy 83), Berg, Khizanishvili (Vanoli 69), Ball, Burke (Ostenstad 69), Ricksen, Hughes, Lovenkrands, Capucho, Mols.

FINAL TABLE

	P	W	D	L	F	A	Pts
MANCHESTER UTD.	6	5	0	1	13	2	15
STUTTGART	6	4	0	2	9	6	12
Panathinaikos	6	1	1	4	5	13	4
Rangers	6	1	1	4	4	10	4

GROUP F

September 16, 2003
Partizan Belgrade 1 (Delibasic 54), **FC Porto** 1 (Costinha). Att: 32,000.
Real Madrid 4 (Roberto Carlos 29, Ronaldo 34, 56, Figo 61 pen). **Marseille** 2 (Drogba 25, Van Buyten 83). Att: 65,000.

October 1, 2003
FC Porto 1 (Costinha 7), **Real Madrid** 3 (Helguera 28, Solari 37, Zidane 67). Att: 37,506.
Marseille 3 (Drogba 62, 68, 85), **Partizan Belgrade** 0. Att: 58,000.

October 22, 2003
Marseille 2 (Drogba 24, Marlet 82), **FC Porto** 3 (Maniche 31, Derlei 36, Alenitchev 80). Att: 59,000.
Real Madrid 1 (Raul 38), **Partizan Belgrade** 0. Att: 48,000.

November 4, 2003
FC Porto 1 (Alenitchev 21), **Marseille** 0. Att: 33,215.
Partizan Belgrade 0, **Real Madrid** 0. Att: 32,700.

November 26, 2003
FC Porto 2 (McCarthy 25, 49), **Partizan Belgrade** 1 (Delibasic 90). Att: 22,177.
Marseille 1 (Mido 64), **Real Madrid** 2 (Beckham 35, Ronaldo 73). Att: 59,000.

December 9, 2003
Partizan Belgrade 1 (Delibasic 79), **Marseille** 1 (Mido 61). Att: 30,000.
Real Madrid 1 (Solari 9), **FC Porto** 1 (Derlei 34 pen). Att: 25,000.

FINAL TABLE

	P	W	D	L	F	A	Pts
REAL MADRID	6	4	2	0	11	5	14
FC PORTO	6	3	2	1	9	8	11
Marseille	6	1	1	4	9	11	4
Partizan Belgrade	6	0	3	3	3	8	3

GROUP G

September 16, 2003
Besiktas 0, **Lazio** 2 (Stam 37, Fiore 77). Att: 28,000.
Sparta Prague 0, **Chelsea** 1 (Gallas 85). Att: 18,997.
Chelsea (4-3-1-2): Cudicini, Johnson, Desailly, Gallas, Bridge, Geremi, Makelele, Petit (Lampard 46), Veron, Mutu (Duff 47), Crespo (Hasselbaink 72).

October 1, 2003
Chelsea 0, **Besiktas** 2 (Yalcin 25, 29). Att: 32,957.
Chelsea (3-1-4-2): Cudicini, Terry, Desailly, Gallas, Makelele, Geremi, Lampard, Veron, Babayaro (Bridge 23), Mutu (Duff 46), Crespo (Hasselbaink 46).
Lazio 2 (Inzaghi 46, 60 pen), **Sparta Prague** 2 (Sioko 27, Poborsky 35). Att: 30,000.

October 22, 2003
Chelsea 2 (Lampard 57, Mutu 65), **Lazio** (Inzaghi 39). Att: 40,405.
Chelsea (4-3-1-2): Cudicini, Johnson, Gallas, Terry, Bridge, Lampard, Makelele, Veron (Gronkjaer 64), Duff (Geremi 79), Mutu (Cole 87), Gudjohnsen.
Sparta Prague 2 (Zelenka 58, Poborsky 85), **Besiktas** 1 (Pancu 60 pen). Att: 14,512.

November 4, 2003
Besiktas 1 (Guiaro 82), **Sparta Prague** 0. Att: 25,000.
Lazio 0, **Chelsea** 4 (Crespo 15, Gudjohnsen 70, Duff 75, Lampard 80). Att: 48,500.
Chelsea (4-3-1-2): Cudicini, Johnson, Gallas, Terry, Bridge, Lampard, Makelele, Veron (Cole 74), Duff, Mutu (Gronkjaer 57), Crespo (Gudjohnsen 66). **Sent-off:** Johnson.

November 26, 2003
Chelsea 0, **Sparta Prague** 0. Att: 40,152.
Chelsea (4-1-3-2): Cudicini, Melchiot, Gallas, Terry, Bridge, Makelele, Lampard, Cole (Geremi 72), Duff, Crespo (Gudjohnsen 72), Mutu.
Lazio 1 (Muzzi 55), **Besiktas** 1 (Pancu 45 pen). Att: 49,000.

December 9, 2003
Besiktas 0, **Chelsea** 2 (Hasselbaink 77, Bridge 88). Att: 55,350 (played in Gelsen-kirchen).
Chelsea (3-4-1-2): Cudicini, Gallas, Desailly, Terry, Johnson, Lampard, Makelele, Babayaro (Bridge 83), Geremi, Gronkjaer (Duff 72), Hasselbaink.
Sparta Prague 1 (Kincl 90), **Lazio** 0. Att: 12,000.

FINAL TABLE

	P	W	D	L	F	A	Pts
CHELSEA	6	4	1	1	9	3	13
SPARTA PRAGUE	6	2	2	2	5	5	8
Besiktas	6	2	1	3	5	7	7
Lazio	6	1	2	3	6	10	5

GROUP H

September 16, 2003
AC Milan 1 (Inzaghi 66), **Ajax** 0. Att: 48,000.
Bruges 1 (Saeternes 83), **Celta Vigo** 1 (Juanfran 50). Att: 25,000.

October 1, 2003
Ajax 2 (Sonck 11, 54), **Bruges** 0. Att: 49,371.
Celta Vigo 0, **AC Milan** 0. Att: 28,000.

October 22, 2003
AC Milan 0, **Bruges** 1 (Mendoza 33). Att: 43,823.
Ajax 1 (Ibrahimovic 53), **Celta Vigo** 0.

November 4, 2003
Celta Vigo 3 (Luccin 25 pen, Milosevic 38, Vagner 62), **Ajax** 2 (Sonck 53, Van der Vaart 81). Att: 20,000.
Bruges 0, **AC Milan** 1 (Kaka 85). Att: 28,000.

November 26, 2003
Ajax 0, **AC Milan** 1 (Shevchenko 51). Att: 50,210.
Celta Vigo 1 (Mostovoi 73), **Bruges** 1 (Lange 90). Att: 22,000.

December 9, 2003
AC Milan 1 (Kaka 41), **Celta Vigo** 2 (Jesuli 42, Jose Ignacio 71). Att: 36,207.
Bruges 2 (Lange 27, Saeternes 83), **Ajax** 1 (Sonck 41 pen). Att: 28,041.

FINAL TABLE

	P	W	D	L	F	A	Pts
AC MILAN	6	3	1	2	4	3	10
CELTA VIGO	6	2	3	1	7	6	9
Bruges	6	2	2	2	5	6	8
Ajax	6	2	0	4	6	7	6

FIRST KNOCKOUT ROUND

FIRST LEG

February 24, 2004
Bayern Munich 1 (Makaay 75), **Real Madrid** 1 (Roberto Carlos 83). Att: 59,000.
Celta Vigo 2 (Luis Edu 27, Jose Ignacio 64), **Arsenal** 3 (Edu 18, 58, Pires 80). Att: 21,000.
Arsenal (4-4-2): Lehmann, Lauren, Toure, Campbell, Clichy (Cygan 90), Ljungberg (Bentley 90), Vieira, Edu, Pires, Henry, Reyes (Kanu 78).
Lokomotiv Moscow 2 (Izmailov 32, Maminov 59), **Monaco** 1 (Morientes 69). Att: 28,000.
Sparta Prague 0, **AC Milan** 0. Att: 20,640.

February 25, 2004
Deportivo La Coruna 1 (Luque 36), **Juventus** 0. Att: 28,000.
FC Porto 2 (McCarthy 29, 78), **Manchester Utd.** 1 (Fortune 14). Att: 49,977.
Manchester Utd. (4-4-2): Howard, P. Neville (O'Shea 70), G. Neville, Brown, Fortune, Scholes, Keane, Butt, Giggs, Van Nistelrooy, Saha (Ronaldo 76). **Sent-off:** Keane.
Real Sociedad 0, **Lyon** 1 (Schurrer 18 og). Att: 29,000.
Stuttgart 0, **Chelsea** 1 (Meira 12 og). Att: 50,000.
Chelsea (4-4-2): Cudicini, Johnson, Gallas, Terry, Bridge, Geremi, Makelele, Lampard, Gronkjaer (Duff 66), Gudjohnsen (Hasselbaink 76), Crespo (Cole 88).

SECOND LEG

March 9, 2004
Chelsea 0, **Stuttgart** 0. Att: 36,657 (**Chelsea** won 1-0 on agg).
Chelsea (4-5-1): Cudicini, Johnson (Desailly 30), Gallas, Terry, Bridge, Gronkjaer, Makelele, Lampard, Parker (Geremi 61), Duff (Mutu 82), Crespo.

Juventus 0, **Deportivo La Coruna** 1 (Pandiani 12). Att: 24,680 (**Deportivo La Coruna** won 2-0 on agg).
Lyon 1 (Juninho 77), **Real Sociedad** 0. Att: 38,914 (**Lyon** won 2-0 on agg).
Manchester Utd. 1 (Scholes 32), **FC Porto** 1 (Costinha 90). Att: 67,029 (**FC Porto** won 3-2 on agg).
Manchester Utd. (4-2-3-1): Howard, P. Neville, Brown, G. Neville, O'Shea, Djemba Djemba (Saha 46), Butt, Fletcher (Ronaldo 74, Solskjaer 82), Scholes, Giggs, Van Nistelrooy.

March 10, 2004
AC Milan 4 (Inzaghi 45, Shevchenko 67, 79, Gattuso 85), **Sparta Prague** 1 (Jun 59). Att: 50,000 (**AC Milan** won 4-1 on agg).
Arsenal 2 (Henry 14, 34), **Celta Vigo** 0. Att: 35,402 (**Arsenal** won 5-2 on agg).
Arsenal (4-4-2): Lehmann, Lauren, Toure, Campbell, Cole, Ljungberg, Vieira, Edu (Gilberto Silva 70), Pires (Reyes 70), Bergkamp (Kanu 77), Henry.
Monaco 1 (Prso 60), **Lokomotiv Moscow** 0. Att: 16,500 (agg 2-2, **Monaco** won on away goals).
Real Madrid 1 (Zidane 32), **Bayern Munich** 0. Att: 78,000 (**Real Madrid** won 2-1 on agg).

QUARTER-FINALS

FIRST LEG

March 23, 2004
AC Milan 4 (Kaka 45, 49, Shevchenko 46, Pirlo 53), **Deportivo La Coruna** 1 (Pandiani 11). Att: 60,335.
FC Porto 2 (Deco 44, Carvalho 71), **Lyon** 0. Att: 46,910.

March 24, 2004
Chelsea 1 (Gudjohnsen 53), **Arsenal** 1 (Pires 59). Att: 40,778.
Chelsea (4-4-2): Ambrosio, Gallas, Terry, Desailly, Bridge, Parker (J. Cole 72), Lampard, Makelele, Duff, Gudjohnsen (Melchiot 86), Mutu (Crespo 72). **Sent-off:** Desailly.
Arsenal (4-4-2): Lehmann, Lauren, Campbell, Toure, A. Cole, Ljungberg (Reyes 78), Vieira, Edu, Pires, Bergkamp (Gilberto Silva 72), Henry.
Real Madrid 4 (Pavon 51, Zidane 69, Figo 76, Ronaldo 81), **Monaco** 2 (Squillaci 43, Morientes 83). Att: 70,000.

SECOND LEG

April 6, 2004
Arsenal 1 (Reyes 45), **Chelsea** 2 (Lampard 51, Bridge 87). Att: 35,486 (**Chelsea** won 3-2 on agg).
Arsenal (4-4-2): Lehmann, Lauren, Toure, Campbell, A. Cole, Ljungberg, Vieira, Edu, Pires, Reyes, Henry (Bergkamp 81).
Chelsea (4-4-2): Ambrosio, Melchiot, Gallas, Terry, Bridge, Parker (Gronkjaer 46), Lampard, Makelele, Duff (J. Cole 83), Hasselbaink (Crespo 83), Gudjohnsen.
Monaco 3 (Giuly 45, 66, Morientes 48), **Real Madrid** 1 (Raul 35). Att: 18,000 (agg 5-5, **Monaco** won on away goals).

April 7, 2004
Deportivo La Coruna 4 (Pandiani 5, Valeron 34, Luque 44, Fran 76 pen), **AC Milan** 0. Att: 29,000 (**Deportivo La Coruna** won 5-4 on agg),
Lyon 2 (Luyindula 14, Elber 89), **FC Porto** 2 (Maniche 6, 46). Att: 40,000 (**FC Porto** won 4-2 on agg).

SEMI-FINALS

FIRST LEG

April 20, 2004
Monaco 3 (Prso 17, Morientes 78, Nonda 83), **Chelsea** 1 (Crespo 22). Att: 15,000.
Chelsea (4-4-2): Ambrosio, Melchiot (Hasselbaink 61), Desailly, Terry, Bridge, Parker (Huth 68), Makelele, Lampard, Gronkjaer (Veron 46), Gudjohnsen, Crespo.

April 21, 2004
FC Porto 0, **Deportivo La Coruna** 0. Att: 50,818.

SECOND LEG

May 4, 2004
Deportivo La Coruna 0, **FC Porto** 1 (Derlei 60 pen). Att: 34,600 (**FC Porto** won 1-0 on agg).

May 5, 2004
Chelsea 2 (Gronkjaer 22, Lampard 44), **Monaco** 2 (Ibarra 45, Morientes 60). Att: 37,132 (**Monaco** won 5-3 on agg).
Chelsea (4-1-3-2): Cudicini (Johnson 64), Melchiot, Gallas, Terry, Bridge, Geremi (Parker 69), Gronkjaer, Lampard, Cole, Hasselbaink (Crespo 69), Gudjohnsen.

EUROPEAN CUP FINAL

FC PORTO 3, MONACO 0

Gelsenkirchen, (52,000), Wednesday, May 26, 2004

FC Porto (4-3-1-2): Vitor Baia, Paulo Ferreira, Jorge Costa (capt), Ricardo Carvalho, Nuno Valente, Mendes, Costinha, Maniche, Deco (Pedro Emanuel 85), Carlos Alberto (Alenichev 60), Derlei (McCarthy 78). **Subs not used:** Nuno, Ricardo Costa, Jankauskas, Bosingwa. **Scorers:** Carlos Alberto (39), Deco (71), Alenichev (75). **Booked:** Nuno Valente, Carlos Alberto, Jorge Costa. **Coach:** Jose Mourinho.

Monaco (4-1-3-2): Roma, Ibarra, Givet (Squillaci 73), Rodriguez, Evra, Zikos, Cisse (Nonda 64), Bernardi, Rothen, Giuly (capt) (Prso 23), Morientes. **Subs not used:** Sylva, Plasil, Adebayor, El-Fakiri. **Booked:** Bernardi. **Coach:** Didier Deschamps

Referee: K.Milton Nielsen (Denmark). **Half-time:** 1-0.

Leading scorers: 9 Morientes (Monaco); 7 Prso (Monaco); 6 Makaay (Bayern Munich), Pandiani (Deportivo La Coruna); 5 Drogba (Marseille), Hakan Sukur (Galatasaray), Henry (Arsenal), Juninho (Lyon); 4 Giuly (Monaco), Kaka (AC Milan), Lampard (Chelsea), Luque (Deportivo La Coruna), McCarthy (FC Porto), Pires (Arsenal), Ronaldo (Real Madrid), Shevchenko (AC Milan), Sonck (Ajax), Trezeguet (Juventus), Van Nistelrooy (Manchester Utd.).

EUROPEAN CUP FINALS

| 1956 | Real Madrid 4, Rheims 3 (Paris) |
| 1957 | Real Madrid 2, Fiorentina 0 (Madrid) |

1958†	Real Madrid 3, AC Milan 2 (Brussels)
1959	Real Madrid 2, Rheims 0 (Stuttgart)
1960	Real Madrid 7, Eintracht Frankfurt 3 (Glasgow)
1961	Benfica 3, Barcelona 2 (Berne)
1962	Benfica 5, Real Madrid 3 (Amsterdam)
1963	AC Milan 2, Benfica 1 (Wembley)
1964	Inter Milan 3, Real Madrid 1 (Vienna)
1965	Inter Milan 1, Benfica 0 (Milan)
1966	Real Madrid 2, Partizan Belgrade 1 (Brussels)
1967	Celtic 2, Inter Milan 1 (Lisbon)
1968†	Manchester Utd. 4, Benfica 1 (Wembley)
1969	AC Milan 4, Ajax 1 (Madrid)
1970†	Feyenoord 2, Celtic 1 (Milan)
1971	Ajax 2, Panathinaikos 0 (Wembley)
1972	Ajax 2, Inter Milan 0 (Rotterdam)
1973	Ajax 1, Juventus 0 (Belgrade)
1974	Bayern Munich 4, Atletico Madrid 0 (replay Brussels, after a 1-1 draw, Brussels)
1975	Bayern Munich 2, Leeds Utd. 0 (Paris)
1976	Bayern Munich 1, St. Etienne 0 (Glasgow)
1977	Liverpool 3, Borussia Moenchengladbach 1 (Rome)
1978	Liverpool 1, Brugge 0 (Wembley)
1979	Nott'm. Forest 1, Malmo 0 (Munich)
1980	Nott'm. Forest 1, Hamburg 0 (Madrid)
1981	Liverpool 1, Real Madrid 0 (Paris)
1982	Aston Villa 1, Bayern Munich 0 (Rotterdam)
1983	SV Hamburg 1, Juventus 0 (Athens)
1984†	Liverpool 1, AS Roma 1 (Liverpool won 4-2 on penalties) (Rome)
1985	Juventus 1, Liverpool 0 (Brussels)
1986†	Steaua Bucharest 0, Barcelona 0 (Steaua won 2-0 on penalties) (Seville)
1987	Porto 2, Bayern Munich 1 (Vienna)
1988†	PSV Eindhoven 0, Benfica 0 (PSV won 6-5 on penalties) (Stuttgart)
1989	AC Milan 4, Steaua Bucharest 0 (Barcelona)
1990	AC Milan 1, Benfica 0 (Vienna)
1991†	Red Star Belgrade 0, Marseille 0 (Red Star won 5-3 on penalties) (Bari)
1992	Barcelona 1, Sampdoria 0 (Wembley)
1993	Marseille 1, AC Milan 0 (Munich)
1994	AC Milan 4, Barcelona 0 (Athens)
1995	Ajax 1, AC Milan 0 (Vienna)
1996†	Juventus 1, Ajax 1 (Juventus won 4-2 on penalties) (Rome)
1997	Borussia Dortmund 3, Juventus 1 (Munich)
1998	Real Madrid 1, Juventus 0 (Amsterdam)
1999	Manchester Utd. 2, Bayern Munich 1 (Barcelona)
2000	Real Madrid 3, Valencia 0 (Paris)
2001	Bayern Munich 1, Valencia 1 (Bayern Munich won 5-4 on penalties) (Milan)
2002	Real Madrid 2, Bayer Leverkusen 1, (Glasgow)
2003†	AC Milan 0, Juventus 0 (AC Milan won 3-2 on penalties) (Manchester)
2004	FC Porto 3, Monaco 0 (Gelsenkirchen)

(† After extra time)

UEFA CUP 2003-04

PRE-TOURNAMENT INTERTOTO CUP (SELECTED RESULTS)

FIRST ROUND

Gloria Bistrita 6, **Bangor City** 2 (5-2h, 1-0a); Shakhtyor Soligorsk 8, **Omagh Town** 1 (1-0h, 7-1a); **Shamrock Rov.** 3, Odra Wodzislaw 1 (1-0h, 2-1a).

SECOND ROUND

Liberec 4, **Shamrock Rov.** 0 (2-0h, 2-0a).

FINALS

Perugia 3, Wolfsburg 0 (1-0h, 2-0a); Schalke 2, Superfund 0 (0-0h, 2-0a); Villarreal 2, Heerenveen 1 (0-0h, 2-1a).

QUALIFYING ROUND, FIRST LEG

Apoel Nicosia 2 (Kowiczyk 21, Okkarides 54), **Derry City** 1 (Beckett 43). Att: 9,000. **Coleraine** 2 (Gaston 9, Hammill 45), Uniao Leiria 1 (Manuel 42). Att: 1,700. **Cwmbran** 0, Maccabi Haifa 3 (Tal 9, Zanberg 29, Lopez 89). Att: 1,052. Malmo 4 (Mattisson 23, Yngvesson 29, 57, Skoog 78), **Portadown** 0. Att: 5,941. **Manchester City** 5 (Sinclair 14, Wright-Phillips 51, Sun Jihai 60, Sommeil 74, Anelka 87), **TNS** 0. Att: 34,103. Vega Olimpija 1 (Jusufbegovic 73), **Shelbourne** 0. Att: 2,000. Vllaznia Shkoder, **Dundee** 2 (Lovell 44, Novo 50). Att: 10,000.

QUALIFYING ROUND, SECOND LEG

Derry City 0, Apoel Nicosia 3 (Malekos 36, Charalambides 80, Papandreou 90). Att: 2,200 (Apoel Nicosia won 5-1 on agg). **Dundee** 4 (Novo 2, 89, Sara 40, Rae 50), Vllaznia Shkoder 0. Att: 8,254 (**Dundee** won 6-0 on agg). Maccabi Haifa 3 (Katan 36, Rosso 45, Zanberg 61), **Cwmbran** 0. Att: 3,000 (Maccabi Haifa won 6-0 on agg). **Portadown** 0, Malmo 2 (Ijeh 60, 62). Att: 3,000 (Malmo won 6-0 on agg). **Shelbourne** 2 (Cahill 14, J. Byrne 90), Vega Olimpija 3 (Jusufbegovic 9, Zlogar 45, Kmetec 56). Att: 3,500 (Vega Olimpija won 4-2 on agg). **TNS** 0, **Manchester City** 2 (Negouai 43, Huckerby 81). Att: 10,123 (**Manchester City** won 7-0 on agg). Uniao Leiria 5 (Ludemar 58, 79, Edson 73, 76, Caico 90), **Coleraine** 0. Att: 4,000 (Uniao Leiria won 6-2 on agg).

QUALIFYING ROUND (ON AGGREGATE)

AIK Athens 1, Fylkir 0; Artmedia Petrzalka 2, Dudelange 0; Brondby 5, Dinamo Minsk 0; Cementamic 1, Dospel Katowice 1 (Cementamica won on away goal); Crvena Zvezda 8, Nistru Otaci 2; Dinamo Bucharest 6, Metalurgs 3; Dnipro 2, Vaduz 0; Esbjerg 9, Santa Coloma 1; Ferencvaros 6, Birkirkara 0; Groclin Dyskobolia 6, Atlantas 1; Hajduk Split 2, Haka 2 (Hajduk Split won on away goals); Hapoel Tel Aviv 3, Banants 2; Kamen Ingrad 9, Etzella Ettelbruck 1; Karnten 3, Grindavik 2; Lens 5, Torpedo Kutaisi 0; Levski Sofia 6, Atyrau 1; Lokeren 7, Dinamo Tirana 1; Lyn Oslo 9, Runavik 1; Molde 6, Klaksvik 0; MyPa 5, Young Boys 4; Neuchatel Xamax 4, Valletta 1; Nordsjaelland 6, Shirak 0; Odense 4, Tallinn 1; Publikum 12, Belasica 2; Puchov 6, Sioni Bolnisi 0; Sartid 4, Sarajevo 1; Steaua Bucharest 1, Neman-Belcard 1 (Steaua Bucharest won on away goal); Torpedo Moscow 9, Domagnano 0; Varteks 6, Levadia Maardu 3; Ventspils 3, Wisla Plock 3 (Ventspils won on away goals); Viktoria Zizkov 6, Zhenis Astana 1; Zeljeznicar 4, Anorthosis Famagusta 1; Zimbru 2, Liteks Lovech 0;

FIRST ROUND, FIRST LEG

Dundee 1 (Novo 64), Perugia 2 (Di Loreto 50, Fusani 84). Att: 9,911. Genclerbirligi 3 (Skoko 42, Youla 43, 60), **Blackburn Rov.** 1 (Emerton 57). Att: 18,000. **Hearts** 2 (De Vries 28, Webster 60), Zeljeznicar 0. Att: 15,830. **Manchester City** 3 (Sibierski 8, Fowler 77, Anelka 80 pen), Lokeren 2 (Zoundi 14, Kristinsson 40). Att: 29,067. **Newcastle Utd.** 5 (Bellamy 31, 37, Bramble 59, Shearer 77, Ambrose 89), Breda 0. Att: 36,007. Olimpija 1 (Zlogar 66), **Liverpool** 1 (Owen 78). Att: 10,000. **Southampton** 1 (Phillips 52), Steaua Bucharest 1 (Raducanu 20).

FIRST ROUND, SECOND LEG

Blackburn Rov. 1 (Jansen 65), Genclerbirligi 1 (Ozkan 66). Att: 14,573 (Genclerbirligi won 4-2 on agg). **Liverpool** 3 (Le Tallec 30, Heskey 37, Kewell 47), Olimpija 0. Att: 42,880 (**Liverpool** won 4-1 on agg). Lokeren 0, **Manchester City** 1 (Anelka 19 pen). Att: 10,000 (**Manchester City** won 4-2 on agg). Breda 0, **Newcastle Utd.** 1 (Robert 86). Att: 15,564 (**Newcastle Utd.** won 6-0 on agg). Perugia 1 (Margiotta 71), **Dundee** 0 (Perugia won 3-1 on agg). Steaua Bucharest 1 (Raducanu 82), **Southampton** 0. Att: 29,000 (Steaua Bucharest won 2-1 on agg). Zeljeznicar 0, **Hearts** 0. Att: 20,000 (**Hearts** won 2-0 on agg).

FIRST ROUND (ON AGGREGATE)

Aris Salonika 3, Zimbru 2; Auxerre 2, Neuchatel Xamax 0; Barcelona 9, Puchov 1; Basle 3, Malatyaspor 2; Benfica 2, La Louviere 1; Bordeaux 3, Artmedia Petrzalka 2; Brondby 2, Viktoria Zizkov 0; Borussia Dortmund 3, Austria Vienna 1; Crvena Zvezda 6, Odense 5; Debrecen 6, Varteks 3; Dinamo Bucharest 5 Shakhtar Donetsk 2; Dnipro 4, Hamburg 2; Dinamo Zagreb 3, Hungaria 1; FC Copenhagen 2, Ferencvaros 2 (FC Copenhagen won 3-2 on pens); Feyenoord 3, Karnten 1; Gaziantepspor 1, Hapoel Tel Aviv 0; Groclin Dyskobolia 1, Hertha Berlin 0; Hajduk Split 1, Grasshoppers 1 (Hajduk Split won on away goal); Lens 6, Cementarnica 0; Levski Sofia 5, Ramat 0; Maccabi Haifa 4, Publikum 3; Mallorca 6, Apoel Nicosia 3; Molde 3, Uniao Leiria 2; Panionios 3, Nordsjaelland 1; Parma 4, Metalurg Donetsk 1; Roma 5, Vardar 1; PAOK Salonika 3, Lyn Oslo 1; Rosenborg 10, Ventspils 1; Salzburg 2, Udinese 2 (Salzburg won on away goals); Schalke 1, Kamen Ingrad 0; Slavia Prague 4, Sartid 2; Sochaux 3 MyPa 0; Spartak Moscow 3, Esbjerg 1; Sporting Lisbon 3, Malmo 0; Teplice 3, Kaiserslautern 1; Torpedo Moscow 2, CSKA Sofia 2 (Torpedo Moscow won 3-2 on pens); Utrecht 6, Zilina 0; Valencia 2, AIK Athens 0; Valerenga 1, Graz 1 (Valerenga won on away goal); Villareal 3, Trabzonspor 2; Wisla Krakow 4, Nijmegen 2.

SECOND ROUND, FIRST LEG

Basle 2 (Cantaluppi 11, Chipperfield 15), **Newcastle Utd.** 3 (Robert 14, Bramble 37, Ameobi 75). Att: 30,000. Bordeaux 0, **Hearts** 1 (De Vries 78). Att: 15,536. **Manchester City** 1 (Anelka 6), Groclin Dyskobolia 1 (Mila 65). Att: 32,056. Steaua Bucharest 1 (Raducanu 69), **Liverpool** 1 (Traore 23). Att: 25,000.

SECOND ROUND, SECOND LEG

Groclin Dyskobolia 0, **Manchester City** 0. Att: 5,500 (Groclin Dyskobolia won on away goal). **Hearts** 0, Bordeaux 2 (Riera 8, Feindouno 66). Att: 17,587 (Bordeaux won 2-1 on agg). **Liverpool** 1 (Kewell 49), Steaua Bucharest 0. Att: 42,837 (**Liverpool** won 2-1 on agg). **Newcastle Utd.** 1 (Smiljanic 14 og), Basle 0. Att: 40,395 (**Newcastle Utd.** won 4-2 on agg)

SECOND ROUND (ON AGGREGATE)

Auxerre 4, Utrecht 0; Barcelona 5, Panionios 0; Benfica 5, Molde 1; Brondby 3, Schalke 3 (Brondby won 3-1 on pens); Debrecen 1, PAOK Salonika 1 (Debrecen won on away goal); Dnipro 3, Dinamo Zagreb 1; Gaziantepspor 6, Lens 1; Genclerbirligi 4,

Sporting Lisbon 1; Levski Sofia 2, Slavia Prague 2 (Levski Sofia won on away goals); Mallorca 3, FC Copenhagen 2; Parma 9, Salzburg 0; Perugia 3, Aris Salonika 1; Rosenborg 1, Crvena Zvezda 0; Roma 2, Hajduk Split 1; Sochaux 6, Borussia Dortmund 2; Spartak Moscow 5, Dinamo Bucharest 3; Teplice 3, Feyenoord 1; Valerenga 0, Wisla Krakow 0 (Valerenga won 4-3 on pens); Valencia 4, Maccabi Haifa 0; Villarreal 2, Torpedo Moscow 1;

THIRD ROUND, FIRST LEG

Celtic 3 (Larsson 3, 90, Sutton 12), Teplice 0. Att: 48,947. **Liverpool** 2 (Gerrard 67, Kewell 70), Levski Sofia 0. Att: 39,149. Valerenga 1 (Normann 54), **Newcastle Utd.** 1 (Bellamy 39). Att: 17,039.

THIRD ROUND, SECOND LEG

Levski Sofia 2 (Ivanov 27, Simonovic 40), **Liverpool** 4 (Gerrard 7, Owen 11, Hamann 44, Hyypia 67). Att: 40,281 (**Liverpool** won 6-2 on agg). **Newcastle Utd.** 3 (Shearer 19, Ameobi 47, 89), Valerenga 1 (Hagen 25). Att: 38,531 (**Newcastle Utd.** won 4-2 on agg). Teplice 1 (Masek 35), **Celtic** 0. Att: 10,000 (**Celtic** won 3-1 on agg).

THIRD ROUND (ON AGGREGATE)

Auxerre 1, Panathinaikos 0; Barcelona 3, Brondby 1; Benfica 2, Rosenborg 2 (Benfica won on away goals); Bordeaux 5, Groclin Dyskobolia 1; Bruges 1, Debrecen 0; Genclerbirligi 4, Parma 0; Inter Milan 2, Sochaux 2 (Inter Milan won on away goals); Mallorca 3, Spartak Moscow 1; Marseille 1, Dnipro 0; PSV Eindhoven 3, Perugia 1; Roma 2, Gaziantepspor 1; Valencia 5, Besiktas 2; Villarreal 5, Galatasaray 2;

FOURTH ROUND, FIRST LEG

Celtic 1 (Thompson 59), Barcelona 0. Att: 59,539. **Liverpool** 1 (Baros 55), Marseille 1 (Drogba 78). Att: 41,270. **Newcastle Utd.** 4 (Bellamy 67, Shearer 71, Robert 74, Bramble 84), Mallorca 1 (Correa 57). Att: 38.012.

FOURTH ROUND, SECOND LEG

Barcelona 0, **Celtic** 1. Att: 78,000 (**Celtic** won 1-0 on agg). Mallorca 0, **Newcastle Utd.** 3 (Shearer 46, 89, Bellamy 78). Att: 11,500 (**Newcastle Utd.** won 7-1 on agg). Marseille 2 (Drogba 38 pen, Meite 58), **Liverpool** 1 (Heskey 15). Att: 50,000 (Marseille won 3-2 on agg)

FOURTH ROUND (ON AGGREGATE)

Bordeaux 4, Bruges 1; Inter Milan 4, Benfica 3; PSV Eindhoven 4, Auxerre 1; Villarreal 3, Roma 2; Valencia 2, Genclerbirligi 0.

QUARTER-FINALS, FIRST LEG

Bordeaux 1 (Riera 18), Valencia 2 (Baraja 75, Rufete 87). Att: 29,108. **Celtic** 1 (Larsson 64), Villarreal 1 (Josico 9). Att: 58,493. Marseille 1 (Drogba 47), Inter Milan 0. Att: 57,000. PSV Eindhoven 1 (Kezman 15), **Newcastle Utd.** 1 (Jenas 45). Att: 35,000.

QUARTER-FINALS, SECOND LEG

Inter Milan 0, Marseille 1 (Meriem 73). Att: 36,044 (Marseille won 2-0 on agg). **Newcastle Utd.** 2 (Shearer 9, Speed 66), PSV Eindhoven 1 (Kezman 52 pen). Att: 50,083 (**Newcastle Utd.** won 3-2 on agg). Valencia 2 (Pellegrino 51, Rufete 60), Bordeaux 1 (Costa 71). Att: 35,000 (Valencia won 4-2 on agg). Villarreal 2 (Anderson 6, Roger 68), **Celtic** 0. Att: 23,000 (Villarreal won 3-1 on agg).

SEMI-FINALS, FIRST LEG

Newcastle Utd. 0, Marseille 0. Att: 52,004. Villarreal 0, Valencia 0. Att: 23,000.

SEMI-FINALS, SECOND LEG

Marseille 2 (Drogba 18, 82), **Newcastle Utd.** 0 Att: 52,000 (Marseille won 2-0 on agg).
Valencia 1 (Mista 16 pen), Villarreal 0. Att: 55,000 (Valencia won 1-0 on agg).

UEFA CUP FINAL

MARSEILLE 0, VALENCIA 2

Gothenburg, (43,000), Wednesday, May 19, 2004

Marseille (5-2-2-1): Barthez, Ferreira, Beye, Hemdani (capt), Meite, Dos Santos, Flamini (Batlles 71), N'Diaye (Celestini 84), Marlet, Meriem (Gavanon 45), Drogba. **Subs not used:** Christanval, Vachousek, Ecker, Cicut. **Booked:** Marlet, Drogba. **Sent-off:** Barthez (44). **Coach:** Jose Anigo.

Valencia (4-4-2): Canizares, Curro Torres, Ayala, Marchena (Pellegrino 86), Carboni, Rufete (Aimar 64), Albelda (capt), Baraja, Vicente, Angulo (Sissoko 83), Mista. **Subs not used:** Rangel, Sanchez, Garrido, Xisco. **Scorers:** Vicente (45 pen), Mista (47). **Booked:** Vicente, Carboni. **Coach:** Rafael Benitez.

Leading scorers: 6 Anderson (Villarreal), Drogba (Marseille), Kezman (PSV Eindhoven), Shearer (Newcastle Utd.); **5** Bellamy (Newcastle Utd.), Mista (Valencia), Riera (Bordeaux); **4** Brattbakk (Rosenborg), Cassano (Roma), Chamakh (Bordeaux), Eto'o (Mallorca), Frankowski (Wisla Krakow), Frau (Sochaux), Margiotta (Perugia), Riquelme (Villarreal), Ronaldinho (Barcelona), Venhlinskyy (Dnipo).

UEFA CUP FINALS

1972	Tottenham beat Wolves 3-2 on agg. (2-1a, 1-1h)
1973	Liverpool beat Borussia Moenchengladbach 3-2 on agg. (3-0h, 0-2a)
1974	Feyenoord beat Tottenham 4-2 on agg. (2-2a, 2-0h)
1975	Borussia Moenchengladbach beat Twente Enschede 5-1 on agg. (0-0h, 5-1a)
1976	Liverpool beat Brugge 4-3 on agg. (3-2h, 1-1a)
1977	Juventus beat Atletico Bilbao on away goals after 2-2 agg. (1-0h, 1-2a)
1978	PSV Eindhoven beat Bastia 3-0 on agg. (0-0a, 3-0h)
1979	Borussia Moenchengladbach beat Red Star Belgrade 2-1 on agg. (1-1a, 1-0h)
1980	Eintracht Frankfurt beat Borussia Moenchengladbach on away goals after 3-3 agg. (2-3a, 1-0h)
1981	Ipswich Town beat AZ 67 Alkmaar 5-4 on agg. (3-0h, 2-4a)
1982	IFK Gothenburg beat SV Hamburg 4-0 on agg. (1-0h, 3-0a)
1983	Anderlecht beat Benfica 2-1 on agg. (1-0h, 1-1a)
1984	Tottenham beat Anderlecht 4-3 on penalties after 2-2 agg. (1-1a, 1-1h)
1985	Real Madrid beat Videoton 3-1 on agg. (3-0a, 0-1h)
1986	Real Madrid beat Cologne 5-3 on agg. (5-1h, 0-2a)
1987	IFK Gothenburg beat Dundee Utd. 2-1 on agg. (1-0h, 1-1a)
1988	Bayer Leverkusen beat Espanol 3-2 on penalties after 3-3 agg. (0-3a, 3-0h)
1989	Napoli beat VfB Stuttgart 5-4 on agg. (2-1h, 3-3a)
1990	Juventus beat Fiorentina 3-1 on agg. (3-1h, 0-0a)

1991	Inter Milan beat AS Roma 2-1 on agg. (2-0h, 0-1a)
1992	Ajax beat Torino on away goals after 2-2 agg. (2-2a, 0-0h)
1993	Juventus beat Borussia Dortmund 6-1 on agg. (3-1a, 3-0h)
1994	Inter Milan beat Salzburg 2-0 on agg. (1-0a, 1-0h)
1995	Parma beat Juventus 2-1 on agg. (1-0h, 1-1a)
1996	Bayern Munich beat Bordeaux 5-1 on agg. (2-0h, 3-1a)
1997	FC Schalke beat Inter Milan 4-1 on penalties after 1-1 agg. (1-0h, 0-1a)
1998	Inter Milan beat Lazio 3-0 (one match) – Paris
1999	Parma beat Marseille 3-0 (one match) – Moscow
2000	Galatasaray beat Arsenal 4-1 on penalties after 0-0 (one match) – Copenhagen
2001	Liverpool beat Alvaves 5-4 on golden goal (one match) – Dortmund
2002	Feyenoord beat Borussia Dortmund 3-2 (one match) – Rotterdam
2003	FC Porto beat Celtic 3-2 on silver goal (one match) – Seville
2004	Valencia beat Marseille 2-0 (one match) – Gothenburg

FAIRS CUP FINALS

(As UEFA Cup previously known)

1958	Barcelona beat London 8-2 on agg. (2-2a, 6-0h)
1960	Barcelona beat Birmingham 4-1 on agg. (0-0a, 4-1h)
1961	AS Roma beat Birmingham City 4-2 on agg. (2-2a, 2-0h)
1962	Valencia beat Barcelona 7-3 on agg. (6-2h, 1-1a)
1963	Valencia beat Dynamo Zagreb 4-1 on agg. (2-1a, 2-0h)
1964	Real Zaragoza beat Valencia 2-1 (Barcelona)
1965	Ferencvaros beat Juventus 1-0 (Turin)
1966	Barcelona beat Real Zaragoza 4-3 on agg. (0-1h, 4-2a)
1967	Dynamo Zagreb beat Leeds Utd. 2-0 on agg. (2-0h, 0-0a)
1968	Leeds Utd. beat Ferencvaros 1-0 on agg. (1-0h, 0-0a)
1969	Newcastle Utd. beat Ujpest Dozsa 6-2 on agg. (3-0h, 3-2a)
1970	Arsenal beat Anderlecht 4-3 on agg. (1-3a, 3-0h)
1971	Leeds Utd. beat Juventus on away goals after 3-3 agg. (2-2a, 1-1h)

CUP-WINNERS' CUP FINALS

1961	Fiorentina beat Rangers 4-1 on agg. (2-0 Glasgow first leg, 2-1 Florence second leg)
1962	Atletico Madrid beat Fiorentina 3-0 (replay Stuttgart, after a 1-1 draw, Glasgow)
1963	Tottenham beat Atletico Madrid 5-1 (Rotterdam)
1964	Sporting Lisbon beat MTK Budapest 1-0 (replay Antwerp, after a 3-3 draw, Brussels)
1965	West Ham Utd. beat Munich 1860 2-0 (Wembley)
1966†	Borussia Dortmund beat Liverpool 2-1 (Glasgow)
1967†	Bayern Munich beat Rangers 1-0 (Nuremberg)
1968	AC Milan beat SV Hamburg 2-0 (Rotterdam)
1969	Slovan Bratislava beat Barcelona 3-2 (Basle)
1970	Manchester City beat Gornik Zabrze 2-1 (Vienna)
1971†	Chelsea beat Real Madrid 2-1 (replay Athens, after a 1-1 draw, Athens)
1972	Rangers beat Moscow Dynamo 3-2 (Barcelona)
1973	AC Milan beat Leeds Utd. 1-0 (Salonika)
1974	Magdeburg beat AC Milan 2-0 (Rotterdam)

1975	Dynamo Kiev beat Ferencvaros 3-0 (Basle)
1976	Anderlecht beat West Ham Utd. 4-2 (Brussels)
1977	SV Hamburg beat Anderlecht 2-0 (Amsterdam)
1978	Anderlecht beat Austria WAC 4-0 (Paris)
1979†	Barcelona beat Fortuna Dusseldorf 4-3 (Basle)
1980†	Valencia beat Arsenal 5-4 on penalties after a 0-0 draw (Brussels)
1981	Dynamo Tbilisi beat Carl Zeiss Jena 2-1 (Dusseldorf)
1982	Barcelona beat Standard Liege 2-1 (Barcelona)
1983†	Aberdeen beat Real Madrid 2-1 (Gothenburg)
1984	Juventus beat Porto 2-1 (Basle)
1985	Everton beat Rapid Vienna 3-1 (Rotterdam)
1986	Dynamo Kiev beat Atletico Madrid 3-0 (Lyon)
1987	Ajax beat Lokomotiv Leipzig 1-0 (Athens)
1988	Mechelen beat Ajax 1-0 (Strasbourg)
1989	Barcelona beat Sampdoria 2-0 (Berne)
1990	Sampdoria beat Anderlecht 2-0 (Gothenburg)
1991	Manchester Utd. beat Barcelona 2-1 (Rotterdam)
1992	Werder Bremen beat Monaco 2-0 (Lisbon)
1993	Parma beat Royal Antwerp 3-1 (Wembley)
1994	Arsenal beat Parma 1-0 (Copenhagen)
1995†	Real Zaragoza beat Arsenal 2-1 (Paris)
1996	Paris St. Germain beat Rapid Vienna 1-0 (Brussels)
1997	Barcelona beat Paris St. Germain 1-0 (Rotterdam)
1998	Chelsea beat VfB Stuttgart 1-0 (Stockholm)
1999	Lazio beat Real Mallorca 2-1 (Villa Park, Birmingham)

(† After extra time)

INTER-CONTINENTAL CUP

BOCA JUNIORS 1, AC MILAN 1 (aet, Boca Juniors won 3-1 on pens)

Yokohama, (66,757), Sunday, December 14, 2003

Boca Juniors (4-4-2): Abbondanzieri, Perea, Schiavi, Burdisso, Rodriguez, Donnet, Cascini, Battaglia, Cagna, Barros Schelotto (Tevez 73), Iarley. **Scorer:** Donnet, (29).

AC Milan (4-4-2): Dida, Cafu, Costacurta, Maldini, Pancaro, Gattuso (Ambrosini 102), Pirlo, Seedorf, Kaka (Rui Costa 78), Tomasson (Inzaghi 60), Shevchenko. **Scorer:** Tomasson (24).

Referee: V. Ivanov (Russia). **Half-time:** 1-1.

COMPLETE RESULTS

Year	Winners	Runners-up	Score		
1960	Real Madrid (Spa.)	Penarol (Uru.)	0-0	5-1	
1961	Penarol (Uru.)	Benfica (Por.)	0-1	2-1	5-0
1962	Santos (Bra.)	Benfica (Por.)	3-2	5-2	
1963	Santos (Bra.)	AC Milan (Ita.)	2-4	4-2	1-0
1964	Inter Milan (Ita.)	Independiente (Arg.)	0-1	2-0	1-0
1965	Inter Milan (Ita.)	Independiente (Arg.)	3-0	0-0	
1966	Penarol (Uru.)	Real Madrid (Spa.)	2-0	2-0	
1967	Racing (Arg.)	Celtic (Sco.)	0-1	2-1	1-0
1968	Estudiantes (Arg.)	Manchester Utd. (Eng.)	1-0	1-1	

1969	AC Milan (Ita.)	Estudiantes (Arg.)	3-0 1-2
1970	Feyenoord (Hol.)	Estudiantes (Arg.)	2-2 1-0
1971	Nacional (Uru.)	Panathanaikos (Gre.)*	1-1 2-1
1972	Ajax (Hol.)	Independiente (Arg.)	1-1 3-0
1973	Independiente (Arg.)	Juventus (Ita.)*	1-0 #
1974	Atletico Madrid (Spa.)*	Independiente (Arg.)	0-1 2-0
1975	Not played		
1976	Bayern Munich (W.Ger.)	Cruzeiro (Bra.)	2-0 0-0
1977	Boca Juniors (Arg.)	Borussia Mönchengladbach (W.Ger.)*	2-2 3-0
1978	Not played		
1979	Olimpia Asuncion (Par.)	Malmö (Swe.)*	1-0 2-1
1980	Nacional (Arg.)	Nott'm. Forest (Eng.)	1-0
1981	Flamengo (Bra.)	Liverpool (Eng.)	3-0
1982	Penarol (Uru.)	Aston Villa (Eng.)	2-0
1983	Porto Alegre (Bra.)	SV Hamburg (W.Ger.)	2-1
1984	Independiente (Arg.)	Liverpool (Eng.)	1-0
1985	Juventus (Ita.)	Argentinos Juniors (Arg.)	2-2 (aet)
	(Juventus won 4-2 on penalties)		
1986	River Plate (Arg.)	Steaua Bucharest (Rum.)	1-0
1987	Porto (Por.)	Penarol (Arg.)	2-1 (aet)
1988	Nacional (Uru.)	PSV Eindhoven (Hol.)	1-1 (aet)
	(Nacional won 7-6 on penalties)		
1989	AC Milan (Ita.)	Nacional (Col.)	1-0 (aet)
1990	AC Milan (Ita.)	Olimpia Asuncion (Par.)	3-0
1991	Red Star (Yug.)	Colo Colo (Chi.)	3-0
1992	Sao Paulo (Bra.)	Barcelona (Spa.)	2-1
1993	Sao Paulo (Bra.)	AC Milan (Ita.)	3-2
1994	Velez Sarsfield (Arg.)	AC Milan (Ita.)	2-0
1995	Ajax (Hol.)	Gremio (Bra.)	0-0 (aet)
	(Ajax won 4-3 on penalties)		
1996	Juventus (Ita.)	River Plate (Arg.)	1-0
1997	Borussia Dortmund (Ger.)	Cruzeiro (Arg.)	2-0
1998	Real Madrid (Spa.)	Vasco da Gama (Bra.)	2-1
1999	Manchester Utd. (Eng.)	Palmeiras (Bra.)	1-0
2000	Boca Juniors (Arg.)	Real Madrid (Spa.)	2-1
2001	Bayern Munich (Ger.)	Boca Juniours (Arg.)	1-0
2002	Real Madrid (Spa.)	Olimpia Ascuncion (Par.)	2-0
2003	Boca Juniors (Arg.)	AC Milan (Ita.)	1-1
	(Boca Juniors won 3-1 on penalties)		

Played as a single match in Japan since 1980
* European Cup runners-up. # One match only.
Summary: 42 contests; South America 22 wins, Europe 20 wins.

EUROPEAN SUPER CUP

AC MILAN 1, FC PORTO 0

Monaco, (8,000), Friday, August 29, 2003

AC Milan (4-4-2): Dida, Simic, Nesta, Maldini, Pancaro, Rui Costa (Cafu 85), Gattuso, Pirlo, Seedorf (Ambrosini 71), Shevchenko (Rivaldo 76), Inzaghi. **Scorer:** Shevchenko (10). **Booked:** Ambrosini, Pirlo, Seedorf.

FC Porto (4-3-1-2): Vitor Baia, Paulo Ferrreira, Jorge Costa, Ricardo Carvalho, Ricardo Costa (Bosingwa 67), Costinha, Deco, Maniche, Alenichev (Ricardo Fernandes 75), Derlei, McCarthy (Jankauskas 60). **Booked:** Maniche, Ricardo Fernandes.

Referee: G. Barber (England). **Half-time:** 1-0.

EUROPEAN TABLES

FRANCE

		P	W	D	L	F	A	Pts
1	Lyon	38	24	7	7	64	26	79
2	Paris SG	38	22	10	6	50	28	76
3	Monaco	38	21	12	5	59	30	75
4	Auxerre	38	19	8	11	60	34	65
5	Sochaux	38	18	9	11	54	42	63
6	Nantes	38	17	9	12	47	35	60
7	Marseille	38	17	6	15	51	45	57
8	Lens	38	15	8	15	34	48	53
9	Rennes	38	14	10	14	56	44	52
10	Lille	38	14	9	15	41	41	51
11	Nice	38	11	17	10	42	39	50
12	Bordeaux	38	13	11	14	40	43	50
13	Strasbourg	38	10	13	15	43	50	43
14	Metz	38	11	9	18	34	42	42
15	Ajaccio	38	10	10	18	33	55	40
16	Toulouse	38	9	12	17	31	44	39
17	Bastia	38	9	12	17	33	49	39
18	Guingamp	38	10	8	20	36	58	38
19	Le Mans	38	9	11	18	35	57	38
20	Montpellier	38	8	7	23	41	74	31

Leading scorers: 26 Cisse (Auxerre); 20 Frei (Rennes); 19 Drogba (Marseille); 18 Pauleta (Paris SG), Luyindula (Lyon); 17 Frau (Sochaux); 16 Bamogo (Montpellier), 14 Santos (Sochaux); 13 Giuly (Monaco), Manchev (Lille); 12 Ljuboja (Paris SG), Maoulida (Metz).
Cup Final: Paris SG 1, La Berrichonne 0.

GERMANY

		P	W	D	L	F	A	Pts
1	Werder Bremen	34	22	8	4	79	38	74
2	Bayern Munich	34	20	8	6	70	39	68
3	Bayer Leverkusen	34	19	8	7	73	39	65
4	Stuttgart	34	18	10	6	52	24	64
5	Bochum	34	15	11	8	57	39	56
6	Borussia Dortmund	34	16	7	11	59	48	55
7	Schalke	34	13	11	10	49	42	50
8	Hamburg	34	14	7	13	47	60	49
9	Hansa Rostock	34	12	8	14	55	54	44
10	Wolfsburg	34	13	3	18	56	61	42
11	Borussia M'gladbach	34	10	9	15	40	49	39
12	Hertha Berlin	34	9	12	13	42	59	39
13	Freiburg	34	10	8	16	42	67	38
14	Hannover	34	9	10	15	49	63	37
15	Kaiserslautern*	34	11	6	17	39	62	36
16	Eintracht Frankfurt	34	9	5	20	36	53	32
17	1860 Munich	34	8	8	18	32	55	32
18	Cologne	34	6	5	23	32	57	23

* Kaiserslautern had three points deducted for breaching licensing rules.

Leading scorers: 28 Ailton (Werder Bremen); 23 Makaay (Bayern Munich); 20 Max (Hansa Rostock); 16 Berbatov (Bayer Leverkusen), Ewerthon (Borussia Dortmund), Hashemian (Bochum), Koller (Borussia Dortmund); 15 Klimowicz (Wolfsburg); 14 Franca (Bayer Leverkusen); 13 Klasnic (Werder Bremen), Madsen (Bochum).
Cup Final: Werder Bremen 3, Alemannia Aachen 2.

HOLLAND

		P	W	D	L	F	A	Pts
1	Ajax	34	25	5	4	79	31	80
2	PSV Eindhoven	34	23	5	6	92	30	74
3	Feyenoord	34	20	8	6	71	38	68
4	Heerenveen	34	17	7	10	45	35	58
5	Alkmaar	34	17	6	11	65	42	57
6	Roda JC	34	14	11	9	60	41	53
7	Willem II	34	13	10	11	47	54	49
8	Twente	34	15	3	16	56	53	48
9	Breda	34	12	10	12	58	55	46
10	Utrecht	34	13	7	14	42	52	46
11	Waalwijk	34	10	10	14	47	55	40
12	Roosendahl	34	10	10	14	34	47	40
13	Groningen	34	9	10	15	38	53	37
14	Nijmegen	34	10	4	20	44	62	34
15	Den Haag	34	9	7	18	36	61	34
16	Vitesse Arnhem	34	4	16	14	39	56	28
17	Volendam	34	7	6	21	31	79	27
18	Zwolle	34	5	11	18	27	67	26

Leading scorers: 31 Kezman (PSV Eindhoven); 20 Kuijt (Feyenoord); 15 Elkhattabi (Alkmaar), Sibon (Heerenveen); 14 Buffel (Feyenoord), N'Kufo (Twente); 13 Ibrahimovic (Ajax), Redan (Roda JC); 12 Cristiano (Roda JC), Vennegoor (PSV Eindhoven).
Cup Final: FC Utrecht 1, FC Twente 0.

ITALY

		P	W	D	L	F	A	Pts
1	AC Milan	34	25	7	2	65	24	82
2	Roma	34	21	8	5	68	19	71
3	Juventus	34	21	6	7	67	42	69
4	Inter Milan	34	17	8	9	59	37	59
5	Parma	34	16	10	8	57	46	58
6	Lazio	34	16	8	10	52	38	56
7	Udinese	34	13	11	10	44	40	50
8	Sampdoria	34	11	13	10	40	42	46
9	Chievo	34	11	11	12	36	37	44
10	Lecce	34	11	8	15	43	56	41
11	Brescia	34	9	13	12	52	57	40
12	Bologna	34	10	9	15	45	53	39
13	Siena	34	8	10	16	41	54	34
14	Reggina	34	6	16	12	29	45	34
15	Perugia	34	6	14	14	44	56	32
16	Modena	34	6	12	16	27	46	30
17	Empoli	34	7	9	18	26	54	30
18	Ancona	34	2	7	25	21	70	13

Leading scorers: 24 Shevchenko (AC Milan); 23 Gilardino (Parma); 20 Totti (Roma); 19 Chevanton (Lecce); 17 Adriano (Inter Milan); 16 Trezeguet (Juventus); 14 Cassano (Roma), 13 Bazzani (Sampdoria), Vieri (Inter Milan); 12 Baggio (Brescia), Fava (Udinese), Tomasson (AC Milan).
Cup Final: Lazio 4, Juventus 2 (on agg).

PORTUGAL

		P	W	D	L	F	A	Pts
1	Porto	34	25	7	2	63	19	82
2	Benfica	34	22	8	4	62	28	74
3	Sporting	34	23	4	7	60	33	73
4	Nacional	34	17	5	12	56	35	56
5	Sp. Braga	34	15	9	10	36	38	54
6	Maritimo	34	12	12	10	35	33	48
7	Rio Ave	34	12	12	10	42	37	48
8	Boavista	34	12	11	11	32	31	47
9	Moreirense	34	12	10	12	33	33	46
10	U. Leiria	34	11	12	11	43	45	45
11	Beira-Mar	34	11	8	15	36	45	41
12	Gil Vicente	34	10	10	14	43	40	40
13	Academica	34	11	5	18	40	42	38
14	V. Guimarães	34	9	10	15	31	40	37
15	Belenenses	34	8	11	15	35	54	35
16	Alverca	34	10	5	19	33	49	35
17	P. Ferreira	34	8	4	22	27	53	28
18	Est. Amadora	34	4	5	25	22	74	17

Leading scorers: 20 McCarthy (FC Porto); 19 Adriano (Nacional); 15 Evandro (Rio Ave), Liedson (Sporting); 14 Ricardo Sousa (Boavista); 13 Derlei (FC Porto); 12 Simao (Benfica); 11 Ferreira (Gil Vicente), Serginho (Nacional), Sokota (Benfica), Wender (Braga), Ze Manuel (Pacos Ferreira).
Cup Final: Benfica 2, FC Porto 1 (aet).

SPAIN

		P	W	D	L	F	A	Pts
1	Valencia	38	23	8	7	71	27	77
2	Barcelona	38	21	9	8	63	39	72
3	Dept. La Coruna	38	21	8	9	60	34	71
4	Real Madrid	28	21	7	10	72	54	70
5	Athletic Bilbao	38	15	11	12	53	49	56
6	Sevilla	38	15	10	13	56	45	55
7	Atletico Madrid	38	15	10	13	51	53	55
8	Villarreal	38	15	9	14	47	49	54
9	Real Betis	38	13	13	12	46	43	52
10	Malaga	38	15	6	17	50	55	51
11	Mallorca	38	15	6	17	54	66	51
12	Osasuna	38	11	15	12	38	37	48
13	Real Zaragoza	38	13	9	16	46	55	48
14	Albacete	38	13	8	17	40	48	47
15	Real Sociedad	38	11	13	14	49	53	46
16	Espanyol	38	13	4	21	48	64	43
17	Racing Santander*	38	11	10	17	48	63	42
18	Valladolid	38	10	11	17	46	56	41
19	Celta Vigo	38	9	12	17	48	68	39
20	Murcia	38	5	11	22	29	57	26

* One point deducted for player ineligibility

Leading scorers: 24 Ronaldo (Real Madrid); 20 Julio Baptista (Sevilla); 19 Mista (Valencia); Salva (Malaga), Tamudo (Espanyol), Torres (Atletico Madrid); 17 Eto'o (Mallorca), Villa (Real Zaragoza); 15 Ronaldinho (Barcelona); 14 Milosevic (Celta Vigo), Nihat (Real Sociedad), Pandiani (Deportivo La Coruna), Saviola (Barcelona).
Cup Final: Real Zaragoza 3, Real Madrid 2 (aet).

2006 WORLD CUP QUALIFYING

As is the way in international football, no sooner had the sporting world come to terms with Greece's shock victory at Euro 2004 than thoughts immediately turned to the next major tournament.

The World Cup in Germany may not kick-off until 9 June 2006, but many of the FIFA Confederations are well under way with qualification matches to decide the 31 teams who will join the hosts – the only country to qualify automatically – at the competition.

Brazil and Argentina unsurprisingly went into September round of fixtures heading the South American table, although competition was fierce for the two remaining automatic places.

The fifth-placed team will play off against the winners of the Oceania region, where the minnows from the Soloman Islands have surprisingly reached the two-legged final against favourites Australia.

Meanwhile, closer to home, England coach Sven-Goran Eriksson will have to overcome passionate local rivalries to guide his team to Germany after being paired with both Wales and Northern Ireland in qualifying.

England have not played the Welsh side since the 1984 Home Championships – the last before it was discontinued – when Mark Hughes was the toast of Wrexham with the only goal of the game.

And it is more than 17 years since England faced Northern Ireland and beat them home and away while qualifying for the 1988 European Championships.

Elsewhere, Scotland's main rivals in Group Five are Italy, Norway and Slovenia, while the Republic of Ireland face two mouth-watering ties against France.

Only the winners in each of the eight UEFA groups will be guaranteed a place at the World Cup, with the two best runners-up also qualifying automatically and the remaining three places available via the now established play-off route involving the other second-placed sides.

To complete the World Cup party, Africa will provide five teams in Germany, Asia at least four and the CONCACAF region guaranteed three places with another up for grabs in a play-off against an Asian side.

EUROPE

Group One: Andorra, Armenia, Czech Republic, Finland, Netherlands, Macedonia, Romania.

Group Two: Albania, Denmark, Georgia, Greece, Kazakhstan, Turkey, Ukraine.

Group Three: Estonia, Latvia, Liechtenstein, Luxembourg, Portugal, Russia, Slovakia.

Group Four: Cyprus, Faroe Islands, France, Israel, Republic of Ireland, Switzerland.

Group Five: Belarus, Italy, Moldova, Norway, Scotland, Slovenia.

Group Six: Austria, Azerbaijan, England, Northern Ireland, Poland, Wales.

Group Seven: Belgium, Bosnia-Herzogovina, Lithuania, San Marino, Serbia-Montenegro, Spain.

Group Eight: Bulgaria, Croatia, Hungary, Iceland, Malta, Sweden.

AFRICA

GROUP 1

	P	W	D	L	F	A	Pts
Congo	3	2	0	1	4	2	6
Senegal	3	2	0	1	4	3	6
Togo	3	1	1	1	3	2	4
Zambia	3	1	1	1	2	2	4
Liberia	3	1	1	1	3	3	4
Mali	3	0	1	1	1	3	1

GROUP 2

	P	W	D	L	F	A	Pts
South Africa	3	2	0	1	4	4	6
Ghana	3	1	1	1	4	2	4
DR Congo	3	1	1	1	4	4	4
Cape Verde	3	1	1	3	3	4	4
Uganda	3	1	1	1	2	2	4
Burkina Faso	3	1	0	2	3	5	3

GROUP 3

	P	W	D	L	F	A	Pts
Cameroon	3	2	1	0	4	1	7
Ivory Coast	3	2	0	1	4	3	6
Egypt	3	1	1	1	7	5	4
Libya	3	1	1	1	1	2	4
Benin	3	0	2	1	5	6	2
Sudan	3	0	1	2	1	5	1

GROUP 4

	P	W	D	L	F	A	Pts
Nigeria	3	2	0	1	3	1	6
Zimbabwe	3	1	2	0	4	2	5
Angola	3	1	2	0	3	2	5
Rwanda	3	1	0	2	3	5	3
Algeria	3	0	2	1	1	2	2
Gabon	3	0	2	1	4	6	2

GROUP 5

	P	W	D	L	F	A	Pts
Guinea	2	1	1	0	3	2	4
Morocco	2	1	1	0	2	1	4
Tunisia	2	1	0	1	5	3	3
Botswana	3	1	0	2	3	5	3
Malawi	3	0	2	1	2	4	2
Kenya	0	0	0	0	0	0	0

ASIA

GROUP 1

	P	W	D	L	F	A	Pts
Jordan	3	3	0	0	7	0	9
Iran	3	1	0	1	10	2	6
Qatar	3	1	0	2	6	4	3
Laos	3	0	0	3	0	17	0

GROUP 2

	P	W	D	L	F	A	Pts
Uzbekistan	3	2	1	0	5	1	7
Iraq	3	1	2	0	8	3	5
Palestine	3	1	1	1	9	4	4
Chinese Taipei	3	0	0	3	1	15	0

GROUP 3

	P	W	D	L	F	A	Pts
Japan	3	3	0	0	10	1	9
Oman	3	2	0	1	12	2	6
India	3	1	0	2	2	12	3
Singapore	3	0	0	3	1	10	0

GROUP 4

	P	W	D	L	F	A	Pts
China	3	3	0	0	6	0	9
Kuwait	3	2	0	1	6	1	6
Hong Kong	3	1	0	2	3	6	3
Malaysia	3	0	0	3	1	9	0

GROUP 5

	P	W	D	L	F	A	Pts
UAE	3	2	1	0	4	0	7
North Korea	3	1	2	0	5	2	5
Thailand	3	1	0	2	4	5	3
Yemen	3	0	1	2	1	7	1

GROUP 6

	P	W	D	L	F	A	Pts
Bahrain	3	2	1	0	7	1	7
Syria	3	1	1	1	4	4	4
Tajikistan	3	1	1	1	3	3	4
Kyrgyzstan	3	0	1	2	2	8	1

GROUP 7

	P	W	D	L	F	A	Pts
South Korea	3	2	1	0	4	0	7
Lebanon	3	2	0	1	5	2	6
Vietnam	3	1	0	2	4	4	3
Maldives	3	0	1	2	0	7	1

GROUP 8

	P	W	D	L	F	A	Pts
Saudi Arabia	3	3	0	0	7	0	9
Turkmenistan	3	2	0	1	5	4	6
Indonesia	3	1	0	2	3	6	3
Sri Lanka	3	0	0	3	0	4	0

CONCACAF

Qualified for Second Stage: USA, El Salvador, Jamaica, Panama, Costa Rica, Guatemala, Honduras, Canada, Mexico, St Kitts & Nevis, Trinidad & Tobago, St Vincent & Grenadines.

OCEANIA

Qualified for Play-Off match: Australia, Soloman Islands.

SOUTH AMERICA

	P	W	D	L	F	A	Pts
Brazil	7	3	4	0	11	7	13
Argentina	7	3	3	1	11	6	12
Chile	7	3	2	2	9	7	11
Paraguay	7	3	2	2	9	8	11
Ecuador	7	3	1	3	8	7	10
Venezuela	7	3	1	3	6	7	10
Peru	7	2	3	2	9	7	9
Colombia	7	2	1	4	10	10	7
Uruguay	7	2	1	4	12	19	7
Bolivia	7	2	0	5	9	16	6

Results: Ecuador 2 Venezuela 0, Argentina 2 Chile 2, Peru 4 Paraguay 1, Uruguay 5 Bolivia 0, Colombia 1 Brazil 2, Venezuela 0 Argentina 3, Chile 2 Peru 1, Bolivia 4 Colombia 0, Paraguay 4 Uruguay 1, Brazil 1 Ecuador 0, Uruguay 2 Chile 1, Colombia 0 Venezuela 1, Paraguay 2 Ecuador 1, Argentina 3 Bolivia 0, Peru 1 Brazil 1, Venezuela 2 Bolivia 1, Chile 0 Paraguay 1, Ecuador 0 Peru 0, Colombia 1 Argentina 1, Brazil 3 Uruguay 3, Bolivia 0 Chile 2, Argentina 1 Ecuador 0, Uruguay 0 Venezuela 3, Paraguay 0 Brazil 0, Peru 0 Colombia 2, Bolivia 2 Paraguay 1, Venezuela 0 Chile 1, Uruguay 1 Peru 3, Ecuador 2 Colombia 1, Brazil 3 Argentina 1, Ecuador 3 Bolivia 2, Argentina 0 Paraguay 0, Peru 0 Venezuela 0, Colombia 5 Uruguay 0, Chile 1 Brazil 1.

QUOTE – UNQUOTE

'I have never seen so many fans crying at a match' – **Graham Taylor**, Radio Five match summariser, at the end of Millwall's victory over Sunderland in the F.A Cup semi-final.

'As a Millwall fan you don't plan your season around the F.A. Cup Final' – Caller to Six-O-Six who had to return home early from his honeymoon for the big match.

'It's a cancer in the game. It was a European problem, but now it's one for the Premiership to deal with' – **Keith Hackett**, general manager of the Professional Game's Match Officials' Board on players diving.

'It has never happened to me in 31 years of refereeing' – **Neale Barry**, apologising for an accidental 'assist' in Phil Mulryne's winner for Norwich at Reading.

WORLD CUP SUMMARIES 1930-2002

1930 IN URUGUAY

WINNERS: Uruguay. RUNNERS-UP: Argentina. THIRD: U.S.A. FOURTH: Yugoslavia.
Other countries taking part: Belgium, Bolivia, Brazil, Chile, France, Mexico, Paraguay, Peru, Rumania, Yugoslavia. **Total entries:** 13.
Venue: All matches played in Montevideo.
Top scorer: Stabile (Argentina) 8 goals.
Final (30.7.30): **Uruguay 4** (Dorado 12, Cea 55, Iriarte 64, Castro 89), **Argentina 2** (Peucelle 29, Stabile 35). **Att:** 90,000.
Uruguay: Ballesteros; Nasazzi (Capt.), Mascheroni, Andrade, Fernandez, Gestido, Dorado, Scarone, Castro, Cea, Iriarte.
Argentina: Botasso; Della Torre, Paternoster, Evaristo (J.), Monti, Suarez, Peucelle, Varallo, Stabile, Ferreira (Capt.), Evaristo (M.).
Referee: Langenus (Belgium). **Half-time:** 1-2.

1934 IN ITALY

WINNERS: Italy. RUNNERS-UP: Czechoslovakia. THIRD: Germany. FOURTH: Austria.
Other countries in finals: Argentina, Austria, Belgium, Brazil, Egypt, France, Holland, Hungary, Romania, Spain, Sweden, Switzerland, U.S.A. **Total entries:** 29 (16 qualifiers).
Venues: Bologna, Florence, Genoa, Milan, Naples, Rome, Trieste, Turin.
Top scorers: Conen (Germany), Nejedly (Czechoslovakia), Schiavio (Italy), each 4 goals.
Final (Rome, 10.6.34): **Italy 2** (Orsi 82, Schiavio 97), **Czechoslovakia 1** (Puc 70), **after extra time. Att:** 50,000.
Italy: Combi (Capt.); Monzeglio, Allemandi, Ferraris, Monti, Bertolini, Guaita, Meazza, Schiavio, Ferrari, Orsi.
Czechoslovakia: Planicka (Capt.); Zenisek, Ctyroky, Kostalek, Cambal, Krcil, Junek, Svoboda, Sobotka, Nejedly, Puc.
Referee: Eklind (Sweden). **Half-time:** 0-0. **90 mins:** 1-1.

1938 IN FRANCE

WINNERS: Italy. RUNNERS-UP: Hungary. THIRD: Brazil. FOURTH: Sweden.
Other countries in finals: Belgium, Cuba, Czechoslovakia, Dutch East Indies, France, Germany, Holland, Norway, Poland, Rumania, Sweden, Switzerland. **Total entries:** 25 (15 qualifiers).
Venues: Antibes, Bordeaux, Le Havre, Lille, Marseilles, Paris, Reims, Strasbourg, Toulouse.
Top scorer: Leonidas (Brazil) 8 goals.
Final (Paris, 19.6.38): **Italy 4** (Colaussi 6, 36, Piola 15, 81), **Hungary 2** (Titkos 7, Sarosi 65). **Att:** 45,000.
Italy: Olivieri; Foni, Rava, Serantoni, Andreolo, Locatelli, Biavati, Meazza (Capt.), Piola, Ferrari, Colaussi.
Hungary: Szabo; Polgar, Biro, Szalay, Szucs, Lazar, Sas, Vincze, Sarosi (Capt.), Szengeller, Titkos.
Referee: Capdeville (France). **Half-time:** 3-1.

1950 IN BRAZIL

WINNERS: Uruguay. RUNNERS-UP: Brazil. THIRD: Sweden. FOURTH: Spain.
Other countries in finals: Bolivia, Chile, England, Italy, Mexico, Paraguay, Spain, Switzerland, U.S.A., Yugoslavia. **Total entries:** 29 (13 qualifiers).
Venues: Belo Horizonte, Curitiba, Porto Alegre, Recife, Rio de Janeiro, Sao Paulo.
Top scorer: Ademir (Brazil) 9 goals.
Deciding Match (Rio de Janeiro, 16.7.50): **Uruguay 2** (Schiaffino 64, Ghiggia 79), **Brazil 1** (Friaca 47). **Att:** 199,850.

163

(For the only time, the World Cup was decided on a final pool system, in which the winners of the four qualifying groups met in a six-match series. So, unlike previous and subsequent tournaments, there was no official Final as such, but Uruguay v Brazil was the deciding final match in the final pool).

Uruguay: Maspoli; Gonzales, Tejera, Gambetta, Varela (Capt.), Andrade, Ghiggia, Perez, Miguez, Schiaffino, Moran.

Brazil: Barbosa; Augusto (Capt.), Juvenal, Bauer, Danilo, Bigode, Friaca, Zizinho, Ademir, Jair, Chico.

Referee: Reader (England). **Half-time:** 0-0.

1954 IN SWITZERLAND

WINNERS: West Germany. RUNNERS-UP: Hungary. THIRD: Austria. FOURTH: Uruguay.
Other countries in finals: Belgium, Brazil, Czechoslovakia, England, France, Italy, Korea, Mexico, Scotland, Switzerland, Turkey, Uruguay, Yugoslavia. **Total entries:** 35 (16 qualifiers).
Venues: Basle, Berne, Geneva, Lausanne, Lugano, Zurich.
Top scorer: Kocsis (Hungary) 11 goals.
Final (Berne, 4.7.54): **West Germany 3** (Morlock 12, Rahn 17, 84), **Hungary 2** (Puskas 4, Czibor 9). **Att:** 60,000.
West Germany: Turek; Posipal, Kohlmeyer, Eckel, Liebrich, Mai, Rahn, Morlock, Walter (O.), Walter (F.) (Capt.), Schaefer.
Hungary: Grosics; Buzansky, Lantos, Bozsik, Lorant, Zakarias, Czibor, Kocsis, Hidegkuti, Puskas (Capt.), Toth (J.).
Referee: Ling (England). **Half-time:** 2-2.

1958 IN SWEDEN

WINNERS: Brazil. RUNNERS-UP: Sweden. THIRD: France. FOURTH: West Germany.
Other countries in finals: Argentina, Austria, Czechoslovakia, England, Hungary, Mexico, Northern Ireland, Paraguay, Scotland, Soviet Union, Wales, West Germany, Yugoslavia. **Total entries:** 47 (16 qualifiers).
Venues: Boras, Eskilstuna, Gothenburg, Halmstad, Helsingborg, Malmo, Norrkoping, Orebro, Sandviken, Stockholm, Vasteras.
Top scorer: Fontaine (France) 13 goals.
Final (Stockholm, 29.6.58): **Brazil 5** (Vava 10, 32, Pele 55, 88, Zagalo 76), **Sweden 2** (Liedholm 4, Simonsson 83). **Att:** 49,737.
Brazil: Gilmar; Santos (D.), Santos (N.), Zito, Bellini (Capt.), Orlando, Garrincha, Didi, Vava, Pele, Zagalo.
Sweden: Svensson; Bergmark, Axbom, Boerjesson, Gustavsson, Parling, Hamrin, Gren, Simonsson, Liedholm (Capt.), Skoglund.
Referee: Guigue (France). **Half-time:** 2-1.

1962 IN CHILE

WINNERS: Brazil. RUNNERS-UP: Czechoslovakia. THIRD: Chile. FOURTH: Yugoslavia.
Other countries in finals: Argentina, Bulgaria, Colombia, England, Hungary, Italy, Mexico, Soviet Union, Spain, Switzerland, Uruguay, West Germany, Yugoslavia. **Total entries:** 53 (16 qualifiers).
Venues: Arica, Rancagua, Santiago, Vina del Mar.
Top scorer: Jerkovic (Yugoslavia), 5 goals.
Final (Santiago, 17.6.62): **Brazil 3** (Amarildo 17, Zito 69, Vava 77), **Czechoslovakia 1** (Masopust 16). **Att:** 68,679.
Brazil: Gilmar; Santos (D.), Mauro (Capt.), Zozimo, Santos (N.), Zito, Didi, Garrincha, Vava, Amarildo, Zagalo.
Czechoslovakia: Schroiff; Tichy, Novak, Pluskal, Popluhar, Masopust (Capt.), Pospichal, Scherer, Kvasnak, Kadraba, Jelinek.
Referee: Latychev (Soviet Union). **Half-time:** 1-1.

1966 IN ENGLAND

WINNERS: England. RUNNERS-UP: West Germany. THIRD: Portugal. FOURTH: USSR.
Other countries in finals: Argentina, Brazil, Bulgaria, Chile, France, Hungary, Italy, Mexico, North Korea, Soviet Union, Spain, Switzerland, Uruguay. **Total entries**: 53 (16 qualifiers).
Venues: Birmingham (Villa Park), Liverpool (Goodison Park), London (Wembley and White City), Manchester (Old Trafford), Middlesbrough, Sheffield (Hillsborough), Sunderland.
Top scorer: Eusebio (Portugal) 9 goals.
Final (Wembley, 30.7.66): **England 4** (Hurst 19, 100, 120, Peters 78), **West Germany 2** (Haller 13, Weber 89), **after extra time. Att**: 93,802.
England: Banks; Cohen, Wilson, Stiles, Charlton (J.), Moore (Capt.), Ball, Hurst, Hunt, Charlton (R.), Peters.
West Germany: Tilkowski; Hottges, Schnellinger, Beckenbauer, Schulz, Weber, Haller, Held, Seeler (Capt.), Overath, Emmerich.
Referee: Dienst (Switzerland). **Half-time:** 1-1. **90 mins:** 2-2.

1970 IN MEXICO

WINNERS: Brazil. RUNNERS-UP: Italy. THIRD: West Germany. FOURTH: Uruguay.
Other countries in finals: Belgium, Bulgaria, Czechoslovakia, El Salvador, England, Israel, Mexico, Morocco, Peru, Romania, Soviet Union, Sweden, Uruguay. **Total entries**: 68 (16 qualifiers).
Venues: Guadalajara, Leon, Mexico City, Puebla, Toluca.
Top scorer: Muller (West Germany) 10 goals.
Final (Mexico City, 21.6.70): **Brazil 4** (Pele 18, Gerson 66, Jairzinho 71, Carlos Alberto 87), **Italy 1** (Boninsegna 38). **Att**: 107,412.
Brazil: Felix; Carlos Alberto (Capt.), Brito, Piazza, Everaldo, Clodoaldo, Gerson, Jairzinho, Tostao, Pele, Rivelino.
Italy: Albertosi; Burgnich, Facchetti (Capt.), Cera, Rosato, Bertini (Juliano 72), Domenghini, De Sisti, Mazzola, Boninsegna (Rivera 84), Riva.
Referee: Glockner (East Germany). **Half-time:** 1-1.

1974 IN WEST GERMANY

WINNERS: West Germany. RUNNERS-UP: Holland. THIRD: Poland. FOURTH: Brazil.
Other countries in finals: Argentina, Australia, Brazil, Bulgaria, Chile, East Germany, Haiti, Italy, Scotland, Sweden, Uruguay, Yugoslavia, Zaire. **Total entries**: 98 (16 qualifiers).
Venues: Berlin, Dortmund, Dusseldorf, Frankfurt, Gelsenkirchen, Hamburg, Hanover, Munich, Stuttgart.
Top scorer: Lato (Poland) 7 goals
Final (Munich, 7.7.74): **West Germany 2** (Breitner 25 pen., Muller 43), **Holland 1** (Neeskens 2 pen.). **Att**: 77,833.
West Germany: Maier; Vogts, Schwarzenbeck, Beckenbauer (Capt.), Breitner, Bonhof, Hoeness, Overath, Grabowski, Muller, Holzenbein.
Holland: Jongbloed; Suurbier, Rijsbergen (De Jong 69), Haan, Krol, Jansen, Van Hanegem, Neeskens, Rep, Cruyff (Capt.), Rensenbrink (Van der Kerkhof (R.) 46).
Referee: Taylor (England). **Half-time:** 2-1.

1978 IN ARGENTINA

WINNERS: Argentina. RUNNERS-UP: Holland. THIRD: Brazil. FOURTH: Italy.
Other countries in finals: Austria, France, Hungary, Iran, Italy, Mexico, Peru, Poland, Scotland, Spain, Sweden, Tunisia, West Germany. **Total entries**: 102 (16 qualifiers).
Venues: Buenos Aires, Cordoba, Mar del Plata, Mendoza, Rosario.
Top scorer: Kempes (Argentina) 6 goals.

Final (Buenos Aires, 25.6.78): **Argentina 3** (Kempes 38, 104, Bertoni 115), **Holland 1** (Nanninga 82), **after extra time. Att:** 77,000.
Argentina: Fillol; Passarella (Capt.), Olguin, Galvan, Tarantini, Ardiles (Larrosa 66), Gallego, Ortiz (Houseman 74), Bertoni, Luque, Kempes.
Holland: Jongbloed; Krol (Capt.), Poortvliet, Brandts, Jansen (Suurbier 73), Haan, Neeskens, Van der Kerkhof (W.), Rep (Nanninga 58), Van der Kerkhof (R.), Rensenbrink.
Referee: Gonella (Italy). **Half-time:** 1-0. **90 mins:** 1-1.

1982 IN SPAIN

WINNERS: Italy. RUNNERS-UP: West Germany. THIRD: Poland. FOURTH: France.
Other countries in finals: Algeria, Argentina, Austria, Belgium, Brazil, Cameroon, Chile, Czechoslovakia, El Salvador, England, France, Honduras, Hungary, Kuwait, New Zealand, Northern Ireland, Peru, Scotland, Soviet Union, Spain, Yugoslavia. **Total entries:** 109 (24 qualifiers).
Venues: Alicante, Barcelona, Bilbao, Coruna, Elche, Gijon, Madrid, Malaga, Oviedo, Seville, Valencia, Valladolid, Vigo, Zaragoza.
Top scorer: Rossi (Italy) 6 goals.
Final (Madrid, 11.7.82): **Italy 3** (Rossi 57, Tardelli 69, Altobelli 81), **West Germany 1** (Breitner 84). **Att:** 90,089.
Italy: Zoff (Capt.); Bergomi, Scirea, Collovati, Cabrini, Oriali, Gentile, Tardelli, Conti, Rossi, Graziani (Altobelli 18 – Causio 88).
West Germany: Schumacher; Kaltz, Stielike, Forster (K-H.), Forster (B.), Dremmler (Hrubesch 63), Breitner, Briegel, Rummenigge (Capt.) (Muller 70), Fischer, Littbarski.
Referee: Coelho (Brazil). **Half-time:** 0-0.

1986 IN MEXICO

WINNERS: Argentina. RUNNERS-UP: West Germany. THIRD: France. FOURTH: Belgium.
Other countries in finals: Algeria, Belgium, Brazil, Bulgaria, Canada, Denmark, England, Hungary, Iraq, Italy, Mexico, Morocco, Northern Ireland, Paraguay, Poland, Portugal, Scotland, South Korea, Soviet Union, Spain, Uruguay. **Total entries:** 118 (24 qualifiers).
Venues: Guadalajara, Irapuato, Leon, Mexico City, Monterrey, Nezahualcoyotl, Puebla, Queretaro, Toluca.
Top scorer: Lineker (England) 6 goals.
Final (Mexico City, 29.6.86): **Argentina 3** (Brown 23, Valdano 56, Burruchaga 85), **West Germany 2** (Rummenigge 74, Voller 82). **Att:** 115,026.
Argentina: Pumpido; Cuciuffo, Brown, Ruggeri, Olarticoechea, Batista, Giusti, Maradona (Capt.), Burruchaga (Trobbiani 89), Enrique, Valdano.
West Germany: Schumacher; Berthold, K-H.Forster, Jakobs, Brehme, Briegel, Eder, Matthaus, Magath (Hoeness 62), Allofs (Voller 45), Rummenigge (Capt.).
Referee: Filho (Brazil). **Half-time:** 1-0.

1990 IN ITALY

WINNERS: West Germany. RUNNERS-UP: Argentina. THIRD: Italy. FOURTH: England.
Other countries in finals: Austria, Belgium, Brazil, Cameroon, Colombia, Costa Rica, Czechoslovakia, Egypt, England, Holland, Rep. of Ireland, Romania, Scotland, Spain, South Korea, Soviet Union, Sweden, United Arab Emirates, U.S.A., Uruguay, Yugoslavia. **Total entries:** 103 (24 qualifiers).
Venues: Bari, Bologna, Cagliari, Florence, Genoa, Milan, Naples, Palermo, Rome, Turin, Udine, Verona.
Top scorer: Schillaci (Italy) 6 goals.
Final (Rome, 8.7.90): **Argentina 0, West Germany 1** (Brehme 85 pen.). **Att:** 73,603.
Argentina: Goycochea; Ruggeri (Monzon 45), Simon, Serrizuela, Lorenzo, Basualdo, Troglio, Burruchaga (Calderon 53), Sensini, Maradona (Capt.), Dezotti. **Sent-off:** Monzon (65), Dezotti (86) – first players ever to be sent off in World Cup Final.

West Germany: Illgner; Berthold (Reuter 75), Buchwald, Augenthaler, Kohler, Brehme, Matthaus (Capt.), Littbarski, Hassler, Klinsmann, Voller.
Referee: Codesal (Mexico). **Half-time:** 0-0.

1994 IN U.S.A.

WINNERS: Brazil. RUNNERS-UP: Italy. THIRD: Sweden. FOURTH: Bulgaria.
Other countries in finals: Argentina, Belgium, Bolivia, Bulgaria, Cameroon, Colombia, Germany, Greece, Holland, Mexico, Morocco, Nigeria, Norway, Rep. of Ireland, Romania, Russia, Saudi Arabia, South Korea, Spain, Switzerland, U.S.A. **Total entries:** 144 (24 qualifiers).
Venues: Boston, Chicago, Dallas, Detroit, Los Angeles, New York City, Orlando, San Francisco, Washington.
Top scorers: Salenko (Russia), Stoichkov (Bulgaria), each 6 goals.
Final (Los Angeles, 17.7.94): **Brazil 0, Italy 0**, after extra time; **Brazil** won 3-2 on pens. **Att:** 94,194.
Brazil: Taffarel; Jorginho (Cafu 21), Aldair, Marcio Santos, Branco, Mazinho, Mauro Silva, Dunga (Capt.), Zinho (Viola 105), Romario, Bebeto.
Italy: Pagliuca; Mussi (Apolloni 35), Baresi (Capt.), Maldini, Benarrivo, Berti, Albertini, D. Baggio (Evani 95), Donadoni, R. Baggio, Massaro.
Referee: Puhl (Hungary).
Shoot-out: Baresi over, Marco Santos saved, Albertini 1-0, Romario 1-1, Evani 2-1, Branco 2-2, Massaro saved, Dunga 2-3, R Baggio over.

1998 IN FRANCE

WINNERS: France. RUNNERS-UP: Brazil. THIRD: Croatia. FOURTH: Holland.
Other countries in finals: Argentina, Austria, Belgium, Bulgaria, Cameroon, Chile, Colombia, Denmark, England, Germany, Holland, Iran, Italy, Jamaica, Japan, Mexico, Morocco, Nigeria, Norway, Paraguay, Romania, Saudi Arabia, Scotland, South Africa, South Korea, Spain, Tunisia, U.S.A., Yugoslavia. **Total entries:** 172 (32 qualifiers).
Venues: Bordeaux, Lens, Lyon, Marseille, Montpellier, Nantes, Paris (St Denis, Parc des Princes), Saint-Etienne, Toulouse.
Top scorer: Davor Suker (Croatia) 6 goals.
Final (Paris St Denis, 12.7.98): **Brazil 0, France 3** (Zidane 27, 45, Petit 90). **Att:** 75,000.
Brazil: Traffarel; Cafu, Junior Baiano, Aldair, Roberto Carlos; Dunga (Capt.), Leonardo (Denilson 46), Cesar Sampaio (Edmundo 74), Rivaldo; Bebeto, Ronaldo.
France: Barthez; Thuram, Leboeuf, Desailly, Lizarazu; Karembeu (Boghossian 56), Deschamps (Capt.), Petit, Zidane, Djorkaeff (Viera 75); Guivarc'h (Dugarry 66). **Sent-off:** Desailly (68).
Referee: S Belqola (Morocco). **Half-time:** 0-2.

2002 IN JAPAN/SOUTH KOREA

WINNERS: Brazil. RUNNERS-UP: Germany. THIRD: Turkey. FOURTH: South Korea.
Other countries in finals: Argentina, Belgium, Cameroon, China, Costa Rica, Croatia, Denmark, Ecuador, England, France, Italy, Japan, Mexico, Nigeria, Paraguay, Poland, Portugal, Republic of Ireland, Russia, Saudi Arabia, Senegal, Slovenia, South Africa, Spain, Sweden, Tunisia, United States, Uruguay.
Venues: Japan – Ibaraki, Kobe, Miyagi, Niigata, Oita, Osaka, Saitama, Sapporo, Shizuoka, Yokohama. **South Korea** – Daegu, Daejeon, Gwangju, Incheon, Jeonju, Busan, Seogwipo, Seoul, Suwon. Ulsan.
Top scorer: Ronaldo (Brazil) 8 goals.
Final (Yokohama, 30.6.02): **Germany 0, Brazil 2** (Ronaldo 67, 79). **Att:** 69,029.
Germany: Kahn (Capt.), Linke, Ramelow, Metzelder, Frings, Jeremies (Asamoah 77), Hamann, Schneider, Bode (Zeige 84), Klose (Bierhoff 74), Neuville.
Brazil: Marcos, Lucio, Edmilson, Roque Junior, Cafu (Capt.) Kleberson, Gilberto Silva, Roberto Carlos, Ronaldinho (Juninho 85), Rivaldo, Ronaldo (Denilson 90).
Referee: Collina (Italy). **Half-time:** 0-0.

BRITISH AND IRISH INTERNATIONALS
2003-04

(*Denotes new cap)

EUROPEAN CHAMPIONSHIP 2004 – QUALIFYING

SERBIA – MONTENEGRO 1, WALES 0
Belgrade, (30,000), Wednesday, August 20, 2003

Serbia & Montenegro (3-4-1-2): Jevric, Gavranic, Krstajic, Stefanovic, Cirkovic, Mladenovic, Stankovic (Djordjevic 81), Dragutinovic, Vukic (Ilic 68), Kovacevic, Kezman (Milosevic 71). **Scorer:** Mladenovic (73). **Booked:** Vukic, Stankovic, Jevric, Milosevic.

Wales (4-3-2-1): Jones (Southampton), Delaney (Aston Villa), Page (Sheffield Utd.), Gabbidon (Cardiff City), Speed (Newcastle Utd.), Davies (Tottenham), Pembridge (Everton), Savage (Birmingham City), Bellamy (Newcastle Utd.), Giggs (Manchester Utd.), Blake (Wolves) (Earnshaw, Cardiff City, 78). **Booked:** Delaney.

Referee: A. Frisk (Sweden). **Half-time:** 0-0.

MACEDONIA 1, ENGLAND 2
Skopje, (20,500), Saturday, September 6, 2003

Macedonia (3-5-2): Milosevski, Stojanovski, Mitrevsi, Stavrevski, Grozdanovski (Braga 56), Trajanaov, Pandev (Gjuzelov 48), Sumulikoski, Sakiri, Naumoski, Hristov (Dimitrovski 88). **Scorer:** Hristov (28). **Booked:** Naumoski, Braga, Hristov, Sakiri.

England (4-4-2): James (West Ham Utd.), G. Neville (Manchester Utd.), Terry (Chelsea), Campbell (Arsenal), Cole (Arsenal), Butt (Manchester Utd.), Beckham (Real Madrid), Lampard (Chelsea) (Heskey, Liverpool, 46), Hargreaves (Bayern Munich), Rooney (Everton) (P. Neville, Manchester Utd., 86), Owen (Liverpool) (Dyer, Newcastle Utd., 86). **Scorers:** Rooney (53), Beckham (63 pen). **Booked:** Campbell, Beckham.

Referee: F. De Bleeckere (Belgium). **Half-time:** 1-0.

SCOTLAND 3, FAROE ISLANDS 1
Hampden Park, (49,001), Saturday, September 6, 2003

Scotland (4-4-2): Douglas (Celtic), McNamara (Celtic), Wilkie (Dundee), Webster (Hearts), Naysmith (Everton), Devlin (Birmingham City) (McFadden, Everton, 58), Cameron (Wolves), Ferguson (Blackburn Rov.), McCann (Southampton), Dickov (Leicester City) (Rae, Dundee, 67), Crawford (Dunfermline Athletic) (Thompson, Rangers, 74). **Scorers:** McCann (8), Dickov (45), McFadden (74). **Booked:** Crawford.

Faroe Islands (4-4-2): Mikkelsen, J. I. Petersen, Johanessen, J. R. Jacobsen, Thorsteinsson, Johnsson (Danielsen 84), Benjaminsen, J. Petersen, R. Jacobsen, Borg (Holst 84), H. Petersen (Askelsen, 65). **Scorer:** Johnsson (36). **Booked:** Benjaminsen, R. Jacobsen.

Referee: D. Ceferin (Slovenia). **Half-time:** 2-1.

ITALY 4, WALES 0
Milan, (68,000), Saturday, September 6, 2003

Italy (4-4-2): Buffon, Panucci (Oddo 58), Nesta, Cannavaro, Zambrotta, Camoranesi, Perrotta (Fiore 86), Zanetti, Del Piero, Vieri, Inzaghi (Gattuso 74). **Scorers:** Inzaghi (59, 62, 70), Del Piero (76 pen). **Booked:** Buffon.

Wales (4-3-2-1): Jones (Southampton), Davies (Tottenham), Delaney (Aston Villa), Page (Sheffield Utd.), Speed (Newcastle Utd.), Koumas (W.B.A.) (Earnshaw, Cardiff City, 71), Pembridge (Fulham) (Johnson, W.B.A., 79), Savage (Birmingham City), Bellamy (Newcastle Utd.), Giggs (Manchester Utd.), Hartson (Celtic) (Blake, Wolves 82). **Booked:** Savage, Bellamy, Delaney.

Referee: M. Merk (Germany). **Half-time:** 0-0.

UKRAINE 0, NORTHERN IRELAND 0
Donetsk, (24,000), Saturday, September 6, 2003

Ukraine (4-4-2): Shovkovski, Tymoshchuk, Luzhny, Fedorov, Nesmachni, Zubov, Horshkov, Gusin (Gusev 71), Rebrov (Melaschenko 72), Vorobey, Voronin. **Booked:** Nesmachni.

Northern Ireland (4-4-1-1): Taylor (Fulham), Baird (Southampton), A. Hughes (Newcastle Utd.), McCartney (Sunderland), Kennedy (Wigan Athletic), Gillespie (Leicester City), Griffin (Dundee Utd.), Doherty (Bristol City) (Mulryne, Norwich City, 67), Johnson (Birmingham City), M. Hughes (Crystal Palace) (Jones, Crewe Alexandra, 79), Healy (Preston N.E.) (Smith, Glentoran, 62). **Booked:** M. Hughes, Doherty, Griffin.

Referee: W. Stark (Germany). **Half-time:** 0-0.

REPUBLIC OF IRELAND 1, RUSSIA 1
Lansdowne Road, (36,000), Saturday, September 6, 2003

Rep. of Ireland (4-4-1-1): Given (Newcastle Utd.), Carr (Tottenham), Breen (Sunderland), Cunningham (Birmingham City), O'Shea (Manchester Utd.) (Harte, Leeds Utd., 25), Carsley (Everton) (Reid, Blackburn Rov., 46), Holland (Charlton Athletic), Healy (Sunderland), Kilbane (Everton), Duff (Chelsea), Morrison (Birmingham City) (Doherty, Tottenham, 73). **Scorer:** Duff (35). **Booked:** Cunningham, Kilbane.

Russia (4-5-1): Ovchinnikov, Evseev, Ignashevich, Onopko, Sennikov, Gusev, Esipov (Kerzhakov 34), Smertin, Mostovoi, Alenichev (Aldonin 39), Bulykin. **Scorer:** Ignashevich (42). **Booked:** Gusev, Ignashevich, Evseev, Mostovoi.

Referee: L. Michel (Slovakia). **Half-time:** 1-1.

ENGLAND 2, LIECHTENSTEIN 0
Old Trafford, (64,931), Wednesday, September 10, 2003

England (4-3-1-2): James (West Ham Utd.), G. Neville (Manchester Utd.), Terry (Chelsea), Upson (Birmingham City), Bridge (Chelsea), Beckham (Real Madrid) (Hargreaves, Bayern Munich, 58), Gerrard (Liverpool) (P. Neville, Manchester Utd., 58), Lampard (Chelsea), Rooney (Everton) (Cole, Chelsea, 69), Owen (Liverpool), Beattie (Southampton). **Scorers:** Owen (46), Rooney (52). **Booked:** Bridge.

Liechtenstein (4-2-3-1): Jehle, Telser, Hasler, Ritter, Martin Stocklasa (Maierhofer 46), Michael Stocklasa, Gerster, R. Beck (T. Beck 57), Frick, Burgmeier, D'Elia (Buchel 73). **Booked:** Martin Stocklasa, Jehle, Gerster.

Referee: K. Fisker (Denmark). **Half-time:** 0-0.

GERMANY 2, SCOTLAND 1
Dortmund, (67,000), Wednesday, September 10, 2003

Germany (4-4-2): Kahn, Freidrich, Worms, Baumann, Rau, Schneider (Kehl 80), Ramelow, Ballack, Rehmer, Bobic (Klose 75), Kuranyi. **Scorers:** Bobic (25), Ballack (50 pen). **Booked:** Rau.

Scotland (4-4-2): Douglas (Celtic), McNamara (Celtic), Pressley (Hearts), Dailly (West Ham Utd.), Naysmith (Everton), McFadden (Everton) (Rae, Dundee, 53), Lambert (Celtic) (Ross, Rangers, 46), Ferguson (Blackburn Rov.), Cameron (Wolves), Thompson (Rangers), McCann (Southampton). **Scorer:** McCann (60). **Booked:** Dailly, Ross, Pressley, Ferguson. **Sent-off:** Ross (66).

Referee: A. Frisk (Sweden). **Half-time:** 1-0.

WALES 1, FINLAND 1
Millennium Stadium, (70,000), Wednesday, September 10, 2003

Wales (4-3-2-1): Jones (Southampton), Weston (Cardiff City) (Johnson, W.B.A., 73), Melville (Fulham), Page (Sheffield Utd.), Speed (Newcastle Utd.), Davies (Tottenham), Pembridge (Fulham), Koumas (W.B.A.), Earnshaw (Cardiff City) Giggs (Manchester Utd.), Hartson (Celtic) (Blake, Wolves, 82. **Scorer:** Davies (3). **Booked:** Koumas, Melville. **Sent-off:** Koumas (64).

Finland (4-2-3-1): Niemi, Pasanen (Kopteff 82), Tihinen, Hyypia, Saarinen (Reini 46), Riihilahti, Tainio, Nurmela, Kolkka, Vayrynen (Kuqi 57), Forssell. **Scorer:** Forssell (80). **Booked:** Pasanen.

Referee: A. Ibanez (Spain). **Half-time:** 1-0.

NORTHERN IRELAND 0, ARMENIA 1
Windsor Park, (8,616), Wednesday, September 10, 2003

Northern Ireland (4-4-2): Taylor (Fulham), Baird (Southampton), Hughes (Newcastle Utd.), McCartney (Sunderland), McCann (Cheltenham Town), Gillespie (Leicester City) (Jones, Crewe Alexandra, 29), Griffin (Dundee Utd.), Doherty (Bristol City) (Mulryne, Norwich City, 29), Johnson (Birmingham City) Healy (Preston N.E.) (McVeigh, Norwich City, 78), Smith (Glentoran). **Booked:** Johnson.

Armenia (3-5-1-1): Berezovski, Hovsepyan, Zechu, Bilibio, Sarkisian, Petrosyan, (Arman Karamyan 13), Voskanyan, Khachatryan, Melikyan, Artavadz Karamyan (Partiskyan 87), Mousesyan (Hakobyan 75). **Scorer:** Arman Karamyan (27). **Booked:** Melikyan.

Referee: A. Stredak (Slovakia). **Half-time:** 0-1.

TURKEY 0, ENGLAND 0
Istanbul, (42,000), Saturday, October 11, 2003

Turkey (4-3-1-2): Rustu, Fatih, Alpay, Bulent, Ibrahim, Okan (Ilhan 67), Tugay, Emre (Ergun 79), Sergen (Tuncay 61), Nihat, Hakan Sukur. **Booked:** Rustu, Tugay, Hakan Sukur.

England (4-4-2): James (West Ham Utd.), G. Neville (Manchester Utd.), Terry (Chelsea), Campbell (Arsenal), Cole (Arsenal), Beckham (Real Madrid), Butt (Manchester Utd.), Gerrard (Liverpool), Scholes (Manchester Utd.) (Lampard, Chelsea, 90), Heskey (Liverpool) (Vassell, Aston Villa, 68), Rooney (Everton) (Dyer, Newcastle Utd., 73). **Booked:** Butt.

Referee: P.Collina (Italy). **Half-time:** 0-0.

SCOTLAND 1, LITHUANIA 0
Hampden Park, (50,343), Saturday, October 11, 2003

Scotland (4-4-2): Douglas (Celtic), McNamara (Celtic), Pressley (Hearts), Dailly (West Ham Utd.), Naysmith (Everton), Rae (Dundee), Cameron (Wolves) (Fletcher, Manchester Utd., 65), Ferguson (Blackburn Rov.), McFadden (Everton) (Alexander, Preston N.E., 89) Crawford (Dunfermline Athletic), Miller (Wolves) (Hutchison, West Ham Utd., 65). **Scorer:** Fletcher (70). **Booked:** McNamara, Naysmith.

Lithuania (4-4-2): Stauce, Dziaukstas, Zvirgzdauskas, Dedura, Regelskis (Beniusis 85), Barasa, Vencevicius (Maclulevicius 79), Razanauskas, Baravicius (Cesnauskas 46), Jankauskas, Poskus. **Booked:** Vencevicius, Poskus.

Referee: C. Colombo (France. **Half-time:** 0-0.

WALES 2, SERBIA – MONTENEGRO 3
Millennium Stadium, (72,514), Saturday, October 11, 2003

Wales (4-2-3-1): Jones (Southampton), Weston (Cardiff City) (Edwards, Aston Villa, 73), Delaney (Aston Villa), Gabbidon (Cardiff City), Barnard (Grimsby Town), Robinson (Portsmouth) (Oster, Sunderland, 88), Speed (Newcastle Utd.), Earnshaw (Cardiff City), Giggs (Manchester Utd.), Bellamy (Newcastle Utd.), Hartson (Celtic) (Blake, Wolves, 86). **Scorers:** Hartson (24 pen), Earnshaw (90). **Booked:** Bellamy.

Serbia & Montenegro (3-4-1-2): Jevric, Gavrancic, Bunjevcevic, Djordjevic, Cirkovic (Brnovic 75), Mladenovic, Boskovic, Sarac, Vukic, Kovacevic (Ljuboja 79), Kezman (Milosevic 60). **Scorers:** Vukic (4), Milosevic (82), Ljuboja (87). **Booked:** Bunjevcevic, Gavrancic, Kezman, Djordjevic, Kovacevic.

Referee: F. Stuchlik (Austria). **Half-time:** 1-1.

GREECE 1, NORTHERN IRELAND 0
Athens, (12,500), Saturday, October 11, 2003

Greece (3-5-2): Nikopolidis, Dabizas (Venetidis 46), Antzas, Delias, Selyaridis, Giannakopoulos, Bassinas, Tsartas, Fyssas, Charisteas (Nikolaidis 46), Vryzas. **Scorer:** Tsartas (69 pen). **Booked:** Charisteas, Delias.

Northern Ireland (4-5-1): Taylor (Fulham), Baird (Southampton), McCartney (Sunderland), A. Hughes (Newcastle Utd.), Kennedy (Wigan Athletic), Healy (Preston N.E.), Griffin (Dundee Utd.) (Jones, Crewe Alexandra, 85), Whitley (Sunderland), M. Hughes (Crystal Palace), Elliott (Hull City) (Murdock, Hibernian, 70), Gillespie (Leicester City) (Smith, Glentoran, 63). **Booked:** McCartney, Taylor, M. Hughes, Whitley. **Sent-off:** McCartney (68).

Referee: L. Batista (Portugal). **Half-time:** 0-0.

SWITZERLAND 2, REPUBLIC OF IRELAND 0
Basle, (31,006), Saturday, October 11, 2003

Switzerland (4-3-1-2): Stiel, Haas, Murat Yakin, Muller, Spycher, Huggel, Vogel, Wicky, Hakan Yakin (Celestini 56), Frei (Henchoz 92), Chapuisat (Streller 69). **Scorers:** Hakan Yakin (6), Frei (60). **Booked:** Haas, Wicky.

Rep. of Ireland (4-4-2): Given (Newcastle Utd.), Carr (Tottenham), Breen (Sunderland), O'Shea (Manchester Utd.), Harte (Leeds Utd.), Duff (Chelsea), Holland (Charlton Athletic) (Kinsella, Aston Villa, 74), Healy (Sunderland), Kilbane (Everton) (Finnan, Liverpool 74), Keane (Tottenham), Connolly (West Ham Utd.) (Morrison, Birmingham City, 58). **Booked:** Carr, Kinsella, Harte.

Referee: A. Frisk (Sweden). **Half-time:** 1-0.

PLAY-OFFS FIRST LEGS

SCOTLAND 1, HOLLAND 0
Hampden Park, (50,670), Saturday, November 15, 2003

Scotland (4-1-3-2): Douglas (Celtic), McNamara (Celtic), Pressley (Hearts), Wilkie (Dundee), Naysmith (Everton), Dailly (West Ham Utd.), Fletcher (Manchester Utd.), Ferguson (Blackburn Rov.), McCann (Southampton) (*Pearson, Motherwell, 74), Dickov (Leicester City) (Miller, Wolves, 65), McFadden (Everton) (Hutchison, West Ham Utd., 90). **Scorer:** McFadden (22). **Booked:** McFadden, Dailly.

Holland (4-4-1-1): Van der Sar, Ooijer, Stam, F. De Boer, Van Bronckhorst (Seedorf, 46), Van der Meyde, Cocu, Davids (Van der Vaart 60), Overmars, Kluivert (Makaay 76), Van Nistelrooy. **Booked:** Stam, Ooijer.

Referee: T. Hauge (Norway). **Half-time:** 1-0.

RUSSIA 0, WALES 0
Moscow, (29,000), Saturday, November 15, 2003

Russia (4-3-1-2): Ovchinnikov, Evseev, Ignashevitch, Onopko, Sennikov, Smertin (Gusev 59), Mostovoi, Alenichev, Loskov, Sytchev (Izmallov 46), Bulykin. **Booked:** Ovchinnikov, Mostovoi.

Wales: Jones (Southampton), Delaney (Aston Villa), Melville (Fulham), Gabbidon (Cardiff City), Barnard (Grimsby Town), Speed (Newcastle Utd.), Koumas (W.B.A.), Johnson (W.B.A.), Savage (Birmingham City), Giggs (Manchester Utd.), Hartson (Celtic) (Blake, Wolves, 80). **Booked:** Delaney, Koumas, Speed.

Referee: L. Batista (Portugal). **Half-time:** 0-0.

PLAY-OFFS, SECOND LEGS

HOLLAND 6, SCOTLAND 0
Amsterdam, (52,000), Wednesday, November 19, 2003

Holland (3-4-3): Van der Sar, Reiziger, Ooijer (F. De Boer 46), Bouma (Seedorf 66), Cocu, Sneijder, Van der Vaart, Davids, Van der Meyde, Van Nistelrooy (Kluivert 77), Overmars. **Scorers:** Sneijder (13), Ooijer (32), Van Nistelrooy (36, 50, 66), De Boer(64). **Booked:** Davids, Van Nistelrooy.

Scotland (4-4-2): Douglas (Celtic), McNamara (Celtic), Pressley (Hearts), Wilkie (Dundee), Naysmith (Everton) (Ross, Rangers, 46), Fletcher (Manchester Utd.), Rae (Dundee), Ferguson (Blackburn Rov.), McCann (Southampton) (Miller, Wolves, 62), Dickov (Leicester City) (Crawford, Dunfermline Athletic, 46), McFadden (Everton). **Booked:** Naysmith, Pressley, Dickov.

Referee: L. Michel (Slovakia). **Half-time:** 3-0.

WALES 0, RUSSIA 1
Millennium Stadium, (73,800), Wednesday, November 19, 2003

Wales (4-1-4-1): Jones (Southampton), Delaney (Aston Villa), Melville (Fulham), Gabbidon (Cardiff City), Barnard (Grimsby Town), Speed (Newcastle Utd.), Koumas (W.B.A.) (Blake, Wolves, 74), Johnson (W.B.A.) (Earnshaw, Cardiff City, 58), Savage (Birmingham City), Giggs (Manchester Utd.), Hartson (Celtic). **Booked:** Savage, Barnard.

Russia (4-1-4-1): Malafeev, Evseev, Ignashevitch, Onopko, Sennikov, Smertin, Gusev, Titov (Radimov 59), Alenichev, Izmailov, Bulykin. **Scorer:** Evseev (22). **Booked:** Alenichev, Bulykin, Radimov.

Referee: M. Gonzalez (Spain). **Half-time:** 0-1.

FRIENDLY INTERNATIONALS

REPUBLIC OF IRELAND 2, AUSTRALIA 1
Lansdowne Road, (40,000), Tuesday, August 19, 2003

Rep. of Ireland (4-4-2): Colgan (Stockport Co.), Carr (Tottenham) (Harte, Leeds Utd., 57), Breen (Sunderland) (O'Brien, Newcastle Utd., 46), Cunningham (Birmingham City) (Dunne, Manchester City, 84), O'Shea (Manchester Utd.), Finnan (Liverpool) (Kilbane, Sunderland, 66), Kinsella (Aston Villa), Holland (Charlton Athletic) (Healy, Sunderland, 19), Duff (Chelsea) (Quinn, Sheffield Wed., 80), Doherty (Tottenham) (Morrison, Birmingham City, 57), Keane (Tottenham) (Connolly, West Ham Utd., 45). **Scorers:** O'Shea (74), Morrison (81).

Australia (4-4-2): Schwarzer, Neill, Foxe, Popovic, Lazaridis, Emerton, Okon (Grella 66), Bresciano, Tiatto (Vidmar 69), Viduka (Aloisi 78), Chipperfield. **Scorer:** Viduka (49). **Booked:** Okon.

Referee: K. Vidlak (Czech Republic). **Half-time:** 0-0.

ENGLAND 3, CROATIA 1
Portman Road, (28,700), Wednesday, August 20, 2003

England (4-4-2): James (West Ham Utd.) (Robinson, Leeds Utd., 46), P. Neville (Manchester Utd.) (Mills, Leeds Utd., 82), Terry (Chelsea), Ferdinand (Manchester Utd.) (Upson, Birmingham City, 60), A. Cole (Arsenal) (Bridge, Chelsea, 60), Beckham (Real Madrid) (Sinclair, Manchester City, 60), Butt (Manchester Utd.) (Lampard, Chelsea, 27), Scholes (Manchester Utd.) (J. Cole, Chelsea, 60), Gerrard (Liverpool) (Murphy, Liverpool, 82), Owen (Liverpool) (Dyer, Newcastle Utd., 60), Heskey (Liverpool) (Beattie, Southampton, 77). **Scorers:** Beckham (10 pen), Owen (51), Lampard (80). **Booked:** Gerrard.

Croatia (3-5-2): Pletikosa (Butina 70), Tomas, R. Kovac, Simunic, Simic (Babic 46), Leko (Rosso 60), Rapaic (Srna 46), N. Kovac (Agic 73), Zivkovic (Seric 73), Maric (Mornar 46), Olic. **Scorer:** Mornar (78). **Booked:** N.Kovac, R. Kovac.

Referee: C. Larsen (Denmark). **Half-time:** 1-0.

NORWAY 0, SCOTLAND 0
Oslo, (12,858), Wednesday, August 20, 2003

Norway (4-4-1-1): E. Johnsen, Basma (Aas 70), Berg (R. Johnsen 46), Lundekvam, Bergdolmo, (Iversen 68), Andresen, F. Johnsen (Solli 46), Hangeland (Andersen 46), Riise, Solskjaer, Carew (Flo 81). **Booked:** Carew.

Scotland (4-4-2): Douglas (Celtic), Ross (Rangers) (*Fletcher, Manchester Utd., 60), Webster (Hearts) Pressley (Hearts), Dailly (West Ham Utd.), Cameron (Wolves) (Rae, Dundee, 84), Lambert (Celtic), Ferguson (Rangers), Naysmith (Everton), Crawford (Dunfermline) (Devlin, Birmingham City, 80), Hutchison (West Ham Utd.). **Booked:** Pressley, Hutchison.

Referee: M. Vuorela (Finland). **Half-time:** 0-0.

REPUBLIC OF IRELAND 2, TURKEY 2
Lansdowne Road, (27,200), Tuesday, September 9, 2003

Rep. of Ireland (4-3-1-2): Colgan (Stockport Co.) (*Murphy, W.B.A., 72), Finnan (Liverpool), Breen (Sunderland) (Morrison, Birmingham City, 86), O'Brien (Newcastle Utd.) (Dunne, Manchester City, 72), Harte (Leeds Utd.) (Carr, Tottenham, 90), Kinsella (Aston Villa), Healy (Sunderland) (McPhail, Leeds Utd., 86), Kilbane (Everton), Duff (Chelsea) (Reid, Blackburn Rov., 46), Connolly (West Ham Utd.), Doherty (Tottenham). **Scorers:** Connolly (35), Dunne (90).

Turkey (4-4-2): Rustu (Omer 61) (Zafer 86), Fatih, Bulent (Umit Davala 46), Alpay (Okan 46), Ergun, Tayfun (Deniz 46), Tugay (Ahmet 72), Emre (Gokdeniz 61), Hasan Sas (Ibrahim 46), Tuncay (Yilmaz 72), Hakan Sukur (Tumer 86). **Scorers:** Hakan Sukur (51), Yilmaz (86). **Booked:** Alpay, Emre.

Referee: J. Wegereef (Holland). **Half-time:** 1-0.

ENGLAND 2, DENMARK 3
Old Trafford, (64,159), Sunday, November 16, 2003

England (4-3-1-2): James (West Ham Utd.) (Robinson, Leeds Utd., 46), G. Neville (Manchester Utd.) (*Johnson, Chelsea, 16), Terry (Chelsea), Upson (Birmingham City), A. Cole (Arsenal) (Bridge, Chelsea, 46), Beckham (Real Madrid) (Jenas, Newcastle Utd., 66), Butt (Manchester Utd.) (P. Neville, Manchester Utd., 46), Lampard (Chelsea), J. Cole (Chelsea) (Murphy, Liverpool, 76), Rooney (Everton) (*Parker, Charlton Athletic, 66), Heskey (Liverpool) (Beattie, Southampton, 46). **Scorers:** Rooney (5), J. Cole (9). **Booked:** James, Johnson.

Denmark (4-4-2): Sorensen, Helveg (Priske 46), Henriksen, Nielsen (Gaardsoe 71), N. Jensen, Gronkjaer (Lovenkrands 62), Gravesen, Wieghorst (D. Jensen 29), Rommedahl (Perez 20), Sand (Tomasson 46), Jorgensen (Madsen 84). **Scorers:** Jorgensen (8, 30 pen), Tomasson (82). **Booked:** D. Jensen.

Referee: V. Hrinak (Slovakia). **Half-time:** 2-2.

REPUBLIC OF IRELAND 3, CANADA 0
Lansdowne Road, (23,253), Tuesday, November 18, 2003

Rep. of Ireland (4-4-2): Given (Newcastle Utd.) (Colgan, Stockport Co., 82), Carr (Tottenham) (Harte, Leeds Utd., 46), Cunningham (Birmingham City), Dunne (Manchester City), O'Shea (Manchester Utd.) (*Thompson, Nott'm Forest, 87), S. Reid (Blackburn Rov.) (Delap, Southampton, 61), Kavanagh (Cardiff City) (Holland, Charlton Athletic, 11), *A. Reid (Nott'm Forest) (McPhail, Leeds Utd., 73), Duff (Chelsea) (Kilbane, Everton, 87), Doherty (Tottenham) (Morrison, Birmingham City, 46), Keane (Tottenham). **Scorers:** Duff (23), Keane (60, 84).

Canada (4-4-2): Hirschfeld, Stalteri, De Vos (Rogers 82), McKenna, Jazic, Bent, Bircham (Nash 79), Imhof, Hastings (Fenwick 87), Peschisolido (Bernier 75), Radzinski. **Booked:** Bircham.

Referee: M. Whitby (Wales). **Half-time:** 1-0.

PORTUGAL 1, ENGLAND 1
Faro, (27,000), Wednesday, February 18, 2004

Portugal (4-2-3-1): Ricardo, Paulo Ferreira, Fernando Couto (Beto 83), Andrade (Ricardo Carvalho 75), Rui Jorge (Valente 46), Costinha (Deco 46), Petit (Viana 83), Figo (Boa Morte 66), Rui Costa (Tiago 61), Simao (Ronaldo 46), Pauleta (Almeida 78). **Scorer:** Pauleta (70). **Booked:** Petit.

England (4-4-2): James (Manchester City), P. Neville (Manchester Utd.) (Mills, Leeds Utd., 46), Southgate (Middlesbrough), King (Tottenham), A. Cole (Arsenal) (Bridge, Chelsea, 18) (Carragher, Liverpool, 86), Beckham (Real Madrid) (Hargreaves, Bayern Munich, 86), Butt (Manchester Utd.) (Jenas, Newcastle Utd., 86), Scholes (Manchester Utd.) (Dyer, Newcastle Utd., 46), Lampard (Chelsea) (J. Cole, Chelsea, 46), Rooney (Everton) (Heskey, Liverpool, 71), Owen (Liverpool) (Smith, Leeds Utd., 71). **Scorer:** King (47).

Referee: V. Kassai (Hungary). **Half-time:** 0-0.

WALES 4, SCOTLAND 0
Millennium Stadium, (47,124), Wednesday, February 18, 2004

Wales (4-4-2): Crossley (Fulham) (Ward, Nott'm Forest, 46), Edwards (Aston Villa), Melville (West Ham Utd.) (Symons, Crystal Palace, 87), Page (Sheffield Utd.), Gabbidon (Cardiff City), Oster (Sunderland), Savage (Birmingham City) (*C. Fletcher, Bournemouth, 72), Speed (Newcastle Utd.) (Robinson, Portsmouth, 72), Davies (Tottenham) (*Parry, Cardiff City, 33), Earnshaw (Cardiff City), Giggs (Manchester Utd.) (Taylor, Nott'm. Forest, 46). **Scorers:** Earnshaw (1, 35, 58), Taylor (78).

Scotland (4-1-3-2): Douglas (Celtic), McNamara (Celtic), Caldwell (Newcastle Utd.), Ritchie (Walsall), Naysmith (Everton) (*Murty, Reading, 46), Dailly (West Ham Utd.), Fletcher (Manchester Utd.) (Webster, Hearts, 86), Cameron (Wolves) (*Gallagher, Blackburn Rov., 68), Pearson (Celtic) (McFadden, Everton, 46), Miller (Wolves), Dickov (Leicester City).

Referee: M. Ross (Northern Ireland). **Half-time:** 2-0.

NORTHERN IRELAND 1, NORWAY 4
Windsor Park, (11,288), Wednesday, February 18, 2004

Northern Ireland (4-4-2): Taylor (Fulham), Baird (Southampton), A. Hughes (Newcastle Utd.), McCartney (Sunderland), Kennedy (Wigan Athletic) (Jones, Crewe Alexandra, 77), Gillespie (Leicester City) (McVeigh, Norwich City, 73), M. Hughes (Crystal Palace), Griffin (Stockport Co.) (Williams, Wimbledon, 46), Johnson (Birmingham City), Smith (Glentoran), Healy (Preston N.E.). **Scorer:** Healy (56). **Booked:** Gillespie.

Norway (4-4-1-1): Myhre (Holtan 70), El Fakiri, Johnsen, Hangeland, Riise (Hanstveit 70), Helstad (Hoiland 89), Andresen, Hoset, Pedersen (Odegaard 81), Iversen (Tessem 62), Rushfeldt (Flo 46). **Scorers:** Pedersen (17, 35), Iversen (43), Gillespie (57 og).

Referee: C. Thomson (Scotland). **Half-time:** 0-3.

REPUBLIC OF IRELAND 0, BRAZIL 0
Lansdowne Road, (44,000), Wednesday, February 18, 2004

Rep. of Ireland (4-4-2): Given (Newcastle Utd.), Carr (Tottenham), O'Brien (Newcastle Utd.), Cunningham (Birmingham City), O'Shea (Manchester Utd.), Holland (Charlton Athletic), Kavanagh (Cardiff City), Kilbane (Everton), Reid (Nott'm Forest) (McAteer, Sunderland, 64), Morrison (Birmingham City), Keane (Tottenham). **Booked:** Kavanagh.

Brazil (4-2-3-1): Dida, Cafu, Lucio, Roque Junior, Roberto Carlos, Kleberson (Julio Baptista 46), Gilberto Silva (Edmilson 14), Ronaldinho, Kaka, Ze Roberto, Ronaldo. **Booked:** Cafu, Roque Junior.

Referee: A. Frisk (Sweden). **Half-time:** 0-0.

SWEDEN 1, ENGLAND 0
Gothenburg, (40,464), Wednesday, March 31, 2004

Sweden (4-4-2): Isaksson (Kihistedt 46), Lucic, Mellberg, Mjallby (Linderoth 46), Edman, Nilsson, Svensson (Jonson 46), Andersson (Kallstrom 46), Wilhelmsson, Ibramhovic (Ostlund 90), Elmander (Hansson 46). **Scorer:** Ibramovic (54). **Booked:** Mjallby.

England: James (Manchester City), P. Neville (Manchester Utd.), Terry (Chelsea) (*Gardner, Tottenham, 46), Woodgate (Newcastle Utd.) (Southgate, Middlesbrough, 46), Carragher (Liverpool), Hargreaves (Bayern Munich) (Jenas, Newcastle Utd., 60), Butt (Manchester Utd.) (Parker, Chelsea, 78), Gerrard (Liverpool) (Cole, Chelsea, 60), *Thompson (Celtic) (Heskey, Liverpool, 60), Vassell (Aston Villa) (*Defoe, Tottenham, 12), Rooney (Everton) (Smith, Leeds Utd., 60). **Booked:** P. Neville.

Referee: T. Ovebro (Norway). **Half-time:** 0-0.

SCOTLAND 1, ROMANIA 2
Hampden Park, (20,433), Wednesday, March 31, 2004

Scotland (3-5-2): Gallacher (Dundee Utd.), Dailly (West Ham Utd.), Pressley (Hearts), *Kennedy (Celtic) (Crainey, Southampton, 18), Alexander (Preston N.E.), Caldwell (Hibernian), Rae (Rangers), Cameron (Wolves), McCann (Southampton), Miller (Wolves) (McFadden, Everton 51), Thompson (Rangers) (Crawford, Dunfermline Athletic, 63). **Scorer:** McFadden (57).

Romania (4-4-2): Stelea (Lobont 46), Stoican, Iensci, Chivu, Rat, F. Petre (Mitea 46), O. Petre, Pancu (Danciulescu 89), Cernat (Soava 63), Ganea (Cristea 81), Mutu. **Scorers:** Chivu (37), Pancu (51). **Booked:** Mutu, Cernat.

Referee: J. Hyytia (Finland). **Half-time:** 0-1.

HUNGARY 1, WALES 2
Budapest, (15,000), Wednesday, March 31, 2004

Hungary (3-5-2): Babos, Peto, Stark, Komlosi (Dveri 89), Bodnar, Molnar, Lisztes (Toth 52), Gera, Low (Bodor 89), Kenesei (Szabics 46), Torghelle (Sebok 69). **Scorer:** Kenesei (17 pen). **Booked:** Lisztes, Torghelle.

Wales (4-4-2): Jones (Wolves) (Coyne, Leicester City, 46), Gabbidon (Cardiff City), Page (Sheffield Utd.), Melville (West Ham Utd.) *Thatcher (Leicester City) (Edwards, Aston Villa, 64), Koumas (W.B.A.), Savage (Birmingham City), Robinson (Portsmouth) (C. Fletcher, Bournemouth, 89), Vaughan (Crewe Alexandra) (Roberts, Tranmere Rov., 64), Earnshaw (Cardiff City), Taylor (Nott'm Forest). **Scorers:** Koumas (20), Earnshaw (81). **Booked:** Thatcher, Vaughan.

Referee: F. Meyer (Germany). **Half-time:** 1-1.

ESTONIA 0, NORTHERN IRELAND 1
Tallinn, (2,000), Wednesday, March 31, 2004

Estonia (4-4-2): Kaalma, Jaager, Stepanov, Piiroja (Rahn 82), Klavan, Smirnov (Reinumae 85), Reim, Kristal, Kink (Terehov 71), Zeleinski (Teever 64), Rooba (Lindpere 73). **Booked:** Reim, Piiroja, Rahn.

Northern Ireland: Taylor (Birmingham City), Baird (Southampton), Williams (Wimbledon), Craigan (Motherwell), *Capaldi (Plymouth Argyle), Jones (Crewe Alexandra) (McCann, Cheltenham Town, 68), Sonner (Nott'm Forest) (Duff, Cheltenham Town, 78), Whitley (Sunderland), Mulryne (Norwich City), Healy (Preston N.E.), Smith (Glentoran). **Scorer:** Healy (45). **Booked:** Sonner, Healy, Williams.

Referee: P.Kari (Finland). Half-time: 0-1.

REPUBLIC OF IRELAND 2, CZECH REPUBLIC 1
Lansdowne Road, (42,000), Wednesday, March 31, 2004

Rep. of Ireland: Given (Newcastle Utd.) (*Kenny, Sheffield Utd., 82), Maybury (Hearts), Doherty (Tottenham) (*Miller, Celtic, 70), Cunningham (Birmingham City), Harte (Leeds Utd.), Reid (Nott'm Forest) (Delap, Southampton, 66), Holland (Charlton Athletic), Kilbane (Everton), Duff (Chelsea) (Kinsella, W.B.A., 76), Keane (Tottenham), Morrison (Birmingham City) (Lee, Cardiff City, 76). **Scorers:** Harte (52), Keane (90). **Booked:** Kilbane.

Czech Republic: Cech (Vaniak 46), Jiranek (Plasil 69), Bolf (Rozehnal 58), Ujfalusi, Jankulovski, Sioko (Stajner 46), Galasek, Tyce, Nedved (Heinz 46), Baros (Vorisek, 84), Koller (Lovenc 46). **Scorer:** Baros (81). **Booked:** Sionko.

Referee: E. Fisker (Denmark). Half-time: 0-0.

DENMARK 1, SCOTLAND 0
Copenhagen, (22,885), Wednesday, April 28, 2004

Denmark (4-3-3): Sorensen, Helveg, Henriksen (Kroldrup 66), Laursen, N. Jensen (Perez 46), D. Jensen, C. Jensen (Sennels 46), Wieghorst (Retov 80), Gronkjaer (Rasmussen 88), Tomasson (Sand 46), Jorgensen (Rommedahl 66). **Scorer:** Sand (60).

Scotland (4-4-2): Gallacher (Dundee Utd.), Caldwell (Hibernian), Pressley (Hearts), *Mackay (Norwich City), Crainey (Southampton), Cameron (Wolves) (McCann, Southampton, 46), Fletcher (Manchester Utd.), Dailly (West Ham Utd.), Holt (Norwich City) (*Canero, Leicester City, 16), Kyle (Sunderland), McFadden (Everton). **Booked:** Caldwell, McFadden.

Referee: M. Ingvarsson (Sweden). Half-time: 0-0.

NORTHERN IRELAND 1, SERBIA – MONTENEGRO 1
Windsor Park, (9,690), Wednesday, April 28, 2004

Northern Ireland (4-4-2): Taylor (Birmingham City) (Carroll, Manchester Utd., 46), Baird (Southampton), Williams (Wimbledon), Craigan (Motherwell), Capaldi (Plymouth Argyle), Gillespie (Leicester City) (Jones, Crewe Alexandra, 46), Doherty (Bristol City) (Hughes, Crystal Palace, 78), Whitley (Sunderland) (Sonner, Nott'm Forest, 78), Mulryne (Norwich City) (McVeigh, Norwich City, 46), Healy (Preston N.E.) (Hamilton, Portadown, 46), Quinn (Willem 11) (Smith, Glentoran, 78). **Scorer:** Quinn (18). **Booked:** Whitley, Doherty, Quinn.

Serbia & Montenegro (4-5-1): Banovic, Cirkovic (Markoski 82), Petkovic, Krstajic, Dragutinovic (Vitakic 46), Trobok (Ivic 46), Gavrancic, Nadj, Vukic, Paunovic (Kolakovic 69), Kezman. **Scorer:** Paunovic (7). **Booked:** Nadj, Paunovic, Krstajic.

Referee: C. Richards (Wales). Half-time: 1-1.

POLAND 0, REPUBLIC OF IRELAND 0
Bydgoszcz, (18,000), Wednesday, April 28, 2004

Poland (4-1-4-1): Dudek (Boruc 58), Zewlakow (Kaczorowski 83), Klos (Bosacki 80), Glowacki (Hajto 46), Rzasa, Lewandowski, Zurawski, Szymkowiak (Radomski 85), Mila (Smolarek 65), Krzynowek (Kosowski 46), Olisadebe (Niedzielan 46).

Rep. of Ireland (4-4-2): Given (Newcastle Utd.) (Colgan, Hibernian, 70), O'Shea (Manchester Utd.), Doherty (Tottenham) (O'Brien, Newcastle Utd., 80), Cunningham (Birmingham City), Harte (Leeds Utd.) (Maybury, Hearts, 63), S. Reid (Blackburn Rov.), Miller (Celtic), Kinsella (W.B.A.), A. Reid (Nott'm Forest) (*Douglas, Blackburn Rov., 80), Lee (Cardiff City) (Barrett, Coventry City, 63), Morrison (Birmingham City) (*Byrne, Shelbourne, 89.). **Booked:** Maybury, Barrett.

Referee: S. Shebek (Ukraine). Half-time: 0-0.

ESTONIA 0, SCOTLAND 1
Tallinn, (4,000), Thursday, May 27, 2004

Estonia (4-4-2): Kaalma, Allas, Stepanov, Jaager, Klavan, Rahn, Reim, Viikmae, Terehhov (Reinumae 85), Oper, Lindpere (Kink 75). **Booked:** Viikmae, Rahn.

Scotland (4-4-2): Gallacher (Dundee Utd.), *McNamee (Livingston), Pressley (Hearts) (Webster, Hearts, 46), Mackay (Norwich City), *Hughes (Portsmouth),. Caldwell (Hibernian), Holt (Norwich City), *Quashie (Portsmouth), Fletcher (Manchester Utd.), McFadden (Everton), (Kerr, Newcastle Utd., 89), Miller (Wolves) (Crawford, Dunfermline Athletic, 78). **Scorer:** McFadden (76). **Booked:** Caldwell.

Referee: T. Poulsen (Denmark). **Half-time:** 0-0.

NORWAY 0, WALES 0
Oslo, (14,137), Thursday, May 27, 2004

Norway (4-4-2): Myhre, Basma, Berg (Lundekvam 17), Johnsen (Andersen 88), Riise, Helstad (Flo 61), Andresen, Hoset, Pedersen (Bergdolmo 46), Solskjaer (Solli 61), Saeternes (Lange 46). **Booked:** Solskjaer.

Wales (4-4-2): Coyne (Leicester City), Delaney (Aston Villa), *Collins (Cardiff City), Gabbidon (Cardiff City), Thatcher (Leicester City), Oster (Sunderland) (Barnard, Grimsby Town, 90), Fletcher (Bournemouth), Robinson (Portsmouth) Edwards, Aston Villa, 75), Parry (Cardiff City) (G. Roberts, Tranmere Rov., 71), Earnshaw (Cardiff City) (N. Roberts, Wigan Athletic, 71), Bellamy (Newcastle Utd.) (Llewellyn, Wrexham, 80).

Referee: M. Hansson (Sweden). **Half-time:** 0-0.

REPUBLIC OF IRELAND 1, ROMANIA 0
Lansdowne Road, (42,356), Thursday, May 27, 2004

Rep. of Ireland (4-4-2): Given (Newcastle Utd.), Finnan (Liverpool), Cunningham (Birmingham City), O'Brien (Newcastle Utd.), Maybury (Hearts), Miller (Celtic), Roy Keane (Manchester Utd.), Holland (Charlton Athletic), Reid (Nott'm Forest) (*Rowlands, Q.P.R., 78), Robbie Keane (Tottenham), Morrison (Birmingham City) **Scorer:** Holland (85).

Romania (4-4-2): Labont (Stelea 46), Dumitru, Icensi (Barcauan 90), Ghianes, Dancia (M. Petre 78), Radoi (Constianin 84), Plesan (Aliuta 61), Soava (O. Petre 90), Dica (Alexa 78), Danciulescu (Neaga 61), Ganea (Niculae 88).

Referee: J. Jara (Czech Republic). **Half-time:** 0-0.

REPUBLIC OF IRELAND 0, NIGERIA 3 (Unity Cup)
The Valley, (7,438), Saturday, May 29, 2004

Rep. of Ireland (4-4-2): Colgan (Hibernian), Finnan (Liverpool), Doherty (Tottenham), Cunningham (Birmingham City), Maybury (Hearts) (*Clarke, Stoke City, 46), Miller (Celtic) (Rowlands, Q.P.R., 46), Kinsella (W.B.A.), Holland (Charlton Athletic) (Douglas, Blackburn Rov., 67), McPhail (Leeds Utd.), Keane (Tottenham) (Barrett, Coventry City, 84), Lee (Cardiff City).

Nigeria (4-4-2): Rotimi, Abbey (Adamu 90), Olajengbesi, Enakhire, Lawal, Utaka, Olofinjana (Obiefule 86) Obodo, Ekwueme, Martins (Showunmi 84), Ogbeche (Baita 72). **Scorers:** Ogbeche (36, 69), Martins (4).

Referee: A. D'Urso (England). **Half-time:** 0-1.

SCOTLAND 4, TRINIDAD & TOBAGO 1
Easter Road, (16,187), Sunday, May 30, 2004

Scotland (4-4-2): *Gordon (Hearts), McNamara (Celtic), Pressley (Hearts), Mackay (Norwich City) (McNamee, Livingston, 85), *McAllister (Livingston), Quashie (Portsmouth) (Hughes, Portsmouth, 72), G. Caldwell (Hibernian) (S. Caldwell,

Newcastle Utd., 80), Fletcher (Manchester Utd.), Holt (Norwich City), Crawford (Dunfermline Athletic) (Miller, Wolves, 67), McFadden (Everton) (Webster, Hearts, 85). **Scorers:** Fletcher (6), Holt (14), G. Caldwell (23), Quashie (34).

Trinidad & Tobago (3-5-2): Ince, Sancho, Cox, Andrews, Edwards (Theobald 90), Eve (Jermot 82), Dwarika (Nixon 74), Jones (Rojas 46), Mason, John, Glen (Boucard 28). **Scorer:** John (55).

Referee: P. Vink (Holland). **Half-time:** 4-0.

WALES 1, CANADA 0
The Racecourse Ground, (10,805), Sunday, May 30, 2004

Wales (4-4-2): Coyne (Leicester City) (*Margetson, Cardiff City, 46), Delaney (Aston Villa), Collins (Cardiff City), Gabbidon (Cardiff City), Thatcher (Leicester City), Oster (Sunderland), Fletcher (Portsmouth), Robinson (Portsmouth) (Edwards, Aston Villa, 79), Parry (Cardiff City) (Earnshaw, Cardiff City, 67), Bellamy (Newcastle Utd.), Giggs (Manchester Utd.) (Llewellyn, Wrexham, 89). **Scorer:** Parry (21).

Canada (4-4-2): Onstad, Imhof, Watson, De Vos, Jazic, Hulme (Occean 79), De Guzman, Hutchinson (Peschisolido 46), Brennan (Bircham 46), Radzinski (McKenna 72), De Rosario (Klukowski 83).

Referee: P. McKeon (Republic of Ireland). **Half-time:** 1-0.

BARBADOS 1, NORTHERN IRELAND 1
Bridgetown, (8,000), Monday, May 31, 2004

Barbados (4-4-2): Chase, Braithwaite, Parris, James, Burrowes, Hall, Forde, Lovell, Grosvenor, Skinner (Riley 65), Lucas. **Scorer:** Skinner (40).

Northern Ireland (4-4-2): Taylor (Birmingham City), Baird (Southampton) (Jones, Crewe Alexandra, 67), Capaldi (Plymouth Argyle) (Elliott, Hull City, 67), Williams (Wimbledon), Gillespie (Leicester City) (Murdock, Hibernian, 45), Johnson (Birmingham City), Sonner (Nott'm Forest) (McVeigh, Norwich City, 67), Mulryne (Norwich City) (Smith, Glentoran, 45), Quinn (Willem 11), Healy (Preston N.E.), Hamilton (Portadown, 80). **Scorer:** Healy (71). **Sent-off:** Williams (30).

Referee: N. Brizan (Trinidad). **Half-time:** 1-0.

ENGLAND 1, JAPAN 1
City of Manchester Stadium, (38,581), Tuesday, June 1, 2004

England (4-1-2-1-2): James (Manchester City), G.Neville (Manchester Utd.) (P. Neville, Manchester Utd., 87), Terry (Chelsea) (King, Tottenham, 90), Campbell (Arsenal), A. Cole (Arsenal), Lampard (Chelsea) (Butt, Manchester Utd., 83), Beckham (Real Madrid) (J. Cole, Chelsea, 83), Gerrard (Liverpool) (Hargreaves, Bayern Munich, 83), Scholes (Manchester Utd.) (Dyer, Newcastle Utd., 78), Owen (Liverpool) (Vassell, Aston Villa, 78), Rooney (Everton) (Heskey, Birmingham City, 78). **Scorer:** Owen (22).

Japan (3-4-1-2): Narasaki, Tsubol, Miyamoto, Nakazawa, Kaji, Inamoto (Fukunishi 89), Ono, Santos, Nakamura, Kubo (Yanagisawa 59) Tamada (Suzuki 59). **Scorer:** Ono (53).

Referee: R. Rosetti (Italy). **Half-time:** 1-0.

ST KITTS & NEVIS 0, NORTHERN IRELAND 2
Basseterre, (3,500), Wednesday, June 2, 2004

St Kitts & Nevis (4-4-2): Byron (Benjamin 46), Lewis (Riley 46), Eddy (Challenger46), Burton (Jeffers 46), Issac (Hodge 46), Huggins (A. Saddler 46), K. Saddler, Gomez (Sargent 46), Lake (Francis 46), Leader (Lawrence 46), Gumbs.

Northern Ireland (4-4-2): Taylor (Birmingham City), Baird (Southampton), Capaldi (Plymouth Argyle), Craigan (Motherwell), Murdock (Hibernian), McVeigh (Norwich City) (Mulryne, Norwich City, 63), Sonner (Nott'm Forest) (Jones, Crewe Alexandra, 51), Whitley (Sunderland) (Johnson, Birmingham City, 63), Elliott (Hull City) (Gillespie, Leicester City, 63), Hamilton (Portadown) (Healy, Preston N.E., 63), Smith (Glentoran). **Scorers:** Healy (81), Jones (84).

Referee: J. Matthew (St Kitts & Nevis). **Half-time:** 0-0.

REPUBLIC OF IRELAND 1, JAMAICA 0 (Unity Cup)
The Valley, (6,155), Wednesday, June 2, 2004

Rep. of Ireland (4-4-2): Kenny (Sheffield Utd.), Maybury (Hearts), Doherty (Tottenham), O'Brien (Newcastle Utd.), O'Shea (Manchester Utd.) (Clarke, Stoke City, 46), Barrett (Coventry City), Kinsella (W.B.A.), Quinn (Sheffield Wed.) (Holland, Charlton Athletic, 83), A. Reid (Nott'm Forest) (Rowlands, Q.P.R., 77), Morrison (Birmingham City), Lee (Cardiff City) (*McGeady, Celtic, 83). **Scorer:** Barrett (26).

Jamaica (4-3-3): Ricketts, Neil, Stewart, Goodison, G. Reid, Davis, Chin-Sue (Langley 66), Hyde, Burton (Bernard 83), Lisbie (Johnson 83), King (Dobson 85).

Referee: R. Styles (England). **Half-time:** 1-0.

ENGLAND 6, ICELAND 1
City of Manchester Stadium, (43,500), Saturday, June 5, 2004

England (4-4-2): Robinson (Tottenham) (Walker, Leicester City, 62), G. Neville (Manchester Utd.) (P. Neville, Manchester Utd., 46), Carragher (Liverpool) (Defoe, Tottenham, 85), Campbell (Arsenal) (King, Tottenham, 46), A. Cole (Arsenal) (Bridge, Chelsea, 46), Beckham (Real Madrid) (Dyer, Newcastle Utd., 46), Lampard (Chelsea) (Butt, Manchester Utd., 46), Gerrard (Liverpool) (Hargreaves, Bayern Munich, 46), Scholes (Manchester Utd.) (J. Cole, Chelsea, 46), Rooney (Everton) (Heskey, Birmingham City, 46), Owen (Liverpool) (Vassell, Aston Villa, 46). **Scorers:** Lampard (25), Rooney (27, 38), Vassell (57, 77), Bridge (68)

Iceland (3-4-1-2): Arason, Ingimarsson, Marteinsson (K. Sigurdsson 46), Hreidarsson, T. Gudjonsson (Jonsson 78), J. Gudjonsson, Gretarsson, I. Sigurdsson (J. Gudmundsson 78), Gudjohnsen, Helguson (T. Gundmundsson 85), H. Sigurdsson (B. Gudjonsson 69).

Referee: J. Wegereef (Holland). **Half-time:** 3-1.

HOLLAND 0, REPUBLIC OF IRELAND 1
Amsterdam, (43,000), Saturday, June 5, 2004

Holland (4-4-2): Van der Sar, Reiziger (Heitinga 46), Stam, Bouma (Van Hooijdonk 84), Van Bronckhorst, Sneijder (Seedorf 63), Bosvelt 63), Cocu, Van der Vaart, Davids (Robben 63), Van Nistelrooy (Makaay 66), Kluivert (Van der Meyde 46).

Rep. of Ireland (4-4-2); Given (Newcastle Utd.), Finnan (Liverpool), O'Brien (Newcastle Utd.), Cunningham (Birmingham City), Maybury (Hearts) (*Doyle, Coventry City, 88), Barrett (Coventry City), Holland (Charlton Athletic), Quinn (Sheffield Wed.), Reid (Nott'm Forest), Morrison (Birmingham City) (Lee, Cardiff City, 83), Keane (Tottenham). **Scorer:** Keane (45).

Referee: M. Dean (England). **Half-time:** 0-1.

TRINIDAD & TOBAGO 0, NORTHERN IRELAND 3
Bacolet, Tobago, (7,500), Sunday, June 6, 2004

Trinidad & Tobago (3-5-2): Ince, Eve, Sancho (Thomas 45), Cox, Rougier (Roberts 76), Andrews, Bouchard (Fitzwilliams 68), Jemmott, Mason (Yorke 46), Edwards (Theobald 83), John.

Northern Ireland (4-4-2): Taylor (Birmingham City) (*Mannus, Linfield, 82), Baird (Southampton), Capaldi (Plymouth Argyle), Craigan (Motherwell) (Murdock, Hibernian, 46), Williams (Wimbledon), Elliott (Hull City) (Jones, Crewe Alexandra, 46), Johnson (Birmingham City) (Gillespie, Leicester City, 72), Mulryne (Norwich City) (Sonner, Nott'm Forest, 72), Whitley (Sunderland), Healy (Preston N.E.) (McVeigh, Norwich City, 65), Quinn (Willem 11) (Smith, Glentoran, 61). **Scorers:** Healy (5, 65), Elliott (41).

Referee: B. Callender (Barbados). **Half-time:** 0-2.

BRITISH AND IRISH UNDER-21
INTERNATIONALS 2003-04

EUROPEAN U-21 CHAMPIONSHIP QUALIFYING ROUND

SERBIA-MONTENEGRO 3, WALES 0
Novi Sad, (3,000), Tuesday, August 19, 2003

Wales: Brown (Gillingham), Moss (Shrewsbury Town), Price (Scarborough) (Somner, Brentford, 70) Pejic (Wrexham), Rees (Millwall), Tolley (Shrewsbury Town), Pipe (Coventry City) (Powell, Leicester City, 73), Fowler (Coventry City), Collins (Cardiff City) (M. Williams, Manchester Utd., 51), G. Williams (Crystal Palace), Gall (Yeovil Town).

Scorers – Serbia & Montenegro: Matic (10), Lazovic (60), Milobanovic (76). **Half-time:** 1-0.

MACEDONIA 1, ENGLAND 1
Skopje, (2,700), Friday, September 5, 2003

England: Kirkland (Liverpool), Johnson (Chelsea), Clarke (Everton), Konchesky (Charlton Athletic), Jagielka (Sheffield Utd.), Pennant (Arsenal) (Wright-Phillips, Manchester City, 61), Barton (Manchester City), Sidwell (Reading), Tonge (Sheffield Utd.) (Defoe, West Ham Utd., 66), Jeffers (Arsenal), Ameobi (Newcastle Utd.).

Scorers – Macedonia: Stojkovski (62). **England:** Jagielka (35). **Half-time:** 0-1.

ITALY 8, WALES 1
Pavia, (4,000), Friday, September 5, 2003

Wales: Brown (Gillingham), Pejic (Wrexham), Somner (Brentford), Fowler (Coventry City), Rees (Millwall), Collins (Cardiff City) (Powell, Leicester City, 61), Pipe (Coventry City), Brough (Notts Co.), Gall (Yeovil Town), Vaughan (Crewe Alexandra), G. Williams (Crystal Palace) (M. Williams, Manchester Utd., 23).

Scorers – Italy: Gilardino (17, 49, 69, 87), Brighi (20), Sculli (35, 64), Borriello (90). **Wales:** Vaughan (27). **Half-time:** 3-1.

UKRAINE 1, NORTHERN IRELAND 0
Donetsk, (2,500), Friday, September 5, 2003

Northern Ireland: Blayney (Southampton), Hughes (Tottenham), Capaldi (Plymouth Argyle), Buchan (Lisburn), Webb (Ross Co.), Melaugh (Rochdale) (Davis, Aston Villa), Clingan (Wolves), McFlynn (Margate), McEvilly (Rochdale), Feeney (Bournemouth), Davey (UCD) (Clarke, Peterborough Utd.)

Scorer – Ukraine: Danylovsky (58). **Half-time:** 0-0.

REPUBLIC OF IRELAND 2, RUSSIA 0
Waterford, (4,000), Friday, September 5, 2003

Rep. of Ireland: Connor (Waterford), Kelly (Tottenham), Cryan (Sheffield Utd.) (Byrne, Scunthorpe Utd., 81), Thompson (Nott'm Forest), Kohlmann (Borussia Dortmund), Butler (Sunderland), Miller (Celtic), O'Connor (Brentford) (Doyle, Coventry City, 76), Reid (Nott'm Forest), O'Flynn (Cork City) (Elliott, Manchester City, 88), Barrett (Coventry City).

Scorers – Rep. of Ireland: Barrett (65), Rogochiy (81 og). **Half-time:** 0-0.

ENGLAND 1, PORTUGAL 2
Goodison Park, (23,744), Tuesday, September 9, 2003

England: Grant (Derby Co.), Jagielka (Sheffield Utd.), Dawson (Nott'm Forest), Clarke (Everton), Konchesky (Charlton Athletic), Johnson (Chelsea), Barton (Manchester City), Prutton (Southampton) (Defoe, West Ham Utd., 79), Barry (Aston Villa), Amoebi (Newcastle Utd.), Jeffers (Arsenal).

Scorers – England: Barton (37). **Portugal:** Quaresma (4), Postiga (78). **Half-time:** 1-1.

GERMANY 0, SCOTLAND 1
Ahlen, (5,700), Tuesday, September 9, 2003

Scotland: Soutar (Dundee), Caldwell (Newcastle Utd.), Pearson (Motherwell), McCracken (Dundee Utd.), Crainey (Celtic), Williams (Nott'm Forest), Duff (Dundee Utd.), Murray (Hibernian) Kyle (Sunderland), Stewart (Manchester Utd.) (Fletcher, Manchester Utd., 57), Lynch (Preston N.E.) (Maloney, Celtic, 50).

Scorer – Scotland: Maloney (62). **Half-time:** 0-0.

WALES 0, FINLAND 0
Merthyr, (1,311), Tuesday, September 9, 2003

Wales: Brown (Gillingham), Powell (Leicester City), Price (Scarborough), Fowler (Coventry City) (Collins, Cardiff City, 85), Pejic (Wrexham), Morgan (Wrexham), Pipe (Coventry City), Brough (Notts Co.), Gall (Yeovil Town), Williams (Manchester Utd.), Stock (Bournemouth).

NORTHERN IRELAND 3, ARMENIA 1
Ballymena Showgrounds, (250), Tuesday, September 9, 2003

Northern Ireland: Blayney (Southampton), Close (Middlesbrough), Capaldi (Plymouth Argyle), Buchanan (Lisburn), Webb (Ross Co.), Melaugh (Rochdale), McFlynn, Margate, 61), Hughes (Tottenham) (Davis, Aston Villa, 55), Clingan (Wolves), McEvilly (Rochdale), Feeney (Bournemouth) (Clarke, Peterborough Utd., 55), Davey (UCD).

Scorers – Northern Ireland: Feeney (52), McFlynn (72), Davey (87). **Armenia:** Pachajyan (3). **Half-time:** 0-1.

TURKEY 1, ENGLAND 0
Istanbul, (4,000), Friday, October 10, 2003

England: Grant (Derby Co.), Johnson (Chelsea), Davies (Middlesbrough), Jagielka (Sheffield Utd.), Taylor (Portsmouth), Wright-Phillips (Manchester City), Sidwell (Reading) (Reo-Coker, Wimbledon, 61), Jenas (Newcastle Utd.), Prutton (Southampton) (Bent, Ipswich Town, 80), Ameobi (Newcastle Utd.), Defoe (West Ham Utd.). **Sent-off:** Johnson.

Scorer – Turkey: Fatih (2). **Half-time:** 1-0.

SCOTLAND 3, LITHUANIA 2
McDiarmid Park, (5,289), Friday, October 10, 2003

Scotland: Soutar (Dundee), Caldwell (Newcastle Utd.), Hammell (Motherwell), Kennedy (Celtic), McCracken (Dundee Utd.), Williams (Nott'm Forest) (Hughes, Rangers, 63), Canero (Kilmarnock) (McManus, Hibernian, 70), Kerr (Newcastle Utd.), Maloney (Celtic), Stewart (Manchester Utd.), Lynch (Preston N.E.) (Gallagher (Blackburn Rov., 75).

Scorers – Scotland: Hammell (79), Hughes (90, 90). **Lithuania:** Stankevicius (5), Kucys (71 prn)

WALES 0, SERBIA-MONTENEGRO 1
Barry, (1,200), Friday, October 10, 2003

Wales: Brown (Gillingham), Moss (Shrewsbury Town), Price (Scarborough), Collins (Cardiff City), Day (Mansfield Town), Stock (Bournemouth), Pipe (Coventry City), Jones (Wrexham), Gall (Yeovil Town) (Crowell, Wrexham, 58), Tolley (Shrewsbury Town) (Morgan, Wrexham, 63), Williams (Manchester Utd.).

Scorer – Serbia & Montenegro: Matic (30). **Half-time:** 0-1.

GREECE 0, NORTHERN IRELAND 1
Athens, (300), Friday, October 10, 2003

Northern Ireland: Blayney (Southampton), Close (Middlesbrough), Capaldi (Plymouth Argyle), Buchanan (Lisburn), Webb (Ross Co.), Clingan (Wolves), Melaugh (Glentoran) (Hughes, Tottenham), McFlynn (Margate), McEvilly (Rochdale) (Braniff, Millwall), Feeney (Bournemouth), Davey (UCD).

Scorer – Northern Ireland: Feeney (25). **Half-time:** 0-1.

SWITZERLAND 0, REPUBLIC OF IRELAND 2
Neuchatel, (3,652), Friday, October 10, 2003

Rep. of Ireland: Connor (Waterford), Kelly (Tottenham), Thompson (Nott'm Forest), Fitzgerald (Blackburn Rov.), Kohlmann (Borussia Dortmund), Thornton (Sunderland), Keegan (Leeds Utd.), O'Connor (Brentford) (Whelan, Manchester City, 90), Hoolahan (Shelbourne), Elliott (Manchester City), Walters (Bolton Wand.) (Deane, Charlton Athletic, 81).

Scorer – Rep. of Ireland: Walters (61, 74). **Half-time:** 0-0.

PLAY-OFFS

CROATIA 2, SCOTLAND 0
Varazdin, (4,000), Sunday, November 16, 2003

Scotland: Gordon (Hearts), Caldwell (Newcastle Utd.), Hammell (Motherwell), McCracken (Dundee Utd.), Kennedy (Celtic), Kerr (Newcastle Utd.), Canero (Kilmarnock), Murray (Hibernian), Kyle (Sunderland), Stewart (Manchester Utd.) (Hughes, Rangers, 84), McManus (Hibernian) (Maloney, Celtic, 46).

Scorers – Croatia: Babic (6), Ljubojevic (11). **Half-time:** 2-0.

SCOTLAND 1, CROATIA 0
Easter Road, (11,992), Tuesday, November 18, 2003

Scotland: Gordon (Hearts), Duff (Dundee Utd.), Hammell (Motherwell), Williams (Nott'm Forest), Kennedy (Celtic), Kerr (Newcastle Utd.), Canero (Kilmarnock) (Montgomery, Sheffield Utd., 90), Murray (Hibernian), Kyle (Sunderland) (Lynch, Preston N.E., 36), Maloney (Celtic) (Hughes, Rangers, 68), O'Connor (Hibernian).

Scorer – Scotland: O'Connor (11). **Half-time:** 1-0.

FRIENDLIES

ENGLAND 0, CROATIA 3
Upton Park, (20,000), Tuesday, August 19, 2003

England: Murray (Wolves), Johnson (Chelsea), Parnaby (Middlesbrough), Clarke (Everton) (Jagielka, Sheffield Utd., 73), Konchesky (Charlton Athletic), Pennant (Arsenal), Jenas (Newcastle Utd.), Prutton (Southampton), Barry (Aston Villa) (Sidwell, Reading, 46), Jeffers (Arsenal) (C. Cole, Chelsea, 70), Defoe (West Ham Utd.).

Scorers – Croatia: Ljubojevic (12, 52), Pranjic (90). **Half-time:** 0-1.

NORWAY 3, SCOTLAND 1
Skien, (1,144), Tuesday, August 19, 2003

Scotland: McGregor (Rangers) (Gordon, Hearts, 46), Caldwell (Newcastle Utd.), Hammell (Motherwell), McCracken (Dundee Utd.) (Dowie, Rangers, 46), Crainey (Celtic) (Doig, Nott'm Forest, 46), Williams (Nott'm Forest), Duff (Dundee Utd.), Pearson (Motherwell) (Noble, West Ham Utd., 61), Kyle (Sunderland) (Gallagher, Blackburn Rov., 46), Stewart (Manchester Utd.) (Hughes, Rangers, 58), Lynch (Preston N.E.) (McManus, Hibernian, 46) (Kennedy, Celtic, 90).

Scorers – Norway: Pedersen (54, 71), Hoff (87). **Scotland:** Lynch (21). **Half-time:** 0-1.

POLAND 1, REPUBLIC OF IRELAND 5
Gdansk, (2,000), Tuesday, August 19, 2003

Rep. of Ireland: Connor (Waterford), Kelly (Tottenham), Kohlmann (Borussia Dortmund) (Capper, Scarborough, 76), Byrne (Scunthorpe Utd.), Cryan (Sheffield Utd.), Keegan (Leeds Utd.), Gilroy (Scarborough) (Cash, Nott'm Forest 67), Elliott (Manchester City), O'Flynn (Cork City) (Zayed, Bray Wand., 76), O'Connor (Brentford) (Ward, Kidderminster Harr., 80), Hoolahan (Shelbourne).

Scorers – Poland: Abbott (13). **Rep. of Ireland:** Elliott (2, 82, 88), Hoolahan (28), O'Flynn (72). **Half-time:** 1-2.

ENGLAND 3, HOLLAND 2
KC Stadium, Hull, (25,280), Tuesday, February 17, 2004

England: Carson (Leeds Utd.), Hunt (Bolton Wand.) (Hoyte, Arsenal, 46), Johnson (Chelsea), Taylor (Newcastle Utd.), Ridgewell (Aston Villa), Bentley (Arsenal), Reo-Coker (West Ham Utd.) (Chaplow, Burnley, 84), Welsh (Liverpool), Downing (Middlesbrough) (Whittingham, Aston Villa, 69), C. Cole (Chelsea) (Bent, Ipswich Town, 84), Ashton (Crewe Alexandra) (Stead, Blackburn Rov., 69).

Scorers – England: Ashton (23), Bentley (72), Bent (87). **Holland:** Tuyp (47), Huntelaar (74). **Half-time:** 1-0.

SCOTLAND 1, HUNGARY 2
City Stadium, Livingston, (1,544), Wednesday, February 18, 2004

Scotland: Smith (Rangers) (Marshall, Celtic 46), Lawson (Celtic) (Dempster, Rushden & Diamonds, 46), Lappin (St Mirren) (Morrison, Aberdeen, 55), Kennedy (Celtic), Dowie (Rangers) (Diamond, Aberdeen, 46), McCunnie (Ross Co.), Foy (Liverpool) (Wallace (Celtic, 65), Wilson (Dundee Utd.) (Sweeney, Millwall, 46), O'Connor (Hibernian) (Beattie, Celtic, 46), Maloney (Celtic) (Reilly, Wycombe Wand., 83), Prunty (Aberdeen).

Scorers – Scotland: Maloney (31 pen), **Hungary:** Csehi (86), Jovanczai (90). **Half-time:** 1-0.

REPUBLIC OF IRELAND 0, PORTUGAL 0 (Madeira Tournament)
Funchal, (3,000), Monday, February 23, 2004

Rep. of Ireland: Henderson (Aston Villa), Kelly (Tottenham), Fitzgerald (Blackburn Rov.), Paisley (Longford Town) (McStay, Leeds Utd., 46), Kohlmann (Borussia Dortmund), Flood (Manchester City) (Deane, Charlton Athletic, 46), Keegan (Leeds Utd.), Whelan (Manchester City), Foley (Liverpool), Doyle (Cork City) (Murphy, Waterford Utd., 76), Yeates (Tottenham) (Bradley, Arsenal, 78).

REPUBLIC OF IRELAND 1, ITALY 0 (Madeira Tournament)
Funchal, (1,500), Wednesday, February 25, 2004

Rep. of Ireland: Henderson (Aston Villa), Kelly (Tottenham) (Whelan, Manchester City, 46), Cooney (Coventry City), Paisley (Longford Town), Kohlmann (Borussia Dortmund), Flood (Manchester City), Keegan (Leeds Utd.) (Cregg, Arsenal, 46), Foley (Liverpool), Kearney (Cork City), Murphy (Waterford Utd.) (Doyle, Cork City, 68), Bradley (Arsenal) (Deane, Charlton Athletic, 68).

Scorer – Rep. of Ireland: Kearney (81). **Half-time:** 0-0.

REPUBLIC OF IRELAND 4, MADEIRA SELECT 0 (Madeira Tournament)
Funchal, (2,500), Friday, February 27, 2004

Rep. of Ireland: Henderson (Aston Villa) (Doyle, Birmingham City, 83), Kelly (Tottenham), Fitzgerald (Blackburn Rov.), Cooney (Coventry City), Paisley (Longford Town), Flood (Manchester City), Keegan (Leeds Utd.), Whelan (Manchester City), Kearney (Cork City) (Deane, Charlton Athletic, 81), Doyle (Cork City) (Cogan, Millwall, 73), Yeates (Tottenham) (Murphy, Waterford Utd., 46).

Scorers – Rep. of Ireland: Doyle (23, 31), Paisley (54), Flood (79). **Half-time:** 2-0.

SWEDEN 2 ENGLAND 2
Kristianstad, (7,330), Tuesday, March 30, 2004

England: Carson (Leeds Utd.) (Grant, Derby Co., 69), Hoyte (Arsenal), Dawson (Nott'm Forest), Taylor (Newcastle Utd.) (Kilgallon, Leeds Utd., 63), Ridgewell (Aston Villa), Bentley (Arsenal) (Chopra, Newcastle Utd., 79), Tonge (Sheffield Utd.) (Ambrose, Newcastle Utd., 63), Reo-Coker (West Ham Utd.) (Jones, Manchester Utd., 69), Downing (Middlesbrough) (Milner, Leeds Utd., 79), C. Cole (Chelsea), Ashton (Crewe Alexandra) (Stead, Blackburn Rov., 63)

Scorers – Sweden: Nilsson (58), Andersson (70). **England:** Ashton (14), Chopra (90). **Half-time:** 0-1.

SCOTLAND 0, ROMANIA 2
Firhill Stadium, (1,967) Tuesday, March 30, 2004

Scotland: Samson (Kilmarnock), Lawson (Celtic), Lappin (St Mirren), Hutton (Rangers) (Kinniburgh, Motherwell, 56), Dowie (Rangers), Fotheringham (Dundee), Wilson (Dundee Utd.) (Burke, Rangers, 64), McCunnie (Ross Co.), O'Connor (Hibernian) (Boyd, Kilmarnock, 73), Riordan (Hibernian) (Foy, Liverpool, 51), Beattie (Celtic) (Prunty, Aberdeen, 84).

Scorers – Romania: Plesan (5), Florescu (89). **Half-time:** 0-1.

DENMARK 2, SCOTLAND 2
Helsingor, (500), Tuesday, April 27, 2004

Scotland: Marshall (Celtic) (Smith, Rangers, 46), Wilson (Dundee Utd.), Lappin (St Mirren) (Morrison, Aberdeen, 46), Dowie (Rangers), Quinn (Motherwell), Sweeney (Millwall) (Beattie, Celtic, 67), Hutton (Rangers) (Burke, Rangers, 72), Brown (Hibernian) (Fotheringham, Dundee, 55), Boyd (Kilmarnock) (Clarkson, Motherwell, 46), Foy (Liverpool) (Murray, Kilmarnock, 12), Gallacher (Blackburn Rov.).

Scorers – Denmark: Krohn-Delhi (45, 84). **Scotland:** Clarkson (73), Beattie (89). **Half-time:** 1-0.

POLAND 2, REPUBLIC OF IRELAND 2
Grudziadz, (3,000), Tuesday, April 27, 2004

Rep. of Ireland: Henderson (Aston Villa), Kelly (Tottenham), Fitzgerald (Blackburn Rov.), McCarthy (Manchester City), Capper (Scarborough) (Dillon, Longford Town, 19), Potter (Liverpool) (Ward, Bohemians, 74), Whelan (Manchester City), Thornton (Sunderland), Flood (Manchester City), Elliott (Manchester City), Doyle (Cork City) (Mehmet, Dunfermline Athletic, 46)

Scorers – Poland: Pawel Brozek (21), Piotr Brozek (53). **Scotland:** Elliott (66), Fitzgerald (89). **Half-time:** 1-0.

REPUBLIC OF IRELAND 3, SCOTLAND 1
Terryland Park, Galway, (2,000), Tuesday, May 25, 2004

Rep. of Ireland: Henderson (Aston Villa) (Murphy, Swansea City, 46), Kelly (Tottenham), McCarthy (Manchester City), Fitzgerald (Blackburn Rov.), Capper (Scarborough), Foley (Luton Town) (Brennan, Newcastle Utd., 80), Whelan (Manchester City), Potter (Liverpool), Kearney (Cork City) (Foley, Liverpool, 87), Murphy (Waterford Utd.) (Behan, Cork City, 87), Tabb (Brentford) (Zayed, Bray Wand., 70).

Scotland: Samson (Kilmarnock) (Smith, Rangers, 46), Lawson (Celtic) (Murray, Kilmarnock, 71), Lappin (St Mirren), Dowie (Rangers), Robertson (Nott'm Forest), McCunnie (Ross Co.), Wilson (Dundee Utd.), Morrison (Aberdeen) (Sweeney, Millwall, 57), Boyd (Kilmarnock), Prunty (Aberdeen), Beattie (Celtic) (Fotheringham, Dundee, 46).

Scorers – Rep. of Ireland: Fitzgerald (10, 35), McCarthy (20). **Scotland:** Beattie (12). **Half-time:** 3-1.

EUROPEAN U-21 CHAMPIONSHIP QUALIFYING TABLES

GROUP 1

	P	W	D	L	F	A	Pts
France	8	7	1	0	14	0	22
Cyprus	8	5	0	3	12	5	15
Israel	8	3	1	4	6	11	10
Slovenia	8	2	3	3	4	7	9
Malta	8	0	1	7	0	13	1

GROUP 2

	P	W	D	L	F	A	Pts
Norway	8	6	1	1	19	4	19
Denmark	8	6	1	1	24	3	19
Bosnia-Herz.	8	4	1	3	16	10	13
Romania	8	2	1	5	6	7	7
Luxembourg	8	0	0	8	0	31	0

GROUP 3

	P	W	D	L	F	A	Pts
Czech Republic	8	6	0	2	17	4	18
Belarus	8	6	0	2	11	6	18
Austria	8	3	2	3	5	8	11
Holland	8	1	4	3	6	10	7
Moldova	8	0	2	6	3	14	2

GROUP 4

	P	W	D	L	F	A	Pts
Poland	8	6	2	0	24	6	20
Sweden	8	4	2	2	17	13	14
Hungary	8	4	0	4	17	13	12
Latvia	8	3	0	5	11	16	9
San Marino	8	1	0	7	8	29	3

GROUP 5

	P	W	D	L	F	A	Pts
Scotland	6	4	1	1	10	6	13
Germany	6	4	1	1	11	5	13
Luthuania	6	3	0	3	10	10	9
Iceland	6	0	0	6	2	12	0

GROUP 6

	P	W	D	L	F	A	Pts
Spain	8	6	1	1	16	2	19
Greece	8	3	3	2	10	7	12
Ukraine	8	2	5	1	8	5	11
Northern Ireland	8	2	1	5	8	16	7
Armenia	8	1	2	5	5	17	5

GROUP 7

	P	W	D	L	F	A	Pts
Turkey	8	7	1	0	18	5	22
Portugal	8	6	0	2	20	11	18
England	8	3	2	3	14	10	11
Slovakia	8	2	0	6	9	16	6
Macedonia	8	0	1	7	4	23	1

GROUP 8

	P	W	D	L	F	A	Pts
Croatia	6	3	2	1	9	4	11
Belgium	6	3	1	2	10	8	10
Bulgaria	6	3	1	2	7	8	10
Estonia	6	0	2	4	4	10	2

GROUP 9

	P	W	D	L	F	A	Pts
Italy	8	7	0	1	26	5	21
Serbia-Mont.	8	6	1	1	16	8	19
Finland	8	3	2	3	11	9	11
Wales	8	2	1	5	7	16	7
Azerbaijan	8	0	0	8	0	22	0

GROUP 10

	P	W	D	L	F	A	Pts
Switzerland	8	6	1	1	12	6	19
Russia	8	5	0	3	14	8	15
Albania	8	3	1	4	10	10	10
Rep. of Ireland	8	2	2	4	8	11	8
Georgia	8	1	2	5	7	16	5

Play-offs to decide Championship finalists (on agg): Belarus 5, Portugal 1; Croatia 2, **Scotland** 1; Germany 2, Turkey 1; Italy 1, Denmark 1 (Italy won on away goal); Portugal 3, France 3 (aet, Portugal won 4-1 on pens); Serbia-Montenegro 5, Norway 4; Sweden 3, Spain 1; Switzerland 3, Czech Republic 3 (aet, Switzerland won 4-3 on pens).

FINALS – GERMANY (MAY 27-JUNE 8)

GROUP A: Serbia-Montenegro 3, Croatia 2; Italy 1, Belarus 2; Belarus 1, Croatia 1; Italy 2, Serbia-Montenegro 1; Italy 1, Croatia 0; Belarus 1, Serbia-Montenegro 2.

GROUP TABLE

	P	W	D	L	F	A	Pts
ITALY	3	2	0	1	4	3	6
SERBIA-MONT.	3	2	0	1	6	5	6
Belarus	3	1	1	1	4	4	4
Croatia	3	0	1	2	3	5	1

GROUP B: Germany 2, Switzerland 1; Sweden 3, Portugal 1; Germany 1, Sweden 2; Switzerland 2, Portugal 2; Germany 1, Portugal 2; Switzerland 1, Sweden 3.

GROUP TABLE

	P	W	D	L	F	A	Pts
SWEDEN	3	3	0	0	8	3	9
PORTUGAL	3	1	1	1	5	6	4
Germany	3	1	0	2	4	5	3
Switzerland	3	0	1	2	4	7	1

Semi-finals: Italy 3, Portugal 1; Sweden 1, Serbia-Montenegro 1 (aet, Serbia-Montenegro won 6-5 on pens). **Third Place Play-off:** Portugal 3, Sweden 2 (aet, silver goal). **Final** (June 8, 2004, Dusseldorf): Italy 3, Serbia-Montenegro 0.

DEBUT GOAL AFTER 34 SECONDS

Jason Roberts, Wigan's £1.4m. signing from West Brom scored after 34 seconds of his debut, a 4-2 win at Preston.

DEJA VU FOR MILLWALL

It was deja vu for Millwall when they beat Tranmere 2-1 in a replay to earn an FA Cup semi-final against Sunderland. The last time the London side reached the last four was in 1937 – when they faced the same opponents. Sunderland won that match 2-1 and went on to beat Preston 3-1 at Wembley.

OTHER BRITISH & IRISH INTERNATIONAL RESULTS
ENGLAND

v. ALBANIA

		E	A
1989	Tirana (W.C.)	2	0
1989	Wembley (W.C.)	5	0
2001	Tirana (W.C.)	3	1
2001	Newcastle (W.C.)	2	0

v. ARGENTINA

		E	A
1951	Wembley	2	1
1953*	Buenos Aires	0	0
1962	Rancagua (W.C.)	3	1
1964	Rio de Janeiro	0	1
1966	Wembley (W.C.)	1	0
1974	Wembley	2	2
1977	Buenos Aires	1	1
1980	Wembley	3	1
1986	Mexico City (W.C.)	1	2
1991	Wembley	2	2
1998†	St Etienne (W.C.)	2	2
2000	Wembley	0	0
2002	Sapporo (W.C.)	1	0

(* Abandoned after 21 mins. – rain)
(† England lost 3-4 on pens.)

v. AUSTRALIA

		E	A
1980	Sydney	2	1
1983	Sydney	0	0
1983	Brisbane	1	0
1983	Melbourne	1	1
1991	Sydney	1	0
2003	West Ham	1	3

v. AUSTRIA

		E	A
1908	Vienna	6	1
1908	Vienna	11	1
1909	Vienna	8	1
1930	Vienna	0	0
1932	Chelsea	4	3
1936	Vienna	1	2
1951	Wembley	2	2
1952	Vienna	3	2
1958	Boras (W.C.)	2	2
1961	Vienna	1	3
1962	Wembley	3	1
1965	Wembley	2	3
1967	Vienna	1	0
1973	Wembley	7	0
1979	Vienna	3	4

v. BELGIUM

		E	B
1921	Brussels	2	0
1923	Highbury	6	1
1923	Antwerp	2	2
1924	West Bromwich	4	0
1926	Antwerp	5	3
1927	Brussels	9	1
1928	Antwerp	3	1
1929	Brussels	5	1
1931	Brussels	4	1
1936	Brussels	2	3
1947	Brussels	5	2
1950	Brussels	4	1
1952	Wembley	5	0
1954	Basle (W.C.)	4	4
1964	Wembley	2	2
1970	Brussels	3	1
1980	Turin (E.C.)	1	1
1990	Bologna (W.C.)	1	0
1998*	Casablanca	0	0
1999	Sunderland	2	1

(* England lost 3-4 on pens.)

v. BOHEMIA

		E	B
1908	Prague	4	0

v. BRAZIL

		E	B
1956	Wembley	4	2
1958	Gothenburg (W.C.)	0	0
1959	Rio de Janeiro	0	2
1962	Vina del Mar (W.C.)	1	3
1963	Wembley	1	1
1964	Rio de Janeiro	1	5
1969	Rio de Janeiro	1	2
1970	Guadalajara (W.C.)	0	1
1976	Los Angeles	0	1
1977	Rio de Janeiro	0	0
1978	Wembley	1	1
1981	Wembley	0	1
1984	Rio de Janeiro	2	0
1987	Wembley	1	1
1990	Wembley	1	0
1992	Wembley	1	1
1993	Washington	1	1
1995	Wembley	1	3
1997	Paris (T.F.)	0	1
2000	Wembley	1	1
2002	Shizuoka (W.C.)	1	2

v. BULGARIA

		E	B
1962	Rancagua (W.C.)	0	0
1968	Wembley	1	1
1974	Sofia	1	0
1979	Sofia (E.C.)	3	0
1979	Wembley (E.C.)	2	0

		E	B
1996	Wembley	1	0
1998	Wembley (E.C.)	0	0
1999	Sofia (E.C.)	1	1

v. CAMEROON

		E	C
1990	Naples (W.C.)	3	2
1991	Wembley	2	0
1997	Wembley	2	0
2002	Kobe (Japan)	2	2

v. CANADA

		E	C
1986	Vancouver	1	0

v. CHILE

		E	C
1950	Rio de Janeiro (W.C.) ..	2	0
1953	Santiago	2	1
1984	Santiago	0	0
1989	Wembley	0	0
1998	Wembley	0	2

v. CHINA

		E	C
1996	Beijing	3	0

v. C.I.S.
(formerly Soviet Union)

		E	C
1992	Moscow	2	2

v. COLOMBIA

		E	C
1970	Bogota	4	0
1988	Wembley	1	1
1995	Wembley	0	0
1998	Lens (W.C.)	2	0

v. CROATIA

		E	C
1995	Wembley	0	0
2003	Ipswich	3	1
2004	Lisbon (E.C.)	4	2

v. CYPRUS

		E	C
1975	Wembley (E.C.)	5	0
1975	Limassol (E.C.)	1	0

v. CZECH REPUBLIC

		E	C
1998	Wembley	2	0

v. CZECHOSLOVAKIA

		E	C
1934	Prague	1	2
1937	Tottenham	5	4
1963	Bratislava	4	2
1966	Wembley	0	0
1970	Guadalajara (W.C.)	1	0

		E	C
1973	Prague	1	1
1974	Wembley (E.C.)	3	0
1975*	Bratislava (E.C.)	1	2
1978	Wembley (E.C.)	1	0
1982	Bilbao (W.C.)	2	0
1990	Wembley	4	2
1992	Prague	2	2

(* Aband. 0-0, 17 mins. prev. day – fog)

v. DENMARK

		E	D
1948	Copenhagen	0	0
1955	Copenhagen	5	1
1956	W'hampton (W.C.)	5	2
1957	Copenhagen (W.C.)	4	1
1966	Copenhagen	2	0
1978	Copenhagen (E.C.)	4	3
1979	Wembley (E.C.)	1	0
1982	Copenhagen (E.C.)	2	2
1983	Wembley (E.C.)	0	1
1988	Wembley	1	0
1989	Copenhagen	1	1
1990	Wembley	1	0
1992	Malmo (E.C.)	0	0
1994	Wembley	1	0
2002	Niigata (W.C.)	3	0
2003	Manchester Utd.	2	3

v. EAST GERMANY

		E	EG
1963	Leipzig	2	1
1970	Wembley	3	1
1974	Leipzig	1	1
1984	Wembley	1	0

v. ECUADOR

		E	Ec
1970	Quito	2	0

v. EGYPT

		E	Eg
1986	Cairo	4	0
1990	Cagliari (W.C.)	1	0

v. F.I.F.A.

		E	F
1938	Arsenal	3	0
1953	Wembley	4	4
1963	Wembley	2	1

v. FINLAND

		E	F
1937	Helsinki	8	0
1956	Helsinki	5	1
1966	Helsinki	3	0
1976	Helsinki (W.C.)	4	1
1976	Wembley (W.C.)	2	1
1982	Helsinki	4	1
1984	Wembley (W.C.)	5	0
1985	Helsinki (W.C.)	1	1

		E	F
1992	Helsinki	2	1
2000	Helsinki (W.C.)	0	0
2001	Liverpool (W.C.)	2	1

v. FRANCE

		E	F
1923	Paris	4	1
1924	Paris	3	1
1925	Paris	3	2
1927	Paris	6	0
1928	Paris	5	1
1929	Paris	4	1
1931	Paris	2	5
1933	Tottenham	4	1
1938	Paris	4	2
1947	Arsenal	3	0
1949	Paris	3	1
1951	Arsenal	2	2
1955	Paris	0	1
1957	Wembley	4	0
1962	Sheffield Wed. (E.C.)	1	1
1963	Paris (E.C.)	2	5
1966	Wembley (W.C.)	2	0
1969	Wembley	5	0
1982	Bilbao (W.C.)	3	1
1984	Paris	0	2
1992	Wembley	2	0
1992	Malmo (E.C.)	0	0
1997	Montpellier (T.F.)	1	0
1999	Wembley	0	2
2000	Paris	1	1
2004	Lisbon (E.C.)	1	2

v. GEORGIA

		E	G
1996	Tbilisi (W.C.)	2	0
1997	Wembley (W.C.)	2	0

v. GERMANY/WEST GERMANY

		E	G
1930	Berlin	3	3
1935	Tottenham	3	0
1938	Berlin	6	3
1954	Wembley	3	1
1956	Berlin	3	1
1965	Nuremberg	1	0
1966	Wembley	1	0
1966	Wembley (W.C.F.)	4	2
1968	Hanover	0	1
1970	Leon (W.C.)	2	3
1972	Wembley (E.C.)	1	3
1972	Berlin (E.C.)	0	0
1975	Wembley	2	0
1978	Munich	1	2
1982	Madrid (W.C.)	0	0
1982	Wembley	1	2
1985	Mexico City	3	0
1987	Dusseldorf	1	3
1990*	Turin (W.C.)	1	1

		E	G
1991	Wembley	0	1
1993	Detroit	1	2
1996†	Wembley (E.C.)	1	1
2000	Charleroi (E.C.)	1	0
2000	Wembley (W.C.)	0	1
2001	Munich (W.C.)	5	1

(* England lost 3-4 on pens.)
(† England lost 5-6 on pens.)

v. GREECE

		E	G
1971	Wembley (E.C.)	3	0
1971	Athens (E.C.)	2	0
1982	Salonika (E.C.)	3	0
1983	Wembley (E.C.)	0	0
1989	Athens	2	1
1994	Wembley	5	0
2001	Athens (W.C.)	2	0
2001	Manchester Utd. (W.C.)	2	2

v. HOLLAND

		E	H
1935	Amsterdam	1	0
1946	Huddersfield	8	2
1964	Amsterdam	1	1
1969	Amsterdam	1	0
1970	Wembley	0	0
1977	Wembley	0	2
1982	Wembley	2	0
1988	Wembley	2	2
1988	Dusseldorf (E.C.)	1	3
1990	Cagliari (W.C.)	0	0
1993	Wembley (W.C.)	2	2
1993	Rotterdam (W.C.)	0	2
1996	Wembley (E.C.)	4	1
2001	Tottenham	0	2
2002	Amsterdam	1	1

v. HUNGARY

		E	H
1908	Budapest	7	0
1909	Budapest	4	2
1909	Budapest	8	2
1934	Budapest	1	2
1936	Highbury	6	2
1953	Wembley	3	6
1954	Budapest	1	7
1960	Budapest	0	2
1962	Rancagua (W.C.)	1	2
1965	Wembley	1	0
1978	Wembley	4	1
1981	Budapest (W.C.)	3	1
1981	Wembley (W.C.)	1	0
1983	Wembley (E.C.)	2	0
1983	Budapest (E.C.)	3	0
1988	Budapest	0	0
1990	Wembley	1	0
1992	Budapest	1	0
1996	Wembley	3	0
1999	Budapest	1	1

v. ICELAND

		E	I
1982	Reykjavik	1	1
2004	Manchester City	6	1

v. REPUBLIC OF IRELAND

		E	RI
1946	Dublin	1	0
1950	Everton	0	2
1957	Wembley (W.C.)	5	1
1957	Dublin (W.C.)	1	1
1964	Dublin	3	1
1977	Wembley	1	1
1978	Dublin (E.C.)	1	1
1980	Wembley (E.C.)	2	0
1985	Wembley	2	1
1988	Stuttgart (E.C.)	0	1
1990	Cagliari (W.C.)	1	1
1990	Dublin (E.C.)	1	1
1991	Dublin (E.C.)	1	1
1995*	Dublin	0	1

(* Abandoned 27 mins. – crowd riot)

v. ISRAEL

		E	I
1986	Tel Aviv	2	1
1988	Tel Aviv	0	0

v. ITALY

		E	I
1933	Rome	1	1
1934	Arsenal	3	2
1939	Milan	2	2
1948	Turin	4	0
1949	Tottenham	2	0
1952	Florence	1	1
1959	Wembley	2	2
1961	Rome	3	2
1973	Turin	0	2
1973	Wembley	0	1
1976	New York	3	2
1976	Rome (W.C.)	0	2
1977	Wembley (W.C.)	2	0
1980	Turin (E.C.)	0	1
1985	Mexico City	1	2
1989	Wembley	0	0
1990	Bari (W.C.)	1	2
1996	Wembley	0	1
1997	Nantes (T.F.)	2	0
1997	Rome (W.C.)	0	0
2000	Turin	0	1
2002	Leeds	1	2

v. JAPAN

		E	J
1995	Wembley	2	1
2004	Manchester City	1	1

v. KUWAIT

		E	K
1982	Bilbao (W.C.)	1	0

v. LIECHTENSTEIN

		E	L
2003	Vaduz (E.C.)	2	0
2003	Manchester Utd. (E.C.) ..	2	0

v. LUXEMBOURG

		E	L
1927	Luxembourg	5	2
1960	Luxembourg (W.C.)	9	0
1961	Arsenal (W.C.)	4	1
1977	Wembley (W.C.)	5	0
1977	Luxembourg (W.C.)	2	0
1982	Wembley (E.C.)	9	0
1983	Luxembourg (E.C.)	4	0
1998	Luxembourg (E.C.)	3	0
1999	Wembley (E.C.)	6	0

v. MACEDONIA

		E	M
2002	Southampton (E.C.)	2	2
2003	Skopje (E.C.)	2	1

v. MALAYSIA

		E	M
1991	Kuala Lumpur	4	2

v. MALTA

		E	M
1971	Valletta (E.C.)	1	0
1971	Wembley (E.C.)	5	0
2000	Valletta	2	1

v. MEXICO

		E	M
1959	Mexico City	1	2
1961	Wembley	8	0
1966	Wembley (W.C.)	2	0
1969	Mexico City	0	0
1985	Mexico City	0	1
1986	Los Angeles	3	0
1997	Wembley	2	0
2001	Derby	4	0

v. MOLDOVA

		E	M
1996	Kishinev	3	0
1997	Wembley (W.C.)	4	0

v. MOROCCO

		E	M
1986	Monterrey (W.C.)	0	0
1998	Casablanca	1	0

v. NEW ZEALAND

		E	NZ
1991	Auckland	1	0
1991	Wellington	2	0

v. NIGERIA

		E	N
1994	Wembley	1	0
2002	Osaka (W.C.)	0	0

v. NORWAY

		E	N
1937	Oslo	6	0
1938	Newcastle	4	0
1949	Oslo	4	1
1966	Oslo	6	1
1980	Wembley (W.C.)	4	0
1981	Oslo (W.C.)	1	2
1992	Wembley (W.C.)	1	1
1993	Oslo (W.C.)	0	2
1994	Wembley	0	0
1995	Oslo	0	0

v. PARAGUAY

		E	P
1986	Mexico City (W.C.)	3	0
2002	Liverpool	4	0

v. PERU

		E	P
1959	Lima	1	4
1961	Lima	4	0

v. POLAND

		E	P
1966	Everton	1	1
1966	Chorzow	1	0
1973	Chorzow (W.C.)	0	2
1973	Wembley (W.C.)	1	1
1986	Monterrey (W.C.)	3	0
1989	Wembley (W.C.)	3	0
1989	Katowice (W.C.)	0	0
1990	Wembley (E.C.)	2	0
1991	Poznan (E.C.)	1	1
1993	Chorzow (W.C.)	1	1
1993	Wembley (W.C.)	3	0
1996	Wembley (W.C.)	2	1
1997	Katowice (W.C.)	2	0
1999	Wembley (E.C.)	3	1
1999	Warsaw (E.C.)	0	0

v. PORTUGAL

		E	P
1947	Lisbon	10	0
1950	Lisbon	5	3
1951	Everton	5	2
1955	Oporto	1	3
1958	Wembley	2	1
1961	Lisbon (W.C.)	1	1
1961	Wembley (W.C.)	2	0
1964	Lisbon	4	3
1964	Sao Paulo	1	1
1966	Wembley (W.C.)	2	1
1969	Wembley	1	0
1974	Lisbon	0	0
1974	Wembley (E.C.)	0	0
1975	Lisbon (E.C.)	1	1
1986	Monterrey (W.C.)	0	1
1995	Wembley	1	1
1998	Wembley	3	0
2000	Eindhoven (E.C.)	2	3

		E	P
2002	Aston Villa	1	1
2004	Faro	1	1
2004*	Lisbon (E.C.)	2	2

(*England lost 5–6 on pens)

v. ROMANIA

		E	R
1939	Bucharest	2	0
1968	Bucharest	0	0
1969	Wembley	1	1
1970	Guadalajara (W.C.)	1	0
1980	Bucharest (W.C.)	1	2
1981	Wembley (W.C.)	0	0
1985	Bucharest (W.C.)	0	0
1985	Wembley (W.C.)	1	1
1994	Wembley	1	1
1998	Toulouse (W.C.)	1	2
2000	Charleroi (E.C.)	2	3

v. SAN MARINO

		E	SM
1992	Wembley (W.C.)	6	0
1993	Bologna (W.C.)	7	1

v. SAUDI ARABIA

		E	SA
1988	Riyadh	1	1
1998	Wembley	0	0

v. SERBIA-MONTENEGRO

		E	S-M
2003	Leicester	2	1

v. SLOVAKIA

		E	S
2002	Bratislava (E.C.)	2	1
2003	Middlesbrough (E.C.)	2	1

v. SOUTH AFRICA

		E	SA
1997	Manchester Utd.	2	1
2003	Durban	2	1

v. SOUTH KOREA

		E	SK
2002	Seoguipo	1	1

v. SOVIET UNION (see also C.I.S.)

		E	SU
1958	Moscow	1	1
1958	Gothenburg (W.C.)	2	2
1958	Gothenburg (W.C.)	0	1
1958	Wembley	5	0
1967	Wembley	2	2
1968	Rome (E.C.)	2	0
1973	Moscow	2	1
1984	Wembley	0	2
1986	Tbilisi	1	0
1988	Frankfurt (E.C.)	1	3
1991	Wembley	3	1

v. SPAIN

Year	Venue	E	S
1929	Madrid	3	4
1931	Arsenal	7	1
1950	Rio de Janeiro (W.C.)	0	1
1955	Madrid	1	1
1955	Wembley	4	1
1960	Madrid	0	3
1960	Wembley	4	2
1965	Madrid	2	0
1967	Wembley	2	0
1968	Wembley (E.C.)	1	0
1968	Madrid (E.C.)	2	1
1980	Barcelona	2	0
1980	Naples (E.C.)	2	1
1981	Wembley	1	2
1982	Madrid (W.C.)	0	0
1987	Madrid	4	2
1992	Santander	0	1
1996*	Wembley (E.C.)	0	0
2001	Aston Villa	3	0

(* England won 4-2 on pens.)

v. SWEDEN

Year	Venue	E	S
1923	Stockholm	4	2
1923	Stockholm	3	1
1937	Stockholm	4	0
1948	Arsenal	4	2
1949	Stockholm	1	3
1956	Stockholm	0	0
1959	Wembley	2	3
1965	Gothenburg	2	1
1968	Wembley	3	1
1979	Stockholm	0	0
1986	Stockholm	0	1
1988	Wembley (W.C.)	0	0
1989	Stockholm (W.C.)	0	0
1992	Stockholm (E.C.)	1	2
1995	Leeds	3	3
1998	Stockholm (E.C.)	1	2
1999	Wembley (E.C.)	0	0
2001	Manchester Utd.	1	1
2002	Saitama (W.C.)	1	1
2004	Gothenburg	0	1

v. SWITZERLAND

Year	Venue	E	S
1933	Berne	4	0
1938	Zurich	1	2
1947	Zurich	0	1
1949	Arsenal	6	0
1952	Zurich	3	0
1954	Berne (W.C.)	2	0
1962	Wembley	3	1
1963	Basle	8	1
1971	Basle (E.C.)	3	2
1971	Wembley (E.C.)	1	1
1975	Basle	2	1
1977	Wembley	0	0

v. SPAIN (continued)

Year	Venue	E	S
1980	Wembley (W.C.)	2	1
1981	Basle (W.C.)	1	2
1988	Lausanne	1	0
1995	Wembley	3	1
1996	Wembley (E.C.)	1	1
1998	Berne	1	1
2004	Coimbra (E.C.)	3	0

v. TUNISIA

Year	Venue	E	T
1990	Tunis	1	1
1998	Marseille (W.C.)	2	0

v. TURKEY

Year	Venue	E	T
1984	Istanbul (W.C.)	8	0
1985	Wembley (W.C.)	5	0
1987	Izmir (E.C.)	0	0
1987	Wembley (E.C.)	8	0
1991	Izmir (E.C.)	1	0
1991	Wembley (E.C.)	1	0
1992	Wembley (W.C.)	4	0
1993	Izmir (W.C.)	2	0
2003	Sunderland (E.C.)	2	0
2003	Istanbul (E.C.)	0	0

v UKRAINE

Year	Venue	E	U
2000	Wembley	2	0

v. URUGUAY

Year	Venue	E	U
1953	Montevideo	1	2
1954	Basle (W.C.)	2	4
1964	Wembley	2	1
1966	Wembley (W.C.)	0	0
1969	Montevideo	2	1
1977	Montevideo	0	0
1984	Montevideo	0	2
1990	Wembley	1	2
1995	Wembley	0	0

v. U.S.A.

Year	Venue	E	USA
1950	Belo Horizonte (W.C.)	0	1
1953	New York	6	3
1959	Los Angeles	8	1
1964	New York	10	0
1985	Los Angeles	5	0
1993	Boston	0	2
1994	Wembley	2	0

v. YUGOSLAVIA

Year	Venue	E	Y
1939	Belgrade	1	2
1950	Arsenal	2	2
1954	Belgrade	0	1
1956	Wembley	3	0
1958	Belgrade	0	5
1960	Wembley	3	3

		E	Y			E	Y
1965	Belgrade	1	1	1974	Belgrade	2	2
1966	Wembley	2	0	1986	Wembley (E.C.)	2	0
1968	Florence (E.C.)	0	1	1987	Belgrade (E.C.)	4	1
1972	Wembley	1	1	1989	Wembley	2	1

ENGLAND'S RECORD

England's first international was a 0-0 draw against Scotland in Glasgow, on the West of Scotland cricket ground, Partick, on November 30, 1872. Now, 132 years on, their complete International record, at the start of 2004-05, is:

P	W	D	L	F	A
816	457	201	158	1833	837

ENGLAND "B" TEAM RESULTS
(England score shown first)

1949	Finland (A)	4	0	1979	N. Zealand (H)	4	1
1949	Holland (A)	4	0	1980	U.S.A. (H)	1	0
1950	Italy (A)	0	5	1980	Spain (H)	1	0
1950	Holland (H)	1	0	1980	Australia (H)	1	0
1950	Holland (A)	0	3	1981	Spain (A)	2	3
1950	Luxembourg (A)	2	1	1984	N. Zealand (H)	2	0
1950	Switzerland (H)	5	0	1987	Malta (A)	2	0
1952	Holland (A)	1	0	1989	Switzerland (A)	2	0
1952	France (A)	1	7	1989	Iceland (A)	2	0
1953	Scotland (A)	2	2	1989	Norway (A)	1	0
1954	Scotland (H)	1	1	1989	Italy (H)	1	1
1954	Germany (A)	4	0	1989	Yugoslavia (H)	2	1
1954	Yugoslavia (A)	1	2	1990	Rep. of Ireland (H)	1	4
1954	Switzerland (A)	0	2	1990	Czechoslovakia (H)	2	0
1955	Germany (A)	1	1	1990	Algeria (A)	0	0
1955	Yugoslavia (H)	5	1	1991	Wales (A)	1	0
1956	Switzerland (H)	4	1	1991	Iceland (A)	1	0
1956	Scotland (A)	2	2	1991	Switzerland (H)	2	1
1957	Scotland (H)	4	1	1991	Spanish XI (A)	1	0
1978	W. Germany (A)	2	1	1992	France (H)	3	0
1978	Czechoslovakia (A)	1	0	1992	Czechoslovakia (A)	1	0
1978	Singapore (A)	8	0	1992	C.I.S. (H)	1	1
1978	Malaysia (A)	1	1	1994	N. Ireland (H)	4	2
1978	N. Zealand (A)	4	0	1995	Rep. of Ireland (H)	2	0
1978	N. Zealand (A)	3	1	1998	Chile (H)	1	2
1978	N. Zealand (A)	4	0	1998	Russia (H)	4	1
1979	Austria (A)	1	0				

GREAT BRITAIN V. REST OF EUROPE (F.I.F.A.)

		GB	RofE			GB	RofE
1947	Glasgow	6	1	1955	Belfast	1	4

SCOTLAND

v. ARGENTINA

		S	A
1977	Buenos Aires	1	1
1979	Glasgow	1	3
1990	Glasgow	1	0

v. AUSTRALIA

		S	A
1985*	Glasgow (W.C.)	2	0
1985*	Melbourne (W.C.)	0	0
1996	Glasgow	1	0

193

		S	A
2000	Glasgow	0	2

(* World Cup play-off)

v. AUSTRIA

		S	A
1931	Vienna	0	5
1933	Glasgow	2	2
1937	Vienna	1	1
1950	Glasgow	0	1
1951	Vienna	0	4
1954	Zurich (W.C.)	0	1
1955	Vienna	4	1
1956	Glasgow	1	1
1960	Vienna	1	4
1963*	Glasgow	4	1
1968	Glasgow (W.C.)	2	1
1969	Vienna (W.C.)	0	2
1978	Vienna (E.C.)	2	3
1979	Glasgow (E.C.)	1	1
1994	Vienna	2	1
1996	Vienna (W.C.)	0	0
1997	Glasgow (W.C.)	2	0

(* Abandoned after 79 minutes)

2003	Glasgow	0	2

v. BELARUS

		S	B
1997	Minsk (W.C.)	1	0
1997	Aberdeen (W.C.)	4	1

v. BELGIUM

		S	B
1947	Brussels	1	2
1948	Glasgow	2	0
1951	Brussels	5	0
1971	Liege (E.C.)	0	3
1971	Aberdeen (E.C.)	1	0
1974	Brugge	1	2
1979	Brussels (E.C.)	0	2
1979	Glasgow (E.C.)	1	3
1982	Brussels (E.C.)	2	3
1983	Glasgow (E.C.)	1	1
1987	Brussels (E.C.)	1	4
1987	Glasgow (E.C.)	2	0
2001	Glasgow (W.C.)	2	2
2001	Brussels (W.C.)	0	2

v. BOSNIA

		S	B
1999	Sarajevo (E.C.)	2	1
1999	Glasgow (E.C.)	1	0

v. BRAZIL

		S	B
1966	Glasgow	1	1
1972	Rio de Janeiro	0	1
1973	Glasgow	0	1
1974	Frankfurt (W.C.)	0	0
1977	Rio de Janeiro	0	2

		S	B
1982	Seville (W.C.)	1	4
1987	Glasgow	0	2
1990	Turin (W.C.)	0	1
1998	St. Denis (W.C.)	1	2

v. BULGARIA

		S	B
1978	Glasgow	2	1
1986	Glasgow (E.C.)	0	0
1987	Sofia (E.C.)	1	0
1990	Sofia (E.C.)	1	1
1991	Glasgow (E.C.)	1	1

v. CANADA

		S	C
1983	Vancouver	2	0
1983	Edmonton	3	0
1983	Toronto	2	0
1992	Toronto	3	1
2002	Edinburgh	3	1

v. CHILE

		S	C
1977	Santiago	4	2
1989	Glasgow	2	0

v. C.I.S. (formerly Soviet Union)

		S	C
1992	Norrkoping (E.C.)	3	0

v. COLOMBIA

		S	C
1988	Glasgow	0	0
1996	Miami	0	1
1998	New York	2	2

v. COSTA RICA

		S	C
1990	Genoa (W.C.)	0	1

v. CROATIA

		S	C
2000	Zagreb (W.C.)	1	1
2001	Glasgow (W.C.)	0	0

v. CYPRUS

		S	C
1968	Nicosia (W.C.)	5	0
1969	Glasgow (W.C.)	8	0
1989	Limassol (W.C.)	3	2
1989	Glasgow (W.C.)	2	1

v. CZECH REPUBLIC

		S	C
1999	Glasgow (E.C.)	1	2
1999	Prague (E.C.)	2	3

v. CZECHOSLOVAKIA

		S	C
1937	Prague	3	1
1937	Glasgow	5	0

		S	C
1961	Bratislava (W.C.)	0	4
1961	Glasgow (W.C.)	3	2
1961*	Brussels (W.C.)	2	4
1972	Porto Alegre	0	0
1973	Glasgow (W.C.)	2	1
1973	Bratislava (W.C.)	0	1
1976	Prague (W.C.)	0	2
1977	Glasgow (W.C.)	3	1

(* World Cup play-off)

v. DENMARK

		S	D
1951	Glasgow	3	1
1952	Copenhagen	2	1
1968	Copenhagen	1	0
1970	Glasgow (E.C.)	1	0
1971	Copenhagen (E.C.)	0	1
1972	Copenhagen (W.C.)	4	1
1972	Glasgow (W.C.)	2	0
1975	Copenhagen (E.C.)	1	0
1975	Glasgow (E.C.)	3	1
1986	Neza (W.C.)	0	1
1996	Copenhagen	0	2
1998	Glasgow	0	1
2002	Glasgow	0	1
2004	Copenhagen	0	1

v. EAST GERMANY

		S	EG
1974	Glasgow	3	0
1977	East Berlin	0	1
1982	Glasgow (E.C.)	2	0
1983	Halle (E.C.)	1	2
1986	Glasgow	0	0
1990	Glasgow	0	1

v. ECUADOR

		S	E
1995	Toyama, Japan	2	1

v. EGYPT

		S	E
1990	Aberdeen	1	3

v. ESTONIA

		S	E
1993	Tallinn (W.C.)	3	0
1993	Aberdeen	3	1
1996	Tallinn (W.C.)	* No result
1997	Monaco (W.C.)	0	0
1997	Kilmarnock (W.C.)	2	0
1998	Edinburgh (E.C.)	3	2
1999	Tallinn (E.C.)	0	0

(* Estonia absent)

2004	Tallinn	1	0

v. FAROE ISLANDS

		S	F
1994	Glasgow (E.C.)	5	1
1995	Toftir (E.C.)	2	0

		S	F
1998	Aberdeen (E.C.)	2	1
1999	Toftir (E.C.)	1	1
2002	Toftir (E.C.)	2	2
2003	Glasgow (E.C.)	3	1

v. FINLAND

		S	F
1954	Helsinki	2	1
1964	Glasgow (W.C.)	3	1
1965	Helsinki (W.C.)	2	1
1976	Glasgow	6	0
1992	Glasgow	1	1
1994	Helsinki (E.C.)	2	0
1995	Glasgow (E.C.)	1	0
1998	Edinburgh	1	1

v. FRANCE

		S	F
1930	Paris	2	0
1932	Paris	3	1
1948	Paris	0	3
1949	Glasgow	2	0
1950	Paris	1	0
1951	Glasgow	1	0
1958	Orebro (W.C.)	1	2
1984	Marseilles	0	2
1989	Glasgow (W.C.)	2	0
1990	Paris (W.C.)	0	3
1997	St. Etienne	1	2
2000	Glasgow	0	2
2002	Paris	0	5

v. GERMANY/WEST GERMANY

		S	G
1929	Berlin	1	1
1936	Glasgow	2	0
1957	Stuttgart	3	1
1959	Glasgow	3	2
1964	Hanover	2	2
1969	Glasgow (W.C.)	1	1
1969	Hamburg (W.C.)	2	3
1973	Glasgow	1	1
1974	Frankfurt	1	2
1986	Queretaro (W.C.)	1	2
1992	Norrkoping (E.C.)	0	2
1993	Glasgow	0	1
1999	Bremen	1	0
2003	Glasgow (E.C.)	1	1
2003	Dortmund (E.C.)	1	2

v. GREECE

		S	G
1994	Athens (E.C.)	0	1
1995	Glasgow	1	0

v. HOLLAND

		S	H
1929	Amsterdam	2	0
1938	Amsterdam	3	1

195

	S	H
1959 Amsterdam	2	1
1966 Glasgow	0	3
1968 Amsterdam	0	0
1971 Amsterdam	1	2
1978 Mendoza (W.C.)	3	2
1982 Glasgow	2	1
1986 Eindhoven	0	0
1992 Gothenburg (E.C.)	0	1
1994 Glasgow	0	1
1994 Utrecht	1	3
1996 Birmingham (E.C.)	0	0
2000 Arnhem	0	0
2003* Glasgow (E.C.)	1	0
2003* Amsterdam (E.C.)	0	6

(* Qual. Round play-off)

v. HUNGARY

	S	H
1938 Glasgow	3	1
1955 Glasgow	2	4
1955 Budapest	1	3
1958 Glasgow	1	1
1960 Budapest	3	3
1980 Budapest	1	3
1987 Glasgow	2	0

v. ICELAND

	S	I
1984 Glasgow (W.C.)	3	0
1985 Reykjavik (W.C)	1	0
2002 Reykjavik (E.C)	2	0
2003 Glasgow (E.C)	2	1

v. IRAN

	S	I
1978 Cordoba (W.C.)	1	1

v. REPUBLIC OF IRELAND

	S	RI
1961 Glasgow (W.C.)	4	1
1961 Dublin (W.C.)	3	0
1963 Dublin	0	1
1969 Dublin	1	1
1986 Dublin (E.C.)	0	0
1987 Glasgow (E.C.)	0	1
2000 Dublin	2	1
2003 Glasgow (E.C.)	0	2

v. ISRAEL

	S	I
1981 Tel Aviv (W.C.)	1	0
1981 Tel Aviv (W.C.)	3	1
1986 Tel Aviv	1	0

v. ITALY

	S	I
1931 Rome	0	3
1965 Glasgow (W.C.)	1	0
1965 Naples (W.C.)	0	3
1988 Perugia	0	2
1992 Glasgow (W.C.)	0	0
1993 Rome (W.C.)	1	3

v. JAPAN

	S	J
1995 Hiroshima	0	0

v. LATVIA

	S	L
1996 Riga (W.C.)	2	0
1997 Glasgow (W.C.)	2	0
2000 Riga (W.C.)	1	0
2001 Glasgow (W.C.)	2	1

v. LITHUANIA

	S	L
1998 Vilnius (E.C.)	0	0
1999 Glasgow (E.C.)	3	0
2003 Kaunus (E.C.)	0	1
2003 Glasgow (E.C.)	1	0

v. LUXEMBOURG

	S	L
1947 Luxembourg	6	0
1986 Glasgow (E.C.)	3	0
1987 Esch (E.C.)	0	0

v. MALTA

	S	M
1988 Valletta	1	1
1990 Valletta	2	1
1993 Glasgow (W.C.)	3	0
1993 Valletta (W.C.)	2	0
1997 Valletta	3	2

v. MOROCCO

	S	M
1998 St. Etienne (W.C.)	0	3

v. NEW ZEALAND

	S	NZ
1982 Malaga (W.C.)	5	2
2003 Edinburgh	1	1

v. NIGERIA

	S	N
2002 Aberdeen	1	2

v. NORWAY

	S	N
1929 Bergen	7	3
1954 Glasgow	1	0
1954 Oslo	1	1
1963 Bergen	3	4
1963 Glasgow	6	1
1974 Oslo	2	1
1978 Glasgow (E.C.)	3	2
1979 Oslo (E.C.)	4	0
1988 Oslo (W.C.)	2	1
1989 Glasgow (W.C.)	1	1

		S	N
1992	Oslo	0	0
1998	Bordeaux (W.C.)	1	1
2003	Oslo	0	0

v. PARAGUAY

		S	P
1958	Norrkoping (W.C.)	2	3

v. PERU

		S	P
1972	Glasgow	2	0
1978	Cordoba (W.C.)	1	3
1979	Glasgow	1	1

v. POLAND

		S	P
1958	Warsaw	2	1
1960	Glasgow	2	3
1965	Chorzow (W.C.)	1	1
1965	Glasgow (W.C.)	1	2
1980	Poznan	0	1
1990	Glasgow	1	1
2001	Bydgoszcz	1	1

v. PORTUGAL

		S	P
1950	Lisbon	2	2
1955	Glasgow	3	0
1959	Lisbon	0	1
1966	Glasgow	0	1
1971	Lisbon (E.C.)	0	2
1971	Glasgow (E.C.)	2	1
1975	Glasgow	1	0
1978	Lisbon (E.C.)	0	1
1980	Glasgow (E.C.)	4	1
1980	Glasgow (W.C.)	0	0
1981	Lisbon (W.C.)	1	2
1992	Glasgow (W.C.)	0	0
1993	Lisbon (W.C.)	0	5
2002	Braga	0	2

v. ROMANIA

		S	R
1975	Bucharest (E.C.)	1	1
1975	Glasgow (E.C.)	1	1
1986	Glasgow	3	0
1990	Glasgow (E.C.)	2	1
1991	Bucharest (E.C.)	0	1
2004	Glasgow	1	2

v. RUSSIA

		S	R
1994	Glasgow (E.C.)	1	1
1995	Moscow (E.C.)	0	0

v. SAN MARINO

		S	SM
1991	Serravalle (E.C.)	2	0
1991	Glasgow (E.C.)	4	0
1995	Serravalle (E.C.)	2	0

		S	SM
1995	Glasgow (E.C.)	5	0
2000	Serravalle (W.C.)	2	0
2001	Glasgow (W.C.)	4	0

v. SAUDI ARABIA

		S	SA
1988	Riyadh	2	2

v. SOUTH AFRICA

		S	SA
2002	Hong Kong	0	2

v. SOUTH KOREA

		S	SK
2002	Busan	1	4

v. SOVIET UNION
(see also C.I.S. and RUSSIA)

		S	SU
1967	Glasgow	0	2
1971	Moscow	0	1
1982	Malaga (W.C.)	2	2
1991	Glasgow	0	1

v. SPAIN

		S	Sp
1957	Glasgow (W.C.)	4	2
1957	Madrid (W.C.)	1	4
1963	Madrid	6	2
1965	Glasgow	0	0
1975	Glasgow (E.C.)	1	2
1975	Valencia (E.C.)	1	1
1982	Valencia	0	3
1985	Glasgow (W.C.)	3	1
1985	Seville (W.C.)	0	1
1988	Madrid	0	0

v. SWEDEN

		S	Swe
1952	Stockholm	1	3
1953	Glasgow	1	2
1975	Gothenburg	1	1
1977	Glasgow	3	1
1980	Stockholm (W.C.)	1	0
1981	Glasgow (W.C.)	2	0
1990	Genoa (W.C.)	2	1
1995	Solna	0	2
1996	Glasgow (W.C.)	1	0
1997	Gothenburg (W.C.)	1	2

v. SWITZERLAND

		S	Sw
1931	Geneva	3	2
1948	Berne	1	2
1950	Glasgow	3	1
1957	Basle (W.C.)	2	1
1957	Glasgow (W.C.)	3	2
1973	Berne	0	1
1976	Glasgow	1	0
1982	Berne (E.C.)	0	2

		S	Sw
1983	Glasgow (E.C.)	2	2
1990	Glasgow (E.C.)	2	1
1991	Berne (E.C.)	2	2
1992	Berne (W.C.)	1	3
1993	Aberdeen (W.C.)	1	1
1996	Birmingham (E.C.)	1	0

v. TRINIDAD + TOBAGO

		S	T
2004	Hibernian	4	1

v. TURKEY

		S	T
1960	Ankara	2	4

v. U.S.A.

		S	USA
1952	Glasgow	6	0
1992	Denver	1	0
1996	New Britain, Conn	1	2
1998	Washington	0	0

v. URUGUAY

		S	U
1954	Basle (W.C.)	0	7
1962	Glasgow	2	3
1983	Glasgow	2	0
1986	Neza (W.C.)	0	0

v. YUGOSLAVIA

		S	Y
1955	Belgrade	2	2
1956	Glasgow	2	0
1958	Vaasteras (W.C.)	1	1
1972	Belo Horizonte	2	2
1974	Frankfurt (W.C.)	1	1
1984	Glasgow	6	1
1988	Glasgow (W.C.)	1	1
1989	Zagreb (W.C.)	1	3

v. ZAIRE

		S	Z
1974	Dortmund (W.C.)	2	0

WALES

v. ALBANIA

		W	A
1994	Cardiff (E.C.)	2	0
1995	Tirana (E.C.)	1	1

v. ARGENTINA

		W	A
1992	Gifu (Japan)	0	1
2002	Cardiff	1	1

v. ARMENIA

		W	A
2001	Yerevan (W.C.)	2	2
2001	Cardiff (W.C.)	0	0

v. AUSTRIA

		W	A
1954	Vienna	0	2
1955	Wrexham	1	2
1975	Vienna (E.C.)	1	2
1975	Wrexham (E.C.)	1	0
1992	Vienna	1	1

v. AZERBAIJAN

		W	A
2002	Baku (E.C.)	2	0
2003	Cardiff (E.C.)	4	0

v. BELARUS

		W	B
1998	Cardiff (E.C.)	3	2
1999	Minsk (E.C.)	2	1
2000	Minsk (W.C.)	1	2
2001	Cardiff (W.C.)	1	0

v. BELGIUM

		W	B
1949	Liege	1	3
1949	Cardiff	5	1
1990	Cardiff (E.C.)	3	1
1991	Brussels (E.C.)	1	1
1992	Brussels (W.C.)	0	2
1993	Cardiff (W.C.)	2	0
1997	Cardiff (W.C.)	1	2
1997	Brussels (W.C.)	2	3

v. BOSNIA-HERZEGOVINA

		W	B-H
2003	Cardiff	2	2

v. BRAZIL

		W	B
1958	Gothenburg (W.C.)	0	1
1962	Rio de Janeiro	1	3
1962	Sao Paulo	1	3
1966	Rio de Janeiro	1	3
1966	Belo Horizonte	0	1
1983	Cardiff	1	1
1991	Cardiff	1	0
1997	Brasilia	0	3
2000	Cardiff	0	3

v. BULGARIA

		W	B
1983	Wrexham (E.C.)	1	0
1983	Sofia (E.C.)	0	1
1994	Cardiff (E.C.)	0	3
1995	Sofia (E.C.)	1	3

v. CANADA

		W	C
1986	Toronto	0	2
1986	Vancouver	3	0
2004	Wrexham	1	0

v. CHILE

		W	C
1966	Santiago	0	2

v. COSTA RICA

		W	C
1990	Cardiff	1	0

v. CROATIA

		W	C
2002	Varazdin	1	1

v. CYPRUS

		W	C
1992	Limassol (W.C.)	1	0
1993	Cardiff (W.C.)	2	0

v. CZECHOSLOVAKIA (see also R.C.S.)

		W	C
1957	Cardiff (W.C.)	1	0
1957	Prague (W.C.)	0	2
1971	Swansea (E.C.)	1	3
1971	Prague (E.C.)	0	1
1977	Wrexham (W.C.)	3	0
1977	Prague (W.C.)	0	1
1980	Cardiff (W.C.)	1	0
1981	Prague (W.C.)	0	2
1987	Wrexham (E.C.)	1	1
1987	Prague (E.C.)	0	2

v. CZECH REPUBLIC

		S	CR
2002	Cardiff	0	0

v. DENMARK

		W	D
1964	Copenhagen (W.C.)	0	1
1965	Wrexham (W.C.)	4	2
1987	Cardiff (E.C.)	1	0
1987	Copenhagen (E.C.)	0	1
1990	Copenhagen	0	1
1998	Copenhagen (E.C.)	2	1
1999	Anfield (E.C.)	0	2

v. EAST GERMANY

		W	EG
1957	Leipzig (W.C.)	1	2
1957	Cardiff (W.C.)	4	1
1969	Dresden (W.C.)	1	2
1969	Cardiff (W.C.)	1	3

v. ESTONIA

		W	E
1994	Tallinn	2	1

v. FAROE ISLANDS

		W	FI
1992	Cardiff (W.C.)	6	0
1993	Toftir (W.C.)	3	0

v. FINLAND

		W	F
1971	Helsinki (E.C.)	1	0
1971	Swansea (E.C.)	3	0
1986	Helsinki (E.C.)	1	1
1987	Wrexham (E.C.)	4	0
1988	Swansea (W.C.)	2	2
1989	Helsinki (W.C.)	0	1
2000	Cardiff	1	2
2002	Helsinki (E.C.)	2	0
2003	Cardiff (E.C.)	1	1

v. FRANCE

		W	F
1933	Paris	1	1
1939	Paris	1	2
1953	Paris	1	6
1982	Toulouse	1	0

v. GEORGIA

		W	G
1994	Tbilisi (E.C.)	0	5
1995	Cardiff (E.C.)	0	1

v. GERMANY/WEST GERMANY

		W	G
1968	Cardiff	1	1
1969	Frankfurt	1	1
1977	Cardiff	0	2
1977	Dortmund	1	1
1979	Wrexham (E.C.)	0	2
1979	Cologne (E.C.)	1	5
1989	Cardiff (W.C.)	0	0
1989	Cologne (W.C.)	1	2
1991	Cardiff (E.C.)	1	0
1991	Nuremberg (E.C.)	1	4
1995	Dusseldorf (E.C.)	1	1
1995	Cardiff (E.C.)	1	2
2002	Cardiff	1	0

v. GREECE

		W	G
1964	Athens (W.C.)	0	2
1965	Cardiff (W.C.)	4	1

v. HOLLAND

		W	H
1988	Amsterdam (W.C.)	0	1
1989	Wrexham (W.C.)	1	2
1992	Utrecht	0	4
1996	Cardiff (W.C.)	1	3
1996	Eindhoven (W.C.)	1	7

v. HUNGARY

		W	H
1958	Sanviken (W.C.)	1	1
1958	Stockholm (W.C.)	2	1

199

		W	H
1961	Budapest	2	3
1963	Budapest (E.C.)	1	3
1963	Cardiff (E.C.)	1	1
1974	Cardiff (E.C.)	2	0
1975	Budapest (E.C.)	2	1
1986	Cardiff	0	3
2004	Budapest	2	1

v. ICELAND

		W	I
1980	Reykjavik (W.C.)	4	0
1981	Swansea (W.C.)	2	2
1984	Reykjavik (W.C.)	0	1
1984	Cardiff (W.C.)	2	1
1991	Cardiff	1	0

v. IRAN

		W	I
1978	Tehran	1	0

v. REPUBLIC OF IRELAND

		W	RI
1960	Dublin	3	2
1979	Swansea	2	1
1981	Dublin	3	1
1986	Dublin	1	0
1990	Dublin	0	1
1991	Wrexham	0	3
1992	Dublin	1	0
1993	Dublin	1	2
1997	Cardiff	0	0

v. ISRAEL

		W	I
1958	Tel Aviv (W.C.)	2	0
1958	Cardiff (W.C.)	2	0
1984	Tel Aviv	0	0
1989	Tel Aviv	3	3

v. ITALY

		W	I
1965	Florence	1	4
1968	Cardiff (W.C.)	0	1
1969	Rome (W.C.)	1	4
1988	Brescia	1	0
1996	Terni	0	3
1998	Anfield (E.C.)	0	2
1999	Bologna (E.C.)	0	4
2002	Cardiff (E.C.)	2	1
2003	Milan (E.C.)	0	4

v. JAMAICA

		W	J
1998	Cardiff	0	0

v. JAPAN

		W	J
1992	Matsuyama	1	0

v. KUWAIT

		W	K
1977	Wrexham	0	0
1977	Kuwait City	0	0

v. LUXEMBOURG

		W	L
1974	Swansea (E.C.)	5	0
1975	Luxembourg (E.C.)	3	1
1990	Luxembourg (E.C.)	1	0
1991	Luxembourg (E.C.)	1	0

v. MALTA

		W	M
1978	Wrexham (E.C.)	7	0
1979	Valletta (E.C.)	2	0
1988	Valletta	3	2
1998	Valletta	3	0

v. MEXICO

		W	M
1958	Stockholm (W.C.)	1	1
1962	Mexico City	1	2

v. MOLDOVA

		W	M
1994	Kishinev (E.C.)	2	3
1995	Cardiff (E.C.)	1	0

v. NORWAY

		W	N
1982	Swansea (E.C.)	1	0
1983	Oslo (E.C.)	0	0
1984	Trondheim	0	1
1985	Wrexham	1	1
1985	Bergen	2	4
1994	Cardiff	1	3
2000	Cardiff (W.C.)	1	1
2001	Oslo (W.C.)	2	3
2004	Oslo	0	0

v. POLAND

		W	P
1973	Cardiff (W.C.)	2	0
1973	Katowice (W.C.)	0	3
1991	Radom	0	0
2000	Warsaw (W.C.)	0	0
2001	Cardiff (W.C.)	1	2

v. PORTUGAL

		W	P
1949	Lisbon	2	3
1951	Cardiff	2	1
2000	Chaves	0	3

v. QATAR

		W	Q
2000	Doha	1	0

v. R.C.S. (formerly Czechoslovakia)

		W	RCS
1993	Ostrava (W.C.)	1	1
1993	Cardiff (W.C.)	2	2

v. REST OF UNITED KINGDOM

		W	UK
1951	Cardiff	3	2
1969	Cardiff	0	1

v. ROMANIA

		W	R
1970	Cardiff (E.C.)	0	0
1971	Bucharest (E.C.)	0	0
1983	Wrexham	5	0
1992	Bucharest (W.C.)	1	5
1993	Cardiff (W.C.)	1	2

v. RUSSIA (See also Soviet Union)

		W	R
2003*	Moscow (E.C.)	0	0
2003*	Cardiff (E.C.)	0	1
(* Qual. Round play-offs)			

v. SAN MARINO

		W	SM
1996	Serravalle (W.C.)	5	0
1996	Cardiff (W.C.)	6	0

v. SAUDI ARABIA

		W	SA
1986	Dahran	2	1

v. SERBIA + MONTENEGRO

		W	S
2003	Belgrade (E.C.)	0	1
2003	Cardiff (E.C.)	2	3

v. SOVIET UNION (See also Russia)

		W	SU
1965	Moscow (W.C.)	1	2
1965	Cardiff (W.C.)	2	1
1981	Wrexham (W.C.)	0	0
1981	Tbilisi (W.C.)	0	3
1987	Swansea	0	0

v. SPAIN

		W	S
1961	Cardiff (W.C.)	1	2
1961	Madrid (W.C.)	1	1
1982	Valencia	1	1
1984	Seville (W.C.)	0	3
1985	Wrexham (W.C.)	3	0

v. SWEDEN

		W	S
1958	Stockholm (W.C.)	0	0
1988	Stockholm	1	4
1989	Wrexham	0	2
1990	Stockholm	2	4
1994	Wrexham	0	2

v. SWITZERLAND

		W	S
1949	Berne	0	4
1951	Wrexham	3	2
1996	Lugano	0	2
1999	Zurich (E.C.)	0	2
1999	Wrexham (E.C.) .:........	0	2

v. TUNISIA

		W	T
1998	Tunis	0	4

v. TURKEY

		W	T
1978	Wrexham (E.C.)	1	0
1979	Izmir (E.C.)	0	1
1980	Cardiff (W.C.)	4	0
1981	Ankara (W.C.)	1	0
1996	Cardiff (W.C.)	0	0
1997	Istanbul (W.C.)	4	6

v. UKRAINE

		W	U
2001	Cardiff (W.C.)	1	1
2001	Kiev (W.C.)	1	1

v. URUGUAY

		W	U
1986	Wrexham	0	0

v. U.S.A.

		W	USA
2003	San Jose	0	2

v. YUGOSLAVIA

		W	Y
1953	Belgrade	2	5
1954	Cardiff	1	3
1976	Zagreb (E.C.)	0	2
1976	Cardiff (E.C.)	1	1
1982	Titograd (E.C.)	4	4
1983	Cardiff (E.C.)	1	1
1988	Swansea	1	2

NORTHERN IRELAND

v. ALBANIA

		NI	A
1965	Belfast (W.C.)	4	1
1965	Tirana (W.C.)	1	1
1983	Tirana (E.C.)	0	0
1983	Belfast (E.C.)	1	0
1992	Belfast (W.C.)	3	0
1993	Tirana (W.C.)	2	1

		NI	A
1996	Belfast (W.C.)	2	0
1997	Zurich (W.C.)	0	1

v. ALGERIA

		NI	A
1986	Guadalajara (W.C.)	1	1

v. ARGENTINA

		NI	A
1958	Halmstad (W.C.)	1	3

v. ARMENIA

		NI	A
1996	Belfast (W.C.)	1	1
1997	Yerevan (W.C.)	0	0
2003	Yerevan (E.C.)	0	1
2003	Belfast (E.C.)	0	1

v. AUSTRALIA

		NI	A
1980	Sydney	2	1
1980	Melbourne	1	1
1980	Adelaide	2	1

v. AUSTRIA

		NI	A
1982	Madrid (W.C.)	2	2
1982	Vienna (E.C.)	0	2
1983	Belfast (E.C.)	3	1
1990	Vienna (E.C.)	0	0
1991	Belfast (E.C.)	2	1
1994	Vienna (E.C.)	2	1
1995	Belfast (E.C.)	5	3

v. BARBADOS

		NI	B
2004	Bridgetown	1	1

v. BELGIUM

		NI	B
1976	Liege (W.C.)	0	2
1977	Belfast (W.C.)	3	0
1997	Belfast	3	0

v. BRAZIL

		NI	B
1986	Guadalajara (W.C.)	0	3

v. BULGARIA

		NI	B
1972	Sofia (W.C.)	0	3
1973	Sheffield (W.C.)	0	0
1978	Sofia (E.C.)	2	0
1979	Belfast (E.C.)	2	0
2001	Sofia (W.C.)	3	4
2001	Belfast (W.C.)	0	1

v. CANADA

		NI	C
1995	Edmonton	0	2
1999	Belfast	1	1

v. CHILE

		NI	C
1989	Belfast	0	1
1995	Edmonton, Canada	0	2

v. COLOMBIA

		NI	C
1994	Boston, USA	0	2

v. CYPRUS

		NI	C
1971	Nicosia (E.C.)	3	0
1971	Belfast (E.C.)	5	0
1973	Nicosia (W.C.)	0	1
1973	Fulham (W.C.)	3	0
2002	Belfast	0	0

v. CZECHOSLOVAKIA/CZECH REPUBLIC

		NI	C
1958	Halmstad (W.C.)	1	0
1958	Malmo (W.C.)	2	1
2001	Belfast (W.C.)	0	1
2001	Teplice (W.C.)	1	3

v. DENMARK

		NI	D
1978	Belfast (E.C.)	2	1
1979	Copenhagen (E.C.)	0	4
1986	Belfast	1	1
1990	Belfast (E.C.)	1	1
1991	Odense (E.C.)	1	2
1992	Belfast (W.C.)	0	1
1993	Copenhagen (W.C.)	0	1
2000	Belfast (W.C.)	1	1
2001	Copenhagen (W.C.)	1	1

v. ESTONIA

		NI	E
2004	Tallinn	1	0

v. FAROE ISLANDS

		NI	FI
1991	Belfast (E.C.)	1	1
1991	Landskrona, Sw. (E.C.)	5	0

v. FINLAND

		NI	F
1984	Pori (W.C.)	0	1
1984	Belfast (W.C.)	2	1
1998	Belfast (E.C.)	1	0
1999	Helsinki (E.C.)	1	4
2003	Belfast	0	1

v. FRANCE

		NI	F
1951	Belfast	2	2
1952	Paris	1	3
1958	Norrkoping (W.C.)	0	4
1982	Paris	0	4
1982	Madrid (W.C.)	1	4
1986	Paris	0	0
1988	Belfast	0	0
1999	Belfast	0	1

v. GERMANY/WEST GERMANY

		NI	G
1958	Malmo (W.C.)	2	2
1960	Belfast (W.C.)	3	4
1961	Berlin (W.C.)	1	2
1966	Belfast	0	2

		NI	G
1977	Cologne	0	5
1982	Belfast (E.C.)	1	0
1983	Hamburg (E.C.)	1	0
1992	Bremen	1	1
1996	Belfast	1	1
1997	Nuremberg (W.C.)	1	1
1997	Belfast (W.C.)	1	3
1999	Belfast (E.C.)	0	3
1999	Dortmund (E.C.)	0	4

v. GREECE

		NI	G
1961	Athens (W.C.)	1	2
1961	Belfast (W.C.)	2	0
1988	Athens	2	3
2003	Belfast (E.C.)	0	2
2003	Athens (E.C.)	0	1

v. HOLLAND

		NI	H
1962	Rotterdam	0	4
1965	Belfast (W.C.)	2	1
1965	Rotterdam (W.C.)	0	0
1976	Rotterdam (W.C.)	2	2
1977	Belfast (W.C.)	0	1

v. HONDURAS

		NI	H
1982	Zaragoza (W.C.)	1	1

v. HUNGARY

		NI	H
1988	Budapest (W.C.)	0	1
1989	Belfast (W.C.)	1	2
2000	Belfast	0	1

v. ICELAND

		NI	I
1977	Reykjavik (W.C.)	0	1
1977	Belfast (W.C.)	2	0
2000	Reykjavik (W.C.)	0	1
2001	Belfast (W.C.)	3	0

v. REPUBLIC OF IRELAND

		NI	RI
1978	Dublin (E.C.)	0	0
1979	Belfast (E.C.)	1	0
1988	Belfast (W.C.)	0	0
1989	Dublin (W.C.)	0	3
1993	Dublin (W.C.)	0	3
1993	Belfast (W.C.)	1	1
1994	Belfast (E.C.)	0	4
1995	Dublin (E.C.)	1	1
1999	Dublin	1	0

v. ISRAEL

		NI	I
1968	Jaffa	3	2
1976	Tel Aviv	1	1
1980	Tel Aviv (W.C.)	0	0

		NI	I
1981	Belfast (W.C.)	1	0
1984	Belfast	3	0
1987	Tel Aviv	1	1

v. ITALY

		NI	I
1957	Rome (W.C.)	0	1
1957	Belfast	2	2
1958	Belfast (W.C.)	2	1
1961	Bologna	2	3
1997	Palermo	0	2
2003	Campobasso	0	2

v. LATVIA

		NI	L
1993	Riga (W.C.)	2	1
1993	Belfast (W.C.)	2	0
1995	Riga (E.C.)	1	0
1995	Belfast (E.C.)	1	2

v. LIECHTENSTEIN

		NI	L
1994	Belfast (E.C.)	4	1
1995	Eschen (E.C.)	4	0
2002	Vaduz	0	0

v. LITHUANIA

		NI	L
1992	Belfast (W.C.)	2	2
1993	Vilnius (W.C.)	1	0

v. LUXEMBOURG

		NI	L
2000	Luxembourg	3	1

v. MALTA

		NI	M
1988	Belfast (W.C.)	3	0
1989	Valletta (W.C.)	2	0
2000	Ta'Qali	3	0
2000	Belfast (W.C.)	1	0
2001	Valletta (W.C.)	1	0

v. MEXICO

		NI	M
1966	Belfast	4	1
1994	Miami	0	3

v. MOLDOVA

		NI	M
1998	Belfast (E.C.)	2	2
1999	Kishinev (E.C.)	0	0

v. MOROCCO

		NI	M
1986	Belfast	2	1

v. NORWAY

		NI	N
1974	Oslo (E.C.)	1	2
1975	Belfast (E.C.)	3	0

		NI	N
1990	Belfast	2	3
1996	Belfast	0	2
2001	Belfast	0	4
2004	Belfast	1	4

v. POLAND

		NI	P
1962	Katowice (E.C.)	2	0
1962	Belfast (E.C.)	2	0
1988	Belfast	1	1
1991	Belfast	3	1
2002	Limassol (Cyprus)	1	4

v. PORTUGAL

		NI	P
1957	Lisbon (W.C.)	1	1
1957	Belfast (W.C.)	3	0
1973	Coventry (W.C.)	1	1
1973	Lisbon (W.C.)	1	1
1980	Lisbon (W.C.)	0	1
1981	Belfast (W.C.)	1	0
1994	Belfast (E.C.)	1	2
1995	Oporto (E.C.)	1	1
1997	Belfast (W.C.)	0	0
1997	Lisbon (W.C.)	0	1

v. ROMANIA

		NI	R
1984	Belfast (W.C.)	3	2
1985	Bucharest (W.C.)	1	0
1994	Belfast	2	0

v. SERBIA + MONTENEGRO

		NI	S
2004	Belfast	1	1

v. SLOVAKIA

		NI	S
1998	Belfast	1	0

v. SOVIET UNION

		NI	SU
1969	Belfast (W.C.)	0	0
1969	Moscow (W.C.)	0	2
1971	Moscow (E.C.)	0	1
1971	Belfast (E.C.)	1	1

v. SPAIN

		NI	S
1958	Madrid	2	6
1963	Bilbao	1	1
1963	Belfast	0	1
1970	Seville (E.C.)	0	3
1972	Hull (E.C.)	1	1
1982	Valencia (W.C.)	1	0
1985	Palma, Majorca	0	0
1986	Guadalajara (W.C.)	1	2
1988	Seville (W.C.)	0	4
1989	Belfast (W.C.)	0	2
1992	Belfast (W.C.)	0	0

		NI	S
1993	Seville (W.C.)	1	3
1998	Santander	1	4
2002	Belfast	0	5
2002	Albacete (E.C.)	0	3
2003	Belfast (E.C.)	0	0

v. ST KITTS + NEVIS

		NI	SK
2004	Basseterre	2	0

v. SWEDEN

		NI	S
1974	Solna (E.C.)	2	0
1975	Belfast (E.C.)	1	2
1980	Belfast (W.C.)	3	0
1981	Stockholm (W.C.)	0	1
1996	Belfast	1	2

v. SWITZERLAND

		NI	S
1964	Belfast (W.C.)	1	0
1964	Lausanne (W.C.)	1	2
1998	Belfast	1	0

v. THAILAND

		NI	T
1997	Bangkok	0	0

v. TRINIDAD + TOBAGO

		NI	T
2004	Port of Spain	3	0

v. TURKEY

		NI	T
1968	Belfast (W.C.)	4	1
1968	Istanbul (W.C.)	3	0
1983	Belfast (E.C.)	2	1
1983	Ankara (E.C.)	0	1
1985	Belfast (W.C.)	2	0
1985	Izmir (W.C.)	0	0
1986	Izmir (E.C.)	0	0
1987	Belfast (E.C.)	1	0
1998	Istanbul (E.C.)	0	3
1999	Belfast (E.C.)	0	3

v. UKRAINE

		NI	U
1996	Belfast (W.C.)	0	1
1997	Kiev (W.C.)	1	2
2002	Belfast (E.C.)	0	0
2003	Donetsk (E.C.)	0	0

v. URUGUAY

		NI	U
1964	Belfast	3	0
1990	Belfast	1	0

v. YUGOSLAVIA

		NI	Y
1975	Belfast (E.C.)	1	0
1975	Belgrade (E.C.)	0	1

1982	Zaragoza (W.C.)	0	0	1990	Belfast (E.C.)	0	2
1987	Belfast (E.C.)	1	2	1991	Belgrade (E.C.)	1	4
1987	Sarajevo (E.C.)	0	3	2000	Belfast	1	2

REPUBLIC OF IRELAND

v. ALBANIA

		RI	A
1992	Dublin (W.C.)	2	0
1993	Tirana (W.C.)	2	1
2003	Tirana (E.C.)	0	0
2003	Dublin (E.C.)	2	1

v. ALGERIA

		RI	A
1982	Algiers	0	2

v. ANDORRA

		RI	A
2001	Barcelona (W.C.)	3	0
2001	Dublin (W.C.)	3	1

v. ARGENTINA

		RI	A
1951	Dublin	0	1
1979*	Dublin	0	0
1980	Dublin	0	1
1998	Dublin	0	2
(* Not regarded as full Int.)			

v. AUSTRALIA

		RI	A
2003	Dublin	2	1

v. AUSTRIA

		RI	A
1952	Vienna	0	6
1953	Dublin	4	0
1958	Vienna	1	3
1962	Dublin	2	3
1963	Vienna (E.C.)	0	0
1963	Dublin (E.C.)	3	2
1966	Vienna	0	1
1968	Dublin	2	2
1971	Dublin (E.C.)	1	4
1971	Linz (E.C.)	0	6
1995	Dublin (E.C.)	1	3
1995	Vienna (E.C.)	1	3

v. BELGIUM

		RI	B
1928	Liege	4	2
1929	Dublin	4	0
1930	Brussels	3	1
1934	Dublin (W.C.)	4	4
1949	Dublin	0	2
1950	Brussels	1	5
1965	Dublin	0	2
1966	Liege	3	2
1980	Dublin (W.C.)	1	1

		RI	B
1981	Brussels (W.C.)	0	1
1986	Brussels (E.C.)	2	2
1987	Dublin (E.C.)	0	0
1997*	Dublin (W.C.)	1	1
1997*	Brussels (W.C.)	1	2
(* World Cup play-off)			

v. BOLIVIA

		RI	B
1994	Dublin	1	0
1996	East Rutherford, N.J. ...	3	0

v. BRAZIL

		RI	B
1974	Rio de Janeiro	1	2
1982	Uberlandia	0	7
1987	Dublin	1	0
2004	Dublin	0	0

v. BULGARIA

		RI	B
1977	Sofia (W.C.)	1	2
1977	Dublin (W.C.)	0	0
1979	Sofia (E.C.)	0	1
1979	Dublin (E.C.)	3	0
1987	Sofia (E.C.)	1	2
1987	Dublin (E.C.)	2	0

v. CAMEROON

		RI	C
2002	Niigata (W.C.)	1	1

v. CANADA

		RI	C
2003	Dublin	3	0

v. CHILE

		RI	C
1960	Dublin	2	0
1972	Recife	1	2
1974	Santiago	2	1
1982	Santiago	0	1
1991	Dublin	1	1

v. CHINA

		RI	C
1984	Sapporo	1	0

v. CROATIA

		RI	C
1996	Dublin	2	2
1998	Dublin (E.C.)	2	0
1999	Zagreb (E.C.)	0	1

		RI	C
2001	Dublin	2	2

v. CYPRUS

		RI	C
1980	Nicosia (W.C.) ...	3	2
1980	Dublin (W.C.)	6	0
2001	Nicosia (W.C.) ...	4	0
2001	Dublin (W.C.)	4	0

v. CZECHOSLOVAKIA/CZECH REPUBLIC

		RI	C
1938	Prague	2	2
1959	Dublin (E.C.)	2	0
1959	Bratislava (E.C.) .	0	4
1961	Dublin (W.C.)	1	3
1961	Prague (W.C.)	1	7
1967	Dublin (E.C.)	0	2
1967	Prague (E.C.)	2	1
1969	Dublin (W.C.)	1	2
1969	Prague (W.C.)	0	3
1979	Prague	1	4
1981	Dublin	3	1
1986	Reykjavik	1	0
1994	Dublin	1	3
1996	Prague	0	2
1998	Olomouc	1	2
2000	Dublin	3	2
2004	Dublin	2	1

v. DENMARK

		RI	D
1956	Dublin (W.C.)	2	1
1957	Copenhagen (W.C.) ..	2	0
1968*	Dublin (W.C.)	1	1
1969	Copenhagen (W.C.) ..	0	2
1969	Dublin (W.C.)	1	1
1978	Copenhagen (E.C.) ..	3	3
1979	Dublin (E.C.)	2	0
1984	Copenhagen (W.C.) ..	0	3
1985	Dublin (W.C.)	1	4
1992	Copenhagen (W.C.) ..	0	0
1993	Dublin (W.C.)	1	1
2002	Dublin	3	0

(* Abandoned after 51 mins. – fog)

v. ECUADOR

		RI	E
1972	Natal	3	2

v. EGYPT

		RI	E
1990	Palermo (W.C.)	0	0

v. ESTONIA

		RI	E
2000	Dublin (W.C.)	2	0
2001	Tallinn (W.C.) ...	2	0

v. FINLAND

		RI	F
1949	Dublin (W.C.)	3	0
1949	Helsinki (W.C.) ...	1	1
1990	Dublin	1	1
2000	Dublin	3	0
2002	Helsinki	3	0

v. FRANCE

		RI	F
1937	Paris	2	0
1952	Dublin	1	1
1953	Dublin (W.C.)	3	5
1953	Paris (W.C.)	0	1
1972	Dublin (W.C.)	2	1
1973	Paris (W.C.)	1	1
1976	Paris (W.C.)	0	2
1977	Dublin (W.C.)	1	0
1980	Paris (W.C.)	0	2
1981	Dublin (W.C.)	3	2
1989	Dublin	0	0

v. GEORGIA

		RI	G
2002	Tbilisi (E.C.) ..	2	1
2003	Dublin (E.C.) ...	2	0

v. GERMANY/WEST GERMANY

		RI	G
1935	Dortmund	1	3
1936	Dublin	5	2
1939	Bremen	1	1
1951	Dublin	3	2
1952	Cologne	0	3
1955	Hamburg	1	2
1956	Dublin	3	0
1960	Dusseldorf	1	0
1966	Dublin	0	4
1970	Berlin	1	2
1979	Dublin	1	3
1981	Bremen	0	3
1989	Dublin	1	1
1994	Hanover	2	0
1995*	Dublin	1	0
2002	Ibaraki (W.C.) ...	1	1

(*v. W. Germany 'B')

v. GREECE

		RI	G
2000	Dublin	0	1
2002	Athens	0	0

v. HOLLAND

		RI	H
1932	Amsterdam	2	0
1934	Amsterdam	2	5
1935	Dublin	3	5
1955	Dublin	1	0
1956	Rotterdam	4	1
1980	Dublin (W.C.)	2	1
1981	Rotterdam (W.C.) ..	2	2

	RI	H
1982 Rotterdam (E.C.)	1	2
1983 Dublin (E.C.)	2	3
1988 Gelsenkirchen (E.C.)	0	1
1990 Palermo (W.C.)	1	1
1994 Tilburg	1	0
1994 Orlando (W.C.)	0	2
1995* Liverpool (E.C.)	0	2
1996 Rotterdam	1	3
(* Qual. Round play-off)		
2000 Amsterdam (W.C.)	2	2
2001 Dublin (W.C.)	1	0
2004 Amsterdam	1	0

v. HUNGARY

	RI	H
1934 Dublin	2	4
1936 Budapest	3	3
1936 Dublin	2	3
1939 Cork	2	2
1939 Budapest	2	2
1969 Dublin (W.C.)	1	2
1969 Budapest (W.C.)	0	4
1989 Budapest (W.C.)	0	0
1989 Dublin (W.C.)	2	0
1992 Gyor	2	1

v. ICELAND

	RI	I
1962 Dublin (E.C.)	4	2
1962 Reykjavik (E.C.)	1	1
1982 Dublin (E.C.)	2	0
1983 Reykjavik (E.C.)	3	0
1986 Reykjavik	2	1
1996 Dublin (W.C.)	0	0
1997 Reykjavik (W.C.)	4	2

v. IRAN

	RI	I
1972 Recife	2	1
2001* Dublin (W.C.)	2	0
2001* Tehran (W.C.)	0	1
(*Qual. Round play-off)		

v. ISRAEL

	RI	I
1984 Tel Aviv	0	3
1985 Tel Aviv	0	0
1987 Dublin	5	0

v. JAMAICA

	RI	J
2004 Charlton	1	0

v. ITALY

	RI	I
1926 Turin	0	3
1927 Dublin	1	2
1970 Florence (E.C.)	0	3
1971 Dublin (E.C.)	1	2
1985 Dublin	1	2

	RI	I
1990 Rome (W.C.)	0	1
1992 Boston, USA	0	2
1994 New York (W.C.)	1	0

v. LATVIA

	RI	L
1992 Dublin (W.C.)	4	0
1993 Riga (W.C.)	2	0
1994 Riga (E.C.)	3	0
1995 Dublin (E.C.)	2	1

v. LIECHTENSTEIN

	RI	L
1994 Dublin (E.C.)	4	0
1995 Eschen (E.C.)	0	0
1996 Eschen (W.C.)	5	0
1997 Dublin (W.C.)	5	0

v. LITHUANIA

	RI	L
1993 Vilnius (W.C.)	1	0
1993 Dublin (W.C.)	2	0
1997 Dublin (W.C.)	0	0
1997 Zalgiris (W.C.)	2	1

v. LUXEMBOURG

	RI	L
1936 Luxembourg	5	1
1953 Dublin (W.C.)	4	0
1954 Luxembourg (W.C.)	1	0
1987 Luxembourg (E.C.)	2	0
1987 Luxembourg (E.C.)	2	1

v. MACEDONIA

	RI	M
1996 Dublin (W.C.)	3	0
1997 Skopje (W.C.)	2	3
1999 Dublin (E.C.)	1	0
1999 Skopje (E.C.)	1	1

v. MALTA

	RI	M
1983 Valletta (E.C.)	1	0
1983 Dublin (E.C.)	8	0
1989 Dublin (W.C.)	2	0
1989 Valletta (W.C.)	2	0
1990 Valletta	3	0
1998 Dublin (E.C.)	1	0
1999 Valletta (E.C.)	3	2

v. MEXICO

	RI	M
1984 Dublin	0	0
1994 Orlando (W.C.)	1	2
1996 New Jersey	2	2
1998 Dublin	0	0
2000 Chicago	2	2

v. MOROCCO

	RI	M
1990 Dublin	1	0

v. NIGERIA

		RI	N
2002	Dublin	1	2
2004	Charlton	0	3

v. NORWAY

		RI	N
1937	Oslo (W.C.)	2	3
1937	Dublin (W.C.)	3	3
1950	Dublin	2	2
1951	Oslo	3	2
1954	Dublin	2	1
1955	Oslo	3	1
1960	Dublin	3	1
1964	Oslo	4	1
1973	Oslo	1	1
1976	Dublin	3	0
1978	Oslo	0	0
1984	Oslo (W.C.)	0	1
1985	Dublin (W.C.)	0	0
1988	Oslo	0	0
1994	New York (W.C.)	0	0
2003	Dublin	1	0

v. PARAGUAY

		RI	P
1999	Dublin	2	0

v. POLAND

		RI	P
1938	Warsaw	0	6
1938	Dublin	3	2
1958	Katowice	2	2
1958	Dublin	2	2
1964	Cracow	1	3
1964	Dublin	3	2
1968	Dublin	2	2
1968	Katowice	0	1
1970	Dublin	1	2
1970	Poznan	0	2
1973	Wroclaw	0	2
1973	Dublin	1	0
1976	Poznan	2	0
1977	Dublin	0	0
1978	Lodz	0	3
1981	Bydgoszcz	0	3
1984	Dublin	0	0
1986	Warsaw	0	1
1988	Dublin	3	1
1991	Dublin (E.C.)	0	0
1991	Poznan (E.C.)	3	3
2004	Bydgoszcz	0	0

v. PORTUGAL

		RI	P
1946	Lisbon	1	3
1947	Dublin	0	2
1948	Lisbon	0	2
1949	Dublin	1	0
1972	Recife	1	2
1992	Boston, USA	2	0

		RI	P
1995	Dublin (E.C.)	1	0
1995	Lisbon (E.C.)	0	3
1996	Dublin	0	1
2000	Lisbon (W.C.)	1	1
2001	Dublin (W.C.)	1	1

v. ROMANIA

		RI	R
1988	Dublin	2	0
1990*	Genoa	0	0
1997	Bucharest (W.C.)	0	1
1997	Dublin (W.C.)	1	1

(* Rep. won 5-4 on pens.)

v. RUSSIA (See also Soviet Union)

		RI	R
1994	Dublin	0	0
1996	Dublin	0	2
2002	Dublin	2	0
2002	Moscow (E.C.)	2	4
2003	Dublin (E.C.)	1	1

v. SAUDI ARABIA

		RI	SA
2002	Yokohama (W.C.)	3	0

v. SOUTH AFRICA

		RI	SA
2000	New Jersey	2	1

v. SOVIET UNION
(See also Russia)

		RI	SU
1972	Dublin (W.C.)	1	2
1973	Moscow (W.C.)	0	1
1974	Dublin (E.C.)	3	0
1975	Kiev (E.C.)	1	2
1984	Dublin (W.C.)	1	0
1985	Moscow (W.C.)	0	2
1988	Hanover (E.C.)	1	1
1990	Dublin	1	0

v. SPAIN

		RI	S
1931	Barcelona	1	1
1931	Dublin	0	5
1946	Madrid	1	0
1947	Dublin	3	2
1948	Barcelona	1	2
1949	Dublin	1	4
1952	Madrid	0	6
1955	Dublin	2	2
1964	Seville (E.C.)	1	5
1964	Dublin (E.C.)	0	2
1965	Dublin (W.C.)	1	0
1965	Seville (W.C.)	1	4
1965	Paris (W.C.)	0	1
1966	Dublin (E.C.)	0	0
1966	Valencia (E.C.)	0	2
1977	Dublin	0	1

		RI	S
1982	Dublin (E.C.)	3	3
1983	Zaragoza (E.C.)	0	2
1985	Cork	0	0
1988	Seville (W.C.)	0	2
1989	Dublin (W.C.)	1	0
1992	Seville (W.C.)	0	0
1993	Dublin (W.C.)	1	3
2002*	Suwon (W.C.)	1	1
(*Rep. lost 3-2 on pens.)			

v. SWEDEN

		RI	S
1949	Stockholm (W.C.)	1	3
1949	Dublin (W.C.)	1	3
1959	Dublin	3	2
1960	Malmo	1	4
1970	Dublin (E.C.)	1	1
1970	Malmo (E.C.)	0	1
1999	Dublin	2	0

v. SWITZERLAND

		RI	S
1935	Basle	0	1
1936	Dublin	1	0
1937	Berne	1	0
1938	Dublin	4	0
1948	Dublin	0	1
1975	Dublin (E.C.)	2	1
1975	Berne (E.C.)	0	1
1980	Dublin	2	0
1985	Dublin (W.C.)	3	0
1985	Berne (W.C.)	0	0
1992	Dublin	2	1
2002	Dublin (E.C.)	1	2
2003	Basle (E.C.)	0	2

v. TRINIDAD & TOBAGO

		RI	T&T
1982	Port of Spain	1	2

v. TUNISIA

		RI	T
1988	Dublin	4	0

v. TURKEY

		RI	T
1966	Dublin (E.C.)	2	1
1967	Ankara (E.C.)	1	2
1974	Izmir (E.C.)	1	1
1975	Dublin (E.C.)	4	0
1976	Ankara	3	3
1978	Dublin	4	2
1990	Izmir	0	0
1990	Dublin (E.C.)	5	0
1991	Istanbul (E.C.)	3	1
1999	Dublin (E.C.)	1	1
1999	Bursa (E.C.)	0	0
2003	Dublin	2	2

v. URUGUAY

		RI	U
1974	Montevideo	0	2
1986	Dublin	1	1

v. U.S.A.

		RI	USA
1979	Dublin	3	2
1991	Boston	1	1
1992	Dublin	4	1
1992	Washington	1	3
1996	Boston	1	2
2000	Foxboro	1	1
2002	Dublin	2	1

v. YUGOSLAVIA

		RI	Y
1955	Dublin	1	4
1988	Dublin	2	0
1998	Belgrade (E.C.)	0	1
1999	Dublin (E.C.)	2	1

ONE TO FORGET FOR SODJE

Efe Sodje, Huddersfield's Nigerian international defender, had an afternoon to forget, despite his side's 3-2 win over Scunthorpe. Sodje conceded an own goal, gave away a penalty and was later sent off for a second yellow card.

POIGNANT FOR PAUL

Paul Harrison, 19-year-old goalkeeper, was on the Liverpool bench for the first time against Newcastle at Anfield in last season's final match. His father Gary and uncle Stephen were among the 96 victims of the Hillsborough disaster in 1989.

BRITISH & IRISH INTERNATIONAL APPEARANCES SINCE THE WAR (1946-2004)

(As at start of season 2004-05. In year shown, 2004 = season 2003-04 etc.
*Also a pre-war International player. Totals include appearances as substitute).

ENGLAND

A'Court, A. (Liverpool, 1958-9) 5
Adams, T. (Arsenal, 1987-2001) 66
Allen, A. (Stoke City, 1960) 3
Allen, C. (Q.P.R., Tottenham,
  1984-8) 5
Allen, R. (W.B.A., 1952-5) 5
Anderson, S. (Sunderland, 1962) 2
Anderson, V. (Nott'm Forest, Arsenal,
  Manchester Utd., 1979-88) 30
Anderton, D. (Tottenham,
  1994-2002) 30
Angus, J. (Burnley, 1961) 1
Armfield, J. (Blackpool, 1959-66) 43
Armstrong, D. (Middlesbrough,
  Southampton, 1980-4) 3
Armstrong, K. (Chelsea, 1955) 1
Astall, G. (Birmingham City, 1956) ... 2
Astle, J. (W.B.A., 1969-70) 5
Aston, J. (Manchester Utd.,
  1949-51) 17
Atyeo, J. (Bristol City, 1956-7) 6

Bailey, G. (Manchester Utd., 1985) ... 2
Bailey, M. (Charlton Athletic,
  1964-5) 2
Baily, E. (Tottenham, 1950-3) 9
Baker, J. (Hibernian, Arsenal,
  1960-6) 8
Ball, A. (Blackpool, Everton, Arsenal,
  1965-75) 72
Ball, M. (Everton, 2001) 1
Banks, G. (Leicester City, Stoke City,
  1963-72) 73
Banks, T. (Bolton Wand., 1958-9) 6
Bardsley, D. (Q.P.R., 1993) 2
Barham, M. (Norwich City, 1983) 2
Barlow, R. (W.B.A., 1955) 1
Barmby, N. (Tottenham, Middlesbrough,
  Everton, Liverpool, 1995-2002) 23
Barnes, J. (Watford, Liverpool,
  1983-96) 79
Barnes, P. (Manchester City, W.B.A.,
  Leeds Utd., 1978-82) 22
Barrass, M. (Bolton Wand., 1952-3) ... 3
Barrett, E. (Oldham Athletic, Aston Villa,
  1991-3) 3
Barton, W. (Wimbledon, Newcastle Utd.,
  1995) 3
Barry, G. (Aston Villa, 2000-03) 8

Batty, D. (Leeds Utd., Blackburn Rov.,
  Newcastle Utd., Leeds Utd.,
  1991-2000) 42
Baynham, R. (Luton Town, 1956) 3
Beardsley, P. (Newcastle Utd., Liverpool,
  Newcastle Utd., 1986-96) 59
Beasant, D. (Chelsea, 1990) 2
Beattie, J. (Southampton, 2003-4) 5
Beattie, K. (Ipswich Town, 1975-8) ... 9
Beckham, D. (Manchester Utd., Real
  Madrid, 1997-2004) 72
Bell, C. (Manchester City, 1968-76) . 48
Bentley, R. (Chelsea, 1949-55) 12
Berry, J. (Manchester Utd., 1953-6) .. 4
Birtles, G. (Nott'm Forest, 1980-1) ... 3
Blissett, L. (Watford, AC Milan,
  1983-4) 14
Blockley, J. (Arsenal, 1973) 1
Blunstone, F. (Chelsea, 1955-7) 5
Bonetti, P. (Chelsea, 1966-70) 7
Bould, S. (Arsenal, 1994) 2
Bowles, S. (Q.P.R., 1974-7) 5
Bowyer, L. (Leeds Utd., 2003) 1
Boyer, P. (Norwich City, 1976) 1
Brabrook, P. (Chelsea, 1958-60) 3
Bracewell, P. (Everton, 1985-6) 3
Bradford, G. (Bristol Rov., 1956) 1
Bradley, W. (Manchester Utd., 1959) .. 3
Bridge, W. (Southampton, Chelsea,
  2002-4) 17
Bridges, B. (Chelsea, 1965-6) 4
Broadbent, P. (Wolves, 1958-60) 7
Broadis, I. (Manchester City, Newcastle
  Utd., 1952-4) 14
Brooking, T. (West Ham Utd.,
  1974-82) 47
Brooks, J. (Tottenham, 1957) 3
Brown, A. (W.B.A., 1971) 1
Brown, K. (West Ham Utd., 1960) 1
Brown, W. (Manchester Utd.,
  1999-2003) 7
Bull, S. (Wolves, 1989-91) 13
Butcher, T. (Ipswich Town, Rangers,
  1980-90) 77
Butt, N. (Manchester Utd.,
  1997-2004) 35
Byrne, G. (Liverpool, 1963-6) 2
Byrne, J. (Crystal Palace, West Ham
  Utd., 1962-5) 11

NORTHERN IRELAND

Aherne, T. (Belfast Celtic, Luton Town, 1947-50) 4

Anderson, T. (Manchester Utd., Swindon Town, Peterborough Utd., 1973-9) 22

Armstrong, G. (Tottenham, Watford, Real Mallorca, W.B.A., 1977-86) 63

Baird, C. (Southampton, 2003-4) 11

Barr, H. (Linfield, Coventry City, 1962-3) 3

Best, G. (Manchester Utd., Fulham, 1964-77) 37

Bingham, W. (Sunderland, Luton Town, Everton, Port Vale, 1951-64) 56

Black, K. (Luton Town, Nott'm Forest, 1988-94) 30

Blair, R. (Oldham Athletic, 1975-6) ... 5

Blanchflower, R.D. (Barnsley, Aston Villa, Tottenham, 1950-63) 56

Blanchflower, J. (Manchester Utd., 1954-8) 12

Bowler, G. (Hull City, 1950) 3

Braithwaite, R. (Linfield, Middlesbrough, 1962-5) 10

Brennan, R. (Luton Town, Birmingham City, Fulham, 1949-51) 5

Briggs, W. (Manchester Utd., Swansea City, 1962-5) 2

Brotherston, N. (Blackburn Rov., 1980-5) 27

Bruce, W. (Glentoran, 1961-7) 2

Campbell, D. (Nott'm Forest, Charlton Athletic, 1987-8) 10

Campbell, J. (Fulham, 1951) 2

Campbell, R. (Crusaders, 1963-5) 2

Campbell, R. (Bradford City, 1982) ... 2

Campbell, W. (Dundee, 1968-70) 6

Capaldi, A. (Plymouth Argle, 2004) ... 5

Carey, J. (Manchester Utd., 1947-9) .. 7

Carroll, R. (Wigan Athletic, Manchester Utd., 1997-2004) 14

Casey, T. (Newcastle Utd., Portsmouth, 1955-9) 12

Caskey, W. (Derby Co., Tulsa Roughnecks, 1979-82) 7

Cassidy, T. (Newcastle Utd., Burnley, 1971-82) 24

Caughey, M. (Linfield, 1986) 2

Clarke, C. (Bournemouth, Southampton, Q.P.R., Portsmouth, 1986-93) ... 38

Cleary, J. (Glentoran, 1982-5) 5

Clements, D. (Coventry City, Sheffield Wed., Everton, New York City Cosmos, 1965-76) 48

Cochrane, A. (Coleraine, Burnley, Middlesbrough, Gillingham, 1976-84) 26

Cochrane, D. (Leeds Utd., 1947-50) 10

Connell, T. (Coleraine, 1978) 1

Coote, A. (Norwich City, 1999-2000) . 6

Cowan, J. (Newcastle Utd., 1970) 1

Coyle, F. (Coleraine, Nott'm Forest, 1956-8) 4

Coyle, L. (Derry C., 1989) 1

Coyle, R. (Sheffield Wed., 1973-4) ... 5

Craig, D. (Newcastle Utd., 1967-75) 25

Craigan, S. (Partick Thistle, Motherwell, 2003-4) 8

Crossan, E. (Blackburn Rov., 1950-5) . 3

Crossan, J. (Sparta Rotterdam, Sunderland, Manchester City, Middlesbrough, 1960-8) 24

Cunningham, W. (St Mirren, Leicester City, Dunfermline, 1951-62) 30

Cush, W. (Glenavon, Leeds Utd., Portadown, 1951-62) 26

D'Arcy, S. (Chelsea, Brentford, 1952-3) 5

Davison, A. (Bolton Wand., Bradford City C., Grimsby Town, 1996-7) 3

Dennison, R. (Wolves, 1988-97) 18

Devine, J. (Glentoran, 1990) 1

Dickson, D. (Coleraine, 1970-3) 4

Dickson, T. (Linfield, 1957) 1

Dickson, W. (Chelsea, Arsenal, 1951-5) 12

Doherty, L. (Linfield, 1985-8) 2

*Doherty, P. (Derby Co., Huddersfield Town, Doncaster Rov., 1946-50) 6

Doherty, T. (Bristol City, 2003-4) 5

Donaghy, M. (Luton Town, Manchester Utd., Chelsea, 1980-94) 91

Dougan, D. (Portsmouth, Blackburn Rov., Aston Villa, Leicester City, Wolves, 1958-73) 43

Douglas, J. (Belfast Celtic, 1947) 1

Dowd, H. (Glenavon, 1974) 3

Dowie, I. (Luton Town, Southampton, Crystal Palace, West Ham Utd., Q.P.R., 1990-2000) 59

Duff, M. (Cheltenham Town, 2002-4) . 3

Dunlop, G. (Linfield, 1985-90) 4

Eglington, T. (Everton, 1947-9) 6

Elder, A. (Burnley, Stoke City, 1960-70) 40

Elliott, S. (Motherwell, Hull City, 2001-4) 20

Farrell, P. (Everton, 1947-9) 7

Feeney, J. (Linfield, Swansea City, 1947-50) 2

218

SCOTLAND

WALES

Williams, G. (Derby Co., Ipswich Town, 1988-96) 13
Williams, G.E. (W.B.A., 1960-9) 26
Williams, G.G. (Swansea City, 1961-2) 5
Williams, H.J. (Swansea City, 1965-72) 3
Williams, H.T. (Newport, Leeds Utd., 1949-50) 4
Williams, S. (W.B.A., Southampton, 1954-66) 43

Witcomb, D. (W.B.A., Sheffield Wed., 1947) 3
Woosnam, P. (Leyton Orient, West Ham Utd., Aston Villa, 1959-63) 17

Yorath, T. (Leeds Utd., Coventry City, Tottenham, Vancouver Whitecaps, 1970-81) 59
Young, E. (Wimbledon, Crystal Palace, Wolves, 1990-6) 21

REPUBLIC OF IRELAND

Aherne, T. (Belfast Celtic, Luton Town, 1946-54) 16
Aldridge, J. (Oxford Utd., Liverpool, Real Sociedad, Tranmere Rov., 1986-97) 69
Ambrose, P. (Shamrock R., 1955-64) . 5
Anderson, J. (Preston N.E., Newcastle Utd., 1980-9) 16

Babb, P. (Coventry City, Liverpool, Sunderland, 1994-2003) 35
Bailham, E. (Shamrock R., 1964) 1
Barber, E. (Bohemians, Birmingham City, 1966) 2
Barrett, G. (Arsenal, Coventry City, 2003-4) 5
Beglin, J. (Liverpool, 1984-7) 15
Braddish, S. (Dundalk, 1978) 2
Branagan, K. (Bolton Wand., 1997) ... 1
Bonner, P. (Celtic, 1981-96) 80
Brady, L. (Arsenal, Juventus, Sampdoria, Inter-Milan, Ascoli, West Ham Utd., 1975-90) 72
Brady, R. (Q.P.R., 1964) 6
Breen, G. (Birmingham City, Coventry City, West Ham Utd., Sunderland 1996-2004) 60
*Breen, T. (Shamrock R., 1947) 3
Brennan, F. (Drumcondra, 1965) 1
Brennan, S. (Manchester Utd., Waterford, 1965-71) 19
Browne, W. (Bohemians, 1964) 3
Buckley, L. (Shamrock R., Waregem, 1984-5) 2
Burke, F. (Cork Ath., 1952) 1
Butler, P. (Sunderland, 2000) 1
Butler, T. (Sunderland, 2003) 2
Byrne, A. (Southampton, 1970-4) 14
Byrne, J. (Shelbourne, 2004) 1
Byrne, J. (Q.P.R., Le Havre, Brighton & H.A., Sunderland, Millwall, 1985-93) 23
Byrne, P. (Shamrock R., 1984-6) 8

Campbell, A. (Santander, 1985) 3
Campbell, N. (St Patrick's Ath., Fortuna Cologne, 1971-7) 11

Cantwell, N. (West Ham Utd., Manchester Utd., 1954-67) 36
Carey, B. (Manchester Utd., Leicester City, 1992-4) 3
*Carey, J. (Manchester Utd., 1946-53) 21
Carolan, J. (Manchester Utd., 1960) .. 2
Carr, S. (Tottenham, 1999-2004) 30
Carroll, B. (Shelbourne, 1949-50) 2
Carroll, T. (Ipswich Town, 1968-73) . 17
Carsley, L. (Derby Co., Blackburn Rov., Coventry City, Everton, 1997-2004) 29
Cascarino, A. (Gillingham, Millwall, Aston Villa, Chelsea, Marseille, Nancy, 1986-2000) 88
Chandler, J. (Leeds Utd., 1980) 2
Clarke, C. (Stoke City, 2004) 2
Clarke, J. (Drogheda, 1978) 1
Clarke, K. (Drumcondra, 1948) 2
Clarke, M. (Shamrock R., 1950) 1
Clinton, T. (Everton, 1951-4) 3
Coad, P. (Shamrock R., 1947-52) 11
Coffey, T. (Drumcondra, 1950) 1
Colfer, M. (Shelbourne, 1950-1) 2
Colgan, N. (Hibernian, 2002-4) 8
Conmy, O. (Peterborough Utd., 1965-70) 5
Connolly, D. (Watford, Feyenoord, Excelsior, Feyenoord, Wimbledon, West Ham Utd., 1996-2004) 40
Conroy, G. (Stoke City, 1970-7) 27
Conway, J. (Fulham, Manchester City, 1967-77) 20
Corr, P. (Everton, 1949-50) 4
Courtney, E. (Cork Utd., 1946) 1
Coyle, O. (Bolton Wand., 1994) 1
Coyne, T. (Celtic, Tranmere Rov., Motherwell, 1992-8) 22
Crowe, G. (Bohemians, 2003) 2
Cummins, G. (Luton Town, 1954-61) 19
Cuneen, T. (Limerick, 1951) 1
Cunningham, K. (Wimbledon, Birmingham City, 1996-2004) 57
Curtis, D. (Shelbourne, Bristol City, Ipswich Town, Exeter City) 17

Savage, D. (Millwall, 1996) 5
Saward, P. (Millwall, Aston Villa,
  Huddersfield Town, 1954-63) 18
Scannell, T. (Southend Utd., 1954) 1
Scully, P. (Arsenal, 1989) 1
Sheedy, K. (Everton, Newcastle Utd.,
  1984-93) 46
Sheridan, J. (Leeds Utd., Sheffield
  Wed., 1988-96) 34
Slaven, B. (Middlesbrough, 1990-3) ... 7
Sloan, P. (Arsenal, 1946) 2
Smyth, M. (Shamrock R., 1969) 1
Stapleton, F. (Arsenal, Manchester Utd.,
  Ajax, Derby Co., Le Havre, Blackburn
  Rov., 1977-90) 71
Staunton, S. (Liverpool, Aston Villa,
  Liverpool, Crystal Palace, Aston Villa,
  1989-2002) 102
*Stevenson, A. (Everton, 1947-9) 6
Strahan, F. (Shelbourne, 1964-5) 5
Swan, M. (Drumcondra, 1960) 1
Synnott, N. (Shamrock R., 1978-9) 3

Thomas, P. (Waterford, 1974) 2
Thompson, J. (Nott'm Forest, 2004) ... 1
Townsend, A. (Norwich City, Chelsea,
  Aston Villa, Middlesbrough,
  1989-97) 70

Traynor, T. (Southampton, 1954-64) ... 8
Treacy, R. (W.B.A., Charlton Athletic,
  Swindon Town, Preston N.E.,
  Shamrock R., 1966-80) 42
Tuohy, L. (Shamrock R., Newcastle Utd.,
  Shamrock R., 1956-65) 8
Turner, A. (Celtic, 1963) 2

Vernon, J. (Belfast Celtic, 1946) 2

Waddock, G. (Q.P.R., Millwall,
  1980-90) 21
Walsh, D. (W.B.A., Aston Villa,
  1946-54) 20
Walsh, J. (Limerick, 1982) 1
Walsh, M. (Blackpool, Everton, Q.P.R.,
  Porto, 1976-85) 21
Walsh, M. (Everton, Norwich City,
  1982-3) 4
Walsh, W. (Manchester City,
  1947-50) 9
Waters, J. (Grimsby Town, 1977-80) ... 2
Whelan, R. (St Patrick's Ath., 1964) ... 2
Whelan, R. (Liverpool, Southend Utd.,
  1981-95) 53
Whelan, L. (Manchester Utd.,
  1956-7) 4
Whittaker, R. (Chelsea, 1959) 1

INTERNATIONAL GOALSCORERS 1946-2004

(As at start of season 2004-05)

ENGLAND

Charlton, R	49	Barnes, J	11	Charlton, J	6
Lineker	48	Douglas	11	Johnson	6
Greaves	44	Mannion	11	Macdonald	6
Finney	30	Sheringham	11	Mullen	6
Lofthouse	30	Clarke, A	10	Rowley	6
Shearer	30	Flowers, R	10	Vassell	6
Platt	27	Gascoigne	10	Waddle	6
Owen	26	Lee, F	10	Adams	5
Robson, B	26	Milburn	10	Atyeo	5
Hurst	24	Wilshaw	10	Baily	5
Mortensen	23	Beardsley	9	Brooking	5
Channon	21	Bell	9	Carter	5
Keegan	21	Bentley	9	Edwards	5
Peters	20	Hateley	9	Ferdinand, L	5
Haynes	18	Rooney	9	Heskey	5
Hunt, R	18	Wright, I	9	Hitchens	5
Lawton	16	Ball	8	Lampard	5
Taylor, T	16	Broadis	8	Latchford	5
Woodcock	16	Byrne, J	8	Neal	5
Scholes	14	Hoddle	8	Pearce	5
Beckham	13	Kevan	8	Pearson, Stan	5
Chivers	13	Anderton	7	Pearson, Stuart	5
Mariner	13	Connelly	7	Pickering, F	5
Smith, R	13	Coppell	7	Barmby	4
Francis, T	12	Fowler	7	Barnes, P	4
		Paine	7	Bull	4

233

N. IRELAND

Kyle	1
Lambert	1
Linwood	1
Mackay, G	1
MacLeod	1
McAvennie	1
McCall	1
McCalliog	1
McKenzie	1
McKimmie	1
McKinnon	1
McLean	1
McLintock	1
McSwegan	1
Miller, W	1
Mitchell	1
Morgan	1
Mulhall	1
Murray, J	1
Narey	1
Naysmith	1
Ormond	1
Orr	1
Parlane	1
Provan, D	1
Quashie	1
Quinn	1
Ritchie, P	1
Sharp	1
Stewart, R	1
Thornton	1
Wallace, I	1
Weir, A	1
Weir, D	1
Wilkie	1

WALES

Rush	28
Allchurch, I	23
Ford	23
Saunders	22
Hughes, M	16
Charles, John	15
Jones, C	15
Toshack	13
Hartson	11
James, L	10
Davies, R.T	8
Giggs	8
James, R	8
Vernon	8
Davies, R.W	7
Earnshaw	7
Flynn	7
Walsh, I	7
Bellamy	6
Charles, M	6
Curtis, A	6
Griffiths, A	6
Medwin	6
Pembridge	6
Speed	6
Clarke, R	5
Leek	5
Blake	4
Coleman	4
Davies, S	4
Deacy	4
Edwards, I	4
Tapscott	4
Thomas, M	4
Woosnam	4
Allen, M	3
Bodin	3
Bowen, M	3
England	3
Melville	3
Palmer, D	3
Rees, R	3
Robinson, J	3
Davies, G	2
Durban, A	2
Dwyer	2
Edwards, G	2
Giles, D	2
Godfrey	2
Griffiths, M	2
Hodges	2
Horne	2
Jones, Barrie	2
Jones, Bryn	2
Lowrie	2
Nicholas	2
Phillips, D	2
Reece, G	2
Robinson	2
Savage	2
Slatter	2
Symons	2
Yorath	2
Barnes	1
Blackmore	1
Bowen, D	1
Boyle, T	1
Burgess, R	1
Charles, Jeremy	1
Evans, I	1
Foulkes	1
Harris, C	1
Hewitt, R	1
Hockey	1
Jones, A	1
Jones, D	1
Jones, J	1
Koumas	1
Krzywicki	1
Lovell	1
Mahoney	1
Moore, G	1
O'Sullivan	1
Parry	1
Paul	1
Powell, A	1
Powell, D	1
Price, P	1
Roberts, P	1
Smallman	1
Taylor	1
Williams, A	1
Williams, G.E	1
Williams, G.G	1
Young	1

REP. OF IRELAND

Quinn, N	21
Keane, Robbie	20
Stapleton	20
Aldridge	19
Cascarino	19
Givens	19
Cantwell	14
Daly	13
Brady	9
Connolly	9
Harte	9
Keane, Roy	9
Kelly, D	9
Sheedy	9
Curtis	8
Grealish	8
McGrath, P	8
Breen G	7
Fitzsimons	7
Ringstead	7
Staunton	7
Townsend	7
Coyne	6
Duff	6
Houghton	6
McEvoy	6
Martin, C	6
Moran	6
Cummins	5
Fagan, F	5
Giles	5
Holland	5
Lawrenson	5
Morrison	5
Rogers	5
Sheridan	5
Treacy	5
Walsh, D	5
Byrne, J	4
Doherty	4
Dunne, R	4

Irwin	4	Fallon	2	Glynn	1
Kilbane	4	Fitzgerald, P	2	Grimes	1
McGee	4	Foley	2	Healy	1
Martin, M	4	Gavin	2	Holmes	1
O'Neill, K	4	Hale	2	Hughton	1
Robinson	4	Hand	2	Kavanagh	1
Tuohy	4	Hurley	2	Kernaghan	1
Carey, J	3	Kelly, G	2	Mancini	1
Coad	3	Leech	2	McCann	1
Conway	3	McCarthy	2	McPhail	1
Farrell	3	McLoughlin	2	Mooney	1
Fogarty	3	O'Connor	2	Moroney	1
Haverty	3	O'Farrell	2	Mulligan	1
Kennedy, Mark	3	O'Reilly, J	2	O'Callaghan, K	1
Kinsella	3	Reid	2	O'Keefe	1
McAteer	3	Ambrose	1	O'Leary	1
Ryan, R	3	Anderson	1	O'Neill, F	1
Waddock	3	Carroll	1	O' Shea	1
Walsh, M	3	Dempsey	1	Ryan, G	1
Whelan	3	Duffy	1	Slaven	1
Barrett	2	Finnan	1	Sloan	1
Conroy	2	Fitzgerald, J	1	Strahan	1
Dennehy	2	Fullam, J	1	Waters	1
Eglington	2	Galvin	1		

SVEN'S SALARY

F.A. chief executive Mark Palios told the Institute of Chartered Accountants that England coach Sven-Goran Eriksson's salary was "significantly less" than the widely reported £4m. a year. He is contracted to the F.A. until 2008.

BRASSED OFF IN FIRST MATCH AS MANAGER

Chris Brass, the League's youngest manager, was sent off during his first match in charge of York. Brass, 28 when appointed, and Steve Livingstone were dismissed following a clash at Carlisle. The season also ended badly for player-manager Brass, whose team were relegated to the Conference.

FOUR FOR RICHARDS IN 21 MINUTES

Marc Richards scored all four goals for Northampton in 21 minutes in their 4-0 win at Macclesfield. They came after 18, 23, 26 and 39 minutes.

HOME INTERNATIONAL RESULTS

Note: In the results that follow, W.C. = World Cup, E.C. = European Championship. TF = Tournoi de France. For Northern Ireland read Ireland before 1921.

ENGLAND V. SCOTLAND
Played 110; England 45; Scotland 41; drawn 24. Goals: England 192, Scotland 169.

Year	Venue	E	S	Year	Venue	E	S
1872	Glasgow	0	0	1932	Wembley	3	0
1873	The Oval	4	2	1933	Glasgow	1	2
1874	Glasgow	1	2	1934	Wembley	3	0
1875	The Oval	2	2	1935	Wembley	0	2
1876	Glasgow	0	3	1936	Wembley	1	1
1877	The Oval	1	3	1937	Glasgow	1	3
1878	Glasgow	2	7	1938	Wembley	0	1
1879	The Oval	5	4	1939	Glasgow	2	1
1880	Glasgow	4	5	1947	Wembley	1	1
1881	The Oval	1	6	1948	Glasgow	2	0
1882	Glasgow	1	5	1949	Wembley	1	3
1883	Sheffield	2	3	1950	Glasgow (W.C.)	1	0
1884	Glasgow	0	1	1951	Wembley	2	3
1885	The Oval	1	1	1952	Glasgow	2	1
1886	Glasgow	1	1	1953	Wembley	2	2
1887	Blackburn	2	3	1954	Glasgow (W.C.)	4	2
1888	Glasgow	5	0	1955	Wembley	7	2
1889	The Oval	2	3	1956	Glasgow	1	1
1890	Glasgow	1	1	1957	Wembley	2	1
1891	Blackburn	2	1	1958	Glasgow	4	0
1892	Glasgow	4	1	1959	Wembley	1	0
1893	Richmond	5	2	1960	Glasgow	1	1
1894	Glasgow	2	2	1961	Wembley	9	3
1895	Goodison Park	3	0	1962	Glasgow	0	2
1896	Glasgow	1	2	1963	Wembley	1	2
1897	Crystal Palace	1	2	1964	Glasgow	0	1
1898	Glasgow	3	1	1965	Wembley	2	2
1899	Birmingham	2	1	1966	Glasgow	4	3
1900	Glasgow	1	4	1967	Wembley (E.C.)	2	3
1901	Crystal Palace	2	2	1968	Glasgow (E.C.)	1	1
1902	Birmingham	2	2	1969	Wembley	4	1
1903	Sheffield	1	2	1970	Glasgow	0	0
1904	Glasgow	1	0	1971	Wembley	3	1
1905	Crystal Palace	1	0	1972	Glasgow	1	0
1906	Glasgow	1	2	1973	Glasgow	5	0
1907	Newcastle	1	1	1973	Wembley	1	0
1908	Glasgow	1	1	1974	Glasgow	0	2
1909	Crystal Palace	2	0	1975	Wembley	5	1
1910	Glasgow	0	2	1976	Glasgow	1	2
1911	Goodison Park	1	1	1977	Wembley	1	2
1912	Glasgow	1	1	1978	Glasgow	1	0
1913	Stamford Bridge	1	0	1979	Wembley	3	1
1914	Glasgow	1	3	1980	Wembley	2	0
1920	Sheffield	5	4	1981	Wembley	0	1
1921	Glasgow	0	3	1982	Glasgow	1	0
1922	Birmingham	0	1	1983	Wembley	2	0
1923	Glasgow	2	2	1984	Glasgow	1	1
1924	Wembley	1	1	1985	Glasgow	0	1
1925	Glasgow	0	2	1986	Wembley	2	1
1926	Manchester	0	1	1987	Glasgow	0	0
1927	Glasgow	2	1	1988	Wembley	1	0
1928	Wembley	1	5	1989	Glasgow	2	0
1929	Glasgow	0	1	1996	Wembley (E.C.)	2	0
1930	Wembley	5	2	1999	Glasgow (E.C.)	2	0
1931	Glasgow	0	2	1999	Wembley (E.C.)	0	1

ENGLAND V. WALES

Played 97; England won 62; Wales 14; drawn 21. Goals: England 239, Wales 90.

Year	Venue	E	W	Year	Venue	E	W
1879	The Oval	2	1	1932	Wrexham	0	0
1880	Wrexham	3	2	1933	Newcastle	1	2
1881	Blackburn	0	1	1934	Cardiff	4	0
1882	Wrexham	3	5	1935	Wolverhampton	1	2
1883	The Oval	5	0	1936	Cardiff	1	2
1884	Wrexham	4	0	1937	Middlesbrough	2	1
1885	Blackburn	1	1	1938	Cardiff	2	4
1886	Wrexham	3	1	1946	Manchester	3	0
1887	The Oval	4	0	1947	Cardiff	3	0
1888	Crewe	5	1	1948	Villa Park	1	0
1889	Stoke	4	1	1949	Cardiff (W.C.)	4	1
1890	Wrexham	3	1	1950	Sunderland	4	2
1891	Sunderland	4	1	1951	Cardiff	1	1
1892	Wrexham	2	0	1952	Wembley	5	2
1893	Stoke	6	0	1953	Cardiff (W.C.)	4	1
1894	Wrexham	5	1	1954	Wembley	3	2
1895	London	1	1	1955	Cardiff	1	2
1896	Cardiff	9	1	1956	Wembley	3	1
1897	Sheffield	4	0	1957	Cardiff	4	0
1898	Wrexham	3	0	1958	Birmingham	2	2
1899	Bristol	4	0	1959	Cardiff	1	1
1900	Cardiff	1	1	1960	Wembley	5	1
1901	Newcastle	6	0	1961	Cardiff	1	1
1902	Wrexham	0	0	1962	Wembley	4	0
1903	Portsmouth	2	1	1963	Cardiff	4	0
1904	Wrexham	2	2	1964	Wembley	2	1
1905	Anfield	3	1	1965	Cardiff	0	0
1906	Cardiff	1	0	1966	Wembley (E.C.)	5	1
1907	Fulham	1	1	1967	Cardiff (E.C.)	3	0
1908	Wrexham	7	1	1969	Wembley	2	1
1909	Nottingham	2	0	1970	Cardiff	1	1
1910	Cardiff	1	0	1971	Wembley	0	0
1911	Millwall	3	0	1972	Cardiff	3	0
1912	Wrexham	2	0	1972	Cardiff (W.C.)	1	0
1913	Bristol	4	3	1973	Wembley (W.C.)	1	1
1914	Cardiff	2	0	1973	Wembley	3	0
1920	Highbury	1	2	1974	Cardiff	2	0
1921	Cardiff	0	0	1975	Wembley	2	2
1922	Anfield	1	0	1976	Wrexham	2	1
1923	Cardiff	2	2	1976	Cardiff	1	0
1924	Blackburn	1	2	1977	Wembley	0	1
1925	Swansea	2	1	1978	Cardiff	3	1
1926	Selhurst Park	1	3	1979	Wembley	0	0
1927	Wrexham	3	3	1980	Wrexham	1	4
1927	Burnley	1	2	1981	Wembley	0	0
1928	Swansea	3	2	1982	Cardiff	1	0
1929	Stamford Bridge	6	0	1983	Wembley	2	1
1930	Cardiff	4	0	1984	Wrexham	0	1
1931	Anfield	3	1				

ENGLAND V. N. IRELAND

Played 96; England won 74; Ireland 6; drawn 16. Goals: England 319, Ireland 80.

Year	Venue	E	I
1882	Belfast	13	0
1883	Aigburth, Liverpool	7	0
1884	Belfast	8	1
1885	Manchester	4	0
1886	Belfast	6	1
1887	Sheffield	7	0
1888	Belfast	5	1
1889	Goodison Park	6	1
1890	Belfast	9	1
1891	Wolverhampton	6	1
1892	Belfast	2	0
1893	Birmingham	6	1
1894	Belfast	2	2
1895	Derby	9	0
1896	Belfast	2	0
1897	Nottingham	6	0
1898	Belfast	3	2
1899	Sunderland	13	2
1900	Dublin	2	0
1901	Southampton	3	0
1902	Belfast	1	0
1903	Wolverhampton	4	0
1904	Belfast	3	1
1905	Middlesbrough	1	1
1906	Belfast	5	0
1907	Goodison Park	1	0
1908	Belfast	3	1
1909	Bradford (Park Ave)	4	0
1910	Belfast	1	1
1911	Derby	2	1
1912	Dublin	6	1
1913	Belfast	1	2
1914	Middlesbrough	0	3
1919	Belfast	1	1
1920	Sunderland	2	0
1921	Belfast	1	1
1922	West Bromwich	2	0
1923	Belfast	1	2
1924	Goodison Park	3	1
1925	Belfast	0	0
1926	Anfield	3	3
1927	Belfast	0	2
1928	Goodison Park	2	1
1929	Belfast	3	0
1930	Sheffield	5	1
1931	Belfast	6	2
1932	Blackpool	1	0
1933	Belfast	3	0
1935	Goodison Park	2	1
1935	Belfast	3	1
1936	Stoke	3	1
1937	Belfast	5	1
1938	Manchester	7	0
1946	Belfast	7	2
1947	Goodison Park	2	2
1948	Belfast	6	2
1949	Manchester (W.C.)	9	2
1950	Belfast	4	1
1951	Birmingham	2	0
1952	Belfast	2	2
1953	Goodison Park (W.C.)	3	1
1954	Belfast	2	0
1955	Wembley	3	0
1956	Belfast	1	1
1957	Wembley	2	3
1958	Belfast	3	3
1959	Wembley	2	1
1960	Belfast	5	2
1961	Wembley	1	1
1962	Belfast	3	1
1963	Wembley	8	3
1964	Belfast	4	3
1965	Wembley	2	1
1966	Belfast (E.C.)	2	0
1967	Wembley (E.C.)	2	0
1969	Belfast	3	1
1970	Wembley	3	1
1971	Belfast	1	0
1972	Wembley	0	1
1973	*Goodison Park	2	1
1974	Wembley	1	0
1975	Belfast	0	0
1976	Wembley	4	0
1977	Belfast	2	1
1978	Wembley	1	0
1979	Wembley (E.C.)	4	0
1979	Belfast	2	0
1979	Belfast (E.C.)	5	1
1980	Wembley	1	1
1982	Wembley	4	0
1983	Belfast	0	0
1984	Wembley	1	0
1985	Belfast (W.C.)	1	0
1985	Wembley (W.C.)	0	0
1986	Wembley (E.C.)	3	0
1987	Belfast (E.C.)	2	0

(* Switched from Belfast because of political situation in N. Ireland)

SCOTLAND V. WALES

Played 103; Scotland won 60; Wales 20; drawn 23. Goals: Scotland 237, Wales 116.

Year	Venue	S	W	Year	Venue	S	W
1876	Glasgow	4	0	1935	Aberdeen	3	2
1877	Wrexham	2	0	1936	Cardiff	1	1
1878	Glasgow	9	0	1937	Dundee	1	2
1879	Wrexham	3	0	1938	Cardiff	1	2
1880	Glasgow	5	1	1939	Edinburgh	3	2
1881	Wrexham	5	1	1946	Wrexham	1	3
1882	Glasgow	5	0	1947	Glasgow	1	2
1883	Wrexham	3	0	1948	Cardiff (W.C.)	3	1
1884	Glasgow	4	1	1949	Glasgow	2	0
1885	Wrexham	8	1	1950	Cardiff	3	1
1886	Glasgow	4	1	1951	Glasgow	0	1
1887	Wrexham	2	0	1952	Cardiff (W.C.)	2	1
1888	Edinburgh	5	1	1953	Glasgow	3	3
1889	Wrexham	0	0	1954	Cardiff	1	0
1890	Paisley	5	0	1955	Glasgow	2	0
1891	Wrexham	4	3	1956	Cardiff	2	2
1892	Edinburgh	6	1	1957	Glasgow	1	1
1893	Wrexham	8	0	1958	Cardiff	3	0
1894	Kilmarnock	5	2	1959	Glasgow	1	1
1895	Wrexham	2	2	1960	Cardiff	0	2
1896	Dundee	4	0	1961	Glasgow	2	0
1897	Wrexham	2	2	1962	Cardiff	3	2
1898	Motherwell	5	2	1963	Glasgow	2	1
1899	Wrexham	6	0	1964	Cardiff	2	3
1900	Aberdeen	5	2	1965	Glasgow (E.C.)	4	1
1901	Wrexham	1	1	1966	Cardiff (E.C.)	1	1
1902	Greenock	5	1	1967	Glasgow	3	2
1903	Cardiff	1	0	1969	Wrexham	5	3
1904	Dundee	1	1	1970	Glasgow	0	0
1905	Wrexham	1	3	1971	Cardiff	0	0
1906	Edinburgh	0	2	1972	Glasgow	1	0
1907	Wrexham	0	1	1973	Wrexham	2	0
1908	Dundee	2	1	1974	Glasgow	2	0
1909	Wrexham	2	3	1975	Cardiff	2	2
1910	Kilmarnock	1	0	1976	Glasgow	3	1
1911	Cardiff	2	2	1977	Glasgow (W.C.)	1	0
1912	Tynecastle	1	0	1977	Wrexham	0	0
1913	Wrexham	0	0	1977	Anfield (W.C.)	2	0
1914	Glasgow	0	0	1978	Glasgow	1	1
1920	Cardiff	1	1	1979	Cardiff	0	3
1921	Aberdeen	2	1	1980	Glasgow	1	0
1922	Wrexham	1	2	1981	Swansea	0	2
1923	Paisley	2	0	1982	Glasgow	1	0
1924	Cardiff	0	2	1983	Cardiff	2	0
1925	Tynecastle	3	1	1984	Glasgow	2	1
1926	Cardiff	3	0	1985	Glasgow (W.C.)	0	1
1927	Glasgow	3	0	1985	Cardiff (W.C.)	1	1
1928	Wrexham	2	2	1997	Kilmarnock	0	1
1929	Glasgow	4	2	2004	Cardiff	0	4
1930	Cardiff	4	2				
1931	Glasgow	1	1				
1932	Wrexham	3	2				
1933	Edinburgh	2	5				
1934	Cardiff	2	3				

SCOTLAND V. N. IRELAND

Played 93; Scotland won 62; Ireland 15; drawn 16. Goals: Scotland 257, Ireland 81.

Year	Venue	S	I	Year	Venue	S	I
1884	Belfast	5	0	1937	Belfast	3	1
1885	Glasgow	8	2	1938	Aberdeen	1	1
1886	Belfast	7	2	1939	Belfast	2	0
1887	Belfast	4	1	1946	Glasgow	0	0
1888	Belfast	10	2	1947	Belfast	0	2
1889	Glasgow	7	0	1948	Glasgow	3	2
1890	Belfast	4	1	1949	Belfast	8	2
1891	Glasgow	2	1	1950	Glasgow	6	1
1892	Belfast	3	2	1951	Belfast	3	0
1893	Glasgow	6	1	1952	Glasgow	1	1
1894	Belfast	2	1	1953	Belfast	3	1
1895	Glasgow	3	1	1954	Glasgow	2	2
1896	Belfast	3	3	1955	Belfast	1	2
1897	Glasgow	5	1	1956	Glasgow	1	0
1898	Belfast	3	0	1957	Belfast	1	1
1899	Glasgow	9	1	1958	Glasgow	2	2
1900	Belfast	3	0	1959	Belfast	4	0
1901	Glasgow	11	0	1960	Glasgow	5	1
1902	Belfast	5	1	1961	Belfast	6	1
1902	Belfast	3	0	1962	Glasgow	5	1
1903	Glasgow	0	2	1963	Belfast	1	2
1904	Dublin	1	1	1964	Glasgow	3	2
1905	Glasgow	4	0	1965	Belfast	2	3
1906	Dublin	1	0	1966	Glasgow	2	1
1907	Glasgow	3	0	1967	Belfast	0	1
1908	Dublin	5	0	1969	Glasgow	1	1
1909	Glasgow	5	0	1970	Belfast	1	0
1910	Belfast	0	1	1971	Glasgow	0	1
1911	Glasgow	2	0	1972	Glasgow	2	0
1912	Belfast	4	1	1973	Glasgow	1	2
1913	Dublin	2	1	1974	Glasgow	0	1
1914	Belfast	1	1	1975	Glasgow	3	0
1920	Glasgow	3	0	1976	Glasgow	3	0
1921	Belfast	2	0	1977	Glasgow	3	0
1922	Glasgow	2	1	1978	Glasgow	1	1
1923	Belfast	1	0	1979	Glasgow	1	0
1924	Glasgow	2	0	1980	Belfast	0	1
1925	Belfast	3	0	1981	Glasgow (W.C.)	1	1
1926	Glasgow	4	0	1981	Glasgow	2	0
1927	Belfast	2	0	1981	Belfast (W.C.)	0	0
1928	Glasgow	0	1	1982	Belfast	1	1
1929	Belfast	7	3	1983	Glasgow	0	0
1930	Glasgow	3	1	1984	Belfast	0	2
1931	Belfast	0	0	1992	Glasgow	1	0
1932	Glasgow	3	1				
1933	Belfast	4	0				
1934	Glasgow	1	2				
1935	Belfast	1	2				
1936	Edinburgh	2	1				

WALES V. N. IRELAND

Played 90; Wales won 42; Ireland 27; drawn 21. Goals: Wales 182, Ireland 127.

Year	Venue	W	I	Year	Venue	W	I
1882	Wrexham	7	1	1933	Wrexham	4	1
1883	Belfast	1	1	1934	Belfast	1	1
1884	Wrexham	6	0	1935	Wrexham	3	1
1885	Belfast	8	2	1936	Belfast	2	3
1886	Wrexham	5	0	1937	Wrexham	4	1
1887	Belfast	1	4	1938	Belfast	0	1
1888	Wrexham	11	0	1939	Wrexham	3	1
1889	Belfast	3	1	1947	Belfast	1	2
1890	Shrewsbury	5	2	1948	Wrexham	2	0
1891	Belfast	2	7	1949	Belfast	2	0
1892	Bangor	1	1	1950	Wrexham (W.C.)	0	0
1893	Belfast	3	4	1951	Belfast	2	1
1894	Swansea	4	1	1952	Swansea	3	0
1895	Belfast	2	2	1953	Wrexham	3	2
1896	Wrexham	6	1	1954	Wrexham (W.C.)	1	2
1897	Belfast	3	4	1955	Belfast	3	2
1898	Llandudno	0	1	1956	Cardiff	1	1
1899	Belfast	0	1	1957	Belfast	0	0
1900	Llandudno	2	0	1958	Cardiff	1	1
1901	Belfast	1	0	1959	Belfast	1	4
1902	Cardiff	0	3	1960	Wrexham	3	2
1903	Belfast	0	2	1961	Belfast	5	1
1904	Bangor	0	1	1962	Cardiff	4	0
1905	Belfast	2	2	1963	Belfast	4	1
1906	Wrexham	4	4	1964	Swansea	2	3
1907	Belfast	3	2	1965	Belfast	5	0
1908	Aberdare	0	1	1966	Cardiff	1	4
1909	Belfast	3	2	1967	Belfast (E.C.)	0	0
1910	Wrexham	4	1	1968	Wrexham (E.C.)	2	0
1911	Belfast	2	1	1969	Belfast	0	0
1912	Cardiff	2	3	1970	Swansea	1	0
1913	Belfast	1	0	1971	Belfast	0	1
1914	Wrexham	1	2	1972	Wrexham	0	0
1920	Belfast	2	2	1973	*Goodison Park	0	1
1921	Swansea	2	1	1974	Wrexham	1	0
1922	Swansea	1	1	1975	Belfast	0	1
1923	Wrexham	0	3	1976	Swansea	1	0
1924	Belfast	1	0	1977	Belfast	1	1
1925	Wrexham	0	0	1978	Wrexham	1	0
1926	Belfast	0	3	1979	Belfast	1	1
1927	Cardiff	2	2	1980	Cardiff	0	1
1928	Belfast	2	1	1982	Wrexham	3	0
1929	Wrexham	2	2	1983	Belfast	1	0
1930	Belfast	0	7	1984	Swansea	1	1
1931	Wrexham	3	2				
1932	Belfast	0	4				

(* Switched from Belfast because of political situation in N. Ireland)

RECORDS SECTION
Compiled by Albert Sewell

INDEX

GOALSCORING
(† Football League pre 1992-3. * Home team)

Highest: *Arbroath 36, Bon Accord (Aberdeen) 0, in **Scottish Cup** 1st Round, Sept. 12, 1885. On same day, also in Scottish Cup 1st Round, Dundee Harp beat Aberdeen Rov. 35-0.

Internationals: England 15, *France 0, in Paris, 1906 (Amateur); England 13 *Ireland 0, in Belfast, Feb. 18, 1882 (record in U.K.); *England 9, Scotland 3, at Wembley, Apr. 15, 1961; Biggest England win at Wembley: 9-0 v Luxembourg (E.Champ), Dec. 15, 1982.

Other record wins: Scotland: 11-0 v Ireland (Glasgow, Feb. 23, 1901); **Northern Ireland:** 7-0 v Wales (Belfast, Feb. 1, 1930); **Wales:** 11-0 v Ireland (Wrexham, Mar. 3, 1888); **Rep. of Ireland:** 8-0 v Malta (E. Champ., Dublin, Nov. 16, 1983).

Record International defeats: England: 1-7 v Hungary (Budapest, May 23, 1954); **Scotland:** 3-9 v England (Wembley, April 15, 1961); **Ireland:** 0-13 v England (Belfast, Feb. 18, 1882); **Wales:** 0-9 v Scotland (Glasgow, March 23, 1878); **Rep. of Ireland:** 0-7 v Brazil (Uberlandia, May 27, 1982).

World Cup: Qualifying round – Australia 31, American Samoa 0, world record Int. score (April 11, 2001); Australia 22, Tonga 0 (April 9, 2001); Iran 19, Guam 0 (Nov. 25, 2000); Maldives 0, Iran 17 (June 2, 1997). **Finals – highest scores:** Hungary 10, El Salvador 1 (Spain, June 15, 1982); Hungary 9, S. Korea 0 (Switzerland, June 17, 1954); Yugoslavia 9, Zaire 0 (W. Germany, June 18, 1974).

European Championship: Qualifying round – highest scorers: Spain 12, Malta 1 (Seville, Dec. 21, 1983); – France 10, Azberbaijan 0 (Auxerre, Sept. 6, 1995). **Finals – highest score:** Holland 6, Yugoslavia 1 (Quarter-final, Rotterdam, June 25, 2000).

F.A. Cup: *Preston N.E. 26, Hyde 0, 1st Round, Oct. 15, 1887.

League Cup: *West Ham Utd. 10, Bury 0 (2nd Round, 2nd Leg, Oct 25, 1983); *Liverpool 10, Fulham 0 (2nd Round, 1st Leg, Sept. 23, 1986). **Record Aggregates:** Liverpool 13, Fulham 2 (10-0h, 3-2a), Sept. 23-Oct. 7, 1986; West Ham Utd. 12, Bury 1 (2-1a, 10-0h), Oct. 4-25, 1983; Liverpool 11, Exeter City 0 (5-0h, 6-0a), Oct 7-28, 1981.

F.A. Premier League (beginning 1992-3): *Manchester Utd. 9, Ipswich Town 0, Mar. 4, 1995. **Record away win:** Manchester Utd. 8, *Nott'm. Forest 1, Feb. 6, 1999.

Highest aggregate scores in Premier League – 9: Manchester Utd. 9, Ipswich Town 0, Mar. 4, 1995; Nott'm. Forest 1, Manchester Utd. 8, Feb. 6, 1999; Blackburn Rov. 7, Sheff. Wed. 2, Aug. 25, 1997; Southampton 6, Manchester Utd. 3, Oct. 26, 1996; Tottenham 7, Southampton 2, Mar. 11, 2000.

†**Football League (First Division):** *Aston Villa 12, Accrington 2, Mar. 12, 1892; *Tottenham 10, Everton 4, Oct. 11, 1958 (highest 1st Div. aggregate that century); *W.B.A. 12, Darwen 0, Apr. 4, 1892; *Nott'm. Forest 12, Leicester Fosse 0, Apr. 21, 1909. **Record away wins:** Sunderland 9, *Newcastle Utd. 1, Dec. 5, 1908; Wolves 9, *Cardiff City 1, Sept. 3, 1955.

New First Division (beginning 1992-3): *Bolton Wand. 7, Swindon Town 0, Mar. 8, 1997; Sunderland 7, Oxford Utd. 0, Sept. 19, 1998. **Record away win:** Birmingham City 7, *Stoke City 0, Jan. 10, 1998; Birmingham City 7, *Oxford Utd. 0, Dec. 12, 1998.

Record aggregates (11 goals): *Grimsby Town 6, Burnley 5, Oct. 29, 2002; *Burnley 4, Watford 7, Apr. 5, 2003.

†**Second Division:** *Manchester City 11, Lincoln City 3, Mar. 23, 1895; *Newcastle Utd. 13, Newport County 0, Oct. 5, 1946; *Small Heath 12, Walsall Town Swifts 0, Dec. 17, 1892; *Darwen 12, Walsall 0, Dec. 26, 1896; *Small Heath 12, Doncaster Rov. 0, Apr. 11, 1903. **Record away win:** Sheffield Utd. 10, *Burslem Port Vale 0, Dec. 10, 1892.

New Second Division (beginning 1992-3): *Hartlepool Utd. 1, Plymouth Argyle 8, May 7, 1994; *Hartlepool Utd. 8, Grimsby Town 1, Sept. 12, 2003.

†**Third Division:** *Gillingham 10, Chesterfield 0, Sept. 5, 1987; *Tranmere Rov. 9, Accrington Stanley 0, Apr. 18, 1959; *Brighton & H.A. 9, Southend Utd. 1, Nov. 22, 1965; *Brentford 9, Wrexham 0, Oct. 15, 1963. **Record away win:** Fulham 8, *Halifax Town 0, Sept. 16, 1969.

New Third Division (beginning 1992-3): *Barnet 1, Peterborough Utd. 9, Sept. 5, 1998.

†**Third Division (North):** *Stockport Co. 13, Halifax Town 0 (still joint biggest win in F. League – see Div. 2) Jan. 6, 1934; *Tranmere Rov. 13, Oldham Athletic 4, Dec. 26, 1935. *(17 is highest Football League aggregate score).* **Record away win:** Barnsley 9, *Accrington Stanley 0, Feb. 3, 1934.

†**Third Division (South):** *Luton Town 12, Bristol Rov. 0, Apr. 13, 1936; *Gillingham 9, Exeter City 4, Jan. 7, 1951. **Record away win:** Walsall 8, *Northampton Town 0, Apr. 8, 1947.

†**Fourth Division:** *Oldham Athletic 11, Southport 0, Dec. 26, 1962; *Hartlepool Utd. 10, Barrow 1, Apr. 4, 1959; *Wrexham 10, Hartlepool Utd. 1, Mar. 3, 1962. **Record away win:** Rotherham Utd. 8, *Crewe Alexandra 1, Sept. 8, 1973.

Scottish Premier Division – Highest aggregate: 11 goals – Celtic 8, Hamilton 3, Jan. 3, 1987; Motherwell 5, Aberdeen 6, Oct. 20, 1999. **Other highest team scores:** Aberdeen 8, Motherwell 0 (Mar. 26, 1979); Kilmarnock 1, Rangers 8 (Sept. 6, 1980); Hamilton 0, Celtic 8 (Nov. 5, 1988).

Scottish League Div. 1: *Celtic 11, Dundee 0, Oct. 26, 1895. **Record away win:** Hibs 11, *Airdrie 1, Oct. 24, 1959.

Scottish League Div. 2: *Airdrieonians 15, Dundee Wanderers 1, Dec. 1, 1894. (biggest win in history of League football in Britain).

Record modern Scottish League aggregate (12 goals): Brechin City 5, Cowdenbeath 7, Div. 2, Jan. 18, 2003.

Record British score since 1900: Stirling Albion 20, Selkirk 0 (Scottish Cup 1st. Round, Dec. 8, 1984). Winger Davie Thompson (7 goals) was one of 9 Stirling players to score.

LEAGUE GOALS – BEST IN SEASON (Before restructure in 1992)

Div.		Goals	Games
1	W.R. (Dixie) Dean, Everton, 1927-8	60	39
2	George Camsell, Middlesbrough, 1926-7	59	37
3(S)	Joe Payne, Luton Town, 1936-7	55	39
3(N)	Ted Harston, Mansfield Town, 1936-7	55	41
3	Derek Reeves, Southampton, 1959-60	39	46
4	Terry Bly, Peterborough Utd., 1960-1	52	46

(Since restructure in 1992)

Div.		Goals	Games
1	Guy Whittingham, Portsmouth, 1992-3	42	46
2	Jimmy Quinn, Reading, 1993-4	35	46
3	Andy Morrell, Wrexham, 2002-03	34	45

F.A. PREMIER LEAGUE – BEST IN SEASON

Andy Cole **34 goals** (Newcastle Utd. – 40 games, 1993-4); Alan Shearer **34 goals** (Blackburn Rov. – 42 games, 1994-5).

FOOTBALL LEAGUE – BEST MATCH HAULS
(Before restructure in 1992)

Div.		Goals
1	Ted Drake (Arsenal), away to Aston Villa, Dec. 14, 1935	7
	James Ross (Preston N.E.) v Stoke City, Oct 6, 1888	7
2	*Neville (Tim) Coleman (Stoke City) v Lincoln City, Feb. 23, 1957 .	7
	Tommy Briggs (Blackburn Rov.) v Bristol Rov., Feb. 5, 1955	7
3(S)	Joe Payne (Luton Town) v Bristol Rov., April 13, 1936	10
3(N)	Robert ('Bunny') Bell (Tranmere Rov.) v Oldham Athletic, Dec. 26, 1935 – he also missed a penalty	9
3	Barrie Thomas (Scunthorpe Utd.) v Luton Town, April 24, 1965	5
	Keith East (Swindon Town) v Mansfield Town, Nov. 20, 1965	5
	Steve Earle (Fulham) v Halifax Town, Sept. 16, 1969	5
	Alf Wood (Shrewsbury Town) v Blackburn Rov., Oct. 2, 1971	5
	Tony Caldwell (Bolton Wand.) v Walsall, Sept 10, 1983	5
	Andy Jones (Port Vale) v Newport Co., May 4, 1987	5
4	Bert Lister (Oldham Athletic) v Southport, Dec. 26, 1962	6

* Scored from the wing

(SINCE RESTRUCTURE IN 1992)

Div.	Goals
1	**4** in match – John Durnin (Oxford Utd. v Luton Town, 1992-3); Guy Whittingham (Portsmouth v Bristol Rov. 1992-3); Craig Russell (Sunderland v Millwall, 1995-6); Darren Byfield (Rotherham Utd. at Millwall, 2002–03); David Connolly (Wimbledon at Bradford City, 2002–03); Marlon Harewood (Nott'm. F. v Stoke City, 2002–03); Michael Chopra (Watford at Burnley, 2002–03); Robert Earnshaw (Cardiff City v Gillingham, 2003–04).
2	**5** in match – Paul Barnes (Burnley v Stockport Co., 1996-7); Robert Taylor (all 5, Gillingham at Burnley, 1998-9); Lee Jones (all 5, Wrexham v Cambridge Utd., 2001-02).
3	**5** in match – Tony Naylor (Crewe Alexandra v Colchester Utd., 1992-3); Steve Butler (Cambridge Utd. v Exeter City, 1993-4); Guiliano Grazioli (Peterborough Utd. at Barnet, 1998-9).

F.A. PREMIER LEAGUE – BEST MATCH HAUL

5 goals in match: Andy Cole (Manchester Utd. v Ipswich Town, 1994-5); Alan Shearer (Newcastle Utd. v Sheffield Wed., 1999-2000).

SCOTTISH LEAGUE

Div.		Goals
Prem.	Kenny Miller (Rangers) v St. Mirren, Nov. 4, 2000	5
	Paul Sturrock (Dundee Utd.) v Morton, Nov. 20, 1984	5
1	Jimmy McGrory (Celtic) v Dunfermline Athletic, Jan. 14, 1928	8
1	Owen McNally (Arthurlie) v Armadale, Oct. 1, 1927	8
2	Jim Dyet (King's Park) v Forfar Athletic, Jan. 2, 1930, on his debut for the club	8
2	John Calder (Morton) v Raith Rov., April 18, 1936	8
2	Norman Haywood (Raith Rov.) v Brechin, Aug. 20, 1937	8

SCOTTISH LEAGUE – BEST IN SEASON

Prem.	Brian McClair (Celtic, 1986-7)	35
	Henrik Larsson (Celtic, 2000-01)	35
1	William McFadyen (Motherwell, 1931-2)	53
2	*Jimmy Smith (Ayr, 1927-8 – 38 appearances)	66

(*British record)

CUP FOOTBALL

Scottish Cup: John Petrie (Arbroath) v Bon Accord, at Arbroath, 1st Round, Sept. 12, 1885 ...... **13**

F.A. Cup: Ted MacDougall (Bournemouth) v Margate, 1st Round, Nov. 20, 1971 ...... **9**

F.A. Cup Final: Billy Townley (Blackburn Rov.) v Sheffield Wed., at Kennington Oval, 1890; Jimmy Logan (Notts Co.) v Bolton Wand., at Everton, 1894; Stan Mortensen (Blackpool) v Bolton Wand., at Wembley, 1953 ...... **3**

League Cup: Frank Bunn (Oldham Athletic) v Scarborough (3rd Round), Oct. 25, 1989 ...... **6**

Scottish League Cup: Jim Fraser (Ayr) v Dumbarton, Aug. 13, 1952; Jim Forrest (Rangers) v Stirling Albion, Aug. 17, 1966 ...... **5**

Scottish Cup: Most goals in match since war: **10** by Gerry Baker (St. Mirren) in 15-0 win (1st. Round) v Glasgow Univ., Jan 30, 1960; **9** by his brother Joe Baker (Hibernian) in 15-1 win (2nd. Round) v Peebles Rov., Feb. 11, 1961.

AGGREGATE LEAGUE SCORING RECORDS

Goals

* Arthur Rowley (1947-65, WBA, Fulham, Leicester City, Shrewsbury Town) **434**

† Jimmy McGrory (1922-38, Celtic, Clydebank) **410**

Hughie Gallacher (1921-39, Airdrieonians, Newcastle Utd., Chelsea, Derby Co., Notts Co., Grimsby Town, Gateshead) **387**

William ('Dixie') Dean (1923-37, Tranmere Rov., Everton, Notts County) **379**

Hugh Ferguson (1916-30, Motherwell, Cardiff City, Dundee) **362**

■ Jimmy Greaves (1957-71, Chelsea, Tottenham, West Ham Utd.) **357**

Steve Bloomer (1892-1914, Derby Co., Middlesbrough, Derby Co.) **352**

George Camsell (1923-39, Durham City, Middlesbrough) **348**

Dave Halliday (1920-35, St. Mirren, Dundee, Sunderland, Arsenal, Manchester City, Clapton Orient) **338**

John Aldridge (1979-98, Newport, Oxford Utd., Liverpool, Tranmere Rov.) **329**

John Atyeo (1951-66, Bristol City) **315**

Joe Smith (1908-29, Bolton Wand., Stockport Co.) **315**

Victor Watson (1920-36, West Ham Utd., Southampton) **312**

Harry Johnson (1919-36, Sheffield Utd., Mansfield Town) **309**

Bob McPhail (1923–1939, Airdrie, Rangers) **306**

(* **Rowley** scored 4 for WBA, 27 for Fulham, 251 for Leicester City, 152 for Shrewsbury Town. ■ **Greaves's** 357 is record top-division total (he also scored 9 League goals for AC Milan). **Aldridge** also scored 33 League goals for Real Sociedad. † **McGrory** scored 397 for Celtic, 13 for Clydebank.)

Most League goals for one club: 349 – Dixie Dean (Everton 1925-37); **326 – George Camsell** (Middlesbrough 1925-39); **315 – John Atyeo** (Bristol City 1951-66); **306 – Vic Watson** (West Ham Utd. 1920-35); **291 – Steve Bloomer** (Derby Co. 1892-1906, 1910-14); **259 – Arthur Chandler** (Leicester City 1923-35); **255 – Nat Lofthouse** (Bolton Wand. 1946-61); **251 – Arthur Rowley** (Leicester City 1950-58).

Over 500 Goals: Jimmy McGrory (Celtic, Clydebank and Scotland) scored a total of 550 goals in his first-class career (1922-38).

Over 1,000 Goals: Brazil's **Pele** is reputedly the game's all-time highest scorer with 1,282 goals in 1,365 matches (1956-77), but many of them were scored in friendlies for his club, Santos. He scored his 1,000th goal, a penalty, against Vasco da Gama in the Maracana Stadium, Rio, on November 19, 1969. Pele (born Oct. 23, 1940) played regularly for Santos from the age of 16. During his career, he was sent off only once. He played 95 'A' Internationals for Brazil and in their World Cup-winning teams in 1958 and 1970. ● Pele (Edson Arantes do Nascimento) was subsequently Brazil's Minister for Sport. He never played at Wembley, apart from being filmed there scoring a goal for a commercial. Aged 57, Pele received an 'honorary knighthood' (Knight Commander of the British Empire) from the Queen at Buckingham Palace on December 3, 1997.

MOST LEAGUE GOALS IN SEASON: DEAN'S 60

W.R. ('Dixie') Dean, Everton centre-forward, created a League scoring record in 1927-8 with an aggregate of 60 in 39 First Division matches. He also scored three goals in F.A. Cup-ties, and 19 in representative games (total for the season 82).

George Camsell, of Middlesbrough, previously held the record with 59 goals in 37 Second Division matches in 1926-7, his total for the season being 75.

SHEARER'S RECORD 'FIRST'

Alan Shearer (Blackburn Rov.) is the only player to score more than 30 top-division goals in 3 successive seasons since the war: 31 in 1993-4, 34 in 1994-5, 31 in 1995-6.
David Halliday (Sunderland) topped 30 First Div. goals in 4 consecutive seasons with totals of 38, 36, 36 and 49 from 1925-26 to 1928-29.

MOST GOALS IN A MATCH

TOP SCORE by a player in a first-class club match is **13** in the Scottish Cup and **10** in the Football League.
September 12, 1885: John Petrie set the all-time British individual record for a first-class match when, in Arbroath's 36-0 win against Bon Accord (Scottish Cup first round), he scored **13**
April 13, 1936: Joe Payne set the still-existing individual record on his debut as a centre-forward, for Luton Town v Bristol Rov. (Div. III South). In a 12-0 win he scored **10**
December 26, 1935: Robert ('Bunny') Bell for Tranmere Rov. v Oldham Athletic (Div. III North) beat Drake's 12-day-old record in a 13-4 win by scoring **9**
October 6, 1888: James Ross for Preston N.E. (7-0 v Stoke City) set a League record in its first season by scoring all **7**
December 14, 1935: Ted Drake for Arsenal in 7-1 win away to Aston Villa (Div. 1). Scored six goals with his first six shots and in all equalled Ross's top-division record by scoring **7**
February 5, 1955: Tommy Briggs for Blackburn Rov. v Bristol Rov. set Second Division record during 8-3 win by scoring **7**
February 23, 1957: Neville ('Tim') Coleman for Stoke City v Lincoln City (8-0) in Second Division set a record as a winger by scoring **7**

OTHER BIG HAULS

Eric Gemmell for Oldham Athletic v Chester City in Third Division North (11-2), January 19, 1952, and **Albert Whitehurst** for Bradford City v Tranmere Rov. (Third Division North) (8-0), March 6, 1929; both scored **seven**.

W.H. (Billy) Minter scored **seven** goals for St. Albans City in replayed F.A. Cup 4th Qualifying Round against Dulwich Hamlet, November 22, 1922. Dulwich won 8-7, and Minter's seven is still the most goals scored in one match by a player in a losing side.

Denis Law scored **seven** but only one counted and he finished a loser in Manchester City's F.A. Cup 4th Round tie at Luton Town in 1961. The original match on January 28 was washed out (69 mins.) when City led 6-2 (Law 6). He scored a seventh when the game was played again, but Luton won 3-1.

Louis Page, England outside-left, when tried for the first time as centre-forward, accomplished the **double hat-trick** for Burnley in a First Division match against Birmingham, at St. Andrews, April 10, 1926. Burnley won 7-1.

Davie Wilson, Rangers outside-left, scored **six** goals from centre-forward at Falkirk in Scottish League, March 17, 1962. Result: 7-1.

Geoff Hurst was the last player to score **six** in a League match, in West Ham Utd.'s 8-0 win v Sunderland (Div. 1) on October 19, 1968.

ROWLEY'S ALL-TIME RECORD

Arthur Rowley is English football's **top club scorer** with a total of 464 goals for WBA, Fulham, Leicester City and Shrewsbury Town (1947-65). They comprised 434 in the League, 26 F.A. Cup, 4 League Cup.

Jimmy Greaves is second with a total of 420 goals for Chelsea, AC Milan, Tottenham and West Ham Utd., made up of 366 League, 35 F.A. Cup, 10 League Cup and 9 in Europe. He also scored nine goals for Italian club AC Milan.

John Aldridge, Tranmere Rovers manager, retired as a player at the end of the season 1997-98 with a career total of 329 Football League goals for Newport, Oxford Utd., Liverpool and Tranmere Rov. (1997-98). In all competitions for those clubs he scored 410 goals in 737 apps. He also scored 45 goals in 63 games for Spanish club Real Sociedad.

MOST GOALS IN INTERNATIONAL MATCHES

THIRTEEN BY

Archie Thompson for Australia v American Samoa in World Cup (Oceania Group qualifier) at Coff's Harbour, New South Wales, April 11, 2001. Result: 31-0.

SEVEN BY

Stanley Harris for England v France in Amateur International in Paris, November 1, 1906. Result: 15-0.

SIX BY

Nat Lofthouse for Football League v Irish League, at Wolves, September 24, 1952. Result: 7-1.

Joe Bambrick for Ireland against Wales, in Belfast, February 1, 1930. Result: 7-0.

W.C. Jordan in Amateur International for England v France, at Park Royal, March 23, 1908. Result: 12-0.

Vivian Woodward for England v Holland in Amateur International, at Chelsea, December 11, 1909. Result: 9-1.

FIVE BY

Steve Bloomer for England v Wales (Cardiff City) March 16, 1896. Result: 9-1.

Hughie Gallacher for Scotland against Ireland (Belfast), February 23, 1929. Result: 7-3.

Willie Hall for England v Ireland, at Old Trafford, Manchester, November 16, 1938. Five in succession (first three in 3½ mins. – fastest International hat-trick). Result: 7-0.

Malcolm Macdonald for England v Cyprus (Wembley) April 16, 1975. Result: 5-0.

Hughie Gallacher for Scottish League against Irish League (Belfast) November 11, 1925. Result: 7-3.

Barney Battles for Scottish League against Irish League (Firhill Park, Glasgow) October 31, 1928. Result: 8-2.

Bobby Flavell for Scottish League against Irish League (Belfast) April 30, 1947. Result: 7-4.

Joe Bradford for Football League v Irish League (Everton) September 25, 1929. Result: 7-2.

Albert Stubbins for Football League v Irish League (Blackpool) October 18, 1950. Result: 6-3.

Brian Clough for Football League v Irish League (Belfast) September 23, 1959. Result: 5-0.

LAST ENGLAND PLAYER TO SCORE . . .

3 goals: Michael Owen v Germany (5-1), World Cup qual., Munich, Sept. 1, 2001.

4 goals: Ian Wright v San Marino (7-1), World Cup qual., Bologna, Nov. 17, 1993.

5 goals: Malcolm Macdonald v Cyprus (5-0), Eur. Champ. qual., Wembley, Apr. 16, 1975.

INTERNATIONAL TOP SHOTS

		Goals	Games
England	– Bobby Charlton (1958-70)	49	106
N. Ireland	– David Healy (2000-04)	14	35
Scotland	– Denis Law (1958-74)	30	55
	– Kenny Dalglish (1971-86)	30	102
Wales	– Ian Rush (1980-96)	28	73
Rep. of I.	– Niall Quinn (1986-2002)	21	91

ENGLAND'S TOP MARKSMEN
(As at start of season 2004-05)

	Goals	Games
Bobby Charlton (1958-70)	49	106
Gary Lineker (1984-92)	48	80
Jimmy Greaves (1959-67)	44	57
Tom Finney (1946-58)	30	76
Nat Lofthouse (1950-58)	30	33
Alan Shearer (1992-2000)	30	63
Vivian Woodward (1903-11)	29	23
Steve Bloomer (1895-1907)	28	23
David Platt (1989-96)	27	62
Michael Owen (1998-2004)	26	60
Bryan Robson (1979-91)	26	90
Geoff Hurst (1966-72)	24	49
Stan Mortensen (1947-53)	23	25
Tommy Lawton (1938-48)	22	23
Mike Channon (1972-77)	21	46
Kevin Keegan (1972-82)	21	63
Martin Peters (1966-74)	20	67
George Camsell (1929-36)	18	9
'Dixie' Dean (1927-32)	18	16
Johnny Haynes (1954-62)	18	56
Roger Hunt (1962-69)	18	34
Tommy Taylor (1953-57)	16	19
Tony Woodcock (1978-86)	16	42

CONSECUTIVE GOALS FOR ENGLAND

Steve Bloomer scored in **TEN** consecutive appearances (19 goals) for **England** between March 1895 and March 1899.

In modern times, **Paul Mariner** (Ipswich Town) scored in five consecutive **England** appearances (7 goals) between November 1981 and June 1982.

ENGLAND'S TOP FINAL SERIES MARKSMAN

Gary Lineker with 6 goals at 1986 World Cup in Mexico.

MOST GOALS FOR ENGLAND U-21S

13 – Alan Shearer (11 apps.)
Francis Jeffers (13 apps.)

'GOLDEN GOAL' DECIDERS

The Football League, in an experiment to avoid penalty shoot-outs, introduced a new 'golden goal' system in the 1994-95 **Auto Windscreens Shield** to decide matches in the knock-out stages of the competition in which scores were level after 90 minutes. The first goal scored in overtime ended play.

Iain Dunn (Huddersfield Town) became the first player in British football to settle a match by this sudden-death method. His 107th-minute goal beat Lincoln City 3-2 on Nov. 30, 1994, and to mark his 'moment in history' he was presented with a golden football trophy.

The AWS Final of 1995 was decided when **Paul Tait** headed the only goal for Birmingham City against Carlisle Utd. 13 minutes into overtime – the first time a match at Wembley had been decided by the 'golden goal' formula.

First major tournament match to be decided by sudden death was the Final of the **1996 European Championship** at Wembley in which Germany beat Czech Rep. 2-1 by **Oliver Bierhoff's** goal in the 95th minute.

In the **1998 World Cup Finals** (2nd Round), host country France beat Paraguay 1-0 on **Laurent Blanc's** Golden Goal (114 mins.).

France won the **2000 European Championship** with Golden Goals in the semi-final, 2-1 v Portugal (Zinedine Zidane pen, 117 mins), and in the Final, 2-1 v Italy (David Trezeguet, 103 mins).

Galatasaray (Turkey) won the **European Super Cup** 2-1 against Real Madrid (Monaco, August 25, 2000) with a 103rd min Golden Goal, a penalty.

Liverpool won the **UEFA Cup** 5-4 against Alaves with a 117th min Golden Goal, an own goal, in the Final in Dortmund (May 19, 2001).

In the **2002 World Cup Finals**, 3 matches were decided by Golden Goals: in the 2nd Round Senegal beat Sweden 2-1 (Henri Camara, 104 mins) and South Korea beat Italy 2-1 (Ahn Jung – hwan, 117 mins); in the Quarter-final, Turkey beat Senegal 1-0 (Ilhan Mansiz, 94 mins).

France won the 2003 FIFA Confederations Cup Final against Cameroon (Paris, June 29) with a 97th-minute Golden Goal by Thierry Henry.

Doncaster Rov. won promotion to Football League with a 110th-minute Golden Goal winner (3–2) in the Conference Play-off Final against Dagenham & Redbridge at Stoke City (May 10, 2003).

Germany won the **Women's World Cup Final** 2-1 v Sweden (Los Angeles, October 12, 2003) with a 98th-minute Golden Goal.

GOLD TURNS TO SILVER

Starting with the 2003 Finals of the UEFA Cup and Champions' League/European Cup, UEFA introduced a new rule by which a Silver Goal could decide the winners if the scores were 'level' after 90 minutes.

Team leading after 15 minutes' extra time win match. If sides level, a second period of 15 minutes to be played. If still no winner, result to be decided by penalty shoot-out.

UEFA said the change was made because the Golden Goal put too much pressure on referees and prompted teams to play negative football.

Although both 2003 Euro Finals went to extra time, neither was decided by a Silver Goal. The new rule applied in the 2004 European Championship Finals, and Greece won their Semi-final against the Czech Republic with a 105th-minute Silver Goal.

The **International Board** decided (Feb. 28 2004) that the Golden/Silver Goal rule was 'unfair' and that from July 1 competitive International matches level after extra time would, when necessary, be settled on penalties.

PREMIERSHIP TOP SHOTS (1992-2004)

Alan Shearer	243	Ian Wright	113
Andy Cole	164	Thierry Henry	112
Les Ferdinand	149	Dion Dublin	110
Robbie Fowler	143	Jimmy Floyd Hasselbaink	103
Teddy Sheringham	139	Matthew Le Tissier	101
Dwight Yorke	120	(As at start of season 2004-05)	
Michael Owen	118		

LEAGUE GOAL RECORDS

The highest goal-scoring aggregates in the Football League, Premier and Scottish League are as follows:

FOR

	Goals	Games	Club	Season
Prem.	97	38	Manchester Utd.	1999-2000
Div. 1	128	42	Aston Villa	1930-1
New Div. 1	108	46	Manchester City	2001-02
Div. 2	122	42	Middlesbrough	1926-7
New Div. 2	89	46	Millwall	2000-01
Div. 3(S)	127	42	Millwall	1927-8
Div. 3(N)	128	42	Bradford City	1928-9
Div. 3	111	46	Q.P.R.	1961-2
New Div. 3	96	46	Luton Town	2001-02
Div. 4	134	46	Peterborough Utd.	1960-1
Scot. Prem.	105	38	Celtic	2003-04
Scot. L. 1	132	34	Hearts	1957-8
Scot. L. 2	142	34	Raith Rov.	1937-8
Scot. L. 3 (Modern)	87	36	Ross County	1998-9
	87	36	Stranraer	2003-04

AGAINST

	Goals	Games	Club	Season
Prem.	100	42	Swindon Town	1993-4
Div. 1	125	42	Blackpool	1930-1
New Div. 1	102	46	Stockport Co.	2001-02
Div. 2	141	34	Darwen	1898-9
New Div. 2	102	46	Chester City	1992-3
Div. 3(S)	135	42	Merthyr T.	1929-30
Div. 3(N)	136	42	Nelson	1927-8
Div. 3	123	46	Accrington S.	1959-60
New Div. 3	113	46	Doncaster Rov.	1997-8
Div. 4	109	46	Hartlepool Utd.	1959-60
Scot. Prem.	100	36	Morton	1984-5
Scot. Prem.	100	44	Morton	1987-8
Scot. L. 1	137	38	Leith A.	1931-2
Scot. L. 2	146	38	Edinburgh City	1931-2
Scot. L. 3 (Modern)	118	36	East Stirling	2003-04

BEST DEFENSIVE RECORDS – *Denotes under old offside law

Div.	Goals Agst.	Games	Club	Season
Prem.	17	38	Arsenal	1998-9
1	16	42	Liverpool	1978-9
1	*15	22	Preston N.E.	1888-9
New Div. 1	28	46	Sunderland	1998-9
2	18	28	Liverpool	1893-4
2	*22	34	Sheffield Wed.	1899-1900
2	24	42	Birmingham City	1947-8
2	24	42	Crystal Palace	1978-9
New Div. 2	25	46	Wigan Athletic	2002-03
3(S)	*21	42	Southampton	1921-2
3(S)	30	42	Cardiff City	1946-7
3(N)	*21	38	Stockport Co.	1921-2
3(N)	21	46	Port Vale	1953-4
3	30	46	Middlesbrough	1986-7
New Div. 3	20	46	Gillingham	1995-6
4	25	46	Lincoln City	1980-1

SCOTTISH LEAGUE

Div.	Goals Agst.	Games	Club	Season
Prem.	18	38	Celtic	2001-02
1	*12	22	Dundee	1902-3
1	*14	38	Celtic	1913-14
2	20	38	Morton	1966-7
2	*29	38	Clydebank	1922-3
2	29	36	East Fife	1995-6
New Div. 3	21	36	Brechin	1995-6

TOP SCORERS (LEAGUE ONLY)

		Goals	Div.
2003-04	Thierry Henry (Arsenal)	30	Prem
2002-03	Andy Morrell (Wrexham)	34	3
2001-02	Shaun Goater (Manchester City)	28	1
	Bobby Zamora (Brighton & H.A.)	28	2
2000-01	Bobby Zamora (Brighton & H.A.)	28	3
1999-00	Kevin Phillips (Sunderland)	30	Prem.
1998-9	Lee Hughes (W.B.A.)	31	1
1997-8	Pierre van Hooijdonk (Nott'm Forest)	29	1
	Kevin Phillips (Sunderland)	29	1
1996-7	Graeme Jones (Wigan Athletic)	31	3
1995-6	Alan Shearer (Blackburn Rov.)	31	Prem.
1994-5	Alan Shearer (Blackburn Rov.)	34	Prem.
1993-4	Jimmy Quinn (Reading)	35	2
1992-3	Guy Whittingham (Portsmouth)	42	1
1991-2	Ian Wright (Crystal Palace 5, Arsenal 24)	29	1
1990-1	Teddy Sheringham (Millwall)	33	2
1989-90	Mick Quinn (Newcastle Utd.)	32	2
1988-9	Steve Bull (Wolves)	37	3
1987-8	Steve Bull (Wolves)	34	4
1986-7	Clive Allen (Tottenham)	33	1
1985-6	Gary Lineker (Everton)	30	1
1984-5	Tommy Tynan (Plymouth Argyle)	31	3
	John Clayton (Tranmere Rov.)	31	4
1983-4	Trevor Senior (Reading)	36	4
1982-3	Luther Blissett (Watford)	27	1
1981-2	Keith Edwards (Hull City 1, Sheffield Utd. 35)	36	4
1980-1	Tony Kellow (Exeter City)	25	3
1979-80	Clive Allen (Queens Park Rangers)	28	2
1978-9	Ross Jenkins (Watford)	29	3
1977-8	Steve Phillips (Brentford)	32	4
	Alan Curtis (Swansea City)	32	4
1976-7	Peter Ward (Brighton & H.A.)	32	3
1975-6	Dixie McNeil (Hereford)	35	3
1974-5	Dixie McNeil (Hereford)	31	3
1973-4	Brian Yeo (Gillingham)	31	4
1972-3	Bryan (Pop) Robson (West Ham Utd.)	28	1
1971-2	Ted MacDougall (Bournemouth)	35	3
1970-1	Ted MacDougall (Bournemouth)	42	4
1969-70	Albert Kinsey (Wrexham)	27	4
1968-9	Jimmy Greaves (Tottenham)	27	1
1967-8	George Best (Manchester Utd.)	28	1
	Ron Davies (Southampton)	28	1
1966-7	Ron Davies (Southampton)	37	1
1965-6	Kevin Hector (Bradford P.A.)	44	4

1964-5	Alick Jeffrey (Doncaster Rov.)	36	4
1963-4	Hugh McIlmoyle (Carlisle Utd.)	39	4
1962-3	Jimmy Greaves (Tottenham)	37	1
1961-2	Roger Hunt (Liverpool)	41	2
1960-1	Terry Bly (Peterborough Utd.)	52	4

100 LEAGUE GOALS IN SEASON

Manchester City, First Div. Champions in 2001-02, scored 108 goals.

Bolton Wanderers, First Div. Champions in 1996-7, reached exactly 100 goals, the first side to complete a century in League football since 103 by Northampton Town (Div. 4 Champions) in 1986-7.

Last League Champions to reach **100** League goals: **Tottenham** (115 in 1960-1). Last century of goals in the top division: **111** by runners-up **Tottenham** in 1962-3.

Wolves topped 100 goals in four successive First Division seasons (1957-8, 1958-9, 1959-60, 1960-1).

In **1930-1**, the Championship top three all scored a century of League goals: 1 Arsenal (127), 2 Aston Villa (128), 3 Sheffield Wed. (102).

100 GOALS AGAINST

Swindon Town, relegated with 100 goals against in 1993-4, were the first top-division club to concede a century of League goals since **Ipswich Town** (121) went down in 1964. Most goals conceded in the top division: 125 by **Blackpool** in 1930-31, but they avoided relegation.

MOST LEAGUE GOALS ON ONE DAY

A record of 209 goals in the four divisions of the Football League (43 matches) was set on **January 2, 1932**: 56 in Div. 1, 53 in Div. 2, 57 in Div. 3 South and 43 in Div. 3 North. There were two 10-goal aggregates: Bradford City 9, Barnsley 1 in Div. 2 and Coventry City 5, Fulham 5 in Div. 3 South.

That total of 209 League goals on one day was equalled on **February 1, 1936** (44 matches): 46 in Div. 1, 46 in Div. 2, 49 in Div. 3 South and 69 in Div. 3 North. Two matches in the Northern Section produced 23 of the goals: Chester 12, York City 0 and Crewe Alexandra 5, Chesterfield 6.

MOST GOALS IN TOP DIV. ON ONE DAY

This record has stood since December 26, 1963, when **66 goals** were scored in the ten First Division matches played.

MOST F.A. PREMIER LEAGUE GOALS ON ONE DAY

47, in nine matches on May 8, 1993 (last day of season).

FEWEST PREMIERSHIP GOALS IN ONE WEEK-END

10, in 10 matches on November 24/25, 2001.

FEWEST FIRST DIV. GOALS ON ONE DAY

For full/near full programme: **Ten goals,** all by home clubs, in ten matches on April 28, 1923 (day of Wembley's first F.A. Cup Final).

SCORERS IN 10 CONSECUTIVE TOP-DIVISION MATCHES

Ruud van Nistelrooy (Manchester Utd.) March 22-August 23, 2004). He scored 13 goals in last 8 games of season 2002-03 and in first 2 of 2003-04. Since the last war, 3 other players scored in 10 successive matches in the old First Division: **Billy McAdams** (Man. City, 1957-58), **Ron Davies** (Southampton, 1966-67) and **John Aldridge** (Liverpool, May-Oct. 1987).

SCORERS FOR 5 PREMIERSHIP CLUBS

Stan Collymore (Nott'm. F., Liverpool, Aston Villa, Leicester City, Bradford City); **Mark Hughes** (Manchester Utd., Chelsea, Southampton, Everton, Blackburn Rov.); **Nick Barmby** (Tottenham, Middlesbrough, Everton, Liverpool, Leeds Utd.); **Benito Carbone** (Sheff. Wed., Aston Villa, Bradford City, Derby Co., Middlesbrough); **Les Ferdinand** (Q.P.R., Newcastle Utd., Tottenham, West Ham Utd., Leicester City).

SCORERS IN MOST CONSECUTIVE LEAGUE MATCHES

Arsenal broke the record by scoring in 55 successive Premiership fixtures: the last match in season 2000-01, then all 38 games in winning the Championship in 2001–02, and the first 16 in season 2002–03. The sequence ended with a 2–0 defeat away to Man. Utd. on December 7, 2002.

Chesterfield previously held the record, having scored in 46 consecutive matches in Div. 3 (North), starting on Christmas Day 1929 and ending on December 27, 1930.

SIX-OUT-OF-SIX HEADERS

When **Oxford Utd.** beat Shrewsbury Town 6-0 (Div. 2) on April 23, 1996, all six goals were headers.

FIVE IN A MATCH

Latest players to score 5 goals in a top-division match: **Tony Woodcock** (for Arsenal in 6-2 win away to Aston Villa) and **Ian Rush** (Liverpool 6, Luton Town 0), both on October 29, 1983; **Andy Cole** (Manchester Utd. 9, Ipswich Town 0) on March 4, 1995; **Alan Shearer** (Newcastle Utd. 8, Sheffield Wed. 0) on September 19, 1999.

ALL–ROUND MARKSMAN

Alan Cork scored in four divisions of the Football League and in the F.A. Premier League in his 18-season career with Wimbledon, Sheffield Utd., and Fulham (1977-95).

MOST CUP GOALS

F.A. Cup – most goals in one season: 20 by Jimmy Ross (Preston N.E., runners-up 1887-8); 15 by Albert (Sandy) Brown (Tottenham, winners 1900-1).

Most F.A. Cup goals in individual careers: 48 by Harry Cursham (Notts Co. 1880-87); this century: 44 by Ian Rush (39 for Liverpool, 4 for Chester City, 1 for Newcastle Utd. 1979-98). Denis Law was the previous highest F.A. Cup scorer this century with 41 goals for Huddersfield Town, Manchester City and Manchester Utd. (1957-74).

Most F.A. Cup Final goals by individual: 5 by Ian Rush for Liverpool (2 in 1986, 2 in 1989, 1 in 1992).

HOTTEST CUP HOT-SHOT

Geoff Hurst scored 21 cup goals in season 1965-66: 11 League Cup, 4 F.A. Cup and 2 Cup-Winners' Cup for West Ham Utd., and 4 in the World Cup for England.

SCORERS IN EVERY ROUND

Twelve players have scored in **every round** of the F.A. Cup in one season, from opening to Final inclusive: **Archie Hunter** (Aston Villa, winners 1887); **Sandy Brown** (Tottenham, winners 1901); **Harry Hampton** (Aston Villa, winners 1905); **Harold Blackmore** (Bolton Wand., winners 1929); **Ellis Rimmer** (Sheffield Wed., winners 1935); **Frank O'Donnell** (Preston N.E., beaten 1937); **Stan Mortensen** (Blackpool, beaten 1948); **Jack Milburn** (Newcastle Utd., winners 1951); **Nat Lofthouse** (Bolton Wand., beaten 1953); **Charlie Wayman** (Preston N.E., beaten 1954); **Jeff Astle** (W.B.A., winners 1968); **Peter Osgood** (Chelsea, winners 1970).

Blackmore and the next seven completed their 'set' in the Final at Wembley; Osgood did so in the Final replay at Old Trafford.

Only player to score in every **Football League Cup** round possible in one season: **Tony Brown** for W.B.A., winners 1965-6, with 9 goals in 10 games (after bye in Round 1).

TEN IN A ROW

Dixie McNeill scored for Wrexham in **ten successive** F.A. Cup rounds (18 goals): 11 in Rounds 1-6, 1977-8; 3 in Rounds 3-4, 1978-9; 4 in Rounds 3-4, 1979-80.

Stan Mortensen (Blackpool) scored 25 goals in 16 F.A. Cup rounds out of 17 (1946-51).

TOP MATCH HAULS IN F.A. CUP

Ted MacDougall scored nine goals, a record for the competition proper, in the F.A. Cup first round on November 20, 1971, when Bournemouth beat Margate 11-0. On November 23, 1970 he had scored six in an 8-1 first round replay against Oxford City.

Other six-goal F.A. Cup scorers include **George Hilsdon** (Chelsea v Worksop, 9-1, 1907-8), **Ronnie Rooke** (Fulham v Bury, 6-0, 1938-9), **Harold Atkinson** (Tranmere Rov. v Ashington, 8-1, 1952-3), **George Best** (Manchester Utd. v Northampton Town 1969-70, 8-2 away), and **Duane Darby** (Hull City v Whitby, 8-4, 1996-7).

Denis Law scored all **six** for Manchester City at Luton Town (6-2) in an F.A. Cup 4th Round tie on January 28, 1961, but none of them counted — the match was abandoned (69 mins.) because of a waterlogged pitch. He also scored City's goal when the match was played again, but they lost 3-1.

Tony Philliskirk scored **five** when Peterborough Utd. beat Kingstonian 9-1 in an F.A. Cup 1st Round replay on November 25, 1992, but had them wiped from the records. With the score at 3-0, the Kingstonian goalkeeper was concussed by a coin thrown from the crowd and unable to play on. The F.A. ordered the match to be replayed at Peterborough Utd. behind closed doors, and Kingstonian lost 1-0.

● Two players have scored **ten goals** in F.A. Cup preliminary round matches: **Chris Marron** for South Shields against Radcliffe in September 1947; **Paul Jackson**, aged 21, when Sheffield-based club Stocksbridge Park Steels beat Oldham Town 17–1 on August 31, 2002. He scored 5 in each half and all ten with his feet – goal times 6, 10, 22, 30, 34, 68, 73, 75, 79, 84 mins.

QUICKEST GOALS AND RAPID SCORING

Six seconds after kick-off by **Albert Mundy** for Aldershot v Hartlepool Utd., October 25, 1958; **Barrie Jones** for Notts County v Torquay Utd., March 31, 1962; **Keith Smith** for Crystal Palace v Derby Co., December 12, 1964.

9.6 seconds by **John Hewitt** for Aberdeen at Motherwell, 3rd Round, January 23, 1982 (fastest goal in Scottish Cup history).

A goal in **4 seconds** was claimed by **Jim Fryatt**, for Bradford P.A. v Tranmere Rov. (Div. 4, April 25, 1965), and by **Gerry Allen** for Whitstable Town v Danson (Kent League, March 3,1989). Backed by filmed evidence, **Damian Mori** scored in 4 seconds for Adelaide City v Sydney Utd. (Australian National League, December 6, 1995).

Colin Cowperthwaite reputedly scored in 3½ seconds for Barrow v Kettering (Alliance Premier League) on December 8, 1979, but the timing was unofficial.

Phil Starbuck scored for Huddersfield Town only **3 seconds** after entering the field as 54th min. substitute at home to Wigan Athletic (Div. 2) on Easter Monday, April 12, 1993. A corner-kick was delayed, awaiting his arrival, and he scored with a header.

Malcolm Macdonald scored after **5 seconds** (officially timed) in Newcastle Utd.'s 7-3 win in a pre-season friendly at St. Johnstone on July 29, 1972. From the kick-off, the ball was passed to him, and Macdonald, spotting the goalkeeper off his line, smashed a shot over him and into the net.

Scored first kick: Billy Foulkes (Newcastle Utd.) for Wales v England at Cardiff City, October 20, 1951, in his first International match.

Six goals in seven minutes in Preston N.E.'s record 26-0 F.A. Cup 1st Round win v Hyde, October 15, 1887.

Five in 20 minutes: **Frank Keetley** in Lincoln City's 9-1 win over Halifax Town in Div. III (North), January 16, 1932; **Brian Dear** for West Ham Utd. v W.B.A. (6-1, Div.1) April 16, 1965.

Four in five minutes: by **John McIntyre** for Blackburn Rov. v Everton (Div. 1), September 16, 1922; **W.G. (Billy) Richardson** for W.B.A. v West Ham Utd. (Div. 1), November 7, 1931.

Three in three minutes: Billy Lane for Watford v Clapton Orient (Div.3S), December 20, 1933; Johnny Hartburn for Leyton Orient v Shrewsbury Town (Div. 3S), January 22, 1955; Gary Roberts for Brentford v Newport, (Freight Rover Trophy, South Final), May 17, 1985; Gary Shaw for Shrewsbury Town v Bradford City (Div. 3), December 22, 1990.

Fastest hat-trick in League History: 2 mins. 20 secs. By Bournemouth's 84th-minute substitute James Hayter in 6-0 home win v Wrexham (Div. 2) on February 24, 2004 (goal times 86, 87, 88 mins.).

Three in 2½ minutes: Jimmy Scarth for Gillingham v Leyton Orient (Div. 3S), November 1, 1952.

Two in nine seconds: Jamie Bates with last kick of first half, Jermaine McSporran 9 seconds into second half when Wycombe Wand. beat Peterborough Utd. 2-0 at home (Div. 2) on September 23, 2000.

Arsenal scored six goals in 18 minutes (71-89 mins.) in 7-1 home win (Div. 1) v Sheffield Wed., February 15, 1992.

Plymouth Argyle scored five goals in first 18 minutes in 7-0 home win v Chesterfield (Div. 2), January 3, 2004.

Sunderland scored eight goals in 28 minutes at Newcastle Utd. (9-1 Div 1), December 5, 1908. Newcastle went on to win the Championship.

Southend Utd. scored all seven goals in 29 minutes in 7-0 win at home to Torquay Utd. (Leyland Daf Cup, Southern quarter-final), February 26, 1991. Score was 0-0 until 55th. minute.

Six goals in first 19 minutes by Tranmere Rov. when they beat Oldham Athletic 13-4 (Div. 3 North) on December 26, 1935.

Notts Co. scored six second-half goals in 12 minutes (Tommy Lawton 3, Jackie Sewell 3) when they beat Exeter City 9-0 (Div. 3 South) at Meadow Lane on October 16, 1948.

World's fastest goal: 2.8 seconds, direct from kick-off, by Argentinian Ricardo Olivera for Rio Negro v Soriano (Uruguayan League), December 26, 1998.

Fastest International goal: 8.3 secs. by Davide Gualtieri for San Marino v England (World Cup qual., Bologna, November 17, 1993).

Fastest International hat-trick: 3 minutes 15 seconds by Masashi Nakayami for Japan in 9-0 win v Brunei in Macao (Asian Cup), February 16, 2000.

Fastest International hat-trick in British matches: 3½ minutes by Willie Hall for England v N. Ireland at Old Trafford, Manchester, November 16, 1938. (Hall scored 5 in 7-0 win); 4½ minutes by Arif Erdem for Turkey v N. Ireland, European Championship, at Windsor Park, Belfast, on September 4, 1999.

Fastest International goal by substitute: 5 seconds by John Jensen for Denmark v Belgium (Eur. Champ.), October 12, 1994.

Fastest England goals: 17 seconds by Tommy Lawton v Portugal in Lisbon, May 25, 1947. 27 seconds by Bryan Robson v. France in World Cup at Bilbao, Spain on June 16, 1982; 37 seconds by Gareth Southgate v South Africa in Durban, May 22, 2003; 30 seconds by Jack Cock v Ireland, Belfast, October 25, 1919; 30 seconds by Bill Nicholson v Portugal at Goodison Park, May 19, 1951. 38 seconds by Bryan Robson v Yugoslavia at Wembley, December 13, 1989; 42 seconds by Gary Lineker v Malaysia in Kuala Lumpur, June 12, 1991.

Fastest goal by England substitute: 10 seconds by Teddy Sheringham v Greece (World Cup qualifying match) at Old Trafford, October 6, 2001.

Fastest F.A. Cup Final goals: 30 seconds by John Devey, for Aston Villa v W.B.A., 1895; at Wembley: 42 seconds by Roberto di Matteo, for Chelsea v Middlesbrough, 1997.

Fastest goal by substitute in F.A. Cup Final: 96 seconds by Teddy Sheringham for Manchester Utd. v Newcastle Utd. at Wembley, May 22, 1999.

Fastest League Cup Final goal: 3 minutes by Derek Lythgoe for Norwich City v Rochdale, 1962.

Fastest goal in cup final: 4.07 seconds by 14-year-old Owen Price for Ernest Bevin College, Tooting, beaten 3-1 by Barking Abbey in Heinz Ketchup Cup Final at Arsenal Stadium on May 18, 2000. Owen, on Tottenham's books, scored from inside his own half when the ball was played back to him from kick-off.

Fastest F.A. Cup hat-tricks: In 3 minutes by Billy Best for Southend Utd. v Brentford (2nd. Round, December 7, 1968); 2 minutes 20 seconds by Andy Locke for Nantwich v Droylesden (1st. Qual. Round, September 9, 1995).

F.A. Premier League – fastest scoring: Four goals in 4 minutes, 44 seconds by Tottenham at home to Southampton on Sunday, February 7, 1993.

Premiership – fast scoring away: When Aston Villa won 5-0 at Leicester (January 31, 2004), all the goals were scored in 18 second-half minutes (50-68).

Fastest First Division hat-tricks since war: Graham Leggat, 3 goals in 3 minutes (first half) when Fulham beat Ipswich Town 10-1 on Boxing Day, 1963; Nigel Clough, 3 goals in 4 minutes (81, 82, 85 pen) when Nott'm Forest beat Q.P.R. 4-0 on Sunday, December 13, 1987.

Fastest goal in Champions League: 20.07 seconds by Gilbert Silva for Arsenal away to PSV Eindhoven (Group A), September 26, 2002.

F.A. Premier League – fastest hat-trick: 4½ minutes (26, 29, 31) by Robbie Fowler in Liverpool 3, Arsenal 0 on Sunday, August 28, 1994.

Fastest hat-trick of headers: Dixie Dean's 5 goals in Everton's 7–2 win at home to Chelsea (Div. 1) on November 14, 1931 included 3 headers between 5th and 15th-minutes.

Fastest Premier League goals: 10 seconds by Ledley King for Tottenham away to Bradford City, December 9, 2000; 10.4 seconds by Alan Shearer for Newcastle Utd. v Manchester City, January 18, 2003; 11 seconds by Mark Viduka for Leeds Utd. V Charlton Athletic Ath., March 17, 2001; 13 seconds by Chris Sutton for Blackburn Rov. at Everton, April 1, 1995; 13 seconds by Dwight Yorke for Aston Villa at Coventry City, September 30, 1995.

Fastest top-division goal: 7 seconds by Bobby Langton for Preston N.E. v Manchester City (Div. 1), August 25, 1948.

Fastest Premier League goal by substitute: 9 seconds by Shaun Goater, Manchester City's equaliser away to Manchester Utd. (1–1), Feb. 9, 2003.

Four in 13 minutes by Premier League substitute: Ole Gunnar Solskjaer for Manchester Utd. away to Nott'm. Forest, Feb. 6, 1999.

Fastest new-First Division goal: 10 seconds by Keith O'Neill for Norwich City v Stoke City, April 12, 1997.

Fastest Scottish hat-trick: 2½ mins. by Ian St. John for Motherwell away to Hibernian (Scottish League Cup), August 15, 1959.

Fastest all-time hat-trick: Reported at 1 min. 50 secs. by Eduardo Maglioni for Independiente against Gimnasia de la Plata in Argentina First Division, March 18, 1973.

Fastest goal in Women's Football! 7 seconds by Angie Harriott for Launton Ladies v Thame Utd. (Southern League, Prem. Div.), season 1998-9.

FASTEST GOALS IN WORLD CUP FINAL SERIES

10.8 secs. by Hakan Sukur for Turkey against South Korea in 3rd/4th-place match at Taegu, June 29, 2002.

15 secs. by Vaclav Masek for Czechoslovakia v Mexico (in Vina, Chile, 1962).

27 secs. by Bryan Robson for England v France (in Bilbao, Spain, 1982).

TOP MATCH SCORES SINCE WAR

By English clubs: 13-0 by Newcastle Utd. v Newport (Div. 2, Oct. 1946); 13-2 by Tottenham v Crewe Alexandra (F.A. Cup 4th. Rd. replay, Feb. 1960); 13-0 by Chelsea v Jeunesse Hautcharage, Lux. (Cup-Winners' Cup 1st. Rd., 2nd. Leg, Sept. 1971).

By Scottish club: 20-0 by Stirling Albion v Selkirk (E. of Scotland League) in Scottish Cup 1st. Rd. (Dec. 1984). That is the highest score in British first-class football since Preston N.E. beat Hyde 26-0 in F.A. Cup, Oct. 1887.

GOALS BY WINGERS

		Season	Matches	Goals
	Football League	(Div. I)		
Cliff Bastin (Arsenal)		1932-3	42	33
	Scottish League	(Div. I)		
Bob Ferrier (Motherwell)		1929-30	27	32
	Scottish League	(Div. II)		
Ken Dawson (Falkirk)		1935-6	34	39

GOALS BY GOALKEEPERS

Goalkeepers who have scored with long clearances include:

Pat Jennings for Tottenham away to Manchester Utd. (goalkeeper Alex Stepney) in the F.A. Charity Shield on August 12, 1967.

Peter Shilton for Leicester City at Southampton (goalkeeper Campbell Forsyth) on October 14, 1967 (Div. 1).

Ray Cashley for Bristol City at home to Hull City (goalkeeper Jeff Wealands) on September 18, 1973 (Div. 2).

Steve Sherwood for Watford away to Coventry City (goalkeeper Raddy Avramovic) on January 14, 1984 (Div. 1).

Steve Ogrizovic for Coventry City away to Sheffield Wed. (goalkeeper Martin Hodge) on October 25, 1986 (Div. 1).

Andy Goram for Hibernian at home to Morton (goalkeeper David Wylie) on May 7, 1988 (Scottish Premier Div.).

Andy McLean, on Irish League debut, for Cliftonville v Linfield (goalkeeper George Dunlop) on August 20, 1988.

Alan Paterson for Glentoran against Linfield (goalkeeper George Dunlop) on November 30, 1988 (Irish League Cup Final at The Oval, Belfast). His long punt (87 mins) gave Glentoran a 2-1 victory – the only instance of a goalkeeper scoring the winning goal in a senior cup final in the UK.

Ray Charles for East Fife at Stranraer (goalkeeper Bernard Duffy) on February 28, 1990 (Scottish Div. 2).

Iain Hesford scored Maidstone's winner (3-2 v Hereford, Div. 4, November 2, 1991) with long kick-out that went first bounce past Tony Elliott in opposite goal.

Chris Mackenzie for Hereford at home to Barnet (goalkeeper Mark Taylor) in Div. 3, August 12, 1995.

Aston Villa's **Mark Bosnich** scored the last goal (a penalty) when Australia beat Solomon Islands 13-0 in World Cup Oceania Zone qualifier in Sydney on June 11, 1997.

With a free-kick from his own half, Notts Co. goalkeeper **Steve Mildenhall** scored past Mansfield Town 'keeper Kevin Pilkington for the winning goal (4-3,away) in the Worthington Cup 1st Round on August 21, 2001.

Mart Poom headed Sunderland's last-seconds equaliser (1-1) away to his former club Derby Co. (goalkeeper Andy Oakes), Div. 1, September 20, 2003.

Brad Friedel (Blackburn Rov.) shot late equaliser against Charlton Athletic 'keeper Dean Kiely at The Valley (Premiership, February 21, 2004) but finished on losing side, 2-3.

Paul Robinson (Leeds Utd.) headed last-minute equaliser (2-2) at home to Swindon Town (Carling Cup, 2nd Round, September 24, 2003). Leeds won 4-3 on penalties.

Most goals by a goalkeeper in a League season: 5 (all penalties) by **Arthur Birch** for Chesterfield (Div. 3 North), 1923-4.

Arthur Wilkie, Reading's goalkeeper at home to Halifax Town (Div. 3) on August 31, 1962, injured a hand, then played as a forward and scored twice in a 4-2 win.

Alex Stepney was Manchester Utd.'s joint top scorer for two months in season 1973-4 with two penalties.

Alan Fettis, N. Ireland goalkeeper, scored twice for Hull City in Div. 2 in season 1994-5: as a substitute in 3-1 home win v Oxford Utd. (Dec. 17) and, when selected outfield, with last-minute winner (2-1) at Blackpool on May 6.

Peter Schmeichel, Manchester Utd.'s goalkeeper, headed an 89th minute equaliser (2-2) from Ryan Giggs' corner in the UEFA Cup 1st. Round, 2nd leg against Rotor Volgograd (Russia) on September 26, 1995, but United lost the tie on away goals.

On October 20, 2001, **Schmeichel** became the first goalkeeper to score in the Premiership when, following a corner, he volleyed Aston Villa's second goal in their 3-2 defeat at Everton.

In League matches for Swansea City, **Roger Freestone** scored with a penalty at Oxford Utd. (Div. 2, April 30, 1995) and, in 1995-6 (Div. 2) with penalties at home to Shrewsbury Town (August 12) and Chesterfield (August 26).

Goalkeeper **Jimmy Glass**, on loan from Swindon Town, scored the winner that kept Carlisle Utd. in the Football League on May 8, 1999. With only ten seconds of injury time left, he went upfield for a corner and shot the goal that beat Plymouth Argyle 2-1 at Brunton Park. It preserved Carlisle Utd.'s League existence since 1928 and sent Scarborough down to the Conference.

Tony Roberts (Dagenham & Redbridge), only known goalkeeper to score from open play in the F.A. Cup, away to Basingstoke in 4th Qual. Round on October 27, 2001. His last-minute equaliser (2-2) forced a replay, which Dagenham won 3-0 and went on to the 3rd Round proper.

Jose Luis Chilavert, Paraguay's Int. goalkeeper, scored a hat-trick of penalties when his club Velez Sarsfield beat Ferro Carril Oeste 6-1 in the Argentine League on November 28, 1999. In all, he scored 8 goals in his 72 Internationals.

OWN GOALS

Most by player in one season: 5 by **Robert Stuart** (Middlesbrough) in 1934-35.

Three in match by one team: Sheffield Wed.'s Vince Kenny, Norman Curtis and Eddie Gannon in 5–4 defeat at home to W.B.A. (Div. 1) on December 26, 1952; **Rochdale's** George Underwood, Kenny Boyle and Danny Murphy in 7–2 defeat at Carlisle (Div. 3 North), December 25, 1954; **Sunderland's** Stephen Wright and Michael Proctor (2) in 24, 29, 32 minutes at home to Charlton Athletic (1–3, Premiership), February 1, 2003.

Two in match by one player: Chris Nicholl (Aston Villa) scored all 4 goals in 2-2 draw away to Leicester City (Div. 1), March 20, 1976; **Jamie Carragher** (Liverpool) in first half at home to Manchester Utd. (2-3) in Premiership, September 11, 1999; **Jim Goodwin** (Stockport Co.) in 1–4 defeat away to Plymouth Argyle (Div. 2), September 23, 2002; **Michael Proctor** (Sunderland) in 1–3 defeat at home to Charlton Athletic Ath. (Premiership), February 1, 2003.

Fastest own goals: 8 seconds by **Pat Kruse** of Torquay Utd., for Cambridge Utd. (Div. 4), January 3, 1977; in **First Division**, 16 seconds by **Steve Bould** (Arsenal) away to Sheffield Wed., February 17, 1990.

Late own-goal man: Frank Sinclair (Leicester City) put through his own goal in the 90th minute of Premiership matches away to Arsenal (L1-2) and at home to Chelsea (D2-2) in August 1999.

Half an own goal each: Chelsea's second goal in a 3-1 home win against Leicester City on December 18, 1954 was uniquely recorded as 'shared own goal'. Leicester City defenders **Stan Milburn** and **Jack Froggatt**, both lunging at the ball in an attempt to clear, connected simultaneously and sent it rocketing into the net.

Match of 149 own goals: When Adama, Champions of Malagasy (formerly Madagascar) won a League match 149–0 on October 31, 2002, all 149 were **own goals** scored by opponents Stade Olympique De L'Emryne. They repeatedly put the ball in their own net in protest at a refereeing decision.

MOST SCORERS IN MATCH

Liverpool set a Football League record with **EIGHT** scorers when they beat Crystal Palace 9-0 (Div.1) on September 12, 1989. Their marksmen were: Steve Nicol (7 and 88 mins), Steve McMahon (16), Ian Rush (45), Gary Gillespie (56), Peter Beardsley (61), John Aldridge pen. (67), John Barnes (79) and Glenn Hysen (82).

Fifteen years earlier, **Liverpool** had gone one better with **NINE** different scorers when they achieved their record win, 11-0 at home to Stromsgodset (Norway) in the Cup-Winners' Cup 1st. round, 1st leg on September 17, 1974.

Eight players scored for **Swansea City** when they beat Sliema, Malta, 12-0 in the Cup-Winners' Cup 1st round, 1st leg on September 15, 1982.

Nine Stirling Albion players scored in the 20-0 win against Selkirk in the Scottish Cup 1st. Round on December 8, 1984.

LONG SCORING RUNS

Tom Phillipson scored in 13 consecutive matches for Wolves (Div. 2) in season 1926-27, which is still an English League record. **Bill Prendergast** scored in 13 successive League and Cup appearances for Chester City (Div. 3 North) in season 1938-39.

Dixie Dean scored in 12 consecutive games (23 goals) for Everton in Div. 2 in 1930-1.

Danish striker **Finn Dossing** scored in 15 consecutive matches (Scottish record) for Dundee Utd. (Div. 1) in 1964-5.

Marco Negri (Rangers) scored in all the first 10 Premier games of 1997-8, a total of 12 goals.

Jermain Defoe, 18, on loan from West Ham Utd., equalled a single-season post-war record by scoring for Bournemouth in 10 consecutive matches (Div. 2), October-January 2000-01. **Billy McAdams** did likewise for Manchester City (1957-8), as did **Ron Davies** for Southampton (1966-7).

John Aldridge (Liverpool) scored in 10 successive First Division matches – the last game of season 1986-7 and the first nine in 1987-8.

Kevin Russell (Wrexham) scored in nine consecutive matches in Div. 4, March-May, 1988.

Ruud van Nistelrooy (Manchester Utd.) holds the new record for scoring in most consecutive Premiership matches in one season – 8 (11 goals) in December-January, 2001-02. He repeated the feat in the last 8 Premiership games (13 goals, including 5 penalties and 2 hat-tricks) of season 2002–03.

Ian Wright scored on 12 successive first-team appearances, including 7 Premiership, for Arsenal (Sept. 15-Nov. 23, 1994).

50-GOAL PLAYERS

With **52** goals for **Wolves** in 1987-8 (34 League, 12 Sherpa Van Trophy, 3 Littlewoods Cup, 3 F.A. Cup), **Steve Bull** became the first player to score 50 in a season for a League club since **Terry Bly** for 4th Division newcomers Peterborough Utd. in 1960-1. Bly's 54 comprised 52 League goals and 2 in the F.A. Cup, and included 7 hat-tricks, still a post-war League record.

Bull was again the country's top scorer with 50 goals in season 1988-9: 37 League, 2 Littlewoods Cup and 11 Sherpa Van Trophy.

Between Bly and Bull, the highest individual scoring total for a season was 49 by two players: Ted MacDougall (Bournemouth 1970-1, 42 League, 7 F.A. Cup) and Clive Allen (Tottenham 1986-7, 33 League, 12 Littlewoods Cup, 4 F.A. Cup).

HOT SHOTS

Jimmy Greaves was First Division top scorer (League goals) six times in 11 seasons: 32 for Chelsea (1958-9), 41 for Chelsea (1960-1) and, for Tottenham, 37 in 1962-3, 35 in 1963-4, 29 in 1964-5 (joint top) and 27 in 1968-9.

Brian Clough (Middlesbrough) was the Second Division's leading scorer in three successive seasons: 40 goals in 1957-8, 42 in 1958-9 and 39 in 1959-60.

John Hickton (Middlesbrough) was top Div. 2 scorer three times in four seasons: 24 goals in 1967-8, 24 in 1969-70 and 25 in 1970-1.

MOST HAT-TRICKS

Nine by **George Camsell** (Middlesbrough) in Div. 2, 1926-7, is the record for one season. Most League hat-tricks in career: 37 by **Dixie Dean** for Tranmere Rov. and Everton (1924-38).

Most **top division** hat-tricks in a season since last war: six by **Jimmy Greaves** for Chelsea (1960-1). **Alan Shearer** scored five hat-tricks for Blackburn Rov. in the Premier League, season 1995-96.

Frank Osborne (Tottenham) scored three consecutive hat-tricks in Div. 1 in October-November 1925, against Liverpool, Leicester City (away) and West Ham Utd.

Tom Jennings (Leeds Utd.) scored hat-tricks in three successive First Div. matches (Sept-Oct, 1926): 3 goals v Arsenal, 4 at Liverpool, 4 v Blackburn Rov. Leeds Utd. were relegated at the end of the season.

Jack Balmer (Liverpool) scored only three hat-tricks in a 17-year career - in successive First Div. matches (Nov. 1946): 3 v Portsmouth, 4 at Derby Co., 3 v Arsenal. No other Liverpool player scored during that 10-goal sequence by Balmer.

Gilbert Alsop scored hat-tricks in three successive matches for Walsall in Div. 3 South in April 1939: 3 at Swindon Town, 3 v Bristol City and 4 v Swindon Town.

Alf Lythgoe scored hat-tricks in three successive games for Stockport Co. (Div. 3 North) in March 1934: 3 v Darlington, 3 at Southport and 4 v Wrexham.

TRIPLE HAT-TRICKS

There have been at least three instances of **3 hat-tricks being scored** for **one team** in a Football League match:-

April 21, 1909: Enoch West, Billy Hooper and Alfred Spouncer scored 3 apiece for Nott'm. Forest (12-0 v Leicester Fosse, Div. 1).

March 3, 1962: Ron Barnes, Wyn Davies and Roy Ambler registered hat-tricks in Wrexham's 10-1 win against Hartlepool Utd. (Div. 4).

November 7, 1987: Tony Adcock, Paul Stewart and David White each scored 3 goals for Manchester City in 10-1 win at home to Huddersfield Town (Div. 2).

For the first time in the Premiership, **three hat-tricks** were completed **on one day** (September 23, 1995): Tony Yeboah for Leeds Utd. at Wimbledon; Alan Shearer for Blackburn Rov. v Coventry City; and Robbie Fowler with 4 goals for Liverpool v Bolton Wand.

In the F.A. Cup, **Jack Carr**, **George Elliott** and **Walter Tinsley** each scored 3 in Middlesbrough's 9-3 first round win against Goole in Jan. 1915. **Les Allen** scored 5, **Bobby Smith** 4 and **Cliff Jones** 3 when Tottenham beat Crewe Alexandra 13-2 in a fourth-round replay in February 1960.

HAT-TRICKS v THREE 'KEEPERS

When West Ham Utd. beat Newcastle Utd. 8-1 (Div.1) at home on April 21, 1986 **Alvin Martin** scored 3 goals against different 'keepers: Martin Thomas injured a shoulder and was replaced, in turn, by outfield players Chris Hedworth and Peter Beardsley.

Jock Dodds of Lincoln City had done the same **against** West Ham Utd. on December 18, 1948, scoring past **Ernie Gregory**, **Tommy Moroney** and **George Dick**. The Hammers lost 3-4.

David Herd (Manchester Utd.) scored against three Sunderland goalkeepers (Jim Montgomery, Charlie Hurley and Johnny Parke) in 5-0 First Division home win on Nov. 26, 1966.

Brian Clark, of Bournemouth, scored against three Rotherham Utd. goalkeepers (Jim McDonagh,, Conal Gilbert and Michael Leng twice) in 7-2 win at Rotherham Utd. (Div. 3) on Oct. 10, 1972.

On Oct. 16, 1993 (Div.3) **Chris Pike** (Hereford) scored a hat-trick against different goalkeepers. Opponents Colchester Utd., beaten 5-0, became the first team in League history to have two 'keepers sent off in the same game.

Joe Bradford of Birmingham City scored three hat-tricks in eight days in September 1929-30 v Newcastle Utd. (won 5-1) on the 21st, 5 for the Football League v Irish League (7-2) on the 25th, and 3 in his club's 5-7 defeat away to Blackburn Rov. on the 28th.

PREMIERSHIP DOUBLE HAT-TRICK

Robert Pires and **Jermaine Pennant** each scored 3 goals in Arsenal's 6–1 win at home to Southampton (May 7, 2003).

TON UP – BOTH ENDS

Manchester City are the only club to **score and concede** a century of League goals in the same season. When fifth in the 1957-8 Championship, they scored 104 goals and gave away 100.

TOURNAMENT TOP SHOTS

Most individual goals in a World Cup Final series: 13 by **Just Fontaine** for France, in Sweden 1958.

Most in European Championship Finals: 9 by **Michel Platini** for France, in France 1984.

MOST GOALS ON CLUB DEBUT

Jim Dyet scored **eight** in King's Park's 12-2 win against Forfar Athletic (Scottish Div. 2, Jan. 2, 1930).

Len Shackleton scored **six** times in Newcastle Utd.'s 13-0 win v Newport County (Div. 2, Oct. 5, 1946) in the week he joined them from Bradford Park Avenue.

MOST GOALS ON LEAGUE DEBUT

Five by **George Hilsdon**, for Chelsea (9-2) v Glossop, Div. 2 Sept. 1, 1906.

Alan Shearer, with three goals for Southampton (4-2) v Arsenal, April 9, 1988, became, at 17, the youngest player to score a First Division hat-trick on his full debut.

CLEAN-SHEET RECORDS

On the way to promotion from Div. 3 in season 1995-6, **Gillingham's** ever-present goalkeeper **Jim Stannard** set a clean-sheet record. In 46 matches, he achieved 29 shut-outs (17 at home, 12 away), beating the 28 by Ray Clemence for Liverpool (42 matches in Div. 1, 1978-9) and the previous best in a 46-match programme of 28 by Port Vale (Div. 3 North, 1953-4). In conceding only 20 League goals in 1995-6, Gillingham created a defensive record for the lower divisions.

Chris Woods, Rangers' England goalkeeper, set a British record in season 1986-7 by going 1,196 minutes without conceding a goal. The sequence began in the UEFA Cup match against Borussia Moenchengladbach on Nov. 26, 1986 and ended when Rangers were sensationally beaten 1-0 at home by Hamilton in the Scottish Cup 3rd. Round on Jan. 31, 1987 with a 70th.-minute goal by Adrian Sprott.

The previous British record of 1,156 minutes without a goal conceded was held by Aberdeen goalkeeper **Bobby Clark** (season 1970-1).

There have been three instances of clubs keeping 11 consecutive clean sheets in the Football League: Millwall (Div. 3 South, 1925-6), York City (Div. 3, 1973-4) and Reading (Div. 4, 1978-9). In his sequence, Reading goalkeeper **Steve Death** set the existing League shut-out record of 1,103 minutes.

Mark Leonard (Chesterfield) kept a clean sheet in 8 consecutive Div.3 away games (Jan./April 1994). Believed an away-match record in British football.

Sasa Ilic remained unbeaten for over 14 hours with 9 successive shut-outs (7 in FL Div. 1, 2 in play-offs) to equal a Charlton Athletic club record in Apr./May 1998. He had 12 clean sheets in 17 first team games after winning promotion from the reserves with 6 successive clean sheets.

Sebastiano Rossi kept a clean sheet in 8 successive away matches for AC Milan (Nov. 1993-Apr. 1994).

A world record of 1,275 minutes without conceding a goal was set in 1990-1 by **Abel Resino**, the Atletico Madrid goalkeeper. He was finally beaten by Sporting Gijon's Enrique in Atletico's 3-1 win on March 19, 1991.

In International football, the record is held by **Dino Zoff** with a shut-out for Italy (Sept. 1972 to June 1974) lasting 1,142 minutes.

LOW SCORING

Fewest goals by any club in season in Football League: **24** by **Stoke City** (Div. 1, 42 matches, 1984-5); **24** by **Watford** (Div. 2, 42 matches, 1971-2). In 46-match programme, **27** by **Stockport Co.** (Div. 3, 1969-70).

Arsenal were the lowest Premier League scorers in its opening season (1992-3) with 40 goals in 42 matches, but won both domestic cup competitions. In subsequent seasons the lowest Premier League scorers were **Ipswich Town** (35) in 1993-4, **Crystal Palace** (34) in 1994-5, **Manchester City** (33) in 1995-6 and **Leeds Utd.** (28) in 1996-7 until **Sunderland** set the Premiership's new fewest-goals record with only 21 in 2002-03.

LONG TIME NO SCORE

The world International non-scoring record was set by **Northern Ireland** when they played 13 matches and 1,298 minutes without a goal. The sequence began against Poland on Feb. 13, 2002 and ended 2 years and 5 days later when David Healy scored against Norway (1-4) in Belfast on Feb. 18, 2004.

Longest non-scoring sequences in Football League: 11 matches by **Coventry City** in 1919-20 (Div. 2); 11 matches by **Hartlepool Utd.** in 1992-3 (Div. 2). After beating Crystal Palace 1-0 in the F.A. Cup 3rd round on Jan. 2, they went 13 games and 2 months without scoring (11 League, 1 F.A. Cup, 1 Autoglass Trophy). The sequence ended after 1,227 blank minutes with a 1-1 draw at Blackpool (League) on March 6.

In the **Premier League** (Oct.-Jan. season 1994-5) Crystal Palace failed to score in nine consecutive matches.

The British non-scoring club record is held by **Stirling Albion**: 14 consecutive matches (13 League, 1 Scottish Cup) and 1,292 minutes play, from Jan. 31, 1981 until Aug. 8, 1981 (when they lost 4-1 to Falkirk in the League Cup).

In season 1971-2, **Mansfield Town** did not score in any of their first nine home games in Div. 3. They were relegated on goal difference of minus two.

F.A. CUP CLEAN SHEETS

Most consecutive F.A. Cup matches without conceding a goal: 11 by **Bradford City**. The sequence spanned 8 rounds, from 3rd. in 1910-11 to 4th. Round replay in 1911-12, and included winning the Cup in 1911.

ATTENDANCES

GREATEST WORLD CROWDS

World Cup, Maracana Stadium, Rio de Janeiro, July 16, 1950. Final match (Brazil v Uruguay) attendance 199,850; receipts £125,000.

Total attendance in three matches (including play-off) between Santos (Brazil) and AC Milan for the Inter-Continental Cup (World Club Championship) 1963, exceeded 375,000.

BRITISH RECORD CROWDS

Most to pay: 149,547, Scotland v England, at Hampden Park, Glasgow, April 17, 1937. This was the first all-ticket match in Scotland (receipts £24,000).

At Scottish F.A. Cup Final: 146,433, Celtic v Aberdeen, at Hampden Park, April 24, 1937. Estimated another 20,000 shut out.

For British club match (apart from a Cup Final): 143,470, Rangers v Hibernian, at Hampden Park, March 27, 1948 (Scottish Cup semi-final).

F.A. Cup Final: 126,047, Bolton Wand. v West Ham Utd., at Wembley, April 28, 1923. Estimated 150,000 in stadium.

World Cup Qualifying Ties: 120,000, Cameroon v Morocco, Yaounde, November 29, 1981; 107,580, Scotland v Poland, Hampden Park, October 13, 1965.

European Cup: 135,826, Celtic v Leeds Utd. (semi-final, 2nd. leg) at Hampden Park, Glasgow, April 15, 1970.

European Cup Final: 127,621, Real Madrid v Eintracht Frankfurt, at Hampden Park, Glasgow, May 18, 1960.

European Cup-Winners' Cup Final: 100,000, West Ham Utd. v TSV Munich, at Wembley, May 19, 1965.

Scottish League: 118,567, Rangers v Celtic, January 2, 1939.

Scottish League Cup Final: 107,609, Celtic v Rangers, at Hampden Park, October 23, 1965.

Football League old format: First Div.: 83,260, Manchester Utd. v Arsenal, January 17, 1948 (at Maine Road); **Second Div.**: 70,302 Tottenham v Southampton, February 25, 1950; **Third Div. South**: 51,621, Cardiff City v Bristol City, April 7, 1947; **Third Div. North**: 49,655, Hull City v Rotherham Utd., December 25, 1948; **Third Div.**: 49,309, Sheffield Wed. v Sheffield Utd., December 26, 1979; **Fourth Div.**: 37,774, Crystal Palace v Millwall, March 31, 1961.

F.A. Premier League: 67,758, Manchester Utd. v Southampton, January 31, 2004.

Football League – New Div. 1: 41,214, Sunderland v Stoke City, April 25, 1998; **New Div. 2**: 32,471, Manchester City v York City, May 8, 1999; **New Div. 3**: 22,319 Hull City v Hartlepool Utd., December 26, 2002.

In English Provinces: 84,569, Manchester City v Stoke City (F.A. Cup 6th Round), March 3, 1934.

Record for Under-21 International: 32,865 England v France at Derby Co., February 9, 1999.

Record for friendly match: 104,679, Rangers v Eintracht Frankfurt, at Hampden Park, Glasgow, October 17, 1961.

Record Football League aggregate (season): 41,271,414 (1948-9) – 88 clubs.

Record Football League aggregate (single day): 1,269,934, December 27, 1949, previous day, 1,226,098.

Record average home League attendance for season: 67,640 by Manchester Utd. in 2003-04.

Long-ago League attendance aggregates: 10,929,000 in 1906-07 (40 clubs); 28,132,933 in 1937-8 (88 clubs).

Last 1m. crowd aggregate, League: 1,007,200, December 27, 1971.

Record Amateur match attendance: 100,000 for F.A. Amateur Cup Final, Pegasus v Harwich & Parkeston at Wembley, April 11, 1953.

Record Cup-tie aggregate: 265,199, at two matches between Rangers and Morton, in the Scottish Cup Final, 1947-8.

Abandoned match attendance records: In England – 63,480 at Newcastle Utd. v Swansea City F.A. Cup 3rd round, Jan. 10, 1953, abandoned 8 mins (0-0), fog.

In Scotland: 94,596 at Scotland v Austria (4-1), Hampden Park, May 8, 1963. Referee Jim Finney ended play (79 minutes) after Austria had two players sent off and one carried off.

What is still **Colchester Utd.'s** record crowd (19,072) was for the F.A. Cup 1st round tie v Reading on Nov. 27, 1948, abandoned 35 minutes (0-0), fog.

SMALLEST CROWDS

Smallest League attendances: 13, Stockport Co. v Leicester City (Div. 2, May 7, 1921; played at Old Trafford – Stockport ground closed); 469, Thames v Luton Town (Div. 3 South, December 6, 1930).

Lowest post-war League attendance: 450 Rochdale v Cambridge Utd. (Div. 3, February 5, 1974).

Lowest F.A. Premier League crowd: 3,039 for Wimbledon v Everton, Jan. 26, 1993 (smallest top-division attendance since war).

Lowest Saturday post-war top-division crowd: 3,231 for Wimbledon v Luton Town, Sept. 7, 1991 (Div. 1).

Lowest Football League crowds, new format – Div. 1: 849 for Wimbledon v Rotherham Utd., (Div. 1) October 29, 2002 (smallest att. in top two divisions since war); 1,054 Wimbledon v Wigan Athletic (Div. 1), Sept. 13, 2003 in club's last home match when sharing Selhurst Park; **Div. 2:** 1,077, Hartlepool Utd. v Cardiff City, March 22, 1994; **Div. 3:** 739, Doncaster Rov. v Barnet, March 3, 1998.

Other low First Division crowds since the war: 3,121 for Wimbledon v Sheffield W., Oct. 2, 1991; 3,231 for Wimbledon v Luton Town, Sept. 7, 1991; 3,270 for Wimbledon v Coventry City, Dec. 28, 1991; 3,496 for Wimbledon v Luton Town, Feb. 14, 1990.

Lowest top-division crowd at a major ground since the war: 4,554 for Arsenal v Leeds Utd. (May 5, 1966) – fixture clashed with live TV coverage of Cup-Winners' Cup Final (Liverpool v Borussia Dortmund).

Smallest League Cup attendances: 612, Halifax Town v Tranmere Rov. (1st Round, 2nd Leg) September 6, 2000; 664, Wimbledon v Rotherham Utd. (3rd Round), November 5, 2002.

Smallest League Cup attendance at top-division ground: 1,987 for Wimbledon v Bolton Wand. (2nd Round, 2nd Leg) Oct. 6, 1992.

Smallest Wembley crowds for England matches: 15,628 v Chile (Rous Cup, May 23, 1989 – affected by Tube strike); 20,038 v Colombia (Friendly, Sept. 6, 1995); 21,432 v Czech. (Friendly, Apr. 25, 1990); 21,142 v Japan (Umbro Cup, June 3, 1995); 23,600 v Wales (British Championship, Feb. 23, 1983); 23,659 v Greece (Friendly, May 17, 1994); 23,951 v East Germany (Friendly, Sept. 12, 1984); 24,000 v N. Ireland (British Championship, Apr. 4, 1984); 25,756 v Colombia (Rous Cup, May 24, 1988); 25,837 v Denmark (Friendly, Sept. 14, 1988).

Smallest Int. modern crowd: 221 for Poland v N. Ireland (4-1, friendly) at Limassol, Cyprus, on February 13, 2002. Played at neutral venue at Poland's World Cup training base.

Smallest Int. modern crowds at home: N.Ireland: 2,500 v Chile (Belfast, May 26, 1989 – clashed with ITV live screening of Liverpool v Arsenal Championship decider); **Scotland:** 7,843 v N.Ireland (Hampden Park, May 6, 1969); **Wales:** 2,315 v N.Ireland (Wrexham, May 27, 1982).

Smallest attendance for post-war England match: 2,378 v San Marino (World Cup) at Bologna (Nov. 17, 1993). Tie clashed with Italy v Portugal (World Cup) shown live on Italian TV.

Smallest paid attendance for British first-class match: 29 for Clydebank v East Stirling, CIS Scottish League Cup 1st Round, July 31, 1999. Played at Morton's Cappielow Park ground, shared by Clydebank, the match clashed with the Tall Ships Race which attracted 200,000 to the area.

NO SPECTATORS

F.A. Cup 3rd. Round, 2nd. Replay, March 3, 1915: Norwich City 0, Bradford City 2, at Lincoln. Played behind closed doors, so that vital war work was not disrupted.

Cup-Winners' Cup, 1st. Round, 2nd. Leg, October 1, 1980: West Ham Utd. 5, Castilla (Spain) 1. UEFA ordered match to be played behind closed doors after misconduct by West Ham Utd. fans in 1st. Leg in Madrid (Castilla 3, West Ham 1).

European Championship, Qualifying Round, April 2, 2003: Slovakia 4, Liechtenstein 0 at Spartak Stadium, Trnava. UEFA ordered match to be played behind closed doors following racial abuse of England players by Slovakia crowd in Bratislava, October 12.

F.A. CUP CROWD RECORD (OUTSIDE FINAL)

The first F.A. Cup-tie shown on closed-circuit TV (5th. Round, Saturday, March 11, 1967, kick-off 7pm) drew a total of 105,000 spectators to Goodison Park and Anfield. This is the biggest attendance for a single F.A. Cup match other than the Final. At Goodison, 64,851 watched the match 'for real', while 40,149 saw the TV version on eight giant screens at Anfield. Everton beat Liverpool 1-0.

LOWEST SEMI-FINAL CROWD

The smallest F.A. Cup semi-final attendance since the war was 17,987 for Manchester Utd. v Crystal Palace replay, at Villa Park on April 12, 1995. Crystal Palace supporters largely boycotted tie after a fan died in car-park clash outside pub in Walsall before first match. Previous lowest: 25,963 for Wimbledon v Luton Town, at Tottenham on April 9, 1988.

Lowest quarter-final crowd since the war: 8,735 for Chesterfield v Wrexham on March 9, 1997.

Smallest F.A. Cup 3rd. Round attendances for matches between League clubs: 1,833 for Chester City v Bournemouth (at Macclesfield Town) Jan. 5, 1991; 1,966 for Aldershot v Oxford Utd., Jan. 10, 1987.

PRE-WEMBLEY CUP FINAL CROWDS

AT CRYSTAL PALACE

1895	42,560	1902	48,036	1908	74,967
1896	48,036	Replay	33,050	1909	67,651
1897	65,891	1903	64,000	1910	76,980
1898	62,017	1904	61,734	1911	69,098
1899	73,833	1905	101,117	1912	54,434
1900	68,945	1906	75,609	1913	120,028
1901	110,802	1907	84,584	1914	72,778

AT OLD TRAFFORD

1915	50,000

AT STAMFORD BRIDGE

1920	50,018	1921	72,805	1922	53,000

RECEIPTS RECORDS

Wembley Stadium underwent its first considerable alteration during 1962-3 in preparation for the World Cup in 1966. Higher admission fees at the 1963 F.A. Cup Final resulted in 100,000 spectators paying a record £89,000.
This is how Wembley's receipts records subsequently rose:

1968 F.A. Cup Final (Everton v W.B.A.)	£110,000
1968 European Cup Final (Manchester Utd. v Benfica)	£120,000
1976 F.A. Cup Final (Southampton v Manchester Utd.)	£420,000
1978 F.A. Cup Final (Ipswich Town v Arsenal)	£500,000
1981 England v Hungary (World Cup)	£671,000
1982 F.A. Cup Final (Tottenham v Q.P.R.)	£886,000
(plus £605,000 for replay)	
1984 F.A. Cup Final (Everton v Watford)	£919,000
*1985 F.A. Cup Final (Manchester Utd. v Everton)	£1,100,000
1986 F.A. Cup Final (Liverpool v Everton)	£1,100,000
†1987 League Cup Final (Arsenal v Liverpool)	£1,000,000
1987 F.A. Cup Final (Coventry City v Tottenham)	£1,286,737
1988 F.A. Cup Final (Wimbledon v Liverpool)	£1,422,814
1989 F.A. Cup Final (Liverpool v Everton)	£1,600,000
1990 League Cup Final (Nott'm Forest v Oldham Athletic)	£1,650,000
1990 F.A. Cup Final (Manchester Utd. v Crystal Palace – first match)	£2,000,000
1991 League Cup Final (Manchester Utd. v Sheffield Wed.)	£2,000,000
1991 F.A. Cup Final (Nott'm F. v Tottenham)	£2,016,000
1992 F.A. Cup Final (Liverpool v Sunderland)	£2,548,174
1993 F.A. Cup Final (Arsenal v Sheffield W. – first match)	£2,818,000
(Replay took receipts for both matches to £4,695,200)	
1994 F.A. Cup Final record (Manchester Utd. v Chelsea)	£2,962,167
1997 League Cup Final record (Leicester City v Middlesbrough)	£2,750,000
1998 League Cup Final record (Chelsea v Middlesbrough)	£2,983,000
•2000 F.A. Cup Final record (Chelsea v Aston Villa)	£3,100,000

(* Britain's first £1m. gate; †First £1m. gate for League Cup Final; • British club match receipts record)

Record England match receipts: £4,100,000 (v. Germany, Wembley, European Championship semi-final, June 26, 1992 - att: 75,862)

EARLY CUP FINAL RECEIPTS

1885 Blackburn Rov. v Queens Park	£442
1913 Aston Villa v Sunderland	£9,406
1923 Bolton Wand. v West Ham Utd., first Wembley Final	£27,776
1939 Portsmouth v Wolves	£29,000
1946 Derby Co. v Charlton Athletic	£45,000

WORLD RECORD MATCH RECEIPTS

£4,300,000 for **World Cup Final**, Argentina v West Germany (Rome, July 8, 1990).

INTERNATIONAL RECORDS
MOST APPEARANCES

Peter Shilton, England goalkeeper, then aged 40, retired from International football after the 1990 World Cup Finals with the European record number of caps – 125. Previous record (119) was set by **Pat Jennings**, Northern Ireland's goalkeeper from 1964-86, who retired on his 41st birthday during the 1986 World Cup in Mexico. Shilton's England career spanned 20 seasons from his debut against East Germany at Wembley on Nov. 25, 1970.

Four players have completed a century of appearances in full International matches for England. **Billy Wright** of Wolves, was the first, retiring in 1959 with a total of 105 caps. **Bobby Charlton,** of Manchester Utd., beat Wright's record in the World Cup match against West Germany in Leon, Mexico, in June 1970 and **Bobby Moore,** of West Ham Utd., overtook Charlton's 106 caps against Italy in Turin, in June 1973. Moore played 108 times for England, a record that stood until **Shilton** reached 109 against Denmark in Copenhagen (June 7, 1989).

Kenny Dalglish became Scotland's first 100-cap International v Romania (Hampden Park, March 26, 1986).

World's most-capped player: Mohamed Al-Deayea (Saudi Arabia goalkeeper), made his 165th International appearance, v Republic of Ireland (World Cup) at Yokohama, Japan, on June 11, 2002.

Most-capped European goalkeeper: Thomas Ravelli, 143 Internationals for Sweden (1981-97).

Gillian Coultard, (Doncaster Belles), England Women's captain, received a special presentation from Geoff Hurst to mark 100 caps when England beat Holland 1-0 at Upton Park on October 30, 1997. She made her Int. debut at 18 in May 1981, and retired at the end of season 1999-2000 with a record 119 caps (30 goals).

BRITAIN'S MOST-CAPPED PLAYERS

(As at start of season 2004-05)

England

Peter Shilton	125
Bobby Moore	108
Bobby Charlton	106
Billy Wright	105
Bryan Robson	90

Scotland

Kenny Dalglish	102
Jim Leighton	91
Alex McLeish	77
Paul McStay	76
Tommy Boyd	72

Wales

Neville Southall	92
Dean Saunders	75
Peter Nicholas	73
Ian Rush	73
Mark Hughes	72
Joey Jones	72

Northern Ireland

Pat Jennings	119
Mal Donaghy	91
Sammy McIlroy	88

Republic of Ireland

Steve Staunton	102
Niall Quinn	91
Tony Cascarino	88
Paul McGrath	83
Pat Bonner	80
Ray Houghton	73
Liam Brady	72
Frank Stapleton	71
Kevin Moran	71
Andy Townsend	70

MOST ENGLAND CAPS IN ROW

Most consecutive International appearances: 70 by **Billy Wright**, for England from October 1951 to May 1959. He played 105 of England's first 108 post-war matches.

England captains most times: Billy Wright and **Bobby Moore**, 90 each.

England captains – 4 in match (v Serbia & Montenegro at Leicester June 3, 2003): **Michael Owen** was captain for the first half and after the interval the armband passed to **Emile Heskey** (for 15 minutes), **Philip Neville** (26 minutes) and substitute **Jamie Carragher** (9 minutes, including time added).

MOST PLAYERS FROM ONE CLUB IN ENGLAND SIDES

Arsenal supplied seven men (a record) to the England team v Italy at Highbury on November 14, 1934. They were: Frank Moss, George Male, Eddie Hapgood, Wilf Copping, Ray Bowden, Ted Drake and Cliff Bastin. In addition, Arsenal's Tom Whittaker was England's trainer.

Since then until 2001, the most players from one club in an England team was six from **Liverpool** against Switzerland at Wembley in September 1977. The side also included a Liverpool old boy, Kevin Keegan (Hamburg).

Seven **Arsenal** men took part in the England – France (0-2) match at Wembley on February 10, 1999. Goalkeeper David Seaman and defenders Lee Dixon, Tony Adams and Martin Keown lined up for England. Nicolas Anelka (2 goals) and Emmanuel Petit started the match for France and Patrick Vieira replaced Anelka.

Manchester Utd. equalled Arsenal's 1934 record by providing England with seven players in the World Cup qualifier away to Albania on March 28, 2001. Five started the match – David Beckham (captain), Gary Neville, Paul Scholes, Nicky Butt and Andy Cole – and two went on as substitutes: Wes Brown and Teddy Sheringham.

INTERNATIONAL SUBS RECORDS

Malta substituted all 11 players in their 1-2 home defeat against England on June 3, 2000. Six substitutes by England took the total replacements in the match to 17, then an International record.

Most substitutions in match by **England**: 11 in second half by Sven Goran Eriksson against Holland at Tottenham on August 15, 2001; 11 against Italy at Leeds on March 27, 2002; Italy sent on 8 players from the bench – the total of 19 substitutions was then a record for an England match; 11 against Australia at Upton Park on February 12, 2003 (entire England team changed at half-time); 11 against Iceland at City of Manchester Stadium on June 5, 2004.

Forty-three players, a record for an England match, were used in the International against Serbia & Montenegro at Leicester on June 3, 2003. England sent on 10 substitutes in the second half and their opponents changed all 11 players.

Up to the end of season 2003-04, **England coach Sven-Goran Eriksson** had used 166 substitutes in 19 Friendly International matches.

The **Republic of Ireland** sent on 12 second-half substitutes, using 23 players in all, when they beat Russia 2-0 in a friendly International in Dublin on February 13, 2002.

First England substitute: Wolves winger **Jimmy Mullen** replaced injured Jackie Milburn (15 mins.) away to Belgium on May 18, 1950. He scored in a 4-1 win.

ENGLAND'S WORLD CUP-WINNERS

At Wembley, July 30, 1966, 4-2 v West Germany (2-2 after 90 mins), scorers Hurst 3, Peters. Team: Banks; Cohen, Wilson, Stiles, Charlton (J.), Moore (Captain), Ball, Hurst, Charlton (R.), Hunt, Peters. Manager **Alf Ramsey** fielded that same eleven in six successive matches (an England record): the World Cup quarter-final, semi-final and Final, and the first three games of the following season. England wore red shirts in the Final and Her Majesty the Queen presented the Cup to Bobby Moore. The players each received a £1,000 bonus, plus £60 World Cup Final appearance money, all less tax, and Ramsey a £6,000 bonus from the F.A. The match was shown live on TV (in black and white).

BRAZIL'S RECORD RUN

Brazil hold the record for the longest unbeaten sequence in International football: 45 matches from 1993-7. The previous record of 31 matches undefeated was held by Hungary between June 1950 and July 1954.

ENGLAND MATCHES ABANDONED

May 17, 1953 v **Argentina** (Friendly, Buenos Aires) after 23 mins. (0–0) – rain.
   Oct. 29, 1975 v **Czechoslovakia** (Eur. Champ. Qual., Bratislava) after 17 mins. (0–0) – fog. Played next day.
   Feb. 15, 1995 v **Rep. of Ireland** (Friendly, Dublin) after 27 mins. (1–0) – crowd disturbance.

ENGLAND POSTPONEMENT

Nov 21, 1979 v **Bulgaria** (Eur. Champ. qual., Wembley postponed for 24 hours – fog.

ENGLAND UNDER COVER

England played indoors for the first time when they beat Argentina 1-0 in the World Cup at the Sapporo Dome, Japan, on June 7, 2002.

ALL-SEATED INTERNATIONALS

The first **all-seated crowd** (30,000) for a full International in Britain saw **Wales** and **West Germany** draw 0-0 at Cardiff City Arms Park on May 31, 1989. The terraces were closed.
   England's first all-seated International at Wembley was against Yugoslavia (2-1) on December 13, 1989 (attendance 34,796). The terracing behind the goals was closed for conversion to seating.
   The first **full-house all-seated** International at Wembley was for England v Brazil (1-0) on March 28, 1990, when a capacity 80,000 crowd paid record British receipts of £1,200,000.
   Cardiff's new **Millennium Stadium** set attendance records for **Wales** in consecutive friendly Internationals: 66,500 v Finland, March 28, 2000, then 72,500 v Brazil, May 23, 2000 – Britain's first indoor International.

ENGLAND 'ON THE ROAD'

Since Wembley Stadium closed in October 2000, England have played home fixtures at 14 club grounds (to end of season 2003-04): Manchester Utd. (4), Aston Villa (2), Liverpool (2), Manchester City (2), Derby, Tottenham, Newcastle, Leeds, Southampton, West Ham, Sunderland, Leicester, Middlesbrough and Ipswich.

FIRST BLACK CAPS

First black player for **England** in a senior International was Nott'm. Forest full-back **Viv Anderson** against Czechoslovakia at Wembley on November 29, 1978.
   Aston Villa's **Ugo Ehiogu** was **England's** first black captain (U-21 v Holland at Portsmouth, April 27, 1993).
   Paul Ince (Manchester Utd.) became the first black player to captain **England** in a full International (v U.S.A., Boston, June 9, 1993).
   First black British International was **Eddie Parris** (Bradford Park Avenue) for Wales against N. Ireland in Belfast on December 5, 1931.

MOST NEW CAPS IN ENGLAND TEAM

6, **by Sir Alf Ramsey** (v Portugal, April 3, 1974).
   6, by Sven-Goran Eriksson (v Australia, February 12, 2003; 5 at half-time when 11 changes made).

PLAYED FOR MORE THAN ONE COUNTRY

Multi-nationals in senior International football include: **Johnny Carey** (1938-53) – caps Rep. of Ireland 29, N. Ireland 7; **Ferenc Puskas** (1945-62) – caps Hungary 84, Spain 4; **Alfredo di Stefano** (1950-6) – caps Argentina 7, Spain 31; **Ladislav Kubala** (1948-58) – caps, Hungary 3, Czechoslovakia 11, Spain 19, only player to win full Int. honours with 3 countries. Kubala also played in a fourth Int. team, scoring twice for FIFA v England at Wembley in 1953.

Eleven players, including Carey, appeared for both N. Ireland and the Republic of Ireland in seasons directly after the last war.

Cecil Moore, capped by N. Ireland in 1949 when with Glentoran, played for USA v England in 1953.

Hawley Edwards played for England v Scotland in 1874 and for Wales v Scotland in 1876.

Jack Reynolds (Distillery and W.B.A.) played for both Ireland (5 times) and England (8) in the 1890s.

Bobby Evans (Sheffield Utd.) had played 10 times for Wales when capped for England, in 1910-11. He was born in Chester of Welsh parents.

In recent years several players have represented USSR and one or other of the breakaway republics. The same applies to Yugoslavia and its component states. **Josip Weber** played for Croatia in 1992 and made a 5-goal debut for Belgium in 1994.

3-GENERATION INTERNATIONAL FAMILY

When Bournemouth striker **Warren Feeney** was capped away to Liechtenstein on March 27, 2002, he became the third generation of his family to play for N. Ireland. He followed in the footsteps of his grandfather James (capped twice in 1950) and father Warren Snr. (1 in 1976).

FATHERS & SONS CAPPED BY ENGLAND

George Eastham senior (pre-war) and **George Eastham** junior; **Brian Clough** and **Nigel Clough**; **Frank Lampard** senior and **Frank Lampard** junior.

FATHER & SON SAME-DAY CAPS

Iceland made father-and-son Int. history when they beat Estonia 3-0 in Tallin on April 24, 1996. Arnor Gudjohnsen (35) started the match and was replaced (62 mins.) by his 17-year-old son Eidur.

LONGEST UNBEATEN START TO ENGLAND CAREER

By **Steven Gerrard**, 21 matches (W16, D5) 2000–03.

SUCCESSIVE ENGLAND HAT-TRICKS

The last player to score a hat-trick in consecutive England matches was **Dixie Dean** on the summer tour in May 1927, against Belgium (9-1) and Luxembourg (5-2).

POST-WAR HAT-TRICKS v ENGLAND

November 25, 1953, scorer **Nandor Hidegkuti** (England 3, Hungary 6, Wembley); May 11, 1958, scorer **Aleksandar Petakovic** (Yugoslavia 5, England 0, Belgrade); May 17, 1959, scorer **Juan Seminario** (Peru 4, England 1, Lima); June 15, 1988, scorer **Marco Van Basten** (Holland 3, England 1, European Championship, Dusseldorf).

NO-SAVE GOALKEEPERS

Chris Woods did not have one save to make when England beat San Marino 6-0 (World Cup) at Wembley on February 17, 1993. He touched the ball only six times throughout the match.

Gordon Banks had a similar no-save experience when England beat Malta 5-0 (European Championship) at Wembley on May 12, 1971. Malta did not force a goal-kick or corner, and the four times Banks touched the ball were all from back passes.

FOOTBALL'S GOVERNING BODIES

By June 2003, a total of 204 National Associations were members of the Federation Internationale de Football Association (F.I.F.A., founded May, 1904), and the Union of European Football Associations (U.E.F.A., founded June, 1954) embraced 52 countries.
The seven original members of the F.I.F.A. were Belgium, Denmark, France, Holland, Spain, Sweden and Switzerland.

FIFA WORLD YOUTH CHAMPIONSHIP (UNDER-20)

Finals: 1977 (Tunis) Soviet Union 2, Mexico 2 (Soviet won 9-8 on pens.); **1979** (Tokyo) Argentina 3, Soviet Union 1; **1981** (Sydney) W. Germany 4, Qatar 0; **1983** (Mexico City) Brazil 1, Argentina 0; **1985** (Moscow) Brazil 1, Spain 0; **1987** (Santiago) Yugoslavia 1, W. Germany 1 (Yugoslavia won 5-4 on pens.); **1989** (Riyadh) Portugal 2, Nigeria 0; **1991** (Lisbon) Portugal 0, Brazil 0 (Portugal won 4-2 on pens.); **1993** (Sydney) Brazil 2, Ghana 1; **1995** (Qatar) Argentina 2, Brazil 0; **1997** (Kuala Lumpur) Argentina 2, Uruguay 1; **1999** (Lagos) Spain 4, Japan 0; **2001** (Buenos Aires) Argentina 3, Ghana 0; **2002**, tournament not played; **2003** (Dubai) Brazil 1, Spain 0.

FAMOUS CLUB FEATS

The Double: There have been ten instances of a club winning the Football League/Premiership title and the F.A. Cup in the same season. **Manchester Utd.** and **Arsenal** have each done so three times:-
Preston N.E. 1888-89; **Aston Villa** 1896-97; **Tottenham** 1960-61; **Arsenal** 1970-71, 1997-98, 2001-02; **Liverpool** 1985-86; **Manchester Utd.** 1993-94, 1995-96, 1998-99.
The Treble: Liverpool were the first English club to win three major competitions in one season when in 1983-84, Joe Fagan's first season as manager, they were League Champions, League Cup winners and European Cup winners.
Alex Ferguson's **Manchester Utd.** achieved an even more prestigious treble in 1998-99, completing the domestic double of Premiership and F.A. Cup and then winning the European Cup.
Liverpool completed a unique treble by an English club with three cup successes under Gerard Houllier in season 2000-01: the League Cup, F.A. Cup and UEFA Cup.
Liverpool the first English club to win five major trophies in one calendar year (February-August 2001): League Cup, F.A. Cup, UEFA Cup, Charity Shield, UEFA Super Cup.
As Champions in season 2001-02, **Arsenal** set a Premiership record by winning the last 13 matches. They were the first top-division club since Preston N.E. in the League's inaugural season (1888-9) to maintain an unbeaten away record.
(See Scottish section for treble feats by Rangers and Celtic.)
Home Runs: Sunderland lost only one home Div. 1 game out of 73 in five seasons, 1891 to 1896. **Brentford** won all 21 home games in 1929-30 in the Third Division (South). Others have won all home games in a smaller programme.
Record Home Run: Liverpool went 85 competitive first-team games unbeaten at home between losing 2-3 to Birmingham City on January 21, 1978 and 1-2 to Leicester City on January 31, 1981. They comprised 63 in the League, 9 League Cup, 7 in European competition and 6 F.A. Cup. Leicester were relegated that season.
Millwall were unbeaten at home in the League for 59 consecutive matches from 1964-67.
Third to First: Charlton Athletic, in 1936, became the first club to advance from the Third to First Division in successive seasons. **Queen's Park Rangers** were the second club to achieve the feat in 1968, and **Oxford Utd.** did it in 1984 and 1985 as Champions of

each division. Subsequently, **Derby Co.** (1987), **Middlesbrough** (1988), **Sheffield Utd.** (1990) and **Notts Co.** (1991) climbed from Third Division to First in consecutive seasons.

Watford won successive promotions from the modern Second Division to the Premier League in 1997-8, 1998-9. **Manchester City** equalled the feat in 1998-9, 1999-2000.

Fourth to First: Northampton Town, in 1965 became the first club to rise from the Fourth to the First Division. **Swansea City** climbed from the Fourth Division to the First (three promotions in four seasons), 1977-8 to 1980-1. **Wimbledon** repeated the feat, 1982-3 to 1985-6 **Watford** did it in five seasons, 1977-8 to 1981-2. **Carlisle Utd.** climbed from Fourth Division to First, 1964-74.

Non-League to First: When **Wimbledon** finished third in the Second Division in 1986, they completed the phenomenal rise from non-League football (Southern League) to the First Division in nine years. Two years later they won the F.A. Cup.

Tottenham, in 1960-1, not only carried off the First Division Championship and the F.A. Cup for the first time that century but set up other records by opening with 11 successive wins, registering most First Division wins (31), most away wins in the League's history (16), and equalling Arsenal's First Division records of 66 points and 33 away points. They already held the Second Division record of 70 points (1919-20).

Arsenal, in 1993, became the first club to win both English domestic cup competitions (F.A. Cup and League Cup) in the same season. **Liverpool** repeated the feat in 2000-01.

Preston N.E., in season 1888-9, won the first League Championship without losing a match and the F.A. Cup without having a goal scored against them. Only other English clubs to remain unbeaten through a League season were **Liverpool** (Div. 2 Champions in 1893-4) and **Arsenal** (Premiership Champions 2003-04).

Bury, in 1903, also won the F.A. Cup without conceding a goal.

Everton won Div. 2, Div. 1 and the F.A. Cup in successive seasons, 1930-1, 1931-2, 1932-3.

Liverpool won the League Championship in 1964, the F.A. Cup in 1965 and the Championship again in 1966. In 1978 they became the first British club to win the European Cup in successive seasons. **Nott'm. Forest** repeated the feat in 1979 and 1980.

Liverpool won the League Championship six times in eight seasons (1976-83) under **Bob Paisley's** management.

Sir Alex Ferguson's **Manchester Utd.** have won the F.A. Premier League in eight of its twelve seasons (1993-2004). They were runners-up twice and third twice.

Most Premiership wins in season: 28 by Manchester Utd. (1999-2000).

Biggest points-winning margin by League Champions: 18 by Manchester Utd. (1999-2000).

COVENTRY UNIQUE

Coventry City are the only club to have played in the Premier League, all four previous divisions of the Football League and in both sections (North and South) of the old Third Division.

Grimsby Town were the other club to play in the four divisions of the Football League and its two Third Division sections.

FAMOUS UPS & DOWNS

Sunderland: Relegated in 1958 after maintaining First Division status since their election to the Football League in 1890. They dropped into Division 3 for the first time in 1987.

Aston Villa: Relegated with **Preston N.E.** to the Third Division in 1970.

Arsenal up: When the League was extended in 1919, Woolwich Arsenal (sixth in Division Two in 1914-15, last season before the war) were elected to Division One. Arsenal have been in the top division ever since.

Tottenham down: At that same meeting in 1919 Chelsea (due for relegation) retained their place in Division One but the bottom club (Tottenham) had to go down to Division Two.

Preston N.E. and Burnley down: Preston N.E., the first League Champions in season 1888-9, dropped into the Fourth Division in 1985. So did Burnley, also among the League's original members in 1888. In 1986, Preston N.E. had to apply for re-election.

Wolves' fall: Wolves, another of the Football League's original members, completed the fall from First Division to Fourth in successive seasons (1984-5-6).

Lincoln City out: Lincoln City became the first club to suffer automatic demotion from the Football League when they finished bottom of Div. 4, on goal difference, in season 1986-7. They were replaced by Scarborough, champions of the GM Vauxhall Conference. Lincoln City regained their place a year later.

Swindon Town up and down: In the 1990 play-offs, Swindon Town won promotion to the First Division for the first time, but remained in the Second Division because of financial irregularities.

MOST CHAMPIONSHIP WINS

Liverpool, by winning the First Division in 1976-7, established a record of 10 Championship victories. They later increased the total to 18. **Manchester Utd.** are second with 15 League titles (7 Football League, 8 Premier League) and **Arsenal** third with 13 (10 Football League, 3 Premier League).

LONGEST CURRENT MEMBERS OF TOP DIVISION

Arsenal (since 1919), **Everton** (1954), **Liverpool** (1962), **Manchester Utd.** (1975), **Southampton** (1978).

CHAMPIONS: FEWEST PLAYERS

Liverpool used only 14 players (five ever-present) when they won the League Championship in season 1965-6. **Aston Villa** also called on no more than 14 players to win the title in 1980-81, with seven ever-present.

UNBEATEN CHAMPIONS

Only two clubs have become Champions of England with an unbeaten record: **Preston N.E.** as the Football League's first winners in 1888-9 (22 matches) and **Arsenal,** Premiership winners in 2003-04 (38 matches).

LEAGUE HAT-TRICKS

Huddersfield Town created a record in 1924-5-6 by winning the League Championship three years in succession.

Arsenal equalled this League hat-trick in 1933-4-5, **Liverpool** in 1982-3-4 and **Manchester United** in 1999-2000-01.

'SUPER DOUBLE' WINNERS

Since the war, there have been three instances of players appearing in and then managing F.A. Cup and Championship-winning teams:

Joe Mercer: Player in Arsenal Championship teams 1948, 1953 and in their 1950 F.A. Cup side; manager of Manchester City when they won Championship 1968, F.A. Cup 1969.

Kenny Dalglish: Player in Liverpool Championship-winning teams 1979, 1980, 1982, 1983, 1984, player-manager 1986, 1988, 1990; player-manager when Liverpool won F.A. Cup (to complete Double) 1986; manager of Blackburn Rov., Champions 1995.

George Graham: Played in Arsenal's Double-winning team in 1971, and as manager took them to Championship success in 1989 and 1991 and the F.A. Cup – League Cup double in 1993.

BACK FIRST TIME

The following clubs won promotion the season after losing their position in the First Division of the League (*as Champions):

Sheffield Wed. *1899-1900, *1951-2, *1955-6, *1958-9, 1990-1; **Bolton Wand.** 1899-1900, *1908-9, 1910-11; **W.B.A.** *1901-2; **Manchester City** *1902-3, *1909-10, 1950-1; **Burnley** *1897-8.
Small Heath 1902-3; **Liverpool** *1904-5; **Nott'm. Forest** *1906-7; **Preston N.E.** *1912-13, 1914-15; **Notts Co.** *1913-14; **Derby Co.** *1914-15.
Tottenham *1919-20, 1977-8; **Leeds Utd.** 1927-8, 1931-2; **Middlesbrough** *1928-9; **Everton** *1930-1; **Manchester Utd.** 1937-8, *1974-5; **Huddersfield Town** 1952-3.
Aston Villa *1959-60, 1987-8; **Chelsea** 1962-3; *1988-9; **Norwich City** 1974-5, 1981-2, *1985-6; **Wolves** 1976-7, 1982-3; **Birmingham City** 1979-80, 1984-5.

West Ham Utd., relegated in 1992, won promotion to the **Premier League** in 1993; *Crystal Palace** and **Nott'm. Forest** both returned to the **Premiership** in 1994, a year after relegation; so did **Leicester City** in 1996, *Bolton Wand.** in 1997, *Nott'm Forest** and **Middlesbrough** in 1998, *Charlton Athletic** in 2000 *Manchester City** in 2002, **Leicester City** in 2003 and **W.B.A.** in 2004.

ORIGINAL TWELVE

The original 12 members of the Football League (formed in 1888) were: **Accrington, Aston Villa, Blackburn Rov., Bolton Wand., Burnley, Derby Co., Everton, Notts Co., Preston N.E., Stoke City, W.B.A.** and **Wolves.**
   Results on the opening day (September 8, 1888): Bolton Wand. 3, Derby Co. 6; Everton 2, Accrington 1; Preston N.E. 5, Burnley 2; Stoke City 0, W.B.A. 2; Wolves 1, Aston Villa 1. Preston N.E. had the biggest first-day crowd: 6,000. Blackburn Rov. and Notts Co. did not play that day. They kicked off a week later (September 15) – Blackburn Rov. 5, Accrington 5; Everton 2, Notts Co. 1.

FASTEST CLIMBS

Three promotions in four seasons by two clubs – **Swansea City:** 1978 third in Div.4; 1979 third in Div.3; 1981 third in Div.2; **Wimbledon:** 1983 Champions of Div.4; 1984 second in Div.3; 1986 third in Div.2.

MERSEYSIDE RECORD

Liverpool is the only city to have staged top-division football – through Everton and/or Liverpool – in **every season** since League football began in 1888.

EARLIEST RELEGATIONS POST-WAR

From top division: **Q.P.R.** went down from the old First Division on March 29, 1969. From modern First Division: **Stockport Co.** on March 16, 2002, with 7 matches still to play; **Wimbledon** on April 6, 2004, with 7 matches to play.

LEAGUE RECORDS

MOST POINTS IN A SEASON

The following records applied before the introduction of three points for a win in the Football League in 1981-2.
Lincoln City set a **Football League** record in season 1975-6 with 74 points from 46 games (including 32 victories) in **Division 4.**
First Division: Liverpool (1978-9), 68 points from 42 matches.
Second Division: Tottenham (1919-20), 70 points from 42 matches.
Third Division: Aston Villa (1971-2) 70 points from 46 matches.
Since 3 points for win (pre-Premier League):
First Division: Everton (1984-5) and Liverpool (1987-8) 90 points: **Second Division:** Chelsea (1988-9) 99 points; **Third Division:** Bournemouth (1986-7) 97 points; **Fourth Division:** Swindon Town (1985-6) 102 points.
Since change of League format:

Premier League: Manchester Utd. (1993-4) 92 points; **First Division**: Sunderland (1998-9) 105 points (record for any division); **Second Division**: Fulham (1998-9) 101 points; **Third Division**: Plymouth Argyle (2001-02) 102 points.
Fewest Points: Doncaster Rov. 8 points (of possible 68) in Second Division, 1904-5. Stirling Albion 6 points (of possible 60) in Scottish League Division A, 1954-5.

DOUBLE CHAMPIONS

Nine men have played in and managed League Championship-winning teams:
Ted Drake Player – Arsenal 1934, 1935, 1938. Manager – Chelsea 1955.
Bill Nicholson Player – Tottenham 1951. Manager – Tottenham 1961.
Alf Ramsey Player – Tottenham 1951. Manager – Ipswich Town 1962.
Joe Mercer Player – Everton 1939, Arsenal 1948, 1953. Manager – Manchester City 1968.
Dave Mackay Player – Tottenham 1961. Manager – Derby Co. 1975.
Bob Paisley Player – Liverpool 1947. Manager – Liverpool 1976, 1977, 1979, 1980, 1982, 1983.
Howard Kendall Player – Everton 1970. Manager – Everton 1985, 1987.
Kenny Dalglish Player – Liverpool 1979, 1980, 1982, 1983, 1984. Player-manager – Liverpool 1986, 1988, 1990. Manager – Blackburn Rov. 1995.
George Graham Player – Arsenal 1971. Manager – Arsenal 1989, 1991.

MOST LEAGUE CHAMPIONSHIP MEDALS

Kenny Dalglish: 9 – 8 for Liverpool (5 as player, 1979-80-82-83-84; 3 as player-manager, 1986-88-90); 1 for Blackburn Rov. (as manager, 1995). As a player he also won 4 Scottish Championship medals with Celtic (1972-73-74-77). **Phil Neal**: 8 for Liverpool (1976-77-79-80-82-83-84-86); **Alan Hansen**: 8 for Liverpool (1979-80-82-83-84-86-88-90); **Ryan Giggs**: 8 for Manchester Utd. (1993–94–96–97–99–2000–01–03); **Sir Alex Ferguson**: 8 as Manchester Utd. manager (1993-94-96-97-99-2000-01-03).

CANTONA'S FOUR-TIMER

Eric Cantona played in four successive Championship-winning teams: Marseille 1990-1, Leeds Utd. 1991-2, Manchester Utd. 1992-3 and 1993-4.

ARRIVALS AND DEPARTURES

The following are the Football League arrivals and departures since 1923:

Year	In	Out
1923	Doncaster Rov. New Brighton	Stalybridge Celtic
1927	Torquay Athletic	Aberdare Athletic
1928	Carlisle Utd.	Durham City
1929	York City	Ashington
1930	Thames	Merthyr Tydfil
1931	Mansfield Town Chester City	Newport County Nelson
1932	Aldershot Newport County	Thames Wigan Borough
1938	Ipswich Town	Gillingham
1950	Colchester Utd. Gillingham Scunthorpe Utd. Shrewsbury Town	
1951	Workington	New Brighton
1960	Peterborough Utd.	Gateshead
1962	Oxford Utd.	Accrington Stanley (resigned)
1970	Cambridge Utd.	Bradford P.A.
1972	Hereford Utd.	Barrow
1977	Wimbledon	Workington

276

1978	Wigan Athletic	Southport
1987	Scarborough	Lincoln City
1988	Lincoln City	Newport County
1989	Maidstone Utd.	Darlington
1990	Darlington	Colchester Utd.
1991	Barnet	
1992	Colchester Utd.	Aldershot, Maidstone (resigned)
1993	Wycombe Wand.	Halifax Town
1997	Macclesfield Town	Hereford Utd.
1998	Halifax Town	Doncaster Rov.
1999	Cheltenham Town	Scarborough
2000	Kidderminster Harriers	Chester City
2001	Rushden & Diamonds	Barnet
2002	Boston Utd.	Halifax Town
2003	Yeovil Town, Doncaster Rov.	Exeter City, Shrewsbury Town
2003	Chester City, Shrewsbury Town	Carlisle Utd., York City

Leeds City were expelled from Div. 2 in October, 1919; Port Vale took over their fixtures.

EXTENSIONS TO FOOTBALL LEAGUE

Clubs	Season	Clubs	Season
12 to 14	1891-2	44 to 66+	1920-1
14 to 28*	1892-3	66 to 86†	1921-2
28 to 31	1893-4	86 to 88	1923-4
31 to 32	1894-5	88 to 92	1950-1
32 to 36	1898-9	92 to 93	1991-2
36 to 40	1905-6	(Reverted to 92 when Aldershot closed,	
40 to 44	1919-20	March 1992)	

* Second Division formed. + Third Division (South) formed from Southern League clubs.
† Third Division (North) formed.
Football League reduced to 70 clubs and three divisions on the formation of the F.A. Premier League in 1992; increased to 72 season 1994-5, when Premier League reduced to 20 clubs.

RECORD RUNS

Nott'm. Forest hold the record unbeaten sequence in the English League – 42 matches spanning the last 26 of season 1977-8 and the first 16 of 1978-9. The run began on 19, November 1977 and ended on December 9, 1978 when Forest lost 0-2 at Liverpool. Their sequence comprised 21 wins and 21 draws.

Arsenal start Premiership season 2004-5 within 2 games of Forest's record, having played 40 games (W28, D12) since last beaten (2-3 at home to Leeds on May 4, 2003).

Best debuts: Ipswich Town won the First Division at their first attempt in 1961-2. **Peterborough Utd.** in their first season in the Football League (1960-1) not only won the Fourth Division but set the all-time scoring record for the League of 134 goals. **Hereford Utd.** were promoted from the Fourth Division in their first League season, 1972-3. **Wycombe Wand.** were promoted from the Third Division (via the play-offs) in their first League season, 1993-4.

Record winning sequence in a season: 14 consecutive League victories (all in Second Division): **Manchester Utd.** 1904-5, **Bristol City** 1905-6 and **Preston N.E.** 1950-1.

Best winning start to League season: 13 successive victories in Div. 3 by **Reading**, season 1985-6.

Best starts in 'old' First Division: 11 consecutive victories by **Tottenham** in 1960-1; 10 by **Manchester Utd.** in 1985-6. **Newcastle Utd.** won their first 11 matches in the **'new' First Division** in 1992-3.

Longest unbeaten sequence (all competitions): 40 by **Nott'm. Forest**, March-December 1978. It comprised 21 wins, 19 draws (in 29 League matches, 6 League Cup, 4 European Cup, 1 Charity Shield).

Longest unbeaten starts to League season: 38 matches (26 wins, 12 draws) in **Arsenal's** undefeated Premiership season, 2003-4; 29 matches – **Leeds Utd.,** Div. 1 1973-4 (19 wins, 10 draws, goals 51-16); **Liverpool,** Div. 1 1987-8 (22 wins, 7 draws, goals 67-13).

Most consecutive League matches unbeaten in a season: 38 **Arsenal** Premiership season 2003-4 (see above); 30 **Burnley** (21 wins, 9 draws, goals 68-17), September 6, 1920 – March 25, 1921, Div. 1.

Longest winning sequence in Div. 1: 13 matches by **Tottenham** – last two of season 1959-60, first 11 of 1960-1.

Longest winning one-season sequences in Championship: 13 matches by **Preston N.E.** in 1891-2 (September 12–January 2); 13 by **Sunderland,** also in 1891-2 (November 14–April 2).

Premier League – best starts to season: (before **Arsenal** unbeaten through season 2003-4): 12 games unbeaten – **Nott'm. Forest** in 1995-6, **Arsenal** in 1997-8, **Aston Villa** in 1998-9, **Liverpool** 2002-03.

Premier League – most consecutive wins (two seasons): 14 by **Arsenal,** February-August, 2002.

Premier League's record unbeaten run: 40 matches (W28, D12) by **Arsenal** (May 7, 2003–May 15, 2004). **In one season,** all 38 matches by Arsenal (W26, D12) in 2003-4.

Premier League – longest unbeaten away run: 23 matches (W16, D7) by **Arsenal** (Aug. 18, 2001–Sept. 28, 2002); and by **Arsenal** again (W13, D10), April 5 2003–May 15, 2004.

Record home-win sequences: Bradford Park Avenue won 25 successive home games in Div. 3 North – the last 18 in 1926-7 and the first 7 the following season. Longest run of home wins in the top division is 21 by **Liverpool** – the last 9 of 1971-2 and the first 12 of 1972-3.

British record for successive League wins: 25 by **Celtic** (Scottish Premier League), August 16, 2003–February 29, 2004.

WORST SEQUENCES

Cambridge Utd. experienced the longest run without a win in Football League history in season 1983-4: 31 matches (21 lost, 10 drawn) between October 8 and April 23. They finished bottom of the Second Division.

Previous worst no-win League sequence was 30 by **Crewe Alexandra** (Div. 3 North) in season 1956-7.

Worst losing start to a League season: 12 consecutive defeats by **Manchester Utd.** (Div. 1) in 1930-1.

Worst Premier League start: Swindon Town 15 matches without win (6 draws, 9 defeats), 1993-4.

Worst Premier League sequence: Sunderland 20 matches without win (2 draws, 18 defeats) 2002-03.

Premier League – most consecutive defeats: Sunderland last 15 matches, season 2002-03.

Longest non-winning start to League season: 25 matches (4 draws, 21 defeats) by **Newport County,** Div. 4 (Aug. 15, 1970 – Jan. 9, 1971). Worst no-win League starts since then: 16 matches by **Burnley** (9 draws, 7 defeats in Div. 2, 1979-80); 16 by **Hull City** (10 draws, 6 defeats in Div. 2, 1989-90); 16 by **Sheffield Utd.** (4 draws, 12 defeats in Div. 1, 1990-91).

Most consecutive League defeats: 18 by **Darwen** (Div. 2) 1898-9. **In modern times:** 17 by **Sunderland** (15 Prem., 2 Div. 1), January 18–August 16, 2004.

Most League defeats in season: 34 by **Doncaster Rov.** (Div. 3) 1997-8; 33 by **Wimbledon** (Div. 1) 2003-4.

Fewest League wins in season: 1 by **Loughborough Town** (Div. 2, season 1899-1900). They lost 27, drew 6, goals 18-100 and dropped out of the League. (See also Scottish section).

Fewest home League wins in season: 1 by **Loughborough Town** (Div. 2, 1899-1900); **Notts Co.** (Div. 1, 1904-5), **Woolwich Arsenal** (Div. 1, 1912-13), **Blackpool** (Div. 1, 1966-7), **Rochdale** (Div. 3, 1973-4).

Most home League defeats in season: 18 by **Cambridge Utd.** (Div. 3, 1984-5).

Away League defeats record: 24 in row by **Nelson** (Div. 3 North) – 3 in April 1930 followed by all 21 in season 1930-31. They then dropped out of the League.

Biggest defeat in Champions' season: During Newcastle Utd.'s Championship-winning season in 1908-9, they were beaten 9-1 at home by Sunderland on December 5.

WORST START BY EVENTUAL CHAMPIONS

Sunderland took only 2 points from their first 7 matches in season 1912-13 (2 draws, 5 defeats). They won 25 of the remaining 31 games to clinch their fifth League title.

SUNDERLAND'S FOUR-TIME WORST

Sunderland were relegated to the Nationwide League at the end of season 2002–03 as the worst-ever team in the Premiership: fewest wins (4), fewest points (19), fewest goals (21) and with the longest run of consecutive defeats (15).

UNBEATEN LEAGUE SEASON

Only three clubs have completed an English League season unbeaten: **Preston N.E.** (22 matches in 1888-9, the League's first season), **Liverpool** (28 matches in Div. 2, 1893-4) and **Arsenal** (38 matches in Premiership, 2003-4).

100 PER CENT HOME RECORDS

Five clubs have won every home League match in a season, four of them in the old Second Division: **Liverpool** (14) in 1893-4, **Bury** (15) in 1894-5, **Sheffield Wed.** (17) in 1899-1900 and **Small Heath**, subsequently Birmingham (17) in 1902-3. The last club to do it, **Brentford**, won all 21 home games in Div. 3 South in 1929-30.

Rotherham Utd. just failed to equal that record in 1946-7. They won their first 20 home matches in Div. 3 North, then drew the last 3-3 v Rochdale.

WORST HOME RUNS

Most consecutive home League defeats: 8 by **Rochdale**, who took only 11 points in Div. 3 North in season 1931-2; 8 by **Stockport Co.** (Div.1) in season 2001-02; 8 by **Sunderland** (Premiership), season 2002–03.

Between November 1958 and October 1959 **Portsmouth** drew 2 and lost 14 out of 16 consecutive home games.

West Ham Utd. did not win in the Premiership at Upton Park in season 2002–03 until the 13th. home match on January 29.

MOST AWAY WINS IN SEASON

Doncaster Rovers won 18 of their 21 away League fixtures when winning Div. 3 North in 1946-7.

AWAY WINS RECORD

Most **consecutive away League wins: 10** by **Tottenham** (Div. 1) – 8 at start of 1960-1, after ending previous season with 2 away victories.

100 PER CENT HOME WINS ON ONE DAY

Div. 1 – All 11 home teams won on Feb. 13, 1926 and on Dec. 10, 1955. **Div. 2** – All 12 home teams won on Nov. 26, 1988. **Div. 3**, all 12 home teams won in the week-end programme of Oct. 18-19, 1968.

NO HOME WINS IN DIV. ON ONE DAY

Div. 1 – 8 away wins, 3 draws in 11 matches on Sept. 6, 1986. **Div. 2** – 7 away wins, 4 draws in 11 matches on Dec. 26, 1987. **Premier League** – 6 away wins, 5 draws in 11 matches on Dec. 26, 1994.

The week-end **Premiership** programme on Dec. 7-8-9, 1996 produced no home win in the ten games (4 aways, 6 draws). There was again no home victory (3 away wins, 7 draws) in the week-end **Premiership** fixtures on September 23-24, 2000.

MOST DRAWS IN A SEASON (FOOTBALL LEAGUE)

23 by **Norwich City** (Div. 1, 1978-9), **Exeter City** (Div. 4, 1986-7). **Cardiff City** and **Hartlepool Utd.** (both Div. 3, 1997-8). Norwich City played 42 matches, the others 46.

MOST DRAWS IN ONE DIV. ON ONE DAY

On September 18, 1948 **nine** out of 11 First Division matches were drawn.

MOST DRAWS IN PREMIER DIV. PROGRAMME

Over the week-ends of December 2-3-4, 1995, and September 23-24, 2000, seven out of the ten matches finished level.

FEWEST DRAWS IN SEASON (46 MATCHES)

3 by **Reading** (Div. 3 South, 1951–2); **Bradford City Park Avenue** (Div. 3 North, 1956–7); **Tranmere Rov.** (Div. 4, 1984–5); **Southend Utd.** (Div. 3, 2002–3).

HIGHEST-SCORING DRAWS IN LEAGUE

Leicester City 6, Arsenal 6 (Div. 1 April 21, 1930) and **Charlton Athletic 6, Middlesbrough 6** (Div 2. October 22, 1960)
   Latest 6-6 draw in first-class football was between Tranmere Rov. and Newcastle Utd. in the Zenith Data Systems Cup 1st. Round on October 1, 1991. The score went from 3-3 at 90 minutes to 6-6 after extra time, and Tranmere Rov. won 3-2 on penalties.
   Most recent 5-5 draws in top division: Southampton v Coventry City (Div. 1, May 4, 1982); Q.P.R. v Newcastle Utd. (Div. 1, Sept. 22, 1984).

DRAWS RECORDS

Most consecutive drawn matches in Football League: 8 by **Torquay Utd.** (Div. 3), Oct. 25 – Dec. 13, 1969.
   Longest sequence of draws by the same score: six 1-1 results by **Q.P.R.** in season 1957-8.
   Tranmere Rov. became the first club to play **five consecutive 0-0 League draws**, in season 1997-8.

IDENTICAL RECORDS

There is only **one instance** of two clubs in one division finishing a season with identical records. In 1907-8, **Blackburn Rov.** and **Woolwich Arsenal** were bracketed equal 14th. in the First Division with these figures: P38, W12, D12, L14, Goals 51-63, Pts. 36.
   The total of **1195 goals** scored in the Premier League in season 1993-4 was **repeated** in 1994-5.

CHAMPIONS OF ALL DIVISIONS

Wolves and **Burnley** are the only clubs to have won the Championships of the old **Divisions 1, 2, 3** and **4**. Wolves were also **Champions** of the **Third Division North**.

UPS & DOWNS RECORD

Northampton Town went from **Fourth Division** to **First** and back again in nine seasons (1961-9). **Carlisle Utd.** did the same from 1974-87.

MAJOR POINTS DEDUCTIONS

Season 2000–01: Chesterfield (Div. 3) had 9 points deducted (plus £20,000 fine) for breach of transfer regulations and under-reporting gate receipts. They finished in third (promotion) place.
   Season 2002–03: Boston Utd. entered the Football League under a double penalty. On charges of contractual irregularities, they were fined £100,000 by the F.A. and deducted 4 points.

NIGHTMARE STARTS

Most goals conceded by a goalkeeper on League debut: 13 by **Steve Milton** when Halifax Town lost 13-0 at Stockport Co. (Div. 3 North) on January 6, 1934.

Post-war: 11 by Crewe Alexandra's new goalkeeper **Dennis Murray** (Div. 3 North) on September 29, 1951, when Lincoln City won 11-1.

RELEGATION ODD SPOTS

In season 1937-8, **Manchester City** were the highest-scoring team in the First Division with 80 goals (3 more than Champions Arsenal), but they finished in 21st place and were relegated – a year after winning the Championship. They scored more goals than they conceded (77).

That season produced the **closest relegation battle** in top-division history, with only 4 points spanning the bottom 11 clubs in Div. 1. WBA went down with Manchester City.

Twelve years earlier, in 1925-6, City went down to Division 2 despite totalling 89 goals – still the most scored in any division by a relegated team. Manchester City also scored 31 F.A. Cup goals that season, but lost the Final 1-0 to Bolton Wanderers.

Cardiff City were relegated from Div. 1 in season 1928-9, despite conceding fewest goals in the division (59). They also scored fewest (43).

On their way to relegation from the First Division in season 1984–85, **Stoke City** twice lost ten matches in a row.

RELEGATION TREBLES

Two Football League clubs have been relegated three seasons in succession. **Bristol City** fell from First Division to Fourth in 1980-1-2, and **Wolves** did the same in 1984-5-6.

CHRISTMAS 'CERTAINTY'

Wolves' demotion in May 2004 maintained the pattern that no club bottom of the Premiership at Christmas has ever avoided relegation.

OLDEST CLUBS

Oldest Association Football Club is **Sheffield F.C.** (formed in 1857). The original minute book is still in existence.

The oldest Football League clubs are **Notts Co.**, 1862; **Nott'm. Forest**, 1865; and **Sheffield Wed.**, 1866.

FOUR DIVISIONS

In **May, 1957**, the Football League decided to re-group the two sections of the Third Division into Third and Fourth Divisions in **season 1958-9**.

The Football League was reduced to three divisions on the formation of the F.A. Premier League in **1992**.

THREE UP – THREE DOWN

The Football League Annual General Meeting of June 1973 agreed to adopt the promotion and relegation system of three up and three down.

The **new system** came into effect in **season 1973-4** and applied only to the first three divisions; four clubs were still relegated from the Third and four promoted from the Fourth.

It was the first change in the promotion and relegation system for the top two divisions in 81 years.

PLAY-OFF FINALS
HIGHEST SCORES

Div. 1	1993	(Wembley)	Swindon Town 4, Leicester City 3
	1995	(Wembley)	Bolton Wand. 4, Reading 3
	1998	(Wembley)	Charlton Athletic 4, Sunderland 4 (Charlton Athletic won 7–6 on pens.)

Div. 2	1993	(Wembley)	W.B.A. 3, Port Vale 0
	2000	(Wembley)	Gillingham 3, Wigan Athletic 2
	2001	(Cardiff)	Walsall 3, Reading 2
Div. 3	2003	(Cardiff)	Bournemouth 5, Lincoln City 2

BIGGEST ATTENDANCES

Div. 1	1998	(Wembley)	Charlton Athletic v Sunderland	77,739
Div. 2	1999	(Wembley)	Manchester City v Gillingham	76,935
Div. 3	1997	(Wembley)	Northampton Town v Swansea City	46,804

MOST LEAGUE APPEARANCES

Players with more than 700 Football League apps. (as at end of season 2003-04):

1005   **Peter Shilton** 1966-97 (286 Leicester City, 110 Stoke City, 202 Nott'm. Forest, 188 Southampton, 175 Derby Co., 34 Plymouth Argyle, 1 Bolton Wand., 9 Leyton Orient).

931   **Tony Ford** 1975-2002 (423 Grimsby Town, 9 Sunderland, 112 Stoke City, 114 W.B.A., 5 Bradford City, 76 Scunthorpe Utd., 103 Mansfield Town, 89 Rochdale).

824   **Terry Paine** 1956-77 (713 Southampton, 111 Hereford).

795   **Tommy Hutchison** 1968-91 (165 Blackpool, 314 Coventry City, 46 Manchester City, 92 Burnley, 178 Swansea City). In addition, 68 Scottish League apps. for Alloa 1965-68, giving career League app. total of 863.

790   **Neil Redfearn** 1982-2004 (35 Bolton Wand., 100 Lincoln City, 46 Doncaster Rov., 57 Crystal Palace, 24 Watford, 62 Oldham Athletic, 292 Brnsley, 30 Charlton Athletic, 17 Bradford City, 22 Wigan Athletic, 42 Halifax Town, 54 Boston Utd., 9 Rochdale).

782   **Robbie James** 1973-94 (484 Swansea City, 48 Stoke City, 87 Q.P.R., 23 Leicester City, 89 Bradford City, 51 Cardiff City).

777   **Alan Oakes** 1959-84 (565 Manchester City, 211 Chester City, 1 Port Vale).

773   **Dave Beasant** 1980-2003 (340 Wimbledon, 20 Newcastle Utd., 6 Grimsby Town, 4 Wolves, 133 Chelsea, 88 Southampton, 139 Nott'm. F., 27 Portsmouth, 16 Brighton).

770   **John Trollope** 1960-80 (all for Swindon Town, record total for one club).

764   **Jimmy Dickinson** 1946-65 (all for Portsmouth).

761   **Roy Sproson** 1950-72 (all for Port Vale).

760   **Mick Tait** 1974-97 (64 Oxford Utd., 106 Carlisle Utd., 33 Hull City, 240 Portsmouth, 99 Reading, 79 Darlington, 139 Hartlepool Utd.).

758   **Billy Bonds** 1964-88 (95 Charlton Athletic, 663 West Ham Utd.).

758   **Ray Clemence** 1966-88 (48 Scunthorpe Utd., 470 Liverpool, 240 Tottenham).

757   **Pat Jennings** 1963-86 (48 Watford, 472 Tottenham, 237 Arsenal).

757   **Frank Worthington** 1966-88 (171 Huddersfield Town, 210 Leicester City, 84 Bolton Wand., 75 Birmingham City, 32 Leeds Utd., 19 Sunderland, 34 Southampton, 31 Brighton & H.A., 59 Tranmere Rov., 23 Preston N.E., 19 Stockport Co.).

749   **Ernie Moss** 1968-88 (469 Chesterfield, 35 Peterborough Utd., 57 Mansfield Town, 74 Port Vale, 11 Lincoln City, 44 Doncaster Rov., 26 Stockport Co., 23 Scarborough, 10 Rochdale).

746   **Les Chapman** 1966-88 (263 Oldham Athletic, 133 Huddersfield Town, 70 Stockport Co., 139 Bradford City, 88 Rochdale, 53 Preston N.E.).

744   **Asa Hartford** 1967-90 (214 W.B.A., 260 Manchester City, 3 Nott'm. F., 81 Everton, 28 Norwich City, 81 Bolton Wand., 45 Stockport Co., 7 Oldham Athletic, 25 Shrewsbury Town).

743   **Alan Ball** 1963-84 (146 Blackpool, 208 Everton, 177 Arsenal, 195 Southampton, 17 Bristol Rov.).

743   **John Hollins** 1963-84 (465 Chelsea, 151 Q.P.R., 127 Arsenal).

743   **Phil Parkes** 1968-91 (52 Walsall, 344 Q.P.R., 344 West Ham Utd., 3 Ipswich Town).

737	**Steve Bruce** 1979-99 (205 Gillingham, 141 Norwich City, 309 Manchester Utd. 72 Birmingham City, 10 Sheffield Utd.).	
732	**Mick Mills** 1966-88 (591 Ipswich Town, 103 Southampton, 38 Stoke City).	
731	**Ian Callaghan** 1959-81 (640 Liverpool, 76 Swansea City, 15 Crewe Alexandra).	
731	**David Seaman** 1982-2003 (91 Peterborough Utd, 75 Birmingham City, 141 Q.P.R., 405 Arsenal, 19 Manchester City).	
725	**Steve Perryman** 1969-90 (655 Tottenham, 17 Oxford Utd., 53 Brentford).	
722	**Martin Peters** 1961-81 (302 West Ham Utd., 189 Tottenham, 207 Norwich City, 24 Sheffield Utd.).	
718	**Mike Channon** 1966-86 (511 Southampton, 72 Manchester City, 4 Newcastle Utd., 9 Bristol Rov., 88 Norwich City, 34 Portsmouth).	
718	**Phil Neal** 1968-89 (186 Northampton Town, 455 Liverpool, 77 Bolton Wand.).	
716	**Ron Harris** 1961-83 (655 Chelsea, 61 Brentford).	
716	**Mike Summerbee** 1959-79 (218 Swindon Town, 357 Manchester City, 51 Burnley, 3 Blackpool, 87 Stockport Co.).	
714	**Glenn Cockerill** 1976-98 (186 Lincoln City, 26 Swindon Town, 62 Sheffield Utd., 387 Southampton, 90 Leyton Orient, 40 Fulham, 23 Brentford).	
705	**John Wile** 1968-86 (205 Peterborough Utd., 500 W.B.A.).	
701	**Neville Southall** 1980-2000 (39 Bury, 578 Everton, 9 Port Vale, 9 Southend, 12 Stoke, 53 Torquay, 1 Bradford City).	

● **Stanley Matthews** made 701 League apps. 1932-65 (322 Stoke City, 379 Blackpool), incl. 3 for Stoke City at start of 1939-40 before season abandoned (war).
● Goalkeeper **John Burridge** made a total of 771 League appearances in a 28-season career in English and Scottish football (1968-96). He played 691 games for 15 English clubs (Workington, Blackpool, Aston Villa, Southend Utd., Crystal Palace, Q.P.R., Wolves, Derby Co., Sheffield Utd., Southampton, Newcastle Utd., Scarborough, Lincoln City, Manchester City and Darlington) and 80 for 5 Scottish clubs (Hibernian, Aberdeen, Dumbarton, Falkirk and Queen of the South).

LONGEST LEAGUE APPEARANCE SEQUENCE

Harold Bell, centre-half of Tranmere Rov., was ever-present for the first nine post-war seasons (1946-55), achieving a League record of 401 consecutive matches. Counting F.A. Cup and other games, his run of successive appearances totalled 459.

The longest League sequence since Bell's was 394 appearances by goalkeeper **Dave Beasant** for Wimbledon, Newcastle Utd. and Chelsea. His nine-year run began on August 29, 1981 and was ended by a broken finger sustained in Chelsea's League Cup-tie against Portsmouth on October 31, 1990. Beasant's 394 consecutive League games comprised 304 for Wimbledon (1981-8), 20 for Newcastle Utd. (1988-9) and 70 for Chelsea (1989-90).

Phil Neal made 366 consecutive First Division appearances for Liverpool between December 1974 and September 1983, a remarkable sequence for an outfield player in top-division football.

EVER-PRESENT DEFENCE

The **entire** defence of Huddersfield Town played in all 42 Second Division matches in season 1952-3, namely, Bill Wheeler (goal), Ron Staniforth and Laurie Kelly (full-backs), Bill McGarry, Don McEvoy and Len Quested (half-backs). In addition, Vic Metcalfe played in all 42 League matches at outside-left.

FIRST SUBSTITUTE USED IN LEAGUE

Keith Peacock (Charlton Athletic), away to Bolton Wand. (Div. 2) on August 21, 1965.

FROM PROMOTION TO CHAMPIONS

Clubs who have become Champions of England a year after winning promotion: **Liverpool** 1905, 1906; **Everton** 1931, 1932; **Tottenham** 1950, 1951; **Ipswich Town** 1961, 1962; **Nott'm. Forest** 1977, 1978. The first four were placed top in both seasons: Forest finished third and first.

PREMIERSHIP'S FIRST MULTI-NATIONAL LINE-UP

Chelsea made history on December 26, 1999 when they started their Premiership match at Southampton without a single British player in the side. They won 2–1.

Fulham's Unique XI: In the Worthington Cup 3rd. Round at home to Bury on November 6, 2002, **Fulham** fielded 11 players of 11 different nationalities. Ten were full Internationals, with Lee Clark an England U–21 cap.

THREE-NATION CHAMPION

Trevor Steven earned eight Championship medals, in three countries: two with Everton (1985, 1987); five with Rangers (1990, 1991, 1993, 1994, 1995) and one with Marseille in 1992.

LEEDS NO-WAY AWAY

Leeds Utd., in 1992-3, provided the first instance of a club failing to win an away League match as reigning Champions.

PIONEERS IN 1888 AND 1992

Three clubs among the twelve who formed the Football League in 1888 were also founder members of the F.A. Premier League: **Aston Villa**, **Blackburn Rov.** and **Everton**.

CHAMPIONS (MODERN) WITH TWO CLUBS – PLAYERS

Francis Lee (Manchester City 1968, Derby Co. 1975); **Ray Kennedy** (Arsenal 1971, Liverpool 1979, 1980, 1982); **Archie Gemmill** (Derby Co. 1972, 1975, Nott'm. F. 1978); **John McGovern** (Derby Co. 1972, Nott'm. F. 1978) **Larry Lloyd** (Liverpool 1973, Nott'm. F. 1978); **Peter Withe** (Nott'm. F. 1978, Aston Villa 1981); **John Lukic** (Arsenal 1989, Leeds Utd. 1992); **Kevin Richardson** (Everton 1985, Arsenal 1989); **Eric Cantona** (Leeds Utd. 1992, Manchester Utd. 1993, 1994, 1996, 1997); **David Batty** (Leeds Utd. 1992, Blackburn Rov. 1995), **Bobby Mimms** (Everton 1987, Blackburn Rov. 1995), **Henning Berg** (Blackburn Rov. 1995, Manchester United 1999, 2001).

TITLE TURNABOUTS

In January 1996, Kevin Keegan's **Newcastle Utd.** led the Premier League by 13 points. They finished runners-up to Manchester Utd.

At Christmas 1997, **Arsenal** were 13 points behind leaders Manchester Utd. and still 11 points behind at the beginning of March 1998. But a run of 10 wins took the title to Highbury.

On March 2, 2003, **Arsenal**, with 9 games left, went 8 points clear of Manchester Utd., who had a match in hand. United won the Championship by 5 points.

● In March 2002, **Wolves** were in second (automatic promotion) place in Nationwide Div. 1, 11 points ahead of W.B.A., who had 2 games in hand. They were overtaken by Albion on the run-in, finished third, then failed in the play-offs. A year later they won promotion to the Premiership via the play-offs.

CLUB CLOSURES

Four clubs have left the Football League in mid-season: **Leeds City** (expelled Oct. 1919); **Wigan Borough** (Oct. 1931, debts of £20,000); **Accrington Stanley** (March 1962, debts £62,000); **Aldershot** (March 1992, debts £1.2m.). **Maidstone Utd.**, with debts of £650,000, closed August 1992, on the eve of the season.

FOUR-DIVISION MEN

In season 1986-7, goalkeeper **Eric Nixon,** became the first player to appear in **all four divisions** of the Football League **in one season.** He served two clubs in Div. 1: Manchester City (5 League games) and Southampton (4); in Div. 2 Bradford City (3); in Div. 3 Carlisle Utd. (16); and in Div. 4 Wolves (16). Total appearances: 44.

Harvey McCreadie, a teenage forward, played in four divisions over two seasons inside a calendar year – from Accrington (Div. 3) to Luton Town (Div. 1) in January 1960, to Div. 2 with Luton Town later that season and to Wrexham (Div. 4) in November.

Tony Cottee played in all four divisions in season 2000-01, for Leicester City (Premiership), Norwich City (Div. 1), Barnet (Div. 3, player-manager) and Millwall (Div. 2).

FATHERS & SONS

When player-manager **Ian Bowyer** (39) and **Gary Bowyer** (18) appeared together in the **Hereford Utd.** side at Scunthorpe Utd. (Div.4, April 21, 1990), they provided the first instance of father and son playing in the same team in a Football League match for 39 years. Ian Bowyer played as substitute, and Gary scored Hereford's injury-time equaliser in a 3-3 draw.

Alec (39) and **David** (just 17) **Herd** were the previous father-and-son duo in League football – for **Stockport Co.,** 2-0 winners at Hartlepool Utd. (Div.3 North) on May 5, 1951.

When **Preston N.E.** won 2-1 at Bury in Div. 3 on January 13, 1990, the opposing goalkeepers were brothers: **Alan Kelly** (21) for Preston N.E. and **Gary** (23) for Bury. Their father, **Alan Kelly Senior** (who kept goal for Preston N.E. in the 1964 F.A. Cup Final and won 47 Rep. of Ireland caps) flew from America to watch the sons he taught to keep goal line up on opposite sides.

George Eastham Snr. (manager) and son **George Eastham Jnr.** were inside-forward partners for Ards in the Irish League in season 1954-5.

FATHER & SON BOTH CHAMPIONS

John Aston Snr. won a Championship medal with Manchester Utd. in 1952 and **John Aston Jnr.** did so with Utd. in 1967.

FATHER & SON RIVAL MANAGERS

When **Bill Dodgin senior** took Bristol Rov. to Fulham for an F.A. Cup 1st Round tie in Nov. 1970, the opposing manager was his son, **Bill junior.**

FATHER & SON ON OPPOSITE SIDES

It happened for the first time in F.A. Cup history (1st. Qual. Round on Sept. 14, 1996) when 21-year-old **Nick Scaife** (Bishop Auckland) faced his father **Bobby** (41), who played for Pickering. Both were in midfield. Home side Bishops won 3-1.

THREE BROTHERS IN SAME SIDE

Southampton provided the first instance for 65 years of three brothers appearing together in a First Division side when **Danny Wallace** (24) and his 19-year-old twin brothers **Rodney** and **Ray** played against Sheffield Wed.on October 22, 1988. In all, they made 25 appearances together for Southampton until September 1989.

A previous instance in Div. 1 was provided by the Middlesbrough trio, **William, John** and **George Carr** with 24 League appearances together from January 1920 to October 1923.

The **Tonner** brothers, **Sam, James** and **Jack,** played together in 13 Second Division matches for Clapton Orient in season 1919-20.

Brothers **David, Donald** and **Robert Jack** played together in Plymouth Argyle's League side in 1920.

TWIN TEAM-MATES (see also **Wallace twins** above)

Twin brothers **David** and **Peter Jackson** played together for three League clubs (Wrexham, Bradford City and Tranmere Rov.) from 1954-62.

The **Morgan** twins, **Ian** and **Roger**, played regularly in the Q.P.R. forward line from 1964-68.

W.B.A's **Adam** and **James Chambers**, 18, were the first twins to represent England (v Cameroon in World Youth Championship, April 1999). They first played together in Albion's senior team, aged 19, in the League Cup 2nd. Round against Derby Co. in September 2000.

SIR TOM DOES THE HONOURS

Sir Tom Finney, England and Preston N.E. legend, opened the Football League's new headquarters on their return to Preston on Feb. 23, 1999. Preston had been the League's original base for 70 years before they moved to Lytham St. Annes in 1959.

SHORTENED MATCHES

The 0-0 score in the **Bradford City v Lincoln City Third Division fixture** on May 11, 1985, abandoned through fire after 40 minutes, was subsequently confirmed as a result. It is the shortest officially completed League match on record, and was the fourth of only five instances in Football League history of the score of an unfinished match being allowed to stand.

The other occasions: **Middlesbrough 4, Oldham Athletic 1** (Div. 1, April 3, 1915), abandoned after 55 minutes when Oldham Athletic defender Billy Cook refused to leave the field after being sent off; **Barrow 7, Gillingham 0** (Div. 4, Oct. 9, 1961), abandoned after 75 minutes because of bad light, the match having started late because of Gillingham's delayed arrival.

A crucial **Manchester derby** (Div.1) was abandoned after 85 minutes, and the result stood, on April 27, 1974, when a pitch invasion at Old Trafford followed the only goal, scored for City by Denis Law, which relegated Manchester Utd., Law's former club.

Only instance of a first-class match in England being abandoned **'through shortage of players'** occurred in the First Division at Bramall Lane on March 16, 2002. Referee Eddie Wolstenholme halted play after 82 minutes because **Sheffield Utd.** were reduced to 6 players against **W.B.A.** They had had 3 men sent off (goalkeeper and 2 substitutes), and with all 3 substitutes used and 2 players injured, were left with fewer than the required minimum of 7 on the field. Promotion contenders W.B.A. were leading 3-0, and the League ordered the result to stand.

The last 60 seconds of **Birmingham City v Stoke City** (Div. 3, 1-1, on Feb. 29, 1992) were played behind locked doors. The ground had been cleared after a pitch invasion.

A First Division fixture, **Sheffield Wed. v Aston Villa** (Nov. 26, 1898), was abandoned through bad light after 79½ mins. with Wed. leading 3-1. The Football League ruled that the match should be completed, and the remaining 10½ minutes were played **four months later** (Mar. 13, 1899), when Wed. added another goal to make the result 4-1.

F.A. CUP RECORDS

(See also Goalscoring section)

CHIEF WINNERS

Eleven Times: Manchester Utd.
Nine Times: Arsenal.
Eight Times: Tottenham.
Seven Times: Aston Villa.
Three Times in Succession: The Wanderers (1876-7-8) and Blackburn Rov. (1884-5-6).
Trophy Handed Back: The F.A. Cup became the Wanderers' absolute property in 1878, but they handed it back to the Association on condition that it was not to be won outright by any club.
In Successive Years by Professional Clubs: Blackburn Rov. (in 1890 and 1891); Newcastle Utd. (in 1951 and 1952); Tottenham (in 1961 and 1962); Tottenham again (in 1981 and 1982) and Arsenal (in 2002 and 2003).
Record Final-tie score: Bury 6, Derby Co. 0 (1903).

Most F.A. Cup wins at Wembley: Manchester Utd. 9, Arsenal 7, Tottenham 6, Newcastle Utd. 5, Liverpool 5.

F.A. CUP: SECOND DIVISION WINNERS

Notts Co. (1894), Wolves (1908), Barnsley (1912), West Bromwich Albion (1931), Sunderland (1973), Southampton (1976), West Ham Utd. (1980). When Tottenham won the Cup in 1901 they were a Southern League club.

'OUTSIDE' SEMI-FINALISTS

Wycombe Wand., in 2001, became only the eighth team from outside the top two divisions to reach the semi-finals, following Millwall (1937), Port Vale (1954), York City (1955), Norwich City (1959), Crystal Palace (1976), Plymouth Argyle (1984) and Chesterfield (1997). None reached the Final.

FOURTH DIVISION QUARTER-FINALISTS

Oxford Utd. (1964), Colchester Utd. (1971), Bradford City (1976), Cambridge Utd. (1990).

F.A. CUP – FOUR TROPHIES

The latest F.A. Cup, first presented at Wembley in 1992, is a replica of the one it replaced, which had been in existence since 1911. 'It was falling apart and was not going to last much longer,' said the FA.

The new trophy is the fourth F.A. Cup. These were its predecessors:

1895 First stolen from shop in Birmingham while held by Aston Villa. Never seen again.

1910 Second presented to Lord Kinnaird on completing 21 years as F.A. president.

1992 Third 'gracefully retired' after 80 years' service (1911-91).

There are three F.A. Cups currently in existence. The retired model is still used for promotional work. The present trophy stays with the winners until the following March. A third, identical Cup is secreted in the F.A. vaults as cover against loss of the existing trophy.

FINALISTS RELEGATED

Four clubs have reached the F.A. Cup Final in a season of relegation, and all lost at Wembley: Manchester City 1926, Leicester City 1969, Brighton & H.A. 1983, Middlesbrough 1997.

GIANT-KILLING IN F.A. CUP

(* Home team; R = Replay; Season 2004 = 2003-04)

2004 *Hornchurch 2	Darlington 0
2004 *Scarborough 1	Doncaster Rov. 0
2004 *Port Vale 0	Scarborough 1
2004 *Scarborough 1	Southend Utd. ... 0R
2004 *Accrington 1	Huddersfield T. 0
2004 *Accrington 0	Bournemouth 0R
(Accrington won on pens).	
2004 *Stevenage 2	Stockport Co. 1
2004 *Torquay Utd. 1	Burton Alb. 2
2004 *Telford 3	Brentford 0
2004 *Crewe Alex. 0	Telford 1
2004 *Colchester Utd. ... 3	Coventry City 1R
2004 *Bolton Wand. 1	Tranmere Rov. 2R
2004 *Gillingham 3	Charlton Ath. 1
2003 *Chesterfield 1	Morecambe 2
2003 *Colchester Utd. ... 0	Chester City 1
2003 *Southport 4	Notts Co. 2
2003 Margate 1	Leyton Orient 0R
(at Dover)	
2003 *Q.P.R. 1	Vauxhall Mot .... 1 R
(Vauxhall won on pens.)	
2003 *Shrewsbury T. 2	Everton 1
2003 *Dagenham & R. .. 2	Plymouth .... 0 R
2003 *Darlington 2	Farnborough 3
2003 *Rochdale 2	Coventry City 0
2003 *Liverpool 0	Crystal Palace 2
2003 *Sunderland 0	Watford 1
2002 *Wigan Athletic ... 0	Canvey Island 1
2002 *Canvey Island 1	Northampton T. ... 0
2002 *Dagenham & R .. 3	Exeter City 0R
2002 *Cardiff City 2	Leeds Utd. 1
2002 *Derby Co. 1	Bristol Rov. 3
2001 *Wycombe Wand. .. 2	Wolves 1
2001 *Wimbledon 2	Wycombe Wand. . 2R
(Wycombe Wand. won on pens).	
2001 *Leicester City 1	Wycombe Wand. . 2
2001 *Brentford 1	Kingstonian 3
2001 *Yeovil 5	Colchester Utd. ... 1

Year	Home		Away	
2001	*Southend Utd.	0	Kingstonian	1
2001	*Nuneaton	1	Stoke City	0R
2001	*Hull City	0	Kettering	1R
2001	*Northwich Vic.	1	Bury	0R
2001	*Port Vale	1	Canvey Island	2R
2001	*Lincoln City	0	Dagenham & R.	1
2001	*Morecambe	2	Cambridge Utd.	1
2001	*Blackpool	0	Yeovil	1
2001	*Everton	0	Tranmere Rov.	3
2001	*Tranmere Rov.	4	Southampton	3R
2000	*Rushden & D	2	Scunthorpe Utd.	0
2000	*Chesterfield	1	Enfield	2
2000	*Hereford	1	York City	1
2000	*Ilkeston Town	2	Carlisle Utd.	1
2000	*Hereford	1	Hartlepool Utd.	2
1999	*Bedlington T	4	Colchester Utd.	1
1999	*Hednesford	3	Barnet	1
1999	*Mansfield Town	1	Southport	2
1999	*Rushden & D	1	Shrewsbury Town	0
1999	*Southend Utd.	1	Doncaster Rov.	1
1999	*Yeovil Town	2	Northampton T	0
1999	*Aston Villa	0	Fulham	2
1998	*Hull City	0	Hednesford	2
1998	Lincoln City	3	Emley	3R
(at Huddersfield; Emley won on pens.)				
1998	*Leyton O	0	Hednesford	1R
1998	*Swindon Town	1	Stevenage	2
1998	*Stevenage	2	Cambridge Utd.	1
1997	*Millwall	0	Woking	1R
1997	*Brighton & H.A.	1	Sudbury Town	1R
(Sudbury won on pens).				
1997	*Blackpool	0	Hednesford	1
1997	*Cambridge Utd.	0	Woking	2
1997	*Leyton O.	1	Stevenage	2
1997	*Hednesford	3	York City	0
1997	*Chesterfield	1	Nott'm. Forest	0
1996	*Hitchin	2	Bristol Rov.	1
1996	*Woking	2	Barnet	1R
1996	*Bury	2	Blyth Spartans	0
1996	*Gravesend	2	Colchester Utd.	0
1995	*Kingstonian	2	Brighton & H.A.	1
1995	*Enfield	1	Cardiff City	2
1995	*Marlow	2	Oxford Utd.	0
1995	*Woking	1	Barnet	0R
1995	*Hitchin	4	Hereford	1
1995	*Torquay Utd.	0	Enfield	1R
1995	*Altrincham	0	Wigan Athletic	0
1995	*Wrexham	2	Ipswich Town	1
1995	*Scarborough	1	Port Vale	0
1994	*Colchester Utd.	3	Sutton	4
1994	*Yeovil	1	Fulham	0
1994	*Torquay Utd.	0	Sutton	1
1994	*Halifax Town	2	W.B.A.	1
1994	*Birmingham C.	1	Kidderminster	2
1994	*Stockport Co.	1	Q.P.R.	4
1994	*Liverpool	0	Bristol City	1R
1994	*Arsenal	2	Bolton Wand.	3R
1994	*Leeds Utd.	2	Oxford Utd.	3R
1994	*Luton Town	2	Newcastle Utd.	0R
1994	*Kidderminster	1	Preston N.E.	0
1994	*Cardiff City	1	Manchester City	0
1993	*Hereford	1	Yeovil	2R
1993	*Torquay Utd.	2	Yeovil	5
1993	*Altrincham	2	Chester City	0R
1993	*Cardiff City	2	Bath	3
1993	*Chesterfield	2	Macclesfield	2R
(Macclesfield Town won on pens).				
1993	*Marine	4	Halifax Town	1
1993	*Stafford	2	Lincoln City	1R
1993	*Hartlepool Utd.	1	Crystal Palace	0
1993	*Liverpool	2	Bolton Wand.	2R
1992	*Fulham	0	Hayes	2
1992	*Crawley	4	Northampton	2
1992	*Telford	2	Stoke City	1R
1992	*Aldershot	0	Enfield	1
1992	*Halifax Town	1	Witton A.	2R
1992	*Maidstone	1	Kettering	2
1992	*Walsall	0	Yeovil	1R
1992	*Farnborough	4	Torquay Utd.	3
1992	*Wrexham	2	Arsenal	1
1991	*Scarborough	0	Leek	2
1991	*Northampton	0	Barnet	1R
1991	*Hayes	1	Cardiff City	0R
1991	*Chorley	2	Bury	1
1991	*Shrewsbury T	1	Wimbledon	0
1991	*W.B.A.	2	Woking	4
1990	*Aylesbury	1	Southend Utd.	0
1990	*Scarborough	0	Whitley Bay	1
1990	*Welling	1	Gillingham	0R
1990	*Whitley Bay	2	Preston N.E.	0
1990	*Northampton	2	Coventry City	0
1990	*Cambridge Utd.	1	Millwall	0R
1989	*Sutton	2	Coventry City	1
1989	*Halifax Town	2	Kettering	3R
1989	*Kettering	2	Bristol Rov.	1
1989	*Bognor	2	Exeter City	1
1989	*Leyton Orient	0	Enfield	1R
1989	*Altrincham	3	Lincoln City	2
1989	*Wrexham	2	Runcorn	3R
1988	*Sutton	3	Aldershot	0
1988	*Peterborough	0	Sutton	3
1988	*Carlisle Utd.	2	Maccesfield	1
1988	*Macclesfield	4	Rotherham Utd.	0
1988	*Chester City	0	Runcorn	1
1988	*Cambridge Utd.	0	Yeovil	1
1987	*Caernarfon	1	Stockport Co.	0
1987	Chorley	3	Wolves	0R
(at Bolton)				
1987	*Telford	3	Burnley	0
1987	*York City	3	Caernarfon	2R
1987	*Aldershot	3	Oxford Utd.	0
1987	*Wigan Athletic	1	Norwich City	0
1987	*Charlton Ath.	1	Walsall	2
1986	*Stockport Co.	0	Telford	1
1986	*Wycombe W.	2	Colchester Utd.	0
1986	*Dagenham	2	Cambridge Utd.	1
1986	*Blackpool	1	Altrincham	2
1986	*Birmingham C.	1	Altrincham	2

1986	*Peterborough 1	Leeds Utd. 0
1985	*Telford 2	Lincoln City 1
1985	*Preston N.E. 1	Telford 4
1985	*Telford 2	Bradford City 1
1985	*Telford 3	Darlington 0R
1985	*Blackpool 0	Altrincham 1
1985	*Wimbledon 1	Nott'm. Forest ... 0R
1985	*Orient 2	W.B.A. 1
1985	*Dagenham 1	Peterborough 0
1985	*Swindon Town 1	Dagenham 2R
1985	*York City 1	Arsenal 0
1984	*Halifax Town 2	Whitby 3
1984	*Bournemouth 2	Manchester Utd. .. 0
1984	*Telford 3	Stockport Co. 0
1984	*Telford 3	Northampton 2R
1984	Telford 4	*Rochdale 1
1983	*Cardiff City 2	Weymouth 3
1981	*Exeter City 3	Leicester City 1R
1981	*Exeter City 4	Newcastle Utd. .. 0R
1980	*Halifax Town 1	Manchester City .. 0
1980	*Harlow 1	Leicester City 0R
1980	*Chelsea 0	Wigan Athletic 1
1979	*Newport 2	West Ham Utd. ... 1
1978	*Wrexham 4	Newcastle 1R
1978	*Stoke City 2	Blyth Spartans 3
1976	*Leeds Utd. 0	Crystal Palace 1
1975	*Brighton & H.A. .. 0	Leatherhead 1
1975	*Burnley 0	Wimbledon 1
1972	*Hereford 2	Newcastle 1R
1971	*Colchester Utd. .. 3	Leeds Utd. 2
1969	*Mansfield Town .. 3	West Ham Utd. ... 0
1967	*Swindon Town ... 3	West Ham Utd. . 0R
1967	*Manchester U. ... 1	Norwich City 2
1966	*Ipswich Town ... 2	Southport 3R
1965	*Peterborough 2	Arsenal 1
1964	*Newcastle Utd. .. 1	Bedford Town 2
1964	*Aldershot 2	Aston Villa 1R
1961	*Coventry City 1	Kings Lynn 2
1961	*Chelsea 1	Crewe Alex. 2
1960	*Manchester City . 1	South'ton 5
1959	*Norwich City 3	Manchester U 0
1959	*Worcester 2	Liverpool 1
1959	*Tooting 3	Bournemouth 1
1959	*Tooting 2	Northampton 1
1958	*Newcastle Utd. .. 1	Scunthorpe Utd. .. 3
1957	*Wolves 0	Bournemouth 1
1957	*Bournemouth 3	Tottenham 1
1957	*Derby Co. 1	New Brighton 3
1956	*Derby Co. 1	Boston United 6
1955	*York City 2	Tottenham 1
1955	*Blackpool 0	York City 2
1954	*Arsenal 1	Norwich City 2
1954	*Port Vale 2	Blackpool 0
1952	*Everton 3	Leyton Orient 3
1949	*Yeovil Town 2	Sunderland 1
1948	*Colchester Utd. .. 1	Huddersfield 0
1948	*Arsenal 0	Bradford P.A. 1
1938	*Chelmsford 4	Southampton 1
1933	*Walsall 2	Arsenal 0
1922	*Everton 0	Crystal Palace 6

YEOVIL TOP GIANT-KILLERS

Yeovil's victories over Colchester Utd. and Blackpool in season 2000-01 gave them a total of 20 F.A. Cup wins against League opponents. They set another non-League record by reaching the third round 13 times.

This is Yeovil's triumphant Cup record against League clubs: 1924-5 Bournemouth 3-2; 1934-5 Crystal Palace 3-0; Exeter City 4-1; 1938-9 Brighton & H.A. 2-1; 1948-9 Bury 3-1, Sunderland 2-1; 1958-9 Southend Utd. 1-0; 1960-1 Walsall 1-0; 1963-4 Southend Utd. 1-0, Crystal Palace 3-1; 1970-1 Bournemouth 1-0; 1972-3 Brentford 2-1; 1987-8 Cambridge Utd. 1-0; 1991-2 Walsall 1-0; 1992-3 Torquay Utd. 5-2, Hereford 2-1; 1993-4 Fulham 1-0; 1998-9 Northampton 2-0; 2000-01 Colchester Utd. 5-1, Blackpool 1-0.

NON-LEAGUE BEST IN F.A. CUP

Since League football began in 1888, three non-League clubs have reached the F.A. Cup Final. **Sheffield Wed.** (Football Alliance) were runners-up in 1890, as were **Southampton** (Southern League) in 1900 and 1902. **Tottenham** won the Cup as a Southern League team in 1901.

Otherwise, the **furthest progress** by non-League clubs has been to the **5th. Round** on 5 occasions: Colchester Utd. 1948, Yeovil 1949, Blyth Spartans 1978, Telford 1985 and Kidderminster 1994.

Greatest number of non-League sides to reach the **3rd. Round** is 6 in 1978: Blyth, Enfield, Scarborough, Tilbury, Wealdstone and Wigan Athletic. Since then, 5 in 1988: Bath City, Macclesfield Town, Maidstone, Sutton and Yeovil.

Most to reach **Round 4**: 3 in 1957 (Rhyl, New Brighton, Peterborough Utd.) and 1975 (Leatherhead, Stafford and Wimbledon).

Five non-League clubs reaching **Round 3** in 2001 was a Conference record. They were Chester City, Yeovil, Dagenham & Redbridge, Morecambe and Kingstonian.

In season 2002–3, **Team Bath** became the first University-based side to reach the F.A. Cup 1st. Round since Oxford University (Finalists in 1880).

NON-LEAGUE 'LAST TIMES' IN F.A. CUP

Last time no non-League club reached Round 3: 1951. Last time only one did so: 1969 (Kettering Town). Last time only two: 2000 (Hereford and Rushden & Diamonds) and 2002 (Canvey Island and Dagenham & Redbridge).

TOP-DIVISION SCALPS

Victories in F.A. Cup by non-League clubs over top-division teams since 1900 include:-
1900-1 (Final, replay); **Tottenham** 3, Sheffield Utd. 1 (Tottenham then in Southern League); 1919-20 **Cardiff City** 2, Oldham Athletic 0, and Sheffield Wed. 0, **Darlington** 2; 1923-4 **Corinthians** 1, Blackburn Rov. 0; 1947-8 **Colchester Utd.** 1, Huddersfield Town 0; 1948-9 **Yeovil Town** 2, Sunderland 1; 1971-2 **Hereford Utd.** 2, Newcastle Utd. 1; 1974-5 Burnley 0, **Wimbledon** 1; 1985-6 Birmingham City 1, **Altrincham** 2; 1988-9 **Sutton Utd.** 2, Coventry City 1.

MOST WEMBLEY FINALS

Eight players appeared in five F.A. Cup Finals at Wembley, replays excluded:-
- Joe Hulme (Arsenal: 1927, lost; 1930 won; 1932 lost; 1936 won; Huddersfield Town: 1938 lost).
- Johnny Giles (Manchester Utd.: 1963 won; Leeds Utd.: 1965 lost; 1970 drew at Wembley, lost replay at Old Trafford; 1972 lost; 1973 lost).
- Pat Rice (all for Arsenal: 1971 won; 1972 lost; 1978 lost; 1979 won; 1980 lost).
- Frank Stapleton (Arsenal: 1978 lost; 1979 won; 1980 lost; Manchester Utd.: 1983 won; 1985 lost).
- Ray Clemence (Liverpool: 1971 lost; 1974 won; 1977 lost; Tottenham: 1982 won; 1987 lost).
- Mark Hughes (Manchester Utd.: 1985 won; 1990 won; 1994 won; 1995 lost; Chelsea: 1997 won).
- John Barnes (Watford: 1984 lost; Liverpool: 1988 lost; 1989 won; 1996 lost; Newcastle Utd.: 1998, sub, lost): he was the first player to lose Wembley F.A. Cup Finals with three different clubs.
- Roy Keane (Nott'm Forest: 1991 lost; Manchester Utd.: 1994 won; 1995 lost; 1996 won; 1999 won).

Stapleton, Clemence and Hughes also played in a replay, making six actual F.A. Cup Final appearances for each of them.
Glenn Hoddle also made six F.A. Cup Final appearances at Wembley: 5 for Tottenham (incl. 2 replays), in 1981, 1982 and 1987, and 1 for Chelsea as sub in 1994.
▲Paul Bracewell played in four F.A. Cup Finals without being on the winning side – for Everton 1985, 1986, 1989, Sunderland 1992.

MOST WEMBLEY/CARDIFF FINAL APPEARANCES

6 by **Roy Keane** (Nott'm F: 1991 lost; Manchester Utd.: 1994 won; 1995 lost; 1996 won; 1999 won; 2004 won).

5 by **David Seaman** and **Ray Parlour** (Arsenal): 1993 won; 1998 won; 2001 lost; 2002 won; 2003 won; **Dennis Wise** (Wimbledon 1988 won; Chelsea 1994 won; 1997 won; 2000 won; Millwall 2004 lost).

F.A. CUP-WINNING GOALKEEPER-CAPTAINS

1988 **Dave Beasant** (Wimbledon); 2003 **David Seaman** (Arsenal).

MOST-WINNING MANAGER

Sir Alex Ferguson (Man. Utd.) 5 times (1990, 1994, 1996, 1999, 2004).

PLAYER-MANAGERS IN F.A. CUP FINAL

Kenny Dalglish (Liverpool, 1986); **Glenn Hoddle** (Chelsea, 1994); **Dennis Wise** (Millwall, 2004).

F.A. CUP DEBUTS IN FINAL

Alan Davies (Manchester Utd. v Brighton & H.A., 1983); **Chris Baird** (Southampton v Arsenal, 2003); **Curtis Weston** (Millwall substitute v Manchester Utd., 2004).

F.A. CUP SEMI-FINALS AT WEMBLEY

1991 Tottenham 3, Arsenal 1; **1993** Sheffield Wed. 2, Sheffield Utd. 1; Arsenal 1, Tottenham 0; **1994** Chelsea 2, Luton 0; Manchester Utd. 1, Oldham 1; **2000** Aston Villa beat Bolton 4-1 on pens. (after 0-0); Chelsea 2, Newcastle Utd 1.

FIRST F.A. CUP ENTRANTS (1871-2)

Barnes, Civil Service, Crystal Palace, Clapham Rov., Donnington School (Spalding), Hampstead Heathens, Harrow Chequers, Hitchin, Maidenhead, Marlow, Queen's Park (Glasgow), Reigate Priory, Royal Engineers, Upton Park and Wanderers. Total 15. Three scratched. **Record F.A. Cup entry 674 in 1921.**

CUP 'FIRSTS'

Out of country: Cardiff City, by defeating Arsenal 1-0 in the 1927 Final at Wembley, became the first and only club to take the F.A. Cup out of England.

All-English Winning XI: First club to win the F.A. Cup with all-English XI: Blackburn Olympic in 1883. Others since: W.B.A. in 1888 and 1931, Bolton Wand. (1958), Manchester City (1969), West Ham Utd. (1964 and 1975).

Non-English Winning XI: Liverpool in 1986 (Mark Lawrenson, born Preston N.E., was a Rep. of Ireland player).

Won both Cups: Old Carthusians won the F.A. Cup in 1881 and the F.A. Amateur Cup in 1894 and 1897. **Wimbledon** won Amateur Cup in 1963, F.A. Cup in 1988.

MOST GAMES NEEDED TO WIN F.A. CUP

Barnsley played a record 12 matches (20 hours' football) to win the F.A. Cup in season 1911-12. All six replays (one in Rd. 1, three in Rd. 4 and one in each of semi-final and Final) were brought about by goalless draws.

Arsenal played 11 F.A. Cup games when winning the trophy in 1979. Five of them were in the 3rd. Rd. against Sheffield Wed..

LONGEST F.A. CUP TIES

6 matches (11 hours): **Alvechurch v Oxford City** (4th. qual. round, 1971-2). Alvechurch won 1-0.

5 matches (9 hours, 22 mins – record for competition proper): **Stoke City v Bury** (3rd. round, 1954-5). Stoke City won 3-2.

5 matches: **Chelsea v Burnley** (4th. round, 1955-6). Chelsea won 2-0.

5 matches: **Hull City v Darlington** (2nd. round, 1960-1). Hull City won 3-0.

5 matches: **Arsenal v Sheffield Wed.** (3rd. round, 1978-9). Arsenal won 2-0.

Other marathons (qualifying comp., all 5 matches, 9 hours): **Barrow v Gillingham** (last qual. round, 1924-5) – winners Barrow; **Leyton v Ilford** (3rd. qual. round, 1924-5) – winners Leyton; **Falmouth Town v Bideford** (3rd. qual. round, 1973-4) – winners Bideford.

End of Cup Final replays: The F.A. decided that, with effect from 1999, there would be no Cup Final replays. In the event of a draw after extra time, the match would be decided on penalties.

F.A. Cup marathons ended in season 1991-2, when the penalty shoot-out was introduced to decide ties still level after one replay and extra time.

- In 1932-3 **Brighton & H.A.** (Div. 3 South) played 11 F.A. Cup games, including replays, and scored 43 goals, without getting past Rd 5. They forgot to claim exemption and had to play from 1st Qual. Round.

LONGEST ROUND

The longest round in F.A. Cup history was the **third round** in **season 1962-3**. It took 66 days to complete, lasting from January 5 to March 11, and included 261 postponements because of bad weather.

LONGEST UNBEATEN F.A. CUP RUN

23 matches by **Blackburn Rov.** In winning the Cup in three consecutive years (1884-5-6), they won 21 ties (one in a replay), and their first Cup defeat in four seasons was in a first round replay of the next competition.

RE-STAGED F.A. CUP TIES

Sixth round, March 9, 1974: Newcastle Utd. 4, Nott'm. Forest 3. Match declared void by F.A. and ordered to be replayed following a pitch invasion after Newcastle Utd. had a player sent off. Forest claimed the hold-up caused the game to change its pattern. The tie went to two further matches at Goodison Park (0-0, then 1-0 to Newcastle Utd.).

Third round, January 5, 1985: Burton Albion 1, Leicester City 6 (at Derby Co.). Burton goalkeeper Paul Evans was hit on the head by a missile thrown from the crowd, and continued in a daze. The F.A. ordered the tie to be played again, behind closed doors at Coventry City (Leicester City won 1- 0).

First round replay, November 25, 1992: Peterborough Utd. 9 (Tony Philliskirk 5), Kingstonian 1. Match expunged from records because, at 3-0 after 57 mins, Kingstonian were reduced to ten men when goalkeeper Adrian Blake was concussed by a 50 pence coin thrown from the crowd. The tie was re-staged on the same ground behind closed doors (Peterborough Utd. won 1-0).

Fifth round: Within an hour of Cup-holders Arsenal beating Sheffield Utd. 2-1 at Highbury on February 13, 1999, the Football Association took the unprecedented step of declaring the match void because an unwritten rule of sportsmanship had been broken. With United's Lee Morris lying injured, their goalkeeper Alan Kelly kicked the ball into touch. Play resumed with Arsenal's Ray Parlour throwing it in the direction of Kelly, but Nwankwo Kanu took possession and centred for Marc Overmars to score the 'winning' goal. After four minutes of protests by manager Steve Bruce and his players, referee Peter Jones confirmed the goal. Both managers absolved Kanu of cheating but Arsenal's Arsene Wenger offered to replay the match. With the F.A. immediately approving, it was re-staged at Highbury ten days later (ticket prices halved) and Arsenal again won 2-1.

F.A. CUP PRIZE FUND

The makeover of the F.A. Cup competition took off in 2001-02 with the introduction of prize money round by round (semi-finals excepted) Later-round payments remained the same in 2002-03-04: 3rd Round £50,000; 4th Round £75,000; 5th Round £150,000; 6th Round £400,000; Runners-up £1m; Winners £2m.

F.A. CUP FOLLIES 1999-2000

The F.A. broke with tradition by deciding the 3rd. Round should be moved from its regular January date and staged before Christmas. Criticism was strong, gates poor and the 3rd. Round in 2001-01 reverted to the New Year.

By allowing the holders Manchester Utd. to withdraw from the 1999-2000 Cup competition in order to play in FIFA's inaugural World Club Championship in Brazil in January, the F.A. were left with an odd number of clubs in the 3rd. Round. Their solution was a **'lucky losers'** draw among clubs knocked out in Round 2. Darlington, beaten at Gillingham, won it to re-enter the competition, then lost 2-1 away to Aston Villa.

WAR-TIME MARATHON

Match of 203 minutes: Stockport Co.'s second-leg tie with Doncaster Rov. in the Third Division North Cup, March 30, 1946, lasted 203 minutes and a replay was still necessary. Both legs were drawn 2-2 and Doncaster won the replay 4-0.

F.A. CUP FINAL HAT-TRICKS

There have been only three in the history of the competition: **Billy Townley** (Blackburn Rov., 1890), **Jimmy Logan** (Notts Co., 1894) and **Stan Mortensen** (Blackpool, 1953).

FIVE WINNING MEDALS

The Hon. Arthur Kinnaird (The Wanderers and Old Etonians), **Charles Wollaston** (The Wanderers) and **Jimmy Forrest** (Blackburn Rov.) each earned five F.A. Cup winners' medals. Kinnaird, later president of the F.A., played in nine of the first 12 F.A. Cup Finals, and was on the winning side three times for The Wanderers, in 1873 (captain), 1877, 1878 (captain), and twice as captain of Old Etonians (1879, 1882).

MOST F.A. CUP WINNERS' MEDALS AT WEMBLEY

4 – **Mark Hughes** (3 for Manchester Utd., 1 for Chelsea).

3 – 18 players: **Dick Pym** (3 clean sheets in Finals), **Bob Haworth, Jimmy Seddon, Harry Nuttall, Billy Butler** (all Bolton Wand.); **David Jack** (2 Bolton Wand., 1 Arsenal); **Bob Cowell, Jack Milburn, Bobby Mitchell** (all Newcastle Utd.); **Dave Mackay** (Tottenham); **Frank Stapleton** (1 Arsenal, 2 Manchester Utd.); **Bryan Robson** (3 times winning captain), **Arthur Albiston, Gary Pallister** (all Manchester Utd.); **Bruce Grobbelaar, Steve Nicol, Ian Rush** (all Liverpool); **Roy Keane, Peter Schmeichel; Dennis Wise** (1 Wimbledon, 2 Chelsea).

• Arsenal's **David Seaman** and **Ray Parlour** have each earned 4 winners' medals (2 at Wembley, 2 at Cardiff) as has Manchester Utd's **Roy Keane** (3 at Wembley, 1 at Cardiff).

MOST F.A. CUP APPEARANCES

88 by **Ian Callaghan** (79 for Liverpool, 7 for Swansea City, 2 for Crewe Alexandra); 87 by **John Barnes** (31 for Watford, 51 for Liverpool, 5 for Newcastle Utd.); 86 by **Stanley Matthews** (37 for Stoke City, 49 for Blackpool); 86 by **Peter Shilton** for six clubs (Leicester City, Stoke City, Nott'm. Forest, Southampton, Derby Co. and Plymouth Argyle); 84 by **Bobby Charlton** (80 for Manchester Utd., 4 for Preston N.E.); 82 by **David Seaman** (5 for Peterborough Utd., 5 for Birmingham City, 17 for Q.P.R., 54 for Arsenal, 1 for Manchester City.

THREE-CLUB FINALISTS

Four players have appeared in the F.A. Final for three clubs: **Harold Halse** for Manchester Utd. (1909), Aston Villa (1913) and Chelsea (1915); **Ernie Taylor** for Newcastle Utd. (1951), Blackpool (1953) and Manchester Utd. (1958); **John Barnes** for Watford (1984), Liverpool (1988, 1989, 1996) and Newcastle Utd. (1998); **Dennis Wise** for Wimbledon (1988), Chelsea (1994, 1997, 2000), Millwall (2004)..

CUP MAN WITH TWO CLUBS IN SAME SEASON

Stan Crowther, who played for Aston Villa against Manchester Utd. in the 1957 F.A. Cup Final, appeared for both Aston Villa and United in the 1957-8 competition. United signed him directly after the Munich air crash and, in the circumstances, he was given special dispensation to play for them in the Cup, including the Final.

CAPTAIN'S CUP DOUBLE

Martin Buchan is the only player to have captained Scottish and English F.A. Cup-winning teams – Aberdeen in 1970 and Manchester Utd. in 1977.

MEDALS BEFORE AND AFTER

Two players appeared in F.A. Cup Final teams before and after the war: **Raich Carter** was twice a winner (Sunderland 1937, Derby Co. 1946) and **Willie Fagan** twice on the losing side (Preston N.E. 1937, Liverpool 1950).

DELANEY'S COLLECTION

Scotland winger **Jimmy Delaney** uniquely earned Scottish, English, N. Ireland and Rep. of Ireland cup medals. He was a winner with Celtic (1937), Manchester Utd. (1948) and Derry City (1954) and a runner-up with Cork City (1956).

STARS WHO MISSED OUT

Internationals who never won an F.A. Cup winner's medal include: **Tommy Lawton, Tom Finney, Johnny Haynes, Gordon Banks, George Best, Terry Butcher, Peter Shilton, Martin Peters, Nobby Stiles, Alan Ball** and **Malcolm Macdonald**.

CUP WINNERS AT NO COST

Not one member of **Bolton's** 1958 F.A. Cup-winning team cost the club a transfer fee. Five were Internationals and the eleven each joined the club for a £10 signing-on fee.

ALL-INTERNATIONAL CUP WINNERS

In **Manchester Utd.'s** 1985 Cup-winning team v Everton, all 11 players were full Internationals, as was the substitute who played. So were ten of Everton's team.
   Arsenal's Cup-winning line-ups in the 2002 and 2003 Finals were all full Internationals, as were all 14 players who appeared for **Manchester Utd.** in the 2004 final.

NO-CAP CUP WINNERS

Sunderland, in 1973, were the last F.A. Cup-winning team not to include an International player, although some were capped later.

11-NATIONS LINE-UP

Liverpool fielded a team of 11 different nationalities in the F.A. Cup 3rd Round at Yeovil on Jan. 4, 2004.

HIGH-SCORING SEMI-FINALS

The **record team score** in F.A. Cup semi-finals is 6: 1891-2 WBA 6, Nott'm. Forest 2; 1907-8 Newcastle Utd. 6, Fulham 0; 1933-4 Manchester City 6, Aston Villa 1.
   Most goals in semi-finals (aggregate): 17 in 1892 (4 matches) and 1899 (5 matches). In modern times: 15 in 1958 (3 matches, including Manchester Utd. 5, Fulham 3 – highest-scoring semi-final since last war); 16 in 1989-90 (Crystal Palace 4, Liverpool 3; Manchester Utd. v Oldham Athletic 3-3, 2-1. **All 16 goals** in those three matches were scored by **different players**.
   Last hat-trick in an F.A. Cup semi-final was scored by **Alex Dawson** for Manchester Utd. in 5-3 replay win against Fulham at Highbury in 1958.

F.A. CUP SEMI-FINAL VENUES

Aston Villa Park has staged more such matches (53 including replays) than any other ground. Next is Hillsborough (33).

FOUR SPECIAL AWAYS

For the only time in F.A. Cup history, **all four quarter-finals** in season 1986-7 were won by the away team.

F.A. CUP – DRAWS RECORD

In season 1985-6, **seven** of the eight F.A. Cup 5th. Round ties went to replays – a record for that stage of the competition.

LUCK OF THE DRAW

In the F.A. Cup on Jan. 11, 1947, eight of **London**'s ten Football League clubs involved in the 3rd. Round were drawn at home (including Chelsea v Arsenal). Only Crystal Palace played outside the capital (at Newcastle Utd.).

Contrast: In the 3rd. Round in Jan. 1992, Charlton Athletic were the only London club drawn at home (against Barnet), but the venue of the Farnborough v West Ham Utd. tie was reversed on police instruction. So Upton Park staged Cup-ties on successive days, with West Ham Utd. at home on the Saturday and Charlton Athletic (who shared the ground) on Sunday.

Arsenal were drawn away in every round on the way to reaching the F.A. Cup Finals of 1971 and 1972. **Manchester Utd.** won the Cup in 1990 without playing once at home.

The 1999 F.A. Cup finalists **Manchester Utd.** and **Newcastle Utd.** were both drawn at home every time in Rounds 3-6.

On their way to the semi-finals of both domestic Cup competitions in season 2002–03, **Sheffield Utd.** were drawn at home ten times out of ten and won all ten matches – six in the League's Worthington Cup and four in the F.A. Cup.

F.A. CUP: ALL TOP-DIVISION VICTIMS

Only instance of an F.A. Cup-winning club meeting top-division opponents in every round was provided by Manchester Utd. in 1947-8. They beat Aston Villa, Liverpool, Charlton Athletic, Preston N.E., then Derby Co. in the semi-final and Blackpool in the Final.

In **contrast**, these clubs have reached the Final without playing top-division opponents on the way: West Ham Utd. (1923), Bolton Wand. (1926), Blackpool (1948), Bolton Wand. (1953), Millwall (2004).

HOME ADVANTAGE

For the first time in F.A. Cup history, all eight ties in the 1992-3 5th. Round were won (no replays) by the **clubs drawn at home**. Only other instance of eight home wins at the 'last 16' stage of the F.A. Cup was in 1889-90, in what was then the 2nd. Round.

FEWEST TOP-DIVISION CLUBS IN LAST 16 (5TH. ROUND)

5 in 1958; **6** in 1927, 1970, 1982; **7** in 1994, 2003; **8** in 2002, 2004.

SIXTH-ROUND ELITE

For the first time in F.A. Cup 6th. Round history, dating from 1926, when the format of the competition changed, **all eight quarter-finalists** in 1995-6 were from the top division.

F.A. CUP SEMI-FINAL – DOUBLE DERBIES

There have been only two instances of both F.A. Cup semi-finals in the same year being local derbies: **1950** Liverpool beat Everton 2-0 (Maine Road), Arsenal beat Chelsea 1-0 after 2-2 draw (both at Tottenham); **1993** Arsenal beat Tottenham 1-0 (Wembley), Sheffield Wed. beat Sheffield Utd. 2-1 (Wembley).

TOP CLUB DISTINCTION

Since the Football League began in 1888, there has never been an F.A. Cup Final in which **neither club** represented the top division.

SPURS OUT – AND IN

Tottenham were banned, pre-season, from the 1994-5 F.A. Cup competition because of financial irregularities, but were readmitted on appeal and reached the semi-finals.

BROTHERS IN F.A. CUP FINAL TEAMS (Modern Times)

1950 Denis and Leslie Compton (Arsenal); **1952** George and Ted Robledo (Newcastle Utd.); **1967** Ron and Allan Harris (Chelsea); **1977** Jimmy and Brian Greenhoff (Manchester Utd.); **1996** and **1999** Gary and Phil Neville (Manchester Utd.)

F.A. CUP – FIRST SPONSORS

Littlewoods Pools became the first sponsors of the F.A. Cup in season 1994-5 in a £14m., 4-year deal.

French insurance giants **AXA** took over (season 1998-9) in a sponsorship worth £25m. over 4 years.

TRADITION RETURNS

With effect May, 2003, the F.A. Cup Final reverted to being played on the last Saturday of the season.

FIRST GOALKEEPER-SUBSTITUTE IN CUP FINAL

Paul Jones (Southampton), who replaced injured Antti Niemi against Arsenal in 2003.

FINAL LOSERS LACK FINISH

In the last 11 F.A. Cup Finals to 2004, ten of the losing sides failed to score.

LEAGUE CUP RECORDS
(See also Goalscoring section)

Highest scores: West Ham Utd. 10-0 v Bury (2nd. Rd., 2nd. Leg 1983-4; agg. 12-1); Liverpool 10-0 v Fulham (2nd. Rd., 1st. Leg 1986-7; agg. 13-2).

Most League Cup goals (career): 49 Geoff Hurst (43 West Ham Utd., 6 Stoke City, 1960-75); 49 Ian Rush (48 Liverpool, 1 Newcastle Utd., 1981-98).

Highest scorer (season): 12 Clive Allen (Tottenham 1986-7 in 9 apps).

Most goals in match: 6 Frank Bunn (Oldham Athletic v Scarborough, 3rd. Rd., 1989-90).

Fewest goals conceded by winners: 3 by Leeds Utd. (1967-8), Tottenham (1970-1), Aston Villa (1995-6).

Most winner's medals: 5 Ian Rush (Liverpool).

Most appearances in Final: 6 Kenny Dalglish (Liverpool 1978-87), Ian Rush (Liverpool 1981-95).

Alan Hardaker Man of the Match Award was introduced in the 1990 Final, in recognition of the League's late secretary who proposed the competition in 1960.

League Cup sponsors: Milk Cup 1981-6, Littlewoods Cup 1987-90, Rumbelows Cup 1991-2, Coca-Cola Cup 1993-8. Worthington Cup 1999-2003, Carling Cup from season 2003-4.

Norwich City unique: In 1985, Norwich City became (and they remain) the only club to win a major domestic cup and be relegated in the same season. They won the League's Milk Cup and went down from the old First Division.

Liverpool's League Cup records: Winners a record 7 times. **Ian Rush** only player to win 5 times. Rush also first to play in 8 winning teams in Cup Finals **at Wembley,** all with Liverpool (F.A. Cup 1986-89-92; League Cup 1981-82-83-84-95).

Britain's first under-cover Cup Final: Worthington (League) Cup Final 2002 between Blackburn Rov. and Tottenham at Cardiff's Millennium Stadium on Sunday, February 24, 2002. With rain forecast, the retractable roof was closed on the morning of the match.

DISCIPLINE

SENDINGS-OFF

Season 2003-4 set an **all-time record** of 504 players sent off in English domestic football competitions. They comprised 58 in the Premiership, 390 Nationwide League, 28 F.A. Cup (excluding non-League dismissals), 22 League Cup, 2 in Nationwide play-offs, 4 in LDV Vans Trophy. Previous highest red-card total was 437 in season 2001-02, followed by 436 in 2002-03.

The 58 Premiership red cards in 2003-04 was 13 fewer than the record English **top-division** total of 71 in 2002-03. **Bolton Wand.** were the only club in the English divisions without a player sent off in any first-team competition last season.

Worst day for dismissals in English football history was December 13, 2003 with 19 red cards (2 Premiership and the 17 in the Nationwide League setting a **Football League record** for one day).

Previous worst overall total was 18 on November 16, 2002 (1 Premier League, 5 Nationwide League, 12 in F.A. Cup 1st. Round – 7 of those non-League). That equalled the **F.A. Cup's worst disciplinary day** (12 dismissals in 1st. Round on November 20, 1982).

Most players ordered off in **Anglo-Scottish football on one day**: 25, all League, on Oct. 16, 1999 (14 in England, 11 in Scotland).

● In the entire first season of post-war League football (1946-7) only 12 players were sent off, followed by 14 in 1949-50, and the total League dismissals for the first nine seasons after the war was 104.

The worst pre-war total was 28 in each of seasons 1921-2 and 1922-3.

ENGLAND SENDINGS-OFF

Alan Smith became the ninth player England have had sent off in their International history (1872 to date) when he was shown the red card in the last minute of the European Championship qualifier against Macedonia at Southampton on October 16, 2002.

June 5, 1968 **Alan Mullery**	v Yugoslavia (Florence, Eur. Champ.)
June 6, 1973 **Alan Ball**	v Poland (Chorzow, World Cup qual.)
June 15, 1977 **Trevor Cherry**	v Argentina (Buenos Aires, friendly)
June 6, 1986 **Ray Wilkins**	v Morocco (Monterrey, World Cup Finals)
June 30, 1998 **David Beckham**	v Argentina (St. Etienne, World Cup Finals)
Sept. 5, 1998 **Paul Ince**	v Sweden (Stockholm, Eur. Champ. qual.)
June 5, 1999 **Paul Scholes**	v Sweden (Wembley, Eur. Champ. qual.)
Sept. 8, 1999 **David Batty**	v Poland (Warsaw, Eur. Champ. qual.)
Oct. 16, 2002 **Alan Smith**	v Macedonia (Southampton, Eur. Champ. qual.)

Other countries: Most recent sendings-off of players representing the other Home Countries: **N. Ireland** – **Mark Williams** v Barbados (Friendly, Bridgetown, May 2004); **Scotland** – **Maurice Ross** v Germany (European Champ., Dortmund, Sept. 2003); **Wales** – Jason Koumas v Finland (European Champ., Cardiff, September 2003); **Rep. of Ireland** – **Gary Kelly** v Holland (World Cup qual., Dublin, September 2001).

England dismissals at other levels:-
U-23 (4): **Stan Anderson** (v Bulgaria, Sofia, May 19, 1957); **Alan Ball** (v Austria, Vienna, June 2, 1965); **Kevin Keegan** (v E. Germany, Magdeburg, June 1, 1972); **Steve Perryman** (v Portugal, Lisbon, Nov. 19, 1974).
U-21 (12): **Sammy Lee** (v Hungary, Keszthely, June 5, 1981); **Mark Hateley** (v Scotland, Hampden Park, April 19, 1982); **Paul Elliott** (v Denmark, Maine Road, Manchester, March 26, 1986); **Tony Cottee** (v W. Germany, Ludenscheid, September 8, 1987); **Julian Dicks** (v Mexico, Toulon, France, June 12, 1988); **Jason Dodd** (v Mexico, Toulon, May 29, 1991; 3 Mexico players also sent off in that match); **Matthew Jackson** (v France, Toulon, May 28, 1992); **Robbie Fowler** (v Austria, Kafkenberg, October 11, 1994); **Alan Thompson** (v Portugal, Oporto, September 2, 1995); **Terry Cooke** (v Portugal, Toulon, May 30, 1996); **Ben Thatcher** (v Italy, Rieti, October 10, 1997); **John Curtis** (v Greece, Heraklion, November 13, 1997); **Jody Morris** (v Luxembourg, Grevenmacher, October 13, 1998); **Stephen Wright** (v Germany, Derby Co., October 6, 2000); **Alan Smith** (v Finland, Valkeakoski, October 10, 2000); **Luke Young** and **John Terry** (v Greece, Athens, June 5, 2001); **Shola Ameobi** (v Portugal, Rio Maior, March 28, 2003); **Jermaine Pennant** (v Croatia, Upton Park, August 19, 2003); **Glen Johnson** (v Turkey, Istanbul, October 10, 2003).
England 'B' (1): **Neil Webb** (v Algeria, Algiers, December 11, 1990).

MOST DISMISSALS IN INTERNATIONAL MATCHES

19 (10 Chile, 9 Uruguay), June 25, 1975; **6** (2 Mexico, 4 Argentina), 1956; **6** (5 Ecuador, 1 Uruguay), Jan. 4, 1977 (4 Ecuadorians sent off in 78th min., match abandoned, 1-1); **5** (Holland 3, Brazil 2), June 6, 1999 in Goianio, Brazil.

INTERNATIONAL STOPPED THROUGH DEPLETED SIDE

Portugal v Angola (5-1), friendly International in Lisbon on November 14, 2001, abandoned (68 mins) because Angola were down to 6 players (4 sent off, 1 carried off, no substitutes left).

MOST 'CARDS' IN WORLD CUP FINALS MATCH

18 (16 yellow, 2 red, both colours equally shared) in Germany v Cameroon group qualifier, Shizuoka, Japan, June 11, 2002.

FIVE OFF IN ONE MATCH

For the first time since League football began in 1888, **five** players were sent off in one match (two Chesterfield, three Plymouth Argyle) in Div. 2 at Saltergate on **Feb. 22, 1997.** Four were dismissed (two from each side) in a goalmouth brawl in the last minute.

Second instance of **five** sent off in a League match was on **Dec. 2, 1997:** 4 Bristol Rov. players, 1 Wigan Athletic in Div. 2 match at Wigan. Four of those dismissals came in the 45th minute.

Only the third instance of **five** players sent off in an English League match occurred on **Nov. 23, 2002:** Exeter City 3, Cambridge Utd. 2 – all in the last minute.

There have been eleven instances of **four** Football League club players being sent off in one match:

Jan. 8, 1955 Crewe Alexandra v Bradford City (Div. 3 North), two players from each side.

Dec. 13, 1986 Sheffield Utd. (1 player) v Portsmouth (3) in Div. 2.

Aug. 18, 1987 Port Vale v Northampton Town (Littlewoods Cup 1st. Round, 1st. Leg), two players from each side.

Dec. 12, 1987 Brentford v Mansfield Town (Div. 3), two players from each side.

Sept. 6, 1992 First instance in British first-class football of **four players from one side** being sent off in one match. Hereford Utd.'s seven survivors, away to Northampton Town (Div. 3), held out for a 1-1 draw.

Mar. 1, 1977 Norwich City v Huddersfield Town (Div. 1), two from each side.

Oct. 4, 1977 Shrewsbury Town (1 player), Rotherham Utd. (3) in Div. 3.

Aug. 22, 1998 Gillingham v Bristol Rov. (Div. 2), two from each side, all after injury-time brawl.

Mar. 16, 2001 Bristol City v Millwall (Div. 2), two from each side.

Aug. 17, 2002 Lincoln City (1 player), Carlisle (3) in Div. 3; **Aug. 26, 2002** (Wycombe Wand. v Q.P.R. (Div. 2), two from each side.

Four Stranraer players were sent off away to Airdrie (Scottish Div. 1) on Dec. 3, 1994, and that Scottish record was equalled when **four Hearts men** were ordered off away to Rangers (Prem. Div.) on **Sept. 14, 1996.** Albion Rov. had **four** players sent off (3 in last 8 mins) away to Queen's Park (Scottish Div. 3) on **August 23, 1997.**

In the **Island Games** in Guernsey (July 2003), five players (all from Rhodes) were sent off against Guernsey for violent conduct and the match was abandoned by referee Wendy Toms.

Modern instances of **three players from one side** being sent off:

Dec. 13, 1986 Portsmouth (away to Sheffield Utd., Div. 2); **Aug. 23, 1989** Falkirk (home to Hearts, Scottish Skol Cup 3rd. Round); **Apr. 20, 1992** Newcastle Utd. (away to Derby Co., Div. 2); **May 2, 1992** Bristol City (away to Watford, Div. 2); **Nov. 23, 1996** Wycombe Wand. (home to Preston N.E., Div. 2); **Feb. 8, 1997** Darlington (away to Scarborough, Div. 3); **Oct. 4, 1997** Rotherham Utd. (away to Shrewsbury Town, Div. 3); **Mar. 28, 1998** Barnsley (home to Liverpool, Premiership); **Sept. 26, 1998** Southend Utd. (away to Swansea City, Div. 3); **May 1, 1999** West Ham Utd. (home to Leeds Utd., Premiership); **Oct. 9, 1999** Torquay Utd. away to Northampton Town (Div. 3); **Dec. 28, 1999** Cardiff City away to Cambridge Utd. (Div. 2); **Apr. 29, 2000** Halifax Town away to York City (Div. 3); **Apr. 16, 2001** Carlisle Utd. away to Scunthorpe Utd. (Div. 3); **Apr. 1, 2002** Kidderminster away to Bristol Rov. (Div. 3); **Mar. 16, 2002** Sheffield Utd. home to W.B.A. (Div.1); **Dec. 13, 2003** Southend Utd. away to Swansea City.

Aug. 24, 1994: Three Sheffield Utd. players, and one from Udinese, were sent off in the Anglo-Italian Cup at Bramall Lane on Aug. 24, 1994. In addition, Utd. manager Dave Bassett was ordered from the bench.

Most dismissals one team, one match: Five players of America Tres Rios in first ten minutes after disputed goal by opponents Itaperuna in Brazilian cup match in Rio de Janeiro on Nov. 23, 1991. Tie then abandoned and awarded to Itaperuna.

Eight dismissals in one match: Four on each side in S. American Super Cup quarter-final (Gremio, Brazil v Penarol, Uruguay) in Oct. 1993.

Five dismissals in one season – Dave Caldwell (2 with Chesterfield, 3 with Torquay Utd.) in 1987-88.

First instance of **four dismissals in Scottish match**: three **Rangers** players (all English – Terry Hurlock, Mark Walters, Mark Hateley) and **Celtic's** Peter Grant in Scottish Cup quarter-final at Parkhead on Mar. 17, 1991 (Celtic won 2-0).

Four players (3 Hamilton, 1 Airdrie) were sent off in Scottish Div. 1 match on Oct. 30, 1993.

Four players (3 Ayr, 1 Stranraer) were sent off in Scottish Div. 1 match on Aug. 27, 1994.

In Scottish Cup first round replays on Dec. 16, 1996, there were two instances of **three players of one side sent off**: Albion Rov. (away to Forfar) and Huntly (away to Clyde).

FASTEST SENDINGS-OFF

World record – **10 secs: Giuseppe Lorenzo** (Bologna) for striking opponent in Italian League match v Parma, December 9, 1990.

Domestic – **13 secs: Kevin Pressman** (Sheffield Wed. goalkeeper at Wolves, Div. 1, Sunday, Aug. 14, 2000); **15 secs: Simon Rea** (Peterborough Utd. at Cardiff, Div. 2, Nov. 2, 2002). **19 secs: Mark Smith** (Crewe Alexandra goalkeeper at Darlington, Div. 3, Mar. 12, 1994). **In Div. 1** – **85 secs: Liam O'Brien** (Manchester Utd. at Southampton, Jan. 3, 1987). **Premier League** – **72 secs: Tim Flowers** (Blackburn Rov. goalkeeper v Leeds Utd., Feb. 1, 1995).

In World Cup – **55 secs: Jose Batista** (Uruguay v Scotland at Neza, Mexico, June 13, 1986).

In European competition – **90 secs: Sergei Dirkach** (Dynamo Moscow v Ghent UEFA Cup 3rd round, 2nd leg, December 11, 1991).

Fastest F.A. Cup dismissal – **52 secs: Ian Culverhouse** (Swindon Town defender, deliberate hand-ball on goal-line, away to Everton, 3rd. Round, Sunday Jan. 5, 1997).

Fastest League Cup dismissal – **33 secs: Jason Crowe** (Arsenal substitute v Birmingham City, 3rd Round, Oct. 14, 1997).

Fastest Sending-off on debut: See Jason Crowe (above).

Fastest Sending-off of substitute – **0 secs: Walter Boyd** (Swansea City) for striking opponent before ball in play after he went on (83 mins) at home to Darlington, Div. 3, Nov. 23, 1999.

MOST SENDINGS-OFF IN CAREER

21 – **Willie Johnston** (Rangers 7, WBA 6, Vancouver Whitecaps 4, Hearts 3, Scotland 1)

21 – **Roy McDonough** (13 in Football League – Birmingham City, Walsall, Chelsea, Colchester Utd., Southend Utd., Exeter City, Cambridge Utd. + 8 non-league).

13 – **Steve Walsh** (Wigan Athletic, Leicester City, Norwich City, Coventry City).

13 – **Martin Keown** (Arsenal, Aston Villa, Everton).

12 – **Dennis Wise** (Wimbledon, Chelsea, Leicester City, Millwall).

12 – **Vinnie Jones** (Wimbledon, Leeds Utd., Sheffield Utd., Chelsea, Q.P.R.).

12 – **Mark Dennis** (Birmingham City, Southampton, Q.P.R.).

12 – **Roy Keane** (Manchester Utd., Rep. of Ireland).

11 – **Alan Smith** (Leeds Utd., England U-21, England).

9 – **Patrick Vieira** (Arsenal).

Most Premiership Sendings-off: Patrick Vieira 9, Vinnie Jones 7, Roy Keane 7.

● **Carlton Palmer** holds the unique record of having been sent off with each of his five Premiership clubs: Sheffield Wed., Leeds Utd., Southampton, Nott'm. Forest and Coventry City.

WEMBLEY SENDINGS-OFF

Manchester Utd.'s **Kevin Moran** is the only player to be sent off in the F.A. Cup Final (v Everton, 1985). His dismissal was one of 22 in major matches at Wembley:

Aug. 1948 **Branko Stankovic** (Yugoslavia) v Sweden, Olympic Games.
July 1966 **Antonio Rattin** (Argentina captain) v England, World cup q-final.
Aug. 1974 **Billy Bremner** (Leeds Utd.) and **Kevin Keegan** (Liverpool), Charity Shield.
Mar. 1977 **Gilbert Dresch** (Luxembourg) v England, World Cup.
May 1985 **Kevin Moran** (Manchester Utd.) v Everton, F.A. Cup Final.
Apr. 1993 **Lee Dixon** (Arsenal) v Tottenham, F.A. Cup semi-final.
May 1993 **Peter Swan** (Port Vale) v W.B.A., Div. 2 Play-off Final.
Mar. 1994 **Andrei Kanchelskis** (Manchester Utd.) v Aston Villa, League Cup Final.
May 1994 **Mike Wallace** and **Chris Beaumont** (Stockport Co.) v Burnley, Div. 2 Play-off
    Final.
June 1995 **Tetsuji Hashiratani** (Japan) v England, Umbro Cup.
May 1997 **Brian Statham** (Brentford) v Crewe Alexandra, Div. 2 Play-off Final.
Apr. 1998 **Capucho** (Portugal) v England, friendly.
Nov. 1998 **Ray Parlour** (Arsenal) and Tony Vareilles (Lens), Champions League.
Mar. 1999 **Justin Edinburgh** (Tottenham) v Leicester City, League Cup Final.
June 1999 **Paul Scholes** (England) v Sweden, European Championship qual.
Feb. 2000 **Clint Hill** (Tranmere) v Leicester City, League Cup Final.
Apr. 2000 **Mark Delaney** (Aston Villa) v Bolton Wand., F.A. Cup semi-final.
May 2000 **Kevin Sharp** (Wigan Athletic) v Gillingham, Div. 2 Play-off Final.
Aug. 2000 **Roy Keane** (Manchester Utd. captain) v Chelsea, Charity Shield.

WEMBLEY'S SUSPENDED CAPTAINS

Suspension prevented four **club captains** playing at Wembley in modern finals, in successive years.

Three were in F.A. Cup Finals – Glenn Roeder (Q.P.R., 1982), **Steve Foster** (Brighton & H.A., 1983) and **Wilf Rostron** (Watford, 1984) – and Sunderland's **Shaun Elliott** was barred from the 1985 Milk Cup Final.

Roeder was banned from Q.P.R.'s 1982 Cup Final replay against Tottenham, and Foster was ruled out of the first match in Brighton & H.A.'s 1983 Final against Manchester Utd.

BOOKINGS RECORDS

Most players of one Football League club booked in one match is **TEN** – members of the Mansfield Town team away to Crystal Palace in 'F.A. Cup third round, January 1963.

Fastest bookings – 3 seconds after kick-off, **Vinnie Jones** (Chelsea, home to Sheffield Utd., F.A. Cup fifth round, February 15, 1992); 5 seconds after kick-off: **Vinnie Jones** (Sheffield Utd., away to Manchester City, Div. 1, January 19, 1991). He was sent-off (54 mins) for second bookable offence.

FIGHTING TEAM-MATES

Charlton Athletic's **Mike Flanagan** and **Derek Hales** were sent off for fighting each other five minutes from end of F.A. Cup 3rd Round tie at home to Southern League Maidstone on Jan. 9, 1979.

Bradford City's **Andy Myers** and **Stuart McCall** had a fight during the 1-6 Premiership defeat at Leeds on Sunday, May 13, 2001.

On Sept. 28, 1994 the Scottish F.A. suspended Hearts players **Graeme Hogg** and **Craig Levein** for ten matches for fighting each other in a pre-season 'friendly' v Raith.

FOOTBALL'S FIRST BETTING SCANDAL

A Football League investigation into the First Division match which ended Manchester Utd 2, Liverpool 0 at Old Trafford on Good Friday, April 2, 1915 proved that the result had been 'squared' by certain players betting on the outcome. Four members of each team were suspended for life, but some of the bans were lifted when League football resumed in 1919 in recognition of the players' war service.

PLAYERS JAILED

Ten professional footballers found guilty of conspiracy to fraud by 'fixing' matches for betting purposes were given prison sentences at Nottingham Assizes on Jan. 26, 1965.

Jimmy Gauld (Mansfield Town), described as the central figure, was given four years. Among the others sentenced, Tony Kay (Sheffield Wed., Everton & England), Peter Swan (Sheffield Wed. & England) and David 'Bronco' Layne (Sheffield Wed.) were suspended from football for life by the F.A.

LONG SUSPENSIONS

The longest suspension (8 months) in modern times for a player in British football has been imposed on two Manchester Utd. footballers. First, French international captain **Eric Cantona**, following his attack on a spectator as he left the pitch after being sent off at Crystal Palace (Prem. League) on Jan. 25, 1995.

The club immediately suspended him to the end of the season and fined him 2 weeks' wages (est. £20,000). Then, on a disrepute charge, the F.A. fined him £10,000 (February 1995) and extended the ban to September 30 (which FIFA confirmed as world wide).

A subsequent 2-weeks' jail sentence on Cantona for assault was altered, on appeal, to 120 hours' community service, which took the form of coaching schoolboys in the Manchester area.

On December 19, 2003 on F.A. commission, held at Bolton F.C., suspended **Rio Ferdinand** (Manchester Utd. & England) from football for 8 months (plus £50,000 fine) for failing to take a random drug test at the club's training ground on September 23. The ban operated from January 12, 2004.

Mark Dennis, the Q.P.R. defender, was sent off for the 11th time in his career away to Tottenham (Div. 1) on November 14, 1987. (Two of those dismissals were for after-match tunnel offences; in addition, Dennis had then been cautioned 64 times in ten seasons and answered two disrepute charges concerning newspaper articles).

On December 10, the F.A. imposed on him a 53-day suspension, which was amended on appeal (January 25) to an 8-match ban. This was the longest suspension of a Football League player since **Kevin Keegan** (Liverpool) and **Billy Bremner** (Leeds Utd.) were each banned for 5 weeks (10 matches) after being sent off in the F.A. Charity Shield at Wembley in August 1974.

On December 6, 1988 Dennis was sent off for **12th. time** (Q.P.R. v Fulham reserves) and fined £1,000.

Steve Walsh (Leicester City) wassent off 13 times in his 18-season career (4 times with Wigan Athletic, 9 with Leicester City; 11 times in League, twice in F.A. Cup; 12 times away, once at home).

Before the disciplinary points system was introduced in season 1972-73, offenders were suspended for a specific number of weeks. Other lengthy suspensions imposed by the F.A. for on-field offences:

November 1969: Derek Dougan (Wolves) 8 weeks; **John Fitzpatrick** (Manchester Utd.) 8 weeks.

January 1970: Ronnie Rees (Nott'm Forest) 6 weeks; **George Best** (Manchester Utd.) 6 weeks.

January 1971: Peter Osgood (Chelsea) 8 weeks, following second trio of cautions in a year.

December 1971: Kevin Lewis (Manchester Utd.) 5 months; **Denis Hollywood** and **Brian O'Neil** (both Southampton) 9 weeks.

October 1987: Steve Walsh (Leicester City) 9 matches − original ban of 6 games (following the sixth sending-off of his career) increased to 9 when he reached 21 disciplinary points.

April 1988: Chris Kamara (Swindon Town) suspended to end of season (6 matches).

October 1988: Paul Davis (Arsenal) suspended for 9 matches, and fined a record £3,000, for breaking jaw of Glen Cockerill (Southampton) − off-ball incident caught on video.

January 1992: Frank Sinclair (Chelsea) suspended for 9 matches (fined £600) after being found guilty of assault on referee Paul Alcock (clash of heads) while playing for W.B.A. on loan.

January 1993: Alan Gough, Fulham goalkeeper, suspended for 42 days for assaulting referee in Autoglass Trophy match at Gillingham on December 8.

November 1994: Andy Townsend (Aston Villa) suspended for 6 matches (3 for 21 discip. points, 3 for sending-off).

October 26, 1997: Emmanuel Petit (Arsenal) pushes referee Paul Durkin when sent off at home to Aston Villa (Prem.). F.A. impose 3-match ban and £1,000 fine.

August 1998: F.A. suspend **David Batty** (Newcastle Utd.) for first 6 Prem. matches of season 1998-9 and fine him £1,500 for pushing referee David Elleray when sent off at Blackburn Rov. in last game of previous season.

October 1998: Paolo Di Canio (Sheff. Wed.) banned for 11 matches and fined £10,000 for pushing referee Paul Alcock after being sent off at home to Arsenal (Prem.), Sept. 26.

October 2002: F.A. suspend **Roy Keane** (Manchester Utd.) for 5 matches and fine him a record £150,000 on disrepute charges following publication of his autobiography.

Seven-month ban: Frank **Barson**, 37-year-old Watford centre-half, sent off at home to Fulham (Div. 3 South) on September 29, 1928, was suspended by the F.A. for the remainder of the season.

Twelve-month ban: Oldham Athletic full-back **Billy Cook** was given a 12-month suspension for refusing to leave the field when sent off at Middlesbrough (Div. 1), on April 3, 1915. The referee abandoned the match with 35 minutes still to play, and the score (4-1 to Middlesbrough) was ordered to stand.

Long Scottish bans: September 1954: Willie Woodburn, Rangers and Scotland centre-half, suspended for rest of career after fifth sending-off in 6 years.

Billy McLafferty, Stenhousemuir striker, was banned (April 14) for 8½ months, to Jan. 1, 1993, and fined £250 for failing to appear at a disciplinary hearing after being sent off against Arbroath on Feb. 1.

Twelve-match ban: On May 12, 1994 Scottish F.A. suspended Rangers forward **Duncan Ferguson** for 12 matches for violent conduct v Raith on Apr. 16. On Oct. 11, 1995, Ferguson (then with Everton) sent to jail for 3 months for the assault (served 44 days); Feb. 1, 1996 Scottish judge quashed 7 matches that remained of SFA ban on Ferguson.

On September 29, 2001 the SFA imposed a **17-match suspension** on Forfar Athletic's former Scottish International **Dave Bowman** for persistent foul and abusive language when sent off against Stranraer on September 22. As his misconduct continued, he was shown **5 red cards** by the referee.

FINES ETC. – MODERN

2000 (January) F.A. fine Notts Co. manager **Gary Brazil** £250 and Bournemouth manager Mel Machin £100 for comments to referee Jeff Winter after F.A. Cup 1st Round replay, November 9. Football League fine **Barnet** £2,500 for late arrival at Hartlepool, November 2. F.A. ban **Ben Thatcher** (Wimbledon) for 2 matches for elbowing Sunderland's Nicky Summerbee, January 3 – on video evidence (player not sent off). F.A. fine West Ham Utd. captain **Steve Lomas** £6,000 for comments to officials after match at Chelsea, November 7. F.A. fine **Hull City** £2,500 for failing to assist with enquiries into running of club. F.A. suspend referee **Rob Harris** for month for 'not applying the rules' at Tranmere v Sunderland F.A. Cup (4), January 8, Tranmere having replaced a sent-off player with a substitute.

2000 (March) F.A. fine **Paul Gascoigne** (Middlesbrough) £5,000, with 3-match ban, for elbowing offence v Aston Villa (February 14) in which Gascoigne broke an arm (charged on video evidence – incident missed by match officials). F.A. fine **Paolo Di Canio** (West Ham Utd.) £5,000 for making gesture to opponent v Aston Villa (January 15). UEFA fine **Chelsea** £7,500 and **Marseille** £37,000 for spectator misconduct (Champions League, February 29). F.A. fine **Leeds Utd.** and **Tottenham** £150,000 each for mass player-brawl at Elland Road (Premier League), February 12. F.A. fine Wolves striker **Ade Akinbiyi** £2,000 with 4-match suspension for head-butting Nott'm Forest player, February 26. Seven **Leicester City** men – players and officials, past or present – collectively fined £75,000 by F.A. for misconduct relating to distribution of tickets for 1999 Worthington Cup Final.

2000 (April) Football League fine **Bolton Wand.** £45,000 for poaching manager Sam Allardyce from Notts Co. F.A. fine **Emmanuel Petit** (Arsenal) £5,000 for obscene gesture to Aston Villa fans, March 5. F.A. fine **Steve Claridge** £900 for breach of rules when betting on his team to beat Barnsley, January 29 (they did by 3-0, Claridge hat-trick). F.A. fine **Chelsea** £50,000 for players' part in tunnel brawl at home to Wimbledon, February 12 (see also May). F.A. fine Chelsea captain **Dennis Wise** £7,500 for 'insulting behaviour' in same incident. F.A. fine Tranmere Rov. manager **John Aldridge** £750 for incident at Worthington Cup Final v Leicester and for comments to match officials after League matches v Birmingham and Portsmouth.

2000 (May) F.A. fine **Wimbledon** £50,000 and captain **Kenny Cunningham** £5,000 for their part in tunnel brawl at Chelsea, February 12 (see April).

2000 (July) UEFA fine **Portuguese F.A. £70,300** and ban 3 of their players from all **European** competitions, club and country, as sequel to fracas when France awarded penalty (handball by Everton's **Abel Xavier**) for Golden Goal decider in Euro 2000 semi-final. Suspensions: **Xavier** 9 months, **Nuno Gomes** 8 months, **Paulo Bento** 6 months. F.A. fine **Bryan Robson** (Middlesbrough manager) £7,500 for confrontation with referee after defeat at Coventry, April 15. F.A. fine **John Hartson** (Wimbledon) £5,000 on charge of abusive language to referee away to Bradford City, April 30.

2000 (October) F.A. fine **Paul Ince** (Middlesbrough) £15,000 for misconduct (abusive language at home to Derby Co., Sept. 6. F.A. fine **Gilles Grimandi** (Arsenal) £3,000 (1-match ban) for stamping on Gary McAllister (Liverpool), August 21. F.A. fine Swindon Town manager **Colin Todd** £2,500 for verbal assault on referee at Exeter (Worthington Cup, Sept. 5). UEFA fine **David Beckham** £4,000 for spitting towards referee in Manchester Utd.'s Champions League defeat away to PSV Eindhoven, Sept. 26. F.A. give Arsenal manager **Arsene Wenger** 12-match touchline ban and fine him 4 weeks' wages after 'tunnel row' with fourth official at Sunderland, August 19 (Wenger to appeal – see Feb. 2001). F.A. fine **Ipswich Town** £2,500 for sub-standard floodlights v Manchester Utd., August 22. F.A. fine **Neil Lennon** (Leicester City) £4,000 for ticket-selling offences (1999 Worthington Cup Final). F.A. fine **Crystal Palace** £20,000. **Nott'm. Forest** £15,000 for players' mass confrontation at Selhurst Park, August 28. UEFA fine **Arsenal** £8,300 for offences at Champions League match away to Lazio. Oct. 17.

2000 (November) F.A. fine **Norwich City** £30,000 (reduced on appeal to £12,000 plus £12,000 suspended) and **Blackpool** £6,000 for players' mass brawl at Norwich (Worthington Cup, Sept. 19). F.A. fine Tranmere Rov. manager **John Aldridge** £2,500 with 14-day touchline ban for throwing water bottle away to Barnsley, Oct. 17. F.A. fine **Preston N.E.** and **Sheffield Utd.** £15,000 each after 19-player brawl at Preston, August 19 (Sheffield Utd. manager **Neil Warnock** fined £2,000). F.A. ban **Stan Collymore** (Bradford City) 3 matches for stamping on Paul Gascoigne when playing for Leicester City v Everton, Sept. 29 (incident investigated by F.A. video panel).

2000 (December) UEFA fine **Manchester Utd.** £2,000 for players' misconduct v PSV Eindhoven (Champions League), Oct. 18.

2001 (January) F.A. fine **Paul Jewell** (Sheffield Wed. manager) £1,000 for comments to referee at Birmingham (Worthington Cup), December 12.

2001 (February) Arsenal manager **Arsene Wenger's** appeal (see October) upheld – reprimanded and fine reduced to £10,000. **Patrick Vieira** fined £10,000 by F.A. (1-match ban) for kicking Olivier Dacourt, Leeds Utd., Nov. 26. **Matt Elliott** (Leicester City) fined £5,000 by F.A. and **Hassan Kachloul** (Southampton) £2,000 on 'improper conduct' charges F.A. fine **Colin Todd** (Derby Co. assistant-manager) £2,500, with 3-match touchline ban, for verbal abuse of match official when Swindon Town manager.

2001 (March) F.A. fine **Gary Neville** (Manchester Utd.) £30,000, with 2-match ban, for foul and abusive language to assistant-referee after F.A. Cup defeat v West Ham Utd., Jan. 28 (see April re appeal). F.A. fine **Jim Magilton** (Ipswich Town) £5,000, with 1-match ban, for comments to referee at Chelsea, Jan. 20. F.A. fine Wimbledon manager **Terry Burton** £2,000, with 2-match touchline ban, for comments to assistant-referee at F.A. Cup 4th Round replay v Wycombe Wand., Feb. 20.

2001 (April) F.A. fine Wycombe Wand. manager **Lawrie Sanchez** £2,000, with 3-match touchline ban, for comments to assistant-referee at F.A. Cup 6th Round win at Leicester, March 10. F.A. fine Ipswich Town defender **Hermann Hreidarsson** £1,500 for jumping into crowd to celebrate goal v Bradford City, March 4. F.A. fine **Gillingham** £15,000 and **Crystal Palace** £5,000 following 12-player brawl at Gillingham, Dec. 26. Football League tribunal docks **Chesterfield** (Div. 3 leaders) 9 points, plus £20,000 fine, for breach of transfer regulations and under-reporting gate receipts (subsequent appeal turned down). F.A. fine **Nott'm. Forest** and **Preston N.E.** £5,000 each after mass confrontation of players at Nottingham, November 4. F.A. Appeal Board reduce fine on **Gary Neville** (Manchester Utd.) – see March – to £7,000; 2-match ban stays. FIFA ban Scotland captain **Colin Hendry** from 6 Int. matches (reduced to 3 on appeal) for elbowing a San Marino player in World Cup qualifier at Hampden Park, March 28.

2001 (May) F.A. fine **Lee Hendrie** (Aston Villa) £5,000 for 'over-exuberant' celebration of winning goal at home to Leicester City, April 4.

2001 (August) F.A. impose fines (suspended to end of season) for poor disciplinary records in 2000-01: **Derby Co.** £100,000; **Everton** and **Sheffield Wed.** £50,000; **Millwall** and **Bury** £25,000; **Torquay Utd.** and **Exeter City** £12,500.

2001 (September) F.A. find **Martin Keown** (Arsenal) £10,000 with 1-match ban for striking Mark Viduka (Leeds Utd.) at Highbury, May 5. UEFA fine **English F.A.** £2,400 for 4 England U-21 players being booked v Germany, August 31, UEFA fine **Newcastle Utd.** £2,800 for 3 bookings v Troyes (InterToto Cup). F.A. fine Birmingham City manager **Trevor Francis** £1,500 for protests at play-off semi-final v Preston N.E. in May.

2001 (November) F.A. fine **Mark Wright**, Oxford Utd. manager, £1,750 with 4-match touchline ban for abusive language to referee v Scunthorpe Utd., October 20.

2001 (December) F.A. fine Watford £5,000 and W.B.A. £2,500 for 16-player brawl, September 15.

2002 (January) F.A. find **David Ginola** (Aston Villa) £22,000 with 2-match ban for confrontation with 4th official when sent off v Leicester City, December 1. Football League fines: **Carlisle Utd.** £25,000 for fielding ineligible player v Mansfield Town, November 10; **Luton Town** £20,000 for failing to fulfil fixture at Kidderminster, December 1 (claiming 20 players ill or injured).

2002 (February) F.A. fines: **Portsmouth** £10,000 after 15 bookings in less than a month; **Wolves** £2,500 for players' misconduct v W.B.A., December 2; managers **Mark McGhee** (Millwall) £7,500 and **Steve Bruce** (Birmingham City) £5,000 for confrontations with referee, January 10.

2002 (March) F.A. fines: **Everton** £25,000 for disorderly conduct at Fulham, December 8 (£30,000 Fulham fine subsequently rescinded); **Mauricio Taricco** (Tottenham) £5,000 for improper conduct v Chelsea (Worthington Cup semi-final, 2nd leg). F.A. ban **Thierry Henry** (Arsenal) 3 domestic matches for improper conduct towards referee v Newcastle Utd., December 18. Premier League fine **Liverpool** £20,000 for illegal approach when signing **Christian Ziege** from Middlesbrough, August 2000; Ziege fined £20,000 for breach of rules.

2002 (April) F.A. fine Blackburn Rov. manager **Graeme Souness** £10,000 (1-match touchline ban) for verbal abuse of referee at Middlesbrough (F.A. Cup 5th Round, February 16).

2002 (May) F.A. fines: Derby Co. manager **John Gregory** £5,000 for improper conduct at Premiership match v Newcastle Utd., April 13. **Sheffield Utd.** £10,000 for players' misconduct at abandoned match v W.B.A., March 16; manager **Neil Warnock** £2,000, with 2-match ban for misconduct; 3 players punished – **Patrick Suffo** £3,000, with 3-match ban, **Keith Curle** £500 (2-match ban), **George Santos** 2-match ban. Wales F.A. fine **Cardiff City** £20,000 for crowd trouble v Leeds Utd. (F.A. Cup 3rd Round, January 6). N. Ireland manager **Sammy McIlroy** and assistant **Jim Harvey** each banned for 1 match and fined £4,000 by FIFA for misconduct at World Cup qualifier away to Malta, October 6.

2002 (July) F.A. fine new League club **Boston Utd.** £100,000 (with 4 points deduction) for contractual irregularities.

2002 (August) **Robbie Savage** (Birmingham City) fined £10,000 by F.A. for 'improper conduct' (using referee's toilet before Leicester City's home match v Aston Villa, April 20).

2002 (August) F.A. fines for poor disciplinary records, season 2001–02: **Arsenal** £50,000, suspended for year, (9 domestic sendings-off); **Portsmouth** £30,000 (suspended for year) for 6 red, 95 yellow cards; **Derby Co.** £15,000, **Tranmere Rov.** £15,000, **Sheff. Wed.** £5,000, **Sheff. Utd.** £5,000. Other F.A. fines: **Geoff Horsfield** (Birmingham City) £3,000 for off-ball incident in play-off s-final v Millwall, April 18; **George Boateng** (Mid'bro') £2,500 for throwing boot into crowd with former club Aston Villa at Leicester City, April 20).

2002 (September) F.A. fine Burnley manager **Stan Ternent** £2,500 (with 2-match touchline ban) for abusive language to referee at home to Wolves, March 30.

2002 (October) F.A. fine **Roy Keane** (Manchester Utd.) record £150,000 (with 5-match suspension) on disrepute charges following publication of autobiography. **Graeme Souness** (Blackburn Rov. manager) fined £15,000 (with 3-match touchline ban) after being 'sent off' by referee v Liverpool, August 28. Arsenal captain **Patrick Vieira** fined £25,000 (with 2-match suspension) for 'insulting language' to referee when sent off at Chelsea (Premier, September 1).

2002 (November) F.A. fine **Rotherham Utd.** £4,000 and **Sheff. Utd.** £2,000 for player incidents at end of match at Bramall Lane, September 14.

2002 (December) F.A. fines: **Birmingham City** £25,000 for spectator misconduct v Aston Villa, September 16; **Dennis Bergkamp** (Arsenal) £5,000 for misconduct, home to Blackburn Rov., October 26; **Trevor Francis** (Crystal Palace manager) £1,000 for cuffing reserve 'keeper Alex Kolinko (on bench) for laughing when Bradford City scored at Selhurst Park, August 13; Norwich City manager **Nigel Worthington** £500 (with 1-match touchline ban) after being ordered from bench, home to Sheff. Utd., September 7. UEFA fine **English F.A.** £9,000 and **Slovakian F.A.** £27,000 (reduced to £9,000 on appeal) because of crowd trouble at Eur. Champ. Qual. Match, Bratislava, October 12.

2003 (January) F.A. fine **Ashley Cole** (Arsenal) £2,000 (with 2-match ban) for 'insulting words' to match official at Southampton, November 23. **Bristol City** fined £50,000 by Football League (£25,000 suspended for 2 years) and ordered to pay Gillingham £50,000 compensation for illegal approach to manager Tony Pulis, June 1999. F.A. fine former Boston Utd. Manager **Steve Evans** £8,000, ban him from management for 18 months following July inquiry into club's financial affairs; former Boston Utd. chairman **Pat Malkinson** fined £5,250 and banned for 13 months from involvement in football.

2003 (February) F.A. suspend **Steven Gerrard** (Liverpool) for 3 matches for violent conduct (two-footed tackle) at home to Everton, December 22 (conviction on TV evidence). F.A. fine **Martin Keown** (Arsenal) £5,000 for 'confrontation' with Ruud van Nistelrooy away to Manchester Utd., December 7.

2003 (March) F.A. fines: Derby Co. manager **John Gregory** £7,500 (with 5-match touchline ban) for 'abusive language' to fourth official at Portsmouth, February 8; **Dennis Bergkamp** (Arsenal) £7,500 for elbowing Lee Bowyer (West Ham Utd.) at Highbury, January 19; **Paul Hart** (Nott'm. Forest manager) £500 for 'improper conduct' to match officials, home to Reading, December 21.

2003 (April) F.A. fine **Craig Bellamy** (Newcastle Utd.) £5,000 (with 1-match ban) for 'insulting remarks' to referee at Mid'bro', March 5.

2003 (May) F.A. fines: **Christophe Dugarry** (Birmingham City) £12,500 for spitting incident away to Aston Villa, March 3; **Dion Dublin** (Aston Villa) £6,000 for 'improper behaviour' after being sent off v Birmingham City, March 3. UEFA fines: **English F.A.** £68,000 following pitch invasions and racist chanting at England–Turkey Eur. Champ. qual. match, Sunderland, April 2; **Sir Alex Ferguson** £4,800 for 'improper statements', alleging that Champion's League quarter-final draw was 'fixed' so that Man. Utd. met Real Madrid; Arsenal captain **Patrick Vieira** £2,300 for alleging UEFA not tough enough in dealing with racism after Champions League match away to Valencia, March 19.

2003 (August) F.A. fine **Aston Villa** and **Birmingham City** £5,000 each – sequel to player-brawl at Villa Park, March 3. Prem. League fine **Manchester City** £25,000 for allocating Southampton fewer than stipulated 3,000 tickets for final match at Maine Road, May 11.

2003 (September) UEFA fine **Man. Utd.** and Real Madrid £14,000 each for fans' misconduct at Champions League match at Bernabeu, April 8. **Newcastle Utd.** fined £2,100 for 5 player-cautions in Champions League qualifier away v Partizan Belgrade, August 13.

2003 (October) F.A. fine **Sol Campbell** (Arsenal) £20,000 on 'improper behaviour' charge in Community Shield match v Man. Utd., August 10. F.A. fine Portsmouth manager **Harry Redknapp** £3,000 with 2-match touchline ban for abusive language to match officials at Wolves, August 30. F.A. fine Man. Utd. manager **Sir Alex Ferguson** £10,000 with 2-match touchline ban on 'improper conduct' charge at Newcastle, August 23. On October 30, as sequel to fracas away to Man. Utd. (September 21), F.A. fine **Arsenal** £175,000 and punish 5 Arsenal players: **Lauren** 4-match ban, £40,000 fine; **Keown** 3-match ban, £20,000 fine; **Vieira** 1-match ban, £20,000 fine; **Parlour** 1-match, £10,000 fine; **Cole** £10,000 fine. UEFA fine **English F.A.** £4,400 and Turkish **F.A.** £13,300 for half-time tunnel melee at European Champ. Qualifying match in Istanbul, October 11.

2003 (December) F.A. fine Manchester Utd. players **Ryan Giggs** £7,500 and **Cristiano Ronaldo** £4,000 for 'improper conduct' v. Arsenal, September 21 (see Arsenal punishments above). F.A. ban **Joe Cole** (Chelsea) for 2 Christmas matches, with

£15,000 fine, for his involvement as West Ham Utd. captain in fracas at Bolton last April 19. F.A. fine **Luis Boa Morte** (Fulham) £4,000 with 1-match ban for stamping on opponent v Leicester City, October 4.

2004 (January) F.A. ban **Alan Smith** (Leeds Utd.) 2 matches for throwing plastic bottle back into crowd at Carling Cup match v Manchester Utd., October 28.

2004 (February) F.A. fine Arsenal goalkeeper **Jens Lehmann** £10,000 for throwing ball at **Kevin Phillips** (Southampton), December 29 (Phillips Later fined £2,000 for treading on Lehmann's foot). F.A. fine Leicester City manager **Micky Adams** £500 for confrontation with referee v Birmingham City, December 13.

2004 (March) F.A. fine Burnley manager **Stan Ternent** £3,000, with 4-match touchline ban, for 'improper conduct' at F.A. Cup 4th round tie v Gillingham, January 24.

2004 (April) F.A. fine **Duncan Ferguson** £10,000 and add 4-match suspension for 'violent conduct' when sent off at Leicester, March 20. F.A. fine Millwall player-manager **Dennis Wise** £3,000 for 'abusive words' to referee at Sheffield Utd., March 2. F.A. fine **Stockport Co.** and **Brighton & H.A.** £5,000 each following players incident at Stockport (Div. 2), February 28.

2004 (May) F.A. fine Blackburn Rov. manager **Graeme Souness** £10,000 for 'abusive/insulting language' to referee v Tottenham, November 29.

2004 (June) F.A. fine **Millwall** and **Sheffield Utd.** £8,000 each for 'failure to control their players' (Div. 1) at Bramall Lane, March 2.

TOP FINES

Clubs: £1,500,000 (increased from original £600,000) Tottenham, Dec. 1994; **£175,000** Arsenal, Oct 2003; **£150,000** Leeds Utd., Mar. 2000; **£150,000** Tottenham, Mar. 2000; **£105,000** Chelsea, Jan. 1991; **£100,000** Boston Utd., July 2002; **£90,000** Tottenham, Jan. 1996; **£75,000** Chelsea, July 1988; **£75,000** Everton, Apr. 1994; **£60,000** Wimbledon, Jan. 1996; **£55,000** Birmingham City, Feb. 1994; **£50,000** Norwich City, June 1989; **£50,000** Arsenal, Nov. 1990; **£50,000** Barnet, Nov. 1992; **£50,000** Middlesbrough, Jan. 1997; **£50,000** Arsenal, Aug. 1997; **£50,000** Everton, July 1999; **£50,000** Chelsea, Apr. 2000; **£50,000** Wimbledon, May 2000; **£50,000** Arsenal, Aug. 2002; **£50,000** Bristol City, Jan. 2003.

Players: £150,000 Roy Keane (Manchester Utd.); Oct. 2002; **£45,000** Patrick Vieira (Arsenal), Oct. 1999; **£40,000** Lauren (Arsenal), Oct 2003; **£32,000** Robbie Fowler (Liverpool), Apr. 1999; **£25,000** Patrick Vieira (Arsenal); Oct. 2002; **£22,000** David Ginola (Aston Villa), Jan. 2002; **£20,000** Vinnie Jones (Wimbledon), Nov. 1992; **£20,000** Patrick Vieira (Arsenal), Dec. 1998; **£20,000** John Hartson (Wimbledon – offence when with West Ham Utd.), Jan. 1999; **£20,000** Christian Ziege (ex-Liverpool), Mar. 2002; **£20,000** Sol Campbell (Arsenal), Oct. 2003; **£20,000** Martin Keown (Arsenal), Oct. 2003; **£20,000** Patrick Vieira (Arsenal), Oct. 2003.

● In eight seasons with Arsenal (1996-2004) Patrick Vieira was fined a total of £122,000 by the F.A. for offences that included six sendings-off.

Managers: £15,000 Graeme Souness (Blackburn), Oct. 2002. **£10,000** Arsene Wenger (Arsenal), Feb. 2001; **£10,000** Graeme Souness (Blackburn) Apr. 2002; **£10,000** Sir Alex Ferguson (Manchester Utd.), Oct. 2003; **£10,000** Graeme Souness (Blackburn), May 2004; **£7,500** Bryan Robson (Middlesbrough), July 2000; **£7,500** Mark McGhee (Millwall), Feb. 2002; **£7,500** John Gregory (Derby). Mar. 2003; **£5,000** Brian Clough (Nott'm. Forest), Feb. 1989; **£5,000** Ruud Gullit (Newcastle Utd.), Sept. 1999; **£5,000** John Gregory (Aston Villa), Nov. 1999; **£5,000** Steve Bruce (Birmingham), Feb. 2002; **£4,800** Sir Alex Ferguson (Manchester Utd.) by UEFA, May 2003.

Football Association: £68,000 by UEFA, May 2003; **£9,000** by UEFA, Dec. 2002; **£4,400** by UEFA, Oct. 2003.

MANAGERS

INTERNATIONAL RECORDS
(As at start of season 2004-05)

	P	W	D	L	F	A
Sven-Goran Eriksson	42	22	13	7	82	42
(England – appointed Coach Jan. 2001)						
Lawrie Sanchez	6	3	2	1	9	6
(N. Ireland – appointed Jan. 2004)						
Berti Vogts	26	8	4	14	25	44
(Scotland – appointed Feb. 2002)						
Mark Hughes	37	11	13	13	39	43
(Wales – appointed Aug. 1999)						
Brian Kerr	18	11	5	2	22	12
(Rep. of Ireland – appointed Jan. 2003)						
Sammy McIlroy	29	5	7	17	19	40
(N. Ireland, Final Record)						
Jan. 2000 – Oct. 2003						

ENGLAND'S MANAGERS

		P	W	D	L
1946-62	**Walter Winterbottom**	139	78	33	28
1963-74	**Sir Alf Ramsey**	113	69	27	17
1974	**Joe Mercer**, caretaker	7	3	3	1
1974-77	**Don Revie**	29	14	8	7
1977-82	**Ron Greenwood**	55	33	12	10
1982-90	**Bobby Robson**	95	47	30	18
1990-93	**Graham Taylor**	38	18	13	7
1994-96	**Terry Venables**, coach	23	11	11	1
1996-99	**Glenn Hoddle**, coach	28	17	6	5
1999	**Howard Wilkinson**, caretaker	1	0	0	1
1999-2000	**Kevin Keegan**, coach	18	7	7	4
2000	**Howard Wilkinson**, caretaker	1	0	1	0
2000	**Peter Taylor**, caretaker	1	0	0	1
2001-2004	**Sven-Goran Eriksson**, coach	42	22	13	7

INTERNATIONAL MANAGER CHANGES

England: Walter Winterbottom 1946-62 (initially coach); **Alf Ramsey** (Feb. 1963-May 1974); **Joe Mercer** (caretaker May 1974); **Don Revie** (July 1974-July 1977); **Ron Greenwood** (Aug. 1977-July 1982); **Bobby Robson** (July 1982-July 1990); **Graham Taylor** (July 1990-Nov. 1993); **Terry Venables**, coach (Jan. 1994-June 1996); **Glenn Hoddle**, coach (June 1996-Feb. 1999); **Howard Wilkinson** (caretaker Feb. 1999); **Kevin Keegan** coach (Feb. 1999-Oct. 2000); **Howard Wilkinson** (caretaker Oct. 2000); **Peter Taylor** (caretaker Nov. 2000); **Sven-Goran Eriksson** (from Jan. 2001).

N. Ireland (modern): **Billy Bingham** (1967-Aug. 1971); **Terry Neill** (Aug. 1971-Mar. 1975); **Dave Clements** (player-manager Mar. 1975-1976); **Danny Blanchflower** (June 1976-Nov. 1979); **Billy Bingham** (Feb. 1980-Nov. 1993); **Bryan Hamilton** Feb. 1994-Feb. 1998); **Lawrie McMenemy** (Feb. 1998-Nov. 1999); **Sammy McIlroy** (Jan. 2000-Oct. 2003); **Lawrie Sanchez** (since Jan. 2004).

Scotland (modern): **Bobby Brown** (Feb. 1967-July 1971); **Tommy Docherty** (Sept. 1971- Dec. 1972); **Willie Ormond** (Jan. 1973-May 1977); **Ally MacLeod** (May 1977-Sept.1978); **Jock Stein** (Oct. 1978-Sept. 1985); **Alex Ferguson** (caretaker Oct. 1985-June 1986); **Andy Roxburgh**, coach (July 1986-Sept. 1993); **Craig Brown** (Sept. 1993-Oct. 2001); **Berti Vogts** (since Feb. 2002).

Wales (modern): **Mike Smith** (July 1974-Dec. 1979); **Mike England** (Mar. 1980-Feb. 1988); **David Williams** (caretaker Mar. 1988); **Terry Yorath** (Apr. 1988-Nov. 1993); **John**

Toshack (Mar. 1994, one match); **Mike Smith** (Mar. 1994-June 1995); **Bobby Gould** (Aug. 1995-June 1999); **Mark Hughes** (since Aug. 1999).

Rep. of Ireland (modern): **Liam Tuohy** (Sept. 1971-Nov. 1972); **Johnny Giles** (Oct. 1973-Apr. 1980, initially player-manager); **Eoin Hand** (June 1980-Nov. 1985); **Jack Charlton** (Feb. 1986-Dec. 1995); **Mick McCarthy** (Feb. 1996-Oct. 2002); **Brian Kerr** (since Jan. 2003).

FIRST BLACK ENGLAND MANAGER

Chris Ramsey, 36, in charge of England's U-20 squad for the World Youth Championship in Nigeria, April 1999. He was Brighton & H.A.'s right-back in the 1983 F.A. Cup Final v Manchester Utd.

YOUNGEST LEAGUE MANAGERS

Ivor Broadis, 23, appointed player-manager of Carlisle Utd., August 1946; **Chris Brass**, 27, appointed player-manager of York City, June 2003; **Terry Neill**, 28, appointed player-manager of Hull City, June 1970;

Graham Taylor, 28, appointed manager of Lincoln City, December 1972.

LONGEST-SERVING LEAGUE MANAGERS – ONE CLUB

Fred Everiss, secretary-manager of W.B.A. for 46 years (1902-48); since last war, **Sir Matt Busby**, in charge of Manchester Utd. for 25 seasons (1945-69, 1970-71); **Jimmy Seed** at Charlton Athletic for 23 years (1933-56).

LAST ENGLISH MANAGER TO WIN CHAMPIONSHIP

Howard Wilkinson (Leeds Utd.), season 1991–92.

1,000-TIME MANAGERS

Only four have managed in more than 1,000 English League games: **Alec Stock**, **Brian Clough**, **Jim Smith** and **Graham Taylor**. **Sir Matt Busby**, **Dario Gradi**, **Dave Bassett**, **Lennie Lawrence** and **Alan Buckley** have each managed more than 1,000 matches in all competitions.

SHORT-TERM MANAGERS

		Departed
3 Days	Bill Lambton (Scunthorpe Utd.)	April 1959
7 Days	Tim Ward (Exeter City)	March 1953
7 Days	Kevin Cullis (Swansea City)	February 1996
10 Days	Dave Cowling (Doncaster Rov.)	October 1997
10 Days	Peter Cormack (Cowdenbeath)	December 2000
13 Days	Johnny Cochrane (Reading)	April 1939
13 Days	Micky Adams (Swansea City)	October 1997
16 Days	Jimmy McIlroy (Bolton Wand.)	November 1970
20 Days	Paul Went (Leyton Orient)	October 1981
27 Days	Malcolm Crosby (Oxford Utd.)	January 1998
28 Days	Tommy Docherty (Q.P.R.)	December 1968
32 Days	Steve Coppell (Manchester City)	November 1996
41 Days	Steve Wicks (Lincoln City)	October 1995
44 Days	Brian Clough (Leeds Utd.)	September 1974
44 Days	Jock Stein (Leeds Utd.)	October 1978
48 Days	John Toshack (Wales)	March 1994
48 Days	David Platt (Sampdoria coach)	February 1999
49 Days	Brian Little (Wolves)	October 1986
49 Days	Terry Fenwick (Northampton Town)	February 2003
61 Days	Bill McGarry (Wolves)	November 1985
63 Days	Dave Booth (Peterborough Utd.)	January 1991

● In May 1984, Crystal Palace named **Dave Bassett** as manager, but he changed his mind four days later, without signing the contract, and returned to Wimbledon.

● In an angry outburst after a play-off defeat in May 1992, Barnet chairman Stan Flashman sacked manager **Barry Fry** and re-instated him a day later.

EARLY-SEASON MANAGER SACKINGS

2003 Glenn Roeder (West Ham) 15 days; **2000** Alan Buckley (Grimsby Town) 10 days; **1997** Kerry Dixon (Doncaster Rov.) 12 days; **1996** Sammy Chung (Doncaster Rov.) on morning of season's opening League match; **1996** Alan Ball (Manchester City) 12 days; **1994** Kenny Hibbitt (Walsall) and Kenny Swain (Wigan Athletic) 20 days; **1993** Peter Reid (Manchester City) 12 days; **1991** Don Mackay (Blackburn Rov.) 14 days; **1989** Mick Jones (Peterborough Utd.) 12 days; **1980** Bill McGarry (Newcastle Utd.) 13 days; **1979** Dennis Butler (Port Vale) 12 days; **1977** George Petchey (Leyton O.) 13 days; **1977** Willie Bell (Birmingham City) 16 days; **1971** Len Richley (Darlington) 12 days.

FEWEST MANAGERS

West Ham Utd. have had only ten managers in their 105-year history: Syd King, Charlie Paynter, Ted Fenton, Ron Greenwood, John Lyall, Lou Macari, Billy Bonds, Harry Redknapp, Glenn Roeder and Alan Pardew.

RECORD START FOR MANAGER

Arsenal were unbeaten in 17 League matches from the start of season 1947-8 under new manager Tom Whittaker.

MANAGER CHOSEN BY POLL

A month after being sacked by Third Division promotion winners Hartlepool Utd., **Mike Newell** became manager of Luton Town in June 2003. He was appointed via a telephone poll which the club, under a new board, conducted among fans, players, shareholders and season-ticket holders.

MANAGER DOUBLES

Four managers have won the League Championship with different clubs: **Tom Watson**, secy-manager with Sunderland (1892-3-5) and Liverpool (1901); **Herbert Chapman** with Huddersfield Town (1923-4, 1924-5) and Arsenal (1930-1, 1932-3); **Brian Clough** with Derby Co. (1971-2) and Nott'm. Forest (1977-8); **Kenny Dalglish** with Liverpool (1985-6, 1987-8, 1989-90) and Blackburn Rov. (1994-5).

Managers to win the F.A. Cup with different clubs: **Billy Walker** (Sheffield Wed. 1935, Nott'm. Forest 1959; **Herbert Chapman** (Huddersfield Town 1922, Arsenal 1930).

Kenny Dalglish (Liverpool) and **George Graham** (Arsenal) completed the Championship/F.A. Cup double as both player and manager with a single club. **Joe Mercer** won the Championship as a player with Everton, the Championship twice and F.A. Cup as a player with Arsenal and both competitions as manager of Manchester City.

FIRST CHAIRMAN-MANAGER

On December 20, 1988, after two years on the board, Dundee Utd. manager **Jim McLean** was elected chairman, too. McLean, Scotland's longest-serving manager (appointed by Utd. on November 24, 1971), resigned at end of season 1992-3 (remained chairman).

Ron Noades was chairman-manager of Brentford from July 1998 – March 2001.

TOP DIVISION PLAYER–MANAGERS

Les Allen (Q.P.R. 1968-9); **Johnny Giles** (W.B.A. 1976-7); **Howard Kendall** (Everton 1981-2); **Kenny Dalglish** (Liverpool, 1985-90); **Trevor Francis** (Q.P.R., 1988-9); **Terry Butcher** (Coventry City, 1990-1); **Peter Reid** (Manchester City, 1990-93); **Trevor Francis** (Sheffield Wed., 1991-4), **Glenn Hoddle**, (Chelsea, 1993-5); **Bryan Robson** (Middlesbrough, 1994-7), **Ray Wilkins** (Q.P.R., 1994-6); **Ruud Gullit** (Chelsea, 1996-8); **Gianluca Vialli** (Chelsea, 1998-2000).

FOREIGN TRIUMPHS

Former Dutch Int. **Ruud Gullit** became the first foreign manager to win a major English competition when Chelsea took the F.A. Cup in 1997.

In season 1997-8 Chelsea won the Coca-Cola Cup and the Cup-Winners' Cup for Gullit's successor, the Italian **Gianluca Vialli**; Arsenal won the Premiership and F.A. Cup double under Frenchman **Arsene Wenger**; Dutchman **Wim Jansen** took Celtic to triumph in the Scottish Championship and Coca-Cola Cup.

Under Frenchman **Gerard Houllier**, Liverpool achieved a triple success in 2000-01, winning the Worthington Cup, F.A. Cup and UEFA Cup. They won the Worthington Cup again in 2003.

In 2001-02 **Arsene Wenger** took Arsenal to his second Premiership – F.A. Cup double in five seasons, followed by his third F.A. Cup success in 2002–03 and a third Premiership triumph (Arsenal unbeaten) in 2003-04.

Arsene Wenger and **Gerard Houllier** became the first foreign managers to receive recognition when they were awarded honorary OBEs in the Queen's Birthday Honours in June 2003 'for their contribution to English football and Franco–British relations.'

In 1998-9 Rangers completed the Scottish treble under Dutchman **Dick Advocaat**.In 1999-2000 Chelsea won the F.A. Cup under **Vialli** and Rangers completed the Scottish Premier League and S.F.A. Cup double for **Advocaat**.

MANAGERS OF POST-WAR CHAMPIONS (*Double Winners)

1947 George Kay (Liverpool); **1948** Tom Whittaker (Arsenal); **1949** Bob Jackson (Portsmouth); **1950** Bob Jackson (Portsmouth); **1951** Arthur Rowe (Tottenham); **1952** Matt Busby (Manchester Utd.); **1953** Tom Whittaker (Arsenal).

1954 Stan Cullis (Wolves); **1955** Ted Drake (Chelsea); **1956** Matt Busby (Manchester Utd.); **1957** Matt Busby (Manchester Utd.); **1958** Stan Cullis (Wolves); **1959** Stan Cullis (Wolves); **1960** Harry Potts (Burnley).

1961 *Bill Nicholson (Tottenham); **1962** Alf Ramsey (Ipswich Town); **1963** Harry Catterick (Everton); **1964** Bill Shankly (Liverpool); **1965** Matt Busby (Manchester Utd.); **1966** Bill Shankly (Liverpool); **1967** Matt Busby (Man Utd.).

1968 Joe Mercer (Manchester City); **1969** Don Revie (Leeds Utd.); **1970** Harry Catterick (Everton); **1971** *Bertie Mee (Arsenal); **1972** Brian Clough (Derby Co.); **1973** Bill Shankly (Liverpool); **1974** Don Revie (Leeds Utd.).

1975 Dave Mackay (Derby Co.); **1976** Bob Paisley (Liverpool); **1977** Bob Paisley (Liverpool); **1978** Brian Clough (Nott'm. Forest); **1979** Bob Paisley (Liverpool); **1980** Bob Paisley (Liverpool); **1981** Ron Saunders (Aston Villa).

1982 Bob Paisley (Liverpool); **1983** Bob Paisley (Liverpool); **1984** Joe Fagan (Liverpool); **1985** Howard Kendall (Everton); **1986** *Kenny Dalglish (Liverpool – player/manager); **1987** Howard Kendall (Everton).

1988 Kenny Dalglish (Liverpool – player/manager); **1989** George Graham (Arsenal); **1990** Kenny Dalglish (Liverpool); **1991** George Graham (Arsenal); **1992** Howard Wilkinson (Leeds Utd.); **1993** Alex Ferguson (Manchester Utd.).

1994 *Alex Ferguson (Manchester Utd.); **1995** Kenny Dalglish (Blackburn Rov.); **1996** *Alex Ferguson (Manchester Utd.); **1997** Alex Ferguson (Manchester Utd.); **1998** *Arsene Wenger (Arsenal); **1999** *Alex Ferguson (Manchester Utd.); **2000** Sir Alex Ferguson (Manchester Utd.); **2001** Sir Alex Ferguson; **2002** *Arsene Wenger (Arsenal); **2003** Sir Alex Ferguson (Manchester Utd.); **2004** Arsene Wenger (Arsenal).

SIR ALEX IS TOPS

With 26 major prizes **Sir Alex Ferguson** has the most successful managerial record with Scottish and English clubs combined. At **Aberdeen** (1978-86) he won ten top prizes: 3 Scottish Championships, 4 Scottish Cups, 1 Scottish League Cup, 1 Cup-Winners' Cup, 1 European Super Cup.

Manchester Utd. winning the Premiership in 2001 made Sir Alex the outright most successful manager in English football, the first to win seven League titles, the first to win three in a row. He achieved an eighth Premiership success in 2003.

His fifth F.A. Cup success in 2004 was United's 16th major trophy in the last 15 seasons: 1990 F.A. Cup, 1991 Cup-Winners' Cup, 1992 League Cup, 1993 League Championship, 1994 League Championship and F.A. Cup, 1996 Championship and F.A. Cup; 1997 Championship; 1999 Championship; F.A. Cup and European Cup; 2000 Championship; 2001 Championship; 2003 Championship; F.A. Cup 2004.

United are unbeaten in 10 domestic semi-finals (F.A. Cup 6, League Cup 4) under Sir Alex.

Aged 57, he signed a new 3-year contract with United (May 4, 1999), making him **Britain's highest-paid manager**, reputedly at £1.67m. a year. When that contract ended in 2002, he changed his mind about retiring and signed to stay in charge at Old Trafford for a further 3 years to June 2005, (reported at £3.5m. a year).

BOB PAISLEY'S HONOURS

Bob Paisley won 13 major competitions for Liverpool (1974-83): 6 League Championships, 3 European Cups, 3 League Cups, 1 UEFA Cup.

MANAGERS WITH MOST F.A. CUP SUCCESSES

5 Sir Alex Ferguson (Manchester Utd.); **3** Charles Foweraker (Bolton Wand.), John Nicholson (Sheffield Utd.), Bill Nicholson (Tottenham), Arsene Wenger (Arsenal).

RECORD FEE FOR MANAGER

Tottenham paid Leeds Utd. £3m. compensation when they appointed **George Graham** In October 1998.

HOLE-IN-ONE MANAGER

Three days after appointing **Bobby Williamson** manager, from Hibernian, **Plymouth Argyle** clinched promotion and the Second Division Championship by beating Q.P.R. 2-1 on April 24, 2004.

RELEGATION 'DOUBLES'

Managers associated with two clubs relegated in same season: **John Bond** in 1985-6 (Swansea City and Birmingham City); **Ron Saunders** in 1985-6 (W.B.A. – and their reserve team – and Birmingham City); **Bob Stokoe** in 1986-7 (Carlisle Utd. and Sunderland); **Billy McNeill** in 1986-7 (Manchester City and Aston Villa); **Dave Bassett** in 1987-8 (Watford and Sheffield Utd.); **Mick Mills** in 1989-90 (Stoke City and Colchester Utd.).

MANAGER DEPARTURES – REPORTED TOP PAY-OFFS

£3.7m David O'Leary (Leeds Utd., June 2002); **£1.75m** Claudio Ranieri (Chelsea, May 2004); **£1.5m** Terry Venables (Leeds Utd., March 2003); **£1.2m**. Gerard Houllier (Liverpool, May 2004); **£1m** Harry Redknapp (West Ham Utd., May 2001); **£1m** John Gregory (Derby Co., May 2003); **£900,000** Howard Wilkinson (Leeds Utd., September 1996); **£750,000** Graeme Souness (Torino, October 1997); **£700,000** George Graham (Tottenham, March 2001); **£600,000** Kenny Dalglish (Director of Football, Celtic, June 2000); **£600,000** Peter Reid (Leeds Utd., November 2003); **£500,000** Ossie Ardiles (Tottenham, November 1994); **£500,000** Roy Evans (Liverpool, November 1998); **£500,000** Glenn Hoddle (England manager, February 1999); **£500,000** Joe Kinnear (Wimbledon, June 1999); **£500,000** John Toshack (Real Madrid, November 1999); **£500,000** John Barnes (Celtic, February 2000); **£500,000** Stuart Gray (Southampton, October 2001); **£422,000** Joe Royle (Manchester City, May 2001).

● **Sam Hammam**, owner of Wimbledon, departed in April 2000 reputedly richer by £36m. **Ken Bates** resigned as Chelsea chairman in March 2004 with a pay-off from the Roman Abramovich takeover reported at £17.1m.

WEMBLEY STADIUM

When Wembley Stadium closed after England's World Cup qualifying match against Germany in October 2000, demolition was due to begin within weeks and 'new Wembley' scheduled to open in 2004. The reality was two years of frustration and embarrassment for the Football Association, the F.A.-owned Wembley National Stadium Ltd. and the Government after plans for a £430m. loan from City banks fell through.

The finances eventually agreed included a £426m. loan from West Deutsche Landesbank, the German finance house, a minimum £100m. from the Football Association and £120m. previously given by Sport England. Building is contracted to the Australian-based construction company Multiplex.

After the two-year delay, the bulldozers and giant excavator Goliath moved into Wembley in September 2002. By December, the crowns atop the symbolic concrete towers were removed and placed in storage, to be exhibited in the Wembley Experience Museum.

That will be among the attractions when, after a 39 months' building programme, the £757m., 90,000-seat stadium, designed by Lord Foster, opens with a showpiece England match against, possibly, Brazil or Germany, preceding the return of the F.A. Cup Final to its traditional home in May 2006.

By mid-June 2004 the giant steel arch, iconic centre piece of the rebuilt stadium, was in place, bringing a spectacular new dimension to London's skyline. Its highest point is 439 ft., its span 1040 ft. (the length of 3 football pitches) and at 4 times the height of the old towers will make Wembley the tallest stadium in the world. The arch weighs 1,700 tonnes and stands at an angle to avoid shadows on the pitch.

A £70m.-a-year income is predicted for the stadium, and for 30 years from 2006 the Wembley schedule will include all England Internationals, F.A. Cup semi-finals and Final, the League Cup Final, Play-off Finals, F.A. Community Shield and the Rugby League Challenge Cup Final.

INVASION DAY

Memorable scenes were witnessed at the **first F.A. Cup Final at Wembley, April 28, 1923**, between **Bolton** and **West Ham**. An accurate return of the attendance could not be made owing to thousands breaking in, but there were probably more than 200,000 spectators present. The match was delayed for 40 minutes by the crowd invading the pitch. Official attendance was 126,047.

Gate receipts totalled £27,776. The two clubs and the Football Association each received £6,365 and the F.A. refunded £2,797 to ticket-holders who were unable to get to their seats. Cup Final admission has since been by ticket only.

REDUCED CAPACITY

Capacity of the all-seated **Wembley Stadium** was 78,000. The last 100,000 attendance was for the 1985 F.A. Cup Final between Manchester Utd. and Everton.

WEMBLEY'S FIRST UNDER LIGHTS

November 30, 1955 (England 4, Spain 1), when the floodlights were switched on after 73 minutes (afternoon match played in damp, foggy conditions).

First Wembley International played throughout under lights: England 8, N. Ireland 3 on evening of November 20, 1963 (att: 55,000).

MOST WEMBLEY APPEARANCES BY PLAYER

57 by Peter Shilton (52 England, 2 League Cup Finals, 1 F.A. Cup Final, 1 Charity Shield, 1 Football League XI).

WEMBLEY HAT-TRICKS

Three players have scored hat-tricks in major cup finals at Wembley: **Stan Mortensen** for Blackpool v Bolton Wand. (F.A. Cup Final, 1953), **Geoff Hurst** for England v West Germany (World Cup Final, 1966) and **David Speedie** for Chelsea v Manchester City (Full Members Cup, 1985).

ENGLAND'S WEMBLEY DEFEATS

England have lost 18 matches to foreign opponents at Wembley:

Nov.	1953	3-6 v Hungary	Apr.	1972	1-3 v W. Germany
Oct.	1959	2-3 v Sweden	Nov.	1973	0-1 v Italy
Oct.	1965	2-3 v Austria	Feb.	1977	0-2 v Holland

Mar.	1981	1-2 v Spain	Sept.	1991	0-1 v Germany
May	1981	0-1 v Brazil	June	1995	1-3 v Brazil
Oct.	1982	1-2 v W. Germany	Feb.	1997	0-1 v Italy
Sept.	1983	0-1 v Denmark	Feb.	1998	0-2 v Chile
June	1984	0-2 v Russia	Feb.	1999	0-2 v France
May	1990	1-2 v Uruguay	Oct.	2000	0-1 v Germany

A further defeat came in **Euro 96**. After drawing the semi-final with Germany 1-1, England went out 6-5 on penalties.

FASTEST GOALS AT WEMBLEY

In first-class matches: **38 seconds** by **Bryan Robson** in England's 2-1 win against Yugoslavia on December 13, 1989; **44 seconds** by **Bryan Robson** for England in 4-0 win v N. Ireland on February 23, 1982; **42 seconds** by **Roberto di Matteo** for Chelsea in the 1997 F.A. Cup Final v Middlesbrough.

Fastest goal in **any** match at Wembley: **20 seconds** by **Maurice Cox** for Cambridge University against Oxford on December 5, 1979.

FOUR WEMBLEY HEADERS

When **Wimbledon** beat Sutton Utd. 4-2 in the F.A. Amateur Cup Final at Wembley on May 4, 1963, Irish centre-forward **Eddie Reynolds** headed all four goals.

WEMBLEY ONE-SEASON DOUBLES

In 1989, **Nott'm. Forest** became the first club to win two Wembley Finals in the same season (Littlewoods Cup and Simod Cup).

In 1993, **Arsenal** made history there as the first club to win the League (Coca-Cola) Cup and the F.A. Cup in the same season. They beat Sheffield Wed. 2-1 in both finals.

SUDDEN DEATH DECIDERS

First Wembley Final decided on sudden death (first goal scored in overtime): April 23, 1995 – **Birmingham City** beat Carlisle Utd. (1-0, Paul Tait 103 mins.) to win Auto Windscreens Shield.

First instance of a 'golden goal' deciding a major International tournament was at Wembley on June 30, 1996, when **Germany** beat the Czech Republic 2-1 in the European Championship Final with Oliver Bierhoff's goal in the 95th. minute.

MILLENNIUM STADIUM, CARDIFF

Wales' new national stadium is the ground its chairman **Glanmor Griffiths** proudly built. On the site of Cardiff Arms Park, world-famous home of Welsh Rugby, it cost £130m. (£46m. from Lottery grants), took two years to build with retractable roof and a 73,434 all-seated capacity. Facilities include 126 hospitality boxes, 380 wheelchair spaces, 112 turnstiles, 38 food outlets and 17 public bars.

The stadium opened on June 26, 1999 with Wales beating the reigning World rugby champions South Africa. The first soccer international there was Wales v Finland on March 29, 2000.

The first 11 soccer matches played at the Millennium Stadium were won by the team using the North dressing-room. Stoke City ended the sequence when they beat Brentford 2-0 in the Div. 2 play-off Final on May 11, 2002.

The Millennium Stadium has solved English football's problem caused by the closure of Wembley, staging all the major domestic Finals in seasons 2000-01-02-03-04.

In the F.A. Charity Shield fixture on Sunday, August 12, 2001, Liverpool and Manchester Utd. became the first British clubs to meet under a closed-in roof.

The retractable roof has been closed for three major Finals: Worthington Cup, 2002 and 2003, F.A. Cup, 2003.

SHADOWS OVER SOCCER

DAYS OF TRAGEDY – CLUBS

Season 1988-9 brought the worst disaster in the history of British sport, with the death of *95 Liverpool supporters (200 injured) at the **F.A. Cup semi-final** against Nott'm. Forest at **Hillsborough, Sheffield**, on Saturday, April 15. The tragedy built up in the minutes preceding kick-off, when thousands surged into the ground at the Leppings Lane end. Many were crushed in the tunnel between entrance and terracing, but most of the victims were trapped inside the perimeter fencing behind the goal. The match was abandoned without score after six minutes' play. The dead included seven women and girls, two teenage sisters and two teenage brothers. The youngest victim was a boy of ten, the oldest 67-year-old Gerard Baron, whose brother Kevin played for Liverpool in the 1950 Cup Final. (*Total became 96 in March 1993, when Tony Bland died after being in a coma for nearly four years).

The two worst disasters in one season in British soccer history occurred at the end of 1984-5. On May 11, the last Saturday of the League season, 56 people (two of them visiting supporters) were burned to death – and about 200 taken to hospital – when fire destroyed the main stand at the **Bradford City-Lincoln City** match at Valley Parade.

The wooden, 77-year-old stand was full for City's last fixture before which, amid scenes of celebration, the club had been presented with the Third Division Championship trophy. The fire broke out just before half-time and, within five minutes, the entire stand was engulfed.

Eighteen days later, on May 29, at the European Cup Final between **Liverpool** and **Juventus** at the Heysel Stadium, Brussels, 39 spectators (31 of them Italian) were crushed or trampled to death and 437 injured. The disaster occurred an hour before the scheduled kick-off when Liverpool supporters charged a Juventus section of the crowd at one end of the stadium, and a retaining wall collapsed.

The sequel was a 5-year ban by UEFA on English clubs generally in European competition, with a 6-year ban on Liverpool.

On May 26, 1985 ten people were trampled to death and 29 seriously injured in a crowd panic on the way into the **Olympic Stadium, Mexico City** for the Mexican Cup Final between local clubs National University and America.

More than 100 people died and 300 were injured in a football disaster at **Nepal's national stadium** in Katmandu in March 1988. There was a stampede when a violent hailstorm broke over the capital. Spectators rushed for cover, but the stadium exits were locked, and hundreds were trampled in the crush.

In South Africa, on January 13, 1991 40 black fans were trampled to death (50 injured) as they tried to escape from fighting that broke out at a match in the gold-mining town of Orkney, 80 miles from Johannesburg. The friendly, between top teams **Kaiser Chiefs** and **Orlando Pirates**, attracted a packed crowd of 20,000. Violence erupted after the referee allowed Kaiser Chiefs a disputed second-half goal to lead 1-0.

Disaster struck at the French Cup semi-final (May 5, 1992) with the death of 15 spectators and 1,300 injured when a temporary metal stand collapsed in the Corsican town of Bastia. The tie between Second Division **Bastia** and French Champions **Marseille** was cancelled. **Monaco**, who won the other semi-final, were allowed to compete in the next season's Cup-Winners' Cup.

A total of 318 died and 500 were seriously injured when the crowd rioted over a disallowed goal at the National Stadium in Lima, Peru, on May 24, 1964. **Peru** and **Argentina** were competing to play in the Olympic Games in Tokyo.

That remained sport's heaviest death toll until October 20, 1982, when (it was revealed only in July 1989) 340 Soviet fans were killed in Moscow's Lenin Stadium at the UEFA Cup second round first leg match between **Moscow Spartak** and **Haarlem (Holland)**. They were crushed on an open stairway when a last-minute Spartak goal sent departing spectators surging back into the ground.

Among other crowd disasters abroad: **June 1968** – 74 died in **Argentina**. Panic broke out at the end of a goalless match between River Plate and Boca Juniors at Nunez, Buenos Aires, when Boca supporters threw lighted newspaper torches on to fans in the tiers below.

February 1974 – 49 killed in **Egypt** in crush of fans clamouring to see Zamalek play Dukla Prague.

September 1971 – 44 died in **Turkey**, when fighting among spectators over a disallowed goal (Kayseri v Siwas) led to a platform collapsing.

The then worst disaster in the history of British football, in terms of loss of life, occurred at Glasgow Rangers' ground at **Ibrox Park**, January 2, 1971.

Sixty-six people were trampled to death (100 injured) as they tumbled down Stairway 13 just before the end of the **Rangers v Celtic** New Year's match. That disaster led to the 1975 Safety of Sports Grounds legislation.

The Ibrox tragedy eclipsed even the Bolton disaster in which 33 were killed and about 500 injured when a wall and crowd barriers collapsed near a corner-flag at the **Bolton Wand. v Stoke City** F.A. Cup sixth round tie on March 9, 1946. The match was completed after half an hour's stoppage.

In a previous crowd disaster at **Ibrox** on April 5, 1902, part of the terracing collapsed during the Scotland v England International and 25 people were killed. The match, held up for 20 minutes, ended 1-1, but was never counted as an official International.

Eight leading players and three officials of **Manchester Utd.** and eight newspaper representatives were among the 23 who perished in the air crash at Munich on February 6, 1958, during take-off following a European Cup-tie in Belgrade. The players were Roger Byrne, Geoffrey Bent, Eddie Colman, Duncan Edwards, Mark Jones, David Pegg, Tommy Taylor and Liam Whelan, and the officials were Walter Crickmer (secretary), Tom Curry (trainer) and Herbert Whalley (coach). The newspaper representatives were Alf Clarke, Don Davies, George Follows, Tom Jackson, Archie Ledbrooke, Henry Rose, Eric Thompson and Frank Swift (former England goalkeeper of Manchester City).

On May 14, 1949, the entire team of Italian Champions **Torino**, 8 of them Internationals, were killed when the aircraft taking them home from a match against Benfica in Lisbon crashed at Superga, near Turin. The total death toll of 28 included all the club's reserve players, the manager, trainer and coach.

On February 8, 1981, 24 spectators died and more than 100 were injured at a match in **Greece**. They were trampled as thousands of the 40,000 crowd tried to rush out of the stadium at Piraeus after Olympiakos beat AEK Athens 6-0.

On November 17, 1982, 24 people (12 of them children) were killed and 250 injured when fans stampeded at the end of a match at the Pascual Guerrero stadium in **Cali, Colombia**. Drunken spectators hurled fire crackers and broken bottles from the higher stands on to people below and started a rush to the exits.

On December 9, 1987, the 18-strong team squad of **Alianza Lima**, one of Peru's top clubs, were wiped out, together with 8 officials and several youth players, when a military aircraft taking them home from Puccalpa crashed into the sea off Ventillana, ten miles from Lima. The only survivor among 43 on board was a member of the crew.

On April 28, 1993, 18 members of **Zambia's International** squad and 5 ZFA officials died when the aircraft carrying them to a World Cup qualifying tie against Senegal crashed into the Atlantic soon after take-off from Libreville, Gabon.

On October 16, 1996, 81 fans were crushed to death and 147 seriously injured in the 'Guatemala Disaster' at the World Cup qualifier against Costa Rica in Mateo Flores stadium. The tragedy happened an hour before kick-off, allegedly caused by ticket forgery and overcrowding – 60,000 were reported in the 45,000-capacity ground – and safety problems related to perimeter fencing.

On July 9, 1996, 8 people died, 39 injured in riot after derby match between **Libya's two top clubs** in Tripoli. Al-Ahli had beaten Al-Ittihad 1-0 by a controversial goal.

On April 6, 1997, 5 spectators were crushed to death at **Nigeria's national stadium** in Lagos after the 2-1 World Cup qualifying victory over Guinea. Only two of five gates were reported open as the 40,000 crowd tried to leave the ground.

It was reported from the **Congo** (October 29, 1998) that a bolt of lightning struck a village match, killing all 11 members of the home team Benatshadi, but leaving the opposing players from Basangana unscathed. It was believed the surviving team wore better-insulated boots.

On January 10, 1999 eight fans died and 13 were injured in a stampede at **Egypt's Alexandria Stadium**. Some 25,000 spectators had pushed into the ground. Despite the tragedy, the cup-tie between Al-Ittihad and Al-Koroum was completed.

Three people suffocated and several were seriously injured when thousands of fans forced their way into **Liberia's national stadium** in Monrovia at a goalless World Cup qualifying match against Chad on April 23, 2000. The stadium (capacity 33,000) was reported 'heavily overcrowded'.

On Sunday, July 9, 2000 12 spectators died from crush injuries when police fired tear gas into the 50,000 crowd after South Africa scored their second goal in a World Cup group qualifier against Zimbabwe in **Harare**. A stampede broke out as fans scrambled to leave the national stadium. Players of both teams lay face down on the pitch as fumes swept over them. FIFA launched an investigation and decided that the result would stand, with South Africa leading 2-0 at the time of the 84th-minute abandonment.

On April 11, 2001, at one of the biggest matches of the South African season, 43 died and 155 were injured in a crush at **Ellis Park, Johannesburg**. After tearing down a fence, thousands of fans surged into a stadium already packed to its 60,000 capacity for the Premiership derby between top Soweto teams Kaizer Chiefs and Orlando Pirates. The match was abandoned at 1-1 after 33 minutes. In January 1991, 40 died in a crowd crush at a friendly between the same clubs at Orkney, 80 miles from Johannesburg.

On April 29, 2001, seven people were trampled to death and 51 injured when a riot broke out at a match between two of Congo's biggest clubs, Lupopo and Mazembe at **Lubumbashi**, southern Congo.

On May 6, 2001, two spectators were killed in Iran and hundreds were injured when a glass fibre roof collapsed at the over-crowded Mottaqi Stadium at **Sari** for the match between Pirouzi and Shemshak Noshahr.

On May 9, 2001, in Africa's worst football disaster, 123 died and 93 were injured in a stampede at the national stadium in **Accra, Ghana**. Home team Hearts of Oak were leading 2-1 against Asante Kotoko five minutes from time, when Asanti fans started hurling bottles on to the pitch. Police fired tear gas into the stands, and the crowd panicked in a rush for the exits, which were locked. It took the death toll at three big matches in Africa in April/May to 173.

On August 12, 2001, two players were killed by lightning and ten severely burned at a **Guatemala** Third Division match between Deportivo Culquimulilla and Pueblo Nuevo Vinas.

On November 1, 2002, two players died from injuries after lightning struck Deportivo Cali's training ground in **Colombia**.

On March 12, 2004, five people were killed and more than 100 injured when spectators stampeded shortly before the Syrian Championship fixture between Al-Jihad and Al-Fatwa in **Qameshli**, Northern Syria. The match was cancelled.

DAYS OF TRAGEDY – PERSONAL

Sam Wynne, Bury right-back, collapsed five minutes before half-time in the First Division match away to Sheffield Utd. on April 30, 1927, and died in the dressing-room.

In the Rangers v Celtic League match on September 5, 1931, **John Thomson**, the 23-year-old Celtic and Scotland goalkeeper, sustained a fractured skull when diving at an opponent's feet just before half-time and died the same evening.

Sim Raleigh (Gillingham), injured in a clash of heads at home to Brighton & H.A. (Div. 3 South) on December 1, 1934, continued to play but collapsed in second half and died in hospital the same night.

James Thorpe, 23-year-old Sunderland goalkeeper, was injured during the First Division match at home to Chelsea on February 1, 1936 and died in a diabetic coma three days later.

Derek Dooley, Sheffield Wed. centre-forward and top scorer in 1951-52 in the Football League with 46 goals in 30 matches, broke a leg in the League match at Preston N.E. on February 14, 1953, and, after complications set in, had to lose the limb by amputation.

John White (27), Tottenham's Scottish International forward, was killed by lightning on a golf course at Enfield, North London in July, 1964.

Two players were killed by lightning during the **Army Cup Final** replay at Aldershot in April, 1948.

Tommy Allden (23), Highgate Utd. centre-half was struck by lightning during an Amateur Cup quarter-final with Enfield Town on February 25, 1967. He died the following day. Four other players were also struck but recovered.

Roy Harper died while refereeing the York City–Halifax Town (Div. 4) match on May 5, 1969.

Jim Finn collapsed and died from a heart attack while refereeing Exeter City v Stockport Co. (Div. 4) on September 16, 1972.

Scotland manager **Jock Stein**, 62, collapsed and died at the end of the Wales–Scotland World Cup qualifying match (1-1) at Ninian Park, Cardiff on September 10, 1985.

David Longhurst, 25-year-old York City forward, died after being carried off two minutes before half-time in the Fourth Division fixture at home to Lincoln City on September 8, 1990. The match was abandoned (0-0). The inquest revealed that Longhurst suffered from a rare heart condition.

Mike North collapsed while refereeing Southend Utd. v Mansfield Town (Div. 3) on April 16, 2001 and died shortly afterwards. The match was abandoned and re-staged on May 8, with the receipts donated to his family.

Marc-Vivien Foe, 28, on his 63rd appearance in Cameroon's midfield, collapsed unchallenged in the centre circle after 72 minutes of the FIFA Confederations Cup semi-final against Colombia in Lyon, France, on June 26, 2003, and despite the efforts of the stadium medical staff he could not be revived. He had been on loan to Manchester City from Olympique Lyonnais in season 2002–03, and poignantly scored the club's last goal at Maine Road.

Reto Gafner, 32-year-old goalkeeper, died on November 4, 2003 from head injuries sustained in collision with an opponent when playing for FC Greifensee v Wiedikon (Swiss Div. 2).

Miklos Feher, 24, Hungarian Int. striker, died after collapsing on pitch at end of Benfica's 1-0 win away to Vitoria Guimaraes (Portuguese League) on January 25, 2004.

Jiang Tao, 18-year-old Chinese player, died when struck by lightning while training with Singapore S-League club Sinchi FC on March 10, 2004.

GREAT SERVICE

'For services to Association Football', **Stanley Matthews** (Stoke City, Blackpool and England), already a C.B.E., became the first professional footballer to receive a knighthood. This was bestowed in 1965, his last season.

Before he retired and five days after his 50th birthday, he played for Stoke City to set a record as the oldest First Division footballer (v. Fulham, February 6, 1965).

Over a brilliant span of 33 years, he played in 886 first-class matches, including 54 full Internationals (plus 31 in war time), 701 League games (including 3 at start of season 1939-40, which was abandoned on the outbreak of war) and 86 F.A. Cup-ties, and scored 95 goals. He was never booked in his career.

Sir Stanley died on February 23 2000, three weeks after his 85th birthday. His ashes were buried under the centre circle of Stoke's Britannia Stadium. After spending a number of years in Toronto, he made his home back in the Potteries in 1989, having previously returned to his home town, Hanley, Stoke-on-Trent in October, 1987 to unveil a life-size bronze statue of himself.

The inscription reads: 'Sir Stanley Matthews, CBE. Born Hanley, 1 February 1915. His name is symbolic of the beauty of the game, his fame timeless and international, his sportsmanship and modesty universally acclaimed. A magical player, of the people, for the people.'

On his home-coming in 1989, Sir Stanley was made President of Stoke City, the club he joined as a boy of 15 and served as a player for 20 years between 1931 and 1965, on either side of his spell with Blackpool.

In July 1992 FIFA honoured him with their 'Gold merit award' for outstanding services to the game.

Former England goalkeeper **Peter Shilton** has made more first-class appearances (1,387) than any other footballer in British history. He played his 1,000th. League game in Leyton Orient's 2-0 home win against Brighton & H.A. on Dec. 22, 1996 and in all played 9 times for Orient in his final season. He retired from International football after the 1990 World Cup in Italy with 125 caps, then a world record.

Shilton's career spanned 32 seasons, 20 of them on the International stage. He made his League debut for Leicester City in May 1966, two months before England won the World Cup.

His 1,387 first-class appearances comprise a record 1,005 in the Football League, 125 Internationals, 102 League Cup, 86 F.A. Cup, 13 for England U-23s, 4 for the Football League and 52 other matches (European Cup, UEFA Cup, World Club Championship, Charity Shield, European Super Cup, Full Members' Cup, Play-offs, Screen Sports Super Cup, Anglo-Italian Cup, Texaco Cup, Simod Cup, Zenith Data Systems Cup and Autoglass Trophy).

Shilton appeared more times at Wembley (57) than any other player: 52 for England, 2 League Cup Finals, 1 F.A. Cup Final, 1 Charity Shield match, and 1 for the Football League. He passed a century of League appearances with each of his first five clubs: Leicester City (286), Stoke City (110), Nott'm. Forest (202), Southampton (188) and Derby Co. (175) and subsequently played for Plymouth Argyle, Bolton Wand. and Leyton Orient.

His club honours, all gained with Nott'm. Forest: League Championship 1978, League Cup 1979, European Cup 1979 and 1980, PFA Player of Year 1978.

Five other British footballers have made more than 1,000 first-class appearances:

Ray Clemence, formerly with Tottenham, Liverpool and England, retired through injury in season 1987-8 after a goalkeeping career of 1,119 matches starting in 1965-6. Clemence played 50 times for his first club, Scunthorpe Utd.; 665 for Liverpool; 337 for Tottenham; his 67 representative games included 61 England caps.

A third great British goalkeeper, **Pat Jennings**, ended his career (1963-86) with a total of 1,098 first-class matches for Watford, Tottenham, Arsenal and N. Ireland. They were made up of 757 in the Football League, 119 full Internationals, 84 F.A. Cup appearances, 72 League/Milk Cup, 55 European club matches, 2 Charity Shield, 3 Other Internationals, 1 Under-23 cap, 2 Texaco Cup, 2 Anglo-Italian Cup and 1 Super Cup. Jennings played his 119th. and final International on his 41st birthday, June 12, 1986, against Brazil in Guadalajara in the Mexico World Cup.

Yet another outstanding 'keeper, **David Seaman**, passed the 1,000 appearances milestone for clubs and country in season 2002–03, reaching 1,004 when aged 39, he captained Arsenal to F.A. Cup triumph against Southampton.

With Arsenal, Seaman won 3 Championship medals, the F.A. Cup 4 times, the Double twice, the League Cup and Cup-Winners' Cup once each. After 13 seasons at Highbury, he joined Manchester City (June 2003) on a free transfer. He played 26 matches for City before a shoulder injury forced his retirement in January 2004, aged 40.

Seaman's 22-season career composed 1,046 first-class matches: 955 club apps. (Peterborough Utd. 106, Birmingham City 84, Q.P.R. 175, Arsenal 564, Manchester City 26); 75 senior caps for England, 26 'B' caps and 10 at U-21 level.

Defender **Graeme Armstrong**, 42-year-old commercial manager for an Edinburgh whisky company and part-time assistant-manager and captain of Scottish Third Division club Stenhousemuir, made the 1000th first team appearance of his career in the Scottish Cup 3rd Round against Rangers at Ibrox on January 23, 1999. He was presented with the Man of the Match award before kick-off.

Against East Stirling on Boxing Day, he had played his 864th League game, breaking the British record for an outfield player set by another Scot, Tommy Hutchison, with Alloa, Blackpool, Coventry City, Manchester City, Burnley and Swansea City.

Armstrong's 24-year career, spent in the lower divisions of the Scottish League, began as a 1-match trialist with Meadowbank Thistle in 1975 and continued via Stirling Albion, Berwick Rangers, Meadowbank and, from 1992, Stenhousemuir.

Tony Ford became the first English outfield player to reach 1000 senior appearances in Rochdale's 1-0 win at Carlisle (Auto Windscreens Shield) on March 7, 2000. Grimsby-born, he began his 26-season midfield career with Grimsby Town and played for 7 other League clubs: Sunderland (loan), Stoke City, W.B.A., Bradford City (loan), Scunthorpe Utd., Mansfield Town and Rochdale. He retired, aged 42, in 2001 with a career record of 1072 appearances (121 goals) and his total of 931 League games is exceeded only by Peter Shilton's 1005.

NINE KNIGHTS OF SOCCER

In the Queen's Birthday Honours on June 12, 2004, **Trevor Brooking**, 55, was awarded a knighthood for 'services to sport.' The former West Ham Utd. and England player chaired Sport England before becoming the F.A. Director of Football Development. He is the ninth football personality to be knighted.

The elite list reads: **Stanley Matthews** (1965), **Alf Ramsey** (1967), **Matt Busby** (1968), **Bobby Charlton** (1994), **Tom Finney** (1998), **Geoff Hurst** (1998), **Alex Ferguson** (1999), **Bobby Robson** (2002) and **Trevor Brooking** (2004).

PENALTIES

The **penalty-kick** was introduced to the game, following a proposal to the Irish F.A. in 1890 by William McCrum, son of the High Sheriff for Co. Omagh, and approved by the International Football Board on June 2, 1891.

First penalty scored in a first-class match in England was by John Heath, for Wolves v Accrington Stanley (5-0 in Div. 1, September 14, 1891).

The greatest influence of the penalty has come since the 1970s, with the introduction of the shoot-out to settle deadlocked ties in various competitions.

Manchester Utd. were the first club to win a competitive match in British football via a shoot-out (4-3 away to Hull City, Watney Cup semi-final, August 1, 1970); in that penalty contest, George Best was the first player to score, Denis Law the first to miss.

The shoot-out was adopted by FIFA and UEFA the same year (1970).

In season 1991-2, penalty shoot-outs were introduced to decide **F.A. Cup ties** still level after one replay and extra time.

Wembley saw its first penalty contest in the 1974 Charity Shield. Since then many major matches across the world have been settled in this way, including:

1974	**F.A. Charity Shield** (Wembley): Liverpool beat Leeds Utd. 6-5 (after 1-1).
1976	**Eur. Champ. Final** (Belgrade): Czech. beat W. Germany 5-3 (after 2-2).
1980	**Cup-Winners' Cup Final** (Brussels): Valencia beat Arsenal 5-4 (0-0).
1980	**Eur. Champ. 3rd/4th place play-off** (Naples): Czechoslovakia beat Italy 9-8 (after 1-1).
1982	**World Cup s-final** (Seville): West Germany beat France 5-4 (after 3-3).
1984	**European Cup Final** (Rome): Liverpool beat AS Roma 4-2 (after 1-1).
1984	**UEFA Cup Final**: Tottenham (home) beat Anderlecht 4-3 (2-2 agg.).
1984	**Eur. Champ. s-final** (Lyon, France): Spain beat Denmark 5-4 (after 1-1).
1986	**European Cup Final** (Seville): Steaua Bucharest beat Barcelona 2-0 (0-0). Barcelona's four penalties were all saved.
1986	**World Cup q-finals** (in Mexico): France beat Brazil 4-3 (after 1-1); West Germany beat Mexico 4-1 (after 0-0); Belgium beat Spain 5-4 (after 1-1).
1987	**Freight Rover Trophy Final** (Wembley): Mansfield Town beat Bristol City 5-4 (after 1-1).
1987	**Scottish League (Skol) Cup Final** (Hampden Park): Rangers beat Aberdeen 5-3 (after 3-3).
1988	**European Cup Final** (Stuttgart): PSV Eindhoven beat Benfica 6-5 (after 0-0).
1988	**UEFA Cup Final**: Bayer Leverkusen (home) beat Espanyol 3-2 after 3-3 (0-3a, 3-0h).
1990	**Scottish F.A. Cup Final** (Hampden Park): Aberdeen beat Celtic 9-8 (0-0).
1990	**World Cup** (in Italy): 2nd. Round: Rep. of Ireland beat Romania 5-4 (after 0-0); q-final: Argentina beat Yugoslavia 3-2 (after 0-0); s-finals: Argentina beat Italy 4-3 (after 1-1); West Germany beat England 4-3 (1-1).
1991	**European Cup Final** (Bari): Red Star Belgrade beat Marseille 5-3 (after 0-0).
1991	**Barclays League Play-off** (4th. Div. Final – Wembley): Torquay Utd. beat Blackpool 5-4 (after 2-2).
1992	**F.A. Cup s-final** replay (Villa Park): Liverpool beat Portsmouth 3-1 (after 0-0).
1992	**Barclays League Play-off** (4th. Div. Final – Wembley): Blackpool beat Scunthorpe Utd. 4-3 (after 1-1).
1992	**Eur. Champ. s-final** (Gothenburg): Denmark beat Holland 5-4 (after 2-2).

1993	**Barclays League Play-off:** (3rd Div. Final – Wembley): York City beat Crewe Alexandra 5-3 (after 1-1).

1993 **Barclays League Play-off:** (3rd Div. Final – Wembley): York City beat Crewe Alexandra 5-3 (after 1-1).

1993 **F.A. Charity Shield** (Wembley): Manchester Utd. beat Arsenal 5-4 (after 1-1).

1994 **League (Coca-Cola) Cup s-final:** Aston Villa beat Tranmere Rov. 5-4 (after 4-4, 1-3a, 3-1h).

1994 **Autoglass Trophy Final** (Wembley): Swansea City beat Huddersfield Town 3-1 (after 1-1).

1994 **World Cup** (in U.S.A.): **2nd. Round:** Bulgaria beat Mexico 3-1 (after 1-1); q-final: Sweden beat Romania 5-4 (after 2-2); **Final:** Brazil beat Italy 3-2 (after 0-0).

1994 **Scottish League (Coca-Cola) Cup Final** (Ibrox Park): Raith beat Celtic 6-5 (after 2-2).

1995 **Cup-Winners' Cup s-final:** Arsenal beat Sampdoria away 3-2 (5-5 agg.)

1995 **Copa America Final** (Montevideo): Uruguay beat Brazil 5-3 (after 1-1).

1996 **European Cup Final** (Rome): Juventus beat Ajax 4-2 (after 1-1).

1996 **European U-21 Champ. Final** (Barcelona): Italy beat Spain 4-2 (after 1-1).

1996 **Eur. Champ. q-finals:** England beat Spain (Wembley) 4-2 after 0-0; France beat Holland (Anfield) 5-4 after 0-0; **s-finals:** Germany beat England (Wembley) 6-5 after 1-1; Czech Republic beat France (Old Trafford) 6-5 after 0-0.

1997 **Auto Windscreens Shield Final** (Wembley): Carlisle Utd. beat Colchester Utd. 4-3 (after 0-0)

1997 **UEFA Cup Final:** FC Schalke beat Inter Milan 4-1 (after 1-1 agg.).

1998 **Nationwide League play-off** (1st Div. Final Wembley): Charlton Athletic beat Sunderland 7-6 (after 4-4).

1998 **World Cup Finals:** Argentina beat England (2nd Round) 4-3 (after 2-2); France beat Italy (Q-final) 4-3 (after 0-0; Brazil beat Holland (S-final) 4-2 (after 1-1).

1999 **Nationwide League play-offs Div. 1 s-final:** Watford beat Birmingham City 7-6 away (after 1-1); **Div. 2 Final (Wembley):** Manchester City beat Gillingham 3-1 (after 2-2).

1999 **Women's World Cup Final** (Rose Bowl, Pasedena, California) U.S.A. beat China 5-4 (after 0-0). **Third/Fourth place play-off** (same venue): Brazil beat Norway 5-4 (after 0-0).

2000 **African Nations Cup Final** (Lagos): Cameroon beat Nigeria 4-3 (after 0-0).

2000 **F.A. Cup s-final** (Wembley): Aston Villa beat Bolton Wand. 4-1 (after 0-0).

2000 **UEFA Cup Final** (Copenhagen): Galatasaray beat Arsenal 4-1 (after 0-0).

2000 **Eur. Champ. s-final** (Amsterdam): Italy beat Holland 3-1 (after 0-0). Holland missed 5 penalties in match – 2 in normal play, 3 in shoot-out. Italy survived with ten men after 33rd minute sending-off.

2000 **Olympic Final** (Sydney): Cameroon beat Spain 5-3 (after 2-2). Spain led 2-0, then had 2 men sent off.

2001 **League (Worthington) Cup Final** (Millennium Stadium, Cardiff): Liverpool beat Birmingham City 5-4 (after 1-1).

2001 **Champions League Final** (Milan): Bayern Munich beat Valencia 5-4 (after 1-1).

2002 **Eur. U-21 Champ. Final** (Basle): Czech Republic beat France 3-1 (after 0-0).

2002 **Nationwide League** play-off (1st Div. Final, Millennium Stadium, Cardiff): Birmingham City beat Norwich City 4-2 (after 1-1).

2002 **World Cup Finals:** Spain beat Rep. of Ireland (2nd Round) 3-2 (after 1-1); South Korea beat Spain (Q-final) 5-3 (after 0-0).

2003 **Champions League Final** (Old Trafford): AC Milan beat Juventus 3–2 (after 0–0).

2003 **F.A. Community Shield** (Millennium Stadium, Cardiff): Manchester Utd. beat Arsenal 4-3 (after 1-1).

2004 **Nationwide League play-off s-finals – Div. 1:** Crystal Palace beat Sunderland 5-4 away (after 4-4 agg.); Div. 2; Brighton & H.A. beat Swindon Town 4-3 home (after 2-2 agg.); Div. 3; Mansfield Town beat Northampton Town 5-4 home (after 3-3 agg.). **Div. 3 Final** (Millennium Stadium, Cardiff): Huddersfield Town beat Mansfield Town 4-1 (after 0-0).

2004 **Eur. Champ. q-finals:** Portugal beat England (Lisbon) 6-5 after 2-2; Holland beat Sweden (Faro) 5-4 after 0-0.

Footnote: Highest-recorded score in a penalty shoot-out between Football League clubs was **Aldershot's 11-10** victory at home to **Fulham** after their 1-1 draw in the Freight Rover Trophy Southern quarter-final on February 10, 1987. Seven spot-kicks were missed or saved in a record 28-penalty shoot-out at senior level.

In South America in 1992, in a 26-shot competition, **Newell's Old Boys** beat America 11-10 in the Copa Libertadores.

Longest-recorded penalty contest in first-class matches was in Argentina in 1988 – from 44 shots, **Argentinos Juniors** beat **Racing Club 20-19**. **Genclerbirligi** beat **Galatasaray** 17-16 in a Turkish Cup-tie in 1996. Only one penalty was missed.

Highest-scoring shoot-outs in **Int. football:** North Korea beat Hong Kong 11-10 (after 3-3 draw) in an Asian Cup match in 1975; and Ivory Coast beat Ghana 11-10 (after 0-0 draw) in African Nations Cup Final, 1992.

Most penalties needed to settle an adult game in Britain: 44 in Norfolk Primary Cup 4th Round replay, December 2000. Aston Village side **Freethorpe** beat Foulsham 20-19 (5 kicks missed). All 22 players took 2 penalties each, watched by a crowd of 20. The sides had drawn 2-2, 4-4 in a tie of 51 goals.

Penalty that took 24 days: That is how long elapsed between the award and the taking of a penalty in an Argentine Second Division match between **Atalanta** and **Defensores** in 2003. A riot ended the original match with 5 minutes left, and the game was resumed on 30 April behind closed doors with the penalty that caused the abandonment. Lucas Ferreiro scored it to give Atalanta a 1–0 win.

ENGLAND'S CRUCIAL PENALTY SHOOT-OUTS

1990 World Cup Semi-final: Beaten 4-3 by West Germany.
1996 European Champ. Q-final: Beat Spain 4-2
1996 European Champ. S-final: Beaten 6-5 by Germany
1998 World Cup (2nd Round): Beaten 4-3 by Argentina.
2004 European Champ. Q-final: Beaten 6-5 by Portugal.

INTERNATIONAL PENALTIES, MISSED

Four penalties out of five were missed when **Colombia** beat **Argentina** 3-0 in a Copa America group tie in Paraguay in July 1999. Martin Palmeiro missed three for Argentina and Colombia's Hamilton Ricard had one spot-kick saved.

In the European Championship semi-final against Italy in Amsterdam on June 29, 2000, **Holland** missed five penalties – two in normal time, three in the penalty contest which Italy won 3-1 (after 0-0). Dutch captain Frank de Boer missed twice from the spot.

F.A. CUP SHOOT-OUTS

In **13 seasons** since the introduction of this method to settle F.A. Cup ties (from Round 1) that are level after two matches, a total of **60 ties** in the competition proper have been decided by such means (5 in 1991-2, 6 in 1992-3, 4 in 1993-4, 4 in 1994-5, 4 in 1995-6; 3 in 1996-7, 12 in 1997-8, 5 in 1998-9, 4 in 1999-2000, 2 in 2000-01, 3 in 2001-02, 5 in 2002-03, 3 in 2003-04).

The **first** penalty contest in the F.A. Cup took place in **1972**. In days of the play-off for third place, the match was delayed until the eve of the following season when losing semi-finalists **Birmingham City** and **Stoke City** met at St. Andrew's on Aug. 5. The score was 0-0 and Birmingham City won 4-3 on penalties.

Highest recorded F.A. Cup shoot-out went to 24 kicks, with Macclesfield Town beating Forest Green Rov. (away) 11-10 in 1st Round replay on November 28, 2001.

Shoot-out abandoned: The F.A. Cup 1st Round replay between Oxford City and Wycombe Wand. at Wycombe on November 9, 1999 was abandoned (1-1) after extra time because, as the penalty shoot-out was about to begin, a fire broke out under a stand. Wycombe won the second replay 1-0 at Oxford Utd.'s ground.

Closest the **F.A. Cup Final** has come to a shoot-out was in 1993. Arsenal's Wembley replay against Sheffield Wed. went to extra time and was into its last minute when Andy Linighan headed their winner.

F.A. CUP SEMI-FINAL SHOOT-OUTS

1992 Liverpool beat Portsmouth 3–1 at Villa Park. **2000** Aston Villa beat Bolton Wanderers 4–1 at Wembley.

MISSED CUP FINAL PENALTIES

John Aldridge (Liverpool) became the first player to miss a penalty in the F.A. Cup Final at Wembley – and the second in the competition's history (previously Charlie Wallace, of Aston Villa, in the 1913 Final against Sunderland at Crystal Palace) – when Wimbledon's Dave Beasant saved his shot in May 1988. Seven previous penalties had been scored in this Final at Wembley.

Another crucial penalty miss at Wembley was by Arsenal's **Nigel Winterburn,** Luton Town's Andy Dibble saving his spot-kick in the 1988 Littlewoods Cup Final, when a goal would have put Arsenal 3–1 ahead. Instead, they lost 3–2.

Winterburn was the third player to fail with a League Cup Final penalty at Wembley, following **Ray Graydon** (Aston Villa) against Norwich City in 1975 and **Clive Walker** (Sunderland), who shot wide in the 1985 Milk Cup Final, also against Norwich City (won 1–0). Graydon had his penalty saved by Kevin Keelan, but scored from the rebound and won the cup for Aston Villa (1–0).

Tottenham's **Gary Lineker** saw his penalty saved by Nott'm. Forest goalkeeper Mark Crossley in the 1991 F.A. Cup Final.

Derby Co.'s Martin Taylor saved a penalty from **Eligio Nicolini** in the Anglo-Italian Cup Final at Wembley on March 27, 1993, but Cremonese won 3–1.

LEAGUE PENALTIES RECORD

Most penalties in Football League match: Five – 4 to Crystal Palace (3 missed), 1 to Brighton & H.A. (scored) in Div. 2 match at Selhurst Park on March 27 (Easter Monday), 1989. Crystal Palace won 2–1. Three of the penalties were awarded in a 5-minute spell. The match also produced 5 bookings and a sending-off.

Other teams missing 3 penalties in a match: **Burnley** v Grimsby Town (Div. 2), February 13, 1909; **Manchester City** v Newcastle Utd. (Div. 1), January 17, 1912.

HOTTEST MODERN SPOT-SHOT

Matthew Le Tissier ended his career in season 2001-02 with the distinction of having netted 48 out of 49 first-team penalties for Southampton. He scored the last 27 after his only miss when Nott'm. Forest keeper Mark Crossley saved in a Premier League match at The Dell on March 24, 1993.

SPOT-KICK HAT-TRICKS

Right-back **Joe Willetts** scored three penalties when Hartlepool Utd. beat neighbours Darlington 6–1 (Div. 3N) on Good Friday 1951.

Danish International **Jan Molby**'s only hat-trick in English football, for Liverpool in a 3-1 win at home to Coventry City (Littlewoods Cup, 4th round replay, Nov. 26, 1986) comprised three goals from the penalty spot.

It was the first such hat-trick in a major match for two years – since **Andy Blair** scored three penalties for Sheffield Wed. against Luton Town (Milk Cup 4th. round, Nov. 20 1984).

Portsmouth's **Kevin Dillon** scored a penalty hat-trick in the Full Members Cup (2nd rd.) at home to Millwall (3–2) on Nov. 4, 1986.

Alan Slough scored a hat-trick of penalties in an away game and was on the losing side, when Peterborough Utd. were beaten 4-3 at Chester City (Div. 3, Apr. 29, 1978).

Penalty hat-tricks in **International football**: Dimitris Saravakos (in 9 mins.) for Greece v Egypt in 1990. He scored 5 goals in match; **Henrik Larsson**, among his 4 goals in Sweden's 6-0 home win v Moldova in World Cup qualifying match, June 6, 2001.

MOST PENALTY GOALS (LEAGUE) IN SEASON

Thirteen out of 13 by **Francis Lee** for Manchester City (Div. 1) in 1971-2. His goal total for the season was 33. In season 1988-9, **Graham Roberts** scored 12 League penalties for Second Division Champions Chelsea.

PENALTY-SAVE SEQUENCES

Ipswich Town goalkeeper **Paul Cooper** saved eight of the ten penalties he faced in 1979-80. **Roy Brown** (Notts Co.) saved six in a row in season 1972-3.

Andy Lomas, goalkeeper for Chesham Utd. (Diadora League) claimed a record eight consecutive penalty saves – three at the end of season 1991-2 and five in 1992-3.

Mark Bosnich (Aston Villa) saved five in two consecutive matches in 1993-4: three in Coca-Cola Cup semi-final penalty shoot-out v Tranmere Rov. (Feb. 26), then two in Premiership at Tottenham (Mar. 2).

MISSED PENALTIES SEQUENCE

Against Wolves in Div. 2 on Sept. 28, 1991, **Southend Utd.** missed their seventh successive penalty (five of them the previous season).

SCOTTISH RECORDS
(See also under 'Goals' & 'Discipline')

RANGERS' MANY RECORDS

Rangers' record-breaking feats include:-
League Champions: 50 times (once joint holders) – world record.
Winning every match in Scottish League (18 games, 1898-9 season).
Major hat-tricks: Rangers have completed the domestic treble (League Championship, League Cup and Scottish F.A. Cup) a record seven times (1948-9, 1963-4, 1975-6, 1977-8, 1992-3, 1998-9, 2002-3).
League & Cup double: 16 times.
Nine successive Championships (1989-97). Four men played in all nine sides: Richard Gough, Ally McCoist, Ian Ferguson and Ian Durrant.
105 major trophies: Championships 50, Scottish Cup 31, League Cup 23, Cup-Winners' Cup 1.

CELTIC'S GRAND SLAM

Celtic's record in 1966-7 was the most successful by a British club in one season. They won the **Scottish League**, the **Scottish Cup**, the **Scottish League Cup** and became the first British club to win the **European Cup**. They also won the **Glasgow Cup**.

Celtic have 3 times achieved the Scottish treble (League Championship, League Cup and F.A. Cup), in 1966-7, 1968-9 and 2000-01 (in Martin O'Neill's first season as their manager). They became Scottish Champions for 2000-01 with a 1-0 home win against St. Mirren on April 7 – the earliest the title had been clinched for 26 years, since Rangers' triumph on March 29, 1975.

They have won the Scottish Cup 32 times, and have completed the League and Cup double 13 times.

Celtic won nine consecutive Scottish League titles (1966-74) under Jock Stein.

They set a **British record** of 25 consecutive League wins in season 2003-04 (Aug. 15 to Mar. 14). They were unbeaten for 77 matches (all competitions) at Celtic Park from August 22, 2001, to April 21, 2004.

UNBEATEN SCOTTISH CHAMPIONS

Celtic and **Rangers** have each won the Scottish Championship with an unbeaten record: Celtic in 1897-98 (P18, W15, D3), Rangers in 1898-99 (P18, W18).

LARSSON SUPREME

After missing most of the previous campaign with a broken leg, Swedish International **Henrik Larsson**, with 53 goals in season 2000-01, set a post-war record for Celtic and equalled the Scottish Premier League record of 35 by Brian McClair (Celtic) in 1986-7. Larsson's 35 earned him Europe's Golden Shoe award.

His 7 seasons as a Celtic Player ended, when his contract expired in May 2004, with a personal total of 242 goals in 315 apps. (third-highest scorer in the club's history). He helped Celtic win 4 League titles, and at 32 he moved to Barcelona (free) on a 2-year contract.

SCOTTISH CUP HAT-TRICKS

Aberdeen's feat of winning the Scottish F.A. Cup in 1982-3-4 made them only the third club to achieve that particular hat-trick.

Queen's Park did it twice (1874-5-6 and 1880-1-2), and **Rangers** have won the Scottish Cup three years in succession on three occasions: 1934-5-6, 1948-9-50 and 1962-3-4.

SCOTTISH CUP FINAL DISMISSALS

Three players have been sent off in the Scottish F.A. Cup Final: **Jock Buchanan** (Rangers v. Kilmarnock, 1929), **Roy Aitken** (Celtic v Aberdeen, 1984) and **Walter Kidd** (Hearts captain v Aberdeen, 1986).

RECORD SEQUENCES

Celtic hold the Scottish League record run of success with 62 matches undefeated, from November 13, 1915 to April 21, 1917, when Kilmarnock won 2-0 at Parkhead.

Greenock Morton in 1963-4 were undefeated in home League matches, obtained a record 67 points out of 72 and scored 135 goals, clinching promotion from Div. 2 as early as February 29.

Queen's Park did not have a goal scored against them during the first seven seasons of their existence (1867-74, before the Scottish League was formed).

WORST HOME SEQUENCE

After gaining promotion to Div. 1 in 1992, **Cowdenbeath** went a record 38 consecutive home League matches without a win. They ended the sequence (drew 8, lost 30) when beating Arbroath 1-0 on April 2, 1994, watched by a crowd of 225.

ALLY'S RECORDS

Ally McCoist became the first player to complete 200 goals in the Premier Division when he scored Rangers' winner (2-1) at Falkirk on December 12, 1992. His first was against Celtic in September 1983, and he reached 100 against Dundee on Boxing Day 1987.

When McCoist scored twice at home to Hibernian (4-3) on December 7, 1996, he became Scotland's record post-war League marksman, beating Gordon Wallace's 264.

Originally with St. Johnstone (1978-81), he spent two seasons with Sunderland (1981-3), then joined Rangers for £200,000 in June 1983.

In 15 seasons at Ibrox, he scored 355 goals for Rangers (250 League), and helped them win 10 Championships (9 in succession), 3 Scottish Cups and earned a record 9 League Cup winner's medals. He won the European Golden Boot in consecutive seasons (1991-2, 1992-3).

His 9 Premier League goals in three seasons for Kilmarnock gave him a career total of 281 Scottish League goals when he retired at the end of 2000-01.

FIVE IN A MATCH

Paul Sturrock set an individual scoring record for the Scottish Premier Division with 5 goals in Dundee Utd.'s 7-0 win at home to Morton on November 17, 1984. **Marco Negri** equalled the feat with all 5 when Rangers beat Dundee Utd. 5-1 at Ibrox (Premier Division) on August 23, 1997, and **Kenny Miller** scored 5 in Rangers' 7-1 win at home to St. Mirren on November 4, 2000.

SEATS MILESTONE FOR CELTIC

In season 1998-9, **Celtic** became the first British club with an **all-seated** capacity of 60,000. That figure was exceeded by **Manchester Utd.** (61,629) in 1999-2000.

NEGRI'S TEN-TIMER

Marco Negri scored in Rangers' first ten League matches (23 goals) in season 1997-8 – a Premier Division record. The previous best sequence was 8 by Ally MacLeod for Hibernian in 1978.

DOUBLE SCOTTISH FINAL

Rangers v Celtic drew **129,643** and **120,073** people to the Scottish Cup Final and replay at Hampden Park, Glasgow, in 1963. Receipts for the two matches totalled £50,500.

MOST SCOTTISH CHAMPIONSHIP MEDALS

13 by **Sandy Archibald** (Rangers, 1918-34). Post-war record: **10** by **Bobby Lennox** (Celtic, 1966-79).

Alan Morton won **nine** Scottish Championship medals with Rangers in 1921-23-24-25-27-28-29-30-31. **Ally McCoist** played in the Rangers side that won nine successive League titles (1989-97).

Between 1927 and 1939 **Bob McPhail** helped Rangers win nine Championships, finish second twice and third once. He scored 236 League goals but was never top scorer in a single season.

SCOTTISH CUP – NO DECISION

The **Scottish F.A.** withheld their Cup and medals in 1908-9 after Rangers and Celtic played two drawn games in the Final. Spectators rioted.

FEWEST LEAGUE WINS IN SEASON

Clydebank won only one of 36 matches in Div. 1, season 1999-2000. That victory did not come until March 7 (2-1 at home to Raith).

HAMPDEN'S £63M. REDEVELOPMENT

On completion of redevelopment costing £63m. **Hampden Park**, home of Scottish football and the oldest first-class stadium in the world, was re-opened full scale for the Rangers-Celtic Cup Final on May 29, 1999.

Work on the 'new Hampden' (capacity 52,000) began in 1992. The North and East stands were restructured (£12m.); a new South stand and improved West stand cost £51m. The Millennium Commission contributed £23m. and the Lottery Sports Fund provided a grant of £3.75m.

DEMISE OF AIRDRIE AND CLYDEBANK

In May 2002, First Division **Airdrieonians**, formed in 1878, went out of business. They had debts of £3m. Their place in the Scottish League was taken by **Gretna**, from the English Unibond League, who were voted into Div. 3. Second Division **Clydebank** folded in July 2002 and were taken over by the new **Airdrie United** club.

GREAT SCOTS

In February 1988, the Scottish F.A. launched a national **Hall of Fame**, initially comprising the first 11 Scots to make 50 International appearances, to be joined by all future players to reach that number of caps. Each member receives a gold medal, invitation for life at all Scotland's home matches, and has his portrait hung at Scottish F.A. headquarters in Glasgow.

MORE CLUBS IN 2000

The **Scottish Premier League** increased from 10 to 12 clubs in season 2000-1.

The **Scottish Football League** admitted two new clubs – Peterhead and Elgin City from the Highland League – to provide three divisions of 10 in 2000-1.

NOTABLE SCOTTISH 'FIRSTS'

- The father of League football was a Scot, **William McGregor**, a draper in Birmingham City. The 12-club Football League kicked off in September 1888, and McGregor was its first president.
- **Hibernian** were the first British club to play in the European Cup, by invitation. They reached the semi-final when it began in 1955-6.
- **Celtic** were Britain's first winners of the European Cup, in 1967.
- Scotland's First Division became the **Premier Division** in season 1975-6.
- Football's **first International** was staged at the West of Scotland cricket ground, Partick, on November 30, 1872: Scotland 0, England 0.
- Scotland introduced its **League Cup** in 1945-6, the first season after the war. It was another 15 years before the Football League Cup was launched.
- The Scottish F.A. Cup has been **sponsored** by Tennents for the last 15 seasons.
- Scotland pioneered the use in British football of **two substitutes** per team in League and Cup matches.
- The world's **record football score** belongs to Scotland: Arbroath 36, Bon Accord 0 (Scottish Cup first round) on September 12, 1885.
- The Scottish F.A. introduced the **penalty shoot-out** to their Cup Final in 1990.
- On Jan. 22, 1994 all six matches in the **Scottish Premier Division** ended as draws.
- Scotland's new Premier League introduced a **3-week shut-down** in January 1999 — first instance of British football adopting the winter break system that operates in a number of European countries. The SPL ended its New Year closure after 2003.
- **Rangers** made history at home to St. Johnstone (Premier League, 0-0, March 4, 2000) when fielding a team entirely without Scottish players.

SCOTTISH CUP SHOCK RESULTS

1885-86 (1) Arbroath 36, Bon Accord 0
1921-22 (F) Morton 1, Rangers 0
1937-38 (F) East Fife 4, Kilmarnock 2 (replay, after 1-1)
1960-61 (F) Dunfermline 2, Celtic 0 (replay, after 0-0)
1966-67 (1) Berwick Rangers 1, Rangers 0
1979-80 (3) Hamilton 2, Keith 3
1984-85 (3) Stirling Albion 20, Selkirk 0
1984-85 (3) Inverness Thistle 3, Kilmarnock 0
1986-87 (3) Rangers 0, Hamilton 1
1994-95 (4) Stenhousemuir 2, Aberdeen 0
1998-99 (3) Aberdeen 0, Livingston 1
1999-2000 (3) Celtic 1, Inverness Caledonian Thistle 3
2002-03 (5) Inverness Caledonian Thistle 1, Celtic 0

Scottish League (Coca-Cola) Cup Final shock
1994-95   Raith 2, Celtic 2 (Raith won 6-5 on pens.)

SCOTTISH DISCIPLINE (MODERN) – MAJOR PUNISHMENTS

1989 (June) fine **Hearts** £93,000, following TV infringement at UEFA Cup q-final.
1994 (August) Scottish League fine **Celtic** record £100,000 for poaching manager Tommy Burns from Kilmarnock.
1996 (November) UEFA fine **Celtic** £42,000 and **Alan Stubbs** £28,000 for using unlicensed agents in summer transfer from Bolton Wanderers.
1999 (August) Scottish Premier League fine **Celtic** £45,000 for their part in disturbances at home match with Rangers, May 2.
2000 (April) Scottish League deduct a record 15 points from **Hamilton Academical**, following their players (in protest over unpaid wages) refusing to turn up for Div. 2 fixture at Stenhousemuir on April 1. As a result, Hamilton relegated at end of season.

MISCELLANEOUS

NATIONAL ASSOCIATIONS FORMED

F.A. on Oct. 26 .... **1863**
F.A. of Wales **1876**
Scottish F.A. **1873**
Irish F.A. **1904**
Federation of International Football Associations (FIFA) **1904**

NATIONAL & INTERNATIONAL COMPETITIONS LAUNCHED

F.A. Cup **1871**
Welsh Cup **1877**
Scottish Cup **1873**
Irish Cup **1880**
Football League **1888**
F.A. Premier League **1992**
Scottish League **1890**
Scottish Premier League **1998**
Scottish League Cup **1945**
Football League Cup **1960**
Home International Championship **1883-4**
World (Jules Rimet) Cup, at Montevideo **1930**
European Championship **1958**
European Cup **1955**
Fairs/UEFA Cup **1955**
Cup-Winners' Cup **1960**
Youth International (16-18 age-groups) **1946-7**
Olympic Games Tournament, at Shepherd's Bush **1908**

INNOVATIONS

Size of Ball: Fixed in **1872**.

Shinguards: Introduced and registered by Sam Weller Widdowson (Nott'm. Forest & England) in **1874**.

Referee's Whistle: First used on Nott'm. Forest's ground in **1878**.

Professionalism: Legalised in England in the summer of **1885** as a result of agitation by Lancashire clubs.

Goal-nets: Invented and patented in **1890** by Mr. J. A. Brodie of Liverpool. They were first used in the North v South match in January, **1891**.

Referees and Linesmen: Replaced umpires and referees in January, **1891**.

Penalty-kick: Introduced at Irish F.A.'s request in the season **1891-2**. The penalty law ordering the goalkeeper to remain on the goal-line came into force in September, **1905**, and the order to stand on his goal-line until the ball is kicked arrived in **1929-30**.

White ball: First came into official use in **1951**.

Floodlighting: First F.A. Cup-tie (replay), Kidderminster Harriers v Brierley Hill Alliance, **1955**.

Heated pitch to beat frost tried by Everton at Goodison Park in **1958**.

First Soccer Closed-circuit TV: At Coventry City ground in October **1965** (10,000 fans saw their team win at Cardiff City, 120 miles away).

Substitutes (one per team) were first allowed in Football League matches at the start of season **1965-6**. Three substitutes (one a goalkeeper) allowed, two of which could be used, in Premier League matches, **1992-93**. The Football League introduced three substitutes for **1993-94**.

Three points for a win: This was introduced by the Football League in **1981-2**, by FIFA in World Cup games in 1994, and by the Scottish League in the same year.

Offside law amended, player 'level' no longer offside, and 'professional foul' made sending-off offence, **1990**.

Penalty shoot-outs introduced to decide F.A. Cup ties level after one replay and extra time, **1991-2**.
New back-pass rule – goalkeeper must not handle ball kicked to him by team-mate, **1992**.
Linesmen became 'referees' assistants', **1998**.
Goalkeepers not to hold ball longer than 6 seconds, **2000**.
Free-kicks advanced by ten yards against opponents failing to retreat, **2000**.

CUP AND LEAGUE DOUBLES

League Championship and F.A. Cup: Preston N.E., 1889; Aston Villa, 1897; Tottenham, 1961; Arsenal, 1971; Liverpool 1986; Manchester Utd. 1994, 1996; Arsenal 1998; Manchester Utd. 1999; Arsenal 2002.
F.A. Cup and Promotion: W.B.A., 1931.
F.A. Cup and Football League Cup: Arsenal, 1993; Liverpool, 2001 (also won UEFA Cup).
League Championship and Football League Cup: Nott'm Forest, 1978; Liverpool, 1982; Liverpool, 1983; Liverpool, 1984 (also won European Cup).
Scottish League Championship and Cup Double: Rangers, (16): 1928-30-34-35-49-50-53-63-64-76-78-92-93-96-2000-2003. Celtic, (13): 1907-8-14-54-67-69-71-72-74-77-88-2001-04. Aberdeen, (1): 1984.
Scottish Treble (Championship, Cup, League Cup): Rangers 7 times (1949-64-76-78-93-99, 2003); Celtic 3 times (1967-69-2001) (also won European Cup in 1967).

DERBY DAYS: COMPLETE LEAGUE RESULTS

Arsenal v Tottenham: Played 134 (all top div.); Arsenal 54 wins, Tottenham 45, Drawn 35.
Aston Villa v Birmingham City: Played 100; Aston Villa 39, Birmingham City 34, Drawn 27.
Everton v Liverpool: Played 170 (all top div.); Liverpool 62, Everton 54, Drawn 54.
Ipswich Town v Norwich City: Played 72; Ipswich Town 34, Norwich City 26, Drawn 12.
Manchester City v Manchester Utd.: Played 130; United 50, City 34, Drawn 46.
Middlesbrough v Newcastle Utd.: Played 102; Newcastle Utd. 42, Middlesbrough 33, Drawn 27.
Newcastle v Sunderland: Played 126; Newcastle Utd. 46, Sunderland 41, Drawn 39 (incl. 1990 play-offs – Sunderland win and draw).
Middlesbrough v Sunderland: Played 122; Sunderland 53, Middlesbrough 38, Drawn 31.
Nott'm. Forest v Notts Co.: Played 86; Forest 35, County 28, Drawn 23.
Sheffield Utd. v Sheffield Wed.: Played 104; United 39, Wednesday 32, Drawn 33.
Port Vale v Stoke City: Played 44; Stoke City 16, Port Vale 14, Drawn 14.
Bristol City v Bristol Rovers: Played 86; City 33, Rovers 25, Drawn 28.
Celtic v Rangers: Played 272; Rangers 105, Celtic 87, Drawn 80.
Dundee v Dundee Utd.: Played 119; United 57, Dundee 36, Drawn 26.
Hearts v Hibernian: Played 231; Hearts 94, Hibernian 68, Drawn 69.

YOUNGEST AND OLDEST

Youngest Caps   *Age*
Norman Whiteside (N. Ireland v Yugoslavia, June 17, 1982)   **17** years **41** days
Ryan Green (Wales v Malta, June 3, 1998)   **17** years **226** days
Wayne Rooney (England v Australia, February 12, 2003)   **17** years **111** days
Johnny Lambie (Scotland v Ireland, March 20, 1886)   **17** years **92** days
Jimmy Holmes (Rep. of Ireland v Austria, May 30, 1971)   **17** years **200** days
England's youngest cap (pre-Rooney) since 1900: Michael Owen (v Chile, Wembley, February 11, 1998) 18 years 59 days.
Youngest England scorer: Wayne Rooney (17 years, 317 days) v Macedonia, Skopje, September 6, 2003.
Youngest England captains: Bobby Moore (v Czech., Bratislava, May 29, 1963), 22 years, 47 days; Michael Owen (v Paraguay, Anfield, April 17, 2002), 22 years, 117 days.
Youngest England players to reach 50 caps: Michael Owen (23 years, 6 months) v Slovakia at Middlesbrough, June 11, 2003; Bobby Moore (25 years, 7 months) v Wales at Wembley, November 16, 1966.

Youngest player in World Cup Final: Pele (Brazil) aged 17 years, 237 days v Sweden in Stockholm, June 12, 1958.

Youngest player to appear in World Cup Finals: Norman Whiteside (N. Ireland v Yugoslavia in Spain – June 17, 1982, age 17 years and 42 days.

Youngest First Division player: Derek Forster (Sunderland goalkeeper v Leicester City, August 22, 1964) aged 15 years, 185 days.

Youngest First Division scorer: At 16 years and 57 days, schoolboy Jason Dozzell (substitute after 30 minutes for Ipswich Town at home to Coventry City on February 4, 1984). Ipswich Town won 3-1 and Dozzell scored their third goal.

Youngest F.A. Premier League player: Aaron Lennon (Leeds Utd. sub. v Tottenham, August 23, 2003, 16 years, 129 days.

Youngest F.A. Premier League scorer: James Milner (Leeds Utd. away to Sunderland, December 26, 2002), 16 years, 357 days.

Youngest player sent off in Premier League: Wayne Rooney (Everton, away to Birmingham City, December 26, 2002) aged 17 years, 59 days.

Youngest First Division hat-trick scorer: Alan Shearer, aged 17 years, 240 days, in Southampton's 4-2 home win v Arsenal (April 9, 1988) on his full debut. Previously, Jimmy Greaves (17 years, 309 days) with 4 goals for Chelsea at home to Portsmouth (7-4), Christmas Day, 1957.

Youngest to complete 100 Football League goals: Jimmy Greaves (20 years, 261 days) when he did so for Chelsea v Manchester City, November 19, 1960.

Youngest Football League scorer: Ronnie Dix (for Bristol Rov. v Norwich City, Div. 3 South, March 3, 1928) aged 15 years, 180 days.

Youngest players in Football League: Albert Geldard (Bradford Park Avenue v Millwall, Div. 2, September 16, 1929) aged 15 years, 158 days; Ken Roberts (Wrexham v Bradford Park Avenue, Div. 3 North, September 1, 1951) also 15 years, 158 days.

Youngest player in Scottish League: Goalkeeper Ronnie Simpson (Queens Park) aged 15 in 1946.

Youngest player in F.A. Cup: Andy Awford, Worcester City's England Schoolboy defender, aged 15 years, 88 days when he substituted in second half away to Boreham Wood (3rd. qual. round) on October 10, 1987.

Youngest player in F.A. Cup proper: Schoolboy Lee Holmes (15 years, 277 days) for Derby Co. away to Brentford in 3rd. Round on January 4, 2003.

Youngest Wembley Cup Final captain: Barry Venison (Sunderland v Norwich City, Milk Cup Final, March 24, 1985 – replacing suspended captain Shaun Elliott) – aged 20 years, 220 days.

Youngest F.A. Cup-winning captain: Bobby Moore (West Ham Utd., 1964, v Preston N.E.), aged 23 years, 20 days.

Youngest F.A. Cup Final captain: David Nish aged 21 years and 212 days old when he captained Leicester City against Manchester City at Wembley on April 26, 1969.

Youngest F.A. Cup Final player: Curtis Weston (Millwall sub. last 3 mins v Manchester Utd., 2004) aged 17 years, 119 days.

Youngest F.A. Cup Final scorer: Norman Whiteside (Manchester Utd. v Brighton & H.A. in 1983 replay at Wembley), aged 18 years, 19 days.

Youngest F.A. Cup Final managers: Stan Cullis, Wolves (33) v Leicester City, 1949; Steve Coppell, Crystal Palace (34) v Manchester Utd., 1990; Ruud Gullit, Chelsea (34) v Mid'bro', 1997.

Youngest player in Football League Cup: Kevin Davies (Chesterfield sub at West Ham Utd., 2nd Round, 2nd Leg on September 22, 1993) aged 16 years, 180 days.

Youngest Wembley scorer: Norman Whiteside (Manchester Utd. v Liverpool, Milk Cup Final, March 26, 1983) aged 17 years, 324 days.

Youngest Wembley Cup Final goalkeeper: Chris Woods (18 years, 125 days) for Nott'm Forest v Liverpool, League Cup Final on March 18, 1978.

Youngest Wembley F.A. Cup Final goalkeeper: Peter Shilton (19 years, 219 days) for Leicester City v Manchester City, April 26, 1969.

Youngest senior International at Wembley: Salomon Olembe (sub for Cameroon v England, November 15, 1997), aged 16 years, 342 days.

Youngest winning manager at Wembley: Roy McDonough, aged 33 years. 6 months, 24 days as player-manager of Colchester Utd., F.A. Trophy winners on May 10, 1992.

Youngest scorer in full International: Mohamed Kallon (Sierra Leone v Congo, African Nations Cup, April 22, 1995), reported as aged 15 years, 192 days.

Youngest player sent off in World Cup Final series: Rigobert Song (Cameroon v Brazil, in USA, June 1994) aged 17 years, 358 days.

Youngest F.A. Cup Final referee: Kevin Howley, of Middlesbrough, aged 35 when in charge of Wolves v Blackburn Rov., 1960.

Youngest player in England U-23 team: Duncan Edwards (v. Italy, Bologna, January 20, 1954), aged 17 years, 112 days.

Youngest player in England U-21 team: Lee Sharpe (v. Greece, away, February 7, 1989), aged 17 years, 254 days.

Youngest player in Scotland U-21 team: Christian Dailly (v Romania, Hampden Park, Sept. 11, 1990), aged 16 years, 330 days.

Youngest player in senior football: Cameron Campbell Buchanan, Scottish-born outside right, aged 14 years, 57 days when he played for Wolves v W.B.A. in War-time League match, September 26, 1942.

Youngest player in peace-time senior match: Eamon Collins (Blackpool v Kilmarnock, Anglo-Scottish Cup quarter-final 1st. leg, September 9, 1980) aged 14 years, 323 days.

World's youngest player in top-division match: Centre-forward Fernando Rafael Garcia, aged 13, played for 23 minutes for Peruvian club Juan Aurich in 3-1 win against Estudiantes on May 19, 2001.

Oldest player to appear in Football League: New Brighton manager Neil McBain (51 years, 120 days) as emergency goalkeeper away to Hartlepool Utd. (Div. 3 North, March 15, 1947).

Other oldest post-war League players: Sir Stanley Matthews (Stoke City, 1965, 50 years, 5 days); Peter Shilton (Leyton Orient 1997, 47 years, 126 days); Dave Beasant (Brighton & H.A. 2003, 44 years, 46 days); Alf Wood (Coventry City, 1958, 43 years, 199 days); Tommy Hutchison (Swansea City, 1991, 43 years, 172 days).

Oldest Football League debutant: Andy Cunningham, for Newcastle Utd. at Leicester City (Div. 1) on February 2, 1929, aged 38 years, 2 days.

Oldest post-war debutant in English League: Defender David Donaldson (35 years, 7 months, 23 days) for Wimbledon on entry to Football League (Div. 4) away to Halifax Town, August 20, 1977.

Oldest player to appear in First Division: Sir Stanley Matthews (Stoke City v Fulham, February 6, 1965), aged 50 years, 5 days – on that his last League appearance, the only 50-year-old ever to play in the top division.

Oldest players in Premier League: Goalkeepers John Burridge (Manchester City v Q.P.R., May 14, 1995), aged 43 years, 5 months, 11 days; Steve Ogrizovic (Coventry City v Sheffield Wed., May 6, 2000), aged 42 years, 7 months, 24 days; Neville Southall (Bradford City v Leeds Utd., March 12, 2000), aged 41 years, 5 months, 26 days. Outfield: Gordon Strachan (Coventry City v Derby Co., May 3, 1997) aged 40 years, 2 months, 24 days.

Oldest player for British professional club: John Ryan (owner-chairman of Conference club Doncaster Rov., played as substitute for last minute in 4–2 win at Hereford on April 26, 2003), aged 52 years, 11 months, 3 weeks.

Oldest F.A. Cup Final player: Walter (Billy) Hampson (Newcastle Utd. v Aston Villa on April 26, 1924), aged 41 years, 257 days.

Oldest F.A. Cup-winning team: Arsenal 1950 (average age 31 years, 2 months). Eight of the players were over 30, with the three oldest centre-half Leslie Compton 37, and skipper Joe Mercer and goalkeeper George Swindin, both 35.

Oldest World Cup-winning captain: Dino Zoff, Italy's goalkeeper v W. Germany in 1982 Final, aged 40 years, 92 days.

Oldest player capped by England: Stanley Matthews (v. Denmark, Copenhagen, May 15, 1957), aged 42 years, 103 days.

Oldest England scorer: Stanley Matthews (v N. Ireland, Belfast, October 6, 1956), aged 41 years, 248 days.

Oldest British International player: Billy Meredith (Wales v England at Highbury, March 15, 1920), aged 45 years, 229 days.

Oldest 'new caps': Goalkeeper Alexander Morten, aged 41 years, 113 days when earning his only England Cap against Scotland on March 8, 1873; Arsenal centre-half Leslie Compton, at 38 years, 64 days when he made his England debut in 4-2 win against Wales at Sunderland on November 15, 1950. **For Scotland:** Goalkeeper Ronnie Simpson (Celtic) at 36 years, 186 days v England at Wembley, April 15, 1967.

Longest Football League career: This spanned 32 years and 10 months, by Stanley Matthews (Stoke City, Blackpool, Stoke City) from March 19, 1932 until February 6, 1965.

Smallest F.A. Cup-winning captain: 5ft. 4in. – Bobby Kerr (Sunderland v Leeds Utd., 1973).

SHIRT NUMBERING

Numbering players in Football League matches was made compulsory in 1939. Players wore numbered shirts (1-22) in the F.A. Cup Final as an experiment in 1933 (Everton 1-11 v Manchester City 12-22).

Squad numbers for players were introduced by the F.A. Premier League at the start of season 1993-4. They were optional in the Football League until made compulsory in 1999-2000.

Names on shirts: For first time, players wore names as well as numbers on shirts in League Cup and F.A. Cup Finals, 1993.

SUBSTITUTES

In **1965**, the Football League, by 39 votes to 10, agreed that **one substitute** be allowed for an injured player at any time during a League match. First substitute used in Football League: Keith Peacock (Charlton Athletic), away to Bolton Wand. in Div. 2, August 21, 1965.

Two substitutes per team were approved for the League (Littlewoods) Cup and F.A. Cup in season 1986-7 and two were permitted in the Football League for the first time in 1987-8.

Three substitutes (one a goalkeeper), two of which could be used, introduced by the Premier League for 1992-3. The Football League followed suit for 1993-4.

Three substitutes (one a goalkeeper) were allowed at the World Cup Finals for the first time at US '94.

Three substitutes (any position) introduced by Premier League and Football League in 1995-6.

First substitute to score in F.A. Cup Final: Eddie Kelly (Arsenal v Liverpool, 1971).

The **first recorded use of a substitute was in 1889** (Wales v Scotland at Wrexham on April 15) when Sam Gillam arrived late – although he was a Wrexham player – and Allen Pugh (Rhostellyn) was allowed to keep goal until he turned up. The match ended 0-0.

When Dickie Roose, the Welsh goalkeeper, was injured against England at Wrexham, March 16, 1908, Dai Davies (Bolton Wand.) was allowed to take his place as substitute. Thus Wales used 12 players. England won 7-1.

END OF WAGE LIMIT

Freedom from the maximum wage system – in force since the formation of the Football League in 1888 – was secured by the Professional Footballers' Association in 1961. About this time Italian clubs renewed overtures for the transfer of British stars and Fulham's **Johnny Haynes** became the first British player to earn £100 a week.

THE BOSMAN RULING

On December 15, 1995 the **European Court of Justice** ruled that clubs had no right to transfer fees for out-of-contract players, and the outcome of the 'Bosman case' irrevocably changed football's player-club relationship. It began in 1990, when the contract of 26-year-old **Jean-Marc Bosman**, a midfield player with FC Liege, Belgium, expired. French club Dunkirk wanted him but were unwilling to pay the £500,000 transfer fee, so Bosman was compelled to remain with Liege. He responded with a lawsuit against his club and UEFA on the grounds of 'restriction of trade', and after five years at various court levels the European Court of Justice ruled not only in favour of Bosman but of all professional footballers.

The end of restrictive labour practices revolutionised the system. It led to a proliferation of transfers, rocketed the salaries of elite players who, backed by an increasing army of agents, found themselves in a vastly improved bargaining position as they moved from team to team, league to league, nation to nation. Removing the limit on the number of foreigners clubs could field brought an increasing ratio of such signings, not least in England and Scotland.

Bosman's one-man stand opened the way for footballers to become millionaires, but ended his own career. All he received for his legal conflict was 16 million Belgian francs (£312,000) in compensation, a testimonial of poor reward and martyrdom as the man who did most to change the face of football.

Celtic were the first British club to lose out, when Scottish International John Collins moved to Monaco in June 1996. Subsequent Bosman-free transfers involving British clubs include: Gianluca Vialli, Juventus to Chelsea (7/96); Michael Hughes, Strasbourg to West Ham Utd. (7/96); Gustavo Poyet, Real Zaragoza to Chelsea (5/97); David Connolly, Watford to Feyenoord (7/97); Jonathan Gould, Bradford City to Celtic (8/97); Brian Laudrup, Rangers to Chelsea (6/98); Shaka Hislop, Newcastle Utd. to West Ham Utd. (7/98); Gerry Taggart, Bolton Wand. to Leicester City (7/98); Mikael Forssell, HJK Helsinki to Chelsea (11/98); Steve McManaman, Liverpool to Real Madrid (7/99); Andy Melville, Sunderland to Fulham (5/99); Peter Schmeichel, Manchester Utd. to Sporting Lisbon (6/99); Markus Babbel, Bayern Munich to Liverpool (1/00); Pegguy Arphexad, Leicester City to Liverpool (7/00); Gary McAllister, Coventry City to Liverpool (7/00); Paul Okon, Fiorentina to Middlesbrough (7/00); Benito Carbone, Aston Villa to Bradford City (8/00); Winston Bogarde, Barcelona to Chelsea (8/00); Jari Litmanen, Barcelona to Liverpool (1/01); Teddy Sheringham, Manchester Utd. to Tottenham (6/01); Nelson Vivas, Arsenal to Inter Milan (6/01); Sol Campbell, Tottenham to Arsenal (6/01); Laurent Blanc, Inter Milan to Man. Utd. (8/01) ; Jamie Redknapp, Liverpool to Tottenham (4/02); Peter Schmeichel, Aston Villa to Manchester City (7/02); Enriqe de Lucas, Espanyol to Chelsea (7/02); Jay Jay Okocha, Paris SG. to Bolton Wand. (7/02); Shaka Hislop, West Ham Utd. to Portsmouth (7/02); Youri Djorkaeff, Kaiserslautern to Bolton Wand. (7/02); Denis Irwin, Manchester Utd. to Wolves (7/02); Paul Ince, Mid'bro' to Wolves (8/02); Ronny Johnsen, Manchester Utd. to Aston Villa (8/02); David Seaman, Arsenal to Manchester City (7/03); Teddy Sheringham, Tottenham to Portsmouth (7/03); Les Ferdinand, West Ham Utd. to Leicester City (7/03); Gary Breen, West Ham Utd. to Sunderland (8/03); Steve Staunton, Aston Villa to Coventry City (8/03); Paolo di Canio, West Ham Utd. to Charlton Athletic (8/03); Michael Gray, Sunderland to Blackburn Rov. (1/04); Andy Impey, Leicester City to Nott'm. F. (5/04); Muzzy Izzet, Leicester City to Birmingham City (6/04); Michael Bridges, Leeds Utd. to Bolton Wand. (6/04); Michael Ricketts, Middlesbrough to Leeds Utd. (6/04); Henrik Larsson, Celtic to Barcelona (7/04).

GREATEST SHOCKS

Excluding such tragedies as the Munich air crash (Feb. 1958), the Bradford City fire disaster (May 1985), Heysel (May 1985) and Hillsborough (April 1989), here in date order are, arguably, the greatest shocks in football history:

(1) Jan. 1933   F.A. Cup 3rd. Round: Walsall 2, Arsenal 0.
(2) Jan. 1949   F.A. Cup 4th. Round: Yeovil 2, Sunderland 1.
(3) June 1950   World Cup Finals: U.S.A. 1, England 0 (Belo Horizonte, Brazil).
(4) Nov. 1953   England 3, Hungary 6 (Wembley).
(5) Sept. 1962   Cup-Winners' Cup 1st. Round, 1st. Leg: Bangor 2, Napoli 0.
(6) Mar. 1966   World Cup stolen in London (found a week later).
(7) June 1966   World Cup Finals: N. Korea 1, Italy 0 (Middlesbrough).
(8) Jan. 1967   Scottish Cup 1st. Round: Berwick Rangers 1, Glasgow Rangers 0.
(9) Mar. 1969   League Cup Final: Swindon Town 3, Arsenal 1.
(10) Feb. 1971   F.A. Cup 5th. Round: Colchester Utd. 3, Leeds Utd. 2.
(11) Jan. 1972   F.A. Cup 3rd. Round: Hereford Utd. 2, Newcastle Utd. 1.
(12) May 1973   F.A. Cup Final: Sunderland 1, Leeds Utd. 0.
(13) July 1974   Bill Shankly retires as Liverpool manager.
(14) May 1976   F.A. Cup Final: Southampton 1, Manchester Utd. 0.
(15) July 1977   England manager Don Revie defects to coach Utd. Arab Emirates.
(16) June 1982   World Cup Finals: Algeria 2, West Germany 1 (Gijon, Spain).
(17) Jan. 1984   F.A. Cup 3rd. Round: Bournemouth 2, Manchester Utd. (holders) 0.
(18) May 1988   F.A. Cup Final: Wimbledon 1, Liverpool 0 .

(19)	June 1990	World Cup Finals: Cameroon 1, Argentina (World Champions) 0 (Milan).
(20)	Sept. 1990	European Championship (Qual. Round): Faroe Islands 1, Austria 0.
(21)	Feb. 1991	Kenny Dalglish resigns as Liverpool manager.
(22)	Jan. 1992	F.A. Cup 3rd. Round: Wrexham 2, Arsenal 1.
(23)	June 1992	European Championship Final: Denmark 2, Germany (World Champions) 0.
(24)	June 1993	U.S. Cup '93: U.S.A. 2, England 0 (Foxboro, Boston).
(25)	July 1994	World Cup Finals: Bulgaria 2, Germany 1 (New York City).
(26)	Feb. 1998	Concacaf Gold Cup: U.S.A. 1, Brazil 0 (Los Angeles).
(27)	July 1998	World Cup Q-final: Croatia 3 Germany 0.
(28)	July 1996	Olympic s-final (Athens, Georgia): Nigeria beat Brazil 4-3 with extra-time 'golden goal' (Brazil led 3-1 with 13 mins. left).
(29)	Feb. 2000	Scottish Cup 3rd. Round: Celtic 1, Inverness Cal. Thistle 3.
(30)	Nov. 2000	Scotland 0, Australia 2 (friendly, Hampden Park)
(31)	June 2001	Confed. Cup 3rd place play-off: Australia 1, Brazil 0 (Ulsan, S. Korea).
(32)	July 2001	Honduras 2, Brazil 0 (Copa America quarter-final).
(33)	Oct. 2002	European Championship (Qual. Round): England 2, Macedonia 2.
(34)	Feb. 2003	England 1, Australia 3 (friendly, Upton Park).
(35)	Mar. 2003	Scottish Cup 5th. Round: Inverness Cal. Thistle 1, Celtic 0.

OTHER INTERNATIONAL SHOCKS

(Read in conjunction with Greatest Shocks above)

1982	Spain 0, N. Ireland 1 (World Cup Finals in Spain).
1990	Scotland 0, Costa Rica 1 (World Cup Finals in Italy).
1990	Sweden 1, Costa Rica 2 (World Cup Finals in Italy).
1993	Argentina 0, Colombia 5 (World Cup qual. round).
1993	France 2, Israel 3 (World Cup qual. round).
1993	San Marino score fastest goal in Int. records: 8.3 secs. v England (World Cup qual. round).
1994	Moldova 3, Wales 2; Georgia 5, Wales 0 (both Euro. Champ. qual. round).
1995	Belarus 1, Holland 0 (European Champ. qual. round).
2001	Australia 1, France 0 (Confed. Cup, S. Korea). France won tournament.
2001	German 1, England 5 (World Cup qual. round).
2002	France 0, Senegal 1 (World Cup Finals, opening match, in S. Korea).
2002	France, World Cup holders, out without scoring.
2002	World Cup joint hosts South Korea beat Italy with Golden Goal, then Spain on penalties.
2004	Portugal 1, Greece 2 (European Champ. opening match).
2004	France 0, Greece 1 (European Champ. quarter-final).
2004	Greece 1, Czech Republic 0 (European Champ. semi-final).
2004	Portugal 0, Greece 1(European Champ. final).

GREAT RECOVERIES

On December 21, 1957, Charlton Athletic were losing 5-1 against Huddersfield Town (Div. 2) at The Valley with only 28 minutes left, and from the 15th minute, had been reduced to ten men by injury, but they won 7-6, with left-winger Johnny Summers scoring five goals. Huddersfield Town (managed by Bill Shankly) remain the only team to score six times in a League match and lose.

Among other notable comebacks: on November 12, 1904 (Div. 1), Sheffield Wed. were losing 0-5 at home to Everton, but drew 5-5. At Anfield on December 4, 1909 (Div.1), Liverpool trailed 2-5 to Newcastle Utd. at half-time, then won 6-5. On Boxing Day, 1927, in Div. 3 South, Northampton Town won 6-5 at home to Luton Town after being 1-5 down at half-time. On September 22, 1984 (Div. 1), Q.P.R. drew 5-5 at home to Newcastle Utd. after trailing 0-4 at half-time. On April 12, 1993 (Div. 1) Swindon Town were 1-4 down at Birmingham City with 30 minutes left, but won 6-4.

Other astonishing turnabouts in Div.1 include: Grimsby Town (3-5 down) won 6-5 at W.B.A. on Apr. 30, 1932; and Derby Co. beat Manchester Utd. 5-4 (from 1-4) on Sept. 5, 1936.

With 5 minutes to play, Ipswich Town were losing 3-0 at Barnsley (Div. 1, March 9, 1996), but drew 3-3.

On Sunday, Jan. 19, 1997 (Div. 1), Q.P.R. were 0-4 down away to Port Vale at half-time and still trailing 1-4 with 5 minutes left. They drew 4-4.

Celtic trailed 0-2, 1-3 and 2-4 away to Dunfermline (Scottish First Div., Nov. 19,1966) but won 5-4 with a last-minute penalty.

Tranmere Rov. retrieved a 3-0 half-time deficit to beat Southampton 4-3 in an F.A. Cup fifth round replay at home on Feb. 20, 2001.

Premier League comebacks: Jan. 4, 1994 – Liverpool were 3 down after 24 mins. at home to Manchester Utd., drew 3-3; Nov. 8, 1997 – Derby Co. led 3-0 after 33 mins. at Elland Road, but Leeds Utd. won 4-3 with last-minute goal; Sept. 29, 2001 – Manchester Utd. won 5-3 at Tottenham after trailing 3-0 at half-time.

Season 2003-04 produced some astonishing turn-rounds. **Premiership** (Oct. 25): In bottom-two clash at Molineux, Wolves were 3 down at half-time v Leicester City, but won 4-3. Feb. 22: Leicester City, down to 10 men, rallied from 3-1 down at Tottenham to lead 4-3. Result 4-4.

First Division (Nov. 8): West Ham Utd. led 3-0 after 18 mins at home to WBA, but lost 4-3.

F.A. Cup 4th **Round replay** (Feb. 4): At half-time, Tottenham led 3-0 at home to Manchester City, but City, reduced to 10 men, won 4-3.

Other Tottenham debacles: on Dec. 3, 1960 (Div. 1) they led 4-0 at home to Burnley at half-time. Result 4-4. On March 19, 1966 (Div. 1) Tottenham led 5-1 at home to Aston Villa after 50 mins. Result 5-5.

In the 1966 World Cup quarter-final (July 23) at Goodison Park, North Korea led Portugal 3-0, but Eusebio scored 4 times to give Portugal a 5-3 win.

GOALS THAT WERE WRONGLY GIVEN

Tottenham's last-minute winner at home to Huddersfield (Div. 1) on April 2, 1952: Eddie Baily's corner-kick struck referee W.R. Barnes in the back, and the ball rebounded to Baily, who centred for Len Duquemin to head into the net. Baily had infringed the Laws by playing the ball twice, but the result (1-0) stood. Those two points helped Spurs to finish Championship runners-up; Huddersfield were relegated.

The second goal (66 mins) in **Chelsea's** 2-1 home win v Ipswich Town (Div. 1) on Sept. 26, 1970: Alan Hudson's low shot from just beyond the penalty-area hit the stanchion on the outside of goal and the ball rebounded on to the pitch. But instead of the goal-kick, referee Roy Capey gave a goal, on a linesman's confirmation. TV pictures proved otherwise. But the Football League quoted from the Laws of the Game: 'The referee's decision on all matters is final.' And though it was wrong, the goal stood and sent Chelsea on the way to victory.

MATCHES OFF

Worst day for postponements: Feb. 9, 1963, when 57 League fixtures in England and Scotland were frozen off. Only 7 Football League matches took place, and the entire Scottish programme was wiped out

Worst other weather-hit days:

Jan. 12, 1963 and Feb. 2, 1963 – on both those Saturdays, only 4 out of 44 Football League matches were played.

Jan. 1, 1979 – 43 out of 46 Football League fixtures postponed.

Jan. 17, 1987 – 37 of 45 scheduled Football League fixtures postponed; only 2 Scottish matches survived.

Feb. 8-9, 1991 – only 4 of the week-end's 44 Barclays League matches survived the freeze-up (4 of the postponements were on Friday night). In addition, 11 Scottish League matches were off.

Jan. 27, 1996 – 44 Cup and League matches in England and Scotland were frozen off. The ten fixtures played comprised 3 F.A. Cup (4th. Round), 1 in Div. 1, 5 in Scottish Cup (3rd. Round), 1 in Scottish Div. 2.

Fewest matches left on one day by postponements was during the Second World War – Feb. 3, 1940 when, because of snow, ice and fog only one out of 56 regional league fixtures took place. It resulted Plymouth Argyle 10, Bristol City 3.

The Scottish Cup second round tie between Inverness Thistle and Falkirk in season 1978-9 was **postponed 29 times** because of snow and ice. First put off on Jan. 6, it was eventually played on Feb. 22. Falkirk won 4-0.

Pools Panel's busiest days: Jan. 17, 1987 and Feb. 9, 1991 – on both dates they gave their verdict on 48 postponed coupon matches.

FEWEST 'GAMES OFF'

Season 1947-8 was the best since the war for Football League fixtures being played to schedule. Only **six** were postponed.

LONGEST SEASON

The latest that League football has been played in a season was **June 7, 1947** (six weeks after the F.A. Cup Final). The season was extended because of mass postponements caused by bad weather in mid-winter.

The latest the F.A. Cup competition has ever been completed was in season 1981-2, when Tottenham beat Q.P.R. 1-0 in a Final replay at Wembley on May 27.

Worst winter hold-up was in season 1962-3. The Big Freeze began on Boxing Day and lasted until March, with nearly 500 first-class matches postponed. The F.A. Cup 3rd. Round was the longest on record – it began with only three out of 32 ties playable on January 5 and ended 66 days and 261 postponements later on March 11. The Lincoln City-Coventry City tie was put off 15 times. The Pools Panel was launched that winter, on January 26, 1963.

HOTTEST DAYS

The Nationwide League kicked off season 2003-04 on August 9 with pitch temperatures of 102 degrees recorded at Luton Town v Rushden & Diamonds and Bradford City v Norwich City.

On the following day, there was a pitch temperature of 100 degrees for the Community Shield match between Manchester Utd. and Arsenal at Cardiff's Millennium Stadium.

FOOTBALL LEAGUE SECRETARIES

Harry Lockett (1888-1902), **Tom Charnley** (1902-33), **Fred Howarth** (1933-57), **Alan Hardaker** (1957-79), **Graham Kelly** (1979-88), **David Dent** (1989-2001). Andy Williamson succeeded David Dent in June 2001, with the title Head of Operations

Football League Chairman: Sir Brian Mawhinney (appointed December 2002).

F.A. Premier League: Secretary: Mike Foster. Chairman: David Richards (Sheffield Wed.). Chief Executive: Richard Scudamore.

FOOTBALL ASSOCIATION SECRETARIES/ CHIEF EXECUTIVES

Ebenezer Morley (1863-66), **Robert Willis** (1866-68), **R.G. Graham** (1868-70), **Charles Alcock** (1870-95, paid from 1887), 1895-1934 **Sir Frederick Wall**, 1934-62 **Sir Stanley Rous**, 1962-73 **Denis Follows**, 1973-89 **Ted Croker** (latterly chief executive), 1989-99 **Graham Kelly** (chief executive), 2000-02 **Adam Crozier** (chief executive). Since May 2003 **Mark Palios** (chief executive).

F.A. Chairman: Geoffrey Thompson (appointed June, 1999).

FOOTBALL'S SPONSORS

Football League: Canon 1983-6; Today Newspaper 1986-7; Barclays 1987-93; Endsleigh Insurance 1993-6; Nationwide Building Society 1996-2001 then extended to 2004; Coca-Cola 2004-7.

League Cup: Milk Cup 1982-6; Littlewoods 1987-90; Rumbelows 1991-2; Coca-Cola Cup 1993-8; Worthington Cup 1998-2003; Carling Cup 2003-6.

Premier League: Carling 1993-2001; Barclaycard 2001-04.

F.A. Cup: Littlewoods 1994-8; AXA 1998-2002.

SOCCER HEADQUARTERS

Football Association: 25 Soho Square, London W1D 4FA (moved from Lancaster Gate, London W2, September 2000). Chief Executive: Mark Palios.

F.A. Premier League: 11 Connaught Place, London W1 2ET. Chief Executive: Richard Scudamore. Secretary: Mike Foster.

Football Foundation: 25 Soho Square, London W1D 4FF. Chief Executive: Peter Lee.

Football League: Edward VII Quay, Navigation Way, Preston PR2 2YF. Head of Operations: Andy Williamson. **London Office:** 11 Connaught Place, London W2 2ET.

Professional Footballers' Association: 2 Oxford Utd. Court, Bishopsgate, Manchester M2 3WQ. Chief Executive: Gordon Taylor.

Scottish Football Association: Hampden Park, Glasgow G42 9AY. Chief Executive: David Taylor.

Scottish Premier League: National Stadium, Hampden Park, Glasgow G42 9EB. Secretary: Iain Blair.

Scottish Football League: Hampden Park, Glasgow G42 9EB. Secretary: Peter Donald.

Irish Football Association: 20 Windsor Avenue, Belfast BT9 6EG. Secretary: David Bowen.

Irish Football League: 96 University Street, Belfast BT7 1HE. Secretary: Harry Wallace.

League of Ireland: 80 Merrion Square, Dublin 2. Secretary: Eamonn Morris.

Republic of Ireland F.A.: 80 Merrion Square, Dublin 2. Secretary:

Welsh Football Association: 3 Westgate Street, Cardiff CF1 1DD. Secretary: David Collins.

Football Conference: Collingwood House, Schooner Court, Crossways, Dartford, Kent DA2 6QQ.

FIFA: P.O. Box 85, 8030 Zurich, Switzerland.

UEFA: Route de Geneve, CH-1260, Nyon, Geneva, Switzerland.

WORLD'S LARGEST STADIA

(Source: *FIFA NEWS*)

Capacity **165,000:** Maracana, Rio de Janeiro, Brazil; **150,000** Rungnado Stadium, Pyongyang, North Korea; **125,000** Magalhaes Pinto Stadium, Belo Horizonte, Brazil; **120,000** Morumbi Stadium, Sao Paulo, Brazil; Stadium of Light, Lisbon, Portugal; Krirangan Stadium, Salt Lake, Calcutta; Senayan Stadium, Jakarta, Indonesia; **119,000** Castelao Stadium, Fortaleza, Brazil; **115,000** Arrudao Stadium, Recife, Brazil; Azteca Stadium, Mexico City; Nou Camp, Barcelona, Spain; **114,000** Bernabeu Stadium, Madrid; **100,000** Nasser Stadium, Cairo, Egypt; Azadi Stadium, Tehran, Iran; Red Star Stadium, Belgrade, Yugoslavia; Central Stadium, Kiev, USSR.

F.A. NATIONAL FOOTBALL CENTRE

Situated at Burton-upon-Trent, it was scheduled to open in August 2003, but a year later its future remained uncertain. The original plan (350 acres, construction cost £50m) comprised 14 pitches, sports science clinic, swimming pools, indoor training facilities and luxury accommodation for England teams at all levels to train there.

NEW HOMES OF SOCCER

Newly-constructed League grounds in England since the war: 1946 Hull City (Boothferry Park); 1950 Port Vale (Vale Park); 1955 Southend Utd. (Roots Hall); 1988 Scunthorpe Utd. (Glanford Park); 1990 Walsall (Bescot Stadium); 1990 Wycombe Wand. (Adams Park); 1992 Chester City (Deva Stadium, Bumpers Lane); 1993 Millwall (New Den); 1994 Huddersfield Town (Alfred McAlpine Stadium, Kirklees); 1994 Northampton Town (Sixfields Stadium); 1995 Middlesbrough (Riverside Stadium); 1997 Bolton Wand. (Reebok Stadium); 1997 Derby Co. (Pride Park); 1997 Stoke City (Britannia Stadium); 1997 Sunderland (Stadium of Light); 1998 Reading (Madejski Stadium); 1999 Wigan Athletic (JJB Stadium); 2001 Southampton (St. Mary's Stadium); 2001 Oxford Utd. (Kassam Stadium); 2002 Leicester City (Walkers Stadium); 2002 Hull City (Kingston Communications Stadium); 2003 Manchester City (City of Manchester Stadium); 2003 Darlington (Reynolds Arena).

GROUND-SHARING

Crystal Palace and Charlton Athletic (Selhurst Park, 1985-91); Bristol Rov. and Bath City (Twerton Park, Bath, 1986-96); Partick Thistle and Clyde (Firhill Park, Glasgow, 1986-91; in seasons 1990-1, 1991-2 Chester City shared Macclesfield Town's ground (Moss Rose). Crystal Palace and Wimbledon shared Selhurst Park, from season 1991-2, when Charlton Athletic (tenants) moved to rent Upton Park from West Ham Utd. Clyde moved to Douglas Park, Hamilton Academicals' home, in 1991-2. Stirling Albion shared Stenhousemuir's ground, Ochilview Park, in 1992-3. In 1993-4, Clyde shared Partick's home until moving to Cumbernauld. In 1994-5, Celtic shared Hampden Park with Queen's Park (while Celtic Park was redeveloped); Hamilton shared Partick's ground. Airdrie shared Clyde's Broadwood Stadium. Bristol Rov. left Bath City's ground at the start of season 1996-7, sharing Bristol Rugby Club's Memorial Ground. Clydebank shared Dumbarton's Boghead Park from 1996-7 until renting Greenock Morton's Cappielow Park in season 1999-2000. Brighton shared Gillingham's ground in seasons 1997-8, 1998-9. Fulham shared Q.P.R.'s home at Loftus Road in seasons 2002–3, 2003–4, returning to Craven Cottage in August 2004.

Inverness Caledonian Thistle moved to share Aberdeen's Pittodrie Stadium in 2004-5 after being promoted to the SPL.

ARTIFICIAL TURF

Q.P.R. were the first British club to install an artificial pitch, in 1981. They were followed by Luton Town in 1985, and Oldham Athletic and Preston N.E. in 1986. Q.P.R. reverted to grass in 1988, as did Luton Town and promoted Oldham Athletic in season 1991-2 (when artificial pitches were banned in Div. 1). Preston N.E. were the last Football League club playing 'on plastic' in 1993-4, and their Deepdale ground was restored to grass for the start of 1994-5.

Stirling Albion were the first Scottish club to play on plastic, in season 1987-8.

F.A. SOCCER SCHOOL

The Football Association's national soccer school, at Lilleshall, aimed at providing the backbone of England's World Cup challenge in the 1990s, was opened by the Duke of Kent (President) on September 4, 1984. It was sponsored by GM Motors, and the first intake comprised 25 boys aged fourteen.

The School of Excellence produced England Internationals Nick Barmby, Andy Cole, Sol Campbell, Ian Walker and Michael Owen. It closed in 1999, to be replaced nationwide by academies at leading clubs.

DOUBLE RUNNERS-UP

There have been nine instances of clubs finishing runner-up in both the League Championship and F.A. Cup in the same season: 1928 Huddersfield Town; 1932 Arsenal; 1939 Wolves; 1962 Burnley; 1965 and 1970 Leeds Utd.; 1986 Everton; 1995 Manchester Utd; 2001 Arsenal.

CORNER-KICK RECORDS

Not a single corner-kick was recorded when Newcastle Utd. drew 0-0 at home to Portsmouth (Div.1) on December 5, 1931.

The record for most corners in a match for one side is believed to be Sheffield Utd.'s 28 to West Ham Utd.'s 1 in Div.2 at Bramall Lane on October 14, 1989. For all their pressure, Sheffield Utd. lost 2-0.

Nott'm. Forest led Southampton 22-2 on corners (Premier League, Nov. 28, 1992) but lost the match 1-2.

Tommy Higginson (Brentford, 1960s) once passed back to his own goalkeeper from a corner kick.

When Wigan Athletic won 4–0 at home to Cardiff City (Div. 2) on February 16, 2002, all four goals were headed in from corners taken by N. Ireland International Peter Kennedy.

Steve Staunton (Rep. of Ireland) is believed to be the only player to score direct from a corner in two Internationals.

OFFSIDES NIL

Not one offside decision was given in the **Brazil-Turkey** World Cup semi-final at Saitama, Japan, on June 26, 2002.

'PROFESSIONAL FOUL' DIRECTIVE

After the 1990 World Cup Finals, F.I.F.A. dealt with the **'professional foul'**, incorporating this directive into the Laws of the Game: 'If, in the opinion of the referee, a player who is moving towards his opponents' goal, with an obvious opportunity to score, is intentionally impeded by an opponent through unlawful means – thus denying the attacking player's team the aforesaid goalscoring opportunity – the offender should be sent from the field of play.'

SACKED AT HALF-TIME

Leyton Orient sacked **Terry Howard** on his 397th. appearance for the club – at half-time in a Second Division home defeat against Blackpool (Feb. 7, 1995) for 'an unacceptable performance'. He was fined two weeks' wages, given a free transfer and moved to Wycombe Wanderers.

Harald Schumacher, former Germany goalkeeper, was sacked as Fortuna Koln coach when they were two down at half-time against Waldhof Mannheim (Dec. 15, 1999). They lost 5-1.

MOST GAMES BY 'KEEPER FOR ONE CLUB

Alan Knight made 683 League appearances for Portsmouth, over 23 seasons (1978-2000), a record for a goalkeeper at one club. The previous holder was Peter Bonetti with 600 League games for Chelsea (20 seasons, 1960-79).

PLAYED TWO GAMES ON SAME DAY

Jack Kelsey played full-length matches for both club and country on Wed., November 26, 1958. In the afternoon he kept goal for Wales in a 2-2 draw against England at Villa Park, and he then drove to Highbury to help Arsenal win 3-1 in a prestigious floodlit friendly against Juventus.

On the same day, winger **Danny Clapton** played for England (against Wales and Kelsey) and then in part of Arsenal's match against Juventus.

On November 11, 1987, **Mark Hughes** played for Wales against Czechoslovakia (European Championship) in Prague, then flew to Munich and went on as substitute that night in a winning Bayern Munich team, to whom he was on loan from Barcelona.

On February 16, 1993 goalkeeper **Scott Howie** played in Scotland's 3-0 U-21 win v Malta at Tannadice Park, Dundee (k.o. 1.30pm) and the same evening played in Clyde's 2-1 home win v Queen of South (Div. 2).

Ryman League **Hornchurch**, faced by end-of-season fixture congestion, played **two matches on the same night** (May 1, 2001). They lost 2-1 at home to Ware and drew 2-2 at Clapton.

GOING PUBLIC

Manchester Utd. became the fourth British club (after Tottenham, Hibernian and Millwall) to 'go public' with a share issue in June 1991. Many other clubs have since "floated" on the Stock Exchange.

MEDIA INVEST IN TOP CLUBS

In season 1999-2000, satellite broadcaster **BSkyB** bought 9.9% share stakes in Manchester Utd. (£84m), Chelsea (£40m), Leeds Utd. (£13.8m), Manchester City (£12m) and a 5% share in Sunderland (£6.5m). **Granada TV** bought a £22m. stake in Liverpool. Cable giants **NTL** acquired 9.9% shares/sponsorship investment in Newcastle Utd. (£35m) and Aston Villa (£26m) and Leicester City (£12.5m). They agreed a £31m. sponsorship with Rangers.

RECORD CLUB LOSSES

Fulham, brokered by Harrods owner Mohamed Al Fayed, made British football's then record loss of £23.3m. in the year to June 30, 2001 (in which they won promotion to the Premiership as Div. 1 Champions). The club's debts rose to £61.7m. Previous highest loss was £18.7m. by **Newcastle Utd.** in 2000. In September 2002, **Leeds Utd.** reported a new record British club loss of £33.9m for the year ending June 30. It took their debts to £77m. A year later, in October 2003, **Leeds** declared another British record loss of £49.5m. (debts £78m).

FIRST 'MATCH OF THE DAY'

BBC TV (recorded highlights): Liverpool 3, Arsenal 2 on August 22, 1964. **First complete match to be televised:** Arsenal 3, Everton 2 on August 29, 1936. **First League match televised in colour:** Liverpool 2, West Ham Utd. 0 on November 15, 1969.

'MATCH OF THE DAY' – BIGGEST SCORES

Football League: Tottenham 9, Bristol Rov. 0 (Div. 2, 1977-8). **Premier League:** Nott'm Forest 1, Manchester Utd. 8 (1998-9).

FIRST COMMENTARY ON RADIO

Arsenal 1, **Sheffield Utd.** 1 (Div. 1) broadcast on BBC, January 22, 1927.

OLYMPIC SOCCER WINNERS

1908 Great Britain (in London); **1912** Great Britain (Stockholm); **1920** Belgium (Antwerp); **1924** Uruguay (Paris); **1928** Uruguay (Amsterdam); **1932** No soccer in Los Angeles Olympics. **1936** Italy (Berlin); **1948** Sweden (London); **1952** Hungary (Helsinki); **1956** USSR (Melbourne); **1960** Yugoslavia (Rome); **1964** Hungary (Tokyo); **1968** Hungary (Mexico); **1972** Poland (Munich); **1976** E. Germany (Montreal); **1980** Czechoslovakia (Moscow); **1984** France (Los Angeles); **1988** USSR (Seoul); **1992** Spain (Barcelona); **1996** Nigeria (Atlanta); **2000** Cameroon (Sydney).
Highest scorer in Final tournament: Ferenc Bene (Hungary) 12 goals, 1964.
Record crowd for Olympic Soccer Final: 108,800 (France v Brazil, Los Angeles 1984).

MOST AMATEUR CUP WINS

Bishop Auckland set the F.A. Amateur Cup record with 10 wins, and in 1957 became the only club to carry off the trophy in three successive seasons. Five wins: Clapton and Crook Town. The competition was discontinued after the Final on April 20, 1974. (Bishop's Stortford 4, Ilford 1, at Wembley).

FOOTBALL FOUNDATION

This was formed (May 2000) to replace the **Football Trust**, which had been in existence since 1975 as an initiative of the Pools companies to provide financial support at all levels, from schools football to safety and ground improvement work throughout the game. The Foundation, chaired by **Tom Pendry** and with representatives of the Government, F.A. and Premier League on board, was empowered to distribute 5% of the Premiership's TV money to football's grass-roots level.

TESTIMONIALS

The first £1m. testimonial was **Sir Alex Ferguson's** at Old Trafford on October 11, 1999, when a full-house crowd of 54,842 saw a Rest of the World team beat Manchester Utd. 4-2. United's manager pledged that a large percentage of the receipts would go to charity.

Two nights after Manchester Utd. completed the Double in May, 1994, 42,079 packed Old Trafford for **Mark Hughes'** testimonial (1-3 Celtic). The estimated proceeds of £500,000 equalled the then testimonial record of **Ally McCoist's** match (Rangers 1, Newcastle Utd. 2) on August 3, 1993.

The match for **Bryan Robson**, Manchester Utd. and England captain, against Celtic at Old Trafford on Tuesday, November 20, 1990 was watched by a crowd of 41,658, and receipts of £300,000 were a then record for a testimonial.

Kenny Dalglish's testimonial (Liverpool v Real Sociedad) at Anfield on August 14, 1990 attracted 30,461 spectators, with receipts estimated at £150,000.

On December 4, 1990, **Willie Miller's** testimonial (Aberdeen v World XI) packed Pittodrie to its 22,500 capacity, and raised an estimated £150,000.

The match for 82-year-old **Sir Matt Busby**, between Manchester Utd. and a Rep. of Ireland XI at Old Trafford on Sunday, August 11, 1991 was watched by 35,410 (estimated benefit £250,000).

Ian Rush's testimonial brought an estimated £250,000 from a 25,856 crowd at Anfield on December 6, 1994 (Liverpool 6, Celtic 0).

Three lucrative testimonials were staged in May 1996. Arsenal's **Paul Merson** earned a reported £400,000 (a percentage to charity) from his match against an Int. XI at Highbury (May 9, att: 31,626); the Republic of Ireland's new manager **Mick McCarthy** received an estimated £300,000 from a 40,000 crowd who saw Celtic beaten 3-0 at Lansdowne Road, Dublin on May 26; and **Stuart Pearce** benefited by some £200,000 from a turn-out of 23,815 when Nott'm. Forest beat Newcastle Utd. 6-5 at the City Ground on May 8.

Testimonial sums reported in season 1996-7 included: **Bryan Gunn**, Norwich City goalkeeper, £250,000 for 21,000 sell-out v Manchester Utd., Nov. 4; **Brian McClair**, Manchester Utd., £380,000 v Celtic, April 14.

Among testimonials in 1997-8: A full-house 50,000, at Ibrox paid an estimated £500,000 for retiring manager **Walter Smith** (Rangers 1, Liverpool 0) on March 3, 1998.

Paul McGrath's testimonial at Lansdowne Road, Dublin (May 17, 1998) produced record receipts of £600,000. A crowd of 39,000 saw Jack Charlton's XI beat a Rep. Of Ireland XI 3-2.

A crowd of 49,468 attended Ibrox (Rangers 4, Middlesbrough 4) on March 2, 1999 for former Rangers player **Alan McLaren's** testimonial. His fund benefited by an estimated £500,000.

A capacity crowd of 36,733 packed St. James' Park, paying an estimated £250,000, for **Peter Beardsley's** testimonial (Newcastle Utd. 1, Celtic 3) on Jan. 27, 1999.

Among testimonials in 2000-01: **Denis Irwin** (Manchester Utd.) estimated receipts £1m. from Manchester Utd. 2, Manchester City 0, Old Trafford, (att. 45,158) August 16; **David Seaman** (Arsenal 0, Barcelona 2, (att. 33,297), May 22. He donated part of the £600,000 estimated receipts to the Willow Foundation Charity, set up by Bob Wilson, his goalkeeping coach at Highbury. The testimonial for **Tom Boyd** (Celtic) against Manchester Utd. (May 15, 2001) attracted a 57,000 crowd with receipts estimated at £1m.

In season 2001-02: For **Ryan Giggs**, a full-house 66,967 (record Testimonial attendance) paid £1m. to see Manchester Utd. 3, Celtic 4 on August 1. Undisclosed sums were donated to charities.

Receipts estimated at £500,000 were produced by the 35,887 crowd at Tottenham v Fiorentina (August 8) for **Bill Nicholson**, who managed Tottenham from 1958-74.

Gary Kelly's Testimonial (Leeds Utd. 1, Celtic 4) drew 26,440 at Elland Road on May 7, 2002, and receipts of £600,000 were donated to cancer charities.

Tony Adams' second Testimonial (1-1 v Celtic on May 13, 2002) two nights after Arsenal completed the Double, was watched by 38,021 spectators. Of £1m. receipts, he donated a substantial percentage to Sporting Chance, the charity that helps sportsmen/women with drink, drug, gambling problems.

Another one-club player, **Matthew Le Tissier**, ended his playing career at Southampton with 31.904 spectators (receipts £500,000) watching a 9-9 draw with an England XI on May 14, 2002.

On the same night, Sunderland and a Republic of Ireland XI drew 0-0 in front of 35,702 at the Stadium of Light. The beneficiary, **Niall Quinn**, was donating his entire Testimonial proceeds, estimated at £1m., to children's hospitals in Sunderland and Dublin, and to homeless children in Africa and Asia.

On May 17, 2004, two days after Arsenal completed a Championship-winning unbeaten season, **Martin Keown's** farewell to Highbury (6-0 v England XI) was watched by a full-house 38,000 and produced £500,000 for his Testimonial.

WHAT IT USED TO COST

Minimum admission to League football was one shilling in 1939. After the war, it was increased to 1s. 3d. in 1946; 1s. 6d. in 1951; 1s. 9d. in 1952; 2s. in 1955; 2s. 6d. in 1960; 4s. in 1965; 5s. in 1968; 6s. in 1970; and 8s. (40p) in 1972. After that, the fixed minimum charge was dropped.

Wembley's first Cup Final programme in 1923 cost three pence (1¼p in today's money). The programme for the 'farewell' F.A. Cup Final in May, 2000 was priced £10.

WHAT THEY USED TO EARN

In the 1930s, First Division players were on £8 a week (£6 in close season) plus bonuses of £2 win, £1 draw. The maximum wage went up to £12 when football resumed post-war in 1946 and had reached £20 by the time the limit was abolished in 1961.

ENGLAND TOP EURO-PRIZE WINNERS

There have been **134 European club competitions** since what is now the Champions' League was launched in season 1955-6; 49 for the European Cup, 46 for the Fairs/UEFA Cup and 39 for the Cup-Winners' Cup, which ended in 1999.

Despite the five-year enforced absence that followed the Heysel disaster in 1985, **English clubs** jointly head the prize list, Liverpool's success in the 2001 UEFA Cup taking the total to 27 triumphs: 9 in the Champions' Cup, 8 in the Cup-Winners' Cup and 10 in the Fairs/UEFA Cup.

Italy joined England on 27 Euro successes in 2003, followed on that total by Spain, whose clubs won both the European Cup and UEFA Cup in 2004. The 134 winners represent 17 countries.

England's 27 prizes are shared among 13 clubs: Liverpool 7 (4 EC, 3 UEFA); Manchester Utd. 3 (2 EC, 1 CWC); Tottenham 3 (1 CWC, 2 UEFA); Chelsea 2 (2 CWC); Leeds Utd. 2 (2 UEFA); Nott'm. Forest 2 (2 EC); Arsenal 2 (1 UEFA, 1 CWC); Aston Villa 1 (EC); Everton 1 (CWC); Ipswich Town 1 (UEFA); Manchester City 1 (CWC); Newcastle Utd. 1 (UEFA); West Ham Utd. 1 (CWC).

Scotland's three successes have been achieved by Celtic (EC); Rangers and Aberdeen (both CWC).

EUROPEAN TRIUMPHS, COUNTRY BY COUNTRY

	European Cup/ Champions League	Cup-Winners' Cup	Fairs Cup/ UEFA Cup	Total
England	9	8	10	27
Italy	10	7	10	27
Spain	11	7	9	27
West Germany/Germany	6	4	6	16
Holland	6	1	4	11
Portugal	3	1	1	5
Belgium	–	3	1	4
Scotland	1	2	–	3
USSR	–	3	–	3
France	1	1	–	2
Sweden	–	–	2	2
Yugoslavia	1	–	1	2
Czechoslovakia	–	1	–	1
East Germany	–	1	–	1
Hungary	–	–	1	1
Romania	1	–	–	1
Turkey	–	–	1	1
Total:	49	39	46	134

EUROPEAN TROPHY WINNERS – SUMMARY

European Cup (49 competitions, 21 different winners): **9** Real Madrid; **6** AC Milan; **4** Ajax Amsterdam, Liverpool; Bayern Munich; **2** Benfica, Inter Milan, Juventus, Manchester Utd., Nott'm. Forest, FC Porto; **1** Aston Villa, Barcelona, Borussia Dortmund, Celtic, Feyenoord, Hamburg SV, Marseille, PSV Eindhoven, Red Star Belgrade, Steaua Bucharest.

Cup-Winners' Cup (39 competitions, 32 different winners): **4** Barcelona; **2** Anderlecht, Chelsea, Dynamo Kiev, AC Milan; **1** Aberdeen, Ajax Amsterdam, Arsenal, Atletico Madrid, Bayern Munich, Borussia Dortmund, Dynamo Tbilisi, Everton, Fiorentina, Hamburg SV, Juventus, Lazio, Magdeburg, Manchester City, Manchester Utd., Mechelen, Paris St. Germain, Parma, Rangers, Real Zaragoza, Sampdoria, Slovan Bratislava, Sporting Lisbon, Tottenham, Valencia, Werder Bremen, West Ham Utd.

UEFA Cup (orig. Fairs Cup) (46 competitions, 29 different winners): **3** Barcelona, Inter Milan, Juventus, Liverpool, Valencia; **2** Borussia Moenchengladbach, Feyenoord, IFK Gothenburg, Leeds Utd., Parma, Real Madrid, Tottenham; **1** Ajax Amsterdam, Anderlecht, Arsenal, Bayer Leverkusen, Bayern Munich, Dynamo Zagreb, Eintracht Frankfurt, PSV Eindhoven, Ferencvaros, Ipswich Town, Napoli, Newcastle Utd., Real Zaragoza, AS Roma, FC Schalke, Galatasaray, FC Porto.

- Four clubs have won all three trophies – Barcelona, Bayern Munich, Juventus and Ajax.
- The Champions League was introduced into the European Cup in 1992-3 to counter the threat of a European Super League.

BRITAIN'S 30 TROPHIES IN EUROPE

Liverpool's success in the 2001-01 UEFA Cup took the number of **British** club triumphs in European Football to 30:

European Cup (10)	Cup-Winners' Cup (10)	Fairs/UEFA Cup (10)
1967 Celtic	1963 Tottenham	1968 Leeds Utd.
1968 Manchester Utd.	1965 West Ham Utd.	1969 Newcastle Utd.
1977 Liverpool	1970 Manchester City	1970 Arsenal
1978 Liverpool	1971 Chelsea	1971 Leeds Utd.
1979 Nott'm Forest	1972 Rangers	1972 Tottenham
1980 Nott'm Forest	1983 Aberdeen	1973 Liverpool
1981 Liverpool	1985 Everton	1976 Liverpool
1982 Aston Villa	1991 Manchester Utd.	1981 Ipswich Town
1984 Liverpool	1994 Arsenal	1984 Tottenham
1999 Manchester Utd.	1998 Chelsea	2001 Liverpool

END OF CUP-WINNERS' CUP

The **European Cup-Winners' Cup**, inaugurated in 1960-61, terminated with the 1999 final. The competition merged into a revamped, 121-club **UEFA Cup**.

Also with effect from season 1999-2000, the **European Cup/Champions League** was increased by 8 clubs to 32.

From its inception in 1955, the **European Cup** comprised only championship-winning clubs until 1998-9, when selected runners-up were introduced. Further expansion came in 1999-2000 with the inclusion of clubs finishing third in certain leagues and fourth in 2002.

EUROPEAN CLUB COMPETITIONS – SCORING RECORDS

European Cup – Record aggregate: 18-0 by Benfica v Dudelange (Lux) (8-0a, 10-0h), prelim. round, 1965-6.
Record single-match score: 12-0 by Feyenoord v KR Reykjavik (Ice), 1st. round, 1st. leg, 1969-70 (aggregate was 16-0).

Champions League – highest match aggregates: 11 goals – Monaco 8, Deportivo La Coruna 3 (Nov. 5, 2003); 9 goals – Paris St. Germain 7, Rosenborg 2 (Oct. 24. 2000).

Cup-Winners' Cup – *Record aggregate: 21-0 by Chelsea v Jeunesse Hautcharage (Lux) (8-0a, 13-0h), 1st. round, 1971-2.
 Record single-match score: 16-1 by Sporting Lisbon v Apoel Nicosia, 2nd. round, 1st. leg, 1963-4 (aggregate was 18-1).

UEFA Cup (prev. Fairs Cup) – *Record aggregate: 21-0 by Feyenoord v US Rumelange (Lux) (9-0h, 12-0a), 1st. round, 1972-3.
 Record single-match score: 14-0 by Ajax Amsterdam v Red Boys (Lux) 1st. round, 2nd leg, 1984-5 (aggregate also 14-0).

Record British score in Europe: 13-0 by **Chelsea** at home to Jeunesse Hautcharage (Lux) in Cup-Winners' Cup 1st. round, 2nd. leg, 1971-2. Chelsea's overall 21-0 win in that tie is highest aggregate by British club in Europe.

Individual scoring record for European tie (over two legs): **10 goals** (6 home, 4 away) by **Kiril Milanov** for Levski Spartak in 19-3 agg. win CWC 1st round v Lahden Reipas, 1976-7. Next highest: **8 goals** by **Jose Altafini** for AC Milan v US Luxembourg (European Cup, prelim. round, 1962-3, agg. 14-0) and by **Peter Osgood** for Chelsea v Jeunesse Hautcharage (Cup-Winners' Cup, 1st. round 1971-2, agg. 21-0). Altafini and Osgood each scored 5 goals at home, 3 away.

Individual single-match scoring record in European competition: **6** goals by **Mascarenhas** for Sporting Lisbon in 16-1 Cup-Winner's Cup 2nd. round, 1st. leg win v Apoel, 1963-4; **6** by **Lothar Emmerich** for Borussia Dortmund in 8-0 CWC 1st. round, 2nd. leg win v Floriana 1965-6; **6** by **Kiril Milanov** for Levski Spartak in 12-2 CWC 1st. round, 1st. leg win v Lahden Reipas, 1976-7.

Most goals in single European campaign: 15 by **Jurgen Klinsmann** for Bayern Munich (UEFA Cup 1995-6).

Most goals by British player in European competition: 30 by Peter Lorimer (Leeds Utd., in 9 campaigns).

Most European Cup goals by individual player: 49 by **Alfredo di Stefano** in 58 apps. for Real Madrid (1955-64).

(*Joint record European aggregate)

First European 'Treble': Clarence Seedorf is the only player to win the European Cup with three clubs: Ajax in 1995, Real Madrid in 1998 and AC Milan in 2003.

EUROPEAN FOOTBALL – BIG RECOVERIES

In the 49-year history of European competition, only four clubs have survived a **4-goal** deficit after the first leg had been completed:

1961-2 (Cup-Winners' Cup 1st. Rd.): Leixoes (Portugal) beat Chaux de Fonds (Luxembourg) 7-6 on agg. (lost 2-6a, won 5-0h).

1962-3 (Fairs Cup 2nd. Rd.): Valencia (Spain) beat **Dunfermline** 1-0 in play-off in Lisbon after 6-6 agg. (Valencia won 4-0h, lost 2-6a).

1984-5 (UEFA Cup 2nd. Rd.): Partizan Belgrade beat **Q.P.R.** on away goals (lost 2-6 away, at Highbury, won 4-0 home).

1985-6 (UEFA Cup 3rd. Rd.): Real Madrid beat Borussia Moenchengladbach on away goals (lost 1-5a, won 4-0h) and went on to win competition.

In the **Champions League** quarter-final, 2003-04, Deportivo La Coruna lost the first leg 4-1 away to Inter Milan, then won the return match 4-0 to go through 5-4 on agg. This was the first instance in the 12-year history of the Champions League of a team over-turning a 3-goal deficit.

In the **European Cup**, there are eight instances of clubs reaching the next round after **arrears of three goals** in the first leg:

1958-9 (Prel. Rd.) Schalke beat KB Copenhagen (0-3, 5-2, 3-1).

1965-6 (Q-final) Partizan Belgrade beat Sparta Prague (1-4, 5-0).

1970-1 (S-final) Panathinaikos beat Red Star Belgrade on away goal (1-4, 3-0).

1975-6 (2nd. Rd.) Real Madrid beat **Derby Co.** (1-4, 5-1).

1985-6 (S-final) Barcelona beat IFK Gothenburg on pens. (0-3, 3-0).

1988-9 (1st. Rd.) Werder Bremen beat Dynamo Berlin (0-3, 5-0).
1988-9 (2nd. Rd.) Galatasaray (Turkey) beat Neuchatel Xamax (Switz.) (0-3, 5-0).
1992-3 (1st. Rd.) **Leeds Utd.** beat VfB Stuttgart 2-1 in play-off in Barcelona. Over two legs, VfB won on away goal (3-0h, 1-4 away) but a third match was ordered because they broke 'foreigners' rule in team selection.

In the **Cup-Winners' Cup**, six clubs survived a **3-goal** deficit:
1963-4 (Q-final) Sporting Lisbon beat **Manchester Utd.** (1-4, 5-0).
1963-4 (S-final) MTK Budapest beat **Celtic** (0-3, 4-0).
1978-9 (2nd. Rd.) Barcelona beat Anderlecht on pens. (0-3, 3-0).
1980-1 (1st. Rd.) Carl Zeiss Jena beat AS Roma (0-3, 4-0).
1984-5 (Q-final) Rapid Vienna beat Dynamo Dresden (0-3, 5-0).
1989-90 (1st. Rd.) Grasshoppers (Switz.) beat Slovan Bratislava (0-3, 4-0).

In the **Fairs Cup/UEFA Cup**, there have been more than 20 occasions when clubs have survived a deficit of **3 goals**, the most notable example being the 1988 UEFA Cup Final, which Bayer Leverkusen won 3-2 on pens., having lost the first leg 0-3 away to Espanol and won the return 3-0 to level the aggregate.

Apart from Leeds Utd., two other British clubs have won a European tie from a 3-goal, first leg deficit: **Kilmarnock** 0-3, 5-1 v Eintracht Frankfurt (Fairs Cup 1st. Round, 1964-5); **Hibernian** 1-4, 5-0 v Napoli (Fairs Cup 2nd. Round, 1967-8).

English clubs have three times gone out of the **UEFA Cup** after leading 3-0 from the first leg: 1975-6 (2nd. Rd.) **Ipswich Town** lost 3-4 on agg. to Bruges; 1976-7 (Q-final) **Q.P.R.** lost on pens. to AEK Athens after 3-3 agg; 1977-8 (3rd. Rd.) **Ipswich Town** lost on pens. to Barcelona after 3-3 agg.

HEAVIEST ENGLISH-CLUB DEFEATS IN EUROPE

(Single-leg scores)
European Cup: Ajax 5, Liverpool 1 (2nd. Rd.), Dec. 1966 (agg. 7-3); Real Madrid 5, Derby Co. 1 (2nd. Rd.), Nov. 1975 (agg. 6-5).
Cup-Winners' Cup: Sporting Lisbon 5, Manchester Utd. 0 (Q-final), Mar. 1964 (agg. 6-4).
Fairs/UEFA Cup: Bayern Munich 6, Coventry City 1 (2nd. Rd.), Oct. 1970 (agg. 7-3). Combined London team lost 6-0 (agg. 8-2) in first Fairs Cup Final in 1958.

SHOCK ENGLISH-CLUB DEFEATS

1968-69 (E. Cup, 1st. Rd.): Manchester City beaten by Fenerbahce, 1-2 agg.
1971-72 (CWC, 2nd. Rd.): Chelsea beaten by Atvidaberg on away goals.
1993-94 (E. Cup, 2nd. Rd.): Manchester Utd. beaten by Galatasaray on away goals.
1994-95 (UEFA Cup, 1st. Rd.): Blackburn Rov. beaten by Trelleborgs, 2-3 agg.
2000-01 (UEFA Cup, 1st. Rd.): Chelsea beaten by St. Gallen, Swit. 1-2 agg.

FIFA'S HALL OF CHAMPIONS

Ten retired players, honoured for 'sporting success that contributed to the positive image of the game' – Sir Stanley Matthews, Sir Bobby Charlton (England), Pele (Brazil), Franz Beckenbauer (W. Germany), Johan Cruyff (Holland), Alfredo di Stefano (Argentina), Eusebio (Portugal), Michel Platini (France), Ferenc Puskas (Hungary), Lev Yashin (Soviet Union). Managers: Sir Matt Busby (Manchester Utd.), Rinus Michels (Ajax Amsterdam).
The names were announced in January 1998.

P.F.A. FAIR PLAY AWARD (Bobby Moore Trophy from 1993)

1988	Liverpool	1997	Crewe Alexandra
1989	Liverpool	1998	Cambridge Utd.
1990	Liverpool	1999	Grimsby Town
1991	Nott'm. Forest	2000	Crewe Alexandra
1992	Portsmouth	2001	Crewe Alexandra
1993	Norwich City	2002	Crewe Alexandra
1994	Crewe Alexandra	2003	Crewe Alexandra
1995	Crewe Alexandra	2004	Crewe Alexandra
1996	Crewe Alexandra		

RECORD MEDALS SALE

West Ham Utd. bought (June 2000) the late **Bobby Moore's** collection of medals and trophies for £1.8m. at Christie's auction in London. It was put up for sale by his first wife Tina and included his World Cup winner's medal.

A No. 6 duplicate red shirt made for England captain **Bobby Moore** for the 1966 World Cup Final fetched £44,000 at an auction at Wolves' ground in Sept. 1999. Moore kept the shirt he wore in that Final and gave the replica to England physio Harold Shepherdson.

Sir Geoff Hurst's 1966 World Cup-winning shirt fetched a record £91,750 at Christie's on September 28, 2000. His World Cup Final cap fetched £37,600 and his Man of the Match trophy £18,800. Proceeds totalling £274,410 from the 129 lots went to Hurst's three daughters and charities of his choice, including the Bobby Moore Imperial Cancer Research Fund.

In August 2001, Sir Geoff sold his World Cup-winner's medal to his former club West Ham Utd. (for their museum) for a reported £150,000.

'The **Billy Wright Collection**' – caps, medals and other memorabilia from his illustrious career – fetched over £100,000 at Christie's in Glasgow on Nov. 21, 1996.

At the sale in Oct. 1993, trophies, caps and medals earned by **Ray Kennedy**, former England, Arsenal and Liverpool player, fetched a then record total of £88,407. Kennedy, suffering from Parkinson's Disease, received £73,000 after commission.

The P.F.A. paid £31,080 for a total of 60 lots – including a record £16,000 for his 1977 European Cup winner's medal – to be exhibited at their Manchester museum. An anonymous English collector paid £17,000 for the medal and plaque commemorating Kennedy's part in the Arsenal Double in 1971.

Previous record for one player's medals, shirts etc. collection: £30,000 (**Bill Foulkes**, Manchester Utd. in 1992). The sale of **Dixie Dean**'s medals etc. in 1991 realised £28,000.

In March 2001, **Gordon Banks**' 1966 World Cup-winner's medal fetched a new record £124,750, and at auctions in season 2001-02: In London on Sept. 21, TV's Nick Hancock, a Stoke City fan, paid £23,500 for **Sir Stanley Matthews**' 1953 F.A. Cup-winner's medal. He also bought one of Matthews' England caps for £3,525 and paid £2,350 for a Stoke Div. 2 Championship medal (1963).

Dave Mackay's 1961 League Championship and F.A. Cup winner's medals sold for £18,000 at Sotherby's. Tottenham bought them for their museum.

A selection of England World Cup-winning manager **Sir Alf Ramsey**'s memorabilia – England caps, championship medals with Ipswich Town etc. – fetched more than £80,000 at Christie's. They were offered for sale by his family, and his former clubs Tottenham and Ipswich Town were among the buyers.

Ray Wilson's 1966 England World Cup-winning shirt fetched £80,750. Also in March 2002, the No. 10 shirt worn by **Pele** in Brazil's World Cup triumph in 1970 was sold for a record £157,750 at Christies. It went to an anonymous telephone bidder.

In October 2003, **George Best's** European Footballer of the Year (1968) trophy was sold to an anonymous British bidder for £167,250 at Bonham's, Chester. It was the most expensive item of sporting memorabilia ever auctioned in Britain.

England captain **Bobby Moore's** 1970 World Cup shirt, which he swapped with Pele after Brazil's 1-0 win in Mexico, was sold for £60,000 at Christie's in London in March 2004.

LONGEST UNBEATEN CUP RUN

Liverpool established the longest unbeaten Cup sequence by a Football League club: 25 successive rounds in the League/Milk Cup between semi-final defeat by Nott'm. Forest (1-2 agg.) in 1980 and defeat at Tottenham (0-1) in the third round on October 31, 1984. During this period Liverpool won the tournament in four successive seasons, a feat no other Football League club has achieved in any competition.

NEAR £1M. RECORD DAMAGES

A High Court judge in Newcastle (May 7, 1999) awarded Bradford City's 28-year-old striker **Gordon Watson** record damages for a football injury: £909,143. He had had his right leg fractured in two places by Huddersfield Town's Kevin Gray on Feb. 1, 1997.

Huddersfield Town were 'proven negligent for allowing their player to make a rushed tackle'. The award was calculated at £202,643 for loss of earnings, £730,500 for 'potential career earnings' if he had joined a Premiership club, plus £26,000 to cover medical treatment and care.

Watson, awarded £50,000 in an earlier legal action, had a 6-inch plate inserted in the leg. He resumed playing for City in season 1998-9.

BIG HALF-TIME SCORES

Tottenham 10, Crewe Alexandra 1 (F.A. Cup 4th. Rd. replay, Feb. 3, 1960; result 13-2); Tranmere Rov. 8, Oldham Athletic 1 (Div. 3N., Dec. 26, 1935; result 13-4); Chester City 8, York City 0 (Div. 3N., Feb. 1, 1936; result 12-0; believed to be record half-time scores in League football).

Nine goals were scored in the first half – Burnley 4, Watford 5 in Div. 1 on April 5, 2003. Result: 4–7.

Stirling Albion led Selkirk 15-0 at half-time (result 20-0) in the Scottish Cup 1st. Rd., Dec. 8, 1984.

World record half-time score: 16-0 when Australia beat American Samoa 31-0 (another world record) in the World Cup Oceania qualifying group at Coff's Harbour, New South Wales, on April 11, 2001.

● On March 4, 1933 Coventry City beat Q.P.R. (Div. 3 South) 7-0, having led by that score at half-time. This repeated the half-time situation in Bristol City's 7-0 win over Grimsby Town on Dec. 26, 1914.

● Only instance of club failing to win League match after leading 5-0 at half-time: Sheffield Wed. 5, Everton 5 (Div. 1, Nov. 12, 1904; Wed. scored 5 in first half, Everton 5 in second).

TOP SECOND-HALF TEAM

Most goals scored by a team in one half of a League match is eleven. Stockport Co. led Halifax Town 2-0 at half-time in Div. 3 North on Jan. 6, 1934 and won 13-0.

FIVE NOT ENOUGH

Last team to score 5 in League match and lose: Reading, beaten 7-5 at Doncaster Rov. (Div. 3, Sept. 25, 1982).

LONG SERVICE WITH ONE CLUB

Bill Nicholson, OBE, has been associated with Tottenham for 66 years – as a wing-half (1938-55), then the club's most successful manager (1958-74) with 8 major prizes, subsequently chief advisor and scout. Now 85, he is club president, is an honorary freeman of the borough, still lives close to the ground, has an executive suite named after him at the club, and the stretch of roadway from Tottenham High Road to the main gates has the nameplate Bill Nicholson Way.

Ted Bates, the Grand Old Man of Southampton with 66 years of unbroken service to the club, was awarded the Freedom of the City in April, 2001. He joined Saints as an inside-forward from Norwich City in 1937, made 260 peace-time appearances for the club, became reserve-team trainer in 1953 and manager at The Dell for 18 years (1955-73), taking Southampton into the top division in 1966. He was subsequently chief executive, director and club president. He died in October 2003, aged 85.

Dario Gradi, MBE, 62, is the longest-serving manager in British football, having completed 21 seasons and more than 1,000 matches in charge of Crewe Alexandra (appointed June 1983). Never a League player, he previously managed Wimbledon and Crystal Palace. At Crewe, where he is also a director, his policy of finding and grooming young talent has earned the club more than £15m. in transfer fees.

Bob Paisley was associated with Liverpool for 57 years from 1939, when he joined them from Bishop Auckland, until he died in February 1996. He served them as player, trainer, coach, assistant-manager, manager, director and vice-president.

Ronnie Moran, who joined Liverpool in as a player 1952, retired from the Anfield coaching staff in season 1998-9.

Ernie Gregory served West Ham Utd. for 52 years as goalkeeper and coach. He joined them as boy of 14 from school in 1935, retired in May 1987.

Ted Sagar, Everton goalkeeper, 23 years at Goodison Park (1929-52, but only 16 League seasons because of War).

Alan Knight, goalkeeper, played 23 seasons (1977-2000) for his only club, Portsmouth.

Roy Sproson, defender, played 21 League seasons for his only club, Port Vale (1950-71).

Allan Ball, goalkeeper, 20 seasons with Queen of the South (1963-83).

Pat Bonner, goalkeeper, 19 seasons with Celtic (1978-97).

Danny McGrain, defender, 17 years with Celtic (1970-87).

TIGHT AT HOME

Fewest home goals conceded in League season (modern times): 4 by **Liverpool** (Div. 1, 1978-9); 4 by **Manchester Utd.** (Premier League, 1994-5) – both in 21 matches.

FOOTBALL POOLS

Littlewoods launched them in 1923 with a capital of £100. Coupons were first issued (4,000 of them) outside Manchester Utd.'s ground, the original 35 investors staking a total of £4-7s.-6d (pay-out £2-12s).

Vernons joined Littlewoods as the leading promoters. The Treble Chance, leading to bonanza dividends, was introduced in 1946 and the Pools Panel began in January 1963, to counter mass fixture postponements caused by the Big Freeze winter.

But business was hard hit by the launch of the National Lottery in 1994. Dividends slumped, the work-force was drastically cut and in June 2000 the Liverpool-based Moores family sold Littlewoods Pools in a £161m. deal.

The record prize remains the £2,924,622 paid to a Worsley, Manchester, syndicate in November 1994.

Fixed odds football – record pay-out: £654,375 by Ladbrokes (May 1993) to Jim Wright, of Teignmouth, Devon. He placed a £1,000 each-way pre-season bet on the champions of the three Football League divisions – Newcastle Utd. (8–1), Stoke City (6–1) and Cardiff City (9–1).

Record for match accumulator: **£164,776** to £4 stake on 18 correct results, October 5, 6, 7, 2002. The bet, with Ladbrokes in Colchester, was made by Army chef Mark Simmons.

TRANSFER DEADLINE

This was introduced by the Football League in 1911, to prevent clubs in contention for honours or fighting relegation gaining an unfair advantage in the closing weeks.

The original deadline was March 16. It is now 5 p.m. on the fourth Thursday in March, after which only in exceptional circumstances (e.g. if a side has no fit goalkeeper) can a transferred player appear for his new club that season.

After the last war, frantic spending was the norm on deadline day, but in recent years last-day business has dwindled to a comparative trickle.

TRANSFER WINDOW

This was introduced to Britain in September 2002 via FIFA regulations to bring uniformity across Europe (the rule previously applied in a number of other countries). The transfer of contracted players is restricted to two periods: June 1–August 31 and January 1–31).

On appeal, Football League (Nationwide) clubs continued to sign/sell players through seasons 2002–03, 2003-04 (excluding deals with Premiership clubs).

TEMPORARY TRANSFERS

These were introduced (originally limited to two per club) as 'permit loan transfers' by the Football League in 1967.

PROGRAMME PIONEERS

Chelsea pioneered football's magazine-style programme when they introduced a 16-page issue for their First Division match against Portsmouth on Christmas Day 1948. It cost sixpence (2½p).

TRIBUNAL-FEE RECORDS

Top tribunal fee: £2.5m for **Chris Bart-Williams** (Sheffield Wed. to Nott'm. Forest, June 1995).

Biggest discrepancy: Andy Walker, striker, Bolton Wand. to Celtic, June 1994: Bolton Wand. asked £2.2m, Celtic offered £250,000. Tribunal decided £550,000.

LONGEST THROW-IN?

That by Notts Co.'s **Andy Legg** was measured (season 1994-5) at 41 metres (45 yards) and claimed as the longest throw by any footballer in the world, until 1997-8, when **Dave Challinor** (Tranmere Rov.) reached 46.3 metres (50½ yards).

BALL JUGGLING: WORLD RECORD CLAIMS

Sam Ik (South Korea) juggled a ball non-stop for 18 hours, 11 minutes, 4 seconds in March 1995. Thai footballer **Sam-Ang Sowanski** juggled a ball for 15 hours without letting it touch the ground in Bangkok in April 2000.

Milene Domingues, wife of Brazilian star Ronaldo and a player for Italian women's team Fiammamonza, Milan, became the 'Queen of Keepy Uppy' when for 9 hours, 6 minutes she juggled a ball 55,187 times.

SUBS' SCORING RECORD

Barnet's 5-4 home win v Torquay Utd. (Div. 3, Dec. 28, 1993) provided the first instance of **all four substitutes** scoring in a major League match in England.

FOOTBALL'S OLDEST ANNUAL

Now in its 118th edition, this publication began as the 16-page *Athletic News Football Supplement & Club Directory* in 1887. From the long-established *Athletic News*, it became the *Sunday Chronicle Annual* in 1946, the *Empire News* in 1956, the *News of the World & Empire News* in 1961 and, since 1965, the *News of the World Annual*.

TRANSFER TRAIL

For space reasons, it is no longer possible to include every million-pound transfer involving British clubs since the first such deal: **Trevor Francis** from Birmingham City to Nott'm. Forest (£1,180,000) in Feb. 1979. For the same reason, deals below £6m are not included.

★	=	British record fee at that time	H	=	Record winger import
A	=	Record all-British deal	J	=	Record received for winger
B	=	British record for goalkeeper	K	=	Record for teenager
C	=	World record for defender	L	=	Most expensive foreign import
D	=	Record deal between English and Scottish clubs	M	=	Record English-club signing
			N	=	British record for striker
E	=	Record fee paid by Scottish club	P	=	Record British export
F	=	Record fee to Scottish club	(• Re dates, 1/00 = Jan 2000 etc)

	Player	From	To	Date	£
★CAM	Rio Ferdinand	Leeds Utd.	Manchester Utd.	7/02	28,250,000
★L	Juan Sebastian Veron	Lazio	Manchester Utd.	7/01	28,100,000
P	David Beckham	Manchester Utd.	Real Madrid	7/03	23,300,000
★	Nicolas Anelka	Arsenal	Real Madrid	8/99	22,500,000
J	Marc Overmars	Arsenal	Barcelona	7/00	22,000,000
N	Ruud van Nistelrooy	PSV Eindhoven	Manchester Utd.	4/01	19,000,000
AC	Rio Ferdinand	West Ham Utd.	Leeds Utd.	11/00	18,000,000
	Damien Duff	Blackburn Rov.	Chelsea	7/03	17,000,000
	Hernan Crespo	Inter Milan	Chelsea	8/03	16,800,000
	Claude Makelele	Real Madrid	Chelsea	9/03	16,000,000
	Adrian Mutu	Parma	Chelsea	8/03	15,800,000
★	Alan Shearer	Blackburn Rov.	Newcastle Utd.	7/96	15,000,000
	Jimmy F. Hasselbaink	Atl. Madrid	Chelsea	6/00	15,000,000
	Juan Sebastian Veron	Manchester Utd.	Chelsea	8/03	15,000,000
	Djibril Cisse	Auxerre	Liverpool	7/04	14,000,000
	Paulo Ferreira	Porto	Chelsea	7/04	13,500,000
	Jaap Stam	Manchester Utd.	Lazio	8/01	13,300,000
	Robbie Keane	Coventry City	Inter Milan	7/00	13,000,000
	Sylvain Wiltord	Bordeaux	Arsenal	8/00	13,000,000
	Nicolas Anelka	Paris St. Germain	Manchester City	5/02	13,000,000
	Louis Saha	Fulham	Manchester Utd.	1/04	12,825,000
	Dwight Yorke	Aston Villa	Manchester Utd.	8/98	12,600,000
K	Cristiano Ronaldo	Sporting Lisbon	Manchester Utd.	8/03	12,240,000
	Juninho	Middlesbrough	Atl. Madrid	7/97	12,000,000
	Jimmy F. Hasselbaink	Leeds Utd.	Atl. Madrid	8/99	12,000,000
DE	Tore Andre Flo	Chelsea	Rangers	11/00	12,000,000
	Robbie Keane	Inter Milan	Leeds Utd.	12/00	12,000,000
	Arjen Robben	PSV Eindhoven	Chelsea	4/04	12,000,000
	Steve Marlet	Lyon	Fulham	8/01	11,500,000
	Sergei Rebrov	Dynamo Kiev	Tottenham	5/00	11,000,000
	Frank Lampard	West Ham Utd.	Chelsea	6/01	11,000,000
	Robbie Fowler	Liverpool	Leeds Utd.	11/01	11,000,000
	Jaap Stam	PSV Eindhoven	Manchester Utd.	5/98	10,750,000
	Thierry Henry	Juventus	Arsenal	8/99	10,500,000
	Laurent Robert	Paris St. Germain	Newcastle Utd.	8/01	10,500,000
	Chris Sutton	Blackburn Rov.	Chelsea	7/99	10,000,000
	Emile Heskey	Leicester City	Liverpool	2/00	10,000,000
	El Hadji Diouf	Lens	Liverpool	6/02	10,000,000

	Scott Parker	Charlton Athletic	Chelsea	1/04	10,000,000
	Juan Pablo Angel	River Plate (Arg.)	Aston Villa	1/01	9,500,000
	Jonathan Woodgate	Leeds Utd.	Newcastle Utd.	1/03	9,000,000
F	Giovanni van Bronckhorst	Rangers	Arsenal	6/01	8,500,000
★	Stan Collymore	Nott'm Forest	Liverpool	6/95	8,500,000
	Hugo Viana	Sporting Lisbon	Newcastle Utd.	6/02	8,500,000
	Dean Richards	Southampton	Tottenham	9/01	8,100,000
	Massimo Maccarone	Empoli	Middlesbrough	7/02	8,100,000
	Andrei Kanchelskis	Everton	Fiorentina	1/97	8,000,000
	Dietmar Hamann	Newcastle Utd.	Liverpool	7/99	8,000,000
	Ugo Ehiogu	Aston Villa	Middlesbrough	10/00	8,000,000
	Francis Jeffers	Everton	Arsenal	6/01	8,000,000
	Andy Cole	Manchester Utd.	Blackburn Rov.	12/01	8,000,000
B	Fabien Barthez	Monaco	Manchester Utd.	5/00	7,800,000
	Jesper Gronkjaer	Ajax Amsterdam	Chelsea	10/00	7,800,000
★	Dennis Bergkamp	Inter Milan	Arsenal	6/95	7,500,000
	Kevin Davies	Southampton	Blackburn Rov.	6/98	7,500,000
	John Hartson	West Ham Utd.	Wimbledon	1/99	7,500,000
	Emmanuel Petit	Barcelona	Chelsea	6/01	7,500,000
	Diego Forlan	Independiente (Arg.)	Manchester Utd.	1/02	7,500,000
	Barry Ferguson	Rangers	Blackburn Rov.	8/03	7,500,000
	Olivier Dacourt	Lens	Leeds Utd.	5/00	7,200,000
	Jose Reyes	Sevilla	Arsenal	1/04	7,100,000
★	Andy Cole	Newcastle Utd.	Manchester Utd.	1/95	7,000,000
	Fabrizio Ravanelli	Juventus	Middlesbrough	7/96	7,000,000
	Stan Collymore	Liverpool	Aston Villa	5/97	7,000,000
H	Marc Overmars	Ajax Amsterdam	Arsenal	6/97	7,000,000
	Duncan Ferguson	Everton	Newcastle Utd.	11/98	7,000,000
	Lauren	Real Mallorca	Arsenal	5/00	7,000,000
	Carl Cort	Wimbledon	Newcastle Utd.	7/00	7,000,000
	Edwin Van der Sar	Juventus	Fulham	8/01	7,000,000
	Boudewijn Zenden	Barcelona	Chelsea	8/01	7,000,000
	Seth Johnson	Derby Co.	Leeds Utd.	10/01	7,000,000
	Robbie Keane	Leeds Utd.	Tottenham	8/02	7,000,000
	Wayne Bridge	Southampton	Chelsea	7/03	7,000,000
	Jermain Defoe	West Ham Utd.	Tottenham	2/04	7,000,000
	Alan Smith	Leeds Utd.	Manchester Utd.	5/04	7,000,000
	Geremi	Real Madrid	Chelsea	7/03	6,900,000
	Petr Cech	Rennes	Chelsea	7/04	6,900,000
	Gabriel Heinze	Paris St. Germain	Manchester Utd.	6/04	6,900,000
	Paul Merson	Middlesbrough	Aston Villa	8/98	6,750,000
	Corrado Grabbi	Ternana (It.)	Blackburn Rov.	6/01	6,750,000
	Tore Andre Flo	Rangers	Sunderland	8/02	6,750,000
	Faustino Asprilla	Parma	Newcastle Utd.	2/96	6,700,000
	David Platt	Bari	Juventus	6/92	6,500,000
	Olivier Dacourt	Everton	Lens	6/99	6,500,000
	Kieron Dyer	Ipswich Town	Newcastle Utd.	7/99	6,500,000
	Craig Bellamy	Coventry City	Newcastle Utd.	6/01	6,500,000
	Gareth Southgate	Aston Villa	Middlesbrough	7/01	6,500,000
	Michael Ball	Everton	Rangers	8/01	6,500,000
	John Hartson	Coventry City	Celtic	8/01	6,500,000
	Helder Postiga	FC Porto	Tottenham	6/03	6,250,000

	William Gallas	Marseille	Chelsea	5/01	6,200,000
	Paul Ince	Manchester Utd.	Inter Milan	6/95	6,000,000
	Les Ferdinand	Q.P.R.	Newcastle Utd.	6/95	6,000,000
	Les Ferdinand	Newcastle Utd.	Tottenham	7/97	6,000,000
	Faustino Asprilla	Newcastle Utd.	Parma	1/98	6,000,000
	Robbie Keane	Wolves	Coventry City	8/99	6,000,000
	Marc-Vivien Foe	West Ham Utd.	Lyon	5/00	6,000,000
	Chris Sutton	Chelsea	Celtic	7/00	6,000,000
	Mark Viduka	Celtic	Leeds Utd.	7/00	6,000,000
	Nick Barmby	Everton	Liverpool	7/00	6,000,000
	Emmanuel Petit	Arsenal	Barcelona	7/00	6,000,000
	Richard Wright	Ipswich Town	Arsenal	7/01	6,000,000
	Bosko Balaban	Dynamo Zagreb	Aston Villa	8/01	6,000,000
	Glen Johnson	West Ham Utd.	Chelsea	7/03	6,000,000
	Joe Cole	West Ham Utd.	Chelsea	8/03	6,000,000
	Mikel Arteta	Barcelona	Rangers	7/02	5,800,000
	Nick Barmby	Middlesbrough	Everton	10/96	5,750,000
	Dion Dublin	Coventry City	Aston Villa	11/98	5,750,000
	Eyal Berkovic	West Ham Utd.	Celtic	7/99	5,750,000
	Neil Lennon	Leicester City	Celtic	12/00	5,700,000
	Mario Stanic	Parma	Chelsea	6/00	5,600,000
★	David Platt	Aston Villa	Bari	7/91	5,500,000
★	Paul Gascoigne	Tottenham	Lazio	6/92	5,500,000
	Fabrizio Ravanelli	Middlesbrough	Marseille	9/97	5,500,000
	Gary Speed	Everton	Newcastle Utd.	2/98	5,500,000
	Georgi Kinkladze	Manchester City	Ajax	5/98	5,500,000
	Andrei Kanchelskis	Fiorentina	Rangers	7/98	5,500,000
	Steve Stone	Nott'm Forest	Aston Villa	3/99	5,500,000
	Robert Pires	Marseille	Arsenal	7/00	5,500,000
	Christian Ziege	Middlesbrough	Liverpool	8/00	5,500,000
	Igor Biscan	Dynamo Zagreb	Liverpool	12/00	5,500,000
	Tomas Repka	Fiorentina	West Ham Utd.	9/01	5,500,000
	David Dunn	Blackburn Rov.	Birmingham City	7/03	5,500,000
	Pierluigi Casiraghi	Lazio	Chelsea	5/98	5,400,000
	Christian Dailly	Derby Co.	Blackburn Rov.	8/98	5,300,000
	Nick Barmby	Tottenham	Middlesbrough	8/95	5,250,000
	Dietmar Hamann	Bayern Munich	Newcastle Utd.	7/98	5,250,000
	David Platt	Juventus	Sampdoria	7/93	5,200,000

BRITISH RECORD TRANSFERS FROM FIRST £1,000 DEAL

Player	From	To	Date	£
Alf Common	Sunderland	Middlesbrough	2/1905	1,000
Syd Puddefoot	West Ham Utd.	Falkirk	2/22	5,000
Warney Cresswell	S. Shields	Sunderland	3/22	5,500
Bob Kelly	Burnley	Sunderland	12/25	6,500
David Jack	Bolton Wand.	Arsenal	10/28	10,890
Bryn Jones	Wolves	Arsenal	8/38	14,500
Billy Steel	Morton	Derby Co.	9/47	15,000
Tommy Lawton	Chelsea	Notts Co.	11/47	20,000
Len Shackleton	Newcastle Utd.	Sunderland	2/48	20,500
Johnny Morris	Manchester Utd.	Derby Co.	2/49	24,000
Eddie Quigley	Sheffield Wed.	Preston N.E.	12/49	26,500

Trevor Ford	Aston Villa	Sunderland	10/50	30,000
Jackie Sewell	Notts Co.	Sheffield Wed.	3/51	34,500
Eddie Firmani	Charlton Athletic	Sampdoria	7/55	35,000
John Charles	Leeds Utd.	Juventus	4/57	65,000
Denis Law	Manchester City	Torino	6/61	100,000
Denis Law	Torino	Manchester Utd.	7/62	115,000
Allan Clarke	Fulham	Leicester City	6/68	150,000
Allan Clarke	Leicester City	Leeds Utd.	6/69	165,000
Martin Peters	West Ham Utd.	Tottenham	3/70	200,000
Alan Ball	Everton	Arsenal	12/71	220,000
David Nish	Leicester City	Derby Co.	8/72	250,000
Bob Latchford	Birmingham City	Everton	2/74	350,000
Graeme Souness	Middlesbrough	Liverpool	1/78	352,000
Kevin Keegan	Liverpool	Hamburg	6/77	500,000
David Mills	Middlesbrough	W.B.A.	1/79	516,000
Trevor Francis	Birmingham City	Nott'm. Forest	2/79	1,180,000
Steve Daley	Wolves	Manchester City	9/79	1,450,000
Andy Gray	Aston Villa	Wolves	9/79	1,469,000
Bryan Robson	W.B.A.	Manchester Utd.	10/81	1,500,000
Ray Wilkins	Manchester Utd.	AC Milan	5/84	1,500,000
Mark Hughes	Manchester Utd.	Barcelona	5/86	2,300,000
Ian Rush	Liverpool	Juventus	6/87	3,200,000
Chris Waddle	Tottenham	Marseille	7/89	4,250,000
David Platt	Aston Villa	Bari	7/91	5,500,000
Paul Gascoigne	Tottenham	Lazio	6/92	5,500,000
Andy Cole	Newcastle Utd.	Manchester Utd.	1/95	7,000,000
Dennis Bergkamp	Inter Milan	Arsenal	6/95	7,500,000
Stan Collymore	Nott'm. Forest	Liverpool	6/95	8,500,000
Alan Shearer	Blackburn Rov.	Newcastle Utd.	7/96	15,000,000
Nicolas Anelka	Arsenal	Real Madrid	8/99	22,500,000
Juan Sebastian Veron	Lazio	Manchester Utd.	7/01	28,100,000
Rio Ferdinand	Leeds Utd.	Manchester Utd.	7/02	28,250,000

• **World's first £1m. transfer:** Guiseppe Savoldi, Bologna to Napoli, July 1975.

TOP FOREIGN SIGNINGS

Player	From	To	Date	£
Zinedine Zidane	Juventus	Real Madrid	7/01	47,200,000
Luis Figo	Barcelona	Real Madrid	7/00	37,200,000
Hernan Crespo	Parma	Lazio	7/00	35,000,000
Ronaldo	Inter Milan	Real Madrid	8/02	33,000,000
Gianluigi Buffon	Parma	Juventus	7/01	32,600,000
Christian Vieri	Lazio	Inter Milan	6/99	31,000,000
Alessandro Nesta	Lazio	AC Milan	8/02	30,200,000
Hernan Crespo	Lazio	Inter Milan	8/02	29,000,000
Gaizka Mendieta	Valencia	Lazio	7/01	28,500,000
Pavel Nedved	Lazio	Juventus	7/01	25,000,000
Rui Costa	Fiorentina	AC Milan	7/01	24,500,000
Gabriel Batistuta	Fiorentina	Roma	5/00	22,000,000
Lilian Thuram	Parma	Juventus	6/01	22,000,000
Nicolas Anelka	Real Madrid	Paris St. Germain	7/00	21,700,000
Filippo Inzaghi	Juventus	AC Milan	7/01	21,700,000
Denilson	Sao Paulo	Real Betis	7/97	21,400,000

Marcio Amoroso	Udinese	Parma	6/99	21,000,000
Ronaldinho	Paris St Germain	Barcelona	7/03	21,000,000
Antonio Cassano	Bari	Roma	3/01	20,000,000
Javier Saviola	River Plate	Barcelona	7/01	20,000,000
Juan Sebastian Veron	Parma	Lazio	6/99	19,800,000
Hidetoshi Nakata	Roma	Parma	7/01	19,100,000
Ronaldo	Barcelona	Inter Milan	6/97	18,000,000
Francesco Toldo	Fiorentina	Inter Milan	7/01	18,000,000
Christian Vieri	Atletico Madrid	Lazio	8/98	17,500,000
David Trezeguet	Monaco	Juventus	6/00	17,500,000
Savo Milosevic	Real Zaragoza	Parma	7/00	17,000,000
Andrei Shevchenko	Dynamo Kiev	AC Milan	6/99	15,700,000
Vincenzo Montella	Sampdoria	Roma	6/99	15,300,000
Clarence Seedorf	Real Madrid	Inter Milan	12/99	15,000,000
Walter Samuel	Roma	Real Madrid	5/04	15,000,000
Mathias Almeyda	Lazio	Parma	7/00	14,800,000
Ronald de Boer	Ajax	Barcelona	1/99	14,000,000
Frank de Boer	Ajax	Barcelona	1/99	
Claudio Lopez	Valencia	Lazio	7/00	14,000,000
Shabani Nonda	Rennes	Monaco	6/00	13,500,000
Gianluigi Lentini	Torino	AC Milan	7/92	13,000,000
Walter Samuel	Boca Juniors	Roma	6/00	13,000,000
Geovanni	Cruzeiro	Barcelona	6/01	12,700,000
Jose Mari Romero	Atletico Madrid	AC Milan	12/99	12,700,000
Gianluca Vialli	Sampdoria	Juventus	6/92	12,500,000
Ronaldo	PSV Eindhoven	Barcelona	7/96	12,500,000
Rivaldo	Dep. La Coruna	Barcelona	8/97	12,500,000

WORLD RECORD GOALKEEPER FEE

£32.6m for **Gianluigi Buffon** (Parma to Juventus, July 2001).

RECORD CONFERENCE FEE

£250,000: Andy Clarke, Barnet to Wimbledon, Feb 1991; **Barry Hayles**, Stevenage Borough to Bristol Rov., Aug. 1997; **Jason Roberts**, Hayes to Wolves, Sept. 1997.

RECORD FEE BETWEEN NON-LEAGUE CLUBS

£180,000 for **Justin Jackson**, Morecambe to Rushden & Diamonds (Conference), June 2000.

WORLD RECORD FEE FOR TEENAGER

£19m. for **Antonio Cassano**, 18, Bari to Roma, March 2001.

BRITISH RECORD FEES FOR TEENAGERS

£12.24m. for **Cristiano Ronaldo**, aged 18, Sporting Lisbon to Manchester Utd., Aug. 2003
£8.5. for **Hugo Viana,** aged 19, Sporting Lisbon to Newcastle Utd., June 2002.
£6m. for **Robbie Keane**, aged 19, Wolves to Coventry City, Aug. 1999.

FINAL WHISTLE – OBITUARIES 2003–04

JULY

JOHN ASHTON, Snr, 81, one of Matt Busby's first signings, was left-back in Manchester United's F.A. Cup-winning team in 1948 and in their successful Championship side 4 years later. He partnered Johnny Carey in one of the outstanding full-back pairings of the early post-war years and was capped 17 times by England (1948–50). His one-club career of 282 League and Cup apps. (30 goals) ended in 1954 when he was diagnosed with tuberculosis, but on recovery he continued at Old Trafford in a coaching capacity until 1972. His was a proud Wembley presence in 1968 when his son, John Jnr., starred as United became the first English club to win the European Cup.

AUGUST

CLIVE CHARLES, 51, West Ham United and Cardiff City full-back (1971–76), died at his home in Portland, Oregon, after a long battle with cancer..He coached the U.S. men's team to the semi-finals of the 2002 Olympics in Sydney.

KEN COOTE, 75, played a club-record 514 League games as 'the best full-back Brentford ever had.' A one-club man, he was the mainstay of their defence for 15 seasons (1949–63), was never booked and captained the side to the Fourth Division title in 1963.

JIMMY DAVIS, 21, highly promising Manchester United winger on loan to Watford, was killed in a motorway crash in Oxfordshire in the early hours of August 9. As a mark of respect Watford's home game v Coventry City that day was postponed. He made 1 senior app. for United and played 15 games on loan at Swindon Town in 2002–03. His memory was touchingly commemorated at the 2004 F.A. Cup Final which ended with all the United players changing into shirts with 'Davis' on the back before they received the trophy and medals.

LOTHAR EMMERICH, 61, powerful West Germany left-winger (5 caps) whose career was defined by the 1966 World Cup. In the group stage, he scored with an 'impossible' shot from the byline, and in the Final against England his driven free-kick led to the last-minute goal that took the match into extra-time. Weeks earlier, he was in the Borussia Dortmund side that beat Liverpool 2–1 in the European Cup-Winners' Cup Final at Hampden Park. Between 1963–69 he scored 115 goals in 183 Bundesliga games for Dortmund, whom he left to play in Belgium for VAC Beerschott.

RAY HARFORD, 58, one of the game's most respected managers/coaches over two decades, died of cancer on the season's opening day. His 6-club playing career (1964–76) took in Charlton Athletic, Exeter City, Lincoln City, Mansfield Town, Port Vale and Colchester United. In management, he also served 6 clubs, starting with Fulham (1984–86). He took Luton Town to their first major success in the 1988 League Cup against Arsenal. He next managed unfashionable Wimbledon (1990–91) and was assistant to Kenny Dalglish when Blackburn Rovers won promotion to the Premier League in 1992 and the Premiership title in 1995. He managed Blackburn from 1995–97, then W.B.A. in 1997, Q.P.R. 1997–98 and finally coached Millwall.

FRANK LARGE, 63, who died in Ireland, was a bustling, crowd-pleasing centre-forward whose career spanned 9 clubs and an aggregate of 210 goals in 563 League apps. For Halifax Town, Q.P.R., Northampton Town, Swindon Town, Carlisle United, Oldham Athletic, Leicester City, Fulham and Chesterfield. Leeds-born, he was discovered by Halifax Town and served 3 spells with Northampton Town.

HELMUT RAHN, 73, was the dribbling, hard-shooting outside-right who became a national hero when he shot West Germany's winning goal in the 1954 World Cup Final against Hungary in Switzerland. For a winger, he had the remarkable strike rate of 21 goals in 40 Internationals (1951–60). With Rot-Weiss Essen, he won the German Cup (1953) and Championship (1955), then played for FC Koln, Enschede (Holland) and SV Duisberg.

TREVOR SMITH, 67, son of the Black Country, was the solid, uncompromising centre-half who played 430 games for Birmingham City (1951–64) and twice for England in 1959. He was also capped at U-23 and 'B' levels. He was a bastion in Birmingham City's Second Division-winning team in 1955, played in their last F.A. Cup Final in 1956 and in the two-leg League Cup Final victory against Aston Villa in 1963. He concluded his career with 2 seasons at Walsall (1964–66).

GUY THYS, 80, was the legendary and most successful manager of Belgium's national team. He twice held the position (1976–89 and 1990–91) and was in charge for 114 International matches, a Belgium record. He chain-smoked them to the 1980 European Championship Final against West Germany and, among 3 World Cup qualifications, to the 1986 semi-final against Argentina.

SEPTEMBER

JACK BURKITT, 77, was captain of Nottingham Forest's 1959 F.A. Cup-winning team. A wing-half and one-club man, he made more than 500 apps. for Forest between 1948–61.

RON (TOT) LEVERTON, 77, was a Nottingham Forest inside-forward in the early Post-war years (104 League apps., 36 goals, 1946–53). He later played for Notts County (1953–55) and Walsall (1956–57).

JOE McDONALD, 73, left-back, in Nottingham Forest's F.A. Cup triumph in 1959, pre-deceased the captain of that side, Jack Burkitt, by a few days. Originally with Falkirk, he played for Sunderland from 1953–58 and for Forest (1958–60).

OCTOBER

JOE BAKER, 63, Liverpool-born of Scottish parentage, was one of the most dynamic centre-forwards of the 1960s. By the age of 21 he had scored 159 goals in 4 seasons for Hibernian, including a club record 42 in the Scottish League in season 1959–60. He won the first of 8 England caps at 18, and after an unsettled spell in Italy with Torino, the 5ft. 8 in. striker returned to British football with a £70,000 transfer to Arsenal (101 goals in 157 apps., 1962–65). He subsequently played for Nottingham Forest (1965–68), Sunderland (1969–70), returned to Hibernian and retired with Raith Rovers in 1974. After two spells in management with Albion Rovers, he became a publican and later worked in the building trade. He died after collapsing while playing golf at Lanark.

STEVE DEATH, 54, signed from West Ham United for £20,000, was Reading's goalkeeper in 537 first-team matches from 1969–82. Though only 5ft. 7in., he set the still-existing English League record of 1103 minutes without conceding a goal (including 11 consecutive clean sheets) in Division Four in season 1978–79.

NOVEMBER

TED BATES, 85, was the most influential figure in Southampton's history. He served the club for two-thirds of a century in the widest possible range – player, coach, manager, chief executive, director and president. He presided over Saints' rise from the old Third Division South in the Fifties to the top division in 1966, saw them return to the First Division after relegation, subsequently as ever-present members of the Premier League since its formation in 1992, and played a significant part in the club's relocation from his beloved Dell to St. Mary's. He joined Southampton from Norwich City on his 19th. birthday in May 1937. Despite a war-interrupted career, he made 202 League apps. At inside-forward (64 goals) in the company of Alf Ramsey, Charlie Wayman and Don Roper and was appointed manager from reserve coach in September 1955. He took Saints to the Third Division title (106 goals) in 1960 and into the First Division for the first time in 1966. Among players he discovered were Terry Paine, Derek Reeves, Martin Chivers and Mick Channon. His proudest moments were to see the F.A. Cup won by his successor Lawrie McMenemy in 1976 and, personally, to be awarded the MBE in 2001.

PROF. SIR ROLAND SMITH, 75, former chairman of Manchester United plc. He helped oversee the club's flotation on the Stock Exchange and to establish them as the world's richest club.

DECEMBER

REDFERN FROGGATT, 79, served an exemplary career at inside-forward for Sheffield Wednesday, his only club, from 1946–59. He scored 140 goals in 434 League apps. And was capped 4 times by England on the left wing in 2 of those Internationals by his cousin, Portsmouth's Jack Froggatt.

GIL REECE, 61, was a fast, clever winger capped 29 times by Wales from 1965–75. Cardiff-born, he began in League football with Newport County, then played 210 League games (58 goals) for Sheffield United (1965–72). Three seasons with Cardiff City followed, and his League career ended with a brief spell at Swansea City.

JANUARY 2004

JOHN BONNAR, 80, was Celtic's goalkeeper in 180 matches (49 clean sheets) after joining them from Arbroath in August 1948. He helped them win the League and Cup double in 1954, and after short spells with Dumbarton and St Johnstone retired in 1960.

CHARLIE ELLIOTT, 91, an able defender who played 95 League games for Coventry City (1931–48), was also a prominent cricketer, scoring more than 12,000 runs for Derbyshire (1932–56). He was subsequently a first-class umpire and Test selector.

MIKLOS FEHER, 24, Benfica's Hungarian International striker, died of a heart attack after collapsing on the field during a 1–0 League win against Vitoria Guimaraes. He had gone on as substitute after 60 minutes.

THOMAS (T.G.) JONES, 86, whose career was denied full acclaim by the Second World War, was one of the best footballing centre-halves of his time. He won a Championship medal with Everton in 1939, 17 full caps for Wales (1938–50) and played in 14 wartime Internationals. Signed from Wrexham for £8,000 in 1936, he made 176 League and Cup apps. for Everton, ultimately as captain, and retired at 32. In 2000 he was named Everton's 'Millennium Giant of the 1940s.'

LEONIDAS DA SILVA, 90, Brazil's 'Black Diamond,' was reckoned to be the first exponent of the bicycle kick. He scored 25 goals in 26 Internationals, 8 of them in 4 matches at the 1938 World Cup in France (4 in a 6–5 win against Poland). Born in Rio de Janeiro, he began with Penarol of Uruguay and returned to Brazil to play for Vasco da Gama, Botafogo, Flamengo and Sao Paulo.

MIKE McCULLAGH, 67 was chairman of Middlesbrough for 3 turbulent years in the 1980s when, from debts of £1.8m., the club survived liquidation and rose from Third to First Division in successive years (1987–88).

REG (J.R.) SMITH, 91, was a pre-war left-winger who played 138 games for Millwall (26 goals) and was capped twice by England in 1939. South Africa-born, he did war service with the RAF and subsequently helped Dundee win the Scottish League Cup twice (1952, 1953). He managed Falkirk to Scottish Cup success in 1957 and returned to The Den as Millwall manager from 1959–61.

FEBRUARY

JOHN CHARLES, 72, was a colossus of British football, unarguably Wales' greatest player and the best-value English-club player to go abroad. Of powerful build at 6ft. 2in. and nearly 15st, he excelled at both ends of the field – Billy Wright described him as 'the best centre-forward' he played against while to Nat Lofthouse he was 'the finest centre-half I ever faced.' Never cautioned or sent off in his career, he was, to Juventus supporters, 'Il Buono Gigante' (the 'Gentle Giant'). Raised in the Welsh valleys, he joined Swansea Town's groundstaff and moved to Leeds United as a 16-year-old in 1947. He scored 42 Second Division goals for Leeds in season 1953–54, inspired them to the top division in 1955–56 and outscored all other First Division marksmen with 38 goals in 1956–57. In April 1957 a record British transfer fee of £65,000 took him to Juventus, for whom he scored 105 goals in 178 matches, helping them to 3 Italian League titles and 2 Cup successes. The first of his 38 caps (15 goals) at 18 years, 71 days in 1950 made him the then youngest Wales International, and he inspired them to reach their only World Cup Final series in Sweden (quarter-finalists) in 1958. He went back to Leeds (£53,000) in 1962, but after only 11 Second Division games returned briefly to Italy with Roma. He ended his League career with 3 seasons at Cardiff City (1963–66), then player-managed non-League Hereford United for 5 years and finished in the game as manager of Merthyr Tydfil for one season. He was belatedly appointed CBE in 2001 and received the freedom of his home town, Swansea City. Back in Leeds, he battled Alzheimer's for his last two years. Last January, he suffered a heart attack in an Italian TV studio. Juventus flew him home by air ambulance and he died in Wakefield Hospital on February 21. At his funeral, 5,000 Leeds supporters paid tribute as the hearse moved slowly round the Elland Road pitch, and more than 600 people attended a memorial service in Swansea. His widow Glenda bequeathed his ashes to be incorporated into a statue to be erected at Swansea City's new White Rock Stadium. Sir Bobby Robson, Newcastle United manager, said: 'John was not only one of the greatest footballers who ever lived. He was one of the greatest men ever to play the game.'

HENRY COCKBURN, 80, was a perpetual-motion, 5ft. 5in. wing-half for Manchester United and England in the immediate post-war years. He won the first of 13 International caps (in a 7–2 win against N. Ireland in Belfast, Sept. 1946) after making only 7 First Division Apps. He played in United's F.A. Cup triumph in 1948 and their Championship success in 1952. He made a total of 275 apps. For the club and completed his career with 35 League games for Bury (1954–56).

TOMMY EGLINGTON, 81, was Everton's outside-left in the first post-war decade and a dual Irish International, winning 24 caps for the Republic (1946–56) and 6 for Northern Ireland (1947–49) at a time when the Irish F.A. selected players from south of the border. Originally with Shamrock Rovers, he made 394 League apps. for Everton (76 goals) and remained on Merseyside to play 172 games for Tranmere Rovers (36 goals) from 1957–61.

ALLY MacLEOD, 72, was the larger-than-life manager of Scotland's team at the 1978 World Cup. 'Ally's Army' went 25,000 strong to Hampden Park to cheer the squad aboard an open-top bus before they flew to Argentina, where a 3–1 defeat against Peru and a 1–1 draw with Iran ended Scotland's hopes, despite Holland being beaten 3–2 in the final game. A left-winger with Blackburn Rovers (1960 F.A. Cup Final) and Hibernian, MacLeod began in management with Ayr, then Aberdeen (League Cup winners 1977) and after 17 months in charge of Scotland managed Motherwell, Airdrie, Ayr again and Queen of the South. He returned to Hampden Park in July 2003 to receive a crystal decanter from the Tartan Army 'in appreciation of his services to the national team and to Scottish football in general.'

ROQUE MASPOLI, 86, was Uruguay's outstanding goalkeeper in their shock World Cup triumph over Brazil in Rio in 1950, watched by the all-time world record crowd of 200,000. As a player he helped Penarol win 6 League titles in the 1940s, and as coach guided them to 5 more Championship successes.

BOB STOKOE, 73, managed Sunderland to their famous 1973 F.A. Cup Final victory over then-mighty Leeds United – the first such triumph for a Second Division side in 42 years. At the final whistle, Stokoe sprinted across the Wembley turf to embrace Jim Montgomery for his extraordinary double save that clinched Sunderland's first (and still latest) Cup success since 1937. Stokoe thus became a dual Cup hero in the north-east, having played centre-half in Newcastle United's winning team in 1955. He signed for them in 1947 and after 287 apps. in the famous black and white captained, coached and player-managed Bury from 1961–65. In all he managed 6 clubs over 25 years: Charlton Athletic, Sunderland, 3 stints at Carlisle United and 2 at each of Bury, Rochdale, and Blackpool.

GEOFF TWENTYMAN, 74, began his career with Carlisle United (1946–53) and was Liverpool's centre-half (170 League apps.) from 1953–59. He was the father of Geoff Jnr., who played for Preston North End and Bristol Rovers in the 1980s.

MARCH

JOE MELLING, 57, widely-respected football editor of the *Mail on Sunday* and a former chairman of the Football Writers' Association, died after a year-long battle against cancer. He was a son of Preston North End, his idol Tom Finney.

JIMMY MITCHELL, former Aberdeen captain (184 apps., 1952–58).

APRIL

GEORGE HARDWICK, 84, was Middlesbrough's stylish left-back whose England caps were all won as captain in the first 13 matches after the war (10 wins, 2 draws, 1 defeat, 1946–48). He played in 17 wartime Internationals and in two wartime Wembley finals as a guest for Chelsea. He joined Middlesbrough' for a £5 signing-on fee in April 1937 and made 166 apps. for them, followed by 190 games as player-manager of Oldham Athletic (1950–56). After coaching PSV Eindhoven and the Dutch national team, he returned to England in 1961 as Middlesbrough's youth team coach and managed Sunderland in 1964–65.

EDDIE HOPKINSON, 68, who made the still-record 519 League apps. for Bolton Wanderers from 1956–69, was England's goalkeeper in 14 Internationals (1957–60). His agility and daring at the feet of opponents amply compensated for his lack of reach at 5ft. 9in. and he earned an F.A. Cup winner's medal in the 1958 Final against Manchester United. From playing as an amateur for Oldham Athletic, he signed professional for Bolton in November 1952. He retired through injury at 34 in 1969, subsequently serving Bolton as reserve, youth and goalkeeping coach. His son Paul kept goal for Stockport County in 1975–76.

RONNIE SIMPSON, 73, had a widely successful goalkeeping career, representing Great Britain in the 1948 Olympics in London, winning the F.A. Cup with Newcastle United (1952, 1955) and playing in Celtic's historic victory over Inter Milan in 1967 as the first British winners of the European Cup. He began as a Queens Park amateur, played next for Third Lanark and moved to Newcastle (£8,750) in February 1951. After 9 years and 295 apps. In the Tyneside club's last golden era, he returned to Scotland with Hibernian. They sold him to Celtic for £4000, and at 32 the most glorious chapter in his career was still to come. He helped the Hoops win 4 League titles, 3 League Cups and the Scottish Cup. With 5 caps, he became, at 36 years and 197 days, the oldest Scottish player to make his International debut – in the 3–2 Wembley win against World Cup winners England in

April 1967 just before receiving Scotland's Footballer of the Year award. He retired in his 40th year after 188 matches and 91 clean sheets for Celtic.

WILLIE WATSON, 84, who died in Johannesburg, belonged to a rare and now extinct sporting breed as both a top-class footballer (4 England caps at wing-half, 1950–51) and cricketer (23 Tests, 1951–59, as a Yorkshire and Leicestershire left-hand batsman). Son of the famous Billy Watson, who played in Huddersfield Town's F.A. Cup-winning team of 1922 and for their Championship hat-trick side of 1924–25–26, Willie played pre-war for Huddersfield and then, via an £8,000 transfer, in the first 8 postwar seasons (1946–54) for Sunderland (211 League apps.). He became player-manager of Halifax Town in the mid-1950s, returned there as manager in 1964, and, after managing Bradford City in 1966–68, settled in South Africa, where he managed the Wanderers club in Johannesburg.

MAY

ORVAR BERGMARK, 73, played right-back in the Sweden side that, as hosts, reached the 1958 World Cup Final against Brazil. He won 94 caps and was national coach from 1966–70. Clubs as player: AIK Solna, Orebro, Roma.

JESUS GIL, 71, was the tempestuous millionaire owner of Atletico Madrid. As president from 1987, he appointed 40 managers in 15 years, 6 of them in 1993. They included Cesar Menotti, Arrigo Sacchi, Ron Atkinson and Claudio Ranieri. His philosophy: 'I pay the bills, so the coach has to agree with my ideas about the team.' He celebrated the club's League/Cup double in 1996 by bathing in champagne and riding through Madrid on a white horse.

DANNY McLENNAN, 79, went from a modest playing background as a defender with Rangers, Dundee and East Fife, and then managing Berwick Rangers and Stirling Albion to a world-wide coaching career spanning 9 countries: Zimbabwe, Iran, Iraq and Malawi from 1970–84 and 5 other national teams – Libya, the Philippines, Bahrain, Mauritius twice and Fiji. He also coached club sides in Kenya, Tanzania, Saudi Arabia, Jordan, Palestine, Norway and Malta. He retired in 2000 back home in the fishing village of Crail in Fife.

IAN McWILLIAM, 52, Celtic defender (joined 1977) died after suffering 8 years with leukaemia. At 6 ft. 5in. he was the tallest man to play for the Hoops.

DENNIS WILSHAW, 78, was a free-scoring inside-forward in the Fifties, averaging a goal every 2 games with a career total of 112 in 219 apps. For Wolves. He signed professional at Molineux in 1944 and spent 2 years on loan at Third Division Walsall (1946–48). He scored 25 goals in Wolves' Championship success in 1953–54 and his 10 goals in 12 matches for England included 4 in the 7–2 beating of Scotland at Wembley in April 1955. He left Wolves for home-town club Stoke City (£10,000) in December 1957. After a broken leg in the F.A. Cup 5th. Round at Newcastle in February 1961 ended his football, he pursued a successful teaching career in Stoke.

JUNE

STEPHEN SMITH, 28, an England and Wolves fan, was stabbed to death by a pickpocket while quietly celebrating with friends outside a Lisbon bar a few hours after England's 4–2 European Championship group win against Croatia.

RON ASHMAN, 78, the manager who introduced Kevin Keegan to professional football, died after a short illness. During the first of two spells in charge of Scunthorpe United, he brought Keegan to the Old Show Ground in 1968 as a 17-year-old, selling him to Bill Shankly's Liverpool for £30,000 in 1971. Ashman made 662 appearances for Norwich City, later managed the club and also managed Grimsby Town. After leaving football he went into the travel business.

MILESTONES OF SOCCER

1848 First code of rules compiled at Cambridge Univ.
1857 Sheffield F.C., world's oldest football club, formed.
1862 Notts Co. (oldest League club) formed.
1863 Football Association founded – their first rules of game agreed.
1871 F.A. Cup introduced.
1872 First official International: Scotland 0, England 0. Corner-kick introduced.
1873 Scottish F.A. formed; Scottish Cup introduced.
1874 Shinguards introduced. Oxford v Cambridge, first match.
1875 Crossbar introduced (replacing tape).
1876 F.A. of Wales formed.
1877 Welsh Cup introduced.
1878 Referee's whistle first used.
1880 Irish F.A. founded; Irish Cup introduced.
1883 Two-handed throw-in introduced.
1885 Record first-class score (Arbroath 36, Bon Accord 0 – Scottish Cup). Professionalism legalised.
1886 International Board formed.
1887 Record F.A. Cup score (Preston N.E. 26, Hyde 0).
1888 Football League founded by Wm. McGregor. First matches on Sept. 8.
1889 Preston N.E. win Cup and League (first club to complete Double).
1890 Scottish League and Irish League formed.
1891 Goal-nets introduced. Penalty-kick introduced.
1892 Inter-League games began. Football League Second Division formed.
1893 F.A. Amateur Cup launched.
1894 Southern League formed.
1895 F.A. Cup stolen from Birmingham shop window – never recovered.
1897 First Players' Union formed. Aston Villa win Cup and League.
1898 Promotion and relegation introduced.
1901 Maximum wage rule in force (£4 a week). Tottenham first professional club to take F.A. Cup South. First six-figure attendance (110,802) at F.A. Cup Final.
1902 Ibrox Park disaster (25 killed). Welsh League formed.
1904 F.I.F.A. founded (7 member countries).
1905 First £1,000 transfer (Alf Common, Sunderland to Middlesbrough).
1907 Players' Union revived.
1908 Transfer fee limit (£350) fixed in January and withdrawn in April.
1911 New F.A. Cup trophy – in use to 1991. Transfer deadline introduced.
1914 King George V first reigning monarch to attend F.A. Cup Final.
1916 Entertainment Tax introduced.
1919 League extended to 44 clubs.
1920 Third Division (South) formed.
1921 Third Division (North) formed.
1922 Scottish League (Div. II) introduced.
1923 Beginning of football pools. First Wembley Cup Final.
1924 First International at Wembley (England 1, Scotland 1). Rule change allows goals to be scored direct from corner-kicks.
1925 New offside law.
1926 Huddersfield Town complete first League Championship hat-trick.
1927 First League match broadcast (radio): Arsenal v Sheff. Utd. (Jan 22). First radio broadcast of Cup Final (winners Cardiff City). Charles Clegg, president of F.A., becomes first knight of football.
1928 First £10,000 transfer – David Jack (Bolton Wand. to Arsenal). W.R. ('Dixie') Dean (Everton) creates League record – 60 goals in season. Britain withdraws from F.I.F.A.
1930 Uruguay first winners of World Cup.
1931 W.B.A. win Cup and promotion.

1933 Players numbered for first time in Cup Final (1-22).

1934 Sir Frederick Wall retires as F.A. secretary; successor Stanley Rous. Death of Herbert Chapman (Arsenal manager).

1935 Arsenal equal Huddersfield Town's Championship hat-trick record. Official two-referee trials.

1936 Joe Payne's 10-goal League record (Luton Town 12, Bristol Rov. 0).

1937 British record attendance: 149,547 at Scotland v England match.

1938 First live TV transmission of F.A. Cup Final. F.A.'s 75th anniversary. Football League 50th Jubilee. New pitch marking – arc on edge of penalty-area. Laws of Game re-drafted by Stanley Rous. Arsenal pay record £14,500 fee for Bryn Jones (Wolves).

1939 Compulsory numbering of players in Football League. First six-figure attendance for League match (Rangers v Celtic, 118,567). All normal competitions suspended for duration of Second World War.

1944 Death of Sir Frederick Wall (84), F.A. secretary 1896-1934.

1945 Scottish League Cup introduced.

1946 British associations rejoin F.I.F.A. Bolton Wand. disaster (33 killed) during F.A. Cup tie with Stoke City. Walter Winterbottom appointed England's first director of coaching.

1947 Great Britain beat Rest of Europe 6-1 at Hampden Park, Glasgow. First £20,000 transfer – Tommy Lawton, Chelsea to Notts Co.

1949 Stanley Rous, secretary F.A., knighted. England's first home defeat outside British Champ. (0-2 v Eire).

1950 Football League extended from 88 to 92 clubs. World record crowd (203,500) at World Cup Final, Brazil v Uruguay, in Rio. Scotland's first home defeat by foreign team (0-1 v Austria).

1951 White ball comes into official use.

1952 Newcastle Utd. first club to win F.A. Cup at Wembley in successive seasons.

1953 England's first Wembley defeat by foreign opponents (3-6 v Hungary).

1954 Hungary beat England 7-1 in Budapest.

1955 First F.A. Cup match under floodlights (prelim. round replay, Sept. 14): Kidderminster Harriers v Brierley Hill Alliance.

1956 First F.A. Cup ties under floodlights in competition proper (Jan. 7). First League match by floodlight (Feb. 22, Portsmouth v Newcastle Utd.). Real Madrid win the first European Cup.

1957 Last full Football League programme on Christmas Day. Entertainment Tax withdrawn.

1958 Manchester Utd. air crash at Munich (Feb. 6). League re-structured into four divisions.

1959 Football League establish fixtures copyright; pools must pay for use.

1960 Record transfer fee: £55,000 for Denis Law (Huddersfield Town to Manchester City). Wolves win Cup, miss Double and Championship hat-trick by one goal. For fifth time in ten years F.A. Cup Final team reduced to ten men by injury. F.A. recognise Sunday football. Football League Cup launched.

1961 Tottenham complete the first Championship-F.A. Cup double this century. Maximum wage (£20 a week) abolished in High Court challenge by George Eastham. First British £100-a-week wage paid (by Fulham to Johnny Haynes). First £100,000 British transfer – Denis Law, Manchester City to Torino. Sir Stanley Rous elected president of F.I.F.A.

1962 Manchester Utd. raise record British transfer fee to £115,000 for Denis Law.

1963 F.A. Centenary. Football League's 75th anniversary. Season extended to end of May due to severe winter. First points panel. English "retain and transfer" system ruled illegal in High Court test case.

1964 Rangers' second great hat-trick – Scottish Cup, League Cup and League. Football League and Scottish League guaranteed £500,000 a year in new fixtures copyright agreement with Pools. First televised 'Match of the Day' (BBC2): Liverpool 3, Arsenal 2 (August 22).

1965 Bribes scandal – ten players jailed (and banned for life by F.A.) for match-fixing 1960-3. Stanley Matthews knighted in farewell season. Arthur Rowley (Shrewsbury

Town) retires with record of 434 League goals. Substitutes allowed for injured players in Football League matches (one per team).

1966 England win World Cup (Wembley).

1967 Alf Ramsey, England manager, knighted; O.B.E. for captain Bobby Moore. Celtic become first British team to win European Cup. First substitutes allowed in F.A. Cup Final (Tottenham v Chelsea) but not used. Football League permit loan transfers (two per club).

1968 First F.A. Cup Final televised live in colour (BBC2 – W.B.A. v Everton). Manchester Utd. first English club to win European Cup.

1970 F.I.F.A./U.E.F.A approve penalty shoot-out in deadlocked ties.

1971 Arsenal win League Championship and F.A. Cup.

1973 Football League introduce 3-up, 3-down promotion/relegation between Divisions 1, 2 and 3 and 4-up, 4-down between Divisions 3 and 4.

1974 First F.A. Cup ties played on Sunday (Jan. 6). League football played on Sunday for first time (Jan. 20). Last F.A. Amateur Cup Final. Joao Havelange (Brazil) succeeds Sir Stanley Rous as F.I.F.A. president.

1975 Scottish Premier Division introduced.

1976 Football League introduce goal difference (replacing goal average) and red/yellow cards.

1977 Liverpool achieve the double of League Championship and European Cup. Don Revie defects to United Arab Emirates when England manager – successor Ron Greenwood.

1978 Freedom of contract for players accepted by Football League. P.F.A. lifts ban on foreign players in English football. Football League introduce Transfer Tribunal. Viv Anderson (Nott'm. Forest) first black player to win a full England cap. Willie Johnston (Scotland) sent home from World Cup Finals in Argentina after failing dope test.

1979 First all-British £500,000 transfer – David Mills, M'bro' to W.B.A. First British million pound transfer (Trevor Francis – B'ham to Nott'm. Forest). Andy Gray moves from Aston Villa to Wolves for a record £1,469,000 fee.

1981 Tottenham win 100th F.A. Cup Final. Liverpool first British side to win European Cup three times. Three points for a win introduced by Football League. Q.P.R. install Football League's first artificial pitch. Sept. 29, death of Bill Shankly, manager-legend of Liverpool 1959-74. Record British transfer – Bryan Robson (W.B.A. to Manchester Utd.), £1,500,000.

1982 Aston Villa become sixth consecutive English winners of European Cup. Tottenham retain F.A. Cup – first club to do so since Tottenham 1961 and 1962. Football League Cup becomes the (sponsored) Milk Cup.

1983 Liverpool complete the League Championship-Milk Cup double for second year running. Manager Bob Paisley retires. Aberdeen first club to do Cup-Winners' Cup and domestic Cup double. Football League clubs vote to keep own match receipts. Football League sponsored by Canon, Japanese camera and business equipment manufacturers – 3-year agreement starting 1983-4. Football League agree 2-year contract for live TV coverage of ten matches per season (5 Friday night, BBC, 5 Sunday afternoon, ITV).

1984 One F.A. Cup tie in rounds 3, 4, 5 and 6 shown live on TV (Friday or Sunday). Aberdeen take Scottish Cup for third successive season, win Scottish Championship, too. Tottenham win UEFA Cup on penalty shoot-out. Liverpool win European Cup on penalty shoot-out to complete unique treble with Milk Cup and League title (as well as Championship hat-trick). N. Ireland win the final British Championship. France win European Championship – their first honour. F.A. National Soccer School opens at Lilleshall. Britain's biggest score this century: Stirling Alb. 20, Selkirk 0 (Scottish Cup).

1985 Bradford City fire disaster – 56 killed. First £1m. receipts from match in Britain (F.A. Cup Final). Kevin Moran (Manchester Utd.) first player to be sent off in F.A. Cup Final. Celtic win 100th Scottish F.A. Cup Final. European Cup Final horror (Liverpool v Juventus, riot in Brussels) 39 die. UEFA ban all English clubs indefinitely from European competitions. No TV coverage at start of League season – first time since 1963 (resumption delayed until January 1986). Sept: first ground-sharing in League history – Charlton Athletic move from The Valley to Selhurst Park (Crystal Palace).

1986 Liverpool complete League and Cup double in player-manager Kenny Dalglish's first season in charge. Swindon Town (4th Div. Champions) set League points record (102). League approve reduction of First Division to 20 clubs by 1988. Everton chairman Philip Carter elected president of Football League. July 18, death of Sir Stanley Rous (91). 100th edition of *News of the World* Football Annual. League Cup sponsored for next three years by Littlewoods (£2m.). Football League voting majority (for rule changes) reduced from ¾ to ⅔. Wales move HQ from Wrexham to Cardiff City after 110 years. Two substitutes in F.A. Cup and League (Littlewoods) Cup. Two-season League/TV deal (£6.2m.):- BBC and ITV each show seven live League matches per season, League Cup semi-finals and Final. Football League sponsored by *Today* newspaper. Luton Town first club to ban all visiting supporters; as sequel are themselves banned from League Cup. Oldham Athletic and Preston N.E. install artificial pitches, making four in F. League (following Q.P.R. and Luton Town).

1987 May: League introduce play-off matches to decide final promotion/relegation places in all divisions. Re-election abolished – bottom club in Div. 4 replaced by winners of GM Vauxhall Conference. Two substitutes approved for Football League 1987-8. Red and yellow disciplinary cards (scrapped 1981) re-introduced by League and F.A. Football League sponsored by Barclays. First Div. reduced to 21 clubs.

1988 Football League Centenary. First Division reduced to 20 clubs.

1989 Soccer gets £74m. TV deal: £44m. over 4 years, ITV; £30m. over 5 years, BBC/BSB. But it costs Philip Carter the League Presidency. Ted Croker retires as F.A. chief executive; successor Graham Kelly, from Football League. Hillsborough disaster: 95 die at F.A. Cup semi-final (Liverpool v Nott'm. Forest). Arsenal win closest-ever Championship with last kick. Peter Shilton sets England record with 109 caps.

1990 Nott'm. Forest win last Littlewoods Cup Final. Both F.A. Cup semi-finals played on Sunday and televised live. Play-off finals move to Wembley; Swindon Town win place in Div. 1, then relegated back to Div. 2 (breach of financial regulations) – Sunderland promoted instead. Pools betting tax cut from 42½ to 40%. England reach World Cup semi-final in Italy and win F.I.F.A. Fair Play Award. Peter Shilton retires as England goalkeeper with 125 caps (world record). Graham Taylor (Aston Villa) succeeds Bobby Robson as England manager. Int. Board amend offside law (player 'level' no longer offside). F.I.F.A. make "pro foul" a sending-off offence. English clubs back in Europe (Manchester Utd. and Aston Villa) after 5-year exile.

1991 First F.A. Cup semi-final at Wembley (Tottenham 3, Arsenal 1). Bert Millichip (F.A. chairman) and Philip Carter (Everton chairman) knighted. End of artificial pitches in Div. 1 (Luton Town, Oldham Athletic). Scottish League reverts to 12-12-14 format (as in 1987-8). Penalty shoot-out introduced to decide F.A. Cup ties level after one replay.

1992 Introduction of fourth F.A. Cup (previous trophy withdrawn). F.A. launch Premier League (22 clubs). Football League reduced to three divisions (71 clubs). Record TV-sport deal: BSkyB/BBC to pay £304m. for 5-year coverage of Premier League. ITV do £40m., 4-year deal with F. League. Channel 4 show Italian football live (Sundays). F.I.F.A. approve new back-pass rule (goalkeeper must not handle ball kicked to him by team-mate). New League of Wales formed. Record all-British transfer, £3.3m.: Alan Shearer (Southampton to Blackburn Rov.). Charlton Athletic return to The Valley after 7-year absence.

1993 Barclays end 6-year sponsorship of F. League. For first time both F.A. Cup semi-finals at Wembley (Sat., Sun.). Arsenal first club to complete League Cup/F.A. Cup double. Rangers pull off Scotland's domestic treble for fifth time. F.A. in record British sports sponsorship deal (£12m. over 4 years) with brewers Bass for F.A. Carling Premiership, from Aug. Brian Clough retires after 18 years as Nott'm. Forest manager; as does Jim McLean (21 years manager of Dundee Utd.). Football League agree 3-year, £3m. sponsorship with Endsleigh Insurance. Premier League introduce squad numbers with players' names on shirts. Record British transfer: Duncan Ferguson, Dundee Utd. to Rangers (£4m.). Record English-club signing: Roy Keane, Nott'm. Forest to Manchester Utd. (£3.75m.). Graham Taylor resigns as England manager after World Cup exit (Nov.). Death in Feb. of Bobby Moore (51), England World-Cup winning captain 1966.

1994 Death of Sir Matt Busby (Jan.). Terry Venables appointed England coach (Jan.). Manchester Utd. complete the Double. Last artificial pitch in English football goes – Preston N.E. revert to grass, summer 1994. Bobby Charlton knighted. Scottish League format changes to four divisions of ten clubs. Record British transfer: Chris Sutton, Norwich City to Blackburn Rov. (£5m.). Sept: F.A. announce first sponsorship of F.A. Cup – Littlewoods Pools (4-year, £14m. deal, plus £6m. for Charity Shield). Death of Billy Wright, 70 (Sept).

1995 New record British transfer: Andy Cole, Newcastle Utd. to Manchester Utd. (£7m.). First England match abandoned through crowd trouble (v Rep. of Ireland, Dublin). Blackburn Rov. Champions for first time since 1914. Premiership reduced to 20 clubs. British transfer record broken again (June): Stan Collymore, Nott'm. Forest to Liverpool (£8½m.). Starting season 1995-6, teams allowed to use 3 substitutes per match, not necessarily including a goalkeeper. Dec: European Court of Justice upholds Bosman ruling, barring transfer fees for players out of contract and removing limit on number of foreign players clubs can field.

1996 Death in Feb. of Bob Paisley (77), ex-Liverpool, most successful manager in English Football. F.A. appoint Chelsea manager Glenn Hoddle to succeed Terry Venables as England coach after Euro 96. Manchester Utd. first English club to achieve Double twice (and in 3 seasons). Football League completes £125m., 5-year TV deal with BSkyB starting 1996-7. England stage European Championship, reach semi-finals, lose on pens to tournament winners Germany. Keith Wiseman succeeds Sir Bert Millichip as F.A. Chairman. Linesmen become known as "referees' assistants". Coca-Cola Cup experiment with own disciplinary system (red, yellow cards). Alan Shearer football's first £15m. player (Blackburn Rov. to Newcastle Utd.). Nigeria first African country to win Olympic soccer. Nationwide Building Society sponsor Football League in initial 3-year deal worth £5.25m. Peter Shilton first player to make 1000 League apps.

1997 Howard Wilkinson appointed English football's first technical director. England's first home defeat in World Cup (0-1 v Italy). Ruud Gullit (Chelsea) first foreign coach to win F.A. Cup. Rangers equal Celtic's record of 9 successive League titles. Manchester Utd. win Premier League for fourth time in 5 seasons. New record World Cup score: Iran 17, Maldives 0 (qual. round). Season 1997-8 starts Premiership's record £36m., 4-year sponsorship extension with brewers Bass (Carling).

1998 In French manager Arsene Wenger's second season at Highbury, Arsenal become second English club to complete the Double twice. Chelsea also win two trophies under new player-manager Gianluca Vialli (Coca-Cola Cup, Cup Winners' Cup). France win 16th World Cup competition. In breakaway from Scottish League, top ten clubs form new Premiership under SFA, starting season 1998-9. Football League celebrates its 100th season, 1998-9. New F.A. Cup sponsors – French insurance giants AXA (25m., 4-year deal). League Cup becomes Worthington Cup in £23m., 5-year contract with brewers Bass. Nationwide Building Society's sponsorship of Football League extended to season 2000-1.

1999 F.A. buy Wembley Stadium (£103m.) for £320m., plan rebuilding (Aug. 2000-March 2003) as new national stadium (Lottery Sports fund contributes £110m.) Scotland's new Premier League takes 3-week mid-season break in January. Sky screen Oxford Utd. v Sunderland (Div. 1, Feb. 27) as first pay-per-view match on TV. F.A. sack England coach Glenn Hoddle; Fulham's Kevin Keegan replaces him at £1m. a year until 2003. Sir Alf Ramsey, England's World Cup-winning manager, dies aged 79. With effect 1999, F.A. Cup Final to be decided on day (via penalties, if necessary). Hampden Park re-opens for Scottish Cup Final after £63m. refit. Alex Ferguson knighted after Manchester Utd. complete Premiership, F.A. Cup, European Cup treble. Starting season 1999-2000, UEFA increase Champions League from 24 to 32 clubs. End of Cup-Winners' Cup (merged into 121-club UEFA Cup). F.A. allow holders Manchester Utd. to withdraw from F.A. Cup to participate in FIFA's inaugural World Club Championship in Brazil in January. Chelsea first British club to field an all-foreign line-up at Southampton (Prem, Dec. 26). F.A. vote (December) in favour of streamlined 14-man board of directors to replace its 92-member council.

2000 Scot Adam Crozier takes over as F.A. chief executive, Jan. 1. Wales move to Cardiff City's £125m. Millennium Stadium (v Finland, March 29). Brent Council approve plans for new £475m. Wembley Stadium (completion target spring 2003); demolition of old stadium to begin after England v Germany (World Cup qual., Oct. 7). Fulham Ladies become Britain's first female professional team. F.A. Premiership and Nationwide League to introduce (season 2000-01) rule whereby referees advance free-kick by 10 yards and caution player who shows dissent, delays kick or fails to retreat 10 yards. Scottish football increased to 42 League clubs in 2000-01 (12 in Premier League and 3 division of ten; Peterhead and Elgin City elected from Highland League). France win eleventh European Championship – first time a major Int. tournament has been jointly hosted (Holland/Belgium). England's £10m. bid to stage 2006 World Cup fails; vote goes to Germany. England manager Kevin Keegan resigns (Oct. 7) after 1-0 World Cup defeat by Germany in Wembley's last International. Oct. 30: Lazio's Swedish coach Sven Goran Eriksson agrees to become England head coach.

2001 January: Scottish Premier League experiment with split into two 5-game mini leagues (6 clubs in each) after 33 matches completed. July: New transfer system agreed by FIFA/UEFA is ratified. August: Barclaycard begin £48m., 3-year sponsorship of the Premiership, and Nationwide's contract with the Football League is extended by a further 3 years (£12m.). ITV, after winning auction against BBC's Match of the Day, begin £183m., 3-season contract for highlights of Premiership matches; BSkyB's live coverage (66 matches per season) for next 3 years will cost £1.1bn. BBC and BSkyB pay £400m. (3-year contract) for live coverage of F.A. Cup and England home matches. ITV and Ondigital pay £315m. to screen Nationwide League and Worthington Cup matches. In new charter for referees, top men can earn up to £60,000 a season in Premiership. Real Madrid break world transfer record, buying Zinedine Zidane from Juventus for £47.2m. F.A. introduce prize money, round by round, in F.A. Cup.

2002 February: Scotland appoint their first foreign manager, Germany's former national coach Bertie Vogts replacing Craig Brown. April: Collapse of ITV Digital deal, with Football League owed £178m., threatens lower-division clubs. May: Arsenal complete Premiership/F.A. Cup Double for second time in 5 seasons, third time in all. June: Newcastle Utd. manager Bobby Robson knighted in Queen's Jubilee Honours. Brazil win World Cup for fifth time. July: New record British transfer and world record for defender, £28.25m. Rio Ferdinand (Leeds Utd. to Manchester Utd.). August: Transfer window introduced to British football. F.A. Charity Shield renamed F.A. Community Shield. September: After 2-year delay, demolition of Wembley Stadium begins. October: Adam Crozier, F.A. chief executive, resigns.

2003 January: F.A. Cup draw (from 4th. Round) reverts to Monday lunchtime. March: Scottish Premier League decide to end mid-winter shut-down. May: Mark Palios appointed F.A. chief executive. For first time, two Football League clubs demoted (replaced by two from Conference). June: Ban lifted on loan transfers between Premiership clubs. July: David Beckham becomes record British export (Man. Utd. to Real Madrid, £23.3m.). Biggest takeover in British football history – Russian oil magnate Roman Abramovich buys control of Chelsea for reported £150m. September: Wimbledon leave rented home at Selhurst Park, become England's first franchised club in 68-mile move to Milton Keynes.

2004 Arsenal first club to win Premiership with unbeaten record and only the third in English football history to stay undefeated through League season. June: Trevor Brooking knighted in Queen's Birthday Honours. Wimbledon change name to Milton Keynes Dons. July: Greece beat hosts Portugal to win European Championship as biggest outsiders (80-1 at start) ever to succeed in major Int. tournament. August: New contracts – Premiership in £57m. deal with Barclays, seasons 2004-07. Coca-Cola replace Nationwide as Football League sponsors (£15m. over 3 years), rebranding Div. 1 as Football League Championship, with 2nd. and 3rd. Divs. becoming Divs 1 and 2. After 3 years, BBC Match of the Day wins back Premiership highlights from ITV with 3-year, £105m. contract (2004-07).

ENGLISH LEAGUE ROLL-CALL

REVIEWS, APPEARANCES & SCORERS 2003-04

(Figures in brackets = appearances as substitute)

F.A. BARCLAYCARD PREMIERSHIP

ARSENAL

Immortality, Arsene Wenger's claim for his team, was by no means over the top. Arsenal remained unbeaten throughout the 38-match campaign to win the title for the second time in three years. The fact that they did it with such poise and panache meant the achievement took on even greater significance. A stoppage-time penalty miss by Ruud van Nistelrooy amid unpleasant scenes at Old Trafford proved a close thing. And back-to-back defeats by Manchester United in the F.A. Cup and Chelsea in the Champions League could have undermined them. But Thierry Henry hat-tricks against Liverpool and Leeds then left no room for doubt and his team finished 11 points clear of Chelsea. Henry claimed the Golden Boot with 30 goals, Robert Pires had another productive season, while Patrick Vieira was the heartbeat of a fine team.

Aliadiere, J .... 3(7)	Gilberto Silva .... 29(3)	Ljungberg, F .... 27(3)
Bentley, D 1	Henry, T 37	Parlour, R .... 16(9)
Bergkamp, D .... 21(7)	Hoyte, J .... –(1)	Pires, R .... 33(3)
Campbell, S 35	Kanu, N .... 3(7)	Reyes, J .... 7(6)
Clichy, G .... 7(5)	Keown, M .... 3(7)	Toure, K .... 36(1)
Cole, A 32	Lauren .... 30(2)	Vieira, P 29
Cygan, P .... 10(8)	Lehmann, J 38	Wiltord, S .... 8(4)
Edu .... 13(17)		

League goals (73): Henry 30, Pires 14, Bergkamp 4, Gilberto Silva 4, Ljungberg 4, Vieira 3, Wiltord 3, Edu 2, Reyes 2, Campbell 1, Kanu 1, Toure 1, Opponents 4.
F.A. Cup goals (15): Ljungberg 4, Henry 3, Reyes 2, Toure 2, Bentley 1, Bergkamp 1, Edu 1, Pires 1. **Carling Cup goals (9):** Aliadiere 4, Kanu 2, Edu 1, Fabregas, F 1, Wiltord 1. **Champions League goals (16):** Henry 5, Pires 4, Edu 3, Ljungberg 2, Cole 1, Reyes 1. **Community Shield goals (1):** Henry 1.
Average home League attendance: 38,079. **Player of Year:** Thierry Henry.

ASTON VILLA

David O'Leary breathed new life into a team that flirted uncomfortably with relegation during the previous season. From a low point of third from bottom after 13 matches, Villa climbed steadily and convincingly, missing out on a UEFA Cup spot only through a 2-0 home defeat by Manchester United in the final game. O'Leary insisted he would have settled for sixth place – and would be happy with a repeat in the campaign ahead. No-one responded more to the manager's guidance than Juan Pablo Angel, who scored 16 goals in the League and seven in the Carling Cup as Villa reached the semi-finals before losing to Bolton.

Allback, M .... 7(8)	Hadji, M .... –(1)	Moore, S .... 2(6)
Alpay .... 4(2)	Hendrie, L 32	Postma, S .... –(2)
Angel, J P 33	Hitzlsperger, T ...... 22(10)	Ridgewell, L .... 5(6)
Barry, G 36	Johnsen, R .... 21(2)	Samuel, J 38
Crouch, P .... 6(10)	Kinsella, M 2	Solano, N 10
De La Cruz, U .... 20(8)	McCann, G 28	Sorensen, T 38
Delaney, M .... 23(2)	Mellberg, O 33	Vassell, D .... 26(6)
Dublin, D .... 12(11)	Moore, L .... –(7)	Whittingham, P .... 20(12)

League goals (48): Angel 16, Vassell 9, Crouch 4, Barry 3, Dublin 3, Hitzlsperger 3, Hendrie 2, Samuel 2, Allback 1, Alpay 1, Johnsen 1, Mellberg 1, Moore, S 1, Opponents 1.
F.A. Cup goals (1): Barry 1. **Carling Cup goals (15):** Angel 7, Hitzlsperger 2, McCann 2, Samuel 1, Vassell 1, Whittingham 1, Opponents 1.
Average home League attendance: 36,622. **Player of Year:** Juan Pablo Angel.

BIRMINGHAM CITY

When Steve Bruce's side put four past Leeds at the end of March, they were within a point of a Champions League place and the manager was calling it 'nothing short of a miracle.' In the end it didn't happen, because on-loan Mikael Forssell's goals dried up and there were not enough coming from other areas. Birmingham did not win another match, but tenth place was still a commendable achievement in their second season of Premiership football, particular as record-signing David Dunn was injured for almost half of it. With Forssell staying for another season and new record-buy Emile Heskey brought in to play alongside him, Birmingham are determined to continue moving up in the world.

Barrowman, A ....–(1)	Dunn, D ....20(1)	Kirovski, J ....–(6)
Bennett, I ....4(2)	Figueroa, L ....–(1)	Lazaridis, S ....25(5)
Carter, D ....1(4)	Forssell, M 32	Morrison, C ...19(13)
Cisse, A ....5(10)	Grainger, M ....3(1)	Purse, D 9
Clapham, J ....22(3)	Horsfield, G ....2(1)	Savage, R 31
Clemence, S ....32(3)	Hughes, B ....17(9)	Taylor, Maik 34
Cunningham, K 36	John, S ....7(22)	Taylor, Martin ....11(1)
Devlin, P ....–(2)	Johnson, D 35	Tebily, O ....17(10)
Dugarry, C ....12(2)	Kenna, J ....14(3)	Upson, M 30

League goals (43): Forssell 17, John 4, Morrison 4, Hughes 3, Savage 3, Clemence 2, Dunn 2, Kenna 2, Lazaridis 2, Dugarry 1, Grainger 1, Johnson 1, Taylor, Martin 1.
F.A. Cup goals (6): Forssell 2, Hughes 2, Clemence 1, Morrison 1. **Carling Cup goals:** None.
Average home League attendance: 29,078. **Player of Year:** Mikael Forssell.

BLACKBURN ROVERS

A difficult season was threatening to become desperate when Blackburn succumbed to a tenth home defeat against Leeds, who joined them on 31 points as a result. But as relegation beckoned, they pulled off a dramatic 4-3 victory at Fulham thanks to a late goal by Jon Stead. Then, the 21-year-old, signed from Huddersfield for £1.2m., came up with the winner against both Everton and Manchester United, took his tally to six in 11 games and dragged his new side to safety. First stage defeats in the F.A. Cup, Carling Cup and UEFA Cup compounded the problems of a side who had lost Damien Duff and David Dunn and had Barry Ferguson and Lorenzo Amoruso struck by long-term injuries.

Amoruso, L ....11(1)	Flitcroft, G ....29(2)	Neill, L ....30(2)
Andresen, M 11	Friedel, B 36	Reid, S ....9(7)
Babbel, M ....23(2)	Gallagher, P .....12(14)	Short, C 19
Baggio, D ....–(9)	Grabbi, C ....–(5)	Stead, J 13
Cole, A ....27(7)	Gray, M 14	Taylor, M ....10(1)
Danns, N ....–(1)	Gresko, V ....22(2)	Thompson, D ......10(1)
Douglas, J 14	Jansen, M ....9(10)	Todd, A 19
Emerton, B ....31(6)	Johansson, N-E .....7(7)	Tugay ....30(6)
Enckelman, P 2	Mahon, A ....1(2)	Yorke, D ....15(8)
Ferguson, B ....14(1)		

League goals (51): Cole 11, Stead 6, Yorke 4, Amoruso 3, Babbel 3, Flitcroft 3, Gallagher 3, Emerton 2, Jansen 2, Neill 2, Tugay 1, Baggio 1, Douglas 1, Ferguson 1, Friedel 1, Gresko 1, Short 1, Thompson 1, Opponents 4.

F.A. Cup goals: None. **Carling Cup goals (3):** Yorke 2, Ferguson 1. **UEFA Cup goals (2):** Emerton 1, Jansen 1.
Average home League attendance: 24,376. **Player of Year:** Tugay.

BOLTON WANDERERS

Defeat by Middlesbrough in the Carling Cup Final took nothing away from a highly-satisfactory season for Bolton, whose eighth-place finish was the club's best for 44 years. Heavy defeats early on at Manchester United, Portsmouth and Manchester City did not augur well, but ironically it was the away form of Sam Allardyce's side that was to stand them in good stead. Eight victories came on their travels, including a particularly notable one at Stamford Bridge. There was also a record run of five victories at the end, and the satisfaction of being the only team not to have had a player sent off. Strangely, however, Jay-Jay Okocha was unable to decorate his considerable contribution with a single League goal.

Ba, I .... –(9)	Giannakopoulos,	Moreno, J .... 1(7)
Barness, A .... 11(4)	S .... 17(14)	N'Gotty, B .... 32(1)
Campo, I .... 37(1)	Howey, S .... 2(1)	Nolan, K 37
Charlton, S .... 28(3)	Hunt, N .... 28(3)	Okocha, J-J .... 33(2)
Davies, K 38	Jaaskelainen, J 38	Otsemobor, J 1
Djorkaeff, Y .... 24(3)	Jardel, M ....–(7)	Pedersen, H .... 19(14)
Facey, D .... –(4)	Laville, F 5	Thome, E .... 25(1)
Frandsen, P .... 22(11)	Little, G ....–(4)	Vaz Te, R .... –(1)
Gardner, R .... 20(2)		

League goals (48): Davies 9, Djorkaeff 9, Nolan 9, Pedersen 7, Campo 4, Giannakopoulos 2, N'Gotty 2, Frandsen 1, Hunt 1, Opponents 4.
F.A. Cup goals (2): Nolan 1, Shakes, R 1. **Carling Cup goals (15):** Jardel 3, Okocha 2, Giannakopoulos 2, Nolan 2, Pedersen 2, Davies 1, Djorkaeff 1, N'Gotty 1.
Average home League attendance: 26,795. **Player of Year:** Kevin Davies.

CHARLTON ATHLETIC

Hanging on to a European place was probably too much to ask of a side who have made something of a habit of falling away in the final quarter of the season. Charlton, however, could be happy with seventh, their highest in top-flight football for 51 years. Long-term injuries sidelined the likes of Richard Rufus, Gary Rowett and Kevin Lisbie, while the loss of Scott Parker to Chelsea was a major blow. On the plus-side, a hat-trick by Lisbie, when he was fit, in a 3-2 win over Liverpool and a 4-2 victory over Chelsea had The Valley rocking. With the £10m. received for Parker earmarked for general team-strengthening, the club look well-placed to make further progress.

Bartlett, S .... 13(6)	Hreidarsson, H 33	Perry, C .... 25(4)
Campbell-Ryce, J ...... –(2)	Jensen, C .... 27(4)	Powell, C .... 11(5)
Cole, C .... 8(13)	Johansson, J .... 16(10)	Rowett, G 1
Di Canio, P .... 23(8)	Kiely, D 37	Royce, S 1
Euell, J .... 24(7)	Kishishev, R .... 30(3)	Stuart, G .... 23(5)
Fish, M 23	Konchesky, P .... 17(4)	Svensson, M .... 1(2)
Fortune, J .... 21(7)	Lisbie, K .... 5(4)	Thomas, J .... –(1)
Holland, M 38	Parker, S 20	Young, L .... 21(3)

League goals (51): Euell 10, Holland 6, Bartlett 5, Cole 4, Di Canio 4, Jensen 4, Johansson 4, Lisbie 4, Stuart 3, Fortune 2, Hreidarsson 2, Parker 2, Perry 1.
F.A. Cup goals (2): Cole 1, Opponents 1. **Carling Cup goals (4):** Di Canio 1, Jensen 1, Lisbie 1, Parker 1.
Average home League attendance: 26,293. **Player of Year:** Dean Kiely.

CHELSEA

A season which began with football's biggest-ever spending spree ended with an emotional farewell to the man who had been the beneficiary of it – more than 40,000 fans acclaiming Claudio Ranieri on a lap of Stamford Bridge after the final match against Leeds. Ranieri took his side to the runners-up spot behind Arsenal and into the semi-finals of the Champions League. But it was not enough for owner Roman Abramovich or his chief executive Peter Kenyon, for whom the final straw proved to be Ranieri's tactical mistakes in the first leg of that semi-final against ten-man Monaco which left too much to do in the return. While some overseas signings failed to justify the outlay, England's Frank Lampard proved a model of consistency, playing in every Premiership, F. A. Cup and Champions League match and scoring 15 times. All eyes will be on Ranieri's replacement, Jose Mourinho, in the season ahead.

Ambrosio, M 8	Geremi .... 19(6)	Mutu, A .... 21(4)
Babayaro, C .... 5(1)	Gronkjaer, J .... 19(12)	Nicolas, A .... 1(1)
Bridge, W 33	Gudjohnsen, E .... 17(9)	Oliveira, F .... –(1)
Cole, J .... 18(17)	Hasselbaink, J .... 22(8)	Parker, S .... 7(4)
Crespo, H .... 13(6)	Huth, R .... 8(8)	Petit, E .... 3(1)
Cudicini, C 26	Johnson, G .... 17(2)	Stanic, M .... –(2)
Desailly, M 15	Lampard, F 38	Sullivan, N 4
Duff, D .... 17(6)	Makelele, C .... 26(4)	Terry, J 33
Gallas, W .... 23(6)	Melchiot, M .... 20(3)	Veron, J .... 5(2)

League goals (67): Hasselbaink 12, Crespo 10, Lampard 10, Gudjohnsen 6, Mutu 6, Duff 5, Johnson 3, Gronkjaer 2, Melchiot 2, Terry 2, Babayaro 1, Bridge 1, Cole 1, Geremi 1, Parker 1, Veron 1, Opponents 3.
F.A. Cup goals (8): Mutu 3, Gudjohnsen 2, Hasselbaink 1, Lampard 1, Terry 1. **Carling Cup goals (6):** Cole 2, Gudjohnsen 2, Hasselbaink 2. **Champions League goals (21):** Lampard 4, Gudjohnsen 3, Bridge 2, Crespo 2, Hasselbaink 2, Duff 1, Gallas 1, Gronkjaer 1, Huth 1, Johnson 1, Mutu 1, Opponents 1.
Average home League attendance: 41,234. **Player of Year:** Frank Lampard.

EVERTON

Twelve months earlier, all the talk was about David Moyes restoring some pride to the blue half of the city after a seventh-place finish. This time, the manager admitted to being 'embarrassed' by a troubled season in which Everton finished one above the relegation zone. The team were largely the same and a mid-table spot at the half-way point offered some promise. But only three more victories were secured. Goals became increasingly hard to come by and the last six matches yielded only two points, with a 5-1 last-day defeat by Manchester City confirming the manager's intention to undertake a rebuilding job during the summer.

Campbell, K .... 8(9)	Li Tie .... 4(1)	Radzinksi, T .... 28(6)
Carsley, L .... 15(6)	Linderoth, T .... 23(4)	Rooney, W .... 26(8)
Chadwick, N .... 1(2)	Martyn, N .... 33(1)	Simonsen, S 1
Clarke, P 1	McFadden, J .... 11(12)	Stubbs, A .... 25(2)
Ferguson, D .... 13(7)	Naysmith, G .... 27(2)	Unsworth, D .... 22(4)
Gravesen, T .... 29(1)	Nyarko, A .... 7(4)	Watson, S .... 22(2)
Hibbert, T .... 24(1)	Osman, L .... 3(1)	Weir, D .... 9(1)
Jeffers, F .... 5(13)	Pembridge, M 4	Wright, R 4
Kilbane, K .... 26(4)	Pistone, A .... 20(1)	Yobo, J .... 27(1)

League goals (45): Rooney 9, Radzinksi 8, Ferguson 5, Watson 5, Kilbane 3, Unsworth 3, Gravesen 2, Naysmith 2, Yobo 2, Campbell 1, Carsley 1, Osman 1, Opponents 3.
F.A. Cup goals (5): Ferguson 2, Jeffers 2, Kilbane 1. **Carling Cup goals (4):** Ferguson 2, Chadwick 1, Linderoth 1.
Average home League attendance: 38,837. **Player of Year:** Nigel Martyn.

FULHAM

Chris Coleman's Fulham derived considerable satisfaction in upsetting the odds. The manager was made a clear favourite to become the season's first casualty. His team were tipped by many to face a relegation struggle. Instead, they achieved the club's highest-ever placing of ninth, despite losing some impetus after leading scorer Louis Saha moved to Manchester United in mid-January with the side sixth. High-spot was a 3-1 victory at Old Trafford, where later their F.A. Cup run ended at the quarter-final stage after Steed Malbranque's penalty had threatened a second upset there. Another boost for supporters is a return home to a redeveloped Craven Cottage after two seasons at Loftus Road.

Boa Morte, L .... 32(1)	Harley, J .... 3(1)	Melville, A 9
Bocanegra, C 15	Hayles, B .... 10(16)	Pearce, I .... 12(1)
Bonnissel, J 16	Inamoto, J .... 15(7)	Pembridge, M .... 9(3)
Buari, M .... 1(2)	John, C .... 3(5)	Petta, B .... 3(6)
Clark, L 25	Knight, Z .... 30(1)	Pratley, D .... –(1)
Crossley, M 1	Leacock, D 3	Rehman, Z .... –(1)
Davis, S .... 22(2)	Legwinski, S .... 30(2)	Saha, L .... 20(1)
Djetou, M .... 19(7)	Malbranque, S 38	Sava, F .... –(6)
Goma, A 23	Marlet, S 1	Van der Sar, E 37
Green, A 4	McBride, B .... 5(10)	Volz, M .... 32(1)

League goals (52): Saha 13, Boa Morte 9, Malbranque 6, Davis 5, Hayles 4, John 4, McBride 4, Clark 2, Inamoto 2, Marlet 1, Pembridge 1, Sava 1.
F.A. Cup goals (9): Malbranque 2, Saha 2, Boa Morte 1, Davis 1, Hayles 1, Inamoto 1, McBride 1. **Carling Cup goals:** None.
Average home League attendance: 16,342. **Player of Year:** Edwin van der Sar.

LEEDS UNITED

If 2002-03 was a traumatic season at Elland Road, then this one was a whole lot worse. Record losses, managerial and boardroom upheavals, constant take-over talk and more player-sales were followed by relegation for a club who just three years earlier had been a power in Europe. Peter Reid was dismissed in November, Eddie Gray filled the caretaker role until the last game of the season and Kevin Blackwell became the latest in the hot-seat. Back-to-back victories over Leicester and Blackburn raised a flicker of hope that the drop could be avoided. But Mark Viduka's dismissal against Leicester deprived Leeds of his services in a crunch match against Portsmouth, and he was sent off again in a 4-1 defeat at Bolton which left them with no hope.

Bakke, E .... 8(2)	Harte, I .... 21(2)	Olembe, S .... 8(4)
Barmby, N .... 1(5)	Johnson, Seth .... 24(1)	Pennant, J .... 34(2)
Batty, D .... 10(2)	Johnson, Simon .... 1(4)	Radebe, L .... 11(3)
Bridges, M .... 1(9)	Kelly, G 37	Richardson, F .... 2(2)
Caldwell, S 13	Kilgallon, M .... 7(1)	Robinson, P 36
Camara, Z 13	Lennon, A .... –(11)	Roque Junior 5
Carson, S .... 2(1)	Matteo, D 33	Sakho, L .... 9(8)
Chapuis, C .... –(1)	McPhail, S .... 8(4)	Smith, A 35
Domi, D .... 9(3)	Milner, J .... 27(3)	Viduka, M 30
Duberry, M 19	Morris, J .... 11(1)	Wilcox, J 3

League goals (40): Viduka 11, Smith 9, Duberry 3, Milner 3, Johnson, Seth 2, Kilgallon 2, Matteo 2, Pennant 2, Bakke 1, Caldwell 1, Camara 1, Harte 1, McPhail 1, Sakho 1.
F.A. Cup goals (1): Viduka 1. **Carling Cup goals (4):** Roque Junior 2, Harte 1, Robinson 1.
Average home League attendance: 36,666. **Player of Year:** Alan Smith.

LEICESTER CITY

Forced to rely largely on free-transfers to bolster the side that came up, Leicester were always struggling to avoid relegation for the second time in three years. Their problems were compounded by the demoralising events at a training camp in La Manga and by a tendency to surrender what should have been points-winning leads. Losing 4-3 at Wolves, after being 3-0 up at half-time, and conceding two last-minute goals in a 3-3 draw at Middlesbrough were prime examples. At home, Leicester went six months without a win, an eventual 3-1 success over Portsmouth coming too late to save them. Few of that team will remain when Leicester start the new campaign back in Division One.

Benjamin, T .... 2(2)	Elliott, M .... 3(4)	McKinlay, W .... 15(1)
Bent, M .... 28(5)	Ferdinand, L .... 20(9)	Nalis, L .... 11(9)
Brooker, P .... –(3)	Freund, S .... 13(1)	Rogers, A .... 7(1)
Canero, P .... 2(5)	Gillespie, K .... 7(5)	Scimeca, R .... 28(1)
Coyne, D .... 1(3)	Guppy, S .... 9(6)	Scowcroft, J .... 33(2)
Curtis, J .... 14(1)	Heath, M 13	Sinclair, F .... 11(3)
Dabizas, N 18	Hignett, C .... 3(10)	Stewart, J .... 16(9)
Davidson, C .... 8(5)	Howey, S 13	Taggart, G 9
Deane, B .... –(5)	Impey, A .... 11(2)	Thatcher, B .... 28(1)
Dickov, P .... 28(7)	Izzet, M 30	Walker, I 37

League goals (48): Ferdinand 12, Dickov 11, Bent 9, Scowcroft 5, Izzet 2, Hignett 1, Howey 1, Nalis 1, Scimeca 1, Sinclair 1, Stewart 1, Thatcher 1, Opponents 2.
F.A. Cup goals (3): Bent 1, Dickov 1, Ferdinand 1. **Carling Cup goals (1):** Dickov 1.
Average home League attendance: 30,983. **Player of Year:** Les Ferdinand.

LIVERPOOL

Another modest season by Anfield's standards cost Gerard Houllier his job and brought in Valencia's Rafael Benitez to try to restore some of the good times. The task is a major one after Liverpool finished 30 points behind champions Arsenal and were grateful to claim the fourth Champions League place ahead of Newcastle. Had it not been for the efforts of Steven Gerrard, it is doubtful if they would have managed that. Gerrard, replacing Sami Hyypia as captain, almost ran himself into the ground in an effort to spark the team. Elsewhere, Liverpool fell to Portsmouth in the fifth round of the F.A. Cup and Marseille in round four of the UEFA Cup.

Baros, M .... 6(7)	Hamann, D 25	Murphy, D .... 19(12)
Biscan, I .... 27(2)	Henchoz, S .... 15(3)	Otsemobor, J 4
Carragher, J 22	Heskey, E .... 25(10)	Owen, M 29
Cheyrou, B .... 9(3)	Hyypia, S 38	Riise, J.A .... 22(6)
Diao, S .... 2(1)	Jones, P 2	Sinama-Pongolle, F . 3(12)
Diouf, E-H .... 20(6)	Kewell, H 36	Smicer, V .... 15(5)
Dudek, J 30	Kirkland, C 6	Traore, D 7
Finnan, S .... 19(3)	Le Tallec, A .... 3(10)	Welsh, J .... –(1)
Gerrard, S 34	Luzi, P .... –(1)	

League goals (55): Owen 16, Heskey 7, Kewell 7, Murphy 5, Gerrard 4, Hyypia 4, Smicer 3, Cheyrou 2, Hamann 2, Sinama-Pongolle 2, Baros 1, Opponents 2.
F.A. Cup goals (5): Cheyrou 2, Heskey 1, Murphy 1, Owen 1. **Carling Cup goals (6):** Heskey 2, Murphy 2, Kewell 1, Smicer 1. **UEFA Cup goals (14):** Kewell 3, Gerrard 2, Heskey 2, Owen 2, Baros 1, Hamann 1, Hyypia 1, Le Tallec 1, Traore 1.
Average home League attendance: 42,677.

MANCHESTER CITY

A remarkable F.A. Cup fourth round replay at White Hart Lane summed up City's topsy-turvy season. Trailing Tottenham 3-0 and reduced to ten men when Joey Barton was sent off, they stormed back to win 4-3 with a last-minute Jon Macken goal. In their new stadium, Kevin Keegan's side scored big wins over Aston Villa, Bolton, Everton and, most significantly, Manchester United. But interspersed with these results were many more indifferent performances. The pressure intensified with a run of seven matches without a win in late March and April, which left City looking nervously over their shoulder before victory over Newcastle left them safe.

Anelka, N	31(1)	James, D	17	Sommeil, D	18
Barton, J	24(4)	Jordan, S	–(2)	Stuhr-Ellegaard, K	2(2)
Berkovic, E	1(3)	Macken, J	7(8)	Sun Jihai	29(4)
Bosvelt, P	22(3)	McManaman, S	20(2)	Tarnat, M	32
Distin, S	38	Reyna, C	19(4)	Tiatto, G	1(4)
Dunne, R	28(1)	Seaman, D	19	Van Buyten, D	5
Elliott, S	–(2)	Sibierski, A	18(15)	Wanchope, P	12(10)
Fowler, R	23(8)	Sinclair, T	20(9)	Wright-Phillips, S	32(2)

League goals (55): Anelka 16, Fowler 7, Wright-Phillips 7, Wanchope 6, Sibierski 5, Tarnat 3, Distin 2, Barton 1, Macken 1, Reyna 1, Sinclair 1, Sommeil 1, Sun Jihai 1, Opponents 3.
F.A. Cup goals (12): Anelka 4, Macken 2, Bosvelt 1, Distin 1, Fowler 1, Sibierski 1, Tarnat 1, Wright-Phillips 1. **Carling Cup goals (4):** Wright-Phillips 2, Fowler 1, Macken 1.
UEFA Cup goals (12): Anelka 4, Fowler 1, Huckerby, D 1, Negouai, C 1, Sibierski 1, Sinclair 1, Sommeil 1, Sun Jihai 1, Wright-Phillips 1.
Average home League attendance: 46,834. **Player of Year:** Shaun Wright-Phillips.

MANCHESTER UNITED

Victory over Millwall in the F.A. Cup Final only partially compensated for Premiership and European disappointments in a season which brought almost as many problems off the field as on it. United were top, three points ahead of Arsenal in mid-season, but lost their defensive stability when Rio Ferdinand began an eight-month ban for missing a routine drugs test and were never the same force again. Nine League defeats told their own story. Even so, United were unlucky to go out of the Champions League at the first knock-out stage, Paul Scholes having a perfectly good goal disallowed by a Russian linesman and FC Porto sneaking through with a last-minute strike by Costinha. Major plusses were the growing maturity of Cristiano Ronaldo and Darren Fletcher.

Bellion, D	4(10)	Fortune, Q	18(5)	O'Shea, J	32(1)
Brown, W	15(2)	Giggs, R	29(4)	Ronaldo, C	15(14)
Butt, N	12(9)	Howard, T	32	Saha, L	9(3)
Carroll, R	6	Keane, R	25(3)	Scholes, P	24(4)
Djemba-Djemba, E	10(5)	Kleberson	10(2)	Silvestre, M	33(1)
Ferdinand, R	20	Neville, G	30	Solskjaer, O	7(6)
Fletcher, D	17(5)	Neville, P	29(2)	Van Nistelrooy, R	31(1)
Forlan, D	10(14)				

League goals (64): Van Nistelrooy 20, Scholes 9, Giggs 7, Saha 7, Forlan 4, Ronaldo 4, Keane 3, Bellion 2, Kleberson 2, Neville, G 2, O'Shea 2, Butt 1, Opponents 1.
F.A. Cup goals (15): Van Nistelrooy 6, Scholes 4, Ronaldo 2, Forlan 1, Silvestre 1, Opponents 1. **Carling Cup goals (3):** Bellion 1, Djemba-Djemba 1, Forlan 1. **Champions League goals (15):** Van Nistelrooy 4, Forlan 2, Fortune 2, Butt 1, Djemba-Djemba 1, Giggs 1, Neville, P 1, Scholes 1, Silvestre 1, Solskjaer 1.
Community Shield goals (1): Silvestre 1.
Average home League attendance: 67,641.

MIDDLESBROUGH

Middlesbrough's 128-year wait for a major trophy came to an end with victory in the Carling Cup and a place in Europe. A best-ever Premiership finish also beckoned until four defeats at the end of the season, the final one a 5-1 reversal at Portsmouth. It left Steve McClaren's side 11th and the manager promising to make every effort to bolster his attacking options with a major signing after too many points were dropped at home. High spot in the League came when Juninho, smallest player on the pitch, headed two goals in a 3-2 victory at Old Trafford, the day Manchester United started to lose ground on Arsenal.

Boateng, G	35	Cooper, C	17(2)	Doriva	19(2)
Christie, M	7(3)	Davies, A	8(2)	Downing, S	7(13)

Ehiogu, U 16	Mendieta, G .... 30(1)	Ricketts, M .... 7(16)
Greening, J .... 17(8)	Mills, D 28	Riggott, C .... 14(3)
Job, J-D .... 19(5)	Morrison, J .... –(1)	Schwarzer, M 36
Jones, B 1	Nash, C 1	Southgate, G 27
Juninho .... 26(5)	Nemeth, S .... 17(15)	Stockdale, R .... –(2)
Maccarone, M ..... 13(10)	Parnaby, S .... 8(5)	Wright, A 2
Marinelli,C 2	Queudrue, F 31	Zenden, B 31

League goals (44): Nemeth 9, Juninho 8, Job 5, Maccarone 6, Zenden 4, Mendieta 2, Ricketts 2, Christie 1, Greening 1, Marinelli 1, Southgate 1, Opponents 4.
F.A. Cup goals (3): Job 1, Zenden 1, Opponents 1. **Carling Cup goals (9):** Zenden 2, Christie 1, Job 1, Juninho 1, Maccarone 1, Mendieta 1, Ricketts 1, Opponents 1.
Average home League attendance: 30,398. **Player of Year:** Juninho.

NEWCASTLE UNITED

Newcastle's season-by-season progress under Sir Bobby Robson stalled after a dreadful start to the 2003-04 campaign and a run of injuries to key players at the end of it. They were always playing catch-up after failing to win any of their opening six matches, and also went out in the qualifying round of the Champions League to Partizan Belgrade. Alan Shearer's goals helped turn things round, but the loss of Craig Bellamy, Jonathan Woodgate, Kieron Dyer and Jermaine Jenas proved too big a handicap when they pursued the fourth Champions League spot and UEFA Cup success. Newcastle fell at the semi-final hurdle to Marseille, but had some consolation on the final day of the campaign when a draw at Anfield took them into next season's competition.

Ambrose, D .... 10(14)	Caldwell, S .... 3(2)	O'Brien, A .... 27(1)
Ameobi, S .... 18(8)	Chopra, M .... 1(5)	Robert, L .... 31(4)
Bellamy, C .... 13(3)	Dyer, K 25	Shearer, A 37
Bernard, O 35	Given, S 38	Solano, N .... 8(4)
Bowyer, L .... 17(7)	Griffin, A 5	Speed, G .... 37(1)
Bramble, T .... 27(2)	Hughes, A 34	Taylor, S 1
Bridges, M .... –(6)	Jenas, J .... 26(5)	Viana, H .... 5(11)
Brittain, M .... –(1)	LuaLua, L .... 2(5)	Woodgate, J 18

League goals (52): Shearer 22, Ameobi 7, Robert 6, Bellamy 4, Speed 3, Ambrose 2, Bowyer 2, Jenas 2, Bernard 1, Dyer 1, O'Brien 1, Opponents 1.
F.A. Cup goals (4): Dyer 2, Robert 2. **Carling Cup goals (1):** Robert 1. **Champions League goals (1):** Solano 1. **UEFA Cup goals (24):** Shearer 6, Bellamy 3, Ameobi 3, Bramble 3, Robert 3, Ambrose 1, Jenas 1, Speed 1, Opponents 1.
Average home League attendance: 51,440.

PORTSMOUTH

A catalogue of injuries coupled to a failure to win away from home threatened to send Portsmouth straight back to Division One. There were times when Harry Redknapp was struggling to name a full squad of senior players. Then the tide turned with a settled side and a single goal success over arch-rivals Southampton which launched a run of 21 points from their final ten matches, including victory over Manchester United which had the Pompey Chimes celebrating imminent survival. It ended with a 5-1 defeat of Middlesbrough, four of the goals coming from the Nigerian striker Aiyegbeni Yakubu, who took his tally to 11 in those ten games and 16 for the season.

Berger, P 20	Harper, K .... –(7)	Primus, L .... 19(2)
Berkovic, E .... 10(1)	Hislop, S 30	Quashie, N .... 17(4)
Burton, D .... –(1)	Hughes, R .... 8(3)	Roberts, J .... 4(6)
Curtis, J .... 5(1)	LuaLua, L .... 10(5)	Robinson, C .... –(1)
De Zeeuw, A 36	Mornar, I .... 3(5)	Schemmel, S .... 12(2)
Duffy, R .... –(1)	O'Neil, G 3	Sheringham, T ...... 25(7)
Faye, A 27	Pasanen, P .... 11(1)	Sherwood, T .... 7(6)
Foxe, H .... 8(2)	Pericard, V .... –(6)	Smertin, A .... 23(3)

Srnicek, P	 3	Taylor, M	..... 18(12)	Yakubu, A	..... 35(2)
Stefanovic, D	 32	Todorov, S	 1	Zivkovic, B	..... 17(1)
Stone, S	..... 29(3)	Wapenaar, H	 5		

League goals (47): Yakubu 16, Sheringham 9, Berger 5, LuaLua 4, Stefanovic 3, O'Neil 2, Stone 2, Berkovic 1, De Zeeuw 1, Foxe 1, Mornar 1, Quashie 1, Roberts 1.
F.A. Cup goals (7): Taylor 3, Hughes 1, Schemmel 1, Sheringham 1, Yakubu 1. **Carling Cup goals (9):** Roberts 3, Sherwood 2, Yakubu 2, Taylor 1, Opponents 1.
Average home League attendance: 20,108. **Player of Year:** Arjan De Zeeuw.

SOUTHAMPTON

Gordon Strachan's decision to take a sabbatical came with three months left of a season which opened with an unbeaten run of six matches but had then started to meander towards a mid-table position. His side also lost to Steaua Bucharest in the first round of the UEFA Cup and were soundly beaten at home by Newcastle in the F.A. Cup, a shortage of goals having proved an increasing problem. Paul Sturrock's move from Plymouth to replace Strachan seemed to have the biggest impact on Kevin Phillips. After struggling to recapture his old scoring form at Sunderland, Phillips blossomed to finish with 12 goals for the League campaign when providing much-needed support for James Beattie.

Baird, C	..... 1(3)	Griffit, L	..... 2(3)	Oakley, M	 7
Beattie, J	..... 32(5)	Hall, F	..... 7(4)	Ormerod, B	..... 14(8)
Blayney, A	 2	Higginbotham, D	.... 24(3)	Pahars, M	..... 6(8)
Crainey, S	 5	Jones, P	 8	Phillips, K	..... 28(6)
Cranie, M	.....	Kenton, D	..... 3(4)	Prutton, D	..... 22(5)
Delap, R	..... 26(1)	Le Saux, G	 19	Svensson, A	..... 17(13)
Delgado, A	..... –(4)	Lundekvam, C	 31	Svensson, M	 26
Dodd, J	..... 27(1)	Marsden, C	..... 9(4)	Telfer, P	..... 33(4)
Fernandes, F	..... 21(6)	McCann, N	..... 9(9)	Tessem, J	..... 1(2)
Folly, Y	 9	Niemi, A	 28		

League goals (44): Beattie 14, Phillips 12, Ormerod 5, Griffit 2, Pahars 2, Svensson, M 2, Delap 1, Fernandes 1, Lundekvam 1, Prutton 1, Opponents 3.
F.A. Cup goals: None. **Carling Cup goals (5):** Beattie 3, Le Saux 1, Ormerod 1. **UEFA Cup goals (1):** Phillips 1.
Average home League attendance: 31,703. **Player of Year:** Antti Niemi.

TOTTENHAM HOTSPUR

Tottenham's love affair with Glenn Hoddle ended six games into the season when Southampton, the club he left to return to White Hart Lane as manager, took great delight in winning 3-1 there. Under caretaker David Pleat, the campaign continued to slide and at the half-way point they were in the bottom three. The introduction of Jermain Defoe helped spark a run of five wins out of six during which the team were scoring for fun. But talk of a challenge for a place in Europe gave away to another slump, arrested only by wins over Blackburn and Wolves in the final two games. Surrendering a 3-0 lead to Manchester City and losing the F.A. fourth round replay 4-3 probably summed up their campaign. Supporters will be looking to Jacques Santini for a big improvement.

Anderton, D	..... 16(4)	Jackson, J	..... 9(2)	Postiga, H	..... 9(10)
Blondel, J	..... –(1)	Kanoute, F	..... 19(8)	Poyet, G	..... 12(8)
Brown, M	 17	Keane, R	..... 31(3)	Redknapp, J	..... 14(3)
Bunjevcevic, G	..... 3(4)	Keller, K	 38	Richards, D	 23
Carr, S	 32	Kelly, S	..... 7(4)	Ricketts, R	..... 12(12)
Dalmat, S	..... 12(10)	King, L	..... 28(1)	Taricco, M	..... 31(1)
Davies, S	 17	Konchesky, P	..... 10(2)	Yeates, M	 1
Defoe, J	..... 14(1)	Mabizela, M	..... –(6)	Zamora, R	..... 6(10)
Doherty, G	..... 16(1)	Marney, D	..... 1(2)	Ziege, C	..... 7(1)
Gardner, A	 33				

League goals (47): Keane 14, Defoe 7, Kanoute 7, Dalmat 3, Poyet 3, Davies 2, Anderton 1, Brown 1, Carr 1, Jackson 1, King 1, Mabizela 1, Postiga 1, Redknapp 1, Ricketts 1, Taricco 1, Opponents 1.
F.A. Cup goals (7): Kanoute 3, Doherty 1, Keane 1, King 1, Ziege 1. **Carling Cup goals (8):** Anderton 2, Kanoute 2, Keane 1, Postiga 1, Ricketts 1, Zamora 1.
Average home League attendance: 34,876. **Player of Year:** Robbie Keane.

WOLVERHAMPTON WANDERERS

From the opening day of the season, it was evident that promoted Wolves were in for a hard time. They kicked off with a 5-1 defeat at Blackburn and were four goals down to Charlton within 33 minutes of a Premiership debut at Molineux. There were the odd bright moments, notably when beating Leicester 4-3 after trailing 3-0 and overcoming Manchester United with a Kenny Miller goal. But although Dave Jones finally found a reliable strike partnership in Henri Camara and Carl Cort, his side scored fewer goals than any side. They were bottom at Christmas and a 2-0 defeat at Tottenham on the final day of the season meant they finished there on goal difference.

Andrews, K 1	Ganea, I .... 6(10)	Miller, K .... 17(8)
Blake, N .... 10(3)	Gudjonsson, J .... 5(6)	Murray, M 1
Butler, P 37	Ince, P 32	Naylor, L .... 37(1)
Camara, H .... 29(1)	Irwin, D .... 30(2)	Newton, S .... 20(8)
Cameron, C .... 25(5)	Iversen, S .... 11(5)	Oakes, M 21
Clyde, M .... 6(3)	Jones, P 16	Okoronkwo, I 7
Cooper, K .... –(1)	Kachloul, H .... –(4)	Rae, A .... 27(6)
Cort, C .... 13(3)	Kennedy, M .... 28(3)	Silas .... 2(7)
Craddock, J .... 31(1)	Luzhny, O .... 4(2)	Sturridge, D .... 2(3)

League goals (38): Camara 7, Cort 5, Rae 5, Cameron 4, Iversen 4, Ganea 3, Ince 2, Kennedy 2, Miller 2, Blake 1, Butler 1, Craddock 1, Opponents 1.
F.A. Cup goals (4): Miller 2, Ganea 1, Rae 1. **Carling Cup goals (5):** Rae 2, Craddock 1, Gudjonsson 1, Miller 1.
Average home League attendance: 28,874. **Player of Year:** Henri Camara.

NATIONWIDE LEAGUE – FIRST DIVISION

BRADFORD CITY

Bradford City greeted Bryan Robson with a stirring comeback against Millwall, overturning a two-goal, half-time deficit to win 3-2. Then, they presented the new manager with the stark reality of their situation by losing the next five games without scoring a goal. A surprise victory at leaders Norwich offered another glimmer of hope, but when the club went into administration for the second time at the end of February, relegation looked inevitable. Robson who had replaced Nicky Law, as manager, lost several players and his team lost touch with those directly above them to the extent that they finished the season 15 points adrift of safety.

Armstrong, A 6	Evans, P .... 20(3)	Paston, M 13
Atherton, P 27	Farrelly, G 14	Penfold, T .... 3(1)
Beresford, M 5	Forrest, D .... 2(11)	Sanasy, K .... 2(3)
Bower, M .... 11(3)	Francis, S .... 25(5)	Standing, M .... 2(4)
Branch, P .... 29(4)	Gavin, J .... 37(1)	Summerbee, N .... 33(2)
Cadamarteri, D ...... 14(4)	Gray, A 33	Vaesen, N 6
Combe, A 21	Heckingbottom, P 43	Wallwork, R 7
Cornwall, L .... 2(1)	Jacobs, W .... 11(2)	Wetherall, D 34
Davies, C .... 1(1)	Kearney, T .... 13(4)	Windass, D .... 34(2)
Edds, G .... 19(4)	McHugh, F 3	Wolleaston, R .... 6(8)
Emmanuel, L .... 18(10)	Muirhead, B .... 12(16)	

League goals (38): Branch 6, Windass 6, Gray 5, Wallwork 4, Cadamarteri 3, Evans 3, Atherton 2, Emanuel 2, Muirhead 2, Armstrong 1, Sanasy 1, Summerbee 1, Wetherall 1, Wolleaston 1.
F.A. Cup goals (1): Gray 1. **Carling Cup goals:** None.
Average home League attendance: 11,377. **Player of Year:** Paul Heckingbottom.

BURNLEY

Stan Ternent, third longest-serving manager in the division, paid the price for another frustrating season. A 3-0 defeat by Rotherham proved the final straw and Ternent was dismissed before the final game after six years in charge. With Robbie Blake scoring 19 times, his team had been generally good for goals, but only bottom-of-the-table Wimbledon conceded more. A 5-3 home defeat by Norwich, even allowing for the strength of the opposition, seemed to sum up the campaign, with Burnley surrendering the lead on three occasions. Ternent was replaced by the former Cheltenham and Stoke manager, Steve Cotterill.

Adebola, D	–(3)	Jensen, B	46	Orr, B	1(3)
Blake, R	44(1)	Johnrose, L	4(3)	Pilkington, J	–(1)
Branch, G	30(8)	Little, G	33(1)	Roche, L	21(4)
Camara, M	45	May, D	34(1)	Scott, P	–(2)
Chadwick, L	23(13)	McEveley, J	–(4)	Todd, A	7
Chaplow, R	30(9)	Moore, A	5(8)	Townsend, R	–(1)
Facey, D	12(2)	Moore, I	38(2)	Weller, P	22(8)
Farrelly, G	9(3)	McGregor, M	20(3)	West, D	25(7)
Gnohere, A	12(2)	O'Neill, M	–(4)	Wood, N	8(2)
Grant, A	34(3)				

League goals (60): Blake 19, Moore, I 9, Chadwick 5, Chaplow 5, Facey 5, May 4, Branch 3, Little 3, Adebola 1, Gnohere 1, McGregor 1, Roche 1, West 1, Wood 1, Opponents 1.
F.A. Cup goals (5): Moore, I 3, Blake 2. **Carling Cup goals (3):** Blake 1, Chadwick 1, Moore, I 1.
Average home League attendance: 12,541. **Player of Year:** Robbie Blake.

CARDIFF CITY

Robert Earnshaw enjoyed another productive season as Cardiff consolidated after winning promotion through the play-offs. The Wales striker scored four against Gillingham on his way to 21 for the season, despite a barren run of seven matches at the end of it. Peter Thorne's campaign was also moving along nicely, with a purple patch of nine goals in eight matches until injury ruled him out from late February onwards. And Paul Parry made an impression after stepping up from Conference football with Hereford, not only for his new club but also while Wales.

Alexander, N	24(1)	Earnshaw, R	44(2)	Margetson, M	22
Barker, C	33(6)	Fleetwood, S	–(2)	Maxwell, L	–(1)
Boland, W	33(4)	Gabbidon, D	41	Parry, P	14(3)
Bonner, M	14(6)	Gordon, G	7(8)	Prior, S	4(3)
Bowen, J	–(2)	Gray, J	5(4)	Robinson, J	31(3)
Bullock, L	4(6)	Kavanagh, G	27	Thorne, P	19(4)
Campbell, A	6(19)	Langley, R	39(5)	Vidmar, T	45
Collins, J	15(5)	Lee, A	17(6)	Weston, R	23(1)
Croft, G	23(4)	Lee-Barrett, A	–(1)	Whalley, G	16(6)

League goals (68): Earnshaw 21, Thorne 13, Kavanagh 7, Langley 6, Bullock 3, Gabbidon 3, Lee 3, Campbell 2, Robinson 2, Whalley 2, Collins 1, Croft 1, Gordon 1, Parry 1, Vidmar 1, Opponents 1.
F.A. Cup goals: None. **Carling Cup goals (6):** Earnshaw 5, Campbell 1.
Average home League attendance: 15,614. **Player of Year:** Tony Vidmar.

COVENTRY CITY

Three managers and a failed bid for the play-offs was the story of Coventry's season. Gary McAllister resigned in January to look after his sick wife, Eric Black was sacked two days after a 5-2 win at Gillingham in the penultimate match and Peter Reid came in with the task of turning the team into contenders for a move back to the Premiership in 2004-05. Under Black, they came within striking distance of a top-six place after a run of five wins in six matches. Then, one victory in the next seven, left them trailing and cost Black the job he had held for less than four months.

Adebola, D .... 15(13)	Jackson, J .... 2(3)	Olszar, S .... 1(4)
Arphexad, P 5	Joachim, J .... 27(2)	Pead, C .... 6(11)
Barrett, G .... 20(11)	Jorgensen, C .... 4(4)	Pitt, C 1
Clarke, P 5	Kerr, B .... 5(4)	Safri, Y 31
Davenport, C .... 31(2)	Konjic, M .... 36(6)	Shaw, R .... 11(8)
Deloumeaux, E 19	Lowe, O .... 1(1)	Shearer, C .... 29(1)
Doyle, M .... 38(2)	Mansouri, Y .... 9(5)	Staunton, S .... 34(1)
Giddings, S .... –(1)	McAllister, G 14	Suffo, P .... 20(7)
Gordon, D .... 3(2)	McSheffrey, G .... 16(3)	Ward, G 12
Grainger, M 7	Morrell, A .... 19(11)	Warnock, S .... 42(2)
Gudjonsson, B ...... 17(1)	O'Neill, K .... –(1)	Whing, A .... 26(2)

League goals (67): McSheffrey 11, Morrell 9, Joachim 8, Suffo 7, Doyle 5, Gudjonsson 3, McAllister 3, Staunton 3, Warnock 3, Adebola 2, Barrett 2, Jackson 2, Konjic 2, Deloumeaux 1, Lowe 1, Pead 1, Shaw 1, Whing 1, Opponents 2.
F.A. Cup goals (4): Joachim 3, McSheffrey 1. **Carling Cup goals (2):** Adebola 1, Barrett 1.
Average home League attendance: 14,816. **Player of Year:** Julian Joachim.

CREWE ALEXANDRA

Steve Jones and Dean Ashton proved one of the division's most prolific strike partnerships as Crewe had a mixed season on their return to the First Division. They contributed 34 goals for a side who climbed to ninth early in the New Year, but who started to slip after losing a bizarre match 6-4 at Ipswich. While Jones experienced a leaner time in front of goal from then on, Ashton claimed a hat-trick against Wigan and went on to score five times in the final six games when his team edged away from relegation trouble to finish 18th.

Ashton, D .... 43(1)	Jones, B .... 23(4)	Sorvel, N .... 26(5)
Barrowman, A .... 3(1)	Jones, S .... 43(2)	Symes, M .... 1(3)
Bell, L .... –(3)	Lunt, K .... 43(2)	Tomlinson, S .... –(1)
Brammer, D 16	McCready, C .... 15(7)	Tonkin, A .... 20(6)
Cochrane, J .... 37(2)	Moses, A .... 15(6)	Varney, L .... 5(3)
Edwards, P .... 2(8)	Rix, B .... 18(8)	Vaughan, D .... 29(2)
Foster, S 45	Roberts, J .... –(2)	Walker, R .... 17(3)
Higdon, M .... 7(3)	Robinson, J .... 1(8)	Williams, B 10
Hignett, C .... 11(4)	Smart, A .... –(6)	Wright, D 40
Ince, C 36		

League goals (57): Ashton 19, Jones, S 15, Lunt 7, Foster 2, Rix 2, Barrowman 1, Brammer 1, Higdon 1, Jones, B 1, Robinson 1, Symes 1, Varney 1, Walker 1, Wright 1, Opponents 3.
F.A. Cup goals: None. **Carling Cup goals (2):** Ashton 1, Jones, S 1.
Average home League attendance: 7,741. **Player of Year:** Steve Jones.

CRYSTAL PALACE

Even Iain Dowie could hardly believe it as Palace completed a rags-to-riches rise to the Premiership. They were 19th when Dowie left Oldham to become their sixth manager in just over three years, four days before Christmas. Five months later a transformed team were celebrating a 1-0 win over West Ham in front of a 72,000 Play-off Final crowd. Along the way they were indebted to Andrew Johnson's flood of goals, a last-minute

Brian Deane equaliser for West Ham at Wigan which enabled Palace to squeeze into sixth place, and a stoppage-time goal by substitute Darren Powell which sent their semi-final against Sunderland into extra-time and eventually to penalties.

Berthelin, C 17	Gray, J 24	Powell, D 10
Black, T .... 12(13)	Heeroo, G .... –(1)	Riihilahti, A .... 24(7)
Borrowdale, G ...... 14(9)	Hudson, M 14	Routledge, W ... 32(12)
Butterfield, D 45	Hughes, M 34	Shipperley, N 40
Clarke, M 4	Johnson, A .... 40(2)	Smith, J .... 13(2)
Derry, S .... 25(12)	Leigertwood, M ...... 7(5)	Soares, T .... –(3)
Edwards, R .... 6(1)	Mullins, H 10	Symons, K .... 12(3)
Fleming, C .... 15(2)	Myhre, T 15	Vaesen, N 10
Freedman, D ...... 20(15)	Popovic, T 34	Watson, B .... 8(8)
Granville, D 21		

Play-offs – appearances: Butterfield 3, Granville 3, Hughes 3, Johnson 3, Leigertwood 3, Popovic 3, Riihilahti 3, Routledge 3, Shipperley 3, Vaesen 3, Gray 2, Derry 1(2), Powell –(3), Freedman –(1).
League goals (72): Johnson 27, Freedman 13, Shipperley 8, Routledge 6, Butterfield 4, Granville 3, Gray 3, Hughes 3, Derry 2, Edwards 1, Popovic 1, Watson 1. **Play-offs – goals (5):** Shipperley 2, Butterfield 1, Johnson 1, Powell 1.
F.A. Cup goals: None. **Carling Cup goals (6):** Johnson 4, Freedman 2.
Average home League attendance: 17,344. **Player of Year:** Andrew Johnson.

DERBY COUNTY

Saddled with huge debts and having no money to spend in the transfer market, Derby were always going to be faced with another difficult season. Survival represented success and George Burley's mixture of emerging young talent, like Tom Huddlestone, and seasoned professionals achieved it with a point – and a superior goal difference – to spare. The key was their consistent form, since the turn of the year, at Pride Park, where eight out of 11 matches were won, including a 4-2 success against Nottingham Forest, watched by a crowd of more than 32,000, in which two goals by new-signing Paul Peschisolido took his tally to four in three outings.

Boertien, P .... 10(8)	Hunt, L 1	Oakes, A 10
Bolder, A .... 11(13)	Jackson, R .... 34(2)	Osman, L 17
Bradbury, L 7	Johnson, M 39	Peschisolido, P 11
Caldwell, G .... 6(3)	Junior .... 6(6)	Reich, M .... 9(4)
Costa, C .... 23(11)	Kenna, J 9	Svensson, M .... 9(1)
Dichio, D 6	Kennedy, P 5	Taylor, I 42
Doyle, N .... 1(1)	Labarthe Tome, G .... –(3)	Tudgay, M .... 20(9)
Edwards, R .... 10(1)	Manel .... 12(3)	Valakari, S .... 14(6)
Elliott, S .... 2(2)	Mawene, Y 30	Vincent, J 7
Grant, L 36	McLeod, I .... 4(6)	Walton, D .... 3(2)
Holmes, L .... 17(6)	Mills, P .... 13(6)	Whelan, N .... 3(5)
Huddlestone, T 42 (1)	Morris, L .... 21(2)	Zavagno, L .... 16(1)

League goals (53): Taylor 11, Tudgay 6, Morris 5, Junior 4, Peschisolido 4, Manel 3, Osman 3, Svensson 3, Holmes 2, Bolder 1, Costa 1, Dichio 1, Edwards 1, Johnson 1, Kennedy 1, McLeod 1, Reich 1, Vincent 1, Zavagno 1, Opponents 2.
F.A. Cup goals: None. **Carling Cup goals (1):** Taylor 1.
Average home League attendance: 22,199. **Player of Year:** Youl Mawene.

GILLINGHAM

Player-manager Andy Hessenthaler described it as the longest week of his long career – the time between a 5-2 home defeat by Coventry which had relegation written all over it and the last match of the season at Stoke that would decide his team's fate. As it was, Gillingham stayed up with a slightly superior goal difference after a goalless draw, while down the M6 Walsall's 3-2 win over Rotherham was not enough to keep them up.

Hessenthaler used six goalkeepers during an injury-hit season and it was the last of those, Steve Banks, who did most to earn that vital point with some outstanding saves.

Agyemang, P 20	Hessenthaler, A ...... 27(9)	Pouton, A .... 14(5)
Ashby, B .... 22(1)	Hills, J .... 27(2)	Rose, R .... 12(5)
Banks, S 13	Hirschfeld, L 2	Saunders, M .... 8(13)
Bartram, V 1	Hope, C 37	Shaw, P .... 20(1)
Benjamin, T .... 1(3)	James, K .... 12(5)	Sidibe, M .... 34(7)
Bossu, B .... 3(1)	Jarvis, M .... 2(8)	Smith, P .... 31(2)
Brown, J 22	Johnson, L .... 18(2)	Southall, N .... 34(1)
Brown, W 4	Johnson, T .... 6(9)	Spiller, D .... 32(7)
Cox, I .... 32(1)	King, M .... 9(2)	Vaesen, N 5
Crofts, A .... 1(7)	Nosworthy, N .... 26(1)	Wales, G .... 3(3)
Henderson, D 4	Perpetuini, D .... 14(6)	Wallace, R .... 10(4)

League goals (48): Agyemang 6, Shaw 6, Spiller 6, Sidibe 5, King 4, Hope 3, Johnson, T 3, Hessenthaler 2, Hills 2, Nosworthy 2, Perpetuini 2, Ashby 1, Benjamin 1, Brown, W 1, James 1, Saunders 1, Wales 1, Wallace 1.
F.A. Cup goals (4): Henderson 1, Johnson, T 1, Sidibe 1, Smith 1. **Carling Cup goals (4):** Hills 1, King 1, Nosworthy 1, Saunders 1.
Average home League attendance: 8,517. **Player of Year:** Danny Spiller.

IPSWICH TOWN

Bottom after six games and labelled by some critics the worst side in the club's history, Ipswich displayed commendable powers of recovery to force their way into the Play-offs at the end of a roller-coaster season. Darren Bent scored the only goal of the semi-final first leg, but West Ham proved too strong in the return at Upton Park, winning 2-0. Ipswich scored more times (84) than any team in the division, but also conceded more than most (72). A 6-4 win over Crewe captured their strengths and weaknesses, until the introduction of Matt Elliott from Leicester stemmed the flow of goals against to some extent.

Armstrong, A .... 5(2)	Kuqi, S .... 29(7)	Naylor, R .... 28(11)
Bart-Williams, C ..... 23(3)	Magilton, J 46	Price, L 1
Bent, D .... 32(5)	Mahon, A .... 7(4)	Reuser, M .... 3(14)
Bent, M 4	Makin, C 5	Richards, M .... 41(3)
Bowditch, D .... 7(9)	McGreal, J 18	Santos, G .... 28(6)
Counago, P .... 18(11)	Miller, T .... 27(7)	Westlake, I .... 30(9)
Davis, K 45	Mitchell, S .... –(2)	Wilnis, F 41
Diallo, M .... 16(3)	Nash, G .... –(1)	Wright, J .... 42(3)
Elliott, M 10		

Play-offs – appearances: Bent, D 2, Davis 2, Elliott 2, Magilton 2, Miller 2, Naylor 2, Richards 2, Westlake 2, Wilnis 2, Wright 2, Kuqi 1(1), McGreal 1, Armstrong –(1), Bart-Williams –(1), Bowditch –(1), Reuser –(1).
League goals (84): Bent, D 15, Counago 11, Kuqi 11, Miller 11, Westlake 6, Naylor 5, Wright 5, Bowditch 4, Reuser 3, Armstrong 2, Bart-Williams 2, Bent, M 1, Magilton 1, Mahon 1, McGreal 1, Richards 1, Santos 1, Opponents 2. **Play-offs – goals (1):** Bent, D 1.
F.A. Cup goals (4): Kuqi 1, Miller 1, Naylor 1, Reuser 1. **Carling Cup goals (2):** Bowditch 1, Counago 1.
Average home League attendance: 24,519. **Player of Year:** Ian Westlake.

MILLWALL

Millwall's first-ever F.A. Cup Final came at a price – and after a 3-0 defeat by Manchester United, player-manager Dennis Wise questioned whether it was one worth paying. When his side beat Sunderland in the semi-finals with a goal by Tim Cahill, they were not only in the top six but had games in hand on their rivals. But, distracted by the big day ahead, they failed to win any of the next seven games, and victory over Bradford on the final day of the season was not enough to restore a place in the Play-offs. Even so, Wise had exceeded all expectations after replacing Mark McGhee – and being sent off in his first match in charge.

Braniff, K .... 6(10)	Hearn, C .... 3(4)	Robinson, P .... 7(3)
Cahill, T 40	Ifill, P .... 29(4)	Robinson, T .... –(1)
Chadwick, N .... 11(4)	Juan .... 2(1)	Ryan, R .... 28(2)
Cogan, B .... –(3)	Lawrence, M .... 34(2)	Sadlier, R .... –(2)
Craig, T .... 8(1)	Livermore, D .... 35(1)	Sutton, J .... 2(2)
Dichio, D 15	Marshall, A 16	Sweeney, P .... 21(8)
Dolan, J .... –(1)	McCammon, M .... 3(3)	Ward, D 46
Dunne, A .... 4(4)	Muscat, K 27	Warner, T 28
Elliott, M .... 14(7)	Nethercott, S .... 11(3)	Weston, C .... –(1)
Fofana, A .... 9(7)	Peeters, B .... 16(4)	Whelan, N .... 8(7)
Gueret, W .... 2(1)	Quigley, M .... –(1)	Wise, D .... 26(5)
Harris, N .... 26(12)	Roberts, A .... 29(4)	

League goals (55): Cahill 9, Harris 9, Ifill 8, Dichio 7, Chadwick 4, Whelan 4, Peeters 3, Ward 3, Sweeney 2, Braniff 1, Livermore 1, Nethercott 1, Roberts 1, Wise 1, Opponents 1.

F.A. Cup goals (8): Cahill 3, Braniff 1, Dichio 1, Harris 1, Ifill 1, Wise 1. **Carling Cup goals:** None.

Average home League attendance: 10,496. **Player of Year:** Darren Ward.

NORWICH CITY

Honest, organised, hard-working – that was how Nigel Worthington described his championship-winning side. The description could also have been applied to the manager, who had targeted the Premiership in three years after being appointed in January 2001 and duly delivered. A rock-solid defence, unchanged for much of the season, proved the foundation for success, enabling Worthington to concentrate his efforts on strengthening other areas. The acquisition of Darren Huckerby, after a spell on loan, proved crucial, while Leon McKenzie and Matt Svensson came in to make valuable contributions. Eight wins in the last nine matches kept Norwich clear of all rivals, with veteran Iwan Roberts bowing out in style on the final day when scoring twice against Crewe.

Abbey, Z .... 1(2)	Francis, D .... 39(2)	McKenzie, L .... 12(6)
Brennan, J .... 7(8)	Green, R 46	McVeigh, P .... 36(8)
Briggs, K .... 1(2)	Hammond, E .... –(4)	Mulryne, P .... 14(20)
Cooper, K .... 6(4)	Harper, K 9	Nielsen, D 2
Crouch, P .... 14(1)	Henderson, I .... 14(5)	Notman, A .... –(1)
Drury, A 42	Holt, G 46	Rivers, M .... 7(5)
Easton, C .... 8(2)	Huckerby, D 36	Roberts, I .... 13(28)
Edworthy, M .... 42(1)	Jarvis, M .... –(12)	Shackell, J .... 4(2)
Fleming, C 46	Mackay, M 45	Svensson, M .... 16(4)

League goals (79): Huckerby 14, McKenzie 9, Roberts 8, Francis 7, Svensson 7, McVeigh 5, Crouch 4, Henderson 4, Mackay 4, Rivers 4, Fleming 3, Mulryne 3, Easton 2, Brennan 1, Holt 1, Jarvis 1, Opponents 2.

F.A. Cup goals (1): Brennan 1. **Carling Cup goals:** None.

Average home League attendance: 18,986. **Player of Year:** Craig Fleming.

NOTTINGHAM FOREST

The transformation in Forest's fortunes after the sacking of manager Paul Hart was remarkable. Joe Kinnear inherited a side sliding into the bottom three after going 14 matches without a win, and by the end of the season had experienced defeat in just two of his 17 games in charge. No wonder he did not want it to end. Kinnear began to coax goals out of Gareth Taylor and Marlon King, while the return of David Johnson from a broken leg showed how much he had been missed. Johnson scored five times in the last four fixtures, all against promotion-chasing teams, with more than 29,000 watching the last home game against Wigan.

Barmby, N 6	Impey, A .... 15(1)	Roche, B .... 6(2)
Bopp, E .... 9(6)	Jess, E .... 21(13)	Rogers, A 12
Cash, B .... –(1)	Johnson, D .... 10(7)	Sonner, D .... 19(9)
Chopra, M .... 3(2)	King, M .... 23(1)	Stewart, M .... 11(2)
Dawson, M 30	Louis-Jean, M ...... 37(1)	Taylor, G .... 28(6)
Doig, C .... 7(3)	McPhail, S .... 13(1)	Thompson, J .... 26(6)
Evans, P 8	Morgan, W .... 30(2)	Walker, D .... 23(2)
Gardner, R .... 1(1)	Oyen, D 4	Ward, D 32
Gerrard, P 8	Reid, A 46	Westcarr, C .... –(3)
Gunnarsson, B ..... 9(4)	Robertson, G ...... 12(4)	Williams, G .... 38(1)
Harewood, M 19		

League goals (61): Reid 13, Harewood 12, Taylor 8, Johnson 7, Williams 6, King 5, Jess 2, Morgan 2, Barmby 1, Bopp 1, Dawson 1, Impey 1, Louis-Jean 1, Thompson 1.
F.A. Cup goals (1): King 1. **Carling Cup goals (2):** Bopp 2.
Average home League attendance: 24,750. **Player of Year:** Andy Reid.

PRESTON NORTH END

A productive mid-winter run of seven unbeaten matches, starting with a 4-1 win over Crystal Palace and ending with a 2-1 success at West Ham, lifted Craig Brown's side to fifth in the table. But after injuries began to take their toll and the defence starting leaking goals, such results became harder to come by. West Bromwich Albion were seen off 3-0, but after beating Reading in early March, Preston won only one of their final 13 matches – against struggling Bradford – and finished below half-way.

Abbott, P .... 2(7)	Fuller, R .... 37(11)	Lucas, D .... 1(1)
Alexander, G 45	Gemmill, S 7	Lucketti, C 37
Briscoe, L 2	Gould, J 37	Lynch, S .... 6(12)
Broomes, M 30	Healy, D .... 27(11)	McCormack, A .... 2(3)
Burley, C .... 1(3)	Jackson, Mark ...... –(1)	McKenna, P 39
Cartwright, L ...... 2(10)	Jackson, Michael ... 41(3)	Mears, T .... 11(1)
Cresswell, R .... 41(4)	Keane, M .... 21(9)	O'Neil, N .... 27(2)
Davis, C .... 16(6)	Koumantarakis, G .... 1(6)	Skora, E .... –(2)
Edwards, R .... 16(8)	Lewis, E .... 26(7)	Smith, J .... –(5)
Etuhu, D .... 23(8)	Lonergan, A 8	

League goals (69): Fuller 17, Healy 15, Alexander 9, Lewis 6, McKenna 6, Etuhu 3, Abbott 2, Cresswell 2, Davis 1, Gemmill 1, Keane 1, Koumantarakis 1, Lucketti 1, Lynch 1, Mears 1, O'Neil 1, Opponents 1.
F.A. Cup goals (6): Fuller 2, Cresswell 1, Etuhu 1, Koumantarakis 1, O'Neil 1. **Carling Cup goals:** None.
Average home League attendance: 14,150. **Player of Year:** David Healy.

READING

Between Alan Pardew's controversial departure for West Ham and the arrival of Brighton's Steve Coppell as his replacement, Reading won only one of six matches. The sequence undermined their bright start to the season, and at the end of it there were supporters arguing that it had cost the team a place in the Play-offs. Certainly, there was no escaping the fact that they came within four points of the top six. At the same time, Reading did not score enough goals, particularly in the final half-dozen games after a sweet home win over West Ham had offered them every chance of qualifying.

Ashdown, J 10	Daley, O .... –(6)	Hahnemann, M 36
Brooker, P .... 5(6)	Forster, N .... 28(2)	Harper, J .... 35(4)
Brown, S 19	Goater, S .... 30(4)	Henderson, D .... –(1)
Butler, M .... –(3)	Gordon, D .... –(3)	Hughes, A .... 42(1)

Ingimarsson, I .... 24(1)	Newman, R .... 25(5)	Sidwell, S 43
Kitson, D .... 10(7)	Owusu, L .... 11(5)	Tyson, N .... –(8)
Mackie, J .... 7(2)	Salako, J .... 32(5)	Watson, K .... 10(12)
Morgan, D .... 3(10)	Savage, B .... 6(9)	Williams, A 33
Murray, S .... 25(9)	Shorey, N 35	Young, J .... –(1)
Murty, G .... 37(1)		

League goals (55): Goater 12, Sidwell 8, Forster 7, Kitson 5, Murray 5, Owusu 4, Hughes 3, Salako 3, Shorey 2, Harper 1, Ingimarsson 1, Mackie 1, Morgan 1, Williams 1, Opponents 1.
F.A. Cup goals (4): Goater 2, Opponents 2. **Carling Cup goals (7):** Forster 4, Harper 1, Salako 1, Sidwell 1.
Average home League attendance: 15,095. **Player of Year:** Graeme Murty.

ROTHERHAM UNITED

Another scramble for survival was on the cards when Rotherham scored only once in their opening seven matches, albeit a Darren Byfield goal which accounted for West Ham. But Ronnie Moore again pulled it off with the help of several signings during the course of the season, among them Martin Butler who gave their attack a much-needed edge. His two goals in a 3-0 win over Stoke lifted spirits. Then a run of 20 points from eight matches up to Boxing Day eased his team clear of the bottom three. Butler netted a hat-trick in a 4-4 draw with Norwich and finished with 15 to his credit after four in four games at the end ensured they stayed clear of trouble.

Barker, R .... 12(20)	Hurst, P .... 23(5)	Proctor, M .... 16(1)
Barker, S 36	Lee, A 1	Robins, M .... 2(7)
Baudet, J .... 8(3)	McIntosh, M 18	Robinson, C 14
Branston, G .... 7(1)	Minto, S .... 28(4)	Scott, R .... 8(2)
Butler, M .... 36(1)	Monkhouse, A ...... 17(10)	Sedgwick, C 40
Byfield, D .... 26(2)	Montgomery, G .... 3(1)	Stockdale, R 16
Daws, N .... 3(1)	Morris, J .... 9(1)	Swailes, C 43
Garner, D .... 10(3)	Mullin, J .... 35(3)	Talbot, S .... 19(4)
Gilchrist, P 10	Pollitt, M 43	Warne, P .... 23(12)
Hoskins, W .... –(4)		

League goals (53): Butler 15, Byfield 7, Proctor 6, Mullin 4, Monkhouse 3, Swailes 3, Barker, S 2, Hoskins 2, McIntosh 2, Sedgwick 2, Barker, R 1, Hurst 1, Morris 1, Stockdale 1, Talbot 1, Warne 1, Opponents 1.
F.A. Cup goals (2): Barker, R 1, Hurst 1. **Carling Cup goals (4):** Sedgwick 2, Byfield 1, Swailes 1.
Average home League attendance: 7,137. **Player of Year:** Shaun Barker.

SHEFFIELD UNITED

Maintaining the momentum from a season in which they reached they reached the Final of the Play-offs and the semi-finals of both the F.A. Cup and Worthington Cup was always going to be difficult. The loss of Neil Warnock's No 2, Kevin Blackwell, and midfield man Michael Brown also had to be overcome. Yet United maintained a promotion push until faltering during the run-in and finishing two points away from the top six. There was another good F.A. Cup run, with victories over Cardiff, Nottingham Forest and Colchester before a 1-0 defeat at Sunderland in the sixth round.

Allison, W .... 14(25)	Francis, S .... 4(1)	Lester, J .... 25(7)
Armstrong, C .... 4(8)	Gerrard, P 16	McCall, S 37
Baxter, L 1	Gray, A 14	McLeod, I .... 1(6)
Boussatta, D .... 3(3)	Harley, J 5	Montgomery, N ...... 32(4)
Brown, M .... 14(1)	Jagielka, P 43	Morgan, C 32
Cryan, C .... –(1)	Kabba, S .... –(1)	Ndlovu, P .... 28(8)
Fettis, A .... 2(1)	Kenny, P 27	Page, R 30
Forte, J .... 1(6)	Kozluk, R 42	Parkinson, A .... 3(4)

Peschisolido, P .... 12(15) Shaw, P .... 4(9)   Ward, A .... 20(3)
Rankine, M .... 6(7) Sturridge, D .... 2(2)   Whitlow, M .... 13(4)
Robinson, C .... 4(1) Tonge, M 46   Wright, A 21
Sestanovich, A .... –(2)

League goals (65): Lester 12, Gray 9, Ndlovu 9, Peschisolido 8, Gray 7, Tonge 4, Ward 4, Jagielka 3, Montgomery 3, Brown 2, McCall 2, Allison 1, Armstrong 1, Kozluk 1, Morgan 1, Page 1, Shaw 1, Whitlow 1, Wright 1, Opponents 1.
F.A. Cup goals (5): Allison 2, Lester 1, Morgan 1, Peschisolido 1. **Carling Cup goals (2):** Lester 2.
Average home League attendance: 21,645. **Player of Year:** Chris Morgan.

STOKE CITY

Having saved a struggling side from an immediate return to Division Two in the previous season, Tony Pulis enjoyed another satisfactory achievement as Stoke finished in the top half of the table. Pulis brought in, among others, Gifton Noel-Williams and Carl Asaba to operate a muscular strike force in tandem with Ade Akinbiyi. Between them, they scored enough goals to reach the fringes of the top six before running dry in the final quarter of the campaign. The best scoring performance, however, came from Peter Hoekstra, whose hat-trick delivered a 3-0 win over Reading.

Akinbiyi, A .... 23(7)   Hall, M .... 34(1)   Owen, G .... 1(2)
Andrews, K 16   Halls, J 34   Palmer, J .... –(3)
Asaba, C .... 26(11)   Henry, K .... 14(6)   Richardson, F 6
Clarke, C .... 41(1)   Hill, C .... 9(3)   Russell, D 46
Commons, K .... 14(19)   Hoekstra, P .... 20(4)   Svard, S .... 9(4)
Cutler, N .... 9(4)   Iwelumo, C .... 3(6)   Taggart, G 21
De Goey, E 37   Johnson, R .... 3(4)   Thomas, W 39
Eustace, J 26   Marteinsson, P 3   Wilkinson, A .... 1(2)
Goodfellow, M .... –(4)   Neal, L .... 6(13)   Williams, P .... 16(3)
Greenacre, C .... 8(5)   Noel-Williams, G .... 40(2)   Wilson, B .... –(2)
Gunnarsson, B .... 1(2)

League goals (58): Akinbiyi 10, Noel-Williams 10, Asaba 8, Eustace 5, Commons 4, Hoekstra 4, Russell 4, Clarke 3, Thomas 3, Greenacre 2, Taggart 2, Neal 1, Richardson 1, Svard 1.
F.A. Cup goals (1): Eustace 1. **Carling Cup goals (2):** Goodfellow 1, Iwelumo 1.
Average home League attendance: 14,424. **Player of Year:** Ade Akinbiyi.

SUNDERLAND

Sunderland regrouped after relegation and the departure of players like Kevin Phillips, Michael Gray, Claudio Reyna and Tore Andre Flo. They proved the most consistent side after Norwich and West Bromwich Albion and were seconds away from the Final of the Play-offs when Darren Powell scrambled a goal to give Crystal Palace the impetus for a successful penalty shoot-out. In the F.A. Cup, Tommy Smith's goals were the key to progress to the semi-finals with wins over Hartlepool – in front of a 40,000 crowd at the Stadium of Light – Ipswich, Birmingham and Sheffield United, before missed chances contributed heavily to a 1-0 defeat by Millwall.

Arca, J 31   Gray, M .... –(1)   Poom, M 43
Babb, P 22   Healy, C .... 16(4)   Proctor, M .... 4(13)
Bjorklund, J .... 19(6)   James, C 1   Quinn, S .... 5(1)
Black, C .... –(1)   Kilbane, K 5   Robinson, C .... 6(1)
Breen, G 32   Kyle, K .... 36(8)   Smith, T .... 22(13)
Butler, T .... 7(5)   McAteer, J 18   Stewart, M .... 28(12)
Byfield, D .... 8(9)   McCartney, G ...... 40(1)   Thirlwell, P .... 21(8)
Clark, B .... 2(3)   Myhre, T .... 3(1)   Thornton, S .... 14(8)
Cooper, C .... –(4)   Oster, J .... 35(3)   Whitley, J 33
Downing, S 7   Piper, M .... 4(5)   Williams, D .... 24(5)

Wright, S .... 20(2)

Play-offs – appearances: Babb 2, Breen 2, Kyle 2, McAteer 2, McCartney 2, Oster 2, Poom 2, Stewart 2, Whitley 2, Bjorklund 1(1), Thornton 1(1), Robinson 1(1), Williams 1, Smith –(2).
League goals (62): Stewart 14, Kyle 10, Byfield 5, Oster 5, Arca 4, Breen 4, Smith 4, Thornton 4, Downing 3, McAteer 2, Whitley 2, Poom 1, Proctor 1, Robinson 1, Wright 1, Opponents 1. **Play-offs – goals (4):** Kyle 2, Stewart 2.
F.A. Cup goals (7): Smith 4, Arca 2, Kyle 1. **Carling Cup goals (4):** Kyle 3, Opponents 1.
Average home League attendance: 27,119. **Player of Year:** Julio Arca.

WALSALL

Walsall celebrated on the opening day of the season after a 4-1 win over West Bromwich Albion. They were drowning their sorrows when it drew to a close, with two penalties conceded and a player sent off in a 3-2 victory over Rotherham which proved not enough to prevent relegation on goal difference because of the point gained by Gillingham at Stoke. Five successive defeats when safety looked to have been secured were the problem. Colin Lee was sacked after the second of those for talking to Plymouth about their managerial vacancy, Paul Merson taking temporary charge before being confirmed in the job

Andrews, K 10	Dinning, T .... 2(3)	Osborn, S .... 39(4)
Aranalde, Z .... 29(7)	Emblen, N .... 27(12)	Petterson, A 3
Baird, C 10	Fryatt, M .... 4(7)	Ritchie, P 33
Bazeley, D .... 35(4)	Hay, D .... 14(2)	Roper, I 33
Bennett, J .... –(1)	Lawrence, J .... 8(9)	Samways, V 29
Birch, G .... 25(10)	Leitao, J .... 29(10)	Taylor, K .... 5(6)
Bradbury, L .... 7(1)	Matias, P .... 6(9)	Vincent, J 12
Burley, C 5	McSporran, J .... 2(4)	Wales, G .... 5(2)
Burton, D .... 2(1)	Merson, P .... 31(3)	Walker, J 43
Carbon, M .... 7(1)	O'Neil, G 7	Wrack, D .... 23(4)
Corica, S .... 17(2)	Oakes, S .... 1(4)	Wright, M .... 3(8)

League goals (45): Leitao 7, Wrack 6, Emblen 5, Birch 4, Merson 4, Osborn 3, Andrews 2, Corica 2, Samways 2, Wright 2, Bradbury 1, Fryatt 1, Lawrence 1, Matias 1, Ritchie 1, Taylor 1, Wales 1, Opponents 1.
F.A. Cup goals (1): Leitao 1. **Carling Cup goals (3):** Merson 2, Leitao 1.
Average home League attendance: 7,852. **Player of Year:** Paul Ritchie.

WATFORD

The death in a car crash of 21-year-old Jimmy Davis on the eve of the season cast a shadow over the club. So too did only one win in their first nine matches after the opening fixture against Coventry had been postponed as a mark of respect for the on-loan Manchester United player. It remained a difficult season, but Watford gathered sufficient victories against other teams in the bottom half of the table to steer clear of trouble. High spots were a 2-1 win at Norwich and a third round F.A. Cup tie against Chelsea, who were held 2-2 at Vicarage Road before winning the replay 4-0.

Ardley, N .... 35(3)	Dyche, S .... 22(3)	Mahon, G 32
Baird, C 8	Dyer, B .... 18(13)	Mayo, P 12
Blizzard, D .... 1(1)	Fisken, G .... –(1)	McNamee, A .... –(2)
Bouazza, H .... 6(3)	Fitzgerald, S .... 28(16)	Pidgeley, L .... 26(1)
Brown, W 12	Gayle, M 32	Robinson, P 10
Chamberlain, A .... 20(1)	Hand, J .... 16(6)	Smith, J .... 16(1)
Cook, L .... 20(21)	Helguson, H .... 20(2)	Vernazza, P .... 17(12)
Cox, N 35	Hyde, M .... 28(5)	Webber, D .... 24(3)
Devlin, P 39	Ifil, J .... 9(1)	Young, A .... –(5)
Doyley, L .... 7(2)	Kelly, S 13	

League goals (54): Fitzgerald 10, Helguson 8, Cook 7, Webber 5, Cox 4, Devlin 3, Dyer 3, Young 3, Mahon 2, Smith 2, Ardley 1, Blizzard 1, Bouazza 1, Gayle 1, Hyde 1, Opponents 2.
F.A. Cup goals (2): Helguson 1, Mahon 1. **Carling Cup goals (1):** Fitzgerland 1.
Average home League attendance: 14,943. **Player of Year:** Gavin Mahon.

WEST BROMWICH ALBION

Gary Megson led the club straight back to the Premiership and believes they are much better equipped for the task of staying there than the first time around. The season had an inauspicious start with a 4-1 defeat at Walsall, but for most of it Albion and Norwich were having their own private duel for the championship, which was still in doubt with three games left. Megson's side then faltered, losing to Reading, Stoke and Nottingham Forest, while Norwich stayed on course to finish eight points clear of their rivals. For drama, nothing matched Albion's 4-3 win at West Ham after trailing 3-0 inside 20 minutes.

Berthe, S .... 2(1)	Haas, B 36	Murphy, J .... 2(2)
Chambers, J .... 14(3)	Horsfield, G 20	N'Dour, A 2
Clement, N .... 25(10)	Hoult, R 44	O'Connor, A .... 27(3)
Dichio, D .... 5(6)	Hughes, L .... 21(11)	Robinson, P .... 30(1)
Dobie, S .... 14(17)	Hulse, R .... 29(4)	Sakiri, A .... 6(19)
Dyer, L .... 2(15)	Johnson, A .... 33(5)	Sigurdsson, L 5
Facey, D .... 2(7)	Kinsella, M .... 15(3)	Skoubo, M .... –(2)
Gaardsoe, T 45	Koumas, J .... 37(5)	Volmer, L .... 10(5)
Gilchrist, P .... 16(1)	Moore, D .... 20(2)	Wallwork, R .... 4(1)
Gregan, S .... 40(3)		

League goals (64): Hughes 11, Hulse 10, Koumas 10, Horsfield 7, Dobie 5, Gaardsoe 4, Clement 2, Dyer 2, Johnson 2, Moore 2, Gregan 1, Haas 1, Kinsella 1, Sakiri 1, Opponents 5.
F.A. Cup goals: None. **Carling Cup goals (10):** Hulse 3, Dobie 2, Haas 2, Clement 1, Hughes 1, Opponents 1.
Average home League attendance: 24,764. **Player of Year:** Thomas Gaardsoe.

WEST HAM UNITED

A season which offered the prospect of an immediate return to the Premiership and a measure of financial salvation ended in bitter disappointment. West Ham were second best to a resurgent Crystal Palace in the Play-off Final, leaving Alan Pardew with the prospect of another rebuilding job at Upton Park. Pardew's first came with his arrival, in acrimonious circumstances, from Reading after Glenn Roeder's dismissal and Trevor Brooking's spell as caretaker. He brought in nine new players, selling David James and Jermain Defoe along the way, and although never seriously threatening to close the gap on Norwich and West Bromwich Albion, West Ham looked a good bet for the third promotion place.

Alexandersson, N ...... 5(3)	Garcia, R .... 2(5)	Mullins, H 27
Brevett, R 2	Harewood, M 28	Noble, D .... –(3)
Bywater, S 17	Harley, J 15	Nowland, A .... 2(9)
Carole, S .... –(1)	Horlock, K .... 23(4)	Pearce, I 24
Carrick, M .... 34(1)	Hutchison, D .... 10(14)	Quinn, W 22
Cohen, G .... 1(6)	James, D 27	Reo-Coker, N .... 13(2)
Connolly, D .... 37(2)	Kilgallon, M .... 1(2)	Repka, T 40
Dailly, C 43	Lee, K .... 12(4)	Sofiane, Y .... –(1)
Deane, B .... 9(17)	Lomas, S 5	Srnicek, P .... 2(1)
Defoe, J 19	McAnuff, J .... 4(8)	Stockdale, R .... 5(2)
Etherington, M ...... 34(1)	Mellor, N .... 8(8)	Zamora, R .... 15(2)
Ferdinand, A .... 9(11)	Melville, A .... 11(3)	

Play-offs – appearances: Bywater 3, Carrick 3, Connolly 3, Dailly 3, Etherington 3, Harewood 3, Lomas 3, Melville 3, Mullins 3, Repka 3, Zamora 3, Deane –(3), Reo-Coker –(3), Hutchison –(1), McAnuff –(1).
League goals (67): Harewood 13, Defoe 11, Connolly 10, Deane 6, Etherington 5, Zamora 5, Dailly 3, Hutchison 3, Mellor 2, Reo-Coker 2, Carrick 1, Harley 1, Horlock 1, McAnuff 1, Pearce 1, Opponents 2. **Play-offs – goals (2):** Dailly 1, Etherington 1.
F.A. Cup goals (5): Connolly 2, Deane 1, Harewood 1, Mullins 1. **Carling Cup goals (6):** Defoe 4, Connolly 2.
Average home League attendance: 31,167. **Player of Year:** Matthew Etherington.

WIGAN ATHLETIC

Fooball can be a cruel game, as Wigan found to their cost on the final day of the season. Having led West Ham for almost an hour with a goal from Neil Roberts in front of a record 20,669 crowd for the JJB Stadium, they were within seconds of a Play-off place when Brian Deane headed an equaliser which delivered it instead to Crystal Palace. Paul Jewell's promoted side were left to reflect on the irony of Palace going on to reach the Premiership – and the fact that they took only three points from their last four matches. But Wigan and their manager deserved plenty of credit for achieving more than many expected.

Baines, L .... 23(3)	Filan, J 45	McCulloch, L .... 31(10)
Breckin, I .... 43(2)	Flynn, M .... 1(7)	McMillan, S .... 13(1)
Bullard, J 46	Horsfield, G 16	Mitchell, P .... 1(11)
Burchill, M .... 1(3)	Jackson, M .... 23(1)	Roberts, J 14
De Vos, J .... 25(2)	Jarrett, J .... 33(8)	Roberts, N .... 9(19)
Dinning, T .... 11(2)	Kennedy, J .... 10(2)	Rogers, A 5
Eaden, N 46	Lawrence, J .... –(4)	Teale, G .... 15(13)
Ellington, N .... 43(1)	Liddell, A .... 35(5)	Walsh, G .... 1(2)
Farrelly, G .... 3(4)	Mahon, A .... 13(1)	

League goals (60): Ellington 18, Liddell 9, Roberts, J 8, Horsfield 7, McCulloch 6, Bullard 2, De Vos 2, Roberts, N 2, Teale 2, Jackson 1, Jarrett 1, Kennedy 1, Mahon 1.
F.A. Cup goals (1): Opponents 1. **Carling Cup goals (4):** Bullard 1, Ellington 1, Jarrett 1, McCulloch 1.
Average home League attendance: 9,526. **Player of Year:** John Filan.

WIMBLEDON

Forced by the administrators to sell all their best players, Wimbledon never stood a chance of preserving First Division football at the club's new home in Milton Keynes. They finished 22 points adrift at the bottom and there are fears that the slide may continue in the season ahead. Through it all, manager Stuart Murdoch won widespread admiration for maintaining a dignified stance in the most difficult of circumstances. There were also odd occasions when the Wimbledon spirit of old came to the surface – victories at West Bromwich Albion and Wigan and an unlucky 1-0 defeat at Birmingham in the fourth round of the F.A. Cup.

Agyemang, P .... 23(3)	Heald, P 10	McKoy, N .... 1(2)
Banks, S 24	Herzig, N .... 18(1)	Morgan, L .... 2(1)
Barton, W 5	Holdsworth, D ...... 14(14)	Nowland, A .... 24(1)
Bevan, S 10	Holloway, D .... 8(5)	Ntimban-Zeh, H .... 9(1)
Campbell-Ryce, J ...... 3(1)	Jarrett, A .... 3(6)	Oyedele, S 9
Chorley, B .... 33(2)	Kamara, M .... 15(12)	Puncheon, J .... 6(2)
Darlington, J .... 40(1)	Leigertwood, M 27	Reo-Coker, N 25
Gier, R .... 24(1)	Lewington, D 28	Small, W .... 23(4)
Gordon, M .... 8(11)	Mackie, J .... 8(5)	Smith, G .... 10(1)
Gray, W .... 20(12)	Martin, D 2	Tapp, A .... 12(2)
Harding, B .... 10(5)	McAnuff, J .... 25(2)	Williams, M 11
Hawkins, P .... 16(2)	McDonald, S .... –(2)	Worgan, L .... –(3)

League goals (41): Agyemang 6, McAnuff 5, Gray 4, Reo-Coker 4, Holdsworth 3, Nowland 3, Smith 3, Chorley 2, Kamara 2, Leigertwood 2, Small 2, Darlington 1, Lewington 1, Tapp 1, Williams 1, Opponents 1.
F.A. Cup goals (2): Nowland 2. **Carling Cup goals:** None.
Average home League attendance: 4,750. **Player of Year:** Dean Lewington.

NATIONWIDE LEAGUE – SECOND DIVISION

BARNSLEY

All change again at Oakwell, where the former Leeds chairman Peter Ridsdale led a second takeover of the club in successive seasons and Paul Hart became the sixth manager in five years. A month after being sacked by Nottingham Forest, Hart took over from Gudjon Thordarson, whose eight months in charge came to an end after a 6-1 defeat at Grimsby at the end of February. By then, Barnsley had slipped out of the top six and by the time of Hart's first win, 1-0 over leaders Plymouth in early April, they were too far behind to get back.

Alcock, D .... –(1)	Gallimore, A 20	Neil, A .... 17(14)
Atkinson, R .... –(1)	Gibbs, P .... –(3)	O'Callaghan, B .... 25(4)
Austin, N .... 32(5)	Gorre, D .... 16(3)	Rankin, I .... 9(11)
Baker, T .... –(1)	Handyside, P 28	Rocastle, C .... 4(1)
Beresford, M 14	Hayward, S .... 24(8)	Shuker, C 9
Betsy, K .... 42(3)	Ilic, S 25	Stallard, M 10
Birch, G 8	Ireland, C 43	Tonge, D .... –(1)
Boulding, M .... 5(1)	Kay, A .... 39(4)	Turnbull, R 3
Burns, J .... 16(6)	Lumsdon, C .... 17(11)	Walters, J .... 7(1)
Caig, A 3	Monk, G .... 14(3)	Ward 1
Carson, S .... 9(2)	Mulligan, D .... 2(2)	Warhurst, P .... 3(1)
Crooks, L .... 20(3)	Murphy, D 10	Williams, R .... 3(1)
Davies, A .... 1(3)	Nardiello, D .... 14(2)	Wroe, N .... 1(1)
Fallon, R .... 12(4)		

League goals (54): Betsy 10, Gorre 7, Nardiello 7, Rankin 5, Fallon 4, Ireland 3, Kay 3, Lumsdon 3, Murphy 2, Birch 2, Neil 2, Burns 1, Carson 1, Hayward 1, Stallard 1, Williams 1, Wroe 1.
F.A. Cup goals (4): Betsy 1, Kay 1, Monk 1, Rankin 1. **Carling Cup goals (1):** Gorre 1. **LDV Vans Trophy goals:** None.
Average home League attendance: 9,619. **Player of Year:** Antony Kay.

BLACKPOOL

Blackpool won the LDV Vans Trophy for the second time in three seasons, beating Southend 2-0 at the Millennium Stadium. They also went close to causing an upset in the F.A. Cup, losing unluckily to a last-minute Portsmouth goal at Fratton Park. Form in the League, however, was again up and down, along with Steve McMahon's position as manager. After resigning in January, then changing his mind, McMahon parted company with the club two days before the final match. He was replaced during the summer by former Scotland stalwart and managerial newcomer Colin Hendry.

Barnes, P 19	Donnelly, C .... 8(1)	Jones, B 5
Blinkhorn, M .... 4(8)	Douglas, J .... 15(1)	Jones, L 21
Bullock, M .... 33(11)	Edge, L 1	Mangan, A .... –(2)
Burns, J .... 3(8)	Elliott, S 28	Matias, P 7
Clancy, S .... 1(1)	Evans G .... 21(2)	McMahon, S .... 7(5)
Clarke, C .... 11(7)	Flynn, M .... 29(1)	Murphy, J .... 27(3)
Coid, D .... 30(5)	Grayson, S .... 28(5)	Richardson, L .... 24(4)
Danns, N 12	Hessey, S .... 4(2)	Sheron, M .... 28(10)
Davis, S .... 22(7)	Hilton, K .... 12(2)	Southern, K .... 15(13)
Dinning, T 10	Jaszczun, T .... 5(2)	Taylor, S .... 30(1)
Doherty, S .... –(1)	Johnson, S .... 3(1)	Walker, R .... 3(6)

Wellens, R .... 40(1)   Wiles, S .... –(4)

League goals (58): Taylor 16, Murphy 9, Sheron 8, Coid 3, Dinning 3, Douglas 3, Wellens 3, Danns 2, Southern 2, Blinkhorn 1, Bullock 1, Clarke 1, Davis 1, Flynn 1, Grayson 1, Hilton 1, Johnson 1, Matias 1.
F.A. Cup goals (10): Taylor 6, Burns 1, Coid 1, Richardson 1, Southern 1. **Carling Cup goals (4):** Taylor 3, Southern 1. **LDV Vans Trophy goals (13):** Murphy 4, Sheron 3, Coid 2, Taylor 2, Blinkhorn 1, Southern 1.
Average home League attendance: 6,326. **Player of Year:** Richie Wellens.

BOURNEMOUTH

A 6-0 win over Wrexham, in which late substitute James Hayter scored the fastest-ever Football League hat-trick in two minutes and 20 seconds, kept Bournemouth in the running for the final Play-off place until momentum was lost in the wake of a 2-1 defeat by the team who went on to claim it, Hartlepool. They were held at home by struggling Chesterfield two days later, then fell right away after a 5-1 home reversal against Tranmere. With goals becoming increasingly hard to come by, Bournemouth recorded only one win in the final eight fixtures to finish seven points adrift in ninth position.

Broadhurst, K .... 36(3)	Fletcher, C 40	O'Connor, G .... 28(9)
Browning, M .... 41(1)	Fletcher, S .... 40(1)	Purches, S 42
Buxton, L .... 24(2)	Hayter, J .... 37(7)	Stock, B .... 11(8)
Connell, A .... 1(6)	Holmes, D .... 10(16)	Thomas, D .... 2(8)
Cooke, S 3	Jorgensen, C .... 16(1)	Tindall, J .... 2(17)
Cummings, W 42	Maher, S .... 23(6)	Williams, G .... –(1)
Elliott, W .... 23(16)	Moss, N 46	Young, N .... 5(5)
Feeney, W .... 34(6)		

League goals (56): Hayter 14, Feeney 12, Fletcher, S 9, Elliott 3, Purches 3, Stock 3, Cummings 2, Fletcher, C 2, Holmes 2, O'Connor 2, Broadhurst 1, Maher 1, Opponents 2.
F.A. Cup goals (2): Browning 1, Elliott 1. **Carling Cup goals:** None. **LDV Vans Trophy goals:** None.
Average home League attendance: 6,913. **Player of Year:** James Hayter.

BRENTFORD

Martin Allen's managerial style can border on the eccentric. But it certainly struck a chord with relegation-threatened Brentford, who were second from bottom when Allen controversially resigned his job at Barnet to take over after the dismissal of Wally Downes. The effect on a side with only one win in their previous 19 matches was considerable. Allen began with a 3-2 defeat of Rushden – a result which accelerated that team's slide towards Division Three – and the momentum was maintained until the last kick of the season, by which time Brentford were clear of danger having collected 18 points from nine games.

Beadle, P 1	Hunt, S .... 38(2)	Roget, L 15
Blackman, L .... –(3)	Hutchinson, E 36	Rougier, A .... 29(2)
Bull, R 20	Julian, A 13	Smith, J .... 12(5)
Dobson, M 42	Kitamirike, J .... 21(1)	Smith, P 24
Evans, S .... 14(11)	May, B .... 38(3)	Somner, M .... 30(9)
Fieldwick, L .... 4(1)	Nelson, S 9	Sonko, I .... 42(1)
Fitzgerald, S 9	O'Connor, K .... 36(7)	Tabb, J .... 22(14)
Frampton, A .... 10(6)	Olugbodi, J .... –(2)	Talbot, S 14
Harrold, M .... 5(8)	Peters, M .... 2(7)	Wells, D .... –(1)
Hughes, S .... 1(8)	Rhodes, A .... –(3)	Wright, T .... 18(7)

League goals (52): Hunt 11, Tabb 9, May 7, Hutchinson 5, Rougier 4, Sonko 3, Wright 3, Evans 2, Harrold 2, Talbot 2, Dobson 1, O'Connor 1, Rhodes 1, Opponents 1.
F.A. Cup goals (7): Harrold 3, Frampton 1, O'Connor 1, Rougier 1, Opponents 1. **Carling Cup goals:** None. **LDV Vans Trophy goals (5):** Hunt 2, Tabb 2, Dobson 1.
Average home League attendance: 5,541. **Player of Year:** Jay Tabb.

BRIGHTON & HOVE ALBION

Leon Knight led Brighton back to Division One at the first attempt, scoring his 27th – and most important – goal of the season from the penalty spot with six minutes remaining in the Play-off Final against Bristol City. His team were also indebted to Adam Virgo's header in stoppage-time of extra-time which sent their semi-final against Swindon towards a successful penalty shoot-out. Considering the loss of Steve Coppell to Reading, a subsequent dip in form which new manager Mark McGhee had to address and continuing uncertainty about plans for a new ground, Brighton's achievement was commendable.

Beck, D ....–(1)	Iwelumo, C 10	Piercy, J .... 8(15)
Benjamin, T 10	Jones, N .... 34(2)	Rehman, Z .... 9(2)
Butters, G 43	Jones, S .... 2(1)	Reid, P .... 4(1)
Carpenter, R .... 40(2)	Knight, L .... 43(1)	Roberts, B 32
Cullip, D 40	Kuipers, M .... 9(1)	Robinson, J .... 1(8)
El-Abd, A .... 6(5)	Lee, D .... 1(3)	Rodger, S 7
Flitney, R 3	Marney, D .... –(3)	Virgo, A .... 20(2)
Harding, D .... 17(6)	Mayo, K .... 31(2)	Watson, P .... 14(1)
Hart, G .... 35(7)	McPhee, C .... 17(12)	Wilkinson, S .... –(2)
Henderson, D 10	Oatway, C .... 29(2)	Yeates, M 9
Hinshelwood, A ...... 16(1)	Pethick, R .... 6(8)	

Play-offs – appearances: Butters 3, Carpenter 3, Cullip 3, Harding 3, Iwelumo 3, Knight 3, Jones 3, Oatway 3, Roberts 3, Virgo 3, Reid 2(1), Hart 1(2), Piercy –(1).
League goals (64): Knight 25, Benjamin 5, Carpenter 4, Iwelumo 4, McPhee 4, Piercy 4, Butters 3, Hart 3, Henderson 2, Rehman 2, Cullip 1, Oatway 1, Virgo 1, Opponents 5. **Play-offs – goals (3):** Carpenter 1, Knight 1, Virgo 1.
F.A. Cup goals (1): McPhee 1. **Carling Cup goals (1):** McPhee 1. **LDV Vans Trophy goals (6):** McPhee 3, Carpenter 1, Knight 1, Robinson 1.
Average home League attendance: 6,247. **Player of Year:** Guy Butters.

BRISTOL CITY

When a run of 11 successive victories came to an end with a last-minute defeat by Sheffield Wednesday, Danny Wilson's side still looked good enough for automatic promotion. Instead, form began to fluctuate, goals became harder to come by and Queens Park Rangers edged them out of second place – ironically by winning at Hillsborough on the last day of the season. Then, for the second successive year, City failed in the Play-offs, coming through a nervous semi-final against Hartlepool, but losing to a late Brighton penalty in Cardiff. Wilson paid the price, veteran midfielder Brian Tinnion taking over as player-manager during the summer.

Amankwaah, K .... 4(1)	Doherty, T .... 28(5)	Peacock, L .... 39(2)
Bell, M .... 20(7)	Fortune, C .... 1(5)	Phillips, S 46
Brown, A .... 30(2)	Goodfellow, M .... 7(8)	Roberts, C .... 24(14)
Burnell, J .... 14(3)	Hill, M .... 40(2)	Rougier, A .... 5(1)
Butler, T .... 37(1)	Lita, L .... 2(24)	Tinnion, B .... 36(9)
Carey, L 41	Matthews, L .... 1(7)	Wilkshire, L .... 35(2)
Clist, S 1	Miller, L .... 32(10)	Woodman, C .... 14(7)
Coles, D 45	Murray, S .... 4(2)	

Play-offs – appearances: Butler 3, Carey 3, Coles 3, Doherty 3, Hill 3, Phillips 3, Roberts 3, Rougier 3, Tinnion 3, Woodman 3, Peacock 2, Miller 1, Murray –(3), Goodfellow –(2), Wilkshire –(2), Burnell –(1), Lita –(1).
League goals (58): Peacock 14, Miller 8, Roberts 6, Brown, A 5, Lita 5, Goodfellow 4, Coles 2, Doherty 2, Hill 2, Matthews 2, Tinnion 2, Wilkshire 2, Burnell 1, Butler 1, Carey 1, Rougier 1. **Play-offs – goals (3):** Goodfellow 1, Roberts 1, Rougier 1.
F.A. Cup goals (6): Amankwaah 2, Matthews 1, Roberts 1, Wilkshire 1, Opponents 1.
Carling Cup goals (5): Peacock 2, Bell 1, Coles 1, Miller 1. **LDV Vans Trophy goals:** None.
Average home League attendance: 12,878. **Player of Year:** Tommy Doherty.

CHESTERFIELD

Chesterfield cut it fine for the second successive season, surviving through an 88th minute winner by leading scorer Glynn Hurst against Luton in the final match. They moved out of the bottom four, ahead of Rushden and Grimsby with a point to spare, having lost to both during a miserable start to the season which extended to more than two months before a first victory over Swindon. A 7-0 thrashing at Plymouth was another setback, but by winning six of the next ten games Roy McFarland's team, boosted by Hurst's goals, gave themselves a chance of staying up.

Allott, M	35(5)	Fullarton, J	–(1)	O'Hare, A	40
Blatherwick, S	36	Howson, S	6(3)	Payne, S	20
Brandon, C	39(4)	Hudson, M	32(3)	Reeves, D	18(13)
Burt, J	–(1)	Hurst, G	28(1)	Robinson, M	17(15)
Cade, J	9(1)	Innes, M	17(5)	Rushbury, A	–(5)
Davies, G	18(10)	McMaster, J	4(2)	Searle, D	4(1)
Dawson, K	22(2)	Muggleton, C	46	Smith, A	–(3)
De Bolla, M	3(5)	N'Toya, T	3(3)	Uhlenbeek, G	36(1)
Evatt, I	43	Niven, D	22	Warhurst, P	3(1)
Folan, C	4(3)	O'Halloran, M	1(2)		

League goals (49): Hurst 13, Robinson 6, Evatt 5, Brandon 4, Reeves 4, Allott 2, Blatherwick 2, Cade 2, Hudson 2, McMaster 2, De Bolla 1, Niven 1, O'Hare 1, Payne 1, Rushbury 1, Opponents 2.
F.A. Cup goals (2): Davies 1, Evatt 1. **Carling Cup goals:** None. **LDV Vans Trophy goals (5):** Brandon 2, Cade 1, Robinson 1, Warhurst 1.
Average home League attendance: 4,331. **Player of Year:** Ian Evatt.

COLCHESTER UNITED

Colchester overcame a sticky start to the season, which brought three successive defeats, to achieve another respectable mid-table position. They also enjoyed some long-overdue success in the F.A. Cup, a competition in which non-League teams have often been a source of embarrassment. This time, Colchester overcame Aldershot and Accrington, as well as First Division Coventry on the way to a 1-0 defeat by Sheffield United at Bramall Lane in round five. Progress was also made in the LDV Vans Trophy, before defeat over two legs by Southend in the Southern Section Final.

Andrews, W	32(9)	Fitzgerald, S	22(1)	McKinney, R	5
Baldwin, P	1(3)	Gerken, D	1	Myers, A	21
Bowry, R	18(6)	Hadland, P	–(1)	Pinault, T	31(9)
Brown, J	40	Halford, G	15(3)	Stockley, S	44
Brown, W	16	Izzet, K	43(1)	Tierney, P	2
Cade, J	6(9)	Johnson, G	14(4)	Vine, R	30(5)
Chilvers, L	29(3)	Keith, J	16(12)	White, A	30(3)
Duguid, K	30	McGleish, S	25(9)	Williams, G	5(2)
Fagan, C	30(7)				

League goals (52): Andrews 12, McGleish 10, Fagan 9, Vine 6, Halford 4, Izzet 3, Duguid 2, Keith 2, Williams 2, Johnson 1, White 1.
F.A. Cup goals (8): Vine 4, Keith 2, McGleish 1, Opponents 1. **Carling Cup goals (2):** Fagan 1, Pinault 1. **LDV Vans Trophy goals (14):** McGleish 6, Andrews 2, Vine 2, Brown 1, Izzet 1, Keith 1, Pinault 1.
Average home League attendance: 3,536. **Player of Year:** Alan White.

GRIMSBY TOWN

Grimsby went through three managers, and one of their biggest-ever defeats, on the way to relegation for the second successive season. Needing a win to stay up on the last day, they led at Tranmere but fell away to lose 2-1 to a side playing for the final half-hour with ten men. The worst defensive record in the division came in the wake of an 8-1 defeat early on at Hartlepool, which contributed to the departure of Paul Groves. Nicky

Law came and went before Scarborough's Russell Slade was appointed during the summer and charged with arresting the club's slide.

Anderson, I .... 24(5)	Daws, N 17	Onuora, I .... 18(1)
Antoine-Curier, M ..... 3(2)	Edwards, M .... 32(1)	Parker, W .... –(4)
Armstrong, C 9	Fettis, A 11	Pettinger, A 3
Barnard, D 34	Ford, S .... 21(5)	Pouton, A 5
Bolder, C .... 6(1)	Groves, P .... 7(4)	Rankin, I 12
Boulding, M 27	Hamilton, D .... 20(7)	Rowan, J .... 9(5)
Campbell, S 39	Hockless, G .... 4(9)	Soames, D .... –(10)
Cas, M .... 13(7)	Jevons, P .... 21(8)	Ten Heuvel, L .... 3(1)
Coldicott, S .... 13(1)	Lawrence, J 5	Thorpe, L .... 5(1)
Crane, T 37	Mansaram, D ...... 11(20)	Thorrington, J .... 2(1)
Crowe, J .... 27(5)	McDermott, J 21	Warhurst, P .... 5(2)
Davison, A 32	Nimmo, L .... –(2)	Young, G .... 10(7)

League goals (55): Boulding 12, Jevons 12, Anderson 5, Rankin 4, Crane 3, Onuora 3, Mansaram 3, Barnard 2, Cas 2, Hockless 2, Rowan 2, Armstrong 1, Campbell 1, Edwards 1, Ford 1, Lawrence 1.
F.A. Cup goals (3): Boulding 1, Cas 1, Jevons 1. **Carling Cup goals (2):** Anderson 1, Campbell 1. **LDV Vans Trophy goals (1):** Mansaram 1.
Average home League attendance: 4,730. **Player of Year:** Phil Jevons.

HARTLEPOOL UNITED

How cruel. Despite losing defenders Chris Westwood and Michael Barron to injuries, and with leading scorer Eifion Williams hobbling in his makeshift full-back position, Hartlepool hung on to Anthony Sweeney's potentially-decisive goal in the second leg of their Play-off semi-final against Bristol City until the 88th minute. They conceded another in stoppage-time to lose 3-2 on aggregate, but could still look back with some satisfaction on going so close so soon after promotion. The season also brought one of their biggest-ever wins, 8-1 over Grimsby, and the division's Fair Play award, having been the only team not to have received a red card.

Arnison, P .... 2(2)	Henderson, K .... 1(2)	Robinson, P .... 19(12)
Barron, M 32	Humphreys, R 46	Robson, M .... 17(6)
Boyd, A .... 10(8)	Istead, S .... 1(30)	Shuker, C 14
Brackstone, J .... 5(1)	Jordan, A .... 4(1)	Strachan, G .... 34(2)
Byrne, D 2	McCann, R .... –(4)	Sweeney, A .... 8(3)
Carson, S .... 1(2)	Nelson, M .... 38(2)	Tinkler, M .... 43(1)
Clarke, D .... 23(10)	Porter, J .... 18(9)	Walker, S .... 5(1)
Craddock, D .... 9(1)	Provett, J 45	Westwood, C 45
Danns, N .... 8(1)	Richardson, M 3	Wilkinson, N .... 2(2)
Easter, J .... –(3)	Robertson, H 18	Williams, A 1
Foley, D .... –(1)	Robinson, M 4	Williams, E .... 39(2)
Gabbiadini, M .... 9(6)		

Play-offs – appearances: Barron 2, Boyd 2, Humphreys 2, Nelson 2, Porter 2, Provett 2, Robertson 2, Sweeney 2, Tinkler 2, Westwood 2, Williams, E 2, Clarke –(2), Danns –(2), Robinson –(2).
League goals (76): Williams, E 13, Boyd 12, Robinson 7, Tinkler 6, Clarke 5, Gabbiadini 5, Strachan 5, Robertson 4, Humphreys 3, Nelson 3, Porter 3, Wilkinson 2, Barron 1, Danns 1, Istead 1, Robson 1, Shuker 1, Sweeney 1, Opponents 1. **Play-offs–goals (2):** Porter, Sweeney 1.
F.A. Cup goals (5): Gabbiadini 2, Brackstone 1, Humphreys 1, Porter 1. **Carling Cup goals (3):** Robinson, 2, Istead 1. **LDV Vans Trophy goals (3):** Clarke 2, Williams, E 1.
Average home League attendance: 5,419. **Player of Year:** Jim Provett.

LUTON TOWN

Luton faltered during the run-in after working their way into a top six place, eventually finishing seven points off a Play-off position. To be fair, they could hardly have had a more demanding set of matches after a 3-2 win over Blackpool in mid-March, meeting seven of the leading teams in one eight-match spell. Plymouth and Queens Park Rangers were both held, but by the time of a 3-2 victory over Bristol City, Luton had fallen behind, and the task of winning their final four fixtures was too much. Steve Howard was leading scorer for the third successive year, despite injury denying him a full season.

Bayliss, D 6	Forbes, A .... 21(6)	Neilson, A .... 11(3)
Beckwith, R 13	Hillier, I .... 8(3)	Nicholls, K 21
Beresford, M 11	Holmes, P .... 11(5)	O'Leary, S .... 3(2)
Boyce, E 42	Howard, S 34	Perrett, R .... 5(1)
Brill, D .... 4(1)	Hughes, J .... 20(2)	Pitt, C .... 11(1)
Brkovic, A .... 24(8)	Hyldgaard, M 18	Robinson, S .... 32(2)
Coyne, C 44	Judge, M .... –(1)	Shownunmi, E .... 18(8)
Crowe, D .... –(8)	Keane, K .... 14(1)	Spring, M 24
Davies, C .... 4(2)	Leary, M .... 8(6)	Thorpe, T 2
Davis, S .... 34(2)	Mansell, L .... 12(4)	Underwood, P 1
Foley, K .... 32(1)	McSheffrey, G 18	

League goals (69): Howard 15, Forbes 9, McSheffrey 8, Shownunmi 7, Boyce 4, Holmes 3, Coyne 2, Leary 2, Mansell 2, Nicholls 2, Perrett 2, Robinson 2, Thorpe 2, Brkovic 1, Foley 1, Hughes 1, Keane 1, Neilson 1, O'Leary 1, Spring 1, Opponents 2.
F.A. Cup goals (8): Forbes 5, Boyce 1, Mansell 1, Robinson 1. **Carling Cup goals (8):** Foley 2, Bayliss 1, Coyne 1, Howard 1, McSheffrey 1, Pitt 1, Thorpe 1. **LDV Vans Trophy goals (3):** Judge 1, Leary 1, Shownunmi 1.
Average home League attendance: 6,339. **Player of Year:** Emmerson Boyce.

NOTTS COUNTY

Having one of the division's leading marksmen was no insurance against relegation. Paul Heffernan scored all four goals in a 4-1 win over Stockport and all three in a 3-3 draw against Queens Park Rangers on the way to 20 for the season. But there was little back-up, and by the time Heffernan was in his stride, County were struggling to make up ground, having lost the opening four games. Gary Mills took over as manager when Bill Dearden resigned after a 5-2 defeat by Peterborough early in the New Year to introduce some hope of survival. But two points from the final six games were not enough.

Antoine-Curier, M 4	Garden, S .... 12(1)	Oakes, S 14
Arphexad, P 3	Hackworth, T .... 4(8)	Parkinson, A .... 10(4)
Baldry, S .... 32(3)	Harrad, S .... –(8)	Pipe, D 18
Baraclough, I .... 30(4)	Heffernan, P .... 31(7)	Platt, C 19
Barras, A .... 38(2)	Jenkins, S 17	Rhodes, C .... –(1)
Bewers, J .... –(3)	Livesey, D .... 9(2)	Richardson, I 40
Boertien, P 5	McFaul, S .... 2(4)	Riley, P .... 13(6)
Bolland, P .... 35(4)	McGoldrick, D .... 2(2)	Scoffham, S .... 4(11)
Brough, M .... 5(5)	McHugh, F .... 9(4)	Scully, A .... 6(4)
Caskey, D .... 29(4)	Mildenhall, S 28	Stallard, M .... 18(4)
Deeney, S 3	Murray, A .... 1(2)	Williams, M .... 5(2)
Fenton, N .... 42(1)	Nicholson, K .... 16(7)	Wilson, N .... 2(1)
Francis, W .... –(3)		

League goals (50): Heffernan 20, Stallard 4, Parkinson 3, Platt 3, Richardson 3, Riley 3, Scully 3, Barras 2, Caskey 2, Scoffham 2, Antoine-Curier 1, Baldry 1, Bolland 1, Fenton 1, Opponents 1.
F.A. Cup goals (9): Platt 3, Fenton 2, Barras 1, Heffernan 1, Nicholson 1, Richardson 1. **Carling Cup goals (4):** Stallard 2, Baldry 1, Barras 1. **LDV Vans Trophy goals:** None.
Average home League attendance: 5,939. **Player of Year:** Ian Richardson.

OLDHAM ATHLETIC

Brian Talbot admitted he was taking something of a step in the dark when leaving Rushden after seven years to become manager at Boundary Park. Nearly three months had elapsed since Iain Dowie walked out to join Crystal Palace and Oldham were still hovering just above the relegation area. With three weeks of the season remaining, they were in real danger of going down, until a handsome 4-1 win over champions-elect Plymouth eased the pressure. Another promotion-minded team, Swindon, were also beaten as Oldham finished comfortably clear, having gathered 11 points from the last five matches.

Antoine-Curier, M ..... 5(3)	Haining, W .... 30(1)	Owen, G 15
Barlow, M .... –(1)	Hall, C .... –(1)	Pogliacomi, L 46
Beherall, D 7	Hall, D .... 28(3)	Roca, C .... –(7)
Bonner, M .... 6(1)	Holden, D .... 37(2)	Sheridan, D .... 18(9)
Boshell, D .... 16(6)	Hudson, M 15	Sheridan, J .... 19(3)
Clegg, M .... 28(4)	Johnson, J .... 18(2)	Tierney, M .... –(2)
Cooksey, E ... 22(14)	Killen, C .... 7(6)	Vernon, S .... 28(17)
Crowe, D .... 2(3)	Lomax, K .... –(1)	Walker, R 1
Eyre, J .... 42(1)	Murray, P 41	Wilkinson, W .... 2(3)
Eyres, D .... 22(7)	Ndiwa, K .... 3(1)	Wolfenden, M .... –(1)
Fleming, C .... –(1)	O'Halloran, M ... 2(11)	Zola, C .... 21(4)
Griffin, A .... 25(1)		

League goals (66): Vernon 12, Murray 9, Eyre 6, Johnson 5, Sheridan, J 5, Zola 5, Cooksey 4, Holden 4, Eyres 3, Antoine-Curier 2, Beherall 2, Haining 2, Killen 2, Crowe 1, Griffin 1, Hall, D 1, O'Halloran 1, Owen 1.
F.A. Cup goals (5): Cooksey 2, Eyre 1, Johnson 1, Zola 1. **Carling Cup goals (1):** Antoine-Curier 1. **LDV Vans Trophy goals (4):** Vernon 2, Boshell 1, Zola 1.
Average home League attendance: 6,566. **Player of Year:** Paul Murray.

PETERBOROUGH UNITED

There were not too many half measures about Peterborough's season. Alongside 18 goalless matches, they scored six against Wrexham, five against Notts County and put four past Swindon and Blackpool. That 4-1 victory at Blackpool, achieved in the penultimate game of the season with a team hard hit by injuries, proved crucial for Barry Fry's team, who went into it separated from a bottom four place only by a superior goal difference. It was their seventh success away from home, two more than was achieved throughout the campaign at London Road.

Arber, M .... 43(1)	Jenkins, S .... 6(2)	Rea, S .... 25(3)
Boucard, A .... 7(1)	Kanu, C .... 16(5)	Semple, R .... 1(1)
Branston, G 14	Legg, A .... 38(4)	Shields, T 9
Burton, S .... 27(3)	Logan, R .... 12(17)	St Ledger, S .... 1(1)
Clarke, A .... 28(17)	McKenzie, L 19	Thomson, S .... 28(7)
Farrell, D .... 30(14)	Newton, A .... 28(9)	Tyler, M 43
Fotiadis, A .... –(8)	Nolan, M .... –(1)	Williams, T .... 20(1)
Gill, M .... 27(6)	Pearce, D .... 1(2)	Willock, C .... 22(7)
Green, ... F .... –(3)	Platt, C .... 17(1)	Wood, N .... 2(1)
Jelleyman, G .... 13(4)	Pullen, J 3	Woodhouse, C ...... 26(1)

League goals (58): McKenzie, 10, Clarke 9, Willock 8, Woodhouse 7, Logan 6, Farrell 5, Arber 3, Newton 2, Platt 2, Boucard 1, Burton 1, Rea 1, Thomson 1, Williams 1, Wood 1.
F.A. Cup goals (6): Clarke 2, Logan 1, Newton 1, Thomson 1, Willock 1. **Carling Cup goals:** None. **LDV Vans Trophy goals (7):** McKenzie 3, Clarke 1, Burton 1, Farrell 1, Logan 1.
Average home League attendance: 5,274. **Player of Year:** Curtis Woodhouse.

PLYMOUTH ARGYLE

A team short of individual star quality but rich in collective efficiency and purpose won their second championship in three seasons. Small wonder that Southampton went for Paul Sturrock to replace Gordon Strachan as their manager. Plymouth could easily have been knocked off course by Sturrock's departure with two months of the campaign still remaining. But caretaker Kevin Summerfield maintained a degree of continuity before handing over to Hibernian's Bobby Williamson, whose first match in charge was a title-clinching victory over second-place Queens Park Rangers in front of almost 20,000 at the impressively redeveloped Home Park.

Adams, S .... 25(11)	Friio, D .... 35(1)	Norris, D .... 42(3)
Aljofree, H .... 20(4)	Gilbert, P 40	Phillips, M .... 3(6)
Bent, J .... 13(5)	Hodges, L .... 28(9)	Stonebridge, I .... 21(9)
Beresford, D .... –(1)	Keith, M .... 28(12)	Sturrock, B .... –(24)
Capaldi, T .... 29(4)	Larrieu, R 6	Worrell, D 18
Connolly, P .... 28(2)	Lowndes, N ...... 18(15)	Wotton, P .... 31(7)
Coughlan, G 46	McCormick, L 40	Yetton, S .... –(1)
Evans, M .... 35(9)		

League goals (85): Friio 14, Evans 12, Keith 9, Wotton 9, Lowndes 8, Capaldi 7, Coughlan 6, Norris 5, Stonebridge 5, Hodges 3, Adams 2, Bent 1, Gilbert 1, Phillips 1, Opponents 1.
F.A. Cup goals (2): Friio 1, Stonebridge 1. **Carling Cup goals (1):** Evans 1. **LDV Vans Trophy goals (6):** Lowndes 2, Coughlan 1, Evans 1, Gilbert 1, Keith 1.
Average home League attendance: 12,654. **Player of Year:** Mickey Evans.

PORT VALE

After scoring only three times during the previous season, Stephen McPhee fired Port Vale to within a whisker of the Play-offs with 25 goals, which made him the division's joint top marksman. Two came in a 2-0 victory in the final match against Rushden, who were relegated as a result. But it was not enough, because Swindon and Hartlepool drew 1-1 and those teams filled positions five and six ahead of Vale on goal difference. They had kept up a challenge despite the mid-February departure of manager Brian Horton, who was replaced by long-serving player and coach Martin Foyle.

Armstrong, I .... 4(16)	Brown, R 17	Littlejohn, A ...... 24(12)
Birchall, C .... 1(9)	Burns, L .... 19(8)	McPhee, S 46
Boyd, M .... 20(2)	Collins, S 43	Paynter, B .... 42(2)
Brain, J 32	Cummins, M 42	Pilkington, G 44
Bridge-Wilkinson, M ... 27(6)	Delaney, D 14	Reid, L .... 7(4)
Brightwell, I 2	James, C 8	Rowland, S .... 26(3)
Brisco, N .... 20(7)	Lipa, A .... 27(3)	Walsh, M .... 12(1)
Brooker, S .... 29(3)		

League goals (73): McPhee 25, Paynter 13, Brooker 8, Bridge-Wilkinson 7, Littlejohn 7, Collins 4, Cummins 4, Lipa 2, Armstrong 1, Pilkington 1, Opponents 1.
F.A. Cup goals (4): Burns 1, McPhee 1, Paynter 1, Opponents 1. **Carling Cup goals:** None.
LDV Vans Trophy goals (1): McPhee 1.
Average home League attendance: 5,809. **Player of Year:** Stephen McPhee.

QUEENS PARK RANGERS

Roared on by 9,000 fans – and with nearly as many watching a live screening of the match at Loftus Road – Rangers claimed the second automatic promotion place with a 3-1 win at Sheffield Wednesday on a tense final day of the season. Anything less would have meant Bristol City going up after a neck-and-neck struggle between the two teams for the runners-up spot behind Plymouth. Rangers lost key defender Danny Shittu through injury in January, but Martin Rowlands continued to have a major influence, while Kevin Gallen and Paul Furlong formed one of the division's best strike partnerships.

Ainsworth, G	21(8)	Day, C	29	Oli, D	–(3)
Barton, W	2(1)	Edghill, R	15(5)	Pacquette, R	–(2)
Bean, M	23(8)	Forbes, T	30	Padula, G	36
Bignot, M	6	Furlong, P	31(5)	Palmer, S	24(11)
Bircham, M	36(2)	Gallen, K	44(1)	Rose, M	15(5)
Camp, L	12	Gnohere, A	17(1)	Rowlands, M	41(1)
Carlisle, C	32(1)	Johnson, R	10(1)	Sabin, E	3(7)
Culkin, N	5	Langley, R	1	Shittu, D	18(2)
Cureton, J	2(11)	Marney, D	1(1)	Thorpe, T	22(9)
Daly, W	–(2)	McLeod, K	26(9)	Williams, T	4(1)

League goals (80): Gallen 17, Furlong 16, Rowlands 10, Thorpe 10, Ainsworth 6, Palmer 4, McLeod 3, Padula 3, Bircham 2, Cureton 2, Bean 1, Carlisle 1, Langley 1, Sabin 1, Opponents 3.
F.A. Cup goals: None. **Carling Cup goals (4):** Rowlands 2, Ainsworth 1, Langley 1. **LDV Vans Trophy goals (6):** Gnohere 1, McLeod 1, Pacquette 1, Padula 1, Palmer 1, Thorpe 1.
Average home League attendance: 14,784. **Player of Year:** Martin Rowlands.

RUSHDEN AND DIAMONDS

When the division's second longest-serving manager, Brian Talbot, called time on seven years at Nene Park, Rushden were in the early stages of a slide which was to send them straight back down. From a secure-looking mid-table position, they won only once in 14 games, failing to score in any of the final five. Former Wimbledon coach Ernie Tippett had a thankless task when he was eventually appointed Talbot's successor after a spell as caretaker-manager by defender Barry Hunter, although a last-day victory over Port Vale at home would have saved his team on goal difference.

Ashdown, J	19	Gray, S	33(2)	Mills, G	25(5)
Bell, D	31(6)	Hall, P	28(5)	Okuonghae, M	–(1)
Benjamin, T	5(1)	Hanlon, R	18(9)	Quinn, B	4
Bignot, M	35	Hunter, B	43	Roget, L	16(1)
Burgess, A	32(5)	Jack, R	44(1)	Sambrook, A	14(6)
Darby, D	9(3)	Kelly, M	4(4)	Story, O	–(5)
Dempster, J	11(8)	Kitson, P	18(10)	Talbot, D	3(4)
Duffy, R	4(4)	Lowe, O	24(2)	Turley, W	25
Edwards, A	29	Manangu, E	–(1)	Underwood, P	30
Evans, P	2				

League goals (60): Lowe 15, Jack 12, Gray 5, Kitson 5, Burgess 4, Hunter 4, Edwards 3, Bignot 2, Darby 2, Hall 2, Bell 1, Benjamin 1, Hanlon 1, Mills 1, Talbot 1, Opponents 1.
F.A. Cup goals: None. **Carling Cup goals (1):** Lowe 1. **LDV Vans Trophy goals (2):** Gray 1, Jack 1.
Average home League attendance: 4,456. **Player of Year:** Rodney Jack

SHEFFIELD WEDNESDAY

Chairman Dave Allen apologised for another disappointing season in which his relegated side failed to sustain an early challenge for an immediate return to Division One. Crowds dwarfed all others, but saw fewer goals than anyone, their side lacking the necessary strength and purpose at this level. Wednesday were fourth with two months of the season gone, but failed to win another match until the New Year, were unable to strike any consistency in the second part of the season and finished 16th after losing the final four matches.

Antoine-Curier, M	–(1)	Bromby, L	29	Chambers, A	8(3)
Armstrong, C	5(5)	Brunt, C	8(1)	Cooke, T	19(4)
Barry-Murphy, B	38(3)	Burchill, M	4(1)	Evans, R	5(1)
Beswetherick, J	4(1)	Carr, C	–(2)	Geary, D	41

Haslam, S	16(9)	Ndumbu-Nsungu,		Reddy, M	9(3)
Holt, G	9(8)	G	20(4)	Robins, M	14(1)
Kuqi, S	7	Nixon, E	–(1)	Shaw, J	7(7)
Lee, G	30	Olsen, K	6(4)	Smith, D	41
Lucas, D	17	Owusu, L	12(8)	Smith, P	12(7)
McLaren, P	23(2)	Pressman, K	20(1)	Tidman, O	10
McMahon, L	9(1)	Proudlock, A	26(4)	Wilson, M	3
Mustoe, R	22(3)	Quinn, A	23(1)	Wood, R	9(2)

League goals (48): Ndumbu-Nsungu 9, Kuqi 5, Owusu 5, Quinn 4, Lee 3, Proudlock 3, Robins 3, Brunt 2, Cooke 2, Holt 2, McLaren 2, Shaw 2, Smith, P 2, Bromby 1, Mustoe 1, Reddy 1, Smith, D 1.
F.A. Cup goals (6): Proudlock 3, Holt 1, Ndumbu-Nsungu 1, Owusu 1. **Carling Cup goals (2):** Lee 1, Wood 1. **LDV Vans Trophy goals (9):** Robins 4, Proudlock 3, Lee 1, Reddy 1.
Average home League attendance: 22,336. **Player of Year:** Guylain Ndumbu-Nsungu.

STOCKPORT COUNTY

Sammy McIlroy looked to have swopped one thankless task for another when resigning as Northern Ireland manager to take over at Edgeley Park after Carlton Palmer's dismissal six weeks into the season. Nearly five months into the job, McIlroy had still not moved his side out of the bottom four. Then came a remarkable transformation in their fortunes, starting with a 2-0 victory over promotion-minded Bristol City. It stretched to 11 unbeaten matches, produced 23 points and came to an end only on the last day of the season against Barnsley, by which time County were safe.

Adams, D	12	Goodwin, J	29(5)	Myhill, B	2
Barlow, S	15(15)	Griffin, D	15	Pemberton, M	5(1)
Beckett, L	6(2)	Hardiker, J	38(1)	Robertson, M	9(3)
Byrne, M	1	Heath, M	8	Smith, S	3(3)
Cartwright, L	14(1)	Jackman, D	27	Spencer, J	15
Challinor, D	14(3)	Jones, M	14(2)	Walton, D	7
Clare, R	36	Lambert, R	39(1)	Welsh, A	24(10)
Colgan, N	14(1)	Lescott, A	12(2)	Wilbraham, A	32(9)
Collins, W	–(2)	Lynch, S	9	Williams, Anthony	15
Daly, J	19(6)	McLachlan, F	14(6)	Williams, Ashley	10
Ellison, K	10(4)	Morrison, O	11(11)	Williams, C	4(12)
Gibb, A	23(3)				

League goals (62): Lambert 12, Barlow 8, Wilbraham 8, Beckett 4, Goodwin 4, Clare 3, Daly 3, Lynch 3, McLachlan 3, Williams, C 3, Jackman 2, Jones 2, Byrne 1, Ellison 1, Griffin 1, Morrison 1, Robertson 1, Welsh 1, Opponents 1.
F.A. Cup goals (1): Goodwin 1. **Carling Cup goals (1):** Barlow 1. **LDV Vans Trophy goals (7):** Barlow 3, Goodwin 1, Lambert 1, Morrison 1, Williams, C 1
Average home League attendance: 5,314. **Player of Year:** Ricky Lambert.

SWINDON TOWN

Trailing from their home leg in the Play-off semi-finals, Swindon looked to have turned things round with goals by Sam Parkin and Rory Fallon. Then, with seconds remaining of extra-time, Adam Virgo levelled the tie at 2-2 for Brighton, who went on to prevail in the resulting penalty shoot-out. Parkin had another prolific season, his partnership with Tommy Mooney sparking an unbeaten run off 11 games which produced 29 points and gave their team a glimpse of a two-two place. But in a competitive division, they were not consistent enough in the final quarter of the campaign.

Burton, D	4	Griemink, B	5(1)	Howard, B	21(14)
Duke, D	35(7)	Gurney, A	42	Ifil, J	16
Evans, R	41	Herring, I	1	Igoe, S	33(3)
Fallon, R	6(13)	Hewlett, M	43	Lewis, J	4
Garrard, L	–(1)	Heywood, M	39(1)	Miglioranzi, S	34(1)

Milner, J 6	Parkin, S .... 38(2)	Smith, G .... –(7)
Mooney, T .... 41(4)	Reeves, A .... 17(10)	Stevenson, J .... 1(4)
Nicholas, A .... 28(3)	Robinson, S .... 20(2)	Viveash, A .... 14(1)
O'Hanlon, S .... 17(2)	Ruster, S .... –(2)	

Play-offs – appearances: Evans 2, Gurney 2, Hewlett 2, Heywood 2, Howard 2, Igoe 2, Mooney 2, O'Hanlon 2, Parkin 2, Duke 1, Nicholas 1, Miglioranzi 1, Smith 1(1), Fallon –(2).

League goals (76): Mooney 19, Parkin 19, Gurney 7, Fallon 6, Igoe 5, Howard 4, Miglioranzi 4, Hewlett 3, Milner 2, Burton 1, Duke 1, Heywood 1, Nicholas 1, O'Hanlon 1, Robinson 1, Opponents 1. **Play-offs – goals (2):** Fallon 1, Parkin 1.

F.A. Cup goals (1): Gurney 1. **Carling Cup goals (5):** Parkin 3, Gurney 1, Mooney 1. **LDV Vans Trophy goals (1):** Robinson 1.

Average home League attendance: 7,838. **Player of Year:** Tommy Mooney.

TRANMERE ROVERS

Tranmere might have been forgiven for losing some momentum after the disappointment of defeat by Millwall in an F.A. Cup quarter-final replay, earned when John Achterberg's penalty save from Kevin Muscat capped a fine display of goalkeeping at The Den. Instead, they put together a run of 26 points from 11 subsequent matches to finish a healthy eighth under Brian Little, who had steered them out of trouble after a poor start to the season cost Ray Mathias his job. Rovers counted Bolton among their victims in reaching the last eight for the third time in five seasons.

Achterberg, J 45	Hall, P 9	Loran, T .... 26(2)
Allen, G .... 40(1)	Harrison, D 32	Mellon, M .... 39(4)
Ashton, N .... –(1)	Haworth, S .... 21(1)	Navarro, A .... 9(10)
Beresford, D ...... 13(12)	Hay, A .... 3(16)	Nicholson, S .... 9(7)
Connelly, S .... 33(4)	Howarth, R 1	Onuora, I .... 1(2)
Dadi, E .... 29(9)	Hume, I .... 32(8)	Roberts, G 44
Dagnall, C .... 5(5)	Jennings, S .... 1(3)	Sharps, I .... 25(2)
Goodison, I 12	Jones, G .... 36(6)	Taylor, R .... 21(9)
Gray, K 2	Linwood, P .... 18(2)	

League goals (59): Dadi 16, Hume 10, Jones 9, Haworth 6, Taylor 5, Hall 2, Harrison 2, Nicholson 2, Allen 1, Beresford 1, Dagnall 1, Roberts 1, Sharps 1, Opponents 2.

F.A. Cup goals (11): Hume 3, Dadi 2, Jones 2, Mellon 2, Haworth 1, Taylor 1. **Carling Cup goals (1):** Dadi 1. **LDV Vans Trophy goals (2):** Hume 1, Nicholson 1.

Average home League attendance: 7,605. **Player of Year:** John Achterberg.

WREXHAM

Despite losing 34-goal Andy Morrell and fellow striker Lee Trundle from their promotion-winning team, Wrexham consolidated with a mid-table finish. They held a top six position going into the New Year and were still there six weeks later after more impressive performances away from home. But disciplinary problems together with six-goal defeats by Bournemouth and Peterborough put them out of contention for the Play-offs. Ironically, one of their best performances came when they finished with nine men – holding on for a goalless draw away to leaders Plymouth.

Armstrong, C .... 19(7)	Holmes, S .... 3(10)	One, A .... 2(1)
Barrett, P .... 19(8)	Ingham, M 11	Pejic, S .... 20(1)
Carey, B .... 32(2)	Jones, L .... 13(9)	Roberts, S .... 24(3)
Crowell, M .... 9(6)	Jones, M .... –(13)	Sam, H .... 24(13)
Dibble, A .... 35·	Lawrence, D 45	Spender, S .... 3(3)
Edwards, C 42	Llewellyn, C 46	Thomas, S .... 31(8)
Edwards, P .... 40(1)	Macken, L 1	Whitfield, P .... –(3)
Ferguson, D 39	Morgan, C .... 14(4)	Whitley, J .... 34(2)

League goals (50): Sam 10, Llewellyn 8, Armstrong 5, Edwards, C 5, Jones, L 5, Lawrence 5, Barrett 2, Carey 2, Holmes 2, Thomas 2, Crowell 1, Ferguson 1, Jones, M 1, Opponents 1.
F.A. Cup goals (1): Armstrong 1. **Carling Cup goals:** None. **LDV Vans Trophy goals (8):** Jones, L 3, Sam 2, Armstrong 1, Holmes 1, Jones, M 1.
Average home League attendance: 4,439. **Player of Year:** Dennis Lawrence.

WYCOMBE WANDERERS

Tony Adams could hardly have had a tougher introduction to management after taking over from Lawrie Sanchez in early November. A winner for most of his playing career, the former Arsenal and England stalwart took over a side who were rock bottom – and who stayed there. Adams was offered grounds for optimism in his first match in charge – a 4-1 F.A. Cup first round win over Swindon. But there was no easy fix for Wycombe's League form. They did not manage back-to-back wins until beating Oldham and Port Vale as Easter approached, and by then it was much too late.

Bell, A .... 3(8)	Hole, S .... –(1)	Roberts, S .... 5(11)
Bevan, S 5	Holligan, S .... 8(5)	Rogers, M 15
Bloomfield, M .... 10(2)	Johnson, R 28	Ryan, K .... 10(7)
Branston, G 9	Mapes, C .... 10(5)	Senda, D .... 37(3)
Brown, S .... 18(7)	Marshall, S 8	Simpemba, I .... 17(2)
Bulman, D .... 30(8)	Moore, L 6	Simpson, M 38
Cook, L .... 1(4)	McSporran, J .... 29(4)	Talia, F 17
Currie, D 42	Nethercott, S 22	Taylor, S 6
Dell, S .... 3(1)	Oliver, L .... –(2)	Thomson, A 11
Dixon, J .... 2(6)	Onuora, I 6	Tyson, N 21
Faulconbridge, C .... 11(5)	Patterson, S .... 3(1)	Vinnicombe, C 36
Harding, B .... –(2)	Philo, M .... 4(8)	Williams, S 19
Harris, R .... 6(4)	Reilly, A 5	Worgan, L 2
Henderson, W 3		

League goals (50): Tyson 9, Currie 7, McSporran 7, Moore 4, Bell 3, Mapes 3, Faulconbridge 2, Holligan 2, Johnson 2, Patterson 2, Simpemba 2, Simpson 2, Bloomfield 1, Brown 1, Nethercott 1, Ryan 1, Thomson 1.
F.A. Cup goals (7): McSporran 3, Currie 2, Holligan 1, Thomson 1. **Carling Cup goals (2):** Harris 2. **LDV Vans Trophy goals (5):** McSporran 2, Branston 1, Johnson 1, Thomson 1.
Average home League attendance: 5,291. **Player of Year:** Roger Johnson.

NATIONWIDE LEAGUE – THIRD DIVISION

BOSTON UNITED

Boston achieved a top-half finish in their second season of League football which saw the return of the manager who had first delivered it. Neil Thompson was dismissed in February by new owners of the club and replaced by Steve Evans after the completion of his 20-month F.A. ban for impeding an investigation into contract irregularities, imposed in the wake of their Conference title win. Although lacking a prolific scorer, Boston were a hard-working side who delivered sufficient goals from most departments.

Akinfenwa, A .... 2(1)	Cropper, D .... 4(1)	Logan, R .... 4(4)
Angel, M .... 12(11)	Douglas, S .... 14(15)	Melton, S 9
Balmer, S .... 25(1)	Duffield, P .... 12(17)	Morrow, S .... –(2)
Bastock, P 46	Ellender, P 42	Noble, D 14
Beevers, L 40	Greaves, M .... 34(3)	Potter, G .... 11(1)
Bennett, T 35	Hocking, M .... 16(6)	Redfearn, N .... 19(4)
Boyd, A 14	Hogg, C 10	Rusk, S .... 16(3)
Brown, J .... 3(2)	Holland, C .... 3(2)	Sabin, E 2
Chapman, B .... 33(4)	Hurst, K .... 3(4)	Sutch, D 6
Clarke, R .... 1(3)	Jones, G .... 31(2)	Thomas, D 8

Thompson, L .... 20(15)   Weatherstone, S ..... 14(3)   White, A .... 3(3)

League goals (50): Jones 6, Redfearn 6, Duffield 5, Thompson 5, Boyd 4, Ellender 4, Weatherstone 4, Balmer 3, Thomas 3, Beevers 2, Noble 2, Angel 1, Bennett 1, Cropper 1, Douglas 1, Hurst 1, Melton 1.
F.A. Cup goals: None. **Carling Cup goals (1):** Redfearn 1. **LDV Vans Trophy goals (3):** Akinfenwa 1, Beevers 1, Duffield 1.
Average home League attendance: 2,963. **Player of Year:** Paul Ellender.

BRISTOL ROVERS

Rovers went through five 'managers' and 33 players during a third successive season in which the prospect of relegation had to be confronted. Ray Graydon stepped down in January after less than two years in charge and coach Phil Bater had a brief, unhappy spell at the helm, during which his side slipped to fourth from bottom. Russell Osman and Kevan Broadhurst, brought in as joint-managers with the brief to avoid the drop, used their experience to do just that before handing over to the former Oxford manager Ian Atkins, with the team moving towards a relatively healthy position ten points away from trouble.

Agogo, J .... 28(10)	Gibb, A 8	Quinn, R .... 23(12)
Anderson, I .... 37(2)	Gilroy, D .... 1(3)	Rammell, A .... 1(4)
Anderson, J 8	Haldane, L .... 16(11)	Savage, D .... 37(1)
Arndale, N .... 1(2)	Henriksen, B .... 1(3)	Street, K .... 8(5)
Austin, K .... 21(2)	Hobbs, S .... –(2)	Tait, P .... 28(5)
Barrett, A 45	Hodges, L .... 5(8)	Thorpe, L .... 8(2)
Boxall, D .... 23(1)	Hyde, G .... 33(4)	Twigg, G .... 7(1)
Bryant, S .... 7(5)	Lescott, A 8	Uddin, A 1
Carlisle, W .... 22(3)	Matthews, L 9	Williams, D 6
Clarke, R 2	Miller, K 44	Williams, R .... 15(4)
Edwards, C .... 40(2)	Parker, S .... 13(2)	Willock, C .... –(5)

League goals (50): Tait 12, Carlisle 7, Agogo 6, Haldane 5, Barrett 4, Hodges 2, Hyde 2, Rammell 2, Savage 2, Gibb 1, Parker 1, Quinn 1, Street 1, Thorpe 1, Williams, D 1, Williams, R 1, Opponents 1.
F.A. Cup goals: None. **Carling Cup goals:** None. **LDV Vans Trophy goals (1):** Haldane 1.
Average home League attendance: 7,141. **Player of Year:** Kevin Miller.

BURY

Two goals in the last five minutes by Chris Porter and Simon Whaley set up a 2-0 win over Macclesfield on the final day of the season and lifted Bury to 12th. So congested were the teams around them that defeat would have resulted in the lowest League position in the club's history. It was a satisfactory finish for Graham Barrow, who took over when player-manager Andy Preece was sacked in mid-season after a run of defeats, and for goalkeeper Glyn Garner, who was an ever-present and dominated the Player-of-the-Year awards.

Barrass, M .... 19(3)	Garner, G 46	Singh, H .... 20(8)
Cartledge, J .... 7(4)	Gulliver, P 10	Strong, G 10
Challinor, D 15	Gunby, S .... 1(4)	Swailes, D 42
Charnock, P 3	Kennedy, T .... 22(5)	Thompson, J 1
Clegg, G .... 4(2)	Nugent, D .... 20(6)	Thornley, B 5
Connell, L .... 23(5)	O'Neill, J .... 10(13)	Unsworth, L 27
Daly, J 7	O'Shaughnessy, P ... 21(6)	Whaley, S .... 3(7)
Dunfield, T .... 28(2)	Porter, C .... 19(18)	Whelan, G 13
Duxbury, L .... 36(1)	Preece, A .... 10(4)	Woodthorpe, C 39
Flitcroft, D 17	Seddon, G .... 28(12)	

League goals (54): Seddon 11, Porter 9, Connell 6, Preece 5, Swailes 5, Nugent 3, O'Neill 3, Dunfield 2, Singh 2, Unsworth 2, Barrass 1, Cartledge 1, Daly 1, O'Shaughnessy 1, Whaley 1, Opponents 1.

F.A. Cup goals (1): Porter 1. Carling Cup goals: None. LDV Vans Trophy goals (2): Preece 1, Thompson 1.
Average home League attendance: 2,891. **Player of Year:** Glyn Garner.

CAMBRIDGE UNITED

A flurry of managerial activity towards the end of another modest season brought the Continental touch to Cambridge. John Taylor was sacked with nine matches remaining and replaced, initially, by the former Cameroon and Senegal coach, Claude Le Roy. Less than two months later, the club announced that his No 2, Herve Renard, would take over, with Le Roy becoming director of football. The aim was to use their connections in Europe and bring in some new faces to a side that finished in mid-table for a second successive season, neither threatening the Play-off positions nor in danger of sliding into trouble.

Angus, S .... 39(1)	Goodhind, W .... 25(1)	Revell, A .... 10(10)
Bimson, S .... 21(3)	Guttridge, L 46	Robinson, M .... 1(2)
Bridges, D .... 11(10)	Kitson, D 17	Ruddy, J 1
Chillingworth, D ..... 10(3)	Lockett, K .... 1(1)	Smith 1
Clarke, C .... –(1)	Marshall, S 45	Tann, A .... 31(3)
Daniels, D .... –(1)	McCafferty, N .... 5(1)	Taylor, J .... 6(3)
Duncan, A 37	Murray, F .... 34(4)	Tudor, S .... 30(6)
Dutton, B .... –(3)	Nacca, F .... 2(7)	Turner, J .... 17(19)
Easter, J .... 10(5)	Nicholls, A .... 15(1)	Venus, M 21
Fleming, T .... 17(1)	Opara, L .... 1(7)	Walker, J 23
Fuller, A .... –(1)	Peat, N .... 3(3)	Webb, D .... 19(2)
Gleeson, D .... 3(4)	Quinton, J .... –(1)	Williams, G 4

League goals (55): Guttridge 11, Kitson 10, Chillingworth 7, Revell 3, Tudor 3, Turner 3, Webb 3, Bridges 2, Duncan 2, Easter 2, Tann 2, Angus 1, Fleming 1, Nicholls 1, Opara 1, Walker 1, Williams 1, Opponents 1.
F.A. Cup goals (5): Turner 2, Guttridge 1, Kitson 1, Tann 1. **Carling Cup goals (1):** Walker 1. **LDV Vans Trophy goals:** None.
Average home League attendance: 3,918. **Player of Year:** Luke Guttridge.

CARLISLE UNITED

When Matt Glennon saved a last-minute penalty to protect a 3-2 lead at Mansfield, the possibility of another great escape by Carlisle was still on the cards with two matches to go. But Glennon could do nothing about Kayode Odejayi's 85th minute header which earned Cheltenham a point and sent Carlisle into the Conference in front of a crowd of more than 9,000 at Brunton Park. The fans had responded to the way Paul Simpson, who replaced Roddy Collins as manager, and his team battled against the odds in the second half of the season after taking only five points from their first 21 matches.

Andrews, L .... 33(4)	Glennon, M 44	Murphy, P .... 33(2)
Arnison, P .... 20(6)	Gray, K 25	Preece, A .... 23(2)
Baldacchino, R .... –(1)	Henderson, K .... 10(9)	Raven, P 13
Billy, C 39	Jack, M .... –(3)	Rundle, A .... 6(17)
Birch, M 2	Keen, P .... 2(1)	Russell, C .... 3(3)
Boyd, M 9	Kelly, D .... 9(1)	Schumacher, S 4
Byrne, D .... 9(2)	Langmead, L .... 3(8)	Shelley, B .... 28(3)
Cowan, T 20	Livingstone, S 6	Simpson, P 25
Duffield, P 10	Maddison, L 2	Smith, S 4
Farrell, C .... 21(9)	McDonagh, W .... 23(4)	Summerbell, M .... 4(2)
Foran, R .... 20(3)	McGill, A .... 42(2)	Wake, B .... 2(13)
Fryatt, M .... 9(1)	Molloy, D .... 3(4)	Warhurst, P .... –(1)

League goals (46): Farrell 7, McGill 7, Simpson 6, Foran 4, Duffield 3, Gray 3, Preece 3, Henderson 2, Arnison 1, Billy 1, Boyd 1, Cowan 1, Fryatt 1, Kelly 1, Langmead 1, McDonagh 1, Murphy 1, Raven 1, Opponents 1.

F.A. Cup goals: None. **Carling Cup goals (1):** Russell 1. **LDV Vans Trophy goals (4):** Wake 2, Rundle 1, Schumacher 1.
Average home League attendance: 5,617.

CHELTENHAM TOWN

Although never serious contenders for an immediate return to Division Two, Cheltenham had a significant influence on events at the top and bottom of the table at the end of the season. Kayode Odejayi's late goal consigned Carlisle to the Conference. Then, Shane Duff scored his first of the campaign to earn another 1-1 draw which spoiled Huddersfield's bid for automatic promotion. Under John Ward, who took over in November after Bobby Gould resigned as manager, the team enjoyed a marginally more successful second half of the campaign.

Amankwaah, K ...... 11(1)	Duff, M 42	Hynes, P .... 2(2)
Bird, D .... 18(6)	Duff, S .... 13(2)	Jones, D 14
Book, S .... 4(1)	Finnigan, J .... 32(1)	McCann, G 43
Brayson, P .... 20(10)	Forsyth, R .... 16(11)	Odejayi, K .... 14(16)
Brough, J .... 23(3)	Fyfe, G .... 15(5)	Spencer, D .... 29(7)
Cleverley, B .... 2(6)	Gill, J .... 5(2)	Taylor, R .... 19(9)
Corbett, L .... –(1)	Griffin, A .... 10(5)	Victory, J 44
Cozic, B 7	Henry, K .... 8(1)	Wilson, B 14
Devaney, M .... 32(8)	Higgs, S 42	Yates, M .... 20(1)
Dobson, C .... –(2)	Howells, L .... 7(2)	

League goals (57): Spencer 9, McCann 8, Brayson 7, Taylor 7, Devaney 5, Odejayi 5, Brough 2, Forsyth 2, Victory 2, Yates 2, Cozic 1, Duff, S 1, Finnigan 1, Henry 1, Jones 1, Opponents 3.
F.A. Cup goals (7): McCann 3, Brayson 1, Spencer 1, Taylor 1, Yates 1. **Carling Cup goals (1):** McCann 1. **LDV Vans Trophy goals (1):** Devaney 1.
Average home League attendance: 4,116. **Player of Year:** Shane Higgs.

DARLINGTON

What should have been the start of a new era for Darlington at their new 25,000-seater ground turned sour on and off the pitch. George Reynolds, the man who built it, placed the club in administration, later severed all connections and then had his name removed from the stadium by new owners. Manager Mick Tait stepped down with three months of the season gone and David Hodgson took charge for the third time. His team were second from bottom half-way through and on the way to amassing a total of 11 red cards. But they started to turn things round with six wins out of eight in February/March and managed to keep their heads above water from then on.

Alexander, J .... –(3)	Hutchinson, J .... 38(1)	Nicholls, A .... 25(1)
Bossy, F .... 4(2)	James, C 10	Pearson, G .... 11(7)
Clark, I .... 20(14)	Keltie, C .... 23(8)	Price, M 36
Clarke, M .... 44(1)	Liddle, C 43	Robson, G .... 3(3)
Close, B .... 8(4)	Maddison, N .... 30(2)	Russell, C .... 6(6)
Coghlan, M .... –(3)	Mason, C .... –(1)	Sheeran, N .... –(6)
Collett, A 9	Matthews, L 6	Teggart, N .... 9(6)
Conlon, B .... 38(1)	McGurk, D .... 22(5)	Turnbull, R 1
Convery, M .... 17(8)	Mellanby, D .... 5(2)	Valentine, R .... 33(7)
Graham, J .... 7(2)	Morgan, A .... 4(1)	Wainwright, N .... 30(5)
Hughes, C .... 24(6)		

League goals (53): Conlon 14, Wainwright 7, Clark 4, Clarke 4, Liddle 4, McGurk 4, Convery 2, Graham 2, Hughes 2, Valentine 2, James 1, Keltie 1, Maddison 1, Matthews 1, Morgan 1, Pearson 1, Russell 1, Opponents 1.
F.A. Cup goals: None. **Carling Cup goals:** None. **LDV Vans Trophy goals (1):** Sheeran 1.
Average home League attendance: 5,022. **Player of Year:** Matt Clarke.

401

DONCASTER ROVERS

Doncaster confounded the sceptics by winning promotion for the second successive year – and the Third Division championship into the bargain. They were favourites to go straight back to the Conference, but instead played bright, attacking football under Dave Penney, with only runners-up Hull registering more goals. A crowd of nearly 10,000 saw Rovers become the first side in the four divisions to go up, with a 2-0 win over Cambridge. Key players were Greg Blundell, who scored 18 times and midfielder Michael McIndoe, voted the division's Player of the Season 12 months after winning the Conference's top individual award with champions Yeovil.

Akinfenwa, A .... 4(5)	Foster, S 44	Mulligan, D 14
Albrighton, M .... 27(1)	Gill, R .... –(1)	O'Brien, R 1
Barnes, P .... 2(5)	Green, P .... 38(5)	Paterson, J .... 7(1)
Beech, C 11	Hynes, P .... –(5)	Price, J .... 17(2)
Black, C 1	Maloney, J .... –(1)	Ravenhill, R .... 14(22)
Blundell, G .... 41(3)	Marples, S 16	Rigoglioso, A .... 5(12)
Brown, C .... 17(5)	McGrath, J .... 4(7)	Ryan, T .... 41(1)
Burton, S .... 1(5)	McIndoe, M 45	Tierney, F .... 10(3)
Doolan, J .... 36(3)	Melligan, J 21	Warrington, A 46
Fortune-West, L .... 28(11)	Morley, D .... 15(6)	

League goals (79): Blundell 18, Fortune-West 10, Brown 10, McIndoe 10, Green 8, Akinfenwa 4, Albrighton 3, Ravenhill 3, Tierney 3, Melligan 2, Ryan 2, Foster 1, Hynes 1, Morley 1, Mulligan 1, Paterson 1.
F.A. Cup goals: None. **Carling Cup goals (4):** Blundell 2, Barnes 1, Fortune-West 1. **LDV Vans Trophy goals (1):** Tierney 1.
Average home League attendance: 6,938.

HUDDERSFIELD TOWN

It all came right in the end for Huddersfield after a nightmare finish to the regular season cost them an automatic promotion spot. What had looked like a big enough advantage was finally wiped out in the final match when a misplaced back pass by Pawel Abbott presented Cheltenham with a point and Torquay with third place on goal difference. Peter Jackson's team came from behind to beat Lincoln in the semi-finals of the Play-offs, then held their nerve to win a penalty-shoot out 4-1 against Mansfield in the Final, which had remained goalless through 90 minutes and extra-time. One unwanted record for the season was a total of 13 red cards.

Abbott, P .... 12(1)	Holdsworth, A .... 31(5)	Rachubka, P 13
Ahmed, A .... –(1)	Holland, C .... –(3)	Schofield, D .... 38(2)
Booth, A .... 36(1)	Hughes, I .... 12(1)	Scott, P .... 16(3)
Booty, M .... 3(1)	Lloyd, A .... 30(1)	Senior, P 16
Brown, N .... 13(8)	Mattis, D .... 2(3)	Sodje, E .... 37(2)
Carss, A .... 35(1)	McAliskey, J .... 5(3)	Stead, J 26
Clarke, N .... 25(1)	Mirfin, D .... 15(6)	Thompson, T .... 1(1)
Edwards, R .... 11(6)	Newby, J .... 10(4)	Thorrington, J .... 3(2)
Fowler, L .... 27(2)	Onibuje, F .... –(2)	Worthington, J .... 36(3)
Gray, I 17	Onuora, I .... –(3)	Yates, S 35
Harkins, G .... 1(2)		

Play-offs – appearances: Booth 3, Holdsworth 3, Lloyd 3, Mirfin 3, Rachubka 3, Schofield 3, Sodje 3, Worthington 3, Yates 3, Edwards 2(1), Onuora 2, Abbot 1(1), Carss 1, McAliskey –(2), Fowler –(1), Scott –(1).
League goals (68): Stead 16, Booth 13, Schofield 8, Abbott 5, McAliskey 4, Sodje 4, Lloyd 3, Worthington 3, Carss 2, Mirfin 2, Scott 2, Clarke 1, Edwards 1, Hughes 1, Yates 1, Opponents 2. **Play-offs – goals (4):** Edwards 1, Mirfin 1, Onuora 1, Schofield 1.
F.A. Cup goals: None. **Carling Cup goals (6):** Stead 2, Booth 1, Carss 1, Holdsworth 1, Thorrington 1. **LDV Vans Trophy goals:** None.
Average home League attendance: 10,528. **Player of Year:** Jon Worthington.

HULL CITY

Hull began to realise some of the potential offered by a splendid stadium and huge support by finishing runners-up to Doncaster. Five home matches attracted gates of more than 20,000, topped by the 23,495 who saw a rare goalless draw against Huddersfield in their penultimate home fixture. The team Peter Taylor rebuilt after the disappointments of the previous season were the division's top scorers with 82 goals, Ben Burgess leading the way and Danny Allsopp and Stuart Elliott also reaching double figures.

Allsopp, D .... 31(5)	Green, S .... 38(4)	Musselwhite, P .... 17(1)
Ashbee, I 39	Hinds, R .... 34(5)	Myhill, B 23
Burgess, B 44	Holt, A .... 6(19)	Peat, N .... –(1)
Dawson, A .... 32(1)	Joseph, M 32	Price, J .... 29(4)
Delaney, D 46	Keates, D .... 9(5)	Thelwell, A .... 22(4)
Elliott, S 42	Kuipers, M 3	Walters, J .... 5(11)
Fettis, A 3	Lewis, J 13	Webb, D .... –(4)
Forrester, J .... 6(15)	Marshall, L .... 10(1)	Whittle, J .... 15(3)
France, R .... 7(21)	Melton, S .... –(5)	Wiseman, S .... –(2)

League goals (82): Burgess 18, Allsopp 15, Elliott 14, Price 9, Green 6, Forrester 4, Dawson 3, Ashbee 2, Delaney 2, France 2, Hinds 1, Holt 1, Joseph 1, Lewis 1, Thelwell 1, Walters 1, Opponents 1.
F.A. Cup goals (1): Price 1. **Carling Cup goals:** None. **LDV Vans Trophy goals (4):** Forrester 1, France 1, Williams, R 1, Webb 1.
Average home League attendance: 16,846. **Player of Year:** Damien Delaney.

KIDDERMINSTER HARRIERS

Jan Molby declared his intention to rebuild after a modest season in which Harriers slipped to third from bottom after winning only one their first eight matches of 2004. Molby, who began a second spell at the club when Ian Britton was sacked in October, led them out of trouble with ten points from the next four games and they finished comfortably clear of trouble. High spot of the season came in round three of the F.A. Cup when they were denied victory over Wolves by Alex Rae's 89th minute equaliser and made the Premiership side work hard for a 2-0 win in the replay at Molineux.

Antoine-Curier, M ...... –(1)	Foster, I .... 10(1)	Rickards, S .... 5(8)
Bennett, D .... 34(4)	Gadsby, M .... 23(9)	Sall, A .... 6(1)
Betts, R .... 8(1)	Hatswell, W 32	Shilton, S .... 9(5)
Bishop, A .... 8(3)	Henriksen, B .... 14(8)	Smith, J .... 19(3)
Brock, S 37	Hinton, C .... 41(1)	Stamps, S .... 34(1)
Brown, S 8	Jenkins, L .... 5(2)	Viveash, A 7
Burton, S .... 10(2)	Keates, D 8	Ward, G .... 17(4)
Christiansen, J ..... 11(10)	Lewis, M .... 1(3)	White, A .... 6(1)
Clarke, L .... 3(1)	McHale, C .... –(1)	Williams, D 28
Coleman, K 10	Melligan, J 5	Williams, J .... 28(16)
Danby, J 9	Murray, A .... 19(3)	Willis, A 12
Dyer, L .... 5(2)	Parrish, S .... 16(11)	Yates, M 14
Flynn, S .... 4(2)		

League goals (45): Williams, D 5, Williams, J 4, Bennett 3, Foster 3, Murray 3, Parrish 3, Bishop 2, Brown 2, Gadsby 2, Hatswell 2, Henriksen 2, Keates 2, Yates 2, Christiansen 1, Dyer 1, Hinton 1, Melligan 1, Rickards 1, White 1, Willis 1, Opponents 3.
F.A. Cup goals (6): Bennett 4, Burton 1, Williams, J 1. **Carling Cup goals:** None. **LDV Vans Trophy goals:** None.
Average home League attendance: 2,980. **Player of Year:** Wayne Hatswell.

LEYTON ORIENT

Orient were grateful to have accumulated enough points to offset a wretched finish in which they won only once in 15 matches – a 2-1 victory which condemned York to the Conference in the penultimate fixture. Former player Martin Ling had earlier looked to be steering his side to a respectable position after replacing Paul Brush as manager. Five wins in the first seven matches of 2004 even suggested Orient might close the gap on the Play-off positions. Despite the change in fortunes, Gary Alexander continued to score regularly, finishing with 15 to his credit for the season. But Orient badly needed some back-up.

Akinfenwa, A .... –(1)	Heald, G 4	Newey, T .... 31(3)
Alexander, G 44	Hunt, D .... 35(3)	Peters, M 39
Barnard, D .... 17(6)	Hunt, W 6	Purser, W .... 29(11)
Brazier, M 5	Ibehre, J .... 17(18)	Saah, B .... 4(2)
Cooper, S 9	Jones, B .... 29(2)	Sam, L .... 5(5)
Downer, S .... 1(2)	Joseph, M .... 23(1)	Scott, A 8
Duncan, D .... –(1)	Lockwood, M .... 24(1)	Stephens, K .... –(1)
Ebdon, M .... 10(4)	Mackie, J 20	Tate, C .... 5(19)
Forbes, B .... –(1)	McCormack, A .... 8(2)	Thorpe, L .... 15(2)
Hammond, D .... 6(2)	McGhee, D 10	Toner, C .... 19(8)
Harnwell, J .... 1(2)	Miller, J .... 27(7)	Zakuani, G .... 9(1)
Harrison, L .... 19(1)	Morris, G 27	

League goals (48): Alexander 15, Purser 5, Ibehre 4, Thorpe 4, Lockwood 2, Miller 2, Newey 2, Peters 2, Zakuani 2, Brazier 1, Hunt, D 1, Mackie 1, McGhee 1, Scott 1, Tate 1, Toner 1, Opponents 3.
F.A. Cup goals (3): Alexander 1, Lockwood 1, Purser 1. **Carling Cup goals (1):** Ibehre 1.
LDV Vans Trophy goals (1): Lockwood 1.
Average home League attendance: 4,156. **Player of Year:** Gary Alexander.

LINCOLN CITY

Manager Keith Alexander returned three months after life-saving brain surgery to lead his side into the Play-offs for the second successive season. And they looked to be heading back to the Millennium Stadium when two goals in two minutes by Richard Butcher and Mark Bailey overturned a 2-1 first leg home defeat by Huddersfield in the semi-finals. But Lincoln conceded a controversial penalty after Jamie McCombe challenged Andy Booth with an hour gone and seven minutes from the end a second goal put them out.

Bailey, M .... 34(1)	Liburd, R .... 19(5)	Richardson, M .... 34(4)
Bloomer, M .... 14(13)	Marriott, A 46	Rocastle, C .... –(2)
Butcher, R .... 26(6)	May, R .... 1(4)	Sandwith, K .... 1(2)
Carbon, M 1	Mayo, P .... 31(2)	Sedgemore, B .... 24(3)
Cropper, D .... 5(16)	McCombe, J 8	Wattley, D .... 1(2)
Ellison, K 11	McNamara, N .... 2(8)	Weaver, S 39
Fletcher, G 42	Morgan, P 41	Wilford, A .... –(5)
Futcher, B 43	Pearce, A .... –(3)	Willis, S .... –(1)
Gain, P 42	Remy, E .... –(1)	Yeo, S .... 13(28)
Green, F .... 28(7)		

Play-offs – appearances: Bailey 2, Bloomer 2, Butcher 2, Ellison 2, Fletcher 2, Futcher 2, Gain 2, Marriott 2, Richardson 2, Yeo 2, McCombe 1(1), Weaver 1, Green –(2), Liburd –(1), Wilford –(1).
League goals (68): Fletcher 16, Yeo 11, Richardson 9, Gain 7, Green 7, Butcher 6, Mayo 6, Futcher 3, Bailey 1, Wilford 1, Opponents 1. **Play-offs – goals (3):** Bailey 1, Butcher 1, Fletcher 1.
F.A. Cup goals (3): Bloomer 1, Mayo 1, Yeo 1. **Carling Cup goals:** None. **LDV Vans Trophy goals (7):** Fletcher 2, Bailey 1, Green 1, Mayo 1, Richardson 1, Yeo 1.
Average home League attendance: 4,910. **Player of Year:** Gary Fletcher.

MACCLESFIELD TOWN

Macclesfield were second from bottom, three points adrift and staring at Conference football, when Brian Horton became their third manager of the season after David Moss and John Askey. Horton, who had parted company with Port Vale six weeks earlier, immediately delivered three straight wins over fellow strugglers York, Leyton Orient and Rochdale to ease the pressure, and two own goals conceded by Oxford in their penultimate game confirmed survival. Matthew Tipton, with 16 goals, let the way for a side who finished top of the division's Fair Play table.

Abbey, G .... 23(2)	Harsley, P 16	Potter, G 16
Adams, D 27	Hitchen, S .... 8(1)	Priest, C .... 26(3)
Beresford, D 5	Jones, R 1	Robinson, N .... –(1)
Beswetherick, J .... 3(1)	Little, C .... 18(6)	Ross, N .... 1(5)
Brackenridge, S ..... 2(5)	Macauley, S 16	Smith, D .... 7(3)
Carr, M 7	Miles, J .... 23(6)	Tipton, M .... 34(4)
Carragher, M 18	Munroe, K .... 35(1)	Welch, M .... 33(5)
Carruthers, M ..... 30(9)	Myhill, S 15	Whitaker, D .... 33(3)
Clark, S .... 1(3)	Olsen, J .... –(2)	Widdrington, T .... 34(1)
Flitcroft, D .... 14(1)	Parkin, J 12	Wilson, S .... 31(1)
Haddrell, M .... 4(6)	Payne, S 13	

League goals (54): Tipton 16, Carruthers 8, Miles 6, Little 5, Whitaker 5, Brackenridge 2, Harsley 2, Potter 2, Priest 2, Haddrell 1, Parkin 1, Opponents 4.
F.A. Cup goals (7): Tipton 3, Carruthers 2, Little 1, Miles 1. **Carling Cup goals (1):** Whitaker 1. **LDV Vans Trophy goals (1):** Adams 1.
Average home League attendance: 2,385. **Player of Year:** Matthew Tipton.

MANSFIELD TOWN

Penalties played an influential role as Mansfield narrowly missed out on an immediate return to Division Two. They maintained an interest in the third automatic promotion place until a 3-2 home defeat by Carlisle, sealed by Matt Glennon's last-minute save from Liam Lawrence's spot-kick, in their last-but-one home match. There was success in a 5-4 shoot-out against Northampton after the teams' Play-off semi-final ended all-square after extra-time. But it was Huddersfield who kept their composure after a goalless Final, which could have gone either way, winning this shoot-out 4-1.

Artell, D .... 24(2)	D'Jaffo, L .... 4(4)	Mendes, J .... 36(3)
Baptiste, A .... 14(3)	Day, R .... 40(1)	Mitchell, C .... +–(1)
Beardsley, C .... 2(13)	Dimech, L .... 17(3)	Mulligan, L .... –(1)
Buxton, J 9	Disley, C .... 18(16)	Pacquette, R .... 3(2)
Christie, I .... 24(3)	Eaton, A 3	Pilkington, K 46
Clarke, J .... 11(1)	Hasssell, B .... 33(1)	Vaughan, A 32
Corden, S .... 40(4)	Larkin, C .... 19(18)	White, A .... 2(12)
Curle, K .... –(1)	Lawrence, L 41	Williamson, L .... 29(7)
Curtis, T .... 34(4)	MacKenzie, N .... 25(7)	

Play-offs – appearances: Baptiste 3, Corden 3, Curtis 3, Day 3, Disley 3, Eaton 3, Hassell 3, Lawrence 3, Mendes 3, Pilkington 3, Williamson 3, D'Jaffo –(3), Larkin –(3), MacKenzie –(3).
League goals (76): Lawrence 19, Mendes 11, Christie 8, Corden 8, Larkin 7, Day 6, Disley 5, Artell 3, MacKenzie 2, Vaughan 2, Beardsley 1, Buxton 1, D'Jaffo 1, Dimech 1, Pacquette 1. **Play-offs – goals (3):** Curtis 1, Day 1, Mendes 1.
F.A. Cup goals (10): Lawrence 3, MacKenzie 3, Christie 1, Curtis 1, Larkin 1, Mendes 1.
Carling Cup goals (1): Opponents 1. **LDV Vans Trophy goals (1):** Day 1.
Average home League attendance: 5,206. **Player of Year:** Liam Lawrence.

NORTHAMPTON TOWN

Colin Calderwood came from coaching Tottenham reserves to turn around Northampton's season, only for his team to suffer disappointment when a place in the Final of the Play-offs beckoned. Calderwood, who replaced Martin Wilkinson as manager, lifted them from 19th into a top six spot with a run of only one defeat in 12 matches through to the end of the regular season. There was another recovery when three goals in the space of ten minutes either side of half-time wiped out a 2-0 home defeat by Mansfield in the first leg of the semi-finals. But Mansfield recovered to take the game into extra-time, then won a penalty shoot-out 5-4.

Abidallah, N .... –(1)	Harsley, P .... 5(9)	Smith, M .... 43(1)
Amoo, R .... –(1)	Lincoln, G .... 4(3)	Taylor, J .... 3(5)
Asamoah, D .... 4(27)	Low, J .... 28(5)	Thompson, G .... 7(1)
Burgess, O .... 3(6)	Lyttle, D .... 23(4)	Trollope, P 43
Carruthers, C .... 19(5)	Morison, S .... 2(3)	Ullathorne, R 13
Chambers, L .... 19(5)	Reeves, M .... 9(5)	Vieira, M .... 7(3)
Clark, P 6	Reid, P 33	Walker, R .... 11(1)
Doig, C 9	Richards, M .... 27(14)	Westwood, A .... 8(1)
Dudfield, L .... 12(7)	Sabin, E .... 9(2)	Willmott, C .... 35(1)
Hargreaves, C .... 41(1)	Sadler, M 7	Youngs, T .... 2(10)
Harper, L 39	Sampson, I .... 35(2)	

Play-offs – appearances: Hargreaves 2, Harper 2, Low 2, Richards 2, Sampson 2, Smith 2, Trollope 2, Ullathorne 2, Willmott 2, Asamoah 1(1), Reid 1(1), Sabin 1, Westwood 1, Reeves –(1), Youngs –(1).
League goals (58): Smith 11, Richards 10, Trollope 6, Sabin 5, Walker 4, Asamoah 3, Dudfield 3, Hargreaves 3, Low 3, Reid 2, Sampson 2, Vieira 2, Lincoln 1, Morison 1, Taylor 1, Ullathorne 1, Willmott 1. **Play-offs – goals (3):** Hargreaves 1, Smith 1.
F.A. Cup goals (10): Smith 3, Richards 3, Walker 2, Asamoah 1, Hargreaves 1, Low 1.
Carling Cup goals (3): Dudfield 1, Hargreaves 1, Low 1. **LDV Vans Trophy goals (5):** Dudfield 2, Walker 2, Low 1.
Average home League attendance: 5,305. **Player of Year:** Lee Harper.

OXFORD UNITED

Top of the table at the turn of the year; three points adrift of a play-off place come the end of the season. That was how Oxford's fortunes plummeted, and not even the introduction of Graham Rix after Ian Atkins was dismissed in March when Bristol Rovers announced he was to be their new manager, could stop the rot. Rix did not celebrate a victory until the final day of the campaign when, in his ninth game in charge, Rochdale were beaten 2-0. Before that, Oxford had collected just nine points from 15 matches.

Alsop, J .... 26(3)	Louis, J .... 6(14)	Scott, A .... 2(4)
Ashton, J .... 30(4)	McCarthy, P .... 28(1)	Steele, L .... 3(13)
Basham, S 38	McNiven, S 41	Townsley, D .... 9(2)
Bound, M .... 33(4)	Oldfield, D .... 1(2)	Walker, R .... 3(1)
Brown, D 12	Omoyinmi, E .... 1(2)	Wanless, P 38
Cox, S 5	Pitt, C .... 5(3)	Waterman, D .... 6(7)
Crosby, A .... 41(1)	Quinn, A .... 5(1)	Whitehead, D .... 37(2)
Foran, R .... 3(1)	Rawle, M .... 10(21)	Winters, T .... –(1)
Hackett, C .... 6(16)	Robinson, M 40	Woodman, A 41
Hunt, J .... 36(5)		

League goals (55): Basham 14, Rawle 8, Whitehead 7, Alsop 5, Crosby 5, Wanless 5, Hunt 2, Louis 2, McCarthy 2, Bound 1, Hackett 1, Robinson 1, Steele 1, Opponents 1.
F.A. Cup goals: None. **Carling Cup goals (2):** Basham 1, Louis 1. **LDV Vans Trophy goals:** None.
Average home League attendance: 6,296. **Player of Year:** Dean Whitehead.

ROCHDALE

Steve Parkin's second spell as manager, two years after he left for Barnsley, did not turn out as supporters hoped. Parkin came back when Alan Buckley was sacked at the end of 2003, but Rochdale remained just above the relegation zone and with four games remaining had both York and Carlisle breathing down their neck. Then, successive victories over Leyton Orient and Kidderminster eased the pressure as they finished five points clear of trouble after another disappointing season.

Antoine-Curier, M	5(3)	Flood, W	6	Ndiwa, K	–(1)
Beech, C	9(5)	Gilks, M	12	Patterson, R	3(4)
Bertos, L	40	Grand, S	11(6)	Pemberton, M	1
Betts, R	4(1)	Griffiths, G	29(4)	Redfearn, N	9
Bishop, A	8(2)	Heald, G	10	Shuker, C	14
Brannan, G	11	Hill, S	1	Simpkins, M	25(2)
Burgess, D	33(2)	Holt, G	14	Smith, S	13
Connor, P	21(3)	Jones, G	26	Smith, J	1
Donovan, K	4(3)	Livesey, D	11(2)	Strachan, C	–(1)
Doughty, M	25(6)	McClare, S	33(5)	Townson, K	17(16)
Edwards, N	34	McCourt, P	6(18)	Warner, S	10(4)
Evans, W	45	McEvilly, L	15(15)		

League goals (49): Townson 10, Bertos 9, Connor 6, McEvilly 6, Jones 4, Holt 3, Betts 2, McCourt 2, Antoine-Curier 1, Bishop 1, Brannan 1, Griffiths 1, Heald 1, Shuker 1, Warner 1.
F.A. Cup goals (2): Bertos 1, Townson 1. **Carling Cup goals (1):** Townson 1. **LDV Vans Trophy goals:** None.
Average home League attendance: 3,277. **Player of Year:** Wayne Evans.

SCUNTHORPE UNITED

Steven MacLean, on loan from Rangers, was the division's top scorer – but his team finished in their worst position for 22 years, distracted, perhaps, by an F.A. Cup run which took them to the fourth round before a 2-1 defeat at Portsmouth. Scunthorpe slipped from a seemingly secure mid-table position when winning only one of their final 12 games, and were forced to reinstate Brian Laws as manager, three weeks after his departure amid a boardroom power struggle, when the drop looked a real possibility. MacLean's 23 goals included hat-tricks against Cheltenham, Huddersfield and Cambridge.

Barwick, T	27(3)	Hayes, P	12(23)	Ridley, L	15(3)
Beagrie, P	28(4)	Holloway, D	5	Russell, S	10
Butler, A	33(1)	Hunt, J	–(1)	Sharp, K	37(3)
Byrne, C	39	Jackson, M	15(2)	Smith, J	1
Calvo-Garcia, A	8(4)	Keegan, P	–(2)	Sparrow, M	37(1)
Evans, T	36	Kell, R	21(3)	Stanton, N	31(2)
Featherstone, L	7(4)	Kilford, I	11(7)	Taylor, C	18(2)
Graves, W	12(9)	MacLean, S	37(5)	Torpey, S	42(1)
Groves, P	13	McCombe, J	8(7)	Williams, M	–(1)
Gulliver, P	2	Parton, A	1(3)		

League goals (69): MacLean 23, Beagrie 11, Torpey 11, Groves 3, Sparrow 3, Taylor 3, Butler 2, Calvo-Garcia 2, Hayes 2, Kell 2, Sharp 2, Barwick 1, Byrne 1, Holloway 1, Ridley 1, Opponents 1.
F.A. Cup goals (7): Torpey 3, Hayes 2, McCombe 1, Parton 1. **Carling Cup goals (4):** Hayes 2, Beagrie 1, MacLean 1. **LDV Vans Trophy goals (6):** Hayes 1, Jackson 1, Kell 1, MacLean 1, Sparrow 1, Torpey 1.
Average home League attendance: 3,839. **Player of Year:** Steven MacLean.

SOUTHEND UNITED

A significant improvement in the second half of the season took Southend clear of relegation trouble and brought a place in the LDV Vans Trophy Final. Steve Tilson, confirmed as manager after a spell as caretaker when Steve Wignall was dismissed in November, believes it augurs well for the new campaign. His team were third from bottom going into the New Year, but boosted by 21-goal Leon Constantine they climbed clear of trouble. Drewe Broughton provided some strong support as Southend progressed to the Millennium Stadium, although neither could disturb Blackpool's command of the Final which the Division Two side won 2-0.

Bentley, M	15(6)	Fullarton, J	7	Nightingale, L	–(4)
Bramble, T	16(18)	Gower, M	40	Odunsi, L	12
Broughton, D	27(8)	Hunt, L	23(3)	Pettefer, C	11
Clark, S	2(4)	Husbands, M	3(6)	Petterson, A	1
Constantine, L	40(3)	Jenkins, N	7(9)	Robinson, R	2
Corbett, J	13(4)	Jupp, D	39(1)	Smith, J	16(2)
Cort, L	46	Kightly, M	2(9)	Stuart, J	23(3)
Dudfield, L	13	Maher, K	42	Tilson, S	–(1)
Emberson, C	6	McSweeney, D	16(5)	Warren, M	27(5)
Flahavan, D	37	Nicolau, N	9	Wilson, C	11(3)

League goals (51): Constantine 21, Gower 6, Dudfield 5, Bramble 4, Bentley 2, Broughton 2, Warren 2, Corbett 1, Cort 1, Jenkins 1, Maher 1, McSweeney 1, Odunsi 1, Smith 1, Opponents 2.
F.A. Cup goals (8): Smith 3, Bramble 2, Gower 2, Corbett 1. **Carling Cup goals (2):** Broughton 1, Maher 1. **LDV Vans Trophy goals (15):** Broughton 5, Constantine 4, Bramble 2, Clark 1, Corbett 1, Gower 1, Kightly 1.
Average home League attendance: 4,535. **Player of Year:** Mark Gower.

SWANSEA CITY

Swansea were left with a sense of what might have been . . . . . . if leading scorer Lee Trundle had not been deprived of a bigger tally by injury and his team had not dropped so many points at home. Going into 2004, they were handily placed for a push towards the play-offs, but were unable to sustain it during and after a good FA Cup run in which they reached the fifth round before losing to Tranmere in a tie which could have gone either way. By the time Kenny Jackett replaced Brian Flynn as manager in early April, they had lost touch with the top six.

Britton, L	42	Hylton, L	10(1)	O'Leary, K	28(6)
Byrne, S	2	Iriekpen, E	33(1)	Pritchard, M	1(3)
Coates, J	14(13)	Jenkins, L	8(3)	Rees, M	3
Connolly, K	4(6)	Johnrose, L	21(4)	Rewbury, J	1(1)
Connor, P	12	Jones, S	16(8)	Roberts, S	8(4)
Corbisierso, A	1(4)	Martinez, R	24(3)	Robinson, A	34(3)
Duffy, R	16(2)	Maxwell, L	1(2)	Tate, A	25(1)
Durkan, K	11(4)	Maylett, B	26(7)	Thomas, J	8(8)
Fieldwick, L	4(1)	Murphy, D	11	Trundle, L	29(2)
Freestone, R	35(2)	Nardiello, D	3(1)	Wilson, M	12
Howard, M	25	Nugent, K	31(8)		

League goals (58): Trundle 17, Nugent 8, Robinson 8, Connor 5, Maylett 5, Britton 3, Thomas 3, Wilson 2, Connolly 1, Duffy 1, Durkan 1, Iriekpen 1, Rees 1, Roberts 1, Tate 1.
F.A. Cup goals (10): Trundle 5, Nugent 2, Robinson 2, Durkan 1. **Carling Cup goals (1):** Connolly 1. **LDV Vans Trophy goals (1):** Nardiello 1.
Average home League attendance: 6,853. **Player of Year:** Andy Robinson.

TORQUAY UNITED

Leroy Rosenior, one of the game's bright young coaches, led Torquay to the third automatic promotion place thanks to a productive end-of-season run just when they seemed resigned to a place in the Play-offs. His team recaptured their form to whittle away a five-point lead held by Huddersfield by winning four and drawing one of their last five matches to go up on goal difference. David Graham scored his 22nd goal as Torquay won 2-1 at Southend on the last day of the campaign while Huddersfield were being held at Cheltenham.

Bedeau, A	13(11)	Benefield, J	3(12)	Bernard, N	–(1)

Bond, K .... –(1)	Hazell, R .... 12(7)	Russell, A .... 42(1)
Broad, J .... 4(10)	Hill, K .... 42(3)	Taylor, C 43
Canoville, L .... 32(1)	Hockley, M .... 44(1)	Van Heusden, A 25
Dearden, L .... 21(1)	Killoughery, G .... –(3)	Williamson, M .... 9(2)
Fowler, J .... 24(7)	Kuffour, J .... 33(8)	Wills, K .... 7(16)
Graham, D .... 41(4)	McGlinchey, B 34	Woods, S 46
Gritton, M .... 17(14)	McMahon, D .... –(1)	Woozley, D .... 4(6)
Hankin, S 1	Rosenior, L .... 9(1)	

League goals (68): Graham 22, Kuffour 10, Woods 6, Hill 5, Hockley 5, Gritton 4, Taylor 4, Wills 3, Fowler 2, Russell 2, Bedeau 1, Canoville 1, Hazell 1, Opponents 2.
F.A. Cup goals (1): Benefield 1. **Carling Cup goals (1):** Graham 1. **LDV Vans Trophy goals (2):** Benefield 1, Wills 1.
Average home League attendance: 3,460. **Player of Year:** Alex Russell.

YEOVIL TOWN

So near, yet so far. A last-minute goal by Gavin Williams gave Yeovil a 3-2 victory at Lincoln on the last day of the season but Northampton's win at Mansfield meant they were edged out of a place in the Play-offs on goal difference. Manager Gary Johnson said his players could not have done any more and the Conference champions certainly deserved credit for going so close in their first taste of League football. What proved costly in the end was a run of only one win in eight matches in March/April which left them playing catch-up.

Bishop, A .... 4(1)	Jackson, K .... 19(11)	Rodrigues, H .... 23(11)
Bull, R 7	Johnson, L 45	Skiverton, T .... 25(1)
Collis, S 11	Lindegaard, A .... 12(11)	Stansfield, A .... 7(25)
Crittenden, N .... 20(9)	Lockwood, A 43	Talbot, N .... –(1)
Edwards, J .... 17(10)	Matthews, L .... 2(2)	Terry, P .... 22(12)
El Kholti, A .... 19(4)	O'Brien, R 13	Way, D .... 38(1)
Elam, L .... 6(6)	Pluck, C 36	Weale, C 35
Gall, K .... 39(4)	Reed, S .... 3(2)	Weatherstone, S ..... 11(4)
Giles, C .... –(1)	Rodrigues, D .... 3(1)	Williams, ... 42
Gosling, J .... 4(8)		

League goals (70): Williams 9, Gall 8, Edwards 6, Stansfield 6, Jackson 5, Johnson 5, Way 5, Rodrigues, D 4, Lockwood 4, Pluck 4, Bishop 2, Crittenden 2, Lindegaard 2, Skiverton 2, El Kholti 1, Elam 1, Gosling 1, Rodrigues, H 1, Terry 1, Weatherstone 1.
F.A. Cup goals (9): Williams 3, Edwards 2, Pluck 2, Crittenden 1, Gall 1. **Carling Cup goals (1):** Opponents 1. **LDV Vans Trophy goals (4):** Edwards 2, Gall 1, Williams 1.
Average home League attendance: 6,196. **Player of Year:** Gavin Williams.

YORK CITY

The season got off to a bad start for Chris Brass, at 28 the League's youngest manager, when he was sent off in his first match in charge at Carlisle. Nine months later it ended with York losing their League status after 75 years. The team were only two points off a Play-off place going into the New Year. But after a 2-0 win over Carlisle on January 10, they went into free-fall, failing to win again and accumulating only five points in their last 20 matches. There were six more red cards, the last of them shown to goalkeeper Mark Ovendale in a 2-0 home defeat by Cheltenham.

Arthur, A .... 2(1)	Cooper, R .... 26(12)	Fox, C .... 2(3)
Ashcroft, A .... 1(1)	Crowe, D .... 2(3)	George, L .... 14(7)
Bell, A .... 3(7)	Davies, S .... 6(2)	Haw, R .... –(1)
Brackstone, S .... 4(5)	Dickman, J 2	Hope, R 36
Brass, C 39	Dove, C 1	Law, G .... 2(2)
Browne, G .... 2(3)	Downes, S .... 4(2)	Merris, D .... 42(2)
Bullock, L .... 34(1)	Dunning, D 42	Newby, J .... 6(1)
Coad, M .... –(3)	Edmondson, D .... 26(1)	Nogan, L .... 38(1)

Offiong, R .... 2(2)   Smith, C .... 26(2)   Wilford, A .... 4(2)
Overndale, M 41   Stewart, B .... 2(8)   Wise, S .... 18(1)
Parkin, J .... 9(6)   Walker, J .... 7(2)   Wood, L .... 21(5)
Porter, C 5   Ward, M .... 27(4)   Yalcin, L .... 5(10)
Shaw, J .... 5(3)

League goals (35): Nogan 8, Bullock 7, Dunning 3, George 3, Brackstone 2, Cooper 2, Hope 2, Parkin 2, Wilford 2, Bell 1, Brass 1, Edmondson 1, Wise 1.
F.A. Cup goals (1): Nogan 1. **Carling Cup goals (1):** Merris 1. **LDV Vans Trophy goals (1):** Dunning 1.
Average home League attendance: 3,962.

SCOTTISH LEAGUE ROLL CALL

APPEARANCES & SCORERS 2003-04

(Figures in brackets = appearances as substitute)

BANK OF SCOTLAND PREMIER LEAGUE

ABERDEEN

Ground: Pittodrie Stadium, Aberdeen AB24 5QH. **Capacity:** 22,199.
Telephone: 01224 650400. **Colours:** Red and white. **Nickname:** Dons.

Anderson, R 25   Heikkinen, M 38   O'Leary, R 2
Bird, M .... –(2)   Higgins, C 4   Preece, D 36
Booth, S .... 20(1)   Hinds, L .... 23(7)   Prunty, B .... 6(12)
Buckley, R .... 6(2)   Lombardi, M .... –(1)   Rutkiewicz, K 16
Clark, C .... 18(5)   Mackie, D .... 4(12)   Sheerin, P .... 27(6)
Considine, A 1   McCulloch, M .... 1(2)   Souter, K .... 1(2)
Deloumeaux, E .... 8(3)   McGuire, P .... 16(1)   Stewart, J .... 3(5)
Diamond, A .... 17(2)   McNaughton, K ...... 15(2)   Tarditi, S .... –(1)
Donald, D .... –(1)   McQuilken, J 7   Tiernan, F .... 3(3)
Esson, R 2   Morrison, S .... 26(1)   Tosh, S .... 24(2)
Foster, R .... 12(6)   Muirhead, S .... 24(8)   Zdrilic, D .... 23(8)
Hart, M .... 10(1)

League goals (39): Booth 8, Anderson 5, Hinds 5, Zdrilic 4, Tosh 3, Deloumeaux 2, Diamond 2, McGuire 2, Prunty 2, Clark 1, Foster 1, Morrison 1, Sheerin 1, Opponents 2.
Tennents Cup goals (6): Zdrilic 2, Booth 1, Clark 1, Heikkinen 1, Muirhead 1.
CIS Cup goals (10): Tosh 3, Hinds 2, Zdrilic 2, Booth 1, Muirhead 1, Sheerin 1.

CELTIC

Ground: Celtic Park, Glasgow G40 3RE. **Capacity:** 60,506.
Telephone: 0141 556 2611. **Colours:** Green and white. **Nickname:** Bhoys.

Agathe, D .... 26(1)   Lambert, P .... 9(4)   Mjallby, J .... 10(3)
Balde, B .... 30(1)   Larsson, H .... 36(1)   Pearson, S .... 16(1)
Beattie, C .... 2(8)   Lennon, N 35   Petrov, S .... 33(2)
Crainey, S .... 1(1)   Maloney, S .... 7(10)   Smith, J .... 4(7)
Douglas, R .... 15(1)   Marshall, D 11   Sutton, C 25
Gray, M .... 2(5)   McGeady, A .... 3(1)   Sylla, M .... 5(9)
Hartson, J .... 14(1)   McManus, S 5   Thompson, A 26
Hedman, M 12   McNamara, J .... 26(1)   Valgaeren, J .... 4(3)
Kennedy, J .... 9(3)   Miller, L .... 13(12)   Varga, S 35

Wallace, R .... 4(4)

League goals (105): Larsson 30, Sutton 19, Thompson 11, Hartson 8, Petrov 6, Varga 6, Agathe 5, Maloney 5, Pearson 3, Balde 2, Miller 2, Beattie 1, Kennedy 1, Lambert 1, McGeady 1, McNamara 1, Wallace 1, Opponents 2.
Tennents Cup (12): Larsson 5, Petrov 3, Sutton 2, Hartson 1, Lambert 1. **CIS Cup (3):** Beattie 1, Smith 1, Varga 1. **Champions League goals (18):** Sutton 6, Larsson 3, Miller 3, Agathe 1, Hartson 1, Maloney 1, Petrov 1, Thompson 1, Opponents 1. **UEFA Cup goals (5):** Larsson 3, Sutton 1, Thompson 1.

DUNDEE

Ground: Dens Park, Dundee DD3 7JY. **Capacity:** 12,371.
Telephone: 01382 889966. **Colours:** Navy blue and white. **Nickname:** Dark Blues.

Barrett, N .... 10(2)	Jablonski, N .... 3(9)	Novo, N .... 34(1)
Brady, G .... 35(2)	Kneissl, S .... 5(6)	Rae, G .... 11(2)
Burley, C .... 1(1)	Linn, B .... 3(10)	Ravanelli, F 5
Caballero, F .... 9(4)	Lovell, S .... 15(6)	Robb, S .... 9(6)
Cameron, D .... 6(5)	Mackay, D .... 34(1)	Sancho, B .... 20(1)
Carranza, B .... –(2)	Mair, L 36	Sara, J .... 3(7)
Clark, N .... –(2)	McDonald, C 6	Smith, B .... 27(2)
Cowan, T .... 4(1)	McLean, D .... 3(1)	Soutar, D 1
Fotheringham, M .... 19(5)	McNally, S .... 1(1)	Speroni, J 37
Hegarty, C .... 1(3)	Milne, S .... 15(5)	Wilkie, L 21
Hernandez Santos, J. 27(2)	Nemsadze, G 9	Youngson, A .... 1(1)
Hutchinson, T .... 8(4)		

League goals (48): Novo 19, Milne 8, Lovell 5, Fotheringham 4, Barrett 2, Rae 2, Smith 2, Cowan 1, Hutchinson 1, Kneissl 1, Mair 1, McLean 1, Wilkie 1.
Tennents Cup goals (2): Novo 1, Robb 1. **CIS Cup goals (6):** Ravanelli 3, Linn 1, Novo 1, Wilkie 1. **UEFA Cup goals (7):** Novo 4, Lovell 1, Rae 1, Sara 1.

DUNDEE UNITED

Ground: Tannadice Park, Dundee DD3 7JW. **Capacity:** 14,209.
Telephone: 01382 833166. **Colours:** Tangerine and black. **Nickname:** Terrors.

Archibald, A 38	Gallacher, P 33	McLaren, A .... 26(1)
Bollan, G .... 1(1)	Griffin, D .... 9(4)	Miller, C .... 22(4)
Bullock, T 5	Holmes, G .... –(3)	Paterson, J .... 10(6)
Conway, A .... –(1)	Innes, C 29	Paterson, S .... 2(1)
Coyle, O .... –(3)	Kerr, M .... 30(3)	Robson, B .... 25(3)
Dodds, B .... 23(10)	McCracken, D 32	Samuel, C .... 11(15)
Duff, S .... 10(8)	McInnes, D .... 34(1)	Scotland, J .... 10(11)
Easton, C .... 10(12)	McIntyre, J .... 27(3)	Wilson, M .... 31(1)

League goals (47): Dodds 10, McIntyre 9, Miller 5, Scotland 5, McLaren 4, Robson 3, Wilson 3, Archibald 2, Samuel 2, Innes 1, Kerr 1, McCracken 1, McInnes 1.
Tennents Cup goals (1): McInnes 1. **CIS Cup goals (3):** McIntyre 2, McLaren 1.

DUNFERMLINE ATHLETIC

Ground: East End Park, Dunfermline KY12 7RB. **Capacity:** 12,558.
Telephone: 01383 724295. **Colours:** Black and white. **Nickname:** Pars.

Brewster, C .... 23(3)	Greenhill, G .... –(1)	McGarty, M .... –(1)
Bullen, L .... 19(8)	Grondin, D .... 9(5)	McGroarty, C 2
Byrne, R .... 10(3)	Hunt, N .... 5(8)	McGuire, K .... –(1)
Clark, P .... 1(1)	Kilgallon, S .... 4(7)	Mehmet, B .... 5(13)
Crawford, S .... 33(1)	Labonte, A .... 8(13)	Nicholson, B 36
Dair, J .... –(1)	Mason, G 32	Ruitenbeek, M 1
Dempsey, G .... 15(17)	McDermott, A .... 5(1)	Shields, G .... 15(2)

Skerla, A	35	Tod, A	22(8)	Young, Darren	32
Stillie, D	37	Wilson, C	1	Young, Derek	25(3)
Thomson, Scott	15(1)	Wilson, D	2		

League goals (47): Crawford 13, Brewster 5, Dempsey 5, Nicholson 5, Young, Derek 4, Bullen 2, Hunt 2, Tod 2, Mehmet 1, Shields 1, Thomson, Scott 1, Wilson, S 1, Young, Darren.1. Opponents 4.

Tennents Cup goals (14): Brewster 4, Nicholson 4, Crawford 2, Bullen 1, Byrne 1, Skerla 1, Young, Darren 1. **CIS Cup (4):** Crawford 2, Brewster 1, Young, Darren 1.

HEARTS

Ground: Tynecastle, Edinburgh EH 11 2NL. **Capacity:** 18,000.
Telephone: 0131 200 7200. **Colours:** Maroon and white. **Nickname:** Jam Tarts.

Berra, C	3(3)	Maybury, A	32(1)	Sloan, R	9(4)
Boyack, S	3(5)	McCann, A	6	Stamp, P	23(2)
Gordon, C	29(1)	McKenna, K	22(10)	Tierney, G	1
Hamill, J	12(6)	McMullan, P	1(1)	Valois, J-L	5(6)
Hartley, P	29(1)	Moilanen, T	9	Wales, G	-(1)
Janczyk, N	4(7)	Neilson, R	25(4)	Webster, A	31(1)
Kirk, A	14(10)	Pressley, S	31	Weir, G	7(11)
Kisnorbo, P	28(3)	Severin, S	24(2)	Wyness, D	19(9)
MacFarlane, N	24(5)	Simmons, S	1(6)	De Vries, M	26(5)

League goals (56): De Vries 13, Kirk 7, Wyness 7, McKenna 5, Pressley 5, Hartley 3, Hamill 2, Maybury 2, Stamp 2, Webster 2, Severin 1, Simmons 1, Weir 1, Opponents 5.

Tennents Cup goals (2): Hamill 1, Opponents 1. **CIS Cup goals (2):** Kirk 1, De Vries 1.
UEFA Cup goals (3): De Vries 2, Webster 1.

HIBERNIAN

Ground: Easter Road, Edinburgh EH7 5QG. **Capacity:** 17,500.
Telephone: 0131 661 2159. **Colours:** Green and white. **Nickname:** Hibees.

Andersson, D	38	Kane, J	-(1)	Reid, A	16(4)
Baillie, J	2	McCluskey, J	-(1)	Riordan, D	27(7)
Brown, S	34(2)	McDonald, K	-(1)	Shields, J	1
Brebner, G	22	McManus, T	18(14)	Smith, G	19(1)
Caldwell, G	16(1)	Murdock, C	32	Thomson, K	22
Dobbie, S	7(21)	Murray, J	14	Thomson, S	1
Doumbe, M	33	Nicol, K	11(4)	Whittaker, S	15(13)
Edge, R	20	O'Connor, G	27(6)	Wiss, J	13
Fletcher, S	1(4)	Orman, A	13(5)	Zambernardi, Y	7(1)
Glass, S	9(3)				

League goals (41): Riordan 15, O'Connor 5, Brown 3, McManus 3, Murdock 3, Dobbie 2, Doumbe 2, Brebner 1, Caldwell 1, Murray 1, Nicol 1, Reid 1, Thomson, K 1, Whittaker 1, Opponents 1.

Tennents Cup goals: None. CIS Cup goals (14): Dobbie 4, Riordan 3, O'Connor 2, Brebner 1, Brown 1, Murray 1, Thomson, K 1, Opponents 1.

KILMARNOCK

Ground: Rugby Park, Kilmarnock KA1 2DP. **Capacity:** 18,128.
Telephone: 01563 545300. **Colours:** White and blue. **Nickname:** Killie.

Boyd, K	31(6)	Dillon, S	2	Fulton, S	21
Canero, P	12(1)	Dindeleux, F	33	Greer, G	23(2)
Canning, M	4(1)	Dodds, R	9(2)	Hardie, M	8(8)
Dargo, C	3(9)	Dubourdeau, F	19	Hay, G	30
Di Giacomo, P	4(3)	Fowler, J	25(7)	Hessey, S	7

Innes, C 1
Invincible, D .... 19(3)
Lilley, D 14
Locke, G .... 18(2)
Mahood, A .... 2(3)
McDonald, G .... 15(8)

McLaughlin, B .... 14(2)
McSwegan, G .... 13(18)
Meldrum, C 16
Murray, S .... 22(7)
Naysmith, S .... –(1)

Nish, C .... 15(15)
Samson, C 1
Shields, G 19
Skora, E .... 16(1)
Smith, C .... 2(1)

League goals (51): Boyd 15, Nish 9, Invincible 5, McSwegan 5, Dargo 3, McDonald 3, Skora 3, Canero 2, Canning 1, Dindeleux 1, Hardie 1, Hessey 1, Lilley 1, Shields 1.
Tennents Cup goals (3): McDonald 1, McSwegan 1, Nish 1. **CIS Cup goals:** None.

LIVINGSTON

Ground: City Stadium, Livingston EH54 7DN. **Capacity:** 10,016.
Telephone: 01506 417000. **Colours:** Gold and black. **Nickname:** Livvy's Lions.

Andrews, M 38
Brittain, R .... 5(7)
Camacho, J .... –(6)
Capin, S 2
Dorado, E 28
Fernandez, D ...... 25(2)
Ipoua, G .... –(1)
Kerr, B .... 11(2)
Lilley, D .... 28(7)
Lovell, S .... 24(1)

Main, A 3
Makel, L .... 35(1)
McAllister, J 34
McGovern, J P ..... 12(15)
McKenzie, R 35
McLaughlin, S ...... 8(9)
McMenamin, C ...... 7(8)
McNamee, D .... 29(1)
McPake, J .... –(1)

O'Brien, B .... 28(5)
Pasquinelli, F ...... 16(6)
Quino, F .... 6(6)
Rubio, O .... 36(1)
Snowdon, W .... 1(2)
Toure-Maman, S 1
Whitmore, T .... 2(1)
Wilson, N 4
Xausa, D .... –(1)

League goals (48): Lilley 12, Makel 8, McMenamin 7, O'Brien 6, Fernandez 3, McNamee 3, Pasquinelli 3, Camacho 1, Lovell 1, McAllister 1, McLaughlin 1, Quino 1, Rubio 1.
Tennents Cup goals (8): Lilley 3, Fernandez 2, McMenamin 1, O'Brien 1, Opponents 1.
CIS Cup goals (10): Lilley 3, Makel 3, McAllister 1, Pasquinelli 1, Quino 1, Opponents 1.

MOTHERWELL

Ground: Fir Park, Motherwell ML1 2QN. **Capacity:** 13,742.
Telephone: 01698 333333. **Colours:** Claret and amber. **Nickname:** Well.

Adams, D 31
Bollan, G .... 1(2)
Burns, A .... 29(4)
Clarkson, D .... 32(6)
Corr, B 5
Corrigan, M 38
Cowan, D .... –(1)
Craig, S .... 16(8)
Craigan, S 36

Dair, J .... 19(10)
Fagan, S .... 9(4)
Fitzpatrick, M .... 1(1)
Hammell, S 37
Kinniburgh, W .... –(1)
Lasley, K 33
Leitch, S 20
Marshall, G 33

McDonald, K .... 1(3)
McDonald, S .... 10(5)
McFadden, J .... 2(1)
O'Donnell, P .... 7(2)
Partridge, D 15
Pearson, S .... 17(1)
Quinn, P .... 24(2)
Wright, K .... 2(11)

League goals (42): Clarkson 12, Adams 8, Pearson 4, Craig 3, Lasley 3, McFadden 3, Burns 2, Dair 2, Corrigan 1, Hammell 1, McDonald, S 1, Wright 1, Opponents 1.
Tennents Cup goals (6): Burns 2, Clarkson 2, Adams 1, McDonald, S 1. **CIS Cup goals (3):**
Craig 1, Lasley 1, Pearson 1.

PARTICK THISTLE

Ground: Firhill Stadium, Glasgow G20 7AL. **Capacity:** 14,538.
Telephone: 0141 579 1971. **Colours:** Red, yellow and black. **Nickname:** Jags.

Anis, J Y .... 20(4)
Arthur, K 22
Bonnes, S .... 11(9)
Britton, G .... 15(12)

Cadete, J .... 1(4)
Chiarini, D .... 5(1)
English, T .... –(2)
Fleming, D .... 20(4)

Forrest, E .... 3(2)
Gemmell, J .... –(5)
Gibson, A .... 4(7)
Gibson, B 16

Grady, J .... 32(1)	Milne, K 25	Rowson, D 35
Howie, W .... 5(5)	Mitchell, J .... 30(2)	Strachan, A .... 2(3)
Langfield, J 10	Murray, G 36	Taylor, S .... 6(7)
Lilley, G 15	Panther, E .... –(8)	Thomson, A .... 13(8)
Madaschi, A .... 23(1)	Pinkowski, S 1	Waddell, R .... 3(4)
McBride, J .... 19(2)	Ross, A .... 11(8)	Whyte, D 15
Mikkelsen, J 5	Ross, I .... 15(3)	

League goals (39): Grady 15, Thomson 5, Britton 4, Mitchell 4, Madaschi 2, Rowson 2, Bonnes 1, McBride 1, Milne 1, Ross, A 1, Taylor 1, Waddell 1, Opponents 1.
Tennents Cup (8): Britton 2, Grady 2, Bonnes 1, McBride 1, Mitchell 1, Rowson 1. **CIS Cup (2):** Grady 1, Milne 1.

RANGERS

Ground: Ibrox, Glasgow G51 2XD. **Capacity:** 50,403.
Telephone: 0870 600 1972. **Colours:** Royal blue and white. **Nickname:** Gers.

Adam, C .... 1(1)	Ferguson, B 3	Mols, M .... 29(6)
Arteta, M 23	Fetai, B .... –(1)	Moore, C .... 16(1)
Arveladze, S .... 17(2)	Hughes, S .... 17(5)	Namouchi, H .... 4(3)
Ball, M .... 30(2)	Hutton, A 11	Nerlinger, C .... 11(3)
Berg, H 20	Khizanishvili, Z ...... 25(1)	Ostenstad, E .... 2(9)
Burke, C .... 11(9)	Klos, S 34	Rae, G .... 9(1)
Capucho, N .... 18(4)	Lovenkrands, P .... 22(3)	Ricksen, F .... 29(1)
Davidson, R .... –(1)	MacKenzie, G .... –(2)	Ross, M .... 10(10)
De Boer, F 15	Malcolm, K .... 8(6)	Thompson, S .... 9(7)
De Boer, R .... 12(4)	McCormack, R ...... 1(1)	Vanoli, P .... 14(9)
Duffy, D .... –(1)	McGregor, A 4	Walker, A .... –(2)
Emerson .... 13(1)		

League goals (76): Arveladze 12, Lovenkrands 9, Mols 9, Arteta 8, Thompson 8, Capucho 5, Burke 3, Hughes 3, Namouchi 3, De Boer, F 2, De Boer, R 2, Moore 2, Rae 2, Ball 1, Hutton 1, McCormack 1, Nerlinger 1, Ricksen 1, Ross 1, Vanoli 1, Opponents 1.
Tennents Cup goals (4): Arveladze 2, De Boer, R 1, Lovenkrands 1. **CIS Cup goals (10):** Nerlinger 3, Mols 2, Ostenstad 2, Burke 1, Capucho 1, Lovenkrands 1. **Champions League goals (7):** Lovenkrands 2, Arteta 1, Arveladze 1, Emerson 1, Mols 1, Nerlinger 1.

BELL'S FIRST DIVISION

AYR UNITED

Ground: Somerset Park, Ayr KA8 9NB. **Capacity:** 10,243.
Telephone: 01292 263435. **Colours:** White and black. **Nickname:** Honest Men.

Black, A .... 17(2)	Ferguson, A .... 16(12)	McColl, M .... 2(9)
Brown, G .... 12(3)	Ferguson, S 9	McGrady, S .... 11(6)
Burgess, R 4	Hardy, L 24	Miller, S .... 1(3)
Campbell, M 25	Hillcoat, J .... 1(1)	Mullen, S .... –(5)
Chaplain, S .... 29(5)	Kean, S 36	Ramsay, D 29
Conway, C .... –(6)	Kerr, C .... 5(4)	Roy, L 35
Craig, D 32	Kinniburgh, W 7	Smyth, M .... 31(4)
Crawford, S 1	Latta, J .... 1(1)	Tait, J 11
Doyle, J .... 6(1)	Lyle, W .... 26(4)	Whalen, S .... 7(1)
Dunlop, M .... 18(4)		

League goals (37): Kean 9, Ferguson, A 7, Chaplain 4, Hardy 4, Brown 2, Campbell 2, Dunlop 2, Black 1, Craig 1, Doyle 1, Ramsay 1, Smyth 1, Whalen 1. Opponents 1.
Tennents Cup goals (1): Craig 1. **CIS Cup goals (1):** Smyth 1. **Bell's Cup goals (1):** Kean 1.

BRECHIN CITY

Ground: Glebe Park, Brechin DD9 6BJ. **Capacity:** 3,960.
Telephone: 01356 622856. **Colours:** Red, white and black. **Nickname:** City.

Beith, G .... 2(1)	Gibson, G .... 11(13)	Millar, M 23
Black, R .... 5(2)	Hampshire, S 27	Miller, G .... 3(7)
Boylan, C .... 1(8)	Hay, D .... 16(1)	Mitchell, A .... 27(2)
Budinauckas, K .... 8(1)	Jablonski, N .... 14(1)	Shields, D .... –(2)
Clark, D .... 3(3)	Jackson, C 1	Smith, J .... 26(2)
Clark, R .... –(1)	Johnson,G 25	Soutar, D 12
Davidson, I .... 3(1)	King, C .... 27(6)	Stein, J .... 2(1)
Deas, P 32	McCulloch, M .... 4(3)	Templeman, C .... 22(10)
Dowie, A 15	McCulloch, S .... 22(6)	White, D .... 27(1)
Duffy, D 8	McLeish, K .... 11(7)	Winter, C 10
Fotheringham, K ...... 8(4)		

League goals (37): Templeman 5, Gibson 4, Hampshire 4, Duffy 3, King 3, Fotheringham 2, McCulloch, S 2, McLeish 2, Millar 2, Mitchell 2, Smith 2, White 2, Winter 2, Beith 1, Jablonski 1.
Tennents Cup goals (1): King 1. **CIS Cup goals (5):** Fotheringham 1, Gibson 1, Hampshire 1, Templeman 1, White 1. **Bell's Cup goals (7):** Fotheringham 2, Jablonski 1, Johnson 1, King 1, Templeman 1, White 1.

CLYDE

Ground: Broadwood Stadium, Cumbernauld G68 9NE. **Capacity:** 8,029.
Telephone: 01236 451511. **Colours:** White and red. **Nickname:** Bully Wee.

Doyle, P .... 1(6)	Keogh, P .... 10(13)	McLaughlin, M .... 29(2)
Fotheringham, K ...... 9(2)	Kernaghan, A 22	Mensing, S .... 30(1)
Fraser, J .... 16(2)	Marshall, C .... 24(1)	Millen, A .... 14(1)
Gibson, J .... 26(1)	McCann, A 6	Morrison, A .... 16(1)
Gilhaney, M .... 6(22)	McCluskey, S 2	Potter, J .... 11(1)
Hagen, D .... 22(8)	McConalogue, S ..... 17(4)	Ross, J 35
Halliwell, B 20	McGroarty, C 12	Smith, A .... 24(8)
Harty, I .... 29(5)		

League goals (64): Harty 15, Keogh 12, Smith 10, McConalogue 7, McLaughlin 5, Gibson 4, Fotheringham 2, Gilhaney 2, Marshall 2, Ross 2, Hagen 1, McCluskey 1, Opponents 1.
Tennents Cup goals (3): Smith 2, Ross 1. **CIS Cup goals (4):** Gilhaney 2, Keogh 1, Millen 1. **Bell's Cup goals (2):** Fraser 1, McConalogue 1.

FALKIRK

Ground: Brockville Park, Falkirk FK1 5AX. **Capacity:** 7,576.
Telephone: 01324 624121. **Colours:** Navy blue and white. **Nickname:** Bairns.

Barr, D .... –(1)	Lee, J .... 27(2)	Nicholls, D .... 13(7)
Christie, K 2	MacKenzie, S .... 26(1)	O'Neil, J 30
Colquhoun, D .... 7(8)	MacSween, I .... 5(5)	Rahim, B .... 19(6)
Ferguson, A 17	Manson, S .... –(1)	Ramsay, M .... –(2)
Henry, J .... 5(2)	May, E .... 2(2)	Rodgers, A .... 2(4)
Hill, D .... 19(1)	McAnespie, K ...... 12(10)	Scally, N .... 12(7)
Hughes, J 27	McMenamin, C ..... 13(3)	Sharp, J 30
James, K 13	McPherson, C 35	Twaddle, M .... –(2)
Latapy, R 32	McStay, R .... 2(2)	Xausa, D .... 10(3)
Lawrie, A .... 34(1)		

League goals (43): Lee 8, Latapy 7, Henry 4, McMenamin 4, O'Neil 4, McAnespie 3, Colquhoun 2, Hughes 2, Lawrie 2, Scally 2, James 1, McPherson 1, Nicholls 1, Sharp 1, Opponents 1.

Tennents Cup goals (2): Lee 1, Xausa 1. **CIS Cup goals (5):** Nicholls 2, Latapy 1, McMenamin 1, Rodgers 1. **Bell's Cup goals:** None.

INVERNESS CALEDONIAN THISTLE

Ground: Caledonian Stadium, Inverness IV1 1FF. **Capacity:** 6,280.
Telephone: 01463 222880. **Colours:** Royal blue, red and white. **Nickname:** Caley Thistle.

Bingham, D .... 31(1)	Low, A .... –(1)	McCaffrey, S 34
Brown, M 36	MacKinnon, L .... –(1)	Munro, G .... 8(5)
Christie, C .... 2(1)	MacRae, D .... –(2)	Proctor, D .... 4(5)
Duncan, R 32	Mackie, D .... 5(1)	Ritchie, P .... 23(7)
Golabek, S 34	McMillan, C .... –(7)	Thomson, D .... 7(10)
Hart, R .... 16(5)	Mann, R 33	Tokely, R 34
Hislop, S .... 18(7)	McBain, R 32	Wilson, B .... 26(3)
Keogh, L .... 21(7)		

League goals (67): Ritchie 14, Bingham 13, Wilson 11, Hislop 9, Tokely 4, Keogh 3, McBain 3, McCaffrey 3, Duncan 1, Golabek 1, Hart 1, Mann 1, Munro 1, Thomson 1.
Tennents Cup goals (10): Ritchie 5, Bingham 2, McBain 1, Thomson 1, Wilson 1. **CIS Cup goals (1):** Ritchie 1. **Bell's Cup goals (14):** Hislop 5, Ritchie 3, Bingham 2, Hart 2, Wilson 2.

QUEEN OF THE SOUTH

Ground: Palmerston Park, Dumfries DG2 9BA. **Capacity:** 6,412.
Telephone: 01387 254853. **Colours:** Royal blue and white. **Nickname:** Doonhamers.

Aitken, A .... 24(7)	Jaconelli, E .... 11(4)	Payne, S .... 4(5)
Allan, D .... 15(1)	Lyle, D .... 8(5)	Reid, B 33
Bagan, D .... 29(2)	McAlpine, J .... 19(2)	Samson, C 12
Bowey, S 33	McColligan, B .... 18(5)	Scott, C 10
Burke, A .... 27(6)	McMullan, P .... 3(8)	Talbot, P .... 3(1)
Burns, J .... 23(6)	O'Connor, S .... 19(7)	Thomson, J .... 26(1)
Dodds, J 12	Paton, E 35	Wood, G .... 16(4)
Gibson, W .... 14(1)		

League goals (46): Burke 13, O'Connor 12, Bowey 7, Wood 4, Jaconelli 3, Bagan 2, Paton 2, Lyle 1, McColligan 1, Reid 1.
Tennents Cup goals (3): O'Connor 3. **CIS Cup goals (6):** Burke 3, Bagan 1, Burns 1, Wood 1. **Bell's Cup goals (1):** Lyle 1.

RAITH ROVERS

Ground: Stark's Park, Kirkaldy KY1 1SA. **Capacity:** 10,104.
Telephone: 01592 263514. **Colours:** Navy blue and white. **Nickname:** Rov.

Berthelot, D 14	Glynn, D 1	O'Reilly, C 2
Blackadder, R .... 8(9)	Gonzalez, R .... 17(1)	Paquito, F 33
Bornes, J 13	Hawley, K .... 4(5)	Patino, C 19
Boyle, J .... 3(9)	Henry, J .... 1(1)	Peers, M .... 2(3)
Brady, D .... 24(3)	Irons, S .... –(1)	Pereira, O 10
Brittain, R .... 9(1)	Jack, M 6	Prest, M .... 8(3)
Brown, I .... 13(1)	Langfield, J 5	Raffel, B .... –(1)
Calderon, A .... 26(2)	Leiper, C .... –(1)	Robb, S .... 8(1)
Capin, S .... 11(1)	Malcolm, C .... 1(4)	Smart, J .... 9(2)
Carranza, B 2	Martin, J .... 1(3)	Stanic, G .... 28(1)
Dennis, S 23	Maxwell, R .... 2(5)	Stanley, C .... 18(1)
Dow, A 9	Miller, P .... 1(1)	Sutton, J 20
Evans, D .... 2(5)	Nanou, W 1	Talio, V .... 9(1)
Ferrero, S 12	Nieto, J .... 10(1)	Young, L .... 9(2)

League goals (37): Sutton 13, Pereira 5, Ferrero 4, Calderon 3, Hawley 2, Paquito 2, Blackadder 1, Brittain 1, Brown 1, Dennis 1, O'Reilly 1, Patino 1, Stanley 1, Opponents 1.
Tennents Cup goals (1): Talio 1. **CIS Cup goals:** None. **Bell's Cup goals (10):** Prest 3, Sutton 3, Calderon 1, Peers 1, Stanley 1, Opponents 1.

ROSS COUNTY

Ground: Victoria Park, Dingwall IV15 9QW. **Capacity:** 5,800.
Telephone: 01349 860860. **Colours:** Navy blue and white. **Nickname:** County.

Bayne, G	16(8)	Laughlan, J	17	Ogunmade, D	–(3)
Canning, M	14(1)	Mackay, S	20	Rankin, J	35
Cowie, D	8(10)	Malcolm, S	23(1)	Robertson, H	18(2)
Fridge, L	–(1)	McCulloch, M	33(3)	Smith, G	20
Gethins, C	6(11)	McCunnie, J	35	Stewart, C	16
Hamilton, J	12(8)	MacDonald, N	1	Tait, J	8(1)
Hannah, D	32	McGarry, S	19(7)	Webb, S	12(1)
Higgins, S	15(9)	O'Donnell, S	14(10)	Winters, D	22(8)

League goals (49): Winters 10, Bayne 6, Higgins 6, Hamilton 5, McGarry 5, Rankin 5, O'Donnell 3, Gethins 1, Hannah 1, Mackay 1, Robertson 1, Tait 1, Webb 1, Opponents 3.
Tennents Cup goals: None. **CIS Cup goals (2):** Cowie 1, McGarry 1. **Bell's Cup goals (7):** Winters 3, Hamilton 2, Rankin 1, Opponents 1.

ST JOHNSTONE

Ground: McDiarmid Park, Perth PH1 2SJ. **Capacity:** 10,673.
Telephone: 01738 459090. **Colours:** Royal blue. **Nickname:** Saints.

Baxter, M	11(5)	Hay, C	10(10)	Parker, K	13(15)
Bernard, P	24	Lovering, P	4(1)	Reilly, M	25(1)
Cuthbert, K	29	MacDonald, P	11(3)	Robertson, M	8(1)
Dods, D	24(2)	Malone, E	5(3)	Robertson, J	27
Donnelly, S	35(1)	Maxwell, I	33	Stevenson, R	8(4)
Ferry, M	1	McLaughlin, B	23(6)	Taylor, S	8(1)
Forsyth, R	18(5)	McQuilken, J	15	Vata, R	15
Fotheringham, M	3(3)	Nelson, C	7	Weir, J	9
Fraser, J	2	Paatelainen, M	28(4)		

League goals (59): Paatelainen 11, Hay 9, Donnelly 8, MacDonald 8, Parker 8, McLaughlin 3, Bernard 2, Baxter 1, Dods 1, Fotheringham 1, Malone 1, Maxwell 1, McQuilken 1, Robertson, J 1, Robertson, M 1, Taylor 1, Opponents 1.
Tennents Cup goals: None. **CIS Cup goals (8):** Dods 2, Donnelly 2, Paatelainen 2, MacDonald 1, McLaughlin 1. **Bell's Cup goals (5):** Parker 2, Donnelly 1, Forsyth 1, Paatelainen 1.

ST MIRREN

Ground: St Mirren Park, Paisley PA3 2EJ. **Capacity:** 14,935.
Telephone: 0141 889 2558. **Colours:** Black and white. **Nickname:** Buddies.

Annand, E	6(3)	Lappin, S	23(1)	Millen, A	18
Broadfoot, K	28(3)	Lavety, B	4(8)	Molloy, C	1(1)
Crilly, M	18(6)	MacPherson, A	9	Muir, A	–(3)
Dempsie, M	20(3)	McCay, R	1	Murray, H	27(3)
Dunn, R	11(14)	McGinty, B	23(3)	O'Neil, A	23(5)
Ellis, L	21(1)	McGowne, K	29(1)	Russell, A	17(9)
Gemmill, S	–(3)	McGroarty, C	12	Twaddle, K	1(2)
Gillies, R	33(2)	McKenna, D	1(6)	Walker, S	1
Hinchcliffe, C	28	McKnight, P	–(3)	Woods, S	8

Van Zanten, D .... 32(3)

League goals (39): Gillies 8, McGinty 6, Lappin 4, O'Neil 4, Russell 4, Broadfoot 3, Dunn 2, Murray 2, Van Zanten 2, Crilly 1, McGowne 1, Millen 1, Opponents 1.
Tennents Cup goals (2): Lavety 1, McKenna 1. **CIS Cup goals:** None. **Bell's Cup goals (7):** O'Neil 3, Crilly 1, Gillies 1, McGinty 1, Russell 1.

BELL'S SECOND DIVISION

AIRDRIE UNITED

Ground: Shyberry Excelsior Stadium, Airdrie ML6 8QZ. **Capacity:** 10,171.
Telephone: 01236 622000. **Colours:** White, red and black. **Nickname:** Diamonds.

Black, K 4	McGeown, M 36	Ronald, P .... 7(5)
Christie, K .... 10(2)	McGowan, N 32	Singbo, F .... 3(2)
Coyle, O 23	McKenna, S .... –(1)	Stewart, A 13
Docherty, S 27	McKeown, S .... 10(17)	Vareille, J .... 21(9)
Dunn, D .... 25(2)	McLaren, W .... 18(2)	Wilson, M .... 25(8)
Glancy, M .... 14(11)	McManus, A .... 28(1)	Wilson, S .... 17(3)
Gow, A .... 26(6)	Roberts, M .... 19(10)	Wilson, W .... 20(2)
Lovering, P 18		

League goals (64): Coyle 13, Gow 11, Vareille 10, McLaren 9, McKeown 5, Docherty 4, Dunn 4, Glancy 2, Lovering 2, Christie 1, Roberts 1, Ronald 1, Wilson, S 1.
Tennents Cup goals (5): Coyle 2, McKeown 1, Roberts 1, Stewart 1. **CIS Cup goals (3):** Glancy 1, Roberts 1, Ronald 1. **Bell's Cup goals (8):** Dunn 2, McKeown 2, Gow 1, Roberts 1, Wilson, S 1, Vareille 1.

ALLOA ATHLETIC

Ground: Recreation Park, Alloa FK10 1RR. **Capacity:** 3,142.
Telephone: 01259 722695. **Colours:** Black and gold. **Nickname:** Wasps.

Bolochoweckyj, M 20	Ferguson, B .... 29(1)	Nicolson, I 35
Callaghan, S 35	Hamilton, R 35	Seaton, A 20
Clark, D .... 6(1)	Janczyk, N .... 10(2)	Stevenson, J .... 2(9)
Crabbe, S .... 1(9)	Kelbie, K .... –(7)	Valentine, C 33
Daly, M .... 8(6)	Little, I .... 33(1)	Walker, R 36
Evans, G .... 1(5)	McGlynn, G 32	Walker, S 10
Evans, J .... 4(2)	McGowan, J 34	Watson, G .... –(3)
Ferguson, A 4	McLaughlin, P .... 8(4)	

League goals (55): Hamilton 13, Little 11, Callaghan 6, McGowan 5, Ferguson, B 4, Nicolson 3, Daly 2, Janczyk 2, Stevenson 2, Bolochoweckyj 1, Clark 1, Opponents 1.
Tennents Cup goals (6): Ferguson 2, Hamilton 1, McGowan 1, Walker, R 1, Walker, S 1.
CIS Cup goals: None. **Bell's Cup goals (1):** Callaghan 1.

ARBROATH

Ground: Gayfield Park, Arbroath DD11 1QB. **Capacity:** 6,488.
Telephone: 01241 872157. **Colours:** Maroon and white. **Nickname:** Red Lichties

Browne, P .... 17(4)	Graham, R .... 14(1)	McCulloch, M 20
Cargill, A 25	Farquharson, P .... –(10)	McGlashan, J 34
Collier, J .... –(1)	Heenan, K 1	McMullen, K .... 32(2)
Cusick, J 24	Henslee, G .... 19(10)	Miller, L .... 15(1)
Denham, G 3	Herkes, J .... 6(6)	Mitchell, K 2
Diack, I .... 20(1)	Kerrigan, S .... 3(2)	Peat, M 33
Dow, A 18	King, D 33	Rennie, S 32
Durno, P .... 3(6)	MacLean, D .... 12(4)	Swankie, G .... 16(11)
Graham, E .... 2(3)	McAulay, J .... 8(7)	Woodcock, T 1

League goals (41): McGlashan 10, Cargill 7, Diack 7, MacLean 6, Cusick 5, Dow 2, Durno 1, Henslee 1, McMullen 1, Graham, R 1.
Tennents Cup goals (3): McGlashan 3. **CIS Cup goals (4):** McGlashan 2, Cusick 1, Graham, R 1. **Bell's Cup goals (3):** McGlashan 2, Graham, R 1.

BERWICK RANGERS

Ground: Shielfield Park, Berwick-upon-Tweed TD15 2EF. **Capacity:** 4,131.
Telephone: 01289 307424. **Colours:** Black and gold. **Nickname:** Borderers.

Allan, N 2	Godfrey, R .... 11(1)	McDonald .... –(1)
Bain, K .... –(1)	Gordon, K .... 3(8)	McNicoll, G 32
Bennett, N .... 30(4)	Hampshire, P .... 32(3)	Murie, D 35
Birrill, J .... –(1)	Hilland, P .... 9(4)	Neil, M .... 19(2)
Blackley, D .... –(5)	Hutchison, G 36	Neill, A .... 15(3)
Bracks, K .... –(1)	Inglis, N 25	Noone, D 1
Connell, G .... 25(1)	Kerrigan, S .... –(4)	Robertson, J .... –(1)
Connelly, G .... 27(4)	McAllister, J .... 1(2)	Robertson, M .... –(2)
Cowan, M .... 24(1)	McCormick, M .... –(2)	Smith, D .... 7(9)
Elliot, B .... –(4)	McCutcheon, G ...... 33(1)	Waldie, C .... 11(2)
Forrest, G 18		

League goals (61): Hutchison 22, McCutcheon 14, Forrest 8, Cowan 4, Hampshire 4, Connelly 3, Bennett 2, Hilland 2, McNicoll 1, Neil 1.
Tennents Cup goals (4): Hutchison 3, Opponents 1. **CIS Cup goals:** None. **Bell's Cup goals (1):** McNicoll 1.

DUMBARTON

Ground: Strathclyde Homes Stadium, Dumbarton G82 2JA. **Capacity:** 3,750.
Telephone: 01389 762569. **Colours:** Yellow and black. **Nickname:** Sons.

Bonar, S 35	English, I .... 8(1)	Okoli, J 1
Boyle, C .... 17(8)	Flannery, P .... 8(2)	Renicks, S .... 7(11)
Bradley, M .... 18(6)	Grindlay, S 34	Robertson, K 1
Brittain, C 32	Herd, G .... 11(8)	Rodgers, A .... 7(4)
Collins, N .... 29(1)	Laidler, G .... –(4)	Ronald, P .... 13(1)
Dillon, J .... 31(4)	Mallan, S .... 3(2)	Russell, I .... 26(5)
Dobbins, I .... 12(4)	McEwan, C .... 19(4)	Skjelered, B .... 2(3)
Donald, B .... 24(2)	McKinstry, J 36	Smith, D .... 4(1)
Duffy, C .... 8(1)	Obidile, E .... 8(2)	Wight, J .... –(1)

League goals (56): Russell 10, Dillon 9, Herd 8, Bonar 5, Boyle 4, McEwan 4, Flannery 3, Rodgers 3, Ronald 3, Bradley 2, Collins 2, Brittain 1, English 1, Skjelered 1.
Tennents Cup goals: None. **CIS Cup goals (3):** Bonar 1, Flannery 1, Obidile 1. **Bell's Cup goals:** None.

EAST FIFE

Ground: Bayview Stadium, Methil KY8 3RW. **Capacity:** 2,000.
Telephone: 01333 426323. **Colours:** Gold and black. **Nickname:** Fifers.

Bain, K .... 10(1)	Herkes, J .... 8(7)	McMillan, C 36
Blair, B .... 15(6)	Kelly, P .... 24(1)	Miller, C 6
Byle, L 2	Love, G .... 1(2)	Mitchell, J .... 14(6)
Deuchar, K .... 31(3)	Lumsden, C .... 21(2)	Mortimer, P .... 9(6)
Donaldson, E .... 31(2)	Lynes, C .... 3(3)	Nicholas, S 10
Fairbairn, B .... 10(17)	Mathie, G 16	O'Connor, G 34
Gilbert, G .... 11(6)	MacDonald, A 5	Russell, G .... 9(1)
Graham, J 2	McDonald, G .... 13(1)	Stein, J .... 12(1)
Hall, M 27	McDonald, I .... 22(2)	Stewart, W .... 14(6)

League goals (38): Deuchar 11, McDonald, G 5, McDonald, I 4, Donaldson 3, Fairbairn 3, Hall 2, McMillan 2, Nicholas 2, Gilbert 1, Lynes 1, Mitchell 1, Mortimer 1, Stein 1, Opponents 1.
Tennents Cup goals (6): Deuchar 1, Hall 1, Nicholas 1, Stewart 1, Opponents 2. **CIS Cup goals:** None. **Bell's Cup goals:** None.

FORFAR ATHLETIC

Ground: Station Park, Forfar DD8 3BT. **Capacity:** 4,602.
Telephone: 01307 463576. **Colours:** Sky blue and navy. **Nickname:** Loons.

Bremner, K .... –(1)	Horn, R 28	Rattray, A 23
Brown, M 32	King, M .... 11(4)	Sellars, B .... 28(1)
Byers, K .... 20(4)	Lowring, D .... 16(4)	Shields, P .... 25(6)
Davidson, H .... 33(1)	Lunan, P .... 29(3)	Stewart, D 11
Ferrie, J .... –(1)	Maher, M .... 11(14)	Taylor, S .... 3(9)
Ferrie, N .... 4(2)	McClune, D .... 28(1)	Tosh, P .... 31(1)
Ferry, M .... 11(3)	McNicol, S 12	Vella, S 4
Florence, S .... 8(6)	Ogunmade, D .... 2(3)	Williams, D .... 1(6)
Henderson, D .... 25(1)		

League goals (49): Tosh 19, Shields 9, Davidson 5, Henderson 5, Ferry 4, Rattray 2, Sellars 2, Maher 1, McClune 1, Opponents 1.
Tennents Cup goals (4): Tosh 3, Rattray 1. **CIS Cup goals (4):** Henderson 2, Tosh 2. **Bell's Cup goals (8):** Shields 4, Maher 2, Davidson 1, Tosh 1.

HAMILTON ACADEMICAL

Ground: New Douglas Park, Hamilton ML3 0FT. **Capacity:** 5,300.
Telephone: 01698 286103. **Colours:** Red and white. **Nickname:** Accies.

Aitken, C .... 32(1)	Forbes, B .... 4(2)	McPhee, B 31
Arbuckle, A .... 23(6)	Gemmell, J .... –(7)	Paterson, N .... –(2)
Bailey, J .... 4(2)	Gribben, D .... 4(15)	Quitongo, J .... 14(4)
Blackadder, R .... 10(4)	Hodge, S 31	Sherry, J .... 22(4)
Carrigan, B .... 30(1)	Jellema, R .... –(1)	Thomson, S 36
Convery, M .... 12(4)	Lumsden, T .... 33(1)	Waddell, A .... –(5)
Corcoran, M .... 22(12)	MacLaren, J 1	Waddell, R .... 8(1)
Donnelly, C .... 1(6)	Maxwell, R 2	Walker, J .... 21(2)
Ferguson, D .... 3(1)	McEwan, D 35	Whiteford, A .... 12(5)
Fitter, J 5		

League goals (70): McPhee 18, Carrigan 15, Aitken 8, Quitongo 5, Convery 4, Corcoran 3, Thomson 3, Walker 3, Bailey 2, Gribben 2, Lumsden 2, Whiteford 2, Gemmell 1, Hodge 1, Waddell, R 1.
Tennents Cup goals (4): McPhee 2, Corcoran 1, Quitongo 1. **CIS Cup goals (5):** McPhee 2, Aitken 1, Carrigan 1, Corcoran 1. **Bell's Cup goals (2):** Aitken 1, McPhee 1.

MORTON

Ground: Cappielow Park, Greenock PA15 2TY. **Capacity:** 7,890.
Telephone: 01475 723571. **Colours:** Royal blue, white and yellow. **Nickname:** Ton.

Adam, J .... 2(2)	Hawke, W .... 1(8)	McLeod, C .... 5(1)
Bannerman, S .... 17(8)	Henderson, R .... 20(1)	Millar, C .... 35(1)
Bottiglieri, E .... 32(2)	Hopkin, D .... –(1)	Uotinen, J .... 5(13)
Cannie, P .... 11(8)	McGregor, D .... 25(1)	Walker, P .... 30(2)
Collins, D 28	Maisano, J 29	Weatherson, P 31
Coyle, C 36	Maisano, M .... 28(3)	Wilkie, L 1
Gaughan, P .... 1(1)	McAlistair, J .... 1(5)	Williams, A .... 26(8)
Greacen, S 32	McGlinchey, P .... –(6)	

League goals (66): Weatherson 15, Williams 15, Greacen 7, Maisano, J 7, Walker 5, Bannerman 3, Cannie 3, Maisano, M 3, Millar 3, Bottiglieri 2, Collins 1, Henderson 1, Uotinen 1.
Tennents Cup goals (4): Williams 2, Millar 1, Weatherson 1. **CIS Cup goals (3):** Bannerman 1, Bottiglieri 1, Weatherson 1. **Bell's Cup goals (5):** Weatherson 3, Hawke 1, Maisano, J 1.

STENHOUSEMUIR

Ground: Ochilview Park, Stenhousemuir FK5 5QL. **Capacity:** 2,376.
Telephone: 01324 562992. **Colours:** Maroon and white. **Nickname:** Warriors.

Bonar, P .... 7(5)	Hamilton, S .... 24(2)	McGowan, M .... 9(1)
Booth, M .... 22(5)	Hardie, A 2	McKenna, G .... 17(5)
Brown, A .... 27(5)	Harty, M .... 19(12)	McKenzie, J 16
Cairney, C .... 2(1)	Knox, J .... 4(3)	McQuilter, R 8
Carr, D .... 18(6)	Knox, K 16	Miller, C .... 6(1)
Cosgrove, S .... 11(3)	Johnstone, D .... 1(2)	Morrison, J .... 5(2)
Craig, D .... 3(1)	Kerrigan, S .... 5(1)	Murray 1
Crawford, B .... 1(3)	Lauchlan, M .... 21(5)	Murphy, P .... 19(1)
Donnelly, K .... 4(1)	Mallan, S .... 5(1)	Murphy, S .... 8(1)
Easton, S .... –(1)	McCloy, B .... 4(2)	Savage, J 3
Flannery, P .... 5(4)	McCulloch, C .... 13(2)	Smith, A .... 21(3)
Gaughan, K 15	McCulloch, W 34	Tully, C .... 6(1)
Gillespie, A 1	McDowell, M 2	Waldie, C .... 10(1)

League goals (28): Brown 5, Murphy, S 4, McKenzie 3, Booth 2, Carr 2, Harty 2, Savage 2, Crawford 1, Donnelly 1, Knox, K 1, Lauchlan 1, Mallan 1, McQuilter 1, Opponents 2.
Tennents Cup goals (1): Brown 1. **CIS Cup goals (1):** Harty 1. **Bell's Cup goals:** None.

BELL'S THIRD DIVISION

ALBION ROVERS

Ground: Cliftonhill Stadium, Coatbridge ML5 3RB. **Capacity:** 2,496.
Telephone: 01236 606334. **Colours:** Yellow, red and black. **Nickname:** Wee Rovers.

Bennett, N .... 26(1)	Kerr, S .... 1(1)	Paterson, A .... 29(2)
Bradford, J .... 14(5)	Low, T .... 4(6)	Patrick, R 12
Carr, M 1	Malloy, M .... 2(3)	Potter, K .... 3(2)
Connelly, P .... 2(2)	McAllister, K .... 12(2)	Selkirk, A .... –(2)
Connolly, C .... 3(1)	McBride, K .... 5(6)	Silvestro, C 3
Cormack, P .... 17(4)	McCaig, J .... 21(2)	Skinner, S .... –(2)
Crabbe, S 13	McCaul, G 18	Smith, J .... 27(2)
Diack, I .... 5(7)	McKenzie, M .... 3(8)	Stirling, J .... 31(1)
Fahey, C 9	McManus, P .... 33(1)	Sweeney, S 21
Farrell, D 16	Mercer, J 33	Yardley, M .... 26(1)
Kerr, C .... 5(2)		

League goals (66): McManus 18, Yardley 11, Mercer 10, Stirling 7, Bradford 4, McBride 2, McKenzie 2, Smith 2, Crabbe 1, Diack 1, Farrell 1, McAllister 1, McCaul 1, Patrick 1, Sweeney 1, Opponents 3.
Tennents Cup goals (2): Mercer 1, Opponents 1. **CIS Cup goals (2):** McAllister 1, McManus 1. **Bell's Cup goals (3):** Diack 2, McManus 1.

COWDENBEATH

Ground: Central Park, Cowdenbeath KY4 9QQ. **Capacity:** 4,370.
Telephone: 01383 610166. **Colours:** Royal blue and white. **Nickname:** Blue Brazil.

Campbell, A .... 18(2)	Bristow, S .... –(1)	Buchanan, L .... 8(14)
Boyle, S 1	Brown, G .... 13(1)	Carlin, A 34

Fallon, J .... 4(4)	McCallum, R .... 2(9)	Orhue, P .... –(1)
Fleming, A .... 3(1)	McEwan, M 9	Ritchie, I 30
Fusco, G .... 23(3)	McGuinness, L .... 11(4)	Shand, C .... 30(1)
Gilfillan, B .... 32(1)	McInally, D .... 30(4)	Shields, D .... 31(1)
Gordon, K .... 7(6)	McKeown, J .... 23(1)	Skinner, S .... 7(1)
Kelly, A .... 4(5)	Moffatt, A .... 3(1)	Slaven, J .... –(2)
Matheson, R .... 3(4)	Morris, I 5	Stewart, S .... 4(1)
Mauchlen, I .... 15(9)	Mowat, D .... 34(2)	Winter, C 22

League goals (46): Shields 12, Buchanan 8, Gilfillan 6, Brown 5, Ritchie 4, Morris 2, Skinner 2, Winter 2, Fusco 1, Mauchlen 1, McInally 1, Stewart 1, Opponents 1.
Tennents Cup goals (10): Shields 3, Mauchlen 2, Buchanan 1, Fusco 1, Gilfillan 1, Winter 1, Opponents 1. **CIS Cup goals (3):** McInally 2, Morris 1. **Bell's Cup goals (1):** Brown 1.

EAST STIRLINGSHIRE

Ground: Firs Park, Falkirk FK2 7AY. **Capacity:** 1,632.
Telephone: 01324 623583. **Colours:** Black and white. **Nickname:** Shire.

Baldwin, C .... 23(1)	Lynch, C 2	Mulholland, B .... 12(2)
Boyle, G .... 1(5)	MacKay, J .... 11(3)	Newall, C 15
Connolly, J 19	Maughan, R 26	Oates, S 16
Ford, K .... 8(1)	McAuley, Scott .... 8(1)	Ormiston, D 7
Gilpin, R 4	McAuley, Sean .... 15(4)	Penman, C 1
Hare, R .... 11(4)	McCann, K 2	Polwart, D .... 14(4)
Irvine, S .... 1(1)	McCulloch, G .... 2(1)	Reid, C .... 9(1)
Kane, P .... –(2)	McGhee, G 35	Rodden, P .... 7(9)
Kelly, S .... 20(10)	McLaren, G 30	Todd, C .... 13(1)
Leishman, J .... 14(5)	McLaughlin, P 1	Ure, D .... 26(2)
Livingstone, S .... 29(3)	Miller, D .... 8(2)	

League goals (30): Ure 8, Kelly 6, McAuley, Sean 4, Miller 2, Baldwin 1, Leishman 1, Livingstone 1, Newall 1, Ormiston 1, Polwart 1, Reid 1, Rodden 1, Opponents 2.
Tennents Cup goals: None. **CIS Cup goals (1):** Rodden 1. **Bell's Cup goals (2):** Baldwin 1, Kelly 1.

ELGIN CITY

Ground: Borough Briggs, Elgin IV30 1AP. **Capacity:** 3,900.
Telephone: 01343 551114. **Colours:** Black and white. **Nickname:** Black and Whites.

Addicoat, W 1	Goram, A 3	Pirie, M 27
Allison, J 32	Hamilton, P 3	Ralph, J 1
Anderson, R .... –(1)	Hind, D .... 28(2)	Read, C 1
Bone, A .... 30(2)	Martin, W .... 30(3)	Reid, P .... 1(4)
Bremner, F .... 4(2)	McCormick, S .... 14(2)	Steele, K .... 9(11)
Campbell, Connor 2	McKenzie, J 14	Taylor, R 1
Campbell, Craig 26	McLean, C .... 3(2)	Teasdale, M 1
Coulter, R .... 16(1)	McLean, N .... 18(5)	Thomson, R .... –(1)
Dempsie, A 21	McMillan, A .... 19(2)	Tully, C 17
Dickson, H .... 17(1)	McMullan, R .... 18(9)	Vigurs, I .... 1(1)
Dickson, M .... 1(1)	Murphy, S .... 6(1)	White, J .... 13(3)
Donald .... –(3)	Ogboke, C .... 9(8)	Wood, G .... –(1)
Gallagher, J .... 3(2)		

League goals (48): Bone 15, Martin 8, Ogboke 5, Tully 5, Allison 2, Hind 2, McCormick 2, Steele 2, White 2, Bremner 1, Coulter 1, McKenzie 1, McMillan 1, McMullan 1.
Tennents Cup goals (1): Campbell, Craig 1. **CIS Cup goals:** None. **Bell's Cup goals:** None.

GRETNA

Allan, J	2(4)	Grainger, D	1	O'Neill, P	2
Baldacchino, R	34	Holdsworth, D	28	Prokas, R	28(3)
Birch, M	24	Hore, J	1	Robb, R	1
Cameron, M	25(2)	Irons, D	33(1)	Skelton, G	31(1)
Cohen, G	14(11)	Knox, K	2(1)	Skinner, S	1
Cosgrove, S	–(3)	Lennon, D	3(4)	Spence, C	1
Eccles, M	5(2)	Maddison, L	30	Stevens, I	24(5)
Eeles, S	–(1)	Mathieson, D	36	Summersgill, C	1
Galloway, M	35	May, K	1	Townsley, D	15
Gordon, W	4(13)	McGuffie, R	19(6)	Wake, B	6(5)

League goals (59): Cameron 17, Stevens 10, Townsley 9, Wake 5, Baldacchino 4, Birch 3, Galloway 3, McGuffie 2, Skelton 2, Gordon 1, Irons 1, Maddison 1, Opponents 1.
Tennents Cup goals (9): Stevens 3, Skelton 2, Baldacchino 1, Cohen 1, Gordon 1, Holdsworth 1. **CIS Cup goals (1):** McGuffie 1. **Bell's Cup goals:** None.

MONTROSE

Ground: Links Park, Montrose DD10 8QD. **Capacity:** 4,338.
Telephone: 01674 673200. **Colours:** Royal blue and white. **Nickname:** Gable Endies.

Black, R	10(1)	Gibson, K	19(3)	Smart, C	24(2)
Brash, K	3	Hall, E	1(6)	Smith, E	25
Budd, A	2	Hankinson, M	6(1)	Smith, G	9(4)
Butter, J	30	Henderson, R	4(13)	Spink, D	4(5)
Conway, F	6	Kerrigan, S	32	Stephen, N	1(1)
Coulston, D	2(3)	McQuillan, J	33	Thompson, G	2
Donnachie, B	31(1)	Michie, S	30(1)	Watt, J	1(8)
Farnan, C	6(7)	Sharp, G	13(14)	Webster, K	26(5)
Ferguson, M	1	Simpson, M	9(1)	Wood, M	26(3)
Ferguson, S	36		

League goals (52): Michie 14, Kerrigan 8, Smart 8, Gibson 5, Black 4, Smith, E 4, Webster 2, Wood 2, Farnan 1, Henderson 1, McQuillan 1, Sharp 1, Opponents 1.
Tennents Cup goals (5): Michie 2, Wood 2, Ferguson, S 1. **CIS Cup goals (2):** Kerrigan 1, Smart 1. **Bell's Cup goals:** None.

PETERHEAD

Ground: Balmoor Stadium, Peterhead AB42 1EU. **Capacity:** 3,250.
Telephone: 01779 478256. **Colours:** Royal blue and white. **Nickname:** Blue Toon.

Bain, K	11(2)	Grant, R	4(3)	Robertson, K	16
Bavidge, M	33(1)	Johnston, M	28(4)	Roddie, A	24(2)
Beith, G	9(2)	MacKay, S	11(7)	Shand, R	1
Brash, K	6(2)	Mathers, D	33	Smith, D	11(10)
Buchan, J	15	McGuinness, K	20(3)	Stewart, D	1(5)
Buchanan, R	3	McSkimming, S	20(2)	Stewart, G	4(2)
Duncan, B	20(7)	Milne, K	1(3)	Stewart, I	16(3)
Gibson, K	6	Perry, M	33	Stuart, D	1
Good, I	22(1)	Raeside, R	30(1)	Tindal, K	17(3)

League goals (67): Johnston 18, Bavidge 16, Raeside 6, Stewart, I 6, Buchan 3, Robertson 3, Beith 2, MacKay 2, Roddie 2, Tindal 2, Duncan 1, Gibson 1, Good 1, Perry 1, Smith 1, Stewart, G 1, Opponents 1.
Tennents Cup goals (2): Bavidge 2. **CIS Cup goals (4):** Stewart, I 3, MacKay 1. **Bell's Cup goals (4):** Grant 1, Raeside 1, Stewart, D 1, Stewart, I 1.

QUEEN'S PARK

Ground: Hampden Park, Glasgow G42 9BA. **Capacity:** 52,046.
Telephone: 0141 632 1275. **Nickname:** Spiders.

Agostini, D .... 20(3)	Ferry, D .... 24(2)	Quinn, A .... –(1)
Bonnar, M .... 7(6)	Gallagher, P .... 4(6)	Reilly, S 27
Canning, S .... 25(3)	Graham, A 20	Scrimgour, D 35
Carcary, D .... 16(4)	Harvey, P .... 18(5)	Sinclair, R .... 20(1)
Carrol, F .... 17(7)	Kettlewell, S .... 15(9)	Stewart, C .... 12(2)
Clark, R .... 27(2)	McAuley, S .... 13(2)	Thomson, J .... 4(4)
Conlin, R .... 1(1)	McCallum, D .... 18(1)	Thomson, S 1
Crawford, D .... 1(1)	McCue, B .... –(1)	Trouten, A .... –(1)
Dunning, A .... 12(1)	Menelaws, D .... 3(3)	Weatherston, D .... –(3)
Fallon, S .... 20(1)	Moffat, S .... 8(3)	Whelan, J .... 26(7)

League goals (41): Reilly 7, Carcary 6, McAuley 6, Whelan 5, Canning 3, Carrol 3, Graham 3, Gallagher 2, McCallum 2, Dunning 1, Harvey 1, Stewart 1, Opponents 1.
Tennents Cup goals (1): McAuley 1. **CIS Cup goals (3):** Clark 1, Graham 1, Reilly 1. **Bell's Cup goals (2):** Clark 1, Graham 1.

STIRLING ALBION

Ground: Forthbank Stadium, Stirling FK7 7UJ. **Capacity:** 3,808.
Telephone: 01786 450399. **Colours:** White and navy. **Nickname:** Albion.

Anderson, D .... 25(2)	Hay, P .... 24(6)	Morrison, S 1
Beveridge, R .... 1(3)	Hogarth, M 35	Nugent, P .... 22(1)
Davidson, R .... 21(8)	Kelly, G .... 7(11)	O'Brien, D .... 31(3)
Devine, S .... 20(5)	Lyle, D 19	Rowe, G 36
Elliot, B .... 3(15)	McKinnon, C .... 26(2)	Scotland, C 13
Ferguson, C .... 4(15)	McLean, S .... 30(1)	Smith, A .... 30(1)
Gibson, A .... 15(1)	McNally, M 22	Wilson, D .... 11(8)

League goals (78): McLean 21, McKinnon 11, Lyle 10, O'Brien 10, Davidson 9, Devine 3, Ferguson 3, Rowe 3, Elliot 1, Gibson 1, Hay 1, Kelly 1, Wilson 1, Opponents 3.
Tennents Cup goals (4): Kelly 2, O'Brien 1, Rowe 1. **CIS Cup goals:** None. **Bell's Cup goals (3):** Elliot 2, McLean 1.

STRANRAER

Ground: Stair Park, Stranraer DG9 8BS. **Capacity:** 5,600.
Telephone: 01776 703271. **Colours:** Royal blue and white. **Nickname:** Blues.

Aitken, S .... 31(2)	Grant, A .... 2(7)	McPhee, G .... 1(1)
Collins, L .... 11(1)	Guy, G 1	Moore, M .... 30(1)
Crawford, J .... 2(7)	Henderson, M 35	Sharp, L 35
Cruikshank, C .... 1(5)	Jenkins, A .... 35(1)	Swift, S 36
Essler, G 1	Kerr, P .... 2(4)	Turnbull, D .... 1(10)
Finlayson, K .... 32(1)	Marshall, S .... 1(4)	Wingate, D 36
Gaughan, K .... –(2)	McAllister, T .... 3(7)	Wright, F 34
Graham, D .... 30(2)	McCondichie, A 36	

League goals (87): Moore 24, Graham 19, Finlayson 10, Swift 7, Jenkins 6, Henderson 5, Crawford 3, Sharp 3, Grant 2, Wright 2, Aitken 1, Collins 1, Kerr 1, Turnbull 1, Wingate 1, Opponents 1.
Tennents Cup goals (2): Jenkins 1, Moore 1. **CIS Cup goals:** None. **Bell's Cup goals (2):** Moore 2.

BARCLAYS PREMIERSHIP CLUB DETAILS AND PLAYING STAFFS 2004-05

(At time of going to press)

ARSENAL

Ground: Arsenal Stadium, Highbury, London, N5 1BU.
Telephone: 020 7704 4000. **Club nickname:** Gunners.
First-choice colours: Red white shirts; white shorts; white stockings.
Record transfer fee: £17,400,000 to Seville for Jose Antonio Reyes, January 2004.
Record fee received: £25,000,000 from Barcelona for Marc Overmars, July 2000.
Record attendance: At Highbury: 73,295 v Sunderland March 1935. At Wembley: 73,707 v Lens (Champions League) November 1998.
Capacity for 2004-05: 38,546. **Sponsors:** O_2.
League Championship: winners 1930-31, 1932-33, 1933-34, 1934-35, 1937-38, 1947-48, 1952-53, 1970-71, 1988-89, 1990-91, 1997-98, 2001-02, 2003-04.
F.A. Cup: winners 1930, 1936, 1950, 1971, 1979, 1993, 1998, 2002, 2003.
League Cup: winners 1987, 1993.
European Competitions: winners Fairs Cup: 1969-70, Cup Winners Cup: 1993-94.
Finishing positions in Premiership: 1992-93 10th, 1993-94 4th, 1994-95 12th, 1995-96 5th, 1996-97 3rd, 1997-98 1st, 1998-99 2nd, 1999-2000 2nd, 2000-01 2nd, 2001-02 1st, 2002-03 2nd, 2003-04 1st.
Biggest win: 12-0 v Loughborough Town, Div. 2, 12.3.1900.
Biggest defeat: 0-8 v Loughborough Town, Div. 2, 12.12.1896.
Highest League scorer in a season: Ted Drake, 42, 1934-35.
Most League goals in aggregate: Cliff Bastin, 150, 1930-47.
Most capped player: Kenny Sansom (England) 77.
Longest unbeaten League sequence: 40 matches (May 2004, unbroken).
Longest sequence without a League win: 23 matches (September 1912).

Name	Height ft. in.	Previous club	Birthplace	Birthdate
Goalkeepers				
Lehmann, Jens	6. 3	Borussia Dortmund	Essen	11.10.69
Stack, Graham	6. 2	–	Hampstead	26.09.81
Taylor, Stuart	6. 4	–	Romford	28.11.81
Defenders				
Campbell, Sol	6. 1	Tottenham	Newham	18.09.74
Clichy, Gael	5.11	Cannes	Paris	26.07.85
Cole, Ashley	5. 8	–	Stepney	20.12.80
Cygan, Pascal	6. 5	Lille	Lens	29.04.74
Hoyte, Justin	5.11	–	Waltham Forest	20.11.84
Senderos, Philippe	6. 3	Servette	Switzerland	14.02.85
Svard, Sebastian	5.10	FC Copenhagen	Hvidovre, Den.	15.01.83
Toure, Kolo	5.11	Abidjan	Ivory Coast	19.03.81
Midfielders				
Edu	6. 1	Corinthians	Sao Paulo	15.05.78
Fabregas, Francesc	5.10	Barcelona	Vilessoc, Spain	4.05.87
Gilberto Silva	6. 3	Atletico Mineiro	Lagoada Prata, Bra.	7.10.76
Lauren	5.11	Real Mallorca	Londi Kribi, Cam.	19.01.77
Ljungberg, Fredrik	5.11	Halmstad	Halmstad	16.04.77
Parlour, Ray	5.10	–	Romford	7.03.73
Pennant, Jermaine	5. 9	Notts Co.	Nottingham	5.01.83
Pires, Robert	6. 1	Marseille	Reims	29.10.73
Skulason, Olafur-Ingi	6. 0	–	Reykjavik	1.04.83
Smith, Ryan	5. 9	–	Islington	10.11.86
Vieira, Patrick	6. 4	AC Milan	Dakar, Sen.	23.06.76

Forwards

Name	Height ft. in.	Previous club	Birthplace	Birthdate
Aliadiere, Jeremie	6.0	–	Rambouillet, Fra.	30.03.83
Bentley, David			Peterborough	27.08.84
Bergkamp, Dennis	6.0	Inter Milan	Amsterdam	18.05.69
Henry, Thierry	6.2	Juventus	Paris	17.08.77
Reyes, Jose Antonio	5.9	Seville	Seville	1.09.83
Van Persie, Robin	6.0	Feyenoord	Rotterdam	6.08.83

ASTON VILLA

Ground: Villa Park, Trinity Road, Birmingham, B6 6HE.
Telephone: 0121 327 2299. **Club nickname:** Villans.
First-choice colours: Claret and blue shirts; white shorts; claret and blue stockings.
Record transfer fee: £9,500,000 to River Plate for Juan Pablo Angel, January 2001.
Record fee received: £12,600,000 for Dwight Yorke from Manchester Utd., August 1998.
Record attendance: 76,588 v Derby Co. (F.A. Cup 6) 2 March, 1946.
Capacity for 2004-05: 42,573. **Sponsors:** DWS Investments.
League Championship: winners 1893-94, 1895-96, 1896-97, 1898-99, 1899-1900, 1909-10, 1980-81.
F.A. Cup: winners 1887, 1895, 1897, 1905, 1913, 1920, 1957.
League Cup: winners 1961, 1975, 1977, 1994, 1996.
European Competitions: Winners European Cup 1981-82, European Super Cup 1982-83.
Finishing positions in Premiership: 1992-93 2nd, 1993-94 10th, 1994-95 18th, 1995-96 4th, 1996-97 5th, 1997-98 7th, 1998-99 6th, 1999-2000 6th, 2000-01 8th, 2001-02 8th, 2002-03 16th, 2003-04 6th.
Biggest win: 12-2 v Accrington, Div. 1, 12.3.1892, 11-1 v Charlton Athletic, Div. 2, 24.11.1959, 10-0 v Sheffield Wed., Div. 1, 5.10.1912 and v Burnley, Div. 1, 29.8.1925.
Biggest defeat: 0-7 in five League matches from Blackburn Rov., Div. 1, 19.10.1889 to Manchester Utd., Div. 1, 24.10.1964.
Highest League scorer in a season: 'Pongo' Waring, 49, 1930-31.
Most League goals in aggregate: Harry Hampton, 215, 1904-1915.
Most capped player: Steve Staunton (Rep. of Ireland) 64.
Longest unbeaten League sequence: 15 matches (January 1897, December 1909 and March 1949).
Longest sequence without a League win: 12 matches (November 1973 and December 1986).

Name	Height ft. in.	Previous club	Birthplace	Birthdate
Goalkeepers				
Henderson, Wayne	5.11	–	Dublin	16.09.83
Postma, Stefan	6. 1	De Graafschap	Utrecht	10.06.76
Sorensen, Thomas	6. 4	Sunderland	Odense	12.06.76
Defenders				
Barry, Gareth	6. 0	–	Hastings	23.02.81
Delaney, Mark	6. 1	Cardiff City	Haverfordwest	13.05.76
Laursen, Martin	6. 2	AC Milan	Farvoug, Den.	26.07.77
Mellberg, Olof	6. 1	Racing Santander	Stockholm	9.03.77
Ridgewell, Liam	5.10	–	London	21.07.84
Samuel, Jlloyd	5.11	–	Trinidad	24.05.79
Midfielders				
Davis, Steven	5. 7	–	Ballymena	1.01.85
De la Cruz, Ulises	5.11	Hibernian	Quito	8.02.74
Hendrie, Lee	5.10	–	Birmingham	18.05.77
Hitzlsperger, Thomas	6. 0	Bayern Munich	Munich	5.04.82
Hynes, Peter	5. 9	–	Dublin	28.11.83
McCann, Gavin	5.11	Sunderland	Blackpool	10.01.78
Solano, Nolberto	5. 8	Newcastle Utd.	Lima	12.12.74
Whittingham, Peter	5.10	–	Nuneaton	8.09.84

Forwards

Allback, Marcus	5.11	Heerenveen	Gothenburg	5.07.73
Angel, Juan Pablo	5.11	River Plate	Medellin, Col.	21.10.75
Moore, Luke	5.10	–	Birmingham	13.02.86
Moore, Stefan	5.11	–	Birmingham	28.09.83
Vassell, Darius	5. 7	–	Birmingham	13.06.80

BIRMINGHAM CITY

Ground: St Andrews, Birmingham B9, 4NH.
Telephone: 07091 112 5837. **Club nickname:** Blues.
First-choice colours: Blue shirts; blue shorts; white stockings.
Record transfer fee: £6,250,000 to Liverpool for Emile Heskey, May 2004.
Record fee received: £3,000,000 from Leicester City for Gary Rowett, July 2000.
Record attendance: 66,844 v Everton (F.A. Cup 5) 11 February, 1967.
Capacity for 2004-05: 30,007. **Sponsors:** Phones 4U.
League championship: 6th 1955-56.
F.A. Cup: runners-up 1931, 1956.
League Cup: winners 1963.
European Competitions: runners-up Fairs Cup 1959-60, 1960-61.
Finishing position in Premiership: 2002-03 13th, 2003-04 10th.
Biggest win: 12-0 v Walsall, Div. 2, 17.12.1892, 12-0 v Doncaster Rov., Div. 2, 11.4.1903.
Biggest defeat: 1-9 v Sheffield Wed., Div. 1, 13.12.30. 1-9 v Blackburn Rov., Div. 1, 5.1.1895.
Highest League scorer in a season: Joe Bradford, 29, 1927-28.
Most League goals in aggregate: Joe Bradford, 249, 1920-35.
Most capped player: Malcolm Page (Wales) 28.
Longest unbeaten League sequence: 20 matches (January 1995).
Longest sequence without a League win: 17 matches (January 1986).

Name	Height ft. in.	Previous club	Birthplace	Birthdate
Goalkeepers				
Bennett, Ian	6. 0	Peterborough Utd.	Worksop	10.10.71
Doyle, Colin	6. 5	–	Cork	12.08.85
Taylor, Maik	6. 4	Fulham	Hildeshein, Ger.	4.09.71
Vaesen, Nico	6. 1	Huddersfield Town	Ghent	28.09.69
Defenders				
Cisse, Aliou	6. 0	Montpellier	Zinguinchor, Sen.	24.03.76
Clapham, Jamie	5. 9	Ipswich Town	Lincoln	7.12.75
Cunningham, Kenny	5.11	Wimbledon	Dublin	28.06.71
Grainger, Martin	5.10	Brentford	Enfield	23.08.72
Melchiot, Mario	6. 1	Chelsea	Amsterdam	4.11.76
Sadler, Matthew	5.11	–	Birmingham	26.02.85
Taylor, Martin	6. 4	Blackburn Rov.	Ashington	9.11.79
Tebily, Olivier	6. 0	Celtic	Abidjan, Iv. Coast	19.12.75
Upson, Matthew	6. 1	Arsenal	Eye	18.04.79
Midfielders				
Carter, Darren	6. 2	–	Solihull	18.12.83
Clemence, Stephen	5.11	Tottenham	Liverpool	31.03.78
Dunn, David	5.10	Blackburn Rov.	Blackburn	27.12.79
Gray, Julian	6. 1	Crystal Palace	Lewisham	21.09.79
Gronkjaer, Jesper	6. 1	Chelsea	Nuuk, Den.	12.08.77
Izzet, Muzzy	5.10	Leicester City	Mile End	31.10.74
Johnson, Damien	5.10	Blackburn Rov.	Lisburn	18.11.78
Kilkenny, Neil	5. 8	–		19.12.85
Lazaridis, Stan	5. 9	West Ham Utd.	Perth, Aus.	16.08.72
Motteram, Carl	5. 5	–	Birmingham	3.09.84
Savage, Robbie	5.11	Leicester City	Wrexham	18.10.74

Barrowman, Andrew	6.0	–	Glasgow	27.11.84
Heskey, Emile	6.2	Liverpool	Leicester	11.01.78
John, Stern	6.1	Nott'm Forest	Canefarm, Trin.	30.10.76
Morrison, Clinton	6.1	Crystal Palace	Tooting	14.05.79

BLACKBURN ROVERS

Ground: Ewood Park, Blackburn BB2 4JF.
Telephone: 01254 698888. **Club nickname:** Rovers.
First-choice colours: Blue and white shirts; white shorts; blue and white stockings.
Record transfer fee: £8,000,000 to Manchester Utd. for Andy Cole, December 2001.
Record fee received: £15,000,000 from Newcastle Utd. for Alan Shearer, July 1996.
Record attendance: 62,522 v Bolton Wand., (F.A. Cup 6) 2 March, 1929.
Capacity for 2004-05: 31,367. **Sponsors:** Lonsdale.
League championship: winners 1911-12, 1913-14, 1994-95.
F.A. Cup: winners 1884, 1885, 1886, 1890, 1891, 1928.
League Cup: winners 2002.
European Competitions: Champions League 1st group stage 1995-96.
Finishing positions in Premiership: 1992-93 4th, 1993-94 2nd, 1994-95 1st, 1995-96 7th, 1996-97 13th, 1997-98 6th, 1998-99 19th, 2001-02 10th, 2002-03 6th, 2003-04 15th.
Biggest win: 9-0 v Middlesbrough, Div. 2, 6.11.1954. Also 11-0 v Rossendale, F.A. Cup 1st Rd, 13.10.1884.
Biggest defeat: 0-8 v Arsenal, Div. 1, 25.2.1933.
Highest League scorer in a season: Ted Harper, 43, 1925-26.
Most League goals in aggregate: Simon Garner, 168, 1978-92.
Most capped player: Henning Berg (Norway) 58.
Longest unbeaten League sequence: 23 matches (September 1987).
Longest sequence without a League win: 16 matches (November 1978).

Name	Height ft. in.	Previous club	Birthplace	Birthdate
Goalkeepers				
Enckelman, Peter	6. 2	Aston Villa	Turku, Fin.	10.03.77
Friedel, Brad	6. 3	Liverpool	Lakewood, USA	18.05.71
Yelldell, David	6. 4	Stuttgart	Stuttgart	1.10.81
Defenders				
Amoruso, Lorenzo	6. 2	Rangers	Palese, Ita.	28.06.71
Babbel, Markus	6. 3	Liverpool	Munich	8.09.72
Gray, Michael	5. 7	Sunderland	Sunderland	3.08.74
Gresko, Vratislav	5.11	Parma	Bratislava	24.07.77
Johansson, Nils-Eric	6. 1	Nurnberg	Stockholm	13.01.80
Matteo, Dominic	6. 1	Leeds Utd.	Dumfries	24.04.74
McEveley, James	5.10	–	Liverpool	2.11.85
Neill, Lucas	6. 1	Millwall	Sydney	9.03.78
Short, Craig	6. 2	Everton	Bridlington	25.06.68
Todd, Andy	5.10	Charlton Athletic	Derby	21.09.74
Midfielders				
Danns, Neil	5. 9	–	Liverpool	23.11.82
De Pedro, Javier	5. 8	Real Sociedad	Logrono, Spa.	4.08.73
Donnelly, Ciaran	5.10	–	Blackpool	2.04.84
Douglas, Jonathan	5.11	–	Monaghan	22.11.81
Emerton, Brett	6. 1	Feyenoord	Bankstown, Aus.	22.02.79
Ferguson, Barry	5.10	Rangers	Glasgow	2.02.78
Flitcroft, Garry	6. 0	Manchester City	Bolton	6.11.72
Reid, Steven	6. 1	Millwall	Kingston	10.03.81
Thompson, David	5. 7	Coventry City	Birkenhead	12.09.77
Tugay, Kerimoglu	5. 9	Rangers	Istanbul	24.08.70
Forwards				
Cole, Andy	5.10	Manchester Utd.	Nottingham	15.10.71

Dickov, Paul	5. 6	Leicester City	Livingston	1.11.72
Gallagher, Paul	6. 0		Blackburn	9.08.84
Jansen, Matt	5.11	Crystal Palace	Carlisle	20.10.77
Stead, Jon	6. 3	Huddersfield Town	Huddersfield	7.04.83
Yorke, Dwight	5.10	Manchester Utd.	Canaan, Tob.	3.11.71

BOLTON WANDERERS

Ground: Reebok Stadium, Burnden Way, Lostock, Bolton BL6 6JW.
Telephone: 01204 673673. **Club nickname:** Trotters.
First-choice colours: White shirts; white shorts; white stockings.
Record transfer fee: £3,500,000 to Wimbledon for Dean Holdsworth, October 1997.
Record fee received: £4,500,000 from Liverpool for Jason McAteer, September 1995.
Record attendance: At Reebok Stadium: 28,353 v Leicester City (Premier League) 28 December, 2003. At Burnden Park: 69,912 v Manchester City, (F.A. Cup 5) 18 February, 1933.
Capacity for 2004-05: 28,031. **Sponsors:** Reebok.
League championship: 3rd 1891-92, 1920-21, 1924-25.
F.A. Cup: winners 1923, 1926, 1929, 1958.
League Cup: runners-up 1995, 2004.
Finishing positions in Premiership: 1995-96 20th, 1997-98 18th, 2001-02 16th, 2002-03 17th, 2003-04 8th.
Biggest win: 8-0 v Barnsley, Div. 2, 6.10.1934. Also 13-0 v Sheffield Utd., F.A. Cup 2nd Rd, 1.2.1890.
Biggest defeat: 1-9 v Preston N.E., F.A. Cup 2nd Rd, 10.12.1887.
Highest League scorer in a season: Joe Smith, 38, 1920-21.
Most League goals in aggregate: Nat Lofthouse, 255, 1946-61.
Most capped player: Mark Fish (South Africa) 34.
Longest unbeaten League sequence: 23 matches (October 1990).
Longest sequence without a League win: 26 matches (April 1902).

Name	Height ft. in.	Previous club	Birthplace	Birthdate
Goalkeepers				
Jaaskelainen, Jussi	6. 4	VPS	Vaasa, Fin	17.04.75
Defenders				
Barness, Anthony	5.11	Charlton Athletic	Lewisham	25.03.73
Comyn-Platt, Charlie	6. 2	–	Manchester	2.10.85
Gillan, Michael	5. 9	–	–	12.03.86
Hunt, Nicky	6. 1	–	Bolton	3.09.83
Jaidi, Radhi	6. 3	Esperance	Tunis	30.08.75
Laville, Florent	6. 1	Lyon	Valence, Fra.	7.08.73
Livesey, Daniel	6. 0	–	Salford	31.12.84
N'Gotty, Bruno	6. 2	Marseille	Lyon	10.06.71
Midfielders				
Campo, Ivan	6. 1	Real Madrid	San Sebastian	21.02.74
Nolan, Kevin	6. 1	–	Liverpool	24.06.82
Gardner, Ricardo	5. 9	Harbour View	St Andrews, Jam.	25.09.78
Giannakopoulos, Stelios	5.10	Olympiakos	Greece	12.07.74
Forwards				
Bridges, Michael	6. 1	Leeds Utd.	North Shields	5.08.78
Davies, Kevin	6. 0	Southampton	Sheffield	26.03.77
Djorkaeff, Youri	5.11	Kaiserslautern	Lyon	3.09.68
Ferdinand, Les	5.11	Leicester City	Acton	8.12.66
Jardel, Mario	6. 2	Sporting Lisbon	Fortaleza, Bra.	18.09.73
Okocha, Jay-Jay	5.10	Paris SG	Enugu, Nig.	14.08.73
Pedersen, Henrik	6. 1	Silkeborg	Jutland	10.06.75
Shakes, Ricky	5.10	–	London	25.01.85
Vaz Te, Ricardo	6. 2	Farense	Lisbon	1.10.86

CHARLTON ATHLETIC

Ground: The Valley, Floyd Road, Charlton, London, SE7 8BL.
Telephone: 0208 333 4000. **Club nickname:** Addicks.
First-choice colours: Red and white shirts; white and red shorts; red and white stockings.
Record transfer fee: £4,750,000 to Wimbledon for Jason Euell, July 2001.
Record fee received: £10,000,000 from Chelsea for Scott Parker, January 2004.
Record attendance: 75,031 v Aston Villa (F.A. Cup 5) 12 February, 1938.
Capacity for 2004-05: 26,875. **Sponsors:** all:sports.
League Championship: 2nd 1936-37.
F.A. Cup: winners 1947.
League Cup: 4th rnd 1963, 1966, 1979, 2001.
Finishing positions in Premiership: 1998-99 18th, 2000-01 9th, 2001-02 14th, 2002-03 12th, 2003-04 12th.
Biggest win: 8-1 v Middlesbrough, Div. 1, 12 September 1953.
Biggest defeat: 1-11 v Aston Villa, Div. 2, 14 November 1959.
Highest League scorer in a season: Ralph Allen, 32, Div. 3 (south), 1934-35.
Most League goals in aggregate: Stuart Leary, 153, 1953-62.
Most capped player: Mark Kinsella (Rep. of Ireland) 33.
Longest unbeaten League sequence: 15 matches (December 1980).
Longest sequence without a League win: 16 matches (August 1955).

Name	Height ft. in.	Previous club	Birthplace	Birthdate
Goalkeepers				
Andersen, Stephan	6. 2	AB Copenhagen	Denmark	26.11.81
Kiely, Dean	6. 1	Bury	Salford	10.10.70
Rachubka, Paul	6. 1	Manchester Utd.	San Luis, USA,	21.05.81
Royce, Simon	6. 2	Leicester City	Forest Gate	9.09.71
Defenders				
El Karkouri, Talal	6. 1	Paris St-Germain	Casablanca	8.07.76
Fish, Mark	6. 3	Bolton Wand.	Cape Town	14.03.74
Fortune, Jonathan	6. 2	–	Islington	28.08.80
Hreidarsson, Hermann	6. 1	Ipswich Town	Iceland	11.07.74
Kishishev, Radostin	5.11	Liteks Lovech	Burgas, Bul.	30.07.74
Konchesky, Paul	5.10	–	Barking	15.05.81
Perry, Chris	5. 8	Tottenham	Carshalton	26.04.73
Powell, Chris	5.10	Derby Co.	Lambeth	8.09.69
Turner, Michael	6. 4	–	Lewisham	9.11.83
Young, Luke	6. 0	Tottenham	Harlow	19.07.79
Midfielders				
Campbell-Ryce, Jamal	5.10	Millwall	Lambeth	6.04.83
Holland, Matt	5. 9	Ipswich Town	Bury	11.04.74
Hughes, Bryan	5. 9	Birmingham City	Liverpool	19.06.76
Jensen, Claus	5.11	Bolton Wand.	Nykobing, Den.	29.04.77
Lloyd, Sam	5. 8	–	Leeds	27.09.84
Long, Stacy	5. 8	–	Bromley	11.01.85
McCafferty, Neil	5. 7	–	Londonderry	19.07.84
Stuart, Graham	5. 9	Sheffield Utd.	Tooting	24.10.70
Thomas, Jerome	6. 1	Arsenal	Brent	23.03.83
Forwards				
Bartlett, Shaun	6. 1	FC Zurich	Cape Town	31.10.72
Debolla, Mark	5. 7	–	London	1.01.83
Di Canio, Paolo	5. 9	West Ham Utd.	Rome	9.07.68
Euell, Jason	5.11	Wimbledon	Lambeth	6.02.77
Johansson, Jonatan	6. 2	Rangers	Stockholm	16.08.75
Lisbie, Kevin	5.10	–	Hackney	17.10.78
Rommedahl, Dennis	5.10	PSV Eindhoven	Copenhagen	22.07.79
Varney, Alex	6. 0	–	Farnborough	27.12.84

CHELSEA

Ground: Stamford Bridge Stadium, London SW6 1HS.
Telephone: 0870 300 1212. **Club nickname:** Blues.
First-choice colours: Blue shirts; blue shorts; white stockings.
Record transfer fee: £17,000,000 to Blackburn Rov. for Damien Duff, July 2003.
Record fee received: £12,000,000 from Rangers for Tore Andre Flo, November 2000.
Record attendance: 82,905 v Arsenal (Div. 1) 12 October, 1935.
Capacity for 2004-05: 42,449. **Sponsors:** Emirates.
League Championship: winners 1954-55.
F.A. Cup: winners 1970, 1997, 2000.
League Cup: winners 1965, 1998.
European Competitions: winners Cup Winners' Cup 1970-71, 1997-98.
Finishing positions in Premiership: 1992-93 11th, 1993-94 14th, 1994-95 11th, 1995-96 11th, 1996-97 6th, 1997-98 4th, 1998-99 3rd, 1999-2000 5th, 2000-01 6th, 2001-02 6th, 2002-03 4th, 2003-04 2nd.
Biggest win: 7-0 in four League matches from Lincoln City, Div. 2, 29.10.1910 to Walsall, Div. 2, 4.2.1989. Also 9-2 v Glossop N.E. Div. 2, 1.9.1906.
Biggest defeat: 1-8 v Wolves, Div. 1, 26.9.1923. Also 0-7 v Leeds Utd., Div. 1, 7.10.1967 and v Nott'm. For. Div. 1, 20.4.1991.
Highest League scorer in a season: Jimmy Greaves, 41, 1960-61.
Most League goals in aggregate: Bobby Tambling, 164, 1958-70.
Most capped player: Marcel Desailly (France) 67.
Longest unbeaten League sequence: 27 matches (October 1988).
Longest sequence without a League win: 21 matches (November 1987).

Name	Height ft. in.	Previous club	Birthplace	Birthdate
Goalkeepers				
Ambrosio, Marco	6. 2	Chievo	Brescia	30.05.73
Cech, Petr	6. 5	Rennes	Plzen, Cz.	20.05.82
Cudicini, Carlo	6. 1	Castel Di Sangro	Milan	6.09.73
Macho, Jurgen	6. 4	Sunderland	Vienna	24.08.77
Makalamby, Yves	6. 5	PSV Eindhoven	Belgium	31.01.86
Sullivan, Neil	6. 2	Tottenham	Sutton	24.02.70
Defenders				
Babayaro, Celestine	5. 9	Anderlecht	Kaduna, Nig.	29.08.78
Bridge, Wayne	5.10	Southampton	Southampton	5.08.80
Ferreira, Paulo	6. 0	FC Porto	Lisbon	18.01.79
Gallas, William	6. 1	Marseille	Asnieres, Fra.	17.08.77
Huth, Robert	6. 2	–	Berlin	18.08.84
Johnson, Glen	6. 0	West Ham Utd.	London	23.08.84
Terry, John	6. 1	–	Barking	7.12.80
Midfielders				
Cole, Joe	5. 9	West Ham Utd.	Islington	8.11.81
Duff, Damien	5.10	Blackburn Rov.	Dublin	2.03.79
Geremi	5.11	Real Madrid	Batousam, Cam.	20.12.78
Lampard, Frank	6. 0	West Ham Utd.	Romford	20.06.78
Makelele, Claude	5. 7	Real Madrid	Kinshasa	18.02.73
Nicholas, Alexis	5.10	–	London	13.02.83
Oliveira, Felipe	5.10	FC Porto	Braga, Por.	27.05.84
Parker, Scott	5. 7	Charlton Athletic	Lambeth	13.10.80
Robben, Arjen	5.11	PSV Eindhoven	Bedum, Hol.	23.01.84
Smertin, Alexi	5. 8	Bordeaux	Barnaul, Rus	1.05.75
Stanic, Mario	6. 2	Parma	Sarajevo	10.04.72
Veron, Juan Sebastian	6. 1	Manchester Utd.	Buenos Aires	9.03.75
Forwards				
Cole, Carlton	6. 3	–	Croydon	12.11.83
Crespo, Hernan	6. 1	Inter Milan	Florida, Arg.	5.07.75
Gudjohnsen, Eidur	6. 0	Bolton Wand.	Reykjavik	15.09.78
Forssell, Mickael	6. 0	Helsinki	Steinfurt, Fin.	15.03.81

Kezman, Mateja	5. 9	PSV Eindhoven	Belgrade	12.04.79
Mutu, Adrian	5.11	Parma	Pitesti, Rom.	8.01.79
Zenden, Boudewijn	5.10	Barcelona	Maastricht	15.08.76

CRYSTAL PALACE

Ground: Selhurst Park, London SE25, 6PU.
Telephone: 0208 768 6000. **Club nickname:** Eagles.
First-choice colours: Red and blue shirts; blue shorts; blue stockings.
Record transfer fee: £2,750,000 to Strasbourg for Valerian Ismael, January 1998.
Record fee received: £4,500,000 from Tottenham for Chris Armstrong, June 1995.
Record attendance: 51,482 v Burnley (Div. 2), 11 May, 1979.
Capacity for 2004-05: 26,500. **Sponsors:** Churchill.
F.A. Cup: runners-up 1990.
League Cup: semi-finalists 1993, 1995, 2001.
European Competitions: InterToto Cup 1998.
Finishing positions in Premiership: 1994-95 19th, 1997-98 20th.
Biggest win: 9-0 v Barrow, Div. 4, 11.10.59.
Biggest defeat: 0-9 v Liverpool, Div. 1, 12.9.90; 0-9 v Burnley, F.A. Cup 2 replay, 10.2.09.
Highest League scorer in a season: Peter Simpson, 46, 1930-31.
Most League goals in aggregate: Peter Simpson, 153, 1930-36.
Most capped player: Aleksandrs Kolinko (Latvia) 23.
Longest unbeaten League sequence: 18 matches (August 1969).
Longest sequence without a League win: 20 matches (September 1962).

Name	Height ft. in.	Previous club	Birthplace	Birthdate
Goalkeepers				
Berthelin, Cedric	6. 4	–	Courrieres, Fra.	25.12.76
Cronin, Lance	6. 1	–	Brighton	11.09.85
Kiralry, Gabor	6. 4	Hertha Berlin	Hungary	1.04.76
Speroni, Julian	6. 1	Dundee	Federal, Arg.	18.05.79
Defenders				
Boyce, Emmerson	5.11	Luton Town	Aylesbury	24.09.79
Butterfield, Danny	5.10	Grimsby Town	Boston	21.11.79
Fleming, Curtis	5.11	Middlesbrough	Manchester	8.10.68
Granville, Danny	5.11	Manchester City	Islington	19.01.75
Heeroo, Gavin	6. 0	–	Haringey	2.09.84
Hudson, Mark	6. 3	Fulham	Guildford	30.03.82
Leigertwood, Mikele	6. 2	Wimbledon	Enfield	12.11.82
Popovic, Tony	6. 0	Hiroshima	Sydney	4.07.73
Powell, Darren	6. 3	Brentford	Hammersmith	10.03.76
Smith, Jamie	5. 8	Wolves	Birmingham	17.09.74
Surey, Ben	5.10	–	Camberley	18.12.82
Symons, Kit	6. 2	Fulham	Basingstoke	8.03.71
Togwell, Sam	6. 0	–	Beaconsfield	14.10.84
Midfielders				
Black, Tommy	5. 7	Arsenal	Chigwell	26.11.79
Borrowdale, Gary	6. 0	–	Sutton	16.07.85
Derry, Shaun	5.11	Portsmouth	Nottingham	6.12.77
Hughes, Michael	5. 7	Birmingham City	Larne	2.08.71
Riihilahti, Aki	5.11	Valerenga	Helsinki	9.09.76
Soares, Tom	6. 0	–		10.07.86
Watson, Ben	5.10	–	London	9.07.85
Forwards				
Freedman, Dougie	5. 9	Nott'm Forest	Glasgow	21.01.74
Johnson, Andrew	5. 7	Birmingham City	Bedford	10.02.81
Routledge, Wayne	5.11	–	Sidcup	7.01.85
Shipperley, Neil	6. 1	Wimbledon	Chatham	30.10.74
Williams, Gareth	6. 0	–	Cardiff	10.09.82

EVERTON

Ground: Goodison Park, Liverpool L4 4EL.
Telephone: 0151 330 2200. **Club nickname:** Toffees.
First-choice colours: Blue shirts; white shorts; white stockings.
Record transfer fee: £5,750,000 to Middlesbrough for Nick Barmby.
Record fee received: £8,000,000 from Arsenal for Francis Jeffers, June 2001.
Record attendance: 78,299 v Liverpool (Div. 1) 18 September, 1948.
Capacity for 2004-05: 40,565. **Sponsors:** Chang Beer.
League Championship: winners 1890-91, 1914-15, 1927-28, 1931-31, 1938-39, 1962-63, 1969-70, 1984-85, 1986-87.
F.A. Cup: winners 1906, 1933, 1966, 1984, 1995.
League Cup: runners up 1977, 1984.
European Competitions: winners Cup-Winners' Cup 1984-85.
Finishing positions in Premiership: 1992-93 13th, 1993-94 17th, 1994-95 15th 1995-96 6th 1996-97 15th 1997-98 17th 1998-99 14th, 1999-2000 13th, 2000-01 16th, 2001-02 15th, 2002-03 7th, 2003-04 17th.
Biggest win: 9-1 v Manchester City, Div. 1, 3.9.1906, v Plymouth Argyle, Div. 2, 27.12.1930. Also 11-2 v Derby Co., F.A. Cup 1st rd, 18.1.1890.
Biggest defeat: 4-10 v Tottenham, Div. 1, 11.10.1958.
Highest League scorer in a season: Ralph 'Dixie' Dean, 60, 1927-28.
Most League goals in aggregate: Ralph 'Dixie' Dean, 349, 1925-37.
Most capped player: Neville Southall (Wales) 92.
Longest unbeaten League sequence: 20 matches (April 1978).
Longest sequence without a League win: 14 matches (March 1937).

Name	Height ft. in.	Previous club	Birthplace	Birthdate
Goalkeepers				
Martyn, Nigel	6. 1	Leeds Utd.	St Austell	11.08.66
Turner, Iain	6. 4	Stirling Albion	Stirling	26.01.84
Wright, Richard	6. 2	Arsenal	Ipswich	5.11.77
Defenders				
Clarke, Peter	5.11	–	Southport	3.01.82
Hibbert, Tony	5.10	–	Liverpool	20.02.81
Naysmith, Gary	5.11	Hearts	Edinburgh	16.11.78
Stubbs, Alan	6. 2	Celtic	Kirkby	6.10.71
Pistone, Alessandro	5.11	Newcastle Utd.	Milan	27.07.75
Weir, David	6. 2	Hearts	Falkirk	10.05.70
Yobo, Joseph	6. 2	Marseille	Kano, Nig.	6.09.80
Midfielders				
Carsley, Lee	5. 9	Coventry City	Birmingham	28.02.74
Gravesen, Thomas	5. 9	Hamburg	Vejle, Den.	11.03.76
Kilbane, Kevin	6. 0	Sunderland	Preston	1.02.77
Li Tie	6. 0	Liaoning Bodao	Liaoning, Chi.	18.09.77
Linderoth, Tobias	5. 8	Stabaek	Marseille	21.04.79
Osman, Leon	5. 8	–	Billinge	17.05.81
Watson, Steve	6. 0	Aston Villa	North Shields	1.04.74
Forwards				
Bent, Marcus	6. 2	Ipswich Town	Hammersmith	19.05.78
Campbell, Kevin	6. 1	Trabzonspor	Lambeth	4.02.70
Chadwick, Nick	5.11	–	Stoke	26.10.82
Ferguson, Duncan	6. 4	Newcastle Utd.	Stirling	27.12.71
McFadden, James	5.10	Motherwell	Glasgow	14.04.83
Pascucci, Patrizio	6. 0	Lazio	Rome	25.11.85
Radzinski, Tomasz	5. 9	Anderlecht	Poznan, Pol.	14.12.73
Rooney, Wayne	5.10	–	Liverpool	24.10.85

FULHAM

Ground: Craven Cottage, Stevenage Road, London SW6 6HH.
Telephone: 0870 442 1222. **Club nickname:** Cottagers.
First-choice colours: White shirts; black shorts; white stockings.
Record transfer fee: £11,500,000 to Lyon for Steve Marlet, August 2001.
Record fee received: £3,500,000 from Liverpool for Steve Finnan, June 2003.
Record attendance: 49,335 v Millwall (Div. 2) 8 October, 1938.
Capacity for 2004-05: 22,150. **Sponsors:** Dabs.Com.
League championship: 10th 1959-60.
F.A. Cup: runners-up 1975.
League Cup: 5th Rd. 1968, 1971, 2000.
Finishing positions in Premiership: 2001-02 13th, 2002-03 14th, 2003-04 9th.
Biggest win: 10-1 v Ipswich Town, Div. 1, 26.12.63.
Biggest defeat: 0-10 v Liverpool, League Cup 2nd Rd 1st leg, 23.9.86.
Highest League scorer in a season: Frank Newton, 43, 1931-32.
Most League goals in aggregate: Gordon Davies, 159, 1978-84 and 1986-91.
Most capped player: Johnny Haynes (England) 56.
Longest unbeaten League sequence: 15 matches (January 1999).
Longest sequence without a League win: 15 matches (February 1950).

Name	Height ft. in.	Previous club	Birthplace	Birthdate
Goalkeepers				
Crossley, Mark	6. 0	Middlesbrough	Barnsley	16.06.69
Flitney, Ross	6. 1	Arsenal	Hitchin	1.06.84
Van der Sar, Edwin	6. 6	Juventus	Voorhout, Hol.	29.10.70
Defenders				
Bocanegra, Carlos	6. 0	Chicago Fire	Alta Loma, USA	25.05.79
Bonnissel, Jerome	5.10	Rangers	Montpellier	11.04.73
Djetou, Martin	6. 2	Parma	Ivory Coast	15.12.74
Goma, Alain	6. 0	Newcastle Utd.	Sault, Fra.	5.10.72
Green, Adam	5. 9	–	Hillingdon	12.01.84
Knight, Zat	6. 6	–	Solihull	2.05.80
Leacock, Dean	6. 2	–	Croydon	10.06.84
Pratley, Darren	6. 1	Arsenal	Barking	22.04.85
Midfielders				
Buari, Malik	5.11	–	Accra	24.01.84
Clark, Lee	5. 8	Sunderland	Wallsend	27.10.72
Doherty, Sean	5. 8	Everton	Basingstoke	10.02.85
Inamoto, Junichi	6. 0	Gambia Osaka	Osaka	18.09.79
Legwinski, Sylvain	6. 1	Bordeaux	Clermont-Ferrand	10.06.73
Malbranque, Steed	5. 8	Lyon	Mouscron, Bel.	6.01.80
Rehman, Zesh	6. 2	–	Birmingham	14.10.83
Forwards				
Boa Morte, Luis	5. 9	Southampton	Lisbon	4.08.77
John, Collins	6. 0	FC Twente	Zwandru, Liber.	7.10.85
Hammond, Elvis	5.10	–	Accra	6.10.80
McBride, Brian	6. 1	Columbus	Arlington Hgts, USA	19.06.72
Noble, Stuart	6. 0	–	Edinburgh	14.10.83
Sava, Facundo	6. 1	Gimnasia	Ituzaingo, Arg.	7.03.74

LIVERPOOL

Ground: Anfield Road, Liverpool L4 0TH.
Telephone: 0151 263 2361. **Club nickname:** Reds or Pool.
First-choice colours: Red shirts; red shorts; red stockings.
Record transfer fee: £14,000,000 to Auxerre for Djibril Cisse, July 2004.
Record fee received: £11,000,000 from Leeds Utd. for Robbie Fowler, November 2001.
Record attendance: 61,905 v Wolves, (F.A. Cup 4), 2 February, 1952.

Capacity for 2004-05: 45,364. **Sponsors:** Carlsberg.
League Championship: winners 1900-01, 1905-06, 1921-22, 1922-23, 1946-47,
1963-64, 1965-66, 1972-73, 1975-76, 1976-77, 1978-79, 1979-80, 1981-82,
1982-83, 1983-84, 1985-86, 1987-88, 1989-90.
F.A. Cup: winners 1965, 1974, 1986, 1989, 1992, 2001.
League Cup: winners 1981, 1982, 1983, 1984, 1995, 2001, 2003.
European Competitions: winners European Cup 1976-77, 1977-78, 1980-81, 1983-84
UEFA Cup 1972-73, 1975-76, 2000-01 European Super Cup 1977.
Finishing positions in Premiership: 1992-93 6th, 1993-94 8th, 1994-95 4th, 1995-96
3rd, 1996-97 4th, 1997-98 3rd, 1998-99 7th, 1999-2000 4th, 2000-01 3rd,
2001-02 2nd, 2002-03 5th, 2003-04 4th.
Biggest win: 10-1 v Rotherham Utd., Div. 2, 18.2.1896. Europe: 11-0 v Stromsgodset,
CWC, 17.9.1974.
Biggest defeat: 1-9 v Birmingham City, Div. 2, 11.12.1954.
Highest League scorer in a season: Roger Hunt, 41, 1961-62.
Most League goals in aggregate: Roger Hunt, 245, 1959-69.
Most capped player: Ian Rush (Wales) 67.
Longest unbeaten League sequence: 31 matches (May 1987).
Longest sequence without a League win: 14 (December 1953).

Name	Height ft. in.	Previous club	Birthplace	Birthdate
Goalkeepers				
Dudek, Jerzy	6. 1	Feyenoord	Rybnik, Pol.	23.03.73
Kirkland, Chris	6. 3	Coventry City	Leicester	2.05.81
Luzi, Patrice	6. 3	Monaco	France	8.07.80
Defenders				
Finnan, Steve	5.10	Fulham	Limerick	20.04.76
Carragher, Jamie	6. 1	–	Liverpool	28.01.78
Henchoz, Stephane	6. 1	Blackburn Rov.	Billens, Swi.	7.09.74
Hyypia, Sami	6. 4	Willem II	Porvoo, Fin.	7.10.73
Medjani, Carl	5.11	St Etienne	France	15.05.85
Otsemobor, John	6. 0	–	Liverpool	23.03.83
Traore, Djimi	6. 1	Laval	Saint-Ouen, Fra.	1.03.80
Vignal, Gregory	6. 0	Montpellier	Montpellier	19.07.81
Welsh, John	6. 0	–	Liverpool	10.01.84
Whitbread, Zak	6. 0	–	Liverpool	4.03.84
Midfielders				
Biscan, Igor	6. 3	Croatia Zagreb	Zagreb	4.05.78
Cheyrou, Bruno	6. 1	Lille	Suresnes, Fra.	10.05.78
Diao, Salif	6. 0	Sedan	Senegal	10.02.77
Diarra, Alou	6. 3	Bastia	France	15.07.81
Gerrard, Steven	6. 1	–	Whiston	30.05.80
Hamann, Dietmar	6. 2	Newcastle Utd.	Waldasson, Ger.	27.08.73
Kewell, Harry	6. 0	Leeds Utd.	Sydney	22.09.78
Le Tallec, Anthony	5.11	Le Havre	Hennebont, Fra.	3.10.84
Murphy, Danny	5. 9	Crewe Alexandra	Chester	18.03.77
Potter, Darren	5.10	–	Liverpool	21.12.84
Riise, John Arne	6. 1	Monaco	Molde, Nor.	24.09.80
Smicer, Vladimir	5.10	Lens	Degin, Cz.	24.05.73
Warnock, Stephen	5.10	–	Ormskirk	12.12.81
Forwards				
Baros, Milan	6. 1	Banik Ostrava	Valassake, Cz.	28.10.81
Cisse, Djibril	6. 0	Auxerre	Arles, Fra.	12.08.81
Diouf, El-Hadji	5.11	Lens	Senegal	15.01.81
Mellor, Neil	6. 0	–	Liverpool	4.11.82
Owen, Michael	5. 8	–	Chester	14.12.79
Sinama Pongolle, Florent	5.11	Le Havre	Saint Pierre, Fra.	20.10.84

MANCHESTER CITY

Ground: City of Manchester Stadium, Sportcity, Manchester M11 3FF.
Telephone: 0161 226 2224. **Club nickname:** City.
First-choice-colours: Sky blue shirts; white shorts; sky blue stockings.
Record transfer fee: £13,000,000 to Paris St-Germain for Nicolas Anelka, June 2002
Record fee received: £4,925,000 from Ajax for Georgi Kinkladze, May 1998.
Record attendance: At City of Manchester Stadium: 47,304 v Chelsea (Premier League)
    28 February, 2004. At Maine Road: 84,569 v Stoke City (F.A. Cup 6) 3 March, 1934
    (British record for any game outside London or Glasgow).
Capacity for 2004-05: 48,000. **Sponsors:** Thomas Cook.
League Championship: winners 1936-37, 1967-68.
F.A. Cup: winners 1904, 1934, 1956, 1969.
European Competitions: winners Cup Winners' Cup 1969-70.
Finishing positions in Premiership: 1992-93 9th, 1993-94 16th, 1994-95 17th,
    1995-96 18th, 2000-01: 18th, 2002-03 9th, 2003-04 16th.
Biggest win: 10-1 Huddersfield Town, Div. 2, 7.11.87.
Biggest defeat: 1-9 v Everton, Div. 1, 3,9,1906.
Highest League scorer in a season: Tommy Johnson, 38, 1928-29.
Most League goals in aggregate: Tommy Johnson, 158, 1919-30.
Most capped player: Colin Bell (England) 48.
Longest unbeaten League sequence: 22 matches (April 1947).
Longest sequence without a League win: 17 matches (April 1980).

Name	Height ft. in.	Previous club	Birthplace	Birthdate
Goalkeepers				
De Vlieger, Geert	6. 0	Willem II	Dendermonde, Bel.	16.10.71
Ellegaard, Kevin Stuhr	6. 5	Farum Boldklub	Charlottenlund, Den.	23.05.83
James, David	6. 5	West Ham Utd.	Welwyn Garden City	1.08.70
Schmeichel, Kasper	6. 0	–	Denmark	5.11.86
Weaver, Nicky	6. 3	Mansfield Town	Sheffield	2.03.79
Defenders				
Bischoff, Mikkel	6. 3	AB Copenhagen	Denmark	3.02.82
Distin, Sylvain	6. 4	Paris SG	France	6.12.77
Dunne, Richard	6. 2	Everton	Dublin	21.09.79
Mettomo, Lucien	6. 0	St Etienne	Cameroon	19.04.77
Mills, Danny	6. 0	Leeds Utd.	Norwich	18.05.77
Ritchie, Paul	5.11	Rangers	Kirkcaldy	21.08.75
Sommeil, David	5.11	Bordeaux	Guadeloupe	10.08.74
Sun Jihai	5.10	Dalian Wanda	Dalian, Chi.	30.09.77
Thatcher, Ben	5.10	Leicester City	Swindon	30.11.75
Midfielders				
Barton, Joey	5. 9	–	Huyton	2.09.82
Bosvelt, Paul	5.11	Feyenoord	Doetinchem, Hol.	26.03.70
Jordan, Stephen	6. 0	–	Warrington	6.03.82
McManaman, Steve	6. 0	Real Madrid	Liverpool	11.02.72
Negouai, Christian	6. 4	Charleroi	Martinique	20.01.75
Reyna, Claudio	5. 9	Sunderland	Livingston, New Jersey	20.07.73
Sibierski, Antoine	6. 2	Lens	Lille	5.08.74
Sinclair, Trevor	5.10	West Ham Utd.	Dulwich	2.03.73
Forwards				
Anelka, Nicolas	6. 0	Paris St-Germain	Versailles	14.03.79
Fowler, Robbie	5.11	Leeds Utd.	Liverpool	9.04.75
Huckerby, Darren	5.11	Leeds Utd.	Nottingham	23.04.76
Macken, Jonathan	5.10	Preston N.E.	Manchester	7.09.77
Vuoso, Matias	5. 9	Independiente	Mar del Plata, Arg.	3.11.81
Wanchope, Paulo	6. 4	West Ham Utd.	Costa Rica	31.07.76
Wright-Phillips, Shaun	5. 6	–	Greenwich	25.10.81

MANCHESTER UNITED

Ground: Old Trafford Stadium, Sir Matt Busby Way, Manchester, M16 ORA.
Telephone: 0161 872 1661. **Club nickname:** Red Devils.
First-choice colours: Red shirts; white shorts; black stockings.
Record transfer fee: £29,000,000 to Leeds Utd. for Rio Ferdinand, July 2002.
Record fee received: £25,000,000 from Real Madrid for David Beckham, July 2003.
Record attendance: Club: 70,504 v Aston Villa, 27 December, 1920, F.A. Cup
(semi-final): 76,962, Wolves v Grimsby Town, 25 March, 1939. Note: 83,260 saw
Manchester Utd. v Arsenal, Div. 1, 17 January, 1948 at Maine Road. Old Trafford was
out of action through bomb damage.
Capacity for 2004-05: 68,936. **Sponsors:** Vodafone.
League Championship: winners 1907-08, 1910-11, 1951-52, 1955-56, 1956-7,
1964-65, 1966-67, 1992-93, 1993-94, 1995-96, 1996-97, 1998-99, 1999-
2000, 2000-01.
F.A. Cup: winners 1909, 1948, 1963, 1977, 1983, 1985, 1990, 1994, 1996, 1999,
2004.
League Cup: winners 1992.
European Competitions: winners European Cup 1967-68, 1998-99, Cup-Winners' Cup
1990-91, European Super Cup 1991.
Finishing positions in Premiership: 1992-93 1st, 1993-94 1st, 1994-95 2nd, 1995-96
1st, 1996-97 1st, 1997-98 2nd, 1998-99 1st, 1999-2000 1st, 2000-01 1st,
2001-02 3rd, 2002-03 1st, 2003-04 3rd.
Biggest win: (while Newton Heath) 10-1 v Wolves, Div.1, 15.10.1892, (as Manchester
Utd.) 9-0 v Ipswich Town, FAPL, 4.3.1995. Europe: 10-0 v Anderlecht, European
Cup prelim. round, 26.9.1956.
Biggest defeat: 0-7 v Wolves Div 2, 26.12.1931, v Aston Villa, Div. 1, 27.12.1930 and
v Blackburn Rov. Div. 1, 10.4.1926.
Highest League scorer in a season: Dennis Viollet, 32, 1959-60.
Most League goals in aggregate: Bobby Charlton, 199, 1956-73.
Most capped player: Bobby Charlton (England) 106.
Longest unbeaten League sequence: 26 matches (February 1956).
Longest sequence without a League win: 16 matches (November 1928 and April 1930).

Name	Height ft. in.	Previous club	Birthplace	Birthdate
Goalkeepers				
Carroll, Roy	6. 2	Wigan Athletic	Enniskillen	30.09.77
Howard, Tim	6. 3	NY MetroStars	N. Brunswick, NJ	03.06.79
Ricardo	6. 2	Valladolid	Madrid	31.12.71
Steele, Luke	6. 2	Peterborough Utd.	Peterborough	24.09.84
Defenders				
Bardsley, Phillip	5.10	–	Salford	28.06.85
Brown, Wes	6. 1	–	Manchester	13.10.79
Ferdinand, Rio	6. 2	Leeds Utd.	Peckham	8.11.78
Heinze, Gabriel	5.11	Paris SG	Crespo, Arg.	19.04.78
Lynch, Mark	5.11	–	Manchester	2.09.81
McShane, Paul	5.11	–	Wicklow	6.01.86
Neville, Gary	5.11	–	Bury.	18.02.75
Neville, Phillip	5.11	–	Bury	21.01.77
O'Shea, John	6. 3	Waterford	Waterford	30.04.81
Silvestre, Mikael	6. 0	Inter Milan	Chambray, Fra.	9.08.77
Spector, Jonathan	6. 1	Chicago Sockers	U.S.A.	3.01.86
Midfielders				
Butt, Nicky	5.10	–	Manchester	21.01.75
Djemba-Djemba, Eric	5. 9	Nantes	Douala, Cam.	4.05.81
Eagles, Chris	5.11	–	Hemel Hempstead	19.11.85
Fletcher, Darren	6. 0	–	Edinburgh	1.02.84
Fortune, Quinton	5. 9	Atletico Madrid	Cape Town	21.05.77
Giggs, Ryan	5.11	–	Cardiff	29.11.73
Keane, Roy	5.11	Nott'm Forest	Cork	10.08.71

Name	Height ft. in.	Previous club	Birthplace	Birthdate
Kleberson	5. 9	Paramaense	Urai, Bra.	19.06.79
Miller, Liam	5. 7	Celtic	Cork	13.02.81
Richardson, Kieran	5.10	–	London	21.10.84
Ronaldo, Cristiano	6. 1	Sporting Lisbon	Madeira	5.02.85
Scholes, Paul	5. 7	–	Salford	16.11.74
Tierney, Paul	5.10	–	Salford	15.09.82
Forwards				
Bellion, David	6. 0	Sunderland	Sevres, Fra.	27.11.82
Forlan, Diego	5. 8	Independiente	Montevideo	19.05.79
Johnson, Edward	5.10	–	Chester	20.09.84
Nardiello, Danny	5.11	–	Coventry	22.10.82
Saha, Louis	5.11	Fulham	Paris	8.08.78
Smith, Alan	5. 9	Leeds Utd.	Leeds	28.10.80
Solskjaer, Ole Gunnar	5.10	Molde	Kristiansund, Nor.	26.02.73
Van Nistelrooy, Ruud	6. 2	PSV Eindhoven	Oss, Hol.	1.07.76

MIDDLESBROUGH

Ground: Cellnet Riverside Stadium, Middlesbrough, TS3 6RS.
Telephone: 01642 877700. **Club nickname:** Boro.
First-choice colours: Red and white shirts; red shorts; red stockings.
Record transfer fee: £8,150,000 to Empoli for Massimo Maccarone, July 2002.
Record fee received: £12,000,000 from Atletico Madrid for Juninho, July 1997.
Record attendance: At Riverside Stadium: 34,814 v Newcastle Utd. (Premier League) 5 March, 2003. 35,000 England v Slovakia 11 June, 2003. At Ayresome Park: 53,596 v Newcastle Utd. (Div.1) December 1949.
Capacity for 2004-05: 35,120. **Sponsors:** 888.com.
League Championship: 3rd 1913-14.
F.A. Cup: runners-up 1997.
League Cup: winners 2004.
Finishing positions in Premiership: 1992-93 21th 1995-96 12th, 1996-97 19th 1998-99 9th, 1999-2000 12th, 2000-01 14th, 2001-02 12th, 2002-03 11th, 2003-04 11th.
Biggest win: 9-0 v Brighton & H.A., Div 2, 23.8.1958.
Biggest defeat: 0-9 v Blackburn Rov., Div 2, 6.11.1954.
Highest League scorer in a season: George Camsell, 59, 1926-27.
Most League goals in aggregate: George Camsell, 326, 1925-39.
Most capped player: Wilf Mannion (England) 26.
Longest unbeaten League sequence: 24 matches (September 1973).
Longest sequence without a League win: 19 matches (October 1981).

Name	Height ft. in.	Previous club	Birthplace	Birthdate
Goalkeepers				
Jones, Bradley	6. 3	–	Armadale, Aus.	19.03.82
Nash, Carlo	6. 5	Manchester City	Bolton	26.09.73
Schwarzer, Mark	6. 4	Bradford City	Sydney	6.10.72
Turnbull, Ross	6. 1	–	Bishop Auckland	4.01.85
Defenders				
Cooper, Colin	5.11	Nott'm Forest	Sedgefield	28.02.67
Davies, Andrew	5.11	–	Stockton	17.12.84
Ehiogu, Ugo	6. 2	Aston Villa	Hackney	3.11.72
Queudrue, Franck	5.10	Lens	Paris	27.08.78
Reiziger, Michael	5.10	Barcelona	Amsteveel, Hol.	3.05.73
Riggott, Chris	6. 2	Derby Co.	Derby	1.09.80
Southgate, Gareth	6. 0	Aston Villa	Watford	3.09.70
Midfielders				
Boateng, George	5. 9	Aston Villa	Nkawka, Gha.	5.09.75
Doriva	5. 9	Celta Vigo	Brazil	28.05.72
Downing, Stewart	6. 0	–	Middlesbrough	22.07.84
Juninho	5. 5	Atletico Madrid	Sao Paulo	22.02.73

Name	Height ft. in.	Previous club	Birthplace	Birthdate
Mendieta, Gaizka	5. 8	Lazio	Bilbao	27.03.74
Morrison, James	5.10	–	–	25.05.86
Parnaby, Stuart	5.11	–	Durham	19.07.82
Wilson, Mark	6. 0	Manchester Utd.	Scunthorpe	9.02.79
Forwards				
Christie, Malcolm	6. 0	Derby Co.	Peterborough	11.04.79
Graham, Danny	5.11	–	–	12.08.85
Greening, Jonathan	6. 0	Manchester Utd.	Scarborough	2.01.79
Hasselbaink, Jimmy Floyd	6. 2	Chelsea	Surinam	27.03.72
Job, Joseph-Desire	5.11	Lens	Venissieux, Fra.	1.12.77
Maccarone, Massimo	6. 0	Empoli	Galliate, Ita.	6.09.79
Nemeth, Szilard	5.10	Inter Bratislava	Komarno, Slov.	8.08.77
Viduka, Mark	6. 2	Leeds Utd.	Melbourne	9.10.75

NEWCASTLE UNITED

Ground: St James' Park, Newcastle-upon-Tyne, NE1 4ST.
Telephone: 0191 201 8400. **Club nickname:** Magpies.
First-choice colours: Black and white shirts; black shorts; black and white stockings.
Record transfer fee: £15,000,000 to Blackburn Rov. for Alan Shearer, July 1996.
Record fee received: £8,000,000 from Liverpool for Dietmar Hamann, July 1999.
Record attendance: 68,386 v Chelsea (Div. 1) September 1930.
Capacity for 2004-05: 52,193. **Sponsors:** Northern Rock.
League Championship: winners 1904-05, 1906-07, 1908-09, 1926-27.
F.A. Cup: winners 1910, 1924, 1932, 1951, 1952, 1955.
League Cup: runners-up 1976.
European Competitions: winners Fairs Cup 1968-69, Anglo-Italian Cup 1972-73.
Finishing positions in Premiership: 1993-94 3rd 1994-95 6th 1995-96 2nd 1996-97 2nd 1997-98 13th 1998-99 13th, 1999-2000 11th, 2000-01 11th, 2001-02 4th, 2002-03 3rd, 2003-04 5th.
Biggest win: 13-0 v Newport County, Div. 2, 5.10.1946.
Biggest defeat: 0-9 v Burton Wanderers, Div. 2, 15.4.1895.
Highest League scorer in a season: Hughie Gallacher, 36, 1926-27.
Most League goals in aggregate: Jackie Milburn, 177, 1946-57.
Most capped player: Shay Given (Rep. of Ireland) 51.
Longest unbeaten League sequence: 14 matches (April 1950).
Longest sequence without a League win: 21 matches (January 1978).

Name	Height ft. in.	Previous club	Birthplace	Birthdate
Goalkeepers				
Caig, Tony	6. 0	Hibernian	Whitehaven	11.04.74
Collin, Adam	6. 3	–	Carlisle	9.12.84
Given, Shay	6. 1	Blackburn Rov.	Lifford	20.04.76
Harper, Steve	6. 2	–	Easington	14.03.75
Defenders				
Bernard, Olivier	5. 7	Lyon	Paris	14.10.79
Bramble, Titus	6. 1	Ipswich Town	Ipswich	31.07.81
Elliott, Robbie	5.10	Bolton Wand.	Newcastle	25.12.73
Hughes, Aaron	6. 1	–	Cookstown	8.11.79
O'Brien, Andy	6. 2	Bradford City	Harrogate	29.06.79
Woodgate, Jonathan	6. 2	Leeds Utd.	Middlesbrough	22.01.80
Midfielders				
Ambrose, Darren	5.11	Ipswich Town	Harlow	29.02.84
Bowyer, Lee	5. 9	West Ham Utd.	London	3.01.77
Dyer, Kieron	5. 7	Ipswich Town	Ipswich	29.12.78
Jenas, Jermaine	6. 0	Nott'm Forest	Nottingham	18.02.83
McClen, Jamie	5. 8	–	Newcastle	13.05.79
Milner, James	6. 0	Leeds Utd.	Horsforth	4.01.86
Robert, Laurent	5.10	Paris SG	Saint-Benoit, Fra.	21.05.75
Speed, Gary	5.10	Everton	Deeside	8.09.69

Taylor, Steven	6. 2	–	Greenwich	23.01.86
Viana, Hugo	5.10	Sporting Lisbon	Portugal	15.01.83
Forwards				
Ameobi, Shola	6. 3	–	Zaria, Nig.	12.10.81
Bellamy, Craig	5. 8	Coventry City	Cardiff	13.01.79
Chopra, Michael	5.10	–	Newcastle	23.12.83
Offiong, Richard	5.11	–	South Shields	17.12.83
Shearer, Alan	5.11	Blackburn Rov.	Newcastle	13.08.70

NORWICH CITY

Ground: Carrow Road, Norwich City NR1 1JE.
Telephone: 01603 760760. **Club nickname:** Canaries.
First-choice colours: Yellow shirts; green shorts; yellow stockings.
Record transfer fee: £1,000,000 to Leeds Utd. for Jon Newsome, June 1994.
Record fee received: £5,000,000 from Blackburn Rov. for Chris Sutton, July 1994.
Record attendance: 43,984 v Leicester City (F.A. Cup 6), 30 March, 1963.
Capacity for 2004-05: 24,349. **Sponsors:** Proton and Lotus Cars.
F.A. Cup: semi-finalists 1959, 1989, 1992.
League Cup: winners 1962, 1985.
European Competitions: third round UEFA Cup 1993-94.
Finishing positions in Premiership: 1992-93 3rd, 1993-94 12th, 1994-95 20th.
Biggest win: 10-2 v Coventry City, Div. 3S, 15.3.30; 8-0 v Sutton Utd., F.A. Cup 4, 28.1.89.
Biggest defeat: 2-10 v Swindon Town, Southern League, 5.9.08.
Highest League scorer in a season: Ralph Hunt, 31, 1955-56.
Most League goals in aggregate: Johnny Gavin, 122, 1945-54, 55-58.
Most capped player: Mark Bowen (Wales) 35.
Longest unbeaten League sequence: 20 matches (December 1950).
Longest sequence without a League win: 25 matches (February 1957).

Name	Height ft. in.	Previous club	Birthplace	Birthdate
Goalkeepers				
Crichton, Paul	6. 1	Burnley	Pontefract	3.10.68
Gallacher, Paul	6. 0	Dundee Utd.	Glasgow	16.08.79
Green, Robert	6. 3	–	Chertsey	18.01.80
Defenders				
Brennan, Jim	6. 0	Nott'm Forest	Toronto	8.05.77
Charlton, Simon	5. 8	Bolton Wand.	Huddersfield	25.10.71
Drury, Adam	5.10	Peterborough Utd.	Cambridge	29.08.78
Edworthy, Marc	5.10	Wolves	Barnstaple	24.12.72
Fleming, Craig	5.11	Oldham Athletic	Halifax	6.10.71
Mackay, Malky	6. 3	Celtic	Bellshill	19.02.72
Shackell, Jason	5.11	–	Stevenage	27.09.83
Midfielders				
Briggs, Keith	6. 0	Stockport Co.	Ashton under Lyne	11.12.81
Francis, Damien	6. 2	Wimbledon	Wandsworth	27.02.79
Holt, Gary	5.10	Kilmarnock	Irvine	9.03.73
Mulryne, Phil	5. 8	Manchester Utd.	Belfast	1.01.78
Rivers, Mark	5.10	Crewe Alexandra	Crewe	26.11.75
Safri, Youssef	6. 2	Coventry City	Morocco	1.03.77
Forwards				
Abbey, Zema	6. 1	Cambridge Utd.	Luton	17.04.77
Henderson, Ian	5.11	–	Thetford	24.01.85
Huckerby, Darren	5.10	Manchester City	Nottingham	23.04.76
Jarvis, Ryan	5.11	–	Fakenham	11.07.86
McKenzie, Leon	5.11	Peterborough Utd.	Croydon	17.05.78
McVeigh, Paul	5. 6	Tottenham	Belfast	6.12.77
Svensson, Matt	6. 0	Charlton Athletic	Boras, Swe.	24.09.74

PORTSMOUTH

Ground: Fratton Park, Frogmore Road, Portsmouth, PO4 8RA.
Telephone: 02392 731204. **Club nickname:** Pompey.
First choice colours: Royal blue shirts; white shorts; red stockings.
Record transfer fee: £1,900,000 to Vitesse Arnhem for Dejan Stefanovic, June 2003.
Record fee received: £5,000,000 from Aston Villa for Peter Crouch, March 2002.
Record attendance: 51,385 v Derby Co. (F.A. Cup 6) 26 February, 1949.
Capacity for 2004-05: 20,140. **Sponsors:** Ty Europe.
League Championships: winners 1948-49, 1949-50.
FA Cup: winners 1939.
League Cup: 5th rd. 1961, 1986.
Finishing positions in Premiership: 2003-04 13th.
Biggest win: 9-1 v Notts Co., Div. 1, 09.04.1927.
Biggest defeat: 0-10 v Leicester City, Div. 1, 20.10.1928.
Highest League scorer in a season: Guy Whittingham, 42, Div. 1, 1992-93.
Most League goals in aggregate: Peter Harris, 194, 1946-60.
Most capped player: Jimmy Dickinson (England) 48.
Longest unbeaten League sequence: 15 matches (October 1924).
Longest sequence without a League win: 25 matches (August 1959).

Name	Height ft. in.	Previous club	Birthplace	Birthdate
Goalkeepers				
Ashdown, Jamie	6. 3	Reading	Reading	30.11.80
Hislop, Shaka	6. 4	West Ham Utd.	Hackney	22.02.69
Wapenaar, Harold	6. 1	Utrecht	Vlaardingen, Hol.	10.04.70
Defenders				
Buxton, Lewis	5.11	–	Cowes	10.12.83
Cooper, Shaun	5. 9	–	Newport, IOW	5.10.83
Curtis, John	5.10	Leicester City	Nuneaton	3.09.78
De Zeeuw, Arjan	6. 1	Wigan Athletic	Castricum, Hol.	16.04.70
Duffy, Richard	5. 9	Swansea City	Swansea	30.08.85
Foxe, Hayden	6. 2	West Ham Utd.	Sydney	23.06.77
Griffin, Andy	5. 9	Newcastle Utd.	Billinge	7.03.79
Howe, Eddie	5. 9	Bournemouth	Amersham	29.11.77
Primus, Linvoy	5.11	Reading	Forest Gate	14.07.73
Stefanovic, Dejan	5.11	Vitesse Arnhem	Belgrade	28.10.74
Unsworth, David	6. 1	Everton	Chorley	16.10.73
Midfielders				
Barrett, Neil	5. 9	Chelsea	Tooting	29.12.81
Berger, Patrik	6. 1	Liverpool	Prague	10.11.73
Cooper, Shaun	5.10	–	Isle of Wight	5.10.83
Faye, Amdy	6. 0	Auxerre	Dakar	12.03.77
Harper, Kevin	5..6	Derby Co.	Oldham	15.01.76
Hughes, Richard	5. 9	Bournemouth	Glasgow	25.06.79
O'Neil, Gary	5. 9	–	Beckenham	18.05.83
Quashie, Nigel	6. 0	Nott'm Forest	Peckham	20.07.78
Stone, Steve	5. 8	Aston Villa	Gateshead	20.08.71
Taylor, Matthew	5.11	Luton Town	Oxford	27.11.81
Forwards				
Aiyegbeni, Yakubu	6. 0	Maccabi Haifa	Nigeria	22.11.82
LuaLua, Lomana	5.10	Newcastle Utd.	Zaire	28.12.80
Mornar, Ivica	6. 0	Anderlecht	Split	12.01.74
Todorov, Svetoslav	6. 0	West Ham Utd.	Dobrich, Bul.	30.08.78
Vine, Rowan	5.11	–	Basingstoke	21.09.82

SOUTHAMPTON

Ground: The Friends Provident St Mary's Stadium, Britannia Road, Southampton, SO14 5FP.

Telephone: 0870 220 0000. **Club nickname:** Saints.
First-choice colours: Red and white shirts; black shorts; white stockings.
Record transfer fee: £4,000,000 to Derby Co. for Rory Delap, July 2001.
Record fee received: £8,000,000 from Tottenham for Dean Richards, September 2001.
Record attendance: At St Mary's: 32,151 v Arsenal (Premier League) 29 December, 2003. At The Dell: 31,044 v Manchester Utd. (Div. 1) 8 October 1969.
Capacity for 2004-05: 32,500. **Sponsors:** Friends Provident.
League Championship: 2nd 1983-84.
F.A. Cup: winners 1976.
League Cup: runners-up 1979.
European Competitions: Fairs Cup round 3, 1969-70, Cup-Winners' Cup round 3(QF), 1976-77.
Finishing positions in Premiership: 1992-93 18th, 1993-94 18th, 1994-95 10th, 1995-96 17th, 1996-97 16th, 1997-98 12th, 1998-99 17th, 1999-2000 15th, 2000-01 10th, 2001-02 11th, 2002-03 8th, 2003-04 12th.
Biggest win: 8-0 v Northampton Town, Div. 3S, 24.12.1921.
Biggest defeat: 0-8 v Tottenham, Div. 2, 28.3.1936 and v Everton Div. 1, 20.11.1971.
Highest League scorer in a season: Derek Reeves, 39, 1959-60.
Most League goals in aggregate: Mike Channon, 185, 1966-77, 1979-82.
Most capped player: Peter Shilton (England) 49.
Longest unbeaten League sequence: 19 matches (September 1921).
Longest sequence without a League win: 20 matches (August 1969).

Name	Height ft. in.	Previous club	Birthplace	Birthdate
Goalkeepers				
Niemi, Antti	6. 1	Hearts	Finland	31.05.72
Blayney, Alan	6. 2	–	Belfast	9.10.81
Smith, Paul	6. 4	Brentford	Epsom	17.12.79
Poke, Michael	6. 1	–	Spelthorne	21.11.85
Defenders				
Baird, Chris	5.10	–	Ballymoney	25.02.82
Crainey, Stephen	5. 9	Celtic	Glasgow	22.06.81
Cranie, Martin	6. 0	–	Yeovil	26.09.86
Dodd, Jason	5. 8	–	Bath	2.11.70
Hall, Fitz	6. 5	Oldham Athletic	Walthamstow	20.12.80
Higginbotham, Danny	6. 1	Derby Co.	Manchester	29.12.78
Kenton, Darren	5.11	Norwich City	Wandsworth	13.09.78
Le Saux, Graeme	5.10	Chelsea	Jersey	17.10.68
Lundekvam, Claus	6. 4	SK Brann	Austevoll, Nor.	22.02.73
Mills, Matthew	6. 0	–	Swindon	14.07.86
Svensson, Michael	6. 2	Troyes	Sweden	25.11.75
Van Damme, Jelle	6. 4	Ajax	Lokeren, Bel.	10.10.83
Williams, Paul	5.11	Coventry City	Burton	26.03.71
Midfielders				
Davies, Arron	5. 9	–	Cardiff	22.06.84
Delap, Rory	6. 1	Derby Co.	Sutton Coldfield	6.07.76
Fernandes, Fabrice	5. 9	Rennes	Paris	29.10.79
Folly, Yoann	5.11	St Etienne	Togo	6.06.85
Griffit, Leandre	5. 9	Amiens	Maubeuge, Fra.	21.05.84
Prutton, David	6. 1	Nott'm. Forest	Hull	12.09.81
McCann, Neil	5.10	Rangers	Greenock	8.11.74
Oakley, Matthew	5.10	–	Peterborough	17.08.77
Svensson, Anders	5.10	Elfsborg	Sweden	17.07.76
Telfer, Paul	5. 9	Coventry City	Edinburgh	21.10.71
Tessem, Jo	6. 2	Molde	Orlandet, Nor.	28.02.72
Forwards				
Beattie, James	6. 1	Blackburn Rov.	Lancaster	27.02.78
Best, Leon	6. 1	Notts Co.	Nottingham	19.09.86
Blackstock, Dexter	6. 2	Oxford Utd.	Oxford	20.05.86
Crouch, Peter	6. 6	Aston Villa	Macclesfield	30.01.81

Ormerod, Brett	5.11	Blackpool	Blackburn	18.10.76
Pahars, Marian	5. 8	Skonto Riga	Riga, Lat.	5.08.76
Phillips, Kevin	5. 7	Sunderland	Hitchin	25.07.73

TOTTENHAM HOTSPUR

Ground: 748 High Road, Tottenham, London N17 OAP.
Telephone: 0208 365 5000. **Club nickname:** Spurs.
First-choice colours: White shirts; navy shorts; white stockings.
Record transfer fee: £11,000,000 to Dynamo Kiev for Sergei Rebrov, May 2000.
Record fee received: £5,500,000 from Lazio for Paul Gascoigne, May 1992.
Record attendance: 75,038 v Sunderland (F.A. Cup 6) 5 March 1938.
Capacity for 2004-05: 36,237. **Sponsors:** Thomson.
League Championship: winners 1950-51, 1960-61.
F.A. Cup: winners 1901, 1921, 1961, 1962, 1967, 1981, 1982, 1991.
League Cup: winners 1971, 1973, 1999.
European Competitions: winners Cup-Winners' Cup 1962-63, UEFA Cup 1971-72, 1983-84.
Finishing positions in Premiership: 1992-93 8th, 1993-94 15th, 1994-95 7th, 1995-96 8th, 1996-97 10th, 1997-98 14th, 1998-99 11th, 1999-2000 10th, 2000-01 12th, 2001-02 9th, 2002-03 10th, 2003-04 14th.
Biggest win: 9-0 v Bristol Rov., Div.2, 22.10.1977, F.A. Cup 13-2 v Crewe Alexandra, round four replay, 3.2.1960, Europe 9-0 v Keflavik, UEFA Cup, round one, 28.9.1971.
Biggest defeat: 0-7 v Liverpool, Div.1, 2.9.1979.
Highest League scorer in a season: Jimmy Greaves, 37, 1962-63.
Most League goals in aggregate: Jimmy Greaves, 220, 1961-70.
Most capped player: Pat Jennings (Northern Ireland) 74.
Longest unbeaten League sequence: 22 matches (August 1949).
Longest sequence without a League win: 16 matches (December 1934).

Name	Height ft. in.	Previous club	Birthplace	Birthdate
Goalkeepers				
Burch, Rob	6. 0	–	Yeovil	8.02.84
Robinson, Paul	6. 2	Leeds Utd.	Beverley	15.10.79
Keller, Kasey	6. 1	Rayo Vallecano	Olympia, USA	29.11.69
Defenders				
Bunjevcevic, Goran	6. 2	Red Star Belgrade	Karlovac, Cro.	17.02.73
Carr, Stephen	5. 8	–	Dublin	29.08.76
Doherty, Gary	6. 1	Luton Town	Carndonagh	31.01.80
Gardner, Anthony	6. 5	Port Vale	Stafford	19.09.80
Kelly, Stephen	5.11	–	Dublin	6.09.83
King, Ledley	6. 2	–	Bow	12.10.80
Mabizela, Mbulelo	5.11	Orlando Pirates	South Africa	16.09.80
Richards, Dean	6. 2	Tottenham	Bradford	9.06.74
Taricco, Mauricio	5. 8	Ipswich Town	Buenos Aires	10.03.73
Midfielders				
Brown, Michael	5. 9	Sheffield Utd.	Hartlepool	25.01.77
Davies, Sean	5.11	Fulham	Clapham	20.09.79
Davies, Simon	5.11	Peterborough Utd.	Haverfordwest	23.10.79
Jackson, Johnnie	6. 1	–	Camden	15.08.82
Marney, Dean	5.11	–	Barking	31.01.84
Redknapp, Jamie	6. 0	Liverpool	Barton-on-Sea	25.06.73
Ricketts, Rohan	5.11	Arsenal	Clapham	22.12.82
Forwards				
Barnard, Lee	5.10	–	Romford	18.07.84
Defoe, Jermain	5. 7	West Hanm Utd.	Beckton	7.10.82
Kanoute, Fredi	6. 4	West Ham Utd.	St Foy, Fra.	2.09.77
Keane, Robbie	5. 9	Leeds Utd.	Dublin	8.07.80
Yeates, Mark	5.11	–	Dublin	11.01.85

WEST BROMWICH ALBION

Ground: The Hawthorns, Halfords Lane, West Bromwich B71 4LF.
Telephone: 0121 525 8888. **Club nickname:** Baggies.
First-choice colours: Navy blue and white shirts; white, blue and red shorts; navy blue, white and red stockings.
Record transfer fee: £2,500,000 to Coventry City for Lee Hughes, August 2002.
Record fee received: £5,000,001 from Coventry City for Lee Hughes, August 2001.
Record attendance: 64,815 v Arsenal (F.A. Cup 6), 6 March, 1937.
Capacity for 2004-05: 28,000. **Sponsors:** West Bromwich Building Society.
League championship: winners 1919-20.
F.A. Cup: winners 1888, 1892, 1931, 1954, 1968.
League Cup: winners 1966.
European Competions: quarter-finalists Cup Winners' Cup 1968-69, quarter-finalists UEFA Cup 1978-79.
Finishing positions in Premiership: 2002-03: 19th.
Biggest win: 12-0 v Darwen, Div. 1, 4.4.1892.
Biggest defeat: 3-10 v Stoke City, Div. 1, 4.2.37.
Highest League scorer in a season: Ginger Richardson, 39, 1935-36.
Most League goals in aggregate: Tony Brown, 218, 1963-79.
Most capped player: Stuart Williams (Wales) 33.
Longest unbeaten League sequence: 17 matches (December 1957).
Longest sequence without a League win: 14 matches (February 1996).

Name	Height ft. in.	Previous club	Birthplace	Birthdate
Goalkeepers				
Hoult, Russell	6. 4	Portsmouth	Ashby de la Zouch	22.11.72
Miotto, Simon	6. 1	St Johnstone	Australia	5.09.69
Murphy, Joe	6. 1	Tranmere Rov.	Dublin	21.08.81
Defenders				
Albrechtsen, Martin	6. 2	FC Copenhagen	Denmark	31.03.80
Berthe, Sekou	6. 4	Troyes	Bamako, Mali	7.10.77
Chambers, Adam	5.10	–	West Bromwich	20.11.80
Chambers, James	5.10	–	West Bromwich	20.11.80
Clement, Neil	6. 0	Chelsea	Reading	3.10.78
Gaardsoe, Thomas	6. 2	Ipswich Town	Randers, Den.	23.11.79
Haas, Bernt	6. 1	Sunderland	Vienna	8.04.78
Moore, Darren	6. 2	Portsmouth	Birmingham	22.04.74
Purse, Darren	6. 2	Birmingham City	Stepney	14.02.76
Robinson, Paul	5. 9	Watford	Watford	14.12.78
Scimeca, Riccardo	6. 1	Leicester City	Leamington Spa	13.06.75
Sigurdsson, Larus	6. 0	Stoke City	Akureyri, Ice.	4.06.73
Midfielders				
Brown, Simon	5. 7	–	–	18.09.83
Dyer, Lloyd	5. 8	Aston Villa	Birmingham	13.09.82
Gregan, Sean	6. 0	Preston N.E.	Middlesbrough	29.03.74
Johnson, Andy	6. 1	Norwich City	Bristol	2.05.74
Koumas, Jason	5.10	Tranmere Rov.	Wrexham	25.09.79
Marshall, Lee	6. 2	Leicester City	Islington	21.01.79
O'Connor, James	5. 8	Stoke City	Dublin	1.09.79
Sakiri, Artim	5.11	CSKA Sofia	Macedonia	23.09.73
Wallwork, Ronnie	5.10	Manchester Utd.	Manchester	10.09.77
Forwards				
Dobie, Scott	6. 1	Carlisle Utd.	Workington	10.10.78
Horsfield, Geoff	5.11	Wigan Athletic	Barnsley	1.11.73
Hughes, Lee	5.10	Coventry City	Smethwick	22.05.76
Hulse, Rob	6. 1	Crewe Alexandra	Crewe	25.10.79

COCA-COLA LEAGUE PLAYING STAFFS
2004-05 – CHAMPIONSHIP

BRIGHTON AND HOVE ALBION

Ground: Withdean Stadium, Tongdean Lane, Brighton BN1 5JD.
Telephone: 01273 695400. **Club nickname:** Seagulls.
First-choice colours: Blue and white shirts; white shorts; white stockings.
Main sponsor: Skint. **Capacity for 2004-05:** 6,973.
Record attendance: (Goldstone Ground) 36,747 v Fulham (Div. 2) 27 December, 1958;
   (Withdean Stadium) 6,995 v Halifax Town (Div. 3) 2 December, 2000.

Name	Height ft. in.	Previous club	Birthplace	Birthdate
Goalkeepers				
Kuipers, Michel	6. 2	Bristol Rov.	Amsterdam	26.06.74
Roberts, Ben	6. 1	Charlton Athletic	Bishop Auckland	22.06.75
Defenders				
Blackwell, Dean	6. 1	Wimbledon	Camden	5.12.69
Butters, Guy	6. 3	Gillingham	Hillingdon	30.10.69
Cullip, Danny	6. 0	Brentford	Ascot	17.09.76
El-Abd, Adam	6. 0	–	Brighton	11.09.84
Harding, Daniel	6. 0	–	Gloucester	23.12.83
Hinshelwood, Adam	5.10	–	Oxford	8.01.84
Mayo, Kerry	5. 9	–	Cuckfield	21.09.77
Virgo, Adam	6. 1	–	Brighton	25.01.83
Watson, Paul	5. 8	Brentford	Hastings	4.01.75
Midfielders				
Carpenter, Richard	6. 0	Cardiff City	Sheppey	30.09.72
Hammond, Dean	5.11	–	Sussex	7.03.83
Jones, Nathan	5. 6	Southend Utd.	Cardiff	28.05.73
Lee, David	5.11	Hull City	Basildon	28.03.80
McPhee, Chris	5.10	–	Eastbourne	20.03.83
Oatway, Charlie	5. 7	Brentford	Hammersmith	28.11.73
Piercy, John	5.11	Tottenham	Forest Gate	18.09.79
Reid, Paul	5.10	Bradford City	Sydney	6.07.79
Rodger, Simon	5. 9	Crystal Palace	Shoreham	3.10.71
Forwards				
Hart, Gary	5. 9	Stansted	Harlow	21.09.76
Iwelumo, Chris	6. 3	Stoke City	Coatbridge	1.08.78
Knight, Leon	5. 4	Chelsea	Hackney	16.09.82
Robinson, Jake	5.10	–	Brighton	23.10.86

BURNLEY

Ground: Turf Moor, Harry Potts Way, Burnley BB10 4BX.
Telephone: 0870 4431882. **Club nickname:** Clarets.
First-choice colours: Claret and blue shirts; white shorts; white stockings.
Main sponsor: Hunters Estate Agents. **Capacity for 2004-05:** 22,415.
Record attendance: 54,775 v Huddersfield Town (F.A. Cup 4) 23 February, 1924.

Name	Height ft. in.	Previous club	Birthplace	Birthdate
Goalkeepers				
Jensen, Brian	6. 1	W.B.A.	Copenhagen	8.06.75
Defenders				
Camara, Mohammed	5.11	Wolves	Conakry, Gui.	25.06.75
Duff, Mike	6. 1	Cheltenham Town	Belfast	11.01.78
McGreal, John	5.11	Ipswich Town	Birkenhead	2.06.72

Name	Height ft. in.	Previous club	Birthplace	Birthdate
Roche, Lee	5.10	Manchester Utd.	Bolton	28.10.80
Scott, Paul	5.10	–	Burnley	29.01.85
Midfielders				
Branch, Graham	6. 2	Stockport Co.	Liverpool	12.02.72
Chaplow, Richard	5. 9	–	Accrington	2.02.85
Grant, Tony	5.11	Manchester City	Liverpool	14.11.74
O'Neill, Matthew	5.10	–	Accrington	25.06.84
Pilkington, Joel	5. 8	–	Accrington	1.08.84
Forwards				
Blake, Robbie	5. 9	Bradford City	Middlesbrough	4.03.76
Moore, Ian	5.11	Stockport Co.	Birkenhead	26.08.76

CARDIFF CITY

Ground: Ninian Park, Sloper Road, Cardiff CF11 8SX.
Telephone: 02920 221001. **Club nickname:** Bluebirds.
First-choice colours: Blue shirts; blue shorts; blue stockings.
Main sponsor: Redrow Homes. **Capacity for 2004-05:** 21,500.
Record attendance: 61,566 Wales v England, 14 October, 1961. Club: 57,800 v Arsenal (Div. 1) 22 April, 1953.

Name	Height ft. in.	Previous club	Birthplace	Birthdate
Goalkeepers				
Alexander, Neil	6. 1	Livingston	Edinburgh	10.03.78
Lee-Barrett, Arran	6. 2	Norwich City	Ipswich	28.02.84
Margetson, Martyn	6. 0	Huddersfield Town	West Neath	8.09.71
Warner, Tony	6. 4	Millwall	Liverpool	11.05.74
Defenders				
Barker, Chris	6. 0	Barnsley	Sheffield	02.03.80
Croft, Gary	5. 9	Ipswich Town	Burton	17.02.74
Gabbidon, Daniel	5.10	W.B.A.	Cwmbran	8.08.79
Page, Robert	6. 0	Sheffield Utd.	Llwynpia	3.09.74
Vidmar, Tony	6. 1	Middlesbrough	Adelaide	4.07.70
Weston Rhys	6. 1	Arsenal	Kingston	27.10.80
Midfielders				
Boland, Willie	5. 9	Coventry City	Ennis	6.08.75
Bullock, Lee	6. 1	York City	Stockton	22.05.81
Fleetwood, Stuart	5. 9	–	Gloucester	23.04.86
Langley, Richard	5.10	Q.P.R.	Harlesden	27.12.79
Kavanagh, Graham	5.10	Stoke City	Dublin	2.12.73
Parry, Paul	5.10	Hereford Utd.	Chepstow	19.08.80
Robinson, John	5.10	Charlton Athletic	Bulawayo	29.08.71
Whalley, Gareth	5.10	Bradford City	Manchester	19.12.73
Forwards				
Campbell, Andy	6. 0	Middlesbrough	Middlesbrough	18.04.79
Collins, James	6. 2	–	Newport	23.08.83
Earnshaw, Robert	5. 8	–	Zambia	6.04.81
Lee, Alan	6. 2	Rotherham Utd.	Galway	21.08.78
Thorne, Peter	6. 0	Stoke City	Manchester	21.06.73

COVENTRY CITY

Ground: Highfield Road Stadium, King Richard Street, Coventry CV2 4FW.
Telephone: 0247 623 4000. **Club nickname:** Sky Blues.
First-choice colours: Sky blue, navy and white shirts; sky blue, white and navy shorts; sky blue, navy and white stockings.
Main sponsor: Subaru. **Capacity for 2004-05:** 23,613.
Record attendance: 51,455 v Wolves (Div. 2) 29 April, 1967.

Name	Height ft. in.	Previous club	Birthplace	Birthdate
Goalkeepers				
Brush, Richard	6. 1	–	Birmingham	26.11.84
Shearer, Scott	6. 4	Albion Rov.	Glasgow	15.02.81
Tuffey, Jonathan	6. 0	–	Belfast	20.01.87
Defenders				
Cooney, Sean	6. 3	Inglewood	Perth, Aus.	31.10.83
Davenport, Callum	6. 0	–	Bedford	1.01.83
Shaw, Richard	5. 9	Crystal Palace	Brentford	11.09.68
Staunton, Steve	6. 1	Aston Villa	Drogheda	19.01.69
Whing, Andrew	6. 0	–	Birmingham	20.09.84
Midfielders				
Bates, Tom	5.10	–	Coventry	31.08.85
Deloumeaux, Eric	5.11	Aberdeen	Montbeliard, Fra.	12.05.73
Doyle, Michael	5.10	Celtic	Dublin	8.07.81
Gudjonsson, Bjarni	5. 8	Bochum	Akranes, Iceland	26.02.79
Jorgensen, Claus	5.11	Bradford City	Holstebro, Den.	27.04.76
Hall, Andy	5. 6	–	Northampton	25.01.86
Hughes, Stephen	6. 0	Charlton Athletic	Wokingham	18.09.76
Osbourne, Isaac	5.10	–	Birmingham	22.06.86
Pead, Craig	5. 9	–	Bromsgrove	15.09.81
Sherwood, Tim	6. 0	Portsmouth	St Albans	6.02.69
Forwards				
Adebola, Dele	6. 3	Crystal Palace	Lagos	23.06.75
Barrett, Graham	5.10	Arsenal	Dublin	6.10.81
McSheffrey, Gary	5. 8	–	Coventry	13.08.72
Morrell, Andy	5.11	Wrexham	Doncaster	28.09.74
Suffo, Patrick	6. 0	Sheffield Utd.	Manchester	17.01.78
Wood, Neil	5.10	Manchester Utd.	Manchester	4.01.83

CREWE ALEXANDRA

Ground: Alexandra Stadium, Gresty Road, Crewe CW2 6EB.
Telephone: 01270 213014. **Club nickname:** Railwaymen.
First-choice colours: Red shirts; white shorts; red stockings.
Main sponsor: LC Charles. **Capacity for 2004-05:** 10,104.
Record attendance: 20,000 v Tottenham (F.A. Cup 4) 30 January, 1960.

Name	Height ft. in.	Previous club	Birthplace	Birthdate
Goalkeepers				
Ince, Clayton	6. 2	–	Trinidad	13.07.72
Tomlinson, Stuart	6. 0	–	Chester	10.05.85
Williams, Ben	6. 0	Manchester Utd.	Manchester	27.08.82
Defenders				
Foster, Stephen	5.11	–	Warrington	10.09.80
Jones, Billy	5.11	–	Shrewsbury	24.03.87
McCready, Chris	6. 0	–	Chester	5.07.81
McGowan, Lloyd	5. 9	–	Telford	10.10.84
Morris, Alex	6. 0	–	Stoke	5.10.82
Moses, Adie	5.10	Huddersfield Town	Doncaster	4.05.75
Roberts, Mark	6. 1	–	Northwich	16.10.83
Tonkin, Anthony	5.11	Stockport Co.	Newlyn	17.01.80
Vaughan, David	5. 6	–	St Asaph	18.02.83
Walker, Richard	6. 1	–	Stafford	17.09.80
Midfielders				
Bell, Lee	5.10	–	Crewe	20.11.83
Cochrane, Justin	5.11	Hayes	Hackney	26.01.82
Higdon, Michael	6. 0	–	Liverpool	3.09.83
Lunt, Kenny	5. 8	–	Runcorn	20.11.79

Name	Height ft. in.	Previous club	Birthplace	Birthdate
Rix, Ben	5.10	–	Wolves	11.12.83
Roberts, Gary	5. 9	–	Chester	4.02.87
Robinson, James	5. 9	–	Liverpool	18.09.82
Sorvel, Neil	6. 0	Macclesfield Town	Widnes	2.03.73
White, Andy	6. 4	Mansfield Town	Derby	6.11.81
Forwards				
Ashton, Dean	6. 3	–	Swindon	24.01.83
Edwards, Paul	6. 1	–	Derby	10.11.82
Jones, Steve	5.10	Leigh RMI	Derry	25.10.76
Platt, Matthew	5.11	–	Crewe	15.10.83
Varney, Luke	5.10	Quorn	Leicester	28.09.82
Wilson, Kyle	5.11	–	Wirral	14.11.85

DERBY COUNTY

Ground: Pride Park Stadium, Pride Park, Derby DE24 8XL.
Telephone: 01332 667503. **Club nickname:** Rams.
First-choice colours: White shirts; black shorts; white stockings.
Main sponsor: Marstons Pedigree. **Capacity for 2004-05:** 33,597.
Record attendance: (Baseball Ground) 41,826 v Tottenham (Div. 1) 20 September, 1969. (Pride Park) 33,597 England v Mexico, 25 May, 2001.

Name	Height ft. in.	Previous club	Birthplace	Birthdate
Goalkeepers				
Camp, Lee	5.11	–	Derby	22.08.84
Grant, Lee	6. 2	–	Hemel Hempstead	27.01.83
Oakes, Andy	6. 3	Hull City	Crewe	11.01.77
Defenders				
Boertien, Paul	5.10	Carlisle Utd.	Carlisle	21.01.79
Huddlestone, Tom	6. 1	–	Nottingham	28.12.86
Jackson, Richard	5. 7	Scarborough	Whitby	18.04.80
Johnson, Michael	5.11	Birmingham City	Nottingham	4.07.73
Kenna, Jeff	5.11	Birmingham City	Dublin	27.08.70
Konjic, Mo	6. 4	Coventry City	Bosnia	4.05.70
Mills, Pablo	6. 0	–	Birmingham	27.05.84
Vincent, Jamie	5.10	Portsmouth	London	18.06.75
Walton, Dave	6. 2	Crewe Alexandra	Bedlington	10.04.73
Midfielders				
Bisgaard, Morten	5.10	FC Copenhagen	Randers, Den.	25.06.75
Bolder, Adam	5. 8	Hull City	Hull	25.10.80
Doyle, Nathan	5.11	–	Derby Co.	12.01.87
Holmes, Lee	5. 8	–	Mansfield	2.04.87
Taylor, Ian	6. 1	Aston Villa	Birmingham	4.06.68
Weckstrom, Kris	5. 9	–	Helsinki	26.05.83
Forwards				
Junior	6. 0	Walsall	Fortaleza, Bra.	20.07.76
Labarthe Tome, Gianfranco	5. 9	Huddersfield Town	Lima	20.09.84
McLeod, Izale	6. 1	–	Birmingham	15.10.84
Peschisolido, Paul	5. 7	Sheffield Utd.	Scarborough, Can.	25.05.71
Reich, Marco	6. 0	Kaiserslautern	Germany	30.12.77
Smith, Tommy	5.10	Sunderland	Hemel Hempstead	22.05.80
Tudgay, Marcus	5.10	–	Shoreham	3.02.83

GILLINGHAM

Ground: Priestfield Stadium, Redfern Avenue, Gillingham ME7 4DD.
Telephone: 01634 851854. **Club nickname:** Gills.
First-choice colours: Blue shirts; blue shorts; blue stockings.
Main sponsor: MHS Homes. **Capacity for 2004-05:** 11,000.
Record attendance: 23,002 v Q.P.R. (F.A. Cup 3) 10 January, 1948.

Name	Height ft. in.	Previous club	Birthplace	Birthdate
Goalkeepers				
Banks, Steve	6. 0	Wimbledon	Hillingdon	9.02.72
Bossu, Bertrand	6. 6	Hayes	Calais	11.10.80
Brown, Jason	6. 0	Charlton Athletic	Bermondsey	18.05.82
Knowles, Danny	6. 0	–	Sidcup	7.01.86
Defenders				
Ashby, Barry	6. 2	Brentford	Park Royal	2.11.70
Cox, Ian	6. 0	Burnley	Croydon	25.03.71
Hope, Chris	6. 1	Scunthorpe Utd.	Sheffield	14.11.72
Rose, Richard	5.11	–	Pembury	8.09.82
Midfielders				
Beckwith, Dean	6. 3	–	London	18.09.83
Carew, Ashley	6. 0	–	London	12.12.85
Crofts, Andrew	5.11	–	Chatham	29.05.84
Hessenthaler, Andy	5. 7	Watford	Gravesend	17.06.75
Hills, John	5. 9	Blackpool	Blackpool	21.04.78
Jarvis, Matthew	5. 8	–	Middlesbrough	22.05.86
Johnson, Leon	6. 0	Southend Utd.	Shoreditch	10.05.81
Nosworthy, Nyron	6. 1	–	Brixton	11.10.80
Pouton, Alan	6. 0	Grimsby Town	Newcastle	1.02.77
Perpetuini, David	5. 9	Watford	Hitchin	26.09.79
Saunders, Mark	5.11	Plymouth Argyle	Reading	23.07.71
Smith, Paul	5.11	Brentford	East Ham	18.09.71
Southall, Nicky	5.10	Bolton Wand.	Middlesbrough	28.01.72
Spiller, Daniel	5.10	–	Maidstone	10.01.81
Wallis, Jon	5. 7	–	Gravesend	4.04.86
Forwards				
Agyemang, Patrick	6. 1	Wimbledon	Walthamstow	29.09.80
Awuah, Jones	6. 0	–	Ghana	10.07.83
Henderson, Darius	6. 2	Reading	Sutton	7.09.81
Johnson, Tommy	5.11	Kilmarnock	Newcastle	15.01.71
Roberts, Iwan	6. 3	Norwich City	Bangor	26.06.68
Sidibe, Mamady	6. 4	Swansea City	Mali	18.12.79

IPSWICH TOWN

Ground: Portman Road, Ipswich IP1 2DA.
Telephone: 01473 400500. **Club nickname:** Blues/Town.
First-choice colours: Blue shirts; white shorts; blue stockings.
Main sponsor: Powergen. **Capacity for 2004-05:** 30,000.
Record attendance: 38,010 v Leeds Utd. (F.A. Cup 6) 8 March, 1975.

Name	Height ft. in.	Previous club	Birthplace	Birthdate
Goalkeepers				
Davis, Kelvin	6. 1	Wimbledon	Bedford	29.09.76
Price, Lewis	6. 3	Southampton	Bournemouth	19.07.84
Defenders				
Barron, Scott	5. 9	–	Preston	2.09.85
Collins, Aidan	6. 1	–	Chelmsford	18.10.86
De Vos, Jason	6. 4	Wigan Athletic	Ontario	2.01.74
Diallo, Drissa		Burnley		
Nash, Gerard	6. 1	–	Dublin	11.07.86
Richards, Matthew	5. 8	–	Harlow	26.12.84
Santos, Georges	6. 3	Grimsby Town	Marseilles	15.08.70
Wilnis, Fabian	5.10	De Graafschap	Surinam	23.08.70
Midfielders				
Abidallah, Nabil	5. 7	Ajax	Amsterdam	5.08.82

449

Name		Previous club	Birthplace	Birthdate
Horlock, Kevin	6. 0	West Ham Utd.	Erith	1.11.72
Kuqi, Shefki	6. 2	Sheffield Wed.	Vuqitern, Yug.	10.11.76
Magilton, Jim	6. 0	Sheffield Wed.	Belfast	6.05.69
Miller, Tommy	6. 1	Hartlepool Utd.	Easington	8.01.79
Mitchell, Scott	5.11	–	Ely	2.09.85
Murray, Antonio	5. 8		Cambridge	15.09.84
Reuser, Martijn	5. 9	Vitesse Arnhem	Amsterdam	1.02.75
Westlake, Ian	5.10		Clacton	10.11.83
Forwards				
Bowditch, Dean	5.11	–	Bishop's Stortford	15.06.86
Counago, Pablo	6. 0	Celta Vigo	Pontevedra, Spa.	9.08.79
Naylor, Richard	6. 1	–	Leeds	28.02.77

LEEDS UNITED

Ground: Elland Road, Leeds LS11 0ES.
Telephone: 0113 367 6000. **Club nickname:** Whites.
First-choice colours: White shirts, shorts and stockings.
Main sponsor: Whyte & Mackay. **Capacity for 2004-05:** 40,200.
Record attendance: 57,892 v Sunderland, 15 March 1967.

Name	Height ft. in.	Previous club	Birthplace	Birthdate
Goalkeepers				
Carson, Scott	6. 3	–	Whitehaven	3.09.85
Defenders				
Butler, Paul	6. 0	Wolves	Manchester	2.11.72
Carlisle, Clarke	6. 3	Q.P.R.	Preston	14.10.79
Duberry, Michael	6. 1	Chelsea	Enfield	14.10.75
Kelly, Gary	5. 8	Home Farm	Drogheda	9.07.74
Kilgallon, Matthew	6. 1	–	York	8.01.84
Radebe, Lucas	6. 1	Kaizer Chiefs	Johannesburg	12.04.69
Richardson, Frazer	5.10		Rotherham	29.10.82
Midfielders				
Bakke, Eirik	6. 1	Sogndal	Sogndal, Nor.	13.09.77
Johnson, Seth	5.10	Derby Co.	Birmingham	12.03.79
Keegan, Paul	5.11	–	Dublin	5.07.84
Lennon, Aaron	5. 5	–	Leeds	16.04.87
Pugh, Danny	6. 0	Manchester Utd.	Manchester	18.10.82
Spring, Matthew	5.11	Luton Town	Harlow	17.11.79
Woods, Martin	5. 9	–	Bellshill	1.01.86
Wright, Jermaine	5. 9	Ipswich Town	Greenwich	21.10.75
Forwards				
Cadamarteri, Danny	5. 9	Bradford	Bradford	12.10.79
Joachim, Julian	5. 6	Coventry City	Boston	20.09.74
Johnson, Simon	5. 9	–	West Bromwich	9.03.83
Ricketts, Michael	6. 2	Middlesbrough	Birmingham	4.12.78
Winter, Jamie	5.10	–	Dundee	4.08.85

LEICESTER CITY

Ground: Walkers Stadium, Filbert Way, Leicester, LE2 7FL.
Telephone: 08700 406000. **Club nickname:** Foxes.
First choice colours: Royal blue shirts; white shorts; royal blue stockings.
Main sponsor: Alliance and Leicester. **Capacity for 2004-05:** 32,500.
Record attendance: (Filbert Street) 47,298 v. Tottenham (F.A. Cup 5) 18 February 1928.
(Walkers Stadium) 32,148 v Newcastle Utd. (Premier League) 26 December, 2003.

Name	Height ft. in.	Previous club	Birthplace	Birthdate
Goalkeepers				
Walker, Ian	6. 1	Tottenham	Watford	31.10.71

Defenders

Canero, Peter	5. 9	Kilmarnock	Glasgow	18.01.81
Dabizas, Nikos	6. 2	Newcaste Utd.	Amyndaeo, Gre.	3.08.73
Elliott, Matt	6. 3	Oxford Utd.	Roehampton	1.11.68
Heath, Matt	5.11	–	Leicester	1.11.81

Midfielders

Gillespie, Keith	5.10	Blackburn Rov.	Bangor, NI	18.02.75
Nalis, Lilian	6. 1	Chievo	Nogent, Fra.	29.09.71
Petrescu, Tomi	5.10	–	Jyvaskyia, Fin.	24.07.86
Stewart, Jordan	6. 0	–	Birmingham	3.03.82
Tiatto, Danny	5. 8	Manchester City	Melbourne, Aus.	22.05.73
Wilcox, Jason	6. 0	Leeds Utd.	Bolton	15.07.71
Williams, Gareth	5.11	Nott'm Forest	Glasgow	16.12.81

Forwards

Benjamin, Trevor	6. 2	Cambridge Utd.	Kettering	8.02.79
Dublin, Dion	6. 2	Aston Villa	Leicester	22.04.69
Morris, Lee	5.10	Derby Co.	Blackpool	30.04.80
O'Grady, Chris	6. 0	–	Nottingham	25.01.86
Scowcroft, Jamie	6. 1	Ipswich Town	Bury St Edmunds	15.11.75
Wright, Tommy	5.11	–	Leicester	28.09.84

MILLWALL

Ground: The Den, Zampa Road, London SE16 3LN.
Telephone: 0207 232 1222. **Club nickname:** Lions.
First-choice colours: Blue shirts; blue shorts; blue stockings.
Main sponsor: 24 Seven. **Capacity for 2004-05:** 19,734.
Record attendance: (The Den) 48,672 v Derby Co. (F.A. Cup 5) 20 February, 1937.
   (New Den) 20,093 v Arsenal (F.A. Cup 3) 10 January, 1994.

Name	Height ft. in.	Previous club	Birthplace	Birthdate
Goalkeepers				
Marshall, Andy	6. 2	Ipswich Town	Bury St Edmunds	14.04.75
Defenders				
Clancy, Tim	5.11	–	Trim	8.06.84
Craig, Tony	6. 0	–	Greenwich	20.04.85
Dolan, Joe	6. 3	Chelsea	Harrow	27.05.80
Dunne, Alan	5.10	–	Dublin	23.08.82
Lawrence, Matt	6. 1	Wycombe Wand.	Northampton	19.06.74
Muscat, Kevin	5.11	Rangers	Crawley	7.08.73
Robinson, Paul	6. 1	–	Barnet	7.01.82
Phillips, Mark	6. 2	–	Lambeth	27.01.82
Ward, Darren	6. 3	Watford	Harrow	13.09.78
Midfielders				
Cahill, Tim	5.10	Sydney Utd.	Sydney	6.12.79
Cogan, Barry	5. 9	–	Sligo	4.11.84
Elliott, Marvin	6. 0	–	Wandsworth	15.09.84
Hearn, Charley	5.11	–	Ashford	5.11.83
Livermore, David	6. 0	Arsenal	Edmonton	20.05.80
Morris, Jody	5. 5	Leeds Utd.	Hammersmith	22.12.78
Roberts, Andy	5.10	Wimbledon	Dartford	20.03.74
Weston, Curtis	5.10	–	Greenwich	24.01.87
Wise, Dennis	5. 6	Leicester City	Kensington	16.12.66
Forwards				
Braniff, Kevin	5.11	–	Belfast	4.03.83
Ifill, Paul	6. 0	–	Brighton	20.10.79
Dichio, Danny	6. 3	W.B.A.	Hammersmith	19.10.74
Harris, Neil	5.11	Cambridge City	Orsett	12.07.77
May, Ben	6. 1	–	Gravesend	10.03.84
McCammon, Mark	6. 3	Brentford	Barnet	7.08.78
Peeters, Bob	6. 5	Vitesse Arnhem	Lier, Bel.	10.01.74

| Sutton, John | 6.0 | Raith Rov. | Norwich | 26.12.83 |
| Sweeney, Peter | 6.0 | – | Glasgow | 25.09.84 |

NOTTINGHAM FOREST

Ground: City Ground, Pavilion Road, Nottingham NG2 5FJ.
Telephone: 0115 982 4444. **Club nickname:** Forest.
First-choice colours: Red shirts; white shorts; red stockings.
Main sponsor: Capital One. **Capacity for 2004-05:** 30,602.
Record attendance: 49,945 v Manchester Utd. (Div. 1) 28 October, 1967.

Name	Height ft. in.	Previous club	Birthplace	Birthdate
Goalkeepers				
Gerrard, Paul	6. 2	Everton	Heywood	22.01.73
Roche, Barry	6. 4	–	Dublin	6.04.82
Ward, Darren	5.11	Notts Co.	Worksop	11.05.74
Defenders				
Biggins, James	5. 9	–	Nottingham	6.06.85
Commons, Kris	5. 6	Stoke City	Mansfield	30.08.83
Dawson, Michael	6. 2	–	Northallerton	18.11.83
Doig, Chris	6. 2	–	Dumfries	13.02.81
Impey, Andrew	5. 8	Leicester City	Hammersmith	30.09.71
Louis-Jean, Matthieu	5. 9	Le Havre	Mont-St-Aignan, Fra.	22.02.76
Morgan, Wes	5.11	–	Nottingham	21.01.84
Robertson, Gregor	5.11	–	Edinburgh	19.01.84
Tarka, David	6. 0	Perth Glory	Perth, Aus.	11.02.83
Perch, James	6. 0	–	Mansfield	28.09.85
Rogers, Alan	5.10	Leicester City	Liverpool	3.01.77
Midfielders				
Beaumont, James	5. 7	Newcastle Utd.	Stockton	11.12.84
Bopp, Eugen	6. 0	–	Kiev	5.09.83
Cash, Brian	5.10	–	Dublin	24.11.82
Evans, Paul	5. 8	Bradford City	Oswestry	1.09.74
Gardner, Ross	5. 8	Newcastle Utd.	South Shields	15.02.85
Reid, Andy	5. 7	–	Dublin	29.07.82
Sonner, Danny	5.11	Walsall	Wigan	9.01.72
Thompson, John	6. 1	–	Dublin	12.10.82
Forwards				
James, Kevin	5. 9	Gillingham	Southwark	3.01.80
Jess, Eoin	5.10	Bradford City	Aberdeen	13.12.70
Johnson, David	5. 6	Ipswich Town	Kingston, Jam.	15.08.76
King, Marlon	6. 1	Gillingham	Dulwich	26.04.80
Taylor, Gareth	6. 2	Burnley	Weston-S-Mare	25.02.73
Westcarr, Craig	5.11	–	Nottingham	29.01.85

PLYMOUTH ARGYLE

Ground: Home Park, Plymouth PL2 3DQ.
Telephone: 01752 562561. **Club nickname:** Pilgrims.
First-choice colours: Green shirts; white shorts; green stockings.
Main sponsor: Ginsters. **Capacity for 2004-05:** 20,000.
Record attendance: 42,684 v Aston Villa (Div. 2) 10 October, 1936.

Name	Height ft. in.	Previous club	Birthplace	Birthdate
Goalkeepers				
Larrieu, Romain	6. 2	Valence	Mont de Marsan, Fra.	31.08.76
McCormick, Luke	6. 0	–	Coventry	15.08.83
Defenders				
Adams, Steve	6. 0	–	Plymouth	25.09.80
Aljofree, Hasney	6. 0	Dundee Utd.	Manchester	11.07.78

Name	ft. in.	Previous club	Birthplace	Birthdate
Byrne, Shaun	5. 9	West Ham Utd.	Taplow	21.01.81
Capaldi, Tony	6. 0	Birmingham City	Porsgrunn, Nor.	12.08.81
Coughlan, Graham	6. 2	Livingston	Dublin	18.11.74
Doumbe, Mathias	6. 0	Hibernian	Drancy, Fra.	28.20.79
Gilbert, Peter	5. 9	Birmingham City	Newcastle	31.07.83
Worrell, David	5.11	Dundee Utd.	Dublin	12.01.78
Wotton, Paul	5.11	–	Plymouth	17.08.77
Yetton, Stuart	5. 8	–	Plymouth	27.07.85
Midfielders				
Friio, David	5.10	Valence	Thionville, Fra.	17.02.73
Hodges, Lee	6. 0	Reading	Epping	4.09.73
Lasley, Keith	5. 9	Motherwell	Glasgow	21.09.79
Makel, Lee	5.10	Livingston	Sunderland	11.01.73
Norris, David	5. 7	Bolton Wand.	Stamford	22.02.81
Forwards				
Crawford, Stevie	5.10	Dunfermline	Dunfermline	9.01.74
Evans, Mickey	6. 0	Bristol Rov.	Plymouth	1.01.73
Keith, Marino	6. 0	Livingston	Peterhead	16.12.74
Lowndes, Nathan	5.10	Livingston	Salford	2.06.77
Milne, Steven	5. 7	Dundee	Dundee	5.05.80
Stonebridge, Ian	6. 0	Tottenham	London	30.08.81
Sturrock, Blair	5.11	Dundee Utd.	Dundee	25.08.81

PRESTON NORTH END

Ground: Deepdale, Sir Tom Finney Way, Preston PR1 6RU.
Telephone: 08704 421964. **Club nickname:** Lilywhites.
First-choice colours: White and red shirts; blue shorts; white stockings.
Main sponsor: NewReg. **Capacity for 2004-05:** 21,831.
Record attendance: 42,684 v Arsenal (Div. 1) 23 April, 1938.

	Height			
Name	**ft. in.**	**Previous club**	**Birthplace**	**Birthdate**
Goalkeepers				
Gould, Jonathan	6. 1	Celtic	Paddington	18.07.68
Lonergan, Andy	6. 4	–	Preston	19.10.83
Defenders				
Alexander, Graham	5.11	Luton Town	Coventry	10.10.71
Broomes, Marlon	6. 0	Sheffield Wed.	Birmingham	28.11.77
Davidson, Callum	5.10	Leicester City	Stirling	25.06.76
Davis, Claude	5.11	Portmore Utd.	Jamaica	6.03.79
Lucketti, Chris	6. 0	Huddersfield Town	Littleborough	28.09.71
Midfielders				
Etuhu, Dickson	6. 2	Manchester City	Kano, Nig.	8.06.82
Lewis, Eddie	5.10	Fulham	Cerritos, USA	17.05.74
McCormack, Alan	5. 8	–	Dublin	10.01.84
McKenna, Paul	5. 8	–	Chorley	20.10.77
Mears, Tyrone	5.11	Manchester City	Stockport	18.02.83
O'Neil, Brian	6. 1	Derby Co.	Paisley	6.09.72
Skora, Eric	5.10	–	France	20.08.81
Forwards				
Cresswell, Richard	6. 0	Leicester City	Bridlington	20.09.77
Fuller, Ricardo	6. 3	Tivoli Gardens	Kingston, Jam.	31.10.79
Healy, David	5. 8	Manchester Utd.	Downpatrick	5.08.79
Lynch, Simon	6. 0	Celtic	Montreal	19.05.82
O'Neill, Joe	6. 0	–	Blackburn	28.10.82

QUEENS PARK RANGERS

Ground: Loftus Road Stadium, South Africa Road, London W12 7PA.
Telephone: 0208 743 0262. **Club nickname:** Hoops.
First-choice colours: Blue and white shirts; white shorts; blue and white stockings.

Main sponsor: Binatone. **Capacity for 2004-05:** 19,148.
Record attendance: 35,353 v Leeds Utd. (Div. 1) 27 April, 1974.

Name	Height ft. in.	Previous club	Birthplace	Birthdate
Goalkeepers				
Cole, Jake	6. 0	–	Hammersmith	11.09.85
Culkin, Nick	6. 2	Manchester Utd.	York	6.07.78
Day, Chris	6. 3	Watford	Walthamstow	28.07.75
Defenders				
Bignot, Marcus	5.10	Rushden & D'monds	Birmingham	22.08.74
Edghill, Richard	5. 9	Sheffield Utd.	Oldham	23.09.74
Fletcher, John	6. 0	–	Hammersmith	21.12.86
Gnohere, Arthur	6. 0	Burnley	Ivory Coast	20.11.78
Johnson, Ryan	5.10	–	Dartford	15.01.87
Padula, Gino	5. 9	Wigan Athletic	Buenos Aires	11.07.76
Rose, Matthew	5.11	Arsenal	Dartford	24.09.75
Shittu, Danny	6. 3	Charlton Athletic	Lagos	2.09.80
Midfielders				
Ainsworth, Gareth	5. 9	Cardiff City	Blackburn	10.05.73
Bean, Marcus	5.11	–	Hammersmith	2.11.84
Bircham, Marc	5.10	Millwall	Wembley	11.05.78
Cook, Lee	5. 9	Watford	Hammersmith	3.08.82
Daly, Wesley	5. 9	–	Hammersmith	7.03.84
Johnson, Richard	5.10	Stoke City	Newcastle Aus.	27.04.74
McLeod, Kevin	5.11	Everton	Liverpool	12.09.80
Rowlands, Martin	5. 9	Brentford	Hammersmith	8.02.79
Forwards				
Cureton, Jamie	5. 8	Busan Icons	Bristol	28.08.75
Furlong, Paul	6. 0	Birmingham City	Wood Green	27.01.69
Gallen, Kevin	5.11	Barnsley	Hammersmith	21.09.75
Thorpe, Tony	5. 9	Bristol City	Leicester	10.04.74

READING

Ground: Madejski Stadium, Junction 11 M4, Reading RG2 OFL.
Telephone: 0118 968 1100. **Club nickname:** Royals.
First-choice colours: Blue and white shirts; blue shorts; blue stockings.
Main sponsor: Westcoast. **Capacity for 2004-05:** 24,200.
Record attendance: (Elm Park) 33,042 v Brentford (F.A. Cup 5) 17 February, 1927.
(Madejski Stadium) 24,107 v Chelsea (League Cup 4) 3 December, 2003.

Name	Height ft. in.	Previous club	Birthplace	Birthdate
Goalkeepers				
Hahnemann, Marcus	6. 3	Fulham	Seattle	15.06.72
Young, Jamie	5.11	–	Queensland	25.08.85
Defenders				
Brown, Steve	6. 1	Charlton Athletic	Brighton	13.05.72
Rifat, Ahmet	6. 1	–	London	3.01.86
Shorey, Nicky	5. 9	Leyton Orient	Romford	19.02.81
Sonko, Ibrahima	5.10	Brentford	Bignaola, Sen.	22.01.81
Williams, Adrian	6. 2	Wolves	Reading	16.08.71
Midfielders				
Campbell, Darren	5. 7	–	Huntingdon	16.04.86
Harper, James	5.11	Arsenal	Chelmsford	9.11.80
Hughes, Andy	5.11	Notts Co.	Manchester	2.01.78
Ingimarsson, Ivar	6. 0	Wolves	Iceland	20.08.77
Little, Glen	6. 3	Glentoran	Wimbledon	15.10.75
Morgan, Dean	6. 0	Colchester Utd.	Enfield	3.10.83
Murty, Graeme	5.10	York City	Saltburn	13.11.74
Newman, Ricky	5.10	Millwall	Guildford	5.08.70

Sidwell, Steve	5.10	Arsenal	Wandsworth	14.12.82
Forwards				
Brooker, Paul	5. 8	Leicester City	Hammersmith	25.11.76
Forster, Nicky	5. 9	Birmingham City	Caterham	8.09.73
Goater, Shaun	6. 1	Manchester City	Hamilton, Berm.	25.02.70
Kitson, Dave	6. 3	Cambridge Utd.	Hitchin	21.01.80
Owusu, Lloyd	6. 0	Sheffield Wed.	Slough	12.12.76
Savage, Bas	6. 3	Walton & Hersham	London	7.01.82

ROTHERHAM UNITED

Ground: Millmoor, Rotherham S60 1HR.
Telephone: 01709 512434. **Club nickname:** Millers.
First-choice colours: Red and white shirts; white shorts; red and white stockings.
Main sponsor: Earth Finance. **Capacity for 2004-05:** 9,624.
Record attendance: 25,000 v Sheffield Wed. (Div. 2) 26 January, 1952 and v Sheffield Wed. (Div. 2) 13 December, 1952.

Name	Height ft. in.	Previous club	Birthplace	Birthdate
Goalkeepers				
Montgomery, Gary	6. 2	Coventry City	Leamington Spa	8.10.82
Pollitt, Mike	6. 4	Chesterfield	Bolton	29.02.72
Defenders				
Barker, Shaun	6. 2	–	Notingham	19.09.82
Gilchrist, Phil	5.11	W.B.A.	Stockton	25.08.73
Hurst, Paul	5. 4	–	Sheffield	25.09.74
Minto, Scott	5.10	West Ham Utd.	Heswall	6.09.71
Scott, Rob	6. 1	Fulham	Epsom	15.08.73
Stockdale, Robbie	5.11	Middlesbrough	Redcar	30.11.79
Swailes, Chris	6. 2	Bury	Gateshead	19.10.70
Midfielders				
Daws, Nick	5.11	Bury	Salford	15.03.70
Garner, Darren	5. 9	Plymouth Argyle	Plymouth	10.12.71
McIntosh, Martin	6. 3	Hibernian	East Kilbride	19.03.71
Monkhouse, Andy	6. 0	–	Leeds	23.10.80
Sedgwick, Chris	6. 1	–	Sheffield	28.04.80
Vernazza, Paolo	6. 0	Watford	Islington	1.11.79
Forwards				
Barker, Richard	5.11	Macclesfield Town	Sheffield	30.05.75
Butler, Martin	5.11	Reading	Wordsley	15.09.74
Hoskins, Will	5. 9	–		6.05.86
Mullin, John	6. 0	Burnley	Bury	11.08.75
Proctor, Michael	6. 0	Sunderland	Sunderland	3.10.80
Warne, Paul	5. 8	Wigan Athletic	Norwich	8.05.73

SHEFFIELD UNITED

Ground: Bramall Lane, Sheffield, S2 4SU.
Telephone: 0114 221 5757. **Club nickname:** Blades.
First-choice colours: Red and white shirts; red shorts; red stockings.
Main sponsor: HFS. **Capacity for 2004-05:** 31,031.
Record attendance: 68,287 v Leeds Utd. (F.A. Cup 5) 15 February, 1936.

Name	Height ft. in.	Previous club	Birthplace	Birthdate
Goalkeepers				
Barnes, Phil	6. 1	Blackpool	Sheffield	2.03.79
Kenny, Paddy	6. 1	Sheffield Utd.	Halifax	17.05.78
Defenders				
Armstrong, Chris	5. 9	Oldham Athletic	Newcastle	5.08.82
Bromby, Leigh	6. 0	Sheffield Wed.	Dewsbury	2.06.80

Francis, Simon	6. 0	Bradford City	Nottingham	16.02.85
Jagielka, Phil	5.11	–	Manchester	17.08.82
Kozluk, Robert	5. 7	Derby Co.	Sutton-in-Ashfield	5.08.77
Morgan, Chris	6. 1	Barnsley	Barnsley	9.11.77
Wright, Alan	5. 4	Middlesbrough	Ashton under Lyne	28.09.71
Midfielders				
Gray, Andy	6. 0	Bradford City	Harrogate	15.11.77
Harley, Jon	5. 8	Fulham	Maidstone	26.09.79
McCall, Stuart	5. 7	Bradford City	Leeds	10.06.64
Montgomery, Nick	5. 9	–	Leeds	28.10.81
Ndlovu, Peter	5. 8	Birmingham City	Bulawayo	25.02.73
Quinn, Alan	5. 9	Sheffield Wed.	Dublin	13.06.79
Roma, Dominic	5.10	–	Sheffield	29.11.85
Ross, Ian	5.10	–	Sheffield	23.01.86
Sestanovich, Ashley	6. 3	Hampton	London	18.09.81
Tonge, Michael	5.11	–	Manchester	7.04.83
Forwards				
Forte, Jonathan	6. 0	–	Sheffield	25.07.86
Hayles, Barry	5. 9	Fulham	Lambeth	17.05.72
Kabba, Steve	5. 8	Crystal Palace	Lambeth	7.03.81
Lester, Jack	5.10	Nott'm Forest	Sheffield	8.10.75
Liddell, Andy	5. 7	Wigan Athletic	Leeds	28.06.73
Shaw, Paul	5.11	Gillingham	Burnham	4.09.73
Ward, Ashley	6. 1	Bradford City	Manchester	24.11.70

STOKE CITY

Ground: Britannia Stadium, Stanley Matthews Way, Stoke-on-Trent ST4 7EG.
Telephone: 01782 592222. **Club nickname:** Potters.
First-choice colours: Red and white shirts; white shorts; white stockings.
Main sponsor: Britannia Building Society. **Capacity for 2004-05:** 28,218.
Record attendance: (Victoria Ground) 51,380 v Arsenal (Div. 1) 29 March, 1937.
(Britannia Stadium) 27,109 v Liverpool (League Cup 4) 29 November, 2000.

Name	Height ft. in.	Previous club	Birthplace	Birthdate
Goalkeepers				
De Goey, Ed	6. 6	Chelsea	Gouda, Hol.	20.12.66
Foster, Ben	6. 2	–	Leamington Spa	3.04.83
Simonsen, Steve	6. 3	Everton	South Shields	3.04.79
Defenders				
Clarke, Clive	6. 0	–	Dublin	14.01.80
Hall, Marcus	6. 1	Southampton	Coventry	24.03.76
Halls, John	6. 0	Arsenal	Islington	14.02.82
Hill, Clint	6. 0	Oldham Athletic	Liverpool	19.10.78
Owen, Gareth	6. 1	–	Staffs	21.09.82
Russell, Darel	6. 0	Norwich City	Stepney	22.10.80
Taggart, Gerry	6. 2	Leicester City	Belfast	18.10.70
Thomas, Wayne	6. 2	Torquay Utd.	Gloucester	17.05.79
Wilkinson, Andy	5.11	–	Stone	6.08.84
Williams, Paul	6. 0	Southampton	Burton	26.03.71
Midfielders				
Brammer, Dave	5.10	Crewe Alexandra	Bromborough	28.02.75
Eustace, John	5.11	Coventry City	Solihull	3.11.79
Henry, Karl	6. 1	–	Wolves	26.11.82
Neal, Lewis	5.11	–	Leicester	14.07.81
Forwards				
Akinbiyi, Ade	6. 1	Crystal Palace	Hackney	10.10.74
Asaba, Carl	6. 2	Sheffield Utd.	London	28.01.73
Greenacre, Chris	5.11	Mansfield Town	Halifax	23.12.77
Noel-Williams, Gifton	6. 1	Watford	Islington	21.01.80

SUNDERLAND

Ground: Stadium of Light, Sunderland, Tyne and Wear SR5 1SU.
Telephone: 0191 551 5000. **Club Nickname:** Black Cats.
First-choice colours: Red and white shirts; black shorts, black stockings.
Main sponsor: Reg Vardy. **Capacity for 2004-05:** 49,000.
Record attendance: (Roker Park) 75,118 v Derby Co. (F.A. Cup 6) 8 March, 1933.
(Stadium of Light) 48,305 v Manchester Utd. (Premier League) 13 October, 2001.

Name	Height ft. in.	Previous club	Birthplace	Birthdate
Goalkeepers				
Alnwick, Ben	6. 0	–	Gateshead	1.01.87
Ingham, Michael	6. 4	–	Belfast	7.09.80
Myhre, Thomas				
Poom, Mart	6. 4	Derby Co.	Tallinn, Est.	3.02.72
Defenders				
Arca, Julio	5. 9	Argentinos Jnrs.	Quilmes, Arg.	31.01.81
Breen, Gary	6. 1	West Ham Utd.	London	12.12.73
Caldwell, Stephen	6. 3	Newcastle Utd.	Stirling	12.09.80
Clark, Ben	6. 2	–	Shotley Bridge	24.01.83
McCartney, George	5.11	–	Belfast	28.04.81
Williams, Darren	5.10	York City	Middlesbrough	28.04.77
Wright, Stephen	6. 0	Liverpool	Liverpool	8.02.80
Midfielders				
Healy, Colin	5.11	Celtic	Cork	14.03.80
Kingsberry, Chris	5.10	–	Lisburn	10.09.85
Lawrence, Liam	5. 9	Mansfield Town	Retford	14.12.81
Leadbitter, Grant	5.10	–	Chester-le-Street	7.06.86
Medina, Nicolas	5. 9	Argentinos Jnrs.	Buenos Aires	17.02.82
Oster, John	5. 9	Everton	Boston	8.12.78
Piper, Matthew	6. 1	Leicester City	Leicester	29.09.81
Robinson, Carl	5.10	Portsmouth	Llandrindod Wells	13.10.76
Ryan, Richie	5.10	–	Kilkenny	6.01.85
Thornton, Sean	5.10	Tranmere Rov.	Drogheda	18.05.83
Whitehead, Dean	5.11	Oxford Utd.	Abingdon	12.01.82
Whitley, Jeff	5. 8	Manchester City	Zambia	28.01.79
Forwards				
Elliott, Stephen	5.11	Manchester City	Dublin	6.01.84
Kyle, Kevin	6. 3	Ayr Boswell	Stranraer	7.06.81
Teggart, Neil	6. 2	–	Downpatrick	16.09.84
Stewart, Marcus	5.10	Ipswich Town	Bristol	7.11.72

WATFORD

Ground: Vicarage Road Stadium, Vicarage Road, Watford WD18 0ER.
Telephone: 01923 496000. **Club nickname:** Hornets.
First-choice colours: Yellow shirts; black shorts; black stockings.
Main sponsor: Total. **Capacity for 2004-05:** 20,200.
Record attendance: 34,099 v Manchester Utd. (F.A. Cup 4) February, 1969.

Name	Height ft. in.	Previous club	Birthplace	Birthdate
Goalkeepers				
Chamberlain, Alec	6. 2	Sunderland	March	20.06.64
Lee, Richard	5.11	–	Oxford	5.10.82
Defenders				
Cox, Neil	6. 0	Bolton Wand.	Scunthorpe	8.10.71
Dyche, Sean	6. 0	Millwall	Kettering	28.06.71
Gayle, Marcus	6. 1	Rangers	Hammersmith	27.09.70
Herd, Ben	5.11	–	Welwyn	21.06.85

Name	Height ft. in.	Previous club		Birthplace	Birthdate
Mayo, Paul	5.11	Lincoln City		Lincoln	13.10.81
Smith, Jack	5.11	–		Hemel Hempstead	14.10.83
Midfielders					
Ardley, Neal	5.11	Wimbledon		Epsom	1.09.72
Blizzard, Dominic	6. 2	–		High Wycombe	2.09.83
Devlin, Paul	5. 9	Birmingham City		Birmingham	14.04.72
Doyley, Lloyd	5.10	–		Whitechapel	1.12.82
Ferrell, Andy	5.10	Newcastle Utd.		Newcastle	9.01.84
Gunnarsson, Brynjar	6. 1	Nott'm Forest		Reykjavik, Ice.	16.10.75
Hand, Jamie	5.11	–		Uxbridge	7.02.84
Mahon, Gavin	6. 0	Brentford		Birmingham	2.01.77
McNamee, Anthony	5. 6	–		Kensington	13.07.84
Young, Ashley	5.10	–		Stevenage	9.07.85
Forwards					
Bouazza, Hameur	5.11	–		Evry, Fra.	22.02.85
Dyer, Bruce	6. 0	Barnsley		Ilford	13.04.75
Fitzgerald, Scott	5.11	Northwood		Hillingdon	18.11.79
Helguson, Heidar	5.10	Lillestrom		Akureyri, Ice.	22.08.77
Norville, Jason	5.11	–		Trinidad	9.09.83
Webber, Danny	5. 9	Manchester Utd.		Manchester	25.12.81

WEST HAM UNITED

Ground: Boleyn Ground, Green Street, Upton Park, London E13 9AZ.
Telephone: 0208 548 2748. **Club Nickname:** Hammers.
First-choice colours: Claret and sky blue shirts; white shorts; white stockings.
Main sponsor: Jobserve. **Capacity for 2004-05:** 35,054.
Record attendance: 43,322 v Tottenham, Div. 1, October 1970.

Name	Height ft. in.	Previous club	Birthplace	Birthdate
Goalkeepers				
Bywater, Stephen	6. 3	Rochdale	Manchester	7.06.81
Srnicek, Pavel	6. 2	Portsmouth	Ostrava	10.03.68
Walker, James	5.11	Walsall	Sutton-in-Ashfield	9.07.73
Defenders				
Brevett, Rufus	5. 8	Fulham	Derby	24.09.69
Cohen, Chris	5.11	–	London	5.03.87
Dailly, Christian	6. 0	Blackburn Rov.	Dundee	23.10.73
Ferdinand, Anton	6. 0	–	Peckham	18.02.85
Melville, Andy	6. 0	Fulham	Swansea	29.11.68
Repka, Tomas	6. 2	Fiorentina	Slavicin Zlin, Cz.	2.01.74
Midfielders				
Carrick, Michael	6. 0	–	Wallsend	28.07.81
Etherington, Matt	5.10	Tottenham	Truro	14.08.81
Hutchison, Don	6. 1	Sunderland	Gateshead	9.05.71
Lomas, Steve	6. 0	Manchester City	Hanover	18.01.74
McAnuff, Joel	5.11	Wimbledon	Edmonton	9.11.81
Mullins, Hayden	6. 0	Crystal Palace	Reading	27.03.79
Reo-Coker, Nigel	5. 8	Wimbledon	Thornton Heath	14.05.84
Forwards				
Connolly, David	5. 8	Wimbledon	Willesden	6.06.77
Harewood, Marlon	6. 1	Nott'm Forest	Hampstead	25.08.79
Garcia, Richard	5.11	–	Perth, Aus.	9.04.81
Nowland, Adam	5.11	Wimbledon	Preston	6.07.81
Zamora, Bobby	6. 0	Tottenham	Barking	16.01.81

WIGAN ATHLETIC

Ground: JJB Stadium, Robin Park, Wigan WN5 0UZ.
Telephone: 01942 774000. **Club nickname:** Latics.
First-choice colours: Blue shirts; blue shorts; white stockings.

Main sponsor: JJB Sports. **Capacity for 2004-05:** 25,000.
Record attendance: (Springfield Park) 27,500 v Hereford Utd. (F.A. Cup 2)
12 December, 1953. (JJB Stadium) 20,669 v West Ham Utd. (Div. 1) 9 May, 2004.

Name	Height ft. in.	Previous club	Birthplace	Birthdate
Goalkeepers				
Filan, John	5.11	Blackburn Rov.	Sydney	8.02.70
Walsh, Gary	6. 3	Bradford City	Wigan	21.03.68
Defenders				
Baines, Leighton	5. 7	–		11.12.84
Breckin, Ian	5.11	Chesterfield	Rotherham	24.02.75
Eaden, Nicky	5. 9	Birmingham City	Sheffield	12.12.72
Jackson, Matt	6. 0	Norwich City	Leeds	19.10.71
McMillan, Steve	5. 8	Motherwell	Edinburgh	19.01.76
Mitchell, Paul	5. 9	–	Manchester	26.08.81
Wright, David	5.11	Crewe Alexandra	Warrington	1.05.80
Midfielders				
Bullard, Jimmy	5.10	Peterborough Utd.	Newham	23.10.78
Dinning, Tony	5.11	Wolves	Wallsend	4.12.75
Frandsen, Per	6. 1	Bolton Wand.	Copenhagen	6.02.70
Flynn, Michael	5.11	Barry Town	Newport	17.10.80
Jarrett, Jason	6. 0	Bury	Bury	14.09.79
Mahon, Alan	5. 7	Blackburn Rov.	Dublin	4.04.78
Teale, Gary	5.11	Ayr Utd.	Glasgow	21.07.78
Traynor, Greg	5.10	–	Salford	17.10.84
Forwards				
Ellington, Nathan	5.10	Bristol Rov.	Bradford	2.07.81
Graham, David	5.10	Torquay Utd.	Edinburgh	6.10.78
McCulloch, Lee	6. 1	Motherwell	Bellshill	14.05.78
Roberts, Jason	5.11	W.B.A.	Park Royal	25.01.78
Roberts, Neil	5.10	Wrexham	Wrexham	7.04.78
Vieira, Magno	5.10	–	Brazil	13.02.85

WOLVERHAMPTON WANDERERS

Ground: Molineux Stadium, Wolverhampton, WV1 4QR.
Telephone: 01902 655000. **Club nickname:** Wolves.
First choice colours: Gold and black shirts; black and gold shorts; black and gold
stockings.
Sponsors: Doritos **Capacity for 2004-05:** 28,666.
Record attendance: 61,315 v Liverpool (F.A. Cup 5) 11 February 1939.

Name	Height ft. in.	Previous club	Birthplace	Birthdate
Goalkeepers				
Ikeme, Carl	6. 2	–	Sutton Coldfield	8.06.86
Jones, Paul	6. 4	Southampton	Chirk	18.04.67
Murray, Matt	6. 4	–	Solihull	2.05.81
Oakes, Michael	6. 1	Aston Villa	Northwich	30.10.73
Defenders				
Clyde, Mark	6. 1	–	Limavady	27.12.82
Craddock, Jody	6. 2	Sunderland	Redditch	25.07.75
Lescott, Joleon	6. 2	–	Birmingham	16.08.82
Naylor, Lee	5. 8	–	Walsall	19.03.80
Midfielders				
Andrews, Keith	6. 0	–	Dublin	18.09.80
Cameron, Colin	5. 8	Hearts	Kirkcaldy	23.10.72
Clingan, Sammy	5.11	–	Belfast	13.01.84
Cooper, Kevin	5. 8	Wimbledon	Derby	8.02.75
Ince, Paul	5.11	Middlesbrough	Ilford	21.10.67
Kennedy, Mark	5.11	Manchester City	Dublin	15.05.76

Newton, Shaun	5. 8	Charlton Athletic	Camberwell	20.08.75
Forwards				
Camara, Henri	5. 9	Sedan		10.05.77
Clarke, Leon	6. 2	–	Birmingham	10.02.85
Cort, Carl	6. 4	Newcastle Utd.	Southwark	1.11.77
Ganea, Viorel	5. 9	Stuttgart	Fagara, Rom.	10.08.73
Miller, Kenny	5.10	Rangers	Edinburgh	23.12.79
Silas, Jorge Manuel	5.10	Leiria	Lisbon	1.09.76
Sturridge, Dean	5. 8	Leicester City	Birmingham	26.07.73

LEAGUE ONE

AFC BOURNEMOUTH

Ground: Fitness First Stadium, Dean Court, Bournemouth BH7 7AF.
Telephone: 01202 726300. **Club nickname:** Cherries.
First-choice colours: Red and black shirts; black stockings.
Main sponsor: Seward Motor Group. **Capacity for 2004-05:** 9,230.
Record attendance: 28,799 v Manchester Utd. (F.A. Cup 6) 2 March, 1957.

Name	Height ft. in.	Previous club	Birthplace	Birthdate
Goalkeepers				
Moss, Neil	6. 3	Southampton	New Milton	10.05.75
Stewart, Gareth	6. 0	Blackburn Rov.	Preston	3.02.80
Defenders				
Broadhurst, Karl	6. 1	–	Portsmouth	18.03.80
Cummings, Warren	5. 9	Chelsea	Aberdeen	15.10.80
Maher, Shaun	6. 2	Fulham	Dublin	20.06.78
Purches, Steve	5.11	West Ham Utd.	Ilford	14.01.80
Young, Neil	5. 9	Tottenham	Harlow	31.08.73
Midfielders				
Browning, Marcus	6. 0	Gillingham	Bristol	22.04.71
Elliott, Wade	5. 9	Bashley	Southampton	14.12.78
Fletcher, Carl	5.10	–	Camberley	7.04.80
Tindall, Jason	6. 1	Charlton Athletic	Stepney	15.11.77
Stock, Brian	5.11	–	Winchester	24.12.81
Forwards				
Connell, Alan	5.11	–	Enfield	5.02.83
Fletcher, Steve	6. 2	Hartlepool Utd.	Hartlepool	26.06.72
Hayter, James	5. 9	–	Newport, IOW	9.04.79
Holmes, Derek	6. 0	Ross Co.	Lanark	18.10.78
O'Connor, Garreth	5. 7	Bohemians	Dublin	10.11.78

BARNSLEY

Ground: Oakwell, Barnsley S71 1ET.
Telephone: 01226 211211. **Club nickname:** Tykes.
First-choice colours: Red shirts; white shorts; red stockings.
Main Sponsor: Vodka Kick. **Capacity for 2004-05:** 23,186.
Record attendance: 40,255 v Stoke City (F.A. Cup 5) 15 February, 1936.

Name	Height ft. in.	Previous club	Birthplace	Birthdate
Goalkeepers				
Colgan, Nick	6. 1	Hibernian	Drogheda	19.09.73
Flinders, Scott	6. 0	–	–	12.06.86
Defenders				
Austin, Neil	5.10	–	Barnsley	26.04.83
Carbon, Matt	6. 2	Walsall	Nottingham	8.06.75

Hassell, Bobby	5. 9	Mansfield Town	Derby	4.06.80
Laight, Ryan	6. 0	–	Barnsley	16.11.85
Vaughan, Tony	6. 2	Mansfield Town	Manchester	11.10.75
Williams, Robbie	5.10	–	Pontefract	2.10.84
Williams, Tommy	5.11	Birmingham City	Carshalton	8.07.80
Midfielders				
Betsy, Kevin	6. 1	Fulham	Seychelles	20.03.78
Burns, Jacob	5.10	Leeds Utd.	Sydney	21.04.78
Kay, Antony	5.11	–	Barnsley	21.10.82
Lumsdon, Chris	5.11	Sunderland	Newcastle	15.12.79
McPhail, Stephen	5.10	Leeds Utd.	Westminster	9.12.79
Shuker, Chris	5. 5	Manchester City	Liverpool	9.05.82
Tonge, Dale	5.10	–	Doncaster	7.05.85
Wroe, Nicky	5.11	–	Sheffield	28.09.85
Forwards				
Boulding, Michael	5.10	Grimsby Town	Sheffield	8.02.76
Conlon, Barry	6. 2	Darlington	Drogheda	1.10.78
Rankin, Isaiah	5.10	Bradford City	Edmonton	22.05.78
Stallard, Mark	6. 0	Notts. Co	Derby Co.	24.08.74

BLACKPOOL

Ground: Bloomfield Road, Blackpool FY1 6JJ.
Telephone: 0870 443 1953. **Club nickname:** Seasiders.
First-choice colours: Tangerine shirts; white and tangerine shorts; white and tangerine stockings.
Main sponsor: Pricebusters. **Capacity for 2004-05:** 9,491.
Record attendance: 38,098 v Wolves (Div. 1) 17 September, 1955

Name	Height ft. in.	Previous club	Birthplace	Birthdate
Goalkeepers				
Jones, Lee	6. 3	Stockport Co.	Pontypridd	9.08.70
Defenders				
Flynn, Mike	6. 1	Barnsley	Oldham	23.02.69
Grayson, Simon	6. 0	Blackburn Rov.	Ripon	16.12.69
Hilton, Kirk	5. 7	Manchester Utd.	Flixton	2.04.81
Richardson, Leam	5. 7	Bolton Wand.	Leeds	19.11.79
Midfielders				
Bullock, Martin	5. 4	Barnsley	Derby	5.03.75
Burns, Jamie	5. 9	–	Blackpool	6.03.84
Coid, Danny	5.11	–	Liverpool	3.10.81
Edwards, Paul	5.11	Wrexham	Manchester	1.01.80
Evans, Gareth	6. 0	Huddersfield Town	Leeds	15.02.81
McMahon, Stephen	5. 9	–	Southport	31.07.84
Southern, Keith	5.10	Everton	Gateshead	21.04.84
Wellens, Richard	5. 9	Manchester Utd.	Manchester	26.03.80
Forwards				
Blinkhorn, Matthew	6. 0	–	Blackpool	2.03.85
Murphy, John	6. 2	Chester City	Whiston	18.10.76
Parker, Keigan	5. 7	St Johnstone	Livingston	8.06.82
Sheron, Mike	5.10	Barnsley	St Helens	11.01.72
Taylor, Scott	5.10	Stockport Co.	Chertsey	5.05.76

BRADFORD CITY

Ground: Bradford and Bingley Stadium, Valley Parade, Bradford BD8 7DY.
Telephone: 01274 773355. **Club nickname:** Bantams.
First-choice colours: Claret and amber shirts; white shorts; claret stockings.
Main Sponsor: JCT 600. **Capacity for 2004-05:** 25,136.
Record attendance: 39,146 v Burnley (F.A. Cup 4) 11 March, 1911.

Name	Height ft. in.	Previous club	Birthplace	Birthdate
Goalkeepers				
Defenders				
Atherton, Peter	5.11	Sheffield Wed.	Orrell	6.04.70
Bentham, Craig	5. 9	–	Bradford	7.03.85
Bower, Mark	5.10	–	Bradford	23.01.80
Emanuel, Lewis	5. 8	–	Bradford	4.10.83
Gavin, Jason	6. 0	Middlesbrough	Dublin	14.03.80
Jacobs, Wayne	5. 9	Rotherham Utd.	Sheffield	3.02.69
Swift, John	5. 7	–	–	20.09.84
Wetherall, David	6. 4	Leeds Utd.	Sheffield	14.03.71
Midfielders				
Flynn, Liam	5. 9	–	Bradford	9.11.84
Kearney, Tom	5.11	Everton	Liverpool	7.10.81
Penford, Tom	5.10	–	Leeds	5.01.85
Summerbee, Nicky	5.11	Leicester City	Altrincham	26.08.71
Forwards				
Forrest, Danny	5.11	–	Keighley	23.10.84
Sanasy, Kevin	5. 8	–	Leeds	2.11.84
Windass, Dean	5. 9	Sheffield Utd.	Hull	1.04.69

BRENTFORD

Ground: Griffin Park, Braemar Road, Brentford TW8 0NT.
Telephone: 0870 900 9229. **Club nickname:** Bees.
First-choice colours: Red and white shirts; black shorts; red stockings.
Main sponsor: St George. **Capacity for 2004-05:** 12,750.
Record attendance: 39,626 v Preston N.E. (F.A. Cup 6) 5 March, 1938.

Name	Height ft. in.	Previous club	Birthplace	Birthdate
Goalkeepers				
Julian, Alan	6. 0	–	Ashford	11.03.83
Nelson, Stuart	6. 0	Hucknall Town	–	17.09.81
Defenders				
Dobson, Michael	6. 0	–	Isleworth	9.04.81
Fitzgerald, Scott	6. 0	Colchester Utd.	Westminster	13.08.69
Frampton, Andrew	5.11	Crystal Palace	Wimbledon	3.09.79
Myers, Andy	5.10	Colchester Utd.	Hounslow	3.11.73
Somner, Matt	5.11	–	Isleworth	8.12.82
Midfielders				
Hargreaves, Chris	5.11	Northampton Town	Cleethorpes	12.05.72
Hunt, Stephen	5. 8	Crystal Palace	Port Laoise	1.08.81
Hutchinson, Eddie	6. 1	Sutton Utd.	Kingston	23.02.82
Smith, Jay	5.10	–	Hammersmith	29.12.81
Tabb, Jay	5. 6	–	Tooting	21.02.84
Talbot, Stewart	5.11	Rotherham Utd.	Birmingham	14.06.73
Forwards				
Harrold, Matt		Harlow Town		25.07.84
O'Connor, Kevin	5.11	–	Blackburn	24.02.82
Rankin, Isaiah	5.10	Grimsby Town	Edmonton	22.05.78
Rhodes, Alex	6. 0	Newmarket Town	–	23.01.82

BRISTOL CITY

Ground: Ashton Gate, Bristol BS3 2EJ.
Telephone: 0117 963 0630. **Club nickname:** Robins.
First-choice colours: Red shirts; red shorts; red stockings.
Main sponsor: DAS Legal Services. **Capacity for 2004-05:** 21,479.
Record attendance: 43,335 v Preston N.E. (F.A. Cup 5) 16 February 1935.

Name	Height ft. in.	Previous club	Birthplace	Birthdate
Goalkeepers				
Phillips, Steve	6. 1	–	Bath	6.05.78
Stowell, Mike	6. 2	Wolves	Portsmouth	19.04.65
Defenders				
Amankwaah, Kevin	6. 1	–	Harrow	19.05.82
Bell, Michael	5. 8	Wycombe Wand.	Newcastle	15.11.71
Butler, Tony	6. 2	W.B.A.	Stockport	28.09.72
Carey, Louis	5.10	–	Bristol	20.01.77
Coles, Danny	6. 0	–	Bristol	30.10.81
Fortune, Clayton	5.11	–	Forest Gate	10.11.82
Hill, Matthew	5. 8	–	Bristol	26.03.81
Simpson, Sekani	5.11	–	Bristol	11.03.84
Woodman, Craig	5. 9	–	Tiverton	22.12.82
Midfielders				
Brown, Aaron	5.10	–	Bristol	14.03.80
Doherty, Tom	5. 8	–	Bristol	17.03.79
Hawkins, Darren	5.10	–	Bristol	25.04.84
Murray, Scott	5. 8	Reading	Aberdeen	26.05.74
Orr, Bradley	6. 0	Newcastle Utd.	Liverpool	1.11.82
Tinnion, Brian	6. 2	Bradford City	Durham	23.03.68
Wilkshire, Luke	5. 8	Middlesbrough	Wollongong, Aus.	2.10.81
Forwards				
Goodfellow, Marc	5.10	Stoke City	Burton	20.09.81
Heffernan, Paul	5.10	Notts Co.	Dublin	29.12.81
Lita, Leroy	5. 7	–	Congo	28.12.84
Miller, Lee	5.11	Falkirk	Lanark	18.05.83
Roberts, Christian	5.10	Exeter City	Cardiff	22.10.79

CHESTERFIELD

Ground: Recreation Ground, Chesterfield S40 4SX.
Telephone: 01246 209765. **Club nickname:** Spireites.
First-choice colours: Blue shirts; blue shorts; white stockings.
Main Sponsor: Autoworld Motor Group. **Capacity for 2004-05:** 8,502.
Record attendance: 30,698 v Newcastle Utd. (Div. 2) 7 April, 1939.

Name	Height ft. in.	Previous club	Birthplace	Birthdate
Goalkeepers				
Muggleton, Carl	6. 2	Cheltenham Town	Leicester	13.09.68
Richmond, Andy	6. 0	–	Nottingham	9.01.83
Defenders				
Bailey, Alex	5.11	Arsenal	Newham	21.09.83
Blatherwick, Steve	6. 1	Burnley	Nottingham	20.09.73
Dawson, Kevin	6. 0	Nott'm Forest	Northallerton	18.06.81
Nicholson, Shane	5.10	Tranmere Rov.	Newark	3.06.70
Midfielders				
Davies, Gareth	6. 1	–	Chesterfield	4.02.83
Evatt, Ian	6. 3	Derby Co.	Coventry	19.11.81
Hudson, Mark	5.10	Middlesbrough	Bishop Auckland	24.10.80
Innes, Mark	5.10	Oldham Athletic	Bellshill	27.09.78
Niven, Derek	5.10			
O'Hare, Alan	6. 2	Bolton Wand.	Drogheda	31.07.82
Richardson, Lee	5.11	Huddersfield Town	Halifax	12.03.69
Warne, Stephen	5. 9	–	Sutton-in-Ashfield	27.02.84
Forwards				
Allison, Wayne	6. 1	Sheffield Utd.	Huddersfield	16.10.68
Allott, Mark	5.11	Oldham Athletic	Middleton	3.10.77
Burt, Jamie	5.10	Whitby Town	Blyth	29.09.79

| De Bolla, Mark | 5.7 | Charlton Athletic | London | 1.01.83 |
| Folan, Caleb | 6.1 | Leeds Utd. | Leeds | 26.10.82 |

COLCHESTER UNITED

Ground: Layer Road, Colchester CO2 7JJ.
Telephone: 01206 508800. **Club nickname:** U's.
First-choice-colours: Blue and white shirts; white shorts; white stockings.
Main sponsor: Capacity for 2004-05: 6,169.
Record attendance: 19,072 v Reading (F.A. Cup 1) 27 November, 1948.

Name	Height ft. in.	Previous club	Birthplace	Birthdate
Goalkeepers				
Davison, Aidan	6.1	Grimsby Town	Sedgefield	11.05.68
Gerken, Dean	6.0	–	–	4.08.85
Defenders				
Baldwin, Pat	6.0	Chelsea	London	12.11.82
Brown, Wayne	6.0	Watford	Banbury	20.08.77
Chilvers, Liam	6.2	Arsenal	Chelmsford	6.11.81
Halford, Greg	5.11	–	Chelmsford	8.12.84
Keith, Joey	5.7	West Ham Utd.	Plaistow	1.10.78
Stockley, Sam	5.8	Oxford Utd.	Tiverton	5.09.77
White, John	5.10	–	Colchester	26.07.86
Midfielders				
Bowry, Bobby	5.9	Millwall	Croydon	19.05.71
Crouch, Ross	6.0	–	–	26.03.85
Duguid, Karl	5.11	–	Hitchin	21.03.78
Izzet, Kemal	5.8	Charlton Athletic	Whitechapel	29.09.80
Johnson, Gavin	5.11	Dunfermline	Stowmarket	10.10.70
Johnston, Craig	5.10	–	–	4.12.85
Toney, Tristan	5.11	–	–	26.12.85
Watson, Kevin	6.0	Reading	Hackney	3.01.74
Forwards				
Andrews, Wayne	5.10	Oldham Athletic	Paddington	25.11.77
Cade, Jamie	5.8	Middlesbrough	Durham	15.01.84
Fagan, Craig	5.11	Birmingham City	Birmingham	11.12.82

DONCASTER ROVERS

Ground: Belle Vue, Bawtry Road, Doncaster, DN4 5HT.
Telephone: 01302 539441. **Club nickname:** Rovers.
First-choice colours: Red shirts; white shorts; red stockings.
Main sponsor: Streetwise. **Capacity for 2004-05:** 7,454.
Record attendance: 37,149 v Hull City (Div.3N) 2 October, 1948.

Name	Height ft. in.	Previous club	Birthplace	Birthdate
Goalkeepers				
Warrington, Andy	6.3	York City	Sheffield	10.06.76
Defenders				
Albrighton, Mark	5.11	Telford Utd.	Nuneaton	6.03.76
Beech, Chris	5.9	Rotherham Utd.	Congleton	5.11.75
Black, Chris	6.0	Sunderland	Ashington	7.09.82
Fenton, Nick	6.1	Notts Co.	Preston	23.11.79
Foster, Steve	6.1	Bristol Rov.	Mansfield	3.12.74
Marples, Simon	5.11	Stocksbridge Park	Sheffield	30.07.75
Morley, David	6.2	Oxford Utd.	St Helens	25.09.77
Mulligan, Dave	5.8	Barnsley	Bootle	24.03.82
Price, Jamie	5.9	Leeds Utd.	Normanton	27.10.81
Ryan, Tim	5.10	Southport	Stockport	10.12.74

Midfielders

Name	Height ft. in.	Previous club	Birthplace	Birthdate
Doolan, John	6. 1	Barnet	Liverpool	7.05.74
Green, Paul	5.10	Sheffield Wed.	Sheffield	10.04.83
McGrath, John	5.10	Aston Villa	Limerick	27.03.80
McIndoe, Michael	5. 8	Yeovil Town	Edinburgh	2.12.79
Ravenhill, Ricky	5.10	Barnsley	Doncaster	16.01.81
Tierney, Francis	5.10	Witton Albion	Liverpool	10.09.75

Forwards

Name	Height ft. in.	Previous club	Birthplace	Birthdate
Akinfenwa, Adebayo	6. 0	Rushden & D'monds	London	10.05.82
Blundell, Gregg	6. 0	Northwich Victoria	Liverpool	1.01.76
Coppinger, James	5. 7	Exeter City	Middlesbrough	10.01.81
Fortune-West, Leo	6. 3	Cardiff City	Stratford	9.04.71
McSporran, Jermaine	5.10	Wycombe Wand.	Manchester	1.01.77
Rigoglioso, Adriano	5.11	Morecambe	Liverpool	28.05.79

HARTLEPOOL UNITED

Ground: Victoria Park, Clarence Road, Hartlepool TS24 8BZ.
Telephone: 01429 272584. **Club nickname:** Pool.
First-choice colours: Blue and white shirts; blue shorts; white stockings.
Main Sponsor: Dove Energy. **Capacity for 2004-05:** 7,629.
Record attendance: 17,426 v Manchester Utd. (F.A. Cup 3) 5 January, 1957.

Name	Height ft. in.	Previous club	Birthplace	Birthdate
Goalkeepers				
Konstantopoulos, Dimirios	6. 4	Farense	Greece	29.11.78
Provett, Jim	5.11	–	Trimdon	22.12.82
Defenders				
Barron, Michael	5.11	Middlesbrough	Lumley	22.12.74
Brackstone, John	5.11	–	Hartlepool	9.02.85
Craddock, Darren	6. 0	–	Bishop Auckland	23.02.85
Jordan, Andrew	6. 2	Bristol City	Manchester	14.12.79
Nelson, Michael	5. 9	Bury	Gateshead	15.03.82
Westwood, Chris	5.11	Wolves	Dudley	13.02.77
Midfielders				
Appleby, Andrew	5.10			11.10.85
Clarke, Darrell	5.10	Mansfield Town	Mansfield	16.12.77
Istead, Steven	5. 8	–	South Shields	23.04.86
Robson, Matty	5.10	–	Durham	23.01.85
Robertson, Hugh	5. 9	Ross Co.	Aberdeen	19.03.75
Ross, Jack	6. 1	Clyde	–	5.06.76
Strachan, Gavin	5.11	Southend Utd.	Aberdeen	23.12.78
Sweeney, Anthony	6. 0	–	Stockton	5.09.83
Tinkler, Mark	5.11	Southend Utd.	Bishop Auckland	24.10.74
Wilkinson, Jack	5. 8	Scarborough	Bridlington	12.09.85
Forwards				
Boyd, Adam	5. 9	–	Hartlepool	25.05.82
Foley, David	5. 6	–	South Shields	12.07.87
Humphreys, Richie	5.11	Cambridge Utd.	Sheffield	30.11.77
McCann, Ryan	5. 8	Celtic	Bellshill	15.09.82
Porter, Joel	5. 9	West Adelaide	Sydney	25.12.78
Robinson, Paul	5.11	Blackpool	Sunderland	22.11.78
Williams, Eifion	5.11	Torquay Utd.	Bangor	15.11.75

HUDDERSFIELD TOWN

Ground: McAlpine Stadium, Leeds Road, Huddersfield HD1 6PX.
Telephone: 01484 484100. **Club nickname:** Terriers.
First-choice colours: Blue and white shirts; white shorts; black, blue and white stockings.
Main Sponsor: Prime Time Recruitment. **Capacity for 2004-05:** 24,500.

Record attendance: (Leeds Road) 67,037 v Arsenal (F.A. Cup 6) 27 February, 1932; (McAlpine Stadium) 23,678 v Liverpool (F.A. Cup 3) 12 December, 1999.

Name	Height ft. in.	Previous club	Birthplace	Birthdate
Goalkeepers				
Gray, Ian	6. 2	Rotherham Utd.	Manchester	25.02.75
Martin, Lee	5.11	Macclesfield Town	Huddersfield	9.09.68
Senior, Phil	5.11	–	Huddersfield	30.10.82
Defenders				
Booty, Martyn	5. 8	Chesterfield	Kirby Muxloe	30.05.71
Clarke, Nathan	6. 2	–	Halifax	30.11.83
Edwards, Rob	5. 9	Chesterfield	Manchester	23.02.70
Lloyd, Anthony	5. 7	–	Taunton	14.03.84
McCombe, John	6. 2	–	Pontefract	7.05.85
Mirfin, David	6. 2	–	Sheffield	18.04.85
Sodje, Efe	6. 0	Crewe Alexandra	Greenwich	5.10.72
Midfielders				
Ahmed, Adnan	5.10	–	Burnley	7.06.84
Brandon, Chris	5. 7	Chesterfield	Bradford	7.04.76
Carss, Tony	5.10	Oldham Athletic	Alnwick	31.03.76
Fowler, Lee	5. 7	Coventry City	Cardiff	10.06.83
Holdsworth, Andy	5. 9	–	Pontefract	29.01.84
Worthington, Jon	5. 9	–	Dewsbury	16.04.83
Yates, Steve	5.11	Sheffield Utd.	Bristol	29.01.70
Forwards				
Booth, Andy	6. 1	Sheffield Wed.	Huddersfield	6.12.73
Brown, Nat	6. 2	–	Sheffield	15.06.81
Mendes, Junior	5. 8	Mansfield Town	Balham	15.09.76
Schofield, Danny	5.10	Brodsworth	Doncaster	10.04.80

HULL CITY

Ground: Kingston Communications Stadium, The Circle, Walton Street, Anlaby Road, Hull, HU3 6HU.
Telephone: 0870 837 0003. **Club nickname:** Tigers.
First-choice colours: Amber and black shirts; black and amber shorts; amber and black stockings.
Main Sponsor: Bonus Electrical. **Capacity for 2004-05:** 25,407.
Record attendance: (Boothferry Park) 55,019 v Manchester Utd. (F.A. Cup 6) 28 February, 1949. (Kingston Communications Stadium) 23,495 v Huddersfield Town (Div. 3) 24 April, 2004. 25,280 England U-21 v Holland, 17 February, 2004.

Name	Height ft. in.	Previous club	Birthplace	Birthdate
Goalkeepers				
Leite, Sergio	6. 1	Charlton Athletic	Oporto	16.08.79
Myhill, Boaz	6. 3	Aston Villa	Modesto, Calif.	9.11.82
Defenders				
Cort, Leon	6. 3	Southend Utd.	Bermondsey	11.07.79
Dawson, Andy	5. 9	Scunthorpe Utd.	Northallerton	20.10.78
Delaney, Damien	6. 3	Leicester City	Cork	20.07.81
Edge, Roland	5. 9	Hibernian	Gillingham	25.11.78
Elliott, Stuart	5.10	Motherwell	Belfast	23.07.78
Hinds, Richard	6. 2	Tranmere Rov.	Sheffield	22.08.80
Holt, Andy	6. 1	Oldham Athletic	Stockport	21.05.78
Joseph, Marc	6. 0	Peterborough Utd.	Leicester	10.11.76
Thelwell, Alton	5.11	Tottenham	Holloway	5.09.80
Wiseman, Scott	6. 0	–	Hull	–
Midfielders				
Ashbee, Ian	6. 1	Cambridge Utd.	Birmingham	6.09.76
Barmby, Nick	5. 7	Leeds Utd.	Hull	11.02.74

France, Ryan	5.11	Alfreton	Sheffield	13.12.80
Fry, Russell	6. 0	–	Hull	4.12.85
Green, Stuart	5.10	Newcastle Utd.	Whitehaven	15.06.81
Keane, Michael	5. 4	Preston N.E.	Dublin	29.12.82
Lewis, Junior	6. 3	Leicester City	Wembley	9.10.73
Peat, Nathan	5. 9	–	Hull	19.09.82
Price, Jason	6. 2	Tranmere Rov.	Pontypridd	12.04.77
Forwards				
Allsopp, Danny	6. 0	Notts Co.	Melbourne	10.08.78
Burgess, Ben	6. 3	Stockport Co.	Buxton	9.11.81
Donaldson, Clayton	6. 1	–	Bradford	7.02.84
Facey, Delroy	5.11	W.B.A.	Huddersfield	22.04.80
Walters, Jonathan	6. 1	Bolton Wand.	Birkenhead	20.09.83
Wilbraham, Aaron	6. 3	Stockport Co.	Knutsford	21.10.79

LUTON TOWN

Ground: Kenilworth Stadium, Maple Road, Luton LU4 8AW.
Telephone: 01582 411622. **Club nickname:** Hatters.
First-choice colours: White shirts; black shorts; black stockings.
Main Sponsor: Travel Extras. **Capacity for 2004-05:** 9,640.
Record attendance: 30,069 v Blackpool (F.A. Cup 6) 4 March, 1959.

Name	Height ft. in.	Previous club	Birthplace	Birthdate
Goalkeepers				
Beckwith, Rob	6. 2	–	London	12.09.84
Beresford, Marlon	6. 1	Barnsley	Lincoln	2.09.69
Brill, Dean	6. 2	–	Luton	2.12.85
Defenders				
Barnett, Leon	6. 1	–	Luton	30.11.85
Bayliss, David	5.10	Rochdale	Liverpool	8.06.76
Coyne, Chris	6. 3	Dundee	Brisbane	28.12.78
Davies, Curtis	6. 2	–		15.03.85
Davis, Sol	5. 8	Swindon Town	Cheltenham	4.09.79
Deeney, David	5. 9	–	Balawago, Zim.	12.01.87
Foley, Kevin	5. 9	–	Luton	1.11.84
Perrett, Russell	6. 3	Cardiff City	Barton-on-Sea	18.06.73
Underwood, Paul	5.11	Rushden & Diamonds	Wimbledon	16.08.73
Midfielders				
Hillier, Ian	6. 0	Tottenham	Neath	26.12.79
Holmes, Peter	5.10	Sheffield Wed.	Bishop Auckland	18.11.80
Hughes, Paul	6. 0	Southampton	Hammersmith	19.04.76
Keane, Keith	5. 9	–	Luton	20.11.86
Leary, Michael	5.11	–	Ealing	17.04.83
Neilson, Alan	5.11	Grimsby Town	Wegburg, Ger.	26.09.72
Mansell, Lee	5.10	–	Gloucester	23.09.82
Nicholls, Kevin	5.11	Wigan Athletic	Newham	2.01.79
O'Leary, Stephen	5.10	–	London	12.02.85
Robinson, Steve	5. 9	Preston N.E.	Lisburn	10.12.74
Forwards				
Berkovic, Ahmet	5. 7	Leyton Orient	Dubrovnic	23.09.74
Howard, Steve	6. 2	Northampton Town	Durham	10.05.76
Showunmi, Enoch	6. 5	–	London	–

MILTON KEYNES DONS

Ground: National Hockey Stadium, Silbury Boulevard, Milton Keynes MK9 1FA.
Telephone: 01908 607090. **Club nickname:** Dons.
First-choice colours: White, gold and black shirts; white shorts; white socks.
Main sponsor: Marshall. **Capacity for 2004-05:** 8,500.

Record attendance: (Milton Keynes): 8,118 v West Ham Utd. (Div. 1), 25 November, 2003.

Name	Height ft. in.	Previous club	Birthplace	Birthdate
Goalkeepers				
Bevan, Scott	6. 6	Southampton	Southampton	16.09.79
Defenders				
Chorley, Ben	6. 3	Arsenal	Sidcup	9.09.82
Crooks, Leon	5.11	–	–	21.11.85
Edds, Gareth	5.11	Bradford City	Sydney	3.02.81
Kamara, Malvin	6. 0	–	Southwark	17.11.83
Lewington, Dean	5.11	–	London	18.05.84
Palmer, Steve	6. 1	Q.P.R.	Brighton	31.03.68
Small, Wade	5.10	–	–	23.02.84
Williams, Mark	6. 0	Stoke City	Stalybridge	28.09.70
Midfielders				
Harding, Ben	5.10	–	Carshalton	6.09.84
Herve, Laurent	6. 0	Guingamp	France	19.06.76
Tapp, Alex	5. 9	–	Redhill	7.06.82
Forwards				
Hornuss, Julien	5.11	–	–	12.06.86
Morgan, Lionel	5.11	–	Tottenham	17.02.83
Ntimban-Zeh, Harry	5.10	Sporting Espinho	–	26.09.73

OLDHAM ATHLETIC

Ground: Boundary Park, Oldham OL1 2PA.
Telephone: 0870 753 2000. **Club nickname:** Latics.
First-choice colours: Royal blue shirts; Royal blue shorts; white stockings.
Main sponsor: Horners Motor Group. **Capacity for 2004-05:** 13,695.
Record attendance: 47,761 v Sheffield Wed. (F.A. Cup 4) 25 January, 1930.

Name	Height ft. in.	Previous club	Birthplace	Birthdate
Goalkeepers				
Grange, Chris	6. 2	–	Stockton	24.10.84
Pogliacomi, Leslie	6. 5	–	Australia	3.05.76
Defenders				
Arber, Mark	6. 1	Peterborough Utd.	Johannesburg	9.10.79
Beharall, David	6. 2	Newcastle Utd.	Newcastle	8.03.79
Clegg, Michael	5. 8	Manchester Utd.	Ashton under Lyne	3.07.77
Haining, Will	5.11	–	Glasgow	2.10.82
Hall, Danny	6. 2	–	Ashton under Lyne	14.11.83
Holden, Dean	6. 0	Bolton Wand.	Salford	15.09.79
Tierney, Marc	6. 0	–	Prestwich	23.08.85
Midfielders				
Appleby, Matty	5.10	Barnsley	Middlesbrough	16.04.72
Bonner, Mark	5.10	Cardiff City	Ormskirk	7.06.74
Boshell, Danny	5.10	–	Bradford	30.05.81
Griffin, Adam	5. 7	–	Salford	26.08.84
Johnson, Jermaine	5.11	Bolton Wand.	Kingston, Jam.	25.06.80
Forwards				
Eyre, John	6. 0	Hull City	Hull	9.10.74
Eyres, David	5.11	Preston N.E.	Liverpool	26.02.64
Jack, Rodney	5. 7	Rushden & D'mnds.	St Vincent	28.09.72
Killen, Chris	5.11	Manchester City	Wellington, NZ	8.10.81
Low, Josh	6. 1	Cardiff City	Bristol	15.02.79
Vernon, Scott	6. 1	–	Manchester	13.12.83
Wilkinson, Wes	5. 8	Nantwich	–	1.05.84

PETERBOROUGH UNITED

Ground: London Road Stadium, Peterborough PE2 8AL.
Telephone: 01733 563947. **Club nickname:** Posh.
First-choice colours: Blue shirts; white shorts; blue stockings.
Main sponsor: Capacity for 2004-05: 14,039.
Record attendance: 30,096 v Swansea City (F.A. Cup 5) 20 February, 1965.

Name	Height ft. in.	Previous club	Birthplace	Birthdate
Goalkeepers				
McShane, Luke	6. 1	–	Peterborough	6.11.85
Pullen, James	6. 2	Ipswich Town	Chelmsford	18.03.82
Tyler, Mark	5.11	–	Norwich	2.04.77
Defenders				
Burton, Sagi	6. 2	Crewe Alexandra	Birmingham	25.11.77
Coulson, Mark	5. 8	–	Huntingdon	11.02.86
Jelleyman, Gareth	5.10	–	Holywell	14.11.80
Jenkins, Steve	5. 9	Notts Co.	Merthyr Tydfil	16.07.72
Kanu, Christopher	6. 0	Alaves	Nigeria	4.12.79
Legg, Andrew	5. 8	Cardiff City	Neath	28.07.66
Rae, Simon	6. 1	Birmingham City	Coventry	20.09.76
St Ledger, Sean	6. 0	–	Birmingham	28.12.84
Thomas, Bradley	6. 2	–	Forest Gate	29.03.84
Midfielders				
Boucard, Andre	5.10	Reading	Enfield	10.10.84
Day, Jamie	5. 9	–	High Wycombe	7.05.86
Fry, Adam	5. 8	–	Luton	9.02.85
Newton, Adam	5.10	West Ham Utd.	Ascot	4.12.80
Semple, Ryan	5.11	–	Belfast	14.07.85
Woodhouse, Curtis	5. 8	Birmingham City	Beverley	17.08.80
Forwards				
Clarke, Andy	5.10	Wimbledon	Islington	22.07.67
Clarke, Lee	5.11	Yaxley	Peterborough	28.07.83
Constantine, Leon	6. 2	Southend Utd.	Hackney	24.02.78
Farrell, David	5. 9	Wycombe Wand.	Birmingham	11.11.71
Fotiadis, Andrew	5.11	Luton Town	Hitchin	6.09.77
Logan, Richard	6. 0	Boston Utd.	Bury St Edmunds	4.01.82
Platt, Clive	6. 4	Notts Co.	Wolves	27.10.77
Willock, Callum	6. 0	Fulham	London	29.10.81

PORT VALE

Ground: Vale Park, Hamil Road, Burslem, Stoke-on-Trent ST6 1AW.
Telephone: 01782 655800. **Club nickname:** Valiants.
First-choice colours: White and black shirts; black shorts; black stockings.
Main sponsor: Tricell. **Capacity for 2004-05:** 18,982.
Record attendance: 50,000 v Aston Villa (F.A. Cup 5) 20 February, 1960.

Name	Height ft. in.	Previous club	Birthplace	Birthdate
Goalkeepers				
Goodlad, Mark	6. 0	Nott'm Forest	Barnsley	9.09.80
Defenders				
Brown, Ryan	5. 9	–	Stoke	15.03.85
Burns, Liam	5.11	–	Belfast	30.10.78
Collins, Sam	6. 3	Bury	Pontefract	5.06.77
James, Craig	6. 0	Sunderland	Middlesbrough	15.11.82
Pilkington, George	6. 0	Everton	Rugeley	1.11.81
Rowland, Steve	5.10	–	Wrexham	2.11.81
Smith, Dean	6. 1	Sheffield Wed.	West Bromwich	19.03.71
Walsh, Michael	6. 0	Scunthorpe Utd.	Rotherham	5.08.77

Midfielders

Name	Height ft. in.	Previous club	Birthplace	Birthdate
Birchall, Chris	5. 9	–	Stafford	5.05.84
Cummins, Michael	6. 0	Middlesbrough	Dublin	1.06.78
Lipa, Andreas	6. 1	Xanthi	Vienna	26.04.71
McPhee, Stephen	5. 7	Coventry City	Glasgow	5.06.81
Reid, Levi	5. 5	–	Stafford	19.12.83
Smith, Jeff	5.10	Bolton Wand.	Middlesbrough	28.06.80

Forwards

Name	Height ft. in.	Previous club	Birthplace	Birthdate
Armstrong, Ian	5.11	Liverpool	Fazackerley	16.11.81
Brooker, Stephen	5.10	Watford	Newport Pagnell	21.05.81
Eldershaw, Simon	5.10	–	Stoke	3.12.83
Matthews, Lee	6. 2	Bristol City	Middlesbrough	6.01.79

SHEFFIELD WEDNESDAY

Ground: Hillsborough, Sheffield, S6 1SW.
Telephone: 0114 221 2121. **Club nickname:** Owls.
First-choice colours: Blue and white shirts; black shorts; blue stockings.
Main Sponsor: Napoleons Casinos. **Capacity for 2004-05:** 39,814.
Record attendance: 72,841 v Manchester City (F.A. Cup 5) 17 February, 1934.

Name	Height ft. in.	Previous club	Birthplace	Birthdate
Goalkeepers				
Lucas, David	6. 2	Preston N.E.	Preston	23.11.77
Tidman, Ola	6. 2	Stockport Co.	Sweden	11.05.79
Defenders				
Armstrong, Craig	5.11	Huddersfield Town	South Shields	23.05.75
Branston, Guy	6. 0	Rotherham Utd.	Leicester	9.01.79
Carr, Chris	5.11	Newcastle Utd.	–	14.02.84
Collins, Patrick	6. 2	Sunderland	Newcastle	4.02.85
Heckingbottom, Paul	5.11	Bradford City	Barnsley	17.07.77
Lee, Graeme	6. 2	Hartlepool Utd.	Middlesbrough	31.05.78
Wood, Richard	6. 3	–	Yorkshire	5.07.85
Midfielders				
Brunt, Chris	6. 1	Middlesbrough	Northern Ireland	14.12.84
Evans, Richard	5. 9	Birmingham City	Cardiff	19.06.83
Hamshaw, Matthew	5.10	–	Rotherham	1.01.82
Marsden, Chris	5.11	Southampton	Sheffield	3.01.69
McGovern, Jon-Paul	5.10	Livingston	Glasgow	
McMahon, Lewis	5. 9	–	Doncaster	2.05.85
Smith, Paul	6. 0	Hartlepool Utd.	Leeds	22.07.76
Whelan, Glenn	5.11	Manchester City	Dublin	13.01.84
Forwards				
Bullen, Lee	6. 1	Dunfermline Athletic	Edinburgh	29.03.71
MacLean, Steven	6. 0	Rangers	Edinburgh	23.08.82
Ndumbu-Nsungu, Guylain	6. 3	Amiens	Congo	26.12.82
Olsen, Kim	6. 4	Midtjylland	Denmark	11.02.79
Peacock, Lee	6. 0	Bristol City	Paisley	9.10.76
Proudlock, Adam	6. 0	Wolves	Telford	9.05.81
Shaw, Jon	6. 1	–	Sheffield	10.11.83

STOCKPORT COUNTY

Ground: Edgeley Park, Hardcastle Road, Edgeley, Stockport SK3 9DD.
Telephone: 0161 286 8888. **Club nickname:** County.
First-choice colours: Blue shirts; blue shorts; blue stockings.
Main Sponsor: Skandia. **Capacity for 2004-05:** 10,541.
Record attendance: 27,833 v Liverpool (F.A. Cup 5) 11 February, 1950.

Name	Height ft. in.	Previous club	Birthplace	Birthdate
Goalkeepers				
Cutler, Neil	6. 3	Stoke City	Birmingham	3.09.76
Spencer, James	6. 5	–	Stockport	11.04.85
Defenders				
Adams, Danny	5. 8	Macclesfield Town	Manchester	3.01.76
Goodwin, Jim	5. 9	Celtic	Waterford	20.11.81
Griffin, Danny	5.10	Dundee Utd.	Belfast	10.08.77
Hardiker, John	6. 0	Morecambe	Preston	7.07.82
Jones, Robert	5.11	Gateshead	Stockton	3.11.79
Mair, Lee	6. 0	Dundee	Aberdeen	9.12.80
Pemberton, Martin	5.10	Mansfield Town	Bradford	1.02.79
Midfielders				
Bridge-Wilkinson, Marc	5. 6	Port Vale	Nuneaton	16.03.79
Cartwright, Lee	5. 9	Preston N.E.	Rawtenstall	19.09.72
Clare, Rob	5.10	–	Belper	28.02.83
Gibb, Ali	5. 9	Northampton Town	Salisbury	17.02.76
Jackman, Danny	5. 4	Aston Villa	Worcester	3.01.83
Lambert, Rickie	5.10	Macclesfield Town	Liverpool	16.02.82
Lescott, Aaron	5. 8	Sheffield Wed.	Birmingham	2.12.77
McLachlan, Fraser	5.11	–	Manchester	9.11.82
Robertson, Mark	5. 9	Dundee	Sydney	6.04.77
Forwards				
Barlow, Stuart	5.10	Tranmere Rov.	Liverpool	16.07.68
Beckett, Luke	5.11	Chesterfield	Sheffield	25.11.76
Daly, Jon	6. 3	–	Dublin	8.01.83
Ellison, Kevin	5.11	Leicester City	Liverpool	23.02.79
Holt, David	5.11	–	Gorton	18.11.84
Morrison, Owen	5. 8	Sheffield Utd.	Londonderry	8.12.81
Welsh, Andrew	5.10	–	Manchester	24.01.83
Williams, Chris	5. 7	–	Manchester	26.07.85

SWINDON TOWN

Ground: County Ground, County Road, Swindon SN1 2ED.
Telephone: 01793 333700. **Club nickname:** Robins.
First-choice colours: Red shirts; white shorts; red and white stockings.
Main sponsor: Nationwide. **Capacity for 2004-05:** 14,939.
Record attendance: 32,000 v Arsenal (F.A. Cup 3) 15 January, 1972.

Name	Height ft. in.	Previous club	Birthplace	Birthdate
Goalkeepers				
Evans, Rhys	6. 3	Chelsea	Swindon	27.01.82
Defenders				
Bampton, David	5. 8	–	Swindon	5.05.85
Gurney, Andy	5.11	Reading	Bristol	25.01.74
Heywood, Matthew	6. 3	Burnley	Chatham	26.08.79
Miglioranzi, Stefani	6. 0	Portsmouth	Pocos de Caldas, Bra.	20.09.77
Nicholas, Andrew	6. 2	Liverpool	Liverpool	10.10.83
O'Hanlon, Sean	6. 1	Everton	Liverpool	2.01.83
Reeves, Alan	6. 0	Wimbledon	Birkenhead	19.11.67
Viveash, Adrian	6. 2	Reading	Swindon	30.09.69
Midfielders				
Duke, David	5.10	Sunderland	Inverness	7.11.78
Hewlett, Matt	6. 2	Bristol City	Bristol	25.02.76
Howard, Brian	5. 9	Southampton	Winchester	23.01.83
Igoe, Sammy	5. 6	Reading	Staines	30.09.75
Robinson, Steve	5. 9	Birmingham City	Nottingham	17.10.75
Smith, Grant	6. 1	Sheffield Utd.	Irvine	5.05.80

Fallon, Rory	6.2	Barnsley	Gisbourne, N.Z.	20.03.82
Opara, Lloyd	6.1	Cambridge Utd.	Enfield	6.01.84
Parkin, Sam	6.2	Chelsea	Roehampton	14.03.81

TORQUAY UNITED

Ground: Plainmoor, Torquay TQ1 3PS.
Telephone: 01803 328666. **Club nickname:** Gulls.
First-choice colours: Yellow and royal blue shirts; royal blue and yellow shorts; yellow and royal blue stockings.
Main sponsor: Sparkworld. **Capacity for 2004-05:** 6,283.
Record attendance: 21,908 v Huddersfield Town (F.A. Cup 4) 29 January, 1955.

Name	Height ft. in.	Previous club	Birthplace	Birthdate
Goalkeepers				
Dearden, Kevin	5.11	Wrexham	Luton	8.03.70
Van Heusden, Arjan	6. 3	Mansfield Town	Alphen, Hol.	11.12.72
Defenders				
Canoville, Lee	6. 1	Arsenal	Ealing	14.03.81
Hockley, Matthew	5.11	–	Paignton	5.06.82
Taylor, Craig	6. 1	Plymouth Argyle	Plymouth	24.01.74
Woods, Steve	5.11	Chesterfield	Davenham	5.12.76
Midfielders				
Benefield, Jimmy	5.11	–	Bristol	6.05.83
Broad, Joe	5.11	Plymouth Argyle	Bristol	24.08.82
Fowler, Jason	6. 0	Cardiff City	Bristol	20.08.74
Hill, Kevin	5. 8	Torrington	Exeter	6.03.76
McGlinchey, Brian	5.10	Plymouth Argyle	Londonderry	26.10.77
Russell, Alex	5. 9	Cambridge Utd.	Crosby	17.03.73
Wills, Kevin	5. 9	Plymouth Argyle	Torbay	15.10.80
Forwards				
Bedeau, Tony	5.10	–	Hammersmith	24.03.79
Bond, Kain	5. 8	–	Torquay	19.06.85
Gritton, Martin	6. 1	Plymouth Argyle	Glasgow	1.06.78
Kuffour, Jo	5. 6	Arsenal	Edmonton	17.11.81

TRANMERE ROVERS

Ground: Prenton Park, Prenton Road West, Birkenhead CH42 9PY.
Telephone: 0151 609 3333. **Club nickname:** Rovers.
First-choice colours: White and blue shirts; white and blue shorts; white and blue stockings.
Mian Sponsor: Metropolitan Borough of Wirral. **Capacity for 2004-05:** 16,500.
Record attendance: 24,424 v Stoke City (F.A. Cup 4) 5 February, 1972.

Name	Height ft. in.	Previous club	Birthplace	Birthdate
Goalkeepers				
Achterberg, John	6. 1	PSV Eindhoven	Utrecht	8.07.71
Howarth, Russell	6. 1	York City	York	27.03.82
Palethorpe, Philip	6. 2	–	Wallasey	17.09.86
Defenders				
Ashton, Neil	5.11	–	Liverpool	15.01.85
Goodison, Ian	6. 3	Hull City	Kingston, Jam.	21.11.72
Jackson, Michael	6. 0	Preston N.E.	Runcorn	4.12.73
Linwood, Paul	6. 2	–	Birkenhead	24.10.83
Olsen, James	6. 2	Liverpool	Liverpool	23.10.81
Roberts, Gareth	5. 8	Panionios, Gre.	Wrexham	6.02.78
Sharps, Ian	6. 3	–	Warrington	23.10.80
Taylor, Ryan	5. 8	–	Liverpool	19.08.84

Midfielders

Beresford, David	5. 8	Plymouth Argyle	Middleton	11.11.76
Hall, Paul	5. 9	Rushden & D'monds	Manchester	3.07.72
Harrison, Danny	5.11	–	Liverpool	4.11.82
Jennings, Steven	5. 7	–	Liverpool	28.10.84
Jones, Gary	6. 3	Nott'm Forest	Chester	10.05.75
Loran, Tyrone	6. 2	Manchester City	Amsterdam	29.06.81
Navarro, Alan	5.10	Liverpool	Liverpool	31.05.81
Rankine, Mark	5. 9	Sheffield Utd.	Doncaster	30.09.69
Whitmore, Theodore	6. 2	Livingston	Montego Bay	5.08.72

Forwards

Dadi, Eugene	6. 2	Livingston	Abidjan, Iv. Coast	20.08.73
Dagnall, Chris	5. 8			15.04.86
Haworth, Simon	6. 1	Wigan Athletic	Cardiff	30.03.77
Hume, Iain	5. 7	–	Edinburgh	30.10.83
Robinson, Paul	6. 0	Newcastle Utd.	Newcastle	28.05.84
Zola, Calvin	6. 3	Newcastle Utd.	Zaire	31.12.84

WALSALL

Ground: Bescot Stadium, Bescot Crescent, Walsall WS1 4SA.
Telephone: 01922 622791. **Club nickname:** Saddlers.
First-choice colours: Red shirts; red and white shorts; red and white stockings.
Main Sponsor: Banks's. **Capacity for 2004-05:** 11,200.
Record attendance: (Fellows Park) 25,433 v Newcastle Utd. (Div. 2) 29 August, 1961.
(Bescot Stadium) 11,307 v Wolves (Div. 1) 11 January, 2003.

Name	Height ft. in.	Previous club	Birthplace	Birthdate
Goalkeepers				
McKinney, Richard	6. 2	Colchester Utd.	Ballymoney	18.05.79
Paston, Mark	6. 5	Bradford City	New Zealand	13.12.76
Defenders				
Aranalde, Zigor	6. 1	Logrones	Guipuzcoa, Spa.	28.02.73
Bazeley, Darren	5.11	Wolves	Northampton	5.10.72
Bennett, Julian	6. 1	–	Nottingham	17.12.84
Ritchie, Paul	5.11	Manchester City	Kirkaldy	21.08.75
Willetts, Ryan	5. 9	Coventry City	Coventry	3.11.84
Midfielders				
Birch, Gary	5.10	–	Birmingham	8.10.81
Emblen, Neil	6. 1	Norwich City	Bromley	19.06.71
Corica, Steve	5. 8	Hiroshima	Cairns, Aus.	24.03.73
Jameson, Nathan	5.11	–	Middlesbrough	20.03.85
Osborn, Simon	5. 9	Gillingham	Croydon	19.01.72
Standing, Michael	5.10	Bradford City	Shoreham	20.03.81
Taylor, Daryl	5. 2	Aston Villa	Birmingham	14.11.84
Taylor, Kris	5. 9	Manchester Utd.	Stafford	12.01.84
Wrack, Darren	5. 9	Grimsby Town	Cleethorpes	5.05.76
Wright, Mark	5.11	–	Wolves	24.02.83
Forwards				
Atieno, Taiwo	6. 2	–	Brixton	6.08.85
Fryatt, Matt	5.10	–	Nuneaton	5.03.86
Leitao, Jorge	5.11	Farense	Oporto	14.01.74
Merson, Paul	6. 0	Portsmouth	Harlesden	20.03.68
Onuora, Iffy	6. 1	Tranmere Rov.	Glasgow	28.07.67

WREXHAM

Ground: Racecourse Ground, Mold Road, Wrexham LL11 2AH.
Telephone: 01978 262129. **Club nickname:** Robins.
First-choice-colours: Red shirts; white shorts; red stockings.
Main sponsor: Just Go. **Capacity for 2004-05:** 15,500.

Record attendance: 34,445 v Manchester Utd. (F.A. Cup 4) 26 January, 1957.

Name	Height ft. in.	Previous club	Birthplace	Birthdate
Goalkeepers				
Dibble, Andy	6. 2	Stockport Co.	Cwmbran	8.05.65
Ingham, Michael	6. 4	Sunderland	Preston	9.09.80
Whitfield, Paul	6. 0	–	St Asaph	6.05.82
Defenders				
Carey, Brian	6. 3	Leicester City	Cork	31.05.68
Lawrence, Dennis	5.11	Defence Force	Trinidad	18.01.74
Morgan, Craig	6. 0	–	St Asaph	18.06.85
Pejic, Shaun	6. 1	–	Hereford	16.11.82
Roberts, Stephen	6. 2	–	Wrexham	24.02.80
Midfielders				
Barrett, Paul	5. 9	Newcastle Utd.	Newcastle	13.04.78
Bennett, Dean	5.10	Kidderminstre Harr	Wolverhampton	13.12.77
Crowell, Matt	5. 9	Southampton	Bridgend	3.07.84
Edwards, Carlos	6. 0	Defence Force	Port of Spain, Trin.	24.10.78
Jones, Mark	5.11	–	Wrexham	15.08.83
Smith, Alex	5. 8	Chester City	Liverpool	15.02.76
Whitley, Jim	5. 9	Manchester City	Zambia	14.04.75
Forwards				
Llewellyn, Chris	5.11	Norwich City	Swansea	29.08.79
Sam, Hector	5.10	Financial San Juan	Trinidad	25.02.78
Williams, Danny	6. 1	Kidderminster Harr.	Wrexham	12.07.79

LEAGUE TWO

BOSTON UNITED

Ground: York Street, Boston, PE21 6HN.
Telephone: 01205 364406. **Club nickname:** Pilgrims.
First-choice colours: Amber and black shirts; black shorts; black stockings.
Main sponsor: Chestnut Homes. **Capacity for 2004-05:** 7,646.
Record attendance: 10,086 v Corby Town (Friendly) 1955. League: 5,708 v Lincoln City (Div. 3) 26 December, 2003.

Name	Height ft. in.	Previous club	Birthplace	Birthdate
Goalkeepers				
Bastock, Paul	5.11	Kettering Town	Leamington Spa	19.05.70
Croudson, Steve	6. 0	Grimsby Town	Grimsby	24.11.80
Defenders				
Balmer, Stuart	6. 1	Oldham Athletic	Falkirk	20.09.69
Beevers, Lee	5.10	Ipswich Town	Doncaster	4.12.83
Chapman, Ben	5. 7	Grimsby Town	Scunthorpe	2.03.79
Ellender, Paul	5.10	Scarborough	Scunthorpe	21.10.74
Greaves, Mark	6. 1	Hull City	Hull	22.01.75
McCann, Austin	5. 9	Hearts	Clydebank	21.01.80
Sutch, Daryl	6. 0	Southend Utd.	Lowestoft	11.09.71
Midfielders				
Bennett, Tom	5.11	Walsall	Falkirk	12.12.69
Holland, Chris	5. 9	Huddersfield Town	Clitheroe	11.09.75
Melton, Steve	5.11	Hull City	Lincoln	3.10.78
Rusk, Simon	6. 0	Peterborough Utd.	Peterborough	17.12.81
Thomas, Danny	5. 7	Bournemouth	Leamington Spa	1.05.81
Forwards				
Angel, Mark	5.10	Darlington	Newcastle	23.08.75

Name	Height ft. in.	Previous club	Birthplace	Birthdate
Brown, Jermaine	5.11	Arsenal	Lambeth	12.01.83
Douglas, Stuart	5. 9	Rushden & Diamonds	Enfield	9.04.78
Duffield, Peter	5. 6	York City	Middlesbrough	4.02.69
Kirk, Andy	5.10	Hearts	Belfast	29.05.79
Thompson, Lee	5.10	Sheffield Utd.	Sheffield	25.03.82

BRISTOL ROVERS

Ground: Memorial Ground, Filton Avenue, Horfield, Bristol BS7 0BF.
Telephone: 0117 909 6648. **Club nickname:** Pirates.
First-choice colours: Blue and white shirts; white shorts; blue stockings.
Main sponsor: Cowlin Construction. **Capacity for 2004-05:** 11,679.
Record attendance: (Eastville) 38,472 v Preston N.E. (F.A. Cup 4) 30 January, 1960.
   (Memorial Ground) 11,433 v Sunderland (League Cup 3) 31 October, 2000.

Name	Height ft. in.	Previous club	Birthplace	Birthdate
Goalkeepers				
Clarke, Ryan	6. 3	–	Bristol	30.04.82
Miller, Kevin	6. 1	Exeter City	Falmouth	15.03.69
Defenders				
Anderson, Ijah	5. 8	Brentford	Hackney	30.12.75
Anderson, John	6. 2	Hull City	Greenock	2.10.72
Edwards, Christian	6. 2	Nott'm Forest	Caerphilly	23.11.75
Elliott, Steve	6. 1	Blackpool	Derby	29.10.78
Hinton, Craig	5.11	Kidderminster Harr.	Wolverhampton	26.11.77
Parker, Sonny	5.11	Birmingham City	Middlesbrough	28.02.83
Ryan, Robbie	5.10	Millwall	Dublin	16.05.77
Midfielders				
Campbell, Stuart	5.10	Grimsby Town	Corby	9.12.77
Disley, Craig	5. 1	Mansfield Town	Worksop	24.08.81
Gibb, Alistair	5. 9	Stockport Co.	Salisbury	12.02.76
Hodges, Lee	5. 5	Rochdale	Newham	2.03.78
Hunt, James	5. 8	Oxford Utd.	Derby	17.12.76
Savage, David	6. 1	Oxford Utd.	Dublin	30.07.73
Trollope, Paul	6. 0	Northampton Town	Swindon	3.06.72
Williams, Ryan	5. 5	Hull City	Sutton-in-Ashfield	31.08.78
Forwards				
Agogo, Junior	5.10	Barnet	Accra	8.01.79
Forrester, Jamie	5. 6	Hull City	Bradford	1.11.74
Thorpe, Lee	6. 1	Grimsby Town	Wolves	14.12.75

BURY

Ground: Gigg Lane, Bury BL9 9HR.
Telephone: 0161 764 4881. **Club nickname:** Shakers.
First-choice colours: White shirts; royal blue shorts; white and blue stockings.
Main Sponsor: Bury Metro. **Capacity for 2004-05:** 11,669.
Record attendance: 35,000 v Bolton Wand. (F.A. Cup 3) 9 January, 1960.

Name	Height ft. in.	Previous club	Birthplace	Birthdate
Goalkeepers				
Garner, Glyn	6. 2	Llanelli	Pontypool	9.12.76
Defenders				
Barrass, Matthew	5.11	–	Bury	28.02.80
Cartledge, John	6. 1	Birmingham City	Carshalton	27.11.84
Challinor, Dave	6. 1	Stockport Co.	Chester	2.10.75
Kennedy, Thomas	5.11	–	Bury	24.06.85
Swailes, Danny	6. 3	–	Bolton	1.04.79
Unsworth, Lee	5.11	Crewe Alexandra	Eccles	25.02.73
Woodthorpe, Colin	6. 1	Stockport Co.	Liverpool	13.01.69

Midfielders

Name	Height ft. in.	Previous club	Birthplace	Birthdate
Dunfield, Terry	5. 7	Manchester City	Vancouver	20.02.82
Duxbury, Lee	5.10	Oldham Athletic	Keighley	7.10.69
Flitcroft, David	5.11	Macclesfield Town	Bolton	14.01.74
Mattis, Dwayne	5.11	Huddersfield Town	Huddersfield	31.07.81
Whaley, Simon	5.11	–	Bolton	7.06.85

Forwards

Name	Height ft. in.	Previous club	Birthplace	Birthdate
Douglas-Pringle, Daniel	5.10	Manchester City	Manchester	8.12.84
Jones, Graeme	6. 0	Boston Utd.	Gateshead	13.03.70
Newby, Jon	6. 0	Huddersfield Town	Warrington	28.11.78
Nugent, David	5.11	–	Liverpool	2.05.85
Porter, Chris	6. 1	–	Wigan	12.12.83

CAMBRIDGE UNITED

Ground: Abbey Stadium, Newmarket Road, Cambridge CB5 8LN.
Telephone: 01223 566500. **Club nickname:** U's.
First-choice colours: Amber shirts; black shorts; amber stockings.
Main sponsor: Capital Sports. **Capacity for 2004-05:** 9,001 (7,209 for redevelopment).
Record attendance: 14,000 v Chelsea (Friendly) 1 May, 1970.

Name	Height ft. in.	Previous club	Birthplace	Birthdate
Goalkeepers				
Marshall, Shaun	6. 1	–	Fakenham	3.10.78
Ruddy, John	6. 3	–	St Ives, Cambs.	24.10.86
Defenders				
Angus, Stevland	5.11	West Ham Utd.	Essex	16.09.80
Bimson, Stuart	5.11	Lincoln City	Liverpool	29.09.69
Duncan, Andy	5.11	Manchester Utd.	Hexham	20.10.77
Gleeson, Daniel	6. 3	–	Cambridge	17.02.85
Goodhind, Warren	5.11	Barnet	Johannesburg	16.08.77
Nacca, Francesco	5. 6	–	Valencia	9.11.81
Tann, Adam	6. 1	–	Fakenham	12.05.82
Midfielders				
Guttridge, Luke	5. 6	Torquay Utd.	Barnstaple	27.03.82
El Kholti, Abdou	5.10	Yeovil Town	France	17.10.80
Nicholls, Ashley	5.11	Darlington	Ipswich	30.10.81
Tudor, Shane	5. 7	Wolves	Wolves	10.02.82
Walker, Justin	5.11	Exeter City	Nottingham	6.09.75
Forwards				
Chillingworth, Dan	6. 0	–	Cambridge	13.09.81
Easter, Jermaine	5.10	Hartlepool Utd.	Cardiff	15.01.82
Turner, John	6. 2	–	Harrow	12.02.86
Webb, Daniel	6. 1	Hull City	Poole	2.07.83

CHELTENHAM TOWN

Ground: Whaddon Road, Cheltenham GL52 5NA.
Telephone: 01242 573558. **Club nickname:** Town.
First-choice colours: Red white and black shirts; black shorts; black stockings.
Main Sponsor: George Bence + Sons. **Capacity for 2004-05:** 7,407.
Record attendance: 8,326 v Reading (F.A. Cup 1) 17 November, 1956.

Name	Height ft. in.	Previous club	Birthplace	Birthdate
Goalkeepers				
Higgs, Shane	6. 2	Worcester City	Oxford	13.05.77
Defenders				
Brough, John	6. 0	Hereford Utd.	Ilkeston	8.01.73
Duff, Shane	6. 1	–	Wroughton	2.04.82

Gill, Jerry	5. 7	Northampton Town	Clevedon	8.09.70
Victory, Jamie	5. 8	Bournemouth	London	14.11.75
Wilson, Brian	5.10	Stoke City	Manchester	9.05.83
Midfielders				
Bird, David	5. 8	Cinderford Town	Gloucester	26.12.84
Devaney, Martin	5.11	Coventry City	Cheltenham	1.06.80
Finnigan, John	5. 8	Lincoln City	Wakefield	20.03.76
Fyfe, Graham	5. 6	Raith Rov.	Dundee	7.12.82
Melligan, John	5. 9	Wolves	Dublin	11.02.82
McCann, Grant	5.10	West Ham Utd.	Belfast	14.04.80
Forwards				
Guinan, Steve	6. 1	Hereford Utd.	Birmingham	24.12.75
Murphy, Chris	5. 6	Telford Utd.	Leamington Spa	8.03.83
Odejayi, Kayode	6. 2	Bristol City	Nigeria	21.02.82
Spencer, Damian	6. 1	Bristol City	Ascot	19.09.81

CHESTER CITY

Ground: Deva Stadium, Bumpers Lane, Chester CH1 4LT.
Telephone: 01244 371376. **Club nickname:** Blues.
First-choice colours: Blue and white shirts; blue shorts; blue stockings.
Main sponsor: Truetone. **Capacity for 2004-05:** 6,012.
Record attendance: (Sealand Road): 20,500 v Chelsea (F.A. Cup 3) 16 January 1952.
(Deva Stadium): 5,987 v Scarborough (Conference) 17 April 2004.

Name	Height ft. in.	Previous club	Birthplace	Birthdate
Goalkeepers				
Brown, Wayne	6. 1	Weston-S-Mare	Southampton	14.01.77
MacKenzie, Chris	6. 0	Telford Utd.	Birmingham	14.05.72
Defenders				
Bolland, Phil	6. 0	Oxford Utd.	Liverpool	26.08.76
Collins, Danny	5.11	Buckley Town	Chester	6.08.80
Hessey, Shaun	5.10	Blackpool	Whiston	19.09.78
Ruffer, Carl	5.11	Runcorn	Chester	20.12.74
McIntyre, Kevin	5.10	Doncaster Rov.	Liverpool	23.12.77
Heard, Jamie	5.11	Hull City	Sheffield	11.08.83
Midfielders				
Carden, Paul	5. 9	Doncaster Rov.	Liverpool	29.03.79
Davies, Ben	5.10	Kidderminster Harr.	Walsall	27.05.81
Harris, Andy	5.10	Leyton Orient	Springs, SA,	26.02.77
Forwards				
Branch, Michael	5.10	Bradford City	Liverpool	18.10.78
Clare, Daryl	5. 9	Boston Utd.	Jersey	1.08.78
Rapley, Kevin	5. 9	Colchester Utd.	Reading	21.09.77
Stamp, Darryn	6. 1	Northampton Town	Beverley	21.09.78

DARLINGTON

Ground: The Arena, Hurworth Moor, Neasham Road, Darlington, DL2 1GR.
Telephone: 01325 387000. **Club nickname:** Quakers.
First-choice colours: Black and white shirts; black shorts; black stockings.
Main sponsor: Darlington Building Society. **Capacity for 2004-05:** 25,000.
Record attendance: (Feethams) 21,023 v Bolton Wand. (League Cup 3) 14 November, 1960. (The Arena), 11,600 v Kidderminstre Harr. (Div. 3) 16, August 2003.

Name	Height ft. in.	Previous club	Birthplace	Birthdate
Goalkeepers				
Price, Michael	6. 3	Boston Utd.	Ashington	3.04.83
Russell, Sam	6. 0	Scunthorpe Utd.	–	4.10.82
Defenders				
Hutchinson, Jon	6. 2	Birmingham City	Middlesbrough	2.04.82

Name		Previous club	Birthplace	Birthdate
Liddle, Craig	5.11	Middlesbrough	Chester-le-Street	21.10.71
McGurk, David	5.11		Middlesbrough	30.09.82
Valentine, Ryan	5.10	Everton	Wrexham	19.08.82
Wainwright, Neil	6. 0	Sunderland	Warrington	4.11.77
Midfielders				
Clark, Ian	5.11	Hartlepool Utd.	Stockton	23.10.74
Close, Brian	5.10	Middlesbrough	Belfast	27.01.82
Keltie, Clark	6. 1	–	Newcastle	31.08.83
Maddison, Neil	5.10	Middlesbrough	Darlington	2.10.69
Thomas, Stephen	5.10	Wrexham	Hartlepool	23.06.79
Forwards				
Clarke, Matthew	6. 3	Halifax Town	Leeds	18.12.80
Convery, Mark	5. 6	Sunderland	Newcastle	29.05.81
Russell, Craig	5.10	Carlisle Utd.	Jarrow	4.02.74

GRIMSBY TOWN

Ground: Blundell Park, Cleethorpes, DN35 7PY.
Telephone: 01472 605050. **Club nickname:** Mariners.
First-choice colours: Black and white shirts; black shorts; red stockings.
Main sponsor: Youngs. **Capacity for 2004-05:** 10,033.
Record attendance: 31,651 v Wolves (F.A. Cup 5) 20 February, 1937.

Name	Height ft. in.	Previous club	Birthplace	Birthdate
Goalkeepers				
Defenders				
McDermott, John	5. 7	–	Middlesbrough	3.02.69
Ramsden, Simon	6. 0	Sunderland	Bishop Auckland	17.12.81
Wheeler, Kirk	6. 1	–	Grimsby	13.06.84
Whittle, Justin	6. 1	Hull City	Derby	18.03.71
Young, Greg	6. 2	–	Doncaster	25.04.83
Midfielders				
Coldicott, Stacy	5. 8	W.B.A	Redditch	29.04.74
Crane, Tony	6. 4	Sheffield Wed.	Liverpool	8.09.82
Crowe, Jason	5. 9	Portsmouth	Sidcup	30.09.78
Fleming, Terry	5. 9	Cambridge Utd.	Marston Green	5.01.73
Hildred, Ashley	5. 5	–	Grimsby	9.09.83
Hockless, Graham	5.10	–	Hull	20.10.82
Parkinson, Andy	5. 8	Sheffield Utd.	Liverpool	27.05.79
Forwards				
Carchedi, Giovanni	5. 6	–	Lincoln	10.11.83
Mansaram, Darren	6. 2	–	Doncaster	25.06.84
Nimmo, Liam	6. 0	–	Grimsby	28.12.84

KIDDERMINSTER HARRIERS

Ground: Aggborough Stadium, Hoo Road, Kidderminster DY10 1NB.
Telephone: 01562 823931. **Club nickname:** Harriers.
First-choice colours: Red shirts; white shorts; red stockings.
Main sponsor: Hire-It. **Capacity for 2004-05:** 6,444.
Record attendance: 9,155 v Hereford Utd. (F.A. Cup 1) 27 November, 1948.

Name	Height ft. in.	Previous club	Birthplace	Birthdate
Goalkeepers				
Danby, John	6. 0	–	Stoke	20.09.83
Defenders				
Burton, Steve	6. 1	Hull City	Hull	10.10.82
Hazell, Reuben	5.11	Torquay Utd.	Birmingham	24.04.79
Hatswell, Wayne	6. 0	Chester City	Swindon	8.02.75
Sall, Abdou	6. 4	Toulouse	Senegal	1.11.80

Midfielders

Name	Height ft. in.	Previous club	Birthplace	Birthdate
Bennett, Dean	5.10	Bromsgrove	Wolverhampton	13.12.77
Keates, Dean	5. 6	Hull City	Walsall	30.06.78
Jenkins, Lee	5. 9	Swansea City	Pontypool	28.06.79
Murray, Adam,	5. 9	Notts Co.	Birmingham	30.09.81
Rickards, Scott	5.11	Tamworth	Sutton Coldfield	3.11.81

Forwards

Name	Height ft. in.	Previous club	Birthplace	Birthdate
Christiansen, Jesper	6. 3	Odense	Denmark	18.06.80

LEYTON ORIENT

Ground: Matchroom Stadium, Brisbane Road, London E10 5NE.
Telephone: 0208 926 1111. **Club nickname:** O's.
First-choice colours: Red shirts; red shorts; red stockings.
Main Sponsor: Matchroom Sport. **Capacity for 2004-05:** 5,000 (for development).
Record attendance: 34,345 v West Ham Utd. (F.A. Cup 4) 25 January 1964.

Name	Height ft. in.	Previous club	Birthplace	Birthdate
Goalkeepers				
Harrison, Lee	6. 2	Peterborough Utd.	Billericay	12.09.71
Morris, Glenn	6. 0	–	Woolwich	20.12.83
Defenders				
Barnard, Donny	6. 0	–	Forest Gate	1.07.84
Jones, Billy	6. 0	–	Gillingham	26.06.83
Lockwood, Matthew	5. 9	Bristol Rov.	Rochford	17.10.76
Mackie, John	6. 1	Reading	Enfield	5.07.76
Miller, Justin	6. 0	Ipswich Town	Johannesburg	16.12.80
Newey, Tom	5.10	Leeds Utd.	Sheffield	31.10.82
Peters, Mark	6. 1	Rushden & Diamonds	St Asaph	6.07.72
White, Alan	6. 1	Colchester Utd.	Darlington	22.03.76
Zakuani, Gabriel	6. 1	–	Zaire	31.05.86
Midfielders				
Carlisle, Wayne	6. 0	Bristol Rov.	Lisburn	9.09.79
Duncan, Derek	5. 8	–	–	23.04.87
Hunt, David	5.11	Crystal Palace	Dulwich	10.09.82
Saah, Brian	6. 1	–	Rush Green	16.12.86
Scott, Andy	6. 1	Oxford Utd.	Epsom	2.08.72
Forwards				
Alexander, Gary	6. 0	Hull City	Peckham	15.08.79
Ibehre, Jabo	6. 2	–	Islington	28.01.83
Purser, Wayne	6. 0	Barnet	Basildon	13.04.80
Steele, Lee	5. 8	Oxford Utd.	Liverpool	7.12.73

LINCOLN CITY

Ground: Sincil Bank, Lincoln LN5 8LD.
Telephone: 01522 880011. **Club nickname:** Imps.
First-choice colours: Red and white shirts; black shorts; red and white stockings.
Main sponsor: Siemens. **Capacity for 2004-05:** 10,239.
Record attendance: 23,196 v Derby Co. (League Cup 4) 15 November, 1967.

Name	Height ft. in.	Previous club	Birthplace	Birthdate
Goalkeepers				
Marriott, Alan	6. 0	Tottenham	Bedford	3.09.78
Defenders				
Bloomer, Matthew	6. 1	Hull City	Cleethorpes	30.11.78
Folkes, Peter	6. 0	Bradford City	Birmingham	16.11.84
Futcher, Ben	6. 7	Stalybridge Celtic	Bradford	20.02.81
McCombe, Jamie	6. 5	Scunthorpe Utd.	Scunthorpe	1.01.83
Morgan, Paul	5.11	Preston N.E.	Belfast	23.10.78

Name		Previous club	Birthplace	Birthdate
Sandwith, Kevin	5.11	Halifax Town	Workington	30.04.78
Weaver, Simon	5.11	Nuneaton	Doncaster.	20.12.77
West, Dean	5.10	Burnley	Morley	5.12.72
Midfielders				
Butcher, Richard	6. 0	Kettering	Northampton	22.01.81
Cornelly, Chris	5.10	Ashton Utd.	Huddersfield	7.07.76
Gain, Peter	6. 1	Tottenham	Hammersmith	2.11.76
Forwards				
Fletcher, Gary	6. 0	Leyton Orient	Widnes	4.06.81
Green, Francis	5. 9	Peterborough Utd.	Nottingham	25.08.80
Richardson, Marcus	6. 3	Hartlepool Utd.	Reading	31.08.77
Yeo, Simon	5.10	Hyde Utd.	Stockport	20.10.73

MACCLESFIELD TOWN

Ground: Moss Rose, London Road, Macclesfield SK11 7SP.
Telephone: 01625 264686. **Club nickname:** Silkmen.
First-choice colours: Royal blue shirts; white shorts; royal blue stockings.
Main sponsor: Cheshire Building Society. **Capacity for 2004-05:** 6,208.
Record attendance: 9,003 v Winsford Town (Cheshire Senior Cup 2) 14 February, 1948.

Name	Height ft. in.	Previous club	Birthplace	Birthdate
Goalkeepers				
Fettis, Alan	6. 1	Hull City	Belfast	1.02.71
Wilson, Steve	5.10	Hull City	Hull	24.04.74
Defenders				
Barras, Tony	6. 0	Notts Co.	Billingham	29.03.71
Brightwell, Ian	5.10	Port Vale	Lutterworth	9.04.68
Briscoe, Michael	5.11	Coventry City	Northampton	4.07.83
Carr, Michael	5. 9	–	Crewe	6.12.83
Carragher, Matt	5. 9	Port Vale	Liverpool	14.01.76
Payne, Steve	5.11	Chesterfield	Pontefract	1.08.75
Welch, Michael	6. 3	–	Crewe	11.01.82
Midfielders				
Bailey, Mark	5. 8	Lincoln City	Stoke	12.08.76
Brackenridge, Steve	5. 8	–	Rochdale	31.07.84
Harsley, Paul	5. 8	Northampton Town	Scunthorpe	29.05.78
Potter, Graham	6. 1	Shrewsbury Town	Solihull	20.05.75
Whitaker, Danny	5.10	–	Manchester	14.11.80
Widdrington, Tommy	5. 9	Hartlepool Utd.	Newcastle	1.10.71
Forwards				
Carruthers, Martin	5.11	Scunthorpe Utd.	Nottingham	7.08.72
Miles, John	5.10	Crewe Alexandra	Fazackerley	28.09.81
Parkin, Jonathan	6. 4	York City	Barnsley	30.12.81
Ross, Neil	6. 1	Stockport Co.	Birmingham	10.08.82
Tipton, Matthew	5.10	Oldham Athletic	Bangor	29.06.80

MANSFIELD TOWN

Ground: Field Mill, Quarry Lane, Mansfield NG18 5DA.
Telephone: 0870 756 3160 **Club nickname:** Stags.
First-choice colours: Amber, blue and white shirts; blue and amber shorts; blue and yellow stockings.
Main sponsor: Perry Electrical. **Capacity for 2004-05:** 9,948.
Record attendance: 24,467 v Nott'm. Forest (F.A. Cup 3) 10 January, 1953.

Name	Height ft. in.	Previous club	Birthplace	Birthdate
Goalkeepers				
Pilkington, Kevin	6. 2	Port Vale	Hitchin	8.03.74
White, Jason	6. 2	–	Mansfield	28.01.86

Defenders

Artell, David	6. 0	Rotherham Utd.	Rotherham.	22.11.80
Buxton, Jake	6. 0	–	Sutton-in-Ashfield	4.03.85
Curle, Keith	6. 1	Sheffield Utd.	Bristol	14.11.63
Day, Rhys	6. 1	Manchester City	Bridgend	31.08.82
Eaton, Adam	5. 9	Preston N.E.	Liverpool	2.05.80
Hankey, Dean	5.10	–	Suton-in-Ashfield	23.08.86

Midfielders

Corden, Wayne	5. 9	Port Vale	Leek	1.11.75
Curtis, Tom	5. 8	Portsmouth	Exeter	1.03.73
MacKenzie, Neil	6. 2	Blackpool	Birmingham	15.04.76
Williamson, Lee	5.10	–	Derby	7.06.82

Forwards

Larkin, Colin	5. 9	Wolves	Dundalk	27.04.82

NORTHAMPTON TOWN

Ground: Sixfields Stadium, Upton Way, Northampton NN5 5QA.
Telephone: 01604 757773. **Club nickname:** Cobblers.
First-choice colours: Claret shirts; white shorts; claret stockings.
Main sponsor: Nationwide. **Capacity for 2004-05:** 7,653.
Record attendance: (County Ground) 24,523 v Fulham (Div. 1) 23 April, 1966.
(Sixfields Stadium) 7,557 v Manchester City (Div. 2) 26 September, 1998.

Name	Height ft. in.	Previous club	Birthplace	Birthdate
Goalkeepers				
Bunn, Mark	6. 0	–	London	16.11.84
Harper, Lee	6. 1	Walsall	Chelsea	30.10.71
Defenders				
Amoo, Ryan	5.10	Aston Villa	Leicester	11.10.83
Chambers, Luke	5.11	–	Kettering	29.08.85
Clark, Peter	5.11	Stockport Co.	Romford	10.12.79
Jaszczun, Tommy	5.10	Blackpool	Kettering	16.09.77
Reid, Paul	6. 2	Rangers	Carlisle	18.02.82
Westwood, Ashley	5.11	Sheffield Wed.	Bridgnorth	31.08.76
Willmott, Chris	5.11	Wimbledon	Bedford	30.09.77
Midfielders				
Carruthers, Chris	5.10	–	Kettering	19.08.83
Hicks, David	5.10	Tottenham	–	13.11.85
Low, Josh	6. 1	Oldham Athletic	Bristol	15.02.79
Reeves, Martin	6. 1	Leicester City	Birmingham	7.09.81
Rowson, David	5.10	Partick Thistle	Aberdeen	14.09.76
Forwards				
Asamoah, Derek	5. 6	Slough Town	Ghana	1.05.81
McGleish, Scott	5.10	Colchester Utd.	Barnet	10.02.74
Morison, Steve	6. 2	–	Enfield	29.08.83
Richards, Marc	6. 0	Blackburn Rov.	Wolverhampton	8.07.82
Sabin, Eric	6. 1	Swindon Town	Paris	22.08.75
Smith, Martin	5.11	Huddersfield Town	Sunderland	13.11.74
Youngs, Tom	5. 9	Cambridge Utd.	Bury St Edmunds	31.08.79

NOTTS COUNTY

Ground: Meadow Lane, Nottingham NG2 3HJ.
Telephone: 0115 952 9000. **Club nickname:** Magpies.
First-choice colours: Black and white shirts; black shorts; white stockings.
Main sponsor: Paragon Interiors. **Capacity for 2004-05:** 20,300.
Record attendance: 47,310 v York City (F.A. Cup 6) 12 March, 1955.

Name	Height ft. in.	Previous club	Birthplace	Birthdate
Goalkeepers				
Deeney, Saul	6. 1	Hull City	Londonderry	23.07.81
Mildenhall, Steve	6. 5	Swindon Town	Swindon	13.05.78
Defenders				
Baudet, Julien	6. 2	Rotherham Utd.	Grenoble	13.01.71
Edwards, Mike	6. 1	Grimsby Town	Hessle	25.04.80
McFaul, Shane	6. 0	–	Dublin	23.05.86
Palmer, Chris	5. 7	Derby Co.	Derby	16.10.83
Richardson, Ian	6. 0	Birmingham City	Barking	22.10.70
Ullathorne, Robert	5. 8	Northampton Town	Wakefield	11.10.71
Whitlow, Mike	6. 0	Sheffield Utd.	Northwich	13.01.68
Midfielders				
Bolland, Paul	5.11	Bradford City	Bradford	23.12.79
Gill, Matthew	6. 0	Peterborough Utd.	Cambridge	8.11.80
Oakes, Stefan	6. 1	Walsall	Leicester	6.09.78
Pipe, David	5. 9	Coventry City	Caerphilly	5.11.83
Scully, Tony	5. 7	Peterborough Utd.	Dublin	12.06.76
Forwards				
Gordon, Gavin	6. 3	Cardiff City	Manchester	29.06.79
Harrard, Shaun	5.10	Gresley Rov.	Nottingham	11.12.84
Hurst, Glynn	5.10	Chesterfield	Barnsley	17.01.76
Williams, Matthew	5. 8	Manchester Utd.	St Asaph	5.11.82

OXFORD UNITED

Ground: The Kassam Stadium, Grenoble Road, Oxford OX4 4XP.
Telephone: 01865 337500. **Club nickname:** U's.
First-choice colours: Yellow shirts; blue shorts; blue stockings.
Main Sponsor: Buildbase. **Capacity for 2004-05:** 12,500.
Record attendance: (Manor Ground) 22,730 v Preston N.E. (F.A. Cup 6) 29 February,
1964. (Kassam Stadium) 12,177 v Aston Villa (League Cup 3) 7 November, 2002.

Name	Height ft. in.	Previous club	Birthplace	Birthdate
Goalkeepers				
Cox, Simon	5.11	–	Clapham	24.03.84
Tardif, Chris	6. 1	Portsmouth	Guernsey	19.09.79
Defenders				
Ashton, Jon	6. 0	Leicester City	Nuneaton	4.10.82
Mackay, David	5.11	Dundee	Rutherglen	17.09.75
McNiven, Scott	5.10	Oldham Athletic	Leeds	2.05.78
Quinn, Barry	6. 0	Coventry City	Dublin	9.05.79
Robinson, Matt	5.11	Reading	Exeter	23.12.74
Roget, Leo	6. 1	Rushden & D'mnds.	Ilford	1.08.77
Waterman, David	5.11	Portsmouth	Guernsey	16.05.77
Woozley, David	6. 0	Torquay Utd.	Ascot	6.12.79
Midfielders				
Alexis, Michael	6. 1	–	Oxford	2.01.85
Brooks, Jamie	5. 9	–	Oxford	12.08.80
Brown, Daniel	6. 0	Barnet	London	12.09.80
Hackett, Chris	6. 1	–	Oxford	1.03.83
Oldfield, David	5.11	Peterborough Utd.	Perth, Aus.	30.05.68
Wanless, Paul	6. 1	Cambridge Utd.	Banbury	14.12.73
Forwards				
Alsop, Julian	6. 4	Cheltenham Town	Nuneaton	28.05.73
Basham, Steve	5.11	Preston N.E.	Southampton	2.12.77
Bradbury, Lee	6. 2	Walsall	Isle of Wight	3.07.75
Louis, Jefferson	6. 2	–	Harrow	22.02.79
Mooney, Tommy	5.11	Swindon Town	Billingham	11.08.71

| Rawle, Mark | 5.11 | Southend Utd. | Leicester | 27.04.79 |
| Wolleaston, Robert | 5.11 | Bradford City | London | 21.12.79 |

ROCHDALE

Ground: Spotland, Wilbutts Lane, Rochdale OL11 5DS.
Telephone: 01706 644648. **Club nickname:** Dale.
First-choice colours: Royal blue and white shirts; royal blue and white shorts; royal blue and white stockings.
Main Sponsor: Keytech. **Capacity for 2004-05:** 10,249.
Record attendance: 24,231 v Notts Co. (F.A. Cup 2) 10 December, 1949.

Name	Height ft. in.	Previous club	Birthplace	Birthdate
Goalkeepers				
Edwards, Neil	5. 8	Stockport Co.	Aberdare	5.12.70
Gilks, Matthew	6. 1	–	Rochdale	4.06.82
Defenders				
Bertos, Leo	5.10	Barnsley	Wellington, NZ	'21.12.81
Burgess, Daryl	5.11	Northampton Town	Birmingham	24.01.71
Clarke, Jamie	6. 2	Mansfield Town	Sunderland	18.09.82
Connelly, Sean	5.10	Tranmere Rov.	Sheffield	26.06.70
Evans, Wayne	5.10	Walsall	Welshpool	25.08.71
Griffiths, Gareth	6. 4	Wigan Athletic	Winsford	10.04.70
Heald, Greg	6. 1	Leyton Orient	Enfield	26.09.71
Probets, Ashley	5.11	Arsenal	Bexley	13.12.84
Midfielders				
Brisco, Neil	6. 0	Port Vale	Wigan	26.01.78
Jones, Gary	5.10	Barnsley	Birkenhead	3.06.77
McCourt, Patrick	5.10	–	Derry	16.12.83
Warner, Scott	5.10	–	Rochdale	3.12.83
Forwards				
Armstrong, Chris	6. 1	Leeds Utd.	Durham	8.11.84
Holt, Grant	6. 0	Sheffield Wed.	Carlisle	12.04.81
Tait, Paul	6. 2	Bristol Rov.	Newcastle	24.10.75
Townson, Kevin	5. 6	–	Kirkby	19.04.83

RUSHDEN AND DIAMONDS

Ground: Nene Park, Diamond Way, Irthlingborough NN9 5QF.
Telephone: 01933 652000. **Club nickname:** Diamonds.
First-choice colours: White blue and red shirts; white shorts; white socks.
Main sponsor: Dr Martens. **Capacity for 2004-05:** 6,441.
Record attendance: 6,431 (v Leeds Utd. F.A. Cup 3) 4 January, 1999.

Name	Height ft. in.	Previous club	Birthplace	Birthdate
Goalkeepers				
Turley, Billy	6. 3	Northampton Town	Wolves	15.07.73
Defenders				
Allen, Graham	6. 0	Tranmere Rov.	Bolton	8.04.77
Connelly, Sean	5.10	Tranmere Rov.	Sheffield	26.06.70
Dempster, John	6. 0	–	Kettering	1.04.83
Gray, Stuart	5.10	Reading	Harrogate	18.12.73
Gulliver, Phil	6. 2	Middlesbrough	Bishop Auckland	12.09.82
Hawkins, Peter	6. 0	Wimbledon	Maidstone	19.09.78
Hunter, Barry	6. 4	Reading	Coleraine	18.11.68
Sambrook, Andy	5.10	Gillingham	Chatham	13.07.79
Talbot, Daniel	5. 9	Arsenal	Enfield	30.01.84
Midfielders				
Bell, David	5.10	–	Wellingborough	21.04.84
Burgess, Andy	6. 2	Luton Town	Bedford	10.08.81

Dove, Craig	5. 8	Middlesbrough	Hartlepool	6.08.83
Gier, Rob	5. 9	Wimbledon	Bracknell	6.01.81
Mills, Gary	5. 9	Northampton Town	Sheppey	20.05.81
Wardley, Stuart	5.11	Q.P.R.	Cambridge	10.09.75
Forwards				
Duffy, Robert	6. 1	Swansea City	Swansea	2.12.82
Hay, Alex	5.10	Tranmere Rov.	Birkenhead	14.10.81
Seddon, Gareth	5.11	Bury	Burnley	23.05.80

SCUNTHORPE UNITED

Ground: Glanford Park, Doncaster Road, Scunthorpe DN15 8TD.
Telephone: 01724 747670. **Club nickname:** Iron.
First-choice colours: Claret and blue shirts; claret and blue shorts; blue and claret stockings.
Main sponsor: Mercedes Benz/H & L Garages. **Capacity for 2004-05:** 9,108.
Record attendance: (Old Show Ground) 23,935 v Portsmouth (F.A. Cup 4) 30 January, 1954. (Glanford Park) 8,775 v Rotherham Utd. (Div. 4) 1, May 1989.

Name	Height ft. in.	Previous club	Birthplace	Birthdate
Goalkeepers				
Capp, Adam	6. 2	–	Scunthorpe	17.09.84
Evans, Tom	6. 1	Crystal Palace	Doncaster	13.12.76
Musselwhite, Paul	6. 2	Hull City	Portsmouth	22.12.68
Defenders				
Baraclough, Ian	6. 1	Notts Co.	Leicester	4.12.70
Butler, Andrew	6. 0	–	Doncaster	4.11.83
Byrne, Cliff	6. 0	Sunderland	Dublin	26.04.82
Crosby, Andy	6. 2	Oxford Utd.	Rotherham	3.03.73
Jackson, Mark	5.11	Leeds Utd.	Barnsley	30.09.77
Ridley, Lee	5.10	–	Scunthorpe	5.12.81
Sharp, Kevin	5. 9	Huddersfield Town	Ontario	19.09.74
Stanton, Nathan	5. 9	–	Nottingham	6.05.81
Midfielders				
Barwick, Terry	5.10	–	Doncaster	11.01.83
Beagrie, Peter	5. 9	Bradford City	Middlesbrough	28.11.65
Featherstone, Lee	6. 0	Sheffield Utd.	Chesterfield	20.07.83
Graves, Wayne	5. 8	–	Scunthorpe	18.09.80
Kell, Richard	6. 1	Torquay Utd.	Bishop Auckland	15.09.79
Sparrow, Matthew	5.10	–	London	3.10.81
Taylor, Cleveland	5. 8	Bolton Wand.	Leicester	9.09.83
Forwards				
Hayes, Paul	6. 0	Norwich City	Dagenham	20.09.83
Parton, Andy	5.10	–	Doncaster	29.09.83
Torpey, Steve	6. 3	Bristol City	Islington	8.12.70

SHREWSBURY TOWN

Ground: Gay Meadow, Shrewsbury SY2 5AL.
Telephone: 01743 360111. **Clubcall:** 09068 121194. **Club nickname:** Shrews.
First-choice colours: Royal blue and amber shirts, shorts and stockings.
Main sponsor: RMW Electrical Services. **Capacity for 2004-05:** 8,000.
Record attendance: 18,917 v Walsall (Div. 3) 26 April, 1961.

Name	Height ft. in.	Previous club	Birthplace	Birthdate
Goalkeepers				
Hart, Joe	6. 3	–	–	19.04.87
Howie, Scott	6. 2	Bristol Rov.	Glasgow	4.01.72
Defenders				
Moss, Darren	5.11	Chester City	Wrexham	24.05.81

Name	Height ft. in.	Previous club	Birthplace	Birthdate
Ridler, David	6. 1	Scarborough	Liverpool	12.03.76
Tinson, Darren	6. 0	Macclesfield Town	Connah's Quay	15.11.69
Whitehead, Stuart	5.11	Telford	Bromsgrove	17.07.76
Midfielders				
Aiston, Sam	5. 9	Sunderland	Newcastle	21.11.76
Drysdale, Leon	5. 9	–	Walsall	3.02.81
Edwards, David	5.11	–	Pontesbury	3.02.86
O'Connor, Martin	5. 9	Walsall	Walsall	10.12.67
Sedgemore, Jake	6. 0	Northwich	Wolverhampton	20.10.78
Smith, Ben	5. 9	Hereford Utd.	–	23.11.78
Street, Kevin	5.10	Bristol Rov.	Crewe	25.11.77
Tolley, Jamie	6. 1	–	Shrewsbury	12.05.83
Forwards				
Banim, Jody	5.11	Radcliffe	Manchester	1.04.78
Cramb, Colin	5.11	Fortuna Sittard	Lanark	23.06.74
Darby, Duane	5. 9	Rushden & D'mnds.	Birmingham	17.10.73
Fitzpatrick, Ian	5. 9	Halifax Town	Manchester	22.09.80
Grant, John	5.11	Telford	Manchester	9.08.81
Lowe, Ryan	5.11	Burscough	Liverpool	18.09.78
Rodgers, Luke	5. 6	–	Birmingham	1.01.82

SOUTHEND UNITED

Ground: Roots Hall, Victoria Avenue, Southend SS2 6NQ.
Telephone: 01702 304050. **Club nickname:** Shrimpers.
First-choice colours: Navy shirts; navy shorts; navy stockings.
Main sponsor: Betterview Windows. **Capacity for 2004-05:** 11,500.
Record attendance: 31,033 v Liverpool (F.A. Cup 3) 10 January, 1979.

Name	Height ft. in.	Previous club	Birthplace	Birthdate
Goalkeepers				
Flahavan, Darryl	5.10	Southampton	Southampton	28.11.78
Griemink, Bart	6. 4	Swindon Town	Oss, Hol.	29.03.79
Defenders				
Barrett, Adam	5.10	Bristol Rov.	Dagenham	29.11.79
Bramble, Tesfaye	6. 1	Cambridge City	Ipswich	20.07.80
Edwards, Andy	6. 3	Rushden & Diamonds	Epping	17.09.71
Hunt, Lewis	5.11	Derby Co.	Birmingham	25.08.82
Jupp, Duncan	6. 0	Wimbledon	Guildford	25.01.75
Pettefer, Carl	5. 7	Portsmouth	Burnham	22.03.81
Wilson, Che	5.11	Cambridge City	Ely	17.01.79
Midfielders				
Bentley, Mark	5.10	Dag & Redbridge	–	7.01.78
Gower, Mark	5.11	Barnet	Edmonton	5.10.78
Husbands, Michael	5. 9	Aston Villa	Birmingham	13.11.83
Kightly, Michael	5. 9	–	Basildon	24.01.86
Maher, Kevin	5.11	Tottenham	Ilford	17.10.76
Nicolau, Nicky	5.11	Arsenal	Camden	12.10.83
Smith, Jay	5. 7	Aston Villa	London	24.09.81
Forwards				
Broughton, Drewe	6. 3	Kidderminster Harr.	Hitchin	25.10.78
Corbett, Jim	5. 9	Blackburn Rov.	Hackney	6.07.80
Dudfield, Lawrie	6. 0	Northampton Town	Southwark	7.05.80
Gray, Wayne	5.10	Wimbledon	Camberwell	7.11.80

SWANSEA CITY

Ground: Vetch Field, Swansea SA1 3SU.
Telephone: 01792 633400. **Club nickname:** Swans.
First-choice colours: White and black shirts; white and black shorts; white and black stockings.

Main sponsor: The Travel House. **Capacity for 2004-05:** 13,188.
Record attendance: 32,786 v Arsenal (F.A. Cup 4) 17 February, 1968.

Name	Height ft. in.	Previous club	Birthplace	Birthdate
Goalkeepers				
Murphy, Brian	6. 1	Manchester City	Waterford	7.05.83
Defenders				
Austin, Kevin	6. 0	Bristol Rov.	Hackney	12.02.73
Fieldwick, Lee	5.11	Brentford	Croydon	6.09.82
Howard, Michael	5. 9	Tranmere Rov.	Birkenhead	2.12.78
Hylton, Leon	5. 9	Aston Villa	Birmingham	27.01.83
Iriekpen, Izzy	6. 1	West Ham Utd.	London	10.04.82
Monk, Garry	6. 0	Southampton	Bedford	6.03.79
O'Leary, Kristian	5.11	–	Neath	30.08.77
Ricketts, Sam	6. 1	Telford Utd.	Aylesbury	11.10.81
Tate, Alan	6. 1	Manchester Utd.	Easington	2.09.82
Midfielders				
Britton, Leon	5. 5	West Ham Utd.	London	16.09.82
Corbisiero, Antonio	5.10	–	Exmouth	17.11.84
Fisken, Gary	5.11	Watford	Watford	27.10.81
Jones, Stuart	6. 0	–	Aberystwyth	14.03.84
Martinez, Roberto	5. 9	Walsall	Balaguer, Spa.	13.07.73
Maylett, Bradley	5. 8	Burnley	Manchester	24.12.80
Forwards				
Connor, Paul	6. 1	Rochdale	Bishop Auckland	12.01.79
Forbes, Adrian	5. 8	Luton Town	Ealing	23.01.79
Nugent, Kevin	6. 1	Leyton Orient	Edmonton	10.04.69
Robinson, Andy	5.11	Tranmere Rov.	Birkenhead	15.05.84
Thomas, James	6. 0	Blackburn Rov.	Swansea	16.01.79
Trundle, Lee	5.11	Wrexham	Liverpool	10.10.76

WYCOMBE WANDERERS

Ground: Causeway Stadium, Hillbottom Road, High Wycombe HP12 4HJ.
Telephone: 01494 472100. **Club nickname:** Chairboys.
First-choice colours: Light and dark blue shirts; dark blue shorts; light blue stockings.
Main sponsor: Loans.co.uk. **Capacity for 2004-05:** 10,000.
Record attendance: 9,921 v Fulham (F.A. Cup 3) 8 January, 2002.

Name	Height ft. in.	Previous club	Birthplace	Birthdate
Goalkeepers				
Talia, Frank	6. 1	Reading	Melbourne	20.07.72
Williams, Steve	6. 0	–	Oxford	21.04.83
Defenders				
Burnell, Joe	5.10	Bristol City	Bristol	10.10.80
Johnson, Roger	6. 3	Portsmouth	Ashford	28.04.83
Uhlenbeek, Gus	5. 9	Chesterfield	Surinam	28.07.70
Midfielders				
Bloomfield, Matt	5. 9	Ipswich Town	Ipswich	8.02.84
Ryan, Keith	5.10	Berkhamstead	Northampton	25.06.70
Forwards				
Dixon, Jonny	5. 9	–	Mercia, Spa.	16.01.84
Faulconbridge, Craig	6. 1	Wrexham	Nuneaton	20.04.78
Senda, Danny	5.10	Southampton	Harrow	17.04.81
Tyson, Nathan	6. 0	Reading	Reading	4.05.82

YEOVIL TOWN

Ground: Huish Park, Lufton Way, Yeovil BA22 8YF.
Telephone: 01935 423662. **Club nickname:** Glovers.

First-choice colours: Green and white shirts; white shorts; green socks.
Main sponsor: Bradford Building. **Capacity for 2004-05:** 9,107.
Record attendance: 9,348 v Liverpool (F.A. Cup 3) 4 January, 2004.

Name	Height ft. in.	Previous club	Birthplace	Birthdate
Goalkeepers				
Stephen Collis	6. 0	Nott'm Forest	–	–
Chris Weale	6. 0	–	–	–
Defenders				
Lockwood, Adam	6. 0	Reading	Wakefield	26.10.81
Pluck, Colin	6. 0	Dover		6.09.78
Reed, Stephen	5.11	–	Barnstaple	18.06.85
Skiverton, Terry	6. 1	Welling	London	20.06.75
Midfielders				
Johnson, Lee	5. 6	Watford	Newmarket	7.06.81
Lindegaard, Andy	6. 0	–	Yeovil	10.09.80
O'Brien, Roy	6. 1	Bournemouth	Cork	27.11.74
Terry, Paul	6. 0	Dag & Redbridge	London	3.04.79
Williams, Gavin	5.10	Hereford Utd.	Merthyr Tydfil	3.04.79
Way, Darren	5.11	Norwich City	Plymouth	21.11.79
Forwards				
Gall, Kevin	5. 9	Bristol Rov.	Merthyr Tydfil	4.02.82
Jevons, Phil	5.11	Grimsby Town	Liverpool	1.08.79
Weatherstone, Simon	5.10	Boston Utd.	Reading	26.01.80

BANK OF SCOTLAND PREMIER LEAGUE SQUADS 2004-05

ABERDEEN

Goalkeepers: Ryan Esson, David Preece.
Defenders: Russell Anderson, Alexander Diamond, Michael Hart, Duncan Jones, Murray McCulloch, Phil McGuire, Kevin McNaughton, Scott Morrison, Kevin Rutkiewicz.
Midfielders: Derek Adams, Chris Clark, Richard Foster, Markus Heikkinen, Scott Muirhead, Paul Sheerin, Kevin Souter, Scott Severin, Fergus Tiernan, Steve Tosh.
Forwards: Michael Bird, Steven Craig, Leigh Hinds, Darren Mackie, Scott Michie, Bryan Punty, John Stewart, Stephen Tarditi, Derek Young, David Zdrilic.

CELTIC

Goalkeepers: Rob Douglas, Magnus Hedman, Michael Herbert, David Marshall.
Defenders: Bobo Balde, Stephen Crainey, John Kennedy, Ulrik Laursen, Joos Valgaeren, Stanislav Varga.
Midfielders: Didier Agathe, Paul Lambert, Neil Lennon, Jackie McNamara, Stephen Pearson, Bobby Petta, Stilian Petrov, Jamie Smith, Mohammed Sylla, Alan Thompson, Ross Wallace.
Forwards: Craig Beattie, John Hartson, Shaun Maloney, Aidan McGeady, Chris Sutton.

DUNDEE

Goalkeepers: Derek Soutar.
Defenders: Jonay Hernandez, Tom Hutchinson, Dave Mackay, Callum MacDonald, Lee Mair, Stephen McNally, Brent Sancho, Barry Smith, Lee Wilkie.
Midfielders: Garry Brady, Dougie Cameron, Mark Fotheringham, Chris Hegarty, Neil Jablonski, Steven Robb.
Forwards: Steve Lovell, Glenn Larsen, Bobby Linn.

DUNDEE UNITED

Goalkeepers: Tony Bullock.
Defenders: Alan Archibald, David McCracken, Chris Innes, Scott Paterson.
Midfielders: Stuart Duff, Mark Kerr, Derek McInnes, Jim McIntyre, Charlie Miller, Jim Paterson, Barry Robson, Mark Wilson.
Forwards: Owen Coyle, Billy Dodds, James Grady, Andy McLaren, Colin Samuel, Jason Scotland.

DUNFERMLINE ATHLETIC

Goalkeepers: Derek Stillie.
Defenders: Richie Byrne, Aaron Labonte, Greg Shields, Andrius Skerla, Scott Thomson, Andy Tod, Scott Wilson.
Midfielders: Gary Dempsey, Gary Mason, Barry Nicholson, Darren Young, Derek Young.
Forwards: Craig Brewster, Noel Hunt, Derek Lyle.

HEARTS

Goalkeepers: Craig Gordon, Tepi Moilanen, Jamie MacDonald, Lee Windrum.
Defenders: David Dunn, Patrick Kisnorbo, John Knox, Alan Maybury, Jamie McAllister, Kevin McKenna, Robbie Neilson, Marco Pelosi, Steven Pressley, Jason Thomson, Garry Tierney, Andy Webster.
Midfielders: Liam Fox, Ryan Gay, Paul Hartley, Neil Janczyk, Neil Macfarlane, David McGeown, Paul McMullan, Ross McLeod, Phil Stamp.
Forwards: Mark de Vries, Calum Elliot, Joe Hamill, Ramon Pereira, Robert Sloan, Colin Strickland, Graham Weir, Dennis Wyness.

HIBERNIAN

Goalkeepers: Simon Brown, Andy Reid.
Defenders: Paul Fenwick, Colin Murdock, Alen Orman, Gary Smith, Mark Venus, Steven Whittaker.
Midfielders: Grant Brebner, Stephen Glass, Ian Murray, Kevin Nicol, Kevin Thomson.
Forwards: Scott Brown, Stephen Dobbie, Tom McManus, Garry O'Connor, Derek Riordan, Dean Shiels.

INVERNESS CALEDONIAN THISTLE

Goalkeepers: Mark Brown, Michael Fraser, Jonathan Smith.
Defenders: Stuart Golabek, Stuart McCaffrey, Grant Munro, David Proctor, Ross Tokely.
Midfielders: Russell Duncan, Richard Hart, Liam Keogh, Roy McBain, Darran Thomson, Barry Wilson,
Forwards: Graham Bayne, Steven Hislop.

KILMARNOCK

Goalkeepers: Alan Combe, Colin Meldrum, Craig Samson, Graeme Smith.
Defenders: Sean Dillon, Freddy Dindeleux, Garry Hay, Robbie Henderson, Sean Hessey, Chris Innes, Barry McLaughlin, Greg Shields.
Midfielders: Peter Canero, Mark Canning, James Fowler, Steve Fulton, Martin Hardie, Gary Locke, Alan Mahood, Gary McDonald, Andy McLaren, Stephen Murray, Jose Quitongo, Jesus Garcia Sanjuan.
Forwards: Kris Boyd, Craig Dargo, Paul Di Giacomo, Emillio Jaconelli, Gary McSwegan, David Merdy, Gary Wales.

LIVINGSTON

Goalkeepers: Allan Creer, Alan Main, Roddy McKenzie.
Defenders: Gustave Bahoken, Jason Dair, Emmanuel Dorado, Eamonn Fullerton, David McNamee, James McPake, Oscar Rubio, Will Snowdon, Goran Stanic.
Midfielders: Craig Easton, Stuart Lovell, Scott McLaughlin, Burton O'Brien, Martin Scott, Allan Walker.
Forwards: Robbie Arthur, Steven Boyack, Richard Brittain, Jim Hamilton, Marc Libbra, Colin McMenamin, Fernando Pasquinelli, Stephen Whalen.

MOTHERWELL

Goalkeepers: Barry John Corr, Gordon Marshall, Jamie Ewings.
Defenders: Gary Bollan, Martyn Corrigan, David Cowan, Steven Hammell, Chris Higgins, William Kinniburgh, Graeme Mathie, Barry Neville, David Partridge, Paul Quinn.
Midfielders: Kevin Barkey, Ross Ballantyne, Shaun Fagan, Brian Kerr, Scott Leitch, Phil O'Donnell.
Forwards: Alex Burns, David Clarkson, Richie Foran, Scott McDonald, Andy Scott, Kenny Wright,

RANGERS

Goalkeepers: Stefan Klos, Allan McGregor, Graeme Smith.
Defenders: Marvin Andrews, Michael Ball, Jean-Alain Boumsong, Alan Hutton, Zurab Khizanishvili, Gary MacKenzie, Robert Malcolm, Craig Moore, Gavin Rae, Fernando Ricksen, Maurice Ross, Paolo Vanoli.
Midfielders: Charlie Adam, Chris Burke, Stephen Hughes, Hamed Namouchi, Alex Rae, Alex Walker.
Forwards: Shota Arveladze, Tom Brighton, Robert Davidson, Bajram Fetai, Peter Lovenkrands, Ross McCormack, Nacho Novo, Dado Prso, Steven Thompson,

FIRST FOR SWISS MISS IN UEFA CUP

Nicole Petignat, from Switzerland, became the first woman to referee a UEFA Cup match. The 36-year-old took charge of a qualifying round tie between AIK Solna (Sweden) and Fylkir (Iceland).

MANAGER SEES RED BEFORE YELLOW

Andy Hessenthaler, the Gillingham player-manager, saw red before yellow during his side's 5-0 defeat at Cardiff. Hessenthaler was sent from the dug-out for arguing with the fourth official. Later, he came on as a substitute and was booked for a lunge at John Robinson.

LEAGUE FIXTURES 2004-05

Saturday, 7 August
Coca-Cola League Championship
Burnley v Sheffield Utd.
Coventry City v Sunderland
Crewe Alexandra v Cardiff City
Ipswich Town v Gillingham
Leeds Utd. v Derby Co.
Leicester City v West Ham Utd.
Plymouth Argyle v Millwall
Preston N.E. v Watford
Q.P.R. v Rotherham Utd.
Reading v Brighton & H.A.
Wigan Athletic v Nott'm. Forest

Coca-Cola League One
Bristol City v Torquay Utd.
Chesterfield v Brentford
Doncaster Rov. v Blackpool
Hartlepool Utd. v Bradford City
Hull City v Bournemouth
Luton Town v Oldham Athletic
Milton Keynes Dons v Barnsley
Peterborough Utd. v Tranmere Rov.
Sheffield Wed. v Colchester Utd.
Stockport Co. v Huddersfield Town
Walsall v Port Vale
Wrexham v Swindon Town

Coca-Cola League Two
Boston Utd. v Oxford Utd.
Bury v Yeovil
Darlington v Grimsby Town
Leyton Orient v Macclesfield Town
Mansfield Town v Bristol Rov.
Notts Co. v Chester City
Rushden & D'monds v Kidderminster H.
Scunthorpe Utd. v Rochdale
Shrewsbury Town v Lincoln City
Southend Utd. v Cheltenham Town
Swansea City v Northampton Town
Wycombe Wand. v Cambridge Utd.

Sunday, 8 August
Coca-Cola League Championship
Stoke City v Wolves

Monday, 9 August
Coca-Cola League Championship
Watord v Q.P.R.

Tuesday, 10 August
Coca-Cola League Championship
Brighton & H.A. v Plymouth Argyle
Cardiff City v Coventry City
Gillingham v Leeds Utd.
Millwall v Wigan Athletic
Rotherham Utd. v Burnley
Sheffield Utd. v Stoke City
Sunderland v Crewe Alexandra
West Ham Utd. v Reading

Coca-Cola League One
Barnsley v Bristol City
Blackpool v Sheffield Wed.
Bournemouth v Walsall
Bradford City v Peterborough Utd.
Brentford v Doncaster Rov.
Colchester Utd. v Stockport Co.
Huddersfield Town v Chesterfield
Oldham Athletic v Wrexham
Port Vale v Milton Keynes Dons
Torquay Utd. v Hull City
Tranmere Rov. v Hartlepool Utd.

Coca-Cola League Two
Bristol Rov. v Bury
Cambridge Utd. v Leyton Orient
Cheltenham Town v Scunthorpe Utd.
Chester City v Wycombe Wand.
Grimsby Town v Boston. Utd.
Kidderminster Harr. v Notts Co.
Lincoln City v Southend Utd.
Macclesfield Town v Shrewsbury Town
Northampton T v Rushden & D'monds
Rochdale v Swansea City
Yeovil v Darlington

Wednesday, 11 August
Coca-Cola League Championship
Derby Co. v Leicester City
Nott'm. Forest v Ipswich Town
Wolves v Preston N.E.

490

Coca-Cola League One
Swindon Town v Luton Town

Coca-Cola League Two
Oxford Utd. v Mansfield Town

Friday, 13 August
Coca-Cola League Championship
Cardiff City v Plymouth Argyle

Saturday, 14 August
Barclays Premiership
Aston Villa v Southampton
Blackburn Rov. v W.B.A.
Bolton Wand. v Charlton Athletic
Manchester City v Fulham
Middlesbrough v Newcastle Utd.
Norwich City v Crystal Palace
Portsmouth v Birmingham City
Tottenham v Liverpool

Coca-Cola League Championship
Brighton & H.A. v Coventry City
Derby Co. v Ipswich Town
Gillingham v Preston N.E.
Millwall v Leicester City
Nott'm. Forest v Crewe Alexandra
Rotherham Utd. v Stoke City
Sheffield Utd. v Reading
Sunderland v Q.P.R.
Watford v Burnley
West Ham Utd. v Wigan Athletic
Wolves v Leeds Utd.

Coca-Cola League One
Barnsley v Luton Town
Blackpool v Stockport Co.
Bournemouth v Bristol City
Bradford City v Doncaster Rov.
Brentford v Wrexham
Colchester Utd. v Peterborough Utd.
Oldham Athletic v Walsall
Port Vale v Hull City
Swindon Town v Milton Keynes Dons
Torquay Utd. v Sheffield Wed.
Tranmere Rov. v Chesterfield

Coca-Cola League Two
Bristol Rov. v Notts Co.
Cambridge Utd. v Shrewsbury Town
Cheltenham Town v Leyton Orient
Chester City v Mansfield Town
Grimsby Town v Bury
Kidderminster Harr. v Darlington
Lincoln City v Rushden & D'monds
Macclesfield Town v Swansea City
Northampton Town v Wycombe Wand.

Oxford Utd. v Scunthorpe Utd.
Rochdale v Southend Utd.
Yeovil v Boston Utd.

Sunday, 15 August
Barclays Premiership
Chelsea v Manchester Utd.
Everton v Arsenal

Monday, 16 August
Coca-Cola League One
Huddersfield Town v Hartlepool Utd.

Friday, 20 August
Coca-Cola League Championship
Preston N.E. v Sheffield Utd.

Saturday, 21 August
Barclays Premiership
Birmingham City v Chelsea
Charlton Athletic v Portsmouth
Crystal Palace v Everton
Fulham v Bolton Wand.
Liverpool v Manchester City
Manchester Utd. v Norwich City
Newcastle Utd. v Tottenham
Southampton v Blackburn Rov.

Coca-Cola League Championship
Burnley v Wolves
Coventry City v Millwall
Crewe Alexandra v West Ham Utd.
Ipswich Town v Cardiff City
Leeds Utd. v Nott'm. Forest
Leicester City v Watford
Plymouth Argyle v Sunderland
Q.P.R. v Derby Co.
Reading v Rotherham Utd.
Stoke City v Gillingham
Wigan Athletic v Brighton & H.A.

Coca-Cola League One
Bristol City v Swindon Town
Chesterfield v Colchester Utd.
Doncaster Rov. v Tranmere Rov.
Hartlepool Utd. v Blackpool
Hull City v Oldham Athletic
Luton Town v Torquay Utd.
Milton Keynes Dons v Bournemouth
Peterborough Utd. v Brentford
Sheffield Wed. v Huddersfield Town
Stockport Co. v Bradford City
Walsall v Barnsley
Wrexham v Port Vale

Coca-Cola League Two
Boston Utd. v Macclesfield Town
Bury v Chester City
Darlington v Bristol Rov.
Leyton Orient v Oxford Utd.
Mansfield Town v Kidderminster Harr.
Notts Co. v Yeovil
Rushden & D'monds v Grimsby Town
Scunthorpe Utd. v Lincoln City
Shrewsbury Town v Northampton Town
Southend Utd. v Cambridge Utd.
Swansea City v Cheltenham Town
Wycombe Wand. v Rochdale

Sunday, 22 August
Barclays Premiership
Arsenal v Middlesbrough
W.B.A. v Aston Villa

Tuesday, 24 August
Barclays Premiership
Birmingham City v Manchester City
Crystal Palace v Chelsea

Wednesday, 25 August
Barclays Premiership
Arsenal v Blackburn Rov.
Charlton Athletic v Aston Villa
Fulham v Middlesbrough
Newcastle Utd. v Norwich City
Southampton v Bolton Wand.
W.B.A. v Tottenham

Friday, 27 August
Coca-Cola Championship
Gillingham v Q.P.R.

Coca-Cola League One
Tranmere Rov. v Sheffield Wed.

Coca-Cola League Two
Bristol Rov. v Southend Utd.

Saturday, 28 August
Barclays Premiership
Aston Villa v Newcastle Utd.
Blackburn Rov. v Manchester Utd.
Chelsea v Southampton
Everton v W.B.A.
Manchester City v Charlton Athletic
Middlesbrough v Crystal Palace
Norwich City v Arsenal
Tottenham v Birmingham City

Coca-Cola League Championship
Brighton & H.A. v Preston N.E.
Cardiff City v Stoke City
Derby Co. v Crewe Alexandra
Millwall v Reading
Nott'm. Forest v Coventry City
Rotherham Utd. v Ipswich Town
Sheffield Utd. v Leeds Utd.
Sunderland v Wigan Athletic
Watford v Plymouth Argyle
West Ham Utd. v Burnley
Wolves v Leicester City

Coca-Cola League One
Barnsley v Hull City
Blackpool v Luton Town
Bournemouth v Wrexham
Bradford City v Chesterfield
Brentford v Stockport Co.
Colchester Utd. v Doncaster Rov.
Huddersfield Town v Peterborough Utd.
Oldham Athletic v Milton Keynes Dons
Port Vale v Bristol City
Swindon Town v Hartlepool Utd.
Torquay Utd. v Walsall

Coca-Cola League Two
Cambridge Utd. v Swansea City
Cheltenham Town v Boston Utd.
Chester City v Darlington
Grimsby Town v Mansfield Town
Kidderminster Harr. v Wycombe Wand.
Lincoln City v Notts Co.
Macclesfield Town v Scunthorpe Utd.
Northampton Town v Leyton Orient
Oxford Utd. v Shrewsbury Town
Rochdale v Bury
Yeovil v Rushden & D'monds

Sunday, 29 August
Barclays Premiership
Bolton Wand. v Liverpool

Monday, 30 August
Barclays Premiership
Manchester Utd. v Everton
Portsmouth v Fulham

Coca-Cola League Championship
Burnley v Gillingham
Coventry City v West Ham Utd.
Ipswich Town v Wolves
Leicester City v Brighton & H.A.
Plymouth Argyle v Nott'm. Forest
Preston N.E. v Rotherham Utd.
Stoke City v Derby Co.
Wigan Athletic v Cardiff City

Coca-Cola League One
Bristol City v Brentford
Chesterfield v Port Vale
Doncaster Rov. v Huddersfield Town
Hartlepool Utd. v Colchester Utd.
Luton Town v Bournemouth
Milton Keynes Dons v Torquay Utd.
Peterborough Utd. v Blackpool
Sheffield Wed. v Oldham Athletic
Stockport Co. v Tranmere Rov.
Walsall v Swindon Town
Wrexham v Barnsley

Coca-Cola League Two
Boston Utd. v Chester City
Bury v Kidderminster Harr.
Darlington v Cambridge Utd.
Leyton Orient v Rochdale
Mansfield Town v Yeovil
Notts Co. v Oxford Utd.
Rushden & D'monds v Bristol Rov.
Scunthorpe Utd. v Northampton Town
Shrewsbury Town v Cheltenham Town
Southend Utd. v Macclesfield Town
Swansea City v Lincoln City
Wycombe Wand. v Grimsby Town

Tuesday, 31 August
Coca-Cola League Championship
Crewe Alexandra v Millwall
Leeds Utd. v Watford
Q.P.R. v Sheffield Utd.
Reading v Sunderland

Coca-Cola League One
Hull City v Bradford City

Friday, 3 September
Coca-Cola League One
Tranmere Rov. v Oldham Athletic

Coca-Cola League Two
Wycombe Wand. v Oxford Utd.

Saturday, 4 September
Coca-Cola League One
Blackpool v Wrexham
Bradford City v Port Vale
Brentford v Bournemouth
Chesterfield v Milton Keynes Dons
Colchester Utd. v Swindon Town
Doncaster Rov. v Walsall
Hartlepool Utd. v Barnsley
Peterborough Utd. v Bristol City
Sheffield Wed. v Luton Town
Stockport Co. v Torquay Utd.

Coca-Cola League Two
Boston Utd. v Cambridge Utd.
Bristol Rov. v Shrewsbury Town
Bury v Lincoln City
Chester City v Macclesfield Town
Darlington v Scunthorpe Utd.
Grimsby Town v Rochdale
Kidderminster Harr. v Leyton Orient
Notts Co. v Cheltenham Town
Rushden & D'monds v Southend Utd.
Yeovil v Swansea City

Sunday, 5 September
Coca-Cola League One
Huddersfield Town v Hull City

Coca-Cola League Two
Mansfield Town v Northampton Town

Saturday, 11 September
Barclays Premiership
Aston Villa v Chelsea
Bolton Wand. v Manchester Utd.
Fulham v Arsenal
Liverpool v W.B.A.
Manchester City v Everton
Middlesbrough v Birmingham City
Newcastle Utd. v Blackburn Rov.
Portsmouth v Crystal Palace

Coca-Cola League Championship
Burnley v Crewe Alexandra
Derby Co. v Reading
Gillingham v Sunderland
Leeds Utd. v Coventry City
Nott'm. Forest v Cardiff City
Preston N.E. v Stoke City
Q.P.R. v Plymouth Argyle
Rotherham Utd. v Leicester City
Sheffield Utd. v West Ham Utd.
Watford v Brighton & H.A.
Wolves v Wigan Athletic

Coca-Cola League One
Barnsley v Tranmere Rov.
Bournemouth v Colchester Utd.
Bristol City v Stockport Co.
Hull City v Blackpool
Luton Town v Chesterfield
Milton Keynes Dons v Doncaster Rov.
Oldham Athletic v Hartlepool Utd.
Port Vale v Huddersfield Town
Swindon Town v Peterborough Utd.
Torquay Utd. v Brentford
Walsall v Sheffield Wed.
Wrexham v Bradford City

Coca-Cola League Two
Cambridge Utd. v Mansfield Town
Cheltenham Town v Yeovil
Leyton Orient v Bristol Rov.
Lincoln City v Boston Utd.
Macclesfield Town v Grimsby Town
Northampton Town v Notts Co.
Oxford Utd. v Rushden & D'monds
Rochdale v Darlington
Scunthorpe Utd. v Chester City
Shrewsbury Town v Bury
Southend Utd. v Wycombe Wand.
Swansea City v Kidderminster Harr.

Sunday, 12 September
Barclays Premiership
Tottenham v Norwich City

Coca-Cola League Championship
Ipswich Town v Millwall

Monday, 13 September
Barclays Premiership
Charlton Athletic v Southampton

Tuesday, 14 September
Coca-Cola League Championship
Brighton & H.A. v Wolves
Cardiff City v Watford
Crewe Alexandra v Q.P.R.
Leicester City v Sheffield Utd.
Plymouth Argyle v Leeds Utd.
Reading v Preston N.E.
Stoke City v Ipswich Town
Sunderland v Nott'm. Forest
West Ham Utd. v Rotherham Utd.
Wigan Athletic v Burnley

Wednesday, 15 September
Coca-Cola League Championship
Coventry City v Gillingham

Saturday, 18 September
Barclays Premiership
Arsenal v Bolton Wand.
Birmingham City v Charlton Athletic
Blackburn Rov. v Portsmouth
Crystal Palace v Manchester City
Norwich City v Aston Villa
W.B.A. v Fulham

Coca-Cola League Championship
Brighton & H.A. v Q.P.R.
Cardiff City v Derby Co.
Coventry City v Rotherham Utd.

Crewe Alexandra v Leeds Utd.
Leicester City v Burnley
Millwall v Watford
Plymouth Argyle v Wolves
Reading v Gillingham
Stoke City v Nott'm. Forest
Sunderland v Preston N.E.
West Ham Utd. v Ipswich Town
Wigan Athletic v Sheffield Utd.

Coca-Cola League One
Blackpool v Swindon Town
Bradford City v Bristol City
Brentford v Port Vale
Chesterfield v Walsall
Colchester Utd. v Milton Keynes Dons
Doncaster Rov. v Oldham Athletic
Hartlepool Utd. v Torquay Utd.
Huddersfield Town v Barnsley
Peterborough Utd. v Hull City
Sheffield Wed. v Bournemouth
Stockport Co. v Luton Town
Tranmere Rov. v Wrexham

Coca-Cola League Two
Boston Utd. v Shrewsbury Town
Bristol Rov. v Lincoln City
Bury v Scunthorpe Utd.
Chester City v Cambridge Utd.
Darlington v Northampton Town
Grimsby Town v Leyton Orient
Kidderminster Harr. v Macclesfield Town
Mansfield Town v Rochdale
Notts Co. v Southend Utd.
Rushden & D'monds v Cheltenham Town
Wycombe Wand. v Swansea City
Yeovil v Oxford Utd.

Sunday, 19 September
Barclays Premiership
Chelsea v Tottenham
Everton v Middlesbrough
Southampton v Newcastle Utd.

Monday, 20 September
Barclays Premiership
Manchester Utd. v Liverpool

Friday, 24 September
Coca-Cola League Championship
Leeds Utd. v Sunderland

Saturday, 25 September
Barclays Premiership
Aston Villa v Crystal Palace
Bolton Wand. v Birmingham City

Fulham v Southampton
Liverpool v Norwich City
Manchester City v Arsenal
Middlesbrough v Chelsea
Newcastle Utd. v W.B.A.
Tottenham v Manchester Utd.

Coca-Cola League Championship
Burnley v Stoke City
Derby Co. v Wigan Athletic
Gillingham v Brighton & H.A.
Ipswich Town v Plymouth Argyle
Preston N.E. v Crewe Alexandra
Q.P.R. v Leicester City
Rotherham Utd. v Millwall
Sheffield Utd. v Coventry City
Watford v Reading
Wolves v Cardiff City

Coca-Cola League One
Barnsley v Chesterfield
Bournemouth v Doncaster Rov.
Bristol City v Huddersfield Town
Hull City v Stockport Co.
Luton Town v Peterborough Utd.
Milton Keynes Dons v Hartlepool Utd.
Oldham Athletic v Colchester Utd.
Port Vale v Blackpool
Swindon Town v Bradford City
Torquay Utd. v Tranmere Rov.
Walsall v Brentford
Wrexham v Sheffield Wed.

Coca-Cola League Two
Cambridge Utd. v Grimsby Town
Cheltenham Town v Wycombe Wand.
Leyton Orient v Boston Utd.
Lincoln City v Chester City
Macclesfield Town v Darlington
Northampton Town v Bristol Rov.
Oxford Utd. v Bury
Rochdale v Notts Co.
Scunthorpe Utd. v Mansfield Town
Shrewsbury Town v Yeovil
Southend Utd. v Kidderminster Harr.
Swansea City v Rushden & D'monds

Sunday, 26 September
Barclays Premiership
Portsmouth v Everton

Coca-Cola League Championship
Nott'm. Forest v West Ham Utd.

Monday, 27 September
Barclays Premiership
Charlton Athletic v Blackburn Rov.

Tuesday, 28 September
Coca-Cola League Championship
Burnley v Cardiff City
Gillingham v Leicester City
Ipswich Town v Reading
Leeds Utd. v Stoke City
Preston N.E. v Plymouth Argyle
Q.P.R. v Coventry City
Rotherham Utd. v Crewe Alexandra
Sheffield Utd. v Sunderland
Watford v Wigan Athletic

Wednesday, 29 September
Coca-Cola League Championship
Derby Co. v West Ham Utd.
Nott'm. Forest v Brighton & H.A.

Friday, 1 October
Coca-Cola League Two
Grimsby Town v Cheltenham Town

Saturday, 2 October
Barclays Premiership
Arsenal v Charlton Athletic
Blackburn Rov. v Aston Villa
Everton v Tottenham
Norwich City v Portsmouth
Southampton v Manchester City
W.B.A. v Bolton Wand.

Coca-Cola League Championship
Brighton & H.A. v Sheffield Utd.
Cardiff City v Leeds Utd.
Coventry City v Ipswich Town
Crewe Alexandra v Watford
Leicester City v Preston N.E.
Millwall v Nott'm. Forest
Plymouth Argyle v Gillingham
Reading v Burnley
Stoke City v Q.P.R.
Sunderland v Derby Co.
West Ham Utd. v Wolves
Wigan Athletic v Rotherham Utd.

Coca-Cola League One
Blackpool v Bournemouth
Bradford City v Barnsley
Brentford v Oldham Athletic
Chesterfield v Bristol City
Colchester Utd. v Port Vale
Doncaster Rov. v Wrexham
Hartlepool Utd. v Hull City
Huddersfield Town v Walsall
Peterborough Utd. v Torquay Utd.
Sheffield Wed. v Milton Keynes Dons
Stockport Co. v Swindon Town
Tranmere Rov. v Luton Town

Coca-Cola League Two
Boston Utd. v Scunthorpe Utd.
Bristol Rov. v Oxford Utd.
Bury v Macclesfield Town
Chester City v Swansea City
Darlington v Southend Utd.
Kidderminster Harr. v Cambridge Utd.
Mansfield Town v Lincoln City
Notts Co. v Leyton Orient
Rushden & D'monds v Rochdale
Wycombe Wand. v Shrewsbury Town
Yeovil v Northampton Town

Sunday, 3 October
Barclays Premiership
Birmingham City v Newcastle Utd.
Chelsea v Liverpool
Manchester Utd. v Middlesbrough

Monday, 4 October
Barclays Premiership
Crystal Palace v Fulham

Friday, 8 October
Coca-Cola League Two
Cheltenham Town v Chester City
Southend Utd. v Boston Utd.
Swansea City v Mansfield Town

Saturday, 9 October
Coca-Cola League One
Barnsley v Brentford
Bournemouth v Stockport Co.
Bristol City v Tranmere Rov.
Luton Town v Hartlepool Utd.
Milton Keynes Dons v Bradford City
Port Vale v Doncaster Rov.
Swindon Town v Sheffield Wed.
Torquay Utd. v Huddersfield Town
Walsall v Colchester Utd.
Wrexham v Peterborough Utd.

Coca-Cola League Two
Cambridge Utd. v Bristol Rov.
Leyton Orient v Bury
Lincoln City v Kidderminster Harr.
Macclesfield Town v Notts Co.
Northampton Town v Grimsby Town
Oxford Utd. v Darlington
Rochdale v Yeovil
Scunthorpe Utd. v Wycombe Wand.
Shrewsbury Town v Rushden & D'monds

Sunday, 10 October
Coca-Cola League One
Hull City v Chesterfield
Oldham Athletic v Blackpool

Friday, 15 October
Coca-Cola League Championship
Nott'm. Forest v Wolves

Coca-Cola League Two
Cambridge Utd. v Northampton Town

Saturday, 16 October
Barclays Premiership
Arsenal v Aston Villa
Birmingham City v Manchester Utd.
Blackburn Rov. v Middlesbrough
Bolton Wand. v Crystal Palace
Everton v Southampton
Fulham v Liverpool
Manchester City v Chelsea
W.B.A. v Norwich City

Coca-Cola League Championship
Cardiff City v Rotherham Utd.
Coventry City v Leicester City
Crewe Alexandra v Brighton & H.A.
Derby Co. v Watford
Ipswich Town v Burnley
Leeds Utd. v Preston N.E.
Plymouth Argyle v Wigan Athletic
Q.P.R. v West Ham Utd.
Stoke City v Reading
Sunderland v Millwall

Coca-Cola League One
Blackpool v Colchester Utd.
Bournemouth v Port Vale
Bristol City v Hull City
Doncaster Rov. v Torquay Utd.
Hartlepool Utd. v Chesterfield
Luton Town v Huddersfield Town
Milton Keynes Dons v Brentford
Stockport Co. v Peterborough Utd.
Swindon Town v Oldham Athletic
Tranmere Rov. v Bradford City
Wrexham v Walsall

Coca-Cola League Two
Boston Utd. v Wycombe Wand.
Darlington v Bury
Grimsby Town v Bristol Rov.
Kidderminster Harr. v Scunthorpe Utd.
Leyton Orient v Shrewsbury Town
Mansfield Town v Notts Co.
Oxford Utd. v Lincoln City
Rochdale v Cheltenham Town

Rushden & D'monds v Chester City
Southend Utd. v Swansea City
Yeovil v Macclesfield Town

Sunday, 17 October
Barclays Premiership
Charlton Athletic v Newcastle Utd.

Coca-Cola League Championship
Gillingham v Sheffield Utd.

Coca-Cola League One
Sheffield Wed. v Barnsley

Monday, 18 October
Barclays Premiership
Portsmouth v Tottenham

Tuesday, 19 October
Coca-Cola League Championship
Brighton & H.A. v Cardiff City
Burnley v Coventry City
Leicester City v Ipswich Town
Millwall v Gillingham
Preston N.E. v Q.P.R.
Reading v Leeds Utd.
Rotherham Utd. v Plymouth Argyle
Sheffield Utd. v Nott'm. Forest
Watford v Sunderland
West Ham Utd. v Stoke City
Wigan Athletic v Crewe Alexandra
Wolves v Derby Co.

Coca-Cola League One
Bradford City v Blackpool
Brentford v Hartlepool Utd.
Colchester Utd. v Wrexham
Huddersfield Town v Tranmere Rov.
Oldham Athletic v Bristol City
Peterborough Utd. v Sheffield Wed.
Port Vale v Swindon Town
Torquay Utd. v Bournemouth
Walsall v Luton Town

Coca-Cola League Two
Bristol Rov. v Yeovil
Bury v Boston Utd.
Cheltenham Town v Mansfield Town
Chester City v Kidderminster Harr.
Lincoln City v Rochdale
Macclesfield Town v Cambridge Utd.
Northampton Town v Oxford Utd.
Notts Co. v Darlington
Scunthorpe Utd. v Southend Utd.
Shrewsbury Town v Grimsby Town

Swansea City v Leyton Orient
Wycombe Wand. v Rushden & D'monds

Wednesday, 20 October
Coca-Cola League One
Barnsley v Doncaster Rov.
Chesterfield v Stockport Co.
Hull City v Milton Keynes Dons

Friday, 22 October
Coca-Cola League One
Burnley v Derby Co.

Saturday, 23 October
Barclays Premiership
Aston Villa v Fulham
Chelsea v Blackburn Rov.
Crystal Palace v W.B.A.
Liverpool v Charlton Athletic
Middlesbrough v Portsmouth
Newcastle Utd. v Manchester City
Norwich City v Everton
Tottenham v Bolton Wand.

Coca-Cola League Championship
Brighton & H.A. v Leeds Utd.
Leicester City v Stoke City
Millwall v Cardiff City
Preston N.E. v Nott'm. Forest
Reading v Crewe Alexandra
Rotherham Utd. v Sunderland
Sheffield Utd. v Plymouth Argyle
Watford v Ipswich Town
West Ham Utd. v Gillingham
Wigan Athletic v Coventry City
Wolves v Q.P.R.

Coca-Cola League One
Barnsley v Swindon Town
Bradford City v Sheffield Wed.
Brentford v Blackpool
Chesterfield v Doncaster Rov.
Colchester Utd. v Tranmere Rov.
Huddersfield Town v Milton Keynes Dons
Hull City v Luton Town
Oldham Athletic v Bournemouth
Peterborough Utd. v Hartlepool Utd.
Port Vale v Stockport Co.
Torquay Utd. v Wrexham
Walsall v Bristol City

Coca-Cola League Two
Bristol Rov. v Kidderminster Harr.
Bury v Rushden & D'monds
Cheltenham Town v Cambridge Utd.
Chester City v Grimsby Town

Lincoln City v Leyton Orient
Macclesfield Town v Oxford Utd.
Northampton Town v Rochdale
Notts Co. v Boston Utd.
Scunthorpe Utd. v Yeovil
Shrewsbury Town v Southend Utd.
Swansea City v Darlington
Wycombe Wand. v Mansfield Town

Sunday, 24 October
Barclays Premiership
Manchester Utd. v Arsenal
Southampton v Birmingham City

Friday, 29 October
Coca-Cola League Championship
Crewe Alexandra v Sheffield Utd.

Saturday, 30 October
Barclays Premiership
Arsenal v Southampton
Birmingham City v Crystal Palace
Blackburn Rov. v Liverpool
Charlton Athletic v Middlesbrough
Everton v Aston Villa
Fulham v Tottenham
Portsmouth v Manchester Utd.
W.B.A. v Chelsea

Coca-Cola League Championship
Cardiff City v Leicester City
Coventry City v Reading
Derby Co. v Rotherham Utd.
Gillingham v Wolves
Ipswich Town v Preston N.E.
Nott'm. Forest v Watford
Plymouth Argyle v West Ham Utd.
Q.P.R. v Burnley
Stoke City v Millwall
Sunderland v Brighton & H.A.

Coca-Cola League One
Blackpool v Huddersfield Town
Bournemouth v Barnsley
Bristol City v Colchester Utd.
Doncaster Rov. v Peterborough Utd.
Hartlepool Utd. v Port Vale
Luton Town v Bradford City
Milton Keynes Dons v Walsall
Sheffield Wed. v Chesterfield
Stockport Co. v Oldham Athletic
Swindon Town v Torquay Utd.
Tranmere Rov. v Brentford
Wrexham v Hull City

Coca-Cola League Two
Boston Utd. v Bristol Rov.
Cambridge Utd. v Lincoln City
Darlington v Wycombe Wand.
Grimsby Town v Swansea City
Kidderminster Harr. v Shrewsbury Town
Leyton Orient v Scunthorpe Utd.
Mansfield Town v Bury
Oxford Utd. v Cheltenham Town
Rochdale v Macclesfield Town
Rushden & D'monds v Notts Co.
Southend Utd. v Northampton Town
Yeovil v Chester City

Sunday, 31 October
Barclays Premiership
Bolton Wand. v Newcastle Utd.

Coca-Cola League Championship
Leeds Utd. v Wigan Athletic

Monday, 1 November
Barclays Premiership
Manchester City v Norwich City

Tuesday, 2 November
Coca-Cola League Championship
Cardiff City v West Ham Utd.
Crewe Alexandra v Leicester City
Gillingham v Watford
Ipswich Town v Sheffield Utd.
Leeds Utd. v Burnley
Plymouth Argyle v Reading
Q.P.R. v Millwall
Stoke City v Wigan Athletic
Sunderland v Wolves

Wednesday, 3 November
Coca-Cola League Championship
Coventry City v Preston N.E.
Derby Co. v Brighton & H.A.
Nott'm. Forest v Rotherham Utd.

Friday, 5 November
Coca-Cola League Championship
Millwall v Sunderland

Saturday, 6 November
Barclays Premiership
Aston Villa v Portsmouth
Chelsea v Everton
Crystal Palace v Arsenal
Liverpool v Birmingham City
Newcastle Utd. v Fulham
Norwich City v Blackburn Rov.

Southampton v W.B.A.
Tottenham v Charlton Athletic

Coca-Cola League Championship
Brighton & H.A. v Crewe Alexandra
Burnley v Ipswich Town
Leicester City v Coventry City
Preston N.E. v Leeds Utd.
Reading v Stoke City
Rotherham Utd. v Cardiff City
Sheffield Utd. v Gillingham
Watford v Derby Co.
West Ham Utd. v Q.P.R.
Wigan Athletic v Plymouth Argyle
Wolves v Nott'm. Forest

Coca-Cola League One
Barnsley v Port Vale
Bradford City v Colchester Utd.
Bristol City v Milton Keynes Dons
Chesterfield v Blackpool
Hartlepool Utd. v Doncaster Rov.
Hull City v Walsall
Luton Town v Wrexham
Peterborough Utd. v Bournemouth
Stockport Co. v Sheffield Wed.
Torquay Utd. v Oldham Athletic
Tranmere Rov. v Swindon Town

Coca-Cola League Two
Cheltenham Town v Bury
Chester City v Leyton Orient
Kidderminster Harr. v Boston Utd.
Lincoln City v Northampton Town
Mansfield Town v Macclesfield Town
Notts Co. v Shrewsbury Town
Rochdale v Cambridge Utd.
Rushden & D'monds v Darlington
Scunthorpe Utd. v Grimsby Town
Southend Utd. v Oxford Utd.
Swansea City v Bristol Rov.
Wycombe Wand. v Yeovil

Sunday, 7 November
Barclays Premiership
Manchester Utd. v Manchester City
Middlesbrough v Bolton Wand.

Coca-Cola League One
Huddersfield Town v Brentford

Saturday, 13 November
Barclays Premiership
Birmingham City v Everton
Bolton Wand. v Aston Villa
Charlton Athletic v Norwich City
Fulham v Chelsea

Liverpool v Crystal Palace
Manchester City v Blackburn Rov.
Southampton v Portsmouth
Tottenham v Arsenal

Coca-Cola League Championship
Burnley v Nott'm. Forest
Coventry City v Plymouth Argyle
Gillingham v Derby Co.
Ipswich Town v Leeds Utd.
Leicester City v Sunderland
Preston N.E. v Millwall
Q.P.R. v Wigan Athletic
Reading v Cardiff City
Rotherham Utd. v Wolves
Sheffield Utd. v Watford
Stoke City v Crewe Alexandra
West Ham Utd. v Brighton & H.A.

Sunday, 14 November
Barclays Premiership
Newcastle Utd. v Manchester Utd.
W.B.A. v Middlesbrough

Friday, 19 November
Coca-Cola League Two
Northampton Town v Chester City

Saturday, 20 November
Barclays Premiership
Arsenal v W.B.A.
Chelsea v Bolton Wand.
Crystal Palace v Newcastle Utd.
Everton v Fulham
Manchester Utd. v Charlton Athletic
Middlesbrough v Liverpool
Norwich City v Southampton
Portsmouth v Manchester City

Coca-Cola League Championship
Brighton & H.A. v Burnley
Cardiff City v Preston N.E.
Crewe Alexandra v Gillingham
Derby Co. v Sheffield Utd.
Leeds Utd. v Q.P.R.
Nott'm. Forest v Reading
Plymouth Argyle v Stoke City
Watford v Rotherham Utd.
Wigan Athletic v Leicester City
Wolves v Coventry City

Coca-Cola League One
Blackpool v Tranmere Rov.
Bournemouth v Chesterfield
Brentford v Bradford City
Colchester Utd. v Huddersfield Town

Doncaster Rov. v Stockport Co.
Milton Keynes Dons v Luton Town
Oldham Athletic v Barnsley
Port Vale v Torquay Utd.
Sheffield Wed. v Hartlepool Utd.
Swindon Town v Hull City
Walsall v Peterborough Utd.
Wrexham v Bristol City

Coca-Cola League Two
Boston Utd. v Mansfield Town
Bristol Rov. v Scunthorpe Utd.
Bury v Notts Co.
Cambridge Utd. v Rushden & D'monds
Darlington v Lincoln City
Grimsby Town v Kidderminster Harr.
Leyton Orient v Wycombe Wand.
Macclesfield Town v Cheltenham Town
Oxford Utd. v Rochdale
Shrewsbury Town v Swansea City
Yeovil v Southend Utd.

Sunday, 21 November
Barclays Premiership
Blackburn Rov. v Birmingham City

Coca-Cola League Championship
Millwall v West Ham Utd.
Sunderland v Ipswich Town

Monday, 22 November
Barclays Premiership
Aston Villa v Tottenham

Friday, 26 November
Coca-Cola League Two
Cheltenham Town v Darlington
Southend Utd. v Grimsby Town

Saturday, 27 November
Barclays Premiership
Birmingham City v Norwich City
Bolton Wand. v Portsmouth
Charlton Athletic v Chelsea
Fulham v Blackburn Rov.
Manchester City v Aston Villa
Southampton v Crystal Palace
Tottenham v Middlesbrough
W.B.A. v Manchester Utd.

Coca-Cola League Championship
Burnley v Millwall
Coventry City v Crewe Alexandra
Gillingham v Nott'm. Forest
Ipswich Town v Brighton & H.A.
Leicester City v Plymouth Argyle

Preston N.E. v Derby Co.
Q.P.R. v Cardiff City
Reading v Wigan Athletic
Rotherham Utd. v Leeds Utd.
Sheffield Utd. v Wolves
Stoke City v Sunderland
West Ham Utd. v Watford

Coca-Cola League One
Barnsley v Blackpool
Bradford City v Oldham Athletic
Bristol City v Sheffield Wed.
Chesterfield v Swindon Town
Hartlepool Utd. v Bournemouth
Huddersfield Town v Wrexham
Hull City v Brentford
Luton Town v Doncaster Rov.
Peterborough Utd. v Port Vale
Stockport Co. v Walsall
Torquay Utd. v Colchester Utd.
Tranmere Rov. v Milton Keynes Dons

Coca-Cola League Two
Chester City v Oxford Utd.
Kidderminster Harr. v Northampton Town
Lincoln City v Yeovil
Mansfield Town v Leyton Orient
Notts Co. v Cambridge Utd.
Rochdale v Boston Utd.
Rushden & D'monds v Macclesfield Town
Scunthorpe Utd. v Shrewsbury Town
Swansea City v Bury
Wycombe Wand. v Bristol Rov.

Sunday, 28 November
Barclays Premiership
Liverpool v Arsenal
Newcastle Utd. v Everton

Saturday, 4 December
Barclays Premiership
Arsenal v Birmingham City
Aston Villa v Liverpool
Blackburn Rov. v Tottenham
Chelsea v Newcastle Utd.
Everton v Bolton Wand.
Manchester Utd. v Southampton
Norwich City v Fulham
Portsmouth v W.B.A.

Coca-Cola League Championship
Brighton & H.A. v Rotherham Utd.
Cardiff City v Gillingham
Crewe Alexandra v Ipswich Town
Derby Co. v Coventry City
Leeds Utd. v Leicester City
Millwall v Sheffield Utd.

Nott'm. Forest v Q.P.R.
Plymouth Argyle v Burnley
Sunderland v West Ham Utd.
Watford v Stoke City
Wigan Athletic v Preston N.E.
Wolves v Reading

Sunday, 5 December
Barclays Premiership
Crystal Palace v Charlton Athletic

Monday, 6 December
Barclays Premiership
Middlesbrough v Manchester City

Tuesday, 7 December
Coca-Cola League One
Blackpool v Torquay Utd.
Bournemouth v Bradford City
Brentford v Luton Town
Colchester Utd. v Barnsley
Doncaster Rov. v Bristol City
Milton Keynes Dons v Peterborough Utd.
Oldham Athletic v Chesterfield
Port Vale v Tranmere Rov.
Walsall v Hartlepool Utd.
Wrexham v Stockport Co.

Coca-Cola League Two
Bristol Rov. v Chester City
Bury v Wycombe Wand.
Cambridge Utd. v Scunthorpe Utd.
Darlington v Mansfield Town
Grimsby Town v Notts Co.
Leyton Orient v Southend Utd.
Macclesfield Town v Lincoln City
Northampton Town v Cheltenham Town
Shrewsbury Town v Rochdale
Yeovil v Kidderminster Harr.

Wednesday, 8 December
Coca-Cola League One
Sheffield Wed. v Hull City
Swindon Town v Huddersfield Town

Coca-Cola League Two
Boston Utd. v Rushden & D'monds
Oxford Utd. v Swansea City

Friday, 10 December
Coca-Cola League One
Tranmere Rov. v Bournemouth

Saturday, 11 December
Barclays Premiership
Crystal Palace v Blackburn Rov.
Everton v Liverpool
Manchester City v Tottenham
Newcastle Utd. v Portsmouth
Norwich City v Bolton Wand.
Southampton v Middlesbrough
W.B.A. v Charlton Athletic

Coca-Cola League Championship
Burnley v Preston N.E.
Cardiff City v Sunderland
Crewe Alexandra v Plymouth Argyle
Derby Co. v Nott'm. Forest
Leicester City v Reading
Millwall v Brighton & H.A.
Q.P.R. v Ipswich Town
Rotherham Utd. v Sheffield Utd.
Stoke City v Coventry City
Watford v Wolves
West Ham Utd. v Leeds Utd.
Wigan Athletic v Gillingham

Coca-Cola League One
Blackpool v Bristol City
Bradford City v Walsall
Colchester Utd. v Hull City
Hartlepool Utd. v Stockport Co.
Luton Town v Port Vale
Milton Keynes Dons v Wrexham
Oldham Athletic v Huddersfield Town
Peterborough Utd. v Chesterfield
Sheffield Wed. v Brentford
Swindon Town v Doncaster Rov.
Torquay Utd. v Barnsley

Coca-Cola League Two
Bristol Rov. v Macclesfield Town
Bury v Southend Utd.
Chester City v Shrewsbury Town
Darlington v Leyton Orient
Kidderminster Harr. v Rochdale
Lincoln City v Cheltenham Town
Mansfield Town v Rushden & D'monds
Northampton Town v Boston Utd.
Notts Co. v Wycombe Wand.
Oxford Utd. v Cambridge Utd.
Scunthorpe Utd. v Swansea City
Yeovil v Grimsby Town

Sunday, 12 December
Barclays Premiership
Arsenal v Chelsea
Aston Villa v Birmingham City

Monday, 13 December
Barclays Premiership
Fulham v Manchester Utd.

Friday, 17 December
Coca-Cola League Championship
Brighton & H.A. v Stoke City
Nott'm. Forest v Leicester City

Saturday, 18 December
Barclays Premiership
Birmingham City v W.B.A.
Blackburn Rov. v Everton
Bolton Wand. v Manchester City
Chelsea v Norwich City
Liverpool v Newcastle Utd.
Manchester Utd. v Crystal Palace
Middlesbrough v Aston Villa
Tottenham v Southampton

Coca-Cola League Championship
Coventry City v Watford
Gillingham v Rotherham Utd.
Ipswich Town v Wigan Athletic
Plymouth Argyle v Derby Co.
Preston N.E. v West Ham Utd.
Sheffield Utd. v Cardiff City
Sunderland v Burnley
Wolves v Crewe Alexandra

Coca-Cola League One
Barnsley v Peterborough Utd.
Bournemouth v Swindon Town
Brentford v Colchester Utd.
Bristol City v Luton Town
Chesterfield v Torquay Utd.
Doncaster Rov. v Sheffield Wed.
Huddersfield Town v Bradford City
Hull City v Tranmere Rov.
Port Vale v Oldham Athletic
Stockport Co. v Milton Keynes Dons
Walsall v Blackpool
Wrexham v Hartlepool Utd.

Coca-Cola League Two
Boston Utd. v Darlington
Cambridge Utd. v Bury
Cheltenham Town v Kidderminster Harr.
Grimsby Town v Oxford Utd.
Leyton Orient v Yeovil
Macclesfield Town v Northampton Town
Rochdale v Bristol Rov.
Rushden & D'monds v Scunthorpe Utd.
Shrewsbury Town v Mansfield Town
Southend Utd. v Chester City
Swansea City v Notts Co.
Wycombe Wand. v Lincoln City

Sunday, 19 December
Barclays Premiership
Portsmouth v Arsenal

Coca-Cola League Championship
Leeds Utd. v Millwall
Reading v Q.P.R.

Monday, 20 December
Barclays Premiership
Charlton Athletic v Fulham

Sunday, 26 December
Barclays Premiership
Arsenal v Fulham
Birmingham City v Middlesbrough
Blackburn Rov. v Newcastle Utd.
Chelsea v Aston Villa
Crystal Palace v Portsmouth
Everton v Manchester City
Manchester Utd. v Bolton Wand.
Norwich City v Tottenham
Southampton v Charlton Athletic
W.B.A. v Liverpool

Coca-Cola League Championship
Brighton & H.A. v Gillingham
Cardiff City v Wolves
Coventry City v Sheffield Utd.
Crewe Alexandra v Burnley
Leicester City v Rotherham Utd.
Millwall v Ipswich Town
Plymouth Argyle v Q.P.R.
Reading v Watford
Stoke City v Preston N.E.
Sunderland v Leeds Utd.
West Ham Utd. v Nott'm. Forest
Wigan Athletic v Derby Co.

Coca-Cola League One
Blackpool v Hull City
Bradford City v Wrexham
Brentford v Torquay Utd.
Chesterfield v Luton Town
Colchester Utd. v Bournemouth
Doncaster Rov. v Milton Keynes Dons
Hartlepool Utd. v Oldham Athletic
Huddersfield Town v Port Vale
Peterborough Utd. v Swindon Town
Sheffield Wed. v Walsall
Stockport Co. v Bristol City
Tranmere Rov. v Barnsley

Coca-Cola League Two
Boston Utd. v Lincoln City
Bristol Rov. v Leyton Orient
Bury v Shrewsbury Town

Chester City v Scunthorpe Utd.
Darlington v Rochdale
Grimsby Town v Macclesfield Town
Kidderminster Harr. v Swansea City
Mansfield Town v Cambridge Utd.
Notts Co. v Northampton Town
Rushden & D'monds v Oxford Utd.
Wycombe Wand. v Southend Utd.
Yeovil v Cheltenham Town

Tuesday, 28 December
Barclays Premiership
Aston Villa v Manchester Utd.
Bolton Wand. v Blackburn Rov.
Charlton Athletic v Everton
Fulham v Birmingham City
Liverpool v Southampton
Manchester City v W.B.A.
Middlesbrough v Norwich City
Portsmouth v Chelsea
Tottenham v Crystal Palace

Coca-Cola League Championship
Burnley v Wigan Athletic
Derby Co. v Millwall
Gillingham v Coventry City
Ipswich Town v Stoke City
Leeds Utd. v Plymouth Argyle
Nott'm. Forest v Sunderland
Preston N.E. v Reading
Q.P.R. v Crewe Alexandra
Rotherham Utd. v West Ham Utd.
Sheffield Utd. v Leicester City
Watford v Cardiff City
Wolves v Brighton & H.A.

Coca-Cola League One
Barnsley v Stockport Co.
Bournemouth v Huddersfield Town
Bristol City v Hartlepool Utd.
Luton Town v Colchester Utd.
Milton Keynes Dons v Blackpool
Oldham Athletic v Peterborough Utd.
Port Vale v Sheffield Wed.
Swindon Town v Brentford
Torquay Utd. v Bradford City
Walsall v Tranmere Rov.
Wrexham v Chesterfield

Coca-Cola League Two
Cambridge Utd. v Yeovil
Cheltenham Town v Bristol Rov.
Leyton Orient v Rushden & D'monds
Lincoln City v Grimsby Town
Macclesfield Town v Wycombe Wand.
Northampton Town v Bury
Oxford Utd. v Kidderminster Harr.

Rochdale v Chester City
Scunthorpe Utd. v Notts Co.
Shrewsbury Town v Darlington
Southend Utd. v Mansfield Town
Swansea City v Boston Utd.

Wednesday, 29 December
Barclays Premiership
Newcastle Utd. v Arsenal

Coca-Cola League One
Hull City v Doncaster Rov.

Saturday, 1 January
Barclays Premiership
Aston Villa v Blackburn Rov.
Bolton Wand. v W.B.A.
Charlton Athletic v Arsenal
Fulham v Crystal Palace
Liverpool v Chelsea
Manchester City v Southampton
Middlesbrough v Manchester Utd.
Newcastle Utd. v Birmingham City
Portsmouth v Norwich City
Tottenham v Everton

Coca-Cola League Championship
Burnley v Leicester City
Derby Co. v Cardiff City
Gillingham v Reading
Ipswich Town v West Ham Utd.
Leeds Utd. v Crewe Alexandra
Nott'm. Forest v Stoke City
Preston N.E. v Sunderland
Q.P.R. v Brighton & H.A.
Rotherham Utd. v Coventry City
Sheffield Utd. v Wigan Athletic
Watford v Millwall
Wolves v Plymouth Argyle

Coca-Cola League One
Barnsley v Hartlepool Utd.
Bournemouth v Brentford
Bristol City v Peterborough Utd.
Hull City v Huddersfield Town
Luton Town v Sheffield Wed.
Milton Keynes Dons v Chesterfield
Oldham Athletic v Tranmere Rov.
Port Vale v Bradford City
Swindon Town v Colchester Utd.
Torquay Utd. v Stockport Co.
Walsall v Doncaster Rov.
Wrexham v Blackpool

Coca-Cola League Two
Cambridge Utd. v Boston Utd.
Cheltenham Town v Notts Co.

Leyton Orient v Kidderminster Harr.
Lincoln City v Bury
Macclesfield Town v Chester City
Northampton Town v Mansfield Town
Oxford Utd. v Wycombe Wand.
Rochdale v Grimsby Town
Scunthorpe Utd. v Darlington
Shrewsbury Town v Bristol Rov.
Southend Utd. v Rushden & D'monds
Swansea City v Yeovil

Monday, 3 January
Barclays Premiership
Birmingham City v Bolton Wand.
Blackburn Rov. v Charlton Athletic
Chelsea v Middlesbrough
Crystal Palace v Aston Villa
Everton v Portsmouth
Manchester Utd. v Tottenham
Norwich City v Liverpool
Southampton v Fulham
W.B.A. v Newcastle Utd.

Coca-Cola League Championship
Brighton & H.A. v Watford
Cardiff City v Nott'm. Forest
Coventry City v Leeds Utd.
Crewe Alexandra v Preston N.E.
Leicester City v Q.P.R.
Millwall v Rotherham Utd.
Plymouth Argyle v Ipswich Town
Reading v Derby Co.
Stoke City v Burnley
Sunderland v Gillingham
West Ham Utd. v Sheffield Utd.

Coca-Cola League One
Blackpool v Port Vale
Bradford City v Swindon Town
Brentford v Walsall
Chesterfield v Barnsley
Colchester Utd. v Oldham Athletic
Doncaster Rov. v Bournemouth
Hartlepool Utd. v Milton Keynes Dons
Huddersfield Town v Bristol City
Peterborough Utd. v Luton Town
Sheffield Wed. v Wrexham
Stockport Co. v Hull City
Tranmere Rov. v Torquay Utd.

Coca-Cola League Two
Boston Utd. v Leyton Orient
Bristol Rov. v Northampton Town
Bury v Oxford Utd.
Chester City v Lincoln City
Darlington v Macclesfield Town
Grimsby Town v Cambridge Utd.

Kidderminster Harr. v Southend Utd.
Mansfield Town v Scunthorpe Utd.
Notts Co. v Rochdale
Rushden & D'monds v Swansea City
Wycombe Wand. v Cheltenham Town
Yeovil v Shrewsbury Town

Tuesday, 4 January
Barclays Premiership
Arsenal v Manchester City

Coca-Cola League Championship
Wigan Athletic v Wolves

Saturday, 8 January
Coca-Cola League One
Blackpool v Oldham Athletic
Bradford City v Milton Keynes Dons
Brentford v Barnsley
Chesterfield v Hull City
Colchester Utd. v Walsall
Doncaster Rov. v Port Vale
Hartlepool Utd. v Luton Town
Huddersfield Town v Torquay Utd.
Peterborough Utd. v Wrexham
Sheffield Wed. v Swindon Town
Stockport Co. v Bournemouth
Tranmere Rov. v Bristol City

Coca-Cola League Two
Boston Utd. v Southend Utd.
Bristol Rov. v Cambridge Utd.
Bury v Leyton Orient
Chester City v Cheltenham Town
Darlington v Oxford Utd.
Grimsby Town v Northampton Town
Kidderminster Harr. v Lincoln City
Mansfield Town v Swansea City
Notts Co. v Macclesfield Town
Rushden & D'monds v Shrewsbury Town
Wycombe Wand. v Scunthorpe Utd.
Yeovil v Rochdale

Saturday, 15 January
Barclays Premiership
Aston Villa v Norwich City
Bolton Wand. v Arsenal
Charlton Athletic v Birmingham City
Fulham v W.B.A.
Liverpool v Manchester Utd.
Manchester City v Crystal Palace
Middlesbrough v Everton
Newcastle Utd. v Southampton
Portsmouth v Blackburn Rov.
Tottenham v Chelsea

Coca-Cola League Championship
Burnley v Reading
Derby Co. v Sunderland
Gillingham v Plymouth Argyle
Ipswich Town v Coventry City
Leeds Utd. v Cardiff City
Nott'm. Forest v Millwall
Preston N.E. v Leicester City
Q.P.R. v Stoke City
Rotherham Utd. v Wigan Athletic
Sheffield Utd. v Brighton & H.A.
Watford v Crewe Alexandra
Wolves v West Ham Utd.

Coca-Cola League One
Barnsley v Huddersfield Town
Bournemouth v Sheffield Wed.
Bristol City v Bradford City
Hull City v Peterborough Utd.
Luton Town v Stockport Co.
Milton Keynes Dons v Colchester Utd.
Oldham Athletic v Doncaster Rov.
Port Vale v Brentford
Swindon Town v Blackpool
Torquay Utd. v Hartlepool Utd.
Walsall v Chesterfield
Wrexham v Tranmere Rov.

Coca-Cola League Two
Cambridge Utd. v Chester City
Cheltenham Town v Rushden & D'monds
Leyton Orient v Grimsby Town
Lincoln City v Bristol Rov.
Macclesfield Town v Kidderminster Harr.
Northampton Town v Darlington
Oxford Utd. v Yeovil
Rochdale v Mansfield Town
Scunthorpe Utd. v Bury
Shrewsbury Town v Boston Utd.
Southend Utd. v Notts Co.
Swansea City v Wycombe Wand.

Saturday, 22 January
Barclays Premiership
Arsenal v Newcastle Utd.
Birmingham City v Fulham
Blackburn Rov. v Bolton Wand.
Chelsea v Portsmouth
Crystal Palace v Tottenham
Everton v Charlton Athletic
Manchester Utd. v Aston Villa
Norwich City v Middlesbrough
Southampton v Liverpool
W.B.A. v Manchester City

Coca-Cola League Championship
Brighton & H.A. v Nott'm. Forest
Cardiff City v Burnley

Coventry City v Q.P.R.
Crewe Alexandra v Rotherham Utd.
Leicester City v Gillingham
Millwall v Wolves
Plymouth Argyle v Preston N.E.
Reading v Ipswich Town
Stoke City v Leeds Utd.
Sunderland v Sheffield Utd.
West Ham Utd. v Derby Co.
Wigan Athletic v Watford

Coca-Cola League One
Blackpool v Milton Keynes Dons
Bradford City v Torquay Utd.
Brentford v Swindon Town
Chesterfield v Wrexham
Colchester Utd. v Luton Town
Doncaster Rov. v Hull City
Hartlepool Utd. v Bristol City
Huddersfield Town v Bournemouth
Peterborough Utd. v Oldham Athletic
Sheffield Wed. v Port Vale
Stockport Co. v Barnsley
Tranmere Rov. v Walsall

Coca-Cola League Two
Boston Utd. v Swansea City
Bristol Rov. v Cheltenham Town
Bury v Northampton Town
Chester City v Rochdale
Darlington v Shrewsbury Town
Grimsby Town v Lincoln City
Kidderminster Harr. v Oxford Utd.
Mansfield Town v Southend Utd.
Notts Co. v Scunthorpe Utd.
Rushden & D'monds v Leyton Orient
Wycombe Wand. v Macclesfield Town
Yeovil v Cambridge Utd.

Friday, 28 January
Coca-Cola League Two
Cheltenham Town v Grimsby Town

Saturday, 29 January
Coca-Cola League One
Barnsley v Bradford City
Bournemouth v Blackpool
Bristol City v Chesterfield
Hull City v Hartlepool Utd.
Luton Town v Tranmere Rov.
Milton Keynes Dons v Sheffield Wed.
Oldham Athletic v Brentford
Port Vale v Colchester Utd.
Swindon Town v Stockport Co.
Torquay Utd. v Peterborough Utd.
Walsall v Huddersfield Town
Wrexham v Doncaster Rov.

Coca-Cola League Two
Cambridge Utd. v Kidderminster Harr.
Leyton Orient v Notts Co.
Lincoln City v Mansfield Town
Macclesfield Town v Bury
Northampton Town v Yeovil
Oxford Utd. v Bristol Rov.
Rochdale v Rushden & D'monds
Scunthorpe Utd. v Boston Utd.
Shrewsbury Town v Wycombe Wand.
Southend Utd. v Darlington
Swansea City v Chester City

Tuesday, 1 February
Barclays Premiership
Arsenal v Manchester Utd.
Birmingham City v Southampton
Bolton Wand. v Tottenham
Charlton Athletic v Liverpool
Portsmouth v Middlesbrough
W.B.A. v Crystal Palace

Wednesday, 2 February
Barclays Premiership
Blackburn Rov. v Chelsea
Everton v Norwich City
Fulham v Aston Villa
Manchester City v Newcastle Utd.

Friday, 4 February
Coca-Cola League Two
Northampton Town v Cambridge Utd.
Swansea City v Southend Utd.

Saturday, 5 February
Barclays Premiership
Aston Villa v Arsenal
Chelsea v Manchester City
Crystal Palace v Bolton Wand.
Liverpool v Fulham
Manchester Utd. v Birmingham City
Middlesbrough v Blackburn Rov.
Newcastle Utd. v Charlton Athletic
Norwich City v W.B.A.
Southampton v Everton
Tottenham v Portsmouth

Coca-Cola League Championship
Brighton & H.A. v Derby Co.
Burnley v Leeds Utd.
Leicester City v Crewe Alexandra
Millwall v Q.P.R.
Preston N.E. v Coventry City
Reading v Plymouth Argyle
Rotherham Utd. v Nott'm. Forest
Sheffield Utd. v Ipswich Town

Watford v Gillingham
West Ham Utd. v Cardiff City
Wigan Athletic v Stoke City
Wolves v Sunderland

Coca-Cola League One
Barnsley v Sheffield Wed.
Bradford City v Tranmere Rov.
Brentford v Milton Keynes Dons
Chesterfield v Hartlepool Utd.
Colchester Utd. v Blackpool
Huddersfield Town v Luton Town
Hull City v Bristol City
Oldham Athletic v Swindon Town
Peterborough Utd. v Stockport Co.
Port Vale v Bournemouth
Torquay Utd. v Doncaster Rov.
Walsall v Wrexham

Coca-Cola League Two
Bristol Rov. v Grimsby Town
Bury v Darlington
Cheltenham Town v Rochdale
Chester City v Rushden & D'monds
Lincoln City v Oxford Utd.
Macclesfield Town v Yeovil
Notts Co. v Mansfield Town
Scunthorpe Utd. v Kidderminster Harr.
Shrewsbury Town v Leyton Orient
Wycombe Wand. v Boston Utd.

Friday, 11 February
Coca-Cola League One
Hartlepool Utd. v Peterborough Utd.

Coca-Cola League Two
Southend Utd. v Scunthorpe Utd.

Saturday, 12 February
Barclays Premiership
Arsenal v Crystal Palace
Birmingham City v Liverpool
Blackburn Rov. v Norwich City
Bolton Wand. v Middlesbrough
Charlton Athletic v Tottenham
Everton v Chelsea
Fulham v Newcastle Utd.
Manchester City v Manchester Utd.
Portsmouth v Aston Villa
W.B.A. v Southampton

Coca-Cola League Championship
Cardiff City v Brighton & H.A.
Coventry City v Burnley
Crewe Alexandra v Wigan Athletic
Derby Co. v Wolves
Gillingham v Millwall

Ipswich Town v Leicester City
Leeds Utd. v Reading
Nott'm. Forest v Sheffield Utd.
Plymouth Argyle v Rotherham Utd.
Q.P.R. v Preston N.E.
Stoke City v West Ham Utd.
Sunderland v Watford

Coca-Cola League One
Blackpool v Brentford
Bournemouth v Oldham Athletic
Bristol City v Walsall
Doncaster Rov. v Chesterfield
Luton Town v Hull City
Milton Keynes Dons v Huddersfield Town
Sheffield Wed. v Bradford City
Stockport Co. v Port Vale
Swindon Town v Barnsley
Tranmere Rov. v Colchester Utd.
Wrexham v Torquay Utd.

Coca-Cola League Two
Boston Utd. v Bury
Cambridge Utd. v Macclesfield Town
Darlington v Notts Co.
Grimsby Town v Shrewsbury Town
Kidderminster Harr. v Chester City
Leyton Orient v Swansea City
Mansfield Town v Cheltenham Town
Oxford Utd. v Northampton Town
Rochdale v Lincoln City
Rushden & D'monds v Wycombe Wand.
Yeovil v Bristol Rov.

Saturday, 19 February
Coca-Cola League Championship
Brighton & H.A. v Sunderland
Burnley v Q.P.R.
Leicester City v Cardiff City
Millwall v Stoke City
Preston N.E. v Ipswich Town
Reading v Coventry City
Rotherham Utd. v Derby Co.
Sheffield Utd. v Crewe Alexandra
Watford v Nott'm. Forest
West Ham Utd. v Plymouth Argyle
Wigan Athletic v Leeds Utd.
Wolves v Gillingham

Coca-Cola League One
Barnsley v Bournemouth
Bradford City v Luton Town
Brentford v Tranmere Rov.
Chesterfield v Sheffield Wed.
Colchester Utd. v Bristol City
Huddersfield Town v Blackpool
Hull City v Wrexham

Oldham Athletic v Stockport Co.
Peterborough Utd. v Doncaster Rov.
Port Vale v Hartlepool Utd.
Torquay Utd. v Swindon Town
Walsall v Milton Keynes Dons

Coca-Cola League Two
Bristol Rov. v Boston Utd.
Bury v Mansfield Town
Cheltenham Town v Oxford Utd.
Chester City v Yeovil
Lincoln City v Cambridge Utd.
Macclesfield Town v Rochdale
Northampton Town v Southend Utd.
Notts Co. v Rushden & D'monds
Scunthorpe Utd. v Leyton Orient
Shrewsbury Town v Kidderminster Harr.
Swansea City v Grimsby Town
Wycombe Wand. v Darlington

Tuesday, 22 February
Coca-Cola League Championship
Cardiff City v Millwall
Crewe Alexandra v Reading
Gillingham v West Ham Utd.
Ipswich Town v Watford
Leeds Utd. v Brighton & H.A.
Plymouth Argyle v Sheffield Utd.
Q.P.R. v Wolves
Stoke City v Leicester City
Sunderland v Rotherham Utd.

Coca-Cola League One
Blackpool v Bradford City
Bournemouth v Torquay Utd.
Bristol City v Oldham Athletic
Doncaster Rov. v Barnsley
Hartlepool Utd. v Brentford
Luton Town v Walsall
Milton Keynes Dons v Hull City
Stockport Co. v Chesterfield
Tranmere Rov. v Huddersfield Town
Wrexham v Colchester Utd.

Coca-Cola League Two
Cambridge Utd. v Cheltenham Town
Darlington v Swansea City
Grimsby Town v Chester City
Kidderminster Harr. v Bristol Rov.
Leyton Orient v Lincoln City
Mansfield Town v Wycombe Wand.
Rochdale v Northampton Town
Rushden & D'monds v Bury
Southend Utd. v Shrewsbury Town
Yeovil v Scunthorpe Utd.

Wednesday, 23 February
Coca-Cola League Championship
Coventry City v Wigan Athletic
Derby Co. v Burnley
Nott'm. Forest v Preston N.E.

Coca-Cola League One
Sheffield Wed. v Peterborough Utd.
Swindon Town v Port Vale

Coca-Cola League Two
Boston Utd. v Notts Co.
Oxford Utd. v Macclesfield Town

Saturday, 26 February
Barclays Premiership
Aston Villa v Everton
Chelsea v W.B.A.
Crystal Palace v Birmingham City
Liverpool v Blackburn Rov.
Manchester Utd. v Portsmouth
Middlesbrough v Charlton Athletic
Newcastle Utd. v Bolton Wand.
Norwich City v Manchester City
Southampton v Arsenal
Tottenham v Fulham

Coca-Cola League Championship
Brighton & H.A. v Millwall
Coventry City v Stoke City
Gillingham v Wigan Athletic
Ipswich Town v Q.P.R.
Leeds Utd. v West Ham Utd.
Nott'm. Forest v Derby Co.
Plymouth Argyle v Crewe Alexandra
Preston N.E. v Burnley
Reading v Leicester City
Sheffield Utd. v Rotherham Utd.
Sunderland v Cardiff City
Wolves v Watford

Coca-Cola League One
Barnsley v Torquay Utd.
Bournemouth v Tranmere Rov.
Brentford v Sheffield Wed.
Bristol City v Blackpool
Chesterfield v Peterborough Utd.
Doncaster Rov. v Swindon Town
Huddersfield Town v Oldham Athletic
Hull City v Colchester Utd.
Port Vale v Luton Town
Stockport Co. v Hartlepool Utd.
Walsall v Bradford City
Wrexham v Milton Keynes Dons

Coca-Cola League Two
Boston Utd. v Northampton Town
Cambridge Utd. v Oxford Utd.
Cheltenham Town v Lincoln City
Grimsby Town v Yeovil
Leyton Orient v Darlington
Macclesfield Town v Bristol Rov.
Rochdale v Kidderminster Harr.
Rushden & D'monds v Mansfield Town
Shrewsbury Town v Chester City
Southend Utd. v Bury
Swansea City v Scunthorpe Utd.
Wycombe Wand. v Notts Co.

Saturday, 5 March
Barclays Premiership
Arsenal v Portsmouth
Aston Villa v Middlesbrough
Crystal Palace v Manchester Utd.
Everton v Blackburn Rov.
Fulham v Charlton Athletic
Manchester City v Bolton Wand.
Newcastle Utd. v Liverpool
Norwich City v Chelsea
Southampton v Tottenham

Coca-Cola League Championship
Burnley v Sunderland
Cardiff City v Sheffield Utd.
Crewe Alexandra v Wolves
Derby Co. v Plymouth Argyle
Leicester City v Nott'm. Forest
Millwall v Leeds Utd.
Q.P.R. v Reading
Rotherham Utd. v Gillingham
Stoke City v Brighton & H.A.
Watford v Coventry City
West Ham Utd. v Preston N.E.
Wigan Athletic v Ipswich Town

Coca-Cola League One
Blackpool v Walsall
Bradford City v Huddersfield Town
Colchester Utd. v Brentford
Hartlepool Utd. v Wrexham
Luton Town v Bristol City
Milton Keynes Dons v Stockport Co.
Oldham Athletic v Port Vale
Peterborough Utd. v Barnsley
Swindon Town v Bournemouth
Torquay Utd. v Chesterfield
Tranmere Rov. v Hull City

Coca-Cola League Two
Bristol Rov. v Rochdale
Bury v Cambridge Utd.
Chester City v Southend Utd.

Darlington v Boston Utd.
Kidderminster Harr. v Cheltenham Town
Lincoln City v Wycombe Wand.
Mansfield Town v Shrewsbury Town
Northampton Town v Macclesfield Town
Notts Co. v Swansea City
Oxford Utd. v Grimsby Town
Scunthorpe Utd. v Rushden & D'monds
Yeovil v Leyton Orient

Sunday, 6 March
Barclays Premiership
W.B.A. v Birmingham City

Coca-Cola League One
Sheffield Wed. v Doncaster Rov.

Saturday, 12 March
Coca-Cola League Championship
Burnley v Rotherham Utd.
Coventry City v Cardiff City
Crewe Alexandra v Sunderland
Ipswich Town v Nott'm. Forest
Leeds Utd. v Gillingham
Leicester City v Derby Co.
Plymouth Argyle v Brighton & H.A.
Preston N.E. v Wolves
Q.P.R. v Watford
Reading v West Ham Utd.
Stoke City v Sheffield Utd.
Wigan Athletic v Millwall

Coca-Cola League One
Bristol City v Barnsley
Chesterfield v Huddersfield Town
Doncaster Rov. v Brentford
Hartlepool Utd. v Tranmere Rov.
Hull City v Torquay Utd.
Luton Town v Swindon Town
Milton Keynes Dons v Port Vale
Peterborough Utd. v Bradford City
Sheffield Wed. v Blackpool
Stockport Co. v Colchester Utd.
Walsall v Bournemouth
Wrexham v Oldham Athletic

Coca-Cola League Two
Boston Utd. v Grimsby Town
Bury v Bristol Rov.
Darlington v Yeovil
Leyton Orient v Cambridge Utd.
Mansfield Town v Oxford Utd.
Notts Co. v Kidderminster Harr.
Rushden & D'monds v Northampton Town
Scunthorpe Utd. v Cheltenham Town
Shrewsbury Town v Macclesfield Town
Southend Utd. v Lincoln City

Swansea City v Rochdale
Wycombe Wand. v Chester City

Tuesday, 15 March
Coca-Cola League Championship
Brighton & H.A. v Wigan Athletic
Cardiff City v Ipswich Town
Gillingham v Stoke City
Millwall v Coventry City
Rotherham Utd. v Reading
Sheffield Utd. v Preston N.E.
Sunderland v Plymouth Argyle
Watford v Leicester City
West Ham Utd. v Crewe Alexandra
Wolves v Burnley

Wednesday, 16 March
Coca-Cola League Championship
Derby Co. v Q.P.R.
Nott'm. Forest v Leeds Utd.

Friday, 18 March
Coca-Cola League One
Tranmere Rov. v Peterborough Utd.

Saturday, 19 March
Barclays Premiership
Birmingham City v Aston Villa
Blackburn Rov. v Arsenal
Bolton Wand. v Norwich City
Charlton Athletic v W.B.A.
Chelsea v Crystal Palace
Liverpool v Everton
Manchester Utd. v Fulham
Middlesbrough v Southampton
Portsmouth v Newcastle Utd.
Tottenham v Manchester City

Coca-Cola League Championship
Brighton & H.A. v Reading
Cardiff City v Crewe Alexandra
Derby Co. v Leeds Utd.
Gillingham v Ipswich Town
Millwall v Plymouth Argyle
Nott'm. Forest v Wigan Athletic
Rotherham Utd. v Q.P.R.
Sheffield Utd. v Burnley
Sunderland v Coventry City
Watford v Preston N.E.
West Ham Utd. v Leicester City
Wolves v Stoke City

Coca-Cola League One
Barnsley v Milton Keynes Dons
Blackpool v Doncaster Rov.
Bournemouth v Hull City

509

Bradford City v Hartlepool Utd.
Brentford v Chesterfield
Colchester Utd. v Sheffield Wed.
Huddersfield Town v Stockport Co.
Oldham Athletic v Luton Town
Port Vale v Walsall
Swindon Town v Wrexham
Torquay Utd. v Bristol City

Coca-Cola League Two
Bristol Rov. v Mansfield Town
Cambridge Utd. v Wycombe Wand.
Cheltenham Town v Southend Utd.
Chester City v Notts Co.
Grimsby Town v Darlington
Kidderminster Harr. v Rushden & D'monds
Lincoln City v Shrewsbury Town
Macclesfield Town v Leyton Orient
Northampton Town v Swansea City
Oxford Utd. v Boston Utd.
Rochdale v Scunthorpe Utd.
Yeovil v Bury

Friday, 25 March
Coca-Cola League Two
Bury v Grimsby Town
Southend Utd. v Rochdale
Swansea City v Macclesfield Town

Saturday, 26 March
Coca-Cola League One
Bristol City v Bournemouth
Chesterfield v Tranmere Rov.
Doncaster Rov. v Bradford City
Hartlepool Utd. v Huddersfield Town
Hull City v Port Vale
Luton Town v Barnsley
Milton Keynes Dons v Swindon Town
Peterborough Utd. v Colchester Utd.
Sheffield Wed. v Torquay Utd.
Stockport Co. v Blackpool
Walsall v Oldham Athletic
Wrexham v Brentford

Coca-Cola League Two
Boston Utd. v Yeovil
Darlington v Kidderminster Harr.
Leyton Orient v Cheltenham Town
Mansfield Town v Chester City
Notts Co. v Bristol Rov.
Rushden & D'monds v Lincoln City
Scunthorpe Utd. v Oxford Utd.
Shrewsbury Town v Cambridge Utd.

Monday, 28 March
Coca-Cola League One
Barnsley v Walsall
Blackpool v Hartlepool Utd.
Bournemouth v Milton Keynes Dons
Bradford City v Stockport Co.
Brentford v Peterborough Utd.
Colchester Utd. v Chesterfield
Oldham Athletic v Hull City
Swindon Town v Bristol City
Torquay Utd. v Luton Town
Tranmere Rov. v Doncaster Rov.

Coca-Cola League Two
Bristol Rov. v Darlington
Cambridge Utd. v Southend Utd.
Cheltenham Town v Swansea City
Chester City v Bury
Grimsby Town v Rushden & D'monds
Kidderminster Harr. v Mansfield Town
Lincoln City v Scunthorpe Utd.
Macclesfield Town v Boston Utd.
Northampton Town v Shrewsbury Town
Oxford Utd. v Leyton Orient
Rochdale v Wycombe Wand.

Tuesday, 29 March
Coca-Cola League One
Huddersfield Town v Sheffield Wed.
Port Vale v Wrexham

Coca-Cola League Two
Yeovil v Notts Co.

Friday, 1 April
Coca-Cola League One
Doncaster Rov. v Colchester Utd.

Coca-Cola League Two
Southend Utd. v Bristol Rov.

Saturday, 2 April
Barclays Premiership
Arsenal v Norwich City
Birmingham City v Tottenham
Charlton Athletic v Manchester City
Crystal Palace v Middlesbrough
Fulham v Portsmouth
Liverpool v Bolton Wand.
Manchester Utd. v Blackburn Rov.
Newcastle Utd. v Aston Villa
Southampton v Chelsea
W.B.A. v Everton

Coca-Cola League Championship
Burnley v Watford
Coventry City v Brighton & H.A.
Crewe Alexandra v Nott'm. Forest
Ipswich Town v Derby Co.
Leeds Utd. v Wolves
Leicester City v Millwall
Plymouth Argyle v Cardiff City
Preston N.E. v Gillingham
Q.P.R. v Sunderland
Reading v Sheffield Utd.
Stoke City v Rotherham Utd.
Wigan Athletic v West Ham Utd.

Coca-Cola League One
Bristol City v Port Vale
Chesterfield v Bradford City
Hartlepool Utd. v Swindon Town
Hull City v Barnsley
Luton Town v Blackpool
Milton Keynes Dons v Oldham Athletic
Peterborough Utd. v Huddersfield Town
Sheffield Wed. v Tranmere Rov.
Stockport Co. v Brentford
Walsall v Torquay Utd.
Wrexham v Bournemouth

Coca-Cola League Two
Boston Utd. v Cheltenham Town
Bury v Rochdale
Darlington v Chester City
Leyton Orient v Northampton Town
Mansfield Town v Grimsby Town
Notts Co. v Lincoln City
Rushden & D'monds v Yeovil
Scunthorpe Utd. v Macclesfield Town
Shrewsbury Town v Oxford Utd.
Swansea City v Cambridge Utd.
Wycombe Wand. v Kidderminster Harr.

Tuesday, 5 April
Coca-Cola League Championship
Burnley v West Ham Utd.
Crewe Alexandra v Derby Co.
Ipswich Town v Rotherham Utd.
Leeds Utd. v Sheffield Utd.
Leicester City v Wolves
Plymouth Argyle v Watford
Preston N.E. v Brighton & H.A.
Q.P.R. v Gillingham
Reading v Millwall
Stoke City v Cardiff City
Wigan Athletic v Sunderland

Wednesday, 6 April
Coca-Cola League Championship
Coventry City v Nott'm. Forest

Friday, 8 April
Coca-Cola League One
Tranmere Rov. v Stockport Co.

Coca-Cola League Two
Cheltenham Town v Shrewsbury Town

Saturday, 9 April
Barclays Premiership
Blackburn Rov. v Southampton
Bolton Wand. v Fulham
Chelsea v Birmingham City
Manchester City v Liverpool
Middlesbrough v Arsenal
Norwich City v Manchester Utd.
Portsmouth v Charlton Athletic
Tottenham v Newcastle Utd.

Coca-Cola League Championship
Brighton & H.A. v Leicester City
Cardiff City v Wigan Athletic
Derby Co. v Stoke City
Gillingham v Burnley
Millwall v Crewe Alexandra
Nott'm. Forest v Plymouth Argyle
Rotherham Utd. v Preston N.E.
Sheffield Utd. v Q.P.R.
Sunderland v Reading
Watford v Leeds Utd.
West Ham Utd. v Coventry City
Wolves v Ipswich Town

Coca-Cola League One
Barnsley v Wrexham
Blackpool v Peterborough Utd.
Bournemouth v Luton Town
Brentford v Bristol City
Colchester Utd. v Hartlepool Utd.
Huddersfield Town v Doncaster Rov.
Oldham Athletic v Sheffield Wed.
Port Vale v Chesterfield
Swindon Town v Walsall
Torquay Utd. v Milton Keynes Dons

Coca-Cola League Two
Bristol Rov. v Rushden & D'monds
Cambridge Utd. v Darlington
Chester City v Boston Utd.
Grimsby Town v Wycombe Wand.
Kidderminster Harr. v Bury
Lincoln City v Swansea City
Macclesfield Town v Southend Utd.
Northampton Town v Scunthorpe Utd.
Oxford Utd. v Notts Co.
Rochdale v Leyton Orient
Yeovil v Mansfield Town

Sunday, 10 April
Barclays Premiership
Aston Villa v W.B.A.
Everton v Crystal Palace

Coca-Cola League One
Bradford City v Hull City

Friday, 15 April
Coca-Cola League One
Hartlepool Utd. v Sheffield Wed.

Saturday, 16 April
Barclays Premiership
Arsenal v Everton
Birmingham City v Portsmouth
Charlton Athletic v Bolton Wand.
Crystal Palace v Norwich City
Fulham v Manchester City
Liverpool v Tottenham
Manchester Utd. v Chelsea
Newcastle Utd. v Middlesbrough
Southampton v Aston Villa
W.B.A. v Blackburn Rov.

Coca-Cola League Championship
Burnley v Brighton & H.A.
Coventry City v Wolves
Gillingham v Crewe Alexandra
Ipswich Town v Sunderland
Leicester City v Wigan Athletic
Preston N.E. v Cardiff City
Q.P.R. v Leeds Utd.
Reading v Nott'm. Forest
Rotherham Utd. v Watford
Sheffield Utd. v Derby Co.
Stoke City v Plymouth Argyle
West Ham Utd. v Millwall

Coca-Cola League One
Barnsley v Oldham Athletic
Bradford City v Brentford
Bristol City v Wrexham
Chesterfield v Bournemouth
Huddersfield Town v Colchester Utd.
Hull City v Swindon Town
Luton Town v Milton Keynes Dons
Peterborough Utd. v Walsall
Stockport Co. v Doncaster Rov.
Torquay Utd. v Port Vale
Tranmere Rov. v Blackpool

Coca-Cola League Two
Cheltenham Town v Northampton Town
Chester City v Bristol Rov.
Kidderminster Harr. v Yeovil
Lincoln City v Macclesfield Town

Mansfield Town v Darlington
Notts Co. v Grimsby Town
Rochdale v Shrewsbury Town
Rushden & D'monds v Boston Utd.
Scunthorpe Utd. v Cambridge Utd.
Southend Utd. v Leyton Orient
Swansea City v Oxford Utd.
Wycombe Wand. v Bury

Tuesday, 19 April
Barclays Premiership
Bolton Wand. v Southampton
Middlesbrough v Fulham
Norwich City v Newcastle Utd.
Portsmouth v Liverpool

Wednesday, 20 April
Barclays Premiership
Aston Villa v Charlton Athletic
Blackburn Rov. v Crystal Palace
Chelsea v Arsenal
Everton v Manchester Utd.
Manchester City v Birmingham City
Tottenham v W.B.A.

Saturday, 23 April
Barclays Premiership
Arsenal v Tottenham
Aston Villa v Bolton Wand.
Blackburn Rov. v Manchester City
Chelsea v Fulham
Crystal Palace v Liverpool
Everton v Birmingham City
Manchester Utd. v Newcastle Utd.
Middlesbrough v W.B.A.
Norwich City v Charlton Athletic

Coca-Cola League Championship
Brighton & H.A. v West Ham Utd.
Cardiff City v Reading
Crewe Alexandra v Stoke City
Derby Co. v Gillingham
Leeds Utd. v Ipswich Town
Millwall v Preston N.E.
Nott'm. Forest v Burnley
Plymouth Argyle v Coventry City
Sunderland v Leicester City
Watford v Sheffield Utd.
Wigan Athletic v Q.P.R.
Wolves v Rotherham Utd.

Coca-Cola League One
Blackpool v Chesterfield
Bournemouth v Peterborough Utd.
Brentford v Huddersfield Town
Colchester Utd. v Bradford City
Doncaster Rov. v Hartlepool Utd.

Milton Keynes Dons v Bristol City
Oldham Athletic v Torquay Utd.
Port Vale v Barnsley
Sheffield Wed. v Stockport Co.
Swindon Town v Tranmere Rov.
Walsall v Hull City
Wrexham v Luton Town

Coca-Cola League Two
Boston Utd. v Kidderminster Harr.
Bristol Rov. v Swansea City
Bury v Cheltenham Town
Cambridge Utd. v Rochdale
Darlington v Rushden & D'monds
Grimsby Town v Scunthorpe Utd.
Leyton Orient v Chester City
Macclesfield Town v Mansfield Town
Northampton Town v Lincoln City
Oxford Utd. v Southend Utd.
Shrewsbury Town v Notts Co.
Yeovil v Wycombe Wand.

Sunday, 24 April
Barclays Premiership
Portsmouth v Southampton

Friday, 29 April
Coca-Cola League One
Tranmere Rov. v Port Vale

Saturday, 30 April
Barclays Premiership
Birmingham City v Blackburn Rov.
Bolton Wand. v Chelsea
Charlton Athletic v Manchester Utd.
Fulham v Everton
Liverpool v Middlesbrough
Manchester City v Portsmouth
Newcastle Utd. v Crystal Palace
Southampton v Norwich City
Tottenham v Aston Villa
W.B.A. v Arsenal

Coca-Cola League Championship
Burnley v Plymouth Argyle
Coventry City v Derby Co.
Gillingham v Cardiff City
Ipswich Town v Crewe Alexandra
Leicester City v Leeds Utd.
Preston N.E. v Wigan Athletic
Q.P.R. v Nott'm. Forest
Reading v Wolves
Rotherham Utd. v Brighton & H.A.
Sheffield Utd. v Millwall
Stoke City v Watford
West Ham Utd. v Sunderland

Coca-Cola League One
Barnsley v Colchester Utd.
Bradford City v Bournemouth
Bristol City v Doncaster Rov.
Chesterfield v Oldham Athletic
Hartlepool Utd. v Walsall
Huddersfield Town v Swindon Town
Hull City v Sheffield Wed.
Luton Town v Brentford
Peterborough Utd. v Milton Keynes Dons
Stockport Co. v Wrexham
Torquay Utd. v Blackpool

Coca-Cola League Two
Cheltenham Town v Macclesfield Town
Chester City v Northampton Town
Kidderminster Harr. v Grimsby Town
Lincoln City v Darlington
Mansfield Town v Boston Utd.
Notts Co. v Bury
Rochdale v Oxford Utd.
Rushden & D'monds v Cambridge Utd.
Scunthorpe Utd. v Bristol Rov.
Southend Utd. v Yeovil
Swansea City v Shrewsbury Town
Wycombe Wand. v Leyton Orient

Saturday, 7 May
Barclays Premiership
Arsenal v Liverpool
Aston Villa v Manchester City
Blackburn Rov. v Fulham
Chelsea v Charlton Athletic
Crystal Palace v Southampton
Everton v Newcastle Utd.
Manchester Utd. v W.B.A.
Middlesbrough v Tottenham
Norwich City v Birmingham City
Portsmouth v Bolton Wand.

Coca-Cola League One
Blackpool v Barnsley
Bournemouth v Hartlepool Utd.
Brentford v Hull City
Colchester Utd. v Torquay Utd.
Doncaster Rov. v Luton Town
Milton Keynes Dons v Tranmere Rov.
Oldham Athletic v Bradford City
Port Vale v Peterborough Utd.
Sheffield Wed. v Bristol City
Swindon Town v Chesterfield
Walsall v Stockport Co.
Wrexham v Huddersfield Town

Coca-Cola League Two
Boston Utd. v Rochadale
Bristol Rov. v Wycombe Wand.

Bury v Swansea City
Cambridge Utd. v Notts Co.
Darlington v Cheltenham Town
Grimsby Town v Southend Utd.
Leyton Orient v Mansfield Town
Macclesfield Town v Rushden &
    D'monds
Northampton Town v Kidderminster Harr.
Oxford Utd. v Chester City
Shrewsbury Town v Scunthorpe Utd.
Yeovil v Lincoln City

Sunday, 8 May
Coca-Cola League Championship
Brighton & H.A. v Ipswich Town
Cardiff City v Q.P.R.
Crewe Alexandra v Coventry City
Derby Co. v Preston N.E.
Leeds Utd. v Rotherham Utd.

Millwall v Burnley
Nott'm. Forest v Gillingham
Plymouth Argyle v Leicester City
Sunderland v Stoke City
Watford v West Ham Utd.
Wigan Athletic v Reading
Wolves v Sheffield Utd.

Saturday, 14 May
Barclays Premiership
Birmingham City v Arsenal
Bolton Wand. v Everton
Charlton Athletic v Crystal Palace
Fulham v Norwich City
Liverpool v Aston Villa
Manchester City v Middlesbrough
Newcastle Utd. v Chelsea
Southampton v Manchester Utd.
Tottenham v Blackburn Rov.
W.B.A. v Portsmouth

SCOTTISH LEAGUE FIXTURES 2004-2005

Saturday, 7 August
Bank of Scotland Premier League
Aberdeen v Rangers
Celtic v Motherwell
Dundee v Hearts
Dunfermline v Dundee Utd.
Hibernian v Kilmarnock
Livingston v Inverness CT

Bell's First Division
Airdrie Utd. v St Johnstone
Clyde v Partick
Hamilton v Raith
Queen of South v Ross Co.
St Mirren v Falkirk

Bell's Second Division
Berwick v Morton
Dumbarton v Ayr
Forfar v Brechin
Stirling v Arbroath
Stranraer v Alloa

Bell's Third Division
East Fife v Montrose
Gretna v Albion
Peterhead v East Stirling
Queens Park v Cowdenbeath
Stenhousemuir v Elgin

Saturday, 14 August
Bank of Scotland Premier League
Dundee Utd. v Dundee
Hearts v Aberdeen
Kilmarnock v Celtic
Motherwell v Hibernian
Rangers v Livingston

Bell's First Division
Falkirk v Hamilton
Partick v Airdrie Utd.
Raith v Clyde
Ross Co. v St Mirren
St Johnstone v Queen of South

Bell's Second Division
Alloa v Forfar
Arbroath v Dumbarton
Ayr v Berwick
Brechin v Stirling
Morton v Stranraer

Bell's Third Division
Albion v East Fife
Cowdenbeath v Stenhousemuir
East Stirling v Gretna
Elgin v Queens Park
Montrose v Peterhead

Sunday, 15 August
Bank of Scotland Premier League
Inverness CT v Dunfermline

Saturday, 21 August
Bank of Scotland Premier League
Dundee v Motherwell
Dunfermline v Aberdeen
Hearts v Kilmarnock
Inverness CT v Celtic
Livingston v Dundee Utd.
Rangers v Hibernian

Bell's First Division
Airdrie Utd. v Raith
Clyde v Ross Co.
Hamilton v Partick
Queen of South v Falkirk
St Mirren v St Johnstone

Bell's Second Division
Berwick v Brechin
Dumbarton v Morton
Forfar v Arbroath
Stirling v Alloa
Stranraer v Ayr

Bell's Third Division
East Fife v Cowdenbeath
Gretna v Montrose
Peterhead v Elgin
Queens Park v Albion
Stenhousemuir v East Stirling

Saturday, 28 August
Bank of Scotland Premier League
Aberdeen v Livingston
Celtic v Rangers
Dundee Utd. v Inverness CT
Hibernian v Dundee
Motherwell v Hearts

Bell's First Division
Falkirk v Airdrie Utd.
Queen of South v Clyde
Ross Co. v Partick
St Johnstone v Raith
St Mirren v Hamilton

Bell's Second Division
Arbroath v Stranraer
Ayr v Morton
Brechin v Alloa
Dumbarton v Forfar
Stirling v Berwick

Bell's Third Division
Albion v Peterhead
Cowdenbeath v East Stirling
East Fife v Stenhousemuir
Elgin v Montrose
Queens Park v Gretna

Sunday, 29 August
Bank of Scotland Premier League
Kilmarnock v Dunfermline

Saturday, 4 September
Bell's First Division
Airdrie Utd. v Queen of South
Clyde v St Mirren
Hamilton v St Johnstone
Partick v Falkirk
Raith v Ross Co.

Bell's Second Division
Alloa v Ayr
Berwick v Dumbarton
Forfar v Stirling
Morton v Arbroath
Stranraer v Brechin

Bell's Third Division
East Stirling v Elgin
Gretna v Cowdenbeath
Montrose v Albion
Peterhead v East Fife
Stenhousemuir v Queens Park

Saturday, 11 September
Bank of Scotland Premier League
Celtic v Dundee
Dundee Utd. v Aberdeen
Dunfermline v Motherwell
Hearts v Rangers
Inverness CT v Hibernian
Livingston v Kilmarnock

Bell's First Division
Clyde v Airdrie Utd.
Falkirk v Raith
Queen of South v Hamilton
Ross Co. v St Johnstone
St Mirren v Partick

Bell's Second Division
Ayr v Forfar
Berwick v Alloa
Brechin v Arbroath
Dumbarton v Stranraer
Stirling v Morton

Bell's Third Division
Albion v Stenhousemuir
Cowdenbeath v Elgin
East Fife v East Stirling
Peterhead v Gretna
Queens Park v Montrose

Saturday, 18 September
Bank of Scotland Premier League
Dundee v Livingston
Hibernian v Celtic
Kilmarnock v Aberdeen
Motherwell v Dundee Utd.
Rangers v Inverness CT

Bell's First Division
Airdrie Utd. v Ross Co.
Hamilton v Clyde
Partick v Queen of South
Raith v St Mirren
St Johnstone v Falkirk

Bell's Second Division
Alloa v Dumbarton
Arbroath v Ayr
Forfar v Berwick
Morton v Brechin
Stranraer v Stirling

Bell's Third Division
East Stirling v Queens Park
Elgin v Albion
Gretna v East Fife
Montrose v Cowdenbeath
Stenhousemuir v Peterhead

Sunday, 19 September
Bank of Scotland Premier League
Dunfermline v Hearts

Saturday, 25 September
Bank of Scotland Premier League
Aberdeen v Hibernian
Celtic v Dunfermline
Dundee v Rangers
Hearts v Inverness CT
Kilmarnock v Dundee Utd.
Livingston v Motherwell

Bell's First Division
Falkirk v Clyde
Hamilton v Ross Co.
Raith v Queen of South
St Johnstone v Partick
St Mirren v Airdrie Utd.

Bell's Second Division
Alloa v Morton
Ayr v Brechin
Berwick v Arbroath
Dumbarton v Stirling
Forfar v Stranraer

Bell's Third Division
Albion v East Stirling
East Fife v Queens Park
Gretna v Elgin
Montrose v Stenhousemuir
Peterhead v Cowdenbeath

Saturday, 2 October
Bank of Scotland Premier League
Aberdeen v Dundee
Dundee Utd. v Celtic
Dunfermline v Hibernian
Inverness CT v Motherwell
Rangers v Kilmarnock

Bell's First Division
Airdrie Utd. v Hamilton
Clyde v St Johnstone
Partick v Raith
Queen of South v St Mirren
Ross Co. v Falkirk

Bell's Second Division
Arbroath v Alloa
Brechin v Dumbarton
Morton v Forfar
Stirling v Ayr
Stranraer v Berwick

Bell's Third Division
Cowdenbeath v Albion
East Stirling v Montrose
Elgin v East Fife
Queens Park v Peterhead
Stenhousemuir v Gretna

Sunday, 3 October
Bank of Scotland Premier League
Hearts v Livingston

Saturday, 16 October
Bank of Scotland Premier League
Celtic v Hearts
Dundee v Kilmarnock
Hibernian v Dundee Utd.
Inverness CT v Aberdeen
Livingston v Dunfermline
Motherwell v Rangers

Bell's First Division
Airdrie Utd. v Partick
Clyde v Raith
Hamilton v Falkirk
Queen of South v St Johnstone
St Mirren v Ross Co.

Bell's Second Division
Berwick v Ayr
Dumbarton v Arbroath
Forfar v Alloa
Stirling v Brechin
Stranraer v Morton

Bell's Third Division
East Fife v Albion
Gretna v East Stirling
Peterhead v Montrose
Queens Park v Elgin
Stenhousemuir v Cowdenbeath

Saturday, 23 October
Bank of Scotland Premier League
Aberdeen v Motherwell
Dundee v Dunfermline
Hearts v Hibernian
Kilmarnock v Inverness CT
Livingston v Celtic
Rangers v Dundee Utd.

Bell's First Division
Falkirk v St Mirren
Partick v Clyde
Raith v Hamilton
Ross Co. v Queen of South
St Johnstone v Airdrie Utd.

Bell's Second Division
Alloa v Stranraer
Arbroath v Stirling
Ayr v Dumbarton
Brechin v Forfar
Morton v Berwick

Bell's Third Division
Albion v Gretna
Cowdenbeath v Queens Park
East Stirling v Peterhead
Elgin v Stenhousemuir
Montrose v East Fife

Tuesday, 26 October
Bank of Scotland Premier League
Dundee Utd. v Hearts

Wednesday, 27 October
Bank of Scotland Premier League
Celtic v Aberdeen
Dunfermline v Rangers
Hibernian v Livingston
Inverness CT v Dundee
Motherwell v Kilmarnock

Saturday, 30 October
Bank of Scotland Premier League
Dundee Utd. v Dunfermline
Hearts v Dundee
Inverness CT v Livingston
Kilmarnock v Hibernian
Motherwell v Celtic
Rangers v Aberdeen

Bell's First Division
Airdrie Utd. v Falkirk
Clyde v Queen of South
Hamilton v St Mirren
Partick v Ross Co.
Raith v St Johnstone

Bell's Second Division
Alloa v Brechin
Berwick v Stirling
Forfar v Dumbarton
Morton v Ayr
Stranraer v Arbroath

Bell's Third Division
East Stirling v Cowdenbeath
Gretna v Queens Park
Montrose v Elgin
Peterhead v Albion
Stenhousemuir v East Fife

Saturday, 6 November
Bank of Scotland Premier League
Aberdeen v Hearts
Celtic v Kilmarnock
Dundee v Dundee Utd.
Dunfermline v Inverness CT
Hibernian v Motherwell
Livingston v Rangers

Bell's First Division
Falkirk v Partick
Queen of South v Airdrie Utd.
Ross Co. v Raith
St Johnstone v Hamilton
St Mirren v Clyde

Bell's Second Division
Arbroath v Morton
Ayr v Alloa
Brechin v Stranraer
Dumbarton v Berwick
Stirling v Forfar

Bell's Third Division
Albion v Montrose
Cowdenbeath v Gretna
East Fife v Peterhead
Elgin v East Stirling
Queens Park v Stenhousemuir

Saturday, 13 November
Bank of Scotland Premier League
Aberdeen v Dunfermline
Celtic v Inverness CT
Dundee Utd. v Livingston
Hibernian v Rangers
Kilmarnock v Hearts
Motherwell v Dundee

Bell's First Division
Airdrie Utd. v Clyde
Hamilton v Queen of South
Partick v St Mirren
Raith v Falkirk
St Johnstone v Ross Co.

Bell's Second Division
Alloa v Berwick
Arbroath v Brechin
Forfar v Ayr
Morton v Stirling
Stranraer v Dumbarton

Bell's Third Division
East Stirling v East Fife
Elgin v Cowdenbeath
Gretna v Peterhead
Montrose v Queens Park
Stenhousemuir v Albion

Saturday, 20 November
Bank of Scotland Premier League
Dundee v Hibernian
Dunfermline v Kilmarnock
Hearts v Motherwell
Inverness CT v Dundee Utd.
Livingston v Aberdeen
Rangers v Celtic

Bell's First Division
Clyde v Hamilton
Falkirk v St Johnstone

Queen of South v Partick
Ross Co. v Airdrie Utd.
St Mirren v Raith

Saturday, 27 November
Bank of Scotland Premier League
Aberdeen v Dundee Utd.
Dundee v Celtic
Hibernian v Inverness CT
Kilmarnock v Livingston
Motherwell v Dunfermline
Rangers v Hearts

Bell's First Division
Falkirk v Ross Co.
Hamilton v Airdrie Utd.
Raith v Partick
St Johnstone v Clyde
St Mirren v Queen of South

Bell's Second Division
Ayr v Arbroath
Berwick v Forfar
Brechin v Morton
Dumbarton v Alloa
Stirling v Stranraer

Bell's Third Division
Albion v Elgin
Cowdenbeath v Montrose
East Fife v Gretna
Peterhead v Stenhousemuir
Queens Park v East Stirling

Saturday, 4 December
Bank of Scotland Premier League
Aberdeen v Kilmarnock
Celtic v Hibernian
Dundee Utd. v Motherwell
Hearts v Dunfermline
Inverness CT v Rangers
Livingston v Dundee

Bell's First Division
Airdrie Utd. v St Mirren
Clyde v Falkirk
Partick v St Johnstone
Queen of South v Raith
Ross Co. v Hamilton

Bell's Second Division
Arbroath v Berwick
Brechin v Ayr
Morton v Alloa
Stirling v Dumbarton
Stranraer v Forfar

Bell's Third Division
Cowdenbeath v Peterhead
East Stirling v Albion
Elgin v Gretna
Queens Park v East Fife
Stenhousemuir v Montrose

Saturday, 11 December
Bank of Scotland Premier League
Dundee Utd. v Kilmarnock
Dunfermline v Celtic
Hibernian v Aberdeen
Inverness CT v Hearts
Motherwell v Livingston
Rangers v Dundee

Bell's First Division
Airdrie Utd. v St Johnstone
Clyde v Partick
Hamilton v Raith
Queen of South v Ross Co.
St Mirren v Falkirk

Saturday, 18 December
Bank of Scotland Premier League
Celtic v Dundee Utd.
Dundee v Aberdeen
Hibernian v Dunfermline
Kilmarnock v Rangers
Livingston v Hearts
Motherwell v Inverness CT

Bell's First Division
Falkirk v Queen of South
Partick v Hamilton
Raith v Airdrie Utd.
Ross Co. v Clyde
St Johnstone v St Mirren

Bell's Second Division
Alloa v Arbroath
Ayr v Stirling
Berwick v Stranraer
Dumbarton v Brechin
Forfar v Morton

Bell's Third Division
Albion v Cowdenbeath
East Fife v Elgin
Gretna v Stenhousemuir
Montrose v East Stirling
Peterhead v Queens Park

Sunday, 26 December
Bell's First Division
Falkirk v Airdrie Utd.
Queen of South v Clyde
Ross Co. v Partick
St Johnstone v Raith
St Mirren v Hamilton

Monday, 27 December
Bank of Scotland Premier League
Aberdeen v Inverness CT
Dundee Utd. v Hibernian
Dunfermline v Livingston
Hearts v Celtic
Kilmarnock v Dundee
Rangers v Motherwell

Bell's Second Division
Berwick v Morton
Dumbarton v Ayr
Forfar v Brechin
Stirling v Arbroath
Stranraer v Alloa

Bell's Third Division
East Fife v Montrose
Gretna v Albion
Peterhead v East Stirling
Queens Park v Cowdenbeath
Stenhousemuir v Elgin

Wednesday, 29 December
Bell's First Division
Airdrie Utd. v Queen of South
Clyde v St Mirren
Hamilton v St Johnstone
Partick v Falkirk
Raith v Ross Co.

Saturday, 1 January
Bank of Scotland Premier League
Celtic v Livingston
Dundee Utd. v Rangers
Dunfermline v Dundee
Hibernian v Hearts
Inverness CT v Kilmarnock
Motherwell v Aberdeen

Bell's First Division
Clyde v Airdrie Utd.
Falkirk v Raith
Queen of South v Hamilton
Ross Co. v St Johnstone
St Mirren v Partick

Bell's Second Division
Alloa v Stirling
Arbroath v Forfar
Ayr v Stranraer
Brechin v Berwick
Morton v Dumbarton

Bell's Third Division
Albion v Queens Park
Cowdenbeath v East Fife
East Stirling v Stenhousemuir
Elgin v Peterhead
Montrose v Gretna

Monday, 3 January
Bell's Second Division
Arbroath v Stranraer
Ayr v Morton
Brechin v Alloa
Dumbarton v Forfar
Stirling v Berwick

Bell's Third Division
Albion v Peterhead
Cowdenbeath v East Stirling
East Fife v Stenhousemuir
Elgin v Montrose
Queens Park v Gretna

Saturday, 15 January
Bank of Scotland Premier League
Aberdeen v Celtic
Dundee v Inverness CT
Hearts v Dundee Utd.
Kilmarnock v Motherwell
Livingston v Hibernian
Rangers v Dunfermline

Bell's First Division
Airdrie Utd. v Ross Co.
Hamilton v Clyde
Partick v Queen of South
Raith v St Mirren
St Johnstone v Falkirk

Bell's Second Division
Alloa v Ayr
Berwick v Dumbarton
Forfar v Stirling
Morton v Arbroath
Stranraer v Brechin

Bell's Third Division
East Stirling v Elgin
Gretna v Cowdenbeath
Montrose v Albion

Peterhead v East Fife
Stenhousemuir v Queens Park

Saturday, 22 January
Bank of Scotland Premier League
Aberdeen v Rangers
Celtic v Motherwell
Dundee v Hearts
Dunfermline v Dundee Utd.
Hibernian v Kilmarnock
Livingston v Inverness CT

Bell's First Division
Falkirk v Clyde
Hamilton v Ross Co.
Raith v Queen of South
St Johnstone v Partick
St Mirren v Airdrie Utd.

Bell's Second Division
Ayr v Forfar
Berwick v Alloa
Brechin v Arbroath
Dumbarton v Stranraer
Stirling v Morton

Bell's Third Division
Albion v Stenhousemuir
Cowdenbeath v Elgin
East Fife v East Stirling
Peterhead v Gretna
Queens Park v Montrose

Saturday, 29 January
Bank of Scotland Premier League
Dundee Utd. v Dundee
Hearts v Aberdeen
Inverness CT v Dunfermline
Kilmarnock v Celtic
Motherwell v Hibernian
Rangers v Livingston

Bell's First Division
Airdrie Utd. v Hamilton
Clyde v St Johnstone
Partick v Raith
Queen of South v St Mirren
Ross Co. v Falkirk

Bell's Second Division
Alloa v Dumbarton
Arbroath v Ayr
Forfar v Berwick
Morton v Brechin
Stranraer v Stirling

Bell's Third Division
East Stirling v Queens Park
Elgin v Albion
Gretna v East Fife
Montrose v Cowdenbeath
Stenhousemuir v Peterhead

Saturday, 5 February
Bell's Second Division
Alloa v Morton
Ayr v Brechin
Berwick v Arbroath
Dumbarton v Stirling
Forfar v Stranraer

Bell's Third Division
Albion v East Stirling
East Fife v Queens Park
Gretna v Elgin
Montrose v Stenhousemuir
Peterhead v Cowdenbeath

Saturday, 12 February
Bank of Scotland Premier League
Dundee v Motherwell
Dunfermline v Aberdeen
Hearts v Kilmarnock
Inverness CT v Celtic
Livingston v Dundee Utd.
Rangers v Hibernian

Bell's First Division
Falkirk v Hamilton
Partick v Airdrie Utd.
Raith v Clyde
Ross Co. v St Mirren
St Johnstone v Queen of South

Bell's Second Division
Arbroath v Alloa
Brechin v Dumbarton
Morton v Forfar
Stirling v Ayr
Stranraer v Berwick

Bell's Third Division
Cowdenbeath v Albion
East Stirling v Montrose
Elgin v East Fife
Queens Park v Peterhead
Stenhousemuir v Gretna

Saturday, 19 February
Bank of Scotland Premier League
Aberdeen v Livingston
Celtic v Rangers

Dundee Utd. v Inverness CT
Hibernian v Dundee
Kilmarnock v Dunfermline
Motherwell v Hearts

Bell's First Division
Airdrie Utd. v Raith
Clyde v Ross Co.
Hamilton v Partick
Queen of South v Falkirk
St Mirren v St Johnstone

Bell's Second Division
Berwick v Brechin
Dumbarton v Morton
Forfar v Arbroath
Stirling v Alloa
Stranraer v Ayr

Bell's Third Division
East Fife v Cowdenbeath
Gretna v Montrose
Peterhead v Elgin
Queens Park v Albion
Stenhousemuir v East Stirling

Saturday, 26 February
Bell's Second Division
Alloa v Forfar
Arbroath v Dumbarton
Ayr v Berwick
Brechin v Stirling
Morton v Stranraer

Bell's Third Division
Albion v East Fife
Cowdenbeath v Stenhousemuir
East Stirling v Gretna
Elgin v Queens Park
Montrose v Peterhead

Tuesday, 1 March
Bank of Scotland Premier League
Dundee Utd. v Aberdeen

Wednesday, 2 March
Bank of Scotland Premier League
Celtic v Dundee
Dunfermline v Motherwell
Hearts v Rangers
Inverness CT v Hibernian
Livingston v Kilmarnock

Saturday, 5 March
Bank of Scotland Premier League
Dundee v Livingston
Dunfermline v Hearts
Hibernian v Celtic
Kilmarnock v Aberdeen
Motherwell v Dundee Utd.
Rangers v Inverness CT

Bell's First Division
Falkirk v Partick
Queen of South v Airdrie Utd.
Ross Co. v Raith
St Johnstone v Hamilton
St Mirren v Clyde

Bell's Second Division
Arbroath v Morton
Ayr v Alloa
Brechin v Stranraer
Dumbarton v Berwick
Stirling v Forfar

Bell's Third Division
Albion v Montrose
Cowdenbeath v Gretna
East Fife v Peterhead
Elgin v East Stirling
Queens Park v Stenhousemuir

Saturday, 12 March
Bank of Scotland Premier League
Aberdeen v Hibernian
Celtic v Dunfermline
Dundee v Rangers
Hearts v Inverness CT
Kilmarnock v Dundee Utd.
Livingston v Motherwell

Bell's First Division
Airdrie Utd. v Falkirk
Clyde v Queen of South
Hamilton v St Mirren
Partick v Ross Co.
Raith v St Johnstone

Bell's Second Division
Alloa v Brechin
Berwick v Stirling
Forfar v Dumbarton
Morton v Ayr
Stranraer v Arbroath

Bell's Third Division
East Stirling v Cowdenbeath
Gretna v Queens Park
Montrose v Elgin

Peterhead v Albion
Stenhousemuir v East Fife

Saturday, 19 March
Bank of Scotland Premier League
Aberdeen v Dundee
Dundee Utd. v Celtic
Dunfermline v Hibernian
Hearts v Livingston
Inverness CT v Motherwell
Rangers v Kilmarnock

Bell's First Division
Airdrie Utd. v Clyde
Hamilton v Queen of South
Partick v St Mirren
Raith v Falkirk
St Johnstone v Ross Co.

Bell's Second Division
Alloa v Berwick
Arbroath v Brechin
Forfar v Ayr
Morton v Stirling
Stranraer v Dumbarton

Bell's Third Division
East Stirling v East Fife
Elgin v Cowdenbeath
Gretna v Peterhead
Montrose v Queens Park
Stenhousemuir v Albion

Saturday, 2 April
Bank of Scotland Premier League
Celtic v Hearts
Dundee v Kilmarnock
Hibernian v Dundee Utd.
Inverness CT v Aberdeen
Livingston v Dunfermline
Motherwell v Rangers

Bell's First Division
Clyde v Hamilton
Falkirk v St Johnstone
Queen of South v Partick
Ross Co. v Airdrie Utd.
St Mirren v Raith

Bell's Second Division
Ayr v Arbroath
Berwick v Forfar
Brechin v Morton
Dumbarton v Alloa
Stirling v Stranraer

Bell's Third Division
Albion v Elgin
Cowdenbeath v Montrose
East Fife v Gretna
Peterhead v Stenhousemuir
Queens Park v East Stirling

Saturday, 9 April
Bank of Scotland Premier League
Aberdeen v Motherwell
Dundee v Dunfermline
Hearts v Hibernian
Kilmarnock v Inverness CT
Livingston v Celtic
Rangers v Dundee Utd.

Bell's First Division
Falkirk v Ross Co.
Hamilton v Airdrie Utd.
Raith v Partick
St Johnstone v Clyde
St Mirren v Queen of South

Bell's Second Division
Alloa v Arbroath
Ayr v Stirling
Berwick v Stranraer
Dumbarton v Brechin
Forfar v Morton

Bell's Third Division
Albion v Cowdenbeath
East Fife v Elgin
Gretna v Stenhousemuir
Montrose v East Stirling
Peterhead v Queens Park

Saturday, 16 April
Bank of Scotland Premier League
Celtic v Aberdeen
Dundee Utd. v Hearts
Dunfermline v Rangers
Hibernian v Livingston
Inverness CT v Dundee
Motherwell v Kilmarnock

Bell's First Division
Airdrie Utd. v St Mirren
Clyde v Falkirk
Partick v St Johnstone
Queen of South v Raith
Ross Co. v Hamilton

Bell's Second Division
Arbroath v Berwick
Brechin v Ayr

Morton v Alloa
Stirling v Dumbarton
Stranraer v Forfar

Bell's Third Division
Cowdenbeath v Peterhead
East Stirling v Albion
Elgin v Gretna
Queens Park v East Fife
Stenhousemuir v Montrose

Saturday, 23 April
Bell's First Division
Falkirk v St Mirren
Partick v Clyde
Raith v Hamilton
Ross Co. v Queen of South
St Johnstone v Airdrie Utd.

Bell's Second Division
Alloa v Stirling
Arbroath v Forfar
Ayr v Stranraer
Brechin v Berwick
Morton v Dumbarton

Bell's Third Division
Albion v Queens Park
Cowdenbeath v East Fife
East Stirling v Stenhousemuir
Elgin v Peterhead
Montrose v Gretna

Saturday, 30 April
Bell's First Division
Airdrie Utd. v Partick
Clyde v Raith
Hamilton v Falkirk
Queen of South v St Johnstone
St Mirren v Ross Co.

Bell's Second Division
Berwick v Ayr
Dumbarton v Arbroath
Forfar v Alloa
Stirling v Brechin
Stranraer v Morton

Bell's Third Division
East Fife v Albion
Gretna v East Stirling
Peterhead v Montrose
Queens Park v Elgin
Stenhousemuir v Cowdenbeath

Saturday, 7 May
Bell's First Division
Falkirk v Queen of South
Partick v Hamilton
Raith v Airdrie Utd.
Ross Co. v Clyde
St Johnstone v St Mirren

Bell's Second Division
Alloa v Stranraer
Arbroath v Stirling

Ayr v Dumbarton
Brechin v Forfar
Morton v Berwick

Bell's Third Division
Albion v Gretna
Cowdenbeath v Queens Park
East Stirling v Peterhead
Elgin v Stenhousemuir
Montrose v East Fife

NATIONWIDE CONFERENCE FIXTURES 2004-05

Saturday, 14 August
Accrington v Burton
Aldershot v York
Barnet v Forest Green
Carlisle v Canvey Island
Dag & Red v Stevenage
Exeter v Morecambe
Gravesend v Northwich
Hereford v Farnborough
Leigh v Crawley
Scarborough v Woking
Tamworth v Halifax

Tuesday, 17 August
Burton v Leigh
Canvey Island v Gravesend
Crawley v Hereford
Farnborough v Barnet
Forest Green v Dag & Red
Halifax v Scarborough
Morecambe v Accrington
Northwich v Carlisle
Stevenage v Aldershot
Woking v Exeter
York v Tamworth

Saturday, 21 August
Burton v Dag & Red
Canvey Island v Tamworth
Crawley v Aldershot
Farnborough v Scarborough
Forest Green v Carlisle
Halifax v Barnet
Morecambe v Gravesend
Northwich v Exeter
Stevenage v Accrington
Woking v Leigh
York v Hereford

Saturday, 28 August
Accrington v Crawley
Aldershot v Burton
Barnet v Northwich

Carlisle v Farnborough
Dag & Red v Woking
Exeter v Canvey Island
Gravesend v York
Hereford v Stevenage
Leigh v Halifax
Scarborough v Morecambe
Tamworth v Forest Green

Monday, 30 August
Burton v Scarborough
Canvey Island v Barnet
Crawley v Dag & Red
Farnborough v Exeter
Forest Green v Gravesend
Halifax v Carlisle
Morecambe v Leigh
Northwich v Hereford
Stevenage v Tamworth
Woking v Aldershot
York v Accrington

Saturday, 4 September
Accrington v Woking
Aldershot v Northwich
Barnet v Morecambe
Carlisle v Burton
Dag & Red v York
Exeter v Crawley
Gravesend v Stevenage
Hereford v Halifax
Leigh v Forest Green
Scarborough v Canvey Island
Tamworth v Farnborough

Saturday, 11 September
Crawley v York
Dag & Red v Accrington
Farnborough v Canvey Island
Gravesend v Hereford
Halifax v Forest Green
Leigh v Aldershot
Northwich v Morecambe

Scarborough v Exeter
Stevenage v Burton
Tamworth v Barnet
Woking v Carlisle

Saturday, 18 September
Accrington v Leigh
Aldershot v Dag & Red
Barnet v Gravesend
Burton v Crawley
Canvey Island v Halifax
Carlisle v Tamworth
Exeter v Stevenage
Forest Green v Farnborough
Hereford v Scarborough
Morecambe v Woking
York v Northwich

Tuesday, 21 September
Barnet v Burton
Canvey Island v Crawley
Carlisle v Scarborough
Farnborough v Stevenage
Forest Green v Exeter
Gravesend v Dag & Red
Halifax v Morecambe
Hereford v Aldershot
Northwich v Accrington
Tamworth v Woking
York v Leigh

Saturday, 25 September
Accrington v Gravesend
Aldershot v Carlisle
Burton v York
Crawley v Forest Green
Dag & Red v Halifax
Exeter v Tamworth
Leigh v Hereford
Morecambe v Farnborough
Scarborough v Barnet
Stevenage v Northwich
Woking v Canvey Island

Saturday, 2 October
Barnet v Woking
Canvey Island v Morecambe
Carlisle v Crawley
Farnborough v Accrington
Forest Green v Scarborough
Gravesend v Leigh
Halifax v Exeter
Hereford v Burton
Northwich v Dag & Red
Tamworth v Aldershot
York v Stevenage

Tuesday, 5 October
Accrington v Tamworth
Aldershot v Gravesend
Burton v Halifax
Crawley v Farnborough
Dag & Red v Hereford
Exeter v Barnet
Leigh v Carlisle
Morecambe v York
Scarborough v Northwich
Stevenage v Canvey Island
Woking v Forest Green

Saturday, 9 October
Accrington v Hereford
Barnet v Dag & Red
Burton v Gravesend
Canvey Island v Forest Green
Crawley v Northwich
Exeter v Carlisle
Farnborough v York
Leigh v Stevenage
Morecambe v Tamworth
Scarborough v Aldershot
Woking v Halifax

Saturday, 16 October
Aldershot v Accrington
Carlisle v Barnet
Dag & Red v Leigh
Forest Green v Morecambe
Gravesend v Exeter
Halifax v Farnborough
Hereford v Woking
Northwich v Burton
Stevenage v Crawley
Tamworth v Scarborough
York v Canvey Island

Saturday, 23 October
Barnet v York
Canvey Island v Leigh
Carlisle v Hereford
Exeter v Aldershot
Farnborough v Dag & Red
Forest Green v Northwich
Halifax v Gravesend
Morecambe v Stevenage
Scarborough v Accrington
Tamworth v Crawley
Woking v Burton

Saturday, 6 November
Accrington v Exeter
Aldershot v Morecambe
Burton v Farnborough
Crawley v Woking
Dag & Red v Scarborough

Gravesend v Carlisle
Hereford v Barnet
Leigh v Tamworth
Northwich v Canvey Island
Stevenage v Halifax
York v Forest Green

Saturday, 20 November
Barnet v Accrington
Canvey Island v Hereford
Carlisle v Dag & Red
Exeter v Leigh
Farnborough v Northwich
Forest Green v Burton
Halifax v Aldershot
Morecambe v Crawley
Scarborough v Stevenage
Tamworth v Gravesend
Woking v York

Saturday, 27 November
Accrington v Canvey Island
Aldershot v Barnet
Burton v Exeter
Crawley v Scarborough
Dag & Red v Morecambe
Gravesend v Woking
Hereford v Tamworth
Leigh v Farnborough
Northwich v Halifax
Stevenage v Forest Green
York v Carlisle

Saturday, 4 December
Barnet v Leigh
Canvey Island v Burton
Carlisle v Stevenage
Exeter v York
Farnborough v Aldershot
Forest Green v Accrington
Halifax v Crawley
Morecambe v Hereford
Scarborough v Gravesend
Tamworth v Dag & Red
Woking v Northwich

Tuesday, 7 December
Accrington v Carlisle
Aldershot v Canvey Island
Burton v Morecambe
Crawley v Barnet
Dag & Red v Exeter
Gravesend v Farnborough
Hereford v Forest Green
Leigh v Scarborough
Northwich v Tamworth
Stevenage v Woking
York v Halifax

Saturday, 11 December
Crawley v Burton
Dag & Red v Aldershot
Farnborough v Forest Green
Gravesend v Barnet
Halifax v Canvey Island
Leigh v Accrington
Northwich v York
Scarborough v Hereford
Stevenage v Exeter
Tamworth v Carlisle
Woking v Morecambe

Saturday, 18 December
Accrington v Dag & Red
Aldershot v Leigh
Barnet v Tamworth
Burton v Stevenage
Canvey Island v Farnborough
Carlisle v Woking
Exeter v Scarborough
Forest Green v Halifax
Hereford v Gravesend
Morecambe v Northwich
York v Crawley

Sunday, 26 December
Accrington v Halifax
Aldershot v Forest Green
Burton v Tamworth
Crawley v Gravesend
Dag & Red v Canvey Island
Exeter v Hereford
Leigh v Northwich
Morecambe v Carlisle
Scarborough v York
Stevenage v Barnet
Woking v Farnborough

Tuesday, 28 December
Barnet v Scarborough
Canvey Island v Woking
Carlisle v Aldershot
Farnborough v Morecambe
Forest Green v Crawley
Gravesend v Accrington
Halifax v Dag & Red
Hereford v Leigh
Northwich v Stevenage
Tamworth v Exeter

Saturday, 1 January
Barnet v Stevenage
Canvey Island v Dag & Red
Carlisle v Morecambe
Farnborough v Woking
Forest Green v Aldershot
Gravesend v Crawley

Halifax v Accrington
Hereford v Exeter
Northwich v Leigh
Tamworth v Burton
York v Scarborough

Saturday, 8 January
Accrington v Farnborough
Aldershot v Tamworth
Burton v Hereford
Crawley v Carlisle
Dag & Red v Northwich
Exeter v Halifax
Leigh v Gravesend
Morecambe v Canvey Island
Scarborough v Forest Green
Stevenage v York
Woking v Barnet

Saturday, 22 January
Barnet v Exeter
Canvey Island v Stevenage
Carlisle v Leigh
Farnborough v Crawley
Forest Green v Woking
Gravesend v Aldershot
Halifax v Burton
Hereford v Dag & Red
Northwich v Scarborough
Tamworth v Accrington
York v Morecambe

Saturday, 29 January
Accrington v Northwich
Aldershot v Hereford
Burton v Barnet
Crawley v Canvey Island
Dag & Red v Gravesend
Exeter v Forest Green
Leigh v York
Morecambe v Halifax
Scarborough v Carlisle
Stevenage v Farnborough
Woking v Tamworth

Saturday, 5 February
Accrington v Scarborough
Aldershot v Exeter
Burton v Woking
Crawley v Tamworth
Dag & Red v Farnborough
Gravesend v Halifax
Hereford v Carlisle
Leigh v Canvey Island
Northwich v Forest Green
Stevenage v Morecambe
York City v Barnet

Saturday, 12 February
Barnet v Hereford
Canvey Island v Northwich
Carlisle v Gravesend
Exeter v Accrington
Farnborough v Burton
Forest Green v York
Halifax v Stevenage
Morecambe v Aldershot
Scarborough v Dag & Red
Tamworth v Leigh
Woking v Crawley

Saturday, 19 February
Accrington v Barnet
Aldershot v Halifax
Burton v Forest Green
Crawley v Morecambe
Dag & Red v Carlisle
Gravesend v Tamworth
Hereford v Canvey Island
Leigh v Exeter
Northwich v Farnborough
Stevenage v Scarborough
York v Woking

Saturday, 26 February
Barnet v Aldershot
Canvey Island v Accrington
Carlisle v York
Exeter v Burton
Farnborough v Leigh
Forest Green v Stevenage
Halifax v Northwich
Morecambe v Dag & Red
Scarborough v Crawley
Tamworth v Hereford
Woking v Gravesend

March Fixtures

Saturday, 5 March
Accrington v Forest Green
Aldershot v Farnborough
Burton v Canvey Island
Crawley v Halifax
Dag & Red v Tamworth
Gravesend v Scarborough
Hereford v Morecambe
Leigh v Barnet
Northwich v Woking
Stevenage v Carlisle
York v Exeter

Saturday, 12 March
Barnet v Crawley
Canvey Island v Aldershot
Carlisle v Accrington
Exeter v Dag & Red

Farnborough v Gravesend
Forest Green v Hereford
Halifax v York
Morecambe v Burton
Scarborough v Leigh
Tamworth v Northwich
Woking v Stevenage

Saturday, 19 March
Accrington v Morecambe
Aldershot v Stevenage
Barnet v Farnborough
Carlisle v Northwich
Dag & Red v Forest Green
Exeter v Woking
Gravesend v Canvey Island
Hereford v Crawley
Leigh v Burton
Scarborough v Halifax
Tamworth v York

Friday, 25 March
Burton v Accrington
Canvey Island v Carlisle
Crawley v Leigh
Farnborough v Hereford
Forest Green v Barnet
Halifax v Tamworth
Morecambe v Exeter
Northwich v Gravesend
Stevenage v Dag & Red
Woking v Scarborough
York v Aldershot

Monday, 28 March
Accrington v York
Aldershot v Woking
Barnet v Canvey Island
Carlisle v Halifax
Dag & Red v Crawley
Exeter v Farnborough
Gravesend v Forest Green
Hereford v Northwich
Leigh v Morecambe
Scarborough v Burton
Tamworth v Stevenage

Saturday, 2 April
Burton v Aldershot
Canvey Island v Exeter
Crawley v Accrington
Farnborough v Carlisle
Forest Green v Tamworth
Halifax v Leigh
Morecambe v Scarborough

Northwich v Barnet
Stevenage v Hereford
Woking v Dag & Red
York v Gravesend

Saturday, 9 April
Accrington v Stevenage
Aldershot v Crawley
Barnet v Halifax
Carlisle v Forest Green
Dag & Red v Burton
Exeter v Northwich
Gravesend v Morecambe
Hereford v York
Leigh v Woking
Scarborough v Farnborough
Tamworth v Canvey Island

Saturday, 16 April
Burton v Carlisle
Canvey Island v Scarborough
Crawley v Exeter
Farnborough v Tamworth
Forest Green v Leigh
Halifax v Hereford
Morecambe v Barnet
Northwich v Aldershot
Stevenage v Gravesend
Woking v Accrington
York City v Dag & Red

Saturday, 23 April
Aldershot v Scarborough
Carlisle v Exeter
Dag & Red v Barnet
Forest Green v Canvey Island
Gravesend v Burton
Halifax v Woking
Hereford v Accrington
Northwich v Crawley
Stevenage v Leigh
Tamworth v Morecambe
York v Farnborough

Saturday, 30 April
Accrington v Aldershot
Barnet v Carlisle
Burton v Northwich
Canvey Island v York
Crawley v Stevenage
Exeter v Gravesend
Farnborough v Halifax
Leigh v Dag & Red
Morecambe v Forest Green
Scarborough v Tamworth
Woking v Hereford